2010

Malaysia, Singapore & Brunei

Simon Richmond

Celeste Brash, Adam Karlin, Shawn Low, Brandon Presser

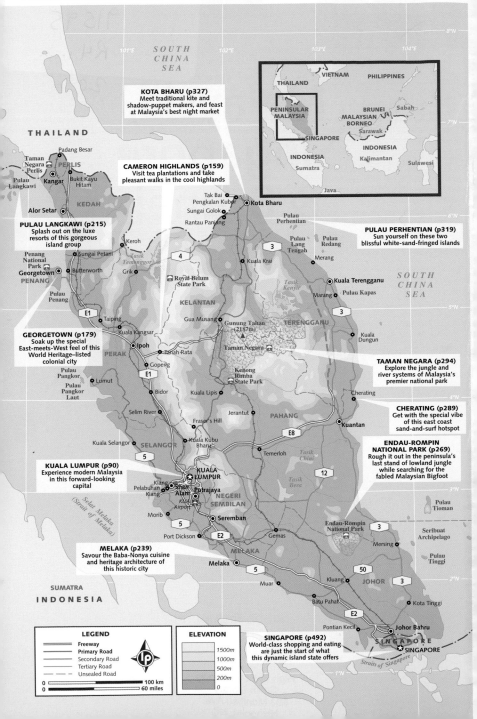

PENINSULAR MALAYSIA & SINGAPORE

KOTA BHARU (p327)
Meet traditional kite and shadow-puppet makers, and feast at Malaysia's best night market

CAMERON HIGHLANDS (p159)
Visit tea plantations and take pleasant walks in the cool highlands

PULAU LANGKAWI (p215)
Splash out on the luxe resorts of this gorgeous island group

PULAU PERHENTIAN (p319)
Sun yourself on these two blissful white-sand-fringed islands

GEORGETOWN (p179)
Soak up the special East-meets-West feel of this World Heritage–listed colonial city

TAMAN NEGARA (p294)
Explore the jungle and river systems of Malaysia's premier national park

CHERATING (p289)
Get with the special vibe of this east coast sand-and-surf hotspot

ENDAU-ROMPIN NATIONAL PARK (p269)
Rough it out in the peninsula's last stand of lowland jungle while searching for the fabled Malaysian Bigfoot

KUALA LUMPUR (p90)
Experience modern Malaysia in this forward-looking capital

MELAKA (p239)
Savour the Baba-Nonya cuisine and heritage architecture of this historic city

SINGAPORE (p492)
World-class shopping and eating are just the start of what this dynamic island state offers

THAILAND

SOUTH CHINA SEA

VIETNAM

PHILIPPINES

PENINSULAR MALAYSIA

BRUNEI
MALAYSIAN
BORNEO
Sabah
Sarawak

SINGAPORE

INDONESIA
Sumatra
Kalimantan
Sulawesi
Java

PERLIS
Padang Besar
Taman Negara Perlis
Pulau Langkawi
Kangar
Bukit Kayu Hitam

KEDAH
Alor Setar

Penang National Park
Georgetown
Butterworth
Sungai Petani
Keroh
PENANG
Pulau Penang
Taiping
Kuala Kangsar
Grik
Tasik Temenggor

Pulau Pangkor
Pulau Pangkor Laut
PERAK
Ipoh
Tanah Rata
Gopeng
Lumut
Bidor
Selim River
Kuala Lipis
Fraser's Hill
Jerantut

Kuala Selangor
SELANGOR
Kuala Kubu Bharu
Klang
Pelabuhan Klang
Shah Alam
KUALA LUMPUR
Putrajaya
KLIA Airport
Morib
NEGERI SEMBILAN
Seremban
Port Dickson
E2
Gemas
MELAKA
Melaka
Muar

Tak Bai
Pengkalan Kubor
Sungai Golok
Rantau Panjang
Kota Bharu
KELANTAN
Gua Musang
Royal Belum State Park
Kuala Krai
Gunung Tahan (2187m)
Taman Negara
Kenong Rimba State Park

Pulau Perhentian
Pulau Redang
Pulau Lang Tengah
Merang
Kuala Terengganu
Marang
Pulau Kapas
TERENGGANU
Kuala Dungun

SOUTH CHINA SEA

Cherating
PAHANG
Kuantan
Temerloh
Tasik Chini
Tasik Bera

Endau-Rompin National Park
Pulau Tioman
Mersing
Seribuat Archipelago
Pulau Tinggi

Kluang
JOHOR
Batu Pahat
Pontian Kecil
Kota Tinggi
Johor Bahru
SINGAPORE
Straits of Singapore

SUMATRA
INDONESIA
Selat Melaka (Strait of Melaka)

THAILAND

SOUTH CHINA SEA

LEGEND
Freeway
Primary Road
Secondary Road
Tertiary Road
Unsealed Road

0   100 km
0   60 miles

ELEVATION
1500m
1000m
500m
200m
0

MALAYSIAN BORNEO & BRUNEI

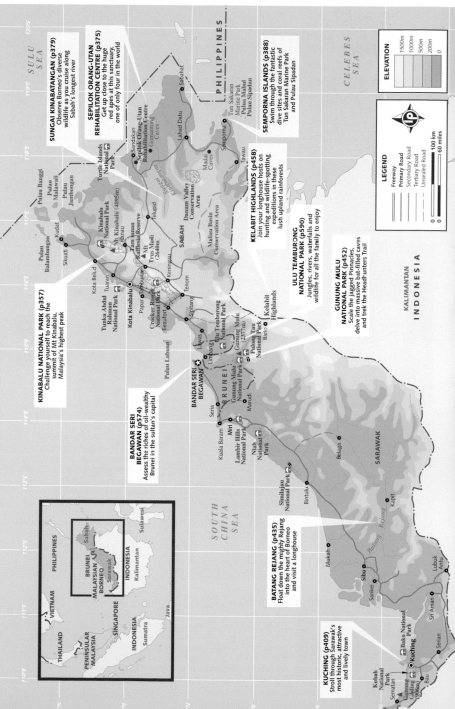

ELEVATION
- 1500m
- 1000m
- 500m
- 200m
- 0

LEGEND
- Freeway
- Primary Road
- Secondary Road
- Tertiary Road
- Unsealed Road

0 _____ 100 km
0 _____ 60 miles

SUNGAI KINABATANGAN (p379)
Observe Borneo's diverse wildlife as you cruise along Sabah's longest river

SEPILOK ORANG-UTAN REHABILITATION CENTRE (p375)
Get up close to the huge red apes at this sanctuary, one of only four in the world

SEMPORNA ISLANDS (p388)
Swim through the fantastic dive sites and coral reefs of Tun Sakaran Marine Park and Pulau Sipadan

KINABALU NATIONAL PARK (p357)
Challenge yourself to reach the summit of Mt Kinabalu, Malaysia's highest peak

KELABIT HIGHLANDS (p458)
Join your longhouse hosts on hunting and wildlife-spotting expeditions in these lush upland rainforests

BANDAR SERI BEGAWAN (p574)
Assess the riches of oil-wealthy Brunei in the sultan's capital

ULU TEMBURONG NATIONAL PARK (p590)
Jungles, rivers, waterfalls and wildlife for all the family to enjoy

GUNUNG MULU NATIONAL PARK (p452)
Scale the jagged Pinnacles, delve into massive bat-filled caves and trek the Headhunters Trail

BATANG REJANG (p435)
Float down the mighty Rejang into the heart of Borneo and visit a longhouse

KUCHING (p409)
Stroll through Sarawak's most historic, attractive and lively town

SULU SEA

CELEBES SEA

PHILIPPINES

SOUTH CHINA SEA

SABAH

SARAWAK

BRUNEI

KALIMANTAN

INDONESIA

VIETNAM

THAILAND

PENINSULAR MALAYSIA

SINGAPORE

INDONESIA

Sumatra

Java

Sulawesi

MALAYSIAN BORNEO

Kalimantan

On the Road

SHAWN LOW Singapore is one orderly place. Every conceivable comfort has been installed in public spaces. From encasing and air-conditioning 'open' streets, to laying down a string of tree-lined passages to connect up parks, to installing an escalator on the side of a hill! I was so amused by the last one I had to ride up and down like a gleeful kid. You'll appreciate the convenience (and so will your sweat glands) when you're attempting to get up this hill to reach the leafy Fort Canning Park (p496).

ADAM KARLIN This is me (on the left) with some friends in Telaga Tujuh (Seven Wells; p219) in Langkawi. There's something about sliding down a waterfall into a pool of cold mountain water that is just, at the end of the day, supremely satisfying in a back-to-boyhood kind of way.

BRANDON PRESSER After a 2am wake-up call, I trudged – like a zombie in a horror flick – up to the top of Mt Kinabalu (p357) for a truly spectacular sunrise. I was quite proud to be the fifth person to reach the summit that morning, especially since I was recovering from a serious bout of food poisoning after eating some questionable critters a few days earlier. This photo was taken at one of the more harrowing moments of the trek – I could hear my heart pounding in my ears! Why do I sign up for these things when I know that I'm afraid of heights?

SIMON RICHMOND
Coordinating Author

My travel buddy and fishing enthusiast Kim had her reservations ('It's like the revenge of the fish', she squealed), but after the initial ticklishness we were both won over by the foot-nibbling sensation of the Foot Master Dr Fish Spa (p107). And we both really enjoyed the authentically painful foot massage that followed.

CELESTE BRASH Most visitors to Pulau Tioman never leave the coast but the interior has some of my favourite jungle walks in the region. While walking across the island from Tekek to Juara (p276) my friends and I oohed and aahed over monstrous trees and spiders, spotted giant black squirrels and monkeys, and finished with a dip in a waterfall. We were exhausted by the time we reached Juara but still managed to visit every hotel on both beaches and go bodysurfing! My bed was on the ground in a tent that night but I slept like a baby.

For full author biographies see p615.

Malaysia, Singapore & Brunei Highlights

On these pages travellers and Lonely Planet staff and authors share their top experiences in Malaysia, Singapore and Brunei. Do you agree with their choices, or have we missed your favourites? Go to lonelyplanet.com and tell us your highlights.

KARL LEHMANN

① CLIMBING MT KINABALU, SABAH

Reaching the summit of Mt Kinabalu (p357) just in time for sunrise made the two-day climb completely worthwhile. Despite the chilly overnight stop midway (we feasted on eggs boiled in a kettle) and the dark, sometimes treacherous, ascent to the top, the sense of achievement and the amazing colours cast by the rising sun were fabulous.

Shona Gold, Lonely Planet Staff

KL DESIGN WEEK 2009

TEMPLE TREE, PULAU LANGKAWI

Pulau Langkawi is famous for its luxury resorts but none of them comes close to the special experience of staying in this collection of vernacular homes (p223) gathered from across the peninsula – the patina of age and experience is retained but the interiors have been updated with modern comforts and a vivid eye for design.

Simon Richmond, Lonely Planet Author, USA

SIMON RICHMOND

4

2 KL DESIGN WEEK

Attending the inaugural KL Design Week (p109) was a highlight of my research trip – the creativity and imagination of local talents was impressive and made me want to discover more about Malaysia's contemporary design scene.

Simon Richmond, Lonely Planet Author, USA

SIMON RICHMOND

3 JUNGLE TREKKING, TAMAN NEGARA

Taman Negara (p294) was a massive highlight of Malaysia for me. We spent a night in Bumbun Kumbang, one of the many jungle hides open to travellers for watching wildlife. We were lucky enough to see a tapir visiting a salt lick, but if you don't manage to spot any wildlife, the night-time glow of the fireflies and the sounds of the jungle are still enough to make it worth the long, hot and rickety journey getting there.

Phillipa Ellis, Lonely Planet Staff

JANE SWEENEY

SNORKELLING, PULAU PERHENTIAN

Pulau Perhentian (p319) was one of the highlights of my first trip to Malaysia. Snorkelling off the beach might yield anemone fish, juvenile reef sharks, Christmas-tree worms, curious parrotfish (they will bite your head!) and a host of other tropical reef critters. You can also hire a local guide to take you by boat to a few key snorkelling spots to see larger sharks and green turtles. In the evenings, settle back in a hammock while getting used to the idea that you're living in a tour-brochure cliché of palm-lined beaches. Then kick off your morning with banana pancakes and lime juice before hitting the reef again.

Janet Brunckhorst, Lonely Planet Staff

5

OLIVIER CIRENDINI

AFTERNOON TEA

Ah… the ritual of tiffin in the midafternoon – one of Malaysia's best colonial hangovers. Sink your choppers into delicious cakes at KL's Carcosa Seri Negara (p112) or cool down with a cuppa and a scone at Fraser's Hill's Ye Olde Smokehouse (p136) – you know it's the pukka thing to do!

Simon Richmond,
Lonely Planet Author, USA

6

SIMON RICHMOND

7

AUN KOH

CENDOL, MELAKA

Nothing beats an ice-cold *cendol* (p71) after a sweaty walk around Melaka's Chinatown (p243). While you can get this weird icy contraption all over Malaysia the especially renowned all-natural palm sugar in Melaka makes this treat even more delicious here. Savour one like a fine wine.

Celeste Brash,
Lonely Planet Author, Tahiti

DELICIOUS HAWKER FOOD, GEORGETOWN, PENANG

In Georgetown walk around Chinatown (p184) – pay particular attention to the old Chinese/colonial shophouses. You can eat almost anywhere and the food is out of this world (p191) – get yourself to one of the hawker centres and point at anything that looks good. Make sure you have some Peranakan food too – it's a great fusion of Chinese, Indian & Malay/Indonesian flavours. Laksa, fish-head curry (sounds revolting but is actually delicious), sambal seafood, *popiah*, porridge and yum cha for breakfast – yum yum yum. I'm hungry now!

**Robert McGowan,
Traveller, UK**

NEIL MCALLISTER/ALAMY

8 BEACH HOPPING, PULAU TIOMAN, MALAYSIA

Don't just cook in one spot on Pulau Tioman (p274), beach hop! Lounge on the beach at Salang one day, hang out at a low-key beach bar at Air Batang the next, then hike over to Juara and go surfing the next. In between you can dive and take boat taxis to other beaches that all have their own personalities.

Celeste Brash, Lonely Planet Author, Tahiti

10

AUN KOH

ERNEST MANEWAL

9 PULAU SIPADAN, SABAH

Stepping off the beach at Pulau Sipadan (p388) I have no idea of the world I am about to enter. The shallow waters of the sandy beach quickly give way to a sheer 900m vertical wall teeming with the most incredible ocean life. Tropical fish and gigantic Pacific green sea turtles brush past while moray eels and leopard sharks patrol the murky depths below. Schools of chevron barracuda, thousands in number, surround me.

Eoin Dunlevy, Lonely Planet Staff

KUCHING MARKET, SARAWAK

Try *roti canai* (flatbread with chickpeas) and *roti telur* (flatbread with eggs) – perfect with the accompanying curry to dip it in. Don't miss the open market in Kuching (Hawker Centre; p419) for cheap, tasty food in a vibrant atmosphere. And whatever you do, try *midin*, a local jungle fern often served stir-fried with *belacan* (shrimp paste).

Leah Schwartz, Traveller

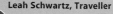

13

PETER SOLNESS

RICHARD I'ANSON

11 ORANG-UTANS, SABAH

Walking down wooden planks through dense jungle you emerge at the crowded feeding station of the Sepilok Orang-Utan Rehabilitation Centre (p375) in Sabah, on the island of Borneo. As we walked down a path a juvenile orang-utan followed us and walked right up to my children; curious he tapped my children on the shoulder. My husband was able to snap a photo right at this incredible moment, a memory that still lasts. Ten years later my children still tell the stories of Borneo, blowpipes and orang-utans.

Jane Bentham, Traveller, USA

WAYNE WALTON

12 OMAR ALI SAIFUDDIEN MOSQUE, BRUNEI

The Omar Ali Saifuddien Mosque (p577) is hard to miss: its minaret soars above all else in Bandar Seri Begawan. The mosque is an exercise in lavish: Italian marble floors, stained-glass windows, plush carpets and a 3.5-million-piece Venetian mosaic inside the main dome. You might struggle to pick your jaw from off the ground.

Shawn Low, Lonely Planet Author, Australia

KEK LOK SI TEMPLE, PENANG

The real highlight of your visit to Penang is Kek Lok Si Temple (p199), where you will see a towering 36m bronze Goddess of Mercy and a panoramic view of the city.

Cschua, Thorn Tree Traveller

JOHN BANAGAN

16

SIMON RICHMOND

14

IMBI MARKET, KUALA LUMPUR

What better way to start a KL day than at Imbi Market (p115), where you can breakfast on a delicious feast of *popiah* rolls, oyster and peanut rice porridge, noodles and creamy egg tarts, washed down with super-strength coffee or frothy *teh tariek*… If you don't know what to choose let the friendly locals point out their favourite stalls.

Simon Richmond, Lonely Planet Author, USA

WAYNE WALTON

15

KAMPONG AYER (WATER VILLAGE), BRUNEI

Brunei's Kampong Ayer (water village; p578) is reportedly the world's largest, where for centuries residents have lived on stilted houses over the Brunei River for relief from the heat and humidity.

Debra Herrmann, Lonely Planet Staff

MICHAEL COYNE

LITTLE INDIA, SINGAPORE

I had all sorts of preconceptions about spotless, controlled, modern Singapore, but Little India (p500) was a real surprise, with its crowded footpaths, prewar buildings with colourful shutters, garlands of fragrant flowers, bins of ochre spices, grocery shops blasting Hindi tunes and corner chapatti-makers. It was hands-down my favourite part of the city.

**Kirsten Rawlings,
Lonely Planet Staff**

19

17

OUTDOOR SINGAPORE

You will love Singapore even if you aren't a city person. It's clean, organised, easy to navigate and has interesting architecture and history, not to mention some of the best food in the world. The Botanic Gardens and National Orchid Garden (p501) are stunning. The Singapore Zoo and the Night Safari (p504) are worth the trip, even though they are touristy. The zoo is unique, there are almost no cages and the animals roam free for the most part. Often the only thing separating you from the animals will be a moat or embankment. Lemurs and mouse deer will literally walk next to you.

Patricia Margaret Wood, Traveller, USA

18

TREKKING, GUNUNG MULU NATIONAL PARK

Discover the Sarawak Chamber in Gunung Mulu National Park (p452), believed to be the largest underground chamber in the world, on a 16-hour caving trip (including extensive hiking). Then watch thousands of bats whirl around in circles and wavy lines to confuse the bat eagles as they leave the Deer Cave each night.

lonelyplanet.com Member

IBAN, SARAWAK

I will never forget hitting the road in search of an independent upriver travel route deep into the lush jungle interior of the Batang Ai National Park (p434) in Sarawak. As we watched residents of a longhouse (p430) carve a freshly slaughtered wild boar for the celebration of a local wedding and talked with an 80-year-old Iban warrior, I was amazed by the authenticity of the cultural exchange.

**Matt Goldberg,
Lonely Planet CEO**

MATT GOLDBERG

22

PHIL WEYMOUTH

20

CHANGI MUSEUM & CHAPEL, SINGAPORE

Singapore's strategically important location positioned it within the sights of ambitious neighbours and inadvertently secured its place in military history as the site of a WWII POW camp during the Japanese occupation. More than 80,000 Allied soldiers and civilian internees including women and children were held here. The museum (p503) records accounts of life inside Changi and manages to retain a positive focus, where stories of heroism, camaraderie and survival prevail.

Debra Herrmann, Lonely Planet Staff

SIMON RICHMOND

21

WALKING THE SOUTHERN RIDGES, SINGAPORE

A late-afternoon stroll along the Southern Ridges route (p507) connecting a string of Singapore's green spaces is a delightful way to not only catch the sea breeze but also experience one of the island's most sensational architectural pieces – the Henderson Waves bridge spanning Henderson Rd.

Simon Richmond, Lonely Planet Author, USA

Contents

Regional Map Contents

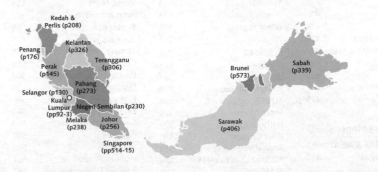

Kedah & Perlis (p208)
Kelantan (p326)
Penang (p176)
Terengganu (p306)
Perak (p145)
Pahang (p273)
Selangor (p130)
Kuala Lumpur (pp92-3)
Negeri Sembilan (p230)
Melaka (p238)
Johor (p256)
Singapore (pp514-15)
Brunei (p573)
Sabah (p339)
Sarawak (p406)

Destination Malaysia, Singapore & Brunei

Entwined by history and shared multi-ethnic populations, Malaysia, Singapore and Brunei are Southeast Asia's terrific trio. Want beautiful beaches and idyllic islands? Crave delicious culinary sensations? Searching for an Indiana Jones–style adventure in steamy jungles or the region's hottest contemporary art, design and fashion creations? From must-see modern architecture to a fascinating range of indigenous peoples, these three countries tick all the boxes on the tropical destination wish list.

Commence your journey in either Malaysia's capital of Kuala Lumpur (KL) or the island state of Singapore and you'll immediately be impressed by how the preserved cultures of the Malay, Chinese and Indian communities connect with a drive to be as innovative and modern as other world metropolises. Trawl street markets, chow down at fabulous hawker stalls, deck yourself out in designer threads from the fanciest shopping malls, and dip into museums highlighting practically every aspect of local life – it's all waiting in these buzzing cities that keep an eye on their past while boldly striding into the future.

Contrasting with the dynamism of urban life is the laid-back charm of the region's rural and coastal escapes. Efficient and reliable transport networks mean it's no drama to access pretty much anywhere – from the deepest recesses of jungle to the peaks of the highest mountains and the depths of coral-reef-packed oceans, much of this protected in national parks.

Recent world economic woes have slashed the previously robust growth rates of this trio of warm, lush and naturally blessed countries, denting local confidence in the process. As far as visitors are concerned this translates into locals who are even more welcoming than ever, and bargain prices, particularly for accommodation, food and transport.

Malaysia

The repercussions of the March 2008 election – in which the United Malays National Organisation (UMNO) and its coalition partners in Barisan Nasional (BN) saw their parliamentary dominance slashed to less than the customary two-thirds majority – continue to ripple through Malaysian political life. Pakatan Rakyat (PR), the opposition People's Alliance, led by the back-from-the-wilderness Anwar Ibrahim (see p43), not only bagged 82 of the parliament's 222 seats but also took control of five out of Malaysia's 13 states including the key economic bases of Selangor and Penang. PR's victory was widely seen as the result of voters' disgust at the excesses of Malaysia's 'money-politics' where bribes are paid to secure political clout and public-sector contracts.

BN's fall guy was mild-mannered but ineffectual prime minister Abdullah Badawi, who resigned in April 2009 in favour of his urbane deputy Mohd Najib bin Tun Abdul Razak (typically referred to as Najib Razak). Son of Abdul Razak, Malaysia's second PM after independence, and nephew of Abdul's successor Hussein Onn, Najib has been groomed for this role ever since he first entered national politics at the age of 23 in 1976.

FAST FACTS:
Malaysia

Population: 27.73 million

GDP per person: US$15,300

Life expectancy: 73.3 years

Inflation: 5.8%

Unemployment: 3.3%

Malaysians who can be awarded the highest honorary rank of Tun: 35

However, the change of guard may be too late to resurrect the fortunes of UMNO, a party seen as corrupt and out of touch with the people according to a survey by the independent Merdeka Center (www.merdeka.org), a point of view publicly agreed with by former PM Dr Mahathir. It hasn't helped that Najib's standing has been undermined not only by his tangential involvement with a high-profile murder case (p44), but also by the political shenanigans in Perak where he was the architect of BN's power grab to recapture control of the state parliament (p146).

So far, to his credit, Najib has resisted playing on tensions between Malaysia's majority Malays and its ethnic-Chinese and Indian minorities. Similar strains also lie beneath the PR's loose alliance of the multiracial Anwar-led Parti Keadilan Rakyat (PKR), secular Chinese-based Democratic Action Party (DAP) and the staunchly Islamic Parti Islam se-Malaysia (PAS). Najib's 1Malaysia policy revolves around mutual respect and trust among Malaysia's different races – how far such respect and trust will extend as BN loses its grip on power after 50 years in the country's driving seat remains to be seen.

Singapore

The People's Action Party (PAP) continues to hold on to power by all means, as it has done since Lee Kuan Yew first led it to victory in 1959. Lee may have retired as prime minister in 1990, but he still keeps a watchful eye on government in his role as the island state's 'Minister Mentor'. His eldest son Lee Hsien Loong has been in the top job since 2004.

The 2009 worldwide economic downturn hit Singapore fairly hard. GDP shrunk by 12.5% in the last quarter of 2008 and growth for 2009 was forecast at -2%. The government dug deep into their S$175 billion reserves and took out S$4.9 billion as part of a S$20 billion economic stimulus package.

Meanwhile the nanny state continues to loosen its paternalistic grip, actively promoting Singapore as an arts hub, allowing two casinos (oops, 'integrated resorts') to operate, and relaxing liquor licensing laws and those relating to public gatherings. This last measure allowed some 2500 pink-clad citizens to gather on 16 May 2009 at Speakers Corner to form a pink dot (www.pinkdot.sg) in support of gay rights.

There has been no relaxation, though, of Singapore's zero tolerance of drugs – one of the few areas where Singapore and Malaysia see eye to eye. A series of ongoing territorial battles have raged between the two since 1965, when Singapore was unceremoniously kicked out of its short-lived union with Malaysia. Negotiations on a replacement for the ageing and congested causeway linking the island with Johor Bahru faltered over Singapore's preconditions that Malaysia provide it with sand for reclamation projects and that Singaporean military jets have access to Malaysian airspace.

Squabbles also continue over payment for water (Singapore gets 40% of its water from Malaysia but plans to make itself self-sufficient by 2061, when the current agreement runs out) and Malaysian Railway land-holdings in Singapore. The sovereignty of Pedra Branca, a tiny outcrop in the South China Sea, is also disputed. The Hague ruled in favour of Singapore in 2008 but Malaysia has promised to keep digging for historical documents in order to challenge the decision.

Brunei

While relations between Malaysia and Singapore are likely to remain touchy for the foreseeable future, those between Malaysia and Brunei are far more cordial. The two countries may have minor disputes over the rights to possible offshore gas and oil exploration sites and over the land border around Limbang, but they share Islam as a common faith and further goodwill was forged in August 2005 when Sultan Hassanal Bolkiah, aged 58, took 26-year-old former TV journalist Azrinaz Mazhar Hakim, a Malaysian, as his third wife. Love must have been in the air in Brunei because in 2004 the 30-year-old Crown Prince Al-Muhtadee Billah Bolkiah married a 17-year-old half-Swiss commoner, Sarah Salleh.

Change is gradually creeping into the world's longest-running absolute monarchy. The legislative council has been restored for the first time in 20 years and an opposition political party has been allowed to form. Millions of dollars were spent to erect a building known as the parliament – however, voting still does not exist. The emphasis on Muslim culture has relaxed slightly, with the Education Minister losing his job in 2005 for pushing unpopular and obscure Islamic studies. The government is also trying to move beyond the oil- and gas-rich nation's habitual economic reliance on hydrocarbons.

FAST FACTS:
Brunei

Population: 390,000

GDP per person: US$51,000

Life expectancy: 76 years

Inflation: 0.4%

Unemployment: 4%

Daily oil production: 193,000 barrels

Getting Started

Trips in Malaysia, Singapore and Brunei can be tailored to suit all budgets. Getting around much of the region is a breeze thanks to the excellent transport infrastructure. More-detailed preparations will be needed to get to the more remote locations of Malaysian Borneo.

WHEN TO GO

See the relevant Climate sections for more information on the weather in Malaysia (p468), Singapore (p559) and Brunei (p590).

Year-round travel is possible. Rain falls fairly evenly throughout the year and the difference between the main October to April rainy season and the rest of the year is not that marked. The exception is the east coast of Peninsular Malaysia, which receives heavy rain from November to mid-February. During these months many east-coast resorts close and boat services dwindle or stop altogether. Travel along the west coast is not affected. The states of Sabah and Sarawak receive high rainfall throughout the year, but it is heaviest from October to March.

Note that the haze from fires in Indonesia (see p80) is at its worst in March, September and October, which could make a holiday across the region during this time a less than pleasant experience.

Celebrations of one kind or another are held throughout the year. Bear in mind, though, that during the major public holidays (see p473, p560 and p591) many locals travel, putting pressure on transport and hotel vacancies. Chinese New Year, Hari Raya and Christmas are all especially busy. During these times it's best to wait until the holiday rush is over before travelling away from the major cities. The main beach and hill resorts get crowded on weekends at any time of year but are often deserted during the week.

The Muslim fasting month of Ramadan is generally not a problem for most travel. Some services in the region may be cut back, especially in the east-coast states of Kelantan and Terengganu, but most transport, hotels and accommodation, restaurants and many businesses function as normal.

COSTS & MONEY

Malaysia is inexpensive by world standards and caters well to all budgets. Singapore and Brunei are pricier, but there are still bargains to be had if you look carefully.

DON'T LEAVE HOME WITHOUT...

- Checking the visa situation (p477, p563 & p592). Those travelling on an Israeli passport cannot enter Malaysia or Brunei.
- Checking government travel advice (p470).
- Proof of vaccination for yellow fever (p595) if coming from infected areas of Africa or South America.
- An umbrella or light raincoat for those sudden showers.
- A torch or head lamp, a pair of binoculars, a mosquito net and leech-proof socks – all essential gear for a jungle trek.
- A sweater or light jacket – but only if you're planning a trip to the cooler highlands (or going to any air-conditioned space in Singapore!).
- Sharp elbows – for battling with the locals over shopping bargains!

Fleapit hotels and hostels where beds can be as cheap as US$3 a night are plentiful. The midrange is well catered for and hotel rooms with air-con and attached bathrooms start at around US$30. Luxury hotels often have promotional rates, especially in Malaysia.

Food generally is inexpensive with the variety and quality excellent; you can usually get away with US$3 for a full meal with a couple of drinks at a food centre or hawker stall – you'll pay even less if you're not that hungry. At the other end of the scale, fancy hotels and restaurants in the main cities offer international cuisine at international prices.

Alcoholic drinks are uniformly pricey. Beer costs about US$2 a small can, almost double in isolated areas. Spirits are about 50% more expensive than beer. With alcohol pretty much unavailable in Brunei, at least you'll save money there.

Transport is generally a bargain. There are plenty of reasonably priced taxis for local travel. Drivers are fairly honest and fares are either fixed or calculated using meters. For long-distance journeys, Malaysia has excellent buses and trains, all at reasonable prices, and even flights need not be too costly if booked far enough in advance.

Besides the travel essentials of food, accommodation and transport you'll find nonessentials and luxuries are moderately priced, even downright cheap.

HOW MUCH?

Midrange hotel double RM100/S$110/B$100

Cup of coffee RM4/ S$4.50/B$4

Bowl of laksa RM5/ S$4/B$4

Restaurant meal RM30/ S$20/B$18

Newspaper RM2/S$1.20/ B$0.80

TRAVELLING RESPONSIBLY

Carbon-cutting overland travel to Peninsular Malaysia and Singapore from Europe and most parts of Asia is possible as long as you have time on your hands – the authoritative **Man in Seat 61** (www.seat61.com/Malaysia.htm) reckons it takes a minimum of 3½ weeks to reach Singapore from London by a combination of trains and buses. However, with no scheduled ferry services from the peninsula, reaching Malaysian Borneo and Brunei is much tougher to do without flying.

Once in the region, making your travels more sustainable can be as simple as taking part in a village homestay program (p467), visiting an organic farm in Singapore (p506) or even buying an eco-basket made by disadvantaged Malaysian women from the folks at **Salaam Wanita** (www .justmarketing.info).

Covered by enormous tracts of rainforest, some of it protected within national parks, it would also seem that Malaysia and Brunei are model countries in which to organise a 'green' vacation. The reality is more complex with best practices in sustainable travel not fully understood or wilfully being flouted as businesses 'green-wash' themselves to appear more environmentally friendly than they really are. As Andrew Sebastian, head of communications for the Malaysian Nature Society (MNS; see p81) says, 'Malaysia is still choking the golden goose of eco-tourism'.

Reality checks are provided by **Green Selipar** (http://greenselipar.com),which does a wonderful job of listing great sustainable travel initiatives around Malaysia, and the pressure group and consultancy **Wild Asia** (www.wildasia .org), which seeks to up standards by handing out sustainable tourism awards in the region. Also see our Sustainable and Green Top Picks (p22), and p478 and p564 for lists of volunteer work opportunities.

TRAVEL LITERATURE

Into the Heart of Borneo (1987) by Redmond O'Hanlon is a hilarious account of author and poet James Fenton's journey into the Bornean interior in search of the fabled Sumatran rhinoceros.

TOP PICKS

EATING & DRINKING

Allow your appetite to lead you around the region for a nonstop feast.

- Join with the locals at one of Kuala Lumpur's vibrant night markets or hawker stall areas such as Jln Alor (p114) or Chinatown's Petaling St (p116)

- Sample the classic Ipoh dishes (p157) of *kway teow* (rice noodles)

- Indulge in a traditional afternoon tea amid the plantations of the Cameron Highlands (p159) or at Brunei's Empire Hotel (p586)

- Slurp the classic spicy-sour *asam* laksa (noodles with prawn paste and tamarind-flavoured gravy) of Penang (p192)

- Discover blue rice, banana *murtabak* (filled *roti canai*) and other local delicacies at Kota Bharu's fantastic night market (p332)

- Tuck into Nonya cuisine, a hybrid of traditional Chinese and Malay culinary styles, in Melaka (p249)

- Get your fingers sticky over chilli crab in Singapore (p536)

- Toast your longhouse host in Sarawak with *tuak*, the rice wine with an alcoholic punch (p430)

SUSTAINABLE & GREEN

Get in touch with nature, local traditions and people at these sustainable and environmentally friendly travel picks.

- Attend the Rainforest World Music Festival in Kuching (p416)

- Explore the giant caves of Niah National Park (p451)

- Take a boat trip down the river deep into Taman Negara (p298), Malaysia's top national park

- Go in search of the giant rafflesia flower and Rajah Brooke Birdwing butterfly with the Semai Orang Asli people of Ulu Geroh in Perak (p159)

- Trek around beautiful Tasik Chini and meet the Jakun people, an Orang Asli tribe (p288)

- Take a tour or arrange a homestay with KOPEL in Penang (p201)

- Study the local language, Bahasa Malaysia (p108) in Kuala Lumpur

- Walk the 7km from Tekek to Juara across the beautiful island of Tioman (p276)

- Spend a weekend helping out at the Ma' Daerah Turtle Sanctuary (p316) on the peninsula's east coast

- Swing through the treetops on the canopy walkway – one of the world's longest – in Brunei's magnificent Ulu Temburong National Park (p590)

OFFBEAT & ODD

Malaysia, Singapore and Brunei have more than their fair share of travel surprises.

- Dip your feet into KL's fish spas (p107)

- Search for Bigfoot in the jungles of Johor (p270)

- Squirm at the body piercings involved in the festival of Thaipusam (p52)

- Pay your respects to the sacred tooth of the Buddha at Singapore's Buddha Tooth Relic Temple (p499)

- Watch kung fu master Dr Ho Eng Hui break through a coconut husk with his index finger at Melaka's Jonker's Walk Night Market (p244)

- Count the multiple cat statues (p414) around Sarawak's evocative capital of Kuching, then get a tribal tattoo or piercing (p420)

- Take a spin in the revolving gallery of the Muzium Padi, a museum devoted to rice, 10km northwest of Alor Setar (p213)

- Glimpse the Ten Courts of Hell at Haw Par Villa in Singapore (p508)

- Check out Brunei's ghostly Jerudong Park Playground (p585), the sultanate's unofficial monument to reckless spending

Ghost Train to the Eastern Star (2008) by Paul Theroux sees the opinionated, perceptive travel writer get laid low by a tummy bug in Penang (holed up at the E&O no less!) then stick the knife into Singapore's Lee Kuan Yew.

Stranger in the Forest (1988) by Eric Hansen follows the intrepid author on his hike from Sarawak to Kalimantan and back with no proper papers, an unreliable map and a slender grasp of the local lingo.

Urban Odysseys (2009) edited by Janet Tay and Eric Forbes is a mixed bag of short stories set in Kuala Lumpur that capture the city's multifaceted, multicultural flavour.

From Majapahit to Putrajaya – Searching for the Other Malaysia (2005) by Farish A Noor is a collection of the local journalist's trenchant observations on the country.

The Golden Chersonese and the Way Thither (1883) by Isabella Bird is a stiff-upper-lip account of the doughty Victorian-era traveller wending her way through the Malaysian jungles of Selangor and Perak, and crossing the Bukit Genting pass on the back of an elephant.

In the Footsteps of Stamford Raffles (1992; also titled *The Duke of Puddle Dock*) by Nigel Barley is part biography and travelogue as the author shadows the journey east made by the founder of Singapore.

Singapore Swing (2007) by John Malathronas exposes the quirkier side of the island state as the author hangs out with paranormal investigators and at brothels and opium dens in his search for Singapore's true soul.

INTERNET RESOURCES

All Malaysia (http://allmalaysia.info) The Star newspaper group's portal into a variety of information sources useful for travellers to the country.

Brunei Tourism (www.tourismbrunei.com) All kinds of tourism information on Brunei is available at the official government-sanctioned site.

Lonely Planet (www.lonelyplanet.com) The Lonely Planet site offers succinct summaries on travelling in Malaysia, Singapore and Brunei, the Thorn Tree bulletin board and much more.

Malaysiakini (www.malaysiakini.com) Find out what's really going on in the country at Malaysia's best online subscriber news site (some content is free to non-subscribers).

Singapore Tourism (www.visitsingapore.com) This is the official site for tourist information, with plenty of links to things to see and do.

Tourism Malaysia (www.tourismmalaysia.gov.my) The official government site for tourist information has events calendars, regional links, background information and listings of domestic and international tourist offices.

LONELY PLANET INDEX

Litre of petrol RM1.80/ S$1.25/B$0.56

Litre of bottled water RM1.50/S$1.50/B$1

Beer – large bottle of Tiger RM11/S$8

Souvenir T-shirt RM20/ S$15/B$20

Street snack – satay stick RM0.50/S$0.40/B$0.25

Itineraries
CLASSIC ROUTES

THE GRAND TOUR   Six Weeks/Kuala Lumpur to Bandar Seri Begawan

Start in **Kuala Lumpur** (KL; p90), for four days of sightseeing and acclimatisation. Next, cool off in the lush **Cameron Highlands** (p159), then warm up again on the beautiful beaches of **Pulau Langkawi** (p215).

Cross the mountainous spine of the peninsula to **Kota Bharu** (p327), a great place to encounter traditional Malay culture. Island- and beach-hop down the east coast, pausing at **Pulau Perhentian** (p319), **Cherating** (p289) and **Pulau Tioman** (p274). Swing inland for a week to explore **Taman Negara** (p294), then return to the west coast to soak up the historic atmosphere of **Melaka** (p239).

Singapore (p492) can easily swallow up a week of shopping, museum viewing and world-class eating. From here you can fly to **Kuching** (p409) in Sarawak, a good base for a longhouse excursion or for arranging a trek in the **Gunung Mulu National Park** (p452). Your next challenge, should you choose to accept it, is to climb **Mt Kinabalu** (p357). Finish up in **Bandar Seri Begawan** (p574), the capital of oil-rich Brunei.

The Grand Tour covers 5000km, taking in the key attractions of Malaysia with stopovers in Singapore and Brunei. A full two months would allow a more leisurely pace.

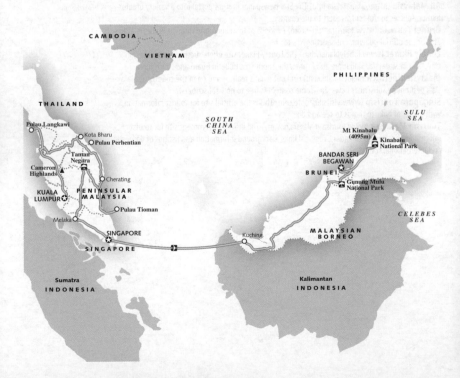

SABAH-SARAWAK SAMPLER   10 Days/Kota Kinabalu to Kuching

Start with Sabah's star attraction, **Mt Kinabalu** (p357). Assaults on Malaysia's highest peak can be launched from the state's government seat, **Kota Kinabalu** (p341) – not the most attractive of places. You'll be obliged to spend a day or two, so why not capital-ise on the flavourful local cuisine and try a day-trip cruise (including buffet dinner) down one of the tea-brown rivers in the **Beaufort Division** (p398), or learn a little about the local culture at the **Mari Mari Cultural Village** (p346)?

Leapfrog by plane from KK to **Miri** (p445) and then on to Mulu for **Gunung Mulu National Park** (p452), home to the world's largest caves, and several memorable jungle treks, including the notorious Headhunters Trail. Pass through Miri once more on a quick flight down to **Kuching** (p409). Sarawak's capital is a real charmer and will easily keep you occupied for several days. Break up your time in town with a visit to **Semenggoh Wildlife Rehabilitation Centre** (p428), **Bako National Park** (p423), and, if you have time, one of the longhouse communities in the **Sri Aman Division** (p433).

Tight on time? We've got you covered. This abridged itinerary offers a sample of Borneo's best – steamy jungles, snaking rivers and smoky longhouse verandahs – while still saving plenty of sights for next time ('cause you know you'll be back for seconds).

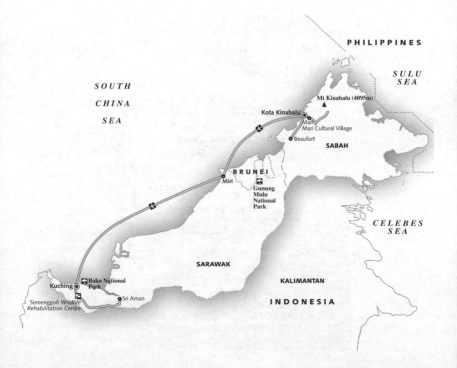

ROADS LESS TRAVELLED

REDISCOVERING MALAYSIA & SINGAPORE

Three Weeks/ Putrajaya to Singapore

From Kuala Lumpur International Airport go directly to **Putrajaya** (p136), the nation's fast-evolving administrative capital and a showcase of modern Malaysian architecture. Then head to the coast to the sleepy old royal capital of **Kuala Selangor** (p140), near to which you can observe the dazzling natural display of fireflies. In the tiny hill station of **Bukit Larut** (p172) there's only accommodation for around 70 visitors – pack your mac, as it's one of the wettest places in Malaysia! The really ambitious could also cram the almost forgotten state of Perlis, on the Thai border, into their first week of travel; the highlight here is **Taman Negara Perlis** (p228).

In week two, if you're up for a rugged jungle experience, dive into either the **Endau-Rompin National Park** (p269) or **Kenong Rimba State Park** (p303). Otherwise take a leisurely tour up the east coast, favouring smaller coastal towns such as **Merang** (p316) or a quiet island such as **Pulau Kapas** (p315). Alternatively rent a houseboat to explore **Tasik Kenyir** (p312).

In week three do some more island-hopping in the **Seribuat Archipelago** (p266) before crossing the causeway into **Singapore** (p492). You might think it impossible that this island state could have any unexplored corners but tourists are light on the ground in **Pulau Ubin** (p504), where cycling is the best way of getting around. Also forgo shopping in favour of bird-spotting in the **Sungei Buloh Wetland Reserve** (p505).

On this 2800km alternative highlights tour of Malaysia and Singapore you'll cover both coasts of the peninsula, trek in the jungle interior and laze on lovely islands – and still avoid the crowds.

ULTIMATE BORNEO   One Month/Kuching to Semporna Archipelago

Initiate yourself into the Bornean lifestyle using **Kuching** (p409), the dreamy riverine capital, to explore the local **longhouses** (p430) and **Bako National Park** (p423). Fly to **Miri** (p445), a lacklustre port city in northern Sarawak, but a great base for trips to the impressive **Niah Caves** (p451); **Gunung Mulu National Park** (p452) for more caves (the world's biggest), the heart-pumping trek to the Pinnacles and a sweat-drenching trek along the Headhunters Trail; and **Bario** (p458), a quiet farming community tucked away in the vine-draped Kelabit Highlands. The really adventurous can tackle a multi-day pilgrimage connecting the dots between hidden runes and far-flung longhouses.

You'll need to pass through Miri yet again to make your way overland to **Bandar Seri Begawan** (p574), Brunei's friendly micro-capital. While here don't miss out on **Ulu Temburong National Park** (p590) in Temburong, Brunei's smaller sliver of jungly land.

Cross back into Malaysia and pause in **Kota Kinabalu** (p341) for some interesting local cuisine before setting your sights on **Mt Kinabalu** (p357). Catch your breath after the climb with some ape love at **Sepilok Orang-Utan Rehabilitation Centre** (p375), followed by a layover in **Sandakan** (p370) for a brief lesson in colonial history. The mighty **Sungai Kinabatangan** (p379) is next, offering wildlife enthusiasts plenty of photo fodder. If you've got the time (and the dime), head deep into Sabah's green interior for a trek through the **Danum Valley Conservation Area** (p384). Finish up by exploring the magnificent dive sites of the **Semporna Archipelago** (p388), accessed by the unremarkable town of **Semporna** (p386).

This itinerary – Borneo's grand tour – tackles the island's top five treks (p356) and leaves plenty of time for some sun, sand, caves and culture. Five or six weeks would be ideal if you really want to take it all in.

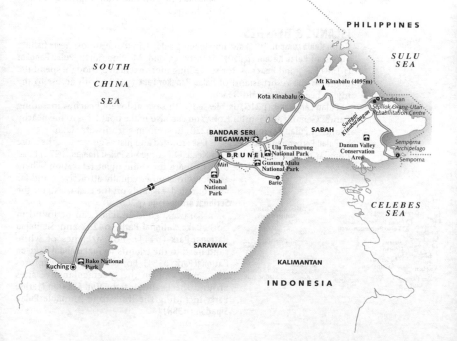

TAILORED TRIPS

COLONIAL FOOTSTEPS

Spend several days soaking up the enduring Portuguese and Dutch influence in World Heritage–listed **Melaka** (p239) before seeing how the British shaped **Kuala Lumpur** (p90) into command central for their adventures in Malaya. A fitting base would be **Carcosa Seri Negara** (p112), former residence of the British government's man in Malaya.

Near the one-time tin boom town of Ipoh is **Kellie's Castle** (p158), the eccentric (and unfinished) Indian-influenced mansion of a wealthy rubber-plantation owner. Savour the mock-Tudor style of Ye Olde Smokehouse in the **Cameron Highlands** (p165) or **Fraser's Hill** (p136).

Kuala Kangsar (p167) was one of the first places the British established control on the peninsula. **Georgetown** (p179) on the island of Penang is the oldest British settlement in Malaysia.

When it comes to grand colonial relics you really shouldn't miss out on **Raffles Hotel** (p496) in Singapore; enjoy sinking a G&T in its Bar & Billiard Room or take high tea in the Tiffin Room.

Over in Borneo, Sarawak's capital **Kuching** (p409) is where you'll find Fort Margherita built by James Brooke, the state's first White Raja. Also follow the heritage trail of colonial-era buildings in **Sandakan** (p370), one-time capital of British North Borneo.

ISLANDS & BEACHES

From **Kuala Lumpur** (p90) start by making a day trip to the atmospheric fishing village of **Pulau Ketam** (p140) for tasty seafood. Moving north, **Pulau Pangkor** (p148) has good beaches; for something more exclusive, though, spend the night on the resort island of **Pulau Pangkor Laut** (p152), with access to the idyllic beach at Emerald Beach.

Pulau Langkawi (p215) is blessed with several lovely beaches including Pantai Cenang and Pantai Kok. You can also make boat trips to the nearby island of **Pulau Dayang Bunting** (p220) to swim in a freshwater lake.

Pulau Perhentian Besar (p319) is less crowded and just as gorgeous as its more popular twin, Pulau Perhentian Kecil. On gorgeous **Pulau Tioman** (p274) head over to Juara for some quiet relaxation. There are numerous other equally attractive – and far less touristed – islands off the east coast; try the **Seribuat Archipelago** (p266).

In Sarawak, good beaches can be found in both **Bako National Park** (p423) and **Similajau National Park** (p444). For stretches of white sand head to the islands in **Tunku Abdul Rahman National Park** (p354). For underwater adventures don't miss out on the spectacular dive sites around the islands of the **Tun Sakaran Marine Park**, including the limestone pinnacle **Pulau Sipadan** (p388).

KIDS' MALAYSIA & SINGAPORE

In **Kuala Lumpur** (p90) keep the kids happy with visits to the **KL Bird Park** (p101) and to the Skybridge at the **Petronas Towers** (p95), where you'll also find the Petrosains interactive science discovery centre. Within day-trip distance of KL are the theme parks at **Sunway Lagoon** (p138) and **Genting Highlands** (p132), both of which are ideal places for all the family to cool down and revive.

Day-trip distance from KL is the **Kuala Gandah Elephant Conservation Centre** (p303), where it's possible to feed the elephants and go for a swim with them. To further experience the wonders of the jungle, head to **Taman Negara** (p294). Even if a long hike in this premier national park is out the question, children can clamber across the canopy walkway or float down the river on an inner tube. Out of the beaches and islands of the east coast, you could choose **Pulau Kapas** (p315) or **Cherating** (p289), slightly more geared towards family holidays.

Singapore (p492) has tonnes of family-friendly diversions including the excellent **zoo and night safari** (p504). Monkeys can easily be spotted on walks around **Bukit Timah Nature Reserve** (p505) and the **MacRitchie Reservoir** (p505). It's fun pedalling around **Pulau Ubin** (p504) and you can hire bikes on **Sentosa Island** (p509), which also boasts a top-class aquarium, dolphin shows, an old fort and OK beaches.

Pulau Kapas
Taman Negara
Cherating
Kuala Gandah
Genting Highlands — Elephant
Conservation Centre
Sunway Lagoon — KUALA LUMPUR

SINGAPORE — Pulau Ubin
Sentosa Island

LAND & SEA ADVENTURES

Top of the list is **Taman Negara** (p294), which includes Gunung Tahan, Peninsular Malaysia's highest peak. The far less tourist-frequented **Endau-Rompin National Park** (p269) has Malaysia's largest population of Sumatran rhinos, although don't count on spotting these elusive beasts.

Pulau Redang (p317) is a spectacular dive site – nine islands surrounded by fine coral reefs and clear water. An alternative dive destination is the much less visited gem of **Pulau Lang Tengah** (p318). The **Seribuat Archipelago** (p266) offers super dive conditions less the crowds; the most accessible islands are Besar, Sibu and Rawa, but the best diving is around Pemanggil and Aur.

Malaysian Borneo has 23 national parks including marine reserves and the rarefied heights of **Mt Kinabalu** (p357); set aside three days to reach the summit. In **Gunung Mulu National Park** (p452) allow four days to tramp the Headhunters Trail and climb to the jagged Pinnacles. A day is sufficient for **Niah National Park** (p450) with its giant caves. Give yourself two days in **Bako National Park** (p423) to hunt out exotic flora and fauna, and to enjoy walks along the rugged coastline.

Don't miss the spectacular **Tun Sakaran Marine Park** (p388) or **Pulau Layang Layang** (p369), part of the famous Borneo Banks, where shallow reefs and impressive drop-offs both play host to shoals of tuna, barracuda and hammerhead sharks. For adventurous trekking both the **Danum Valley** (p384) and the **Crocker Range** (p396) are recommended.

Pulau Lang Tengah
Pulau Redang
Taman Negara

Pulau Layang
Layang
Mt Kinabalu
Crocker Range
Danum Valley
Niah
National
Park
Tun Sakaran
Marine Park
Endau-Rompin — Seribuat
National Park — Archipelago
Gunung Mulu
National
Park
Bako
National
Park

History

As the countries we know today, Malaysia, Singapore and Brunei have been around since 1963, 1965 and 1984 respectively. The region's history, of course, stretches back much further, although pinning down exactly how far back is a moot point due to a lack of archaeological evidence and early written records. What is known for sure is that early civilisation here was shaped by the ebb and flow of the convergent sea trade from China and India. The following sketches in the main events – see the history sections of the destination chapters for more-specific details of each region and p17 for the latest happenings.

Key Malay words like bahasa (language), raja (ruler) and jaya (success) are Sanskrit terms imported to the area by Indian visitors as early as the 2nd century AD.

ORIGINAL PEOPLE

The discovery of a 40,000-year-old skull in the Niah Caves of Sarawak in 1958 (see p450) gives a notional starting point to pre-history in Malaysia. In Peninsular Malaysia, the oldest remains are of the 11,000-year-old skeleton, 'Perak Man', which has genetic similarities to the Negrito who now live in the mountainous rainforests of northern Malaysia. The Negritos were joined by Malaysia's first immigrants, the Senoi, who are thought to have slowly filtered down from central and southern Thailand around 2500 BC.

A third wave, the Proto-Malay, ancestors of today's Malays, came from the Indonesian islands between 1500 and 500 BC. They settled first on the coasts but later were forced upriver into deeper jungle. For more on Malaysia's indigenous people see p38.

It's thought that the word Malay (or Melayu) is based on the ancient Tamil word malia, meaning 'hill'.

EARLY TRADE & EMPIRES

By the 2nd century AD Malaya was known as far away as Europe. Ptolemy, the Greek geographer, labelled it 'Aurea Chersonesus' (Golden Chersonese); it was believed the area was rich in gold. Indian traders also referred to the land as Savarnadvipa (Land of Gold) and were already making regular visits to Malaya in search of the precious metal, tin and aromatic jungle woods. These Indian visitors had a significant impact on Malay social systems, beliefs and culture, introducing them to Hinduism, Buddhism and notions of kingship.

Much more significant was the dominance of the mighty Srivijaya Empire, which held sway from the 7th to the 13th centuries. This Buddhist empire controlled the entire Malacca Straits, Java and southern Borneo, and the great wealth flowing through the area in terms of trade (see p32).

Under the protection of the Srivijayans, a significant Malay trading state grew in the Bujang Valley of Kedah. Relics of temple complexes that house both Buddhist and Hindu artefacts are still being excavated and provide a reminder of the Hindu-Buddhist era in the Malay peninsula.

TIMELINE

c 38,000 BC	c 150AD	200
Earliest evidence of human life in the region is a 40,000-year-old skull found in Sarawak's Niah Caves. These early inhabitants are believed to be related to the aborigines of Australia and New Guinea.	European knowledge of the Malay peninsula is confirmed in Ptolemy's book *Geographia*, which labelled the landmass 'Aurea Chersonesus'. It's likely that Romans visited the region during trading expeditions to India and China.	Langkasuka, one of the first Hindu-Malay kingdoms, is established on the peninsula around the area now known as Kedah. It lasted in one form or another until the 15th century.

THE LOST KINGDOM OF LANGKASUKA

Early Chinese and Malay histories describe an independent kingdom known as Langkasuka, which existed on the Malay peninsula as early as the 2nd century AD. From the descriptions of the lands, it's reckoned that Langkasuka was in the region of Kedah, centred on the sacred mountain Gunung Jerai.

Between the 3rd and 6th centuries, Langkasuka's power dwindled and the Funan Empire, centred on what is now Cambodia, took over control of the region until they were in turn supplanted by the Srivijaya Empire. Langkasuka disappeared from Malaysia's maps although part of its name lingers on the islands of Langkawi. It was also raised as a possible name for an independent Malaya.

THE MELAKA EMPIRE

This history of the Malay state begins in earnest in the late 14th century when Parameswara, a renegade Hindu prince from a little kingdom in southern Sumatra, washed up around 1401 in the tiny fishing village that would become Melaka (p239).

A History of Malaya by Barbara and Leonard Andaya brilliantly explores the evolution of 'Malayness' in Malaysia's history and the challenges of building a multiracial, postindependence nation.

Realising Melaka's potential as a natural deep-water port and that it could never grow without protection from the Thais, Parameswara sent envoys to China to offer tribute. The timing was fortuitous. The Ming emperor had just begun a series of maritime missions to find alternatives to the overland route to the West, and he agreed to offer protection. Melaka became a port of call for the massive Chinese junks that were to ply the oceans for several decades. The junks were also a magnet for the other key traders of the time, the Indians.

Melaka was ideally situated as a halfway point for trade between the two nations. The Indian ships sailed in on the southwest monsoon, berthed in Melaka and waited for the northeast monsoon, which blew in the Chinese junks. Their goods were traded, and the Indians sailed back to India on the same winds that brought in the Chinese. Business boomed as regional ships and *perahus* (traditional Malay boats) arrived to take advantage of trading opportunities.

EARLY ISLAM

The local adoption of Islam is believed to have spread through contact with Indian Muslim traders. The religion gained such respect that by the mid-15th century the third ruler of Melaka, Maharaja Mohammed Shah (r 1424–44), had converted. His son Mudzaffar Shah took the title of sultan and made Islam the state religion.

The Other Malaysia (www.othermalaysia.org) is a resource in which forgotten and sidelined gems of Malaysia's history, politics and culture are gathered together.

As the 15th century progressed, Melaka became Southeast Asia's major entrepôt, attracting Indian Muslim merchants from competing Sumatran ports, and a centre for Islam, disseminating the religion throughout the Indonesian archipelago. The Melakan sultans ruled over the greatest empire

600	**1136**	**1363**
From their base in southern Sumatra, most likely around modern-day Palembang, the Buddhist Srivijaya Empire dominates Malaya, Singapore, Indonesia and Borneo for another six centuries.	The Kedah Annals record that the local Hindu ruler Phra Ong Mahawangsa converted to Islam and took the name Sultan Mudzafar Shah, thus founding the sultanate of Kedah, the oldest on Peninsular Malaysia.	Brunei's first Sultan Awang Alak Betatar takes the name Muhammad Shah on his conversion to Islam, prior to his marriage to a princess from Johor-Temasik.

in Malaysia's history, successfully repelling Siamese attacks. The Malay language became the lingua franca of trade in the region.

Meanwhile across the South China Sea, the first sultan of Brunei, Muhammad Shah, ruled over the kingdom from 1363 to 1402. He converted to Islam in 1363 on the occasion of his marriage to a princess from Johor-Temasik. By the 15th century Sultan Bolkiah reigned over the empire's 'Golden Age': in contrast to the tiny state it is today, at that time Brunei held sway over all of the islands of Borneo and much of the present-day Philippines. Well into the 16th century Bolkiah's armies managed to resist the inroads that Spanish and Portuguese forces tried to make into his territories.

Sejarah Melayu (Malay Annals), a literary work covering the establishment of the Melaka sultanate and 600 years of Malay history, is believed to have been compiled by Tun Sri Lanang, the *bendahara* (chief minister) of the Johor Royal Court in the early 17th century.

THE PORTUGUESE ERA

By the 15th century Europe had developed an insatiable appetite for spices, and the sole suppliers were Venetian merchants, who obtained them from Arab traders, who obtained them from Indian Muslim traders, who obtained them…from Melaka.

The Portuguese were determined to break this chain for 'God, glory and gold'. Their strategy was to build fortresses to control the sea-trade route between Lisbon and Melaka. In 1511 a fleet of 18 heavily armed ships, led

---

A HISTORY OF PIRACY

The lucrative trade routes around the Malay peninsula have long provided rich pickings for pirates. As far back as the Srivijaya Empire, from the 7th to 13th centuries, piracy was a problem. The Srivijayans used the seafaring people the Orang Laut (also known as Sea Gypsies) to police the trade routes, but by the 11th century they had switched sides and become pirates themselves. Parameswara, founder of Melaka, was also a pirate, attacking trading ships from his temporary base of Temasek (Singapore).

A millennium later piracy in the Strait of Melaka, one of the world's busiest waterways, remains a problem. To combat the pirates, Malaysia formed a coast guard that together with forces from Singapore and Indonesia have run coordinated patrols since 2004. They seem to be having an impact as the International Maritime Bureau recorded that attacks in 2008 had dipped to two compared to seven in 2007.

It's not just at sea that the authorities have to keep a lookout for pirates. The street markets of Kuala Lumpur and any number of other cities and towns are packed with pirated copies of DVDs, CDs, computer software and various luxury and brand-name fashion goods. The Business Software Alliance, a Malaysian antipiracy watchdog, reports that over 60% of all software used by businesses are illegal copies. The authorities, keen to preserve Malaysia's growing reputation as a high-tech hub, are cracking down, sending inspectors into businesses and issuing fines to those found using pirated software.

1402	1446	1485
The one-time Hindu prince and pirate Parameswara (1344–1414) founds the great trading port and sultanate of Melaka; seven years later he marries a Muslim princess and adopts the Persian title Iskandar Shah.	A naval force from Siam (Thailand) attacks Melaka. Warded off, the Siamese return in 1456 but are again rebuffed. Such attacks encourage Melaka's rulers to develop closer relations with China.	Under the rule of Sultan Bolkiah Brunei enjoys its 'Golden Age', when it controlled land as far south as present-day Kuching in Sarawak and north towards the islands of the Philippines.

by Viceroy Alfonso de Albuquerque, defeated Melaka's army of 20,000 men
and their war elephants.

The Portuguese immediately built a fortress, the A Formosa, to protect
their new acquisition. Expeditions were sent to the Moluccas, the source of
the spices, where a monopoly agreement was signed with the local sultan.
Within a few years Lisbon had replaced Venice as the greatest trading centre
for Eastern goods.

The 130 years in which the Portuguese held Melaka were fraught with wars
and skirmishes. Their monopolistic attitude to trade and their determination to spread Christianity earned them few friends. The new Johor Empire,
where part of the former sultan's entourage had set up camp, never gave up
hope of recapturing Melaka and continually harassed Portuguese ships in
the Strait of Melaka.

THE DUTCH PERIOD

Johor's fortunes improved drastically with the arrival of the Dutch, who
chose them as allies in the region. Unlike the Portuguese, the Dutch East
India Company had no interest in God or national glory. The company's
aim was solely making money and it focused single-mindedly on wresting
complete control of the spice trade from the Portuguese. The Dutch set up
a base in Batavia (now Jakarta) and negotiated for spices directly with the
sultans of the spice islands.

Together with Johor, the Dutch attacked Melaka and, in January 1641,
captured the city from the Portuguese. In return for their cooperation Johor
was freed from virtually all the tariffs and trade restrictions imposed on other
states by the Dutch. Johor also overcame threats from the Minangkabau
of Sumatra and by the end of the 17th century it was among the strongest
Asian powers in the region.

Despite maintaining control of Melaka for about 150 years, the Dutch
never really realised the full potential of the city. High taxes forced merchants
to seek out other ports and the Dutch choice of Batavia as their regional HQ
meant they were not inclined to invest their full attention on Melaka.

ENTER THE EAST INDIA COMPANY

British interest in the region began with the need by the East India Company
(EIC) for a halfway base for its ships plying the India–China maritime route.
The first base was established on the island of Penang in 1786 (see p176).

Meanwhile, events in Europe were conspiring to consolidate British interests in the Malay peninsula. When Napoleon overran the Netherlands in 1795,
the British, fearing French influence in the region, took over Dutch Java and
Melaka. When Napoleon was defeated in 1818, the British handed the Dutch
colonies back – but not before they had destroyed the walls of A Formosa.

The British lieutenant-governor of Java, Stamford Raffles, had long felt
that Britain, Europe's most powerful nation, should expand its influence

> Sabri Zain's colourful
> website *Sejarah Melayu:
> A History of the Malay
> Peninsula* (www.sabrizain
> .org/malaya) contains a
> wealth of historical info
> including a virtual library
> of nearly 500 books and
> academic papers.

> Peninsular Malaysia was
> Buddhist and Hindu for
> 1000 years before the
> local rulers converted to
> Islam in the 15th century.

1509	**1511**	**1629**
Portuguese traders sail into Melaka. Although at first greeted warmly, acting on the advice of his Indian Muslim councillors, the Melakan sultan later attacks the Portuguese ships, taking 19 prisoners.	Following the Portuguese conquest of Melaka, the sultan and his court flee, establish-ing two new sultanates on the peninsula: Perak to the north and Johor to the south.	The Portuguese in Melaka and the sultanate of Johor bury their differences to successfully defend themselves against the navy of Iskandar Muda, the sultan of Aceh in Sumatra. However, the same year Aceh conquers Kedah.

over Southeast Asia. He bitterly resented handing Java back to the Dutch and eventually managed to persuade the EIC that a settlement south of the Malay peninsula was crucial to the India–China maritime route.

THE RISE OF SINGAPORE

In 1819 Raffles landed on Singapore, at the time part of the Johor Empire. Johor's sultan had died while his elder son was away, and his younger son, aligned with the Dutch, had been proclaimed sultan. In return for supporting the elder son as the rightful sultan Raffles extracted a treaty granting the British sole rights to set up a trading post on Singapore.

'It is impossible to conceive a place combining more advantages…it is the Navel of the Malay countries', wrote a delighted Raffles soon afterwards. The statement proves his foresight because at the time Singapore was little more than an inhospitable swamp surrounded by dense jungle with a population of 150 fishermen and a small number of Chinese farmers. Raffles returned to his post in Bencoolen, Sumatra, but left instructions on Singapore's development as a free port with the new British Resident, Colonel William Farquhar.

In 1822 Raffles returned to Singapore and governed it for one more year. He initiated a town plan that included levelling a hill to form a new commercial district (now Raffles Place) and erecting government buildings around Forbidden Hill (now Fort Canning Hill). Wide streets of shophouses with covered walkways, shipyards, churches and a botanical garden were all built to achieve his vision of a Singapore that would one day be 'a place of considerable magnitude and importance'.

Raffles' blueprint also embraced the colonial practice of administering the population according to neat racial categories, with the Europeans, Indians, Chinese and Malays living and working in their own distinct quarters.

Dutch protests over the original treaty (which was followed up in 1823 by a second treaty fully ceding Singapore to Britain) were set aside when the two nations signed the Anglo-Dutch Treaty in 1824, dividing the region into two distinct spheres of interest: the Dutch controlled what is now Indonesia, and the British had the Malay peninsula and Singapore.

BORNEO DEVELOPMENTS

Britain did not include Borneo in the Anglo-Dutch treaty, preferring that the EIC concentrate its efforts on consolidating their power on the peninsula rather than furthering their geographical scope. This left a path clear for an opportunistic British adventurer, James Brooke (p405), to make his fortune. In 1841, having helped the local viceroy quell a rebellion, Brooke was installed as raja of Sarawak, with the fishing village of Kuching as his capital.

Through brutal naval force and skilful negotiation, James Brooke extracted further territory from the Brunei sultan and eventually brought

---

Read about the rise of Singapore from the man at the centre of it all – Lee Kuan Yew – in his memoirs *The Singapore Story* and *From Third World to First*.

Covering events up to 2001, the second edition of Graham Saunder's *History of Brunei* is the only full-length study of how this tiny country came to be formed.

1641	1786	1790
After a siege lasting several months the Dutch, with the help of the Johor sultanate, wrest Melaka from the Portuguese; this marks the start of Melaka's decline as a major trading port.	Francis Light cuts a deal with the sultan of Kedah to establish a settlement on the largely uninhabited island of Penang. Under a free-trade policy the island's new economy thrives.	The sultan of Kedah's attempt to retake Penang from the British fails. He is forced to cede the island to the British East India Company for 6000 Spanish dollars per annum. In 1800 Province Wellesley on the mainland is added to the deal.

peace to a land where piracy, headhunting and violent tribal rivalry had been the norm. The 'White Raja' dynasty of the Brookes was to rule Sarawak until 1941 and the arrival of the Japanese.

Unlike the British, the White Rajas included tribal leaders in their ruling council. They also discouraged large European companies from destroying native jungle to plant massive rubber plantations. They encouraged Chinese migration, and, without European competition, the Chinese came to dominate the economy.

The once-mighty empire of Brunei continued to shrink. In 1865 the American consul to Brunei persuaded the ailing sultan to grant him what is now Sabah in return for an annual payment. The rights eventually passed to an Englishman, Alfred Dent. In 1881, with the support of the British government, Dent formed the British North Borneo Company to administer the new settlement. To prevent a scramble for Brunei's remains, in 1888 the British government acceded to a request by the sultan to declare his territory a British protectorate.

> Oil was first discovered by the British Resident of the Baran district of Sarawak in 1882 but it wasn't until 1974 that the national oil and gas company Petronas was set up.

BRITISH MALAYA

In Peninsular Malaya, Britain's policy of 'trade, not territory' was challenged when trade was disrupted by civil wars within the Malay sultanates of Negeri Sembilan, Selangor, Pahang and Perak. In this last state, the British were forced to intervene in a succession dispute in 1874; one of the rivals for Perak's throne asked the British to appoint a Resident (or adviser) in return for guaranteeing his position as sultan. From then on the sultan had to consult the Resident on all matters, 'other than those touching on religion and Malay customs'.

The ingenious Resident system preserved the prestige of the sultans but effectively gave the British complete control. Through the late 19th century and into the early 20th century it was gradually introduced into the other states at the same time as the term British Malaya came into use, signalling the Crown's intention to take charge of the whole peninsula. Terengganu was the last state to accept a British Adviser in 1919.

ECONOMIC DEVELOPMENT

The British exploited the peninsula's resources with gusto. Building ports, roads and railways, and selling huge tracts of virgin rainforest, they encouraged entrepreneurs to invest in tin mines, rubber plantations and trading companies. Believing that the Malays were best suited to farming and fishing, they encouraged immigrants from China to work the mines, Indians to tap the rubber trees and build the railways, Ceylonese to be clerks in the civil service, and Sikhs to man the police force.

1819	1823	1826
By backing the elder brother in a succession dispute in Johor, Stamford Raffles gains sole rights to build a trading base on the island of Singapore.	A second treaty is signed in which the Johor sultan fully cedes Singapore to Britain. A year later the Dutch and British carve up the region into what eventually becomes Malaya and Indonesia.	Having swapped Bencoolen on Sumatra for the Dutch-controlled Melaka, the British East India Company combines this with Penang and Singapore to create the Straits Settlements.

F Spencer Chapman's *The Jungle is Neutral* follows a British guerrilla force based in the Malaysian jungles during the Japanese occupation of Malaya and Singapore.

Even though the 'better-bred' Malays were encouraged to join a separate arm of the civil service, there was growing resentment among the vast majority of Malays that they were being marginalised in their own country. A 1931 census revealed that the Chinese numbered 1.7 million and the Malays 1.6 million. Malaya's economy was revolutionised, but the impact of its liberal immigration policy continues to reverberate today. The Singapore Malay Union was formed in 1926 and by the eve of WWII Malays, too, were pushing for their independence.

WWII PERIOD

A few hours before the bombing of Pearl Harbor in December 1941, Japanese forces landed on the northeast coast of Malaya. Within a few months they had taken over the entire peninsula and Singapore. The poorly defended Borneo states fell even more rapidly.

In Singapore, the new governor, General Yamashita, slung the Europeans into the infamous Changi Prison, and Chinese communists and intellectuals, who had vociferously opposed the Japanese invasion of China, were targeted for Japanese brutality. Thousands were executed in a single week. In Borneo, early resistance by the Chinese was also brutally put down.

Noel Barber's *The War of the Running Dogs* is a classic account of the 12-year Malayan Emergency.

The Japanese achieved very little in Malaya. The British had destroyed most of the tin-mining equipment before their retreat, and the rubber plantations were neglected. The Malayan People's Anti-Japanese Army (MPAJA), comprising remnants of the British army and Chinese from the fledgling Malayan Communist Party, waged a weak, jungle-based guerrilla struggle throughout the war.

The Japanese surrendered to the British in Singapore in 1945. Despite the eventual Allied victory, Britain had been humiliated by the easy loss of Malaya and Singapore to the Japanese, and it was clear that their days of controlling the region were now numbered.

Revolusi 48 (http://revolusi48.blogspot.com in Bahasa Malaysia), the documentary sequel to Fahmi Reza's *10 Tahun Sebelum Merdeka* (10 Years Before Merdeka), chronicles the largely forgotten armed revolution for national liberation launched against British colonial rule in Malaya.

FEDERATION OF MALAYA

In 1946 the British persuaded the sultans to agree to the Malayan Union. This amalgamated all the Peninsular Malayan states into a central authority; removed the sovereign rights of the sultans, who would remain as paid 'advisers'; offered citizenship to all residents regardless of race; abolished the special privileges of the Malays (which included favourable quotas in civil service employment and government scholarships); and vested ultimate sovereignty in the king of England. Singapore was to be administered separately. North Borneo and Sarawak became the Crown Colony of British Borneo (the third Raja Brooke realised he could not afford to rebuild after the war).

While the sultans were cajoled and coerced into the Malayan Union, the normally acquiescent Malay population was less easily persuaded. Rowdy pro-

1839	1865	1874
British buccaneer James Brooke lands in Sarawak and helps quell a local rebellion. Two years later in gratitude the Brunei sultanate installs him as the first White Raja of Sarawak.	Brunei's American consul is granted what is now Sabah by the sultan in return for an annual payment. The rights pass to Alfred Dent, an Englishman, who in 1881 forms the British North Borneo Company.	The Pankor Treaty between the British and the sultan of Perak sees the British Empire start to take control of Peninsular Malaysia; the first British Resident of Perak, Sir James Birch, is installed.

test meetings were held throughout the country, and the first Malay political party, the United Malays National Organisation (UMNO), was formed.

After intense meetings between the sultans, British officials and UMNO, the Malayan Union was revoked, and the Federation of Malaya was declared in 1948. The federation upheld the sovereignty of the sultans and the special privileges of the Malays. Citizenship for non-Malays was made more restrictive. Although the Malays were ecstatic about the British climb-down, the Chinese felt they had been betrayed and that their role in resisting the Japanese was poorly appreciated. Many turned to the Malayan Communist Party (MCP), which promised an equitable and just society.

THE EMERGENCY

The ensuing MCP-led insurrection was a full-on civil war (the MCP received little support from the Malays, and their main Chinese supporters were subsistence farmers living along the jungle fringes); it was called an 'Emergency' by the British for insurance purposes, so that claims could still be made on policies that didn't cover riots and civil commotions.

The Emergency hardly touched Malaya's principal cities but caused plantation owners and villagers to live in terror of attacks. Following the assassination of British High Commissioner Sir Henry Gurney in 1951, his successor General Sir Gerald Templer set out to 'win the hearts and minds of the people' through a combination of military tactics and social policies.

Almost 500,000 rural Chinese were resettled into protected New Villages, and guerrilla-free areas had all food restrictions and curfews lifted. Another key move was gaining the support of the jungle-dwelling Orang Asli (see p38). The communists were gradually forced further back into the jungles and towards the Thai border. In 1960 the Emergency was declared over, although sporadic fighting continued and the formal surrender was signed only in 1989.

MERDEKA & MALAYSIA

UMNO led a less militant campaign towards independence. By forming the Parti Perikatan (PP; Alliance Party) with the Malayan Chinese Association (MCA) and the Malayan Indian Congress (MIC), they presented a convincing argument for a racially harmonious, independent nation. In 1955 the British promised independence in two years and held an election to determine the government of the new nation.

PP, led by UMNO's Tunku Abdul Rahman, won a landslide victory, and on 31 August 1957 Merdeka (independence) was declared. A unique solution was found for the problem of having nine state sultans eligible for the position of paramount leader – they would take turns (see p43).

Singapore's politics were dominated by communists and left-leaning trade unions. In 1959 the People's Action Party (PAP) was voted into government.

Anthony Burgess wrote about his experiences in Kelantan as an information officer for the colonial administration in the 1950s in the first volume of his memoirs *Little Wilson and Big God*.

Amir Muhammad's film *The Last Communist* (www.redfilms.com .my/lelakikomunis.htm) was banned in Malaysia in 2006 for allegedly glorifying communism.

For an excellent introduction to the customs and culture of Malaysia's indigenous people, visit the Orang Asli Museum (p132), just north of Kuala Lumpur. Also see the website of the Center for Orang Asli Concerns (www.coac.org.my).

1888	1896	1909
Having lost much territory to the British Empire, Brunei's sultan accepts the inevitable and signs a treaty to make his country a British protectorate. A British Resident is installed in 1906.	Perak, Selangor, Negeri Sembilan and Pahang join as Federated Malay States, their sultans conceding political power to British Residents. In return Britain pledges not to interfere in matters relating to Malay traditions and Islam.	Britain does a deal with the Thai king to gain control of Kelantan, Terengganu, Perlis and Kedah. The final standout Johor succumbs to a British Resident in 1914, completing the set of 'Unfederated Malay States'.

THE ORANG ASLI

According to data published by the Department of Orang Asli Affairs (JHEOA; www.jheoa.gov .my) in December 2004, Peninsular Malaysia has just under 150,000 Orang Asli (Original People), who are generally classified into three groups: the Negrito, the Senoi and the Proto-Malays. These can be further divided into 18 ethnic groups (the smallest being the Orang Kanak with just 87 members, the largest the Semai with 43,505 members), which speak distinctly different languages. The majority remain animists, although there are ongoing attempts to convert them to Islam.

The Orang Asli played important roles in early trade, when products of the jungle were much sought after, but their significance waned as trade products became more sophisticated. During the Malayan Communist Emergency in the 1950s they became 'useful' again. The communists were fighting a jungle guerrilla war, and the Orang Asli were important providers of food, shelter and information. The British Malayan government realised that if they were to win the war, the support of the Orang Asli was crucial. They won them over by setting up jungle 'forts' close to their settlements, which supplied them with medical care and food.

After the communists were thwarted, 'guardianship' of the Orang Asli was undertaken by JHEOA. Originally set up to represent Orang Asli concerns to the government (ie land rights), the department has evolved into a conduit for government decisions. Asli land rights are not recognised, and when logging, agricultural or infrastructure projects require their land, their claims are regarded as illegal.

In Sabah and Sarawak, despite indigenous people being in the majority and Native Customary Rights being legislated, their lack of effective political representation has seriously compromised their land rights. Logging of their rainforests and, more recently, huge oil palm plantations have reduced their land areas considerably. Their enforced isolation from the land and the success of Christian missionaries over the last century has resulted in fragmented communities and the slow disappearance of traditional identity.

In Brunei the indigenous people comprise about 6% of the population. With Brunei's economic interests lying largely in off-shore oil and gas fields, encroachment on the indigenous people's land and rights has been minimal.

Websites that provide information on the Orang Asli peoples are Temiar Web (www.temiar.com) and the Borneo Project (www.borneoproject .org).

It was led by Lee Kuan Yew, a young Cambridge-trained lawyer, who garnered popular support through astute compromises with the trade union leaders. Britain remained responsible for defence and foreign relations.

Although Britain was keen to be rid of its remaining colonies, it was unlikely that it would grant Singapore independence while there was any possibility of a communist government. For Malaya, which was still fighting a rump communist guerrilla force, the thought of an independent communist-dominated Singapore, 'a Cuba across the causeway', was highly unattractive.

In 1961 Tunku Abdul Rahman proposed a merger of Singapore and Malaya. To address the fear that the huge number of Singapore Chinese would tip the racial balance, his plan included the British Borneo territories

1941	1942	1944
Landing at Kota Bharu on Malaya's northeast coast, the Japanese make a lightning dash down the peninsula. Within a month they've taken Kuala Lumpur, and a month later they are at Singapore's doorstep.	The British suffer a humiliating defeat in February as they capitulate Singapore to the Japanese. The occupiers rename it Syonan (Light of the South) and treat all harshly until being defeated themselves in 1945.	A primarily Australian force, Z Special Unit, parachute into Sarawak's Kelabit Highlands and win over the natives. Armed with blowpipes and led by Australian commandos, this unlikely army scores several victories over the Japanese.

in the new nation. Malaysia was born in July 1963 with the fusing of Malaya, Singapore, Sabah and Sarawak.

The new nation immediately faced a diplomatic crisis. The Philippines broke off relations claiming that Sabah was part of its territory. More seriously, Indonesia laid claim to the whole of Borneo and decided the solution to this 'annexation' was 'Konfrontasi'. Indonesian armed forces crossed into Sabah and Sarawak from Kalimantan (Indonesian Borneo), and landings were made in Peninsular Malaysia and even Singapore. Although it was three years before Indonesia officially ended the confrontation, Malaysia was never seriously threatened.

Brunei had been planning to be part of Malaysia but at the eleventh hour Sultan Sri Muda Omar Ali Saifuddien III had second thoughts. He had inherited a fabulously rich country following the discovery of oil in 1929 and, having wrested control of Brunei's internal affairs back from the British, was now determined to use this vast wealth to modernise and develop the infrastructure of the nation rather than see the powers that be in KL take the spoils.

ETHNIC TENSIONS

With Brunei and its tipping balance of Malays out of the picture, the marriage between Singapore and Malaya was doomed from the start. Ethnic Chinese outnumbered Malays in Malaysia, and Singapore's Lee Kuan Yew, knowing this, called for a 'democratic Malaysian Malaysia'.

In August 1965 Tunku Abdul Rahman bowed to the inevitable and booted Singapore out of the federation, leaving Lee publicly sobbing. Within a couple of decades, though, the smile was firmly back on Lee's face. The little island with few natural resources other than its hard-working population had managed to claw its way from obscurity to world admiration for its rapid and successful industrialisation.

Meanwhile, back on the peninsula, the Malaysian government's attempts to develop a Malaysian identity through the Malay language and national education were stymied by Chinese resistance. The Chinese were fiercely protective of their schools, which taught in Mandarin, and were resistant to any moves that might threaten their continued existence.

By the mid-1960s Malays were calling for measures to alleviate the stranglehold that foreign and Chinese companies had on the economy. Malays owned less than 2.5% of corporate wealth and, as they had little capital and know-how, things were not likely to change. Something had to give.

The 1969 general elections were contentious, and racial sentiments were strong. For the first time PP lost its two-thirds majority in parliament. A celebration march by the opposition Democratic Action Party (DAP) and Gerakan (The People's Movement) party in Kuala Lumpur got out of hand,

Brunei's ties with its former colonial master remain strong: UK judges sit in the High Court and Court of Appeal and a British Army Gurkha battalion is permanently stationed in Seria.

Chronicle of Malaysia 1957–2007, edited by Philip Mathews, is a beautifully designed book showcasing 50 years of the country's history in news stories and pictures.

Dr Mahathir Mohamad's first book, *The Malay Dilemma*, in which he postulated that Malay backwardness was due to hereditary and cultural factors, was banned in 1970.

1946	1948	1951
Following public opposition to the proposed Malay Union, the United Malays National Organisation (UMNO) is formed on 1 March, signalling the rise of Malay nationalism and a desire for political independence from Britain.	The start of the period known as the Emergency, when the Malayan Communist Party (MCP) took to the jungles and began fighting a guerrilla war against the British that would last for 12 years.	Sir Henry Gurney, British high commissioner to Malaya, is assassinated by MCP rebels on the road to Fraser's Hill, a terrorist act that alienates many moderate Chinese from the party.

leading to full-scale riots. The government declared a state of emergency, but by the time things quietened down nearly 200 people, mostly Chinese, had been killed. Stunned by the savageness of the riots the government decided that racial harmony could be achieved only if there was economic parity between the races.

NEW ECONOMIC POLICY

In 1970 a 'New Economic Policy' set a target whereby 30% of Malaysia's corporate wealth had to be in the hands of indigenous Malays, or *bumiputra* ('princes of the land'), within 20 years. Malay companies were heavily favoured for government contracts; low-interest *bumiputra* loans were made easily available; and thousands of Malays were sent abroad on government scholarships.

PP invited opposition parties to join them and work from within. The expanded coalition was renamed the Barisan Nasional (BN; National Front), which continues to rule to this day.

To boost the *bumiputra* share in the corporate world, public listed companies were forced to relinquish 30% of their shares to *bumiputra* share-buyers – many of whom bought through *bumiputra* trust funds controlled by government institutions. By its target date of 1990 *bumiputra* corporate wealth had risen to 19%, 11% short of the original target. However, poverty had fallen from 49% to 15%, and a new Malay middle class had emerged.

THE ERA OF MAHATHIR

In 1981 Mahathir Mohamad, a charismatic and outspoken doctor from Langkawi, became prime minister. As a young man Mahathir had been expelled from UMNO for criticising the then prime minister and causing disunity in the party.

During his watch Malaysia's economy went into overdrive, growing from one based on commodities such as rubber to one firmly rooted in industry and manufacturing. Government monopolies were privatised, and heavy industries like steel manufacturing (a failure) and the Malaysian car industry (successful but heavily protected) were encouraged. Multinationals were successfully wooed to set up in Malaysia, and manufactured exports began to dominate the trade figures.

However, Mahathir also presided over a period during which the main media outlets became little more than government mouthpieces. He ended the practice of giving the sultans final assent on legislation, and the once proudly independent judiciary appeared to become subservient to government wishes, the most notorious case being that of Anwar Ibrahim (see opposite). He also permitted widespread use of the Internal Security Act (ISA; see opposite) to silence opposition leaders and social activists, most

Malaysian Politicians Say the Darndest Things Vols 1 & 2 (see www.kinibooks .com) by Amir Muhammad gathers together jaw-dropping statements uttered by the local pollies over the last three decades – stuff like 'If you come across a snake and a man from a certain ethnic community, you should hit the man first'.

1953

Formation of Parti Perikatan (Alliance Party) between UNMO, the Malayan Chinese Association (MCA) and Malayan Indian Congress (MIC). Two years later it wins 80% of the vote in Malaya's first national elections.

1957

On 31 August Merdeka (independence) is declared in Malaya; Tunku Abdul Rahman becomes first prime minister. A year later in Singapore the People's Action Party (PAP) led by Lee Kuan Yew is voted into government.

1963

In July the British Borneo territories of Sabah and Sarawak are combined with Singapore and Malaya to form Malaysia – a move that sparks confrontations with Indonesia and the Philippines.

TROUBLE WITH THE ISA

In July 2009 thousands of people took to the streets of Kuala Lumpur to protest against the Internal Security Act (ISA). This draconian law allows for the arrest and detention of any person without the need for trial under circumstances in which the government deems them to be a threat to national security. Ever since the ISA's enactment in 1960 those circumstances have been wide open to interpretation, with several opposition parties and Amnesty International (www.aimalaysia.org) claiming the law has been much abused by the ruling Barisan Nasional (BN) coalition.

Heading up the protest was opposition leader Anwar Ibrahim, who was jailed under the ISA for 22 months in the early 1970s for championing the cause of poor farmers. More recently, in September 2008, Democratic Action Party (DAP) MP Teresa Kok (http://teresakok.com) was jailed under the ISA for a week for allegedly requesting that a local mosque turn off its loudspeakers broadcasting the call to prayer. Shortly after, law minister Zaid Ibrahim resigned from the Cabinet in support of Kok and others arrested using the ISA.

Detainees, who can be held for 60 days incommunicado, are typically incarcerated at the Kamunting Detention Centre near Taiping, a prison that's become Malaysia's Guantánamo Bay. Apart from Ibrahim, opposition leaders Lim Kit Siang and Karpal Singh have both spent time as inmates there, as has the one-time student activist, journalist and playwright Hishamuddin Rais (http://tukartiub.blogspot.com in Bahasa Malaysia). Rais' play *Bilik Sulit*, about the police interrogation of an ISA detainee, is based on the testimonials of former detainees and has been performed around Malaysia. The tide may be turning on the ISA. Even before the July 2009 protests in which over 400 people were arrested, PM Najib had agreed to review the controversial law.

famously in 1987's Operation Lalang when 106 people were arrested and the publishing licences of several newspapers were revoked.

ECONOMIC & POLITICAL CRISIS

In 1997, after a decade of near constant 10% growth, Malaysia was dragged into the regional currency crisis. Characteristically, Mahathir railed at the West, blaming unscrupulous Western speculators for deliberately undermining the economies of the developing world for their personal gain. Ignoring the advice of the International Monetary Fund, he pegged the Malaysian ringgit to the US dollar, bailed out what were seen as crony companies, forced banks to merge and made it difficult for foreign investors to remove their money from Malaysia's stock exchange. Malaysia's subsequent recovery from the economic crisis, which was more rapid than that of many other Southeast Asian nations, further bolstered Mahathir's prestige.

At odds with Mahathir over how to deal with the economic crisis had been his deputy prime minister and heir apparent, Anwar Ibrahim. Their falling out was so severe that in September 1998 not only was Anwar sacked but he was also charged with corruption and sodomy. Many Malaysians, feeling that

One of Prime Minister Mahathir's favourite mega projects, the Multimedia Super Corridor (www.mscmalaysia.my) stretching from the Kuala Lumpur City Centre to the new KL International Airport at Sepang, was first announced in November 1995. It is still ongoing and in 2006 was extended to cover the whole Klang Valley area.

1965	**1967**	**1969**
In August, following Singapore's 1964 refusal to extend constitutional privileges to the Malays in Singapore and subsequent riots, Singapore is booted out of Malaysia. Lee Kuan Yew becomes Singapore's first prime minister.	Sultan Sri Muda Omar Ali Saifuddien III voluntarily abdicates in favour of his eldest son and the current ruler, the 29th in the unbroken royal Brunei line, Sultan Hassanal Bolkiah.	Following the general election, on 13 March race riots erupt in KL, killing 198. In response the government devises the New Economic Policy of positive discrimination for Malays.

Read about Anwar
Ibrahim in his own words
on the opposition politi-
cian's website – www
.anwaribrahim.com.

Anwar had been falsely arrested, took to the streets chanting Anwar's call for 'Reformasi'. The demonstrations were harshly quelled and in trials that were widely criticised as unfair by Amnesty International, Human Rights Watch and then US Vice President Al Gore, Anwar was sentenced to a total of 15 years' imprisonment. The international community rallied around Anwar, with Amnesty International proclaiming him a prisoner of conscience.

BN felt the impact in the following year's general elections when it suffered huge losses, particularly in the rural Malay areas. The gainers were the fundamentalist Islamic party PAS (Parti Islam se-Malaysia), which had vociferously supported Anwar, and a new political party, Keadilan (People's Justice Party), headed by Anwar's wife Wan Azizah.

THE IMPORTANCE OF ISLAM

Malaysia has two judicial
systems: the federal court
system rules on secular
matters while the *Syariah*
(Islamic) courts have
jurisdiction over Islamic
affairs.

Islam has always played a key role in Malaysian politics, but the rise of PAS, which aims to install an Islamic government in Malaysia, was certainly sparked by the Anwar crisis. More worrying has been the unearthing of radical Islamic groups that the Malaysian government accuses of using deviant teachings to spread militant Islam.

In an effort to outflank PAS's religious credentials, UMNO from its dominant position with the BN has been inching Malaysia closer to becoming more of a conservative Islamic state. Some local authorities have tried to ban or restrict dog ownership (conservative Muslims see dogs as unclean) and prosecute couples for holding hands or kissing in public. There was a move for policewomen, regardless of their religion, to wear the *tudong* (headscarf) at official parades and the whole crazy business over the banning, then unbanning, of the Bible in Iban. There have also been several high-profile demolitions of non-Muslim religious buildings (including a couple of 19th-century Hindu temples) for allegedly not having proper planning permission.

Lawyer and writer Karim
Raslan's *Journeys Through
Southeast Asia: Ceritalah 2*
is worth searching out for
its interesting views on
contemporary Malaysia.

Meanwhile, Brunei, by far the most Islamic nation in the region, has maintained something of a reputation as a model state since its independence in 1984. While the country has always been staunchly Muslim, full Islamic law (including the prohibition of alcohol) was only introduced in 1991. The mid-'90s saw the peak of Brunei's oil wealth – and the worst excesses of the sultan's brother Prince Jefri (see p587), whose consumption seriously damaged the national economy. Traditional and conservative it may be, but there's every sign that Brunei is a nation trying at least to keep in step with the changing demands of modernity (see p18).

ABDULLAH VS MAHATHIR

Prime Minister Mahathir's successor, Abdullah Badawi, was sworn into office in 2003 and went on to lead BN to a landslide victory in the following year's election. In stark contrast to his feisty predecessor, the pious Abdullah

1970	1974	1981
Brunei Town, the country's capital, is renamed Bandar Seri Begawan after the title accorded to the former Sultan Sri Muda Omar Ali Saifuddien III following his abdication.	Following the formation of the Barisan Nasional (BN) in 1973, this new coalition led by Tun Abdul Razak wins the Malaysian general election by a landslide.	The outspoken Dr Mahathir Mohamad becomes prime minister of Malaysia and introduces policies of 'Buy British Last' and 'Look East' in which the country strives to emulate Japan, South Korea and Taiwan.

immediately impressed voters by taking a nonconfrontational, consensus-seeking approach. He set up a royal commission to investigate corruption in the police force (its recommendations have yet to be implemented) and called time on several of the massively expensive mega projects that had been the hallmark of the Mahathir era, including a new bridge across the Straits of Johor to Singapore.

This decision was the straw that broke the doctor's back, causing the former PM to publicly lambaste his successor – an outburst that was largely ignored by the mainstream media. Mahathir turned to the internet to get his views across and raged against press censorship – which many found pretty rich given his own autocratic record while in power. At the same time the ever-outspoken Mahathir found himself at the sharp end of a lawsuit for defamation from Anwar Ibrahim, relating to the since-disproved charges of homosexuality against his former deputy. This case continues to trundle its way through the legal system at the same time as Anwar fights a second round of homosexuality charges.

BN ON THE ROPES

Released from jail in 2004, Anwar returned to national politics in August 2008 on winning the bi-election for the seat vacated by his wife. This was despite sodomy charges again being laid against the politician in June and his subsequent arrest in July. At the time of research, the case had yet to be tried, but appears so full of holes that Amnesty International, Human Rights Watch Asia and Al Gore have again thrown their support behind Anwar.

March 8: The Day Malaysia Woke Up by Kee Thuan Chye is the writer's personal reaction to the politically significant 2008 election and includes interviews with and contributions from a range of notable Malaysians including former law minister Zaid Ibrahim.

Malaysia Today (http:// mt.m2day.org/2008), the popular Malaysian news blog founded by Raja Petra Kamarudin, a former political detainee, receives 1.5 million hits per day.

MALAYSIA'S GOVERNMENT

Malaysia is made up of 13 states and three federal territories (Kuala Lumpur, Pulau Labuan and Putrajaya). Each state has an assembly and government headed by a chief minister (in Malay *Menteri Besar*). Nine of the 13 states have hereditary rulers (sultans), while the remaining four have appointed governors as do the federal territories. In a pre-established order, every five years one of the sultans takes his turn in the ceremonial position of Yang di-Pertuan Agong (king). Since December 2006 the king, who is also the head of state and leader of the Islamic faith, has been the sultan of Terengganu.

Malaysia's current prime minister is Najib Razak, who heads up the BN, a coalition of the United Malays National Organisation (UMNO) and 13 other parties. The official opposition Pakatan Rakyat (PR), its leader being Anwar Ibrahim, is a coalition between Parti Keadilan Rakyat (PKR), the (DAP) and Parti Islam se-Malaysia (PAS). They all sit in a two-house parliament, comprising a 70-member Senate (*Dewan Negara;* 26 members elected by the 13 state assemblies, 44 appointed by the king on the prime minister's recommendation) and a 222-member House of Representatives (*Dewan Rakyat;* elected from single-member districts). National and state elections are held every five years.

1982

Malaysia experiences the worst outbreak of dengue fever in its history, resulting in 35 deaths. The first edition of Lonely Planet's *Malaysia, Singapore & Brunei* is published.

1984

A somewhat reluctant Sultan Hassanal Bolkiah leads Brunei to complete independence from Britain. The country subsequently veers towards Islamic fundamentalism, introducing full Islamic law in 1991.

1990

After more than three decades in the job, Lee Kuan Yew steps down as prime minister of Singapore, handing over to Goh Chok Tong. Lee still keeps an eye on government in his role as 'Minister Mentor'.

Available on DVD (www
.dahuangpictures.com) is
Amir Muhammad's 2009
documentary *Malaysian
Gods*, which commemo-
rates the decade since
the Reformasi movement
began in 1998 with the
sacking of Anwar Ibrahim
as deputy PM.

As the leader of the Pakatan Rakyat (PR; People's Alliance), the opposition coalition that had made sweeping gains against BN in the March 2008
election, Anwar tried – and failed – to persuade some 30 BN MPs to switch
sides so PR could form a new government. Meanwhile, UMNO scrambled to
find a successor to Abdullah, who became the scapegoat for the party's election losses. However, his appointed successor, deputy PM Najib Razak, was
becoming embroiled in a murder and corruption scandal (see below).

Malaysians also took note when Zaid Ibrahim resigned as law minister
in September 2008, partly over the government's practice of detaining its
critics without trial (see the boxed text, p41). The *New York Times* reported
Zaid as saying 'The institutions of government have become so one-sided
it will take years to restore professionalism and integrity', and in criticism
of the economic privileges given to *bumiputra* that Malaysia had 'sacrificed
democracy for the supremacy of one race'.

It's a curious fact, though, that despite such positive discrimination policies being in place now for over 30 years, the position of *bumiputra* in the
economy remains more or less the same. A handful of well-connected
Malays have certainly benefited but the vast majority remain poor. One of

THE CURIOUS CASE OF THE MURDERED MONGOLIAN WOMAN

The annals of Malay history are packed with some pretty incredible tales but few can compete
with that of the murder of Altantuya Shaariibuu, a Mongolian woman who in October 2006 was
shot then blown up in the Malaysian jungle with military-grade explosives.

At a trial which started in June 2007, two Special Branch policemen were charged with Shaariibuu's
murder along with Adbul Razak, a high-profile political analyst and aid to Najib Razak, now prime
minister but at the time deputy PM and defence minister. Abdul, who admitted to an affair with
Shaariibuu, was subsequently acquitted of ordering the policemen to commit the murder.

At the same time Najib, under attack from opposition politicians and high-profile bloggers
(one of whom has since fled the country pending sedition and defamation trials relating to his
accusations), was forced to publicly deny any connection with the killing, stating that he had never
met Shaariibuu. The case became even murkier when the French newspaper *Liberation* published
an article alleging Shaariibuu had acted as an interpreter in a multimillion-dollar deal between
Malaysia and a French arms company over the sale of three submarines. When Shaariibuu had
learned of the commissions (the opposition parties call them bribes) involved in the deal she is
alleged to have tried to blackmail those involved, including Abdul. The article also claimed that
immediately prior to her death Shaariibuu had arrived in KL in the company of a shaman who
would cast a spell over Abdul if he didn't cooperate.

In a second trial the policemen were found guilty and sentenced to death in April 2009 – a
verdict that they are currently appealing against. Shaariibuu's father, who now looks after his
daughter's two young boys, is suing the policemen and the Malaysian government for RM100
million.

1998	2003	2004
Anwar Ibrahim's disagreements with PM Mahathir over how to deal with the Asian currency crisis, as well as his attempts to tackle government corruption, see him sacked, arrested, sent for trial and jailed.	Having announced his resignation the previous year, Dr Mahathir steps down as prime minister in favour of Abdullah Badawi. He remains very outspoken on national policies, recording his views in a blog (http://chedet.co.cc/chedetblog).	A month after the election in which BN takes 199 of 219 seats in the Lower House of parliament, Anwar Ibrahim sees his sodomy conviction overturned and is released from prison.

the few politicians openly advocating the scrapping of the *bumiputra* policy is Anwar Ibrahim.

A MORE RELAXED SINGAPORE

In 1990 Lee Kuan Yew retired, though he still holds the position of 'Minister Mentor'. Lee was followed as prime minister by Goh Chok Tong, who was just keeping the seat warm until Lee's eldest son Lee Hsien Loong was ready to take over the top spot in 2004. Lee Jnr continues to run the country efficiently, if a little less autocratically than his dad. Jailing political dissidents has been replaced with suing them for defamation, but freedom of speech and the press are still tightly controlled.

Conspicuous too has been the relaxation of attempts to control every aspect of Singaporean life. Sugarless chewing gum has been available for some years now and the legalisation of bar-top dancing and deregulation of liquor licensing has led to a boom in Singapore's bar and club scene – Singaporeans are free to blow their high disposable incomes on as many S$15 pints as they like, or indeed gamble it all away once the island's two 'integrated resorts' (ie casinos) open.

Perhaps Singapore's greatest contemporary challenge is to convince its youth – many of whom have enjoyed a lifetime of relative financial security – that continuing restrictions on freedom of speech are appropriate in an era of free global information and communication.

Lee Hsien Loong is the highest-paid head of government in the world, pulling in an annual salary of nearly S$3.8 million (around US$2.8 million) in 2008.

Lee's Law: How Singapore Crushes Dissent by Chris Lydgate is a disturbing and sad account of the rise and systematic destruction of Singapore's most successful opposition politician lawyer JB Jeyaretnam.

2007	2008	2009
As the country celebrates 50 years since independence it is also shaken by two anti-government rallies in November in which tens of thousands take to the streets of KL to protest.	In the March election BN retains power but suffers heavy defeats to the revitalised opposition coalition Pakatan Rakyat (PR); in August Anwar Ibrahim becomes PR leader following his re-election to parliament.	In April Najib Razak, son of Malaysia's second prime minister Tun Abdul Razak, succeeds Abdullah Badawi as prime minister. He announces a 1Malaysia concept with the slogan 'People First, Performance Now'.

The Culture

THE NATIONAL PSYCHE

Although Malaysia, Singapore and Brunei share many cultural similarities, their respective populations do behave differently.

Any discussion about Malaysians (that is, anyone born in Malaysia regardless of ethnic background) immediately leads into issues about the differences between the country's majority Malay population and the sizable Chinese and Indian minorities. The stereotypes of Malays being rural, traditional people and the Chinese being urban and capitalist still hold some credibility but are breaking down, as increasing numbers of rural Malays are attracted by the wealth and jobs of the cities.

The Malay surname is the child's father's first name. This is why Malaysians will use your given name after the Mr or Miss; to use your surname would be to address your father.

The Indians, the next-largest group, are divided by religion and linguistic background. A small, English-educated Indian elite has always played a prominent role in Malaysian society, and a significant merchant class exists, but a large percentage of Indians – imported as indentured labourers by the British – remain a poor working class.

For the most part, despite their differences, everyone gets along, partly because they have to, and also maybe because of the languid, generous spirit of the country – one fostered by a warm climate and a fruitful land. This friendliness and hospitality is what visitors see first and foremost. This said, ethnic tension in Malaysia does exist (see p49). There's also a national obsession with propriety, as evidenced, for example, in the fuss that broke over partially nude photos of the politician Elizabeth Wong leaked on the web in 2009 (see p54).

Status-conscious Malaysians love their honourable titles which include, in order of importance, Tun, Tan Sri, Datuk and Dato'.

Moving from the cities to the more rural, and thus Malay, parts of the country, Islamic culture comes more to the fore, particularly on the east coast of the peninsula. On the whole though you'll find rural Malaysians pretty relaxed and certainly less business-obsessed than their urban brothers. Over in Malaysian Borneo where no one ethnic group holds sway, the cooperation and friendliness factor noticeably rises. You'll be fascinated by the communal lifestyle of the tribes who still live in jungle longhouses – again, here hospitality is a key ingredient of the social mix.

The cultural differences between easy-going Malaysia and fast-paced Singapore are striking. At a simplistic level this can be put down to the ethnic mix being tilted in favour of the Chinese who tend to be more competitive and better educated. Singaporeans can be pushy, but on the whole you're likely to find their straightforward, no-nonsense approach refreshing after travelling in other parts of Asia.

Kiasu, a Hokkien word describing Singaporeans, literally means 'afraid to lose', but embraces a range of selfish and pushy behaviour, where the individual must not lose out at all costs.

Bruneians are exceedingly proud of their country and their sultan whom they adore. They tend to see Malaysia as being poor and corrupt, even though in terms of lifestyle Muslim Bruneians are not that different from their Malay brethren. Out in the longhouses of the country's tiny interior the approach to life is practically indistinguishable from that across the border in Sarawak.

LIFESTYLE

In Southeast Asian terms most Malaysians, Singaporeans and Bruneians lead relatively comfortable lives. Malaysians earn the lowest average monthly salaries of the three (the equivalent of around US$850, compared with US$2714 in Singapore and US$1040 in Brunei) but then the costs of living in Malaysia are not as high.

Increasing Westernisation and the pace of modern life are changing the cultures of the region, but traditional customs and religious values remain strong. Malays in all three countries generally follow Islam devoutly, as well as adhering to older spiritual beliefs and the village-based social system, known as adat. Many aspects of adat are a part of everyday life in the *kampung* (villages), and indeed even in urban areas.

The enduring appeal of the communal *kampung* spirit shouldn't be underestimated – many an urbanite from KL or Singapore hankers after it, despite the affluent Western-style living conditions they are privy to at home. In principle, villagers are of equal status, though a headman is appointed on the basis of his wealth, greater experience or spiritual knowledge. Traditionally the founder of the village was appointed village leader *(penghulu* or *ketua kampung)* and often members of the same family would also become leaders. A *penghulu* is usually a haji, one who has made the pilgrimage to Mecca.

The Muslim religious leader, the imam, holds a position of great importance in the community as the keeper of Islamic knowledge and the leader of prayer. The *pawang* and the *bomoh* are keepers of a spiritual knowledge that is part of an older tradition. Spirits, magic and such things as *keramat* (saint) worship still survive – despite such ideas being at odds with Islamic teachings. Many traditional beliefs and adat customs have adapted to Islam, rather than having been destroyed by it.

Religious customs and superstitions govern much of the Chinese community's home life, from the moment of birth (which is strictly recorded for astrological consultations later in life) to funerals (with many rites and rituals). Most Indians in the region originally come from South India, so the customs and festivals that are more important in the south, especially Tamil Nadu, are the most popular.

All three countries have dabbled, to different degrees, with social and economic policies to shape the lives of their citizens. In Malaysia, the New Economic Policy (NEP; see p40) was designed to promote the position of Malays – it's only been partially successful. In Singapore the government encouraged birth control in the 1970s and 1980s (to stem a booming population), but that plan worked too well and it now provides much encouragement, financial and otherwise (in particular, to educated Chinese Singaporeans) to have more children. In Brunei the Sultan has steered his nation towards Islamic fundamentalism, adopting a national ideology known as Melayu Islam Beraja (MIB).

Adat, with its roots in the region's Hindu period and earlier, is customary law that places great emphasis on collective rather than individual responsibility and on maintaining harmony.

A pawang possesses skills and knowledge about such things as the rice harvest, fishing and rain-making, and knows the rituals needed to ensure their success and appease the necessary spirits.

ECONOMY

The Malaysian economy has enjoyed steady growth since independence. Rubber, tin and timber are no longer the main export earners, and the manufacturing sector dominates, particularly electronics and electrical machinery, which account for nearly 50% of exports in 2007. Seduced by tax incentives, hamstrung trade unions and a very pro-business government,

---

THE POWER OF PETRONAS

Set up in 1974, the Malaysian national oil and gas company Petroliam Nasional Bhd is better known as Petronas (www.petronas.com.my). It has the sole right to develop oil and gas fields across the country, the bulk of which are off the coast of Terengganu, Sarawak and Sabah. In 2008 *Fortune* magazine ranked the company, which had revenues of over US$66,000 million as the 9th-most profitable in the world and the most profitable in Asia. The company contributes more than a third to the Malaysian government's annual budget and employs over 33,000 people worldwide in 103 subsidiaries.

multinationals have poured billions into the Malaysian economy, particularly during Mahathir's premiership (1981–2003).

In recent years there's been less political willingness to prop up national industries such as Proton (a car manufacturer). There's also been a push into the leisure and services industries, with a big success story being AirAsia, the budget airline (purchased from the government for RM1 in 2001 by entrepreneur Tony Fernandes) that has grown from six planes to a fleet of 110, carrying an expected 22 million passengers in 2009.

Malaysian politicians have been known to call in a *bomoh* – a traditional spiritual healer and spirit medium – during election campaigns to assist in their strategy and provide some foresight.

Through the promotion of free trade, and making itself attractive to foreign investors (tax breaks, few currency exchange restrictions and excellent infrastructure), Singapore has famously created a robust dynamic economy. However, manufacturing, for so long the engine room of Singapore's success, is in decline, due in large part to the rapid growth of China and India. In its place, the government is building up sectors like biomedical engineering and multimedia to ensure the country's future. Massive tourism investments such as the Integrated Resorts (p495) are also in the pipeline.

Brunei's economy is also strong, but the country is almost entirely reliant on oil and gas, resources that could run out any time between 2015 and 2030. Production is capped to try to ration the supply, and extensive new deep-sea explorations are planned. The government's attempts to diversify the economy, concentrating on agriculture, technology and banking, have met with some success but attracting the foreign investment necessary for large projects has proved tricky. Foreign labour is limited to protect the domestic workforce, around 60% of whom work in either the civil service or the armed forces.

POPULATION

As of September 2008 Malaysia had a population of 27.7 million people, over 85% of whom live on the peninsula. Malays, including indigenous groups,

THE PERANAKANS

Peranakan means 'half-caste' in Malay, which is exactly what the Peranakans are: descendants of Chinese immigrants who from the 16th century onwards settled in Singapore, Melaka and Penang and married Malay women.

The culture and language of the Peranakans is a fascinating melange of Chinese and Malay traditions. The Peranakans took the name and religion of their Chinese fathers, but the customs, language and dress of their Malay mothers. They also used the terms Straits-born or Straits Chinese to distinguish themselves from later arrivals from China.

Another name you may hear for these people is Baba-Nonyas, after the Peranakan words for men (baba) and women (nonya). The Peranakans were often wealthy traders who could afford to indulge their passion for sumptuous furnishings, jewellery and brocades. Their terrace houses were brightly painted, with patterned tiles embedded in the walls for extra decoration. When it came to the interior, Peranakan tastes favoured heavily carved and inlaid furniture.

Peranakan dress was similarly ornate. Women wore fabulously embroidered kasot manek (beaded slippers) and kebaya (blouses worn over a sarong), tied with beautiful kerasong (brooches), usually of fine filigree gold or silver. Men – who assumed Western dress in the 19th century, reflecting their wealth and contacts with the British – saved their finery for important occasions such as the wedding ceremony, a highly stylised and intricate ritual dictated by adat (Malay customary law).

The Peranakan patois is a Malay dialect but one containing many Hokkien words – so much so that it is largely unintelligible to a Malay speaker. The Peranakans also included words and expressions of English and French, and occasionally practised a form of backward Malay by reversing the syllables.

TALKING THE TALK: THE REGION'S MANY LANGUAGES

As former British colonies Malaysia, Singapore and Brunei are all fantastic countries to visit for English speakers, but linguists will be pleased to tackle the region's multitude of other languages. Malaysia's national language is Bahasa Malaysia. This is often a cause of confusion for travellers, who logically give a literal translation to the two words and call it the 'Malaysian language'. In fact you cannot speak 'Malaysian'; the language is Malay.

Other languages commonly spoken in the region include Tamil, Hokkien, Cantonese and Mandarin, but there are also Chinese dialects, various other Indian and Orang Asli languages, and even, in Melaka, a form of 16th-century Portuguese known as Cristang. All Malaysians speak Malay, and many are fluent in at least two other languages – a humbling thought for those of us who only speak English!

One final thing: you may be slightly confused by the English you do hear – both Malaysia and Singapore have developed their own unique way with the language known respectively as Manglish and Singlish (see p607).

---

make up around 65% of the population, Chinese 26%, Indians 8% and others make up the remaining 1%.

Singapore has a population of 4.8 million, including foreign residents. Chinese are the largest ethnic group (75.2%) followed by Malays (13.6%), Indians (8.8%) and 2.4% from other races.

Brunei's population is 390,000, with Malays and some other indigenous people accounting for around 67%; the Chinese make up 11% of the total; Iban, Dayak and Kelabit people about 6%; the rest are migrant workers and expats.

MULTICULTURALISM

From the ashes of Malaysia's interracial riots of 1969, when distrust between the Malays and Chinese peaked, the country has managed to forge a more tolerant, multicultural society. Though ethnic loyalties remain strong, the emergence of a single 'Malaysian' identity is now a much-discussed and lauded concept, even if it is far from being actually realised.

The government's *bumiputra* policy (see p40) has increased Malay involvement in the economy, albeit largely for an elite. This has helped defuse Malay fears and resentment of Chinese economic dominance, but at the expense of Chinese or Indian Malaysians being discriminated against by government policy. The reality is that the different communities coexist rather than mingle, intermarriage being rare and education still largely split along ethnic lines.

Singaporean government policy has always promoted Singapore as a multicultural nation in which Chinese, Indians and Malays can live in equality and harmony while maintaining their distinct cultural identities. There are imbalances in the distribution of wealth and power among the racial groups, but on the whole multiculturalism seems to work much better in small-scale Singapore than it does in Malaysia.

Similarly Brunei's small scale (not to mention great wealth) has allowed all its citizens, some 30% of whom are not Muslim, to find common goals and live together harmoniously in a state run according to Islamic laws.

MEDIA

Few people are under any illusions about the freedom of the press in the region to report on what they like, how they like. The authorities in Singapore and Brunei keep a tight leash on all media outlets, the Singaporean government going as far as to ban political comment on the internet and in blogs during the 2006 election campaign.

CRUSADING JOURNALIST: STEVEN GAN

In 1999, Steven Gan together with Pramesh Chandran set up the online newspaper **Malaysiakini** (www.malaysiakini.com). It was a gamble for Gan, Malaysiakini's editor, who took a big paycut from his position as a correspondent at Bangkok's *The Nation* newspaper to return to his native country – but one that has ultimately paid off since the site has bucked the trend for online media in being one of the few subscriptions-based services that makes money, averaging 300,000 unique visits a day and an income from subscriptions alone of RM2 million.

Why did you decide to go into online media? There was a lot happening at the time and a need for an alternative news source. Mahathir was still in power, the sacking of Anwar in '98 that precipitated the Reformasi movement was in full swing. A lot more people were interested in politics – but from the mainstream papers they weren't getting the news they wanted to read. It would have been impossible for us to get a print licence, but to launch online was no problem – all we needed was a regular business licence.

What have been your biggest stories? We've consistently reported on police brutality. Those stories eventually forced the government to organize a royal commission on the problem. Our coverage of the VK Lingam affair (when a video clip surfaced, allegedly showing the lawyer Lingam in the process of influencing the appointment of a Malaysian judge) also resulted in a royal commission inquiry.

Why haven't the authorities tried to shut you down? To Mahathir's credit, even though he made sure that the print media towed the government line, he was persuaded that for his pet multimedia supercorridor project to be successful, censorship of the internet was a no-go area. His successors have behaved likewise. We are currently fighting a lawsuit brought against us by the chief minister of Sarawak for our reports on illegal logging deals in his state, but we're confident of winning.

What are your plans for the future of Malaysiakini? We've moved into publishing books on current affairs and our online TV channel is proving a success. We would still like to put out a weekly print magazine, but that's not going to happen under the current government.

In Malaysia, since Mahathir's retirement as prime minister in 2003, there has been noticeably more freedom in what the media covers. The stringent laws haven't changed but the mind-set of journalists has and there's less self-censorship than in the past. In 2006 the government allowed the Qatar-based TV news station Al Jezeera to set up its Asian broadcasting centre in KL (in the Petronas Towers) and the practically unfettered expansion of newspapers and blogs on the web is further proof of a more liberal attitude.

The *Malaysian Insider* (www.themalaysian insider.com) is an online newspaper that offers a largely uncensored take on events and personalities in Malaysia.

RELIGION

Freedom of religion is guaranteed throughout this mainly Islamic region but you'll be hard pressed to find practicing Jews (see boxed text, opposite). Hinduism roots in the region long predate Islam, and the various Chinese religions are also strongly entrenched. Christianity has a presence, more so in Singapore than peninsula Malaysia where it has never been strong. In Malaysian Borneo many of the indigenous people have converted to Christianity, although others still follow their animist traditions.

The cartoonist and artist Lat is a national institution in Malaysia. His witty sketches turn up in the *New Straits Times* newspaper, in advertisements and in books, including *Kampung Boy*.

Islam

Most likely Islam came to Malaysia in the 14th century with the South Indian traders and was not of the more-orthodox Islamic tradition of Arabia. It was adopted peacefully by the coastal trading ports of Malaysia and Indonesia, absorbing rather than conquering existing beliefs. Islamic sultanates replaced Hindu kingdoms, though the Hindu concept of kings remained. The traditions of adat continued (see p47), but Islamic law dominated.

Malay ceremonies and beliefs still exhibit pre-Islamic traditions, but most Malays are ardent Muslims and to suggest otherwise to a Malay would cause great offence. With the rise of Islamic fundamentalism, the calls to introduce Islamic law and purify the practices of Islam have increased, but while the federal government of Malaysia is keen to espouse Muslim ideals, it is wary of religious extremism. *Syariah* (Islamic law) is the preserve of state governments, as is the establishment of Muslim courts of law, which since 1988 cannot be overruled by secular courts.

Chinese Religions

The Chinese in the region usually follow a mix of Buddhism, Confucianism and Taoism. Buddhism takes care of the afterlife, Confucianism looks after the political and moral aspects of life, and Taoism contributes animistic beliefs to teach people to maintain harmony with the universe. But to say that the Chinese have three religions is too simple a view of their traditional religious life. At the first level Chinese religion is animistic, with a belief in the innate vital energy in rocks, trees, rivers and springs. At the second level people from the distant past, both real and mythological, are worshipped as gods. Overlaid on this are popular Taoist, Mahayana Buddhist and Confucian beliefs.

On a day-to-day level most Chinese are much less concerned with the high-minded philosophies and asceticism of the Buddha, Confucius or Lao Zi than they are with the pursuit of worldly success, the appeasement of the dead and the spirits, and the seeking of knowledge about the future. Chinese religion incorporates elements of what Westerners might call 'superstition' – if you want your fortune told, for instance, you go to a temple. The other

---

ANTI-SEMITISM IN MALAYSIA   *Adam Karlin*

Me and a buddy had sank a few beers, but not nearly as many as the locals at the table next to us. One of them came over to our table and refilled our glasses, apropos of nothing – typical Malaysian friendliness. I smiled, gave a heartfelt *'terima kasih'* (thank you).

Then his stumbling drunk friend sat across from us and asked where we were from. My friend said, 'England.' I said, 'America.' He frowned, then said, loudly, 'America is controlled by the Jews.' My friend raised her eyebrows. 'I'm sorry?'

'The Jews! The Yahudi! Control everything!' he continued.

I smiled evenly and said, 'Have you ever met a Jew?'

'No.'

'Well, you have now.'

The drunk started yelling, sputtering and stumbling all at once, before finally getting up and shouting, 'You are not welcome in Malaysia!'

Muslim Malays are some of the friendliest people on earth, but anti-Semitism, ostensibly tied to criticism of Israel, is sadly widespread. If the roots of this anger were just directed at Israel, it would be somewhat understandable (if still one-sided). But with the exception of the (considerable) fact that Israeli passport holders are not permitted to enter Malaysia without clearance from the Ministry of Home Affairs, very few local Muslims differentiate between Israelis and Jews at large. Across the country, banners advocate boycotts of 'Yahudis' (Jews), not just Israel.

Former Prime Minister Mahathir made a 2003 speech to an Islamic leadership conference claiming the USA is a tool of Jewish overlords and once cancelled a planned tour of Malaysia by the New York Philharmonic because the program included work by a Jewish composer.

Not every, or even most, Malaysians would have acted like the (drunk) man above (who was held back by his friends, to their immense credit), but there is an entrenched voice in local media, particularly Muslim media, that is unfriendly to Jews. You may find more acceptance in majority Chinese and Hindu areas, but in the Malay heartland of Terengganu, Perlis, Kedah and Kelantan, Jewish travellers may find it best to keep their religion hidden.

THAIPUSAM

The most spectacular Hindu festival in Malaysia and Singapore is Thaipusam, a wild orgy of seemingly hideous body piercings. The festival happens every year in the Hindu month of Thai (January/February) and is celebrated with the most gusto at the Batu Caves (p131), just outside of Kuala Lumpur.

The greatest spectacle are the devotees who subject themselves to seemingly masochistic acts as fulfilment for answered prayers. Many of the devotees carry offerings of milk in *paal kudam* (milk pots) often connected to the skin by hooks. Even more striking are the *vel kavadi* – great cages of spikes that pierce the skin of the carrier and are decorated with peacock feathers, pictures of deities, and flowers. Some penitents go as far as piercing their tongues and cheeks with hooks, skewers and tridents.

The festival is the culmination of around a month of prayer, a vegetarian diet and other ritual preparations, such as abstinence from sex, or sleeping on a hard floor. While it looks excruciating, a trance-like state stops participants from feeling pain; later the wounds are treated with lemon juice and holy ash to prevent scarring. Like firewalking, only the truly faithful should attempt the ritual. It is said that insufficiently prepared devotees keep doctors especially busy over the Thaipusam festival period with skin lacerations, or by collapsing after the strenuous activities.

Originating in Tamil Nadu (but now banned in India), Thaipusam is also celebrated in Penang at the Nattukotai Chettiar Temple (p187) and the Waterfall Hilltop Temple (p187), and in Johor Bahru at the Sri Thandayuthabani Temple. Ipoh attracts a large number of devotees, who follow the procession from the Sri Mariamar Temple in Buntong to the Sri Subramaniar Temple in Gunung Cheroh. In Singapore, Hindus march from the Sri Srinivasa Perumal Temple (p500) on Serangoon Rd to the Chettiar Hindu Temple (p498).

thing to remember is that Chinese religion is polytheistic. Apart from the Buddha, Lao Zi and Confucius there are many divinities, such as house gods, and gods and goddesses for particular professions.

Hinduism

Hinduism in the region dates back at least 1500 years and there are Hindu influences in cultural traditions, such as *wayang kulit* (see p58) and the wedding ceremony. However, it is only in the last 100 years or so, following the influx of Indian contract labourers and settlers, that it has again become widely practised.

Silat, or *bersilat*, is a Malay martial art that originated in 15th-century Melaka. Today it is a highly refined and stylised activity, more akin to dance than self defence.

Hinduism has three basic practices: *puja* (worship), the cremation of the dead, and the rules and regulations of the caste system. Although still very strong in India, the caste system was never significant in Malaysia, mainly because the labourers brought here from India were mostly from the lower classes.

Hinduism has a vast pantheon of deities although the one omnipresent god usually has three physical representations: Brahma, the creator; Vishnu, the preserver; and Shiva, the destroyer or reproducer. All three gods are usually shown with four arms, but Brahma has the added advantage of four heads to represent his all-seeing presence.

Animism

Among the most popular Chinese deities (or *shen*) are Kuan Yin, the goddess of mercy and Toh Peh Kong, representing the spirit of pioneers and found only outside China.

The animist religions of Malaysia's indigenous peoples – collectively known as the Orang Asli (see p38) – are as diverse as the peoples themselves. While animism does not have a rigid system of tenets or codified beliefs, it can be said of animist peoples that they perceive natural phenomena to be animated by various spirits or deities, and a complex system of practices is used to propitiate these spirits.

Ancestor worship is also a common feature of animist societies and departed souls are considered to be intermediaries between this world and the next. Examples of elaborate burial rituals can still be found in some parts of Sarawak, where the remains of monolithic burial markers and funerary objects still dot the jungle around longhouses in the Kelabit Highlands (p458). However, most of these are no longer maintained and they're being rapidly swallowed up by the fast-growing jungle.

WOMEN IN MALAYSIA, SINGAPORE & BRUNEI

Women had great influence in pre-Islamic Malay society; there were female leaders and the descendants of the Sumatran Minangkabau in Negeri Sembilan still have a matriarchal society. The arrival of Islam weakened the position of women in Malaysia. Nonetheless, women were not cloistered or forced to wear full purdah as in the Middle East, and Malay women today still enjoy more freedom than their counterparts in many other Muslim societies.

As you travel throughout the region you'll see women taking part in all aspects of society, from politics (see boxed text, p54) and big business through to academia and family life. However, no less a figure than Marina Mahathir, prominent women's rights campaigner and daughter of the former prime minister, in 2006 compared the lot of Malaysia's Muslim women to that of blacks under apartheid in South Africa. In Mahathir's view her Muslim sisters are treated as second-class citizens held back by rules that don't apply to non-Muslim women.

Mahathir's outburst followed changes to Malaysia's Islamic family law that make it easier for Muslim men to take multiple wives, to divorce them and to take a share of their wives' property (similar laws already exist in Brunei, where the Sultan has two wives). Female politicians were prompted to vote for the changes by the women's ministry when they were apparently reassured the laws could be amended later.

In Chinese-dominated Singapore women traditionally played a small role in public life. However in recent years, women have started to take up key positions in government and industry.

In Islamic Brunei more women wear the *tudong* (headscarf) than in Malaysia. Many work and there are even one or two female politicians. Since 2002 female Bruneians have been able to legally transfer their nationality to their children, if the father is not Bruneian.

ARTS

Malaysia, Singapore and Brunei are not widely known for their arts, which is a shame as there is much creativity here – particularly in Malaysia and Singapore. Traditional art forms such as *wayang kulit* (shadow puppetry) and *mak yong* (dance and music performances) continue and stand alongside contemporary art, drama and film-making. There's a distinctive look to Malaysia's vernacular architecture as well as a daring and originality in modern constructions. The region is also producing authors who are gaining attention in the wider world.

Singapore has boosted spending on arts across the board with the aim of making the island state the arts hub of the region, in stark contrast to Malaysia where very little public money is assigned to the arts.

Literature

Writers of the calibre of W Somerset Maugham, Joseph Conrad and Noel Coward were inspired by the region in the early 20th century. The classic colonial expat experience is recounted by Anthony Burgess in *The Malayan Trilogy* written in the 1950s. In the late 1960s Paul Theroux lived in Singapore which, together with Malaysia, forms the backdrop to his novel *Saint Jack* and his short-story collection *The Consul's Wife*.

The Singapore Council of Women's Organisations (www.scwo.org.sg) seeks to unite various women's organisations throughout the island state.

Sisters in Islam (sisters inislam.org.my) is the website of a group of professional Malaysian Muslim women who refuse to be bullied by patriarchal interpretations of Islam.

The best source of information for what's currently going on in the Malaysian arts scene is Kakiseni (www.kakiseni .com).

A leading light of the Malaysian literary scene is the London-based Tash Aw (www.tash-aw.com/index2.html), whose debut novel, *The Harmony Silk Factory*, set deep in the heart of Peninsular Malaysia partly during WWII, won the 2005 Whitbread First Novel Award. His 2009 follow-up *Map of the Invisible World*, which focuses of Malaysia and Indonesia in the 1960s, is also garnering great reviews. Hot on Aw's heels are Tan Twan Eng (www .tantwaneng.com) whose literary debut *The Gift of Rain*, long-listed for the 2007 Man Booker Prize, is set in Penang just before and during WWII, and Preeta Samarasan (http://preetasamarasan.com) author of *Evening is the Whole Day*, a novel that focuses on the experiences of an Indian immigrant family living on the outskirts of Ipoh in the early 1980s.

The Singaporean National Arts Council (www.nac .gov.sg) sponsors a huge range of arts and cultural events across the state.

Foreign Bodies and *Mammon Inc* by Hwee Hwee Tan (www.geocities.com /hweehwee_tan) are among the best of contemporary Singaporean fiction. Tan pinpoints the peculiar dilemmas and contradictions facing Singaporean youth. Other celebrated novels by Singaporean writers include *Tigers in Paradise* by Philip Jeyaretnam, *Juniper Loa* by Lin Yutang, *Tangerine* by Colin Cheong and *Playing Madame Mao* by Lau Siew Mai. Short-story fans should read *Little Ironies* by Catherine Lim and *12 Best Singapore Stories* by Goh Sin Tub.

Architecture

Malaysia and Singapore have both made their mark in the world of modern architecture with two iconic buildings: KL's Petronas Towers (p95); and the Esplanade – Theatres on the Bay complex in Singapore (p495). Both have drawn attention to other interesting skyscrapers and civic buildings in the cities that take inspiration from both local culture and the environment –

CAMPAIGNING POLITICIAN: ELIZABETH WONG

A human rights and environmental activist for over 15 years, Elizabeth Wong (http://elizabeth wong.wordpress.com) was elected as a rep of the Pakatan Rakyat (People's Alliance) in the Selangor state election in March 2008. Almost a year later the 39-year-old single woman, Selangor's spokesperson for tourism and environmental issues, found herself at the centre of a media storm after partially naked photos of her, taken by a former lover, were leaked to the press and online. The readiness with which some people used this unwarranted intrusion into Wong's private life to question her character spoke volumes about Malaysia's conservative attitudes on sexual mores and the shady nature of local politics.

What made you stand for election? Because I have a vision of what politics could be like in Malaysia. It's about trying to make it less dirty. We don't have political discourse here; instead it's about smearing each other. No wonder politicians have such a bad reputation! But politics is what drives the economy and sets the social agenda. In particular I want to change young people's perceptions about politicians – that they can be interested in conserving the environment, making the world a safer place for women and so on.

What have your experiences since the election taught you? I've learnt a very important lesson in keeping focus and being patient. By the next election, those aged 45 and under will be the majority of voters – these people want to place their hopes in fresh blood, not those with tainted reputations who are only interested in playing the old style of politics.

What environmental initiatives are you working on? I'm in support of the Green Building Index (GBI) that's been developed by the Architects Association of Malaysia (PAM) and the Civil Engineers' Association (ACEM). If Selangor adopts the GBI as part of the building approvals' code then we will be the first state in Malaysia to do so.

And what about new tourism possibilities in Selangor? The Sultan is planning on opening up his palace in Klang (see p139) and there's also a new environmental interpretive centre out beside the mangroves along the Sungai Sepong, an area that's being labelled as the Sepong Gold Coast as resort development happens around Bagan Lallang beach.

for example the space-age design of Sir Norman Foster's Expo MRT station, which helps combat Singapore's tropical heat. Foster Partners is also responsible for Singapore's equally space-agey Supreme Court.

Vividly painted and handsomely proportioned, traditional wooden Malay houses are also perfectly adapted to the hot, humid conditions of the region. Built on stilts, with high, peaked roofs, they take advantage of even the slightest cooling breeze. Further ventilation is achieved by full-length windows, no internal partitions, and latticelike grilles in the walls. The layout of a traditional Malay house reflects Muslim sensibilities. There are separate areas for men and women, as well as distinct areas where guests of either sex may be entertained.

Although their numbers are dwindling, this type of house has not disappeared altogether. The best places to see examples are in the *kampung* of Peninsular Malaysia, particularly along the east coast in the states of Kelantan and Terengganu. Here you'll see that roofs are often tiled, showing a Thai and Cambodian influence. In KL there's a fantastic example in the grounds of Badan Warisan Malaysia (see p98) as well as the many old traditional wooden homes of the city's Kampung Baru district. Also check out the collection of vernacular houses from across Malaysia at Langkawi's Temple Tree (p223).

In Melaka, the Malay house has a distinctive tiled front stairway leading up to the front verandah – examples can be seen around Kampung Morten (p244). The Minangkabau-style houses found in Negeri Sembilan are the most distinctive of the *kampung* houses, with curved roofs resembling buffalo horns – the design is imported from Sumatra.

Few Malay-style houses have survived Singapore's rapid modernisation – the main place they remain is on Pulau Ubin (p504). Instead, the island state has some truly magnificent examples of Chinese shophouse architecture, particularly in Chinatown, Emerald Hill (off Orchard Rd) and around Katong. There are also the distinctive 'black and white' bungalows built during colonial times; find survivors lurking in the residential areas off Orchard Rd. Most noticeable of all, though, will be the rank upon rank of Housing Development Board (HDB) flats (ww.hdb.gov.sg) – close to a million units so far – that the vast majority of Singaporeans call home. Find out more about Singapore's varied mix of architecture at the Singapore City Gallery (p499).

Despite its oil wealth, there's little that's flashy in the architecture of Brunei's modest capital, Bandar Seri Begawan, where the city's skyline is dominated by the striking Omar Ali Saifuddien Mosque (p577). It's quite a different story, however, out at Jerudong, home to the Sultan's opulent palace and the eye-boggling Empire Hotel (p586).

Drama & Dance

Traditional dramatic forms remain a feature of Malaysia's performing arts scene, particularly on the more-Malay east coast of the country. It's here, in towns such as Kota Bharu and Kuala Terengganu, that you're most likely to see *wayang kulit* – shadow-puppet performances, similar to those of Java in Indonesia, which retell tales from the Hindu epic the *Ramayana*. It's a feat of endurance both for performer and audience since the shadow plays, which often take place at weddings or after the harvest, can last for many hours.

Interesting recent developments on the *wayang kulit* scene include Malaysian composer Yii Kah Hoe's collaboration *Bayang* with the Singapore Chinese Orchestra and the *wayang kulit* troupe Istamuzika performed in Singapore in November 2008. Fahmi Fadzil and Azmyl Yunor also perform their *wayang pasar* – humorous sketches all in Bahasa Malaysia but pretty understandable – at venues such as the bazaar held on KL's CapSquare (see p102) and have also created *wayang pasar* performances using light bulbs: for more info see http://projekway ang.blogspot.com.

To find out more about what people are reading in the region, check local publisher Silverfish (www.silverfishbooks .com); and Bibliobibuli (http://thebookaholic .blogspot.com), the blog of Sharon Bakar, a Malaysia-based British expat.

Peter Carey's *My Life as a Fake* is a great reworking of Frankenstein partly set in Malaysia and wonderfully evoking the sultry side of Kuala Lumpur.

KS Maniam's *The Return* (1994) shines a light on the Indian Malaysian experience, through his character's search for a home on returning from being educated abroad.

Traditional dances include *menora,* a dance-drama of Thai origin performed by an all-male cast dressed in grotesque masks; and the similar *mak yong,* where the participants are female. These performances often take place at Puja Ketek, Buddhist festivals held at temples near the Thai border in Kelantan. The *rodat* is a dance from Terengganu. Often performed at Malay weddings by professional dancers, the *joget* is an upbeat dance with Portuguese origins; in Melaka it's better known as *chakunchak.*

When it comes to contemporary drama and dance Singapore tends to have the edge. Apart from the blockbuster productions that regularly check into the Esplanade – Theatres on the Bay, there's a lot of interesting work by local theatre companies such as Action Theatre (www.action.org.sg), Wild Rice (www.wildrice.com.sg), Toy Factory Ensemble (www.toyfactory.com .sg) and the Singapore Repertory Theatre (www.srt. com.sg).

In Malaysia, head to the Kuala Lumpur Performing Arts Centre (KLPac; p122) to see the latest in Malaysian performing arts; a hit play here in 2009 was *Air Con* by Shannon Shah which picked up several gongs in the annual Cameronian Arts Awards. Also check out any productions by the performing arts collective Five Arts Centre (www.fivearts centre.org).

CHINESE OPERA

In Malaysia and Singapore *wayang* (Chinese opera) is derived from the Cantonese variety, which is seen as a more music hall mix of dialogue, music, song and dance. What the performances lack in literary nuance they make up for with garish costumes and the crashing music that follows the action. The scenery is virtually nonexistent, and props rarely consist of more than a table and chairs, but it is the action that is important.

Performances can go for an entire evening and it is usually easy for the uninitiated to follow the gist of the action. The acting is very stylised, and the music can be searing to Western ears, but seeing a performance is well worthwhile. Street performances are held during important festivals such as Chinese New Year (January/February), the Festival of the Hungry Ghosts (August/September) and the Festival of the Nine Emperor Gods (September/ October). Head to the Chinatown areas of KL and Singapore, or to Melaka or Penang's Georgetown for the best chance of seeing performances.

Music
TRADITIONAL & CLASSICAL

Percussion instruments figure large in traditional Malay music, including the *gendang* (drum), of which there are more than a dozen types, and a variety of gongs made from shells *(cerucap),* coconut shells *(raurau),* and bamboo *(kertuk* and *pertuang).* The *gamelan,* a traditional Indonesian gong orchestra, is found in the state of Kelantan, where a typical ensemble will comprise four different gongs, two xylophones and a large drum. All of these instruments are present in the *nobat* (traditional Malay orchestra) which only plays on ceremonial occasions.

Islamic and Chinese influences are felt in the music of *dondang sayang* (Chinese-influenced romantic songs accompanied by an orchestra), and *hadrah* Islamic chants, sometimes accompanied by dance and music.

The region has a trio of top-class traditional orchestras. In Malaysia, the Malaysian Philharmonic Orchestra plays at the Dewan Filharmonik Petronas (p121) in the Petronas Towers. In Singapore, catch the Singapore Symphony Orchestra (SSO, at the Esplanade – Theatres on the Bay) and the well-respected Singapore Chinese Orchestra which plays not only traditional and symphonic Chinese music but also Indian, Malay and Western pieces.

Malaysia's premier traditional dance troupe, an ensemble of 30 musicians and 60 dancers, is the Petronas Performing Art Group. Its repertoire includes over 100 ethnic dances from across the country.

Singapore's leading dance company, Singapore Dance Theatre (www .singaporedance theatre.com), puts on performances ranging from classical ballet to contemporary dance.

The Nrityalaya Aesthetics Society (www.nas.org .sg) runs Singapore's only full-time troop of Indian dancers and musicians, performs South Indian dance and music and holds an annual drama festival.

POP & ROCK

The Malaysian queen of pop remains the demure Siti Nurhaliza (http://siti zone.com). Other local artists to keep an ear out for include the alternative pop artist Faizal Tahir, runner up of *One in Million*, Malaysia's version of *Idol*; jazz artists Atilia (www.atilia.us) and Shelia Majid (www.sheilamajid .com); the surfer rock music band Kugiran (their *Surfin' with the Legend* CD sees them cover songs by Malaysian icon P Ramlee); songstress Adibah Noor (http://adibah-noor.com), who has a bit of an R&B thing going on; and Zainal Abidin (www.zainalabidin.com), well known on the world music circuit.

Singapore's small band scene includes groups such as Electrico and Ugly in the Morning (www.uglyinthemorning.org), both of whom have released several albums, and jazz artists of an international quality such as pianist Jeremy Montiero and his sister Clarissa. Corrinne May (www.corrinnemay .com) has had success in the US with her four acoustic pop albums. Many successful Singaporean singers are Mandarin or Cantonese exports to the Taiwanese and Hong Kong market. These include Kit Chan, Stefanie Sun, Tanya Chua and Ah Du.

Crafts

Across Malaysia you'll find many traditional crafts still practised. In Brunei, too, crafts (especially *jong sarat* weaving, silverwork and basketry) have traditionally been more important than fine arts.

BATIK

Originally an Indonesian craft, batik – produced by drawing or printing a pattern on fabric with wax and then dyeing the material – has made itself equally at home in Malaysia. You'll find locally produced batik across Malaysia, but Kelantan and Terengganu are its true homes. Batik can be made into clothes, homewares, or simply be created as works of art: the pioneer and master of this was Chuah Thean Teng (1912–2008; see www.yahongart.com).

BASKETRY

The baskets of the Iban, Kayan, Kenyah and Penan are among the most highly regarded in Borneo. Weaving material include rattan, bamboo, swamp nipah grass and pandanus palms. In addition to baskets, related techniques produce sleeping mats, seats and materials for shelters. While each ethnic group has certain distinctive patterns, hundreds or even thousands of years of trade and interaction has led to an intermixing of patterns. Some ethnic groups still produce baskets and other goods in the traditional way and these can be found in some of the markets of Malaysian Borneo. Others may be offered for sale upon a visit to a longhouse.

FABRICS & WEAVINGS

A speciality of Kelantan and Terengganu, *kain songket* is a hand-woven fabric with gold and silver threads through the material. Clothes made from this beautiful fabric are usually reserved for the most important festivals and occasions. *Mengkuang* is a far more prosaic form of weaving using pandanus leaves and strips of bamboo to make baskets, bags and mats.

Pua kumbu is a colourful weaving technique used in Malaysian Borneo to produce both everyday and ceremonial items decorated with a wide range of patterns. A special dyeing process known as ikat is used to produce the colours for *pua kumbu*. Ikat dyeing is performed while the threads of the pattern are already in place on the loom, giving rise to its English name, warp tie-dyeing.

Jit Murad's play *Spilled Gravy on Rice*, a big hit in Malaysia and Singapore, is about child abuse, homosexuality, drugs and Zionism, proving that English-language theatre can escape censorship.

See the blog *Wayang – Fascinating World of Chinese Opera* (http://wayangchineseopera .blogspot.com) for more on local performances.

Malaysia's Dama Orchestra (www.damaorchestra .com) combines modern and traditional Chinese instruments and plays songs that conjure up the smoky elegance of the 1920s and '30s.

MULTICULTURAL MUSICIAN: RESHMONU

Winner of three AIM awards – the Malaysian equivalent of the Grammies – in 2004 for his debut album *Monumental,* singer-songwriter Reshmonu's (www.reshmonu.com) 2009 release *Harapan* (Hope) blends local rhythms and instruments into R&B and Latin grooves such as samba and bossanova. Famous for his distinctive look of braided hair with flowing extensions, the multitalented 32-year-old has opened concerts for the likes of Alicia Keys and the Prodigy and featured on Lonely Planet's TV program *Six Degrees: Kuala Lumpur.*

How did you get into the music business? While I was studying for my degree in engineering I worked as a sound engineer in a club. I had the opportunity to meet many famous musicians and began to understand how the industry works. Singer Prema Lucas heard me sing and said I should be on the stage. I started collecting material which resulted in my fist album.

Your latest album isn't being sold in shops – what's the deal with that? The big labels have pretty much given up on promoting local artists in Malaysia and the record stores take around 50 per cent of the sales price. So I'm always trying new approaches to selling my music. You can buy my music online via www.rrecords.net, my own record label. *Harapan* is also packaged in a denim pouch designed by Key Ng, a favourite Malaysia fashion designer of mine, because it's not just about the music but the complete package.

On your previous albums you sing in English, but Harapan is all in Bahasa Malaysian. Why the change? Dude, I'm Malaysian – I'm not trying to get away from that fact. It was really about finding the right time to launch into the market with a Malay album. Besides, my music has always featured a mix of instruments – the *gendang,* a type of Malay drum; the Indian *tablas* and sitar; and the Chinese *erhu* – it reflects Malaysian society.

What other projects do you have going on? I've set up a recording studio and video production unit and am moving into representing other artists – any type of music, by anyone, from any part of the world – with a scheme to sell single music downloads to mobile phones with a major Malaysian telco.

And about the hair...? Yeah, everyone asks that. I had it done four years ago for a show and have kept it this way ever since – it's my one indulgence. It takes two hairdressers to work on it for four hours every two weeks.

KITES & PUPPETS

Songket Revolution (www.yayasantnz.org) is a beautifully illustrated book showcasing the history of *kain songket* and contemporary fashions using the traditional Malay handwoven fabric.

Crafts most associated with the predominantly Malay states of Kelantan, Terengganu, Kedah and Perlis are the making of traditional kites and *wayang kulit.* The *wau bulan* (moon kite) of Kelantan is a traditional paper and bamboo crescent-shaped kite that can be as large as 3m in length and breadth. Terengganu's *wau kucing* (cat kite) is the logo of Malaysia Airlines. Shadow puppets are made from buffalo hide in the shape of characters from epic Hindu legends.

SILVER & OTHER METALWORK

Kelantan is famed for its silversmiths, who work in a variety of ways and specialise in filigree and repoussé work. In the latter, designs are hammered through the silver from the underside. Kampung Sireh at Kota Bharu is a centre for silverwork. Brasswork is an equally traditional skill in Kuala Terengganu. Objects crafted out of pewter (an alloy of tin) are synonymous with Selangor where you'll find the Royal Selangor Pewter Factory (see p497) as well as other pewter manufacturers.

For more information on popular Malaysian crafts visit the website www .malaysiancraft.com.

WOODCARVING

The Orang Asli tribe of Hma' Meri, who live in a village on Pulau Carey (p140), off the coast of Selangor, are renowned woodcarving craftsmen. In Malaysian Borneo the Kenyah and Kayan peoples are also skilled woodcarvers. In these societies, *kelirieng* (burial columns of up to 2m in diameter and

10m in height, and entirely covered with detailed carvings) were used to bury the remains of headmen. Decaying remnants of *kelirieng* are still uncovered in the rainforest of Sarawak, and an example can be seen in Kuching Municipal Park. Less formidable, but equally beautiful, the Kenyah and Kayan also produced smaller wooden hunting-charms and ornate wooden knife-hilts known as *parang ilang*.

Cinema

Yasmin Ahmad's multi-award-winning *Sepet* (2005), about a Chinese boy and Malay girl falling in love, cut across the country's race and language barriers and in turn upset many devout Malays, as did her follow-up *Gubra* (2006) which dared to take a sympathetic approach to prostitutes. Causing less of a stir was *Talentime* (2009), her film about the run-up to an inter-school performing-arts contest.

Amir Muhammad's work also pushes the boundaries on issues that the government won't allow to be discussed in the public arena. His movie *Lelaki Komunis Terakhir* (The Last Communist Man; 2006) was banned, along with his follow-up movie *Apa Khabar Orang Kampung* (Village People Radio Show; 2007); find out more about them at www.redfilms.com.my.

Muhammad's producer and a pioneer of the Malaysian new wave of directors is James Lee, whose best-known pictures are *Room to Let* (2002) and *Beautiful Washing Machine* (2004). Find out about and purchase some of these films and those of other local indie directors at www.dahuangpictures.com.

Singapore has never been a leading light in film production, but during the 1990s some local movies began to gain international attention, in particular Yonfan's *Bugis Street* and Eric Khoo's *Mee Pok Man,* both released in 1995. Khoo's *12 Storeys* (1997) and more recent *Be with Me* (2005) and *My Magic* (2008) have since featured in competition at Cannes. The last film was nominated for the prestigious Palm d'Or.

The commercially successful, but controversial Royston Tan (www.royston tan.com) continues his love/hate relationship with Singapore's censors. His first feature, *15*, had 27 scenes snipped. In response, he produced the hilarious short music video *Cut* (available on YouTube). His last two films, *881* and *12 Lotus* were Chinese-language features.

Visual Arts

Among the most interesting and internationally successful of contemporary Malaysian artists are Jalaini Abu Hassan ('Jai'), Wong Hoy Cheong, landscape painter Wong Perng Fey, and Yee I-Lann, first recipient of the Australian High Commission Kuala Lumpur residence program. Amron Omar focuses on *silat* (Malaysian martial arts) as a source of inspiration for his paintings – a couple are in KL's National Art Gallery (p103). The capital's commercial galleries (p122) also represent several of these artists and often produce many fine catalogues to support exhibitions.

In Singapore the visual-arts scene is also vibrant, with painting, sculpture and multimedia the vehicles of choice for dynamic explorations into the tensions between Western art practices and the perceived erosion of traditional values. Highly regarded local artists include Da Wu Tang, Vincent Leow, Jason Lim and Zulkifle Mahmod, all of whom took part in the 2007 Venice Biennale.

The Brunei Art Forum in Bandar Seri Begawan promotes local contemporary artists (mostly painters) such as Zakaria Bin Omar, Haji Padzil Haji Ahmad, Pengiran Mohd Roslan Pg Haji Bakar and Teck Kwang Swee, and fosters international links.

The king of Malaysian cinema in the 1950s was P Ramlee who acted in some 70 films in his lifetime and remains a national icon; a road is named after him in KL.

Tsai Ming Liang's *I Don't Want to Sleep Alone,* filmed entirely on location in KL, takes a starkly beautiful but glacially slow look at the tensions in Malaysia's multicultural society.

Your main chance to catch films made in the region is during April's Singapore International Film Festival (www .filmfest.org.sg).

Food & Drink Robyn Eckhardt

Centuries of trade, colonisation, and immigration have left their culinary mark on Malaysia, Singapore and Brunei in the form of cuisines so multi-faceted it would take months of non-stop grazing to truly grasp their breadth. Nowhere else in Asia are the elements of three great culinary traditions – those of China, India and the Malay archipelago – so intertwined. The result is dishes both starkly monocultural (think Chinese wonton noodles and the southern Indian rolled 'pancakes' called *dosa*) and confusingly – but delight-fully – multi-culti (*debal,* a Melakan Eurasian stew, marries European-origi-nated red wine vinegar, Indian black-mustard seeds, Chinese soy sauce and Malay candlenuts). In this region, where the choices are endless, gastronomic malaise is unlikely to be a problem. That's a blessing, but also a curse of sorts – so many dishes, so little time.

In the beautifully photo-graphed book *Inside the Southeast Asian Kitchen* local experts share their knowledge of ingredi-ents, cooking implements and techniques, along with authentic recipes.

FLAVOURS

Malaysia, Brunei and Singapore have similar populations, share a tropical climate and were all at one time home to important trading ports along the spice route. As a result their cuisines are characterised by comparable flavours and are built on a shared foundation of basic ingredients.

Chillies *(cili),* both fresh and dried, are a kitchen staple. (Chilli-phobes need not worry; the region boasts plenty of mild dishes too.) Capsicum stars in sambal, a dip cum relish; its many varieties incorporate ingredients ranging from dried shrimp to fruit and are served alongside humble soup noodles, lavish rice spreads and every meal in between. Chillies are the base of *rempah* (called *bumbu* in Brunei), a pounded paste also containing, at its most basic, garlic and shallots, which forms the foundation of curries, soups and stews.

Herbs and aromatics such as coriander, mint, *daun kesom* (polygonum, a peppery, slightly astringent leaf also known as laksa leaf), celery leaves (from the slender, jade-green Asian variety rather than thick-stemmed, mild-flavoured Western celery) *daun kunyit* (turmeric leaves), curry leaves, lemongrass and wild lime leaves impart a fresh liveliness to curries and noodle dishes. Fragrant pandan leaves are often called 'Southeast Asian vanilla' for the light, slightly sweet essence they lend to sweets. (Pandan is also a natural

---

CULINARY HIGHLIGHTS

Don't leave the region without trying the following:

- *ambuyat* – think of Brunei's sago mash as a blank palette upon which to paint the vibrant flavours of accompanying dishes
- *cendol* – shaved ice, fresh coconut milk, pandan 'pasta' and sweet, smoky palm sugar beat the heat deliciously
- *roti canai* – flaky, crispy griddled bread dipped in curry and dhal and accompanied by a mug of frothy *teh tarik* ('pulled' tea) is one of the world's best ways to wake up
- *char kway teow* – silky rice noodles, plump prawns, briny cockles, chewy Chinese sausage, crispy sprouts, fluffy egg, a hint of chilli – all kissed by the smoke of a red-hot wok. Need we say more?
- Hainanese chicken-rice – tender poached chicken accompanied by rice scented with stock and garlic and a trio of dipping sauces plain and spicy

deodoriser, so don't be surprised to see a bundle of leaves stashed beneath the rear window of your taxi).

Sourness is also an important facet of the region's cuisines. *Asam* (sour) curries and noodle dishes derive piquancy primarily from tamarind and *asam keping,* the flesh of a tart fruit related to the mangosteen that's sliced into thin coins and dried. Malay cooks also make sour soups and sambals with a tiny green fruit called *belimbing,* a relative of the star fruit. Both limes and calamansi, a cross between lime and Mandarin orange, are juiced for salads; slices are served with laksa and other noodle dishes.

Belacan (dried shrimp paste) embodies the Malaysian, Singaporean and Bruneian love of fishy flavours. A black, sticky-sweet version native to Penang, called *hae ko,* dresses vegetable and fruit salad *(rojak)* and is stirred into *asam* laksa, a sour fishy noodle dish, right before serving. Other well-loved condiments made from the fruits of the sea include *cincalok (cencalu* in Brunei), krill mixed with salt and sugar and left to ferment (it's often eaten with rice and eggs) and *budu,* a sludgy long-fermented anchovy sauce favoured by Malay cooks. These piscine condiments lend umami to many a sambal, dipping sauce and curry and, though certainly odiferous, can be addictive; after a few weeks of sampling you may find yourself wishing you could sneak a block of *belacan* past your home country's custom agents.

The region's wet markets devote whole sections to dried seafood, with some stalls specialising in *ikan bilis* – tiny dried anchovies that are deep-fried till crispy and incorporated into sambal or sprinkled atop noodle and rice dishes – and others displaying an array of salted dried fish. Shrimp too, are dried, then ground into *rempah,* fried with vegetables, or tossed into salads and even eaten out of hand as a snack. In Brunei sardines are smoked and then dried in the sun for *tahai,* an ingredient in curries.

No local kitchen is complete without sauces that were originally introduced to the region by the Chinese: soy sauce (and its sweetened cousin *kecap manis*), fermented salted bean paste *(taucu),* oyster sauce and hoisin sauce.

Curries and sweets are made *lemak* (fatty and rich) with coconut milk. Grated coconut is dry-fried, sometimes with dried chillies and other flavourings, to make *kerisik,* a garnish for rice, and is an ingredient in many *kuih* (sweets), where it's often paired with *gula Melaka,* a distinctive dark brown sugar made by boiling the sap collected from cut flower stalks of the coconut palm.

Many restaurants add a 10% service charge. If you see '++' at the bottom of your menu, add 15% for government taxes and service charge.

STAPLES
Rice & Noodles

The locals would be hard-pressed to choose between *nasi* (rice) and *mee* (noodles) – one or the other figures in almost every meal. *Nasi lemak,* an unofficial 'national dish' of Malaysia, is rice steamed with coconut water, and topped with *ikan bilis,* peanuts, sliced cucumber, sweet-hot sambal and half a hard-boiled egg (curry optional). Banana leaf rice – rice served on a banana leaf 'plate' with a choice of curries – is daily Indian fare. In Singapore, Hainanese chicken-rice, a plate of rice flavoured with garlic and broth, tender poached chicken, sliced cucumber and dipping sauces, assumes similar iconic status. Rice is boiled in water or stock to make porridge *(congee* or *bubur),* fried with chillies and shallots for *nasi goreng,* and packed into banana leaf–lined bamboo tubes, cooked, then sliced and doused with coconut-and-vegetable gravy for the Malay speciality *lontong.* Glutinous (sticky) rice – both white and black – is a common *kuih* ingredient; Malays mix glutinous rice with sugar and allow it to ferment for sweet-and-sour, slightly alcoholic *tapai,* which goes nicely with ice cream.

Rice flour, mixed with water and allowed to ferment, becomes the batter for Indian *idli*, steamed cakes to eat with dhal (stewed pulses), and *apam*, crispy-chewy pancakes cooked in special concave pans. Rice flour–based dough is transformed into sweet dumplings like *onde-onde*, coconut flake–dusted, pandan-hued balls hiding a filling of semi-liquid *gula Melaka*.

Many varieties of noodle are made from rice flour. Wide, flat *kway teow* are stir-fried with prawns, cockles, egg and bean sprouts for Malaysia's other 'national dish', the hawker speciality *char kway teow*, and stubby *loh see fun* (literally 'rat-tail noodles') are stewed in a claypot with dark soy sauce. *Meehoon* (or *beehoon*, rice vermicelli) are the noodle of choice for pork noodle soup. *Chee cheong fun* – steamed rice flour sheets – are sliced into strips and topped with curry or sweet brown and red chilli sauces.

When is a fruit not a fruit? When it's a young jackfruit *(nangka muda)*, which Malay cooks treat as a vegetable, stirring it into coconut milk–based curries.

Round yellow noodles are served in soup and stir-fried with curry leaves, bean sprouts and chilli sauce for the Muslim-Indian speciality *mee mamak*. A favourite Chinese dish anywhere in the region is *won ton mee* – wheat-and-egg vermicelli floated in clear meat broth with silky-skinned dumplings, a few leaves of Chinese mustard and sliced roast or barbecued pork.

A primary starch for Bruneians and some indigenous communities in the eastern Malaysian states of Sabah and Sarawak is sago flour, laboriously extracted from the trunk of a variety of palm tree. In Brunei, it's mixed with water and cooked to make *ambuyat* (or *ambulung*), a sticky whitish paste. Served by twisting around chopsticks or long-twined forks, *ambuyat* is usually dipped into *cacah*, a sambal *belacan* and tamarind-based sweet-and-tart sauce, and accompanied by boiled or smoked seafood and salads. Sago flour is also roasted with coconut and mixed with sugar to make *sagun*, a delicious 'dip' for mashed banana slices.

Seafood

Konemann's *Southeast Asian Specialties* provides an overview of Singaporean and Malaysian foods, detailing everything from Sabahan tribal fare to the art of cultivating mushrooms.

Lengthy coastlines and abundant rivers and estuaries mean that seafood forms much of the diet for many of the region's residents. *Ikan* (fish) is left whole, slathered and stuffed with *rempah*, and wrapped in banana leaves (or left naked) and cooked on the grill for *ikan bakar* (grilled fish) or rubbed with turmeric and deep-fried to accompany Indian rice meals. Cut into chunks or steaks, it's cooked in hot and sour stews or coconut curries fragrant with aromatic spices. Whole fish steamed with ginger and garlic is a Chinese favourite. The head and shoulders of large fish are prized; a Chinese cook might steam and serve it smothered in a garlic and *taucu*-based sauce, while an Indian would cook it in spicy and sour curry; Malaysians chop fish heads, deep-fry them, and serve them with *meehoon* in a fish and tomato broth redolent of ginger and rice wine, enriched with evaporated milk. *Sotong* (squid) is deep-fried, stirred into curries or griddle-grilled on a banana leaf with sambal. Shellfish is much adored; Bruneians boil *udang* (prawns) with lemongrass, tamarind and chillies; Singaporeans stir-fry crab with chillies or black pepper; and Malaysians insist that if it doesn't have fresh cockles it's not a real *char kway teow*.

Cradle of Flavor is James Oseland's ode to the Singaporean, Malaysian and Indonesian home-cooking the American food writer and editor fell in love with more than two decades ago.

Meat

Haram (forbidden) to Muslims, *babi* (pork) is the king of meats for Chinese; some hawkers even drizzle noodles with melted lard. Whether roasted till crispy-skinned *(char yoke)* or marinated and barbecued till sweetly charred *(char siew)*, the meat is eaten with rice, added to noodles, and stuffed into steamed and baked buns. Malaysian Hakka (a Chinese dialect group) are renowned for succulent, long-cooked pork dishes like *khaw yoke*, sliced belly seasoned with five spice, layered with sliced taro and steamed.

Chicken *(ayam)* is tremendously popular in Malaysia and Singapore, but more of a special occasion meat in Brunei (as is beef or buffalo). Malay eateries offer a variety of chicken curries, and the meat regularly turns up on skewers, grilled and served with peanut sauce for satay. Another oft-enjoyed fowl is *itik* (duck), roasted and served over rice, simmered in star anise–scented broth and eaten with yellow *mee*, or stewed with aromatics for a spicy Indian-Muslim curry.

Tough local beef *(daging)* is best cooked long and slowly, for dishes like coconut milk–based *rendang*. Chinese-style beef noodles feature tender chunks of beef and springy meatballs in a rich, mildly spiced broth lightened with pickled mustard. Indian Muslims do amazing things with mutton; it's worth searching out *sup kambing,* stewed mutton riblets (and other parts, if you wish) in a thick soup, flavoured with loads of aromatics and chillies that's eaten with sliced white bread.

Vegetables

Vegetable lovers will have a field day. Every rice-based Malay meal includes *ulam,* a selection of fresh and blanched vegetables – wing beans, cucumbers, okra, eggplant and the fresh legume *petai* (or stink bean, so-named for its strong garlicky taste) – and fresh herbs to eat on their own or dip into sambal. Indians cook cauliflower and leafy vegetables such as cabbage, spinach and roselle (sturdy leaves with an appealing sourness) with coconut milk and turmeric. Other greens – *daun ubi* (sweet potato leaves), *kangkong* (water spinach), Chinese broccoli and yellow-flowered mustard – are stir-fried with sambal *belacan* or garlic. The humble jicama is particularly versatile; it's sliced and added raw to *rojak;* grated, steamed, and rolled into *popiah* (soft spring rolls), and mashed, formed into a cake and topped with deep-fried shallots and chillies for Chinese *oh kuih*. Sweet corn is plentiful, sold by vendors grilled or off-the-cob and steamed, at almost every night market.

Tau (soy beans) are consumed in many forms. Soy-milk lovers can indulge in the freshest of the fresh at Chinese wet markets, where a vendor selling deep-fried *crullers* (long fried-doughnut sticks) for dipping is never far away. *Dou fu* (soft fresh bean curd), eaten plain or doused with syrup, makes a great light snack. *Yong tauhu* is a healthy Hakka favourite of firm bean curd and vegetables like okra and eggplant stuffed with ground fish paste and served with chilli sauce. *Fucuk,* which is the chewy skin that forms on the surface of boiling soy milk, is fried golden or eaten fresh in noodle dishes, and absorbent deep-fried *tauhu pok* (bean curd 'puffs') are added to noodles and stews. Malays often cook with *tempeh,* a fermented soy bean cake with a nutty flavour, stir-frying it with *kecap manis,* lemongrass and chillies, and stewing it with vegetables in mild coconut gravy.

Cakes & Desserts

The locals are passionate about sweets; vendors of cakes and pastries lie in wait on street corners, footpaths and in markets. Many *kuih* incorporate coconut, grated or in the form of milk, and palm sugar; among the tastiest are *ketayap,* rice flour 'pancakes' rolled around a mix of the two, and *putu piring* (steamed rice flour 'flapjacks' filled with palm sugar and topped with coconut). Some *kuih* – such as *pulut panggang* (banana leaf–wrapped and grilled glutinous rice-and-coconut tubes filled with grated coconut, chopped dried chillies and dried shrimp) combine sweet and savoury flavours to fantastic effect.

Tong sui (the Chinese name for 'sweet soups'), such as sweet potato and sago pearls in a coconut milk-based broth, are reviving snacks. Perhaps the region's most beloved dessert is *cendol,* a heat-beating mound of shaved ice and chewy mung-bean-flour 'pasta' doused with fresh coconut milk and palm sugar syrup. ABC (for *ais batu campur* or 'mixed ice'), its more flamboyant

Malaysian English-language food 'zine *Flavours* produced three indispensable culinary guides: *Star Street Food Guide,* covering all of Malaysia, *Famous Street Food of Penang,* and the *Perak Good Food Guide.*

INTREPID EATING

Adventurous diners should seek out these specialties:

- *Perut ikan* – this Penang Nonya coconut-milk curry, made with fish innards, pineapple and fresh herbs, is spicy, sweet, sour and – yes – a little fishy.
- *Siat* – when stir-fried, plump sago grubs turn golden and crispy and boast a savoury fattiness recalling pork crackling.
- *Bak kut teh* – order this comforting stewed pork dish 'with everything' and be converted to porcine bits and bobs.
- *Sup torpedo* – Malay bull's penis soup is – like many 'challenging foods' – said to enhance sexual drive.
- *Kerabu beromak* – on Langkawi, coconut milk, chillies and lime juice dress this 'salad' of rubbery but appealingly briny sea-cucumber slices.

---

cousin, is a hillock of shaved ice garnished with fluorescent-coloured (and mostly artificial-tasting) syrups, jellies, red beans, palm seeds and sweet corn. Don't leave the region without investigating the colourful sub-continental *mithai* (sweets) stacked in Little India shop windows; our favourite is creamy, buttery – and, yes, tooth-achingly sweet – milk *halva*.

Fruits

Almost every tropical fruit under the sun can be found at one time of the year or another. Watermelon, pineapple, papaya, crispy sweet-sour guava, and juicy rose apples are year-round treats. *Kedondong* (ambarilla, a small green sour fruit with a single spiky seed), make refreshing juice. Keep an eye out for *ciku*, tan oval fruits whose golden flesh tastes like a honey date. Lychees, rambutan and longan – variations on a white-fleshed, single-seed, juicy and sweetly perfumed theme – are much prized. Try to get past jackfruit's slightly off-putting musky odour, because its sweet flesh – particularly that of the orange-ish honey variety – hints at vanilla. Stinky durian is gag-inducing to some and manna from heaven to others.

DRINKS

Half the fun of taking breakfast in one of Singapore's or Malaysia's Little Indias is watching the tea *wallah* toss-pour an order of *teh tarik* ('pulled' tea) from one cup to the other. Locals love their leaves; tea is also brewed with ginger for *teh halia*, drunk hot or iced, with or without milk *(teh ais* or *teh-o ais)*, and soured with lime juice *(teh limau)*. For an especially rich cuppa head to an Indian cafe and ask for *teh susu kerbau*, hot tea with boiled fresh cow's milk. *Kopi* (coffee) is also extremely popular, and the inky, thick brew owes its distinctive colour and flavour to the fact that its beans are roasted with sugar. *Kopi* is served in Chinese coffee shops (ask for *kopi-o* if you don't want sweetened condensed milk in yours, *kopi gaw* if you want it especially strong, and *kopi bing* if you want it milky and iced) and is an excellent antidote to jet lag.

Caffeine-free alternatives include freshly squeezed or blended vegetable and fruit juices, sticky-sweet fresh sugar-cane juice (nice with a squeeze of calamansi), and *kelapa muda*, or young coconut water, drunk straight from the fruit with a straw. Other, more unusual drinks are *ee bee chui* (barley boiled with water, pandan leaf and rock sugar), *air mata kucing* (made with dried longan), and *cincau* or herbal grass jelly (if you ask for a 'Michael Jackson' yours will include a splash of soy milk). Chinese salted plums add an oddly refreshing dimension to sweetened lime juice, in *asam boi*.

Thanks to sky-high duties, alcohol is pricey in Singapore and Malaysia (and banned or, more accurately, limited to hotels and high-end restaurants in Brunei); for a cheap, boozy night out stick to locally brewed beers such as Tiger, Carlsberg and Guinness. Chinese stores stock a variety of less expensive and sometimes surprisingly palatable hard liquors.

NATIONAL & REGIONAL SPECIALITIES

For Brunei specialities see p584.

Malaysia

PENANG

This northwestern state is the region's gastronomic ground zero; KL residents have been known to make the four-hour drive for a single meal and hungry Singaporeans pack out hotels on weekends. Hawker food is a must. Other than *char kway teow*, don't-miss dishes include the laksa twins: *asam* (round rice noodles in a hot and sour fish gravy topped with slivered pineapple, cucumber, mint leaves and slightly astringent torch ginger flower) and *lemak* (with a coconut milk-based broth that's spicier and lighter than versions served in KL and Singapore). Search out also Hokkien *mee* (also known as prawn *mee*), which consists of rich pork and prawn stock with bean sprouts, sliced pork, shrimp and – if you order like a local – *meehoon* and yellow *mee* mixed.

Penang is home to *nasi kandar*, rice eaten with a variety of curries, a *mamak* (Indian Muslims, many of whom address their seniors with the term *mama*) speciality named after the *kandar* (shoulder pole) from which ambulant vendors once suspended their pots of rice and curry. *Mee goreng* (fried noodles) is served all over the region, but really finds its groove in the hands of Mamak wok jockeys, who make it smokier and spicier than elsewhere and often garnish their noodles with a mound of spicy sautéed squid.

Penang, along with Melaka and Singapore, is also known for its Nonya or Peranakan cuisine, a fusion of Chinese, Malay and Indian ingredients and cooking techniques born of intermarriage between Chinese immigrants and local women (*nonya* are the women descended from these marriages; their male counterparts are *baba*). Penang Nonya dishes, influenced by nearby Thailand, are spicier and tarter than those of Melaka and Singapore; examples are *kerabu beehoon*, rice vermicelli tossed with sambal and lime juice and garnished with fresh herbs, and *otak otak*, curried fish 'custard' steamed in a banana leaf.

PERLIS & KEDAH

Thai culinary influence extends to foods in Malaysia's west-coast states of Perlis and Kedah where fish sauce is as common a seasoning as *belacan*. Here, look for laksa *utara*, a lighter but still spicy and intensely fish-flavoured version of Penang's *asam* laksa. Further south is Ipoh, the mostly Chinese capital of Perak state and a town with a reputation for excellent eating. Pasta lovers rave over Ipoh's rice noodles, said to derive their exceptional silky smoothness from the town's water. Judge for yourself with the local version of Hainanese chicken – served with a side of barely blanched bean sprouts and noodles instead of rice – and *hor fun*, rice noodle soup with shredded chicken breast. Ipoh is also known for its 'white' coffee, made from beans roasted in butter or margarine; it's an exceptionally smooth brew, but be sure to order it at a bona fide old-style coffee shop or you're likely to end up with '3-in-1' coffee powder dissolved in hot water instead of the real thing.

KUALA LUMPUR & NEGERI SEMBILAN

Almost all of Malaysia's specialties can be found in KL, but two dishes in particular are more easily found here than elsewhere: *pan meen* (literally

Renowned Singaporean cook Irene Yeo never found time to write a cookbook. Luckily, her daughter has assembled 100 of her most scrumptious recipes into a slim volume called *Irene's Peranakan Recipes*.

The author of this chapter teams with a professional photographer to publish EatingAsia (http://eating asia.typepad.com), a food blog on Southeast Asian street foods, ingredients and culinary culture, focusing on Malaysia.

'board noodles'), thick and chewy wheat noodles tossed with dark soy and garnished with chopped pork, *ikan bilis,* and shredded cloud ear mushrooms; and *sang har meen* ('fresh sea noodles'), huge freshwater prawns in gravy flavoured with rice wine and prawn fat served over crispy noodles. Klang, a port city an hour south of KL, is home to *bak kut teh,* a truly comforting stew made with pork, garlic, dark soy sauce, and Chinese medicinal herbs; the dish is eaten with rice, Chinese *crullers* and pot after pot of tea (to dissolve the fat, or so locals say). Further south in Negeri Sembilan state, descendents of Minangkabau who immigrated from the Indonesian island of Sumatra hundreds of years ago dish up a mean *nasi padang* – rice accompanied by a parade of fiery curries, *gulai* (fish and vegetables cooked in mild coconut milk gravy), soups and sambals.

MELAKA

There's more Nonya delights to be had in Melaka – think *ayam pong teh* (chicken cooked with *taucu,* dark soy sauce and sugar) and *ikan cili garam* (fish curry) – as well as local specialties of indeterminate origin like satay *celup* (skewered meat, seafood, and vegetables cooked at the table in a tub of peanut-based sauce) and Hainanese chicken served with rice moulded into balls. Often overlooked here is Cristang cuisine, the edible result of intermarriage between Portuguese colonisers and local women and an intriguing blend of Chinese/Peranakan, Indian, Malay and, of course, European ingredients. Its standard bearer is *debal* (devil's curry), a chilli-laden stew flavoured with turmeric and mustard seeds and soured with wine vinegar. A few eateries in Melaka's small Portuguese settlement specialising in *ikan bakar* (grilled fish slathered with sambal) offer Cristang dishes; also check menus at Melaka's many Nonya eateries.

JOHOR

Johor state boasts two tasty Malay noodle specialties: *mee bandung,* yellow noodles topped with a zippy, tomatoey shrimp gravy, and *mee rebus,* the same type of noodles doused with a sweet-savoury sauce thickened with sweet potatoes. The state also has its own variation on the laksa theme, consisting of spaghetti in a thin spicy fish gravy topped with chopped fresh herbs. The small town of Muar is know for *otak otak,* which is nothing like the identically named Penang Nonya dish; here it takes the form of chilli-spiked fish 'sausage' wrapped in banana leaf and grilled.

KELANTAN & TERENGGANU

If you really want to explore Malay cuisine the best place to be is the peninsular east coast. Kelantan state's capital Kota Bahru boasts Malaysia's most beautiful wet market, as well as plenty of places to try specialties like *ayam percik* (chilli paste–marinated chicken, grilled and doused with coconut sauce) and visually arresting *nasi kerabu,* rice tinted blue with natural colouring

'Ketchup' is derived from the Hokkien word *ke-tsiap,* which is a fermented fish sauce brought by Chinese traders to Melaka, where it was encountered by Europeans.

Celine Marbeck's *Cuzinhia Cristang* weaves history and anecdotes with wonderful recipes to tell the story of this sadly disappearing Melakan Eurasian cuisine.

A DISH BY ANY OTHER NAME

In Singapore 'laksa' is a bowl of noodles in coconut curry soup; in Malaysia it could be one of several varieties of noodle. In Penang Hokkien *mee* is a spicy noodle soup with bean sprouts, pork and prawns, but elsewhere in Malaysia it's a mound of thick stir-fried noodles with pork and cabbage in a dark soy sauce. For Indians *apam* is a rice-flour pancake to eat with coconut-and-chilli chutney, while for Chinese it's a spongy griddled cake filled with ground peanuts and sugar. And while *otak otak* is a barbecue-charred, chilli-spiked fish sausage in southern Malaysia, up north on Penang it's a fish custard steamed in banana leaf.

obtained from dried pea flowers, topped with bean sprouts, a lively mixture of chopped herbs, *kerisik,* and sambal. *Kao yam,* a *nasi kerabu* variation, boasts rice coloured green with pandan leaves, tossed with *budu,* raw vegetables and shredded mackerel. The local congee is *nasi air,* a breakfast dish of beef-based rice soup enhanced with cardamom, cinnamon, and coriander seeds and loads of fresh herbs. *Laksam,* the Kelantanese take on laksa, combines fantastically toothsome wide, flat rice noodles doused with *budu*-spiked coconut milk and topped with bean sprouts and herbs. In Terengganu state, a vendor dishing up mounds of red rice signals *nasi dagang.* The slightly nut-flavoured grain is cooked with coconut water and eaten with fried chicken and sambal – essentially *nasi lemak,* Terengganu style. Graze the east coast long enough and you may develop a few cavities; local cooks excel at making all manner of *kuih* and even savoury dishes have a noticeably sweet edge.

SARAWAK & SABAH

Laksa is breakfast food in Sarawak, where residents wake up with spicy, coconut-rich curry soup packed with rice vermicelli, omelette strips, chicken and prawns (truth be told, Sarawak laksa is Malaysia's tastiest). Another popular noodle dish is *kolok mee,* a Hokkien creation of chewy noodles drizzled with lard oil and soy and topped with chopped and sliced barbecued pork. Sarawak's highlanders specialise in dishes cooked in bamboo, such as the chicken dish *ayam pansoh* (a special occasion dish of chicken wrapped in tapioca leaves and cooked with water inside a length of bamboo). Don't leave the area without purchasing some of Sarawak's famed highland rice as a souvenir.

Sabah is home to *midin* (also called 'Sabah veggie'), a sweet green stalk with a whiff of asparagus flavour that's fantastic stir-fried. If you're in Kota Kinabalu, consider splurging on a meal of bounty from the South China Sea, chosen by your own self from a fish tank and cooked to order at one of the city's many seafood restaurants. Two other piscine specialties deserve mention: *umai* (also called *hinava,* and found in Sarawak as well), raw fish seasoned simply with lime juice, coconut milk and chillies, and noodles made of fish paste, served in a magnificent seafood broth with fish balls and chunks of sea bass. For more about Sabah specialities see p350.

Singapore

Singapore's culinary landscape is a near replica of Malaysia's, but in miniature; much of what you eat in the former can be had in the latter and vice versa. Still, Singaporeans do lay special claim to a few dishes – such as crab stir-fried with black pepper and fried carrot cake (squares of radish-flour cake stir-fried with bean sprouts, chilli sauce and salted radish) – that just seem to taste best when prepared at one of the city-state's many squeaky-clean hawker stalls. *Kari kepala ikan* (fish-head curry) was allegedly invented by a Singaporean-Indian cook playing to the Chinese love of fish cheeks. Made with the head and shoulders of large fish such as red snapper or garoupa, the dish is a magnificent melange of fiery chillies, fragrant dry spices, tart tamarind, and unctuous coconut milk. Singaporeans love their *roti prata* (the equivalent of Malaysia's *roti canai*) for breakfast, and have their own version of laksa – called simply 'laksa' – noodles in a prawn and coconut milk–based, highly spiced soup.

If you're looking to splash out you've come to the right place; Singapore's high-end dining scene is second to none in Southeast Asia. Whether you're hankering for handmade papardelle, steak frites, sparklingly fresh sashimi or a molecular gastronomic morsel quick-frozen in liquid nitrogen and bedecked with foam, you'll find it in a posh restaurant there. The city-state's drinks scene is quite happening as well; there's even a restaurant that specialises in pairing cocktails with food.

The forum on makansutra .com is the go to for local recommendations on where to find the best edible everything in Singapore.

FESTIVALS & CELEBRATIONS

As might be expected of a people consumed with food and its pleasures, Singaporeans, Malaysians and Bruneians mark every special occasion with celebratory edibles.

In the weeks leading to Chinese New Year, friends, colleagues and families gather over endless banquets. Every table is graced with *yue sang* (*yee sang* or *yu sheng* – 'fresh fish'), a mound of grated raw vegetables, pickles, pomelo pieces and crispy fried dough pieces topped with sliced raw fish. Diners mix the dish together with their chopsticks, lifting the ingredients high while shouting '*Lo hei!*', Cantonese for 'tossing luck'. Other foods to keep an eye out for at this time of year are pineapple tarts, *nga ku* (deep-fried arrowroot slices, tastier than potato chips), and glutinous rice cakes wrapped in banana leaf *(ti kuih)* that are often sliced, layered with taro and sweet potato, and deep-fried.

During Ramadan special food markets swing into action in the late afternoons, offering a wide variety of Malay treats. As not all vendors are professionals, this is a good opportunity to try Malay foods cooked in home kitchens.

During Deepavali (Diwali), the Indian Festival of Lights, make your way to a Little India, where you'll find stalls selling textiles and household goods, but also special mithai such as *jalebi* (deep-fried fritters soaked in sugar syrup) made on the spot, and savoury snacks like *muruku* (crispy fried coils of curry leaf–studded dough).

The married duo behind website Chubby Hubby (www.chubbyhubby. net/blog) keep readers up-to-date on Singapore's evolving upscale dining scene, with a dash of hawker and *kopitiam* reviews thrown in for good measure.

WHERE TO EAT & DRINK

Many locals would argue that the best (and best-value) food is found at hawker stalls, and who are we to argue? Most of these dishes can't be found in restaurants and when they are, they're rarely as tasty, so hawker stall dining is a must if you really want to appreciate the region's cuisines in all their glory. To partake, simply head to a stand-alone streetside kitchen-on-wheels, coffee shop, or food court (hawker food in Malaysia and Brunei is perfectly safe to eat, but the squeamish may want to start slowly, in one of Singapore's sanitised hawker centres). Place your order with one or a number of different vendors, find a seat (shared tables are common), and pay for each dish as it's delivered. After you're seated you'll be approached by someone taking orders for drinks, which are also paid for separately.

Kopitiam generally refers to old-style, single-owner Chinese coffee shops. These simple fan-cooled establishments serve noodle and rice dishes, strong coffee and other drinks, and all-day breakfast fare like soft-boiled eggs and toast to eat with *kaya* (coconut jam).

Restoran (restaurant) applies to eateries ranging from casual, decades-old Chinese establishments to upscale establishments boasting international fare, slick decor and a full bar. Between the two extremes lie Chinese seafood restaurants where the main course can be chosen live from a tank, as well as the numerous cafes found in Malaysia's many shopping malls.

WESTERN CONNECTION

Don't be surprised to find chops and mushroom soup sharing space with *belacan* fried rice on Singaporean and Malaysian *kopitiam* menus. Introduced to the region by the British but popularised in the early 20th century by the Hainanese immigrants who worked as their cooks and later opened their own restaurants, Western classics like pork chops with roast potatoes and fish and chips are considered local comfort foods. The best versions, usually found in *kopitiam* that predate the end of colonisation, are deliciously authentic to origin.

MOTO ROTI SELLER: NYAMBAR

Motorcycles toting packaged roti (breads and buns), biscuits, sweets, and other edibles are a common sight on Malaysian and Singaporean roadways. We caught up with moto driver Nyambar at a roti depot on the outskirts of KL.

How old are you, and how long have you been a moto roti vendor? I'm 25. Been selling for more than six years.

How did you get your job? My father does the same thing. After I saved for a motorcycle he introduced me to the man who supplies us with roti.

What do you sell? And what's your most popular item? Everything. Breads, *kuih* (sweets), some fruit. *Minum* (drinks) from my cooler. Roti goes first, then fruit.

Do you have a fixed route? Of course. We all keep to one route. I go to building sites. Sometimes I sell to road workers too.

What time do you get off work? And when's your off day? When all is finished I go home. Sometimes I'm out all day, sometimes only seven hours. No regular off day, *lah!* Public holidays only, because there's no building on public holidays.

Consider grazing at one or more *pasar* (markets). Morning markets usually have Chinese-owned stalls selling coffee (a *crull*er maker will be nearby) and Indian-operated *teh tarik* stalls offering freshly griddled roti. Triangular *bungkus* (packages) piled in the middle of tables contain *nasi lemak*; help yourself and pay for what you eat. *Pasar malam* (night markets) are also good hunting grounds, where you'll find everything from laksa to fresh-fried sweet yeast donuts.

VEGETARIANS & VEGANS

Given the inclusion of shrimp paste and other seafood products in many dishes, vegetarians and vegans may find it difficult to negotiate their way around many a menu. Chinese vegetarian restaurants and hawker stalls are a safe bet (signage will include the words '*sayur sayuran*'); they're especially busy on the first and fifteenth of the lunar month, when many Buddhists adopt a vegetarian diet for 24 hours. Look also for Chinese stalls and eateries displaying rows of stainless steel pans and advertising 'economy rice'; some of these are pure veg every day. South Indian restaurants are another haven, for snacks like *idli* to eat with dhal, *dosa* (crispy pancakes sometimes filled with potato curry), and thali (full meals consisting of rice or bread with numerous small servings of curries and vegetables). Some offer vegetarian banana leaf rice meals and economy rice-like displays of varied 'meat' and 'fish' dishes made with gluten and soy.

EATING WITH KIDS

Those travelling with young ones will find the wide selection of dishes on offer at hawker centres and food courts to be the perfect way to satisfy fussy palates. If familiar flavours are in order, head to one of the many Western fast-food outlets that have cropped up in every corner of the region. The locals love kids and will go to lengths to make them happy so unless you're heading for the poshest white-tablecloth establishment in town your children are likely to be welcomed with open arms.

HABITS & CUSTOMS

To those of us used to 'three squares' it might seem as if Malaysians, Singaporeans and Bruneians never stop eating. In fact, five or six meals and snacks is more the order of the day than strict adherence to the breakfast-lunch-dinner trilogy. And except for maybe toast and soft-boiled eggs and dim sum, what's eaten for breakfast can often be eaten for dinner and vice versa.

'Laksa' is derived from 'laksha', the original Persian word for noodle. It's believed that Arab or Indian Muslim traders introduced pasta to Malaysia in the 13th century.

DINING DOS & DON'TS

If eating with your hands:

- Wash your hands first; in Malay restaurants use water from the 'teapot' on the table while holding your fingers over the tray.
- Use only your right hand, and scoop food up with your fingers.
- Serve yourself from the communal plate with utensils, never your fingers.

Don't make these mistakes:

- Don't offer alcohol or pork to Muslims (and don't mention pork to Muslims).
- Don't stick your chopsticks upright in a bowl of rice; it symbolises death to Chinese.

The first meal is often taken on the run, something quick like *nasi lemak*, *roti canai*, or toast and eggs. In fact, almost any hawker food can be purchased *ta pao* (to go); it's not unusual to see customers toting an order (or five) of noodles apportioned into separate bags of starch, soup and veggie. Come late morning a snack is in order – perhaps a *karipap* (deep-fried pastry filled with spiced meat) or a *kuih*. Lunch begins around 12.30pm, something to keep in mind if you plan to eat at a popular establishment.

The British left behind a strong attachment to afternoon tea, consumed here in the form of tea or coffee and a sweet or savoury snack such as *tong sui*, various Indian fritters, battered and fried slices of cassava, sweet potato, and banana and – of course – *kuih*. Mamak stalls and hawker areas see a jump in business a few hours after dinner as locals head out in search of a treat to tide them over until morning.

> When the Portuguese conquered Melaka with a fleet launched from Goa they brought along vindaloo, which morphed into the Cristang speciality *debal*.

Fork and spoon are the cutlery of choice, except in Western-oriented establishments or *kopitiam* serving chops and fish and chips, where you might get a knife too. Don't put the fork in your mouth, but use it to gently nudge food onto your spoon. Chinese noodles and dishes served in Chinese restaurants are usually eaten with chopsticks (though fork and spoon are available on request). Malays and Indians eat rice-based meals with their right hand only, using thumb to manoeuvre rice onto the balls of the fingers and then into the mouth. (This is easier done if you moisten your rice with curries and side dishes and mash the lot together.) Wash your hands before and after with water from the teapot-like container on the table (Malay eateries) or at a communal sink at the side or rear of the room. Napkins are a rarity so it's always a good idea to carry a pack of tissues.

> Friedchillies.com is a goldmine of unbiased information – in the form of a lively forum, focused articles and videos – on Malaysian food and eateries.

In some Chinese eateries you'll be given a basin of hot water containing saucers, chopsticks, bowls and cutlery. This is meant to allow for hygiene concerns; remove the items and dry them off or shake them dry.

EAT YOUR WORDS
Useful Phrases

These Malay phrases may help in off-the-beaten track eating adventures – at most places in the region English will be understood. For guidelines on pronunciation see p606.

Where's a ... ?	*... di mana?*
restaurant	*Kedai makan*
hawker centre	*Pusat penjaja*
Can I see the menu?	*Minta senarai makanan?*
I'd like ...	*Saya mau ...*
What's in this dish?	*Ini termasuk apa?*

Not too spicy, please.	*Kurang pedas.*
I like it hot and spicy!	*Saya suka pedas lagi!*
The bill/check, please.	*Minta bon.*
Thank you, that was delicious.	*Sedap sekali, terima kasih.*
I don't want any meat at all.	*Saya tak mau daging.*
I'm a vegetarian.	*Saya hanya makan sayuran.*

Food Glossary

achar	vegetable and/or fruit pickle
ais kacang	dessert of ice shavings topped with syrups, coconut milk, red beans, seeds and jelly
aloo gobi	Indian potato-and-cauliflower dish
ambuyat	whitish paste made from sago flour eaten with curries and side dishes
ayam	chicken
ayam goreng	fried chicken
bak chang	rice dumpling filled with savoury or sweet meat and wrapped in leaves
bak kut teh	pork ribs and parts stewed with garlic and Chinese medicinal herbs (Malaysia) or garlic and white pepper (Singapore)
belacan	fermented prawn paste
belacan kangkong	water convolvulus stir-fried in prawn paste
bhindi	okra (lady's fingers)
biryani	steamed basmati rice oven-baked with spices and meat, seafood or vegetables
brinjal	aubergine (eggplant)
carrot cake	firm radish cake cubed and stir-fried with egg, garlic, chilli, soy sauce, and bean sprouts; also known as *chye tow kway*
cendol	dessert of shaved ice and mung-bean-flour 'pasta' doused with coconut milk and liquid palm sugar
chapati	griddle-fried wholewheat bread
char kway teow	wide rice noodles stir-fried with cockles, prawns, Chinese sausage, eggs, bean sprouts, and soy and chilli sauces
char siew	sweet and sticky barbecued pork fillet
char yoke	crispy-skinned roasted pork fillet
chicken-rice	steamed chicken, served with rice boiled or steamed in chicken stock, slices of cucumber and a chilli-ginger sauce
chilli padi	extremely hot small chilli
choi sum	popular Chinese green vegetable, served steamed with oyster sauce
claypot rice	rice cooked in a clay pot with chicken, mushroom, Chinese sausage and soy sauce
congee	Chinese porridge
daun kunyit	turmeric leaf
daun pisang	banana leaf, often used as a plate in Malaysia
daun salam	leaves used much like bay leaves in cooking
dhal	dish of puréed lentils
dim sum	sweet and savoury minidishes served at breakfast and lunch; also known as *dian xin* or *yum cha*
dosa	large, light, crispy pancake
dow see	fermented, salted black beans
fish sauce	liquid made from fermented anchovies and salt
fish-head curry	head and 'shoulders' of large fish such as red snapper in curry sauce; also known as *kepala ikan*

gado gado	cold dish of bean sprouts, potatoes, long beans, bean curd, rice cakes and prawn crackers, topped with a spicy peanut sauce
galangal	ginger-like root used to flavour various dishes
garam masala	sweet, mild mixture of freshly ground spices
garoupa	white fish popular in Southeast Asia
ghee	clarified butter
gingko nut	meaty nut used in soups and desserts or roasted and chopped for sauces, salads and meat dishes
gula jawa	brown palm-sugar sold in thin blocks
halal	food prepared according to Muslim dietary laws
hoisin sauce	thick sweet-spicy sauce made from soya beans, red beans, sugar, flour, vinegar, salt, garlic, sesame, chillies and spices
Hokkien mee	yellow noodles fried with sliced meat, boiled squid, prawns and strips of fried egg; in Penang, hot and spicy prawn and pork noodle soup
idli	steamed rice cake
ikan asam	fried fish in sour tamarind curry
ikan bilis	small deep-fried anchovies
kangkong	water convolvulus; thick-stemmed type of spinach
kari ayam	curried chicken
kecap	soy sauce
keema	spicy minced meat
kepala ikan	fish head, usually in curry or grilled
kofta	minced-meat or vegetable ball
kopi-o	black coffee
korma	mild Indian curry with yoghurt sauce
kueh melayu	sweet pancakes filled with peanuts, raisins and sugar
kueh mueh	Malay cakes
kway teow	broad rice-noodles
laksa	noodles in a spicy coconut soup with bean sprouts, quail eggs, prawns, shredded chicken and dried bean curd; also called Nonya laksa to differentiate it from Penang laksa (or *asam* laksa), a version that has a prawn paste and tamarind-flavoured gravy
lassi	yoghurt-based drink
lombok	type of hot chilli
lontong	rice cakes in spicy coconut-milk gravy topped with grated coconut and, sometimes, bean curd and egg
lor mee	noodles with slices of meat, eggs and a dash of vinegar in a dark brown sauce
masala dosa	thin pancake rolled around spicy vegetables with *rasam* on the side
mee	noodles
mee goreng	fried noodles
mee pok	flat noodles made with egg and wheat
mee rebus	yellow noodles served in a thick sweetish sauce made from sweet potatoes and garnished with sliced hard-boiled eggs and green chillies
mee siam	white thin noodles in a sweet and sour gravy made with tamarind
mee soto	noodle soup with shredded chicken
murtabak	*roti canai* filled with pieces of mutton, chicken or vegetables
naan	tear-shaped leavened bread baked in a clay oven
nasi	rice
nasi biryani	saffron rice flavoured with spices and garnished with cashew nuts, almonds and raisins
nasi campur	buffet of curried meats, fish and vegetables, served with rice
nasi goreng	fried rice
nasi lemak	rice boiled in coconut milk, served with *ikan bilis*, peanuts and a curry dish

nasi padang	Malay rice and accompanying meat and vegetable dishes
pakora	vegetable fritter
pan meen	wide, thick wheat noodles tossed with dark soy and topped with ground pork, *ikan bilis* and shredded cloud ear mushrooms
pappadam	Indian cracker
phrik	chillies
pilau	rice fried in ghee and mixed with nuts, then cooked in stock
pisang goreng	banana fritter
popiah	similar to a spring roll, but not fried
pudina	mint sauce
raita	side dish of cucumber, yoghurt and mint
rasam	spicy soup
rendang	spicy coconut curry with beef or chicken
rijsttafel	literally 'rice table'; a buffet of Indonesian dishes
rogan josh	stewed mutton in a rich sauce
rojak	salad doused in a peanut-sauce dressing that may contain shrimp paste
roti canai	unleavened flaky bread cooked with ghee on a hotplate; eaten dipped in dhal or curry; also known as *paratha* or *roti prata*
saag	spicy chopped-spinach dish
sambal	sauce of chilli, onions and prawn paste that has been fried
sambal udang	hot curried prawns
sambar	fiery mixture of vegetables, lentils and split peas
samosa	pastry filled with vegetables or meat
santan	coconut milk
satay	pieces of chicken, beef or mutton that are skewered and grilled
Sichuan	region in south central China famous for its spicy cuisine
soto ayam	spicy chicken soup with vegetables and potatoes
steamboat	meat, seafood and vegetables cooked at the table by being dipped into a pot of boiling clear stock
tamarind	large bean from the tamarind tree with a brittle shell and a dark brown, sticky pulp; used for its sweet-sour taste
tandoori	Indian style of cooking in which marinated meat is baked in a clay oven
taro	vegetable with leaves like spinach, stalks like asparagus and a starchy root similar in size and taste to the potato
tauhu goreng	fried bean curd and bean sprouts in peanut sauce
teh kosong	tea without milk or sugar
teh tariek	tea made with evaporated milk, which is literally pulled or stretched *(tariek)* from one glass to another
teh-o	tea without milk
tikka	small pieces of meat or fish served off the bone and marinated in yoghurt before baking
tom yam	tomato-red hot-and-sour spicy seafood soup
umai	raw fish marinated and served with onions
won ton mee	soup dish with shredded chicken or braised beef
yong dou fu	bean curd stuffed with minced meat
you char kway	baton-shaped deep-fried *cruller* eaten for breakfast, as a snack, or with *bak kut teh* and congee/porridge
yu tiao	deep-fried pastry eaten for breakfast or as a dessert
yu yuan mian	fish-ball soup

Environment

THE LAND
Malaysia

Covering a total of 329,758 sq km, Malaysia consists of two distinct regions. Peninsular Malaysia is the long finger of land extending south from Asia as if pointing towards Indonesia and Australia. Much of the peninsula is covered by dense jungle, particularly its mountainous, thinly populated northern half. On the western side of the peninsula there is a long, fertile plain running down to the sea, while on the eastern side the mountains descend more steeply and the coast is fringed with sandy beaches.

The other part of the country, comprising more than 50% of its area, is Malaysian Borneo – the northern part of the island of Borneo (the larger, southern part is the Indonesian state of Kalimantan). Malaysian Borneo is divided into the states of Sarawak and Sabah, with Brunei a small enclave between them. Both states are covered by dense jungle, with many large river systems, particularly in Sarawak. Mt Kinabalu (4095m) in Sabah is Malaysia's highest mountain.

Singapore

Singapore consists of the main, low-lying Singapore island and 63 much smaller islands within its territorial waters. It is situated just above 1° north in latitude, a mere 137km north of the equator. Singapore island is 42km long and 23km wide; with the other islands, the republic has a total landmass of 700 sq km (and this is growing through land reclamation).

In the centre of Singapore island, Bukit Timah (162m) is the nation's highest point. This central area is an igneous outcrop, containing most of Singapore's remaining forest and open areas. The western part of the island is a sedimentary area of low-lying hills and valleys, while the southeast is mostly flat and sandy. The undeveloped northern coast and the offshore islands are home to some mangrove forest.

Brunei

The sultanate covers just 5765 sq km (the Brunei government–owned cattle farm in Australia is larger than this!). It has no mountain ranges or great rivers, and at its widest the country's larger, western part measures only 120km from side to side. White sandy beaches along the coast give way to low hills rising to around 300m in the interior. The capital, Bandar Seri Begawan, overlooks the estuary of the mangrove-fringed Sungai Brunei (Brunei River), which opens onto Brunei Bay and the separate, eastern part of the country, Temburong. This sparsely populated area of largely unspoilt rainforest consists of a coastal plain drained by Sungai Temburong and rises to a height of 1850m at Bukit Pagon, the highest peak in the country. Western Brunei is divided into the three administrative districts of Brunei-Muara, Tutong and Belait. Approximately 75% of Brunei retains its original forest cover.

WILDLIFE

Malaysia is one of the world's so-called 'mega-diversity' areas. The country's jungle, believed to be 130 million years old and according to government figures covering around 70% of the country, supports a staggering amount of life: around 14,500 species of flowering plant and tree, 210 species of mammal, 600 species of bird, 150 species of frog, 80 species of lizard and thousands of types of insect. Although vast areas of forest have been cleared,

Ria Tan's site Wild Singapore (www .wildsingapore.com) is a blog and a wonderful resource about wildlife and wildlife-related projects in the region.

Pulau Ubin and *Chek Jawa* by Chua Ee Kiam are illustrated with beautiful photographs by Kiam, a dentist who has become one of Singapore's most high-profile environmental activists.

WWF-Malaysia (wwf malaysia.org) is one of the country's leading conservation organisations, running more than 50 projects, from saving endangered species to protecting the natural environment.

some magnificent stands remain mostly protected by a nationwide system of reserves and parks (p78). With patience and some luck, you may encounter the following animals, birds and reptiles in their natural habitat.

Animals

APES & MONKEYS

Around 11,300 orang-utans are thought to live in the forests of Sabah and Sarawak, but their future is threatened by habitat loss; the population has declined by 40% in the last 20 years. Captive orang-utans can be viewed at Sabah's Sepilok Orang-Utan Rehabilitation Centre (p375), the Semenggoh Wildlife Rehabilitation Centre (p428) in Sarawak and the Singapore Zoo (p504).

The Orangutan Foundation (www.orangutan .org.uk) supports conservation projects in Malaysia.

More closely related to apes than monkeys, the tailless and shy gibbons live in the trees, where they feed on fruits such as figs. Their raucous hooting – one of the most distinctive sounds of the Malaysian jungle – helps gibbons establish territories and find mates. Several species inhabit large stands of forest in Peninsular Malaysia and in Borneo.

Malaysia has 10 species of monkey, divided into langurs and macaques. Langurs (leaf monkeys) are mostly tree-dwelling, while pugnacious macaques are the stocky, aggressive monkeys that solicit snacks from tourists at temples and nature reserves. If you are carrying food, watch out for daring raids and be wary of bites – remember these are wild animals and rabies is a potential hazard.

The proboscis monkey is a type of langur and is probably Malaysia's second-most-famous animal, after the orang-utan. The male is an improbable-looking creature with a pendulous nose and bulbous belly; females and youngsters are more daintily built, with quaint, upturned noses. Proboscis monkeys inhabit only the forests of Borneo, where they live almost entirely on leaves. The Sungai Kinabatangan (p379) in Sabah is the best place to look for these monkeys, although there are also colonies in Bako National Park (p423) in Sarawak, and in Brunei.

The pig-tailed macaque, with golden-brown fur and a tail that is merely a dangling stump, is sometimes trained to pick coconuts.

The beautiful silvered leaf monkey is a langur whose fur is frosted with grey tips; observe it at Taman Alam Kuala Selangor (p141) and at Bako National Park (p423).

CATS & CIVETS

In 2004 research proved that the Malayan Tiger – as depicted on the Malaysian coat of arms and only found on the Malay Peninsula – is considered a subspecies of the Indo-Chinese tiger. The exact population is unknown but is considered by the WWF to be around 500, the vast majority of which are found in the states of Pahang, Perak, Terengganu and Kelantan. Hunting and encroachments on their natural habitat by logging operations have put the species under threat.

In March 2009 a proposal to create a 40-hectare tiger park on Penang drew criticism from the Malaysian Conservation Alliance for Tigers, who pointed out that the island had no record of the animals ever having lived there and that the project would very likely undermine government commitments to protect jungle corridors in order to double the wild tiger population to 1000 by 2020.

Find out all about the Malayan Tiger at www .malayantiger.net, the website of the Malaysian Conversation Alliance for Tigers (MYCAT).

Species of leopard including the black panther and the rare clouded leopard are found in Malaysia, as well as smaller species of wild cats, such as the bay cat, a specialised fish-eater, and the leopard cat, which is a bit larger than a domestic cat but with spotted fur.

You may also spot various species of civet cat, a separate family of predators with vaguely catlike features but longer snouts and shaggier coats.

BATS

The Clouded Leopard Project (http://clouded leopard.org) has funded several conservation efforts on Malaysian Borneo for this beautiful animal that may be rarer than the Malayan tiger.

Malaysia has more than 100 species of bat, most of which are tiny, insectivorous (insect-eating) species that live in caves and under eaves and bark. Fruit bats (flying foxes) are only distantly related to insectivorous bats; unlike them they have well-developed eyes and do not navigate by echolocation. There are fruit bats in Taman Negara (p294) and Deer Cave in Gunung Mulu National Park (p452) in Sarawak, where several million insectivorous bats stream out at dusk.

BIRDS

There's excellent bird-watching within a day's travel of Kuala Lumpur; prime locations include Taman Negara (p294), Fraser's Hill (p134) and Taman Alam Kuala Selangor (p141), where you may spot the secretive mangrove pitta, the stately crested serpent eagle and various species of kingfisher.

The Kuala Gandah Elephant Conservation Centre (p303) is the place to learn more about the elephant's plight and see some of the magnificent animals.

Both Sabah and Sarawak have fantastic bird-watching, including some 38 species found nowhere else. Good locations include Gunung Mulu National Park (p452), Mt Kinabalu (p363), Sungai Kinabatangan (p379) and the Danum Valley (p384).

Species to keep an eye out for include brilliantly coloured pittas, trogons, jungle flycatchers, bulbuls, bat hawks, hornbills and the Bornean bristlehead.

In Singapore the Sungei Buloh Wetland Reserve (p505) is home to 140 species of bird.

LAST CHANCE TO SEE...

Habitat loss has placed several of the region's animals in serious danger of extinction. Apart from the orang-utan (p75), tiger (p75) and giant leatherback turtle (opposite), the following are among those most at risk:

- Asian elephant – In 2009 there was great excitement at the announcement that a population of 631 elephants had been found living in Taman Negara (p294). This doesn't detract from the fact that the elephant is highly endangered. Protecting elephants helps safeguard thousands of other species within its habitat since the animals create vital natural pathways by knocking over trees, allowing smaller species to feed, as well as dispersing plant seeds in its dung. However, due to habitat loss, elephants are forced to hunt for food in areas surrounding forests such as plantations, where they raid crops on a massive scale. This leads to them either being shot by farmers or simply dying of starvation.

- Dugong – Found off the coast of Sabah and in the area between Johor and Singapore, these rare herbivorous marine mammals can consume as much as 30kg of seagrasses a day. Their survival is, however, threatened by the destruction of the seagrass beds as well them getting caught up in fishing nets and being hunted.

- Pangolin – Also known as the scaly anteater, the pangolin feeds exclusively on ants and termites and is best known for its tactic of curling up into a ball to escape threats. Pangolin meat is considered a delicacy in the region and its scales are also a popular ingredient in Chinese medicine, causing a lucrative trade in smuggling the creatures out of Malaysia.

- Sumatran rhinoceros – These are found mainly in isolated areas of Sabah and Endau-Rompin National Park (p269) on the peninsula. In Sabah a 2005 report conducted by the WWF found evidence of just 13 of these animals. Since they need at least 10 sq km of rainforest in which to roam, their chance of survival is slim, especially given the rate at which such forest is disappearing. To find out about the project SOS Rhino: Borneo go to www.sosrhino.org/programs/index.php.

- Malayan Tapir – Deforestation is also endangering this extraordinary animal that looks like a cross between a wild pig and a hippo. Growing up to 2m in length and weighing some 300kg, they are herbivorous and are sometimes seen at the salt licks in the further reaches of Taman Negara (p294). For more information see www.tapirs.org.

DON'T DISTURB THE TURTLES

If you're fortunate enough to be around when a turtle is laying its eggs, take the following steps to ensure that the creature is disturbed as little as possible:

■ Stay at least 10m away from any turtle crawling up the beach.

■ Don't use torches (flashlights) or camera flashes.

■ Sit and wait patiently for the turtle to crawl to the top of the dunes – do not impede her. It may be many hours before she is ready to lay eggs.

■ Resist the temptation to take flash photos of hatchlings making their way to the ocean.

REPTILES

Some 250 species of reptile have been recorded, including 140 species of snake. Most snakes are inoffensive, but all should be treated with caution, because if you are bitten by a dangerous one you may find yourself far from help (see p604 for details of what to do if this happens).

Pythons are sometimes seen in national parks and one, the reticulated python, is reputed to grow to 10m in length. Several species of flying snake inhabit the rainforests; they don't literally fly, but glide from trees by extending a flap of loose skin along either side of their bodies. There are also 'flying' lizards and frogs.

The reptile you're most likely to see is the monitor lizard. These carrion-eaters are especially easy to spot on island beaches – Pulau Perhentian Besar (p319) is home to several monsters close to 2m in length. Although they look scary, they generally shy away from humans, unlike their close relative the Komodo dragon.

A Field Guide to the Mammals of Borneo by Junaidi Payne, Charles M Francis and Karen Phillipps and *Pocket Guide to the Birds of Borneo* are both excellent references for travelling naturalists.

TURTLES

Of the world's seven species of turtle, four are native to Malaysia. The hawksbill *(Eretmochelys imbricata)* and the green turtle *(Chelonia mydas)* both have nesting areas within Sabah's Turtle Islands National Park (p379).

Olive ridley *(Lepidochelys olivacea)* and giant leatherback *(Dermochelys coriacea)* turtles, together with the first two, nest on Peninsular Malaysia's east coast. Unfortunately, all four are currently endangered, with leatherback numbers having fallen a staggering 98% since the 1950s; sightings of them are now incredibly rare. It's believed the drop is the result of decades of accidental capture in drift nets, turtle-egg harvesting and marine pollution. Biologists estimate that around one turtle hatchling in every thousand survives the 35 to 50 years it takes to reach maturity; turtle populations simply can't survive years of near-complete egg harvest. See p316 for details of the Ma' Daerah Turtle Sanctuary and sign up for the WWF's Egg = Life campaign at www.saveturtles.my.

While the collection and sale of leatherback eggs have been banned since 1988, in coastal markets it's common to see hundreds of eggs of the smaller green, hawksbill and olive ridley turtles, all of which have seen a marked decline in their populations. It may seem like an uphill battle, but there are some things you can do to help protect these magnificent creatures, such as not buying turtle eggs, turtle meat or anything made from turtle shell.

Wild Malaysia: The Wildlife & Scenery of Peninsular Malaysia by Junaidi Payne and Gerald Cubitt is a lavishly illustrated, large-format coffee-table guide to Malaysian wildlife and habitats.

The turtle's egg-laying process is amazing. After crawling well up the beach, each female leatherback (who can weigh up to 750kg and reach up to 2m in length) digs a deep hole in the sand for her eggs. Into this cavity the turtle, with much huffing and puffing, lays between 50 and 140 eggs. Having covered them, she heads back towards the water. It all takes an enormous effort, and the turtle will pause to catch her breath several times. Back in the water, this heavy, ungainly creature glides off silently into the night.

Plants

The wet, tropical climate of this region produces an amazing range of flora, some unique to the area, such as certain species of orchid and pitcher plants as well as the parasitic rafflesia, which produces the world's largest flower, growing up to 1m across (see p432). The dense rainforest that once covered large swathes of both the peninsula and Borneo has been cleared to make way for vast plantations of oil palms (see below) and other cash crops – what's left is now usually preserved in national parks and other reserves.

Tropical Marine Life of Malaysia & Singapore, Tropical Birds of Malaysia & Singapore, Tropical Fruits of Malaysia & Singapore and *Tropical Plants of Malaysia & Singapore* are some of the titles in Periplus Editions' great series of field guides to the plants and animals of Malaysia.

A single hectare of rainforest (or dipterocarp forest) can support many species of tree, plus a vast diversity of other plants, including many thousands of species of orchid, fungi, fern and moss – some of them epiphytes (plants that grow on other plants). Other important vegetation types include mangroves, which fringe coasts and estuaries and provide nurseries for fish and crustaceans; the stunted rhododendron forests of Borneo's high peaks, which also support epiphytic communities of orchids and hanging lichens (beard moss); and the *kerangas* of Sarawak, which grows on dry, sandy soil and can support many types of pitcher plant.

NATIONAL PARKS & OTHER PROTECTED AREAS

The Malaysian and Bruneian jungles contain some of the world's oldest undisturbed areas of rainforest. It's estimated they've existed for about 100 million years, as they were largely unaffected by the far-reaching climatic changes brought on elsewhere by the Ice Age.

Fortunately, quite large areas of some of the best and most spectacular of these rainforests have been made into national parks, in which all commercial activities are banned. The British established the first national park in Malaysia in 1938 and it is now included in Taman Negara (p294), the crowning glory of Malaysia's network of national parks, which crosses the borders of Terengganu, Kelantan and Pahang. In addition to this and the 27 other national and state parks across the country (23 of them located in Malaysian Borneo), there are various government-protected reserves and sanctuaries for forests, birds, mammals and marine life.

Accommodation is not a problem when visiting most national parks. Various types are available, from hostel to chalet. Transport and accommodation operations are increasingly being handled by private tour companies, who require you to book in advance and pay a deposit.

THE PROBLEM OF PALM OIL

The oil palm *(Elaeis guineensis)*, a native of West Africa and introduced into Malaysia in the 1870s, is probably now the most common tree in Peninsular Malaysia. The country's first oil-palm plantation was established in 1917; today, according to the **Malaysian Palm Oil Council** (www.mpoc.org.my), Malaysia is the world's leading producer of palm oil, accounting for over 40% of global production. The oil is extracted from the orange-coloured fruit, which grows in bunches just below the fronds. It is used primarily for cooking, although it can also be refined into biodiesel – an alternative to fossil fuels.

For all the crops' benefits, there have been huge environmental consequences to the creation of vast plantations that have replaced the native jungle and previously logged forests; in 2003 Friends of the Earth reported that palm-oil production was responsible for 87% of deforestation in Malaysia. The use of polluting pesticides and fertilisers in palm-oil production also undermines the crop's eco credentials.

The **Palm Oil Action Group** (www.palmoilaction.org.au) is an Australian pressure group raising awareness about palm oil and the need to use alternatives. **Roundtable on Sustainable Palm Oil** (www.rspo.org) tries to look at the issue from all sides while seeking to develop and implement global standards. **Proforest** (www.proforest.net) has also been working with **Wild Asia** (www.wildasia.org) on the Stepwise Support Programme, designed to promote sustainability within the palm-oil industry.

MALAYSIA'S TOP 10 NATIONAL PARKS

Park	Features	Activities	Best time to visit	Page reference
Bako National Park	beaches, proboscis monkeys	coastline walks, trekking	May-Sep	p423
Batang Ai	primary forest crawling with wild orang-utan	trekking	year-round	p434
Endau-Rompin National Park	lowland forest, unique plants, Sumatran rhinos, waterfalls and rivers	trekking, wildlife-spotting	Apr-Sep	p269
Gunung Mulu	caves, the Pinnacles, Headhunters Trail	caving, trekking, mountain-climbing	May-Sep	p452
Kinabalu	Mt Kinabalu	mountain-climbing	May-Sep	p357
Niah	caves	caving, trekking	May-Sep	p450
Penang	meromictic lake, monkeys	trekking	Apr-Jul	p202
Perlis	Gua Wang Burma cave, stump-tailed macaques, Malaysia's only semideciduous forest	caving, trekking	Jun-Aug	p228
Taman Negara	canopy walkway, hides, jungle trails, rivers	trekking, wildlife-spotting, river trips	Apr-Sep	p294
Tun Sakaran	sand-fringed islands, technicolour reefs	snorkelling, diving	year-round	p388

Singapore's **National Parks Board** (Nparks; www.nparks.gov.sg) manages 10% of the island's total land area, which comprises over 50 major parks and four nature reserves, including Singapore Botanic Gardens (p501), Bukit Timah Nature Reserve (p505) and Sungei Buloh Wetland Reserve (p505).

For details of Brunei's national parks, see p574.

Marine Parks

Malaysia's marine parks range from inaccessible islands with no tourist facilities to tourist meccas like Pulau Tioman. In order to protect their fragile underwater environments, no potentially destructive activities like fishing or motorised water sports are allowed. This makes these parks ideal for activities such as snorkelling, diving or just lazing around on the beach. There is a RM5 entry fee for all marine parks, but its collection is inconsistent.

Some of the more accessible marine parks:

- Pulau Kapas (p315)
- Pulau Payar (p220)
- Pulau Perhentian (p319)
- Pulau Redang (p317)
- Pulau Tioman (p274)
- Seribuat Archipelago (p266)
- Tun Sakaran (p388)
- Tunku Abdul Rahman (p354)
- Turtle Islands (p379)

ENVIRONMENTAL ISSUES

Malaysia's government maintains that it is doing its best to balance out the benefits of economic development with environmental protection and conservation. Others, including a long list of wildlife and environmental-protection

The local Friends of the Earth organisation is Sahabat Alam Malaysia (SAM); check out its various campaigns on www .foe-malaysia.org.

The Encyclopaedia of Malaysia: The Environment edited by Sham Sani, one volume of an excellent illustrated series of encyclopaedias, covers all you may wish to know about Malaysia's environment.

agencies and pressure groups, beg to differ, pointing out how big business continues to have the ear of government when decision time rolls around.

In contrast, in Singapore strict laws control littering and waste emissions are policed vigilantly. The **Singapore Green Plan 2012** (www.mewr.gov.sg/sgp2012), a 10-year blueprint for environmental sustainability, was updated in 2006; it focuses on waste management, clean air, water supply and ecology. Though little of the island's original wilderness is left, growing interest in ecology has seen new bird sanctuaries and parkland areas created, with new parks in the Marina Bay development as well as a series of park connectors that link up numerous existing parks and gardens around the island.

For up-to-date news and information on environmental issues affecting Malaysian Borneo check out the website of Rengah Sarawak (Sarawak News; www.rengah.c2o.org).

However, massive government effort doesn't necessarily translate to environmental awareness on the ground level. Some locals still love their plastic bags when shopping and getting domestic helpers to wash their cars daily. Having said that, Singaporeans are encouraged to recycle but aren't provided with an easy means to do so (all waste in housing development board flats still go into one central bin).

With few roads and much of its tiny area covered by forest, car emissions are the least of Brunei's problems. However, like much of the region, it suffers the effects of smoke haze (see below) from Indonesia.

Deforestation

Malaysia's logging and palm-oil businesses provide hundreds of thousands of jobs, yet they also wreak untold ecological damage (see p78) and have caused the displacement of many tribal people and the consequent erosion of their unique cultures.

Regional Environmental Awareness Cameron Highlands (REACH; www.reach.org.my) has been working since 2001 to preserve, restore and maintain this region as an environmentally sustainable agricultural area and tourist resort within a permanent nature reserve.

There's a disparity between government figures and those of environmental groups, but it's probable that more than 60% of Peninsular Malaysia's rainforests have been logged, with similar figures applying to Malaysian Borneo. Government initiatives such as the National Forestry Policy have led to deforestation being reduced to 900 sq km a year, a third slower than previously. The aim is to reduce the timber harvest by 10% each year, but even this isn't sufficient to calm many critics who remain alarmed at the rate at which Malaysia's primary forests are disappearing.

Sustained campaigning seems to be producing results: the gazetting of the 117,500 hectare Royal Belum State Park in 2007 was a major victory for the Malaysian Nature Society, which continues to campaign for similar protection to be extended to the neighbouring Temengor Forest Reserve. In Sarawak and Sabah several national parks and reserves have recently been created or extended, such as the Maliau Basin Conservation Area and the Pulong Tau National Park. However, the effects of logging are still clearly being felt in the region, which now suffers unusually long floods during the wet season.

One way forward perhaps lies in Sarawak, ironically the state where Malaysia's primary forests are most under threat. Here Kuching is the base for the **Sarawak Biodiversity Centre** (www.sbc.org.my), an organisation that aims to assist drug companies in their search for valuable medical compounds

BEWARE THE HAZE

The region's environment faces an ongoing threat from the so-called 'haze' – the smoke from fires in the Indonesian states of Kalimantan and Sumatra. Most of these fires are set by Indonesian farmers and plantation companies in order to clear land for agricultural purposes. The haze is at its worst in Singapore and parts of Malaysia usually around March and September and October, just before the rainy season – check the web (such as Singapore's National Environment Agency site http://app2.nea.gov.sg/index.aspx) for up-to-date reports.

LAWYERING FOR NATURE: ANDREW SEBASTIAN

Established in 1940, the Malaysian Nature Society (MNS), the country's oldest and longest-running environmental NGO, with around 4000 members, is an advocate of strict ecotourism policies and environmental policies. It also runs the Taman Alam Kuala Selangor Nature Park (p141) and the Dark Cave at Batu Caves (p131). London-trained lawyer Andrew Sebastian is their head of communications.

How did you come to be involved with the MNS? I grew up at FRIM (p132), where my father worked for the forestry department, so that gave me a love of nature. I've now worked for the MNS for the past 12 years.

What's your major campaign at present? A campaign started by the MNS in 1993 resulted in the protection of 117,500 hectares of old-growth forest in the Royal Belum State Park (in Perak) in 2007. But the job is only partially done since the neighbouring area of Temengor is being logged as we speak – getting this 300,000-hectare area similarly protected will be our focus for the next year, since the logging affects large animals who are falling prey to poachers, not to mention the viability of hornbills – all 10 species that exist in Malaysia – who make their homes in the old trees. If they go, there goes your ecotourism opportunity.

And what else are you working on? We are keen to establish a code of conduct for ecotourism practitioners in Pulau Langkawi (p215), particularly those who take part in the feeding of sea eagles and Brahminy kites – there are reports of the birds being fed chicken entrails rather than their natural diet of fish and seafood, which is possibly having long-term detrimental effects. We're also concerned about the proposals to set up a tiger park on Penang. The island should instead be marketing itself to tourists for its unique culture and world heritage history and for its potentially beautiful beaches, many of which need to be cleaned up.

What have been among your successes? We've been instrumental in getting the government to realise that bird tourism is a big opportunity for the country by helping identify sites that are important so that they can be protected and developed sensitively – we're focusing on three main sites: Fraser's Hill, the Panum valley in Sabah and Taman Negara. We've also had some success in lobbying for the sustainable development of the marine park islands, in particular on Pulau Tioman, where our campaign against the proposed new airport has seen the project taken completely off the shelf.

Could the government be doing more? The national ecotourism master plan drawn up in the 1990s remains a guideline – it's a great idea but many of the suggestions need to be put into law if they're really going to work.

from the rainforest. If the multimillion-dollar cure for cancer or AIDS can be found in these forests, it might just be their partial saviour.

For more on what the government is doing in relation to forest management, see the websites of the forestry departments of **Peninsular Malaysia** (www.forestry.gov.my), **Sarawak** (www.forestry.sarawak.gov.my) and **Sabah** (www.forest.sabah.gov.my). For the alternative point of view, read William W Bevis's award-winning *Borneo Log: The Struggle for Sarawak's Forests,* an evocative narrative that starkly outlines the environmental and human impacts of the logging that goes on in Sarawak, and the website **What Rainforest?** (whatrainforest.com).

Ian Buchanan spent eight years creating the exquisite illustrations and text for *Fatimah's Kampung* (http://en.cap.org.my), a parable about how Malaysia is in the process of sacrificing nature and traditional values for economic development.

Overdevelopment

Wherever you go in Malaysia you're sure to see plenty of construction. Overdevelopment of land for commercial and residential use is taking a toll, not just on the environment.

Economically unnecessary and environmentally unsound dam-construction projects are top of the list of concerns, the most controversial being Sarawak's Bakun Dam (p443). Plagued by financing difficulties since its inception, the still-to-be-completed dam has so far forced up to 11,000 indigenous people from their homes. Such projects are indicative of how the land rights of indigenous peoples are consistently ignored in Malaysia. Particularly affected have been the nomadic Penan of Sarawak, who to some extent have resisted government moves to have them resettle.

On hillsides in Peninsular Malaysia, overdevelopment married to poor construction standards has caused several disastrous landslides, one of the most recent being in December 2008 in Bukit Antarabangsar when four people died as 14 luxury homes tumbled down. The collapse of a 12-storey building in Selangor in December 1993 killed 49 people. The government has toughened up construction codes, but development of such precariously sited facilities continues apace in the cooler highland areas within easy reach of KL, such as the Cameron Highlands.

The marina being constructed in Tekek on Pulau Tioman (p276) has aggravated environmentalists who argue it will damage coral reefs in the area. It has already forced a few hotel operations to close and at the time of writing was an ugly construction site. The proposed second (offshore) airstrip at Pulau Tioman has also drawn fire for similar reasons, although it appears this project may have been postponed.

Some 75% of Kelantan's coast is also under attack from erosion; in the worst cases the shoreline is retreating by up to 10m a year.

Outdoor Activities

For the active traveller Malaysia, Singapore and Brunei are top-class destinations. Nature lovers and rugged adventurers can undertake a wide range of treks, from simple strolls along marked paths to multi-day marathons practically hacking through virgin jungle. Thrillseekers can go rock-climbing, mountain-biking and white-water rafting or don masks and fins to explore the coral reefs and aquatic environments of many marine parks. More sedate activities include golf and bird-spotting.

The following highlights the main outdoor activities in Malaysia; see the Singapore (p492) and Brunei (p572) chapters for details of activities there.

BIRD-WATCHING

Malaysia's tropical jungles and islands are home to over 600 species of birds; see p76 for a brief overview. The principal twitching destinations are:

Cape Rachado Forest Reserve (p234)
Endau-Rompin National Park (p269)
Fraser's Hill (p134)
Gunung Gading National Park (p429)
Gunung Mulu National Park (p452)
Kenong Rimba State Park (p303)
Mt Kinabalu (p363)
Royal Belum State Park (p169)
Similajau National Park (p444)
Taman Negara (p294)

BOATING

If you just want to paddle around an ornamental lake that's easily achieved in KL (see p102 and p103). In Melaka boat cruises along the Melaka River (p246) are a popular diversion, as are the cruises across the lake in Putrajaya (p137), which in 2009 hosted its first international dragon boat race (www .putrajayadragonboat.com).

For more serious sailors the **Royal Langkawi Yacht Club** (☎ 04-966 4078; www .langkawiyachtclub.com) in Kuah (p216) is a useful starting point. The **Royal Selangor Yacht Club** (☎ 03-3168 6964; www.rsyc.com.my) at Pelabuhan Klang (p139) also offers a variety of courses for beginners through to more experienced sailors.

CAVING

Malaysia's limestone hills are riddled with caves (*gua*) to lure spelunkers. Some of these, such as the Batu Caves (p131), near KL, are easily accessible and can be visited with little special equipment or preparation, while others are strictly the terrain of the experienced caver.

The most challenging caves include Gua Charas (p288) and Gua Musang (p336), as well as those found in Taman Negara (p294) and Gunung Mulu National Park (p452).

CYCLING

Malaysia's excellent roads make it one of the best places in Southeast Asia for bike touring. Perhaps the most popular route is the one up the east coast of Peninsular Malaysia, with its relatively quiet roads. However, if you're fit and energetic, you may prefer the hillier regions of the peninsula's interior or Malaysian Borneo – ideal for mountain-biking. Attracting some of the world's top cyclists is **Le Tour De Langkawi** (www.ltdl.com.my), a week-long

The inaugural Standard Chartered KL Marathon (www.kl-marathon.com) took place in June 2009 and included a 5km fun run and half marathon as well as the full 42.195km race.

Malaysian Fishing Net (www.fishing.net.my) has some useful links for those who are interested in fishing through Malaysia.

race generally held in February, which despite its name actually follows a 1000km route around the peninsula stretching from the Genting Highlands to Melaka.

DIVING & SNORKELLING

Reasonable prices, an excellent variety of dive sites and easy access make Malaysia a great diving choice for both first-timers and old hands. The main centres include:

Pulau Perhentian (p320)
Pulau Redang (p317)
Pulau Tioman (p275)
Seribuat Archipelago (p266)
Semporna Archipelago (Sipadan in particular; p388)
Pulau Layang Layang (p369).

MTB Asia (www.mtbasia.com/Links/links1.htm) is a portal with links to several mountain-biking related sites covering both Peninsular Malaysia and Borneo.

Island-based boat dives are the most common, but a few areas, like Sabah's Pulau Sipadan (p388), have some cracking sites right off the beach. You may also come across live-aboard boats to get you to more remote spots.

The standards of diving facilities in Malaysia are generally quite high and equipment rental is widely available. Most places offer the universally recognised Professional Association of Diving Instructors (PADI) certification. While it is possible simply to show up and dive at some of the larger dive centres like Pulau Tioman, it's a good idea to make arrangements in advance, if only to avoid waiting a day or two before starting. Diving at Sipadan is capped at 120 divers per day (see p341 for information about pre-planning in Sabah).

Most dive centres charge around RM180 to RM250 for two dives, including equipment rental. A three-dive day trip at Sipadan costs RM250 to RM450. PADI open-water courses average around RM800. Many resorts and dive operators also offer all-inclusive dive packages, which vary widely in price.

The northeast monsoon brings strong winds and rain to the east coast of Peninsular Malaysia from early November to late February, during which time most dive centres simply shut down. Visibility improves after the monsoon, peaking in August and September. On the west coast conditions are reversed and the best diving is from September to March. In Malaysian Borneo the monsoons are less pronounced and rain falls more evenly throughout the year.

GOLF

It is a *serious* health risk to fly within 24 hours of your last dive. It's also unsafe to dive directly after flying due to poorly pressurised cabins and dehydration.

Welcome to the home of flood-lit golf – playing at night when it's cooler is a favourite pastime in Malaysia. KL offers over 40 courses in and around the city, including the **Royal Selangor Golf Course** (Map pp92-3; ☎ 9206 3333; www.rsgc.com.my; Jln Kelab Golf, off Jln Tun Razak; green fees from RM60). There are world-class courses elsewhere on the peninsula – see p188, p217 and p219.

If you want to tee off in a cooler environment head to Fraser's Hill (p135) or the Cameron Highlands (p159).

KAYAKING & WHITE-WATER RAFTING

Malaysia's mountains plus rainforests equals fast flowing rivers providing ideal opportunities for river-rafting and kayaking enthusiasts. On the peninsula, Kuala Kubu Bharu (p133) has become the white-water hot spot with rafting and kayaking organised along the Sungai Selangor.

In Gopeng on Sungai Kampar, 20 minutes' drive north of Ipoh, rafting trips and other outdoor adventures are offered at the **MY Gopeng Resort** (☎ 019-542 3773; www.mygopeng resort.com).

RESPONSIBLE DIVING

Please consider the following tips when diving or snorkelling, and help preserve the ecology and beauty of the reefs:

■ Do not use anchors on the reef, and take care not to ground boats on coral. Encourage dive operators and regulatory bodies to establish permanent moorings at popular dive sites.

■ Avoid touching living marine organisms with your body, or dragging equipment across the reef. Polyps can be damaged by even the gentlest contact. Never stand on coral, even if it looks solid and robust. If you must hold onto the reef, touch only exposed rock or dead coral.

■ Be conscious of your fins. Even without contact the surge from heavy fin strokes near the reef can damage delicate organisms. When treading water in shallow reef areas, take care not to kick up clouds of sand. Settling sand can easily smother the delicate organisms of the reef.

■ Practise and maintain proper buoyancy control. Major damage can be done by divers descending too fast and colliding with the reef. Be aware that buoyancy can change over the period of an extended trip: initially you may breathe harder and need more weight; a few days later you may breathe more easily and need less weight.

■ Resist the temptation to collect or buy coral or shells. Apart from the ecological damage, taking home marine souvenirs depletes the beauty of a site and spoils the enjoyment of others. The same goes for marine archaeological sites (mainly shipwrecks). Respect their integrity; some sites are even protected from looting by law.

■ Ensure that you take home all your rubbish and any litter you may find. Plastics in particular are a serious threat to marine life. Turtles can mistake plastic for jellyfish and eat it.

■ Resist the temptation to feed fish and discourage snorkel operators from baiting marine life. You may disturb their normal eating habits, encourage aggressive behaviour or feed them food that is detrimental to their health.

White-water rafting has become quite the craze in Sabah, with KK-based operators taking travellers south of the city to the Beaufort Division (p398) for some Grade 3–4 rapids on the Sungai Padas (Padas River). Calmer water at Sungai Kiulu near Mt Kinabalu is a tamer option for beginners.

Kayaking is offered by **Kuching Kayak** (☎ 082-253005; www.kuchingkayak.com; 269 Jln Padungan) in Kuching.

For a list of golf clubs around the country and other information see the website of the Malaysian Golf Association (☎ 03-9283 7300; www.mga online.com.my).

MOUNTAIN CLIMBING

Mt Kinabalu (p357) is an obvious choice – and it's recently got a tad more challenging thanks to the addition of a *via ferrata* descent; see p359 for details.

Borneo's blockbuster is not the only mountain worth climbing in Malaysia. Sabah's Mt Trus Madi (p396) is a far more difficult peak to ascend than Mt Kinabalu. Sarawak's Gunung Mulu (p456) is a challenging four-day climb, while on the peninsula, there are several good climbs in Taman Negara, including Gunung Tahan (p298), which stands at 2187m. There are also a few lesser peaks scattered around that make pleasant day outings.

SURFING

Wannabe Layne Beachleys and Kelly Slaters should haul their boards to Cherating (p289) and Juara on Pulau Tioman (p274), Malaysia's surfing hot spots – see p291 for further details.

Keen mountain-climbers should try to pick up a copy of *Mountains of Malaysia – A Practical Guide and Manual* by John Briggs.

TREKKING

In Malaysia's national parks there are treks to suit all levels of ability, from 20-minute jaunts to 10-day expeditions: see p79 for our top national park

Thrillseekers can set their pulses racing on the Flying Fox and anti-gravity G-Force X rides run in and around KL by AJ Hackett (www.ajhackett.com/malaysia).

trekking recommendations, as well as p356. Even in the heart of KL it's possible to stretch your legs in the Bukit Nanas Forest Reserve (p98); alternatively head a little north of the city to find a fantastic network of forest trails and the suspended walkway at the Forestry Research Institute of Malaysia (FRIM; p132).

Responsible Trekking

Most treks in national parks and similar areas require a guide, and when they aren't required, it is often quite handy to recruit one. A good guide will be able to gauge your abilities and push you a little, rather than taking the easiest way as a matter of course. Try a shorter guided hike before

---

JUNGLE-TREKKING TIPS

Hiking through rainforest in hot, humid and sometimes wet conditions can be exhausting – like doing jumping jacks in a Turkish sauna – you'll be continuously sweaty no matter how fit you are. Oh, and don't forget about the critters – leech and mozzie bites are pretty much guaranteed. The rewards, however, are priceless – from alpine vistas to backwoods longhouses, your jungle jaunt will undoubtedly provide the perfect chitchat fodder at your next cocktail party.

The following guidelines will help to make the experience as painless as possible. See p602 for information on how to deal with leeches.

- Throw fashion out the window – comfortable, loose-fitting clothing is paramount. On overnight trips, bring two sets of loose-fitting clothing: one for hiking and one to put on at the end of the day (keep your night kit in a plastic bag so that it stays dry). Lightweight cotton is ideal. Within minutes of starting out, your hiking kit will be drenched and it will stay that way throughout your trip. If you'll be travelling through dense vegetation, wear long trousers and a long-sleeved shirt. Otherwise, shorts and a T-shirt will suffice.
- A breathable oversized rain jacket (read: not a garbage bag!) will be extremely handy – you are, after all, trekking through a *rain*forest.
- Contrary to popular belief, it's better to navigate the jungle in sturdy running shoes rather than expensive hiking boots (although most locals prefer *kampung adidas*; p352). Thongs are handy for going in and out of longhouses.
- Invest in some leech-proof socks – they look like little Christmas stockings minus the decorative fur. They can be hard to come by in some parts of Malaysia, so consider buying them online before your trip.
- Drink plenty of water. If you're going long distances, bring a water filter or, if you want to keep your carrying weight down, a water purification agent like iodine.
- Get in shape long before your trek and start slowly – try a day hike before setting out on a longer trek.
- Take a guide if you're setting off on a longer and/or lesser-travelled trek.
- Bring talcum powder to cope with the chafing caused by wet undergarments. Wearing loose underwear (or better yet, no underwear at all) will also help prevent chafing.
- If you wear glasses, treat them with an anti-fog solution (ask at the shop where you buy your glasses). Otherwise, you may find yourself blinded by steamed-up glasses soon after setting out.
- Consider adding a Tupperware (or equivalent) container to your packing list to protect your camera and/or binoculars from the elements.
- Other must-haves include sunscreen, insect repellent, a water bottle (stainless steel seems to be the trendiest sustainable option these days) and a torch (preferably a headlamp to keep your hands free). If you are worried about dehydration, electrolyte sachets (RM1) are available at local pharmacies all over the region.

setting off on an overnight adventure to get a sense of how you fare in tropical trekking conditions. Hiring a local guide is the best way to make sure you're in touch with local customs and concerns as you move through tribal lands.

Remember the golden rule of rubbish: if you carried it in, carry it out. Don't overlook easily forgotten or inconvenient items, such as plastic wrapping, cigarette butts, water bottles, sanitary napkins and so forth. Never bury your rubbish – it may be out of sight, but it won't be out of reach of animals.

Where there's a toilet, use it. Where there isn't one, bury your waste. Dig a small hole 15cm deep and at least 100m from any watercourse. Consider carrying a lightweight trowel for this purpose. Cover the waste with soil and a rock. Use toilet paper sparingly and bury it as well. If the area is inhabited, ask locals if they have any concerns about your chosen toilet site.

While your guide may happily hack his way through the undergrowth if necessary, you should always stick to the marked trails, however indistinct they may be. Carving your own path through the jungle can disrupt local people, not to mention the plants and wildlife.

Malaysia

GREG ELMS

Kuala Lumpur

Kuala Lumpur's metamorphosis from the jungle hovel of tin prospectors to a gleaming 21st-century city of high-rises and highways seems like a triumph of man over nature. However, peer down on KL (as it's commonly known) from the bird's-eye height of Menara KL and it's clear that nature continues to fight back: this remains one of the greenest cities in Southeast Asia and is all the better for it.

The blueprint was set early by the British who, in their colonial wisdom, crafted the Lake Gardens. This lush lung remains intact, as does the hillock of rainforest on which Menara KL rests and the old cricket field (now Merdeka Square) on which independence was declared back in 1957. The iconic Petronas Towers were developed alongside a beautifully landscaped park and to the north of the city more greenery surrounds Lake Titiwangsa.

In its built environment, few cities can compare to KL for diversity and daring. Imagine Fritz Lang's *Metropolis* crossed with an Arabian Nights Moorish fantasy and you begin to grasp a place where Chinese, Indian, Malay and contemporary structures coalesce into a fascinating whole.

The cream of Malaysian creativity can be experienced here also in the traditional crafts and cutting-edge art, design and fashion that can be found in KL's abundant malls and markets. Each ethnic community brings something to the table – most importantly in a delicious array of cuisines that make dining out the stellar experience in this star Southeast Asian urban performer.

HIGHLIGHTS

- Discovering vibrant **Chinatown** (p105) on a walking tour
- Marvelling at the steel-clad **Petronas Towers** (p95) and the swank Suria KLCC mall
- Breakfasting at **Imbi Market** (p115) and enjoying supper at **Jln Alor** (p114)
- Reviving in the greenery of the **Lake Gardens** (p102), with its showpiece **KL Bird Park** (p101)
- Admiring the beauty of Islamic art at the **Islamic Arts Museum** (p102)
- Paying respects to the heavenly mother at the **Thean Hou Temple** (p104)

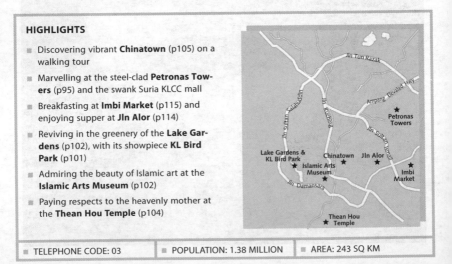

- TELEPHONE CODE: 03   - POPULATION: 1.38 MILLION   - AREA: 243 SQ KM

HISTORY

In 1857, 87 Chinese prospectors in search of tin landed at the apex of the Klang and Gombak Rivers and imaginatively named the place Kuala Lumpur, meaning 'muddy confluence'. Within a month all but 17 of the prospectors had died of malaria and other tropical diseases, but the tin they discovered in Ampang attracted more miners and KL quickly became a brawling, noisy, violent boomtown.

As in other parts of the Malay Peninsula, the local sultan appointed a proxy (known as Kapitan China) to bring the unruly Chinese fortune-seekers and their secret societies into line. The successful candidate Yap Ah Loy (Kapitan China from 1868 to 1885) took on the task with such ruthless relish that he's now credited as the founder of KL.

Loy had barely established control, however, when fighting broke out between local sultans for the throne of Perak. KL was swept up in the conflict and burnt to the ground in 1881. This allowed the British government representative Frank Swettenham to push through a radical new town plan that transferred the central government here, from Klang. By 1886 a railway line linked KL to Klang; by 1887 several thousand brick buildings had been built; and in 1896 the city became the capital of the newly formed Federated Malay States.

After occupation by Japanese forces during WWII (when many Chinese were tortured and killed, and many Indians sent to work on Burma's 'Death Railway'), the British temporarily returned, only to be ousted when Malaysia declared its independence here in 1957.

KL's darkest hour came on 13 May 1969 when race riots mainly between the Malays and Chinese communities claimed hundreds, perhaps thousands, of lives. A year later local government elections were suspended – ever since KL's mayor has been appointed by the Federal Territories Minister. In 1974 the sultan of Selangor ceded the city's land to the state so it could officially become the Federal Territory of Kuala Lumpur. The city has prospered ever since as Malaysia's political and commercial capital.

CLIMATE

Temperature ranges from 21°C to 33°C and the average humidity exceeds 82%. Although there's rain throughout the year, March to April and September to November are the wettest months.

ORIENTATION

Central KL is quite compact, even though its hilly terrain, multilane highways and paucity of footpaths conspire against walkers.

The city's colonial heart is Merdeka Sq. Southeast from here is bustling Chinatown, while immediately south, across a band of highways and train tracks, are the Masjid Negara (National Mosque), historic KL Train Station and the peaceful Lake Gardens. South of the Lake Gardens is KL Sentral, a regional and international train terminus with direct connections to the airport. KL Sentral is part of the area known as Brickfields. On the other side of the tracks further south is Bangsar Baru, a nucleus of trendy shops, restaurants and bars.

Another major arrival and departure point is the Puduraya long-distance bus station. East of Puduraya, the intersection of Jln Sultan Ismail and Jln Bukit Bintang marks the heart of the Golden Triangle, KL's premier business, shopping and entertainment district. Stacked with hotels, the Golden Triangle encompasses an area that stretches north to the Kuala Lumpur City Centre (KLCC) development anchored by the Petronas Towers. Back at Merdeka Sq, if you head against the one-way traffic northeast along Jln Tuanku A Rahman (commonly called Jln TAR) you'll soon hit Little India, and further north, Chow Kit, a red-light area famed for its lively market. Immediately west of Chow Kit is the old Malay area of Kampung Baru. Jln Raja Laut runs almost parallel to Jln TAR and takes the northbound traffic towards Jln Tun Razak marking the outer northern boundary of the city centre; around here you'll find Lake Titiwangsa and the National Art Gallery, Library and Theatre.

INFORMATION

Bookshops

Borders (Map p96; ☎ 2141 0288; Level 2, Berjaya Times Sq, Jln Imbi; ☸ 10am-10pm)

Kinokuniya (Map p96; ☎ 2164 8133; Level 4, Suria KLCC, Jln Ampang; ☸ 10am-10pm) Excellent range of English-language titles.

MPH Bookstores (www.mph.com.my) Bangsar (Map p118; ☎ 2287 3600; 2nd fl Bangsar Village II, 2 Jln Telawi 1; ☸ 10.30am-10.30pm); Golden Triangle (Map p96; ☎ 2142 8231; Ground fl, BB Plaza, Jln Bukit Bintang; ☸ 10.30am-9.30pm)

Silverfish Books (Map p118; ☎ 2284 4837; www .silverfishbooks.com; 58-1 Jln Telawi, Bangsar; ☸ 10am-8pm Mon-Fri, 10am-6pm Sat) Publisher of contemporary Malaysian literature.

KUALA LUMPUR

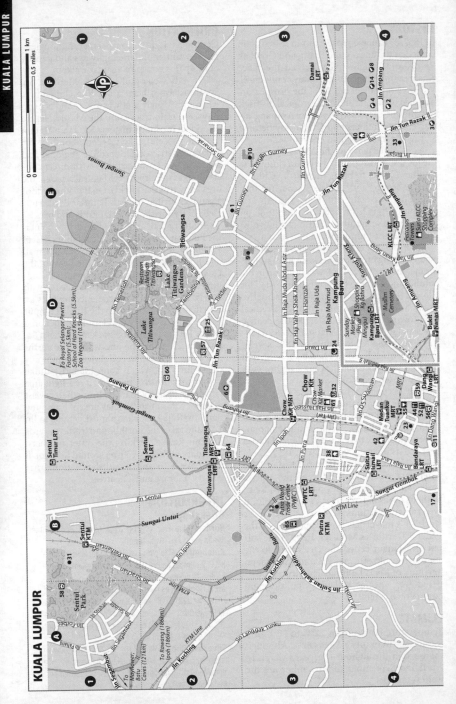

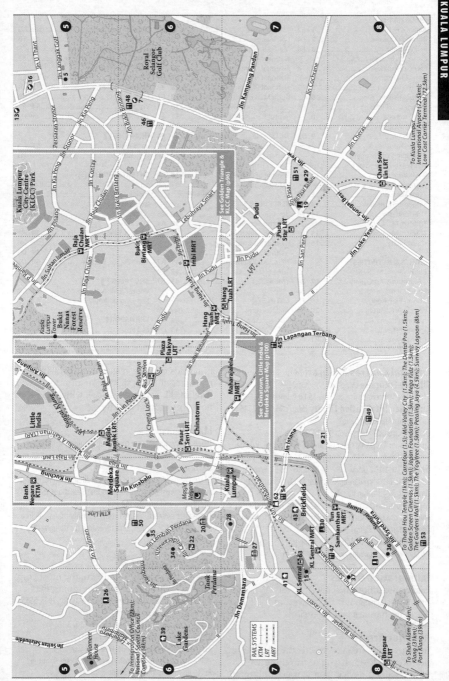

KUALA LUMPUR

Cultural Centres & Libraries

Alliance Française (Map pp92–3; ☎ 2694 7880; http://kl.alliancefrancaise.org.my; 15 Lg Gurney)
Australian Information Library (Map p96; ☎ 2146 5555; 6 Jln Yap Kwan Seng)
British Council (Map p96; ☎ 2723 7900; www .britishcouncil.org/malaysia; Ground fl, West Block, Wisma Selangor Dredging, 142C Jln Ampang)
Goethe Institut (Map pp92–3; ☎ 2164 2011; www .goethe.de/ins/my/kua/deindex.htm; 6th fl Menara See Hoy Chan, 374 Jln Tun Razak).
Japan Foundation (off Map pp92–3; ☎ 2284 6228; www.jfkl.org.my; 18th fl Northpoint, Block B, Mid-Valley City, Medan Syed Putra)
National Library of Malaysia (Map pp92–3; ☎ 2687 1700; www.pnm.gov.my; 232 Jln Tun Razak)

Immigration Offices

Immigration Office (off Map pp92–3; ☎ 2095 5077; Block I, Pusat Bandar Damansara) It's 2km west of the Lake Gardens; handles visa extensions.

Internet Access

Internet cafes are everywhere; the going rate per hour is RM3. If you're travelling with a wi-fi–enabled device, you can get online at hundreds of cafes, restaurants, bars and several hotels for free; sign up for an account with **Wireless@KL** (www.wirelesskl.com), which has 1500 hot spots around the city.

Media

Juice (www.juiceonline.com) Free clubbing-orientated monthly magazine available in top-end hotels, restaurants and bars.
KLue (www.klue.com.my; RM5) Excellent local listings magazine, with many interesting features about what's going on in and around the city.
Time Out (www.timeoutkl.com) Monthly magazine in a globally familiar format; sign up online for their weekly what's-going-on digest.

Medical Services

Pharmacies are all over town; the most common is Guardian, in most shopping malls.
Hospital Kuala Lumpur (Map pp92–3; ☎ 2615 5555; www.hkl.gov.my; Jln Pahang)
Tung Shin Hospital (Map p96; ☎ 2072 1655; http://tungshin.com.my; 102 Jln Pudu)
Twin Towers Medical Centre KLCC (Map p96; ☎ 2382 3500; www.ttmcklcc.com.my; Level 4, Suria KLCC, Jln Ampang; ⊙ 8.30am-6pm Mon-Sat)

Money

You'll seldom be far from a bank/ATM. Moneychangers offer better rates than banks for changing cash and (at times) travellers cheques; they're usually open later hours and on weekends and are found in shopping malls.

Post

Following are details for the main post office, and other useful branches around town.

Little India (Map pp92-3; Jln TAR) Near the crossing with Jln Sultan Ismail.

Main post office (Map p100; Jln Raja Laut; 🕒 8.30am-6pm Mon-Sat, closed 1st Sat of month) Across the river from the Central Market. Has poste restante and packaging is available for reasonable rates at the post-office store.

Sungei Wang Plaza (Map p96; 3rd fl, Jln Sultan Ismail)

Suria KLCC (Map p96; basement, Suria KLCC, Jln Ampang)

Telephone & Fax

Many internet cafes offer competitive netphone and fax services.

Telekom Malaysia (Map p100; Jln Raja Chulan; 🕒 8.30am-4.30pm Mon-Fri, 8.30am-12.30pm Sat) You can make international calls and send faxes.

Tourist Information

Malaysian Tourist Centre (MaTiC; Map p96; ☎ 9235 4900; www.mtc.gov.my; 109 Jln Ampang; 🕒 8am-10pm) Housed in a mansion built in 1935 for rubber and tin tycoon Eu Tong Seng, and almost a tourist attraction in its own right, this is KL's most useful tourist office; it hosts good cultural performances (see p122).

Tourism Malaysia (www.tourismmalaysia.gov.my) KL Sentral (Map pp92-3; ☎ 2274 5823; 🕒 9am-6pm); Kuala Lumpur International Airport (KLIA; ☎ 8776 5651; International Arrival Hall, Sepang); Putra World Trade Centre (Map pp92-3; ☎ 2615 8188; Level 17, 45 Jln Tun Ismail; 🕒 9am-6pm Mon-Sat)

SIGHTS

Six-lane highways and flyovers may slice up the city, but even so, the best way to get a feel for KL's vibrant atmosphere is to walk. The city centre is surprisingly compact – from Chinatown to Little India takes little more than 10 minutes on foot – and some sights are so close together that it's often quicker to walk than take public transport or grab a cab (which can easily become snarled in traffic and KL's tortuous one-way system). For a couple of walking routes, see p105. Apart from the major sights listed here, also explore some of the city's eye-boggling shopping malls (p123) – all part of the essential KL experience.

Golden Triangle

PETRONAS TOWERS & KLCC

Anchoring the huge Kuala Lumpur City Centre (KLCC) urban development (with a park, convention and shopping centre and world-class concert hall) are the iconic **Petronas Towers** (Map p96; www.petronastwintowers .com.my; KLCC, Jln Ampang). A visit to KL just isn't complete unless you've been here.

KUALA LUMPUR IN...

Two Days

Head to **Imbi Market** (p115) for breakfast then move on to the Kuala Lumpur City Centre (KLCC) to secure one of the limited free tickets for the skybridge of the **Petronas Towers** (above). Althernatively head up **Menara KL** (p98) and get your bearings of the city from the revolving restaurant **Seri Angkasa** (p114). Spend the afternoon at the **National Museum** (p102). Go souvenir shopping at the **Central Market** (p123), then explore **Chinatown** (p98), ending up at **Jln Petaling** (p98) for food and the night market.

On day two experience the avian orchestra tuning up in the Lake Gardens' **KL Bird Park** (p101). Cool down inside the **Islamic Arts Museum** (p102) followed by late-afternoon tea at **Carcosa Seri Negara** (p112). Enjoy cocktails at **SkyBar** (p120), then trawl the night food stalls of **Jln Alor** (p114).

Three Days

Start day three with a gentle stroll around **Lake Titiwangsa** (p103) and a visit to the **National Art Gallery** (p103). Amble through the Malay area of **Kampung Baru** (p103) or **Little India** (p102), then take a taxi to the splendid **Thean Hou Temple** (p104). Choose one of the many restaurants in the basement of **Starhill Gallery** (p124) for dinner, followed by a concert at the **Dewan Filharmonik Petronas** (p121) or **No Black Tie** (p121), and a nightcap at **Palate Palette** (p120).

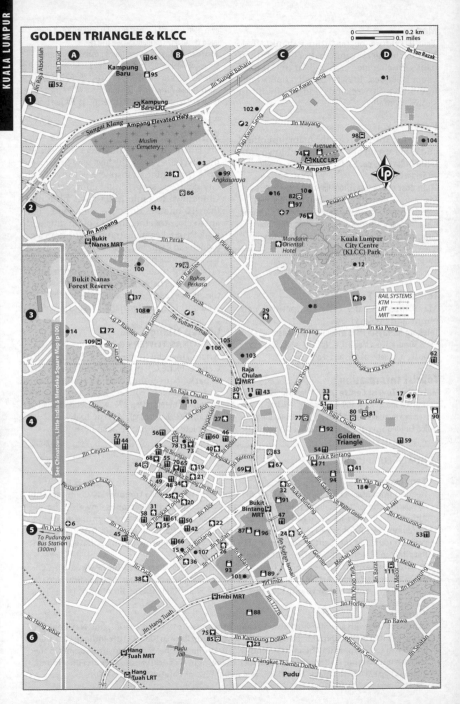

GOLDEN TRIANGLE & KLCC

Opened in 1998, the 88-storey steel-clad twin towers rise up 451.9m. They are the headquarters of the national oil and gas company Petronas (p47) and also house several other companies, as well as Al Jazeera's Asian broadcasting centre. Designed by Argentinian architect Cesar Pelli, the twin towers' floor plan is based on an eight-sided star that echoes arabesque patterns. Islamic influences are also evident in each tower's five tiers – representing the five pillars of Islam – and in the 63m masts that crown them, calling to mind the minarets of a mosque and the Star of Islam.

The highest you can go is the 41st-floor **Skybridge** (Map p96; 9am-1pm & 2.30-7pm Tue-Sun) connecting the two towers, a modest 170m above ground. Only 1640 free tickets are issued daily, so be in line at the ticket counter in the basement as soon as you can after it opens at 8.30am to ensure your place. Also avoid visiting on weekends and public holidays.

Apart from shopping or dining in the Suria KLCC (p123) at the base of the towers, there are still plenty of other things of interest. The spacious **KLCC park** (Map p96) has a great kids' playground, paddling pools and syncronised fountains. All the family will enjoy both the interactive science discovery centre **Petrosains** (Map p96; 2331 8181; www.petrosains.com.my; Level 4, Suria KLCC; adult/child RM12/4; 9.30am-4pm Tue-Fri, 9.30am-5pm Sat, Sun & holidays) and the well-stocked **Aquaria KLCC** (Map p96; 2333 1888; www.klaquaria .com; Concourse Level, Kuala Lumpur Convention Centre; adult/child RM38/26; 11am-8pm) where you can view sand tiger sharks and giant groupers in a 90m-long underwater tunnel.

Galeri Petronas (Map p96; 2051 7770; www .galeripetronas.com; 3rd fl, Suria KLCC; admission free; 10am-8pm Tue-Sun) offers top-class exhibitions of contemporary photography and paintings. Consider booking a ticket for a classical-music concert in the Dewan Filharmonik Petronas (p121) to see inside the beautiful state-of-the-art hall.

MENARA KL & BUKIT NANAS FOREST RESERVE

Built atop the **Bukit Nanas Forest Reserve**, the 421m **Menara KL** (KL Tower; Map p96; 2020 5448; www.menarakl.com.my; 2 Jln Punchak; adult/child RM38/28; 9am-10pm; last tickets up 9.30pm) easily trumps the Petronas Towers when it comes to providing the highest view you're going to get of the city, bar chartering a helicopter. The tower's bulbous pinnacle is inspired by a Malaysian spinning top and, inside, the **viewing deck** is, at 276m, at least 100m higher than the Petronas Towers' skybridge. One floor higher, you can have a meal or afternoon tea at the revolving restaurant Seri Angkasa (p114).

A **shuttle bus** (free; 9am-9.30pm) runs up every 15 minutes to the tower from the gate on Jln Punchak opposite the PanGlobal building. Alternatively get a workout climbing the short and well-labelled nature trails that run through the lowland dipterocarp forest reserve, which you can either explore alone or on a free guided tour starting from the entrance to the tower at 11am, 12.30pm, 2.30pm and 4.30pm daily and lasting about 45 minutes. There are also good displays and leaflets in the **Forest Information Centre** (Map p100; 2026 4741; www.forestry.gov.my; Jln Raja Chulan; 9am-5pm) at the base of the hill.

Also at the entrance to the tower, sign up for the **Flying Fox Park** (Map p96; 2020 5145; www .aj-hackett.com; adult/child R30/15; 11am-7pm) if you fancy being strapped in a harness and sent flying down a 100m wire rope stung down one side of the hill.

BADAN WARISAN MALAYSIA & RUMAH PENGHULU

Find out about the work of built heritage preservation society **Badan Warisan Malaysia** (Heritage of Malaysia Trust; Map p96; 2144 9273; www.badan warisan.org.my; 2 Jln Stonor; 10am-5.30pm Mon-Sat) at its head office in a 1925 colonial bungalow in the shadow the Petronas Towers. The property's grounds contain the **Rumah Penghulu**, a handsome example of a restored Malay-style wooden house from Kedah. Tours of the house are held at 11am and 3pm Monday to Saturday (suggested donation of RM5). The trust also holds exhibitions in the bungalow, where you'll find a good bookshop and an excellent gift store stocking wooden antique furniture and local handcrafted items.

Chinatown & Merdeka Square

Just strolling around bustling Chinatown, with it's daily market along Jln Petaling, is an experience (p105). Immediately northwest is Merdeka Square, the heart of colonial KL.

JALAN PETALING

The commercial heart of Chinatown is one of the most colourful and busiest shopping

PROTECTING THE PAST: ELIZABETH CARDOSA

Malaysia's National Heritage Act is supposed to protect outstanding pieces of the nation's architecture, but with development rampant it doesn't always work, as proved by the destruction of KL's historic Bok House in 2006. Fighting to save other heritage buildings is Elizabeth Cardosa, Executive Director of Badan Warisan Malaysia, a nongovernmental organization that is Malaysia's equivalent of the UK's National Trust.

What does Badan Warisan do? Its principal aim is to promote the preservation of Malaysia's built heritage. We do this in a number of ways – by advocacy, trying to have an impact on official policy from top-level government down to the local level; by influencing public opinion through our publications; and by education – going into schools and getting people involved at the community level. We also provide practical conservation and heritage consultancy services.

What are among your successes? As lead conservation consultants, we recently won a Unesco award for excellence for our work on restoring Stadium Merdeka (Map p100) – it was purpose built for the declaration of independence in 1957 and is the only building of its type in Southeast Asia. We're managing 8 Heeren St in Melaka (p243), where we've also designed a walking tour highlighting the city's endangered trades. We're also hoping to take over the management of the recently restored Suffolk House in Penang (p187).

What's on the danger list? More modest buildings that form part of the streetscape – alone they may not be outstanding, but together they define the character of the area. For example, plans are afoot to redevelop part of Kampung Baru (p103) – local government has an area plan but there's a lot of conflict resolution needed to get an outcome that pleases everyone. It's hard getting the conservation message across, that such buildings have a value for society. For droughts or air pollution, these are problems that affect and resonate with everyone. But when it comes to saving old buildings, unless someone has a personal connection to the structure it's difficult to convince them of the worth of preservation.

parades in KL, particularly at night when stalls cram the covered **street** (Map p100; ☼ 10am-11pm). It offers everything from fresh fruit and cheap clothes and shoes to copies of brand-name watches and handbags, and pirated CDs and DVDs. Be prepared to bargain hard.

SRI MAHAMARIAMMAN TEMPLE

This large and ornate South Indian Hindu **temple** (Map p100; 163 Jln Tun HS Lee; ☼ 8am-8pm), dating from 1873, houses a large silver chariot that's paraded to the Batu Caves (p131) during the Thaipusam festival in January or February each year. Its polychromatic, deity-clad *gopurum* (entrance gate) was under wraps for renovations when we recently passed by, so it should be looking even more dazzling than ever when you show up.

SZE YA TEMPLE

Squashed between Jln Tun HS Lee and Lebuh Pudu (a position apparently determined by feng shui) is this fascinating Taoist **temple** (Map p100; ☼ 8am-8pm). Its construction was organised in 1864 by 'Kapitan China' Yap Ah Loy (see p91); you can see a small statue of the man to the left of the altar. Near here you

could also go shopping or grab something to eat in the Central Market (p123).

MERDEKA SQUARE

This one-time cricket field formerly known as the Padang is where Malaysia's independence (Merdeka) was proclaimed at midnight on 31 August 1957. As such it's hallowed ground to many Malaysians and is speared by a 100m-high freestanding flagpole – claimed to be the world's tallest. Crowds gather here for New Year's Eve and on National Day to watch the parades (see p109).

The square is surrounded by a handsome architectural ensemble. On the west side is the **Royal Selangor Club** (Map p100; www.rscweb.my), an extended mock-Tudor building that was the social centre for high society in KL's tin-boom days of the 1890s, and remains a gathering place for the city's elite. It's also where the, now worldwide, running and drinking club the Hash House Harriers kicked off in 1938.

Opposite the club, across Jln Raja Laut, is the fantasy-like **Sultan Abdul Samad Building** (Map p100) with its distinctive copper-plated cupolas. This blend of Victorian, Moorish and Mogul architecture is typical of many of KL's

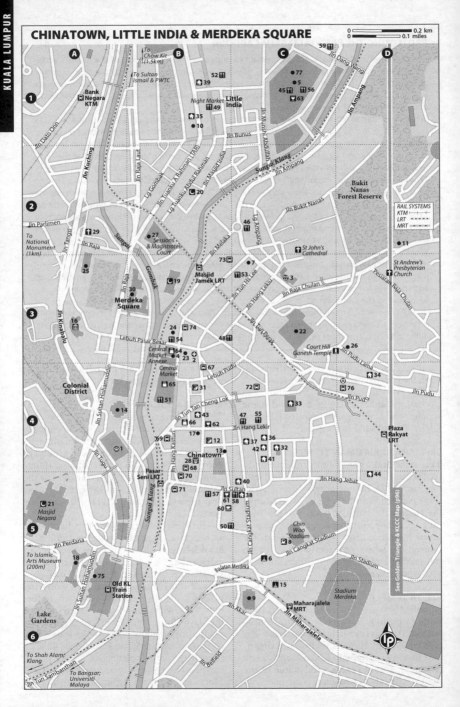

colonial buildings. Designed by AC Norman (an associate of AB Hubbock, architect of the KL Train Station) and built between 1894 and 1897, it was once the Secretariat Building for the British administration and now houses a branch of Malaysia's High Court. It looks particularly attractive at night when fairy lights illuminate its exterior.

At the square's north end are low **memorial arches** inscribed with 'Dataran Merdeka' (Merdeka Sq) and across the road is another of AC Norman's creations, **St Mary's Cathedral** (Map p100), dating from 1894 and housing a fine pipe-organ dedicated to Sir Henry Gurney, the British high commissioner to Malaya, assassinated in 1951 during the Emergency (see p37).

Lake Gardens & Around
Southwest of Chinatown, Lake Gardens – 92-hectares of landscaped hillside gardens originally laid out by the British – seems cut off by railway lines and highways, but it is possible to walk here: take the pedestrian bridge across from the Central Market to Kompleks Dayabumi and then head south around the back of the post office to the underpass leading to the Masjid Negara.

Alternatively, the KL Hop-On-Hop-Off Bus (p109) stops at Masjid Negara, KL Bird Park, the National Monument and the National Museum. Once in the Lake Gardens you're at the mercy of taxi drivers, who insist on charging RM15 to RM18 to cover the short distance back to the city and refuse to use the meter.

KL BIRD PARK
The highlight of the Lake Gardens is undoubtedly the **KL Bird Park** (Map pp92-3; ☎ 2272 1010; www.klbirdpark.com; adult/child RM39/29; ⏱ 9am-6pm), the world's largest walk-in aviary with some 200 (mostly Southeast Asian) species of birds. Check the website for different birds' feeding times throughout the day. The park's **Hornbill Restaurant** (Map pp92-3 ☎ 2693 8086; ⏱ 9am-10pm) is also good for an inexpensive feed, its balcony providing a great view into the treetops.

ISLAMIC ARTS MUSEUM

Containing one of best collections of Islamic decorative arts in the world is KL's outstanding **Islamic Arts Museum** (Muzium Kesenian Islam Malaysia; Map pp92-3; ☎ 2274 2020; www.iamm.org .my; Jln Lembah Perdana; adult/child RM12/6; ⏰ 10am-6pm). Aside from the quality of the exhibits, which include fabulous textiles, carpets, jewellery, calligraphy-inscribed pottery and an amazing reconstruction of an ornate Ottoman room, the building itself is a stunner, with beautifully decorated domes and glazed tilework. There's a Lebanese restaurant offering a set lunch (RM43; closed Monday) and a well-stocked shop selling beautiful high-quality crafts products and art books.

NATIONAL MUSEUM

A major renovation and creation of an entirely new gallery has breathed new life into the **National Museum** (Muzium Negara; Map pp92-3; ☎ 2282 6255; www.muziumnegara.gov.my; Jln Damansara; adult/child RM2/free; ⏰ 9am-6pm), which is packed with interesting displays on Malaysia's history, economy, arts, crafts and various cultures. It's worth timing your visit to coincide with one of the free **guided tours** (English 11am Tue, Thu & Sat; French 9am & noon Thu). The building has a distinctive Minangkabau-styled roof and two beautiful front murals made of Italian mosaic glass depicting Malaysian life. A walkway over the highway connects the museum with the southern stretch of the Lake Gardens.

LAKE GARDENS

Elsewhere in the Lake Gardens you'll find thousands of butterflies fluttering through the **Taman Rama Rama** (Butterfly Park; Map pp92-3; ☎ 2693 4799; Jln Cendarasari; adult/child RM15/8, to take photos extra RM1; ⏰ 9am-6pm). Exit through an insect gallery and marvel at the size of the spiders awaiting you in the Cameron Highlands.

Nearby are the **Taman Orkid** (Orchid Garden; Map pp92-3; admission free; ⏰ 9am-6pm) and the adjacent **Taman Bunga Raya** (Hibiscus Garden; Map pp92-3; admission free; ⏰ 9am-6pm).

The quirky **National Planetarium** (Map pp92-3; ☎ 2273 5484; 53 Jln Perdana; admission RM1; ⏰ 10am-4pm Tue-Sun) shows short generic international science films (RM1 to RM6) in the theatre at regular intervals throughout the day. It's an interesting place to take children for a fun educational experience.

In the garden's northern quarter the massive **National Monument** (Map pp92–3), sculpted in bronze in 1966 by Felix de Weldon, the creator of the Iwo Jima monument in Washington, DC, commemorates the communist defeat in 1950.

At the centre of the gardens lies **Tasik Perdana** (Premier Lake). You can rent boats on weekends and watch t'ai chi practitioners in the early morning.

West of lake and accessed via Persiaran Mahameru is the luxury hotel Carcosa Seri Negara (p112), which was once the official residence of the British government representative.

MASJID NEGARA

The contemporary-styled **Masjid Negara** (National Mosque; Map p100; Jln Perdana; ⏰ 9am-12.30pm, 2-3.30pm & 5-6.30pm) is distinguished by a spikey 73m-high minaret and star-shaped main dome, its 18 points symbolising the 13 states of Malaysia and the five pillars of Islam. The overall design was inspired by the Grand Mosque in Mecca. To go inside you must remove your shoes and dress appropriately (no shorts or skimpy clothing).

KL TRAIN STATION

The British architect AB Hubbock's Moorish- and Mogul-inspired fantasy, **Kuala Lumpur Station** (Map p100) dates from 1911. Sadly, the station is looking shabby and forlorn especially since KL Sentral took over most of its services. This said, it's still a visually handsome building and is best seen from the forecourt of the superb **Malayan Railway Administration Building** (Map p100) opposite; step inside this building to admire the soaring central stairwell. An underpass from here leads you across the busy highway to inside the station where KTM Komuter trains still stop.

Little India & Around

Little India is another area that is best explored on foot (see p107). The best time to visit is late Saturday afternoon when Lg TAR fills up with the area's **pasar malam** (Map p100; night market; ⏰ 4pm-midnight).

A new focus of the area is **CapSquare** (Map p100; www.capsquare.com.my), an attractive complex for business, residential and entertainment purposes bordered by Jln Munshi Abdullah, Jln Dang Wangi and the muddy Sungai Kelang (Kelang River) – head here on the first and third weekends of the month for a bazaar featuring food, fashion and interesting knick-knacks.

Yet to open at the time of research but looking very promising is the **Bank Negara Malaysia Museum & Art Gallery** (Map pp92-3; http://museum.bnm .gov.my), located in a futuristically designed metal-clad complex west of Jln Kuching and within walking distance of Bank Negara train station.

LOKE MANSION

Rescued from the brink of dereliction by the law firm Cheang & Ariff, **Loke Mansion** (Map pp92-3; ☎ 2691 0803; www.cheangariff.com; 273A Jln Medan Tuanku) was once the home of self-made tin tycoon Loke Yew, although the original part of the structure was built in the 1860s by another rich merchant Cheow Ah Yeok. The Japanese high command also set up base here in 1942. After years of neglect, the mansion has been beautifully restored; it's possible to gain access by appointment only, although there's nothing to stop you walking by and admiring the whitewashed exterior.

MASJID JAMEK

Set in a grove of palm trees is KL's most delightful mosque, **Masjid Jamek** (Friday Mosque; Map p100; off Jln Tun Perak; ☒ 8.30am-12.30pm & 2.30-4pm, closed 11am-2.30pm Fri). Built in 1907, the mosque is a tranquil creation of onion domes and minarets of layered pink and cream bricks. Designed again by AB Hubbock, who sought inspiration from Mogul mosques in India, it stands at the confluence of the Sungai Klang and Sungai Gombak – where KL's founders first set foot. Dress appropriately if you wish to enter.

Kampung Baru & Chow Kit
KAMPUNG BARU

The charm of this Malay area (Map pp92-3) lies in just wandering the streets. Somehow the district has managed to retain its sleepy village atmosphere in the midst of the city: traditional Malay wooden houses stand amid leafy gardens and people go quietly about their daily lives – with the exception of Saturday night when a lively *pasar malam* (night market) takes over the area close to the Kampung Baru Light Rail Transit (LRT) station.

A stroll in the area could be combined with a visit to Chow Kit Market (right) to the west. Head east along Jln Raja Alang from Jln TAR and you'll soon pass the impressive **Sikh Temple** (Map pp92-3), the largest in Southeast

Asia and spiritual home of KL's 75,000 Sikhs. Further along the road is the focus of the area's Muslim faithful, the **Masjid Kampung Baru** (Map pp92-3), built in 1924, with its gateway decorated in beautiful glazed tiles. Explore the streets around here at the junction with Jln Daud to find many old wooden houses. Even outside of Saturday night, this is a great area to come for tasty home-cooked Malay food at unpretentious roadside cafes and stalls.

CHOW KIT MARKET

It's sensory overload at this lively **market** (Map pp92-3; 469-473 Jln TAR; ☒ 6am-8pm), where tightly jammed stalls sell clothes, toys, buckets, stationary, noodles, spices, fresh meat and live, flapping fish, as well as a staggering array of weird and wonderful tropical fruit. Shops in the lanes around the market, particularly Jln Haji Hussein, specialise in made-to-order *songkok*, the traditional Malay-style fez.

Northern Kuala Lumpur
LAKE TITIWANGSA

For a picture-postcard view of the city skyline head to Lake Titiwangsa (Map pp92-3) and the relaxing park that surrounds it. If you're feeling energetic, hire row boats, pedal boats and canoes (per hour from RM3) to glide across the lake, or go for a jog. The park is a favourite spot for courting Malaysian couples – and religious police on the lookout for improper behaviour!

Lake Titiwangsa is an 800m walk east of the Titiwangsa monorail station. Buses 101, 102 and 103 run between Titiwangsa and Medan Pasar, while bus 104 runs here from KLCC.

NATIONAL ART GALLERY

Squashed between Jln Tun Razak and the park is the worthwhile **National Art Gallery** (Balai Seni Lukis Negara; Map pp92-3; ☎ 4026 7000; www.art gallery.org.my; 2 Jln Temerloh, off Jln Tun Razak; admission free; ☒ 10am-6pm). A striking mural, Graffiti, by Mahadhir Masri, covers the walkway wall leading up the gallery, the interior of which is dominated by a swirly Guggenheim Museum–style staircase. Among the works to look out for in the gallery's permanent collection, which was only started in 1958, are paintings by Zulkifi Moh'd Dohalan, Wong Hoi Cheong, Ahad Osman and the renowned batik artist Chuah Than Teng. The gallery also hosts many temporary exhibitions.

ISTANA BUDAYA

Looming over the gallery is its neighbour, the **Istana Budaya** (National Theatre; see p122), with its blue-tiled roof reminiscent of an enormous piece of origami. Designed by Mohammed Ka'amur Yaakub, the building's giant roof is based on a traditional Malay floral decoration of betel leaves, while its footprint resembles a *wau bulan* (moon kite). Every Saturday from 6pm to 11pm, there's the Laman Santai – free live music and dance performances staged in front of the theatre – along with cheap food stalls.

Southern Kuala Lumpur

THEAN HOU TEMPLE

Off Jln Syed Putra, the multilayered and highly ornate **Thean Hou Temple** (off Map pp92–3; ☎ 2274 7088; www.hainannet.com; 65 Persiaran Endah; admission free; ☺ 9am-6pm) is one of the most visually impressive in Malaysia. It's dedicated to the Heavenly Mother, Thean Hou. Her statue takes centre stage in the main hall, with Guanyin (the Buddhist Goddess of Mercy) on her right and Shuiwei Shengniang (the Goddess of the Waterfront) to her left. Statues of Milefo (the laughing Buddha), Weituo and Guandi further contribute to this Taoist/Buddhist hodgepodge.

There are great views from the temple's upper decks, while at its base are tourist restaurants and shops. To reach the temple, 3km south of the centre of town, either take a taxi or bus 27 or 52 from Klang bus station (Map p100) and then walk up the hill (ask to be dropped off near the temple). Another route is to take the monorail to Tun Sambanthan station, cross Jln Syed Putra using the overpass and walk up the hill.

BRICKFIELDS

Dragons fly off the corners of the **Sam Kow Tong Temple** (Map pp92–3; ☎ 2274 1239; 16 Jln Thambapillai), just around the corner from the monorail terminus in Brickfields, making for a striking contrast with the soaring hotel towers above KL Sentral.

Other interesting buildings to be seen in this distinctly Indian area include the Buddhist Pagoda (see Meditation, p108), the Temple of Fine Arts (p108), and Wei-Ling Gallery (p122).

PUDU MARKET

Arrive early to experience KL's largest wet (produce) **market** (Map pp92–3; Jln Pasar Baharu; ☺ 6am-2pm) at its most frantic. Here you can get every imaginable type of fruit, vegetable, fish and meat – from the foot of a chicken slaughtered and butchered on the spot to a stingray fillet or a pig's penis. Attached is Pusat Makanan Peng Hwa, an old-fashioned 24-hour food court where you can join locals and market traders wolfing down rice porridge, noodle soup or chicken rice (all under RM10).

The market is five minutes' walk from Pudu LRT station; from the station go south along Jln Pudu, right onto Jln Pasar, then right down Jln Pasar Baharu, passing the colourful **Choon Wan Kong** (Map pp92–3), a Chinese temple dating from 1879.

ACTIVITIES
Gyms & Yoga

Many gyms have classes including yoga. Enquire about short-term membership deals for the gyms; these can work out far cheaper than the usual day-rate of RM50.

California Fitness (Map p96; ☎ 2145 1000; www .californiafitness.com; Lot 10, 50 Jln Sultan Ismail; ☺ 6.30am-midnight Mon-Fri, 8am-8pm Sat & Sun) Also branches at Mid Valley and Sunway Pyramid.

Fitness First (Map p96; ☎ 2711 3299; www.fitness first.com.my; Wisma SPK, 22 Jln Sultan Ismail; ☺ 6.30am-11pm Mon-Fri, 7am-7pm Sat & Sun) It also has a branch in Menara Maxis at the KLCC (Map p96).

Lightworks (Map p96; ☎ 2143 2966; www.lightworks .com.my; 19 Jln Mesui) New Age centre that offers hatha yoga classes with an expat instructor. Drop-in classes are R50 per session and are held Tuesday at noon or Wednesday at 7pm.

Vivekananda Ashram (Map pp92–3; ☎ 2272 5051; 220 Jln Tun Sambanthan, Brickfields) This historic Indian ashram is part of the global Ramakrishna movement. Call for details of kundalini yoga classes.

Yoga 2 Health (Map p118; ☎ 2282 3866; www.yoga2 health.com.my; 1st fl, 21A Jln Telawi 3, Bangsar Baru) Membership is RM35 and its RM35 per class.

Spas, Massage Parlours & Reflexology

The top-end spas are competitively priced (anything from around RM150 for a standard massage to RM700 for a three-hour pamper package) but if your budget is limited there are plenty of alternatives. There's an abundance of Chinese massage and reflexology places scattered throughout the city, with a concentration along Jln Bukit Bintang

---

QUIRKY KUALA LUMPUR

- Join the **Tugu Drum Circle** at the National Monument (Map pp92–3) in the Lake Gardens from 5.30pm to 8.30pm every Sunday, when they gather to make percussive music.

- Discover a little piece of Japan and beautiful *koi carp* at the **Sentul Park Koi Centre** (Map pp92-3; ☎ 4045 1311; www.sentulpark-koi.com; Jln Strachan; ☼ 9am-6pm).

- Catch the changing of the guards on the hour outside the gates of the **Istana Negara** (Map pp92-3; Jln Istana).

- Check out the **'space rocks'** and **scale model of Stonehenge** on the way to the Planetarium in the Lake Gardens (p102).

- Have your fortune told, along with a bubble tea or mango shake, at the **Sixty Nine Bistro** (p119).

- Go paddling at KL's numerous 'fish spas' (p107).

(Map p96), south of BB Plaza. The pricing is fairly consistent (an hour-long full-body massage RM65), but because of the intense competition, you can usually bargain this down to about RM50. In Brickfields there are several operations manned by blind masseurs along Jln Thambapillai; here the rates can drop as low as RM40 per hour. Expect to pay no more than RM30 for 30 minutes of foot reflexology.

Asianel Reflexology Spa (Map p96; ☎ 2142 1397; www.asianel.com; Pamper Level, Starhill Gallery, 181 Jln Bukit Bintang; ☼ 10am-10pm) Upmarket reflexology spa RM148 for foot, shoulder and neck massage.

Donna Spa (☎ 2141 8999; www.donnaspa.net) One of many massage operations on the same floor as Asianel, Donna Spa is Balinese style.

JoJoBa Spa (Map p96; ☎ 2141 7766; www.jojoba.com.my; 15th fl, East Wing Tower, Berjaya Times Sq, 1 Jln Imbi; ☼ 11am-midnight) Claims to be Malaysia's largest tourist spa.

Old Asia (Map p96; ☎ 2143 9888; 14 Jln Bukit Bintang; ☼ 10am-10pm) One of the more pleasantly designed places on the strip, offering spa treatments as well as massages.

Senjakala (Map p100; ☎ 2031 8082; www.senjakala.com; 20 Jln Pudu Lama; ☼ noon-10pm) Tastefully designed men-only spa. Treatment options include barbering and body-hair trimming. Discount available for massage and scrub packages on Tuesday and Thursday.

Spa Village (Map p96; ☎ 2142 8000; Ritz Carlton Hotel, 168 Jln Imbi; ☼ 8am-9pm) Indoor and outdoor beauty and massage treatments, a sensory room, and a second outdoor pool with waterfalls. Health club facilities include 24-hour fitness centre, sauna, steam room and whirlpool.

Starhill Spa (Map p96; ☎ 2719 8342; www.ytlhotels.com; Starhill Gallery, Jln Bukit Bintang; ☼ 6.30am-10pm

Mon-Sat, to 8pm Sun) Award-winning spa and gym featuring more than 40 bath and body treatments.

Swimming

Better for splashing around rather than swimming is the Sunway Lagoon (p138).

Bangsar Sports Complex (off Map p118; ☎ 2284 6065; 3 Jln Terasek Tiga, Bangsar Baru; admission RM3; ☼ 9.30am-noon, 2-4.30pm, 6-8:30pm, closed Sun mornings) Twenty-five-metre pool, which can get crowded. Also has tennis courts, and squash and badminton facilities.

Chin Woo Stadium Swimming Pool (Map p100; off Jln Hang Jebat; adult/child RM4/1.50; ☼ 2-8pm Mon-Fri, 9am-8pm Sat & Sun) Quiet 50m outdoor pool.

WALKING TOURS

These walking tours of the central KL are a great way to gain an insight into daily city life and the interaction between each of the city's main ethnic groups.

Chinatown Walk

Walk south from the station along Jln Benteng, which runs beside the Sungai Klang, across which you'll get a great view of **Masjid Jamek (1**; p103). When you reach the junction with the south end of Lebuh Ampang, you'll be at **Medan Pasar (2)**, site of KL's original market square. In the centre stands a clock tower built in 1937 to commemorate the coronation of King George IV. Note the **painted shophouses (3)**, at Nos 2 to 8, dating from 1906; you could pause for breakfast or coffee at **Sing Seng Nam (4**; p115).

Where Medan Pasar meets Lebuh Pasar Besar you'll see the **OCBC Building (5)**, a graceful Art Deco structure built in 1938 for the

Overseas Chinese Banking Company. Turn east along Lebuh Pasar Besar, to the corner with Jln Tun HS Lee, where you'll find **MS Ally Company (6)**, a pharmacy in business since 1909. Twenty metres down Jln Tun HS Lee on your right is the ornate, colourful but time-ravaged **Bank Simpanan Building (7)**, bearing the date 1914.

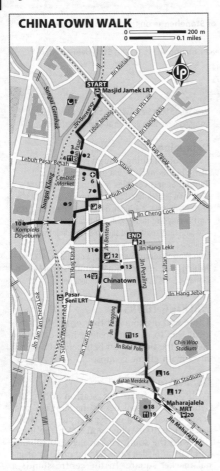

CHINATOWN WALK

Cross Lebuh Pudu, turn right, and after 25m duck left into an alleyway leading to the atmospheric **Sze Ya Temple (8**; p99), KL's oldest Taoist temple. Note the two gilded sedan chairs, dating from 1893 and encased in glass, flanking the temple's main entrance.

Exit the way you came in, cross the street and walk through the alley opposite the **Central Market (9**; p123). Previously the city's produce market, the Central Market, designed by TY Lee, is a fine Art Deco building that was saved by preservationists and refurbished as a centre for handicraft, antique and art sales, as well as a venue for art exhibitions and cultural shows.

Use the pedestrian bridge over the Sungai Klang to get a closer look at the 35-storey marble-clad **Kompleks Dayabumi (10)**. Designed by Nik Mohammed, the previous headquarters of Petronas is one of KL's most graceful buildings, with Islamic arches and recurring motifs.

Return to the southern end of Central Market. Head a short distance south, turn left onto Jln Cheng Lock, then right onto Jln Tun HS Lee. The shophouses along here are among Chinatown's oldest; note the unique feature of a 5ft way (pavement) lower than the road level. The competing scents of dried fish, herbs and fresh flowers hit you as you continue down to the junction with Jln Hang Lekir. On the south corner is the pale yellow-painted Art Deco–styled **Lee Rubber Building (11)**, occupied by Popular bookstore on the ground floor.

Further south along Jln Tun HS Lee, you won't miss the bright-red, incense-wreathed **Guandi Temple (12)**, which is also known as the Kwong Siew Free School. The figure at the rear of the temple is Guandi – the Taoist God of War – and on the altar in front of him are an impressive sword and halberd. Next door, duck into **Jln Sang Guna (13)**, a covered arcade housing Chinatown's atmospheric wet- and fresh-produce market.

Having taken note of the fish, pigs' trotters and tofu at the market, return to Jln Tun HS Lee to admire the 22m-high gate tower to the **Sri Mahamariamman Temple (14**; p99), and to breathe in the sweet jasmine of the flower sellers outside. Continue south after exploring the temple to Jln Sultan, where you turn left and then right onto Jln Panggong, which sweeps around into Jln Balai Polis; along here is **Old China Café (15**; p115), one of the nicest places to eat in Chinatown.

FEEDING THE DOCTOR FISH

Often combined with foot reflexology operations, fish spas are all the rage in KL and bring a new meaning to feeding the fish. Immerse your feet in a tank filled with the small *Garra rufa* and *Cyprinion macrostomus*, also known as Doctor Fish, and allow the flapping podiatrists to gently nibble away at the dead skin. It's an initially ticklish, but not wholly unpleasant, experience lasting 30 minutes (or as long as you can stand it!).

Among the places you can sample this service, which costs RM20 to RM30, are the KLCC aquarium (see p98) and the following:

Foot Master Dr Fish Spa (Map p96; ☎ 2144 3319; 6th fl, Berjaya Times Square; ☺ 10am-10pm)
Morino Kaze (Map p96; www.morinokaze.com.my; ☎ 2141 1916; 2nd fl Piccolo Galleria, 101 Jln Bukit Bintang; ☺ 1pm-1am) They also have a branch in Bangsar Baru (Map p118; ☎ 2288 1916; 9 Jln Telawi 3, Bangsar Baru; ☺ noon-midnight).

Don't stop yet, though, as there are a couple more temples to check out further south around the busy traffic roundabout of Bulatan Merdeka: the ornate ancestral **Chan See Shu Yuen Temple (16)** and, across Jln Stadium, the **Koon Yam (Guanyin) Temple (17)**, dedicated to the Goddess of Mercy. The central effigy inside is Sakyamuni, to whose right is a statue of the South Sea Guanyin (complete with flashing halo); to Sakyamuni's left is a Qianshou (Thousand Arm) Guanyin.

Over the footbridge is the **Chinese Assembly Hall (18)**; plays and musical performances occasionally happen here, and at the back is the **Purple Cane Tea Restaurant (19**; p115).

The **Maharajalela monorail station (20)** is close by if you want to finish your walk here. However, if it's evening, return to **Jln Petaling (21)** to experience the visceral excitement of the night market.

Little India Walk

Starting from Masjid Jamek LRT Station walk one block southeast to Lebuh Ampang. This atmospheric street, lined with moneychangers, Indian cafes, and street vendors selling Indian sweets and flower garlands, has long been the preserve of the Chettiars from South India. Note the striking **old shophouses (1)** at Nos 16 to 18 and Nos 24 to 30, and the ceramic peacock tiles on the **Chettiar House (2)** at No 85.

Return to the station, next to which you'll find the **Masjid Jamek (3**; p103). If you're dressed appropriately, enter the compound to experience the calm core of this pretty mosque. Next to the mosque on the corner of Jln Tun Perak and Jln Tuanku Abdul Rahman (TAR) is the Mogul-inspired **Sessions and Magistrates Courts (4)** building.

Turn right onto Jln TAR, then turn right again onto Jln Melayu and proceed towards the covered arcade of market stalls at the pedistrianised end of Jln Masjid India. Pick your way through the tightly packed stalls to find the Indian Muslim-style mosque **Masjid India (5)**, after which the street is named. You're now in the thick of KL's Little India, an energetic area defined by its preponderance of sari and scarf stalls, gold jewellers and DVD and CD shops playing Bollywood soundtracks at full blast.

The bazaar-like atmosphere of the streets is enhanced every Saturday from late afternoon when a *pasar malam* (night market) sets up along Lg TAR, the lane sandwiched between Jln TAR and Jln Masjid India.

A colonial relic surviving at the south end of Jln TAR is the **Coliseum Hotel (6**; p110), where Somerset Maugham once drank; stop here for a reviving beer or even a meal at the Coliseum Café. The Coliseum Cinema next door is of the same era and screens the latest Bollywood extravaganzas, while heading north along along Jln TAR you'll pass scores of fabric shops including the Art Deco beauty (highlighted with gold and flamingo pink) at No 126, home of **Euro Moda (7)**.

Another Art Deco movie house, the **Odeon (8)**, is on the corner of Jln Dang Wangi and Jln TAR, opposite Sogo department store. Head east along Jln Dang Wangi, then take the first road on the left: on the next corner, opposite the car park, you'll get a glimpse of the grand colonial era **Loke Mansion (9**; p103).

The parallel street to the east is Jln Doraisamy, a restored strip of shophouses turned into bars, clubs and restaurants and rebranded Asian Heritage Row. You could grab a coffee and cake at **Bisou (10**; p116), ending your walk at the nearby Medan Tuanku

KUALA LUMPUR

LITTLE INDIA WALK

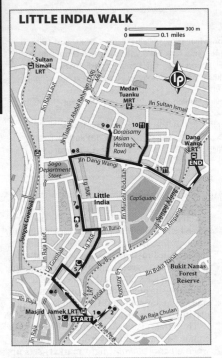

WALK FACTS

Start Masjid Jamek LRT station
Finish Medan Tuanku monorail or Dang Wangi LRT station
Distance 1.5km
Duration 1½ hours

monorail stop. It's better, though, to continue down Jln Dang Wangi to the venerable *kopitiam* **Yut Kee** (**11**, p116) to finish up at Dang Wangi LRT.

COURSES

Check directly with each of the listings for prices and exact course times and details.

ARTS & CRAFTS

C Works Design (Map p100; ☎ 012-257 2344; Ground fl, Central Market Annex; ☺ 10am-9pm) Paint your own batik panel from RM15. Choose a prepared design or create your own. It also has an outlet at Kompleks Budaya Kraf.
Kompleks Budaya Kraf (Map p96; ☎ 2162 7533; www.malaysiancraft.com; Jln Conlay; ☺ 9am-8pm Mon-Fri, to 7pm Sat & Sun) Try your hand at traditional Malay

crafts such as batik or pottery at the craft village in the grounds of this one-stop crafts complex. See also p123.
School of Hard Knocks (off Map pp92-3; ☎ 4145 6122; www.visitorcentre.royalselangor.com; Royal Selangor Pewter Factory, 4 Jln Usahawan 6, Setapak Jaya) This famous pewter centre offers entertaining 30-minute classes where you make your own pewter bowl; advance booking required.

COOKING

LaZat Malaysian Home Cooking Class (☎ 019-238 1198; www.malaysia-klcookingclass.com) Held on Tuesday & Saturday mornings, a 25 min drive from central KL; check the website for the different menus on offer.
Rohani Jelani (www.rohanijelani.com) Book online for courses with cookbook author Rohani Jelani in her kitchen out at Sungai Penchala, 10km southwest of KL.

LANGUAGES

YMCA (Map pp92-3; ☎ 2274 1439; www.ymcakl.com; 95 Jln Padang Belia, Brickfields) Offers Bahasa Malaysia classes as well as courses studying Thai, Mandarin/Cantonese, and Japanese. You can also study martial arts and different types of dancing here.

MEDITATION

Buddhist Maha Vihar (Map pp92-3; ☎ 2274 1141; www.buddhistmahavihara.com; 123 Jln Berhala) Built in the 1800s by Sinhalese Buddhists from Sri Lanka, this Brickfields landmark offers a variety of courses at its institute. Meditation and chanting classes are held daily.

MUSIC & DANCE

Kuala Lumpur Performing Arts Centre (KLPac; Map pp92-3; ☎ 4047 9060; www.klpac.com; Sentul Park, Jln Strachan) A variety of performing-arts courses are offered here, including courses in traditional instruments such as the gamelan.
Sutra Dance Theatre (Map pp92-3; ☎ 4021 1092; www.sutradancetheatre.com; 12 Persiaran Titiwangsa 3, Titiwangsa) Study Odissi and other forms of classical Indian dance at this cultural centre near Taman Tasik Titiwangsa. See also p122.
Temple of Fine Arts (Map pp92-3; ☎ 2274 3709; www.tfa.org.my; 114-116 Jln Berhala, Brickfields) Offers courses in classical Indian dance, song and music. Stage shows take place here throughout the year.

KUALA LUMPUR FOR CHILDREN

There are dozens of attractions around KL set up specifically to keep little ones entertained. A good starting point is the Lake Gardens, particularly the KL Bird Park (p101), the Butterfly Park (Taman Rama Rama; p102) and the playground and boating pond in the Lake Gardens Park. The waterfall splash pool in the KLCC Park (p98) is also great for waterbabies, as is the adjacent adventure playground and the Aquaria KLCC (p98).

Kids will also enjoy KL's malls. Berjaya Times Square (p123) has shops for kids of all ages, plus an indoor theme park. For younger kids, try **Megakidz** (off Map pp92-3; ☎ 2282 9300; www .megakidz.com.my; 3rd fl, North Court, Mid Valley Megamall; admission weekday/weekend RM19/25) in the Mid Valley Megamall – there are storytelling sessions, art activities and an indoor adventure playground, and the centre provides a crèche service (RM30 to RM35 for two hours) for kids aged four and over.

There are more theme parks dotted around KL, including the indoor and outdoor parks at Genting Highlands (p132) and the wet and wild park at Sunway Lagoon (p138). For nature activities, head to Zoo Negara (p132) or the canopy walkway at the Forest Research Institute of Malaysia (p132).

TOURS

Going Places Tours(Map p100; ☎ 2078 4008; www .goingplaces-kl.com; Original Backpackers Inn, 60a Jln Sultan, Chinatown) Offers tours tailored to the backpacker market, including adventurous options such as rafting, caving and rock-climbing.

KL Hop-On Hop-Off (☎ 2166 6162; www.myhopon hopoff.com; adult/child RM38/17; ◷ 8.30am-8.30pm) This double-decker air-con tourist bus makes a circuit of the main tourist sites half-hourly throughout the day. Stops include the KLCC, Jln Bukit Bintang, Menara KL, Chinatown, Merdeka Square and the attractions of Lake Gardens. Tickets, which can be bought on the bus, last all day and you can get on and off as often as you like.

Tour 51 Malaysia(Map p96; ☎ 2161 8830; MaTiC, 109 Jln Ampang) Runs a decent selection of half-day city tours (RM60) and day trips to places such as Putrajaya, Kuala Selangor and Pulau Ketam (RM150-180).

FESTIVALS & EVENTS

The capital is a good venue for Malaysia's major holidays and festivals, including Chinese New Year and Deepavali; see p470 for more information.

City Day KL commemorates becoming a federal territory on 1 February, typically with celebrations at Tasik Perdana and Lake Titiwangsa.

KL Design Week (www.kldesignweek.com) Events were held at CapSquare, MaTIC, Menara KL, the Annexe Gallery and the National Art Gallery for the inaugural design week in March 2009 – it's a great opportunity to catch up on the latest in design from Malaysia and the region.

Malaysian Grand Prix (www.malaysiangp.com.my) End March-early April sees special shopping promotions and other events in the city to accompany the annual Formula 1 race at Sepang (p138).

KL Festival (www.klfestival.org.my) July is a month of events showcasing Malaysian art, dance, theatre and music.

National Day At midnight on 31 August join the crowds in Merdeka Sq to celebrate the anniversary of Malaysia's independence in 1957. There are parades and festivities the next morning, usually at Commonwealth Stadium.

Freedom Film Fest (http://freedomfilmfest.komas.org) Local independent film makers get to show their cutting-edge and controversial docos and shorts in this festival with a political/social theme.

KL International Tower Jump (www.kltowerjump .com) The only time you'll be able to see people legally flinging themselves off the Menara KL is when the international BASE-jumping fraternity are in town in October.

KL International Film Festival (www.sinemamalaysia .com.my) Catch screenings and symposiums on local and international films in November.

SLEEPING

KL is awash with both budget and luxury hotels, although many of the cheapies are grubby flea-pits offering windowless boxy rooms, appealing only for their rock-bottom rates. Characterful midrange options are thin on the ground.

Always ask about special deals as practically all midrange and top-end places offer promotions that can substantially slash rack rates. The only time you should book ahead to be sure of accommodation is public holidays, when room discounts will not apply. Chinatown is crammed with budget places (most pretty awful) but there's also a very healthy backpacker scene in the Golden Triangle – this is where you'll find the pick of budget guesthouses and hostels. The best places will fill up quickly, so book ahead. If other locations are full, Little India and the seedy Chow Kit area further north also have plenty of low-priced accommodation, although many places are brothels, or close enough.

In KL budget means hostels offering a dorm bed and budget hotels offering a double room with attached bathroom for under RM100 net; midrange properties have double rooms with attached bathrooms for RM100 to RM400 net; top-end places charge over RM400 to which you'll also need to add 10% service and 5% tax (expressed as ++).

Budget
CHINATOWN

Wheelers Guest House (Map p100; ☎ 2070 1386; www .backpackerskl.com/wheelers.htm; Level 2, 131-133 Jln Tun HS

Lee; dm/r with shared bathroom RM10/25, r with bathroom RM50; 🖂 🖵) One of KL's quirkier hostels, Wheeler's has a mini-aquarium, gay-friendly staff and great rooftop terrace where free Friday night dinners are hosted. We also love that it offers home-made yoghurt and muesli for breakfast.

Original Backpackers Travellers Inn (Map p100; ☎ 2078 2473; www.backpackerskl.com; 60B Jln Sultan; dm/s/d with shared bathroom RM11/28/30, r with bathroom from RM54; 🖂 🖵) The highlight of this long-established and well-run hostel with perfunctory rooms is its rooftop bar where you can get breakfast as well as hook up with fellow travellers. It also runs a travel agency and can arrange a variety of trips (see p109).

Grocer's Inn (Map p100; ☎ 2078 7906; www.grocers inn.com.my; 78 Jln Sultan; dm/s/d from RM13/35/45; 🖂 🖵) Occupying a handsome century-old building that was once home to the Grocers' Association, this backpackers has a decent range of fan and air-con rooms as well as a rooftop dorm and balconies overlooking Chinatown's bustle. The entrance is in an alley, just off Jln Sultan.

YWCA (Map p100; ☎ 2070 1623; ywcamalaysia.org /accommodations_KL.html; 12 Jln Hang Jebat; s/d/tr with shared bathroom RM30/50/70) A throwback to another generation, this quiet establishment tucked away east of Chinatown offers plain but very acceptable rooms with fan, desk and wardrobe. Only for women, couples and families.

Hotel China Town Inn (Map p100; ☎ 2070 4008; www.chinatowninn.com; 52-54 Jln Petaling; r from RM79; 🖂 🖵) Even though it's in the thick of Chinatown, a calm atmosphere reigns at this well-managed, good-value hotel. All rooms have attached showers and TV (DVD players can be hired). The more expensive deluxe rooms with windows overlook noisy Jln Petaling market.

Also recommended:

Lee Mun Guest House (Map p100; ☎ 2078 0639; 5th fl, 109 Jln Petaling; dm/s/d RM10/25/35; 🖂) No-frills cheapie where the cardboard partition walls are covered with a colourful collage of magazine clippings. The entrance is on Jln Sultan.

Hotel Lok Ann (Map p100; ☎ 2078 9544; 113A Jln Petaling; s/d RM50/60; 🖂) Good value standard hotel, offering clean, spacious rooms with windows, TV, phone and large shower rooms.

GOLDEN TRIANGLE & KLCC
Red Palm (Map p96; ☎ 2143 1279; www.redpalm-kl.com; 5 Tingkat Tong Shin; dm/s/d/tr with breakfast & shared bath-

room RM25/50/70/105; 🖵) Its rooms are tiny and separated by thin walls, but with its friendly management and colourful, comfy communal areas Red Palm feels more like a home than a hostel.

Green Hut Lodge (Map p96; ☎ 2142 3339; www .thegreenhut.com; 48 Tingkat Tong Shin; dm/s/d with breakfast & shared bathroom RM25/50/65, d with breakfast & bathroom RM90; 🖂 🖵) A classic traveller's choice, complete with towel-draped 12-bed dorm, noticeboards and staff that speak Bahasa Backpacker. It's spotless and the jungle mural on the lobby wall is rather eye-catching.

Trekker Lodge (Map p96; ☎ 2142 4633; www .thetrekkerlodge.com; 1-1 Jln Angsoka; dm/s/d with shared bathroom RM25/50/65; d with bathroom RM90; 🖂 🖵) In an old apartment block, this place offers pretty much the same deal as the Green Hut Lodge – no surprise, since it's owned by the same people.

Bedz KL (Map p96; ☎ 2144 2339; www.bedzkl.com; 58 Changkat Bukit Bintang; dm RM30; 🖂 🖵) There are only dorms at this smart new choice, shielded from busy Changkat Bukit Bintang by a grove of bamboo. Rain showers, fussball, plenty of internet terminals and souvenir T-shirts are also part of the package.

our pick Classic Inn (Map p96; ☎ 2148 8648; www .classicinn.com.my; Lorong 1/77A, Changkat Thambi Dollah; dm/s/d R35/88/118; 🖂 🖵) Occupying a smartly renovated, yellow-painted shophouse on the southern edge of the Golden Triangle, this is a retro-charming choice with dorms and private rooms (all with windows), a small grassy garden and welcoming staff.

Lodge Paradise Hotel (Map p96; ☎ 2142 0122; www .lodgeparadize.com; 2 Jln Tengah; dm/r RM35/100; 🅿 🖂 🖵) Although its kidney-shaped swimming pool is currently just for show, this revamped hotel in a four-storey 1940s building couldn't be better placed and promises to offer a great deal once its renovation is complete.

LITTLE INDIA & CHOW KIT
Ben Soo Homestay (Map pp92-3; ☎ 2691 8096, 012-675 6110; bensoohome@yahoo.com; 2nd fl, 61B Jln Tiong Nam; s/d without air-con RM35/40, with use of air-con RM40/46; 🖂 🖵) Down-at-heel but quirkily charming, this homestay offers just two plain clean rooms with wooden floors and shared bathrooms, and the family who runs it is very welcoming.

Coliseum Hotel (Map p100; ☎ 2692 6270; 98-100 Jln TAR; s/d RM38/45; 🖂) If high-ceilinged rooms with ancient electric switches and furnishings are your thing, you'll consider staying here money well spent. All bathrooms are shared. Book well in advance, as it's often full.

BRICKFIELDS

YMCA (Map pp92-3; ☎ 2274 1439; www.ymcakl.com; 95 Jln Padang Belia; d/tr RM80/100; ❄) Close to KL Sentral, the rooms here are spotless and come with TV, telephone and that rarity in a cheap KL hotel: a wardrobe in which to hang your clothes.

Midrange
CHINATOWN

Citin Hotel (Map p100; ☎ 2031 7777; www.citinhotels .com; 38 Jln Pudu; r with breakfast from RM145; ❄ 🖳) You could hardly get closer to Puduraya bus station, which ensures a steady flow of customers for this cut-above-the-average hotel on an otherwise downmarket strip.

5 Elements Hotel (Map p100; ☎ 2031 6888; www .the5elementshotel.com.my; Lot 243 Jln Sultan; s/d from RM149.50/184; ❄ 🖳) With rates that include breakfast and a good range of rooms, some with views towards KL Tower, this new hotel makes a credible stab at boutique stylings. We particularly liked the sensuous design motif snaking its way across the corridor and bedroom walls.

Swiss-Inn (Map p100; ☎ 2072 3333; www.swissinn kualalumpur.com; 62 Jln Sultan; d with breakfast from RM150; ❄ 🖳) Comfortable, clean and centrally located, this is a justly popular choice. The cheapest rooms are windowless but still appealing, with blonde-wood fittings and pastel coverings over spacious beds.

AnCasa Hotel and Spa Kuala Lumpur (Map p100; ☎ 2026 6060; www.ancasa-hotel.com; Jln Tun Tan Cheng Lock; d from RM350; ❄ 🖳) Promotions slash the rack rates by more than half at one of Chinatown's best midrange option, which recently added a Balinese-style spa. Comfortable rooms feature satellite TV, small fridge, kettle and in-room safe.

GOLDEN TRIANGLE

Number Eight Guesthouse (Map p96; ☎ 2144 2050; www.numbereight.com.my; 8-10 Tingkat Tong Shin; d with shared bathroom RM90, with bathroom RM120-140, both with breakfast; ❄ 🖳) Although it's starting to look a little worn, Number Eight's minimalist design remains super-stylish and its value-for-money rooms, some with TVs and DVD players, leave most competitors standing. It does its bit for the environment with solar-heated water.

41 Berangan (Map p96; ☎ 2144 8691; www.41berangan .com; 41 Jln Berangan; d with breakfast from RM120; ❄ 🖳) This sleek new property offers zen-style simplicity and innovation: the two courtyard rooms have been built inside shipping crates. There are a couple of cheaper rooms with shared bathrooms.

Alpha Genesis (Map p96; ☎ 2141 2000; www.alphagenesis hotel.com; 45 Tingkat Tong Shin; r with breakfast from RM170; ❄ 🖳) The rooms are spacious with contemporary furnishings that verge on boutique territory. The deluxe rooms at the front have great views towards the Petronas Towers, and you can rent DVD players (RM25 per day).

Radius International Hotel (Map p96; ☎ 2715 3888; www.radius-international.com; 51A Changkat Bukit Bintang; r with breakfast from RM200; ❄ 🖳) Excellently located for the bars and restaurants of Changkat Bukit Bintang, this pleasant hotel offers some great promotions and high standards as well as a decent-sized pool.

Hotel Capitol (Map p96; ☎ 2143 7000; www.fhihotels .com; Jln Bulan; s/d from RM210; ❄ 🖳) Go online to get the best rates for this pleasing contemporary-styled hotel. Check out its loft-style and premium corner rooms for their hip furnishings and good views. Guests have access to the nearby Federal Hotel's swimming pool.

Piccolo Hotel (Map p96; ☎ 2303 8000; www.the piccolohotel.com; 101 Jln Bukit Bintang; r from RM287.50; ❄ 🖳) Striking marine images decorate the rooms at this new hotel that's going after the boutique crowd. Practically perpetual promotional rates and an excellent location make it a fine choice for business or pleasure.

Royale Bintang Kuala Lumpur (Map p96; ☎ 2143 9898; www.royale-bintang-hotel.com.my; 17-21 Jln Bukit Bintang; r from RM310; ❄ 🖳 🏊) Stylish property offering spacious, comfortable rooms (with high-speed internet access, cable TV, complimentary newspaper), a bar, restaurant, and reasonable-sized gym and pool.

Prince Hotel & Residence Kuala Lumpur (Map p96; ☎ 2170 8888; www.princehotelkl.com.my; 4 Jln Conlay; d/ apt from RM370/480; ❄ 🖳 🏊) The Prince offers outstanding value for its modern, cream-coloured rooms. Some nice facilities include a kids' club, and its serviced apartments are good for long-term stays.

Also recommended:

Bintang Warisan Hotel (Map p96; ☎ 2148 8111; www.bintangwarisan.com; 68 Jln Bukit Bintang; r RM170; ❄) Attractive small hotel with a pre-Independence façade but modern rooms.

Coronade Hotel (Map p96; ☎ 2148 6888; www.coro nade.com; Jln Walter Grenier; d from RM276; ✂ 🖵 🔊) Behind Lot 10, but with good views from upper floors.

Swiss-Garden Hotel (Map p96; ☎ 2141 3333; www .swissgarden.com; 117 Jln Pudu; d with breakfast RM276; ✂ 🖵 🔊) High-standard rooms and facilities.

LITTLE INDIA

Tune Hotel (Map pp92-3; ☎ 7962 5888; www.tunehotels .com; 316 Jln TAR; r RM50-150; ✂ 🖵 🔊) This innovative operation uses the low-cost approach of local budget airline AirAsia: book online well in advance and it's possible to snag a room with a bathroom for under RM50. The basic rate, however, just gets you the room – air-con, toiletries, wi-fi access are extra. Each floor is sponsored, which means you'll find yourself gazing at an ad for, say, McDonald's, Maggi or Nippon Paints in your room and along the corridors. There's also a branch next to the LCC-T (Low Cost Carrier Terminal).

Hotel Noble (Map p100; ☎ 2711 7111; www.hotel noble.com; 165 Jln TAR; d with breakfast RM150; ✂ 🖵) Staff are polite and the ambience is smart, clean and comfortable at this modern hotel on the doorstep of Little India. Rooms with a bathroom come with minibar, safety deposit box, coffee-/tea-making facilities and TV.

Top End

GOLDEN TRIANGLE & KLCC

Impiana (Map p96; ☎ 2147 1111; www.impiana.com; 13 Jln Pinang; d with breakfast from RM450; ✂ 🖵 🔊) The chic Impiana offers spacious rooms with parquet floors and lots of seductive amenities, including an infinity pool with a view across to the Petronas Towers partly marred by construction of yet another luxe hotel in the KLCC quadrant.

Pacific Regency Hotel Suites (Map p96; ☎ 2332 7777; www.pacific-regency.com; Menara Panglobal, Jln Puncak; apt from R450; P ✂ 🖵 🔊) These upmarket self-catering studios and serviced apartments are fine value compared to rooms of a similar standard at KL's other five-star properties. Head to the roof to enjoy the rooftop pool and Luna (p119), one of the city's best bars.

Westin Kuala Lumpur (Map p96; ☎ 2731 8333; www .westin.com/kualalumpur; 199 Jln Bukit Bintang; d/apt from RM525/1250; P ✂ 🖵 🔊) The Westin's spacious rooms are modern and appealing, and it's easy to see why long-term residents love its serviced apartments, which have full kitchens and glassed-in balconies. It also has a good gym and stylish restaurants and bars.

---

our pick Traders Hotel Kuala Lumpur (Map p96; ☎ 2332 9888; www.tradershotels.com; KLCC, off Jln Kia Peng; r/ste from RM610/890; P ✂ 🖵 🔊) Lovely as it is inside, you're going to want to opt for a room with a view across to the Petronas Towers at this contemporary-design addition to KL's portfolio of luxe hotels.

Shangri-La Hotel (Map p96; ☎ 2032 2388; www .shangri-la.com; 11 Jln Sultan Ismail; r/ste from RM660/1910; P ✂ 🖵 🔊) A jaw-droppingly opulent hotel with an impressive range of facilities and several top-class restaurants. The rooms are spacious and well equipped.

Hotel Maya (Map p96; ☎ 2711 8866; www.hotel maya.com.my; 138 Jln Ampang; r/ste with breakfast from RM700/1000; P ✂ 🖵 🔊) Even though it remains one of KL's most stylish hotels, the Maya is beginning to show wear and tear in its sleek timber-floored studios and suites. Rates include airport transfers, as well as a host of other goodies.

Hotel Istana (Map p96; ☎ 2141 9988; www.hotel istana.com.my; 73 Jln Raja Chulan; r/ste from RM1100/3500; P ✂ 🖵 🔊) The Istana's soothing rooms – where beds sport batik throws and there are fresh flowers – stand in contrast to the high glitz of its lobby, which boasts giant columns and Malay motifs. There's also a good-sized swimming pool in a garden setting.

KL SENTRAL & LAKE GARDENS

Hilton Kuala Lumpur (Map pp92-3; ☎ 2264 2264; www .kuala-lumpur.hilton.com; 3 Jln Stesen Sentral; r/ste RM455/850; P ✂ 🖵 🔊) The super-stylish Hilton's contemporary 'innovation rooms' boast 42-inch plasma TV screens, with X-boxes and Playstations available if you happen to have left your own at home. Sweeping city and Lake Garden views and on-the-spot access to KL Sentral are pluses, along with a fab range of restaurants and bars.

Carcosa Seri Negara (Map pp92-3; ☎ 2295 0888; www.ghmhotels.com; Taman Tasik Perdana; ste from RM1100; P ✂ 🖵 🔊) Secluded in the lush greenery of the Lake Gardens this heritage property is split b_ween two colonial mansions: Carcosa, once the residence of British government representative Sir Frank Swettenham; and Seri Negara, the official guesthouse. There are 13 conservatively designed, spacious suites, very much suited to non–rock star VIPs. For a taste of how the other half live consider splashing out on a meal in the Dining Room (p117) or on the hotel's traditional afternoon tea (RM69).

EATING

From Malay and Nonya dishes to practically every permutation of Chinese, Indian, Southeast Asian and European, KL is a nonstop feast. You can dine in incredible elegance or mingle with locals at thousands of street stalls – it's all good and it's seldom heavy on the pocket.

Whether you're on a budget or not, most often the best food is from the hawker stalls, cheap cafes (called *kopitiam*) and inexpensive restaurants (*restoran*). Hygiene standards at hawker stalls are generally good and you should have little to fear from eating at them. However, if this is not your thing – or you just want air-con with your meal – then KL's many food courts, usually located in shopping malls, offer an answer.

If you need more options than those listed below, we highly recommend the website **Fried Chillies** (www.friedchillies.com), which includes spot-on reviews by some of the most enthusiastic foodies we've met, as well as video clips. *Time Out Kuala Lumpur* (see p94) also compiles a monthly top 40 of its favourite culinary picks.

Golden Triangle & KLCC
CHINESE

Blue Boy Vegetarian Food Centre (Map p96; ☎ 2144 9011; Jln Tong Shin; meals RM5-10; ✕ 7.30am-9.30pm) It's hard to believe that everything prepared at this spotless place at the base of a backstreet apartment block is vegetarian, but it's true. The *char kway teow* (broad noodles fried in chilli and black-bean sauce) is highly recommended.

Crystal Jade La Mian Xiao Long Bao (Map p96; ☎ 2148 2338; Annex Block, Lot 10, 50 Jln Sultan Ismail; meals RM20-40; ✕ 11am-10.30pm Mon-Fri, 10.30am-10.30pm Sat & Sun) Avidly patronised chain that turn out ex-

cellent hand-cut noodles and dim sum (sweet and savoury minidishes), with a photographic menu whose pictures actually resemble the delicious food you're served.

Hakka (Map p96; ☎ 2143 1908; meals RM80-100; 90 Jln Raja Chulan; ✕ noon-3pm, 6-11pm) Specialising in Hakka-style cuisine: try the stuffed crabs and tofu dishes. The outdoor section – atmospheric and hung with fairy lights that complement the view of the illuminated Petronas Towers – is only open in the evenings.

EUROPEAN & FUSION

Loaf (Map p96; ☎ 2145 3036; www.theloaf.net; Level 3 & 4 Pavilion KL, 168 Jln Bukit Bintang; meals RM10-20; ✕ 10am-10pm) This Euro-style bakery cafe and bistro (in which ex-PM Dr Mahathir is an investor) is a Malaysian take on a Japanese baked-goods shop. Huh? No matter – the baked goods are divine and we love the mini cheesecakes for a quick snack.

Chiaroscuro (Map p96; ☎ 2144 8006; Ground fl 38 Bidara, 30, Jln Bedara; meals RM50; ✕ noon-3pm, 6.30-11pm Mon-Fri, 6.30-11pm Sat) Tuck into fantastic pizza and other Italian dishes at this relaxed trattoria tucked behind the Istana Hotel.

Magnificent Fish & Chip Bar (Map p96; ☎ 2142 7021; 28 Changkat Bukit Bintang; meals RM60-80; ✕ 8.30am-1am Mon-Fri, 10.30am-1am Sat & Sun) The high quality of the fish (at least eight types, including barramundi) explains the relatively high price you'll pay for the newspaper-wrapped fish and chips at this thoroughly English operation.

Twentyone Kitchen & Bar (Map p96; ☎ 2142 0021; www.twentyone.com.my; 20-1 Changkat Bukit Bintang; meals RM60-80; ✕ noon-3am) Lots of interesting choices on the menu here, several of which you can sample together on taster plates. The bar upstairs, with a deck overlooking the street, gets cranking at weekends when a DJ spins chill and dance tunes.

our pick **Frangipani** (Map p96; ☎ 2144 3001; www .frangipani.com.my; 25 Changkat Bukit Bintang; meals RM100-150; ✕ 7.30-10.30pm Tue-Sun) Indulge in delicious, creative fusion-style dishes at this outstanding fine-dining restaurant. The dining room, which surrounds a reflecting pool, is divine, and there's an equally stylish upstairs bar.

Stylish **Neroteca** (Map p96; ☎ 2070 0530; www .neroteca.com; the Somerset, 8 Lg Ceylon; meals RM50-100; ✕ 10am-midnight Wed-Mon, 6pm-midnight Tue) is the cosy stablemate of nearby **Nerovivo** (Map p96; ☎ 2070 3120; www.nerovivo.com; 3A Jln Ceylon; meals RM50-100; ✕ noon-midnight Sun-Fri, 6pm-midnight Sat) and is equally adept at turning out delicious, authentic Italian staples.

A pork lovers' heaven, **Elcerdo** (Map p96; ☎ 2145 0511; www.elcerdokl.com; 43-45 Changkat Bukit Bintang; meals RM80-100; ⏰ noon-3pm, 6.30-11pm) is a classy 'nose to tail eating' joint. Next door is its tapas bar, El Cerdito, while across the road the restaurant-bar **Werner's on Changkat** (☎ 2142 5670; www.wernerskl.com; 50 Changkat Bukit Bintang) completes the German owner's hat trick.

INDIAN

Restoran Nagansari Curry House (Map p96; Jln Nagansari; meals RM5-10; ⏰ 24hrs) This simple place gets the thumbs up for its authentic banana-leaf meals, including a vegetarian set lunch for RM4.50.

Vansh (Map p96; ☎ 2142 6162; Lower ground fl, Starhill Gallery, 181 Jln Bukit Bintang; meals RM80; ⏰ noon-1am) Tasty and nicely presented Indian food is served at this super-stylish restaurant.

JAPANESE

Rakuzen (Map p96; ☎ 2145 6200; Chulan Sq, 92 Jln Raja Chulan; meals RM50-70; ⏰ lunch & dinner) Great value and nicely presented traditional dishes can be found at this smart place with some Japanese-style rooms at the rear.

Fukuya (Map pp92-3; ☎ 2144 1022 www.fukuya .com.my; 9 Jln Delima; meals R100; ⏰ noon-2.30pm, 6.30-10.30pm Mon-Sat) Based in a quiet suburban area of downtown KL, this 'house of happiness' is where chef Takao Ando makes diners smile with his impeccable *kaiseki* (Japanese fine dining) cuisine.

MALAY & NONYA

Betty's Café (Map p96; ☎ 2031 7880; www.bettys group.com; Wisma Conway, Jln Raja Chulan; meals RM8-15; ⏰ 10am-6pm) Cutely designed canteen offering simple local dishes such as curry laksa, prawn mee noodles and Ipoh *koay teow* soup. There's also a branch in CapSquare (Map p100; ☎ 2691 7880; G49, CapSquare Centre, Capital Square, 8 Jln Munshi Abdullah; ⏰ 10am-10pm).

Little Penang Kafé (Map p96; ☎ 2163 0215; Level 4, Suria KLCC, Jln Ampang; meals RM15-20; ⏰ 10am-10pm) Set meals (RM13.50) let you sample several of the Nonya dishes that Penang is famous for, including *lobak* (deep-fried tofu-rolled chicken strips) and the spicy Siamese *lemak* laksa (using coconut milk), only available Friday to Sunday.

Bijan (Map p96; ☎ 2031 3575; www.bijanrestaurant .com.my; 3 Jln Ceylon; meals RM60-80; ⏰ noon-2.30pm,

6-10.30pm Mon-Sat, 4-11pm Sun) Skilfully cooked traditional dishes in a sophisticated environment. The durian cheesecake is a surprisingly pleasant way of sampling the pungent fruit.

Top Hat (Map p96; ☎ 2142 8611; www.top-hat-restaurant .com; 3 Jln Stonor; meals RM60-110; ⏰ noon-10.30pm) Serves both traditional British – think oxtail stew and bread-and-butter pudding – and local dishes, such as Nyonya Laksa (R28), which all come with signature 'top hats' (pastry shells filled with sliced veggies) and choice of local dessert.

Seri Angkasa (Map p96; ☎ 2020 5055; www .serimelayu.com; Menara KL, Jln Puncak; meals RM70-100; ⏰ noon-11.30pm) Watch KL pass by from this revolving restaurant atop Menara KL (KL Tower). The very decent lunch buffet (noon and 2.30pm) is RM66.70. Book for evening meals, especially for sunset dining. There's a dress code, but the staff will provide men wearing shorts with a sarong (to cover the legs).

Enak (Map p96; ☎ 2141 8973; www.enakkl.com; Feast fl, Starhill Gallery, 181 Jln Bukit Bintang; meals RM70-100; ⏰ noon-1am) Finely presented Malay cuisine with a sophisticated twist, as befits the trendy Starhill Gallery.

Ibunda (Map pp92-3; ☎ 2142 8488; www.ibunda -finedine.com.my; 251 Jln Bukit Bintang; meals RM80-120; ⏰ 11.30am-2.30pm, 6.30-10.30pm Mon-Sat) In a restored colonial mansion Ibunda makes a valiant attempt at Malay-fusion fine dining, serving up eye-popping creations with subtle flavours and textures.

THAI & VIETNAMESE

Sao Nam (Map p96; ☎ 2144 1225; www.saonam.com.my; 25 Tingkat Tong Shin; meals RM50; ⏰ noon-2.30pm, 6-11pm Tue-Sun) Great Vietnamese cuisine served in a colourful, propaganda-art setting.

our pick **Mythai Jim Thompson** (Map p96; ☎ 2148 6151; www.jimthompson.com; Feast fl, Starhill Gallery, 181 Jln Bukit Bintang; meals RM60-80; ⏰ noon-11.30pm) As you'd expect for a Jim Thompson operation, the decor here is lovely, with silk cushions and other decorative items that can be purchased at the store on the gallery's 3rd floor. The food is equally fab and includes dishes that you'd rarely find outside Thailand.

HAWKER STALLS & FOOD COURTS

Jln Alor is lined with some of the best hawker stalls and restaurants in KL. Locals complain that the prices are on the high side, but it's

---

SISTERS ARE DOING IT FOR THEMSELVES: MEI LIM

Mei Lim is obviously doing something right since her Sisters Crispy Popiah stalls can be found in KL's Mid Valley mall, PJ's Sunway Pyramid mall and Putrajaya's Amandala mall, as well as at its humble original location in the Imbi Market.

How long have you been rolling popiah? I've been in this business over 20 years.

What are the ingredients in the roll? I use egg frost – flakes of deep fried egg; crushed peanuts; fried shallots; slivers of cucumber and carrot; and turnip boiled in soy sauce and garlic. I prepare this in the afternoon so it has time to rest overnight – that way it tastes better.

What's the secret to your rolls? There is a secret, but I'm not telling you.

---

still great value and a wonderful atmosphere. Most stalls open around 5pm and close late, although a few are open all day. We list standout options below.

For food courts you can't go wrong with those in the malls. Suria KLCC (Map p96) has two: Signatures on level two specialises in international food, while Rasa Food Arena on level four has more local selections. Pavilion KL's (Map p96) basement level Food Republic food court also offers outstanding choice and swank surroundings.

Ngau Kee Beef Ball Noodles (Map p96; Jln Tingkat Tong Shin; meals RM5-10; 24hr) The dish at this venerable street stall comes in two parts: dry, steamed noodles topped with a thick soysauce mince, and the chunky beef balls in a clear soup. Delicious!

our pick Imbi Market (Map p96; Jln Kampung; meal RM10; 7-11am) The official name is Pasar Baru Bukit Bintang, but everyone knows it simply as Imbi Market. Breakfast is like a party here with all the friendly and curious locals happily recommending their favourite stalls. We like Sisters Popiah (see above); Teluk Intan Chee Cheung Fun, which serves a lovely oyster and peanut congee (rice porridge), and Bunn Choon for the creamy mini-egg tarts.

1 + 1 (Map p96; 21A Jln Alor; meals R10-15; 24hr) One of the few round-the-clock operations on this eats street that does good dim sum for breakfast and lunch. Opposite is the frog porridge stall (per bowl RM7; open 5pm to 2am). You can choose to have 'spicy', where the frogs legs (RM7) are served separately, or 'non-spicy', where they're mixed in with the tasty rice gruel.

our pick Wong Ah Wah (Map p96; Jln Alor; meals RM15-20; 4pm-4am) At the southern end of the street, and justly famous for its seriously addictive chicken wings, this is an ideal spot for a late-night snack with a bottle of beer.

Chinatown & Around

CHINESE

West Lake Restoran (Map p100; ☎ 2072 3350; 15 Jln Sultan; meals RM10-20; 11am-midnight) Simple eatery known for its *yong dou fu* (bean curd stuffed with minced fish) and *mee* (noodle) dishes.

Purple Cane Tea Restaurant (Map p100; ☎ 2272 3090; 1 Jln Maharajalela; meals RM20-30; 11am-10pm) Tucked behind the Chinese Assembly Hall is this relaxing place where tea is used in many of the dishes, including a chicken version of *bak kut the* (a soup normally made with pork rib).

EUROPEAN & FUSION

Café Café (Map pp92-3; ☎ 2141 8141; www.cafecafekl.com; 175 Jln Maharajalela; meals RM80-100; 6-11pm) Flickering candles and twinkling crystal decoration conjure a romantic atmosphere at this quirky French-Italian restaurant. Avoid the fancy fois gras dishes, stick to simpler concoctions and you'll do fine.

MALAY & NONYA

Sing Seng Nam (Map p100; 2 Medan Pasar; meals RM10; 7am-5pm Mon-Sat) KL is fast filling up with new 'old-style' *kopitiam*, but this is the genuine object, busy with lawyers from the nearby courts enjoying breakfast of *kaya* toast and runny boiled egg or a *kopi peng* (iced coffee with milk).

our pick Old China Café (Map p100; ☎ 2072 5915; www.oldchina.com.my; 11 Jln Balai Polis; meals RM40-50; 11.30am-10pm) The old guild hall of the Selangor & Federal Territory Laundry Association is the atmospheric home for this fine cafe specialising in Nonya dishes from Melaka and Penang – its speciality is the spicy coconut-milk soup, laksa.

Precious (Map p100; ☎ 2273 7372; 1st fl, Central Market, Jln Hang Kasturi; meals RM60; 11.30am-10pm) Decorated with beautiful antiques (most for sale) and modern Chinese art, this sister establishment to the Old China Café offers a more upscale environment in which to enjoy trademark Nonya cuisine, as well as a bar.

NEPALI

Khukri (Map p100; ☎ 2072 0663; www.malayanepal.com; Jln Silang; meals RM20; ☯ 9am-9pm) Something of a gathering point for Nepalis in KL, this simple restaurant serves authentic Nepalese cuisine, including great *momos* (dumplings), steamed or fried, and spicy chicken and mutton dishes.

HAWKER STALLS & FOOD COURTS

There's a good food court on level two of **Central Market** (Map p100; Jln Hang Kasturi), but if you want to see all of Chinatown's action, you need to get out on the streets. The easy touristy option is to take a seat at one of the tables outside the Chinese restaurants on Jln Hang Lekir, between Jln Petaling and Jln Sultan.

Better is to join locals enjoying spicy fish and seafood dishes from the **Ikan panggang stall** (Map p100; ☎ 019-315 9448; ☯ 5-11pm Tue-Sun) outside Hong Leong Bank, unsigned and tucked behind the stalls on the corner of Jln Petaling and Jln Hang Lekir. Order ahead – it generally takes 20 minutes for your foil-wrapped pouch of seafood to cook, allowing time to explore the market. Wash the meal down with a glass of *mata kucing* (cat's eye), a refreshing Asian fruit drink, also bought from a stall on the same corner.

Set back from the main drag is the old-style **Tang City Food Court** (Map p100; Jln Hang Lekir). Head to the back to find spicy Burmese noodle dishes served at **Boe Jet Kei** (☯ 4-11.30pm).

Little India, Kampung Baru & Northern Kuala Lumpur

CHINESE

Yut Kee (Map p100; ☎ 2698 8108; 35 Jln Dang Wangi; meals RM10-15; ☯ 7.30am-4.45pm) It doesn't matter how busy it gets at this much beloved Hainanese *kopitiam*, the staff remain calm and polite. Skip the Western dishes and go for the house specialities such as *roti babi* (deep-fried bread filled with shredded pork and onions) or the fried Hokkien mee noodles.

EUROPEAN

Bisou (Map pp92-3; ☎ 2693 0131; www.bisou.com.my; 58 Jln Doraisamy; meals RM10; ☯ 8am-9pm Mon-Fri, 10am-9pm Sat) One of the cheapest and least pretentious places on Asian Heritage Row. It's a cute spot to grab a Western-style breakfast, sandwich or yummy iced cupcake.

Coliseum Café (Map p100; ☎ 2692 6270; 100 Jln TAR; meals RM30; ☯ 10am-10pm) Come for its legendary sizzling steaks and the stuck-in-time colonial-era ambience.

INDIAN

Bilal Restoran (Map p100; ☎ 2078 0804; 33 Jln Ampang; meals RM10; ☯ 8am-10pm) No points for ambience, but the Bilal is highly popular for its South Indian Muslim dishes. There's a large range of *roti canai* (unleavened, flaky flat bread), including egg and *bawang* (onion), plus *ikan* (fish) and *kambing* (mutton) curries.

Sagar (Map p100; ☎ 2691 3088; Semua House, Jln Masjid India; meals RM10; ☯ 8am-8pm) Enjoy the good-value *thali* meals (rice or bread served with assorted vegetables and curries; RM8.80 to RM9.80) at this sidewalk cafe, and soak up the street life of Little India. There's also an air-con section inside.

Sangeetha (Map p100; ☎ 2032 3333; 65 Lebuh Ampang; meals RM10; ☯ 8am-11pm) This well-run vegetarian restaurant serves lots of South Indian delights such as *idli* (savoury, soft, fermented-rice-and-lentil cakes) and *masala dosa* (rice-and-lentil crepes stuffed with spiced potatoes).

Restoran Buharry (Map pp92-3; ☎ 2697 7798; www.buharrybistro.com; 22-24 Jln Doriaswamy; meals RM10-15; ☯ 6am-2am Mon, to 4am Tue-Thu, to 5am Fri & Sat, 8.30am-1am Sun) Popular hangout for office workers on Asian Heritage Row. All the usual *mamak* (Muslim Indian) favourites are on offer, plus excellent *tom yam* (hot and sour) soup and delicious mango smoothies.

JAPANESE & THAI

Yu Ri Tei (Map pp92-3; ☎ 4044 0422; Sentul Park Koi Centre, Jln Strachan; meals RM15-20; ☯ 11am-9pm) Beside the Sentul Park Koi Centre is this charming tea-house serving simple Japanese dishes such as noodles. Combine a meal here with a visit to the adjacent Kuala Lumpur Performing Arts Centre (KLPac; p122).

Thai-la (Map p100; ☎ 2698 4933; Ground fl, CapSquare, Persiaran CapSquare; ☯ noon-10pm Mon-Sat) One of the more interesting dining options at the new CapSquare complex. The food is tasty, the decor has a chic charm and Zaki, the entertainingly camp owner, can talk the hind legs off a donkey.

HAWKER STALLS

The best time to visit Little India is during the Saturday *pasar malam* on Lg Tuanku Abdul Rahman, the alley between Jln TAR and Jln Masjid India. From mid-afternoon, this narrow lane becomes crammed with food stalls serving excellent Malaysian Indian and Chinese food.

Kampung Baru's Saturday *pasar malam* – called the **Sunday Market** (Pasar Minggu; Map pp92-3) because it runs into the early hours of Sunday morning – is also worth attending. The main action here is focused at the end of Jln Raja Alang, not far from the LRT station, where you'll find the stall **Warong Perasan** (Map p96) serving a good selection of Malay dishes.

Ikan Bakar Berempah (Map p96; cnr Jln Raja Muda Musa & Jln Raja Abdullah; meals RM5-10; 24hr) If you can't make it to Kampung Baru for the night market, head to this stall serving a wonderful range of barbecued fish daily.

Lake Gardens, Brickfields & Southern Kuala Lumpur

Brickfield's Indian community makes it a top spot for Indian cuisine.

CHINESE

Siu Siu (Map pp92-3; 016 370 8555; 15-11 Lg Syed Putra Kiri; mains R40-60; 11am-11pm Tue-Sun) On the way to the Tian How Temple, this is a deserved local favourite. Order the milk curry prawns with buns to soak up the tasty gravy or any type of fish.

Chynna (Map pp92-3; 2264 2266; Hilton Kuala Lumpur, 3 Jln Stesen Sentral, Brickfields; meals RM100; noon-2.30pm, 6.30-10.30pm) The big hit among the Hilton's 'Studio' concept restaurants, ranged around Frank Woo's striking giant sculpture *Dancing Shadow*. Chynna offers tasty Cantonese dishes in a Shanghai-chic setting, in opulent reds and golds. A herbal doctor is on hand to balance your chi.

EUROPEAN

Yogitree (off Map pp92-3; 2282 6763; www.yogi tree.com; 1st fl, Gardens Mid Valley, Jln Syed Putra; meals RM20-70; 10am-10pm) We love anywhere that serves breakfast until 6pm. This 'real food' cafe and yoga clothes boutique uses plenty of organic produce in its mix-and-match local and Western food menu.

Dining Room (Map pp92-3; 2295 0813; Carcosa Seri Negara, Taman Tasik Perdana; meals RM200; noon-

2pm, 7-11pm) A masterclass in understated luxury and sublime French-style cuisine. You won't regret treating yourself to the set lunch here (RM126.50), while for a real celebration there's the eight-course degustation dinner (RM322).

INDIAN

Annalakshmi (Map pp92-3; 2272 3799; www.annalakshmi .com.my; Temple of Fine Arts, 116 Jln Berhala, Brickfields; by donation; 11.30am-3pm, 6.30-10pm Tue-Sun) Eat as you wish, give as you feel is the mantra at this vegetarian Indian restaurant. There's a dress code, probably to deter free-loaders.

Vishal (Map pp92-3; 2274 0502; 15 Jln Scott, Brickfields; meals RM5; 7am-10.30pm) Punters sit at two long rows of tables for the great banana-leaf meals served up at this long-running Brickfields favourite.

Gem Restaurant (Map pp92-3; 2260 1373; www .gemrestaurant.com.my; 124 Jln Tun Sambanthan, Brickfields; meals RM10-20; lunch & dinner) One of the most consistently good Indian restaurants in Brickfields. Come for its *thali*, the chunky chicken tikka and the great range of vegetarian options, including creamy Indian-style veg.

HAWKER STALLS

Kompleks Makan Tanglin (Map pp92-3; Jln Cendarasari; meals RM10; 7am-4pm Mon-Sat) Yet another good reason for hanging out in the Lake Gardens is the chance to grab a meal at this popular hawker stall complex – Ikan Bakar Pak Din's stall is a popular one.

Ikan Bakar Jalan Bellamy (Map pp92-3; Jln Bellamy; meals RM10; 11am-11pm Mon-Sat) People drive from all over to frequent the three barbecued fish hawker stalls on the hill behind the royal palace – even the king occasionally sends his minions to get an order of grilled stingray.

Bangsar Baru

Haunt of expats and KL's well-to-do, Bangsar Baru also has fantastic hawker-stall options over in the area known as Taman Lucky (Lucky Gardens) and a great *pasar malam* on Sunday nights. To get there, take the LRT to Bangsar station, then either walk (10 minutes) or jump into a taxi (RM3).

CHINESE

Reunion (Map p118; 2287 3770; 2nd fl Bangsar Village II, Jln Telawi 1; meals RM80-100; noon-3pm, 6-10.30pm)

KUALA LUMPUR

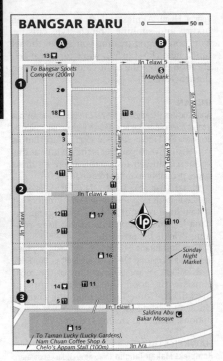

BANGSAR BARU
0 ————— 50 m

Elegantly designed contemporary Chinese restaurant that's ideal for a business dinner or an intimate date.

EUROPEAN & FUSION

Delicious (Map p118; ☎ 2287 1554; www.delicious.com.my; Ground fl, Bangsar Village II, Jln Telawi 1; meals RM40-50; ⏱ 11am-10.30pm Mon-Thu, 9am-10.30pm Fri-Sun) Stylish delicious cafes are popping up all over KL; this is one of the biggest branches, serving its trademark chunky sandwiches, big salads, pastas, scrumptious cakes and other desserts. The afternoon tea set (RM69 for two) is a good deal.

Alexis Bistro (Map p118; ☎ 2284 2880; www.alexis .com.my; 29 Jln Telawi 3; meals RM40-60; ⏱ lunch & dinner) Asian favourites such as laksa mix it up with more European fare at Alexis, another Bangsar brand that's spread its wings around the city; check the website for details of branches at Ampang's Great Eastern Mall and the Gardens, Mid Valley.

La Bodega (Map p118; ☎ 2287 8318; www.bodega .com.my; 14 & 16 Jln Telawi 2; meals RM40-60; ⏱ 8am-1am) This popular, trendy place is four venues in one: an all-day deli cafe serving good sand-wiches, a chilled-out tapas bar, a formal dining room, and a lively lounge bar. Good wine and authentic tapas and paella complete the Spanish mood. The new branch at Pavilion KL (Map p96; ☎ 2148 8018; Level 3, Pavilion KL, 168 Jln Bukit Bintang; open 7am to 3am) is known for its great cooked breakfast.

INDIAN

Sri Nirwana Maju (Map p118; ☎ 2287 8445; 43 Jln Telawi 2; meals RM10-20; ⏱ 7am-2am) There are certainly flashier Indian restaurants in Bangsa, but who cares about the decor when you can tuck into food this good and this reasonably priced? Serves it all from roti for breakfast to banana-leaf curries throughout the day.

MALAY

Chawan (Map p118; ☎ 2287 5507; 69-G Jln Telawi 3; meals RM5-10; ⏱ 8am-midnight) Hard to fault this chic contemporary take on a *kopitiam*. It offers mega-strength coffees from all of the country's states to wash down dishes such as beef *rendang* and a brown paper–wrapped *nasi lemak* (see p61).

Nasi Lemak Antarabangsa (Map p118; ☎ 2284 3366; www.nasilemakantarabangsa.com; 51 Jln Telawi 3; meal RM10; ⏱ 8am-1am) A spiffed-up spin-off from the original *nasi lemak* joint that's been dishing up the rice and trimmings in Kampung Baru since 1973.

HAWKER STALLS

Sunday night's *pasar malam*, held in the parking lot opposite the mosque on Jln Telawi 1, is an institution; you'll find all manner of tempting take-away food stalls, including ones offering *otak otak* (spicy fish paste grilled in banana leaves) and the crepe-like *apam balik*. We can recommend the stall that sells sweet-sour *asam laksa* (a version of laksa with prawn paste and tamarind-flavoured gravy).

Devi's Corner (Map p118; 14 Jln Telawi 2; meals RM10; ✹ 24hr) A pavement-cafe mood prevails at this food court facing the Bangsar Village II mall. The tray curries are excellent, with plenty of fish, prawns and other seafood. You can get *dosa*, biriyani and great satay here.

Nam Chuan Coffee Shop (off Map p118; Lorong Kiri 2; ✹ 8am-10pm) Nam Chuan Coffee Shop is the name of this food court – inside are many individually run stalls, including Christina Jong's which serves Sarawak laksa from 8am to 3pm Thursday to Tuesday. As with other food courts come at different times of the day and you'll find different operators running each of the stalls – some doing the breakfast and lunch, others just working in the evening.

Chelo's Appam Stall (off Map p118; Lucky Gardens Hawker Stalls, 2 Lorong Ara Kiri 3; meals RM5; ✹ 7am-10pm Mon-Sat) Sample freshly made vegan Indian delights, including the sweet *appam* (coconut-milk pancakes). Also in this hawker stall area you'll find Anwar dishing up an amazing fish-head curry.

Self-Catering

You'll find most of what you need at the following central supermarkets; all are open 10am to 9.30pm.

Cold Storage (Map p96; Suria KLCC, Jln Ampang)
Isetan (Map p96; Lot 10, Jln Sultan Ismail)
Mercado (Map p96; Pavilion KL, 168 Jln Bukit Bintang)
UO Supermarket (Map p100; cnr Jln Sultan & Jln Tun HS Lee)

DRINKING

You want bubble tea, iced kopi-o, a frosty beer or a flaming Lamborghini? KL's cafes, teahouses and bars can deliver it all. The Golden Triangle is the main deal with Changkat Bukit Bintang being the hottest strip; if you're into bars packed with testosterone-challenged males and lusty ladies then Jln P Ramlee delivers. The boil has gone off Asian Heritage Row (Jln Doraisamy) near the Medan Tuanku mono-rail station, just as the possibilities for sophisticates and the indie-inclined have heated up at nearby CapSquare. Bangsar continues to hold its own for classy expat bars and cafes.

Unless otherwise noted standard opening hours are 5pm to 2am.

Golden Triangle
CAFES & TEAHOUSES

The Apartment Downtown (Map p96; ✆ 2166 2257; www.atheapartment.com; 1st fl, Suria KLCC, Jln Ampang; ✹ 11am-10pm) Imagine you actually live at the KLCC at this convivial lounge-like cafe-bar space with outdoor seating overlooking the park – it's a lovely spot to revive after a hard day's shopping at the mall.

J Co Donuts & Coffee (Map p96; ✆ 2141 7761; www.jcodonuts.com; basement, Pavilion KL, 168 Jln Bukit Bintang; ✹ 10am-10pm) The wacky donut creations may have cheesy names (Tira Miss U or Mona Pisa anyone?), but they look so damn tasty that it's difficult to pass this fried dough and coffee operation by.

Lecka Lecka (Map p96; ✆ 6201 9000; www.leckalecka.com.my; 181 Jln Bukit Bintang; ✹ 10am-3am) Among the several pavement cafe-bars lining Bintang Walk, Lecka Lecka, outside Starhill Gallery, seduces with its wafting chiffon curtains, soft seats and trademark ice creams. Alternatively, puff on a hubble bubble or sip a cocktail.

Luk Yu Tea House (Map p96; ✆ 2782 3850; Feast fl, Starhill Gallery, 181 Jln Bukit Bintang; ✹ 10-1am) Swing by Starhill Gallery for a premium brew inside a charming traditional Chinese teahouse.

Olé Café (Map p96; ✆ 2148 9007; 48 Changkat Bukit Bintang; ✹ lunch & dinner) One of the few bona fide chill-out spots along a busy strip, this quiet cafe has free internet access, nice teas and coffees, and cakes.

Sixty Nine Bistro (Map p96; ✆ 2144 3369; 14 Jln Kampung Dollah; ✹ noon-midnight) Worth checking out for its eclectic junkshop–chic furnishings, milk and fruit shakes, and resident fortune-tellers and tarot-card readers.

BARS

Ceylon Bar (Map p96; ✆ 2145 7689; 20-2 Changkat Bukit Bintang) Convivial bar with cane chairs on its verandah, sofas and board games at the rear and free wi-fi.

Luna (Map p96; ✆ 2332 7777; Menara PanGlobal, Jln Puncak) Staff can't mix a dirty martini, but you certainly get the twinkling view of KL's skyline at this super-sophisticated rooftop bar surrounding a swimming pool. On

KUALA LUMPUR

GAY & LESBIAN KL

Check out www.utopia-asia.com and www.fridae.com for the latest on KL's small but friendly gay scene. **Prince World KL** (www.princeworldkl.com) organises big gay dance parties several times a year – they're usually held at Oblique, Garçon and **Orange Club** (Map p96; ☎ 2141 49291, Jln Kia Peng).

Frangipani Bar (Map p96; ☎ 2144 3001; 25 Jln Changkat Bukit Bintang; cover Fri RM30; ☯ 5pm-1am Tue-Thu & Sun, 5pm-3am Fri & Sat) Friday is the official gay night at this fab DJ bar, above the restaurant of the same name (p113). On other nights of the week you'll find a very gay-friendly crowd here too.

Oblique (Map p96; www.princeworldkl.com; Jln P Ramlee; cover RM25; ☯ 10pm-3am Sat) Non-straight club that sees a twinky crowd feverishly juggling their stuff to hard house and techno. You'll find it beneath Modestos.

Garçon (☎ 2381 2088; 8 Jln Yap Ah Shak; ☯ 9pm-3am Sun) For Sunday-night gay clubbers this session at the glam Maison (p122) is the place to be seen.

Blue Boy (Map p96; ☎ 2142 1067; 54 Jln Sultan Ismail; ☯ 8.30pm-2am) The workhorse of the KL gay scene just keeps on going. Come before 11pm if you wish to sing karaoke with the winking lady boys. Later it gets packed with rent boys and their admirers.

Thermos (Map p96; ☎ 3214 4968; www.daythermos.com; 40-6 Jln Sultan Ismail; cover RM28; ☯ 2-11pm) If you're just looking to hook up, try this relatively stylish and clean sauna with mini-gym and internet lounge. It's near Blue Boy on an alley running parallel to Jln Sultan Ismail.

Friday and Saturday nights there's a RM50 cover charge.

ourpick Palate Palette (Map p96; ☎ 2142 2148; www.palatepalette.com; 21 Jln Mesui; ☯ noon-midnight Tue-Thu, noon-2am Fri & Sat) Gotta love a place that offers curry popcorn and a drink called Kick in the Nuts. Colourful, creative, quirky and super-cool this cafe-bar is a great place to eat (mains RM10 to RM30), drink, play board games, and check out KL's boho crowd.

Quattro (Map p96; ☎ 2166 6566; www.clubquattro .com; Ave K, 156 Jln Ampang) Drift from spring, through summer, autumn and winter at this season-themed bar, lounge, restaurant and club complex. On the hour you can make a dash through an indoor rain shower – umbrellas are provided! They also have live music Tuesday to Saturday.

SkyBar (Map p96; ☎ 2332 9888; Level 33, Traders Hotel, KLCC; ☯ 7pm-1am, to 3am Fri & Sat) Head to the rooftop pool area of this hotel for a grand circle view across to the Petronas Towers – it's the perfect spot for sundowner cocktails or late-night flutes of bubbly.

Village Bar (Map p96; ☎ 2782 3852; Feast fl, Starhill Gallery, 181 Jln Bukit Bintang; ☯ noon-1am) Like Ali Baba's Bazaar, this enticing bar is hung with myriad coloured-glass lampshades.

Also recommended are a couple of long-running expat bars:

Finnegan's Golden Triangle (Map p96; ☎ 2145 1930; 51 Jln Sultan Ismail); Bangsar Baru (Map p118; ☎ 2284 9024; 6 Jln Telawi 5) Identikit Irish bar with live sports coverage and a decent menu.

Green Man (Map p96; ☎ 2141 9924; 40 Changkat Bukit Bintang) Offering a pool table, simple food and outside seating.

Chinatown
CAFES & TEAHOUSES

Ikopi (Map p100; 1st fl, 6 Jln Panggong; ☯ noon-10pm Wed-Mon) Caffine addicts should seek out this place where coffees from around the world are brewed in mad-scientist contraptions.

Purple Cane Tea House (Map p100; ☎ 2072 1349; 3rd fl, 6 Jln Panggong; ☯ 11am-8pm) Upstairs from Ikopi is this tea drinkers' heaven, while around the corner its shop (Map p100; ☎ 2031 1877; 11 Jln Sultan; open 10am to 10pm) provides a full selection of teas and tea-making implements.

BARS

OM (Map p100; ☎ 2072 7700; Central Market Annexe, Jln Hang Kasturi; ☯ 10am-10pm) Standing for Old Malaya the breezy OM cafe-bar is decorated with antique painted-tin poster ads and has a bar inlaid with a great collection of cigarette packets from around the world.

Reggae Bar (Map p100; ☎ 2026 7690; http://reggaebarkl .com.my; 158 Jln Tun HS Lee; ☯ noon-2am) 'Love all, feed all' is the catchphrase of the red, yellow and green bedecked bar, which is knee-deep in travellers and has Bob Marley on constant rotation.

Little India
Bar Savanh (Map pp92-3; ☎ 2697 1180; www.indochine -group.com; 62-64 Jln Doraisamy) Singapore's Indochine group sprinkles its Vietnamese magic on Asian Heritage Row; after finishing dinner at CoChine, head downstairs to this bar, which often has live music at weekends.

   Urban Attic (Map p100; ☎ 2693 3808; www.attickl .com; C7 Persiaran CapSquare, CapSquare; ☿ 5pm-3am Mon-Sat) Shaping up to be CapSquare's social hub is this partially open-air bar and live-music space. It's a fine hangout and has hosted KL's sporadic Pecha Kucha (www.pecha-kucha .org/cities/kuala-lumpur) nights – show-and-tell sessions with local creatives – in the past, too.

Bangsar Baru & Brickfields
Bar Upstairs (Map p118; ☎ 2284 2881; www.alexis .com.my; 29A Jln Telawi 3, Bangsar Baru) Above Alexis Bistro is this supreme chill-out venue boasting subdued red lighting, opaque furniture and soothing sounds. See the website for details of live music performances here and at other branches.

   Social (Map p118; ☎ 2282 2260; 57-59 Jln Telawi 3, Bangsar Baru; ☿ 10-2am) Classy sports bar offering pool tables and good food as well as the booze. There's also a branch on Changkat Bukit Bintang (see Map p96; ☎ 2142 7021; 28 Changkat Bukit Bintang).

   Zeta Bar (Map pp92-3; ☎ 2264 2264; www.kl-studio .com; Hilton Kuala Lumpur; 3 Jln Stesen Sentral, Brickfields) The classy and expensive Zeta pulls in the well-to-do and hip 30s to 40s crowd.

ENTERTAINMENT
Cinemas
Mainstream movies are screened at the multiplexes in the malls. Contact the cultural centres (see p94) about the art-house films they occasionally screen. Tickets are around RM12.

Cosmo's World Theme Park Theatre (Map p96; ☎ 2117 3046; www.timessquarekl.com/imax.html; 10th fl, Berjaya Times Sq, 1 Jln Imbi) Movies screened on a screen five storeys high.

Golden Screen Cinemas Berjaya Times Square (Map p96; ☎ 8312 3456; www.gsc.com.my; 3rd fl, Berjaya Times Square, 1 Jln Imbi); Mid Valley (off Map pp92-3; ☎ 8312 3456; www.gsc.com.my; Mid Valley Megamall, Mid Valley City); Pavilion KL (Map p96; ☎ 8312 3456;

Level 6, Pavilion KL, 168 Jln Bukit Bintang) Book a seat in Gold Class (RM40) for La-Z-boy–style reclining chairs and drinks service.

Tanjung Golden Village (Map p96; ☎ 7492 2929; www.tgv.com.my; Level 3, Suria KLCC)

Music
The Istana Budaya (p122) sometimes also hosts concerts.

CLASSICAL
Dewan Filharmonik Petronas (Map p96; ☎ 2051 7007; www.malaysianphilharmonic.com; Box Office, Tower 2, Petronas Towers, KLCC; tickets from RM10-210) Don't miss the chance to attend a concert at this gorgeous concert hall at the base of the Petronas Towers. The polished Malaysian Philharmonic Orchestra plays here (usually Friday and Saturday evenings and Sunday matinees, but also other times) as do other local and international ensembles. There is a dress code.

JAZZ
No Black Tie (Map p96; ☎ 2142 3737; www.noblacktie .com.my; 17 Jln Mesui; cover RM20-50; ☿ 5pm-2am Tue-Sun) Small, chic, jazz and live-music venue and bar with an eclectic line-up of artists; the stage is hidden behind a heavy wood door to the rear. Once a month *Time Out* also hosts its On the Up event here, showcasing local singers and bands doing their own material.

ROCK & POP
Also check out the bands playing at Urban Attic (left) and the Laundry out at the Curve (see p138).

   Cloth and Clef (Map p96; ☎ 2143 3034; www .clothandclef.com; 30 Changkat Bukit Bintang) Live music and DJ bar that's trying to do something a bit different and more edgy; play DJ at their monthly 'It's My iPod' events.

   Wings (Map p96; ☎ 2144 3309; www.wingsmusicafe .com; 16 Jln Kampung Dollah, off Jln Pudu; ☿ 6.30pm-1.30am) Relaxed cafe-bar where emerging local artists perform pop, rock and the rest, mainly in Chinese and Bahasa Malaysia.

Clubs
Places come and go in KL's lively but fluid clubbing scene; stay up to date by reading *KLue* or *Time Out* (see p94). On weekend nights a DJ spins dance tunes at the bars at Frangipani (p113) and Twentyone Kitchen & Bar (p113).

Clubs are typically open Wednesday to Sunday and usually charge a cover (including one drink) of RM20 to RM40 Thursday to Saturday.

Loft (Map pp92-3; ☎ 2694 2888; Unit 28-40 Asian Heritage Row, Jln Doraisamy) Together with its sister club Cynna, to which its linked by a common balcony, Loft is the most enduring of Asian Heritage Row's clubbing offerings. A catwalk allows podium queens to showcase their dance moves.

Maison (Map pp92-3; ☎ 2381 2088; www.maison.com.my; 8 Jln Yap Ah Shak) Five shophouses have been knocked together to form a great space for this club where house music, in all its forms, rules.

Zouk (Map p96; ☎ 2171 1997; www.zoukclub.com.my; 113 Jln Ampang) KL's top club offers spaces to suit everyone and a line-up of local and international DJs. As well as the two-level main venue, there's the more sophisticated Velvet Underground, with a dance floor that's glitter-ball heaven; Phuture for hip-hop groovers; and the cutting-edge Bar Sonic, home to the indie-dance event Koko Asia (www.kokoasia.com). Glimpse KL's gilded youth passing by from the outdoor Relish@Terrace Bar.

Dance & Cultural Shows

Central Market (Map p100; ☎ 2031 0399; www.centralmarket.com.my; Jln Hang Kasturi) Hosts a regular programme of free events, including Malay dance, Indian classical dance, Chinese dance and t'ai chi performances. Check the website to see what's on.

Malaysian Tourist Centre (MaTiC; Map p96; ☎ 9235 4900; 109 Jln Ampang; ☒ 3pm Mon, Tue, Thu & Sat) Professionally staged traditional dance and music performances (adult/child under 12 RM5/free) are held regularly in the mini-auditorium to the rear of MaTiC. It also has a similar dance show at 8.30pm daily in the attached restaurant Saloma (☎ 2161 0122; show only RM40, buffet and show RM75).

Seri Melayu (Map p96; ☎ 2145 1833; www.serimelayu.com; 1 Jln Conlay) Traditional Malay music and dance performances (show only RM31.75 Malaysian buffet and show RM70) run from 8.30pm to 9.15pm. Its Malaysian buffet (open 6pm to 10.30pm) is extensive.

Sutra Dance Theatre (Map pp92-3; ☎ 4021 1092; www.sutradancetheatre.com; 12 Persiaran Titiwangsa 3, Titiwangsa) The home of Malaysian dance legend Ramli Ibrahim has been turned into a showcase for Indian classical dance as well as a dance studio, gallery and cultural centre near Lake Titiwangsa. See the website for upcoming shows.

Theatre & Comedy

Istana Budaya (National Theatre; Map pp92-3; ☎ 4026 5555; www.istanabudaya.gov.my; Jln Tun Razak) Big-scale drama and dance shows are staged here, as well as music performances by the National Symphony Orchestra and National Choir. There's a dress code: no shorts, and men must wear long-sleeved shirts.

Kuala Lumpur Performing Arts Centre (KLPac; Map pp92-3; ☎ 4047 9000; www.klpac.com; Sentul West, Jln Strachan) Lots of interesting work is staged at this modern performing-arts complex set in the landscaped grounds of Sentul West in the north of the city.

Time Out Comedy Thursday (Map p96; ☎ 2166 6650; www.timeoutkl.com; Little Havana, Changkat Bukit Bintang; cover RM20; ☒ 9pm first Thu of month) It's always a packed house for this monthly stand-up gig by some of the funniest guys (and occasional girl) in KL.

SHOPPING

KL has everything from street markets proffering fake-label goods to glitzy shopping mall packed with the real deal. Clothing, camera gear, computers and electronic goods are all competitively priced. You'll also find original handicrafts from all over the country as well as interesting contemporary art.

For bookshops, see p91.

Art Galleries

Annexe Gallery (Map p100; ☎ 2070 1137; www.annexegallery.com; Central Market Annex, Jln Hang Kasturi; ☒ 11am-7pm) Nonprofit centre for contemporary arts that does a bit more than just hang works on the wall. Film screenings, theatre and dance workshops, talks and launches are also on the agenda.

Valentine Willie Fine Art (Map p118; ☎ 2284 2348; www.vwfa.net; 1st fl, 17 Jln Telawi 3, Bangsar Baru; ☒ noon-8pm Mon-Fri, noon-6pm Sat) One of KL's best galleries has frequent shows and represents some of the country's top artists.

Wei-Ling Gallery (Map pp92-3; ☎ 2260 1106; www.weiling-gallery.com; 8 Jln Scott, Brickfields; ☒ noon-7pm Mon-Fri, 10am-5pm Sat) The top two floors of this old shophouse have been imaginatively turned into a contemporary gallery to showcase local artists.

Crafts & Souvenirs

Central Market (Pasar Seni; Map p100; ☎ 2031 0399; www.centralmarket.com.my; Jln Hang Kasturi; ☯ 10am-9pm) It's easy to spend an hour or more wandering around this treasure house of souvenirs, batik, kites, clothes and jewellery. Asian artifacts and antiques are also available, but you'll need to bargain hard to get good deals; try Art House Gallery Museum of Ethnic Arts in the annex for interesting pieces from Borneo and Tibet.

Kompleks Budaya Kraf (Map p96; ☎ 2162 7533; www .malaysiancraft.com; Jln Conlay; ☯ 9am-8pm Mon-Fri, to 7pm Sat & Sun) Large handicrafts complex stocking a big variety of locally produced batiks, carved wooden artifacts, pewter utensils, woven baskets, furniture, glassware and ceramics. A highlight of this place is the chance to meet craftsmen and artists in the surrounding gardens. The complex also has a small museum and offers batik-making courses.

Jendela (Map p96; ☎ 2144 9189; www.jendela-kl.com; Explore fl, Starhill Gallery, 181 Jln Bukit Bintang) Beautiful traditional and modern batik prints used for homewares and clothing. There's also a branch at CapSquare.

Peter Hoe Evolution (Map p100; ☎ 2026 0711; 2 Jln Hang Lekir; ☯ 10am-7pm) Peter Hoe's original batik designs on sarongs, shirts and dresses are the main drawcard here, but you'll find many tastefully arranged Malaysian and imported Asian home goods, too. There's also a much bigger store (Peter Hoe Beyond; Map p100; ☎ 2026 9788; 2nd floor Lee Rubber Building, 145 Jln Tun HS Lee; open 10am to 7pm) with a pleasant cafe around the corner on the 2nd floor of the old Lee Rubber Building.

Pucuk Rebung (Map p96; ☎ 2382 0769; Level 3, Suria KLCC, Jln Ampang; ☯ 10am-10pm) This upmarket and pricey arts-and-craft store doubles as a gallery – it specialises in all kinds of Malaysian handmade goods.

Royal Selangor Pewter Factory (off Map pp92-3; ☎ 4145 6122; www.royalselangor.com.my; 4 Jln Usahawan Enam, Setapak Jaya; ☯ 9am-5pm) Located 8km northeast of the city centre is Malaysia's leading manufacturer of pewter. As well as traditional tankards and the like, it has commissioned modern designers to produced some very appealing gifts. For RM50 you can try your own hand at creating a pewter dish (see p108). Take the LRT to Wangsa Maju station and then a taxi (RM3). Alternatively, visit its main outlet (☎ 3182 0240) on level one of Suria KLCC.

Fashion

Sungei Wan Plaza (p124) is a great place for teen fashions and up-and-coming designers such as **Melinda Looi** (www.melindalooi.com), and the Gardens Mall (see below) is also worth a browse too.

Aseana (Map p96; ☎ 2382 9988; Ground fl, Suria KLCC, Jln Ampang; ☯ 10am-10pm) Stylish and extensive selection of local fashion, plus a cafe serving good Malay food and drinks.

iKARRTiNi (Map p96; ☎ 2382 2833; www.ikarrtini .com; level 2, Suria KLCC; ☯ 10am-10pm) Check out the separate men's and women's stores selling their own batik design print fashions on fine silk and cotton.

Markets

The major daily produce markets are those at Chow Kit (p103) and Pudu (p104). For clothes, bags, DVDs and souvenirs check out Chinatown's Jln Petaling (p98).

The following are the major *pasar malam* (night markets):

Bangsar Baru (off Jln Telawi 1; ☯ Sun) See p119.

Kampung Baru (along Jln Raja Muda; ☯ Sat) See p117.

Little India (Lg TAR; ☯ Sat) See p117.

Shopping Malls

You'll find most of what you need at these shopping malls, all open 10am to 10pm.

Bangsar Village I & II (Map p118; ☎ 2282 1808; Jln Telawi 1, Bangsar Baru) These connected malls form the shopping hub of Bangsar; the newer Village II complex is packed with international and local fashion shops, restaurants and cafes.

Berjaya Times Square (Map p96; ☎ 2117 3081; www .timesquarekl.com; 1 Jln Imbi) Mammoth mall with a huge Borders bookstore, an indoor amusement park and a multiplex cinema.

Mid Valley Megamall (off Map pp92-3; ☎ 2938 3333; www.midvalleycity.com; Mid Valley City, Lingkaran Syed Putra) This colossal complex, next to KL Komuter Mid Valley station, is indeed mega and probably the best one-stop shopping, dining and entertainment experience in KL. In a separate building you'll find the Gardens Mall, a more luxe environment embracing designer international brands as well as a hotel and serviced apartments. On level 2, check out local designers at 2201 Fashion Avenue and KN Key Ng (www.keyng .com.my).

Pavilion KL (Map p96; ☎ 2118 8833; www.pavilion -kl.com; 168 Jln Bukit Bintang) Over 450 retail shops spread across seven levels in KL's latest shopping extravaganza – it gives the Suria KLCC a run for its money with its shiny ambience and wide range of international labels.

Starhill Gallery (Map p96; ☎ 2716 8615; www.ytlcommunity.com/starhill; 181 Jln Bukit Bintang) Break out your platinum charge card – this glitzy mall is where you'll find Louis Vuitton, Gucci and many other luxury brands, plus a great range of restaurants in the basement, and spas on the 5th floor.

Suria KLCC (Map p96; ☎ 2382 2828; www.suriaklcc.com.my; KLCC, Jln Ampang) This fine shopping complex at the foot of the Petronas Towers is strong on both local and international brands.

Sungei Wang Plaza (Map p96; ☎ 2148 6109; www.sungeiwang.com; Jln Sultan Ismail) and **BB Plaza** (Map p96; ☎ 2148 7411; Jln Bukit Bintang) are two interlinked malls in which it's easy to lose yourself for hours exploring. Sungei Wang is particularly good for youthful fashion and accessories.

Plaza Low Yat (Map p96; ☎ 2148 3651; 7 Jln 1/77, off Jln Bukit Bintang) and **Imbi Plaza** (Map p96; ☎ 2148 7425; Jln Imbi) are the places to head to for digital and electronic goods, including computers, cameras and mobile phones.

GETTING THERE & AWAY
Air
KL's main airport is **Kuala Lumpur International Airport** (KLIA; ☎ 8777 8888; www.klia.com.my), 75km south of the city centre at Sepang. All of AirAsia's flights are handled by the nearby **Low Cost Carrier Terminal** (LCC-T; ☎ 8777 8888; www.lcct.com.my).

Firefly and Berjaya Air flights go from **Sultan Abdul Aziz Shah Airport** (☎ 7845 3245; www.malaysiaairports.com.my) at Subang, around 20km west of the city centre. For transport options into town, see p126.

At KLIA's international arrival hall you'll find a useful **Tourism Malaysia office** (☎ 8776 5651; ☉ 7am-11pm), a Celcom stand selling prepaid SIM cards for your mobile phone (open 7am to 11pm), and counters for several car-rental firms.

AirAsia's tickets are purchased online (www.airasia.com); it has a small information office in **KL Sentral station** (☎ 1300 889 933; ☉ 8am-10pm). Other airlines with offices in the city:

Berjaya Air (Map p96; ☎ 2141 0088; www.berjaya-air.com; 6th fl, Berjaya Times Square, 1 Jln Imbi)

Cathay Pacific Airways (Map p96; ☎ 2035 2777; www.cathaypacific.com; Suite 22, Level 1, Menara IMC, 8 Jln Sultan Ismail)

China Airlines (Map p96; ☎ 2148 9417; www.china-airlines.com; Amoda Bldg, 22 Jln Imbi)

Garuda Indonesian Airlines (Map p96; ☎ 2162 2811; www.garuda-indonesia.com; Block D, Megan Ave II, 12 Jln Yap Kwan Seng)

Japan Airlines (Map p96; ☎ 1800-813 366; www.jal.com; Level 20, Menara Citibank, 165 Jln Ampang)

Lufthansa (Map p96; ☎ 2052 3428; www.lufthansa.com; 18th fl, Kenanga International, Jln Sultan Ismail)

Malaysia Airlines (Map p96; ☎ 1300 883 000; www.malaysiaair.com; Bangunan MAS, Jln Sultan Ismail)

Royal Brunei Airlines (Map p96; www.bruneiair.com; ☎ 3230 6628; Menara UBN, 10 Jln P Ramlee)

Singapore Airlines (Map p100; ☎ 2698 7033; www.singaporeair.com; 10th fl, Menara Multi-Purpose, Cap-Square, 8 Jln Munshi Abdullah)

Thai Airways International (Map p96; ☎ 2034 6999; www.thaiair.com; 30th fl, Wisma Goldhill, 67 Jln Raja Chulan)

Bus
KL has several bus stations, the main one being Puduraya, just east of Chinatown. From here services fan out all over Peninsular Malaysia as well as to Singapore and Thailand. The only long-distance destinations that Puduraya doesn't handle are Kuala Lipis and Jerantut (for access to Taman Negara), buses to these places leave from Pekeliling bus station; and Kota Bharu and Kuala Terengganu, buses for which leave from Putra bus station.

Other bus services to Singapore, typically taking five hours, are operated by the following:

Aeroline (Map p96; ☎ 6258 8800; www.aeroline.com.my) Offers at least seven services daily (double-/single-

INTERSTATE BUS FARES FROM KUALA LUMPUR		
Destination	**Fare (RM)**	**Duration**
Alor Setar	39.10	5hr
Butterworth	31.30	5hr
Cameron Highlands	30	4hr
Ipoh	117.40	2½hr
Johor Bahru	31.30	5hr
Kuantan	22	4hr
Lumut	24.50	4hr
Melaka	12.40	2hr
Mersing	29.90	5½hr
Penang	35	5hr
Singapore	39.10	5½hr
Sungai Petani	34.20	5hr
Taiping	22.70	3½hr

decker buses RM90/60) from outside the Corus Hotel, Jln Ampang, just east of KLCC.

Nice (Map p100; ☎ 2272 1586; www.nice-coaches.com .my) Services run three times daily from outside the Old KL Train Station on Jln Sultan Hishamuddin to Singapore (RM88). It also offers five daily services to Butterworth (RM68) and six to Johor Bahru (RM68).

Transtar Travel (Map p96; ☎ 2141 1771; www.transtar .com.sg) Offers luxury services to Singapore (RM99) on 16- to 31-seater buses leaving from the Pasarakyat Bus Terminal, Jln Melati, off Jln Imbi.

KLANG BUS STATION

From the Klang bus station (Map p100), near the Pasar Seni LRT station in Chinatown, frequent buses include U18 to Shah Alam (RM2), 710 to Klang (RM3) and 51 for Pelabuhan Klang (Port Klang; RM3.80), as well as buses 66 and 75 to Petaling Jaya (RM2).

PEKELILING BUS STATION

In the north of the city, just off Jln Tun Razak next to Titiwangsa LRT and monorail stations, is **Pekeliling bus station** (Map pp92–3; ☎ 4042 7256). There's a **left-luggage counter** (per bag per day RM3; ◷ 8am-8pm).

Transnasional Express (☎ 4256 8218; www.ktb.com .my) has departures to Kuala Lipis (RM14.60, four hours, six daily) and Raub (RM10.80, 2½ hours, six daily). Several companies including **Plusliner** (Map p100; ☎ 4042 1256; www.plusliner.com) run services to Kuantan (RM22, four hours), which leave at two-hourly intervals between 8am and 8pm; many go via Temerloh (RM10). Buses to Jerantut (RM15, three hours) also go via Temerloh. Buses to Genting Highlands (RM6) leave every half-hour between 6.30am and 9pm.

PUDURAYA BUS STATION

Stay alert at Puduraya (Map p100), a clamorous bus-and-taxi station centrally located on Jln Pudu, next to the Plaza Rakyat LRT station; a few travellers have reported being robbed late at night. Close to the main entrance is an information counter. At the rear is a **left-luggage counter** (per day per bag RM2; ◷ 8am-11pm), as well as the tourist police.

Inside are dozens of bus company ticket-windows. Staff will shout out destinations, but check to be sure the departure time suits you, as they sometimes try to sell tickets for buses that aren't leaving for many hours. Buses leave from numbered platforms in the basement, and note that you'll have to look

for the name of the bus company rather than your destination.

On the main runs, services are so numerous that you can sometimes just turn up and get a seat on the next bus. However, tickets should preferably be booked at least the day before, and a few days before during peak holiday periods, especially to the Cameron Highlands and east-coast destinations.

Government-owned **Transnasional Express** (☎ 2070 3300; www.ktb.com.my) is the largest operation here, with buses to almost all major destinations. Outside the terminal, on Jln Pudu, there are at least another dozen private companies handling tickets for buses to Thailand, Singapore and some Malaysian destinations.

There are only a few daily services to the Cameron Highlands and east-coast destinations, but there are frequent departures to most other places during the day, and at night to the main towns. For the latter, try to leave as late as possible; otherwise, shortened travel times on the Lebuhraya tollway mean you'll arrive at your destination too early in the morning.

For typical adult fares and journey times from KL, see opposite.

PUTRA BUS STATION

Though Puduraya handles buses to the east coast, there are also a number of large-company coach services leaving from the quieter and less intimidating **Putra bus station** (Map pp92–3; Jln Kuching; ☎ 4042 9530), opposite PWTC station (easily reached by taking the LRT to PWTC, or a KTM Komuter train to Putra station).

There are services to Kota Bharu (RM42.90, eight hours, 9.30am and 9.30pm), Kuantan (RM22, four hours, four daily) and Kuala Terengganu (RM39, seven hours, 10.30am and 10pm).

FIXED FARES FOR WHOLE TAXI	
Destination	**Fare**
Fraser's Hill	RM280
Cameron Highlands (Tanah Rata)	RM350
Genting Highlands	RM80
Ipoh	RM280-300
Johor Bahru	RM500
Lumut	RM300
Melaka	RM300
Penang	RM600

Car

KL is the best place to hire a car for touring the peninsula; for sample rates see p486. However, navigating the city's complex (and mostly one-way) traffic system is not for the timid.

All the major companies have offices at the airport. City offices, which are generally open 9am to 5.30pm Monday to Friday and 9am to 1pm Saturday, include the following companies:

Avis (Map p96; ☎ 2144 4487; www.avis.com.my; Angkasa Raya, Jln Ampang)

Hertz (Map p96; ☎ 2148 6433; www5.hertz.com; Ground fl, Kompleks Antarabangsa, Jln Sultan Ismail)

Mayflower (Off Map pp92-3; ☎ 6253 1888; www.mayflowercarrental.com; 18 Jln Segambut Pusat)

Orix (Map p96; ☎ 2142 3009; www.orixauto.com.my; Ground fl, Federal Hotel, 35 Jln Bukit Bintang)

Taxi

Long-distance taxis – often no faster than taking a bus – depart from upstairs at Puduraya bus station (Map p100). Early in the morning the chances are reasonable of finding other passengers waiting to share on the main west-coast runs to Johor Bahru, Melaka, Ipoh and Penang. Otherwise you will usually have to wait to get a full complement of four passengers, or you could charter a whole taxi for fares that are the highest in Malaysia.

Prices should include toll charges. For fares, see p125.

Train

Kuala Lumpur is the hub of the **KTM** (☎ 2267 1200; www.ktmb.com.my) national railway system, with all long-distance trains departing

TRAIN FARES FROM KUALA LUMPUR

Destination	Premier	Superior	Economy
Padang Besar	-	RM40	RM22
Butterworth	-	RM30	RM17
Taiping	-	RM24	RM14
Ipoh	-	RM18	RM10
Tapah Rd	-	RM15	RM8
Seremban	RM19	RM13	RM7
Tampin	RM27	RM17	RM9
Johor Bahru	RM64	RM33	RM22
Singapore	RM68	RM34	RM23
Jerantut	-	RM25	RM15
Kuala Lipis	-	RM29	RM18
Wakaf Baharu	-	RM38	RM28
Tumpat	-	RM39	RM29

TOUCH 'N GO

If you're going to be in KL or Malaysia for an extended period and plan to use public transport or the highways a lot it's perhaps worth taking the time to get yourself a **Touch 'n Go card** (☎ 7628 5115; www.touchngo.com.my). These electronic credit storage cards can be used on all public transport in the Klang Valley, at highway toll booths across the country and at selected parking sites. The cards, which cost RM10 and can be reloaded with values from RM20 to RM500, can be purchased at KL Sentral and the central LRT stations KLCC, Masjid Jamek and Dang Wangi.

---

from KL Sentral (Map pp92–3). The KTM **information office** (⏰ 10am-7pm) in the main hall can advise on schedules and check seat availability. A **ticket delivery service** (☎ 2267 1200; ⏰ 8.30am-4.30pm Mon-Sat) can get your ticket to you for RM4.

There are daily departures for Butterworth, Wakaf Baharu (for Kota Baharu and Jerantut), Johor Bahru, Thailand and Singapore; fares are cheap, especially if you opt for a seat rather than a berth (for which there are extra charges), but journey times are slow. For further information see p488. KTM Komuter trains also link KL with the Klang Valley and Seremban (see opposite).

GETTING AROUND

KL Sentral (Map pp92–3) is the hub of a rail-based urban network consisting of the KTM Komuter, KLIA Ekspres, KLIA Transit, LRT and Monorail systems. Unfortunately the systems – all built separately – remain largely unintegrated. Different tickets generally apply for each service, and at stations where there's an interchange between the services they're rarely conveniently connected. This said, you can happily get around much of central KL on a combination of rail and monorail services, thus avoiding the traffic jams that plague the inner-city roads.

To/From the Airports

KLIA

The fastest way of reaching KL from KLIA is on the **KLIA Ekspres** (☎ 2267 8000; www.kliaekspres.com; adult/child 1-way RM35/15, return RM70/30); it takes

28 minutes and departs every 15 minutes between 5am and 1am. From KL Sentral you can continue to your destination by KMT Komuter, LRT, Monorail or taxi.

The **KL Transit train** (adult/child 1-way RM35/15) also connects KLIA with KL Sentral, but stops at three other stations en route (Salak Tinggi, Putrajaya and Cyberjaya, and Bandar Tasik Selatan), taking about 35 minutes.

If flying from KL on Malaysia Airlines, Cathay Pacific, Royal Brunei or Emirates you can check your baggage in at KL Sentral before making your way to KLIA.

The cheapest option is the **Airport Coach** (☎ 87873894; www.airportcoach.com.my; 1-way/return RM10/18), which takes an hour to KL Sentral; for RM18, however, it will also take you to any central KL hotel from KLIA and pick-up for the return journey for RM25. The bus stand is clearly signposted inside the terminal.

Taxis from KLIA operate on a fixed-fare coupon system. Standard taxis cost RM67.10 (up to three people), premier taxis for four people RM93.40, and family-sized minivans seating up to eight RM180.40. The journey will take around one hour. Buy your taxi coupon before you exit the arrivals hall, to avoid the aggressive pirate taxis that hassle you to pay a few hundred ringgit for the same ride. Going to the airport by taxi, make sure that the agreed fare includes tolls; expect to pay RM65 from Chinatown or Jln Bukit Bintang.

If you're changing to a flight on AirAsia, there's a shuttle bus between KLIA and the LCC-T – it runs every 20 minutes from 6am to midnight and the fare is RM1.50. Penny-pinchers can use this bus to get to Nilai (RM3.50) to connect with the KTM Komuter train to KL Sentral (RM4.70). A taxi between the two airports costs RM33.

LCC-T

To reach the LCC-T (Low Cost Carrier Terminal) from KL Sentral and vice versa, jump on either the **Skybus** (www.skybus.com.my; RM9) or the slightly cheaper **Aerobus** (adult/child 1-way RM8/4); services depart at least every 15 minutes from 4.30am to 12.45pm. Travelling from the LCC-T, prepaid taxis charge RM62 to Chinatown or Jln Bukit Bintang (50% more from midnight to 6am). Buy your coupon at the desk near the arrival hall exit. A taxi from the city to LCC-T will cost around RM65.

SULTAN ABDUL AZIZ SHAH AIRPORT

The easiest way to reach the Sultan Abdul Aziz Shah Airport is to take a taxi (around RM40).

Bus

Although there are several smaller companies, most buses in KL are provided by either **Rapid KL** (☎ 1800-388 228; www.rapidkl.com.my) or **Metrobus** (☎ 5635 3070). There's an **information booth** (Map p100; ☺ 7am-9pm) at the Jln Sultan Mohammed bus stop in Chinatown.

KL buses are the easiest to use as destinations are clearly displayed. KL buses are divided into four classes, and tickets are valid all day on the same class of bus. Bas Bandar (routes starting with B, RM2) services run around the city centre. Bas Utama (routes starting with U, RM2) buses run from the centre to the suburbs. Bas Tempatan (routes starting with T, RM1) buses run around the suburbs. Bas Ekspres (routes starting with E, RM4) are express buses to distant suburbs. You can also buy an all-day ticket covering all non-express buses (RM4) and a ticket covering all Rapid KL buses and trains (RM7).

Local buses leave from half a dozen small bus stands around the city – useful stops in Chinatown include Jln Sultan Mohamed (by Pasar Seni), Klang bus station (south of Pasar Seni), Bangkok Bank (on Lebuh Pudu), Medan Pasar (on Lebuh Ampang), Central Market (on Jln Hang Kasturi), Lebuh Ampang and the Kota Raya department store (on Jln Cheng Lock); see Map p100.

Since KL's inexpensive taxis and reliable LRT systems are more efficient, not prone to get stuck in traffic and air-conditioned, there's little point in using buses except for trips to outlying areas, such as the Batu Caves (p131).

KL Monorail

KL's zippy **monorail** (☎ 2273 1888; www.klmonorail .com.my; RM1.20-2.50; ☺ 6am-midnight) runs between KL Sentral in the south to Titiwangsa in the north. It's a very handy service linking up many of the city's sightseeing areas and providing a cheap air-con tour as you go.

KTM Komuter Trains

KTM Komuter (☎ 2267 1200; www.ktmb.com.my) train services use KL Sentral as a hub. There are two lines: Rawang to Seremban and Sentul to Pelabuhan Klang. Useful stops include Mid Valley (for the Mid Valley Megamall), Subang

Jaya (for Sunway Lagoon), Nilai (for the cheap local bus to the airports) and Pelabuhan Klang (for ferry services to Sumatra). Trains run every 15 to 20 minutes from approximately 6am to 11.45pm. Tickets start from RM1 for one stop.

Light Rail Transit (LRT)

As well as the buses, **Rapid KL** (☎ 1800-388 228; www.rapidkl.com.my) runs the Light Rail Transit (LRT) system. There are three lines: Ampang/Sentul Timur, Sri Petaling/Sentul Timur and Kelana Jaya/Terminal Putra. However, the network is poorly integrated because the lines were constructed by different companies. As a result, you need a new ticket to change from one line to another, and you may also have to follow a series of walkways, stairs and elevators, or walk several blocks down the street.

An electronic control system checks tickets as you enter and exit via turnstiles. Single-journey fares range from RM1 to RM2.80, or you can buy an all-day pass for RM7, which also covers you for Rapid KL buses. You can buy tickets from the cashier or electronic ticket machines. Trains run every six to 10 minutes from 6am to 11.45pm. If you're going to be in KL for a while, consider investing in a monthly combined travel card (RM90 or RM125 including Rapid KL buses).

Taxi

KL has plenty of taxis, and fares are cheap, starting at RM2 for the first kilometre, with an additional 10 sen for each 200m. From midnight to 6am there's a surcharge of 50% on the metered fare, and extra passengers (more than two) are charged 20 sen each. Luggage placed in the boot costs an extra RM1. If you book a cab, it also costs RM1 extra.

Not all taxi drivers follow the law, which says they must use their meter for all journeys. Taxi drivers lingering outside luxury hotels or in tourist hot spots such as the Lake Gardens are especially guilty of this behaviour. At some taxi ranks (ie outside BB Plaza on Jln Bukit Bintang) you'll also pay over the odds for taxis using a pre-paid coupon system. The one place where the pre-paid coupon systems does seem to work reasonably well is KL Sentral.

For reference, by meter it costs no more than RM10 to go right across the central city area, even in moderate traffic. Always ask for a receipt and check to see they haven't included spurious extra charges, such as for baggage you don't have. Be aware that taxis will often only stop at the numerous officially signposted taxi stands, and although it is possible to wave one down, some drivers are reluctant to stop.

Selangor

Surrounding KL, Selangor has developed rapidly into Malaysia's most urbanised, industrialised and prosperous state. Here you'll find great day trips such as those to the Batu Caves and the Forestry Research Institute of Malaysia, as well as rewarding stopovers, including the pleasantly cool hill station of Fraser's Hill (Bukit Fraser) and the old royal capital of Kuala Selangor, with its wildlife-watching and *kampung* (village) atmosphere.

Cutting a broad commercial swathe west from KL to the coast is Klang Valley, featuring the sprawling commuter residences of Petaling Jaya, which is also home to gargantuan shopping malls, the vast Sunway Pyramid and the enormous wave pool at Sunway Lagoon. Fast-flowing freeways and railways will speed you into Selangor's state capital, Shah Alam, notable for its beautiful blue mosque, and Klang, with its reminders of the old sultanate and vibrant Little India – a gourmand's mecca. On the coast discover the Hma' Meri villages of Pulau Carey hidden amid vast palm-oil plantations or take a ferry to the sleepy fishing community of Pulau Ketam.

South of KL, Malaysia's administrative capital of Putrajaya, less than two decades in the making, is packed with striking architecture and makes for a fascinating day trip. Heading northeast up into the highlands of the Banjaran Titiwangsa mountain range, there are the contrasting delights of Genting Highlands, a purpose-built gambling resort that has its moments, and Kuala Kubu Bharu (KKB), one of the most charming small towns in Malaysia and a great base for trekking and river rafting adventures. For more ideas check out the state's tourism website (www.tourismselangor.org).

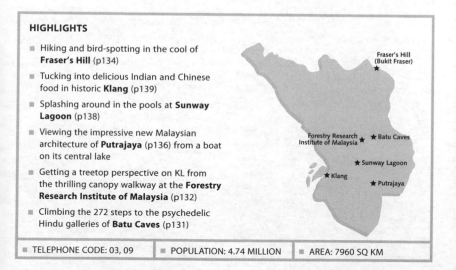

HIGHLIGHTS

- Hiking and bird-spotting in the cool of **Fraser's Hill** (p134)
- Tucking into delicious Indian and Chinese food in historic **Klang** (p139)
- Splashing around in the pools at **Sunway Lagoon** (p138)
- Viewing the impressive new Malaysian architecture of **Putrajaya** (p136) from a boat on its central lake
- Getting a treetop perspective on KL from the thrilling canopy walkway at the **Forestry Research Institute of Malaysia** (p132)
- Climbing the 272 steps to the psychedelic Hindu galleries of **Batu Caves** (p131)

Fraser's Hill (Bukit Fraser) ★
Forestry Research Institute of Malaysia ★ ★ Batu Caves
★ Sunway Lagoon
★ Klang
★ Putrajaya

- TELEPHONE CODE: 03, 09   - POPULATION: 4.74 MILLION   - AREA: 7960 SQ KM

History

In the 15th century, Selangor was under the control of Melaka's great *bendahara* (chief minister), Tun Perak. Once Melaka fell to the Portuguese, control of Selangor was hotly contested, partly because of its rich tin reserves. The Minangkabau settlers, who had migrated from Sumatra 100 years earlier, were displaced by Buginese immigrants from Celebes (present-day Sulawesi), who aided Dutch colonisation by hiring themselves out as mercenaries. By the middle of the 18th century, the Buginese had established the current sultanate, based at Kuala Selangor.

A century later the success of the tin trade and the growing wealth of the Chinese communities in the fledgling city of Kuala Lumpur led to conflicts both among and between the Selangor chiefs and the miners. The outcome was a prolonged civil war, which slashed tin production and saw the destruction of KL. In 1874, with the civil war over, the British made their move to take control. The sultan was forced to accede to the installation of a British Resident at Klang, and for the next 25 years the state prospered, largely on the back of another boom in tin prices.

The most famous of all of the British Residents was Frank Swettenham who, evincing more tolerance and cultural insight than his colleagues, smoothed relations between the sultan and the local chiefs. He cajoled the sultans of four states (Perak, Selangor, Negeri Sembilan and Pahang) into an alliance

that eventually became the Federated Malay States in 1896.

The federation was centrally administered from a phoenix-like KL, which had become a well-ordered and prosperous city by the turn of the 20th century. In 1974 Selangor's sultan ceded KL as a federal territory, and Shah Alam took over the role of state capital. In the late 1990s the federal administrative capital of Putrajaya was also cleaved off from Selangor.

Climate
Lowland Selangor has a tropical climate, with daily temperatures hovering between 21°C and 32°C year-round. There is occasional rain throughout the year. Temperatures at Fraser's Hill and in the Genting Highlands are much cooler, ranging between 12°C and 22°C. Rainfall here is much heavier and more prolonged. Humidity averages about 85% to 90%.

Parks & Reserves
The Taman Alam Kuala Selangor (p141) is an important wetland and forest reserve some 75km northwest of KL, and is home to a large number of rare bird species. Closer to KL you'll find the Bukit Lagong Forest Reserve (p132) 16km northwest, and 22km north of the city the 1200-hectare tract of primary rainforest enclosed in Templer Park, named after the last British high commissioner of Malaysia.

Getting There & Away
Selangor's transport hub is KL – see p124 for full details. Kuala Lumpur International Airport (KLIA) and the Low Cost Carrier Terminal (LCC-T), at Sepang in the state's southeast corner, have road and rail links to the capital and Putrajaya. The Lebuhraya (North–South Hwy), from Johor Bahru to the Thai border, runs the length of the state. Ferries to Sumatra depart from Pelabuhan Klang (p140).

Getting Around
Trains and buses radiate out from KL to destinations around the state; see p124 for details.

NORTH OF KUALA LUMPUR
Batu Caves
Just 13km north of the capital, a short distance off the Ipoh road, a towering limestone outcrop is home to the impressive **Batu Caves** (admission free; car park RM2; ☉ 8am-9pm). The caves were officially discovered around 120 years ago by American naturalist William Hornaday. A short time later a small Hindu shrine was built in the vast open space, later known as Temple Cave.

An enormous golden statue of Muruga, also known as Lord Subramaniam, to whom the caves are dedicated, stands at the foot of a flight of 272 steps leading up to Temple Cave. Beyond the towering main cavern, the space opens to an atrium-like cave at the rear. Monkeys scamper around the shrines, which are dwarfed by the scale of the cave.

Each year in late January or early February a million pilgrims converge here during the three days of Thaipusam (p52). Lord Muruga's silver chariot takes pride of place as it makes its way from the Sri Mahamariamman Temple (p99) in KL's Chinatown to the caves. Get here by dawn if you want to see anything amid the crowds, and bring food and water with you.

DARK CAVE
At step 204, a path branches off to the **Dark Cave** (www.darkcave.com.my; adult/child RM35/25). On the 30-minute guided tour you can explore some 2km of surveyed passageways with seven different chambers. There are some dramatic limestone formations but the caves are damp and muddy – a head torch and wellington boots are provided. See the website about organising a more challenging two- to three-hour tour that involves crawling through the cave's narrow tunnels.

CAVE VILLA
The commercialisation of the caves continues at the base where you now have to pay to enter the previously free **Cave Villa** (☎ 012 910 8389; www.cavevilla.com.my; adult/child RM15/7; ☉ 9am-6pm), fronted by a pond packed with koi carp. It's worth paying to see the psychedelically painted sculptures of various Hindu gods arranged to tell parables from the *Bhagavad Gita* and other Hindu scriptures inside the cave. Outside the cave there's a small bird sanctuary, an area containing over 100 different species of reptiles (including a 7.6m-long python) and classical Indian dance shows on the half hour.

GETTING THERE & AWAY
Take bus 11 (RM2, 45 minutes) to the caves from where Jln Tun HS Lee meets Jln Petaling

---

OFF THE BEATEN TRACK: RIMBU DAHAN

It's worth checking the website of **Rimbun Dahan** (☎ 6038-3690; www.rimbundahan.org /home.html), a private property about 20 minutes' drive west of Kepong and one hour from KL, for times when it's possible to visit. There's a gallery inside this centre for developing traditional and contemporary art, as well as buildings designed by Hijjas Kasturi, the architect of the striking Tabung Haji (Map pp92–3) and Menara Maybank (Map p100) buildings in KL. The property also boasts a 19th-century traditional Malay house and an indigenous garden.

(Map p100), just south of Medan Pasar in KL. The bus also stops along Jln Raja Laut in the Chow Kit area. A taxi from KL shouldn't cost more than RM20.

Forestry Research Institute of Malaysia (FRIM)

Birdsong and wall-to-wall greenery replaces the drone of traffic and air-conditioning at the **Forestry Research Institute of Malaysia** (FRIM; ☎ 03-6279 7525; www.frim.gov.my; admission RM1, cars RM5; ⏰ 8am-6.30pm). The highlight of this 600-hectare jungle park at Kepong, part of the Bukit Lagong Forest Reserve 16km northwest of KL, is its **Canopy Walkway** (adult/child RM5/1; ⏰ 9.30am-2.30pm Tue-Thu, Sat & Sun).

The 200m walkway, hanging a vertigo-inducing 30m above the forest floor, is reached by a streep trail from FRIM's **information centre** (⏰ 8am-5pm Mon-Fri, 9am-4pm Sat & Sun), where you should go first to register and to pick up maps of the other trails in the park. Heading down from the walkway, the trail picks its way through the jungle (follow the water pipe) to a shady picnic area where you can cool off in a series of shallow waterfalls. The return hike incorporating the walkway takes around two hours. Bring water with you.

Elsewhere in the park there's a charming tearoom, a couple of handsome traditional wooden houses, relocated from Melaka and Terengganu, and a **museum** (⏰ 9am-4pm Tue-Sun), which has some interesting displays explaining the rainforest habitat and the forest-related research carried out by FRIM. Several arboreta highlight different types of trees, and there's also a wetland area.

GETTING THERE & AWAY

Take a KTM Komuter train to Kepong (RM1.30) and then a taxi (RM5); arrange for the taxi to pick you up again later. It's a good idea to bring a picnic to enjoy in the park; failing that the FRIM's canteen is open all day and serves decent home-cooked Malay food (around RM10 including a drink).

Orang Asli Museum

In the sleepy village of Gombak, 25km north of KL, the **Orang Asli Museum** (☎ 03-6189 2122; www.jheoa.gov.my/web/guest/25; Jln Pahang; admission free; ⏰ 9am-5pm Sat-Thu) is a fine introduction to the customs and culture of Malaysia's aboriginal people (see p38). The fascinating exhibits include clothes made from the bark of terap and ipoh trees, personal adornments, musical instruments and hunting implements, all accompanied by informative descriptions of the various Orang Asli cultures and ways of life. The helpful staff will play video documentaries on the Orang Asli, if you ask.

The museum's shop sells the striking wood carvings of the Hma' Meri people who live on Pulau Carey (see p140), as well as *tongkat ali*, a kind of ginseng that's marketed as Malaysian Viagra.

To get here take bus 174 (RM2, 1½ hours) from the Lebuh Ampang bus station (Map p100) in Kuala Lumpur.

Zoo Negara

Laid out over 62 hectares around a central lake, **Zoo Negara** (National Zoo; ☎ 03-4108 3422; www .zoonegara.org.my; adult/child RM15/6; ⏰ 9am-5pm), 13km northeast of KL, is home to a wide variety of native wildlife, including tigers, as well as other animals from Asia and Africa. Though a good zoo by the region's standards, some of the animal enclosures look cramped. Animal shows take place throughout the day, but a better way of interacting with the creatures here is to spend some time as a volunteer at the zoo – the website has details about how to arrange this.

Taxis charge around RM30 from central KL or you can take Metrobus 16 (RM2) from Central Market (Map p100) in Chinatown.

Genting Highlands

☎ 03

Opened in 1972, **Genting Highlands** (www.genting .com.my), 50km north of KL on the Pahang border, is in stark contrast to the Old English style of other Malaysian hill stations, its *raison d'être* being a glitzy casino – the only one in the country. It can get very busy here; the resort's five hotels have beds for 10,000 people and three times as many punters usually turn up each day.

In its slender favour is its cool weather; at 2000m above sea level there's no need for air-conditioning. The 3.4km-long **Genting Skyway** (one-way RM5; 7.30am-11pm Mon-Thu, 7.30am-midnight Fri-Sun) is a gentle 11-minute cable-car glide above the dense rainforest. Kids will also enjoy the **indoor and outdoor theme parks** (outdoor park adult/child from RM38/27; indoor park RM26/24, both parks RM51/36); they include water slides, thrill rides, a climbing wall, Snow World and a fierce wind tunnel for a simulated skydive!

To find out about the resort's history drop by the **Visitors Galleria** (10am-8pm) in the lobby of the Genting Hotel.

SLEEPING & EATING

Genting is an easy day trip from KL, but if you do decide to stay, the resort has a choice of five hotels, none of which is particularly outstanding. Rates vary enormously, the most expensive nights generally being Saturday and all public holidays; check on the website (www .genting.com.my) or with the KL **booking office** (Map p96; 03-2718 1118; Wisma Genting, 28 Jln Sultan Ismail; 8.30am-6pm Mon-Fri, 8.30am-1pm Sat). There's no shortage of places to eat, including cheap fast-food outlets and noisy food courts.

First World Hotel (r from RM120;) With 6500 beds, this is Malaysia's largest hotel. The plain but quite acceptable rooms are Genting's cheapest accommodation deal.

Genting Hotel (r from RM255;) High rollers should enquire about the luxury rooms on the Maxims floors of Genting's most luxurious hotel.

Olive (610 1118; Genting Hotel; meals R70; lunch & dinner) This is the pick of the fine-dining options, serving fusion cuisine in (for Genting) surprisingly classy surroundings.

Coffee Terrace (Genting Hotel; lunch/dinner RM55/65; lunch & dinner) A reasonably good buffet-style restaurant offering a range of food including Malay, Nonya, Thai, Western and Indian dishes.

GETTING THERE & AWAY

Buses leave at hourly (and sometimes half-hourly) intervals from 7.30am to 8.30pm from KL's Puduraya bus station (Map p100; adult/child RM8.50/6.80, 1½ hours) and on the hour from 8am to 7pm from KL Sentral (RM8.30/6.70); the price includes the Skyway cable car. A taxi from KL will cost around RM60.

A great deal is the Go Genting Golden Package (RM42), which includes return transport from KL, an all park unlimited ride pass or buffet lunch at the Coffee Terrace. Buy the pass from Genting's ticket office at KL Sentral (Map pp92–3) or from its **main sales office** (Map p96; 03-2718 1118; Wisma Genting, 28 Jln Sultan Ismail; 8.30am-6pm Mon-Fri, 8.30am-1pm Sat), where you can also book resort accommodation.

Kuala Kubu Bharu

03

Known simply as KKB, the charming town of Kuala Kubu Bharu, 72km north of KL, is easily accessible via its new KTM Komuter station. You'll pass through here en-route to Fraser's Hill (p134).

Apart from its stuck-in-time atmosphere, the principal attraction of KKB is as a base for activities such as rafting and kayaking on the Selangor Dam, Sungai Selangor and Sungai Chiling. Among the outfits you can organise this with are local operators **Box Tracks Adventures** (www .tracksadventures.com.my) and **Pierose Swiftwater** (www.raftmal aysia.com).

Jungle trekking is also possible here, the most popular route being to the 20m-tall **Chiling Waterfall** on Sungai Chiling. This is a 1½ hour walk from the so-called Rainbow Bridge on route 55 leading up to Fraser's Hill. The route is clearly marked, but it's a good idea to hire a guide to get you there, since you have to cross the river five times and it's important to be aware of flash flooding. Guides include KKB-based **Eddie** (012 213 2678; eyap48@gmail.com) and **Happy Yen** (017 369 7831; www.happyyen.webs.com), who organises tours to the falls from KL.

SLEEPING & EATING

Accommodation in KKB itself is limited. You could also use Fraser's Hill as a base.

Rumah Rehat Seri Teratai (6064 1971, 019-350 7735; 1A Jln Teratai, Taman Seni Teratai; d RM100) There are just five rooms at this simple Malay guesthouse a few kilometres from the heart of KKB.

Flying Rhino Guesthouse (☎ 6064 2188; theflying rhino@gmail.com; Lot 5 Jln Dato Tabal; d RM148; ☐) At the time of research this excellent new guesthouse, run by a lovely expat couple, was temporarily closed.

ourpick **Sekeping Serendah Retreat** (☎ 012-324 6552; www.serendah.com; Serendah; mud/glass cabins from RM500/650; ☒) If you have wheels this forest-bound ecoretreat outside the town of Serendah, 35km south of KKB, is a gem. Two partly mud-walled cabins each sleep two, while the double-storey glass, steel and wood units, with self-catering facilities, can house up to six each. All the cabins have outdoor showers and there's a fantastic, purpose-built swimming pool, as well as a gurgling stream running through the property. A caretaker is on hand to provide a simple breakfast (RM3) or dinner (RM20).

In KKB, delicious Chinese food is available for lunch at **Restoran Vilet** (15 Jln Kamaraddin; meal RM8; ☯ 11am-4pm) while **Kedai Makanan Govindamah** (☎ 017-362 7790; 9 Jln Abd Hamid, Kuala Kubu Bharu; meal RM5.50; ☯ 7-1am) dishes up palatable veg and non-veg Indian food.

GETTING THERE & AWAY
KKB is a station on the KL-Ipoh train line (RM5 to RM9 from Sentral KL, one hour, four daily). From the station a taxi to the town centre costs around RM5. The No 43 Metrobus service from beside the Bangkok Bank stop (Map p100) in KL runs to Rawang (RM2, every 20 minutes). From Rawang (also on the KTM train line) the No 36 Metrobus goes to KKB (RM3, every 20 minutes).

Fraser's Hill (Bukit Fraser)
☎ 09
Of all the hill stations, Fraser's Hill (Bukit Fraser), 103km north of KL, retains the most colonial charm. Situated across seven densely forested hills at a cool altitude of 1524m, this quiet and relatively undeveloped place, dotted with a mix of stone bungalows and more modern complexes, attracts only a fraction of the visitors of Genting or the Cameron Highlands. In 2009 many of the buildings and accommodation options, owned by the Fraser's Hill Development Corporation, were undergoing a much-needed renovation, so the whole place should be looking freshly spruced up by now.

There's relatively little to do here besides relax in the cool air, enjoy a forest stroll and

indulge in a spot of bird-watching. Should you choose to make it more than just a day trip from KL, there's plenty of accommodation; on weekends and public holidays you will need to book ahead. Like the Genting Highlands, Fraser's Hill is on the Selangor/Pahang border, but almost all visitors come through Selangor, and the state border actually cuts right through the station. For online information check the website of **Pahang Tourism** (www.pahangtou rism.com.my).

INFORMATION
The hill station's focal point is the tiny village at the western end of the golf course.
Fraser's Hill Development Corporation office (FHDC; ☎ 362 2201; www.pkbf.org.my; ☯ 8am-5pm Mon-Fri) Currently sharing premises with the offices for the mosque but likely to move into new digs by the central clock. Provides information, maps and brochures; staff can book accommodation and help arrange hiking guides.
Maybank (Jln Lady Guillemard; ☯ 9.15am-4.30pm Mon-Thu, 9.15am-4pm Fri) Small branch at Shahzan Inn; accepts credit cards, exchanges foreign currency and travellers cheques. Nearest ATM is back in Kuala Kubu Bharu (KKB) opposite the bus station.

SIGHTS & ACTIVITIES
Fraser's Hill's main attraction is its abundant flora and fauna, in particular its **birdlife**. With its lush, damp environment Fraser's Hill supports some 265 species of birds, including the Malaysian whistling thrush, the Kinabalu friendly warbler, the brilliantly coloured green

---

NAMING THE STATION
Fraser's Hill is named after Louis James Fraser, an adventurous Scotsman who migrated to Malaysia in the 1890s after failing in attempts to prospect for gold in Australia. Trying his luck in the country's booming tin-mining industry, Fraser set up a mule-train operation to transport the ore across the hills and is also rumoured to have run gambling and opium dens. These had vanished (along with Fraser himself) by 1917, when Bishop Ferguson-Davie of Singapore came looking for Fraser. Recognising the area's potential as a hill station, the bishop wrote a report to the High Commissioner on his return to Singapore. A couple of years later this 'little England' in the heart of the Malaysian jungle began to be developed.

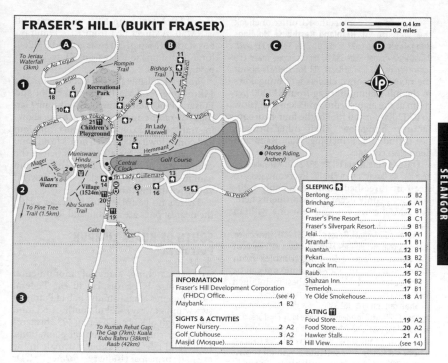

FRASER'S HILL (BUKIT FRASER)

SLEEPING
Bentong	5	B2
Brinchang	6	A1
Cini	7	B1
Fraser's Pine Resort	8	C1
Fraser's Silverpark Resort	9	B1
Jelai	10	A1
Jerantut	11	B1
Kuantan	12	B1
Pekan	13	B2
Puncak Inn	14	A2
Raub	15	B2
Shahzan Inn	16	B2
Temerloh	17	B1
Ye Olde Smokehouse	18	A1

EATING
Food Store	19	A2
Food Store	20	A2
Hawker Stalls	21	A1
Hill View	(see 14)	

INFORMATION
Fraser's Hill Development Corporation (FHDC) Office	(see 4)	
Maybank	1	B2

SIGHTS & ACTIVITIES
Flower Nursery	2	A2
Golf Clubhouse	3	A2
Masjid (Mosque)	4	B2

SELANGOR

magpie, and the long-tailed broadbill with its sky-blue chest. The high point of the local twitchers' calendar is June, when the hill station hosts its International Bird Race, in which teams of bird spotters compete to record the highest number of species.

Pick up a leaflet from the Fraser's Hill Development Corporation Office outlining the hill station's various hikes, most pretty straightforward and signposted. The **Hemmant Trail**, which takes only 30 minutes, is about 1km and leads from the mosque to Victory Bungalow. You'll need to arrange a guide for the 5km-long **Pine Tree Trail**, which takes around six hours and crosses three mountain peaks, including 1505m Pine Tree Hill; a recommended guide is **Mr Durai** (☎ 013-983 1633; durefh@hotmail.com), who charges around RM30 per hour.

At the picturesque nine-hole **golf course** (☎ 362 2129; Jln Genting; green fees Mon-Fri/Sat & Sun RM30/40, hire of half/full set of clubs RM15/30) you'll most likely see dusky leaf monkeys wandering about as well as the occasional wild boar. At the paddock to the east of the golf course, you can go **horse riding** (RM3 to RM7) or practice **archery** (RM5 to RM6). Alternatively hire a paddleboat

(RM6 per 15 minutes) to explore **Allan's Waters**, a small lake next to the flower nursery.

About 5km northwest of the town centre, along Jln Air Terjun, is **Jeriau Waterfall**, with a swimming pool fed from the falls. It's a 20-minute climb up from the road to reach them.

SLEEPING

Musty, damp hotel rooms and cottages go with the territory at Fraser's Hill. At the topend places you can expect to pay 20 to 40% more on weekends and public holidays. Rates typically include breakfast and all the hotels have wi-fi (but no public internet terminal).

Many places were closed for renovation when we visited, including the FHDC-run budget hotel option **Puncak Inn** (☎ 362 2201), the FHDC's three rental bungalows (Kuantan and Cini with three bedrooms and Bentong with two bedrooms) and the Selangor state government's **Rumah Rehat Gap** (☎ 362 2227) at the Gap, 8km south of Fraser's Hill. Bookings for the FHDC properties can be made via its website (www.pkbf.org.my) or at the hillstation office (see opposite).

You can also contact the KL office or check the website of **Highland Resthouse Holdings Bungalows** (Map pp92-3; ☎ 03-2164 8937 in KL; www .hrhbungalows.com; Suite 38A-1, 38th fl, Empire Tower, City Square Centre, 182 Jln Tun Razak, KL) for details about the range of rooms, chalets and bungalows in the hill station, starting from RM300 per room at the eight-bedroom Pekan bungalow to RM2000 for full hire of the four-bedroom Jerantut bungalow. Their other properties include the Brinchang, Jelai, Raub and Temerloh cottages.

Fraser's Pine Resort (☎ 362 2122; www.thepines .com.my; Jln Quarry; r from RM110) Everyone gets to sleep in three-bedroom, reasonably well-kept but plainly decorated apartments here. For RM50 extra you can rent one with an equipped kitchen.

Fraser's Silverpark Resort (☎ 362 2888; www.frasers silverpark.com.my; Jln Lady Maxwell; r from RM150) Not the most attractive-looking complex from the outside, but the views looking out can be spectacular from what are the best maintained self-catering apartments in Fraser's.

Shahzan Inn (☎ 362 3300; www.shahzaninn.com.my; Jln Lady Guillemard; garden/golf course view r incl breakfast from RM145/168) Overlooking the golf course, this is one of the most attractive places to stay. There's a kettle and satellite TV in all rooms and a 20% discount is available to guests at the golf club.

Ye Olde Smokehouse (☎ 362 2226; www.thesmoke house.com.my; Jln Jeriau; d/ste from RM308/385) Exposed beams, log fires, four-poster beds and chintz – the Smokehouse goes for broke on its English-charm offensive. Even if you don't stay here, drop by for a well-made pie or roast at lunch or afternoon tea (RM18) on the garden terrace.

EATING
There a couple of small stores as you come into Fraser's for self-catering supplies and all the hotels have restaurants, Ye Olde Smokehouse's being the best. At the time of research a new complex for hawker stalls was being built beside the kid's playground.

Hill View (☎ 362 2231; mains from RM10; ⏲ 9.30am-9pm) Both passable Western and Chinese food is available at this simple eatery, which has been run by a locally based family for a couple of generations.

GETTING THERE & AWAY
The route to Fraser's Hill is via Kuala Kubu Bharu (KKB); for details of how to get there, see p134. A taxi from KKB to Fraser's Hill is RM50. A direct taxi from KL's Puduraya bus station (Map p100) costs around RM280; for a return taxi journey from KL reckon on paying RM700.

Since a landslide has put out of action the 11km-long road via the Tamil school and Fraser's Pine Resort, the old 8km-long Gap road to Fraser's operates as it once did, allowing traffic to go up on the odd hours from 7am and come down on the even hours from 6am: the road is open for 40 minutes before the change over of direction. Between 8pm and 6am it's a free-for-all, so take it very slowly if you drive during this time.

There's no petrol station in Fraser's Hill; the nearest ones are at Raub and KKB.

SOUTH OF KUALA LUMPUR
Putrajaya
☎ 03

An eye-catching array of monumental architecture is on display in the Federal Government's administrative hub of Putrajaya (www.ppj.gov.my), 25km south of KL and 20km north of KLIA. Covering 4932 hectares of former rubber and palm-oil plantations, this brand new city was but a twinkle in the eye of its principal visionary – former PM, Dr Mahathir – back in the early 1990s. Designed as a garden city, the heart of Putrajaya is a 600-hectare man-made lake fringed by landscaped parks and an eclectic mix of buildings and bridges, which in themselves are the city's chief tourist attraction.

It's worth noting that less than 10% of government workers in Putrajaya are non-Malays. Several huge mosques have already appeared, but there are no major religious monuments for any other ethnic groups – fuelling claims of bias against Indian and Chinese Malaysians by the Malay-dominated government.

SIGHTS & ACTIVITIES
Putrajaya Architecture
Putrajaya cannot be faulted as a showcase of urban planning and vaulting architectural ambition. The main boulevard is Persiaran Perdana, which runs from the elevated spaceship-like **Putrajaya Convention Centre** (☎ 8887 6000; www.pcc.gov.my; Presint 5), worth visiting for the views, to the circular **Dataran Putra** (Putra Square), passing the Mogulesque **Istana Kehakiman** (Palace of Justice) and the modernist Islamic gateway fronting the

Kompleks Perdadanan Putrajaya (Putrajaya Corporation Complex).

Framing Dataran Putra on two sides are **Perdana Putra**, housing the offices of the prime minister, and the handsome **Putra Mosque** (for non-Muslims 9am-1.30pm & 3-6pm Sat-Thu, 3-6pm Fri), which has space for 15,000 worshippers and an ornate pink-and-white-patterned dome, influenced by Safavid architecture from Iran. Appropriately dressed non-Muslim visitors are welcome outside of prayer times.

There are nine bridges, all in different styles. The longest, at 435m, is the **Putra Bridge**, which mimics the Khaju Bridge in Esfahan, Iran. Also worthy of a photo is the futurist sail-like **Wawasan Bridge** connecting Presint 2 and 8.

Lake Cruise

The bridges and buildings look their best viewed from Putrajaya Lake. **Cruise Tasik Putrajaya** (8888 3769; www.cruisetasikputrajaya.com; 10am-7pm), located just beneath the Dataran Putra end of the Putra Bridge, offers up two options: the gondola-like Dondang Sayang Perahu boats (adult/child RM20/12) departing anytime for a 30-minute trip around the lake, or a 45-minute air-con cruise on the Belimbing boat (adult/child RM30/20) leaving hourly from 1pm Monday to Friday and from 11am to 7pm at weekends.

Taman Botani

North of Perdana Putra, near the prime minister's official residence, the 93-hectare **Taman Botani** (Botanic Gardens; 8888 9090; Presint 1; admission free; 9am-7pm daily) features attractive tropical gardens, a visitors centre, a beautifully tiled Moroccan pavilion and a lakeside restaurant. A tourist tram (RM3) trundles between the flower beds and trestles, and you can hire bicycles for RM4 for two hours (RM4 for one hour on weekends).

Taman Wetland

Further north is the serene **Taman Wetland** (Wetland Park; 8889 4373; Presint 13; admission free; 7am-7pm; visitors centre 9am-6pm Mon-Fri, 9am-7pm Sat & Sun), a contemplative space with peaceful nature trails, a colony of flamingos, fluttering butterflies and picnic tables overlooking the lake. Canoeing and boating trips can be arranged here.

SLEEPING & EATING

Pullman Putrajaya Lakeside (8890 0000; www.pullmanputrajaya.com; 2 Jln P5/5, Presint 5; r from RM260;) Close to the Convention Centre and beside the lake, this large new resort complex incorporates traditional Malaysian architectural elements into its design. The rooms and resort facilities are good and include an alfresco seafood restaurant built over the lake.

Putrajaya Shangri-la (8887 8888; www.shangri-la.com; Taman Putra Perdana, Presint 1; r from RM390;) This very classy hotel has a great hillside view across to the lake. Good-value weekend packages are available and its Azur restaurant serves up an impressive Malaysian set lunch (RM40)

Alamanda (www.alamanda.com.my; Presint 1; meals RM10; 9am-9pm) Putrajaya's swish shopping mall is home to several restaurants as well as an excellent food court where you can join the local bureaucrats for a meal.

Selera Putra (Presint 1; meals RM10; 9am-7pm Mon-Fri, 9am-9pm Sat & Sun) Head to this food court beneath Dataran Putra and enjoy the lakeside view while sampling a wide range of inexpensive Malaysian dishes.

GETTING THERE & AWAY

KLIA transit trains from KL Sentral (Map pp92–3) and KLIA stop at the Putrajaya-Cyberjaya station (from KL Sentral it costs RM9.50 one way and takes 20 minutes).

Bus 200 runs from the train station to Dataran Putra (50 sen); a taxi there is RM9 while hiring one for an hour to tour the sights (the recommended option) is a fixed RM30. The city's planned monorail/metro is unlikely to be completed within the next five years.

KLANG VALLEY

Heading southwest of KL along the Klang Hwy, the **Kota Darul Ehsan** ceremonial arch marks the transition between the city and Selangor. Just over the boundary, Petaling Jaya blends into Shah Alam, the state capital, which blends into Klang, the old royal capital – pretty much all in one seamless stretch of housing estates and industrial parks. Efficient public transport to and from KL makes for easy day trips.

Petaling Jaya

03

Many of the people you'll meet in KL actually live in the neighbouring city of Petaling Jaya

SELANGOR

SEPANG CIRCUIT

The **Sepang Circuit** (☎ 03-8778 2222; www.sepangcircuit.com), 65km south of KL and a 10-minute drive east of KLIA, is where Formula One holds the Malaysian Grand Prix every March or April. Tickets go for as little as RM100, which in 2009 included access to an after-race party headlined by top international music acts. During the three days of the grand prix, plenty of special train and bus transport to the circuit is on offer, from around RM80 return from KL city centre.

At other times of the year there's an **auto museum** (admission free; ☼ 9am-6pm), and you can call ahead to book a tour of the facilities. Also check the website for track days when the circuit is open to wannabe Michael Schumachers, who want to rev up their own cars (RM200) or motor-bikes (below 250cc RM70, over 250cc RM100).

(PJ). This sprawling community is defined by its giant shopping malls. Apart from these, there's not a whole lot else to detain you here.

SUNWAY LAGOON & SUNWAY PYRAMID

There are few more fun ways of cooling down on a sticky day than splashing around at **Sunway Lagoon** (☎ 5639 0000; www.sunwaylagoon.com; 3 Jln PJS, 11/11 Bandar Sunway; adult/child from RM45/30, incl water park RM60/45; ☼ 11am-6pm Mon & Wed-Fri, 10am-6pm Sat & Sun). Built on the site of a former tin mine and quarry, the highlight of this multi-zone theme park are the water slides, and the world's largest man-made surf beach. There's also a Wild West–themed section with all the regular thrill rides, an interactive wildlife zoo (ie, you're allowed to stroke the giant tortoises and cuddle the hamsters) and an extreme park with all-terrain vehicles, a rock-climbing wall and paintball fights.

The park is behind the vast **Sunway Pyramid** (☎ 7494 3100; www.sunwaypyramid.com) mall distinguished by its giant lion gateway, faux Egyptian walls and crowning pyramid! Inside is a **skating rink** (admission incl skate hire Mon-Fri RM13, Sat & Sun RM16; ☼ 9am-8pm) as well as a bowling alley, a multiplex cinema and the usual plethora of shops and dining outlets.

Sunway Lagoon is so close to KL that staying over isn't necessary. However, the site does have several appealing accommodation options gathered together in the **Sunway Resort Hotel & Spa** (☎ 7492 8000; http://kualalumpur.sunway hotels.com; rm/villa from RM450/1800; ℗ ☒ ☐ ☎): the **Pyramid Tower** is a modern and quirkily designed business hotel; the **Duplex** offers 12 townhouses, each with three chicly designed bedrooms and fully equipped kitchens – ideal for families; and the **Villas** are 17 contemporary Asian-styled residences, each with their own infinity-style plunge pools, sunken baths and rain showers – great for a romantic getaway.

The easiest way to get to Sunway is take the Putra LRT to Kelana Jaya (RM2.10), then the feeder bus T623 (RM1) or a taxi (RM11) to the Sunway Pyramid. Shuttle buses U63, U67 and U756 run here from Subang Jaya station on the KTM Komuter line. A taxi all the way from central KL will cost around RM21.

THE CURVE

It's got Ikea, it's got Tescos, and it's got oodles more shops and restaurants. However, there are other reasons for heading to **The Curve** (☎ 7710 6868; www.thecurve.com.my; Mutiara Damansara; ☎ 10am-10pm), about 15km west of the centre in Petaling Jaya. One of the best is to attend concerts by up-and-coming local bands at **Laundry Bar** (☎ 7728 1715; www.laundrybar.net; G75 & 76 Western Courtyard; ☼ 11-1am), which has also been hosting the monthly Popcorn & Soda Sunday afternoon film sessions showcasing shorts by local film-makers and feature-length French movies. A free shuttle bus runs three times a day between the mall and the Royale Bintang Hotel (Map p96) on Jln Bukit Bintang (see the Curve website for details). Otherwise catch Metrobus 99 here from KL's Central Market (Map p100).

Shah Alam
☎ 03

Thirty years ago Selangor's state capital was just a rubber-and-palm plantation, but in the late 1970s a massive building program spawned a well-developed infrastructure, huge public buildings and a rapidly growing population. It's a staunchly Muslim city, dominated by the showpiece **Masjid Sultan Salahuddin Abdul Aziz Shah** (☎ 5159 9988; Persiaran Masjid; ☼ 10am-noon & 2-4pm Sat-Thu), one of the largest mosques in Southeast Asia.

Called the Blue Mosque for its azure dome (larger than that of London's St Paul's

Cathedral) covered in a rosette of verses from the Quran, the building accommodates up to 24,000 worshippers. Its four minarets, looking like giant rockets, are the tallest in the world (over 140m). You'll need to be appropriately dressed if you want to look inside. Once you've seen the mosque there isn't a huge amount else to do, so it's best to combine a visit here with a trip out to Klang and the coast.

Bus U18 goes to Shah Alam from KL's Klang bus station (Map p100; RM2, one hour) and will drop you in front of the PKNS Plaza mall, from where it's a short walk to the mosque. Frequent Komuter trains also run from KL to Shah Alam (RM2.50, 45 minutes), but from there it's another bus or taxi ride to the mosque.

Klang & Pelabuhan Klang
☎ 03

About 10km west of Shah Alam is Klang, once the royal capital of Selangor and a mecca for food lovers. This is where the British installed their first Resident in 1874. Its few sights should take no more than a couple of hours to see, leaving you plenty of time to enjoy the real reason for heading here: satisfying your stomach in Klang's vibrant Little India.

Five stops futher down the line the KTM Komuter trains terminate at ramshackle Pelabuhan Klang, once KL's main seaport until the establishment of the modern harbour on Pulau Indah, 17km to the southwest. The main reason for coming here is to either catch a ferry to Sumatra or Pulau Ketam (see p140), or to grab a seafood meal at the nearby waterside village of Bagan Hailan.

SIGHTS
Klang is small enough to see on foot. Heading south from the train station, along Jalan Stesyn, you'll pass several attractive rows of Chinese shophouses (to the right). Running parallel to Jln Stesyn to the right is Jln Tengku Kelana, heart of Klang's colourful **Little India**. Especially frenetic around the Hindu festival of Deepavali, this Little India is more vibrant than that of KL and includes several fortune tellers, who squat on the pavement and predict the future with the aid of green parrots trained to pick out auspicious cards.

Return to Jln Steysn to take a quick look at the grand whitewashed 1909 colonial building housing the **Galeri Diraja Sultan Abdul Aziz** (☎ 3373 6500; www.galeridiraja.com; Bangunan Sultan Suleiman; admission free; ☺ 10am-5pm Tue-Sun). The royal gallery, devoted to the history of the Selangor Sultanate dating back to 1766, contains a wide array of royal regalia, gifts and artifacts, including copies of the crown jewels.

Heading uphill along Jln Istana will bring you to **Istana Alam Shah**, the sultan's palace before the capital was moved to Shah Alam; there are plans to open this to the public. The park opposite gives a pleasant view of the city.

East of the palace, along Jln Kota Raja, the **Masjid Di Raja Sultan Suleiman** is a striking blend of Art Deco and Middle Eastern influences. Opened in 1934, this was once the state mosque and several sultans are buried here. Step inside to admire its stained-glass dome.

EATING
Indian food is Klang's highlight, but it's not the only thing on offer: the town's Chinese community is also famous for inventing *bak kut the* (pork-rib soup with hints of garlic and Chinese five spice). Excellent, reasonably priced seafood is also available at a number of restaurants out at Bagan Hailan, a RM10 taxi ride from Pelabuhan Klang station.

Asoka (Jln Tengku Kelana; meals RM5-10; ☺ 7am-11pm) A vividly orange-and-cream-painted parlour of Indian culinary goodness, including a great selection of sweets, juices and crispy *tosai* pancakes served with coconut chutney.

Jai Hind (Jln Tengku Kelana; meals RM5-10; ☺ 7am-11pm) Also renowned for its sweets, Jai Hind has been in business for over 60 years and is the place to head when it's time for *tiffin* (afternoon snacks).

Sri Barathan Matha Vilas (34-36 Jln Tengku Kelana; meals RM5-10; ☺ 6.30am-10.30pm) It's hard to resist a bowl of this restaurant's signature dish of spicy *mee goreng* fried noodles since the chef prepares them constantly in a giant wok beside the entrance.

Seng Huat Bak Kut Teh (☎ 012-309 8303; 9 Jln Besar; meal RM10; ☺ 7.30am-1pm, 5.30-9pm) Sample the fragrant, flavoursome pork stew at this unpretentious eatery, steps away from the train station, just beneath the Klang Bridge.

Mohana Bistro (☎ 3372 7659; 119 Jln Tengku Kelana; meals RM10-20; ☺ 7am-11pm) Deservedly popular spot for banana leaf curry spreads and spice-ladened biryani rice.

Bagan Seafood (☎ 3176 4546; Lot 4546, Lingkaran Sultan Hishamuddin, off Jalan Pelabuhan Utara, Kg Baru Bagan Hailam; meals RM40; ☺ 11am-3pm, 6-11pm Mon-Fri, 11am-

ISLAND ESCAPES

If you're looking to escape the Klang Valley's urban sprawl, two islands – one reached by ferry, the other by road – make for great day trips.

Chill out on the 30-minute ferry trip (RM6) through the mangroves from Pelabuhan Klang to **Pulau Ketam** (Crab Island), where you'll find a charming fishing village built on stilts over the mudflats. There's little to do here other than wander around the wooden buildings of the village and enjoy a Chinese seafood lunch at one of several restaurants. Air-con ferries depart roughly every hour between 8.45am and 6.30pm (until 7.10pm on weekends); the last ferry back from Pulau Ketam is at 5.45pm (6pm on weekends).

If you don't have your own wheels, hire a taxi to get you out to **Pulau Carey** (from Klang one way/return RM60/130), an island largely covered with palm-oil plantations. Pause either on the way there or back to enjoy a tasty seafood meal at **Kang Guan** (☎ 352 7737; Jln Bandar Lama, Telok Panglima Garang; meals RM30; ⏱ 11.30am-2.45pm & 5.45-11pm) beside the mangroves just before you cross the bridge over to the island.

Your final destination is tiny **Kampung Sungai Bumbon**, home to an Orang Asli tribe known as the Hma' Meri (also written as Mah Meri). Here you can see the woodcarvers who have put the Mah Meri's art on the cultural map. There's also a **community centre** (⏱ 9am-5pm), where you can pick up pretty woven baskets and other products made from dyed pandanus palm leaves as well as an interesting booklet in English about Hma' Meri culture.

Held in August the village's Mystic event, when prayers are made to ancestors and the Hma Meri display their carvings, is worth attending.

midnight Sat & Sun) Brave the long drive out to this seaside eatery to enjoy its super fresh seafood. Order *mantou* (deep-fried bread buns) to mop up the yummy sauces.

GETTING THERE & AWAY
Klang
It's best to come here by train from KL, as the KTM Komuter station is closer to the sights; there are trains every 30 minutes. Klang's bus station is opposite the My Din shopping complex, on the northern side of the river. There are several buses every hour to KL's Klang bus station (Map p100; RM2) or Kuala Selangor (RM2). Express buses between KL and Pelabuhan Klang also stop in Klang. Klang's taxi station is one block east, behind the bus station.

Pelabuhan Klang
Pelabuhan Klang is 41km southwest of KL and 8km past Klang. Buses from KL's Klang bus station (Map p100) run to Pelabuhan Klang via Klang, but they terminate about a kilometre from the port. KTM Komuter trains also run to/from KL and Klang, and the station is just a stone's throw from the ferry terminal.

Ferries to Tanjung Balai (Asahan; one way including tax RM145, 3½ hours, 11am Monday to Saturday) in Sumatra depart from here. Citizens of Australia, America, Britain and several European nations can get a visa on arrival in Indonesia; otherwise you must have an Indonesian visa before boarding. To check on ferry details call **Aero Speed Enterprises** (☎ 3165 2545) at the ferry terminal.

KUALA SELANGOR
☎ 03
Where the Sungai Selangor flows into the sea is the old royal capital of Kuala Selangor. The hilltop fort at this small sleepy town was briefly conquered by the Dutch when they invaded Selangor in 1784; Sultan Ibrahim took it back a year later. The town became embroiled in the Selangor Civil War (1867–73) when the fort was partly destroyed. Later the British built a lighthouse on the hill, which still stands and has become a symbol of the town.

Well off the beaten tourist track, Kuala Selangor has a friendly *kampung* atmosphere and a good wildlife park. It's possible to do as a day trip from KL, or en route to or from Perak state, but an overnight stop is recommended so you can catch the nightly show put on by fireflies along the Sungai Selangor.

Sights & Activities
FIREFLY VIEWING
The main place for viewing the flickering of the fireflies is **Kampung Kuantan**, 9km east of

Kuala Selangor. Malay-style wooden boats row out on the river to the 'show trees' and their dazzling displays. Boats take four people at RM10 each for the 45-minute trip, and leave on demand throughout the evening from around 7pm until midnight. The trips are not recommended on full-moon or rainy nights, when the fireflies are not at their luminous best. Take mosquito repellent.

To reach the village, take the turn-off to Batang Berjuntai, 2km south of Kuala Selangor. A taxi from Kuala Selangor costs RM40 for the return trip.

You can also see the fireflies at the Firefly Park Resort at Kampung Bukit Belimbing (right).

BUKIT MALAWATI

It's a pleasant, short walk through landscaped parklands to the top of Bukit Malawati, with views across the mangrove coastline. The hill has long been an ideal site for monitoring shipping in the Selat Melaka (Strait of Melaka), first for the sultans of Selangor and then for the Dutch, who destroyed the sultan's fort during their invasion in 1784, then rebuilt it, naming it Fort Atlingsburg after their governor general.

All that remains of the old fort today are some sections of wall and cannons. At the summit you'll find the British lighthouse (dating from 1909), a podium for viewing the new moon, and a museum (closed at the time of research). Tame silvered leaf monkeys hang out here too, happy to be fed titbits by visitors.

The road up Bukit Malawati starts one block away from the old bus station in the town centre. It does a clockwise loop of the hill; you can walk up and around in less than an hour.

TAMAN ALAM KUALA SELANGOR NATURE PARK

On the estuary of Sungai Selangor, at the foot of Bukit Malawati and reached by a flight of steps from the hill, is **Taman Alam Kuala Selangor Nature Park** (☎ 3289 2294; www .mns.org.my; Jln Klinik; adult/child RM4/1; ☸ 8am-7pm). Inside the 240-hectare park are three ecosystems – secondary forest, a man-made lake and a mangrove forest with views out to sea – and you can explore them all on a 3km trail that includes a raised walkway above the mangroves.

It's easy to spot the cheeky long-tailed macaques and silvered leaf monkeys at the accommodation huts at the entrance to park. There are also three bird-watching towers and a hide. Around 150 species of birds have been spotted in the park, including mangrove waders such as the rare spoonbilled sandpiper and Nordmann's greenshank, best seen at dawn or dusk. On the lake you might also be lucky enough to see an endangered milky stork; the park cooperated with Zoo Negara on a breeding program and now around four storks still live on the lake. Other fauna you may see includes otters, nocturnal leopard cats and civets.

The **visitors centre** (☸ 8am-6pm) has some interesting displays on the nature in the park as well as a small shop selling Malaysian Nature Society goods and books.

Sleeping

Taman Alam Kuala Selangor Nature Park (☎ 3289 2294; www.mns.org.my; Jln Klinik; r from RM25) Offers simple A-frame huts (RM25) or two-bed (one single, one queen) wooden chalets (RM45) with fan and attached bathroom.

Hotel Kuala Selangor (☎ 3289 2709; 90B Jln Steysen; r from RM33; 🕸) Directly opposite the bus station, this budget option is the best of a few reasonably clean but uninspiring Chinese hotels.

Firefly Park Resort (☎ 3260 1208; www.firefly park.com; Jln Haji Omar, Kg Bukit Belimbing; chalets from RM130; 🕸) This modern resort has plainly decorated, comfortable four-person chalets perched on stilts over the river, and pleasant landscaped grounds. Boat trips to watch the fireflies cost RM15/10 for adults/children, and fishing trips cost RM40 per hour.

De Palma Hotel Kuala Selangor (☎ 3289 7070; www.depalmahotel.com; Jln Tanjung Keramat; r with breakfast from RM200; 🕸 🖳 🕸) Around 1.5km north of the old bus station (follow the signs) is this decent miniresort offering a range of accommodation in nicely furnished and reasonably well-maintained wooden chalets. It rents bicycles (RM5 an hour) and can arrange a trip out to see the fireflies (RM48). The best deal is their two-day, one-night packages (RM120 per person), which include accommodation and the fireflies trip.

Eating

If seafood is what you're after, head to Pasir Penambang, a fishing village on the north side of the river, where a number of atmospheric seafood restaurants are clustered; a taxi from Kuala Selangor costs around RM10.

Auntie Kopitiam (No C3, Jln Sultan Ibrahim; meals RM5-10; ☾ 6am-6pm). Next to the bus station, this old-style coffee shop serves Malaysian favourites such as *nasi lemak* and chicken chop.

Waterfall Café (☎ 3289 2388; 88 Jln Stesen; meals RM6-10; ☾ 10am-9pm) Good food, a picture menu and friendly service make this simple Chinese-run cafe a delight.

Getting There & Away

To reach Kuala Selangor you'll first need to take one of the frequent buses from KL to Klang bus station (see p140), where you'll change to a Kuala Selangor-bound bus (RM5.30, one hour). Heading north from Kuala Selangor to Perak state, first take one of the old rattlers to Sabakbernam (RM7, 1½ hours) for connections to Teluk Intan (see p146).

Buses to and from Klang stop at the old bus station beside Bukit Melawati, but for services to Sabakbernam you will need to go to the new bus station, which is 2km outside the town centre. A local bus from the old to new bus station is 60 sen, or it's a 20-minute walk.

Approximate fares for a taxi ride from Kuala Selangor: KL (RM100), Klang (RM60) and Teluk Intan (RM80).

Perak

The old chestnut, 'What do you prefer, the mountains or the ocean?' goes over pretty well in Perak, peninsular Malaysia's second-largest state. If you're not exploring through limestone hills honeycombed with caves and sprinkled with Chinese temples, you're probably lazing along the Straits of Melaka on Pulau Pangkor. Smooth blue ocean versus jungle peaks patched with tea and strawberry plantations? Decisions, decisions.

There's quite a bit of stuff to see between these altitudinal extremes, though. Perak is one of Malaysia's most historically rich states: the country's former (and still significant) economic engines of tin mining and rubber tapping have their roots, as it were, in Darul Ridzuan, the Land of Grace. Perak's enterprising Chinese population has had a disproportionately huge impact on the evolution of modern Malaysia, while the state's geographic position along the Straits has put it at the centre of much of the national narrative. Thanks to all this heritage there are some pleasantly faded cities well worth your exploration: the royal seat of Kuala Kangsar; the garden metropolis of Taiping; Bukit Larut, the oldest hill station in Malaysia; and sprawling Ipoh, with its colonial architecture and Buddhist cave temples.

Still, with such a varied geography this is, unsurprisingly, a state made for experiencing physical beauty, from Matang Mangrove Forest Reserve to the Cameron Highlands (in Pahang state, but accessible from here), Malaysia's premier hill retreat.

'Perak' means 'silver' in Malay, but historians debate whether the word references the state's tin mines or the fish off its sandy coast. In other words, does Perak's identity come from the mountains, or the ocean? Why not check out both?

PERAK

HIGHLIGHTS

- Polishing off strawberries and tea, and trekking in the **Cameron Highlands** (p159)

- Snacking on delicious street food in **Ipoh** (p157)

- Lazing on one of the fine beaches on **Pulau Pangkor** (p150)

- Soaking up the colonial charm of **Taiping** (p169)

- Getting lost amid the mangroves at **Matang Mangrove Forest Reserve** (p173)

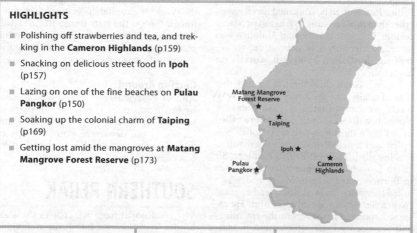

Matang Mangrove Forest Reserve ★
Taiping ★
Ipoh ★
Pulau Pangkor ★
Cameron Highlands ★

■ TELEPHONE CODE: 05   ■ POPULATION: 2.4 MILLION   ■ AREA: 21,005 SQ KM

History

Today's sultanate of Perak dates back to the early 16th century, when the eldest son of the last sultan of Melaka, Sultan Muzaffar Shah, established his own dynasty on the banks of Sungai Perak (Perak River). The state's rich tin deposits quickly made it a target of both covetous neighbours and foreign forces.

Dutch efforts in the 17th century to monopolise the tin trade were unsuccessful, but remains of their forts can still be seen on Pulau Pangkor (Pangkor Island) and at the mouth of Sungai Perak. In the 18th century the Bugis from the south and the Siamese from the north made concerted attempts to dominate Perak, but British intervention in the 1820s trumped them both.

The British had remained reluctant to meddle in the peninsula's affairs, but growing investment in the Strait settlements, along with the rich tin mines of Perak, encouraged their interest. The mines also attracted a great influx of Chinese immigrants, who soon formed rival clan groups allied with local Malay chiefs, all of whom battled to control the mines.

The Perak sultanate was in disarray, and fighting among successors to the throne gave the British their opportunity to step in, making the first real colonial incursion on the peninsula in 1874. The governor, Sir Andrew Clarke, convened a meeting at Pulau Pangkor at which Sultan Abdullah was installed on the throne in preference to Sultan Ismail, the other major contender. The resultant Pangkor Treaty required the sultan accept a British Resident, to be consulted on all issues other than those relating to religion or Malay custom. One year later, Sultan Abdullah was forced, under threat of deposition, to accept administration by British officials on his behalf.

Various Perak chiefs united against this state of affairs, and the Resident, James WW Birch, was assassinated at Pasir Salak in November 1875. Colonial troops were called in to fight a short war, Sultan Abdullah was exiled and a new British-sanctioned sultan was installed. The next British Resident, Sir Hugh Low, had administrative experience in Borneo, was fluent in Malay and was a noted botanist – he even had a pitcher plant (*Nepenthes Lowii*) named after him. He assumed control of taxes from the tin mines and practised greater intervention in state affairs. In 1877 he introduced the first rubber trees to Malaysia, and experimented with planting tea and coffee as well. The sultans, meanwhile, maintained their status, but were increasingly effete figureheads, bought out with stipends.

The first railway in the state, from Taiping to Port Weld (now known as Kuala Sepetang), was built in 1885 to transport the wealth of tin; the result was rapid development in Taiping and Ipoh. In 1896 Perak, along with Selangor, Pahang and Negeri Sembilan, became part of the Federated Malay States. The Resident system persisted, however, even after the Japanese invasion and WWII, ending only when Perak became part of the Federation of Malaya in 1948. Perak joined the new independent state of Malaysia in 1957.

Climate

Perak has a tropical climate, and is hot and humid throughout the year; daily temperatures average between 21°C and 32°C, and humidity levels hover at a steady 90%. There are brief downpours and occasional lighter rain throughout the year, with June and July usually being the driest months. The Cameron Highlands are much cooler; temperatures rarely rising above 21°C. Rainfall is more frequent too.

Getting There & Away

Both the main rail line and the Lebuhraya (E1; North–South Hwy) run the length of the country, from Johor Bahru in the south to the Thai border in the north, giving easy access to the Perak state capital, Ipoh, and other major towns. Ipoh is the state transport hub, with bus connections to most major towns on the peninsula, and has an airport with regular flights to/from Kuala Lumpur.

Getting Around

Almost everywhere in Perak is accessible by bus from Ipoh. Trains are not particularly useful for travelling within the state. Lumut is the departure point for ferries to Pulau Pangkor, and is well served by bus connections.

SOUTHERN PERAK

The road north from KL crosses the state border from Selangor into Perak at Tanjung Malim. If you have your own transport, you

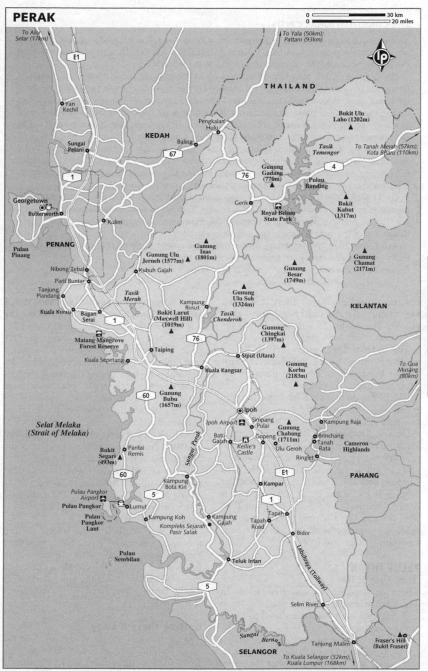

PERAK

0 — 30 km
0 — 20 miles

To Alor Setar (17km)

E1

To Yala (50km); Pattani (93km)

THAILAND

Yan Kechil

Pengkalan Hulu

KEDAH

Baling

67

Sungai Petani

1

Bukit Ulu Laho (1202m) ▲

Tasik Temengor

76

Gunung Gadang (770m) ▲

Pulau Banding

4

To Tanah Merah (57km); Kota Bharu (110km)

Gerik

Royal Belum State Park

Bukit Kabut (1317m) ▲

Georgetown

Butterworth

Kulim

PENANG

Pulau Pinang

Gunung Ulu Jerneh (1577m) ▲

Gunung Inas (1801m) ▲

Gunung Besar (1749m) ▲

Gunung Chamat (2171m) ▲

Nibong Tebal

Parit Buntar

Kubuh Gajah

Tanjung Piandang

Tasik Merah

Kampung Busut

Gunung Ulu Soh (1324m) ▲

KELANTAN

Kuala Kurau

Bagan Serai

1

Bukit Larut (Maxwell Hill) (1019m) ▲

Tasik Chenderoh

Gunung Chingkai (1397m) ▲

Matang Mangrove Forest Reserve

76

Kuala Sepetang

Taiping

Siput (Utara)

Gunung Korbu (2183m) ▲

To Gua Musang (80km)

Kuala Kangsar

60

Gunung Bubu (1657m) ▲

Selat Melaka (Strait of Melaka)

Ipoh

Ipoh Airport

Simpang Pulai

Gunung Chabang (1711m) ▲

Kampung Raja

Batu Gajah

Gopeng

Brinchang

Tanah Rata

Cameron Highlands

Bukit Segari (493m) ▲

Pantai Remis

Kellie's Castle

Ulu Geroh

Ringlet

60

E1

PAHANG

Pulau Pangkor Airport

5

Kampung Bota Kiri

Kampar

Sungai Perak

Pulau Pangkor

Lumut

Pulau Pangkor Laut

Kampung Koh

Kampung Gajah

Kompleks Sejarah Pasir Salak

Tapah

1

Tapah Road

Bidor

Lebuhraya (Tollway)

Pulau Sembilan

Teluk Intan

5

Selim River

Sungai Bernam

Tanjung Malim

Fraser's Hill (Bukit Fraser) ▲▲

SELANGOR

To Kuala Selangor (32km); Kuala Lumpur (168km)

PERAK

PERAK

THE CONSTITUTIONAL CRISIS

A complex power play for state government in Perak has followed 2008's general elections, when the national opposition bloc, Pakatan Rakyat (PR), took over by a slender majority from the Barisan Nasional (BN) coalition, which rules at the federal level.

On 25 January 2009, Nasaruddin Hashim, a BN member, made public his desire to cross the floor to PR. One good defection deserved another, or three: three PR representatives then declared their seats were 'independent,' but that they intended to support BN in confidence matters, thus tipping the balance of power in BN's favour. Nasaruddin went back to his old party in the name of preserving the peace. Even so, state Sultan Azlan Shah dismissed the PR government led by Mohammad Nizar Jamaluddin, and asked BN to form a government.

That decision lead to protests around the state. State Assembly Speaker (and PR member) V Sivakumar tried to hold an emergency sitting of the assembly on 3 March 2009; when BN ignored the meeting, Sivakumar held a session anyways under a tree, which has since become known as the Democracy Tree, complete with website (www.democracytree.org).

On 11 May 2009, the Kuala Lumpur High Court ruled Sultan Shah was not constitutionally permitted to dismiss Nizar, which raised questions from BN as to how much power the courts could exert over the democratic process. In the meantime, PR supporters have called for the dissolution of the state assembly and new snap elections.

As of June 2009, the legitimacy of the state government of Perak still remained in doubt. However most commentators agree on one point: the way the Perak Constitutional Crisis is handled will be a benchmark for the viability of Malaysian democracy.

can get off the Lebuhraya tollway at Tanjung Malim and take the old Hwy 1 through a number of small towns, although there is little to detain you for long. The first of these towns is **Selim River**, where British forces made an unsuccessful last-ditch attempt to halt the Japanese advance through the peninsula during WWII.

The first main town is **Bidor**, famous for its guava and odorous *petai* beans, where you can turn off for Teluk Intan, 42km to the southwest. **Kampung Pasir Salak**, 25km north of Teluk Intan, is a small village of some historical interest (see opposite). From this village, you can follow the valley of Sungai Perak to **Kampung Bota Kiri**. This river valley was the original home of the Perak sultanate and is dotted with royal graves. From Kampung Bota Kiri, you can take the road to Lumut on the coast or travel northeast through a series of *kampung* (villages) to Ipoh.

TELUK INTAN
☎ 05 / pop 62,320

There are two things a traveller can do in Teluk Intan: catch a bus to the next town and clap eyes on a Malaysian rival to Pisa's famous tower.

Well…maybe not so much, but that's what the locals would like you to think after seeing their pride and joy: the **jam besar** (clock tower; admission free; ☺ 8am-5pm Mon-Thu, 8am-12.15pm & 2.45-5pm Fri, 9am-6pm Sat & Sun). Located near the bus station, the 25.5m-high tower was built in 1885 as a potable-water storage tank. A pesky underground river gives the tower a lean (although it's not quite Pisa), and its designer, Mr Leong Choong Cheong, gave it its eight-storey, pagoda-esque appearance (there are actually only three floors).

Colonial buildings and Chinese temples and shophouses are found throughout town; most look on the verge of collapse. The **Istana Raja Muda Perak** is the crumbling palace of the next in line to the sultanate of Perak.

If you're staying the night, the standard midrange option **Hotel Anson** (☎ 622 6166; Jln Sekolah; s/d from RM75/100; 🕸), on the main road south of the bus station, is the best place in town (not saying much).

The usual stalls line the streets around the clock tower and bus station. **Keng Heng Kopitiam** (mains around RM3; ☎ lunch & dinner), a small Chinese cafe stuffed with old photos that rival the small exhibit inside the *jam besar*, serves locally famous *nasi kandar* (rice with small side curries).

Getting There & Away

The central bus station is just south of the clock tower. There are direct buses to/from Ipoh (RM5.80, three daily) and KL's Puduraya bus station (RM10.90, three hours, every 30 minutes), as well as express buses to Lumut (RM6.20, five daily), Kota Bharu (RM34, one daily) and Johor Bahru (RM35, one daily). Local buses to Klang in Selangor (RM9, three daily) depart from the side street next to the post office, just west of the clock tower.

KOMPLEKS SEJARAH PASIR SALAK

Kampung Pasir Salak is both a sleepy riverside village and the birthplace of Malay nationalism, a site steeped in symbology and patriotic myth-making. This was where James WW Birch, the first British Resident of Perak, was speared to death in 1875 while taking a bath. The event is memorialized in the **Kompleks Sejarah Pasir Salak** (Pasir Salak Historical Complex; ☎ 631 1462; adult/child RM3/1; ☒ 10am-5pm Sat-Thu, 10am-noon & 2.45-5pm Fri) museum.

Birch's killers, Maharaja Lela (a local chief), Dato' Sagor and Pandak Indut, have since been enshrined as national heroes (the truth is a bit more murky, see below), and the memorial dedicated to them takes the shape of the traditional *sundang* (knife). Replicas of Maharaja Lela's **fort** and **house** are nearby.

There are several restored traditional houses–cum–museums in the complex; the two most interesting ones feature, respectively, exhibits on traditional Malay weddings and an only slightly cheesy 'time tunnel' of historical dioramas depicting Perak from prehistoric times to independence.

Pasir Salak is a remote and awkward place to get to, with no direct public transport links. A chartered taxi from Teluk Intan to Pasir Salak costs roughly RM80 return, though you'll need to negotiate if you want the driver to wait while you look around.

TAPAH
☎ 05 / pop 80,000

The only reason to come to the small town of Tapah is for bus connections to the Cameron Highlands (p159). If you have to overnight, **Hotel Utara** (☎ 401 2299; 35 Jln Stesyen; r RM30-45; ☒) and **NH Hotel** (☎ 401 7288; 24 Jln Stesyen; r RM50; ☒) are decent options with private bathrooms – luxury by Tapah standards. Local buses make the corkscrewing journey to Tanah Rata in the Cameron Highlands roughly every hour from 8am to 6pm (RM5.70, two hours). Taxis to Tanah Rata (RM80) leave from the taxi station 100m further down Jln Raja, away from the main road.

From the bus station there are a few departures to KL and Penang, but most express long-distance buses leave from **Restoran Caspian** (9 Jln Besar) to Ipoh (RM15.50, two hours, hourly); Johor Bahru/Singapore (RM82/102, nine/10 hours, three daily); KL (RM33, 2½ hours, hourly until 6.15pm); Kuala Terengganu (RM65, nine hours, 9pm); Kuantan (RM54, seven hours, 10am and 9pm); Lumut (RM23, three hours, 11am); Melaka (RM44, 3½ hours, 10am); and Penang (RM70, five hours, five daily). All these buses can also be booked at **CS Travel & Tours** (☎ 491 1200; www.cstravel.com.my; 47 Jln Besar) in Tanah Rata.

The nearest train station, known as **Tapah Road** (☎ 418 1345), is 9km west of town, with one daily service in each direction to KL (RM15, three hours) and Butterworth (RM18, seven hours). A taxi to Tapah Road station from Tapah is around RM20.

LUMUT
☎ 05 / pop 31,882

Most visitors see little beyond the bus station and the ferry terminal, which is the

---

THE MURKY MURDER OF JAMES BIRCH

In Pasir Salak, James WW Birch, first British Resident of Perak, is widely portrayed as an intolerant man, unable to speak Malay and insensitive to Malay customs. His killers, a Malay nobleman and his helpers, are depicted as nationalist heroes. The truth is far murkier. At the time, Birch 'resided' under the terms of the Treaty of Pangkor, which still granted local Perak monarchs nominal autonomy. Birch, sensing (rightly) that he had the power, if not the support, to do as he pleased in Perak, went ahead and reorganised elements of the kingdom's judicial and revenue-collecting system; written accounts from the time suggest he held traditional Malay customs in low regard. This sounds insufferably arrogant, but one of the 'customs' Birch abolished was the then-existing practice of slavery, going so far as to actively help slaves escape and shelter them, thus depriving local sultans of a major source of income. This practice technically violated the terms of the Pangkor Treaty, and that violation, more than latent nationalism, was the justification a group of Malay conspirators needed to plot Birch's death.

departure point for Pulau Pangkor. If you do stay, the waterfront recreation park on the northern side of town, near the yacht club, is an agreeable spot for picnics and relaxing, and there are some decent out-of-town beaches, but not much else. Teluk Batik, around 7km out of town, is one of the more popular beaches. There is no bus service, but a taxi will cost you RM18 one way. Otherwise, this town is primarily populated by Malaysian sailors; the nation's principal naval base is nearby.

Information

Maybank (Jln Sultan Idris Shah)

Moneychanger (Jln Sultan Idris Shah) Next door to the Tourism Malaysia office. You'll get better rates here than on Pulau Pangkor.

Tourism Malaysia office (☎ 683 4057; Jln Sultan Idris Shah; ☼ 9am-5pm Mon-Fri, 9am-1.45pm Sat) Midway between the jetty and the bus station.

Sleeping & Eating

If you're marooned on your way to Pangkor, Lumut has a few decent hotels.

Era Backpackers Hotel (☎ 013-598 3005, 683 8910; 7-9 Jln Raja Muda Musa; dm with shared bathroom from RM15, r with shared bathroom RM25-50; ☒) Opposite the bus station, this hostel, sporting bright, spotless rooms, is Lumut's best budget choice.

Swiss-Garden Golf Resort & Spa Damai Laut (☎ 683 5555; www.damailaut.com; Jln Damai Laut; r/ste from RM230/600; ☒ ☒) North of the centre, this is the top place to stay, with over 300 posh rooms overlooking the sea, a golf course, a spa, etc. That said, why shell out the money when you could stay on Pangkor? Nonguests can putt on the hotel's golf course (nine/18 holes RM100/150).

Getting There & Away

BUS

The most frequent buses take the highway to/from Ipoh (RM5.70, hourly). Direct buses run roughly hourly to/from KL (RM18.80). Other destinations include Butterworth (RM12.70, five daily), Johor Bahru/Singapore (RM40/RM42, six daily), Kota Bharu (RM29.40) and Taiping (RM7, five daily).

TAXI

Long-distance taxis from Lumut can be scarce late in the day. Typical fares per car are Butterworth (RM300), Ipoh (RM200) and KL (RM320).

PULAU PANGKOR

☎ 05 / pop 25,000

Sometimes the name of a destination has a bit of mystery. Not Pulau Pangkor, the 8 sq km 'beautiful island'. As descriptions go, that's as succinct and accurate as it gets. Just a skipped stone (OK, 40-minute ferry ride) from Lumut, this is white-sand paradise par excellence, low-key, very friendly, and if developed in places, still quiet enough to feel untethered to the rat race. The jungly interior, in particular, is wild, unexplored and isolated. Although the beaches get swollen with domestic tourists on weekends, during the week you've got the sand to yourself, and when its raining on other islands, it somehow stays sunny here.

Pangkor has been a pirate hideout and bit-player in the battle to control the Selat Melaka (Strait of Melaka). In the 17th century, the Dutch built a fort here in their bid to monopolise the Perak tin trade, but were driven out by a local ruler before returning briefly some 50 years later. In 1874 a contender for the Perak throne sought British backing and the Pangkor Treaty was signed, ushering in British Residents and the colonial period.

Orientation

The island's east coast is a continuous village strip, comprising Sungai Pinang Kecil (SPK), Sungai Pinang Besar (SPB) and Pangkor Town, the main population centre. Fishing and dried-fish products are a major industry here; tourism is not.

The road that runs along the east coast turns west at Pangkor Town and runs directly across the island to Pasir Bogak. From there it runs north to the village of Teluk Nipah, where you'll find most budget accommodation. It then goes to the northern end of the island, past the airport, to Pangkor's luxury resorts. The road from there back to the eastern side of the island is winding and steep in parts, but it's sealed all the way.

Information

The island's hospital and police station are just west of Pangkor Town, on the road towards Pasir Bogak.

Badrul Hasil Laut Internet Zone (Teluk Nipah; per hr RM6) Most budget hotels at Teluk Nipah also provide internet access.

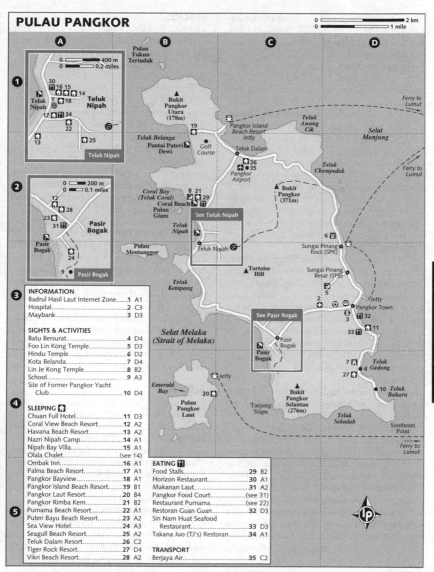

PULAU PANGKOR

INFORMATION
Badrul Hasil Laut Internet Zone	**1**	A1
Hospital	**2**	C3
Maybank	**3**	D3

SIGHTS & ACTIVITIES
Batu Bersurat	**4**	D4
Foo Lin Kong Temple	**5**	D3
Hindu Temple	**6**	D2
Kota Belanda	**7**	D4
Lin Je Kong Temple	**8**	B2
School	**9**	A3
Site of Former Pangkor Yacht Club	**10**	D4

SLEEPING
Chuan Full Hotel	**11**	D3
Coral View Beach Resort	**12**	A2
Havana Beach Resort	**13**	A2
Nazri Nipah Camp	**14**	A1
Nipah Bay Villa	**15**	A1
Olala Chalet	(see 14)	
Ombak Inn	**16**	A1
Palma Beach Resort	**17**	A1
Pangkor Bayview	**18**	A1
Pangkor Island Beach Resort	**19**	B1
Pangkor Laut Resort	**20**	B4
Pangkor Rimba Kem	**21**	B2
Purnama Beach Resort	**22**	A1
Puteri Bayu Beach Resort	**23**	A2
Sea View Hotel	**24**	A3
Seagull Beach Resort	**25**	A2
Teluk Dalam Resort	**26**	C2
Tiger Rock Resort	**27**	D4
Vikri Beach Resort	**28**	A2

EATING
Food Stalls	**29**	B2
Horizon Restaurant	**30**	A1
Makanan Laut	**31**	A2
Pangkor Food Court	(see 31)	
Restaurant Purnama	(see 22)	
Restoran Guan Guan	**32**	D3
Sin Nam Huat Seafood Restaurant	**33**	D3
Takana Juo (TJ's) Restoran	**34**	A1

TRANSPORT
Berjaya Air	**35**	C2

PERAK

Maybank (Pangkor Town) In the same building as Min Lian Hotel, it's open the usual hours and has an ATM. For travellers cheques and cash, the moneychanger (see opposite) in Lumut offers better rates.

www.pangkor.com.my For online information on the island.

www.pulau-pangkor.com Another source of information.

Sights

Pulau Pangkor lends itself well to exploration by motorcycle, bicycle or foot. Spend a day doing a loop of the island, following the sealed road all the way around. By motorcycle it takes about two hours with stops, around three or four hours by bicycle, or you could walk it in a very long day. Locals on motorcycles seem oblivious to road rules, and accidents are not uncommon. The road from Pasir Bogak to Teluk Nipah is hilly and has several blind corners, so be careful if you decide to walk.

Along the western side are the main beaches of Pasir Bogak, Teluk Nipah and Coral Beach, and most of the tourist accommodation. On the northern edge of Coral Beach, look out for the small, psychedelic **Lin Je Kong Temple**, adorned with statues of giant mushrooms, a turtle, a mermaid and, of course, Donald Duck. From here, the road heads inland past Pangkor airport and, to the north, the Pangkor Island Beach Resort at Teluk Belanga. Continuing eastwards, the road skirts Teluk Dalam, with its luxury resort, and crosses over the headland. This is a steep and twisting road through some superb **jungle**. It's quite deserted and travellers have been robbed here – though thankfully this is rare.

On the eastern side, from SPK it's a nearly continuous village strip on to grotty Pangkor Town. Mmm – smells like dried fish! Come to town for genuine Malaysian food, as in genuinely cheap and tasty, from the hawker stalls. A South Indian **Hindu temple** makes for a small, colourful Dravidian explosion, while in SPB, the **Foo Lin Kong temple**, on the side of the hill west of the main road, has a mini version of the Great Wall of China climbing behind it.

At Teluk Gedong, 3km south of Pangkor Town, is the **Kota Belanda** (Dutch Fort), built in 1670 (*danke*, Dutch) and sacked in 1690 (*terimah kasih*, Malay). The Dutch managed to rebuilt the fort in 1743; only five years later they abandoned it for good after local warrior chiefs repeatedly attacked them. The old fort was totally swallowed by jungle until 1973, when it was reconstructed as far as the remaining bricks would allow, which wasn't much.

On the waterfront 100m beyond the fort, **Batu Bersurat** is a mammoth stone carved with the symbol of the Dutch East India Company (Vereenigde Oost-Indische Compagnie; VOC) and other graffiti, including a faint depiction of a tiger stealing a kid. Supposedly, the child of a local European dignitary disappeared while playing near the rock; the Dutch liked the idea of a tiger abduction, although she was more likely nabbed by disenchanted locals.

The road ends just past the fishing village of Teluk Gedong and the defunct Pangkor Yacht Club.

BEACHES

The beach at **Pasir Bogak** is a lovely, if rather narrow, stretch of sand. It's fine for swimming, but during holidays it can get crowded. To the north, **Teluk Nipah** has a wider, better beach, with more water-sports activities to hand.

The best beach on this side of the island is at **Coral Bay**, just north of Teluk Nipah. The water is a clear, emerald-green colour due to the presence of limestone, and the beach is usually quite clean and pretty.

In May, June and July turtles used to lay their eggs at night on **Teluk Ketapang** beach, north of Pasir Bogak. Increasing numbers of gawking tourists have seriously affected turtle numbers, and sightings are increasingly rare. For more information on turtles, see p77.

At the northern end of the island at Teluk Belanga, **Pantai Puteri Dewi** (Golden Sands Beach) is pleasant, but access is restricted to Pangkor Beach Resort guests. Day-trippers have to pay a ridiculous RM50. In between, there are a number of virtually deserted beaches that you can reach by boat, motorcycle or on foot.

On nearby Pulau Pangkor Laut, **Emerald Bay** is a beautiful little horseshoe bay with clear water, fine coral and a gently sloping beach. You'll have to be a guest at the exclusive Pangkor Laut Resort, though, to enjoy it.

Activities

Snorkel gear, boats and jet skis can be hired at hotels or on the beach at Pasir Bogak and Teluk Nipah. A small boat to take you **snorkelling** at small nearby islands costs around RM40 after negotiation, depending on how many of you there are. Boats can also be hired for trips to Pulau Sembilan, nine white-sand-ringed dots that are popular for **sports fishing**, about 1½ hours southwest of Pangkor.

There's good **walking** here, arguably better than on any other Malaysian island. A four-hour trail crosses the island from Teluk Nipah and emerges near the Foo Lin Kong temple; another trail goes from Teluk Ketapang to Bukit Pangkor before joining the east-coast road. Walking trails are often overgrown. Take a guide, a *parang* (bush knife) and water, and protect yourself against leeches and ticks (see p602 and p603). Most guesthouses have lots of information and can organise a guide. Don't be deceived by the relatively small size of the island; several visitors have gotten lost after attempting to traverse the jungle alone.

Sleeping

Teluk Nipah has the best beach and biggest choice of accommodation on Pangkor. Plenty of hostels are here, but they share space with blocky midrange hotels. To the south, Pasir Bogak has bigger, pricier midrange resorts, a few restaurants and not much else. It's especially busy on weekends. The other developments on Pangkor are luxury resorts on isolated beaches.

Rates at most places vary, often substantially, between peak (Friday and/or Saturday and Sunday, plus holidays) and off-peak seasons; the following prices quoted are 'off-peak', available from Monday to Friday (or Sunday to Thursday) and in the low season. Finding a bed at any price during major holidays, such as Chinese New Year, can be near impossible without advance reservations. Budget rooms have shared bathrooms unless stated otherwise, pricier places all have private bathrooms.

TELUK NIPAH

The most lively of Pangkor's beaches is Teluk Nipah. Hotels on the main road experience a fair bit of noise from local youths racing their motorbikes into the wee hours.

Budget

These options are pricier than elsewhere in Malaysia. There are dirt cheap chalets in Pangkor that run for around RM30 for a chalet, but we found conditions to be pretty dire; you've been warned.

Nazri Nipah Camp (☎ 685 2014, 012-5760267; rozie1982@hotmail.com; dm/r from RM10/40) At the edge of the jungle, there's (surprise) a chilled-out reggae theme going on here. Accommodation ranges from simple A-frames to more comfortable chalets with bathrooms. It also has a secluded beer garden and TV lounge.

Purnama Beach Resort (☎ 685 3530; www.purnama .com.my; r RM30-80; ✵ 🖳 💁) This spiffy complex of chalets includes some fairly simple (and simply lovely) fan huts and neat, motel-style doubles. There's a good restaurant, a very small pool and breakfast included – nice.

Olala Chalet (☎ 685 5112; s/d RM50/70; ✵) For chalets with air-con and TV these are pretty good deals, but some cabins are in worse shape than others, so ask to see a few. Attracts a lot of domestic tourists.

Midrange

Ombak Inn (☎ 685 5223; http://ombakinn.tripod.com; r/f from RM70/100; ✵) This quiet hotel has a variety of options, including battered A-frame huts and sparkling fan/air-con bungalows with attached bathrooms that sort of look like the guest room in your grandma's house (and are just as cosy).

Seagull Beach Resort (☎ 685 2878; www.seagull beachvillageresort.com; r RM70-100; ✵ 🖳) You don't have to be on the beach to score good budget rooms on Pangkor. Seagull is set back in the jungle and is endowed with all kinds of backpacker goodness: simple, freestanding huts prowled by cheeky monkeys (seriously, watch your wallet), table tennis, a dartboard and karaoke. The owners have their stuff together, and book great trips throughout the island and beyond.

Palma Beach Resort (☎ 685 3693; r RM75-95; ✵) Reasonably priced midrange option, with attractive wooden chalets with TVs and bathrooms and somewhat blander, but probably more comfortable hotel style rooms.

Nipah Bay Villa (☎ 685 2198; www.pangkornipahbay .com; r RM80-160; ✵ 🖳) One of the oldest accommodation options on the island. Mr and Mrs Sabtu, the owners, are incredibly friendly and have seen it all on Pangkor. There are lots of good chalets and the usual backpacker comforts: common room, laundry, etc.

Havana Beach Resort (☎ 685 3333; www.havana .com.my; s & d from RM110, tr/ste from RM150/250; ✵) Havana has a glut of clean rooms in a compound at the southern edge of the beach strip. They're a little overpriced, but all have TVs and hot showers.

Pangkor Bayview (☎ 685 3540; www.pangkorbayview .com; r from RM160; ✵) This more upmarket place has an assortment of accommodation as wide as an ocean; have a look around before settling and figure on getting what you pay for. Upstairs hotel rooms have balconies overlooking the lane, and there are chalets in the back garden.

PASIR BOGAK

The rest of Pangkor's accommodation possibilities are grouped at each end of the beach at Pasir Bogak. Most places are midrange, and compared to Teluk Nipah it's a very sedate place, primarily geared towards weekending Malaysian families.

Vikri Beach Resort (☎ 685 4258; r RM90-170; ✵) Vikri has a dozen simple but cosy wooden and brick chalets located in scrappy gardens across the road from the beach. It's a peaceful, homely environment, with a kitchen

PERAK

serving up home-cooked Indian food and a very friendly, almost motherly staff.

Sea View Hotel (☎ 685 1605; svhotel@tm.net.my; r from RM130; ✖ ✉) This beachfront place has that old school, seafront holiday vibe you may recall from family vacations (and indeed, most guests are Malaysian families). There's an inviting, palm-fringed pool, though the spartan brick chalets have a somewhat institutional feel.

Coral View Beach Resort (☎ 685 5111; www.pangkorcoralbay.com.my/index.htm; r from RM130; ✖ ✉) One of Pasir Bogak's cheapest options, this is a dowdy and ageing place, though the simple chalet rooms aren't too bad for the price. They're set back from the beach, with views of the forested interior.

Puteri Bayu Beach Resort (☎ 685 1929; www.puteribayu.com; r/ste from RM170/310; ✖ ✉) This luxurious complex has a choice of standard hotel rooms and more appealing chalets set in landscaped gardens (the garden huts are quite nice, and have reduced prices) and on the beach.

PANGKOR TOWN

Chuan Full View Hotel (☎ 685 1123; 60 Jln Besar; r RM25-35; ✖) As the main attraction of Pangkor is its beaches, there is little point in staying in Pangkor Town. But if you get stuck, this place has dated but acceptable rooms, as well as a TV lounge and a verandah at the back overlooking the waterfront. The sign outside says 'Chuan Fu', and for the record, the views aren't all that.

ELSEWHERE ON THE ISLAND

Pangkor Rimba Kem (☎ 685 5523, 013-510 9384; r RM80-150) The only accommodation on Coral Beach is this small collection of standard chalets, which sleep up to four people. It also has tents (RM10), which can also accommodate four. If you bring your own tent, you can pitch it here for RM6. There's a restaurant on site, but annoyingly, it's only open to pre-booked groups.

Teluk Dalam Resort (☎ 685 5000; www.pangkorresorts.com; r from RM230; ✖ ✉ ✉) Fronting a wide bay at the northern end of the island is this peaceful four-star resort. The rustic wooden chalets and bungalows are set in landscaped gardens overlooking the sea. It's a little isolated and the beach isn't great, but there's a tennis court and a children's pool as well as organised trips and activities. Day visitors can use the hotel facilities for RM50.

Pangkor Island Beach Resort (☎ 685 1091; www.pangkorislandbeach.com; r/ste from RM480/900; ✖ ✉ ✉) This large, secluded resort is located on a private sandy bay at Teluk Belanga, at the northern end of the island, and is the most luxurious spot on Pangkor proper by far. The traditionally styled 'sea villas' at RM1100 are superb. Recreational facilities include two pools, tennis courts, and a spa, and there are organised activities for children.

Tiger Rock Resort (☎ 685 4154; www.tigerrock.info; full board from RM570/684; ✖ ✉ ✉) Rebecca Duckett and Owen Wilkinson are the creative geniuses behind this collection of three houses, each one decked out in the individual design tastes and assorted knick-knacks of the owners. The result is a lodgings that can come off as bohemian or tropical or colonially classy, and sometimes all three at once. Whichever house you stay in, there's always a feeling of jungly isolation thanks to the secluded location of the 12.5 acre grounds. The inhouse meals are exceptional, and children are well looked after.

PANGKOR LAUT

The tiny, private island of Pangkor Laut, just opposite Pasir Bogak, is occupied by one of Malaysia's most exclusive tourist developments.

our pick **Pangkor Laut Resort** (☎ 699 1100; www.pangkorlautresort.com; r/ste from US$350/900; ✖ ✉ ✉) Well, it's nice to have your own island, right? This ridiculously luxurious resort is speckled with hillside and seafront villas stocked with king-sized beds, balconies and huge bathrooms, and private 'estates' (uniquely designed houses, with two to four bedrooms, private pools and gardens, on a secluded bay away from the main resort). Every conceivable amenity is to hand, and the resort boasts several fine restaurants, tennis courts and a spa village.

Eating

TELUK NIPAH

Several of Teluk Nipah's guesthouses have restaurants, though these often close outside the high season. There are some basic food stalls along the beach.

Restaurant Purnama (mains from RM4; ☯ breakfast, lunch & dinner) In the guesthouse of the same name, this restaurant offers a cheap menu of Malay standard fare, seafood and a few Western dishes, as well as set breakfasts.

Takana Juo (TJ's) Restoran (mains from RM6; breakfast, lunch & dinner) A family-run Indonesian restaurant at the bungalows of the same name. TJ's serves delicious, cheap food, though the staff certainly take their time serving it. It's regularly full, so you'll need to get here early.

Horizon Restaurant (mains RM9-28; breakfast, lunch & dinner) This place has sunset views, alfresco dining and a mix of Chinese and Malaysian seafood and curries. Prices are relatively high and opening times can be unpredictable.

PASIR BOGAK & PANGKOR TOWN

All the hotels have restaurants and there are a few other places to eat. All are open for breakfast, lunch and dinner, although usually only in the high season.

Opposite the Golden Beach Hotel, **Pangkor Food Court** (Pasir Bogak; mains from RM7) offers cheaper snack food, while next door **Makanan Laut** (Pasir Bogak; mains from RM10) is a popular restaurant specialising in fresh seafood. There are some great Chinese *kedai kopi* (coffee shops) in Pangkor town. **Restoran Guan Guan** (Jln Besar, Pangkor Town; mains from RM5; lunch & dinner) is an old favourite for seafood, and prices are posted on the wall-sized English menu. Opposite the Chuan Full Hotel, the friendly **Sin Nam Huat Seafood Restaurant** (685 2819; 51 Jln Besar, Pangkor Town; mains RM10-35; lunch & dinner) is a good place for crab, lobster and prawn dishes, and it serves beer late into the night.

Getting There & Away

AIR

Berjaya Air (685 5828; Pangkor Airport) has flights every day except Tuesday and Thursday between KL's Subang airport and Pangkor airport (one way RM275). Flights leave Pangkor at 10.30am.

BOAT

Mesra Feri (683 5800), which also runs Duta Pangkor Ferry (two boats, same operator) runs boats every 30 minutes/45 minutes on an alternating basis between 7am and 8.30pm. Boats leave Pangkor starting at 6:30am. Many ferries from Lumut stop at SPK before reaching Pangkor Town, so don't hop off too soon.

Return tickets cost RM10; just check which service is leaving first.

The Pangkor Island Beach Resort and Teluk Dalam Resort at the northern end of the island are served by their own ferry service from Lumut, running seven times a day in both directions (RM16).

There are four rather pricey ferries daily between Lumut and Pangkor Laut (adult/child RM50/25), though these are only for the use of bona fide guests.

BUS

There's a **bus agent** (Jln Besar, Pangkor Town) next to Chuan Full Hotel that handles bookings for express buses originating from Lumut on the mainland.

Getting Around

There are no public buses available to tourists, so you will be obliged to use Pangkor's candy-pink minibus taxis, which operate between 6.30am and 9pm. Set-fare services for up to four people from the jetty in Pangkor Town include Pasir Bogak (RM4), Teluk Nipah (RM10), Pangkor Island Beach Resort (RM18), the airport (RM18) and around the island (RM40). Travel between Teluk Nipah and Pasir Bogak will cost you RM10.

An ideal way to see the island is by motorcycle or bicycle (see p149). There are numerous places at Pangkor Town, Pasir Bogak and Teluk Nipah that rent motorcycles from around RM35 per day and bicycles for RM15 – look out for signs advertising bikes at the guesthouses in Teluk Nipah. Cars must be left on the mainland; there are a number of carparks in Lumut, all charging around RM10 per day.

IPOH

05 / pop 637,200

Ipoh is one of Malaysia's more pleasant midsized cities, chock full of colonial architecture, faded tropical mansions and a few pleasant green lungs. Even Ipoh's 'New Town', a chaotic outgrowth of ramshackle Chinese shopfronts, has a bit of the romance of Old Asia, albeit with a fair bit of edge thrown in. The elegant layout and design of (old) Ipoh speaks to the wealth once generated here from the Kinta valley tin mine; in its day, the city was one of the wealthiest in Southeast Asia. Named for the poisonous ipoh tree (*Antiaris Toxicaria*) that once grew in profusion here, today Ipoh

PERAK

IPOH

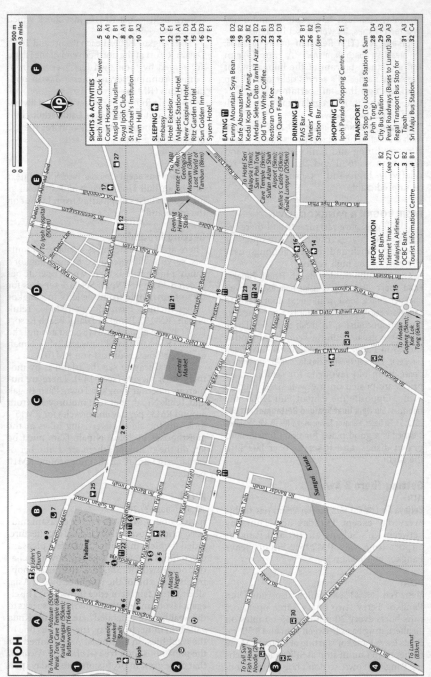

SIGHTS & ACTIVITIES	
Birch Memorial Clock Tower	5 B2
Court House	6 A1
Masjid India Muslim	7 B1
Royal Ipoh Club	8 A1
St Michael's Institution	9 B1
Town Hall	10 A2

SLEEPING 🏠	
Embassy	11 C4
Hotel Excelsior	12 E1
Majestic Station Hotel	13 A1
New Caspian Hotel	14 D3
Ritz Garden Hotel	15 D4
Sun Golden Inn	16 D3
Syuen Hotel	17 E1

EATING 🍴	
Funny Mountain Soya Bean	18 D2
Kafe Abamaashre	19 B2
Kedai Kopi Kong Meng	20 B2
Medan Selera Dato Tawhil Azar	21 D2
Old Town White Coffee	22 B1
Restoran Onn Kee	23 D3
Xin Quan Fang	24 D3

DRINKING 🍸	
FMS Bar	25 B1
Miners' Arms	26 B2
Station Bar	(see 13)

SHOPPING 🛍	
Ipoh Parade Shopping Centre	27 E1

TRANSPORT	
Bus Stop (To Local Bus Station & Sam Poh Tong)	28 D4
City Bus Station	29 A3
Perak Roadways (Buses to Lumut)	30 A3
Regal Transport Bus Stop for Tapah	31 A3
Sri Maju Bus Station	32 C4

INFORMATION	
HSBC Bank	1 B2
Internet Imax	(see 27)
Malaysia Airlines	2 C1
OCBC Bank	3 B2
Tourist Information Centre	4 B1

calls itself the 'Bougainvillea City', which much better captures the vibe of the place.

Give yourself a day at least to amble through this historic town before changing buses to rush off to Pulau Pangkor or the Cameron Highlands. Ipoh is also the sensible base for exploring nearby Buddhist cave temples, the royal town of Kuala Kangsar (p167) and Kellie's Castle (p158).

Orientation

The Old Town is where you'll find the bus and train stations, but otherwise this is a quiet area dominated by colonial architecture, government buildings and banks. Traffic-clogged New Town east of the river is home to most of the hotels and restaurants.

Information

HSBC Bank (Jln Tun Sambathan)

http://ipoh.com.my Useful resource for the city.

Internet Imax (3rd fl, Ipoh Parade Shopping Centre, Jln Sultan Abdul Jalil; per hr RM3; ☉ 10am-midnight Mon-Thu, 10am-2am Fri & Sat, 5pm-midnight Sun)

Ipoh Echo (www.ipohecho.com.my; 30 sen) English-language newspaper featuring good journalism. Arguably the only real community newspaper in the country.

Ipoh Hospital (☎ 253 2533; http://hipoh.moh.gov.my; Jln Hospital)

OCBC Bank (Jln Dato' Maharajah Lela)

Perak Tourist Newspaper Free monthly magazine with useful details on tourist attractions in Perak; available from the tourist information centre and some hotels.

Tourist information centre (☎ 241 2959, 529 0894; Jln Tun Sambathan; ☉ 8am-5pm Mon-Fri)

www.perak.gov.my Information on Perak.

Sights

COLONIAL ARCHITECTURE

Ipoh's grand colonial architecture, a mixture of gleaming whitewash and romantic dilapidation, is found in the Old Town. Known locally as the 'Taj Mahal', the **train station**, dating from 1915, is a blend of Moorish and Victorian architecture designed in the 'Raj' style you see everywhere in India. It houses the wonderfully old-fashioned Majestic Station Hotel. Directly opposite, the **Town Hall** (Dewan Bandaran; 1916) and the **Court House** (Mahkanah Tinggi; 1928) are suitably impressive white neoclassical buildings of grand proportions. All three were built by government architect AB Hubbock.

Nearby on Jln Dato' Sagor, the **Birch Memorial Clock Tower** (1909) was erected in memory

of James WW Birch, Perak's first British Resident, who was murdered at Pasir Salak. The friezes on the clock tower are meant to illustrate the growth of civilisation, featuring figures such as Moses, Buddha, Shakespeare and Charles Darwin. A figure representing Mohammed has since been erased. The road on which this memorial stands has been renamed for one of Birch's killers, who are seen today as nationalists.

The mock-Tudor **Royal Ipoh Club** (1895) overlooks the playing fields of the *padang* (field), and is still a centre of exclusivity. On the *padang's* northern flank is **St Michael's Institution**, a neo-Gothic three-storey colonial school with arched verandahs, founded by the Catholic La Sallean brothers in 1927. Nearby, the green-and-white **Masjid India Muslim** (India Muslim Mosque; 1908) was built in the Mogul style for the local Indian population.

Old Town is also criss-crossed with rows of rickety **Chinese shophouses**, though those in the New Town area east of the river are actually in better condition. After Georgetown in Penang, Ipoh has one of the most extensive areas of later shophouse architecture in Malaysia.

CAVE TEMPLES

Ipoh is set among jungle-clad limestone hills that spectacularly jut out from the valley. The hills are riddled with caves that are believed to be a great source of spiritual power, and over the years meditation grottoes became large-scale temples. These still attract significant numbers of worshippers, but tourists are also welcome to look around. Remember these caves are regarded as holy by the pilgrims, so behave and dress respectfully.

Perak Tong

Founded in 1926 by a Buddhist priest, **Perak Tong** (☎ 546 5387; ☉ 8am-5pm) temple complex extends back into an impressive complex of caverns and grottoes with amazing murals on the interior walls, including some interesting juxtapositions of Theravada Buddhas from Southeast Asia and Chinese Buddhas and Buddhist saints. A staircase and a security guard were crushed by a rockfall here in 2009, but the temple has since reopened.

The cave is located 6km north of Ipoh. From the city bus station, Reliance Bus 141 stops at Perak Tong and then continues on to Kuala Kangsar.

PERAK

Sam Poh Tong

A few kilometres south of Ipoh, **Sam Poh Tong** (☎ 605 3120; ☉ 8am-5pm) is the largest cave temple in Malaysia, although it's less popular than Perak Tong. The main attraction here is the turtle pond, where locals bring turtles to release in the hope of balancing their karma.

Inside the temple is a huge cavern with a small reclining Buddha, and smaller vases set about it. The ornamental garden in front of the temple is quite scenic, and pomelo (a citrus fruit) stalls line the highway.

The temple can be reached by Kinta bus 66 (bound for Kampar) or 73 from Ipoh's local bus station (70 sen).

Kek Lok Tong

To get off the beaten path, you can visit the smaller, more serene **Kek Lok Tong** (☉ 7.30am-7.30pm; donations requested). From Sam Poh Tong backtrack to the T-junction and turn right. Walk for 15 minutes, then turn right again before the first traffic light and follow the signs for Kek Lok Tong. At the cave temple's entrance, climb up to the Three Sages in the central cavern. At the back is a fat Chinese Buddha of Future Happiness sitting in the company of three other Bodhisattvas. Behind the cave is an ornamental garden with ponds and pagodas.

MUSEUMS

North of the *padang*, the **Muzium Darul Ridzuan** (☎ 242 6906; 2020 Jln Panglima Gantang; admission free; ☉ 9am-5pm) is housed in a 1926 villa built for a wealthy Chinese tin miner. The less than inspiring displays recount the history of tin mining (downstairs) and forestry (upstairs) in Perak. The occasional temporary exhibitions are more interesting. There are two concrete air-raid shelters in the garden, erected in 1941.

Sleeping

Most of Ipoh's hotels are to be found in New Town on the eastern side of Sungai Kinta, with a few of the better budget options in the southeast of the city around Jln Che Tak and Jln Ali Pitchay. There are several modern and reliable midrange hotels catering to business travellers, but the city has more than its share of old and downright seedy establishments, dingy little 'hotels' that are actually brothels.

All the options listed here have private bathrooms.

BUDGET

Embassy (☎ 254 9496; 19 Jln CM Yusuf; r from RM25; ✹) This is as cheap and cheerful as Ipoh gets (it does get cheaper, but definitely not more cheery). There's not a lot of character, but rooms are clean and the air-con is cold.

New Caspian Hotel (☎ 243 9254; 20-26 Jln Ali Pitchay; r RM35-60; ✹) Welcoming little budget hotel with adequate rooms, which all have TVs and refrigerators. Not to be confused with the less appealing hotel of the same name on Jln Jubilee.

Sun Golden Inn (☎ 243 6255; 17 Jln Che Tak; r RM40-80; ✹) One of Ipoh's better budget choices, the Sun Golden Inn is a clean and friendly Chinese hotel, with good management who are used to dealing with Westerners.

MIDRANGE

Majestic Station Hotel (☎ 255 4242; www.majesticstationhotel.com; Jln Panglima Bukit Gantang Wahab; s & d from RM88, f from RM130; ✹) The venerable colonial Majestic Station Hotel in Ipoh's magnificently faded, Moorish-style train station has plenty of character. Rooms are furnished in contemporary style, and while they're nice, they don't quite meet the luxurious promise implied by the premises. Do be a dear and take high tea on the long, tiled verandah.

Seri Malaysia (☎ 241 2936; luckyhot@tm.net.my; Lot 10406 Jln Sturrock; s/d RM120/140; ✹ ▣) This branch of the reliable Seri Malaysia chain offers good businessman comfort and crisp, attentive service. Sometimes, you need a bed and some cable TV, and in this regard, Seri more than adequately provides.

Ritz Garden Hotel (☎ 242 7777; www.ritzgardenhotel.com; 86 Jln Yang Kalsom; r/ste from RM160/400; ✹ ▣) The Ritz is one of Ipoh's better midrange choices, with a business centre, a restaurant, and free broadband access in every room. Only the priciest suites (starting at RM2300) have access to the tiny pool and sauna, though. Book online for serious discounts.

TOP END

Hotel Excelsior (☎ 253 6666; www.hotelexcelsior.com.my; 43 Jln Sultan Abdul Jalil; s/d/ste RM200/210/260; ✹) This towering city-centre monolith offers the usual comforts aimed at business travellers, including the regulation conservatively styled rooms, restaurants and gym. There's also a nightclub.

Syuen Hotel (☎ 253 8889; www.syuenhotel.com.my; 88 Jln Sultan Abdul Jalil; r/ste from RM300/600; ✹ ▣ ▣)

The colossal four-star, 290-room Syuen Hotel is the city's top hotel, with all the requisite facilities, including a business centre, cocktail bar, restaurants and a rooftop tennis court and gym. She looks like a grand old dame, but cheaper rooms look out onto internal air shafts and are consequently rather dark. Sizeable discounts on the published rates are available.

Eating

Ipoh is famous for its street food. There's something in the water: folks believe deposits from the rich karst formations around town seep into the groundwater and make Ipoh food unique. Malaysians will tell you Ipoh does the best *kway teow* (a rice noodle dish) in the country. Other tasty local specialities include pomelos – a football-sized citrus fruit – local bean sprouts and Ipoh white coffee, made with palm-oil margarine and served with condensed milk. It's very sweet stuff.

Medan Selera Dato Tawhil Azar (Jln Raja Musa Aziz) Better-known as the Children's Playground, this large food centre has stalls arranged around a small square filled with slides and swings. It's a popular place for Malay food in the evening, it's open late and, of course, kids love it.

MBI Terrace (off Jln Sultan Abdul Jalil; 7pm-midnight) Essentially attached to the city's municipal sports complex, in the evening MBI serves the best *kway teow* in town, according to many Ipoh residents.

Kafe Abarnaashre (29 Jln Tun Sambathan; mains from RM2; lunch & dinner) This simple halal Indian cafe facing the *padang* offers superb value. The menu, which includes lots of vegetarian dishes, is displayed on the wall, with roti and *dosa* starting from as little as RM1.

Funny Mountain Soya Bean (255 6861; 49 Jln Theatre; under RM3; lunch & dinner) Besides having one of the best business names in Malaysia, Funny Mountain is immensely popular for its one dish: soya bean and bean curd pudding. This is a millennia-old Chinese recipe brought to Ipoh direct from the Middle Kingdom; the curd is both delicious and a piece of Asian history.

Restoran Onn Kee (253 1652; 51 Jln Yau Tet Shin; mains from RM3; 1:30pm-3am) Onn Kee is widely recognised as serving the best *ayam taugeh* (bean-sprout chicken) in Perak, if not Malaysia. The chicken comes boiled, soft and fragrant, the sprouts are particularly fat and crunchy, and the combined texture and flavour is surpassingly joyous.

Old Town White Coffee (2 Jln Tun Sambathan; mains from RM3; breakfast & lunch Mon, breakfast, lunch & dinner Tue-Sun) This upmarket coffee house facing the *padang* seems to be forever crowded. Simple chicken rice dishes prevail, and unsurprisingly, the coffee is pretty good.

Kedai Kopi Kong Meng (65 Jln Bandar Timah; mains from RM4; breakfast & lunch, closed Sun) Ipoh eaters swear by the Hakka (southeastern Chinese) cuisine in Kong Meng, which has been in business for almost 70 years. Your best bet in this scruffy, friendly little cafe is the beef noodle soup with some of the special home-made chilli sauce.

Xin Quan Fang (174 Jln Sultan Iskandar Shah; mains from RM4; breakfast & lunch) You better come early (seriously, like 7:15am) for the curry noodles and the pork and bean sprouts. Those two dishes, by the way, are pretty much all Xin Quan Fang churns out, but ohmygod are they good, as testified to by the lines that stretch around the block for this family-run favourite.

Full Sun Fish Head Noodle (off Jln Ng Weng Hup; mains from RM4; breakfast) Fish head noodle soup for breakfast? Hey, break free from those eggs and do as the locals do. The rich, fishy goodness in the cheek meat says 'Good morning!'; that glassy fish eye staring back at you from the soup says, 'Good choice, foodie'.

Drinking

Chinese coffee shops and food centres all across town serve beer and stout.

FMS Bar (2 Jln Sultan Idris Shah) This Ipoh institution was closed for renovation during our visit. Hopefully open by the time you read this, the Federated Malay States bar has been going since 1906, and was the favoured haunt of colonial planters and miners. It still attracts a gaggle of colourful local characters and expats.

Miners' Arms (243 4531; 8 Jln Dato' Maharajah Lela) A popular British-style pub, which also serves fish and chips, and steak dinners. There's live music on Friday and Saturday evenings.

Station Bar (Jln Panglima Bukit Gantang Wahab; noon-midnight) On the ground floor of the Majestic Station Hotel, this quiet bar is a rather murky, gloomy place, but it has a kind of rough-edged charm, if you like that kind of thing.

Getting There & Away

AIR

Firefly (☎ (37-845 4543; www.fireflyz.com.my) As of research, the only flights to Ipoh were four times a week from Singapore (not KL) for RM177.

BUS

Ipoh is on the main KL–Butterworth road; 205km north of the capital and 164km south of Butterworth. The long-distance bus station is at **Medan Gopeng** (☎ 312 2844; Jln Raja Dr Nazrin Shah), 5km south of the city centre and linked by frequent shuttle buses to the city bus station (RM1.30). Numerous bus companies operate from the long-distance bus station.

Destinations and standard fares include Alor Setar (RM17), Butterworth (RM14.70), Hat Yai in Thailand (RM65), Johor Bahru (RM37), Kota Bharu (RM25.40), KL (RM13.40), Lumut (RM6) and Melaka (RM22.70).

The city bus station is off a roundabout south of the train station. Buses depart from here for destinations in Perak, such as Batu Gajah (RM1.80), Gopeng (RM1.50; for Kellie's Castle), Kuala Kangsar (RM6), Taiping (RM8) and Teluk Intan (RM5.80), as well as Tanah Rata in the Cameron Highlands (RM10.30). Note that buses to Tapah (RM4.70), operated by Regal Transport, depart from a stop across the road from the bus station.

Perak Roadways has a separate terminus on Jln Tun Abdul Razak, with regular buses to Lumut (RM5.70, 1¾ hours).

The private **Sri Maju bus company** (☎ 253 8898) has its own bus station on Jln Bendahara, from where it runs 'luxury' buses to KL (RM16, every 45 minutes), Butterworth (RM13.50, nine daily) and Singapore (RM55, six to eight daily).

TAXI

Long-distance taxis depart from in front of the long-distance bus station, and there is another stand at the city bus station. They're rip offs. Whole-taxi fares include Butterworth (RM200), Cameron Highlands (RM180) and Ipoh airport (RM18).

TRAIN

Ipoh's **train station** (☎ 254 0481; Jln Panglima Bukit Gantang Wahab) is on the main Singapore–Butterworth line. There are daily trains (including very frequent intercity service to the former) to both KL (RM12, 4½ hours) and

Butterworth (RM17, five hours), the latter continuing to Hat Yai in Thailand (RM30, 10 hours).

AROUND IPOH

Lost World of Tambun

At the base of forested limestone cliffs 8km northeast of Ipoh, the **Lost World of Tambun** (☎ 542 8888; www.sunway.com.my/lostworldoftambun; 1 Psn Lagun Sunway 1; adult/child RM25/19; ⏰ 11am-6pm Mon & Wed-Fri, 10am-6pm Sat & Sun) is a huge waterpark, especially popular with local families at weekends. There are various pools, waterslides, wave generators and the like, as well as natural hot springs, artificial 'ruins' to explore and a tiger enclosure.

Regular buses from Ipoh's city bus station to Tanjung Rambutan (RM1.50) pass the Lost World.

Kellie's Castle

Also known as Kellie's Folly, **Kellie's Castle** (☎ 605 3668; adult/child RM5/2; ⏰ 8.30am-6pm) is one of those leftovers of British eccentricity you occasionally find scattered in some random corner of the old empire. Here's the story: wealthy Scottish rubber-plantation owner and lover-of-all-things-India William Kellie Smith commissioned the building to be the home of his son. Not only bricks, but artisans and labourers were sourced from India to build what would have been, if finished, one of the most magnificent residences in Malaysia. Poor Smith died in 1926 and the house was abandoned; today, the remaining six-storey structure is a well-tended tourist site. The best-preserved rooms are the guest bedrooms, adorned with fine figurative plasterwork, and there are splendid views of the surrounding countryside from the roof terrace. Tales of secret passageways and ghosts have added to the air of mystery that surrounds this place.

About 500m from the castle is a **Hindu temple**, built for the artisans by Smith when a mysterious illness decimated the workforce and the remaining workers believed the gods needed to be appeased. To show their gratitude to Smith, the workers placed a figure of him, dressed in a white suit and pith helmet, among the Hindu deities on the temple roof. The temple is now semi-derelict but still in use, and the resident priest will point out the statue of Smith.

Kellie's Castle is inconvenient to reach without your own transport. From Ipoh's city

---

RAFFLESIA & BUTTERFLY SPOTTING

About 30km from Ipoh and 12km from Gopeng, a wonderful ecotourism opportunity exists in the Ulu Geroh community of Semai Orang Asli people. As part of the Malaysian Nature Society's **Rafflesia Conservation Project** (www.mns .my/artabout.php?aid=25) some of the locals have formed SEMAI (standing for Sahabat Ekopelancungan Memuliraan Alam Indah, or Friends of Ecotourism and Conservation and Beautiful Tourism), a programme to guide day-trip visitors through the forests looking for the Rafflesia, the world's largest flower, and beautiful butterflies, including the Rajah Brooke Birdwing. For details check the web link above or call ☎ 012-645 6254 or 012-470 1251

---

bus station you can take either the frequent bus 66 to Gopeng (RM1.50) or buses 36 and 37 to Batu Gajah, which leave every 20 minutes (RM1.80). Bus 67 runs approximately every hour in either direction between Batu Gajah and Gopeng, passing in front of Kellie's Castle. You can also charter a taxi from Ipoh (RM50 to RM60 return); a taxi from Batu Gajah costs RM8.

CAMERON HIGHLANDS
☎ 05

OK traveller, you've been sweating through the jungles, beaches and lowlands of Malaysia for weeks now. Another sticky day will make your clothes unwearable. Another sweaty night and you'll lose the ability to sleep. We grant you a reprieve. Come to the Cameron Highlands.

This is Malaysia's most extensive hill station, an alpinescape of blue peaks, green humps, fuzzy tea plantations, small towns and white waterfalls cutting throughout. With an altitude of 1300m to 1829m, the temperature rarely drops below 10°C or climbs above 21°C. The Highlands are inside the state borders of Pahang, but easiest access is via Tapah in Perak. The road winds through Ringlet, then the main towns of Tanah Rata, Brinchang and beyond.

Trekking, tea tasting and visiting local agro-tourism sites is the done thing here; you can also meet other travellers, especially backpackers, as this is one of the major nodes on the Banana Pancake Trail.

Unfortunately development, erosion and poorly planned agriculture have taken their environmental toll on the highlands. Landslips and floods have been the tragic by-product of the above. On the plus side, Ringlet Lake, which had essentially become a mud pie as of 2005, has been restored to, if not it's old clear beauty, then something approaching a life-sustaining body of water. And Malaysians in general seem to be more aware of green issues. On the downside, increased ease of access to the highlands from Ipoh is only going to spur more development. Tourists are the backbone of the economy here, and their purchasing power will have a huge impact on what the Cameron Highlands eventually become: blighted blockhouses scarring the hills, or the cultivated, beautiful heart of the upland Malaysian peninsula.

Orientation
Though the Cameron Highlands lie just over the Perak state border in Pahang, it is accessed from Perak. From the turn-off at Tapah it's 47km up to Ringlet, the first village of the Highlands. It's an ugly, modern place, offering no real inducement to stop. On the way you'll pass the eye-catching waterfall **Lata Iskandar** at the Km 20 marker (20km from Tapah).

Soon after Ringlet you skirt the reservoir created by Sultan Abu Bakar. Tanah Rata, about 13km past Ringlet, is the main town of the Highlands, where restaurants and shops line busy Jln Besar (Main Rd). Most visitors stay here for its lively atmosphere and transport links.

A few kilometres past Tanah Rata many of the Highlands' more luxurious hotels cluster around a gold course (natch). Past here, at Km 65, is Brinchang, dominated by Chinese Malays and resorts catering for domestic tourists. Although closer to many attractions, it has less character than Tanah Rata and is not so well served by public transport.

The road continues to Kampung Raja, a tea-estate village, and the Blue Valley Tea Estate at Km 90. Flower gardens, strawberry stalls and butterfly farms are on this stretch of road, as is the turn-off to Sungai Palas Tea Estate and Gunung Brinchang (Mt Brinchang; 2031m).

Information
The post office, hospital, police and bus and taxi stations are all on Jln Besar in Tanah Rata. Most guesthouses offer internet access for around RM5 per hour.

PERAK

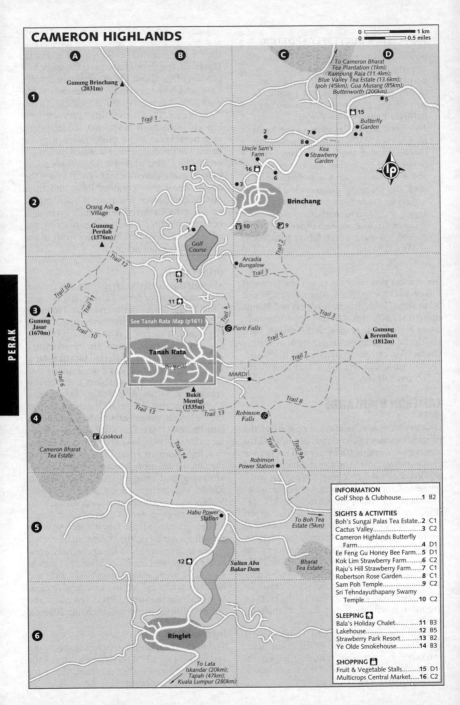

CAMERON HIGHLANDS

PERAK

To Cameron Bharat
Tea Plantation (1km);
Kampung Raja (11.4km);
Blue Valley Tea Estate (13.6km);
Ipoh (45km); Gua Musang (85km);
Butterworth (200km)

Gunung Brinchang
(2031m)

Trail 1

Butterfly
Garden

Uncle Sam's
Farm

Kea
Strawberry
Garden

Brinchang

Orang Asli
Village

Gunung
Perdah
(1576m)

Golf
Course

Gunung
Jasar
(1670m)

Arcadia
Bungalow

Trail 2

Trail 3

Trail 12

Trail 10

Trail 11

Trail 4

Trail 3

Gunung
Beremban
(1812m)

See Tanah Rata Map (p161)

Parit Falls

Trail 5

Tanah Rata

Jln Besar

MARDI

Trail 7

Trail 8

Trail 10

Trail 6

Bukit
Mentigi
(1535m)

Trail 13

Robinson
Falls

Trail 13

Robinson
Power Station

Trail 9

Trail 9A

Lookout

Cameron Bharat
Tea Estate

Trail 14

Habu Power
Station

To Boh Tea
Estate (5km)

Sultan Abu
Bakar Dam

Bharat
Tea Estate

Ringlet

To Lata
Iskandar (20km);
Tapah (47km);
Kuala Lumpur (280km)

INFORMATION
Golf Shop & Clubhouse............**1** B2

SIGHTS & ACTIVITIES
Boh's Sungai Palas Tea Estate..**2** C1
Cactus Valley......................**3** C2
Cameron Highlands Butterfly
    Farm.............................**4** D1
Ee Feng Gu Honey Bee Farm...**5** D1
Kok Lim Strawberry Farm.......**6** C2
Raju's Hill Strawberry Farm....**7** C1
Robertson Rose Garden..........**8** C1
Sam Poh Temple..................**9** C2
Sri Tehndayuthapany Swamy
    Temple..........................**10** C2

SLEEPING
Bala's Holiday Chalet............**11** B3
Lakehouse.......................**12** B5
Strawberry Park Resort..........**13** B2
Ye Olde Smokehouse.............**14** B3

SHOPPING
Fruit & Vegetable Stalls.........**15** D1
Multicrops Central Market.....**16** C2

CS Travel & Tours (Map p161; ☎ 491 1200; www .cstravel.com.my; 47 Jln Besar) Organises coach tours of the Highlands and books bus and air tickets.

Dobi Highlands Laundry (Map p161; 62A Persiaran Camellia 3; per 4kg RM6; ☉ 9am-8pm Mon-Sat, 1-8pm Sun)

HSBC Bank (Map p161; Jln Besar)

Maybank (Map p161; Persiaran Camellia 4)

Pusat Computer CL (Map p161; ☎ 491 2907; 1st fl, 55C Persiaran Camellia 3; per hr RM2.80; ☉ 10am-10pm) The cheapest internet access in Tanah Rata.

Regional Environmental Awareness Cameron Highlands (☎ 491 4950, 012-589 8684; www.reach .org.my) Local environmental group. Volunteers are welcome to join its reforestation and recycling programmes, and the website has up-to-date information on local eco issues.

Tourist information centre (Map p161; ☎ 491 4560; mctic@tm.net.my; Public Library Complex; ☉ 8.30am-12.30pm & 1.30-5pm Mon-Fri, 8.30am-2pm Sat) This small tourist office near the park has a few brochures.

www.cameronhighlands.com An overview of the Highlands, plus information on accommodation and attractions.

www.ewarns.com.my Current information on landslip hazards in the Highlands.

Sights
TEA PLANTATIONS

The first tea was planted here in 1929 by JA Russell, who founded the Boh Tea Estate. When the first tea tour was held we cannot say, but they're certainly the most popular thing to do around here now.

The **Boh Sungai Palas Tea Estate** (Map p160; admission free; ☉ 9am-4.30pm Tue-Sun) is up in the hills north of Brinchang, off the road to Gunung Brinchang. The approach road leads past worker housing and a Hindu temple (tea pickers are predominantly Indian) to the modern visitor centre, where you can watch a video on the history of the estate. There's also a gift shop selling every version of Boh tea you can imagine and a pleasant cafe where you can sip tea while looking out over the lush plantations below. Free 15-minute tours showing the tea-making process are conducted during opening hours. Wait for a staff member to collect you from the visitor centre.

Public buses running between Tanah Rata and Kampung Raja pass the turn-off to Gunung Brinchang. From there it's 4km along the winding road past **Robertson Rose**

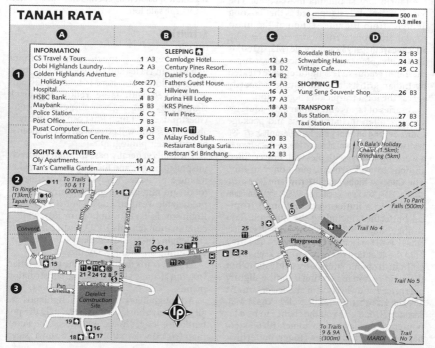

TANAH RATA

0 _____ 500 m
0 _____ 0.3 miles

INFORMATION		
CS Travel & Tours	1	A3
Dobi Highlands Laundry	2	A3
Golden Highlands Adventure Holidays	(see 27)	
Hospital	3	C2
HSBC Bank	4	B3
Maybank	5	B3
Police Station	6	C2
Post Office	7	B3
Pusat Computer CL	8	A3
Tourist Information Centre	9	C3

SIGHTS & ACTIVITIES		
Oly Apartments	10	A2
Tan's Camellia Garden	11	A2

SLEEPING 🛏		
Camlodge Hotel	12	A3
Century Pines Resort	13	D2
Daniel's Lodge	14	B2
Fathers Guest House	15	A3
Hillview Inn	16	A3
Jurina Hill Lodge	17	A3
KRS Pines	18	A3
Twin Pines	19	B3

EATING 🍴		
Malay Food Stalls	20	B3
Restaurant Bunga Suria	21	A3
Restoran Sri Brinchang	22	B3

Rosedale Bistro	23	B3
Schwarbing Haus	24	A3
Vintage Cafe	25	C2

SHOPPING 🛍		
Yung Seng Souvenir Shop	26	B3

TRANSPORT		
Bus Station	27	B3
Taxi Station	28	C3

To Ringlet (13km); Tapah (60km)

To Trails 10 & 11 (200m)

To Bala's Holiday Chalet (1.5km); Brinchang (5km)

To Parit Falls (500m)

Trail No 4

Convent

Jln Gereja

Jln Lembah Jaya

Ye Perdah

Psn Camellia 3

Psn 1

Psn Camellia 4

Psn Camellia 2

Derelict Construction Site

Jln Menteng

Jln Besar

Tanzack Merch

Jln Dayang Endah

Jln Masjid

Playground

Trail No 5

To Trails 9 & 9A (300m)

MARDI

Trail No 7

PERAK

Garden (worth a detour for its hilltop views) to the plantation entrance, after which it's another 15 minutes' walk downhill to the visitors centre.

You can also visit other tea estates, but guided tours are usually given only for organised groups. One exception is **Boh Tea Estate** (off Map p160; www.boh.com.my), southeast of Tanah Rata and 8km off the main road up to the Highlands. From the end of jungle trail 9A (see opposite), it's only a 45-minute walk to the plantation, and tours are given approximately hourly from 10am to 3.30pm.

The **Cameron Bharat Tea Plantation** (off Map p160; ☎ 491 1133; www.bharattea.com.my) has a teahouse, attractively set overlooking the estate, around 3km north of Brinchang.

OTHER SIGHTS

As unexpected sites in the hills go, a temple to a Chinese eunuch and naval officer just about tops the list. The **Sam Poh Temple** (Map p160), just below Brinchang about 1km off the main road, is a brilliant pastiche of imperial Chinese regalia, statuary dedicated to medieval admiral and eunuch Zheng Ho and, allegedly, the fourth-largest Buddha in Malaysia. The Sam Poh temple is signposted as the 'Tokong Temple' from the intersection at the main road in front of the Iris House Hotel. Nearby **Sri Tehndayuthapany Swamy Temple** (Map p160) is an equally colourful Hindu place of worship – the Tamil Nadu–style sculptures were created by Indian aritists, and the temple primarily serves the local tea-picking population.

A series of farms and similar agro-tourism sites are often included in bus and package tours. **Ee Feng Gu Honey Bee Farm** (Map p160; ☎ 496 1951; www.eefenggu.com; admission free; ☉ 8am-7pm) is a working apiary, with pleasant, flower-filled gardens to walk around, and honey to buy. The **Cameron Highlands Butterfly Farm** (Map p160; ☎ 496 1364; Kea Farm; adult/child RM8/5; ☉ 8am-6pm) is home to a fluttering collection of tropical butterflies, including the majestic Raja Brooke. **Raju's Hill Strawberry Farm** (Map p160; ☎ 491 4649; Kea Farm, Brinchang; admission free) may hold the attention of anyone with a keen interest in hydroponic strawberry cultivation, but the main reason for visiting is for the slightly overpriced strawberry jam and ice cream. At **Kok Lim Strawberry Farm** (Map p160; ☎ 491 4481, Brinchang) RM20 gets you the chance to be a labourer for the day and go home with 0.5kg of hand-picked strawberries. Honey, butterflies,

strawberries…how about some cacti? Oh, sweet: here's **Cactus Valley** (Map p160; ☎ 491 5640; Pekan Lama, Brinchang; adult/child RM4/2; ☉ 8am-6pm), where you can wander along tiered terraces filled with various local flowers, fruits and vegetables, as well as cacti. There are potted plants for sale too.

Activities
HIKING

Besides getting in touch with your inner Englishman via tea and strawberries, the main thing to do around here is hike. Trailheads are marked with large yellow-and-black signboards that are sometimes obscured. Guesthouses in Tanah Rata can arrange reliable guides, who will possess an official license bearing their photograph.

The trails generally pass through relatively unspoiled jungle, and the cool weather makes hiking a pleasure. Always carry water, some food, and rain gear to guard against the unpredictable weather. Trails 4 and 9A (as far as Robinson Falls) take an hour or less, while a combination of trails 10, 11 and 12 is a more challenging hike. The rest may be tough going, depending on your level of fitness.

Trail 13 starts from behind the Cameronian Inn, but it stops at the concrete construction pylons.

Although hikes around the Highlands are all relatively short, there is obviously the potential for longer hikes. A glance at the Perak map (p145) will indicate what a short, steep

---

JIM THOMPSON

The Cameron Highlands' most famous jungle trekker was a man who never came back from his walk. American Jim Thompson is credited with having founded the Thai silk industry after WWII. He subsequently made a fortune, and his beautiful, antique-packed house beside a canal in Bangkok is a major tourist attraction today. On 26 March 1967, while holidaying in the Highlands, Jim Thompson left his villa for a predinner stroll – never to be seen again. Despite extensive searches, the mystery of his disappearance has never been explained. Kidnapped? Murdered? Or simply a planned disappearance or suicide? Nobody knows for sure. Today, you can follow his trail on a guided walking tour (p164).

distance it is from the Highlands down to Ipoh or the main road. For any hike outside the immediate area, however, the local authorities have to be notified and a guide is necessary; contact the tourist office for details. Trail 6 was closed during our research.

Trail 1
This trail officially starts at white stone marker 1/5 on the summit of Gunung Brinchang (2031m), but this is a steep, muddy, overgrown trail (often closed for repairs) and it is not advisable to make this descent. Instead, start your walk at the end point of the trail, at white stone marker 1/48 just north of Cactus Valley and ascend to the top of Gunung Brinchang. This walk should take around 3½ hours to complete. From the summit take the 7km sealed road back to Brinchang through the tea plantations – a pleasant and relatively easy walk of about two hours.

Trail 2
Starting just before Sam Poh Temple outside Brinchang, this steep, strenuous hike follows a thin, slippery track for 1½ hours before joining Trail 3.

Trail 3
Begins at Arcadia Bungalow southeast of the golf course and climbs towards Gunung Bereman (1812m), getting steeper near the summit. It's a strenuous three-hour hike all the way to the mountain. An easier alternative is to go as far as Trail 5 and take that back to the Malaysian Agricultural Research and Development Institue (Mardi); this too, though, is a steep path. Trail 3 continues onward to meet Trails 7 and 8.

Trail 4
One of the more popular trails starts next to the river just past Century Pines Resort in Tanah Rata. It leads to Parit Falls, but garbage from the nearby village finds its way here, and it's not the most bucolic spot. The falls can also be reached from the road around the southern end of the golf course. Both hikes are about half a kilometre.

Trail 5
Starting at Mardi, take the road inside the complex and follow the sign around to the left. It's a steep 1½-hour hike to the junction with Trail 3 through open country

and forest. It's easier if done downhill from Trail 3.

Trail 6
Trail 6 is prone to neglect, and the path is unclear in places. It goes from the end of the road at the Cameron Bharat Tea Estate and merges with Trail 10 at the summit of Gunung Jasar (1670m). It's a difficult 2½-hour uphill hike – take a guide.

Trail 7
This very difficult trail ascends Gunung Bereman. It starts inside Mardi. You should allow all day – it's at a steady three-hour uphill hike, with a very steep final climb to the summit.

Trail 8
This trail tails off Trail 9 just before Robinson Falls and is another steep three-hour approach to Gunung Bereman. Although slightly easier than Trail 7, it's still strenuous, especially if done in reverse from the mountain.

Trails 9 & 9A
Trail 9 starts 1.5km from the main road in Tanah Rata. Take the road past Mardi and follow it to the right where it ends at a footbridge. From here the trail leads downhill past Robinson Falls to a metal gate, about 15 minutes away. Trail 9, which is not recommended, goes through the gate and follows the water pipeline down a steep, slippery incline through the jungle to the power station. We recommend Trail 9A, which branches to the left before the metal gate and in about an hour arrives at Boh Rd. Follow this to the main road, where you can either head east to Boh Tea Estate or west to Habu Power Station for buses back to Tanah Rata.

Trails 10, 11 & 12
Gunung Jasar is a fairly strenuous hike via Trail 10, starting behind the Oly Apartments in Tanah Rata. Go through Tan's Camellia Garden and uphill to the left. After reaching the summit, you can continue on towards Gunung Perdah (1576m), but to continue on this trail you must bypass the mountain and return by Trail 11, which joins up with Trail 10 halfway back to Tanah Rata. Both these paths are unclear; take a guide. Trail

12 continues from Gunung Perdah towards the weather station, but it is not well marked or maintained.

Trails 13 & 14

Trail 13 starts behind Cameronian Holiday Inn. It's a 1.5 hour walk with a stream that merges with Trail 14, a difficult four-hour jaunt up Gunung Mentigi (1535m) that exits onto Tanah Rata road. You'll want a guide.

Tours

CS Travel & Tours (Map p161; ☎ 491 1200; www .cstravel.com.my; 47 Jln Besar, Tanah Rata) sells tickets for popular half-day 'countryside tours' of the Highlands, leaving around 8.45am and 1.45pm (RM30/25 adult/child). This is a good way of ticking off the bingo checklist of Highlands attractions, which are spread out and difficult to reach by public transport. Longer tours such as the full-day 'discovery tour' (RM90/70 adult/child) take in Gunung Brinchang and an Orang Asli village. The village may only be visited in the company of an official guide, who will have made a prior appointment. You can meet the tribesmen and participate in traditional activities such as archery, but this is a living community, not a staged tourist attraction, so remember you are a guest – ask before taking photographs and listen to the advice of your guide. Guides for the hiking trails can also be arranged.

Fathers Guest House (Map p161; ☎ 491 2888; 25 Jln Gereja) has a resident licensed guide who leads informative nature tours of the Highlands, including a visit to an Orang Asli village (RM60); available to nonguests.

Golden Highlands Adventure Holidays (Map p161; ☎ 490 1880; www.gohighadventure.com; bus station, Tanah Ratah) offers guided walking tours (RM68/45 adult/child) of the trail followed by famous disappeared trekker Jim Thompson (see the boxed text, p162).

Titiwangsa Tours (☎ 491 1452; www.titiwangsatours .com; 36 Jln Besar, Brinchang) runs a few coach trips including the half-day Agro Delight tour (adult/child RM65/55), touring the local flower nurseries, organic farms and orchards. Entrance fees and dinner are included.

Sleeping

The Highlands are at their busiest during the school holidays in April, August and December. During these times you should book accommodation in advance. Tanah Rata is a favourite stopover for backpackers, and most accommodation here is of the budget variety.

Hostel touts will usually meet new arrivals at the bus station, which is actually pretty useful if you don't know where to stay. If you don't see the tout for the guesthouse you're headed to, ring them and most will pick you up free of charge. Don't believe touts who say their hostel has the last couple of rooms available – this is extremely unlikely. If you choose to walk, it's no more than 20 minutes to any place in town.

Midrange options consist of somewhat impersonal business-style high rises, while luxury resorts are mostly located outside town. Many hotels raise their prices on weekends.

Brinchang also has some hotels, but prices are higher, there's little atmosphere and it's an awkward place to stay if you're dependent on public transport.

The following places have shared bathrooms unless otherwise stated.

TANAH RATA

Budget

Daniel's Lodge (Map p161; ☎ 491 5823; danielslodge@ hotmail.com; 9 Lg Perdah; dm/r from RM8/20; ☐) Despite the fact that the common-area whiteboard proudly states 'Fuck the Lonely Planet', we had quite a fun stay in this clean lodge, also known as Kang's. The backpacker force is strong here: French guys roll cigarettes, British gap-yearers get drunk in the back garden and German hikers compare boots…you know what to expect. Management is helpful and good for booking onward travel and tours.

Fathers Guest House (Map p161; ☎ 491 2484; http:// fathers.cameronhighlands.com; 25 Jln Gereja; dm/s/d/tr from RM10/25/30/50; ☐) This very sociable place is situated on a hill at the western edge of town. The old bunker-style British army Nissen huts are clean and cosy, with between eight and 12 closely packed single beds. There are also rooms with private showers in the nearby house (from RM80), a big garden and a TV lounge. Access is via a long, steep flight of steps.

Twin Pines (Map p161; ☎ 491 2169; http://twin pines.cameronhighlands.com; 2 Jln Mentigi; s/d from RM12/20; ☐) Twin Pines is a good option for trekkers wanting backpacker rates with a less backpackery (read: party) atmosphere. The attic rooms are small, but are a steal; other facilities are well-kept, and management is spot on when it comes to organising tours of the Highlands.

Camlodge Hotel (Map p161; ☎ 491 4549; 3rd fl, 55C Persiaran Camellia 3; s/d/tr RM35/45/55) Above Pusat Computer, in the modern shopping complex at the western end of town. The Camlodge is a small guesthouse with neat, clean rooms but not much atmosphere. All rooms have attached bathrooms.

Midrange

KRS Pines (Map p161; ☎ 491 2777; http://twinpines .cameronhighlands.com; 7 Jln Mentigi; s/d from RM60/90; ▣) Owned by the folks at Twin Pines, KRS offers slightly more upscale digs in a squattish tower block. Smaller rooms go for as low as RM35; all accommodation is spic and span, making this a good borderline budget/midrange option.

Jurina Hill Lodge (Map p161; ☎ 491 5522; http:// jurina.cameronhighlands.com; Jln Mentigi; r from RM75) Popular with Malaysian families and tour groups, this is a cosy, modern guesthouse in a quiet area directly behind the Hillview Inn. It offers spacious hillside bungalows and apartments with between three and eight rooms, including kitchens.

Hillview Inn (Map p161; ☎ 491 2915; hillview_inn@ hotmail.com; 17 Jln Mentigi; r RM55-140; ▣) This three-storey villa has large, lovely rooms all with balconies overlooking a derelict construction site (not as bad as it sounds). You'll pay more for a private bathroom, though the communal showers are superior.

Bala's Holiday Chalet (Map p160; ☎ 491 1660; www .balaschalet.com; r/ste from RM120/220; ▣) Charming mock-Tudor style guesthouse, originally built as a boarding school in 1934. It is set in pretty English-style gardens about 1.5km out of Tanah Rata on the road to Brinchang. The colonial ambience has been preserved, making this one of the more pleasant chalets in the hills.

Top End

Century Pines Resort (Map p161; ☎ 491 5115; www .thongsin.com; 42 Jln Masjid; r/ste from RM249/433) Set in landscaped gardens at the eastern edge of town, this stylish hotel has some beautifully furnished rooms with a light, contemporary touch. It boasts a gym, a pub and a restaurant, and a pleasant outdoor seating area.

Ye Olde Smokehouse (Map p160; ☎ 491 1215; www .thesmokehouse.com.my; r from RM460) This characterful old house near the golf course on the outskirts of town looks as if it's been lifted straight from deepest Surrey, complete with a red British phone box outside. Indoors, the exposed beams, open fireplaces and chintzy decor complete the picture. The restaurant serves up traditional English food too. Prices at the Smokehouse rise by a third on weekends.

Lakehouse (Map p160; ☎ 495 6152; www.lakehouse -cameron.com; r/ste from RM528/616) Overlooking the lake 2km north of Ringlet, this English country house–style hotel has just 18 rooms, all with four-poster beds and antique furnishings. The restaurant serves traditional British cuisine, and there's also a cosy pub and reading rooms. It's a little isolated, and you'll need your own transport to stay here.

BRINCHANG
Budget

Hotel Chua Gin (☎ 491 1801; www.chuagin.com; 11 Jln Besar; r from RM35) This simple hotel offers good value for the price, and is about the only real budget option here. A good bet if you're counting the pennies.

Midrange

Hill Garden Lodge (☎ 491 2988; 15-16 Jln Besar; r from RM72) Neat enough little hotel in the town centre, with small, cosy rooms. It gets busy on Saturday and Sunday, but discounts are often available at other times.

Iris House Hotel (☎ 491 1818; 56 Jln Kuari; r from RM110) Big, modern hotel on the edge of town. The rooms are unremarkable, but this is probably among the better midrange options. It's at the turn-off to Sam Poh Temple.

Top End

Strawberry Park Resort (Map p160; ☎ 491 1166; www .strawberryparkresorts.com; r/ste from RM450/650; ▣) A sprawling 'neo-Tudor' resort in the hills west of town, popular with package-tour groups and anyone needing a bit of pampering up in the hills. You'll find a Thai restaurant and a British grill on site.

Eating
TANAH RATA

The cheapest food in Tanah Rata is found in the mainly Malay food stalls (Map p161) stretching down Jln Besar towards the bus and taxi stations.

PERAK

Restoran Sri Brinchang (Map p161; ☎ 491 5982; 25 Jln Besar; mains from RM3; ⊙ breakfast, lunch & dinner) This bright place serves a range of simple Indian fare, including tandoori chicken set meals, fish-head curry and vegetarian dishes.

Vintage Café (Map p161; ☎ 012-329 3431; 13 Jln Besar; mains from RM4; ⊙ breakfast, lunch & dinner) There's not a lot that's terribly 'vintage' about this place per se, but it does serve a decent line-up of Western and Malay staples.

our pick **Restaurant Bunga Suria** (Map p161; ☎ 491 4666; 66A Persiaran Camellia 3; set meals RM5-9; ⊙ breakfast, lunch & dinner) The best value in town is to be had at this truly excellent South Indian joint. Meat, veg, dosa, curry, whatever: it's all good, spicy and served in large portions on a banana leaf.

Rosedale Bistro (Map p161; ☎ 491 1419; 42-A Jln Besar; mains RM5-18; ⊙ breakfast, lunch & dinner) Very popular with travellers, foreign and domestic, the Rosedale's menu spans several cuisines (Chinese, Malay, European, Indian) and is complemented by good coffee and free wi-fi.

Schwarbing Haus (Map p161; ☎ 491 5667; 59B Persiaran Camellia 3; mains RM18-30; ⊙ lunch & dinner) Das is pork knuckles? In *Malaysia*? *Jah*! Satisfy your yearning for Swiss-German food at this upstairs restaurant. On offer is a meaty menu of bratwurst, schnitzel, pork knuckles and sauerkraut, all imported directly from Europe (hence the relatively high prices).

BRINCHANG

Brinchang has a good night market, which sets up in the central square on late Saturday afternoon. A permanent foodstall centre livens up the southern end of the square. Otherwise, there's a load of Chinese restaurants along the main strip that could mix up all their signs tomorrow without you really being able to tell the difference.

Shopping

The best place to pick up local produce is the **Multicrops Central Market** (Map p160; ☎ 491 5188; 1 Arkid Peladang Sungai Burung, Brinchang; ⊙ 9am-6pm), which sells teas, fruits, strawberry jam, honey, potted plants and numerous other things.

Fresh locally grown vegetables and fruit – including Cameronian apples, oranges and passionfruit – can also be purchased from the market stalls beside the Butterfly Garden in Brinchang.

Back in Tanah Rata, **Yung Seng Souvenir Shop** (Map p161; ☎ 491 2223; 29-30 Jln Besar) has a good,

if rather expensive, selection of Orang Asli woodcarvings, as well as cheaper artwork from across Asia.

Getting There & Away

BUS

The road between Ipoh and Tanah Rata via Simpang Pulai is the most direct route here, although landslides continue to be a problem; check the current status before you travel. The 'old road', as it's now known, is a long and winding climb from Tapah; hundreds of bends can make it an uncomfortable journey. The road passes a number of Orang Asli villages and roadside shacks, where their produce is sold.

There are four daily buses from Ipoh to Tanah Rata between 8am and 6pm (RM10.90, three to 3½ hours) operated by Kinta Omnibus. From Tanah Rata, the first and last buses to Ipoh leave at 8am and 6pm.

From Tapah, there are eight daily buses to Tanah Rata also operating between 8am and 6pm (RM5.20, two hours). From Tanah Rata, the first and last buses down to Tapah leave at 8am and 6pm.

CS Travel & Tours (p164) runs minibuses to Kuala Tahan (Taman Negara), via Gua Musang (RM85, eight to nine hours, 10am).

Several direct long-distance services originate from the Tanah Rata bus station for KL (RM23 to RM30, five hours, six daily), Penang (RM23 to RM28, six hours, five daily) and Singapore (RM90, 10 hours, one daily).

TAXI

The taxi station in Tanah Rata (Map p161) is just east of the bus station on Jln Besar. Full-taxi fares are RM80 to Tapah, RM250 to Ipoh, RM300 to Penang and RM650 to RM800 to KL, but are open to negotiation.

Getting Around

While we never recommend hitch-hiking, many travellers do so to get between Tanah Rata and Brinchang and the tea plantations beyond.

BUS

Getting between Tanah Rata and Brinchang is not a problem between 6.30am and 6.30pm, as buses run every hour or so. There are scheduled buses every hour from Tanah

Rata to Kampung Raja, 23km away across the Highlands, but it's more like two or three hours until the next one happens by. It's quite a scenic trip, and you can hop off at various fruit and vegetable farms along the way. These buses also pass the turn-off to Gunung Brinchang and the Sungai Palas Tea Estate.

TAXI

Taxi services from Tanah Rata include Ringlet (per car RM18), Brinchang (RM11), Sungai Palas Estate (RM25) and Boh Tea Estate (RM30). For touring around, a taxi costs about RM40 per hour, or you can go up to Gunung Brinchang and back for RM100.

NORTHERN PERAK

KUALA KANGSAR

☎ 05 / pop 39,000

An easy-going town with a deep-seated sense of Malay ethnic identity, Kuala Kangsar, seat of the sultan of Perak, is one of the most pleasant royal capitals in Malaysia. It has

also sat at the centre of many of the events of the past two centuries that defined modern Malaysia: first foothold of the British, who moved to control the peninsula by installing Residents at the royal courts here in the 1870s; birthplace of Malaysia's rubber industry (p168); and site of the first Durbar, or conference of Malay sultans in 1897. Yet by the 1890s, the rapid growth of Ipoh and Taiping had left Kuala Kangsar a quiet backwater steeped in Malay tradition.

The small town centre is the usual scruffy jumble, but to the southeast the royal district is spacious and quiet. Main sights are few, but they're quite impressive and can easily be explored on a day trip from Taiping or Ipoh.

Information

The town's bank, bus station and post office are northwest of the royal district, off the road towards Taiping and Butterworth.

Sights

Heading out on Jln Istana beside the wide Sungai Perak, the first striking example of the

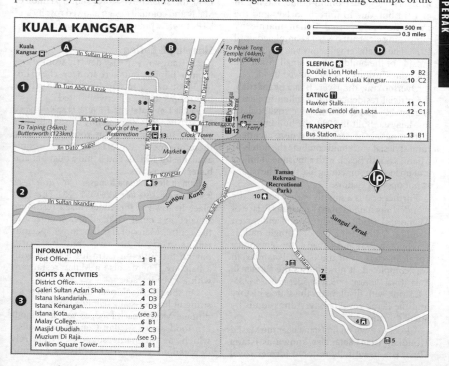

KUALA KANGSAR

SLEEPING 🏨	
Double Lion Hotel	9 B2
Rumah Rehat Kuala Kangsar	10 C2

EATING 🍴	
Hawker Stalls	11 C1
Medan Cendol dan Laksa	12 C1

TRANSPORT	
Bus Station	13 B1

INFORMATION	
Post Office	1 B1

SIGHTS & ACTIVITIES	
District Office	2 B1
Galeri Sultan Azlan Shah	3 C3
Istana Iskandariah	4 D3
Istana Kenangan	5 D3
Istana Kota	(see 3)
Malay College	6 B1
Masjid Ubudiah	7 C3
Muzium Di Raja	(see 5)
Pavilion Square Tower	8 B1

To Perak Tong Temple (44km); Ipoh (50km)

Kuala Kangsar

Jln Sultan Idris

Jln Tun Abdul Razak

Jln Taiping

To Taiping (36km); Butterworth (123km)

Church of the Resurrection

Clock Tower

Jln Temenggong

Jetty
Ferry

Jln Dato' Sagor

Market

Jln Kangsar

Jln Sultan Iskandar

Sungai Kangsar

Taman Rekreasi (Recreational Park)

Sungai Perak

Jln Istana

0 — 500 m
0 — 0.3 miles

PERAK

RUBBERY FACTS

In the late 1870s, a number of rubber trees were planted by British Resident Sir Hugh Low in his gardens in Kuala Kangsar from seed stock allegedly smuggled out of Brazil or taken from London's Kew Gardens. However, it was not until the invention of the pneumatic tyre in 1888, and then the popularity of the motorcar at the start of the 20th century, that rubber suddenly came into demand and rubber plantations sprang up across the country. Almost all of the trees in the new plantations were descended from Low's original rubber trees or from the Singapore Botanic Gardens. You can still see one of those first trees in Kuala Kangsar's **District Office** (Jln Raja Chulan) compound.

wealth of the sultanate is the small but magnificent **Masjid Ubudiah** (Ubudiah Mosque), designed by AB Hubbock, the architect of many of Ipoh's colonial edifices. The mosque, with its huge golden onion-dome, was begun in 1913 but, due to wartime delays and the smashing of imported Italian marble by rampaging elephants, wasn't completed until 1917. The caretaker will show you around the outside of the building for a small donation, but non-Muslims are not allowed inside.

Overlooking the river, **Istana Iskandariah**, the official residence of the sultan of Perak, is arguably the most attractive royal palace in Malaysia. Built in 1933, the building is an intriguing mix of Arab and art deco architectural styles; if you could combine the hotels in Miami's South Beach with a mosque, it might end up looking something like this. The palace is not open to visitors.

Further east is a slightly earlier palace, the wonderfully named **Istana Kenangan** (Palace of Memories), made entirely of wood and woven bamboo, without the use of a single nail. It was built in 1931 and served as the temporary royal quarters until the Istana Iskandariah was completed. It now houses the **Muzium Di Raja** (Royal Museum; 9.30am-5.30pm, closed 12.15-2.45pm Fri), with displays on the state's history and the Perak royal family. Admission is by small donation.

Closer to town on Jln Istana near the Masjid Ubudiah, **Istana Kota**, also known as Istana Hula, is a beautifully restored former royal palace, incorporating Renaissance and neo-classical elements; it could put you in mind of a Mexican villa on a sunny day. Built in 1903, it now hosts the **Galeri Sultan Azlan Shah** (777 5362; adult/child RM4/1; 10am-5pm Sat-Thu, 10am-noon & 2.45-5pm Fri). The Galeri features an exhibition honouring the life of the current sultan of Perak, Sultan Azlan Shah: see his sunglasses, passport, shoes and a separate building that holds his four Rolls Royces, Louis Vuitton luggage and official state gifts. It's a tough life, clearly.

The **Malay College** to the north of town is the most impressive colonial building in Kuala Kangsar. Established in 1905, it was the first Malay school to provide English education for the Malay elite destined for the civil service. It not only provided clerical workers for the British administration but also the nationalist leaders of the conservative 'Malaya for Malays' faction. In the 1950s Anthony Burgess wrote his first book while teaching here.

Opposite the Malay College, **Pavilion Square Tower** is a delightful folly overlooking the surrounding parkland and playing fields. Built in 1930, this small three-storey sports pavilion of Malay and colonial design allowed royalty and VIPs to view polo matches in comfort.

Sleeping & Eating

Kuala Kangsar is an easy day trip from either Ipoh or Taiping, but there are a few cheap hotels if you decide to stay. Rooms have private bathrooms unless otherwise stated.

Double Lion Hotel (776 1010; 74 Jln Kangsar; s/d from RM25/30;) Conveniently close to the bus station. In addition to the rooms with fans, there are more comfortable air-con rooms available for RM70. You'll find a busy bar and bakery downstairs.

Rumah Rehat Kuala Kangsar (776 3872; Jln Bukit Kerajaan; r/ste from RM60/150;) The best place in town is this modernised resthouse situated in a quiet parkland area southeast of the centre. Many of the simple yet spacious rooms overlook the river, and it's worth paying the little bit extra for a room with a balcony. There's also a Malay restaurant with a river terrace.

On the riverbank near the jetty, there's a string of hawker stalls selling a variety of traditional Malay snack food, as well as a modern food court, Medan Cendol dan Laksa, which, as the name suggests, is entirely devoted to various laksa dishes (around

RM2), *cendol* (shaved ice, coconut milk and palm-sugar syrup) and soft drinks. There are numerous coffee shops and fast-food outlets around the town centre.

Getting There & Away

Kuala Kangsar is located 50km northwest of Ipoh, just off the main KL–Butterworth road. It is 123km south of Butterworth and 255km north of KL.

Bus connections include Butterworth (RM10.40, two hours, two daily), Ipoh (RM5.50, one hour, roughly hourly), Kota Bharu (RM22.40, six hours, two daily), KL (RM18.70, 3½ to four hours, eight daily), Lumut (RM9.30, 3½ hours, three daily) and Taiping (RM3, 40 minutes, every 20 to 40 minutes).

Taxis leave from next to the bus station for Butterworth (RM90), Ipoh (RM60), KL (RM220) and Taiping (RM45).

The **train station** (☎ 776 1094) is located less conveniently to the northwest of town. All KL–Butterworth trains stop here. There is one daily train to KL (RM12, 5½ hours) and one to Butterworth (RM8, four hours).

ROYAL BELUM STATE PARK
☎ 05

In the northernmost corner of Perak is one of peninsular Malaysia's largest stretches of virgin jungle, **Royal Belum State Park**, also known as **Belum Forest Reserve**. This green dream of a wilderness, which constitutes the Belum-Temenggor Forest, fairly seethes with some of the nation's most dramatic megafauna: tapirs, tigers, sun bears, panthers and the endangered Sumatran Rhino, whose preservation was one of the motivating factors behind gazetting the park.

Exploring the park, which is about 100km north of Kuala Kangsar near the town of Gerik, is currently done by staying at the exclusive **Belum Rainforest Resort** (☎ 791 6800; www .belumresort.com; r from RM350; 🗴 🖵). The management of the resort will set you up with guides who will take you on treks into the jungle, but these services don't come cheap: a two-day, one-night excursion package runs a whopping RM800. You can also go on relaxation/fishing trips to manmade **Pulau Banding**, which floats in Temenggor Lake.

The actual resort itself is lovely, all dark wooden floors and crisp white accents with large windows and natural light playing together to give the impression that the resort is a thin shell between you and the outside forest.

Getting here is easiest with your own wheels; Gerik sits on Hwy 76, which continues onward to the Thai border. Buses to Gerik run at least once a day from Kuala Kangsar (RM8.60) and Kota Bharu (in Kelanatan; RM 16).

TAIPING
☎ 05 / pop 200,300

'…the Chinese still need to be kept in check, for they are not allowed to go out at night without passes and lanterns.'

Isabella Bird, The Golden Chersonese
and the Way Thither, 1883

How the times have changed. Once a sort of Chinese version of the bloodiest scenes from *The Godfather*, old Larut (from Isabella's times) is known today as Taiping, the 'Town of Everlasting Peace'…and pensioners – there are a lot of retirees pottering about this fair city. That's a far cry from when Taiping was secret-society central, and Chinese underground groups fought each other for control of the lucrative tin industry, which eventually shifted to Ipoh. Taiping became a quiet town, somewhat analogous to Kuala Kangsar; if that town is Perak's seat of Malaysian royalty and identity, Taiping once seemed to embody Chinese entrepreneurial energy. Though the city has lost its former status, tourist brochures still boast of its '31 Firsts' for Malaysia, including the first museum; first railway; first newspapers in English, Malay and Tamil; and the country's first zoo. Today Taiping is a pleasing, quiet little place with a nice colonial district and great street food.

Information

Discover Internet (☎ 806 9487; 3 Jln Panggong Wayang; per hr RM2)
OCBC Bank (Jln Barrack)
Standard Chartered Bank (Jln Kota)
Taiping Hospital (☎ 808 3333; Jln Taming Sari)
Tourist information centre (☎ 805 3245; Menara Jam, 355 Jln Kota; 🕑 8.30am-5.30pm Mon-Thu, 8.30am-1pm & 2-5.30pm Fri, 8.30am-3pm Sat) Located in the Jam Besar. The tourist information centre sells the useful

PERAK

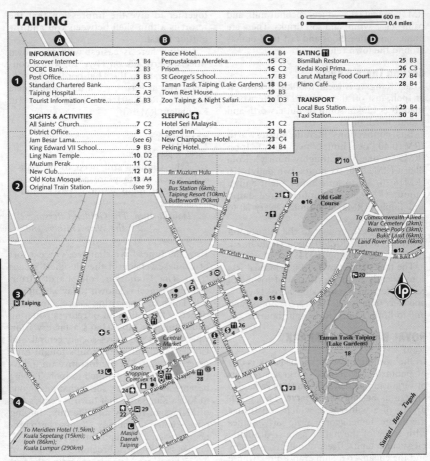

TAIPING

0 _____ 600 m
0 _____ 0.4 miles

Taiping Pocket Guide (RM3) and *Old Taiping* (RM20), a brief history of the town.

Taiping Peace Initiative The Taiping Peace Initiative promotes peace through workshops and through the annual Taiping Peace Awards. Contact the tourist information centre for volunteering opportunities.

www.vintagemalaya.com/Taiping Provides a comprehensive list of Taiping's many heritage buildings.

Sights

TAMAN TASIK TAIPING

Taiping is renowned for its beautiful 62 hectare **Taman Tasik Taiping** (Lake Gardens), built in 1880 on the site of an abandoned tin mine. The gardens owe their lush greenery to the fact that Taiping's annual rainfall is one of the highest in Peninsular Malaysia. In the hills that rise above the gardens is Bukit Larut, the oldest hill station in Malaysia.

The Lake Gardens also hosts the **Zoo Taiping & Night Safari** (☎ 808 6577; www.zootaiping.gov.my; adult/child RM12/8; ☒ 8am-11pm, to midnight Sat), one of the best in the country. If they're not snoozing in the midday heat, you can see all manner of creatures, including elephants, tigers, Malayan sun bears and tapirs lolling about. Feeding time is 10am to noon.

The zoo opens again in the evening for what's billed as Malaysia's first **night safari** (adult/child RM16/10; ☒ 8-11pm, to midnight Sat), when you have a better chance of seeing nocturnal animals beginning to stir, such as fishing bats, slow loris and big cats. It's an eerily atmospheric experience, especially if there are few other visitors.

MUZIUM PERAK
Northwest of the gardens, the **Muzium Perak** (State Museum; ☎ 807 2057; Jln Taming Sari; admission free; ☾ 9am-5pm, closed 12.15-2.45pm Fri) is housed in an impressive colonial building. It's the oldest museum in Malaysia, opening in 1883, and boasts exhibits on subjects as wide-ranging as the Orang Asli and the Outdoors. The cultural collection includes traditional *kris* (daggers), carvings and costumes and is the highlight of the place.

HISTORIC BUILDINGS
The neoclassical **District Office** is on Jln Alang Ahmad. Just around the corner is the **Perpustakaan Merdeka** (Independence Library; 1882). Closer to town on Jln Kota, the **Jam Besar Lama** (Old Clock Tower; 1890) once functioned as Taiping's fire station and now houses the tourist information centre.

Taiping was the starting point for Malaysia's first railway line, now defunct. Opened in 1885, it ran 13.5km to Port Weld (Kuala Sepetang). The original **train station** is a few steps west of gracious, colonial **King Edward VII School** (1905), the classrooms of which were used as torture chambers by the Japanese during WWII. Also on Jln Stesyen are **St George's School** (1915) and the **Town Rest House** (1894), formerly the governor's residence and now the Lagenda Hotel. Another colonial-era landmark is the whitewashed **New Club** building on Jln Bukit Larut, also dating from 1894.

At the western end of town, the **Old Kota Mosque** (1897) is the oldest in Taiping, mainly of note for its hexagonal design.

Taiping has a number of fine old shophouses, such as the **Peace Hotel** on Jln Iskandar. The Peranakan architecture has stucco tiles, stained glass, and beautifully carved bird and flower designs on the upper-wall dividers inside. The coffee shop downstairs is a good spot for a beer, but the scruffy hotel upstairs should be avoided. Opposite the Muzium Perak, the **prison**, built in 1879 to house lawless miners, was used by the Japanese during WWII and later as a rehabilitation centre for captured communists during the Emergency.

Just southwest of the museum and the prison, **All Saints' Church** (1886) is one of the oldest Anglican churches in Malaysia. The cemetery contains the graves of early colonial settlers, most of whom died of tropical diseases or failed to achieve the colonial pension needed to return home to Britain or Australia.

To the north of Muzium Perak, the colourful, gaudy **Ling Nam Temple** is the oldest Chinese temple in Perak. There's sadly not much left apart from a boat figure dedicated to the emperor who built China's first canal.

OTHER SIGHTS
Taiping's **Commonwealth Allied War Cemetery** is just east of the Lake Gardens, with row upon row of headstones for the British, Australian and Indian troops killed during WWII. Further on, down a side road, the **Burmese Pools** are a popular bathing spot by the river.

Sleeping
Taiping has an excellent selection of moderately priced accommodation. Most of the cheap hotels are scattered around the central market, the liveliest (but noisiest) part of town. The better choices are a few streets away. Prices include private bathrooms unless otherwise stated.

Peking Hotel (☎ 807 2975; 2 Jln Idris; r from RM35; 🕸) One of Taiping's great strengths as a destination is its attractive old colonial buildings, so why not sleep in one? The Peking fairly drips with faded character, and was used as a military-police station by the Japanese during WWII. These days it offers fairly basic rooms, which are comfortable enough for the price.

Meridien Hotel (☎ 808 1133; 2 Jln Simpang; r RM60; 🕸) For a businessman's hotel, this is a good deal: clean, cool rooms, plenty of mod-cons and general convenience, if not a lot of character.

New Champagne Hotel (☎ 806 5060; www.new champagnehotel.com; 17 Jln Lim Swee Aun; r from RM63; 🕸) The excellently titled New Champagne sells itself as 'high class budget', which in this case means 'normal midrange'. Not that there's anything wrong with that – it's spic and span and serves its purpose.

Legend Inn (☎ 806 0000; www.legendinn.com; 2 Jln Lg Jafaar; r/ste RM98/155; 🕸) Located across a busy road from the bus station, this modern block has all the requisite midrange amenities, and rooms are large and brightly furnished. It has a good restaurant downstairs too.

Hotel Seri Malaysia (☎ 806 9502; www.serimalaysia .com.my; Jln Taming Sari; r RM120; 🕸 🖾) Spotless chain hotel near the Lake Gardens and, less appealingly, right opposite the prison. It's a grand, and extensive, pink villa complex, offering the usual high standards of comfort and service.

PERAK

Taiping Resort (www.taipingresort.com; Jln Bukit Jana; from r RM120; ✷ ☄) If you'd like to head out of town for some peace, quiet and golf, this little resort tucked into the jungle hills 10km north of the city is quite a steal. Rooms are good in a chain-hotel kind of way, but the pretty location is the main draw. Annoyingly, it only takes online reservations.

Eating

Larut Matang Food Court (off Jln Panggung Wayang; mains from RM3) Come evening time, this is the best place for hawker food (and perhaps food in general) in the city, serving up awesome mee goreng, curry, laksa and the rest.

Kedai Kopi Prima (cnr Jln Kota & Jln Manecksha; mains from RM3; ☺ breakfast, lunch & dinner) This big, busy Chinese coffee shop spills out onto the street in the evenings, which it shares with the near-identical Tang Chen right opposite. Big-screen TVs, music and endless crowds make for a lively atmosphere. Try the *popiah* (delicious thin, wet spring rolls).

Bismillah Restoran (138 Jln Taming Sari; mains from RM3; ☺ lunch & dinner) One of the oldest, and most decrepit-looking, coffee shops, Bismillah is a simple but welcoming place noted for its biryani and roti; the latter is considered the best around.

Piano Café (☎ 807 9007; 7 Jln Panggong Wayang; mains from RM10; ☺ lunch & dinner Tue-Sun) Smart cafe serving Western dishes of the fish-and-chips variety, along with lots of fruit juices but no alcohol. There's occasional live music in the evenings.

Getting There & Away

Taiping is several kilometres off the main KL–Butterworth road. It's 90km south of Butterworth and 291km north of KL. The express-bus station is 7km north of the town centre, at Kemunting. Frequent buses go to Butterworth (RM5.90), Ipoh (RM6.45) and KL (RM19), with less-frequent connections to other destinations like Kota Bharu (RM22.75), Johor Bahru/Singapore (RM52), Kuantan (RM33.35) and Kuala Terengganu (RM45).

There are no hotels nearby, nor any reason to stay in Kemunting – hop on bus 8 (RM1) or take a taxi (RM8) to the town centre. Local buses leave across the street from Masjid Daerah Taiping. From here, buses depart every 15 minutes for Kuala Kangsar (RM3, one hour). There are also buses to Lumut (RM9.90, two hours, three daily).

Taiping's **train station** (☎ 807 5584) is 1km west of the town centre, on the KL–Butterworth line. There is one daily train to KL (RM24, seven hours) and one to Butterworth (RM8, three hours).

Long-distance taxis depart from the centre of town, near the police station.

BUKIT LARUT
☎ 05

Crouched in a wet and cool colonial atmosphere some 1019m above sea level is Bukit Larut (Maxwell Hill), the oldest hill station in Malaysia. It's not nearly as developed as the Cameron Highlands, and while the scenery is a little less dramatic, there's more of a sense of what hill stations were originally about here: elegant bungalows, quiet lanes, sweet-smelling gardens and not much noise but the wind in the leaves. There are no attractions other than the above, which suits some folks just fine.

Few people visit Bukit Larut – in fact, bungalows here only accommodate around 70 visitors. During the school holidays, all are full. Even if you don't stay, Bukit Larut can be an excellent day trip. Getting up to the hill station is half the fun, and once there, you've got fine views over Taiping and the Lake Gardens far below.

Sights & Activities

Most visitors go up and back by Land Rover (RM4.50 return, 7am to 6pm), though the hill is also a favourite with locals who walk up in three to four hours. It's a very scenic path, but don't imagine this is some casual stroll – you need to be fit to complete the walk. You could also choose to take a Land Rover up and walk down.

The first stop is the crumbling **Tea Gardens** checkpoint at the Km 5.5 marker, where a ramshackle guesthouse and a few exotic trees are the only reminder of the former tea estate. Next up, at the KM 9.5 marker, you'll find the Bukit Larut Guesthouse, Bungalow Beringin and a canteen for meals. The Land Rovers stop at the main administration office, where you book for the return journey if you haven't already – very advisable on weekends. There are some tame strolls through the nearby gardens from here.

The Land Rovers usually continue 2km up the hill to Gunung Hijau Rest House. Nearby are the Tempinis and Sri Kanangan bungalows, as well as the **Cendana nursery**, where tulips are grown. From here it's a 30-minute walk along the road, noted for its profusion of butterflies, to the **Telekom transmitter station** at the top of the hill.

The jungle on the hill is superb, but the only real trail for exploring leads off the main road from between the two transmission towers. (It's best to do all your walking in the morning, as afternoon rains cause dangerous, gigantic sparks – large enough to hit your head – along the transmission lines.) The trail follows a practically abandoned path to **Gunung Hijau** (1448m). You can usually only follow the leech-ridden path for about 15 minutes to an old pumping station (now functioning as a small Shiva shrine), but even on this short walk there's a good chance of seeing monkeys and numerous birds. Beyond the shrine the trail is periodically cleared but quickly becomes overgrown; it's advisable to take a guide with you. If you do make it to the summit, on clear days you can see clear out to the Selat Melaka (Strait of Melaka).

Walking back down the road, it takes half an hour from Gunung Hijau Rest House to the main post at Bukit Larut Guesthouse, another hour to the Tea Gardens checkpoint, then another 1½ hours to get to the Land Rover station at the bottom of the hill, 6km from the Taiping Lake Gardens.

Sleeping & Eating

You can book space in one of the bungalows by ringing ☎ 807 7241, or by writing to the Officer in Charge, Bukit Larut Hill Resort, Taiping. If you haven't booked earlier, ring from the Land Rover station at the bottom of the hill.

Bukit Larut Guesthouse (1036m) and **Gunung Hijau Rest House** (1113m) each has four double rooms costing between RM50 and RM60. The bungalows **Beringin** (RM150) at 1036m and **Tempinis** (RM150) at 1143m are equipped with kitchens, so you need to bring provisions. Beringin can accommodate up to eight people; Tempinis up to 10. You pay for the whole bungalow, regardless of how many people are in your party, so coming by yourself is an expensive proposition. Meals are available from the caretakers at the bungalows, but they need advance notice.

There is a basic **camping ground** (per person RM2) below the main resthouse near the Tempinis bungalow.

Next to the upper Land Rover office, the **Bukit Larut Guesthouse** (mains RM3-6) is usually open for meals and has impressive views. Simple rice and noodle dishes are the main menu items.

Getting There & Away

Prior to WWII, you had the choice of walking, riding a pony or being carried up in a sedan chair, as there was no road to the station. Japanese POWs were put to work building a road at the close of the war, and it was opened in 1948.

Private cars are not allowed on the road – it's only open to government Land Rovers, which run a regular service from the station at the foot of the hill, just above the Taiping Lake Gardens. They operate every hour on the hour from 7am to 6pm (until 4pm in the low season), and the trip takes about 40 minutes.

The winding road negotiates 72 hairpin bends on the steep ascent, and there are superb views through the trees on the way up. The Land Rovers going up and those going down pass each other midway at the Tea Gardens. Fares are paid at the bottom of the hill – it's RM2 to the administration office and RM2.50 to Gunung Hijau Rest House. Alternatively, you can walk to the top in three or four hours.

To book a seat in a Land Rover (which is advisable), ring the **station** (☎ 807 7241) at the bottom of the hill. A taxi from central Taiping to this station, about 6km east of the Lake Gardens, should cost RM8.

KUALA SEPETANG
☎ 05

Around 15km west of Taiping, Kuala Sepetang – still shown on some maps under its old name of Port Weld – is a small, scruffy Chinese town of minimal appeal. The main reason for coming out this way is to visit the **Matang Mangrove Forest Reserve** (☎ 858 1762; admission free; ◷ 8am-7pm). The forest, which stretches from here up the coast of Perak towards Seberang Perai (Penang), represents almost half of all Malaysia's gazetted mangrove cover, and is one of the country's most significant nature reserves.

The entrance to the reserve is about 500m outside the town; ask the driver to let you off when you see the big gateway and sign on your right reading 'Pejabat Hutan Kecil Paya Laut'. Here a raised wooden walkway winds its way through a small section of the reserve, allowing you to explore this fascinating ecosystem without getting your feet damp. There are several signs along the route explaining, in English, what plants you are looking at and how it all works. Smooth otters, leopard cats and macaques all inhabit this landscape, though you're unlikely to see much more than the odd bird and scampering lizard unless you're here in the early morning or evening.

If you wish to stay, there are some large **A-frame huts** (from RM38; 🏠), perched on stilts at the water's edge, which sleep between four and eight people. Only one has air-con, and there are shared bathroom blocks. There are also shared tents (RM30), and you can pitch your own here too for around RM10, but make enquiries first as space is limited.

You can explore the mangroves further by charter boat, although it can get quite expensive. The reserve office can set you up with a guide, but expect to pay around RM350 to RM500 for the day.

It may be possible to arrange meals, but there are several basic Chinese restaurants just down the road in Kuala Sepetang. There is also a bank and post office on the main road (Trump Rd), as well as fruit and vegetable stalls and a surprising number of snooker halls, but that's about it.

Getting There & Away

Blue Omnibus 77 runs every 40 minutes from 6.05am to 7pm between Taiping's local bus station and Kuala Sepetang (RM1.90, 30 minutes), with a couple of later departures after that.

Penang

Think of the term 'Southeast Asia'. South and east of what? Essentially, Asia's most influential countries: China and India. And for all the impact these titans have on the continent, there aren't many places where their societies meet in unfiltered, immediate cultural contact.

Then along comes Malaysia's smallest state: Penang. In a teak townhouse, an Indian man places joss sticks in front of a family altar studded with pictures of the Hindu god Rama, the Chinese bodhisattva Kuan Yin and black-and-white photos of his Chinese wife's departed ancestors. Later the couple may eat a curry of cinnamon bark, shallots, tamarind, coriander and chillies – ingredients sourced from Malaysia's mother cultures of Indian, Chinese and Malay.

Local food, by the way, is one of the top draws of the 'Pearl of the Orient,' but the living cultures those dishes stem from are the real reason to visit. Penang is the only one of Malaysia's 13 states to have a Chinese majority population, but rather than feeling mono-ethnic, it exemplifies Asia-as-entrepôt that is this nation at its best. Physical vestiges of the colonial era – low slung townhouses, narrow alleyways, tea shops, temples, Chinese mansions and Little India districts – make a visit to Georgetown eminently rewarding, while beyond lies a landscape of jungle, lakes, beaches, a cosy national park and, yes, a cool hill station.

South of one Asia, east of another, and Asia condensed. This state is about experiencing the continent's culture and history at its oldest and most evolving. And obviously, trying the curry.

HIGHLIGHTS

- Chowing on charred pork on rice while watching life pass by in **Georgetown** (p192)
- Exploring Chinese Assembly Halls and clanhouses like **Khoo Kongsi** (p184)
- Wandering to the top of **Kek Lok Si Temple** (p199).
- Relaxing on the beach at **Batu Ferringhi** (p204)
- Grounding yourself in the state's past in the **Penang Museum** (p184)

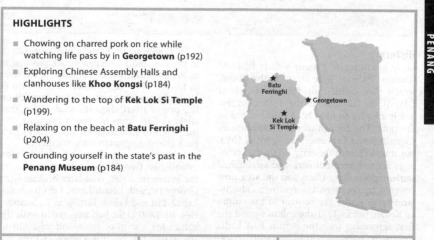

- TELEPHONE CODE: 04   - POPULATION: 1.52 MILLION   - AREA: 1031 SQ KM

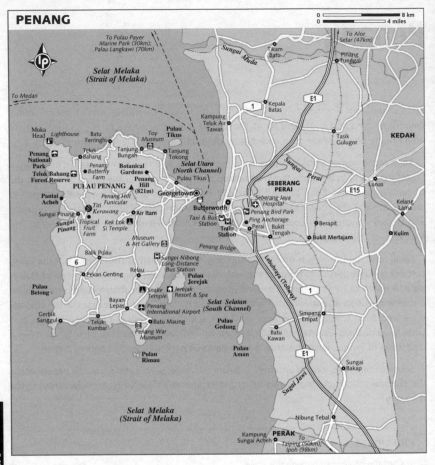

PENANG

History

Little is known of Penang's early history. Chinese seafarers were aware of the island, which they called Pulo Pinang (Betelnut Island), as far back as the 15th century, but it appears to have been uninhabited at the time. The English merchant-adventurer Captain James Lancaster swung by in 1593, but it wasn't until the early 1700s that colonists arrived from Sumatra and established settlements at Batu Uban and the area now covered by southern Georgetown. The island came under the control of the sultan of Kedah, but in 1771 the sultan signed the first agreement with the British East India Company, handing it trading rights in exchange for military assistance against Siam.

In 1786 Captain Francis Light, on behalf of the East India Company, took possession of Penang, which was formally signed over to him in 1791. Light renamed it Prince of Wales Island, as the acquisition date fell on the prince's birthday. It's said Light fired silver dollars from his ship's cannons into the jungle to encourage his labourers to hack back the undergrowth for settlement.

Whatever the truth of the tale, he soon established Georgetown, also named after the Prince of Wales, who later became King George IV, with Lebuh Light, Lebuh Chulia, Lebuh Pitt and Lebuh Bishop as its boundaries. By 1800 Light had negotiated with the sultan for a strip of mainland adjacent to the island; this became known as Province Wellesley, after the governor of India.

Light permitted new arrivals to claim as much land as they could clear, and this, together with a duty-free port and an atmosphere of liberal tolerance, quickly attracted settlers from all over Asia. By the turn of the century Penang was home to over 10,000 people.

The local economy was slow to develop, as mostly European planters set up spice plantations – slow-growing crops requiring a high initial outlay. Although the planters later turned to sugar and coconut, agriculture was hindered by a limited labour force.

In 1805 Penang became a presidency government, on a par with the cities of Madras and Bombay in India, and so gained a much more sophisticated administrative structure.

Penang briefly became the capital of the Straits Settlements in 1826 (including Melaka and Singapore) until it was superseded by the more thriving Singapore. By the middle of the 19th century, Penang had become a major player in the Chinese opium trade, which provided more than half of the colony's revenue. It was a dangerous, rough-edged place, notorious for its brothels and gambling dens, all run by Chinese secret societies.

In 1867 the simmering violence came to a head when large-scale rioting broke out between two rival Chinese secret societies, who had each allied themselves with similar Malay groups. Once the fighting had been brought under control, the British authorities fined each group the then huge sum of $10,000, the proceeds going to establish a permanent police force in the colony.

A royal charter awarded city status to Georgetown in January 1957, just seven months before Malaysian independence, and in the 1960s Penang became a free port. The island enjoyed rapid economic growth in the following decades, but lost its duty-free status to Langkawi in the 1980s. The 2000 repeal of a rent control law led to affordable housing issues that have yet to be totally resolved, as evidenced by Penang's architectural shift over the past few decades from townhouses to high-rise condos.

But this state also has the potential to be a good example of smart growth. Penang's economic engines are tourism and high-tech industries; thanks to the presence of international companies specializing in the latter sector, the 'Pearl of the Orient' is also known as the 'Silicon Valley of the East'. But the sustainability of local tourism rests on preserving at least a facsimile of old Penang.

Residents and tourists have complained about construction development denigrating the island's historical character, and preservation advocates launched a large media campaign in 2004 aimed at conserving the state's unique architectural heritage. Their efforts, to a degree, have succeeded: in 2008 Georgetown (as well as Melaka) was awarded Unesco World Heritage Status. Development issues have not vanished, but they are being addressed with a commendably robust public dialogue.

In 2008, Pakatan Rakyat (PR), the opposition coalition, took control of the state's parliament by 29 seats to Barisan National's (BN) 11, BN's worst performance in Malaysian history. The locally strong Gerakan party, which governed Penang since 1969, was also swept out of power. The platform of two of PR's constituent parties (anti-corruption and a secular, multi-ethnic state) went over well with Penang's large Chinese population, although the margin of the victory was a shock to many analysts.

Orientation

Penang encompasses Pulau Penang, or Penang Island, where all of the state's destinations of note are concentrated, and the mainland. This narrow strip of coast is known as Seberang Perai. There's little to see or do other than change buses or trains in the mainland town of Butterworth, a major transport hub with many more bus connections to other cities in Peninsular Malaysia. Trains running between Kuala Lumpur and Thailand also pass through Butterworth.

Climate

Penang has a tropical climate, with temperatures of between 21°C and 32°C year-round. Brief torrential downpours occur at all times of year, though the period between May and October sees more rain. Humidity is normally 85% to 90%.

SEBERANG PERAI

BUTTERWORTH

☎ 04 / pop 110,000

Butterworth is an industrial town defined to the outside world by its air-force base and ferry terminal. Most travellers use it strictly as a transport hub. The sole point of interest is the **Penang Bird Park** (Taman Burung Pinang; ☎ 399 1899; Jln Todak; adult/child RM20/10; ☻ 9am-7.30pm), 7km east of the ferry terminal across the river. This landscaped park houses more than 300 species of birds, mostly from Southeast Asia, including parrots, hornbills and hawks. If you're waiting for the train (or bus or whatever), a visit to the park is a pleasant way to while the day.

Most of the land transport (buses, taxis) between Penang and other places in Peninsular Malaysia and Thailand leaves from Butterworth's taxi and bus station next to the terminal for ferries going to or from Georgetown.

Sleeping & Eating

'You said the train was in the afternoon!' 'I'm sorry, I can't read military time.' 'Looks like we're stuck here for the night…'

Ambassadress Hotel (☎ 332 7788; 4425 Jln Bagan Luar; r from RM40; ☒) This sleepy Chinese hotel above a cheap *kedai kopi* (coffee shop) of the same name is a fair, if rather timeworn, budget option. Air-con rooms cost RM63, and all have attached bathrooms.

Hotel Berlin (☎ 332 1701; 4802 Jln Bagan Luar; s/d from RM100/120; ☒) A few doors down from the Ambassadress, the Berlin offers a bit more comfort, and discounts are normally available. It has a gym and sauna, and breakfast is included in the price, which is a good deal for Butterworth. We stress, for Butterworth.

Sunway Hotel (☎ 370 7788; www.sh.com.my; 11 Lebuh Tenggiri Dua, Seberang Jaya; s/d RM242/288; ☒ ▢) This modern tower close to the Penang Bird Park in the suburb of Seberang Jaya is aimed primarily at business travellers, with the usual smart international setup. Rooms sport 'oversized beds', and you can even get 'karaoke on demand' through your TV.

There are numerous cheap Chinese cafes scattered around the town centre. As ever, a reliable bet is **Sri Ananda Bahwan Restaurant** (☎ 323 6228; 2982 Jln Bagar Luar; mains from RM3; ☻ breakfast, lunch & dinner), which serves clean and consistently good Indian food (veg and nonveg); you'd be hard-pressed to spend over RM5. It has a particularly good selection of colourful, hand-made Indian sweets, which you can have wrapped up in a box to take away.

Getting There & Away

The mainland strip of Seberang Perai is easily accessed by road and rail from other parts of the peninsula. Butterworth is the transport hub, and the departure point for ferries to Penang, which is also linked to the mainland by road-bridge. For information on bus, ferry and air services, see Getting There & Away in the Georgetown section (p196).

TAXI

Not a good option unless you like being overcharged. Long-distance taxis operate from a depot beside the Butterworth ferry terminal on the mainland. Typical whole-taxi fares (which are negotiable) include such rip-offs as Ipoh (RM210), KL (RM350), Kota Bharu (RM350), Lumut (RM240) and Taiping (RM220).

TRAIN

The **train station** (☎ 323 7962) is next to the ferry terminal and bus and taxi station in Butterworth. One daily train runs to KL and two run in the opposite direction to Hat Yai in Thailand; check with www.ktmb.com.my for the latest info on fares and schedules.

PENANG

☎ 04 / pop 678,000

Penang, or Pulau Pinang, isn't the most physically beautiful island in Malaysia. In fact, it can be downright unsightly in places where the green jungle has been ploughed down by thickets of concrete condos. And having 'only' been inhabited for roughly 300 years, it's relatively young compared with much of Malaysia.

Yet Penang, along with Singapore, Hong Kong and Macau, is arguably one of the most fascinating islands in Asia. That comparison with former island colonies isn't superficial: this is the oldest of the British Straits settlements, predating both Singapore and Melaka. Look at the Straits on a map and their commercial importance vis-à-vis their geography is immediate and obvious: this was the watery road between Asia's two halves and the wet exit to the markets of Europe and the Middle East. As such, Penang straddles the juncture of Asia's two most influential cultures and the colonial empires that conquered them.

The island's mixed population, dominated by the business-savvy Chinese, is the genetic by-product of Penang's geographic location. The unique culture of this little fist of land, forged over decades of colonialism, commercial activity, hosting tourists and preserving backyards, is one Malaysia's most tolerant and cosmopolitan.

GEORGETOWN
☎ 04 / pop 300,000

For many, if not most visitors, Georgetown, the state's historic capital, *is* Penang, to the point that the two names become interchangeable. If your image of Penang is watermarked tumbledown Chinese shopfronts, British Raj–era architecture, trishaw-wide alleys and strings of paper Heavenly Lanterns casting street hawkers from the Malabar Coast to Macau under a blood-red celebratory glow – well, you're right on. That stuff is here.

So too are shopping malls, refurbished Chinese mansions and pubs, boutiques, design studios and cafes that wouldn't be out of place in a Western city centre. Traffic congestion and air pollution aside, it's easy to see why this is one of the most popular expat enclaves in Asia. Forgive us for employing the most overused cliché in the travel writer's phrasebook, but there really is a palpable collision of an older Asia and an Asia-that-will-be (and already is) in these narrow streets. The hotels and shops of Georgetown exemplify this phenomenon; the most popular stores seem to either sell antiques or electronics. The best hotels are gussied-up, well-amenitied heritage houses (see p192).

Georgetown is something of a mainstay on the Southeast Asian backpacker trail, and budget travellers will have no problems finding friends here. All classes of travellers should leave the hotel and hostel ghettoes and wander through the sensory playground that are Georgetown's backstreets: fortune tellers, blue joss smoke, chicken rice, Chinese opera and the sharp roast of a chilli. Eat up – the food here may be the best in Malaysia – and leave having experienced one of Asia's great mini-entrepôts.

Orientation

Georgetown is on the northeastern corner of the island, where the channel between island and mainland is narrowest.

A vehicle- and passenger-ferry service operates across the 3km-wide channel between Georgetown and Butterworth on the mainland. South of the ferry crossing is the Penang Bridge, reputedly the longest in Southeast Asia, which links the island with Malaysia's Lebuhraya (North–South Hwy).

Most places in Georgetown can easily be reached on foot or by trishaw. The old colonial district centres on Fort Cornwallis. Lebuh Pantai is the main street of the 'city', a financial district crammed with banks and stately buildings that once housed the colonial administration. After dark, exercise caution, as this area becomes eerily deserted.

You'll find many of Georgetown's budget hotels and hostels along Lebuh Chulia in Chinatown, where the usual cast of backpackers congregates in restaurants and bars. At the northern end of Lebuh Chulia, Jln Penang is a main thoroughfare and a popular shopping street. In this area are a number of midrange hotels and, at the waterfront end of the street, the venerable Eastern & Oriental (E&O) Hotel.

If you follow Jln Penang south, you'll pass the modern multipurpose Komtar shopping centre, and eventually leave town and continue towards Penang International Airport. If you turn west at the waterfront end of Jln Penang, you'll follow the coastline and eventually come to the northern beaches, including Batu Ferringhi. This road runs right around the island back into town, via the airport.

Finding your way around Georgetown can be slightly complicated. Jln Penang may also be referred to as Jln Pinang or Penang Rd – but there's also a Penang St, which is officially called Lebuh Pinang! (In Malay, 'Jalan' is technically 'road' while 'lebuh' is 'street') Similarly, Chulia St is Lebuh Chulia; Pitt St is sometimes Lebuh Pitt, but is shown on some maps and signposts as Jln Masjid Kapitan Keling. Many streets are still referred to locally by their English names; Lebuh Gereja, for example, is Church St, and Lebuh Pantai is Beach St. Maps are sold at bookshops (below). Don't lose your head over the above; Georgetown is pretty small and finding your way around becomes intuitive after a day or two.

Your feet are a good way of getting around, but if you get tired or the heat just gets to you, trishaws are ideal, particularly at night when travelling this way takes on an almost magical quality. See p198 for more information.

Information
BOOKSHOPS
There are lots of small shops along Lebuh Chulia.

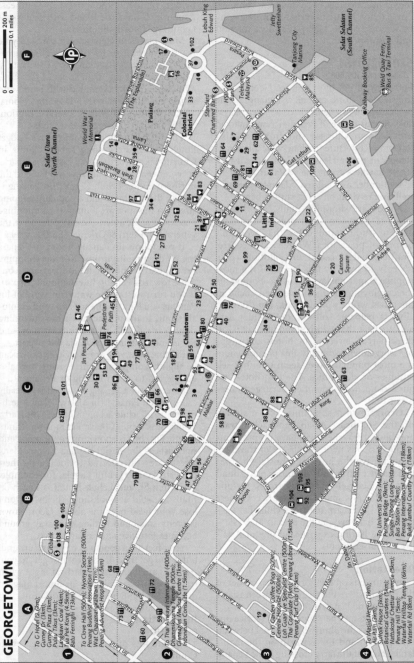

GEORGETOWN

INFORMATION

Eighteen Internet Café...............1 C2
Happy Holidays.........................2 C2
HS Sam Book Store...................3 C2
Immigration Office...................4 F2
Jim's Place............................(see 48)
Main Post Office.......................5 F3
NJ Books Centre.......................6 C2
Penang Heritage Trust...............7 E3
Popular Bookshop.................(see 92)
Silver-Econ Travel.....................8 C2
Stardust ....(see 54)
Tourism Malaysia......................9 F2

SIGHTS & ACTIVITIES

Acheen Street Mosque........ 10 D4
Alpha Utara Gallery.................11 E3
Cathedral of the Assumption.... 12 D2
Cheong Fatt Tze Mansion.........13 D2
City Hall.................................14 E1
Dr Sun Yat Sen's Penang Base.. 15 D3
Fort Cornwallis........................16 F2
Fort Cornwallis Chapel............(see 16)
Fort Cornwallis Lighthouse.......17 F2
Hainan Temple........................18 C2
Jewish Cemetery......................19 A3
Khoo Kongsi............................20 D4
Kuan Yin Teng.........................21 D2
Lim Kongsi...............................22 E3
Loo Pun Hong.........................23 D2
Market...................................24 D3
Masjid Kapitan Keling...............25 D3
Penang Gelugpa Buddhist
   Association.........................(see 23)
Penang Islamic Museum...........26 D3
Penang Museum......................27 D2
Peranakan Museum...............(see 38)
Pinang Gallery.........................28 E2
Pinang Peranakan Mansion......29 E3
Protestant Cemetery................30 C1
Seri Rambai..........................(see 16)
Sri Mariamman Temple............31 D3
St George's Church...................32 E2
State Assembly Building............33 F2
Supreme Court.........................34 E2
Town Hall.................................35 E2
Tua Pek Kong...........................36 D3
Victoria Memorial Clock
   Tower..................................37 F2

SLEEPING

100 Cintra Street......................38 C3
110 Armenian St.......................39 D3
Banana Guesthouse..................40 D3
Blue Diamond Hotel.................41 C2
Broadway Budget Hotel............42 E3
Cathay Heritage.......................43 C2
Cheong Fatt Tze Mansion .....(see 13)
China Tiger..............................44 E3
City Bayview Hotel....................45 D1
Eastern & Oriental Hotel...........46 D1
Hutton Lodge..........................47 B2
Jim's Place..............................48 C2
Malaysia Hotel.........................49 C2
Old Penang Guest House.........50 D2
Oriental Hotel.........................51 C2
SD Guesthouse........................52 D2
Segara Ninda...........................53 C1
Stardust..................................54 C2

EATING

1885....................................(see 46)
Ecco Cafe...............................55 C2
Ee Beng Vegetarian Food.........56 B2
Esplanade Food Centre............57 E1
Hammediyah...........................58 C3
Hawker Stalls..........................59 A2
Hot Wok.................................60 A2
Hui Sin Vegetarian
   Restaurant..........................61 E3
Jing-Si Books & Cafe................62 E3
Jit Seng Duck Rice....................63 C4
Kafeteria Eng Loh....................64 E3
Kayu Nasi Kandar....................65 C2
Khaleel Restaurant..................66 C2
Kheng Pin...............................67 C2
Kissa Koyotei...........................68 A1
Madras New Woodlands
   Restaurant..........................69 E3
Maharaj..................................70 C2
Mr Pot...................................71 C1
New World Park Food Court.....72 A2
Nyonya Baba Cuisine...............73 A2
Opera....................................74 C1
Passage Thru India..................75 C2
Rainforest Bakery....................76 D3
Red Garden Food Paradise &
   Night Market.......................77 C2
Restoran Kapitan.................... 78 D3

Restoran Nasi Padang
   Minang...............................79 B2
Sarkies Corner.....................(see 46)
Sky Hotel................................80 D2
Sri Ananda Bahwan..................81 E3
Thirty Two..............................82 C1

DRINKING

B@92.....................................83 E2
Farquhar's Bar......................(see 46)
Pitt Street Corner.....................84 E2
QEII..85 F3
Slippery Senoritas.................(see 96)
Soho Free House......................86 C1

ENTERTAINMENT

Dome..................................(see 92)
Glo......................................(see 96)

SHOPPING

100 Cintra Street ....(see 38)
Alpha Utara Gallery ....(see 11)
Auntie Sim..............................87 E2
Bee Chin Heong.......................88 C3
Chowraster Bazaar...................89 C3
Fuan Wong..............................90 D3
Hong Giap Hang......................91 C2
Komtar...................................92 B3
Lean Giap Trading....................93 C2
Oriental Arts & Antiques...........94 C1
Prangin Mall...........................95 B3
Renaissance Pewter.................96 D1
Royal Selangor Pewter.............97 E2
Sam's Batik House....................98 C2

TRANSPORT

AirAsia...................................99 D3
Cathay Pacific.........................100 B1
Ekspres Bahagia...................(see 102)
Firefly Airlines......................(see 92)
Hertz...................................101 C1
Langkawi Ferry Service...........102 F2
Local Bus Station....................103 B3
Long Distance Bus Services....104 B3
Malaysia Airlines....................105 B1
Newsia Tours & Travel............106 E4
Pengkalan Weld Bus Stop.......107 E4
Singapore Airlines..................108 B1
TransitLink City Bus Station..... 109 E3

HS Sam Book Store (☎ 262 2705; 473 Lebuh Chulia) One of the best for secondhand books, the 'most organised used bookshop in town' has a fair range of popular paperbacks. Organises car and bike rental, and luggage storage.
NJ Books Centre (☎ 261 6113; 425 Lebuh Chulia) Also buys and sells secondhand books.
Popular Bookshop (Komtar) Stocks novels, travel books, maps and a selection of books on Penang and Malaysia.

IMMIGRATION OFFICES
Immigration office (☎ 250 3410; 29A Lebuh Pantai)

INTERNET ACCESS
Almost every guesthouse along Lebuh Chulia and Love Lane operates a small internet cafe, and it's pretty easy to pick up a wi-fi signal in much of the town. Midrange and top-end hotels (especially the latter) also tend to have their own wi-fi networks. Rates below are RM3 per hour.
Eighteen Internet Café (☎ 264 4754; 18 Lebuh Cintra; ☉ 11am-2pm & 5-9pm Mon-Sat)
Jim's Place (☎ 261 8731; 431 Lebuh Chulia)
Stardust (☎ 263 5723; 370 Lebuh Chulia)

LIBRARIES
Penang Library (☎ 229 3555; 2936 Jln Scotland; ☉ 9am-5pm Tue-Sat, 9am-1pm Sun)

MEDICAL SERVICES
General Hospital (☎ 229 3333; Jln Residensi)

Gleneagles Medical Centre (☎ 227 6111; www
.gleneagles-penang,com; 1 Jln Pangkor)
Loh Guan Lye Specialist Centre (☎ 238 8888; www
.lohguanlye.com; 19 Jln Logan)
Penang Adventist Hospital (☎ 222 7200; www.pah
.com.my; 465 Jln Burma)

MONEY

Branches of major banks are on Lebuh
Pantai and Lebuh Downing near the
main post office, and most have 24-hour
ATMs. There are also ATMs at the base
of Komtar.

At the northwestern end of Lebuh Chulia,
there are numerous moneychangers open
longer hours than the banks and with more
competitive rates. Moneychangers are also
scattered around the banks on Lebuh Pantai
and at the ferry terminal, although you'll
probably get better rates on the mainland
from the moneychangers at the Butterworth
taxi and bus station (Map p176).

TOURIST INFORMATION

Penang Heritage Trust (☎ 264 2631; www.pht.org
.my; 26 Lebuh Gereja; ☯ 9.30am-12.30pm & 2.30-
4.30pm Mon-Fri) Information on the history of Penang,
conservation projects and heritage walking trails.
Tourism Malaysia (☎ 262 0066; 10 Jln Tun Syed Sheh
Barakbah; ☯ 8am-5pm Mon-Fri) Georgetown's main
tourist information office.
www.globalethicpenang.net Information on the
Penang Global Ethic Project, a local interfaith group that
organises talks and exhibitions on religions and peace
issues. See 'Walk of Faith' (p189) for information on the
project's excellent World Religions walking tour.
www.igeorgetownpenang.com An excellent
newsletter aimed at Penang residents that gives good
under-the-skin information on Georgetown.
www.ilovepenang.com Hey, we love you, ilovepenang
.com. Comprehensive information and a nicely designed
website.
www.penang.ws Fairly up-to-date clearing house of
hotel and restaurant listings.
www.penangfoods.com Guess what this website
focuses on?
www.tourismpenang.gov.my Details of sights and
restaurants in Penang.

Also useful is the monthly *Penang Tourist
Newspaper* (RM3), which has comprehensive
listings of shops, tourist attractions and hotel
promotions, as well as detailed pull-out maps.
It's usually available free from tourist offices
and some hotels.

TRAVEL AGENCIES

Most, but not all, of the agencies in
Georgetown are trustworthy. The following
are reliable operators that many travellers use
to purchase discounted airline tickets:
Happy Holidays (☎ 263 6666; www.happyholidays.
com.my; 432 Lebuh Chulia)
Silver-Econ Travel (☎ 262 9882; www.silverecon.com
.my; 438 Lebuh Chulia)

Dangers & Annoyances

Georgetown, like any big city, has its seamy
side. Foreign tourists have been attacked and
mugged in Love Lane and other dimly lit side
streets, and it may be unwise to linger in these
areas alone after dark. There are a lot of public
signs warning of snatch thieves on motorbikes
who pluck away purses, handbags and back-
packs, and prostitutes are considerably more
visible in Georgetown than other parts of the
country. With all of that said, be smart but
not overtly cautious. Penang in general and
Georgetown in particular are reasonably safe,
and given the high number of tourists, police
here tend to be easy to deal with in the unlikely
event that something bad does happen.

Off the street, robberies have occurred
in some backpacker hostels, so you should
never leave valuables, especially your passport,
unattended. There have also been reports of
Peeping Toms spying through the walls of
certain Love Lane hostels. Meanwhile, drug
dealing still occurs in Georgetown, despite
Malaysia's very stiff antidrug laws; don't
get involved.

Sights
COLONIAL DISTRICT

Penang has one of the greatest concentra-
tions of colonial architecture in Asia. Fort
Cornwallis is a good place to start a tour of
the colonial district around the waterfront.
Many of the buildings in the area are marked
with signs explaining their history and significance. You can follow the 'Heritage Trail'
walking tours, which also take in temples
and mosques in Chinatown – pick up a pamphlet of the routes at the tourist office or the
Penang Heritage Trust. There's also a free
bus shuttle (7am to 7pm Monday to Friday,
to 2pm Saturday), which runs between the
jetty and Komtar, winding its way through
the colonial core of Georgetown. It's a good
way to get a quick overview of the town, and
you can get on and off at various numbered

stops. A map of the route is in the *Penang Tourist Newspaper*.

Opposite the southeastern corner of Fort Cornwallis is the **Victoria Memorial Clock Tower**, a gleaming white tower topped by a Moorish dome. Donated by a local Chinese millionaire to honour Queen Victoria's Diamond Jubilee in 1897, it stands 18m (60ft) tall – one foot for each year of her reign. West of the clock tower are the offices of the Penang Heritage Trust on Lebuh Gereja (Church St); Lebuh Gereja, Lebuh Bishop and Lebuh Farquhar were the historical heartland of Penang's Eurasian community, mixed-race Catholic settlers who came here fleeing persecution in other parts of Asia.

A typical feature of Malaysian colonial cities is the *padang*, which is an open playing field surrounded by public buildings. Georgetown's *padang* stretches west from Fort Cornwallis to the **Town Hall** and **City Hall**, two of Penang's most imposing buildings, both of which have fine porticos. The Town Hall, completed in 1880, is Penang's oldest municipal building, and its beautiful restored ballroom is a regular venue for temporary exhibitions. The Town Hall's Hokkien nickname during colonial days was Ang Moh Kong Kuan: 'White Man's Club'. Behind it is the modern **Pinang Gallery** (Lebuh Duke; admission free; ☉ 9am-5pm Mon-Sat), with a rotating display of contemporary local art; it's a hit-or-miss thing, but the air-con is refreshing. The gallery is housed in Dewan Sri Pinang, the island's first multi-purpose hall.

On the southern side of the *padang* is the neoclassical **State Assembly building** (Dewan Undangan Negeri), and northwest along Lebuh Light is the equally impressive **Supreme Court**. In front of the court is a statue of James Richardson Logan, a British lawyer who earned his reputation, and much popularity, for representing non-whites in the 19th century. Logan's work resulted in the official recognition of a number of Chinese secret societies and their festivals, and he pushed for the Transfer of 1867, which resulted in the Straits Settlements becoming their own colony, as opposed to a subset of British India.

Behind the Supreme Court, **St George's Church** (☎ 261 2739; Lebuh Farquhar; ☉ services 8.30am & 10.30am Sun) is the oldest Anglican church in Southeast Asia. This gracefully proportioned building, with its marble floor and towering spire, was built in 1818 with convict labour. In the grounds there is an elegant little pavilion,

housing a memorial plaque to Captain Francis Light. Also on Lebuh Farquhar is the double-spired **Cathedral of the Assumption**, named for the feast day on which its Catholic founders landed here from Kedah.

In the **Protestant Cemetery** on Jln Sultan Ahmad Shah, the mouldering tombs of colonial officials huddle together under a canopy of magnolia trees. Here you'll find the graves of Captain Light and many others, including governors, merchants, sailors and Chinese Christians who had fled the Boxer Rebellion (1900) only to die of fever in Penang. Also here is the tomb of Thomas Leonowens, the young officer who married Anna – the schoolmistress to the King of Siam made famous by Deborah Kerr in the *King and I*. The 1999 remake, *Anna and the King*, was filmed in Malaysia, including some scenes in Penang (partly because the Thai government considered the movie insulting to the Thai monarchy).

Fort Cornwallis

For all its size, **Fort Cornwallis** (☎ 261 0262; Lebuh Light; adult/child RM3/2; ☉ 9am-6.30pm) isn't particularly impressive; only the outer walls stand, enclosing a pleasant park within. The star-shaped structure houses some vaguely informative exhibits, a poor Malaysian man is made to stand in full British colonial uniform at the gate and a speaker system seems to play the *1812 Overture* on repeat loop. It's all wonderfully surreal.

The fort is named for Charles Cornwallis, perhaps best known for surrendering at the Battle of Yorktown to George Washington, effectively ending the American Revolution. Visitors from the USA: have some apple pie. It was at the fort that Captain Light first set foot on the virtually uninhabited island in 1786 and established the free port where trade would, he hoped, be lured from Britain's Dutch rivals. Between 1808 and 1810 convict labour replaced the then-wooden building materials with stone. The star-profile shape of the walls allowed for overlapping fields of fire against enemies.

A bronze statue of Captain Light stands near the entrance, modelled on the likeness of his son, William because no pictures of him could be found. Said son was the founder of Adelaide, so visitors from Australia: have a pie floater. The small **chapel** in the southwest corner was the first to be built in Penang; the first recorded service was the marriage in

1799 of Francis Light's widow, Martina (rumoured to have been Eurasian), to a certain John Timmers.

Seri Rambai, the most important and largest cannon, faces the north coast and was cast in 1603. It has a chequered history; the Dutch gave it to the sultan of Johor, after which it fell into the hands of the Acehnese. It was later given to the sultan of Selangor, and then stolen by pirates before ending up at the fort.

In 2009, the state government announced it was opening tenders to private organisations interested in managing and possibly renovating the fort site, so the situation inside may be very different by the time you read this.

Penang Museum
From the town's foundation site, it's only a short stroll to the **Penang Museum** (☎ 261 3144; www.penangmuseum.com; Lebuh Farquhar; admission RM1; ☺ 9am-5pm Sat-Thu), one of Malaysia's best presented museums. The permanent exhibition is a comprehensive walk-through of Penang's history, festivals and cultures. No settler group is left out and all are admirably described in sympathetic detail, a testament to this state's admirable record of tolerance. Look out for the beautifully carved opium beds, inlaid with mother-of-pearl, and the incredible silk-brocade outfits once worn by the Baba-Nonya (Straits Chinese) population. Temporary exhibitions are eclectic, ranging from galleries of colonial prints to displays on traditional Malay seamanship.

Outside, one of the original Penang Hill funicular railcars is now a kiosk selling souvenirs, including antique costume jewellery and coins; all proceeds benefit the Penang Heritage Trust. The museum's front desk has good information and pamphlets on walking tours of Georgetown.

CHINATOWN
If the imposing profile of the colonial district's buildings represent Penang at its most stately and dignified, the spaghetti of worm-narrow streets clotted to its south is Penang at its most quintessential. Chinatown, which stretches from Lebuh Pantai to Jln Penang, centres on Lebuh Chulia and encloses Little India, Chinese Assembly Halls and the backpacker ghetto. The Penang of tiny tea shops owned by iron Chinese grandmothers, busted Indian stereo systems blaring '*Chuma chuma jai* – blgrfzzzzl' and calls to prayer mingling with the loud slap of mahjong tiles? All right here, folks.

What's there to do? Walk around some, soak up, walk s'more, soak, rinse, repeat. Peek into a temple, haggle at a vegetable market, slurp up some noodle soup and a sweaty bottle of beer with the locals. Political correctness and stereotypes be damned: this is Asia at its most alluring and romantic.

Khoo Kongsi
The *kongsi*, or clanhouse, is a major node of overseas Chinese communities. It is both a benevolent organisation for individuals with the same surname (in this instance, Khoo) and, in its way, an economic collective (indeed, the word as used in modern Chinese means 'company'). But it is also symbolises a deeper social, even spiritual contract between an extended clan, its ancestors and its social obligations. To this end, clanhouses and assembly halls are both the civic and religious backbone for many overseas Chinese, and the most impressive one in Penang is the Khoo clanhouse, or **Khoo Kongsi** (☎ 261 4609; www.khookongsi.com.my; 18 Cannon Sq; adult/child RM5/free; ☺ 9am-5pm), also known as Dragon Mountain Hall.

The Khoo are a successful clan, and they're letting the world know. Stone carvings dance across the entrance hall and pavilions, many of which symbolise, or are meant to attract, good luck and wealth. Note at the entrance a turbaned Sikh guardian watchman. The interior is dominated by incredible murals depicting birthdays, weddings and, most impressively, the 36 celestial guardians (divided into two panels of 18 guardians each). The fiery overhead lighting comes courtesy of enormous paper lamps. Gorgeous ceramic sculptures of immortals, carp, dragons, and carp becoming dragons (a traditional Chinese motif symbolising success) dance across the roof ridges. As impressive as all of this is, Khoo Kongsi was once more ostentatious; the roof caught fire on the night it was completed in 1901, an event put down to divine jealousy. The present *kongsi* dates from 1906.

Kuan Yin Teng
On Lebuh Pitt is the temple of **Kuan Yin Teng** (☺ 9am-6pm) – the goddess of mercy, good fortune, peace and fertility. Built in the early 19th century by the first Hokkien and Cantonese settlers in Penang, the temple is not large or especially impressive, but it's very central

and popular with the Chinese community. It seems to be forever swathed in smoke from the outside furnaces, where worshippers burn paper money, and from the incense sticks waved around inside. It's a very busy place, and Chinese theatre takes place on the goddess' birthday, celebrated on the 19th day of the second, sixth and ninth lunar months.

Cheong Fatt Tze Mansion

Built in the 1880s, the magnificent **Cheong Fatt Tze Mansion** (☎ 262 0006; www.cheongfatttzemansion .com; 14 Lebuh Leith; admission RM12) was commissioned by Cheong Fatt Tze, a Hakka merchant-trader who left China as a penniless teenager and eventually established a vast financial empire throughout east Asia, earning himself the dual sobriquets 'Rockefeller of the East' and the 'last Mandarin'.

The mansion, rescued from ruin in the 1990s, blends Eastern and Western designs, with louvred windows, art nouveau stained glass and beautiful floor tiles, and is a rare surviving example of the eclectic architectural style preferred by wealthy Straits Chinese of the time. The best way to experience the house, now a boutique hotel, is to stay here (see p192); otherwise hour-long guided tours (11am and 3pm Monday to Saturday) give you a glimpse of the beautiful interior.

Acheen Street Mosque

If you're entranced by the call to prayer wafting over the short walk from Khoo Kongsi, the Malay **Acheen Street Mosque** (Lebuh Acheh) is unusual for its Egyptian-style minaret (most Malay mosques have Moorish minarets). Built in 1808 by a wealthy Arab trader, the mosque was the focal point for the Malay and Arab traders in this quarter – the oldest Malay *kampung* (village) in Georgetown. Only Muslims can enter the mosque.

Penang Islamic Museum

The **Penang Islamic Museum** (☎ 262 0172; www. penangislamicmuseum.net; 128 Lebuh Armenian; adult/child RM3/1; ⏰ 9.30am-6pm Wed-Mon) is housed in a restored villa that was once the residence of Syed Alatas, a powerful Acehnese merchant of Arab descent, and later a recycling depot (really) of the Indian Chettiar community. Today it holds a wordy exhibition on the history of Islam in Malaysia and Penang, along with some 19th-century furniture. The main event is an upstairs life-sized diorama of a dock scene that depicts a maritime-oriented *haj* (pilgrimage to Mecca).

Hainan Temple

Probably the coolest feature of this temple is its impressive stone courtyard and the carved pillar work throughout said space, which is bedecked with more red paper lanterns than usual. This duochrome backdrop of slate and crimson looks like it should be the scene of the final fight in a kung fu movie or a *Mortal Kombat* video game. In fact, the **Hainan Temple** (Lebuh Muntri), completed in 1895, is dedicated to Mar Chor, China's patron saint of seafarers.

Tua Pek Kong

The name is ostensibly **Tua Pek Kong** (Lebuh Armenian), but this recently renovated structure, resplendent in red and gold and with polished black columns, has quite a few more aliases: Hock Teik Cheng Sin, Poh Hock Seah, Hokkien Kongsi and Tong Kheng Seah, among others. What's with all the names? Well, besides serving as a temple and assembly hall, this building has also been the registered headquarters of several secret societies (Aside: secret societies register their headquarters? Really? With who?). Each society occupied a different portion of the temple, which became a focal point during the 1867 riots/war between societies. The fighting got so intense a secret passage was built between here and Khoo Kongsi for the purpose of a quick escape. While you search for the corridor, be sure to admire the gilded filigree and lacquered roof beams that give this once underground HQ such an imperial Chinese vibe.

Loo Pun Hong

The tiny **Loo Pun Hong** (70 Love Lane) is one of the most unobtrusive of Penang's Chinese temples. Built in the 1880s, it is dedicated to Lo Pan, legendary inventor of carpentry tools, and is Malaysia's oldest carpenters' guild house. Set back from the lane, it has an ornate altar inside along with a giant drum and bell.

Penang Gelugpa Buddhist Association

This small **Buddhist Temple** (Love Lane), next to Loo Pun Hong, isn't particularly impressive compared to Penang's other religious buildings. But it is unique for being the major representative structure of the Gelugpa (Yellow

Hat) school of Buddhism. The Yellow Hats are a Tibetan order, and as such there are some beautiful Tibetan wall hangings in this temple that you'd be hard-pressed to find outside of a museum.

100 Cintra Street
At the time of research this property was being renovated, but usually the old house at **100 Cintra Street** (☎ 264 3581; adult/child RM5/2.50; ⏰ 11am-6pm Tue-Sun) houses the tiny Peranakan Museum, which celebrates Penang's Baba-Nonya heritage. Furniture, costumes, porcelain and household items are displayed in recreations of late-19th-century interiors (the house itself dates from 1881 and was restored a century later). A small antiques bazaar and a cafe are downstairs. There's accommodation on the middle floor.

Dr Sun Yat Sen's Penang Base
This well-preserved 19th-century **townhouse** (☎ 262 0123; 120 Lebuh Armenian; ⏰ 10am-2pm Mon-Sat) was where the founder of modern China, Dr Sun Yat Sen, organised the Penang Conference and planned the Canton Uprising, which established the Republic of China in 1911. The ground floor, with original tiled floors, furniture and Nonya-style kitchen, is open to visitors by advance reservation.

LITTLE INDIA
As Little Indias go, this one fills all the criteria: it's quite small and it's intensely, well, Indian. Men stand on the street and yell at you to come see their shop/restaurant/stall; pausing to look will result in the inevitable hard sell as folks try to hustle you into their business. Bright lights and scratchy music and purple saris and small Himalayas of spice take turns smashing up your normal dull sensory apparatus. All in all, this is one of the most evocative areas of the city.

Sri Mariamman Temple
Penang, as we have stressed, is a crossroads and cross-pollination of cultures, and to this end, one of the interesting elements of its houses of worship is their emphasis on providing a reference point for expatriates far from home. For local Tamils, the **Sri Mariamman Temple** (Lebuh Pitt; ⏰ 8am-noon & 4-9pm) fulfils the purpose of a Hokkien clanhouse: it's a reminder of the motherland and the community bonds forged within the diaspora. In this case, those bonds don't come from a benevolent society, but a typically South Indian temple, dominated by its entrance tower or *gopuram*. Erupting with sculpture, the tower serves several purposes: it represents Mt Meru, the cosmic mountain that supports the heavens, and delineates the line between this world and the realm of the gods, which begins in the temple compound. Local Tamils pay homage to Tamil Nadu by worshipping Mariamman, a mother goddess popular with diaspora Indians who represents the soil of, if not home, at least the land of sometimes distant origin. This temple was built in 1883 and is Georgetown's oldest Hindu house of worship.

Penang's **Thaipusam** procession begins here (see p189), and in October a wooden chariot takes the temple's deity for a spin around the neighbourhood during **Vijayadasami** festivities.

Pinang Peranakan Mansion
The wealthy Baba-Nonyas of the Straits colonial period had some of the most eclectic tastes of their time; their wealth and their home's position on so many trade routes afforded access to English tilework, Scottish iron embellishments, continental European art and furniture and, of course, the heights of Chinese opulence in interior design. All of the above crash together rather beautifully in the restored **Pinang Peranakan Mansion** (☎ 264 2929; www.pinangperanakanmansion.com.my; 29 Lebuh Gereja; adult/child RM10/free; ⏰ 9:30am-5pm Mon-Sat), former home of Chung Keng Quee, 19th-century merchant, secret-society leader and all-round community pillar. His ornate home is full of antiques and furniture of the period he lived in. There's also an exhibition on Nonya customs, and guided tours take place at 11.30am and 3.30pm.

Masjid Kapitan Keling
Penang's first Indian Muslim settlers (East India Company troops) built **Masjid Kapitan Keling** (⏰ 9am-5.30pm) in 1801 at the junction of Lebuh Buckingham and Lebuh Pitt. The mosque's domes are yellow, in a typically Indian-influenced Islamic style, and it has a single minaret. It looks sublime at sunset. Mosque officials can grant permission to enter.

Alpha Utara Gallery
Housed in an attractively renovated traditional townhouse, **Alpha Utara Gallery** (☎ 262 6840;

www.alpha-utara.com; 83 Lebuh China; admission free; ◷ 10am-6pm Mon-Sat, noon-5pm Sun) is an exhibition space for paintings by contemporary local artists, based around the works of Penang-born artist Khoo Sui Hoe. There are temporary exhibitions spread over two floors, and a bookshop downstairs.

OTHER SIGHTS
Wat Chayamangkalaram & Dhammikarama Temple
An interesting study in the diversity of Buddhist architecture are two temples just off Jln Burma on the main road to Batu Ferringhi. The **Temple of the Reclining Buddha** (Wat Chayamangkalaram; ◷ early morning-5.30pm) is a typically Thai temple with its sharp-eaved roofs and ceiling accents; inside it houses a 33m-long reclining Buddha draped in a gold-leafed saffron robe. The icon represents the Buddha's attainment of nirvana and peaceful passage from this existence, although the claim that it's the third-longest reclining Buddha in the world is dubious. The symbols on the Buddha's feet represent the marks of a true Buddha (a title that means 'enlightened one' as opposed to a name). Also note the entrance and exit; the former is set off by a Naga, a Southeast Asian water dragon, while the latter is marked by a Chinese dragon, the East Asian equivalent of the same mythical animal – another example of two Asias on one island.

The **Dhammikarama Burmese Buddhist Temple** stands opposite and is a rare instance of a Burmese Buddhist temple outside Burma (now Myanmar). There's a series of panel paintings on the life of the Buddha lining the walkways, the characters dressed in typical Burmese costume, while inside typically round-eyed, serene-faced Burmese Buddha statues stare out at worshippers. A pleasant garden and apartments for monks occupy the back grounds, while two large stone elephants flank the gates. Built in 1805, this was Penang's first Buddhist temple; it has been significantly added to over the years.

You can get to both temples on TransitLink bus 202; Minibus 26, 31 or 88; or Hin Bus 93 from Komtar or along Lebuh Chulia.

Penang Buddhist Association
Completed in 1931, this unusual Buddhist temple is situated on Jln Anson about 1km west of town. Instead of the typical colourful design of most Chinese temples, this particular temple shows art deco influences and looks like a frosted cake, all white and pastel. Interior Buddha figures are carved from Italian marble, and glass chandeliers hang above. Penang's Buddhist community gathers here on **Wesak Day** (April/May) to celebrate the triple holy-day of the Buddha's birthday, attainment of enlightenment and death.

Other Mosques & Temples
The glossy, modern **Masjid Negeri** (State Mosque) is at Air Itam, about 1km west of town. It's the biggest in Penang with a striking 50m-high minaret.

Nattukotai Chettiar Temple on Waterfall Rd, near the Botanical Gardens (see p200), is the largest Hindu temple in Penang and is dedicated to Bala Subramaniam, the young incarnation of Murugan, patron deity of Tamil Nadu (where most Malay Indians trace their roots). Further along on the left side is a gate leading up to the **Waterfall Hilltop Temple**, the destination of the Thaipusam procession from Little India's Sri Mariamman Temple.

Northwest of Georgetown, past Gurney Dr out at Tanjung Tokong, **Tua Pek Kong** is dedicated to the Chinese God of Prosperity and dates from 1837.

Suffolk House
On the banks of the Air Itam river, 6.5km west of Georgetown's centre, is the most impressive piece of Anglo-Indian architecture outside of India and one of the flagship causes of the Penang Heritage Trust: **Suffolk House**. This grand home was the original residence of Francis Light, founder of the colony and native of Suffolk, England. Many of the British residences in Penang owe at least some of their features to the ancestral influence of Suffolk House. Paintings of the house in its heyday suggest something like Cotswold-on-Itam.

In 1974 the house was in such poor repair that it was declared structurally unsafe and sealed off. For many years its future looked dire, but in one of Malaysia's rare conservation successes, funds were eventually secured for its full restoration, which was completed in 2007. At the time of research there were plans to open the mansion to the public – check the websites of the **Penang Heritage Trust** (www.pht. org.my) and **Badan Warisan** (www.badanwarisan.org. my) for details.

PENANG

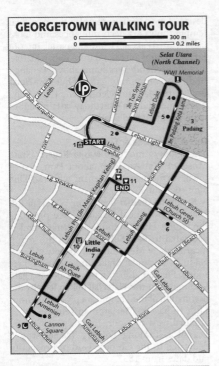

GEORGETOWN WALKING TOUR

0 ——————— 300 m
0 ——————— 0.2 miles

WALK FACTS

Start Penang Museum
Finish Pitt Street Corner
Distance 3.1km
Duration Two to three hours

Activities

Penang has some exceptionally affordable international-standard golf courses. The island's premier course is located at **Bukit Jambul Country Club** (☎ 644 2255; www.bjcc.com.my; 2 Jln Bukit Jambul; 18 holes from RM90) near the airport. *Golf Malaysia* magazine rated it the second most beautiful course in Malaysia; the stunning and very challenging 18 holes were carved straight out of the rocky jungle terrain.

At the **Penang Turf Club** (☎ 229 3233; www.penang turfclub.com; Batu Gantong) horse-racing events take place over two consecutive weekends every two months. Seats are cheap, but gambling is illegal. **Horse riding** is sometimes offered Monday to Friday.

Diving and snorkelling excursions to tiny Pulau Payar, around 32 nautical miles

north of Penang, are run by **Langkawi Coral** (☎ 899 8822; www.langkawicoral.com; 16 Jln Tanjung Tokong; snorkelling/diving RM240/380), which also does day trips to Langkawi (RM300/200 per adult/child).

Walking Tour

It's a tall order, but in one walk we'd like to give you a taste (sometimes literal) of Penang's history, architecture, food and, most importantly, imagery. Don't feel obligated to stick to our exact route; half the fun is exploring little side streets and letting serendipity guide your journey.

The natural starting point is the **Penang Museum** (1; p184), where you can read up on everything you're about to walk past. Head east, then up to the waterfront, passing the **Supreme Court** (2; p183) as you go; check the statue of James Richardson Logan, an advocate for non-whites during the colonial era. Walk up to the not-so-impressive waterfront, then head briefly east before turning down Jln Padang Kota past the green **padang (3)** and the grandiose architecture of the **City Hall** (4; p183) and the **Town Hall** (5; p183). Now proceed east along Lebuh Light, then south on Lebuh Penang. A short detour will pop you into the impressive **Pinang Peranakan Mansion** (6; p186), the old digs of one of Georgetown's great merchant barons.

Continue south into **Little India** (7; p186) and take a deep breath of all that spice and sense of place. If you're hungry, grab a curry. (If you don't like Indian food, there's Chinese just up on Lebuh Gereja. If you don't like either, really, you're in the wrong city). At Lebuh Pasar, head west past rows of shops selling milky Bengali sweets, then south along Lebuh King to the intersection of King and Lebuh Ah Quee.

Pause for a minute and look around. This intersection is our favourite in the city, the most quintessential crossroads in all of Georgetown. To your south is a Chinese Assembly hall and rows of slate-grey, fading Chinese shopfronts, their wooden eaves rotting into water-splotched walls. To your north is a small Indian mosque, and just across the street is a large Malaysian cafeteria where folks watch televised badminton while snacking on *nasi lemak*.

Phew. OK, head west and south on Lebuh Pitt into **Khoo Kongsi** (8; p184), the most impressive Chinese assembly hall in the city,

---

WALK OF FAITH

One of the best walking tours of Penang on offer (and there are many) is Global Ethic Penang's **World Religions Walk**, which takes you past the iconography and houses of worship of Christians, Muslims, Hindus, Sikhs, Buddhists and Chinese traditional religion. Rather than crib the tour here, we'd prefer to direct you to the website: www.globalethicpenang.net/webpages/act_02b.htm. We'd just add (to round out the world's belief systems) Penang's old **Jewish cemetery**, located on Jln Zainal Abidin between Jln Burma and Jln Macalister.

---

then continue a short distance to the Malay **Acheen Street Mosque** (**9**; p185). Head north along Lebuh Pitt to the Hindu **Sri Mariamman Temple** (**10**; p186). And then...enough diversity. You need a beer. Sink one in style at **B@92** (**11**; p195) or opt for the more dive-meets-Chennai vibe of **Pitt Street Corner** (**12**; p195).

Tours

Ping Anchorage (☎ 397 7993; www.pinganchorage.com.my; 25B Jln Todok 2, Seberang Jaya) over on the mainland runs several tours, including the four-hour Hill and Temple tour, which visits Penang Hill and the Kek Lok Si Temple (p199), round-island tours and trips to Penang National Park (p203). Tours cost between RM88 and RM129 (cheaper for groups of three or more), including pick-up from your hotel.

Penang Heritage Trust (☎ 264 2631; www.pht.org.my; 26A Lg Stewart; ⌚ 9.30am-12.30pm & 2.30-4.30pm Mon-Fri) organises a few walking tours, including the 'Little India Experience' and the 'Heritage Trail', taking in the Cheong Fatt Tze Mansion (p185). Both last around three hours and cost RM60, including entry fees. It also has free brochures detailing self-guided walks, such as the 'World Religions Walk' and 'Historic Georgetown Trails'.

Several agents around town book a range of tours at similar prices, including **Happy Holidays** (☎ 263 6666; www.happyholidays.com.my; 432 Lebuh Chulia).

Festivals & Events

All the usual festivals are celebrated in Penang, and are spiced with this island's extraordinary enthusiasm. Current events are listed in the *Penang Tourist Newspaper* and at the website www.igeorgetownpenang.com.

January–February

Thaipusam This masochistic-looking festival is celebrated as fervently here as in Singapore and KL, but without quite the same crowds. The Sri Mariamman (p186), Nattukotai Chettiar (p187) and Waterfall Hilltop (p187) temples are the main centres of activity in Penang.

Chinese New Year Celebrated with particular gusto in Penang. The Khoo Kongsi (p184) is done up for the event, and dance troupes and Chinese opera groups perform all over the city. On the night before the 15th day of the new year, a fire ceremony takes place at Tua Pek Kong (p185) temple. Numerous Chinese mansions and assembly halls throw their doors open to the public at this time as well.

Chap Goh Meh The 15th day of the New Year celebrations, during which local girls throw oranges into the sea from the Esplanade. Traditionally, the girls would chant: 'throw a good orange, get a good husband', while local boys watched and later contacted their dream girl through matchmakers. New Year is also one of the only times to see Baba-Nonya performances of *dondang sayang* (spontaneous and traditional love ballads).

May–August

Penang International Dragon Boat Festival (May/June) A colourful and popular regatta, featuring the traditional dragon boats.

Penang Food & Cultural Festivals (August) Highlights the best of Penang's multi-ethnic heritage.

September–December

Lantern Festival (mid-September) Commemorates the end of Mongol rule in China. It's celebrated by eating moon cakes, Chinese sweets once used to carry secret messages to underground rebel leaders in ancient China.

Deepavali (October) The Hindu 'Festival of Lights' is celebrated with music and dancing at venues in Little India.

Pesta Pulau Penang (November-December) The annual Penang Islands Festival features various cultural events, parades and a fun-fair.

Sleeping

Penang has a variety of accommodation, ranging from dives to big corporate-like block towers to boutique heritage properties. Lebuh Chulia and Love Lane make up the heart of Penang's backpacker land, crammed with cheap hostels and hotels. Quality varies enormously, and it pays to check a few out before parting with your cash. Midrange options are mostly found along Jln Penang, where you'll find a string of high-rises. If you're going top-end, there are some large

PENANG

uber-resorts to choose from (although these tend to be concentrated in Batu Ferrenghi), but we'd recommend opting for one of Penang's excellent heritage-house-cum-hotels.

Be warned that during holidays, most notably Chinese New Year, hotels tend to fill up very quickly and prices can become ridiculously inflated; if you intend to stay at this time, book well in advance.

All budget options listed have shared bathrooms unless otherwise noted, while midrange and top end all have private bathrooms.

BUDGET

Blue Diamond Hotel (☎ 261 1089; 422 Lebuh Chulia; dm/s/d from RM8/20/28; ✗ ▣) The Diamond is set in a beautiful old Chinese warehouse that contains one of…well, the most *memorable* hostels in Malaysia. The owner, a 30-year veteran of Penang's post office, is almost unnaturally friendly and helpful. If you don't mind a bit of grot (especially in your toilets), this is a good bet. If you like to drink, it's a better one: beer and spirits magically coalesce into guests' hands at all hours. The worst cover band in Malaysia often plays in the courtyard; their follow-up show is to hit on every female guest within arms' reach. This may not sound appealing, yet there's an unmistakably fun vibe here, like that crazy uncle you can't help but love, and lots of return backpackers (male and female) swear by this joint. The on-site Mexican restaurant is as good as you'd expect, which is to say: not very. Air-con rooms with private showers cost RM45.

100 Cintra Street (☎ 264 3561/3581; 100 Lebuh Cintra; dm/s/d RM12/28/40) This place puts us in a pickle. Set in a wonderful old Peranakan house that also incorporates a cafe and small museum (p186), this hotel is one of the most atmospheric places to stay in the city (which is saying something). But at the time of research we weren't able to visit due to renovations. However, in the past the simple, striking budget rooms were spare, more Zen minimalist than cheapskate corner-cutting. There was a mattress on a wooden platform with a mosquito net and small fan and, all in all, guests were made to feel like junior agents of the East India Company.

Old Penang Guest House (☎ 263-8805; 53 Love Lane; dm/s/d RM15/26/32.50) This hotel is probably the only budget heritage hotel in town that feels as if its been put through a laundry machine. Particularly a boutique-ish laundry machine.

Hardwood floors, white walls, high ceilings and splashes of red paint add a hip solid-coloured vibe to this hostel, otherwise set in a restored pre-WWII house that could easily serve as set piece in a Maugham or Theroux short story. Air-con rooms cost RM50.

Banana Guest House (☎ 262 6171; www.banana newguesthouse.com; 355 Lebuh Chulia; s/d from RM18/25; ✗ ▣) The Banana Pancake Trail (the Southeast Asian backpacker route) lands very firmly in Banana Guest House, another one of those all-purpose hostels/bars/internet cafes/travel agencies you encounter from Bangkok to Bali. Rooms are OK, although some are sectioned off by the thinnest of walls. Come night this is a good spot to meet other travellers, and the bar staff are the friendliest on the island. Pricier air-con digs come with or without toilet (RM50/60).

SD Guesthouse (☎ 264 3743; 15 Love Lane; s/d/t from RM18/25/35; ✗ ▣) There's creaky floors and cubicle walls, but also free wi-fi and a social vibe; the ups and downs must balance out, because SD is very popular with Georgetown backpackers.

Jim's Place (☎ 016-653 6963, 261 8731; 431 Lebuh Chulia; r RM20-30; ✗ ▣) This handful of fan and air-con rooms are above a popular travellers' cafe. It's the usual backpacker-basic arrangement, with shared bathrooms, and the owner can arrange bus tickets and Thai visas.

Stardust (☎ 263 5723; 370 Lebuh Chulia; s/d from RM25/35; ✗ ▣) Despite having a name that sounds like an ABBA album, Stardust is several cuts above the average Chulia hotel or Love Lane flophouse. Rooms are spotlessly clean and refreshingly airy, and there's wi-fi throughout (plus an internet cafe downstairs).

Hutton Lodge (☎ 263 6003; www.huttonlodge.com; 17 Jln Hutton; dm/s/d from 28/50/60; ✗ ▣) The Hutton's exterior promises a bit more than its interior delivers. From the outside, you see and expect an Old World jaunt with the allure of Asia during the Jazz Age. But the rooms, while comfy and spacious, look like Ikea bed sets for children. It's a decent deal price-wise, but don't expect a heritage-hotel atmosphere a la old Penang.

Broadway Budget Hotel (☎ 262 8550; www.broad waybudgethotel.com; 35 Lebuh Pitt; s/d/t from 35/45/55; ✗ ▣) Hovering between the budget and midrange price categories, the Broadway is a good deal if you want some comfort minus a heck of a lot of atmosphere. Its centrally located, the rooms are large (if bland) and the beds are comfy. There's in-room wi-fi for RM7 a day.

MIDRANGE

Segara Ninda (☎ 262 8748; www.segaraninda.com; 20 Jln Penang; r RM70-110; ⌘ ▯) This elegant century-old villa was once the town residence of Ku Din Ku Meh, a wealthy timber merchant and colonial administrator in what is now southern Thailand. His home has been tastefully renovated, incorporating original features such as the carved wooden ventilation panels and staircase and tiled floors. There are 14 simply furnished rooms of varying sizes, and some are very compact, so it pays to check a few out before deciding.

Malaysia Hotel (☎ 263 3311; www.hotelregalmalaysia. com.my; 7 Jln Penang; s/d from RM108/138; ⌘ ▯) This well-located tower is good for travellers needing the experience of staying in a decently mid-market high-rise. Rooms at the back are quieter and have views of the Cheong Fatt Tze Mansion and the Penang Bridge.

Cathay Heritage (☎ 262 6271; 15 Lebuh Leith; r from RM115; ⌘) Once the Cathay Hotel, the owners of this spot clearly picked up on the marketing trend of the moment and made the appropriate name switch to 'Heritage'. And to be fair, this hotel is set in a very atmospheric Chinese mansion, something like a cross between a traditional assembly hall and a Comfort Inn. Rooms aren't as colourful as the lobby and exterior, but they're perfectly serviceable.

Oriental Hotel (☎ 263 4218/4211; www.oriental.com .my; 105 Jln Penang; r from RM120; ⌘) On the corner of Jln Penang and Lebuh Leith, the Oriental is handily placed and pretty vanilla. The decor doesn't seem to have been changed in decades, which is OK, since rooms are clean and comfortable.

City Bayview Hotel (☎ 263 3161; www.bayviewho tels.com; 25A Lebuh Farquhar; r RM150-185; ⌘ ▯) The Bayview pretty much tops out the corporate-tower genre of Penang hotels, both in terms of quality and price, although seasonal specials keep rates competitive. You know what to expect: a big shiny lobby with glass and steel, several different types of restaurant and quite nicely appointed rooms – the top ones have good views out over the Straits.

TOP END

G Hotel (☎ 238 0000; www.ghotel.com.my; 168 Persiaran Gurney; r from RM295; ⌘ ▯ ▣) The antithesis of the E&O is the G, which exemplifies (and aggregates) the contemporary tides of design, lifestyle and luxury amenities sweeping Malaysia's best hotels. Rooms are studies in minimalist, cubist cool, collections of geometric form set off by swatches of blocky colour. Wi-fi, a yoga studio, a spa and a gym round out an exhaustive list of perks. There's a good crowd of creative and simply successful professionals blowing through the doors, giving the G a vibe that's as Manhattan as it is Malaysia.

Eastern & Oriental Hotel (☎ 222 2000; www.e-o -hotel.com; 10 Lebuh Farquhar; ste from RM1000; ⌘ ▯ ▣) One of the classic grande-dame hotels of the famous Sarkies brothers, hoteliers extraordinaire to the British Empire in Asia, the E&O isn't so much a throwback to the colonial era (the building is not the original hotel) as a concerted effort at recreating that time period within a modern building. All in all, the E&O pulls it off. Porters are deferential and dressed (rather humiliatingly) in white shorts, knee socks and pith helmets; the rooms, decked out with white linens, polished marble floors and earth tone accents, look like the sort of suites where Kipling or Maugham would sip port and smoke cigars. Of course, cleverly concealed within the Victorian facade are modern amenities like cable TV, wi-fi, the works. The sea-facing lawn, where you'll find the biggest and oldest java tree in Penang, is a nice spot for relaxing, sipping your gin rickey and yelling for more ice before waxing your moustache.

Eating

In 2009, Penang was voted by *New York Times* readers one of 44 must-see destinations – and the bulk of public opinion seemed to focus on the state's cuisine, particularly its street food. Well, big surprise: culture combinations tend to produce good food, and Penang's position in the Straits means interesting ingredients were always just the next merchant ship away.

Coming to Penang and not sampling the local food is like going to a Thai island without ever setting foot on the sand or in the sea – you're missing the whole point. And while some menu items might seem a little strange to the uninitiated, in general Penang cooks produce food that is easy even on conservative pallets; you don't need that much daring to enjoy some perfectly prepped chicken-rice.

PENANG

THE BUSINESS OF HERITAGE

Ever since Georgetown's inscription on Unesco's World Heritage list in 2008, dilapidated shop-houses and mansions have been snapped up and fought over as both savvy investors and heritage lovers scrutinise one of the most unique urban landscapes in Malaysia.

Several private investors have followed the lead established over a decade ago by architect Laurence Loh, whose restoration of the **Cheong Fatt Tze Mansion** (see p185; ☎ 262 5289; www .cheongfatttzemansion.com; 14 Lebuh Leith; r from RM250; ✗) resulted in one of the country's most atmospheric boutique heritage hotels. Even if you don't have a clue what feng shui is, by the time you leave you'll realise it's powerful stuff. The house is arranged around a plant-filled central courtyard from which the greatest *chi* energy emanates. Each room is uniquely themed. Wi-fi is available.

The following recommended boutique heritage properties were open, or about to open, during our research:

110 Armenian St (☎ 955 1688; www.bontonresort.com.my; 110 Armenian St; d/house from RM900/1200; ✗ 🖳) Beautifully restored three-bed shophouse in a rapidly gentrifying but still authentic part of the Heritage Zone. The owner is planning on adding several more hotel-style rooms in a row of yet-to-be-converted houses across the street, as well as a shop stocking arty local products.

China Tiger (☎ 012-501 5360; www.tigerrock.info; 25 Lebuh China; d RM 950; ✗ 🖳) This places offers just two suites, but they're wonderful. The two levels are connected by spiral staircases, original art decorates the walls, and guests have access to a serene courtyard. Next door, an art gallery is planned.

Clove Hall (☎ 229 0818; www.clovehall.com; 11 Clove Hall Rd; d RM500; ✗ 🖳 ✗) Standing on land where the Sarkies Brothers had their first home in Penang, this expertly restored 1920s mansion has five suites: three in the main house and two in smaller buildings in the surrounding gardens, which include a lovely pool.

One of the most famous local dishes is *asam* laksa, or Penang laksa, a fish soup with a sour taste from tamarind *(asam)* paste. It's served with special white laksa noodles in street stalls all around the island.

CHINESE
There are so many Chinese restaurants in Georgetown that it's impossible to cover them all here. So, in addition to trying the places listed below, go for a wander, find a place that's crowded, ask a local what's good and order up.

Kafeteria Eng Loh (cnr Jln Gereja & Lebuh Penang; mains from RM2.50; ✗ breakfast, lunch & dinner) A very simple and rather frayed coffee shop, always full of locals chatting over bowls of *kway teow* (broad rice noodles) and chicken-rice.

Jit Seng Duck Rice (☎ 262 2172; 246 Lebuh Carnarvon; RM3-6; ✗ noon-3pm) This hawker stall on Lebuh Carnarvon (Jln Cheong Fatt Tze) has an enviable reputation as one of the best providers of duck-rice in town. For the record, duck-rice is exactly what it sounds like: lovingly seasoned and roasted duck with a crisp, sweet skin, concealing firm, juicy flesh below, served with rice softened by a rich gravy and, often enough, a clean, clear soup. The roast pork is great too. Located by the Star Hotel.

Hui Sin Vegetarian Restaurant (☎ 262 1443; 11 Lebuh China; meals around RM4; ✗ breakfast & lunch Mon-Sat) This excellent value buffet restaurant is the place to go for a filling meat-free lunch. Take what you want from the selection of vegetables, curries and different beancurds on offer, and you'll be charged accordingly. Wash it down with a glass of Chinese tea.

Kheng Pin (80 Jln Penang; mains from RM4; ✗ 7am-3pm, closed Mon) This hawker stand has a few specialities locals swear by, most famously *lorbak* (spiced ground pork wrapped in bean curd dipped in black gravy) and Hainan chicken-rice, one of the great fast foods of East Asia. The latter is deceptively simple – steamed chicken and rice cooked in chicken broth – easy to muck up and so good when executed right, as it is here. The state government sends Kheng Pin's owner to Adelaide in Australia every year to promote Penang cuisine, so you know he's doing something right.

Ee Beng Vegetarian Food (☎ 262 9161; 20 Lebuh Dickens; meals around RM5; ✗ breakfast, lunch & dinner) A popular self-service place for cheap and mostly vegetarian food of the tofu and green vegetables variety. It also serves fish curry

Sky Hotel (☎ 262 2322; 348 Lebuh Chulia; around RM6; ✗ 11.30am-2.30pm) It's incredible that this gem sits in the middle of the greatest concentration of travellers in Georgetown, yet is somehow almost exclusively patronised (in huge, enthusiastic numbers) by locals. People – what's happening? *Sigh*. It is incumbent on you to try the *char siew* (barbecued pork), *siew bak* (pork belly), *siew cheong* (honey-sweetened pork) and roast duck. Order your pork *pun fei sau* (half fat, half lean) to get that proper combination of slightly wet and firm roasted goodness.

Yi Garden Coffee Shop (150 Jln Macalister; mains from RM6; ☽ dinner & late night) There's all kinds of hawker stalls here that serve, according to locals, some of the best *pan mee* (flat, sour noodles) and oyster omelettes in town. Very much a Georgetowner hangout, this is the kind of street food that attracts lots of mothers with children – in case you were worried about catching any kind of bug off the road.

INDIAN

Little India is replete with cheap eating places, especially along Lebuh Pasar and Lebuh Penang, serving up curries, roti, tandoori and biryani. Other places are scattered all around town. Several small restaurants and stalls in this area offer cheap North and South Indian food.

Restoran Kapitan (☎ 264 1191; 93 Lebuh Chulia; mains from RM3; ☽ breakfast, lunch & dinner) Very busy restaurant specialising in tandoori chicken and biryani, along with fish and mutton curries. They do a mean masala tea, too.

Madras New Woodlands Restaurant (☎ 263 9764; 60 Lebuh Penang; mains from RM3; ☽ breakfast, lunch & dinner) One of the best bets for vegetarians offers tasty banana-leaf meals and North Indian specialities, including lots of traditional sweets.

Sri Ananda Bahwan (☎ 264 4204; www.srianandabahwan.com; 55 Lebuh Penang; mains from RM3; ☽ breakfast, lunch & dinner) Basic Indian eatery, seemingly forever full of chatting locals, serving up tandoori chicken, *roti canai* (unleavened flaky flat bread) and *murtabak* (roti canai filled with meat or vegetables). There's an air-con dining hall if you prefer more comfort.

Khaleel Restaurant (☎ 885 1469; 48 Jln Penang; mains from RM4; ☽ 24hr) When you've hit the sauce too hard, there's always Khaleel, a 24-hour curry house that is consistently packed with happy, masticating Tamil customers. In point of fact, the chow is just as good sober as sloshed.

Passage Thru India (☎ 263 0306; 11 Lebuh Leith; mains from RM12; ☽ lunch & dinner) Top-notch Indian

cuisine is on offer at this smart restaurant in a restored townhouse, decked out with traditional carvings and paintings. The feed is what you would expect at a fine Indian dining establishment in a Western city.

Maharaj (☎ 262 0263; 132 Jln Penang; mains from RM14; ☽ lunch & dinner) For a slightly more refined take on your banana-leaf meal, hit up the dark and intimate Maharaj, which serves some fine cuisine with a regional focus on Andhra Pradesh, Kerala and Tamil Nadu, India's spicy south.

MALAY

New World Park (102 Jln Burma; ☽ lunch & dinner) If you're nervous about eating street food, this is the place to come. The famous hawker stalls of Swatow Lane have been moved into this flash pavilion, where gems of the Malaysian street are prepped in a sanitized, almost mall-like atmosphere. Laughing families and friends all line up (seriously line up) for curry *mee* (noodles in a curry-like soup), fishball soup and other specialties, served under indisputably clean and safe conditions.

Hammediyah (164 Lebuh Campbell; mains from RM3; ☽ lunch & dinner) There's lots of halal food available in the kitchen, but you, like all the locals in line, shouldn't leave without trying the *murtabak*, a crepe-esque dish filled with beef and minced onions.

Kayu Nasi Kandar (☎ 264 4767; 216 Jln Penang; mains from RM4; ☽ breakfast, lunch & dinner) Popular food court–style place serving up cheap and tasty Malay and Indian dishes, including fish curry, tandoori chicken and vegetarian options.

Restoran Nasi Padang Minang (☎ 262 9161; 92 Transfer Rd; meals around RM5; ☽ lunch & dinner) Considered the best restaurant in town for Padang food, essentially a large buffet of rice that you scoop selected meats and vegetables onto – think fried fish, fried chicken, veg cooked in chilli paste and the like.

NONYA

Penang, like Melaka and Singapore, was the home of the Straits-born Chinese, or Baba-Nonya, who combined Chinese and Malay traditions, especially in their kitchens. Penang's Nonya cuisine is a tad more fiery due to the island's proximity to Thailand. These days, though, true Nonya cuisine is becoming harder to find and the restaurants are a bit out of the way.

Hot Wok (☎ 227 3368; 124 Jln Burma; mains from RM9; ☽ lunch & dinner Wed-Mon) Located in a grand

Nonya mansion, this restaurant feels slightly upscale but is pretty reasonably priced. Try the *otak-otak* (fish wrapped in banana leaves) and *sambal sotong* (chilli squid).

our pick Nyonya Baba Cuisine (☎ 227 8035; 44 Jln Nagore; mains from RM12; Ⓥ lunch & dinner Wed-Mon, dinner only Tue) Located in a beautiful old Chinese household, this is a great place to sample authentic Nonya food – try the *curry kapitan* (chicken curry) or *hong bak* (pork in thick gravy).

JAPANESE
Kissa Koyotei (☎ 226 6272; 148 Jln Hutton; mains from RM15; Ⓥ lunch & dinner) Get good sushi and ponderous set Japanese lunches in this vaguely surreal restaurant, where the waitresses prance about in pink maid and schoolgirl outfits to loud J-pop.

WESTERN
There's a concentration of smart Western restaurants and coffee bars on the short pedestrianised section of Jln Penang leading up towards the E&O Hotel.

Ecco Cafe (☎ 262 3178; 402 Lebuh Chulia; from RM15; Ⓥ lunch & dinner, closed Sun) We'd normally be wary of a place selling pizza in the heart of backpacker land, but Ecco shows up our prejudice for the small-mindedness it is. Equally popular with hip locals and travellers, there is some damn fine thin-crust European-style pizza on offer in a cosy space that's as contemporary as it is intimate.

Opera (☎ 263 2893; 3E Jln Penang; mains from RM18; Ⓥ lunch & dinner) Cool jazz murmuring in the background, Oriental artworks and crisp linen tablecloths provide a chic atmosphere for some interesting Western and Asian dishes, including 'hazelnut fish and chips' and stir-fried ostrich. The space also doubles as a lifestyle/design store, in case the ostrich wasn't posh enough.

Thirty Two (☎ 262 2232; 32 Jln Sultan Ahmad Shah; mains from RM40; Ⓥ dinner) Some of the finest dining in the city occurs at this genteel restaurant located in an elegant seaside mansion. The menu is upscale haute French with a touch of Asian fusion (mainly in the form of local ingredients); it's all very good stuff. It offers a cocktail bar and live jazz on Friday and Saturday evenings, but don't forget to dress smart casual.

Sarkies Corner (☎ 222 2000; 10 Lebuh Farquhar; lunch buffet RM42, dinner buffet from RM58; Ⓥ lunch & dinner)

Sarkies offers different themed dinner buffets every day of the week; the focus shifts from Asian to Western to fusion to the kitchen sink, and its uniformly good stuff (you'll want to dress up). The lunch buffet is gorgeous – it plucks menu items from across the globe, and if you can't find something you want, you're a very picky eater. Finally, for the nascent colonialist deep in your soul, high tea (RM46) is served in the garden from noon to 3pm every Sunday.

1885 (☎ 261 8333; 10 Lebuh Farquhar; mains from RM45; Ⓥ dinner) The elegant main restaurant of the E&O Hotel serves excellent Western cuisine, such as sea bass with truffle sauce, and roast duck. Open for dinner only, with a smart-casual dress code (no T-shirts, shorts or sandals).

QUICK EATS
We've listed some of Georgetown's best hawker stalls, but there are too many to catalogue in this book. The seafront Esplanade Food Centre is good, as much for delightful sea breezes as the Malay stalls serving delicious Penang specialities. Gurney Drive is packed with cheap and cheerful goodness, and at night the Red Garden behind Hotel Continental offers up stall food and cheesy karaoke – is there a better combination?

Smaller hawker congregations flash up all around town every evening. Lebuh Chulia has a concentration of Western-style cafes catering to backpackers.

Mr Pot (☎ 228-8303; cnr Jln Penang and Jln Sultan Ahmad Shah; mains from RM3; Ⓥ 24hrs) The name of this place suggests it traffics in one of two forms of custom, and seeing as one of those is punishable by death, you can safely assume you will get very fine coffee (especially iced) at all hours, 365 days a year.

Rainforest Bakery (☎ 261 4641; 300 Lebuh Chulia; Ⓥ 11am-7pm) This darling little take-away bakery, run by twin brothers Jesse and Jerry Tan, produces European-style baked treats such as scones, cookies and bagels

Jing-Si Books & Cafe (☎ 261 6561; 31 Lebuh Pantai; RM3; Ⓥ noon-8pm) A stylish oasis of spiritual calm, this outlet for a Taiwanese Buddhist group's teachings is a wonderful place to revive yourself over a pot of one of its interesting teas or coffees (all only RM3).

Komtar has a supermarket and numerous fast-food outlets. On the 5th floor there's a another hawker centre serving all the usual Chinese and Malay dishes, plus some Indian food.

PENANG

Drinking

Most of the backpacker hostels serve beer, but it's not terribly cheap and places tend to shut by 11pm. The exception is Blue Diamond, which seems to close whenever the last person passes out.

ourpick Pitt Street Corner (94 Lebuh Pitt) Pitt Street Corner feels like the offspring of a hipster bar crossed with a sports pub plunked in Tamil Nadu. It's not a dive but it sure isn't posh, either. Basically, it's a friendly spot for Tamil guys to get together, sink some beer, watch some football and Bollywood and sink a few rounds of pool. While we imagine women would be treated fine here, we never saw any inside the bar on any of our visits.

Farquhar's Bar (10 Lebuh Farquhar) Colonial British-style bar inside the E&O Hotel, serving beer, traditional pub food and cocktails; try its signature drink, the Eastern & Oriental Sling (RM16.50) brought to you by a white-coated barman.

Soho Free House (50A Jln Penang; noon-midnight) Rather dimly-lit British-style pub spread out over two floors serving, allegedly, Malaysia's biggest selection of draught beers. It shows live sports on satellite TVs on Saturday and gets rowdy in an expat sort of way some nights.

Slippery Senoritas (The Garage, 2 Jln Penang) Vaguely Spanish-style bar that has occasional live music. The dress code is smart casual and it's popular with Western expats and the Malaysians who love them (or is that the other way round?).

B@92 (92 Lebuh Gereja) Hip bar with a laid-back attitude that features some live acts and hosts a pretty large – and mixed – expat and well-to-do locals crowd. Has an atmosphere somewhere between a British pub, American chain bar and small music venue.

Entertainment

Glo (☎ 261 1066; The Garage, 2 Jln Penang) If you've been longing for superclubs/meat markets while travelling in Malaysia, here's a taste of what you've been missing. Here you'll encounter ear-splitting bass, big lights, lots of smoke, guys with slicked hair and ladies in little dresses. You know the drill.

QEII (☎ 261 2126; 8 Pengkalan Weld) Seemingly surrounded by the Straits, QEII serves passable pizza and better ambience; this spot usually snags a good DJ who keeps funk and slow house grooving over the waterfront views.

Dome (Komtar) This geodesic dome is one of those structures that looked dated the minute it was finished but, in any case, it still hosts some pretty good rock shows and other live acts.

Shopping

Penang is a good place to shop, with plenty of outlets for local crafts and antiques as well as cameras and electronics at competitive prices, although KL has a wider range. Bargaining is usually required, except in department stores. Jln Penang is the best shopping street in Georgetown. A good souvenir is Penang Pewter, a rather more affordable version of the better-known Royal Selangor Pewter, though of equal quality.

ANTIQUES

Lean Giap Trading (☎ 262 0520; 449 Lebuh Chulia; 10.30am-6.30pm Mon-Sat) This jumbled-up little store sells a miscellany of goods, including silverware, Oriental furniture, porcelain and glass. It's got some high quality stuff among the shelves, but you need to poke around with a fair bit of background knowledge.

Oriental Arts & Antiques (☎ 261 2748; 440 Jln Penang; 11am-6pm Mon-Sat) Anything old seems to end up in this place, which has a selection of porcelain, furniture, jewellery, toys and general bric-a-brac.

100 Cintra Street (100 Lebuh Cintra) A small collection of antique stalls occupies the ground floor of this old building. One sells only drinking glasses, others sell porcelain and assorted knick-knacks. For more information about this place, see p186.

ARTS & CRAFTS

Alpha Utara Gallery (☎ 262 6840; www.alpha-utara.com; 83 Lebuh China; admission free; 10am-6pm Mon-Sat, noon-5pm Sun) Penang's best gallery displays the work of native son Khoo Sui Hoe and other excellent local artists like Eaton Tam and Dom Ke Pa.

Auntie Sim (☎ 016-489 4511; 20 Lebuh Pitt; 10am-6pm) The hours aren't exact, but the fortunate might be: Auntie Sim is a reader of cards, palms, your face and the fates. This author, for instance, will apparently be engaged by 30 and is 'not very smart.' Go figure.

Bee Chin Heong (☎ 261 4113; 58 Lebuh Kimberley; 10am-8.30pm) This interesting outlet sells a colourful, bewildering assortment of religious statues, furniture and temple supplies;

PENANG

if you're after a huge Chinese couch, a household shrine or have RM55,000 to spend on a 2m-tall carved wood Buddha, this is the place to come. Even if you're not buying, it's still worth a look round.

Fuan Wong (☎ 262 9079; www.fuanwong.com; 88 Lebuh Armenian; ☺ 11am-6pm Mon-Sat) This small gallery showcases the exquisite fused-glass creations of Penang artist Wong Keng Fuan. Also in the same building is Studio Howard (www.studiohoward.com), which showcases excellent photography of Penang street scenes, architecture, etc.

Hong Giap Hang (☎ 261 3288; 193-195 Jln Penang; ☺ 10am-8pm Mon-Sat, 11am-5pm Sun) If you're looking for pewter products, this place has one of the best ranges in town. It also sells woodcarvings, jewellery, porcelain, crystal and batik.

Renaissance Pewter (☎ 264 5410; the Garage, 2 Jln Penang; ☺ 10.30am-7pm Mon-Sat) Locally made Renaissance pewter is another, much cheaper, alternative to Royal Selangor. Decorative tankards, tea caddies, vases and keyrings can be had here.

Royal Selangor Pewter (☎ 263 6742; 30 Lebuh Light) The top name in Malaysian pewter. This outlet stocks the current range, and pewter-making workshops can be arranged here, costing RM50 for about one hour. Book at least two days in advance.

Sam's Batik House (☎ 261 8528; http://samsbatik house.com; 159 Penang St) When the late Mr Shamdas was dubbed 'Sam' by American soldiers, a legend was born. This is the best place in town for buying sarongs, batik shirts and Indian fabrics and fashions; where else are guys going to find tops that could fit them in on a Bollywood video set?

SHOPPING CENTRES

Chowraster Bazaar (Jln Penang) This shabby old market hall is full of food stalls downstairs, with lots of fruit on display. Upstairs there are clothes stalls, secondhand-book stalls and simple cafes.

Komtar (Jln Penang) A vast modern mall with hundreds of shops selling everything from clothes, shoes and electronics to everyday goods.

Prangin Mall (Jln Penang) Adjoins Komtar and houses a huge number of shops and restaurants, including smarter chain stores such as Parkson Grand, with a wide range of clothes, cosmetics, household goods and suchlike.

Getting There & Away

AIR

In 2007 Firefly Airlines, based out of Penang, threw its hat into the Asia budget airlines stakes.

Airline Offices

AirAsia (☎ 261 5642; 332 Lebuh Chulia, Georgetown)
Cathay Pacific (☎ 226 0411; Menara Boustead, 39 Jln Sultan Ahmad Shah, Georgetown)
Firefly (☎ 250 2000; Komtar, Penang Rd, Georgetown)
Malaysia Airlines (☎ 217 6321/3/6; 38 Jln Sultan Ahmad Shah, Georgetown)
Singapore Airlines (☎ 226 3201; Wisma Penang Gardens, 42 Jln Sultan Ahmad Shah, Georgetown)
Thai Airways International (☎ 226 6000; Wisma Central, 142 Jln Burma, Georgetown)

Domestic Flights

There are several daily connections between Penang and KL, Johor Bahru and Langkawi. Prices vary depending on how far in advance you book, with some fares (for all towns) hovering as low as 38RM (that's basically free with just taxes) and others as expensive as 500RM or more.

International Flights

Penang is a major centre for cheap airline tickets, although international airfares are less competitive than they used to be. For long-running, reliable agents in Georgetown, see p182.

BOAT

Eight ferries constantly run (at least every 15 minutes) from Butterworth to **Pulau Penang** (☎ 310 2377, mainland ferry) from 6am to 12.30am and from 5.30am to 1am from the **island** (☎ 210 2363, island ferry). The fare is adult/child RM1.20/60, with free returns.

Both **Langkawi Ferry Service** (LFS; ☎ 264 3088, 263 1398; www.langkawi-ferry.com; PPC Bldg, Pesara King Edward) and **Ekspres Bahagia** (☎ 263 1943; PPC Bldg, Pesara King Edward) operate a shared ferry service to Medan in Sumatra. Travel agencies will book you into whichever company has open seats, but the boats are all the same. These land in Belawan, and the journey to Medan is completed by bus (included in the price), usually taking about 4¼ hours (but sometimes as long as five or six). The ferry leaves both Sumatra and Georgetown at 9am every day (one way/return RM110/180, child RM60/100).

The same two companies also run daily ferries from Georgetown to Kuah on Langkawi (one way/return RM60/115, child RM45/85, 1¾ to 2½ hours). Boats leave at 8.30am and 8.45am; the second service calls in at Pulau Payar first, but you won't be able to disembark unless you're on a diving or snorkelling package (see p188). Boats return from Langkawi at 2.30pm and 5.30pm. Book a few days in advance to ensure a seat.

BUS

Long-distance bus services leave from the express bus station on Jln Sungei Nibong, just to the south of Penang Bridge. Although travel agents, guesthouses and hotels on Lebuh Chulia sell tickets, it's generally safer to buy them in person at the bus company offices at the station. Taxis to the express bus station cost around RM25 from central Georgetown. You can also take a 303 or 401/401A bus from Komtar mall in central Georgetown (RM2).

From Sungei Nibong there are several daily buses to KL (RM27 to RM60), as well as less frequent buses to Kota Bharu, Melaka, Kuala Terengganu and elsewhere – book well in advance. There are five daily buses to Tanah Rata in the Cameron Highlands (RM23.50 to RM28). Please note that the above prices are especially subject to change.

Many more buses leave from across the channel in Butterworth next to the mainland ferry terminal, and a few long-distance buses also leave from other parts of Georgetown. **Newsia Tours & Travel** (☎ 261 7933; 35-36 Pengkalan Weld) is a major agent.

Many long-distance buses depart in the evening. Typical one-way fares:

Destination	Fare
Alor Setar	RM6.30
Cameron Highlands	RM23.50-28
Ipoh	RM10.70
Johor Bahru	RM49
Kota Bharu	RM27.90-35
Kuala Lumpur	RM27-60
Kuala Perlis	RM9-13
Kuala Terengganu	RM40-53
Kuantan	RM43
Lumut	RM14.90
Melaka	RM36.20
Singapore	RM53
Taiping	RM11.35
Tapah	RM40

From the bus station at Komtar, there are also bus and minibus services to Thailand, including Hat Yai (RM35); Phuket (RM61 to RM70); Ko Pipi (RM88 to RM90); Ko Samui (RM80); and even Bangkok (RM105 to RM120), though it's a long haul and the train is a lot more comfortable. The minibuses don't go directly to some destinations; you'll probably be dumped for a change of vehicle in Hat Yai or Surat Thani, sometimes with significant waiting times. It's better to buy your ticket from a guesthouse that contracts directly with a minibus agency, instead of from bucket shops on Lebuh Chulia. Then, in the case of your minibus showing up two hours late, or not at all, you have someone to hold responsible. However, you might get cheaper tickets if you buy directly at the bus station.

Getting Around

Seberang Perai and Penang are linked by road-bridge and a 24-hour ferry service. Georgetown is well served by bus, and trishaws (see p198) are a popular way to get around the city centre. Buses from Georgetown to other parts of the island are less frequent and getting around the island by road is easiest with your own transport.

TO/FROM THE AIRPORT

Penang International Airport (PEN; ☎ 643 4411) is 18km south of Georgetown. There's a coupon system for taxis from the airport. The fare to Georgetown is RM40.

Taxis take about 45 minutes from the centre of town, while the bus takes at least an hour. Yellow Bus 83 runs to and from the airport (RM1.50) hourly from 6am to 9pm, with stops along Pengkalan Weld, Komtar and Lebuh Chulia.

BOAT

Ferries between Georgetown and Butterworth run roughly every 20 minutes from 6am to 12.30am; boats leave Georgetown from 5.30am to 1am. The journey takes 15 minutes. The adult/child fare is RM1.20/60 sen; cars cost RM7.70 (depending on the size), motorcycles RM2. Return is free.

BUS

As in Kuala Lumpur, the federal, as opposed to state government, runs the locals air-conditioned bus service under the auspices of **Rapid Penang** (☎ 238 1313; www.rapidpg.com.my).

PENANG

Eight colour-coded 'corridors' further divided into 34 routes connect the entire island and the mainland; a comprehensive map can be found at www.rapidpg.com.my/journey-planner/route-maps. Buses tend to run every 20 to 45 minutes, usually from 6am to 11pm daily, but check ahead at the Rapid Penang website. There are stops all around the state, with many concentrated at Georgetown and its ferry points.

Fares are a minimum RM1.40, maximum RM4; most trips shouldn't cost more than RM3. By the time you read this, international tourists should be able to buy a RM20 'passport' that provides unlimited rides for one week. Popular routes and prices from Komtar (Kompleks Tun Abdul Razak, Jln Penang) in central Georgetown are listed below:

Snake Temple 302/401/401E; RM2.70
Kek Lok Si 201/203; RM2
Penang Hill 204; RM2
Teluk Bahang 101; RM2.50
Batu Ferringhi 101; RM2
Butterworth (via Penang Megamall) 704 and 701; RM4.8

Although they are supposedly being replaced by the Rapid Penang fleet, we were able to ride some of the older, non-air conditioned state public buses during research. The fares were similar to Rapid Penang; the only difference seemed to be that the driver didn't mind if passengers smoked out the window.

CAR
Penang Bridge is one of the longest bridges in Asia at 13.5km. If you drive across to the island, there's a RM7 toll payable at the toll plaza on the mainland, but no charge to return.

Rental
Penang's an easy place to rent a car, but you'll probably have to reserve in advance, especially for weekends and holidays or if you need an automatic car. Rates start at around RM100 per day plus insurance, but drop for longer rentals. Good deals can be found at smaller agents, though the main companies are also worth trying for special deals.

There are many car-hire companies in Georgetown:

Avis (☎ 643 9633; Penang International Airport)
Hawk (☎ 881 3886; Penang International Airport)

Hertz Penang International Airport (☎ 643 0209); Georgetown (☎ 263 5914; 38 Lebuh Farquhar)

MOTORCYCLE & BICYCLE
You can hire bicycles from many places, including travellers' guesthouses and shops along Lebuh Chulia, or out at Batu Ferringhi. It costs RM10 to rent a bicycle, and motorcycles start at RM30 per day. Before heading off on a motorcycle, just remember that if you don't have a motorcycle licence, your travel insurance probably won't cover you.

TAXI
Penang's taxi drivers flatly refuse to use their meters, so negotiate the fare before you set off. Typical fares around town cost around RM6 to RM12. Outlying sights serviced by taxi from Georgetown include Pulau Tikus (RM15), Batu Ferringhi (RM45), Botanical Gardens (RM40), Penang Hill Funicular/Kek Lok Si Temple (RM40), Snake Temple (RM35) and Penang International Airport (RM35).

TRISHAW
Bicycle rickshaws are an ideal way to negotiate Georgetown's backstreets and cost around RM30 per hour – but, as with taxis, it's important to make sure you agree on the fare before departure. You won't have any trouble finding a trishaw – more often than not, the drivers will hail you! From the ferry terminal, a trishaw to the hotel area around Lebuh Chulia should cost RM10 (or you can walk there in about 15 minutes).

AROUND THE ISLAND
You can make a circuit of the island by car, motorcycle or bicycle, but it's not possible to circle the whole island by bus. If travelling by motorcycle or car, plan to spend about five hours, with plenty of sightseeing and refreshment stops. If you're on a bicycle, allow all day.

It's 70km all the way round, but only the north-coast road runs beside the beaches. The route takes you from Georgetown around the island clockwise. The road to the airport is congested and built up, but it gets much quieter further around on the island's western side.

Penang Hill (Bukit Bendera)
Rising 821m above Georgetown, the top of Penang Hill (Map p176) provides a cool retreat

from the sticky heat below, being generally about 5°C cooler than at sea level. From the summit there's a spectacular view over the island and across to the mainland. There are some gardens, a simple food court, with one of the original cable-cars kept on show outside, a hotel, police station and post office at the upper funicular station. At the top are an exuberantly decorated **Hindu temple** and a **mosque**. Penang Hill is wonderful at dusk as Georgetown, far below, starts to light up.

Penang Hill was first cleared by Captain Light soon after British settlement in order to grow strawberries (it was originally known as Strawberry Hill). A trail to the top was opened from the Botanical Gardens waterfall and access was by foot, packhorse or sedan chair. The official name of the hill was Flagstaff Hill (now translated as Bukit Bendera), but it is universally known as Penang Hill.

Efforts to make it a popular hill resort were thwarted by difficult access, and the first attempt at a mountain railway, begun in 1897, proved to be a failure. In 1923 a Swiss-built funicular (one way/return RM3/4, every 30 minutes 6.30am to 9.30pm Sunday to Friday, to 11.30pm Saturday) was completed. A tiny **museum** (admission free) inside the station displays some photographs and oddments from those early days. The trip takes a crawling 30 minutes, with a change of carriages at the halfway point. On the way, you pass the bungalows originally built for British officials and other wealthy citizens. Queues on weekends and public holidays can be annoyingly long, with waits of up to 30 minutes.

If you're fit, a number of roads and **walking trails** traverse the hill; you can walk the 5.5km to the Botanical Gardens (Moon Gate; p200) in about three hours from the trail near the upper funicular station. The easier Jeep track from the top also leads to the gardens, just beyond Moon Gate. A signboard on the hill shows walking trails going as far as Teluk Bahang, but these are not well marked and not recommended.

The 11-room **Bellevue Hotel** (☎ 829 9500; penbell@streamyx.com; s & d RM179, f RM219) is the only place to stay here, but while the garden offers some splendid views over Georgetown, it's a little frayed at the edges and very overpriced. The hotel has a restaurant that's nice for a hilltop drink and a small **aviary garden** (adult/child RM4/2; ☯ 9am-6pm) featuring exotic birds.

David Brown's Restaurant (☎ 828 8337; info @penanghillco.com.my; mains from RM15; ☯ 9am-9pm) occupies a hillock on Penang Hill once set aside by Francis Light for strawberry planting. Run by an Anglophone Malay-Chinese (of course), the restaurant serves steak-and-kidney pies, Beef Wellington, bubble and squeak and rainbow trout. No pork bacon, though; we're still in Malaysia.

GETTING THERE & AWAY
From Komtar, or along Lebuh Chulia, you can catch one of the frequent Rt 204 Rapid Penang buses (RM2) to the funicular station at Stesen Bukit Bendera. From Air Itam, walk five minutes to the funicular railway station. A taxi from the ferry terminal in Georgetown to the funicular station is RM40.

The energetic can take one of the walking trails to/from the Botanical Gardens.

Kek Lok Si Temple
The 'Temple of Supreme Bliss' is also the largest Buddhist **temple** (Map p176; ☯ 9am-6pm) in Malaysia and one of the most recognisable buildings in the country, in its way as much a part of the national iconography as the Petronas Towers and the orang-utan. Built by an immigrant Chinese Buddhist in 1890, Kek Lok Si is a cornerstone of the Malay-Chinese community, who provided the funding for its two-decade long construction (and ongoing additions). The temple both stands atop and is carved into the slope of Air Itam, near Penang Hill.

To reach the entrance, walk through a maze of souvenir stalls, past a tightly packed turtle pond and murky fish ponds, until you reach the heart of the complex, where you'll find **Ban Po Thar** (Ten Thousand Buddhas Pagoda; admission RM2), the seven-tier, 30m-high tower that is the 'face' of Kek Lok Si. The design is said to be Burmese at the top, Chinese at the bottom and Thai in between. In another three-storey shrine, there's a large Thai Buddha image that was donated by King Bhumibol of Thailand. There are several other temples here, as well as shops and a **vegetarian restaurant** (☎ 828 8142; mains from RM5; ☯ lunch & dinner Tue-Sun). A **cable-car** (one-way/return RM4/2) whisks you to the highest level, presided over by an awesome 36.5m-high bronze statue of **Kuan Yin**, goddess of mercy. Sixteen highly decorated bronze columns will eventually support a roof over the statue, and 1000

PENANG

2m-high statues of the goddess are planned to surround this area.

Also up here are a couple more temples, a fish pool, extensive gardens and statues of the 12 animals of the Chinese zodiac.

It's an impressive complex, though crowded with tourists and shoppers as much as worshippers. The temple is about a 3km walk from Penang Hill (p198), or you can hop a Rapid Penang bus 201/203 from central Georgetown to Air Itam (RM2), at the foot of the temple.

Botanical Gardens

The 30-hectare **Botanical Gardens** (Map p176; ☎ 227 0428; www.penangbotanicgardens.gov.my; Waterfall Rd; admission free; ◷ 5am-8pm) are also known as the Waterfall Gardens, after the stream that cascades down from Penang Hill. They've also been dubbed the Monkey Gardens for the many long-tailed macaques that scamper around (they've taken over the well-executed website as well). Don't be tempted to feed them; monkeys do bite, and there's a RM500 fine if you're caught. Within the grounds are an orchid house, palm house, bromeliad house, cactus garden and numerous tropical trees, all labelled in English. A path leads to the top of Penang Hill.

TransitLink bus 202 runs past on the way to Teluk Bahang.

Museum & Art Gallery

Six kilometres south of Georgetown, on the sprawling campus of Universiti Sains Malaysia, is the **Museum and Art Gallery** (Map p176; ☎ 261 3144; admission free; ◷ 10am-5pm Sun-Thu, 10am-12.15pm & 2.45-5pm Fri, 10am-1pm Sat). There's a collection of traditional Malaysian and Indonesian musical instruments (including several full gamelan orchestras), aboriginal and Baba-Nonya pieces, and fascinating contemporary Malaysian art and photography.

To get here you'll need to take a 304 bus from Georgetown (RM1.40) to Universiti Sains Malaysia.

Pulau Jerejak

Lying 1.5 nautical miles off Penang's southeast coast, Pulau Jerejak is a thickly forested private island that has been home to a leper colony and a prison in its time, and is today occupied by the **Jerejak Resort & Spa** (Map p176; ☎ 658 7111; www.jerejakresort.com; r RM182-450; ☒ ☒). The resort has some beautifully furnished chalets and a

spa offering various kinds of massage, as well as a less luxurious 'adventure village' complex with simple doubles and dorms, though you will need to book the whole dorm room.

The resort has its own jetty on Penang Island, and day-trippers are welcome. Boats leave roughly every two hours (RM20/16 per adult/child). The price includes a light snack, or one-hour bike rental, and activities on the island include jungle-trekking (one hour, RM20). There's also a suspension-bridge trail (RM15).

No buses run past the jetty; a taxi from Georgetown will cost around RM50.

Snake Temple

Perhaps the most misleadingly named destination in Penang is about 3km before the airport. Not that there's not snakes in the **Snake Temple** (Temple of the Azure Cloud; Map p176; ◷ 9am-6pm). But c'mon – you read 'Snake Temple' and expect beating drums, pythons coiled around lithesome sacrificial virgins, mad monks wielding trained vipers…nah. It's just a temple with some doped up (or seemingly doped up) snakes. It's dedicated to Chor Soo Kong, a Buddhist priest and healer, and was built in 1850 by one of his grateful patients. The several resident venomous Wagler's pit vipers and green tree snakes are said to be slightly stoned by the incense smoke drifting around the temple during the day, but at night they slither down to eat the offerings and apparently throw a huge party, leaving them too messed up to do anything but lay around all the next day. There's a small **snake exhibition** (adult/child RM5/3) with tanks containing various snakes, including pythons and cobras. Persistent snake handlers will charge RM30 for taking your photo holding a snake.

From Georgetown, take a 302 or 401/401E bus to Bayan Lepas (RM2.70) and ask to be let off at the Snake Temple.

Fishing Villages

About 3km after the Snake Temple, you reach the turn-off to the Chinese fishing village of **Batu Maung** (Map p176). The renovated seaside temple here has a shrine dedicated to the legendary Admiral Cheng Ho, also known as Sam Poh. The temple sanctifies a huge 'footprint' on the rock that reputedly belonged to the famous navigator. Devotees pray before his statue and drop coins into the water-filled footprint before catching a bite to eat at Best

---

A KOPEL ECOTOURISM IDEAS

A new ecotourism project is trying to extract tourists from the Georgetown-Northern Beaches region to Balik Pulau and the oft-ignored other sides of Pulau Pinang. KOPEL (Koperasi Pelancongan Pulau Pinang Berhad/Penang Tourism Cooperative Ltd), originally started as a cooperative for trishaw drivers, now puts visitors face to face with many of the traditional folkways that have dominated Malay life. In Balik Pulau this includes tours of traditional handicrafts, a goat farm, paddy fields, seafood markets, palm sap harvesting and the like.

And now KOPEL is sponsoring nine homestays in villages scattered across rarely visited corners of Penang, including the oft-ignored mainland. This is a pretty incredible opportunity for those missing a sense of 'old Asia' to connect to a way of life that is hard to grasp in rapidly modernising Malaysia. Under the auspices of a KOPEL homestay you'll be living life in tune with the rhythms of your hosts, who may be rice farmers, catfish fishermen and the like. Besides being a way of learning about a side of Malay life tourists rarely get to experience, some of the KOPEL homestay sites, like Pulau Betong, a small island off Pulau Penang's coast, are gorgeous, undisturbed slices of nature in their own right.

Rates vary hugely depending on season, length of stay and number of visitors – check the website and get in touch with **KOPEL** (☎ 04-250 5500; www.kopel.com.my) directly for more information on the above.

View seafood restaurant outside. Buses 302 (RM3.40) and 207 (RM4) from Georgetown go past Batu Maung.

Back on the highway, the road climbs up, then drops down to **Teluk Kumbar** (Map p176), from where you can detour to the village of **Gertak Sanggul** (Map p176), which has stalls on the seaside selling fresh fish. You'll pass some pint-sized scenic beaches on the way; none are particularly good for swimming.

Penang War Museum

Heading west of Batu Maung on the road to Teluk Kumbar, you'll soon come upon the **Penang War Museum** (Map p176; ☎ 626 5142; Bukit Batu Maung; adult/child RM25/12.50; ⏰ 9am-7pm), perched on top of the steep Bukit Batu Maung. The former British fort, built in the 1930s, was used as a prison and torture camp by the Japanese during WWII. Today, the crumbling buildings have been restored as a memorial to those dark days. Barracks, ammunition stores, cookhouses, gun emplacements and other structures can be explored in this eerie, atmospheric place, and there are information boards in English all over the site.

Yellow Bus 69 from Georgetown swings by below the hill.

Balik Pulau

☎ 04 / pop 195,000

Balik Pulau (Map p176) is the main town on the island circuit. There are a number of restaurants, food stalls and a daily market here,

but no accommodation – or at least none of note. If you want to stay out here, just walk around with a smile on your face; locals have a habit of offering to put you up for the night. It's a good place for lunch and the local speciality, *laksa balik pulau*, is a must; it's a tasty rice-noodle concoction in a thick fish-broth, with mint leaves, pineapple slivers, onions and fresh chillies.

Balik's Catholic **Holy Name of Jesus Church** was built in 1854, and its twin spires stand impressively against the jungle behind. The town's other claim to fame is its orchards of durian, clove and nutmeg trees.

You can reach Balik Pulau via bus 401/401E or 404 (tickets cost approximately RM4) from Georgetown and Bayan Lepas, bus 501 from Batu Feringghi (RM3.40) and bus 502 from Kek Lok Si (RM2.70).

Sungai Pinang to Pantai Acheh

After Balik Pulau you pass through an area of Malay *kampung* and clove, nutmeg, rubber and durian plantations. Sungai Pinang, a busy Chinese village built along a stagnant river, and Pantai Acheh, an isolated fishing village, are both worth a peek, if only because you'll likely be peeked back at; very few tourists make it out this way.

About 2km further along the road to Teluk Bahang, the **Tropical Fruit Farm** (Map p176; ☎ 227 6223; ⏰ 9am-6pm) cultivates over 140 types of tropical and subtropical fruit trees, native and hybrid. The two-hour tours (RM25/17

PENANG

per adult/child) are pretty educational and include a fruit sampler tasting. Most visitors come on organised trips. Bus 501 from Balik Pulau (RM2) travels past the Tropical Fruit Farm.

Titi Kerawang
☎ 04

After the turn-off to Pantai Acheh, the road starts to climb and twist, offering glimpses of the coast and the sea far below. During durian season, stalls are set up along the road selling the spiky orbs, and you can see nets strung below the trees themselves to protect the precious fruits when they fall.

The jungle becomes denser here before you reach Titi Kerawang. Once the waterfall flowed into a natural swimming pool just off the road, but the nearby dam has left the stream a trickle.

As you descend towards the north coast you'll pass the new dam and come upon the **Teluk Bahang Forest Reserve** (Map p176; ☎ ranger's office 885 1280; ☺ 9am-5pm Tue-Thu, Sat & Sun, 9am-noon & 2.45-5pm Friday). Several kilometres south of Teluk Bahang, it has gentle trails through

the jungle, a few waterfall pools and a small, specialist **Forestry Museum** (☎ 885 2388; admission RM1; ☺ 9am-5pm Tue-Thu, Sat & Sun, 9am-noon & 2.45-5pm Fri).

A little nearer the coast is the **Penang Butterfly Farm** (Map p202; ☎ 885 1253; www.butterfly-insect.com; 830 Jln Teluk Bahang; adult/child RM20/10; ☺ 9am-5.30pm Mon-Fri, 9am-6pm Sat & Sun), with several thousand live butterflies representing over 150 species flapping around like buttery pastel clouds. There are also some fascinating beetles, lizards and spiders crawling about.

From here it's 1km north to the bus stop in Teluk Bahang, passing along the way an **Orchid Garden** (Map p202), where the colourful display of blooms is sure to delight horticulturalists, and **Craft Batik** (Map p202; ☎ 885 1302) factory and shop, a somewhat touristy and overpriced outlet for sarongs and the like.

Teluk Bahang
☎ 04 / pop 2500

If Batu Ferringhi is Penang's version of Cancun, Teluk Bahang is the quiet (sometimes deathly quiet) beach a few kilometres past

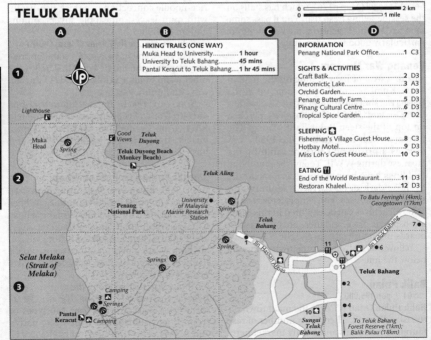

TELUK BAHANG

| 0 | 2 km |
| 0 | 1 mile |

HIKING TRAILS (ONE WAY)
Muka Head to University .... **1 hour**
University to Teluk Bahang .... **45 mins**
Pantai Keracut to Teluk Bahang .... **1 hr 45 mins**

INFORMATION
Penang National Park Office **1** C3

SIGHTS & ACTIVITIES
Craft Batik **2** D3
Meromictic Lake **3** A3
Orchid Garden **4** D3
Penang Butterfly Farm **5** D3
Pinang Cultural Centre **6** D3
Tropical Spice Garden **7** D2

SLEEPING
Fisherman's Village Guest House **8** C3
Hotbay Motel **9** D3
Miss Loh's Guest House **10** C3

EATING
End of the World Restaurant **11** D3
Restoran Khaleel **12** D3

Lighthouse

Good Views

Teluk Duyong

Muka Head   Spring

Teluk Duyong Beach (Monkey Beach)

Teluk Aling

Penang National Park

University of Malaysia Marine Research Station

Spring

Teluk Bahang

To Batu Ferringhi (4km); Georgetown (17km)

Selat Melaka (Strait of Melaka)

Springs

Spring

Jln Hassan Abbas

Jln Teluk Bahang

Teluk Bahang

Camping

Springs

Pantai Keracut   Camping

Sungai Teluk Bahang

To Teluk Bahang Forest Reserve (1km); Balik Pulau (18km)

PENANG

the party. There's not enough beach here for any resorts to crop up, so the main thing to do is tool around **Penang National Park** (Taman Negara Pulau Pinang), which at just 2300 hectares is the smallest in Malaysia. It encompasses the headland, and has some interesting and challenging trails through the jungle.

From Teluk Bahang you can trek down the beach to **Muka Head**, the isolated rocky promontory at the extreme northwestern corner of the island marked by a lighthouse, which is off limits. This is a reasonably easy walk, taking around 3½ hours. The trail passes the University of Malaysia Marine Research Station and the privately owned Teluk Duyong beach, also called Monkey Beach, named for the numerous primates who scamper about here. A **canopy walk** over some of the trees was in the works during our visit, but had yet to be completed.

A more difficult trail heads inland towards **Pantai Keracut**, a beautiful white-sand beach which is a popular spot for picnics. Nearby is the unusual **meromictic lake**, a fascinating rarity as lakes go (bear with us): it's composed of two separate layers of unmixed freshwater on top and seawater below. The resulting layered freshwater and saltwater support a unique ecosystem. Learn more by pitching your tent on the nearby shore.

The small **Penang National Park office** (☎ 881 3530/3500; Jln Hassan Abbas; ☼ 8am-4.30pm Mon-Fri, 8am-noon & 2-4pm Sat & Sun) is near the park entrance in Teluk Bahang. It has a few maps and leaflets. Guides cost RM100 for a full day, although they may be hard to find on weekdays.

The **Pinang Cultural Centre** (☎ 885 1175; Jln Teluk Bahang), down the road from the Penang Mutiara Beach Resort, only opens for large, pre-arranged tour groups. Local handicraft exhibitions, cultural shows and buffets are held here. Your hotel should have the latest details and costs.

Nearby is the **Tropical Spice Garden** (☎ 881 1797; www.tropicalspicegarden.com; Jln Teluk Bahang; adult/child RM14/8; ☼ 9am-6pm), which is not to be confused with Tropical Fruit Farm! This former rubber plantation is now basically one of the best smelling places in the world, overflowing as it is with cinnamon, pepper plants, star anise and everything else culled from your mum's spice rack, growing here in explosive fecundity.

SLEEPING
Rooms have private bathrooms unless otherwise noted.

Miss Loh's Guest House (☎ 885 1227; off Jln Teluk Bahang; dm/s/d with shared bathroom from RM8/15/30; ☒) Miss Loh's is a bit of an anomaly, a throwback to the good old days of long-term backpacking. Her ramshackle guesthouse feels as much run by the guests (most of whom are sticking around for a bit) as anyone else, although we suppose the real masters of the house are the cats and dogs who have the run of the grounds. Rates are negotiable for longer stays, but Miss Loh won't accept telephone reservations. There are communal shower and toilet blocks. To find the guesthouse, look for a store on Teluk Bahang's main street (the one street) that says 'GH Information' – this is your contact into Miss Loh's little world.

Fisherman's Village Guest House (☎ 885 2936; 60 Jln Hassan Abbas, Kampong Nelayan; dm/d from RM7/18; ☒) Fisherman's Village isn't quite as laid-back as Miss Loh's, but that's being pretty relative. This is just the sort of garden spot to fully immerse yourself in some indolent idleness. It feels more like a homestay than anything, and you'll probably be tempted to let yourself get accustomed to the slow pace of life here.

Hotbay Motel (☎ 016-455 9062; 48 Jln Teluk Bahang; r RM65-85; ☒) Situated in the main shopping area east of the roundabout, Hotbay Motel offers fair motel-style rooms, with a communal TV lounge at the front. Rooms with five and seven beds are also available (RM150/210); prices here are pretty negotiable.

EATING
With all those fishing boats in the harbour, fresh and tasty seafood is guaranteed.

Restoran Khaleel (Jln Teluk Bahang; mains from RM4; ☼ breakfast, lunch & dinner). This little food court next to the Hotbay Motel offers the best value along here. The usual Malay specialities like *nasi goreng* and fish-head curry are available.

End of the World Restaurant (☎ 885 1189; mains from RM15; ☼ lunch & dinner) At the western end of the village by the jetty, this restaurant is famous for its fish dishes and huge range of seafood, but it's a little overpriced.

The main shopping area along the road heading east to Batu Ferringhi also has a few coffee shops where travellers can find cheaper Chinese dishes and seafood, as well as a couple of good South Indian places, which sell dishes like *murtabak* and *dosa* (savoury Indian pancakes).

GETTING THERE & AWAY

Bus 101 runs from Georgetown to Teluk Bahang (RM2.50) from roughly 6am to 11pm.

Batu Ferringhi

☎ 04

The road from Teluk Bahang along the coast to Batu Ferringhi is a picturesque stretch of small coves and more beaches. Batu Ferringhi (Foreigner's Rock) is a resort strip stretching along Jln Batu Ferringhi, the main drag, which is lined with big hotels, tourist shops and restaurants. A lot of package resort types end up here, as do an increasing amount of tourists from the Gulf States – you'll likely see men walking shirtless next to women in full *chador* and veil on the beach.

There's a good night market and the **Yahong Art Gallery** (☎ 881 1251; www.yahongart.com; 58D Jln Batu Ferringhi; 9.30am-9pm) sells a vast range of Asian antiques and art, including jewellery, pewter, batik paintings, woodcarvings and, less appealingly, ivory.

The beach is fine for sunbathing, but doesn't compare to Malaysia's best. The water isn't very clear, the sand is more rocky and silty than powdery, and there are too many ATVs roaring up and down the sand, which is hardly relaxing. That said, it's a nice place to get a tan or soak after getting a tan.

ACTIVITIES

There are plenty of watersports outfits along the beach; they tend to rent out waverunners (RM120 for 30 minutes) and run water-skiing (RM100 for 15 minutes) and parasailing (RM80 for 15 minutes) trips.

After which you might need a relaxing massage. All sorts of foot masseuses will offer you their services; expect to pay around RM40 for a 30-minute deep-tissue massage. And yes, they feel heavenly.

SLEEPING

Batu Ferringhi, along with Teluk Bahang, was once a favourite stopover on the budget travellers' trail, and although there's still a clutch of backpacker hostels near the beach, these days the place is dominated by huge luxury developments. Outside high season (roughly December to February), big discounts are often available. Budget places all have shared bath-

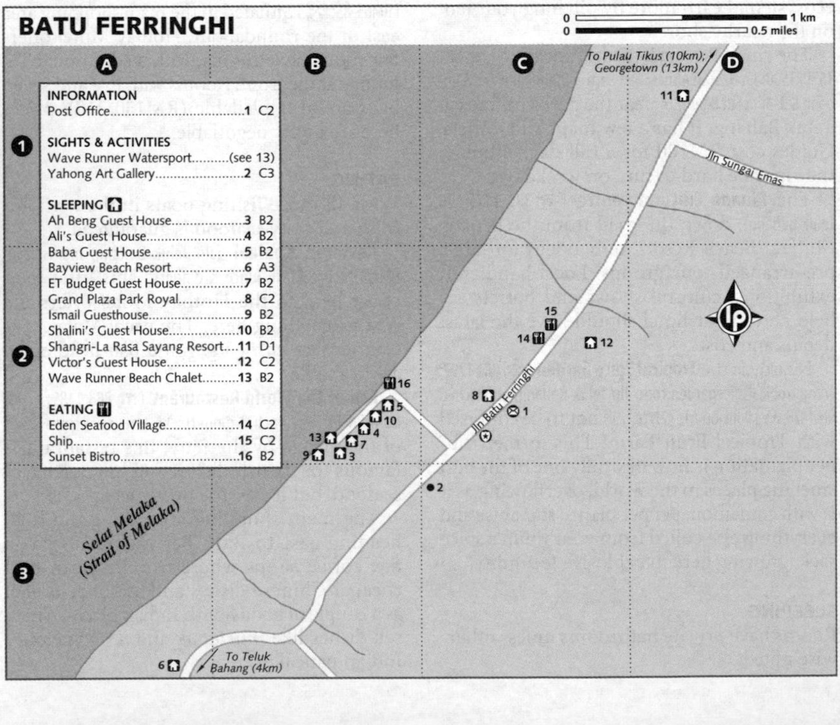
BATU FERRINGHI
0 1 km
0 0.5 miles
A
B
C
D
1
2
3
To Pulau Tikus (10km); Georgetown (13km)
Jln Sungai Emas
Jln Batu Ferringhi
Selat Melaka (Strait of Melaka)
To Teluk Bahang (4km)
INFORMATION
Post Office....1 C2
SIGHTS & ACTIVITIES
Wave Runner Watersport....(see 13)
Yahong Art Gallery....2 C3
SLEEPING
Ah Beng Guest House....3 B2
Ali's Guest House....4 B2
Baba Guest House....5 B2
Bayview Beach Resort....6 A3
ET Budget Guest House....7 B2
Grand Plaza Park Royal....8 C2
Ismail Guesthouse....9 B2
Shalini's Guest House....10 B2
Shangri-La Rasa Sayang Resort....11 D1
Victor's Guest House....12 C2
Wave Runner Beach Chalet....13 B2
EATING
Eden Seafood Village....14 C2
Ship....15 C2
Sunset Bistro....16 B2

rooms except where indicated; midrange and top-end options all have private bathrooms. The budget places here are all practically carbon copies of each other: nice if bland rooms in shared family-run houses, clean conditions and easy access to the beach.

Budget

The following are all practically carbon copies of each other: nice if bland rooms in shared family-run houses, clean conditions and easy access to the beach.

ET Budget Guest House (☎ 881 1553; 47 Batu Ferringhi; r RM25-60; ✖) A double-storey house with basic rooms, most with shared bathroom. The pricier air-con rooms come with TVs and showers.

Victor's Guest House (☎ 881 1005; 399 Jln Batu Ferringhi; r RM30-45; ✖) Down a dusty lane off the main road, Victor's is a friendly Indian guesthouse with large clean rooms upstairs and down. The bare brick walls are a bit cheerless, but it's good value and in a quiet location with chickens pecking about outside.

Baba Guest House (☎ 881 1686; babaguesthouse2000@yahoo.com; 52 Batu Ferringhi; r RM30-60; ✖) Tidy family home with plain rooms, most with shared bathrooms. The dearer air-con rooms come with fridges and showers.

Shalini's Guest House (☎ 881 1859; 56 Batu Ferringhi; r RM30-60, apt 120-200; ✖) This old wooden two-storey house has a friendly family atmosphere. Rooms are basic but neat and some have balconies. The priciest ones have private bathrooms.

Ah Beng Guesthouse (☎ 881 1036; 54C Batu Ferringhi; r RM50-70; ✖) Pricier than most of the beach chalets here, this place has small but comfortable rooms, some with sea-facing balconies. The most expensive rooms have hot water, TVs and fridges.

Ali's Guest House (☎ 881 1316; 53 Batu Ferringhi; r RM60-100; ✖) Simple budget place with a popular open-air restaurant at the front. It's a little pricier and subsequently a little nicer than the above properties, but heads up: no alcohol allowed on site. Breakfast is included.

Midrange

The following rates may be negotiable in low season.

Ismail Guesthouse (☎ 881 2599; Batu Ferringhi; r RM80-160; ✖) Like its next-door neighbour, Wave Runner, Ismail boasts comfy, cool concrete beach chalets plopped right on the sand.

Wave Runner Beach Chalet (☎ 881 4753; 54 Batu Ferringhi; r RM120-150; ✖) Right on the sand, this brick chalet block has just five rooms, so it's often full. Rooms are fresh and clean, with tiled floors, two double beds, TVs, kettles and private showers. There are a few food stalls on the doorstep.

Top End

Grand Plaza Park Royal (☎ 881 1133; www.penang.parkroyalhotels.com; Jln Batu Ferringhi; r/ste from RM284/418; ✖ 🖳 🐾) With 330 rooms, this place still isn't the biggest resort here, but it is one of the better ones. The lobby lounge, with its squashy sofas and piano bar, leads out onto a clean and attractive stretch of beach. Rooms are large and those with sea views are, of course, preferable. Nonguests can use the gardens and pools for RM25 per day, including lunch.

Bayview Beach Resort (☎ 881 2123; www.bayviewbeach.com; Jln Batu Ferringhi; r/ste from RM293/540; ✖ 🖳 🐾) At the western, and quieter, end of the beach, this is a gigantic place set in lovely palm-filled gardens. It has everything you could wish for, including a watersports centre, a gym, squash courts, shops and bars, including one in the middle of the large swimming pool.

Shangri-La Rasa Sayang Resort (☎ 888 8888; www.shangri-la.com; Jln Batu Ferringhi; r from RM650; ✖ 🖳 🐾) A vast luxury resort on a fine stretch of beach. All rooms have balconies, many with sea views. There's a health club, tennis courts, putting green, several restaurants and all the bowing, scraping service and grandiosity you'd expect at such a price.

EATING & DRINKING

Sunset Bistro (☎ 012-553 1313; Batu Ferringhi; mains from RM9; ⏰ noon-1am, to 3am Fri & Sat) Sunset sets the tone for several other beach restaurants in Batu Ferringhi: decent, overpriced executions of pasta, burgers, Chinese, seafood and Malaysian standards. The hiked prices are basically sand-between-your-toes tax.

Ship (☎ 881 2142; www.theship.com.my; 69B Jln Batu Ferringhi; mains from RM15; ⏰ lunch & dinner) You can't miss this one: it's a full-sized replica of a wooden sailing ship, specialising in hefty steaks and seafood. Escargots and oysters are also on the rather overpriced menu. It's quite smart inside, but rather dark.

Eden Seafood Village (☎ 881 1236; 69A Jln Batu Ferringhi; mains from RM20; ⏰ dinner) A huge barn-like place serving seafood plucked from aquariums at the entrance, Cantonese style. Oysters, crab, lobster and a veritable ocean of fish are available. There's a free dance show every evening at 8.30pm. A lot of locals eat here for nice nights out.

There are basic food stalls on the beachfront near the budget guesthouses, where you can enjoy fresh fish. On the corner of Jln Sungai Emas, Global Bay Food Court has cheap Western and Chinese meals.

GETTING THERE & AWAY

Bus 101 runs from Georgetown to Batu Ferringhi (RM2) from roughly 6am to 11pm.

Pulau Tikus

☎ 04

Heading back into Georgetown from Batu Ferringhi, you'll pass **Tanjung Bungah** (Cape of Flowers), the first real beach close to the city, but it's not good for swimming. Even so, big hotels and apartment blocks are cropping up everywhere. Batu Ferringhi is still a better option.

After Tanjung Bungah, you'll enter the Pulau Tikus (Midlands) suburbs, full of discos, wining-and-dining venues, cinemas, and megamalls like Midlands 1-Stop and Island Plaza. A taxi from Lebuh Chulia to Midlands costs RM20.

Pulau Tikus is the beginning of scenic Gurney Dr, with its great sea views and hawker food. Eventually it intersects with Jln Sultan Ahmad Shah, formerly Millionaire's Row, where nouveau riche Chinese in the early 20th century competed to see who could build the most impressive mansion. Many of these mansions have now been demolished or abandoned, or taken over by squatters, fronted by office space or even converted into fast-food outlets.

Buses 101, 104 and 304 all run from Georgetown to Pulau Tikus (RM1.40).

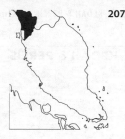

Kedah & Perlis

Tucked into Malaysia's northwest corner are two states that fairly drip with greenness and fertility: Kedah and Perlis. If Kuala Lumpur is Malaysia at its most frenetically developed, and Borneo the nation at its wildest and ruggedest, this is the country's, well, country: not paved, not jungled over, but cultivated, cared for and landscaped into a horizon of looping emerald ridges. Limestone pillars thrust up through this paddyscape and peasants dot it, the latter contributing to the harvest of over half of Malaysia's domestic rice supply.

Not that many foreigners see all this. While it may be one of the most touristed states in Malaysia, most travellers would draw a blank if you asked them anything about 'Kedah.' That's because almost everyone knows it by its biggest island and Malaysia's number one holiday destination: Pulau Langkawi. One of those postcard places where life is a cruise ship commercial starring you, Langkawi is also a living island where there's a fair bit to explore beyond the beach, although no one will fault you for losing a few days (Weeks? Months? Langkawi has that effect…) on the sand. Langkawi's duty-free status also makes it popular with a certain kind of shopper, and it's not uncommon to see folks leaving the island with tanned arms busting with cartons of Marlboros.

Perlis is the smallest state in Malaysia; physically and culturally it borders Kedah. It's also proximate to Thailand, and most travellers rush through here on their way to that kingdom. Their loss: this corner of the country is part of the Malay heartland, which makes it over-whelmingly friendly and culturally significant. The Malays are known as *bumiputra* – sons of the soil – and that soil, physical and cultural, is most fertile in Kedah and Perlis.

HIGHLIGHTS

- Sliding through the seven pools of **Telaga Tujuh** (p219)
- Exploring Kedah's history as a Hindu-Buddhist kingdom at the **Muzium Arkeologi** (p210) in Lembah Bujang
- Deciding between staying in a colonial villa or Chinese mansion at **Temple Tree** (p223) in Langkawi
- Relaxing on one of the stunning beaches of **Pulau Langkawi** (p220)
- Riding the cable car to the top of Langkawi's **Gunung Machinchang** (p219) to enjoy the spectacular views

- **TELEGORE CODE: 04** ■ TELEPHONE CODE: 04
- ■ POPULATION: 2.17 MILLION
- ■ AREA: 10,236 SQ KM

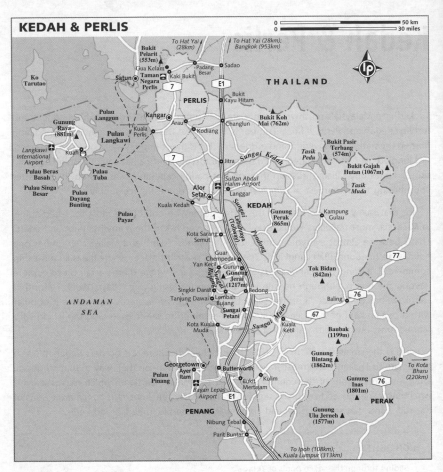

Climate

Kedah and Perlis both enjoy a typical tropical climate, with temperatures between 21°C and 32°C throughout the year. The wettest time of year is between April and October, when the odd tropical storm is expected, whereas there is intermittent rainfall and occasional downpours at other times. Pulau Langkawi tends to see less rain than the mainland. Humidity hovers at around 90%.

National Parks

The tiny state park of Perlis (Taman Negara Perlis; p228) is a remote, 5000-hectare expanse of jungle running along the Thai border. For more details, contact the **park visitors centre** (☎ 945 7898). The entire Langkawi archipelago is a Unesco-designated 'geopark' – the first one to be named so in Southeast Asia – but that status has more publicity than actual protective measures attached to it.

Dangers & Annoyances

Travellers crossing the land border into Malaysia from Thailand have reported a common scam practised by some travel operators. Foreigners are told that at the border crossing they need a certain amount of Malaysian ringgit (RM) to be allowed into the country (usually quite a high amount), and are then obliged to buy Malaysian currency at a highly disadvantageous rate. Don't be taken in by this con – it is not necessary to have a specified amount of Malaysian cash to cross the border.

Langkawi 'beach boys' – local men who make a living off small tourism activities, hustling or flings with foreign women – have a particularly bad reputation for aggression and general sleaziness. We've read many reports of fights between 'beach boys' and male travellers and saw two such incidents during our research. You may just want to be generally careful.

Getting There & Away

The main train line and the Lebuhraya (North–South Hwy) run through Kedah and Perlis, heading southwards to Butterworth and beyond, and northwards to the Thai border. Alor Setar, the state capital of Kedah, is the main transport hub, with bus connections to most major cities on the peninsula. It also has an airport, with regular flights to Kuala Lumpur (KL). Bukit Kayu Hitam in Kedah and Padang Besar in Perlis are the border crossings into Thailand.

Langkawi can be reached by air from KL, Georgetown and Singapore and by ferry from Georgetown, Kuala Kedah and Kuala Perlis and from Satun in Thailand.

Getting Around

Most of the big towns in Kedah and Perlis are easily reached by bus. Trains are infrequent, often leave at inconvenient times and are not particularly useful for travelling within the two states. There is no public transport on Langkawi. You will have to use taxis to get around, unless you rent a car or motorbike.

KEDAH

The iconic man-made geographic feature of Southeast Asia is and ever was the rice paddy. There's something about its flatness and fecundity, all that green suggesting wild, energy and life, yet so expertly and elegantly partitioned off and cultivated. Its nature at its most vibrant, tamed into its most productive.

The paddy field is the eternal horizon of Kedah, Malaysia's 'rice bowl.' Two blocks of colour constantly kiss at the edge of your eyesight: robin's-egg blue on top and deep, alive green on the bottom, with strips of bitumen webbing through. If you find inspiration in the rustic, clean-lined aesthetic

of Asian agriculture, this state is the field of sunflowers to your inner van Gogh.

If not, it's still worth spending some time here meeting Malays. Across the world, rural folk have a reputation for being hard working and hospitable. The cliché holds true in Kedah at least. Here farmers are bent over the ruins of great kingdoms like Srivijaya, and their children seek IT jobs in Alor Setar, but to a man, they're all friendly as hell.

For travellers' purposes there are essentially two Kedahs: the tropical island of Langkawi and its attached islets, and rural, little-visited mainland Kedah. Kedah state's business hours differ from those of most of the peninsula. Banks and government offices are usually closed on Friday, but sometimes open a half-day on Saturday. For information on the state, check out www.visitke dah.com.my.

History

Kedah is one of the most historically significant Malay states. Settlement goes back to the Stone Age, and some of the earliest excavated archaeological sites in the country are near Gunung Jerai. More recent finds in Lembah Bujang date back to the Hindu-Buddhist period in the 4th century AD, and the current royal family can trace its line back directly to this time. Discoveries in Lembah Bujang show that it was the cradle of Hindu-Buddhist civilisation on the peninsula – the society that would become the foundation stone for Malay culture – and one of the first places to come into contact with Indian traders. The latter would eventually bring Islam to Malaysia, a religion whose cultural impact cannot be overstated here.

During the 7th and 8th centuries, Kedah paid tribute to the Srivijaya Empire of Sumatra, but later fell under the influence of the Siamese until the 15th century, when the rise of Melaka led to the Islamisation of the area. In the 17th century Kedah was attacked by the Portuguese, who had already conquered Melaka, and by the Acehnese, who saw Kedah as a threat to their own spice production.

In the hope that the British would help protect what remained of Kedah from Siam, the sultan handed over Penang to the British in the late 18th century. Nevertheless, in the early 19th century Kedah once again came under Siamese control, where it remained, either directly or as a vassal, until early in the 20th century when Siam passed control to the British.

This history of changing hands between the Thai and the British manifests, in places, as a somewhat hybrid Malay-Thai culture.

After WWII, during which Kedah (along with Kelantan) was the first part of Malaya to be invaded by the Japanese, Kedah became part of the Federation of Malaya in 1948, albeit reluctantly.

During the 2008 elections, Kedah, traditionally a breeding ground for leaders of the Barisan National ruling party, came out strongly in favour of the opposition, particularly the Islamist Parti Islam se-Malaysia (PAS).

SUNGAI PETANI

☎ 04

The only reason to stop at 'SP', on the highway between Butterworth and Alor Setar, is for transport connections to Gunung Jerai or the archaeology museum at Lembah Bujang.

If you get stuck, there are a few hotels in the centre. The best is the **Swiss Inn** (☎ 422 3333; www .swissgarden.com; 1 Jln Pahlawan; r/ste RM300/450; ☒ ☒ ☒), a modern chain hotel with large, fresh rooms (nonsmoking) and great facilities. If you book online, rates are half, or even less, of the published prices. Another good choice is the **Seri Malaysia Hotel** (☎ 423 4060; www.serimalaysia.com.my; 21 Jln Pasar; r RM120; ☒), a big, three-storey place opposite the train station.

There are several Chinese and Malay food stalls in the lanes behind the HSBC Bank, just southwest of the clock tower.

Sungai Petani is on Malaysia's main train line, and there is one (7.10pm) daily connection to KL (from RM32, 10 to 11 hours) and two (6.30am and 3.40pm) to Hat Yai, Thailand (from RM16, four to five hours). The local bus station and taxi stand are on Jln Putri, a few hundred metres south of the clock tower and one block west of the main street. The long-distance bus station is also south of the clock tower, but a few blocks east across a small bridge. From there, express buses run to Alor Setar (RM4, hourly).

LEMBAH BUJANG

☎ 04

The source of much of Malay culture, traditions and society were the medieval Hindu-Buddhist kingdoms that traded and conquered across the Indian Ocean centuries ago. The area west of Sungai Petani was home to the most important Hindu-Buddhist kingdom on the peninsula, dating back to the

4th century AD. By the 7th century AD it was part of the large Srivijaya Empire of Sumatra, reaching its architectural peak in the 9th and 10th centuries. Hindu and Buddhist temples were scattered from Gunung Jerai south to Kota Kuala Muda, and in Lembah Bujang alone 50 archaeological sites have already been excavated.

The kingdom traded with India and the Khmer and Srivijaya empires, and was visited by the well-travelled Chinese monk I-Tsing (Yi Jing) in AD 671. In 1025 Srivijaya and Bujang were attacked by the Cholas of India, but the Lembah Bujang kingdom later forged an alliance with the Cholas against the waning Srivijaya Empire. The region continued to trade, but by the 14th century its significance had faded and the temples were deserted with the coming of Islam. They remained buried in the jungle until excavated by British archaeologist HG Quaritch-Wales in 1936.

Along the banks of Sungai Bujang, the **Muzium Arkeologi** (Archaeological Museum; ☎ 457 2005; admission free; ☒ 8am-4.15pm Sun-Thu, 8am-noon & 2.45-4.15pm Fri) chronicles the excavations, and displays stone carvings, pottery and other artefacts. However, most of the carvings have been lost, and only a handful of items are on display, such as a fragment of a wall frieze and a statue of the elephant god, Ganesh. Most numerous are yoni fertility stones.

Though of enormous archaeological significance, the displays don't have the best labelling and it's difficult to fully appreciate the site as presented. The largest temple is the 1000-year-old **Candi Bukit Batu Pahat**. Note the drainage ditches; their presence is testament to strong Indian influence, as locally designed Hindu and Buddhist temples did not have similar outlets.

The archaeological museum is off the Tanjung Dawai road, 2km north of the village of Merbok. From Sungai Petani, take a taxi (RM70) or one of the buses that run roughly every hour to Tanjung Dawai, get off at Merbok (RM2) and walk the 2km to the museum.

GUNUNG JERAI

The forest-clad 1217m Gunung Jerai dominates the surrounding flat plains. It was a sacred mountain in the ancient Hindu period and a landmark for ships sailing from India and Indonesia.

From the base of the mountain, a steep and narrow road snakes its way 13km through a forest recreation park to a sleepy hill resort. From here there are expansive views north across the rice paddies of Kedah and over to Langkawi.

There are few opportunities for hiking or exploring away from the paved road, although a guide can be arranged at the sole resort here. The road itself continues 3km past the resort to the peak and the remains of Candi Telaga Sembilan, a 6th-century Hindu bathing shrine, but the area is the property of the defence ministry and is off limits.

A few kilometres downhill from the resort is a tiny **forestry museum** with exhibits on native trees and their uses, but little on the mountain's flora and fauna. The highlight is an enormous fossilised elephant dropping. From the museum a paved trail leads through the forest to a waterfall and bathing pools.

Sleeping & Eating
Peranginan Gunung Jerai (☎ 423 4345; s & d RM60, f RM110; ❄) The only place to stay, this is a low-key resort with accommodation divided between 20 dated rooms and six larger, and more preferable, chalets. All have hot water and TVs, and you'll find a restaurant and a basic shop at the resort.

Getting There & Away
Gunung Jerai is 30km north of Sungai Petani, and the turn-off is 3km north of Gurun just before Guar Chempedak. From the car park at the bottom of the mountain, minibuses run up to the resort approximately every 45 minutes from 8.30am to 5pm (RM5). Private vehicles can also use the road.

Although the local bus No 2 between Sungai Petani and Alor Setar passes right by the car park on Hwy 1, the express services use the Lebuhraya instead. From Sungai Petani you could also take a taxi or a local Guar Chempedak bus to the car park.

ALOR SETAR
☎ 04
Most travellers use the capital of Kedah, also known as Alor Star, as a hopping-off point to Thailand, Langkawi or southern Malaysia, but there's enough around to keep you exploring for a day. This is a very Malay city, culturally rooted in a conservative mindset that references a fairly strict interpretation of Islam

and reverence for the local monarchy. On the flip side, Alor Setar is a young city where life centres around a very popular mall. Shopping for electronics and clothes is all the rage with Kedah's kids. Austerity, obedience, reverence and consumer capitalism are the odd mix of ingredients that makes up the closest thing Kedah has to an urban scene.

Well, there's some interesting architecture too. The city's long association with Thailand is evident in Thai temples scattered around town, while its relatively small Chinese population lives in a suitably atmospheric (if compact) Chinatown. And the area around the *padang* (town square) is lined with mosques, a sultan's palace and a few colonial administrative buildings, although the town's relatively late transferral to the British (1909) from the Thais reduced the scope of European influence on local buildings.

Orientation
For travellers' purposes, there are three main areas of interest in Alor Setar that form a walkable triangle. The *padang* (town square) is surrounded by most of the city's interesting historical buildings. To the south, in the bend of the Sungai Anak Butik, is the atmospheric, dilapidated Chinatown. East of here, across Sungai Raja, is City Point Plaza, a large mall that anchors the town's commercial district.

Information
There are numerous internet cafes in City Point Plaza; all charge around RM3 per hour.
Maybank (Jln Sultan Badlishah)
Tourist information office (☎ 731 2322; mtpbkdh @tourism.gov.my; Kompleks Pelancongan Negeri Kedah, Jln Raja; ❄ 8am-1pm & 2-4.45pm Sun-Wed, to 4.30pm Thu) South of the town centre.
United Overseas Bank (Jln Raja)

Sights
Note that most businesses and museums are closed from noon to 2pm on Friday for Islamic prayers. This obviously does not extend to Buddhist temples.

PADANG
Some impressive buildings front the town square. The open-sided **Balai Besar** (Royal Audience Hall) was built in 1898 and is still used by the sultan of Kedah for royal and state ceremonies, though it is not open to the

ALOR SETAR

INFORMATION
Maybank..1 B3
Tourist Information Office................2 A3
United Overseas Bank.......................3 B3

SIGHTS & ACTIVITIES
Balai Besar..4 B2
Balai Nobat...5 B2
Balai Seni Negeri (State Art Gallery)...6 B3
Clock Tower...7 B2
High Court...8 B2
Masjid Zahir..9 A2
Menara Alor Star...............................10 B2
Muzium Di Raja.................................11 B3
Rumah Kelahiran Mahathir (Mahathir's
   Birthplace)....................................12 A4
Wat Siam Nikrodharam....................13 C1

SLEEPING
Comfort Motel...................................14 A2
Flora Inn..15 A3
Holiday Villa......................................16 C3
Hotel Regent.....................................17 B3
Hotel Samila......................................18 B2

EATING
Kedai Makanan Laut Haadyai...........19 C1
Pekan Rabu.......................................20 B3
Restoran Rose...................................21 B3
Snack Bars...22 B3

TRANSPORT
Bus Stop for Sungai Petani...............23 B3
Local Bus Station for Shahab Perdana
   Express Bus Station......................24 B3
Taxi Station.......................................25 B3

public. Supported on tall pillars topped with Victorian iron lacework, the building also shows Thai influences in its decoration.

Next to the Balai Besar is the **Muzium Di Raja** (Royal Museum; ☎ 732 7937; Jln Raja; admission free; ☒ 10am-6pm, from 9.30am Fri), which served as the royal palace for the sultan and other members of the family from 1856. Besides housing paraphernalia of the royal family, it's quite enjoyable to wander round the courtyard and admire the buildings.

At the southern edge of the square is the **Balai Seni Negeri**, built in 1893 as a courthouse. Although Kedah was not part of British Malaya at the time, the courthouse is still built in a distinctive, white-columned colonial style. Today it houses the **State Art**

Gallery (☎ 732 5752; Jln Raja; admission free; ☒ 10am-6pm) and displays a decent gallery of contemporary Malaysian art.

To the north, the **Balai Nobat** (Hall of Drums; 1906) is a striking octagonal tower topped by an onion-shaped dome. It's the repository of the *nobat* (royal orchestra), principally composed of percussion instruments; the drums in this orchestra are said to have been a gift from the sultan of Melaka in the 15th century. It isn't open to the public, and the instruments are brought out only on ceremonial occasions such as royal weddings.

Just behind the Balai Nobat is the **High Court**, a classical white colonial building erected in 1922.

The Kedah state mosque, **Masjid Zahir**, is one of the largest and most beautiful mosques in Malaysia. Built in 1912, it has a classical beauty, more of an apparition from *The Thousand and One Nights* than a smoothed-out modern Malaysian mosque. The building encloses the cemetery of Kedah warriors who fought the Thais in 1821. Behind the structure, in contrast to the secular High Court, is the religious s*yariah* (sharia) court complex.

On the opposite side of the lane, the decorative **clock tower**, painted in the same yellow and white livery as the Balai Nobat, was erected in the early 1900s so that the muezzin at the neighbouring mosque would know when to call the faithful to prayer.

If the Petronas Towers weren't enough for you in KL, the second-tallest tower in the country is the **Menara Alor Star** (Telekom Tower; ☎ 720 2234; www.menaraalorstar.com.my; Lebuhraya Darul Aman; adult/child RM6/3; ☒ 9.30am-10pm) which, at 165.5m, is also the tallest structure in town. A glass-sided lift will take you to the observation deck for good views of Alor Setar and the surrounding countryside. There's a revolving restaurant at the top, though it's not always open.

WAT SIAM NIKRODHARAM
Although Alor Setar has weathered Thai occupation, its main Buddhist community is Chinese in heritage. Thus the presence of this cross-cultural *wat* (Buddhist temple): typically Thai with its stupas, fire-in-the-lotus imagery and Angkor Wat–esque wall reliefs, yet scattershot with Chinese Buddhist saints, of import to the Chinese donors who funded the construction of this complex. This is one of those typically Malaysian cultural blends, in this case of Chinese Mahayana and Thai Theravada Buddhism (as mixed up as a Catholic cathedral crossed with a Protestant church).

MUZIUM NEGERI
The **Muzium Negeri** (State Museum; ☎ 733 1162; Lebuhraya Darul Aman; admission free; ☒ 10am-6pm, from 9.30am Fri) is 2km north of the Padang. The small collection includes early Chinese porcelain, artefacts from archaeological excavations at Lembah Bujang and dioramas of royal and rural Malaysian life.

Most local buses from town to the express-bus station pass by the museum. A taxi from the town centre costs RM8.

MAHATHIR'S BIRTHPLACE
Dr Mahathir bin Mohamad, fourth prime minister of Malaysia and longtime keystone of national politics, was born the youngest of nine children in Alor Setar in 1925. His childhood home, **Rumah Kelahiran Mahathir** (Mahathir's Birthplace; ☎ 772 2319; No 18 Lg Kilang Ais; admission free; ☒ 9am-6pm Mon-Sat) is now preserved as a small museum, containing family effects, photos and the politician's old bicycle.

MUZIUM PADI
Muzium Padi (Paddy Museum; ☎ 735 1315; off K351 Hwy; adult/child/camera RM3/1/2; ☒ 10am-6pm, from 9.30am Fri) is all about Kedah's main crop: rice. It's located about 10km northwest of the city, amid, appropriately enough, green rice paddies. The complex, which resembles stacked brass flying saucers, is supposed to emulate the gunny sacks used by rice farmers. Inside…well, if you're *really* into rice, you'll love it. The main event is a top-floor rotating observation deck that looks out onto a mural of the surrounding rice fields (rather than the rather idyllic fields themselves); the gimmick pays homage to Gunung Keriang, a nearby limestone hill that, according to local folklore, is also supposed to rotate.

Sleeping
BUDGET
Flora Inn (☎ 732 2375; http://florainn.tripod.com; 8 Kompleks Medan Raja, Jln Pengkalan Kapal; s/d RM13/65; ☒) Flora Inn is sold as overlooking the 'magnificent' Sungai Kedah, which is little more than algal green glop. That aside, you will find clean, cheap rooms here situated by Chinatown and a small food court, and the management is bend-over-backwards friendly.

Comfort Motel (☎ 734 4866; 2C Jln Kampung Perak; s RM25-40, d RM35-50; ☒) This is a good-value Chinese hotel, located in a renovated wooden house across from the mosque. The rooms all have gleaming tiled floors and TVs, though only the higher-priced ones have private bathrooms.

MIDRANGE
Hotel Regent (☎ 731 1900; www.regentalorsetar.com; 1536 Jln Sultanah Badlishah; s/d RM98/150; ☒) Very much reminiscent of a mid-priced Western motel chain (with slightly dimmer lighting), the Regent comes with the requisite ugly blankets, bad art, comfy rooms and clean facilities. Breakfast included.

Hotel Samila (☎ 731 8888; 27 Jln Kanchut; s/d from RM120/160; ⊠) You pay a little more at this midrange spot and get a little more: comfort, courteous service and quiet. Situated in a good spot for exploring the Padang.

TOP END
Holiday Villa (☎ 734 9999; www.holidayvilla.com.my; 162 Jln Tunku Ibrahim; r from RM310; ⊠ ☒) This towering hotel adjoining the City Point Plaza shopping mall is easily the best place in town. It has spacious, tastefully furnished rooms and a range of facilities, including a gym, a sauna and a few restaurants.

Eating
RESTAURANTS
Restoran Rose (☎ 731 3471; Jln Sultan Baldishah; mains from RM4; ☾ lunch & dinner) Long-running Indian restaurant serving up the usual curries, roti and biryani dishes in the usual slightly tatty if perfectly clean cafeteria atmosphere (or lack thereof).

Kedai Makanan Laut Haadyai (☎ 732 5036; 1915 Jln Stadium; mains from RM10; ☾ 6.30pm-2am) Praised by locals as the best seafood in town, the fish, cockles, lobsters and any damn thing else that once called a body of water home is wonderfully fresh and prepared mainly in Chinese and Thai style. Generally hums to the pleasantly loud mastication of happy local families.

QUICK EATS
Pekan Rabu (Wednesday Market; Jln Langgar; ☾ breakfast, lunch & dinner) This goes on all day, every day, until late at night. Ground-floor outlets offer snack food and drinks while upstairs market stalls sell local products such as *dodol durian* (a gelatinous local sweet made from sticky rice, coconut and durian). The rest of the market is given over to clothes shops.

There are some simple **coffee shops** (Jln Tunku Ibrahim) at the front of City Point Plaza, where you can get noodles and coffee.

Getting There & Away
Alor Setar is 48km from the Bukit Kayu Hitam border to Thailand. Frequent buses go to the border, from where minibus taxis go to Hat Yai (see Bukit Kayu Hitam, p226, for this border crossing). A direct train via the Padang Besar border may be quicker and is certainly more convenient.

AIR
Sultan Abdul Halim Airport is 11km north of town just off the Lebuhraya. Malaysia Airlines, AirAsia and Firefly all offer daily flights; promotional fares to Kuala Lumpur can be as low as RM35 after taxes.

BUS
The tiny bus station on Jln Langgar handles only local buses, including the regular shuttle service to the Shahab Perdana express-bus station on Jln Mergong, 4km north of the town centre (90 sen). A taxi costs RM10. All long-distance buses leave from here.

Frequent buses depart throughout the day for Bukit Kayu Hitam (RM3.20), Kangar (RM3.80) and Kuala Kedah (RM1). There are also regular coaches, operated by several different companies, to KL (RM30), Ipoh (RM17), Butterworth (RM6.30), Melaka (RM35) and Johor Bahru (RM55), as well as to east-coast destinations including Kuantan (RM44.45), Kuala Terengganu (RM41.40) and Kota Bharu (RM28).

Bus services to Sungai Petani (RM3.70, one hour) make a stop on Jln Tunku Ibrahim opposite the Pekan Rabu market. Some buses from the express-bus station stop here too.

TAXI
Rates for a four-passenger taxi from the taxi station include RM40 to Bukit Kayu Hitam, RM65 to Butterworth, RM30 to Kangar, RM18 to Kuala Kedah and RM40 to Padang Besar.

TRAIN
The **train station** (☎ 731 4045; Jln Stesyen) is southeast of the town centre. There is one daily northbound train to Hat Yai in Thailand (from RM12, three hours), and one southbound to KL (from RM35, 11½ hours).

KUALA KEDAH
☎ 04
This busy fishing village 11km from Alor Setar is the southern gateway to Langkawi. If you have time, visit **Kota Kuala Kedah**, a fort built around 1770 opposite the town on the far bank of Sungai Kedah. In one of history's little twists, this Portuguese-built castle became a bastion of Malay independence against warring Siamese, finally falling to invaders in 1821. Try to find 'Meriam Badak Berendam' (The Wallowing Rhino), a cannon stuck in the debris of the collapsed

sea wall, believed to be the abode of the fortress's guardian spirit.

Ferries (☎ 762-6295) to Langkawi leave approximately every half-hour (1½ hours from April to October, the wet season) from 7am to 7pm (adult/child RM23/17).

PULAU LANGKAWI
☎ 04

Langkawi is synonymous with 'tropical paradise': swaying palms, a cool colour contrast of jungle green and ocean blue (offset by brilliant blood red, rich purple and golden mellow come sunset). Despite their immense drawing power, these 99 islands, dominated by 478.5-sq-km Pulau Langkawi, have not been overdeveloped beyond recognition. The district's been duty free since 1986 and roping in tourists well before that. Since 2008 the archipelago's official title is *Langkawi Permata Kedah* (Langkawi, the Jewel of Kedah).

Get just a little ways off the main beaches (themselves pretty pristine) and this is idyllic rural Malaysia, all *kampungs* and oil lamps and admittedly some nice cars (tourists do tend to bring the ringitts with them). And Langkawi, frankly, is fun. Compared to Thailand, Malaysia's islands are dry when it comes to alcohol, but Langkawi is an exception to this rule. You'll still see all sorts of wholesome Malaysian fun happening (hundreds of Malays line dancing on a beach is a sight that sears itself into your eyeballs), but come night, there's a fair amount of booze-fuelled fun about. Past the bad behaviour is a commendable focus on ecosustainability, although this track record isn't perfect.

Orientation
Langkawi is big folks, almost 500 sq km. Kuah, in the southeast corner of the island, is the main town and the arrival point for ferries, but the beaches are elsewhere.

On Langkawi's west coast, the most developed beach is Pantai Cenang, and its southerly appendage of Pantai Tengah. Pantai Kok's lovely beach is lined with luxury resorts and a modern marina. The airport is on the island's central-west coast near Kuala Muda. There are a few isolated resorts here, but the beach is pretty poor. The north coast of the island hides upmarket resorts at Teluk Datai in the west and Tanjung Rhu in the east.

Langkawi International Airport is in the western part of the island, about 5km north of Pantai Cenang.

Information
EMERGENCY
Langkawi Hospital (☎ 966 3333; Jln Bukit Tengah, Kuah)

INTERNET ACCESS
TCY International (☎ 955 2466; Pantai Cenang; per hr RM3) One of the cheaper internet cafes.

INTERNET RESOURCES
www.langkawi-ferry.com Ferry timetables and fares.
www.langkawigeopark.com.my Information on the island's geopark status.
www.langkawi-online.com A comprehensive source of island information.

LEGENDARY LANGKAWI

The name Langkawi combines the old Malay words *helang* (eagle) and *kawi* (strong). Classical Malay literature claims the island as one of the resting places of Garuda, the mythological bird that became Vishnu's vehicle. The whole island is steeped in legends, and the favourite story is of Mahsuri, a maiden who was wrongly accused of infidelity. Before finally allowing herself to be executed, she put a curse on the island for seven generations. As proof of her innocence, white blood flowed from her veins, turning the sands of Langkawi's beaches white. Her mausoleum can be seen near Kuah (p217).

Another legend concerns the naming of places around the island. Pulau Langkawi's two most powerful families became involved in a bitter argument over a marriage proposal. A fight broke out and all the kitchen utensils were used as missiles. The *kuah* (gravy) was spilt at Kuah and seeped into the ground at Kisap, which means 'to seep'. A pot landed at Belanga Perak (Broken Pot) and finally the saucepan of *air panas* (hot water) came to land where Air Hangat village is today. The fathers of these two families got their comeuppance for causing all this mayhem – they are now the island's two major mountain peaks. You can learn more at the intriguing Lagenda Langkawi Dalam Taman (p217).

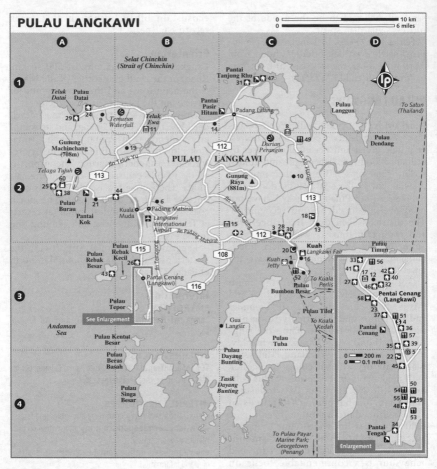

PULAU LANGKAWI

www.mylangkawi.com This website is also worth a look.

MONEY
The only banks are at Kuah, although there are ATMs at the airport and Telaga Harbour Park. There are also moneychangers tucked into and around duty-free shops. There are a couple of moneychangers at Pantai Cenang, but elsewhere most travellers have to rely on the resort hotels, which a) give bad rates and b) might not change money if you are not a guest.

TOURIST INFORMATION
Tourism Malaysia (☎ 966 7789; Jln Persiaran Putra, Kuah; ⏲ 9am-1pm & 2-6pm) Comprehensive information on the whole island.

TRAVEL AGENCIES
Bayu Adventures (☎ 966 0006; Jetty Point Complex, Kuah) Arranges day trips and package trips to Thailand.
Legend Admire Travel & Tours (☎ 966 1368; 50 Persiaran Bunga Raya, Kuah) This leading tour operator runs a variety of trips around the island and to Pulau Payar.
TCY International (☎ 955 2466; Pantai Cenang) Runs tours round Langkawi and Perlis.
Travel Shop (☎ 955 8829; Pantai Cenang) Attached to the Malibest Resort, this place can book an array of island tours.

Sights & Activities
KUAH & AROUND
Kuah is Langkawi's main town, and the main reason to stop here is for banks, ferries or duty-free shopping. There are, however, a few points of interest.

Next to the jetty, the **Lagenda Langkawi Dalam Taman** (☎ 966 4223; Jln Persiaran Putra; admission free; ⏰ 8am-7pm) is a landscaped 'folklore theme park' that stretches along the waterfront. Bright statues dotted amid the lakes illustrate several Langkawi legends – with signboards in English – and there's a narrow, mediocre strip of beach. It's a popular spot for joggers.

Just to the west are the golden onion domes of **Masjid Al-Hana** rising above **CHOGM Park**, which, as a plaque proudly states, was the site of the first-ever international coconut-tree climbing championship in 1987 (won by Sri Lanka). The flags represent members of the Commonwealth, whose leaders met here in 1989.

The international-standard **Gunung Raya Golf Resort** (☎ 966 8148; www.golfgr.com.my; Jln Air Hangat; 9/18 holes RM150/200; ⏰ 7am-7pm), designed by golf guru Max Wexler, is about 8km north of town in a spectacular location in the foothills of Langkawi's highest mountain. Just south of the golf club is the **Kedah Marble** quarry. It's open to visitors.

In the same area you'll find **Langkawi Bird Paradise** (☎ 966 5855; 1485 Jln Kisap, off Jln Air Hangat; adult/child RM15/8; ⏰ 9am-6pm), which touts itself

as Asia's first fully covered wildlife park. There are plenty of animals around (with an emphasis on exotic birds), but we can't say all of them look well cared for.

If you've been wondering what to get former Prime Minister Dr Mahathir Mohamad for his birthday, you could see what everyone else bought at **Galeria Perdana** (☎ 959 1498; Mukim Air Hangat; admission RM10; ⏰ 8.30am-5.30pm). Established by Mahathir himself, the museum displays the sort of weird gifts that get passed between foreign nations and heads of state (F-1 racers, Ming vases painted with Mahathir's face – that sort of thing).

KOTA MAHSURI & PADANG MATSIRAT
Back around 1819 (the date is debated), the Malay princess Mahsuri was unjustly accused of adultery and executed by stabbing. With her dying breath she cursed Langkawi with seven generations of bad luck and expired, supposedly bleeding white blood, a sign of her innocence. Not long after, the Siamese invaded the island, and some 160 years later, in 1987 (that's about seven generations) Langkawi took off as a tourism destination. That's the story anyways, and its been

KEDAH & PERLIS

commemorated by **Kota Mahsuri** (Mahsuri's Fort; ☎ 955 6055; Mukim Ulu Melaka; adult/child RM10/5; 🕑 8am-6pm), a historical complex that includes Mahsuri's Shrine (a fenced-in slab of white stone) as well as a re-creation of a traditional house, a theatre, a 'diorama museum' and some simple food outlets. A fun-in-a-corny-way dinner theatre that focuses on traditional dance takes place from 8pm to 11pm (except Thursday); the cost is RM99.

A result of Mahsuri's curse can still sometimes be seen in the '**field of burnt rice**' at nearby **Padang Matsirat**. There, villagers once burnt their rice fields rather than allow them to fall into the hands of Siamese invaders. It's said heavy rain still sometimes brings traces of burnt grains to the surface.

These sites are west of Kuah, a few kilometres off the road leading to the west-coast beaches and the airport

PANTAI CENANG

Las Vegas has the strip, Bangkok has Khaosan Rd and Langkawi gets Pantai Cenang, 25km west of Kuah. OK, this 2km beach isn't as wild as those other spots, but it is Langkawi's main vein. There are some very fine top-end resorts here, as well as the bulk of Langkawi's budget and midrange accommodation. Come night time, an odd mix of expats, domestic tourists, backpackers and package holiday-makers take to the main road to eat, drink, window shop and generally make merry. That said, Pantai Cenang is fairly sedate in low season.

The beach is gorgeous: white sand, teal water, green palms and all that good stuff. A sandbar sometimes appears at low tide, allowing you to inspect local sea life. Between November and January you can walk across this sandbar to the nearby island of **Pulau Rebak Kecil**, but only for two hours around low tide. The island of **Pulau Tepor** can be reached by hired boat from Pantai Cenang.

At the southern end of Pantai Cenang is the Zon duty-free shopping centre and **Underwater World** (☎ 955 6100; www.underwaterworld langkawi.com.my; adult/child RM38/28; 🕑 9.30am-6.30pm, to 8.30pm Fri-Sun), Malaysia's largest aquarium, featuring 200 different species of marine and freshwater creatures. Some exhibits (especially the rainforest walk) are well executed; some feel like a tropical aquarium in need of a cleaning, but in general it's a great place for the kids.

At the northern end opposite Casa del Mar hotel is **Laman Padi** (Rice Garden; ☎ 955 4312; admission free; 🕑 grounds 7am-midnight, museum 10am-6pm), an 'ecotourism' complex with picturesque rice paddies populated by water buffaloes and ducks. There's also a museum dedicated to rice cultivation, some restaurants, a post office and **Nawa Sari Spa** (☎ 955 4168; http://nawasarispa .com; Laman Padi; 🕑 10am-11pm), where you can contently watch rice paddies sway under the breeze while you're pummelled and oiled by Thai masseurs (massages RM45 to RM100).

If Thai massage isn't your thing, get a different oily rubdown at **Indian Ayurvedic Massage** (☎ 955 9078; www.langkawi-ayurvedic-massage.com), in an unassuming hut 200m off the main road. Customers rave about treatments like *shirodhara*, where a continual flow of warm herbal oil is poured over your forehead as your head and shoulders are massaged. Treatments cost around RM65 to RM195.

Call the above spas to see if they'll provide you with free pick-up service.

PANTAI TENGAH

Head south and Langkawi gets a little more polished; as the road loops around a rocky headland, you're in more upscale Pantai Tengah. There are a few big, all-inclusive resorts here, good restaurants and bars and a few cheaper chalet clusters.

For the traveller in need of some spoiling, the six spa suites at **Ishan Spa** (☎ 955 5585; Pantai Tengah; 🕑 10am-10pm) offer some pretty posh pampering – air treatments, body scrubs, herbal baths and the like – in a space that screams traditional setting (dark wood, frangipani and the like), but also boasts all sorts of modern accents. Rates run from around RM100 to RM350, more for multiday treatments.

PANTAI KOK

On the western part of the island, 12km north of Pantai Cenang, Pantai Kok fronts a beautiful bay surrounded by limestone mountains, jungle and, sadly, a mall. **Telaga Harbour Park** (www.telagaharbour.com) is a yachting marina/harbourfront shopping complex plunked amid some very fine nature.

Heading inland from Pantai Kok you'll come across Oriental Village shopping complex and the station for **Langkawi Cable Car** (☎ 959 4225; adult/child RM25/18; 🕑 10am-6pm Mon-Thu, from noon Wed, 9.30am-7pm Fri-Sun), which will take you on a vertiginous 20-minute trip to the top of the majestic **Gunung Machinchang** (708m). There are some incredible views along the way.

The **Anna & The King Gallery** displays props and costumes from the 1999 film of the same name, which was partly shot at Pantai Kok, but the gallery was closed for maintenance during our visit.

TELAGA TUJUH

If you've been splashing around the ocean, why not add some variety to your life and lounge in some freshwater rock pools? Telaga Tujuh (Seven Wells), located at the top of a waterfall inland from Pantai Kok, is a series of small pools connected by a thin trickle of mountain flow. The smooth rut between pools is slick enough to slide down, especially towards the bottom; doing so is great fun.

You can get here by rented car, motorbike or taxi; drive to the end of the road, about 1km past Pantai Kok, then turn along with the road to the right until you reach the car park. From here it's a steady 10-minute climb through the rainforest (stay to the right) to the wells at the top of the falls. You can make a 2.5 kilometre hike from here to the cable car station; this is a taxing route that requires sound shoes and a good level of physical fitness.

TELUK DATAI

The beaches and jungle around Teluk Datai are some distance off the main road around the island. Here you'll find Langkawi's most exclusive resorts and the **Golf Club Datai Bay** (☎ 959 2700; www.dataigolf.com; 9/18 holes RM300/400), said to be among Malaysia's top 10 courses. The resorts' beautiful beaches are for guests only. The road continues past the resorts to a headland where a short trail takes you through the jungle and down to the sea.

On the way to Teluk Datai is **Langkawi Crocodile Farm** (☎ 959 2559; adult/child RM15/10; ◷ 9am-6pm). If you're not a kid or sympathetic to reptiles you may enjoy the twice-daily 'stunt' shows and hourly feedings, but the small, dirty pools and the fact that many of the farm's residents are turned into meat is a turn-off for many.

Further along where the road turns west along the coast to Teluk Datai is the **Ibrahim Hussein Foundation Museum** (☎ 959 4669; adult/child RM12/free; ◷ 10am-6pm), which displays the abstract and multimedia works of its founder

and namesake. It's good art, especially if you need a break from traditional batik-work and the like.

Temurun Waterfall is halfway between the museum and the resorts. The high falls are worth a look; the turn-off is just east of a huge concrete archway spanning the road.

PANTAI PASIR HITAM

As you head east along the north coast the landscape humps into thickly jungled hills before flattening into a clawed, jagged coast where high tide seems to sweep out the beach. When you can see sand, it appears leopard-spotted and tiger-striped with black; this isn't technically a black-sand beach, but mineral oxides have added their colour scheme to the coast. The beach, Pantai Pasir Hitam, is only a couple of metres wide and located at the foot of a 5m drop, so you can't walk along it.

Before reaching the beach, you'll pass the **Kompleks Kraf Langkawi** (☎ 959 1913; admission free; ◷ 10am-6pm), an enormous handicrafts centre where you can watch demonstrations of traditional crafts and buy any traditional Malaysian product or craft you can imagine. There are also a couple of on-site exhibitions devoted to local legends and wedding ceremonies.

You'll also eventually pass the Kedah cement plant, which stands out like a post-apocalyptic smoke-belching thumb amid the green.

TANJUNG RHU

Just beyond Pasir Hitam at the village of Padang Lalang there's a roundabout with a turn-off to the north to Tanjung Rhu, while the main road continues back to Kuah. Driving toward Tanjung Rhu you'll pass through a corridor of medium-density jungle with a river running to the east lapping at the shore of more hills. It looks like a tempting spot for a swim, but sheer drops make it tough to access the water.

Eventually you'll reach Tanjung Rhu, which has one of Langkawi's wider and better beaches, fronted by magnificent limestone stacks that bend the ocean into a pleasant bay. On clear days, the sunsets here give 'stunning' new meaning. The water is shallow, and at low tide you can walk across the sandbank to the neighbouring islands, except during the monsoon season. Local shops offer mangrove cruises, and kayaks can be hired.

KEDAH & PERLIS

BEST BEACHES

Langkawi's many beaches are among the best in Malaysia. The busiest is the 2km-long strip of sand at **Pantai Cenang**, which has the biggest concentration of hotels, and is popular with everyone from 20-something backpackers to older package tourists. There are watersports activities at hand, and the water is good for swimming, but jellyfish are common, so you might feel a bit tingly when you go for a dip. To the south, **Pantai Tengah** is quieter, with a more family-friendly/honeymooner atmosphere. The beaches at **Pantai Kok** on the west coast are again popular with family groups, but many of the best ones are inside luxury resorts and are inaccessible to nonguests, as are the beautiful sands at **Teluk Datai** on the north. Go to **Tanjung Rhu** for perfect sunsets. The beach on **Pulau Beras Basah** is one of the best for children. It's a small, clean shallow beach, great for swimming and for snorkelling.

Around the promontory, accessible by hired boat, is the **Gua Cerita** (Cave of Legends). Along the coast for a couple of kilometres before the beach, the tiny fish known as *ikan bilis* (anchovies) are spread out on mats to dry in the sun.

GUNUNG RAYA

The tallest mountain on the island (881m) can be reached by a snaking, paved road through the jungle. It's a spectacular drive to the top with views across the island and over to Thailand from a lookout point and a small teahouse (assuming there's no fog). Access to the mountain may occasionally be restricted by the government; the gate at the foot of the mountain will be lowered.

AIR HANGAT VILLAGE

This **village** (☎ 959 1357; culture shows adult/child RM4/2; ⏰ 9am-6pm) is towards the north of the island, not far from the turn-off to Tanjung Rhu, and is known for its hot springs. Apart from watching the water gush along artificial channels and buying souvenirs, there's not much to do, although 'cultural shows' take place occasionally – contact the tourist office to see if anything is lined up. As with so many places on Langkawi, the springs are associated with an intriguing legend (see the box, p215).

DURIAN PERANGIN

Roughly 15km north of Kuah is the turn-off to these waterfalls, which are 3km off the main road. The swimming pools, 10 minutes' walk up through the forest, are always refreshingly cool, although the falls are best seen at the end of monsoon season: late September and early October. In the dry season, naturally, they are not so spectacular.

PULAU DAYANG BUNTING

Tasik Dayang Bunting (Lake of the Pregnant Maiden) is located on the island of the same name. It's a freshwater lake surrounded by craggy limestone cliffs and dense jungle, and its good for swimming. You can rent a pedalo for a spin round the lake, or just sit on the edge of the jetty and have your toes nibbled by the resident catfish.

Legends say a childless couple, after 19 years of trying, had a baby girl after drinking from this lake; since then it's been a popular pilgrimage destination for those wanting children. The lake is also supposedly inhabited by a giant white crocodile. North of the lake is **Gua Langsir** (Cave of the Banshee), which is inhabited by thousands of bats.

The island is best visited on one of the island-hopping tours.

PULAU PAYAR MARINE PARK

Strung out like several green jewels in the teal is this marine park, the focus of Langkawi's dive and snorkeling expeditions. Most trips come to 2km-long Pulau Payar, although you probably won't see the interior of the island – all the action centres on a diving platform and horseshoe-bend of coast. Inquire about the water conditions before you go, as it can be murky. But when it's clear you don't even have to snorkel to be treated to some wonderful views of tropical fish.

Langkawi Coral (☎ 966 7318; www.langkawicoral .com; Lot 1-21 Jetty Point Complex, Kuah) is the main tour operator for Pulau Payar. Trips including snorkelling/diving cost RM240/300. You can also book tickets to the park from Penang (see p188). **East Marine** (☎ 966 3966; www.eastmarine.com .my; Royal Langkawi Yacht Club, Jln Pantai Dato Syed Omar, Kuah) offers the same trip for RM240/340, as does **Pro Dive** (☎ 955 3739; Pantai Cenang). The East

Marine and Pro Dive outfits both offer PADI-certification for around RM1500.

Tours

There are travel agents in Kuah, along Pantai Cenang and at most upmarket resorts that organise tours (see Travel Agencies, p216). Note the following prices are especially subject to change depending on whether meals are included, the number of sites visited etc.

The most popular day trip is the island-hopping tour, offered by most companies (adult/child from RM60/40). The tour usually takes in Pulau Dayang Bunting, Pulau Beras Basah, sea stacks, sea caves and a cruise around mangroves for a look at the local eagles. Pulau Singa Besar might also be visited, with its resident population of mouse deer and crotchety monkeys.

Eagle-feeding tours (adult/child from RM170/110) put customers up close with Langkawi's famous brahminy kites and sea eagles, but there is a significant argument for not feeding the birds. Eagles run the risk of becoming dependent on human handouts and lose their fear of human contact, making them easier prey for hunters. If bad meat is thrown to the eagles (which congregate in large flocks for feeding tours), the health risks to the relatively small population are enormous. Finally, while providing eye candy for tourists, no significant research knowledge is gained from the feeding sessions.

There are several cruise operators in Langkawi, including **Crystal Yacht Holidays** (☎ 955 6545; www.crystalyacht.com), which operates popular sunset dinner cruises (adult/child from RM220/100).

More active trips are run by **Langkawi Canopy Adventures** (☎ 955 4744; www.langkawi.travel/lca.htm) and include jungle trekking (RM120), abseiling through the rainforest (from RM210) and kayak trips (from RM250). The company also operates triathlon/ironman training camps.

Fishing trips are also available, costing from around RM300 for four hours, though prices will depend on when, and for how long, you want to go.

During the monsoon season from July to mid-September, the seas are often too rough and unpredictable for many of the above boat trips.

Diving trips normally concentrate on Pulau Payar (opposite).

Festivals & Events

Langkawi hosts some major events including the **Langkawi International Maritime and Aerospace exhibition** (LIMA; www.limamaritime.com.my) around November, the **Langkawi Arts and Crafts Festival** (LACRAF) in December, the **Langkawi International Water Festival** in April and the biennial **Langkawi International Festival of Arts** (LIFA).

Sleeping

Accommodation options are constantly improving here, especially at the luxury end of the scale. Teak villas and gussied-up traditional huts (with chandelier showerheads, silk sheets and cable TV, natch) strive to outdo each other in the pampering stakes, all to your benefit. Further down the price range you'll end up in decent hotels and chalets, while backpackers will find a decent variety of hostels and dorms. All categories of price are 30% to 50% more expensive than what you'll find on the mainland.

During school holidays and the peak tourist season (November to February), Pulau Langkawi can become crowded, though something can usually still be found. At other times of the year supply far outstrips demand.

KUAH

There's no reason to stay in Kuah unless you *seriously* have a thing for duty-free shopping.

Eagle Bay Hotel (☎ 966 8585; www.eaglebay.com.my; 33 Jln Persiaran Putra; s & d RM125, f RM135; ❊) Right opposite CHOGM Park, this book has a drab cover, but on the inside it's a smart hotel that provides the usual three-star comforts and various package deals.

City Bayview Hotel (☎ 966 1818; www.bayviewhotels .com/langkawi; 1 Jln Pandak Mayah; r/ste from RM185/260; ❊ ▢ ⬚) A reliable choice. This is your standard high-rise chain hotel decked out with stylish rooms and excellent facilities, including a gym, sauna and rooftop pool.

PANTAI CENANG

Pantai Cenang encompasses all the variety of Langkawi accommodation, from veritable jungle villas to backpacker enclaves. As regards the latter, this is the best concentration of budget accommodation on the island. Many places are on the opposite side of the road from the beach and don't have sea views.

KEDAH & PERLIS

Budget

Gecko Guesthouse (☎ 019-428 3801; rebeccafiott@ hotmail.com; dm RM10, r RM25-70; ⚡) 'How long you been here?' 'Two weeks.' 'How long were you going to stay originally?' 'Three days.' 'How long are you staying?' (*Laughs*). Yep – that's the vibe in this most backpacker of backpacker joints. There are a jungly collection of bungalows, chalets and dorms, lotsa dreadlocked folk in the common area, very good chocolate milkshakes behind the bar and a fair bit of popularity – you may want to book early.

Rainbow Lodge (☎ 955 8103; dm RM15, r from RM40) Set a little ways back from the beach, this is a perfectly passable option for those needing a cheap place to rest in between eating, drinking, hangover and more drinking. The dorm looks like a barracks, but it's a good spot for meeting folks.

Sweet Inn (☎ 955 8864; r RM50-70; ⚡ 💻) Super Sweet, actually: a cute yellow building dotted with umbrella-shaded tables, rooms that keep cool in the heat and a friendly common area where meeting fellow congregants at the temple of backpacking is easy and breezy. Just behind but almost sharing the same grounds with Sweet Inn is Daddy's Guest House, where rooms (RM40) are a bit cheaper. It looks a little more like a Malaysian apartment block, but the actual rooms are quite nice, and top-floor ones have sea views.

AB Motel (☎ 955 1300; r RM50-90; ⚡) This is a relatively basic complex of scrubbed-down rooms that gets good reviews from travellers for its cleanliness and extremely easy beach access.

Palms Guest House (☎ 017-631 0121; r from RM65; ⚡ 💻) Run by a friendly English couple, this is an upscale guesthouse, slightly so in terms of price and more so in terms of conditions – rooms feel like the guest suite in a family cottage by the sea. They're clean and centred around a gravel-strewn courtyard shaded by (guess) palms, and there's free wi-fi.

Midrange

Langkapuri Beach Resort (☎ 955 1202; s & d from RM95, f from RM160; ⚡) Pleasant clutch of chalets at the southern end of the beach, near the Zon shopping complex. The chalets are small but clean and comfortable. The pricier ones have sea views and a bit more character.

Malibest Resort (☎ 955 8222; http://langkawi baron-reservations.net; r RM120-230; ⚡) Malibest is a friendly place with a great variety of rooms

set among palm trees right on the sand. These range from slightly older but still comfortable wooden chalets to more modern brick bungalows to the undisputed king of the crop: 'treetop' chalets that sit atop tall wooden pylons and enjoy uninterrupted sea views.

Nadia's Inn Comfort Langkawi (☎ 955 1202; r/ste from RM120/320; ⚡ 🌐) Despite having a name that sounds more like a phrase than a hotel, the rundown on Nadia's is short and sweet: it's a pleasant series of rooms (some of which, admittedly, have horrendous pink lighting – avoid) situated around a faux thatch *kampung* with spacious dimensions, crisp sheets and pleasant-as-you-please service.

Grand Beach Resort (☎ 955 1457; s/d from RM140/180; ⚡) These wooden chalets include what are, essentially, attached cottages that are good for large groups of travellers, but if you're on your own you may want to opt for another option. You'll want to avoid the fan rooms, which get waaay too stuffy.

Langkawi Boutique Resort (☎ 955 7778; www .langkawiholidayresort.co; s & d from RM145, tr from 185; ⚡ 💻 🌐) Hey – nothing says classy like lots of marble in a bathroom, right? There may not be loads of character here, seeing as it's a tower near a pool, some palms and the ocean, but when you're paying a solidly midrange price for an almost-top-end experience, who's complaining?

Top End

Pelangi Beach Resort (☎ 952 8888; www.pelangi beachresort.com; r/ste from RM546/1268; ⚡ 🌐 🌐) This rambling resort towards the northern end of the beach has tastefully furnished chalets in vast, landscaped grounds. It's a family-oriented resort with a full program of kids' activities and sports, restaurants and every imaginable luxury – even electric buggies to take you to your room.

our pick Bon Ton Resort (☎ 955 1688; www.bonton resort.com.my; villas RM590-1160; ⚡ 💻 🌐) The trick of the posh Southeast Asian resort is to present the lodging under the guise of traditional aesthetics, but deck it out with the best modern luxuries, resulting in the best of both worlds. And with that, ladies and gentlemen, we present: the Bon Ton. These eight distinct Malay stilt houses perch over a coconut plantation and a pool, each one decked out with dark wood (wonderful) and positioned to catch the breeze. It's somehow regal and rustic all at once, with its organic accents and traditional craftwork, and very beautiful overall.

Temple Tree (☎ 955 1688; www.templetree.com.my; villa from RM690-1090; ✗ ☐ ☒) This extension of the Bon Ton (above) is a collection of villas that expands on the historical-structure theme; whereas Bon Ton draws inspiration from Malay *kampung*-style stilt houses, Temple Tree references Malaysia as a whole, with Chinese, Penang, colonial-style and other themed residences. The digs are as incredible as the properties at Bon Ton, so it all just depends: do you want to be pampered in a Malaysian village or a colonial villa?

Casa del Mar (☎ 955 2388; www.casadelmar-langkawi .com; r/ste from RM740/1170; ✗ ☐ ☒) Directly opposite the Laman Padi, this is a sumptuous, Spanish villa–style place on a lovely stretch of beach. Several package deals are available, and prices vary dramatically according to occupancy.

PANTAI TENGAH

Larger, midrange resorts dominate Pantai Tengah, though it's still less built up than Pantai Cenang, and is popular with young families.

Zackry Guest House (www.zackryguesthouse.langkawi networks.com; dm/s/d RM20/30/40; ✗ ☐) The best budget accommodation in Tengah is this friendly, sprawling guesthouse, inhabited by happy travellers boozing it up in the common area, Irish owner Neve and her Malaysian boyfriend Chaz and several large, friendly dogs. Rooms are clean and cosy, and there are no phone bookings.

Tropical Resort (☎ 955 4075; from r RM90; ✗) A huddle of modern chalets is set among palm trees in this quiet spot at the back of the beach, just a few minutes' walk from the seashore. It's probably best for singles; families may find the conditions a little cramped.

Sunset Beach Resort (☎ 955 1751; www.sunset beachresort.com.my; r RM160-260; ✗) This is a more upmarket resort, with comfortably furnished chalets surrounded by lush tropical gardens; it has that whole village-cum-resort vibe going on. There's no sea views, although the beach is close.

Frangipani (☎ 955 2020; www.frangipanilangkawi .com; r/ste from RM430/900; ✗ ☐ ☒) All sorts of businesses in Langkawi seek your custom by claiming to prioritise eco issues, but the Frangipani put its money where its mouth is. Treatment plants recycle resort water;

energy-efficient light bulbs are in every room; sustainable building materials provide the setting. And the rooms themselves are easily the match of the best high-end chains: big beds, big spoiling and big views.

Holiday Villa (☎ 955 1701; www.holidayvilla.com.my; r/ste from RM240/810; ✗ ☐ ☒) A vast, modern complex, with tennis courts, a gym, several restaurants and an indoor pool 'exclusively for ladies'. Rooms are airy and brightly furnished, and look out over the lawns and the soft white-sand beach.

PANTAI KOK

Geopark Hotel (☎ 959 2300; www.oriental-inn.com; r from RM184; ✗) Located within the Oriental Village shopping compound inland from Pantai Kok, this modern hotel has large, neatly furnished rooms with the usual mod-cons such as minibars and satellite TVs. It's a bit overpriced considering the distance from the sea.

Mutiara Burau Bay (☎ 959 1061; www.mutiarahotels .com/mutiara_buraubay; s/d from RM480/500; ✗ ☐ ☒) There are huge swathes of rainforest and beach to explore at Mutiara Bay, plus some 150 decked out, cool and comfortable cabanas to stay in. It's a beautiful spot (all 19 acres of the resort), and between your beach hut and the ocean you may run into some resident monkeys.

Berjaya Langkawi Beach & Spa Resort (☎ 959 1888; www.berjayaresorts.com; r/ste from RM550/1000; ✗ ☐ ☒) Past the headland at the northwestern end of the beach, the oversized Berjaya seems to take up the entire northwest coast of the island. There's some 500 rooms spread over a vast area; guests are ferried between reception and their chalets in minibuses. The waterfront suites are the most attractive, while others look out onto the lush rainforest.

Sheraton Langkawi Beach Resort (☎ 952 8000; www.starwoodhotels.com/sheraton; r/ste from RM690/1355; ✗ ☐ ☒) To the southeast of the other resorts, the Sheraton Langkawi has all the usual five-star amenities in an attractively secluded setting on a forested headland by the sea. It's popular with young families.

PULAU REBAK BESAR

Rebak Marina Resort (☎ 966 5566; www.rebakmarina .com; s & d from RM385, f from RM650; ✗ ☐ ☒) Lying just off Pantai Cenang, the small island of Rebak Besar plays host to this exclusive resort, which offers spacious and elegant chalets in beautifully landscaped grounds. It has all the facilities you would expect, including a gym, a spa, tennis courts and restaurants. Transfers from Langkawi airport are included in the price, and there are several different package deals available, as well as an international-standard yachting marina.

TELUK DATAI

Andaman Langkawi (☎ 959 1088; www.theandaman .com; r/ste from RM990/1500; 🟦 🖵 🐾) Just past Golf Club Datai Bay in a grand wooden Malay-style building within the rainforest is this luxurious retreat with a gym, a spa, tennis courts and its own private beach. It has a kids' club and a babysitting service for families.

Datai Langkawi (☎ 959 2500; www.ghmhotels.com; r/ste from RM1530/2550; 🟦 🖵 🐾) The island's most exclusive beach resort, where you can choose between rainforest villas and roomy seafront chalets, many built on stilts over the water. It has a small city's worth of amenities (spas, gyms, yoga, the works) and a knowledgeable jungle-trekking guide on its staff.

TANJUNG RHU

Tanjung Rhu Resort (☎ 959 1033; www.tanjungrhu .com.my; r from RM1400; 🟦 🖵 🐾) Tucked into a secluded cove on the north coast is a glorious golden beach and a cloud of semi-traditional buildings arranged around a central courtyard. This serene resort (one gets the sense the establishment is trying to blend in with, rather than dominate the jungle) is within walking distance of gorgeous Tanung Rhu beach.

Four Seasons Resort (☎ 950 8888; www.fourseasons .com/langkawi; r from RM1850; 🟦 🖵 🐾) Occupying a superb location overlooking the Andaman Sea, the Four Seasons is a truly luxurious amalgamation of 'pavilions' and villas with all the indulgent comforts and mod-cons you would expect from this international chain. The villas come with large, open lounges, marble bathrooms, plasma TVs and gorgeous sea views, while rooms in the two-storey pavilions look onto the gardens.

Eating

KUAH

Eating options in Kuah town consist of several cheap Chinese eateries and outposts of Western chains.

Charlie's Place (☎ 966 4078; www.langkawiyachtclub .com; Jln Pantai Dato Syed Omar; mains from RM20; 🕙 9am-11pm) About 500m uphill from the jetty is the white-gloved ambience and Western-Asian menu of the breezily aristocratic Charlie's.

Barn Thai (☎ 966 6699; Mukim Kisap; mains from RM20; 🕙 lunch & dinner) On the island's east coast, 9km north of Kuah, is this upmarket Thai restaurant with live jazz on some nights (reservations advisable). The setting, at the end of a raised walkway through a mangrove forest reserve, is actually better than the food.

PANTAI CENANG

Many of the hotels at Pantai Cenang have restaurants.

Tomato (☎ 955 5853; mains from RM4; 🕙 24hr) There are some great tomatoes along Cenang beach. This one serves excellent rotis and a standard curry-rice Indian/Malay menu at all hours – take note, nighthawks.

Red Tomato (☎ 955 9118; mains from RM18; 🕙 8am-3pm & 6-11pm Sat-Thu) The second tomato is red and run by expats who crank out some of the best pizza and pasta on the island. Of all the midrange places serving Western standards on the Cenang strip, this is probably your best bet.

our pick Champor-Champor (☎ 955 1449; mains from RM18; 🕙 7-10.30pm) Serves up imaginative regional cuisine such as pan-fried bamakoise (a local fish) with banana, tofu satay and coconut-crusted calamari. The menu descriptions are particularly intriguing – such as the Thai green curry 'with an exotic taste that makes you kinky' – and the tranquil, open-air garden filled with sweet incense and surrounded with plants and native carvings provides a romantic setting to while away a tropical evening.

Putumayo (☎ 953 2233; mains RM30-40; 🕙 7-10.30pm) Excellent service (the waiter folds your napkin in your lap) amid a beautiful open-air courtyard. The cuisine ranges from across Asia, looping from Malaysia through Thailand to China; we highly recommend the fish cooked Nonya style.

Nam (☎ 955 3643; mains RM30-74; 🕙 11am-11pm) At Bon Ton Resort, Nam boasts a well-executed menu of fusion goodness, from pistachio-encrusted haloumi to a nine-course sampler of Straits Chinese cuisine, and at night, amid Bon Ton's starry jungle grounds, the setting is superb. We didn't make it to the also-fusion-focused restaurant in the Straits Club House in nearby Temple Tree, but have heard plenty of glowing reviews from travellers.

There's a *pasar malam* (night market) north of Pantai Cenang held once or twice a week; it's a good place to get authentic Malay food on the cheap.

PANTAI TENGAH

Boom Boom Corner (☎ 012-473 7167; mains from RM4; ✆ 5pm-late) At the northern end of the strip is a bustling food court serving good-value Malay and Pakistani food.

Fat Mum's (☎ 012-470 7863; Jln Teluk Baru; mains from RM8; ✆ 4pm-midnight) Further on, towards Holiday Villa, Fat Mum's serves up Chinese dishes. It's cheap, cheerful and can get pretty boisterous come the evening.

Kantan (☎ 017-480 9722; mains from RM18; ✆ 3-11pm) Supposedly the country's largest restaurant built in traditional Malay style, Kantan looks like a *kampung* house on steroids. Inside, the menu focuses on upscale executions of traditional Malay food like rendang, fish cooked in coconut milk and such, but the spice is very much toned down for foreigners.

PANTAI KOK

The Oriental Village shopping complex has a handful of restaurants, including **Krathong** (☎ 959 2336; mains from RM8; ✆ lunch & dinner Wed-Mon), a quiet Thai restaurant offering traditional curries and fish dishes.

On the seafront, Telaga Harbour Park is home to a few trendy restaurants, including the oddly Marxist-chic themed **Zabinsa's USSR Restaurant** (☎ 012-432 7408; Perdana Quay; mains from around RM12; ✆ noon-midnight), featuring some vaguely Russian specialities.

Drinking

As Langkawi is a duty-free island, it's arguably the best spot for a booze in Malaysia. While you can get alcohol at many restaurants and hotels for half the price on the mainland, there's a good strip of bars here as well. Most bars open around 5pm and close between 11pm or much, much later, depending on how staff are feeling and how many customers are around.

A good place to start is **Bob Marley Bar**, which tends to open around lunchtime. There are beach mats, posters of the great dreaded one, a fairly predictable soundtrack and very good all-round vibe. If you head south along Pantai Cenang past Zon, you'll hit the **1812 Bar**, run by a slightly mad if friendly northern Englishman who, should you be able to take

a tease from him, is one of the best barmen on the island.

As the evening wears on lots of folks end up in Pantai Tengah, where's there's a well-trodden nightspot path. **Reggae Bar** (✆ noon-2am Sat-Thu), a beachside affair, is actually less reggae-oriented than the Bob Marley Bar, while **Sunba Retro Bar** turns into a dancey mega-club open till about 3am. If you're still ready to party after that, **Little Lylia's Chill Out Bar** is, as the name suggests, a laid-back spot that stays open till – oh God, is that the sunrise? Damn.

If you'd prefer to sip a cocktail in more sophisticated surrounds, try the bars at any of the island's upmarket resorts.

Getting There & Away
AIR
Malaysia Airlines (☎ 955 6322), **AirAsia** (☎ 03-2171 9333) and **Firefly** (☎ 03-7845 4543) all have two or three flights daily between Langkawi and KL, with promotional fares going for as low as RM35. Malaysia Airlines and Firefly fly to Penang (RM85) and Tiger Airways and Silk Air fly to Singapore (RM103).

BOAT
All passenger ferries to/from Langkawi operate out of Kuah. From about 8am to 6.30pm, regular ferries operate roughly every hour in either direction between Kuah and the mainland port of Kuala Perlis (RM18, one hour) and every 30 minutes to and from Kuala Kedah (RM23, 1½ hours).

Langkawi Ferry Services (LFS; ☎ 966 9439) and **Ekspres Bahagia** (☎ 966 5784) operate two daily ferries between Kuah and Georgetown (RM60/115 one way/return, 2½ hours) on Penang. Boats depart from Georgetown at 8.30am and 8.45am and leave Kuah at 2.30pm and 5.30pm.

Ferry to Thailand
From the Kuah jetty, LFS makes runs four times a day, between 9.30am and 4pm, to Satun on the Thai coast (RM30, one hour). From the port you can take a taxi to Satun town for connections to Hat Yai or Phuket.

Getting Around
TO/FROM THE AIRPORT
Taxi destinations from the airport include Kuah jetty or Pantai Cenang (RM24), Pantai Kok (RM28), Tanjung Rhu (RM35) and Teluk Datai (RM45). Buy a coupon at the

desk before leaving the airport terminal and use it to pay the driver.

CAR

Cars can be rented cheaply, and touts from the travel agencies at the Kuah jetty will assail you upon arrival. Rates start at around RM60 per day, but drops with bargaining. Cars and Jeeps can also be rented more expensively at the upmarket beach resorts.

MOTORCYCLE & BICYCLE

The easiest way to get around is to hire a motorbike for around RM35 per day. You can do a leisurely circuit of the island (70km) in a day. The roads are excellent, and outside Kuah it's very pleasant and easy riding. Motorbikes can be hired at stands all over the island. A few places also rent mountain bikes for RM15 per day.

TAXI

As there is no public transport available, taxis are the main way of getting around, but fares are relatively high and it may be worth your time to rent your own vehicle. There is a taxi station at the Langkawi Fair mall and at the jetty (☎ 965 2242). From the Kuah jetty, sample set fares include RM5 to Kuah town, RM24 to Pantai Cenang/Pantai Tengah and RM28 to Pantai Kok. A taxi between Pantai Cenang and Pantai Kok will cost you RM26.

BUKIT KAYU HITAM
☎ 04

This is the main border crossing between Malaysia and Thailand, 48km north of Alor Setar. The Lebuhraya handles the vast majority of road traffic between the two countries, and all buses to Hat Yai, Thailand, come this way so immigration processing on both sides of the border can become jammed. Taking the train via Padang Besar is almost always a quicker and more convenient alternative.

At the border post there are a few restaurants, private car-parking facilities and a **Tourism Malaysia Office** (☎ 922 2078, 731 2322; ☽ 9am-5pm). The easiest way to cross the border is to take a through bus all the way to Hat Yai (though when the border opens in the morning, the lines can be horrendous). Buses and taxis from Alor Setar run to the Malaysian customs post. From here it's roughly 2km to the border crossing. Taxis

on the other side run to Sadao, from which there are buses on to Hat Yai.

If arriving from Thailand, ensure that your passport is stamped by the Malaysian border police – otherwise you may be fined for 'illegal entry' when you leave Malaysia.

There is no accommodation on the Malaysian side. Even with the expense of shelling out for a taxi, you'll end up saving money (and headaches) by proceeding immediately to your next destination.

Once in Malaysia, you'll find taxis (RM35) and regular buses (RM5) to Alor Setar, from which frequent buses go to Kuala Kedah (for Langkawi), Butterworth, KL and destinations across the peninsula. Kuala Perlis, the other departure point for Langkawi, is more difficult to reach – first take a bus to Changlun, another to Kangar and then another to Kuala Perlis.

PERLIS

Perlis is Malaysia's smallest state and doesn't tend to register on most travellers' radar except as a transit point to Thailand or Langkawi (via Kuala Perlis). Even Malays tend to regard it as essentially a rice-producing pocket along the Thai border. This isn't an area that's particularly heavy on sites of interest to tourists, but at the risk of stereotyping, as in many rural backwaters the population here is quite friendly. It can be a kick just to hang out with the locals and improve your Bahasa Malaysia (because English definitely isn't widely spoken). Otherwise, small but beautiful Taman Negara Perlis state park is worth exploring. Being a predominantly Muslim state, Perlis observes the same business hours as neighbouring Kedah.

History

Perlis was originally part of Kedah, though it variously fell under Thai and Acehnese sovereignty. After the Siamese conquered Kedah in 1821, the sultan of Kedah made unsuccessful attempts to regain his territory until, in 1842, he agreed to Siamese terms. The Siamese reinstalled the sultan, but made Perlis into a separate vassal principality with its own raja.

As with Kedah, power was transferred from the Thais to the British under the 1909 Anglo-Siamese Treaty, and a British Resident was installed at Arau. A formal treaty between Britain and Perlis wasn't signed until 1930. During the Japanese occupation in WWII, Perlis was 'returned' to Thailand, and then after the war it again returned to British rule until it became part of the Malayan Union, and then the Federation of Malaya in 1957.

KANGAR

☎ 04

Kangar, 45km northwest of Alor Setar, is the state capital of Perlis. As with the state it's the capital of, there's not a heck of a lot to do here besides relax, pray or chat, all of which are fine options for those awaiting an onwards bus.

Sights

Kangar's sole attraction is the **Muzium Negeri Perlis** (National Museum; ☎ 977 1366; Kompleks Warisan Negeri, Jln Kolam; admission free; ⏰ 9am-4pm Sun-Thu, 9am-noon Sat), with dry exhibitions on the history of the state and the royal family.

Around 7km southwest of Kangar, the modern **Muzium Kota Kayang** (☎ 977 0027; admission free; ⏰ 10am-5pm) houses more displays on local history, including Neolithic tools, royal regalia and ceramics. Also at the site are the modest mausoleums of two 16th-century sultans of Kedah. You'll need to catch a taxi from Kangar to get here (RM15).

Sleeping & Eating

Hotel Ban Cheong (☎ 976 1184; 79 Jln Kangar; s/d RM35/60; 🛇) This old Chinese hotel in the town centre has basic singles with fan and shared bathrooms and air-con doubles with private facilities. It's a reasonable budget option for an overnight stay.

Putra Palace (☎ 976 7755; 135 Psn Jubli Emas; r/ste from RM158/308; 🛇 🖵 🔝) This huge, blocky edifice around 1km east of the town centre is Kangar's top hotel. Rooms are furnished to a high standard and have the usual modcons, and there's an excellent restaurant and a gym.

There are many cheap restaurants and cafes sprinkled around the bus station, including **Kedai Kopi Malaysia** (Jln Jubli Perak), attached to the hotel of the same name, and **Embassy** (Jln Jubli Perak), a food court a few doors along, serving standard Chinese fare and beer. They're both open for breakfast, lunch and dinner.

Getting There & Away

The express-bus station is on the southern edge of town, off Jln Jubli Perak. There are departures to KL (RM33, two daily), Butterworth (RM7.60, one daily), Alor Setar (RM3.80, several daily), Ipoh (RM19.70, two daily), Kota Bharu (RM29.50, one daily) and Johor Bahru/Singapore (RM58, one daily, 12 hours), as well as regular buses to Kuala Perlis (RM1.20). Infrequent buses to Kaki Bukit (RM3.20) and Padang Besar (RM3.20) leave from the chaotic local bus station on Jln Tun Abdul Razak.

If you're impatient to get to Langkawi, a taxi to Kuala Perlis from the bus station costs RM18.

KUALA PERLIS

☎ 04

This small port town in the extreme northwest of the peninsula is visited mainly as a departure point for Langkawi. It is also the closest access port to the island from Thailand.

Sleeping & Eating

Pens Hotel (☎ 985 4122; Jln Kuala Perlis; s & d from RM50; 🛇) Probably the best place in town, with neat, comfortable rooms. Along the same street are a few grotty, dirt-cheap hostels.

Near the jetty are several Malay food stalls serving Kuala Perlis' famous special laksa, as well as a few Chinese restaurants.

Getting There & Away

The bus and taxi station is a short walk from the jetty towards town. The frequent bus 56 to Kangar (RM1.20) swings by the jetty before terminating at the station. Less-frequent direct buses depart for Butterworth, Alor Setar, KL and Padang Besar. From the bus station or the jetty, taxis go to Kangar (RM12) and Padang Besar (RM25).

Ferries to Kuah, on Pulau Langkawi, leave at least hourly between 8am and 6pm (RM15).

PADANG BESAR

☎ 04

On the Thai border 35km northeast of Kangar, Padang Besar itself is nothing special, but it's a popular destination for Malaysians because of the duty-free markets in the neutral territory between the two countries. Near the large roundabout are a few banks that will change travellers cheques. Moneychangers will give you even better rates for bank notes (foreign or Thai baht) and have the added advantage of being open longer hours than banks, and open every day.

If arriving from Thailand, ensure that your passport is stamped by the Malaysian border police – otherwise you may be fined for 'illegal entry' when you leave Malaysia.

There's some accommodation on the Malaysian and Thai sides of the border, but you're better off avoiding these mostly dingy budget hotels and heading straight for Kangar or beyond.

Malaysian buses stop near the large roundabout around a kilometre from the large border-crossing complex on the Malaysian side. There are regular buses to/from Kangar (RM4) and, less frequently, to Kaki Bukit. The taxi stand is on the left before you reach the bus stop, and fares are posted for destinations, including Kaki Bukit (RM15) and Kangar (RM20).

Very few people, if any, walk the more than 2km of no-man's land between the Thai and Malaysian sides of the border. Motorcyclists shuttle pedestrian travellers back and forth for about RM5 each way, though bargaining is possible.

There is one daily train connection between Padang Besar and Hat Yai (RM9, 50 minutes). All passengers must disembark to clear customs and immigration (both Thai and Malaysian) before reboarding.

TAMAN NEGARA PERLIS

The small state park of Taman Negara Perlis in the northwest of the state runs for 36km along the Thai border, covering about 5000 hectares. It comprises the Nakawan Range – the longest continuous range of limestone hills in Malaysia – and the Mata Ayer and Wang Mu Forest Reserves.

Information

The **Park Visitor Centre** (☎ 945 7898; psp@pd.jaring .my; Jln Kaki Bukit; ☺ 9am-noon & 2-4pm Mon-Fri) is signposted 3km from the small town of Kaki Bukit. All visitors must register here, and entry to the park is RM2 per day. Guides (RM30 for four

hours) can also be hired at the centre, and are obligatory for many areas.

Sights & Activities

Taman Negara Perlis has heavily forested slopes and numerous cave systems, such as **Gua Wang Burma**, which has intriguing limestone formations. The park is the country's only semi-deciduous forest, and is rich in wildlife; this is the only habitat in Malaysia for the stump-tailed macaque. White-handed gibbons and a rich array of birds can also be found here.

Just outside the park, **Gua Kelam** (Cave of Darkness; admission RM1; ☺ 9am-6pm) is a 370m-long cavern gouged out in tin-mining days; today it's the state's top tourist attraction. A river runs through the cave and emerges in a cascade at a popular swimming spot and a landscaped park. The old tin mine is a short walk from the far end of the cavern. Listen for motorcycles that may be rushing through, and watch out for exploding guano (the build-up of phosphates is highly flammable). The cave is a 1km walk from Kaki Bukit.

The **Wang Kelian Sunday Market** straddles the Malaysia-Thailand border. Fruit, vegetables and clothes from both countries are for sale, and no passport is needed, provided you stay in the market area. The Malaysian side of the market is open every day.

Sleeping

The modern wooden chalets in the **park visitor centre** (dm RM10, chalets RM50-80; 🕄) are very comfortable. You can pitch a tent for RM1.

Getting There & Away

There is no public transport to the park. The nearest town is Kaki Bukit, from which a winding mountain road leads to the tiny village of Kampung Wang Kelian. The park visitor centre is signposted 3km further on.

A taxi to the park from Kangar will cost around RM50 to RM60. Taxis may be harder to find in Kaki Bukit. If you can find one, a taxi from Kaki Bukit to the park will cost roughly RM20 to RM30, but you may be able to negotiate.

Negeri Sembilan

Seat of the Minangkabau people and home to the Cape Rachado Forest Reserve (the last stretch of preserved forest on the west coast of Peninsular Malaysia), Negeri Sembilan (Nine States) has a lot of diversity for its small size. The pedestrian state capital, Seremban, is a slow starter with few notable sights, but within the city's orbit lie the tranquil towns of Sri Menanti, home of the beautifully noble Istana Lama (Old Palace), and Kuala Pilah with its lively night market.

The most popular region of the state is Port Dickson, a long stretch of white beaches chock-full of resorts of every calibre. From here it's an easy day trip to the Cape Rachado Forest Reserve where you can climb up to the ancient lighthouse, descend to empty beaches, search for elusive wildlife and, if you happen to be here between mid-February and mid-April, watch one of the greatest bird shows in the country when thousands of raptors cross low overhead from Sumatra in their annual northward migration.

It's hard to dig up authentic Minangkabau culture today as much has been lost since the people originally settled here from Sumatra in the 15th century, but fortunately the fiery cooking style has lost little of its potency. Search out this cuisine in Seremban and around.

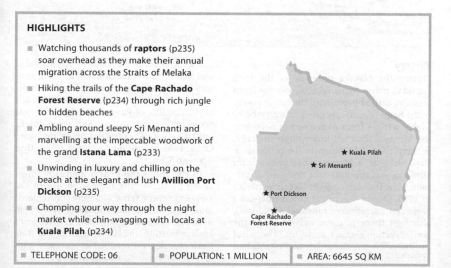

HIGHLIGHTS

- Watching thousands of **raptors** (p235) soar overhead as they make their annual migration across the Straits of Melaka
- Hiking the trails of the **Cape Rachado Forest Reserve** (p234) through rich jungle to hidden beaches
- Ambling around sleepy Sri Menanti and marvelling at the impeccable woodwork of the grand **Istana Lama** (p233)
- Unwinding in luxury and chilling on the beach at the elegant and lush **Avillion Port Dickson** (p235)
- Chomping your way through the night market while chin-wagging with locals at **Kuala Pilah** (p234)

★ Kuala Pilah

★ Sri Menanti

★ Port Dickson

★ Cape Rachado Forest Reserve

| ▪ TELEPHONE CODE: 06 | ▪ POPULATION: 1 MILLION | ▪ AREA: 6645 SQ KM |

NEGERI SEMBILAN

0 — 20 km
0 — 12 miles

To Jerantut (68km)

PAHANG

SELANGOR

To Ipoh (195km)

KUALA LUMPUR

Teriang

Sungai Serting

Serdang
Kajang

B19

N32

Titi

9

Tasik Bera

Semenyih

Sungai Linggi

86

10

Kuala Klawang

11

To Kuantan (125km)

Kampung Langkap

Kampung Parit Tinggi

Mokek

Mantin

Pantai

Bahau

Sungai Muar

Sungai Palong

Kuala Lumpur International Airport (KLIA)

Seremban

Terachi

51

Kuala Pilah

Sri Menanti

Sepang

Pedas

5

E29

Rembau

Lebuhraya (Tollway)

9

1

Gemas

Lukut

Sungai Linggi

Lukut Fort

JOHOR

Port Dickson

Tampin

Teluk Kemang

Pengkalan Kempas

Lubok China

E2

Segamat

Cape Rachado Forest Reserve

Tanjung Tuan Lighthouse (Cape Rachado)

Blue Lagoon

Masjid Tanah

Alor Gajah

MELAKA

Kampung Kuala Linggi

Selat Melaka (Strait of Melaka)

Tanjung Bidara

Durian Tunggal

19

To Johor Bahru (175km)

Jasin

History

During the Melaka sultanate of the 15th century, many Minangkabau people from Sumatra settled here. With the rising power of the Bugis (a seafaring group of warrior-like Malay settlers from Makassar) in Selangor, the Minangkabau felt increasingly insecure, so they turned to Sumatra for protection. Raja Melewar, a Minangkabau prince from Sumatra, was appointed the first *yang di-pertuan besar* (head of state) of Negeri Sembilan in 1773. Out of this initial union emerged a loose confederation of nine *luak* (fiefdoms), although there is some debate about the confederation's exact make-up. The royal capital of Negeri Sembilan was established at Sri Menanti.

Like Selangor to the north, Negeri Sembilan was rich in tin, so for much of the 19th century it suffered unrest and political instability motivated by greed. After Raja Melewar's death, the title of *yang di-pertuan besar* was taken by a succession of Sumatran chiefs, until a series of protracted tin-related wars in 1824–32 led to the severance of political ties with Sumatra.

In the 1880s the British gradually intervened by increasing their influence in the area, and several territories were consolidated into a new confederacy controlled by a British Resident. Becoming part of the Federation of Malaya in 1948, the largely agricultural state has increasingly diversified its economy, with special emphasis on manufacturing.

Climate

The temperature in Negeri Sembilan ranges from 21°C to 33°C and average humidity exceeds 82%. There is rain through the year, with September to November the wettest months.

Getting There & Away

The Lebuhraya (North–South Hwy), connecting Johor Bahru and Kuala Lumpur, is the major road through the state. To get to Negeri Sembilan from KL, see p233; for interstate buses see p234 and p236.

SEREMBAN
☎ 06

A mere 64km southeast of KL, Seremban is the low-key state capital with a bland and busy grid of streets at the centre of town and some lovely gardens and architecture on the city's fringes. Seremban's museums and parks can make an OK outing from KL (if you have a car) or a walk around the Lake Gardens is a pleasant diversion if you're changing buses and have a few hours on your hands.

Minangkabau-style buffalo-horn roofs may adorn many recent buildings, such as the city hall, but the only real access point to Minangkabau culture is at the Muzium Negeri, a component of the Taman Seni Budaya on the outskirts of town. The city itself is home mostly to Chinese and Indian populations.

Information

HSBC (50-52 Jln Dato Bandar Tunggal) Has a 24-hour ATM.
OCBC (cnr Jln Dato Lee Fong Yee & Jln Dato Bandar Tunggal) Has a 24-hour ATM.
Sembilan Internet Library (per hr RM3; ☾ 24hr) Noisy gaming hall; east of the Carlton Star Hotel (p232).

Sights
ARCHITECTURE

Its wonderful multiple roof-points a striking landmark for central Seremban, the **Dewan Undangan Negeri** (State Secretariat Bldg; btwn Jln Dato Abdul Kadir & Jln Dato Abdul Malek) is a fine melding of modern and traditional architecture opposite the **Istana Besar** (Jln Bukit; ☾ closed to the public), home of the sultan of Negeri Sembilan. Directly south and once the offices of the colonial administration, the neoclassical (1912) **State Library** (off Jln Dato Hamzah), west of the Lake Gardens, is Seremban's most imposing colonial building.

Further south, the nine pillars of **Masjid Negeri** (State Mosque; Jln Dato Hamzah) represent the nine original states of Negeri Sembilan.

Seremban's central districts have a few colonial features hidden between lots of more modern buildings. Flee from the heat into the cool, white interior of the Catholic **Church of the Visitation** (85a Jln Yam Tuan), where Mass in English is held on Sunday at 9am, or the more sober **Wesley Methodist Church** (Jln Dato Sheikh Ahmad), built in 1920. The premier colonial school for Seremban's elite, the **King George V School** (Jln Za'aba), still functions as a high school.

Its roof decorated with dragons, the main altar of the **Liesheng Temple** (Jln Dr Samuel; ☾ daylight hr) is dedicated to three Taoist idols, chief among which is Guandi (the God of War). The Chinese characters above the altar mean 'Your needs will be answered'.

LAKE GARDENS

The quaint Lake Gardens are a tame recreation reserve and the place where courting couples go in the evenings. The gardens are at the edge of the green and tranquil colonial district that now mostly houses government quarters.

MUZIUM NEGERI

The **Muzium Negeri** (State Museum; Jln Sungai Ujong; admission free; ☾ 10am-6pm Tue, Wed, Sat & Sun, 8.15am-1pm Thu, 10am-12.15pm & 2.45-6pm Fri), built in the style of a Minangkabau palace, displays handicrafts and historical exhibits. Displays cover the Emergency (see p37), complete with gruesome post-capture portraits of communist leaders. The museum is inside the **Taman Seni Budaya** (Arts & Cultural Park; Jln Sungai Ujong; admission free), which keeps the same hours.

Nearby and also on the museum grounds is the **Rumah Negeri Sembilan**, a less ornate traditional house with a shingle roof showing the hallmark curved-roof style based on the buffalo horn.

Sleeping

While the Kuala Lumpur International Airport (KLIA) is only 20 minutes away, Seremban has a rather depressing selection of hotels. You're better off in KL – even Port Dickson or Melaka are only about an hour away by bus or train and are much better choices. Several of the cheap Chinese flophouses in the centre of town are bordellos; we advise steering clear of those.

NEGERI SEMBILAN

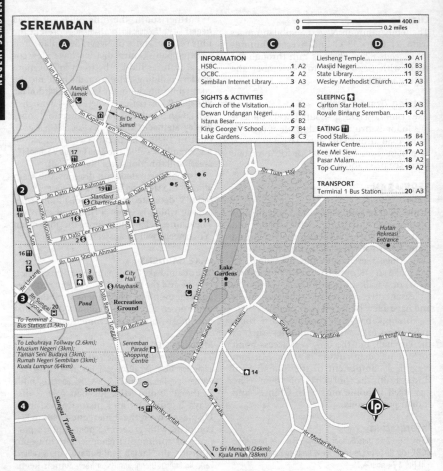

SEREMBAN

0 ————— 400 m
0 ————— 0.2 miles

INFORMATION
HSBC..................................1 A2
OCBC.................................2 A2
Sembilan Internet Library........3 A3

SIGHTS & ACTIVITIES
Church of the Visitation.............4 B2
Dewan Undangan Negeri........5 B2
Istana Besar..........................6 B2
King George V School............7 B4
Lake Gardens.......................8 C3

Liesheng Temple....................9 A1
Masjid Negeri.......................10 B3
State Library.........................11 B2
Wesley Methodist Church......12 A3

SLEEPING
Carlton Star Hotel..................13 A3
Royale Bintang Seremban........14 C4

EATING
Food Stalls...........................15 B4
Hawker Centre......................16 A3
Kee Mei Siew........................17 A2
Pasar Malam.........................18 A2
Top Curry.............................19 A2

TRANSPORT
Terminal 1 Bus Station............20 A3

Carlton Star Hotel (☎ 762 5336; 47 Jln Dato Sheikh Ahmad; r RM75-115; ✗) Safe, freshly painted and within walking distance of Terminal 1 bus station, this hotel has boring but big business-style rooms. The staff is friendly and there's a handy internet cafe across the street.

Royale Bintang Seremban (☎ 766 6666; Jln Dato AS Dawood; www.royalebintang-seremban.com; r/ste from RM250/350; ✗ ☲ ⟲) This four-star resort-style business hotel has uninspiring but comfortable rooms, a good range of restaurants and amenities (swimming pool with water slides, fitness centre, a jogging track to the nearby lake gardens and more) and helpful staff. It's the top choice for Seremban although greater luxury can be found in KL.

Eating

Minangkabau-style dishes worth a try, such as *masak lemak* (fish, meat or vegetables cooked in coconut milk), *rendang* (a thick, dry meat curry usually served with rice cooked in coconut milk) and *dendeng balado* (beef with chilli). It's also said that you haven't been to Seremban if you haven't tried the local *pao* (Chinese-style buns stuffed with meat).

Functional food stalls (generally open from morning to night), serving some Minangkabau fare, are south of the train station (on Jln Tuanku Antah), and at the upstairs **hawker centre** (Jln Lee Sam). The bustling Saturday **pasar malam** (night market; Jln Lee Sam) also has plenty of food stalls.

Kee Mei Siew (24 Jln Dato Bandar Tunggal; ⏳ 8am-6pm) This basic shop is a great place to pick up some of Seremban's famous *pao*.

Top Curry (☎ 767 2294; btw Jln Tuanku Hassan & Jln Dato Abdul Rahman; banana leaf meals RM6.50) Folks from KL come to visit just to eat at this cavernous cafe serving excellent southern Indian curries.

Getting There & Away

Seremban lies on the main north–south rail line from KL to Singapore. KTM Komuter trains, part of KL's city rail network, depart frequently between KL Sentral and Seremban (RM8, last train around 10pm, 45 minutes).

Transnasional buses (☎ 763 8798) leaving from the Terminal 1 bus terminal on Jln Sungai Ujong include departures to KL (RM7, 30 minutes, every 20 minutes), Singapore (RM45, five hours, two per day), Melaka (RM7, 1½ hours, hourly), Kuantan (RM22, six hours), Kuala Pilah (RM4.50, one hour, every 15 minutes) and Kuala Terengganu (RM39.70, six hours). Bus 67 runs to Port Dickson (RM4, one hour). The terminal has a **left-luggage counter** (small/big bag per hr RM1/RM1.50; ⏳ 7.30am-9pm). Long-distance taxis muster upstairs for destinations such as Port Dickson (RM50), KL (RM90), Melaka (RM120) and Sri Menanti (RM40).

Some long distance buses stop at Terminal 2 about 1.5km from town centre – free shuttle buses run from here to Terminal 1.

To reach Seremban from KLIA, first take a bus from the airport to Nilai (RM3) and change to a KTM Komuter train to Seremban (RM2.50).

SEREMBAN TO KUALA PILAH

East from Seremban, the road meanders through the hills to the town of Kuala Pilah, penetrating the heartland of Minangkabau culture around the old royal town of Sri Menanti. Look out for **Minangkabau houses** along the main road, though the traditional thatch of buffalo-horn roofs has been replaced by more utilitarian corrugated iron. The village of **Terachi**, 27km from Seremban at the turn-off to Sri Menanti, has some particularly fine traditional houses, as do villages further north, including **Pantai**, and Sri Menanti itself.

Sri Menanti

☎ 06
Tidy and placid Sri Menanti, 6km off the Seremban–Kuala Pilah road, is the old royal capital, first settled over 400 years ago by Minangkabau immigrants from Sumatra. Swathed in a silence only interrupted by bird song, this sleepy, disengaged hamlet nestles in a highland valley surrounded by green jungle hills, fringed with simple dwellings and scampering chickens.

Just past Sri Menanti's own tiny Lake Gardens is **Istana Besar**, the impressive palace of the sultan of Negeri Sembilan (not open to the public). Originally built in the 1930s, the later addition features a blue-tiled Minangkabau roof.

Just beyond Istana Besar is the magnificent **Istana Lama** (Old Palace; admission free; ⏳ 10am-6pm Sat-Thu, 10am-12.15pm & 2.45-6pm Fri), now a museum. Designed by master craftsmen, the beautiful black hardwood palace is the centrepiece of Sri Menanti. Arranged over four floors, the palace was fashioned without the use of nails in 1908 as a temporary replacement for an even older palace that was razed by British soldiers during the Sungai Ujong wars. The structure is elevated on 99 pillars, many of them carved, each one representing the legendary 99 *luak* (clan) warriors. Inside you can see the king and queen's bedchambers, the children's playroom, a large dining room and huge dining table, as well as kris weaponry and royal regalia. Climb to the top floor for views over the gardens.

Back towards the main road in the compound next to the mosque is the **Makam Di Raja** (Royal Cemetery), which has a distinctive Victorian/Moorish pavilion. The prominent grave of Tuanku Abdul Rahman, the first king of independent Malaysia, is immediately inside the gates.

The two-storey **Sri Menanti Resort** (☎ 497 0577; dm/d RM15/77, chalet RM108-126; 🄿 🏊), next to Istana Lama, has reasonably well-maintained rooms, including 14-bed dorms. Note that room prices rise by RM10 or so on Saturday and Sunday. Nonguests can avail themselves of the swimming pool for RM5.

To reach Sri Menanti from Seremban, take a bus to Kuala Pilah (RM4.50) and then a taxi (return trip around RM30).

Kuala Pilah

☎ 06

Kuala Pilah, a pleasant valley town 40km east of Seremban, is one of the main townships in this strongly Minangkabau region. It's colourfully decorated with brightly painted shophouses.

Its few temples of note include the **Kuil Sri Kanthaswamy** (Jln Melang; ☺ main prayer hall 6.30am-7pm), overflowing with colour and arrayed with deities. The **Sansheng Gong** (Sansheng Temple; Jln Dato Undang Johol) has a skilfully carved boat, from the time of Qing emperor Guangxu, hanging just inside the door. The fierce-looking bearded idol in the centre is Guandi (God of War). There are marvellous carvings along the front of the temple and worn frescoes on the wall. Opposite the temple is an elaborate Chinese-style decorative archway dedicated to Martin Lister, the first British Resident (1889–97) of Negeri Sembilan.

There's no reason to get stranded here, but if you do, Kuala Pilah has several cheap Chinese hotels. The **Desa Inn** (☎ 481 8033; 745 Jln Dato Abdul Manap; d/f RM55/77; ✹) offers clean doubles with tiled floors, air-con, minute TVs, kettle, coffee and small balcony (but you may get woken by the sonorous 6am call to prayer).

For dinner, the lively **night market** (Jln Yam Tuan), near Desa Inn, kicks off at around 6pm daily when the air becomes heavy with the fragrance of satay (from 35 sen) and a medley of Malay and Indian aromas.

There are regular buses from Seremban (RM4.50, one hour, every 15 minutes). In Kuala Pilah, the **bus station** (☎ 288 7207) is hidden away behind the archway opposite the Sansheng Gong. Buses depart for Johor Bahru (RM25) and Kuantan (RM19).

PORT DICKSON

☎ 06

When people talk about Port Dickson (PD) they're usually referring to the long coastline studded with beaches – the actual Port Dickson is a small uninteresting town slightly inland. The beach area is a popular spot for weekend warriors from KL, but during the week it's nearly deserted and is a good place to find a bargain resort and relax poolside for a few days or more. When you feel the need to move, head out to the Cape Rachado Forest Reserve (right) for some fabulous hiking.

For internet access, try **MDS Internet** (3A Km 6.5 Jln Pantai; per hr RM3), 400m south of the Seri Malaysia hotel. A useful moneychanger can be found at the bus station. The post office is opposite the bus station.

Sights & Activities

CAPE RACHADO FOREST RESERVE

The area's highlight is the 80-hectare **Cape Rachado Forest Reserve** (also called the Tanjung Tuan Forest Reserve), the only remaining patch of coastal forest on the west coast of Peninsular Malaysia. This jungle of towering lowland trees has secluded beaches that are ideal turtle laying grounds and is also a stop-over for over 300,000 migratory birds every year (see the boxed text, opposite, for more details). The turn-off to the reserve is near the Km 16 marker (the local bus can let you off here); head down the road for 2km to the Ilham Resort (opposite) and then through the forest reserve for another kilometre to the **Tanjung Tuan lighthouse** (Rumah Api). Unfortunately the lighthouse, which was first built in 1528 by the Portuguese and is the oldest in Malaysia, isn't open to the public. You can, however, walk around to the front of it for great views and on a clear day you can see Sumatra, 38km away across Selat Melaka. A simple network of trails heads into the forest from around the lighthouse and from the road towards the lighthouse to a handful of beaches (bring lots of water – it's a steep climb).

OTHER SIGHTS & ACTIVITIES

The strip of white sand that extends for some 16km along the coast is more popular for it's proximity to KL than anything else, but it's pretty and a pleasant getaway. Unfortunately the water is fairly polluted and the surrounding tourist development looks, for the most part, industrial.

For something beyond jungle and sand, head to the **Port Dickson Ostrich Farm** (☎ 662 7496; Km 14.5 Jln Pantai; adult/child RM8/4; ☺ 9am-5.30pm) for ostrich races (11am and 3.30pm on weekends only), where the birds reach speeds of up to 70kph, as well as ostrich rides and a small farm teeming with crocodiles, goats, peacocks, rabbits and other furry friends.

At the festival of **Navarathiri** (September or October), the goddess Sri Maha Mariamman is conveyed at night on a chariot procession around Port Dickson. The goddess performs

---

IN RAPTURE OF RAPTORS

If you're in Port Dickson around mid-February to mid-April, don't miss the chance to see migrating raptors (birds of prey such as kestrels, falcons and eagles) make the crossing from Sumatra to the Asian continent via the Cape Rachado Forest Reserve. Some 25 species head north for the summer each year and, having used up most of their energy getting across the Straits of Melaka, are tired and fly so low that you can see them stunningly close-up. The birds that arrive late in the afternoon or evening often rest and recuperate at the reserve for the night before heading off again on their long journeys. Without this precious forested rest area, naturalists say that many of the birds would die of exhaustion or starvation.

Sightings are of course not guaranteed and you'll have the best luck seeing the birds from around the Tanjung Tuan Lighthouse between 11am and 3pm when the heat of the day creates thermals for the birds to soar on.

The **Raptor Watch Festival** is held during the height of the migratory period, usually during the first week of March when the lighthouse opens to the public, jungle walks are led by naturalists, live bands come out to the Cape to play and more. For more information and specific dates for the next festival go to www.raptorwatch.org.

---

a similar journey during the **Anniversary Prayers procession** (June or July).

The five-star **Admiral Marina & Leisure Club** (☎ 647 0888; Km 8; www.admiralmarina.com.my) has good dock facilities and is a transit point for racing sailboats.

Sleeping

Rotary Sunshine Camp Holiday Hostel (☎ 647 3798; Km 5 Jln Pantai; dm/r RM7/25) The blue barracks-like buildings behind a chain-link fence look a little depressing on arrival, but this place is so well tended and the staff so friendly that it'll soon win you over. Shower and cooking facilities are shared and it's a short walk to a good beach and cheap food. On weekdays you'll probably have the place to yourself.

Lido Hotel (☎ 662 5273; Km 13 Jln Pantai; d RM45-60; 🅿) It looks like a prison from the outside but inside the rooms are spacious, freshly painted and have attached bathrooms. It's right on the beach.

Casa Rachado (☎ 662 5177; casaranchado@maa .com.my; Tanjung Biru, Km 16 Jln Pantai; r from RM99, ste from RM180; 🅿 🖳) There's a brightly painted Caribbean theme going on at this resort near the Cape Rachado Forest Reserve entrance. Rooms are a little musty but upgrading to a suite gets you an apartment-sized place with a kitchen and views of the sea. Breakfast is included with all room types. There's a tiny mangrove-fringed beach in front and an OK pool. You can also camp here for RM30/50 for two/four people – tent, floor mat and kerosene lantern included.

Corus Paradise Resort (☎ 647 7600; www.corus paradisepd.com; Km 3.5 Jln Pantai; r RM168-418; 🅿 🖳) This is a kitschy kid-friendly choice with a protected artificial lagoon and a big pool with water slides. Rooms are plain but comfortable and there is a handful of mediocre on-site restaurants.

Ilham Resort (☎ 662 6800; www.ilhamresort.com; Tanjung Biru, Km 16 Jln Pantai; r RM180-280, ste RM290-600; 🅿 🖳) Next to Cape Rachado Forest Reserve, Ilham is a massive, elegant resort on a calm bay. The suites are bland and nearly institutional feeling, but rooms have much more style with hardwood floors and muted light. There's a great pool and a quiet stretch of white sand beach.

our pick **Avillion Port Dickson** (☎ 647 6688; www .avillionportdickson.com; Km 5, Jln Pantai; r Sun-Thu RM300-500, r Fri & Sat RM450-950; 🅿 🖳) Beautifully designed and lushly planted with lily ponds, birds of paradise, bromeliads and palms, the accommodation highlight here is the over-the-water chalets that have big terraces you can swim from at high tide. Even the cheapest rooms here are classier than just about anywhere else, with their hardwood floors, elegant wood furnishings, flagstone bathrooms and loads of natural light. Also at hand are several good restaurants, a huge pool with slides, a tennis court and a gym.

Thistle Port Dickson Resort (☎ 662 7878; www .thistle.com.my; Km 16 Jln Pantai, Teluk Kemang; r from RM310; 🅿 🖳) This is a new exclusive hotel (in the refurbished Guoman Resort) set in 90 acres of landscaped grounds with manicured lawns, a private 3km beach, a golf course,

NEGERI SEMBILAN

magnificent pool, beautiful views, a fitness centre and more.

Also recommended:

Kong Ming (Guangming) Hotel (☎ 662 5683; Km 13 Telok Kemang; d Sun-Thu from RM30, Fri & Sat from RM40) Seriously old and rundown but right on the beach, this place is clean, friendly and exudes a gritty, ancient charm.

Selesa Resort (☎ 647 4090; Km 8; superior/deluxe r RM230/290; ❂ ⬛) Minangkabau-style resort with sea-facing rooms, all with small balcony and rather old-style furniture. This is a particularly good stretch of beach.

Seri Malaysia (☎ 647 6070; Km 6; d Sun-Thu RM140, Fri & Sat RM160; ❂ ⬛) Motel-like rooms are right across the street from a good, low-key beach.

Eating

There's a night market with yummy local food stalls in Port Dickson town on the first Saturday of every month, but daily beachside food is limited to a few mediocre food courts, seafood *rumah makan* selling crab by the kilo (around RM22) and restaurants at the resorts.

El Cactus (☎ 012-646 3772; Km 4, Lot 2674, Jln Pantai; meals RM25; ❂ 5.30pm-midnight) is one of PD's few nonhotel bars and a welcoming spot for dinner or a nightcap or two, with outside seating, a music system creatively mounted atop half a Fiat, lounge area, pool table, Latin music and menu (boneless chicken fajitas RM15), plus a relaxed atmosphere.

Getting There & Around

Hourly buses depart for Seremban (RM4, one hour) from where you can get connections to KL, Melaka and beyond. The taxi station is next to the bus station in the centre of town; taxi fares include Melaka (RM120), Seremban (RM50) and KL (RM130).

From Port Dickson town, local buses (RM1) run about every hour and will drop you off wherever you like along the beach. Ubiquitous share taxis are more reliable and convenient and cost RM2 for the first three or four kilometres – expect to pay RM5 to RM15 to get from Port Dickson town to your hotel (depending on the distance). You can flag share taxis down anywhere from the side of the road.

Melaka

Back when Kuala Lumpur was a malaria-ridden swamp and Penang was yet to become the 'Pearl of the Orient,' Melaka was already one of the greatest trading ports in Southeast Asia. Over time it lost favour to Singapore and became a sleepy backwater compared with its high-rolling cousins, but today it's this lost-in-time feel that makes the place so charming.

It's still said that the soul of the country can be glimpsed through the city's mixed Malay, Chinese, Indian and European heritage and the serene *kampung* (villages) scattered among the state's tropical forests, farmlands and beaches. It's true: this is Malaysia's good side and it's no wonder Melaka has become one of the country's most popular destinations. The variations on traditional cuisine, including the famed Malay-Chinese Nonya food, are reason enough to visit and are a delicious way to experience the region's cultural diversity.

While the coastlines of Pulau Besar and Tanjung Bidara don't compare with the country's other beaches, partially due to the water quality of the Strait of Melaka (one of the world's busiest shipping routes), they do make a relaxing getaway or day trip from the state's capital. Other diversions away from the city are manufactured creations: the wildlife and theme park of Ayer Keroh and the golf course and water park of A'Famosa Resort.

HIGHLIGHTS

- Eating Chinese dim sum for breakfast, Nonya food for lunch and Pakistani tandoori for dinner at Melaka's **fabulous restaurants** (p249)
- Catching glimpses of old-time Melaka while leisurely wandering through historic **Chinatown** (p243)
- Snacking, perusing trinket stands and watching Dr Ho Eng Hui pummel his finger into a coconut at the **Jonker Walk Night Market** (p243)
- Feeling like a happy fool while rocking out to 80s dance hits in a wacky Melaka **trishaw** (p253)
- Imagining the past and all its intricacies at the **Baba-Nonya Heritage Museum** (p243)
- Watching freighters move down the Strait of Melaka while lounging on the white sands of **Tanjung Bidara** (p254)

Tanjung Bidara ★

★ Melaka

| ■ TELEPHONE CODE: 06 | ■ POPULATION: 759,000 | ■ AREA: 1652 SQ KM |

MELAKA

History

However the history of the city-state of Melaka is told, the story of the state is inseparable from that of the city for which it was named. Before the late 14th century, Melaka was a simple fishing village.

Parameswara, a Hindu prince from Sumatra, was the founder of Melaka (see the boxed text, opposite). Under Parameswara, the city became a favoured port for waiting out monsoons and resupplying trading ships plying the strategic Selat Melaka. Halfway between China and India, and with easy access to the spice islands of Indonesia, Melaka attracted merchants from all over the East.

In 1405 the Chinese Muslim Admiral Cheng Ho, the 'three-jewelled eunuch prince', arrived in Melaka bearing gifts from the Ming emperor and the promise of protection from Siamese enemies. Chinese settlers followed, who mixed with the local Malays to become known as the Baba and Nonya, the Peranakans or Straits Chinese (see the boxed text, p48). The longest-settled Chinese people in Malaysia, they grafted many Malay customs to their own heritage. By the time of Parameswara's death in 1414, Melaka was a powerful trading state. Its position was consolidated by the state's adoption of Islam in the mid-15th century (see p31).

In 1509 the Portuguese came seeking the wealth of the spice and China trades, but after an initially friendly reception, the Melakans attacked the Portuguese fleet and took a number of prisoners. This prompted an outright assault by the Portuguese, and in 1511 Alfonso de Albuquerque took the city. Under the Portuguese, the fortress of A'Famosa was constructed, and missionaries strove to implant Catholicism. While Portuguese cannons could easily conquer Melaka, they could not force Muslim merchants from Arabia and India to continue trading there, and other ports in the area, such as Islamic Demak on Java, grew to overshadow Melaka.

The period of Portuguese strength in the East was short-lived, as Melaka suffered harrying attacks from the rulers of neighbouring Johor and Negeri Sembilan, as well as from the Islamic power of Aceh in Sumatra. Melaka declined further as Dutch influence in Indonesia grew and Batavia (modern-

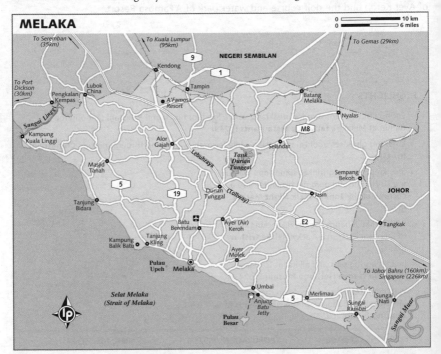

MELAKA

THE PIRATE PRINCE PARAMESWARA

Part legend and part fact, the story of the 14th-century Indonesian Prince Parameswara is the accepted tale of the founding of Melaka. Parameswara was said to be a direct descendent of Alexander the Great, and possessed semi-magical items, some of which were thought to be part of the treasures of Solomon.

After leaving Java and spending time using the island of Temasek (today's Singapore) as a base for his swashbuckling exploits, Parameswara and his faithful band of pirates were forced to flee their new city after an attack by the Siamese. They headed up the Malay Peninsula to the town of Muar in the Johor province, but were soon driven away by a particularly vicious band of monitor lizards. At another short stop, the refugee's freshly built fortress fell into ruins for no apparent reason, making them move on once more.

Not giving up, the group trudged further north and it was here that their luck would change. While hunting at the mouth of the Bertam river, Paremeswara saw a white mouse-deer (*pelanduk*) kick one of his hunting dogs in its defence. The prince was so impressed by the valiant and courageous deer that he decided to build a new city on the spot. He asked one of his servants the name of the tree that was shading them and took the name to christen his town Melaka.

Parameswara later married a Muslim princess which consequently opened the doors of the faith to the rest of the peninsula.

day Jakarta) developed as the key European port of the region. Melaka passed into Dutch hands after an eight-month siege in 1641 and the Dutch ruled Melaka for about 150 years. Melaka again became the centre for peninsular trade, but the Dutch directed more energy into their possessions in Indonesia.

When the French occupied Holland in 1795, the British (as allies of the Dutch) temporarily assumed administration of the Dutch colonies. As traders, the British administrators were essentially opposed to the Dutch policy of trade monopoly and saw the potential for fierce rivalry in Malaysia between themselves and the Dutch. Accordingly, in 1807 they began demolishing the A'Famosa fortress and forcibly removing Melaka's Dutch population to Penang to prevent Melaka rivalling British Malayan centres if Dutch control was restored. Fortunately, Sir Thomas Stamford Raffles, the far-sighted founder of Singapore, stepped in before these destructive policies went too far, and in 1824 Melaka was permanently ceded to the British in exchange for the Sumatran port of Bencoolen (Bengkulu today).

Melaka, together with Penang and Singapore, formed the Straits settlements, the three British territories that were the centres for later expansion into the peninsula. However, under British rule Melaka was eclipsed by other Straits settlements and then superseded by the rapidly growing commercial importance of Singapore. Apart from a brief upturn in the early 20th century when rubber

was an important crop, Melaka returned again to being a quiet backwater, patiently awaiting its renaissance as a tourist drawcard.

Climate
The temperature in Melaka ranges from 21°C to 33°C and average humidity exceeds 82%. There is rain throughout the year, with September to November the wettest months.

Getting There & Away
The Lebuhraya (North-South Highway), linking Johor Bahru and Kuala Lumpur, is the main route through the state. Express buses to KL and Singapore are plentiful and bus connections link with other peninsular destinations. Trains do not stop at Melaka but at Tampin, 38km north of town. Daily boats connect with Dumai in Sumatra. For detailed information on transport, see p252 and p253.

MELAKA CITY
☎ 06
Melaka's Unesco World Heritage Site status, granted in 2008, sealed the town's claim as one as Malaysia's hottest tourist destinations and the development that has ensued is mind-boggling. Unfortunately, as Elizabeth Cardosa of Badan Warisan (see the boxed text, p99) has put it, development so far has mainly come from 'a perceived need to deliver "products" for tourists rather than work to protect the Outstanding

MELAKA CITY

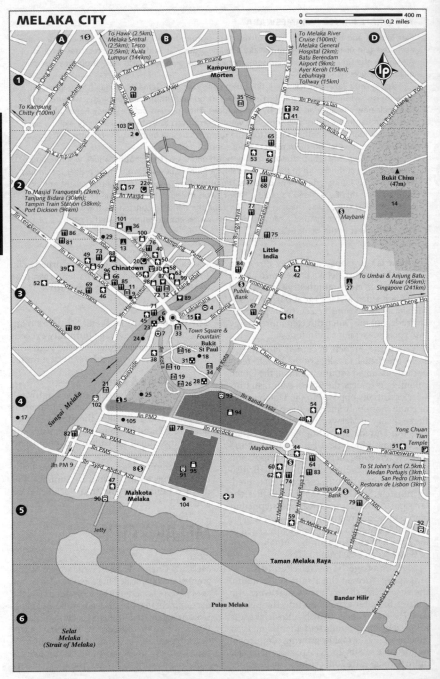

MELAKA

To Hawk (2.5km);
Melaka Sentral
(2.5km); Tesco
(2.5km); Kuala
Lumpur (144km)

To Melaka River
Cruise (100m);
Melaka General
Hospital (2km);
Batu Beréndam
Airport (9km);
Ayer Keroh (15km);
Lebuhraya
Tollway (15km)

Kampung
Morten

Jln Pinang

Jln Tan Chay Yan

Jln Tun Sri Lanang

Jln Peng-ka Jan

Jln Puteri Hang Li Poh

To Kampung
Chitty (100m)

Jln Ong Kim Wee

Jln Ong Kim Wee

Jln Padang

Jln Graha Maju

Jln Hang Tuah

Jln Bukit China

Bukit China
(47m)

To Masjid Tranquerah (2km);
Tanjung Bidara (30km);
Tampin Train Station (38km);
Port Dickson (94km)

Jln Tan Chay Yan

Jln Kampung Hulu

Jln Kubu

Jln Kee Ann

Jln Munshi Abdullah

Jln Bunga Raya

Jln Bendahara

Maybank

Jln Tengkera

Jln Bunga Raya

Jln Kampung Pantai

Little
India

Jln Bukit China

To Umbai & Anjung Batu;
Muar (45km);
Singapore (241km)

Chinatown

Jln Hang Jebat

Jln Tun Tan Cheng Lock

Jln Hang Kasturi

Jln Hang Lekiu

Jln Hang Jebat

Jln Laksamana

Jln Temenggong

Public
Bank

Jln Bukit China

Jln Gereja

Jln Laksamana Cheng Ho

Jln Kota Laksamana

Jln Kota Laksamana

Town Square &
Fountain

Bukit
St Paul

Jln Chan Koon Cheng

Jln Kota

Sungai Melaka

Jln Quayside

Jln Kota

Jln Bandar Hilir

Yong Chuan
Tian
Temple

Jln PM2

Jln PM3

Jln Metdeka

Jln Parameswara

Maybank

To St John's Fort (2.5km);
Medan Portugis (3km);
San Pedro (3km);
Restoran de Lisbon (3km)

Jln PM8

Jln PM4

Jln PM5

Jln Syed Abdul Aziz

Jln PM 9

Mahkota
Melaka

Jln Taman Melaka Raya

Jln TMR

Jln Melaka Raya 3

Bumiputra
Bank

Jetty

Jln Melaka Raya 4

Taman Melaka Raya

Jln Melaka Raya 12

Bandar
Hilir

Pulau Melaka

Selat
Melaka
(Strait of Melaka)

Universal Values for which the site has been inscribed, ie the living cultural heritage of the local communities'. There is still plenty of charm in Chinatown, which is best represented by its resident artists, cooks and creative trishaws, but there is also a slew of gaudy, modern signs on shopfronts and so many photo-snapping tourists that the town is verging on becoming a packaged parody of itself.

It's not quite there yet though, and the modern action still blends in with the surrounding Peranakan, Portuguese and Dutch architecture. With the oldest functioning mosque, Catholic church and Buddhist temple in the country, the city today (as it has for centuries) exudes a tolerance that accepts visitors of every creed and always promises to show them a good time.

And have we mentioned the food? If you're eating local dishes, it's unlikely you'll have a bad meal. From the distinct Peranakan dishes to Eurasian Portuguese cooking and Indian banana leaf shops, the citywide restaurant aromas add further colour to the cultural mosaic that makes Melaka such an astonishing destination.

ORIENTATION

Melaka is a medium-sized town that's easy to navigate and compact enough to explore on foot, bicycle or trishaw.

The colonial areas of Melaka are mainly on the eastern side of the river, focused around Town Sq (which is also known as Dutch Sq) and Christ Church.

MELAKA

Bukit St Paul (St Paul's Hill), the site of the original Portuguese fort of A'Famosa, rises above Town Sq. Located further north is Melaka's tiny Little India, while bustling, scenic Chinatown is to the west.

South of Melaka's old historical quarter are Mahkota Melaka and Taman Melaka Raya, which are two areas built on re-claimed land; bridging Mahkota Melaka to the historic quarter is the Dataran Pahlawan, an enormous new mall and shopping/restaurant complex.

INFORMATION
Bookshops

MPH Bookstores (☎ 283 3050; G73B, Ground fl, Mahkota Parade Shopping Complex, Jln Merdeka; ◷ 9am-10pm) Has the best selection of English-language titles.

Emergency
Melaka Police Hotline (☎ 285 1999)

Immigration Offices
Immigration office (☎ 282 4958; 2nd fl, Wisma Persekutuan, Jln Hang Tuah)

Internet Access

Several cafes in Chinatown have a computer for clients and charge around RM3 per hour.
Fenix Internet Centre (Fenix Inn, 156 Jln Taman Melaka Raya; per hr RM2.50) Also has fax and full business services.

Medical Services

Mahkota Medical Centre (☎ appointments 281 4426/4427, emergency 281 4068/4071; www.mahkotamedical .com; No 3, Mahkota Melaka, Jln Merdeka)
Melaka General Hospital (☎ 282 2344; Jln Pringgit) North of the city centre.

Money

Moneychangers are scattered throughout Chinatown and near the bus stations. There are more ATMs at the shopping malls.
HSBC (Jln Hang Tuah) Has 24-hour ATMs (MasterCard, Visa, Maestro, Cirrus and Plus).
United Overseas Bank (Jln PM5) MasterCard, Visa, Maestro, Cirrus and Plus at its 24-hour ATM.

Post

Post office (Jln Laksamana) This is a small post office off Town Sq.

Tourist Information
Tourism Malaysia (☎ 283 6220; ◷ 9am-10pm) At the Menara Taming Sari tower, it has very knowledgeable, helpful staff.

Tourism Melaka (☎ 281 4803, 1800-889 483; www .melaka.gov.my; Jln Kota; ◷ 9am-1pm & 2-5.30pm) Diagonally across the square from Christ Church, this place was closed for a remodel when we passed.
Tourist Police (☎ 281 4803; Jln Kota; ◷ 8am-11pm)

SIGHTS
Historic Town Centre

This area has a ridiculous number of muse-ums clustered along Jln Kota. A few such as the **Islamic Museum** (admission RM2; ◷ 9am-5.30pm Tue-Sun), the **Architecture Museum** (admission RM2; ◷ 9.30am-5pm Tue-Sun), which focuses on local housing design, and the **Muzium Rakyat** (People's Museum; adult RM2; ◷ 9am-6pm Wed-Mon), which covers everything from *gasing uri* (top-spin-ning) to mutilation for beauty, are worth visiting if you have time on your hands. Most of the others use a bland diorama for-mat where visitors walk through a maze of wordy displays.

STADTHUYS

Melaka's most unmistakable landmark and favourite trishaw pick-up spot is the **Stadthuys** (Town Square; ☎ 282 6526; adult/child RM5/2; ◷ 9am-5.30pm Sat-Thu, 9am-12.15pm & 2.45-5.30pm Fri), the imposing salmon-pink town hall and gover-nor's residence. It's believed to be the oldest Dutch building in the East, built shortly after Melaka was captured by the Dutch in 1641. The vivid colour theme extends to the other buildings around the Town Square and the old clock tower.

To explore inside the Stadthuys you'll need to visit the extensive **History & Ethnography Museum** (◷ guided tours 10.30am & 2.30pm Sat & Sun), which has a number of historical re-creations as well as displays of Chinese and Malay art, weapons and ceramics. Up the hill is the mildly interesting **Literature Museum**, focusing on Malaysian writers. Admission to the above museums (and the **Governor's House** and the **Democratic Government Museum**) is included in the admission price to Stadthuys.

PORTA DE SANTIAGO (A'FAMOSA)

A quick photo stop but a must for anyone visiting Melaka, **Porta de Santiago** was built by the Portuguese as a fortress in 1511. The Dutch were busy destroying the majority of the fort when Sir Stamford Raffles came by in 1810 and saved what remains today. Look for the 'VOC' inscription of the Dutch East India Company on the arch.

In 2006 work on the Menara Taming Sari revolving tower (p245) uncovered another part of the famous wall. The revolving tower was relocated further inland, and the remains of the fortress walls were reconstructed and are now home to the 13m-high **Melaka Malay Sultanate Water Wheel** replica. The original wheel would have been used to channel the river waters for the large number of traders swarming Melaka during the 15th and 16th centuries.

ST PAUL'S CHURCH

St Paul's Church is a breezy sanctuary reached after a steep flight of stairs. Originally built by a Portuguese captain in 1521, the church offers views over Melaka from the summit of Bukit St Paul. Inside the decaying stone interior are intricately engraved tombstones of the Dutch nobility that are buried here. The church was regularly visited by St Francis Xavier, and following his death in China the saint's body was temporarily interred here for nine months before being transferred to Goa, where it remains today. Visitors can look into his ancient tomb (surrounded by a wire fence) in the centre of the church and a marble statue of the saint gazes wistfully over the city.

When the Dutch completed their own Christ Church in 1590 at the base of the hill, St Paul fell into disuse. Under the British a lighthouse was built and the church eventually ended up as a storehouse for gunpowder. The church has been in ruins for more than 150 years.

SULTANATE PALACE

Housing a cultural museum, this wooden replica of a Melaka sultan's **palace** (Jln Kota; admission RM2; ☸ 9am-5.30pm Wed-Mon) is based on descriptions, from the *Malay Annals,* of the original 15th-century palace, built entirely without nails.

MARITIME MUSEUM & NAVAL MUSEUM

Housed in a huge re-creation of the *Flora de la Mar,* a Portuguese ship that sank off the coast of Melaka, the **Maritime Museum** (admission RM2; ☸ 9am-5.30pm) merits a visit. Clamber up for a detailed examination of Melaka's history via faded and dated props. The museum continues in the building next door with more absorbing exhibits featuring local vessels plus an assortment of nautical devices.

Chinatown

Chinatown is the heart of Melaka and is by far the most interesting area to wander around. Stroll along **Jln Tun Tan Cheng Lock**, formerly called Heeren St, which was the preferred address for wealthy Baba (Straits-born Chinese) traders who were most active during the short-lived rubber boom of the early 20th century. The centre street of Chinatown is **Jln Hang Jebat**, formerly known as Jonker St (or Junk St Melaka), that was once famed for its antique shops but is now more of a collection of clothing and crafts outlets and restaurants. On Friday and Saturday nights, the street is transformed into the **Jonker Walk Night Market**, a lively market of food and trinket stalls. Finally, the northern section of **Jln Tokong** (also known as Harmony St) has a handful of authentic Chinese shops selling red and gold lanterns, paper money and funerary preparations.

The following sights are listed in geographical order and could be used as a walking tour: start going northwest on Jln Tun Tan Cheng Lock, follow the map to head southeast down Jln Tokong, then finish by heading northwest again up Jln Hang Jebat.

8 HEEREN STREET

Run by the Heritage Trust of Malaysia, this 18th-century Dutch period residential **house** (admission free; ☸ 11am-4pm Tue-Sat) was restored as a model conservation project. The friendly host will show you around and describe what era each style of the building came from (some as far back as the Portuguese occupation) and what life would have been like inside its walls over the centuries. The project was partially chronicled by Lim Huck Chin and Fernando Jorge in their beautifully designed coffee-table book *Voices from the Street,* which is for sale at the house along with other titles on historical Melaka. You can also pick up an *Endangered Trades: A Walking Tour of Malacca's Living Heritage* (RM5) booklet and map for an excellent self-guided tour of the city centre.

BABA-NONYA HERITAGE MUSEUM

Touring this traditional Peranakan townhouse takes you back to a time when women hid behind elaborate partitions when guests dropped by, and every social situation had its specific location within the house. The captivating **museum** (☎ 283 1273; 48-50 Jln Tun Tan Cheng Lock; adult/child RM8/4, incl tour if enough people; ☸ 10am-12.30pm & 2-4.30pm Wed-Mon) is arranged

COCONUT KUNG FU

While enjoying the Friday and Saturday night Jonker Walk Night Market, don't miss the performance by kung fu master **Dr Ho Eng Hui** (🕒 around 6.30-9pm Fri & Sat) at the southern end of Jln Hang Jebat. He eats fire and throws knives, but the real reason to stick around is to see him pummel his finger into a coconut. If you're not familiar with the strength of a coconut's husk, think back to Tom Hanks in the film *Castaway*. Remember how he spends hours hurling a coconut on the rocks trying to break the damn thing open? Now a soft human finger just shouldn't be able to pierce through a coconut's husk – but this guy really seems to do it and has been entertaining folks by doing so for over 35 years. Dr Ho Eng Hui is in fact a doctor, and the purpose of his performance is to sell a 'miracle oil' (RM10) that cures aches and pains.

to look like a typical 19th-century Baba-Nonya residence. Furniture consists of Chinese hardwoods fashioned in a mixture of Chinese, Victorian and Dutch designs with mother-of-pearl inlay. The highlight is the tour guides who tell tales of the past with a distinctly Peranakan sense of humour.

CHENG HOON TENG TEMPLE

Malaysia's oldest traditional Chinese temple (dating from 1646) remains a central place of worship for the Buddhist community in Melaka. Notable for its carved woodwork, **Cheng Hoon Teng Temple** (Qing Yun Ting, Green Clouds Temple; 25 Jln Tokong; 🕒 7am-7pm) is dedicated to Guanyin, the Goddess of Mercy. All building materials for the temple were imported from China, along with the artisans involved in its construction. A robed effigy of Guanyin can be found within the main temple hall, itself an explosion of black, gold and red. Across the street from the main temple is a traditional opera theatre.

Opposite is the more recently constructed **Xianglin** (Fragrant Forest Temple), which endeavours to follow the layout of a traditional Chinese Buddhist temple.

MASJID KAMPUNG HULU

The oldest functioning **mosque** (Jln Kampung Hulu) ins Malaysia, it was commissioned by the Dutch in 1728. The Portuguese had destroyed all non-Christian establishments during their occupation, but the Dutch had different colonisation tactics and decided to help the locals rebuild their places of worship instead. The resulting mosque is made up of predominantly Javanese architecture with a multitiered roof; at the time of construction, domes and minarets had not yet come into fashion.

KAMPUNG KLING MOSQUE

This hoary **mosque** (Jln Tokong) has a multitiered *meru* roof (a stacked form similar to that seen in Balinese Hindu architecture), which owes its inspiration to Hindu temples, and a Moorish watchtower minaret typical of early mosques in Sumatra.

SRI POYYATHA VINAYAGAR MOORTHI TEMPLE

One of the first Hindu temples built in the country, this **temple** (Jln Tokong) was built in 1781 on the plot donated by the religiously tolerant Dutch and dedicated to the Hindu deity Vinayagar.

CHENG HO CULTURAL MUSEUM

A lengthy paean to Ming Admiral Cheng Ho (Zhenghe), this extensive **museum** (☎ 283 1135; 51 Lg Hang Jebat; adult/child RM20/10; 🕒 9am-6pm Mon-Thu & 9am-7pm Fri-Sun) charts the tremendous voyages of the intrepid eunuch Muslim Chinese seafarer. As a favourite servant of the Chinese emperor's fourth son, Prince Zhu Di, Cheng Ho later became an army officer and ultimately the admiral of China's 'Treasure Fleet', a convoy that solidified China's control over most of Asia during the 15th century. It's a great stop for history buffs, although there's too much information here for anyone expecting a casual visit. The ticket price includes a 15-minute film presentation on Cheng Ho.

Around the City Centre

VILLA SENTOSA

While not an official museum, the 1920s Malay *kampung* house **Villa Sentosa** (Peaceful Villa; ☎ 282 3988; www.travel.to/villasentosa; admission by donation; 🕒 9am-1pm & 2-5pm Sat-Thu, 2.45-5pm Fri), on the Melaka River in Kampung Morten, is well worth a visit. A member of the family will show you around the house. There's a varied collection of objects, including Ming dynasty ceramics and a 100-year-old copy of the *Quran*, but most of all it's an opportunity to wander through a genuine *kampung* house.

ST PETER'S CHURCH

The oldest functioning Catholic church in Malaysia, **St Peter's Church** (Jln Bendahara) was built in 1710 by descendants of early Portuguese settlers. On Good Friday the church comes alive when the Melakans flock here, many of them making it the occasion for a trip home from far-flung parts of the country.

BUKIT CHINA

Besides being the largest **Chinese cemetery** outside of China, Bukit China is also Melaka's best jogging track. Over 12,500 graves, including approximately 20 Muslim tombs, cover the 25 grassy hectares.

In the middle of the 15th century the sultan of Melaka imported the Ming emperor's daughter from China as his bride to seal relations between the two countries. She brought with her a vast retinue, including 500 handmaidens, and the area has been Chinese ever since, the two adjoining hills becoming the burial ground for Chinese traders. At the foot of Bukit China, **Poh San Teng Temple** was built in 1795 and contains images of the Taoist entity Dabo Gong and Guanyin. To the right of the temple is the **Sultan's Well**, a 15th-century well built by Sultan Mansor Shah. It was an important source of water for Melaka and a prime target for opposition forces seeking to take the city.

KAMPUNG CHITTY

Melaka also has a small community of Chitty, or Straits-born Indians, who are the offspring of Indian traders and Malay women. Having arrived in the 1400s, the Chitties are regarded to be older than the Chinese-Malay Peranakan community. Their area of town, known as Kampung Chitty, lies west of Jln Gajah Berang, about a kilometre northwest of Chinatown; look for the archway with elephant sculptures beside the Mutamariman Temple. It's a pretty district in which to wander and see traditional Malay-style houses.

LITTLE INDIA

Across the river from Chinatown is Melaka's surprisingly plain Little India. This busy area along Jln Bendahara and Jln Temenggong is a worthwhile place for soaking in some Indian influence and grabbing an excellent banana leaf meal. During **Deepavali**, a section of Jalan Temenggong closes to traffic to make way for Indian cultural performances and street-side food vendors.

MEDAN PORTUGIS

Roughly 4km east of the city centre on the coast is the **Medan Portugis** (Portuguese Square). The small *kampung* centred on the square is the heart of Melaka's Eurasian community, who are descended from marriages between the colonial Portuguese and Malays 400 years ago. Many of them speak Kristang, a Creole language that mixes Malay with archaic Portuguese. The square, styled after a typical Portuguese *mercado*, wasn't completed until the late 1980s.

The *kampung* is unexceptional and the square is often empty, except on Saturday evenings when cultural events are staged. But the sea breeze is lovely while enjoying a relaxing meal at the many restaurants in and around the square (see p251). Town bus 17 from the local bus station or Panorama Melaka buses will get you here; see Getting Around p253.

ACTIVITIES

For cycling tours to rubber and oil palm plantations out of town, see p246.

Getting High

No we're not suggesting you do anything illegal – Melaka has two very modern activities that give you a bird's-eye view of the city. You have two choices:

Eye on Malaysia, Melaka (child/adult RM10/20; ⏰ 10am-11pm Mon-Thu, 10am-midnight Fri & Sat) This giant gondola-style Ferris wheel spins very slowly for about 20 minutes. At the time of writing the Malaysia International Space Adventure interactive museum (which will include a 4D theatre) was under construction at the site, and a sound and light show on a water screen (that will be highlighted by a fireworks show and water-ski performance) was in the planning stages.

Menara Taming Sari (child/adult RM10/20; ⏰ 10am-10pm) This controversial 80m revolving tower is considered an eyesore by many. Waits can be long and it's all a bit tourist tacky, but is a good way to get your bearings and enjoy great views.

Massage & Reflexology

It seems that reflexology centres have opened up on every corner in Melaka over the last few years. The original, and still one of the best, is **Putuo Traditional Chinese Medical Therapy Centre** (☎ 286 1052; 134 Jln Hang Jebat; 1hr reflexology/qi massage RM38/65; ⊙ 10am-10pm Mon-Thu, 10-midnight Fri-Sun), which offers straightforward, excellent-value services. If you have specific ailments – anything from migraines to water retention – the owner will create a special treatment for you. There are also ear candles, fire cupping, body scrubs and more. The centre's ambience is no-frills Chinese institutional.

TOURS

You can take a DIY city bus tour with Panorama Melaka – see Getting Around, p253.

Boat Trips

Melaka River Cruise (☎ 286 5468; per person RM10) has daily 40-minute riverboat trips (minimum eight people) along the Melaka River from two locations: the 'Spice Garden' on the corner of Jln Tun Mutahii and Jln Tun Sri Lanang in the north of town, and the quay near the Maritime Museum (p243). Cruises don't go out to sea but rather 9km upriver past Kampung Morten and old *godowns* (river warehouses).

Bike Tours

To explore the fascinating landscape around Melaka, join Alias for his three-hour **Eco Bike Tour** (☎ 019-652 5029; www.melakaonbike.com; per person RM80) through 20km of oil palm and rubber tree plantations and delightful *kampung* communities surrounding town. Pick-up is from the Travellers' Lodge (p248). Alias changes the tour around local events or festivals in the area. The tour can leave at either 8am or 3pm any day of the week as long as there are at least two people.

FESTIVALS & EVENTS

Melaka celebrates all the major Malaysian holidays, including Chinese New Year and Thaipusam (see p470).

Easter Good Friday and Easter Sunday processions are held outside St Peter's Church in March/April.

Festa San Pedro In late June, this festival honours the patron saint of the Portuguese fishing community. Celebrations take place at St Peter's Church and normally include a procession from the Porta de Santiago to Medan Portugis and carnival festivities.

Festa San Juan (Festival of St John) This festival is celebrated by Melaka's Eurasian community in late June by the lighting of candles in the Portuguese Settlement.

Dragon Boat Festival This June/July Chinese festival, marked by a dragon-boat race in the Strait of Melaka, commemorates the death, by drowning, of 3rd-century BC Chinese poet and statesman Qu Yuan.

Festa Santa Cruz In mid-September, this festival finishes with a candlelight procession of Melakan and Singaporean Catholics to Malim chapel.

SLEEPING

So many new places are opening up in Melaka that this section is particularly vulnerable to change. The good news is that quality is improving, but the bad news is that there's simply not enough tourism to keep all these places open. Rooms have private showers and dorms have shared bathrooms, unless otherwise stated.

Chinatown

If you have the option of staying in Chinatown, do it. This is what Melaka is all about.

Voyage Guest House (☎ 281 5216; Jln Tukang Besi; dm RM12) Head here for clean, industrial-sized dorm rooms and common areas decorated with a nouveau-heritage Chinatown jazz lounge look. It's run by Voyager Traveller's Lounge (p251).

Sama-Sama Guest House (☎ 305 1980; 26 Jln Tukang Besi; dm RM12, d RM20-40) This place has a great hippy-ish vibe, with a courtyard overflowing with potted plants, mini-ponds and wind chimes. Rooms are intimately linked by creaky wood floors and the breezes that run through the wide walkways. The whole place, including the shared toilets and showers, is kept sparkling clean, but when anyone walks down the hall (usually barefooted) it sounds like they are stomping in combat boots. Not for light sleepers but a fun and quirky place to meet other travellers.

Jalan Jalan Guesthouse (☎ 283 3937; www.jalan jalanguesthouse.com; 8 Jln Tukang Emas; dm/s/d RM12/23/34; 🖳 🛜) This lovely hostel is in a restored old shophouse painted periwinkle blue. Fan-cooled rooms with one shared bathroom are spread out over a tranquil garden inner courtyard. Like some other older places though, noise from your neighbours might keep you awake at night. Internet and wi-fi are free and there's bike rental available.

Ringo's Foyer (☎ 016-354 2223; www.ringosfoyer .com; 46A Jln Portugis; dm/s/d/tr RM12/25/30/40; 🛜) Just far enough out of central Chinatown to be quiet, but close enough to be convenient,

Ringo's is plain and clean, has friendly staff and a relaxing rooftop chill-out area.

Chong Hoe Hotel (☎ 282 6102; 26 Jln Tukang Emas; r with shared bathroom RM25, r with bathroom RM45-75; ☒) Chong Ho has stayed true to its no-frills functional personality and now, after all the years of staying exactly the same, it has an unpretentious charm that's lacking elsewhere. Air-con rooms with bathrooms are some of the cheapest in town and (except when the Kampung Kling Mosque starts blaring) it's a quiet and blissfully unexciting place to catch some Zs.

Kota Lodge (☎ 281 6512; Jln Kota Laksmana; hotelkl8 @streamyx.com; d from RM70; ☒) Heritage not your thing? The brand-new Kota Lodge offers freshly painted characterless rooms, all with good beds, air-con and hot showers. It's stumbling distance from central Chinatown – just follow the signs on Jln Tun Tan Cheng Lock.

Baba House (☎ 281 1216; www.thebabahouse.com .my; 125-127 Jln Tun Tan Cheng Lock; s/d incl breakfast from RM59/75; ☒ 🛜) This elegant Baba building has beautiful tile work, carved panels and a cool, interior courtyard, but rooms, many window-less, aren't nearly as glitzy as the lobby and are dark and worn.

Heeren Inn (☎ 288 3600; heerenin@streamyx.com; 23 Jln Tun Tan Cheng Lock; d RM78-145; ☒ 🖳) Housed in an attractive building, the motel-like window-less rooms here lack the ancient flair of the common areas. Rooms bordering the light-filled central courtyard are the brightest of the bunch.

our pick Number 20 Guesthouse (☎ /fax 281 9761; www.selesalifestyle.com; 20 Jln Hang Jebat; d RM95; ☒ 🖳 🛜) A 1673 Dutch mansion meets urban-Zen chic with dark-wood beam construction, high ceilings, a touch of Chinese art, low opium beds, modern lighting and a common area with elongated windows that look over Jln Hang Jebat. Unfortunately, not all rooms have windows, but you can always get a little air on the rooftop garden. To conform with Melaka city's preservation standards, the guesthouse wasn't allowed to build en suite baths, so all rooms here have shared bathrooms. Breakfast is included and it's gay friendly.

Aldy Hotel – Stadhuys (☎ 283 3232; www.aldy hotel.com.my; 27 Jln Kota; d RM118-280, tr/f incl breakfast RM220/260; ☒ 🖳) This boutique-style hotel opposite the foot of Bukit St Paul is a great choice for families. Worn grey carpet and decades-old decor darken the halls, but things perk up again in the rooms that are newly

remodelled, modern and equipped with satellite TV. The on-site bistro is a great stop for Western favourites and fresh fruit juices.

Heeren House (☎ 281 4241; www.melaka.net/heeren house; 1 Jln Tun Tan Cheng Lock; s/d from RM119/129, f RM259; ☒) The airy, clean and lovely rooms (six in all) in this former warehouse largely overlook the river, with polished floorboards, traditional furniture (some with four-poster beds) and clean showers. This is one of the more unpretentiously restored places in town – it's beautiful in its simplicity. A window-lit cafe (p250) is in the foyer – perfect for trying the daily baked goods over the morning paper.

Hotel Puri (☎ 282 5588; www.hotelpuri.com; 118 Jln Tun Tan Cheng Lock; d/f from RM120/310; ☒ 🖳 🛜) One of Chinatown's gems, Hotel Puri is an elegant creation in a superb old renovated Peranakan manor house. Its elaborate lobby, decked out with beautiful old cane and inlaid furniture, opens to a gorgeous courtyard garden. Standard rooms have butter-yellow walls, crisp sheets, satellite TV and shuttered windows. There's an on-site spa and breakfast is included.

Jalan Taman Melaka Raya & Around

This area is close to some of Melaka's better bars and nightlife, plus it's only a short walk to the historic centre and Chinatown.

Samudra Inn (☎ 282 7441; samudrainn@hotmail .com; 348B Jln Melaka Raya 3; dm/d from RM12/30; ☒) This charmingly homey place is for lovers of peace and quiet. Caged birds chirp softly in the courtyard area, but other than that you won't hear a peep out of anyone. There are kitchen facilities if you want to cook and ex-teacher owners take extra steps to make sure their guests are comfortable, such as taking lone visitors out to dinner.

Shirah's Guest House (☎ 286 1041; shirahgh@tm.ent .my; 207-209, 2nd fl, Jln Melaka Raya 1; fan dm/d RM12/30, air-con d RM45; ☒ 🖳) Brightly painted walls and a gentle Malay welcome make this place sit somewhere between a backpackers and a homestay. Some rooms have balconies and all have high ceilings.

our pick Emily Travellers Home (☎ 012-301 8524; 71 Jln Parameswara; dm/s RM16/24, d RM32-48) Enter the humble entrance off the busy road and it feels like you've stepped into another dimension filled with plants, koi ponds, a bunny hopping around (named Mr Playboy) and happy, mingling people. Every room in the heritage building and its annexes is different, from funky cottages with semi-outdoor 'jungle showers' to simple wooden rooms in the house – the dorm rooms have only two beds apiece. The whole place is decorated with recycled or found objects, including a very cool coffee table that transforms into a barbecue. Rates include breakfast and all-day tea or coffee.

Travellers' Lodge (☎ 226 5709; 214B Jln Melaka Raya 1; d with fan from RM30; 🖳) This is one of the more social and deservedly popular backpacker places in town. The kick-up-your-feet common area has an elevated platform TV lounge with cushions and mats strewn about – perfect for lounging. Rooms are all clean, have windows and tiled floors and the sheltered roof terrace is a boon, dotted with flowers and plants.

Kancil Guesthouse (☎ 281 4044; www.machinta.com .sg/kancil; 177 Jln Parameswara; r RM40-50; 🖳) About a 10-minute hoof from Chinatown, this guesthouse is in an elegant, immaculately kept, open and airy heritage home that offers spacious and comfortable rooms (all with fan). You'll want to wander the house, which is lovely and deep, with a gorgeous garden out back. The owners are pleasant and helpful. Bus 17 goes past here.

Fenix Inn (☎ 281 5511; www.fenixinn.com; 156 Jln Taman Melaka Raya; d RM128-168; 🖳 🖳) Efficiency is the name and business is the game at this crisp hotel. Rooms are small and characterless, but most have a window. A particularly good crop of terminals for internet access make this a good choice for anyone who has to work on the road.

Malacca Straits Hotel (☎ 286 1888; www.malacca straitshotel.com.my; 27 Jln Chan Koon Cheng; r/ste RM168/298; 🖳 🖳 🖳) Smack up against the Hotel Equatorial, this hotel calls itself a 'batik boutique' hotel, and it's not a bad description. Ask to see a room or two here before you decide; all are spacious but only about half have hardwood floors and a handful are furnished with some especially nice teak furniture.

Holiday Inn (☎ 255 9000; Jln Sayed Abdul Aziz; www .melaka.holidayinn.com; r from RM225; 🖳 🖳 🖳) Boldly facing historic Melaka like a gleaming white middle finger, this brand-new Holiday Inn is absurdly tall and doesn't have a single heritage quality about it. Rooms are comfy and carpeted yet bland. Ask for a top-storey room for fantastic views over the Strait of Melaka.

Hotel Equatorial (☎ 282 8333; www.equatorial.com; Jln Parameswara; d RM430-500; 🖳 🖳) The Hotel Equatorial can't be beaten for its location

near the historic centre. While it's a bit frayed around the edges, good discounts online can cut prices nearly in half, making this elegant choice excellent value. It's worth upgrading to a deluxe room, which have either balconies or heaps of extra space. Special packages are available through the hotel, which include tours and specials such as cookery courses. Room prices include a RM88 meal credit at any of the hotel's four restaurants.

Little India to Bukit China

This is one of the busiest and traffic-clogged areas of Melaka, but it's convenient if you're visiting on business and is relatively close to all the sights.

Eastern Heritage Guest House (☎ 283 3026; 8 Jln Bukit China; dm/s/d RM10/28/30) With one foot in Chinatown and the other in Little India, this superb though deteriorating 1918 building, with Peranakan tiling and impressive carved panelling, has lots of open spaces with plenty of natural light. There's a dipping pool, sunroof area, a downstairs common room and breakfast is thrown in. The upstairs dorm is airless and bland, but double and single rooms are brightened up by original murals on the walls.

Tony's Guesthouse (☎ 688 0119; 24 Lg Banda Kaba; r RM24-28; 🖳) This is a scatterbrained, old-school hippy backpacker's place that looks like an appealingly untidy artist's living room. The host couldn't be friendlier and it's a great place to meet other budget road warriors over tea.

Aldy Hotel – Chinatown (☎ 281 3636; www .aldyhotel.com; 148 Jln Bunga Raya; r incl breakfast RM150-260; 🖳 🖳 🖳) While the name says it's in Chinatown, this second location of the Aldy boutique hotel (opened in 2008) is actually outside the main Chinatown heritage centre on the busy thoroughfare of Jln Bunga Raya. The 16 rooms, housed in a 1966 building, are comfortable and verging on trendy.

City Bayview Hotel (☎ 283 9888; www.bayviewintl .com; Jln Bendahara; r RM398; 🖳 🖳) This hotel with a modern edge has a smallish pool, dance club and breakfast included in the room price. The views over the old town from some rooms are quite spectacular. This is a favourite with families, and kids will enjoy the rather weird computerised speaking lift.

Renaissance Melaka Hotel (☎ 284 8888; infomkz @po.jaring.my; Jln Bendahara; d RM470; 🖳 🖳) The Renaissance offers five-star service and old-school luxury. Large windows in the rooms

MELAKA

DON'T LEAVE MELAKA WITHOUT TRYING...

■ laksa – a regional version distinguished by its coconut milk and lemongrass flavours

■ popiah – an uber-spring roll stuffed with shredded carrots, prawns, chilli, garlic, palm sugar and much, much more

■ cendol – a shaved-ice monstrosity with jellies, syrup and coconut milk

■ Nonya pineapple tarts – buttery pastries with a chewy pineapple jam filling

■ chicken rice ball – Hokkien-style chicken and balled-up rice dumplings

■ Assam fish heads – spicy tamarind fish-head stew.

■ satay celup – like fondue but better; you dunk tofu, prawns and more into bubbling soup and cook it to your liking

■ devil curry – a fiery Eurasian chicken curry

---

take advantage of views that sweep over Melaka in all directions, while the spacious rooms, equipped with comfy beds, are modern and chic while incorporating classic Chinese touches. Build up a sweat in the squash courts or at a yoga class then sink a drink in the pub (with regular live music).

Majestic Malacca (☎ 289 8000; www.majestic malacca.com; 188 Jln Bunga Raya; r/ste US$250/650; ☒ ▣ ☎ ▨) This elegant new hotel is an interesting mix: the lobby is in a 1920s colonial-style mansion while the bulk of the hotel is in a modern high-rise built behind. Rooms continue with this old and new theme with hardwood floors, sheer ivory-coloured drapes and heritage-style wood furnishings (including claw-footed bathtubs) – yet all are very modern in their sublime level of comfort. Of course, the place is stacked with amenities including an outdoor swimming pool, a gym, spa and a library.

EATING

Melaka's food mirrors the city's eclectic, multi-cultural DNA. Peranakan cuisine (Nonya; prepared here with a salty Indonesian influence) is the most famous type of cooking here, but there's also Portuguese Eurasian food, Indian, Chinese, Indonesian and more.

Chinatown

On Friday and Saturday nights, Jln Hang Jebat turns into the not-to-be-missed Jonker Walk Night Market.

Poh Piah Lwee (Jln Kubu; ☒ 9am-5pm) An authentic and lively hole in the wall with one specialist cook preparing delicious Hokkien-style *popiah* (RM2), another making near-perfect *rojak* (RM3) while the third whips up a fantastic laksa (RM3).

Low Yong Mow (☎ 282 1235; Jln Tokong; dim sum RM1-6; ☒ 5am-noon, closed Tue) Famous Malaysia-wide for its large and delectably well-stuffed *pao* (steamed pork buns), this place is Chinatown's biggest breakfast treat. With high ceilings, plenty of fans running and a view of Masjid Kampung Kling, the atmosphere oozes all the charms of Chinatown. Take your pick from the endless variety of dumplings, sticky rice dishes and mysterious treats that are wheeled to your table.

Donald & Lily's (☎ 284 8907; Jln Kota Laksmana; snacks RM3; ☒ 9.30am-4pm, closed Tue) Back behind the Heeren Inn, with the staircase entrance hidden by a few hawker stalls selling *cendol*, this is Melaka locals' favourite stop for the regional laksa (RM3) and Nonya *cendol* (RM1.20).

our pick Pak Putra Restaurant (56 Jln Kota Laksmana; tandoori from RM5; ☒ dinner, closed every other Mon) This fabulous Pakistani place cooks up a variety of meats and seafood in clay tandoori ovens perched on the sidewalk. Apart from the tandoori try the taw prawns (cooked with onion, yoghurt and coriander, RM10) or mutton rogan josh (in onion gravy with spices and chilli oil, RM8). Side dishes of veg are around RM5 and a mango lassi costs RM4.

Cafe 1511 (☎ 286 0151; www.cafe1511.com; 52 Jln Tun Tan Cheng Lock; meals RM8; ☒ 10am-6pm Thu-Tue; ▣) Next to the Baba-Nonya Heritage Museum is this high-ceilinged Peranakan cafe, with original tiles along the wall, lovely carved screens, a mishmash of decorative objects from Southeast Asia and a Nonya menu. At the time of writing this place was also planning a guesthouse.

Vegan Salad & Herbs House (☎ 282 9466; 22 Jln Kubu; meals RM10; ☒ 8.30am-4pm Fri-Wed) Around the corner from the Buddhist Guanyin Temple in Chinatown, this health-conscious spot offers a range of uncooked, crisp vegetables, brown rice set lunches and wholemeal bread buns.

Nancy's Kitchen (15 Jln Hang Lekir; meals RM10; ☺ 11am-5.30pm, closed Tue) In a town already known for its graciousness, this home-cooking Nonya restaurant is our favourite for friendly service. The server is as chatty as they come, full of suggestions of what to order and will have you making conversation with the other handful of customers in no time. Try the house speciality: chicken candlenut (RM10).

Hoe Kee Chicken Rice (☎ 283 34751; 4 Jln Hang Jebat; meals RM11; ☺ 8.30am-3pm, closed last Wed of every month) Serving the local speciality of chicken rice ball and Assam fish head (fish heads in a spicy tamarind gravy), you'll need to arrive outside of peak time or expect to wait for a table. The restaurant's setting, with wood floors and ceiling fans, seems to further bring out the exotic flavours.

Heeren House (☎ 281 4241; 1 Jln Tun Tan Cheng Lock; meals around RM12; ☺ 7.30am-6pm) In the hotel of the same name (p247), make this a slot for healthy Western breakfasts, a light meal of quiches and salads (from RM12) and yummy brownies (RM4). You can browse the integrated shop for a wonderful selection of upmarket batik and other crafts from all around Southeast Asia, while you wait for your food to arrive.

To Be Korean Café (☎ 016-635 6501; 58 Jln Tun Tan Cheng Lock; meals around RM25; ☺ 11am-5.30pm Sun-Thu, 11am-10pm Fri & Sat) Traditional Korean pork barbecue (RM23) as well as pages of other specialities (some vegetarian) can be enjoyed here while your feet get the dead skin nibbled off them by little fish – the tables are placed over a pond so can dine with your feet in or out of the water. There's also a selection of 'Korean healthy teas' (from RM3.50) that purport to cure a plethora of ailments.

Harper's Café (2 & 4 Lg Hang Jebat; meals RM40; ☺ lunch & dinner) Perched elegantly over the Sungai Melaka, breezy Harper's serves excellent (though small) Malay-European fusion dishes in a rather stark decor. It's worth visiting for the food, though the service can be slow.

Howard's (☎ 286 8727; 5 Jln Hang Lekir; meals RM40; ☺ lunch & dinner Wed-Mon) A finely crafted ambience of creaseless linen, elegant furniture, black-and-white chequered tile floor, flavoursome international cuisine (lobster bisque, roast rack of lamb) and nonintrusive service, Howard's is a thoroughly unhurried and intimate experience and a top romantic dining choice. Topped off with an impressive wine list, this is definitely Chinatown's swankiest choice.

Jalan Melaka Raya & Around

Serving Chinese food in the main hall and Halal at the back, **Newton Food Court** (Jln Merdeka), just west of the Mahkota Parade shopping complex, is Melaka's newest and most attractive hawker centre. It's under an immense thatched roof and is bordered by palms.

The new jetty over the river in front of the Holiday Inn has a number of semi-upmarket restaurants serving *satay celup* and Western food.

Restoran Amituofoh (☎ 292 6426; 2-20 Jln PM9, Plaza Mahkota, Bandar Hilir; ☺ breakfast, lunch & dinner) This Buddhist vegetarian restaurant – the gift of a Chinese philanthropist – provides food on the house. You should make a contribution, but otherwise there are few conditions: you must wash your own plates and cutlery, and taking food away is not permitted.

Roti Canai Terbang (Jln Melaka Raya 3; roti canai 70 sen-RM3; ☺ breakfast) Get excellent *roti canai* (flaky pancakes) either plain or stuffed with your choice of onion, egg, cheese or all three. This is a huge *roti canai* establishment and it packs in the locals.

Ind Ori (☎ 282 4777; 236 Jln Melaka Raya 1; dishes RM1-15; ☺ 8am-midnight) Mmm, Indonesian Pedang food: fresh and heated in a point and ask buffet. It's just like the real thing but without the flies and dubious sanitation issues. House specialities include avocado juice with chocolate sauce (RM4.50) and *sekotang* (sweet cream and peanut dumplings with green beans and hot ginger; RM5.80).

Ole Sayang (☎ 283 1966; 198 Jln Taman Melaka Raya; meals RM13; ☺ 10am-10pm, closed Wed) Come here for ambient Nonya atmosphere, decorated with old wooden furniture and dim lighting.

Bayonya (☎ 292 2192; 164 Jln Taman Melaka Raya; meals RM15; ☺ 10am-10pm, closed Tue) This authentic eatery is a locals' favourite for its excellent and inexpensive home-cooked Peranakan cuisine. One of the must-tries here is the durian *cendol* (RM5).

Little India to Bukit China

Follow the sounds of a chopping meat cleaver to **Medan Makan Bunga Raya** (Hungry Lane; btwn Jln Bendahara & Jln Bunga Raya), where you can feast on Indian-style curry-pork rice in the evenings or try the local speciality of *gula melaka* (palm sugar) during the day. The

Centrepoint food court (Jln Munshi Abdullah) is the place to seek out Indian and Malay treats for lunch. Further north **Hang Tuah Mall** (Jln Hang Tuah), a pedestrian walk, swarms with open-air food stalls every evening.

our pick Capitol Satay (☎ 283 5508; 41 Lg Bukit China; meals RM8; ☼ from 6pm) Famous for its satay *celup* (a Melaka adaptation of satay steamboat), this place is usually packed to the gills and is one of the cheapest outfits in town. Stainless-steel tables have bubbling vats of soup in the middle where you dunk skewers of okra stuffed with tofu, sausages, chicken, prawns and bok choy.

Selvam (☎ 281 9223; 3 Jln Temenggong; meals RM8; ☼ from 6pm) This is a classic banana leaf restaurant always busy with its loyal band of local patrons ordering tasty and cheap curries, roti and Tandoori chicken sets (RM5.50). Even devout carnivores will second guess their food preferences after trying the Friday-afternoon vegetarian special with 10 varieties of veg for only RM6.

Bulldog Café (☎ 292 1920; 145 Jln Bendahara; meals RM10; ☼ from 6pm) Features Nonya, Chinese, Thai and Western dishes. For cheap snacks, sample the Nonya *popiah* (RM2) or the *pai tee* (RM3), crispy cone-shaped morsels of rice flour stuffed with vegetables.

Medan Portugis

There's really not much reason to head out to this nondescript neighbourhood other than to eat. On Friday and Saturday evenings, head to **Restoran de Lisbon** (Medan Portugis; meals RM30; ☼ dinner Fri & Sat), where you can sample Malay-Portuguese dishes at outdoor tables. Try the delicious local specialities of chilli crabs (RM20) or the distinctly Eurasian devil curry (RM10). Any other time of the week, Medan Portugis has food stalls serving similar dishes to those found at restaurants at seaside tables.

DRINKING

Unlike much of Malaysia, Melaka is studded with watering holes. The Friday- and Saturday-night Jonker Walk Night Market in Chinatown closes down Jln Heng Lekir to traffic and the handful of bars along the lane become a mini street party with tables oozing beyond the sidewalks and live music.

Geographér Café (☎ 281 6813; www.geographer.com .my; 83 Jln Hang Jebat; large Tiger beer RM17.20; ☼ 10am-

1am Wed-Sun; ☐) This ventilated, breezy bar with outside seating and late hours, in a pre-war corner shophouse, is a godsend. A tasty choice of local and Western dishes (meals around RM8) and laid-back, but professional, service round it all off.

Voyager Traveller's Lounge (☎ 281 5216; 40 Lg Hang Jebat; ☐) Ease back into a wicker chair and order a cold beer (and/or an all-day Western-style breakfast) from the glowing bar built out of recycled bottles. Yaksa, the super-helpful young owner, can arrange activities throughout Melaka, and on certain nights there's live music.

Cheng Ho Tea House (Jln Tokong; ☼ 10am-5pm) In an exquisite setting that resembles a Chinese temple garden courtyard, relax here over a pot of fine Chinese tea (from RM15).

ENTERTAINMENT

More entertainment opportunities will be available by 2010 at the site of the Eye on Malaysia, Melaka (see p245).

Sound & Light Show (adult/child RM10/2; ☼ shows 8.30-9.15pm) Held outside the Dataran Pahlawan shopping mall, shows happen only when there's enough demand, and even then they may not be in English. Melaka's history is presented from a strongly nationalistic angle; nevertheless, it's quite good theatre.

Pure Bar (591A Jln Taman Melaka Raya) Popular with locals, this has become Melaka's most fun nightclub/bar. It's also gay friendly.

Arena (The Jetty) At the foot of the jetty in front of the Holiday Inn, this glass-walled night spot has a big stage for live bands and a hopping bar.

Golden Screen Cinemas (☎ 281 0018; 2nd fl Mahkota Parade; tickets RM8) Shows everything from Western blockbusters to Bollywood flicks. There's another branch at Dataran Pahlawan.

SHOPPING

Taking time to browse Chinatown's eclectic mix of shops is an activity in itself. Melakan favourites include Nonya beaded shoes, Nonya 'clogs' (with a wooden base and a single plastic-strip upper), antiques (know your stuff and haggle aggressively), Southeast Asian and Indian clothing, handmade tiles, charms, crystals and more. Peek into the growing array of silent artists studios, where you might see a painter busy at work in a back room.

Dataran Pahlawan (Jln Merdeka) Melaka's largest mall, it has a collection of upmarket designer shops and restaurants on the ground and upper floors and a craft and souvenir market in the basement portion.

Malaqa House (☎ 281 4770; 70 Jln Tun Tan Cheng Lock; ☽ 10am-6pm Mon-Fri, 10am-7pm Sat & Sun) This huge shop is in an elegant building stuffed to the gills with antiques and replicas – it's not cheap, but it's bursting with character.

Top Spinning Academy (79 Jln Tokong; ☽ 10am-4pm) Be prepared for a very enthusiastic traditional top-spinning lesson by *gasing uri* extraordinaire Simpson Wong. You aren't expected to purchase anything, although you probably will if you get the hang of the spin – a top is only RM2.

Orangutan House (59 Lg Hang Jebat; ☽ 10am-6pm Thu-Tue) Also at 96 Jln Tun Tan Cheng Lok and 12 Jln Hang Jebat, these brightly painted T-shirt shops display the work of local artist Charles Cham. Themes span Chinese astrology animals to rather edgy topics (at least for Malaysia) such as 'Use Malaysian Rubber', above a sketch of a condom.

Wan Aik Shoemaker (56 Jln Tokong) Raymond Yeo's beaded Nonya shoes are considered Melaka's finest and begin at a steep but merited RM300. Tiny silk bound-feet shoes (from RM90) are also available, although nowadays they are just a curiosity rather than a necessity.

For practical needs such as camera shops, a pharmacy or electronics store, head to **Mahkota Parade Shopping Complex** (☎ 282 6151; Lot B02, Jln Merdeka).

GETTING THERE & AWAY

Melaka is 144km from Kuala Lumpur, 224km from Johor Bahru and just 94km from Port Dickson.

Air

Recently upgraded Melaka International Airport is 20km north of Melaka in Batu Berendam. **Firefly** (www.fireflyz.com.my) offers flights between Melaka and Singapore (three weekly) and AirAsia is likely to follow suit with routes to Indonesia.

Boat

High-speed ferries make the trip from Melaka to Dumai in Sumatra daily at 10am (one way/ return RM119/170, 1¾ hours). Ferries also run to Pekan Baru (one way/return RM159/269, six hours) in Sumatra at 9.30am on Tuesday, Thursday and Sunday. Tickets are available at the **Tunas Rupat Follow Me Express** (☎ 283 2505; Jln PM2) and other ticket offices near the wharf. **Maxmarine** (☎ 282 0883; G-15 Jln PM 10) runs ferries four days a week to Bengkalis in Sumatra. At all ports in Sumatra, citizens of most countries will have to purchase a one-month visa on arrival (US$25).

Bus

Melaka Sentral, the huge, modern long-distance bus station, is inconveniently located opposite a huge branch of Tesco off Jln Tun Razak, in the north of town. A taxi into town should cost RM15, or you can take bus 17 (RM1) or the Panorama Melaka bus (RM2; see Getting Around, opposite). Frequent buses head to Singapore (RM22, 4½ hours), KL (RM12.40, two hours) and Johor Bahru (RM19, 3½ hours). There are also less frequent departures for Jerantut (RM22.90, five hours via Temerloh), Mersing (RM22.80, 4½ hours), Kota Bharu (RM51.20, 10 hours), Kuala Terengganu (RM42.90, eight hours) and Muar (RM4.70, one hour). Luggage deposit at Melaka Sentral is RM2 per bag. There is also an accommodation reservation counter for hotels in Melaka, a money changer and restaurants.

A-Bus Express (☎ 281 7669; 125 Jln SP1; www.a-bus .com.my) makes about seven trips per day to/ from KLIA International Airport (RM36, two hours). You can book tickets online or at the tourist offices.

Car

Car-hire prices begin at around RM153 per day for a Proton Wira. If driving, Melaka's one-way traffic system requires patience. Try **Hawk** (☎ 283 7878; 52 Jln Cempaka, Taman Seri Cempaka, Peringgit Jaya), north of town.

Taxi

Taxis leave from the long-distance bus station. Taxi rates: Port Dickson (RM120), Johor Bahru (RM250), Mersing (RM280), KL (RM160) and KL airport (RM140).

Train

The nearest **train station** (☎ 441 1034) is 38km north of Melaka at Tampin on the main north–south line from KL to Singapore. Taxis from Melaka cost around RM50 or take the Tai Lye bus (RM4.30, 1½ hours), which leaves every half-hour from Melaka Sentral.

TRICKED OUT TRISHAWS

Nowhere else in Malaysia will you find such wild and crazy a collection of trishaws. Outrageously kitsch, the favourite decorations are plastic flowers, baby doll heads, religious paraphernalia, tinsel, Christmas lights and a sound system. While taking a ride in one of these things might be the most 'I'm a tourist' thing you do in Malaysia, it's good fun and supports an industry that is dying nearly everywhere else in the country. As a spectator, keep an eye out for Singaporean tourists hiring out trishaws en masse: the effect, with several '80s hits blaring at the same time, cameras snapping and all that glitzy decoration, turns the streets of Melaka into a circus-like parade.

GETTING AROUND

Melaka is small enough to walk around, but you can save time and sweat with Panorama Melaka, which offers two types of hop-on, hop-off bus services. A **double-decker bus** (red line; RM5; ◷ 9am-8.30pm) makes a 13-stop run, while a **single-decker bus** (blue line; RM2; ◷ 7am-9.30pm) takes in 23 stops including Melaka Sentral. Both buses run every 30 to 45 minutes – buy your ticket (good all day) on the bus. The red line ticket price includes unlimited passage on the blue line, but not vice versa. Stops for both include the Hang Tua Mall, Jln Hang Jebat (Jonker Walk), the Stadthuys, Hotel Equatorial, Renaissance Melaka Hotel and Kampung Portugis. Route maps and more information about the service are available at the Tourism Malaysia office (p242).

Another useful service is town bus 17, running every 15 minutes from Melaka Sentral to the centre of town, past the huge Mahkota Parade shopping complex, to Taman Melaka Raya and on to Medan Portugis.

Bicycles can be hired at some guesthouses and hotels for around RM10 a day. Taking to Melaka's streets by trishaw is a must (see the boxed text, above) – by the hour they should cost about RM40, or RM15 for any one-way trip within the town, but you'll have to bargain.

Taxis should cost around RM10 for a trip anywhere around town with a 50% surcharge between 1am and 6am.

AROUND MELAKA CITY

AYER KEROH
☎ 06

About 15km northeast of Melaka, Ayer Keroh (also spelled Air Keroh) has several contrived tourist attractions that are largely deserted on weekdays. Kids will like the lushly landscaped **Melaka Zoo** (adult/child RM7/4, night zoo adult/child RM10/5; ◷ 9am-6pm daily, night zoo 8-11pm Fri & Sat), the second-largest zoo in the country (with 200 different species). The best time to go is at night when the nocturnal animals awaken; take the Friday- and Saturday-night shuttle bus (RM12) that picks up at larger hotels. It's also possible to volunteer at the zoo by cleaning cages and helping out with educational activities; those curious should contact the education unit at education@zoomelaka.org.my.

Just across from the zoo is the **Butterfly and Reptile Sanctuary** (adult/child RM5/3; ◷ 9am-6pm), which has a collection of exotic creepy-crawlies, snakes and some sad crocodiles at the reptile park.

But the main attraction in Ayer Keroh is the **Taman Mini Malaysia/Asean** (adult/child RM4/2; ◷ 9am-6pm), a large theme park that has examples of traditional houses from all 13 Malaysian states, as well as neighbouring Asean countries. Also here is **Hutan Rekreasi Air Keroh** (Air Keroh Recreational Forest; admission free), part secondary jungle and part landscaped park with paved trails, a 250m canopy walk, picnic areas and a forestry museum.

Ayer Keroh can be reached on bus 19 from Melaka (RM1.40, 30 minutes), or a taxi will cost around RM35.

PULAU BESAR
☎ 06

The small island of Pulau Besar, 5km off the coast southeast of Melaka, has some interesting graves and meditation caves that are popular pilgrimages for Indian Muslims, but the main reason to come here is for the white beaches and jungle walks. Unfortunately, in 2010 Besar will become the largest independent oil storage terminal in the country, which will surely make the already not-so-great water even more polluted.

The island's only hotel is the **Chandek Kura Resort** (☎ 295 5899; chalet d/tr RM118/138; ✳ ☎) and you can pitch at the **camp site** (☎ 281 8007; per person incl tent rental RM20) next to the resort; call before arrival to secure a site. A handful of basic *kedai kopi* can be found nearby.

Boats (return trip RM40, 30 minutes) depart from the jetty at Anjung Batu (☎ 261 0492) about every two hours from 8am (last boat returns at 10.30pm). The jetty is several kilometres past the old pier at Umbai, southeast of Melaka. Take an SKA bus from Melaka Sentral to Merlimau and ask to be let off at the jetty – it's about a 10-minute walk from the bus stop.

ALOR GAJAH

Just off the road to KL, 24km north of Melaka, is the countryside town of Alor Gajah. In the town centre is the peaceful and grassy Alor Gajah Square, which is bordered by an array of gaily painted shophouses. Most Melaka–KL buses stop in Alor Gajah so it's possible to stop here between the two cities if you're willing to change buses. A taxi to A'Famosa should cost around RM18.

Sights

Right in Alor Gajah Square is the **Museum of Custom and Tradition** (admission RM1; ☯ 9am-5.30pm Wed-Thu & Sat & Sun, 9am-12.15pm & 2.45-5.30pm Fri), which exhibits a modest collection of Malay wedding customs, bridal gifts and ceremonial rites.

Half an hour from Melaka and an hour from KL, the 520-hectare **A'Famosa Resort** (www.afamosa.com) is an all-encompassing resort popular with Malay and Singaporean tourists. Even though the whole place is a little cheesy, you'd be hard pressed not to have fun at the 8-hectare **Water World** (adult/child RM35/27; ☯ 11am-7pm Mon & Wed-Fri, 9am-8pm Sat & Sun), which has two seven-storey-high speed slides, a tube ride and even a man-made beach with a wave pool. **Animal World Safari** (admission with all rides &

shows adult/child RM60/50; ☯ 9am-6pm) spreads over another 60 hectares. The animal shows, with an array of critters dressed in human clothing and doing human activities, aren't something that animal lovers will enjoy. A special rate of adult/child RM75/61 gets you into both the Animal World Safari and Water World. Also within the resort is a 27-hole **golf course** that is rated in the country's top 10.

TANJUNG BIDARA
☎ 06

For a lovely escape, head to white-sand Tanjung Bidara, about 30km northwest of Melaka. It's well away from the main highway, requiring you to take back roads through rice paddies and farms to get to the shore. It's literally deserted midweek, except for maybe one or two fishermen casting from the beach, and only one valiant stall at the beachfront food court is open outside of Saturday and Sunday. The water lapping on the fine sand is brown with sediment and pollution so it's not the best place for swimming, but it's fun to sit against the jungle and watch the massive freighters head down the famous Strait of Melaka.

The main beach area is at **Tanjung Bidara Beach Resort** (☎ 384 2990; fax 384 2995; tw Sun-Thu RM70, Fri & Sat RM100, chalets RM130/150; ☒ ☒), a quiet, relaxing but musty resort with a small swimming pool and restaurant.

Further budget accommodation is strung out over several kilometres along the beach, broken only by a large military camp. There are several simple beachside chalet guesthouses in the friendly Malay village of Kampung Balik Batu.

Buses 42 and 47 from Melaka go to Masjid Tanah, from where a taxi to Tanjung Bidara Beach Resort or Kampung Balik Batu costs RM10.

Johor

Linked to Singapore at the tip of the Asian continent, Johor is the southern gateway to Malaysia. While it's the most populous state in the country, tourism has taken a back seat to economic development (see the boxed text, p257) leaving the state with some great off-the-beaten-path destinations for those who are up to the challenge.

Some of Malaysia's most beautiful islands, within the Seribuat Archipelago, lie off the state's east coast. They attract their fair share of Singaporean weekenders, but remain near empty during the week. Many of these islands are prime dive territory, with similar corals and fish that you'll find at popular Tioman Island (p274) but with fewer crowds. These islands are also blessed with some of the finest white-sand beaches in the country, which fringe flashy turquoise waters and wild jungles.

For more adventure head to Endau-Rompin National Park or climb the eponymous peak at Gunung Ledang National Park. These jungles offer the same rich flora, (very elusive) fauna and swashbuckling action that visitors flock to experience at Taman Negara in Pahang, but once again crowds are rare. Anywhere you go to in the state beyond the capital will involve some determination: either by chartering a boat or joining a tour. The effort, however, is well rewarded.

JOHOR

HIGHLIGHTS

- Swimming, diving and beach bumming it to the max in the **Seribuat Archipelago** (p266)
- Discovering the surprisingly charming waterfront and colonial backstreets of **Johor Bahru** (p257) and realising that the city is outgrowing its bad reputation
- Sweating your way up lofty **Gunung Ledang** (p263)
- Cooling off in the sensational waterfalls of **Endau-Rompin National Park** (p269) after hiking through dense jungle
- Admiring the sultans' treasures at the **Royal Abu Bakar Museum** (p259) in Johor Bahru
- Eating *ikan bakar* (grilled fish) at one of Johor Bahru's busy **hawker centres** (p261)

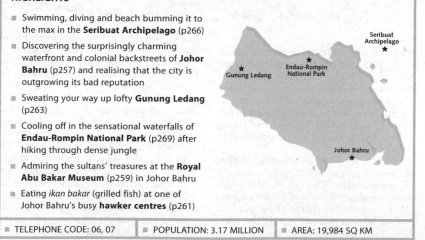

- TELEPHONE CODE: 06, 07
- POPULATION: 3.17 MILLION
- AREA: 19,984 SQ KM

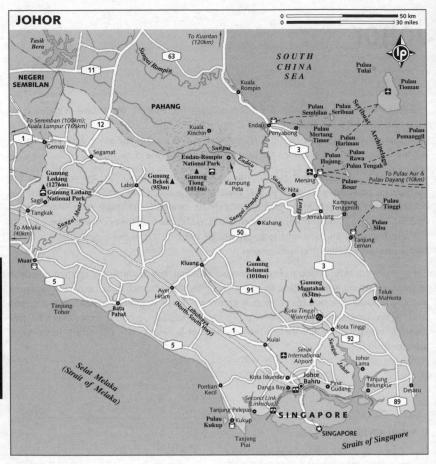

JOHOR

History

With the fall of Melaka to the Portuguese in the 16th century, Johor emerged as the pre-eminent Malay state, its rulers seen as the protectors of the western Malay states. The Portuguese soon attacked Johor, but were eventually content to allow its leaders to rule from their capital on Sungai Johor (Johor River), despite the sultans' impediment to trade in the area.

In 1819 Sir Thomas Stamford Raffles succeeded in gaining Singapore for the British and pensioning off the Malay sultans. Actual power went to the *temenggong* (Malay minister in charge of defence and justice) who continued to rule the state. The most notable among these was the flamboyant Abu Bakar, who elevated himself to the position of Sultan of Johor in 1886. Through his contacts with influential people in London and Singapore, he resisted British attempts to bring Johor closer under its control. Abu Bakar also undertook an ambitious program of modernisation for the state, while continuing to live the high life. Today he is fondly remembered as the Father of Johor.

In 1914 Abu Bakar's successor and son, Ibrahim, was forced by the British to accept a 'general adviser' who had powers similar to those exercised by the British Residents in other states. Sultan Ibrahim was still the ruler of Johor when it became part of the Federation of Malaya in 1948.

THE BRAVE NEW WORLD OF ISKANDAR

Started in 2006 and expected to be completed in 2025, the Iskandar Development Region is a 221,634-hectare area that stretches from Johor Bahru to Senai/Kulai in the north, Tanjung Pelepas at the west and Pasir Gudang at the east. The aim is for the region (which is three times the size of Singapore) to become an international metropolis and liberal trade port not unlike China's Shenzhen and Hong Kong. A 'green theme' is being incorporated with hopes of simultaneously making the area attractive to tourists.

The administrative capital, Kota Iskandar, is literally being built from scratch (with a Moorish-Andalusian architectural theme) and was officially opened by the Sultan of Johor on April 16 2009, with ambitions of having all the administration in the region moved to the new city by the end of 2009.

While the world economic slump inevitably slowed down the development pace for Iskandar, it's still attracting sufficient investors and is moving remarkably well towards its goals. Despite this, the project is harshly criticised by ex-PM Mahathir Mohamad who has warned that the higher cost of living in the region, as well as the fact that most of the land is being sold to foreign investors (many Singaporean), will force out Malaysians. In the end, he prophesises, Iskandar will only be 'an extension of Singapore'.

The Iskandar project has been backed by PM Najib Razak, who believes that growth and foreign investment can only be beneficial for Malaysia and its people. The hopes are that the wealth of Iskandar will spill over to the rest of the country and bring the entire region up to potential.

Climate

The temperature in Johor ranges from 21°C to 32°C, with an average humidity exceeding 82%. Although there is rain through the year, the wettest months are from May to December.

National Parks

Johor's main national parks are Endau-Rompin (p269) and Gunung Ledang (p263). For details of other parks, contact the **Johor National Parks Corporation** (☎ 07-223 7471; www.johorpa rks.com.my).

Getting There & Around

The Lebuhraya (North–South Hwy), connecting Johor Bahru (JB) and Kuala Lumpur, is the main transport artery to the north. Johor Bahru is also connected to Kuala Lumpur (KL) by rail and is accessed from Singapore by rail and road. There are also boat services to ports in Sumatra from Johor Bahru. The airport is 32km northwest of JB, in Senai. At Ayer Hitam on the Lebuhraya, Route 50 splits off east to Mersing. Route 3 in the east connects Mersing to Johor Bahru.

See transport sections in Johor Bahru (p261), Muar (p263) and Mersing (p266) for details of connections to destinations within Johor and to the rest of Peninsular Malaysia.

JOHOR BAHRU

☎ 07

After years of being criticised as a dirty, chaotic border town (and being compared with its glitzy neighbour Singapore), Johor's capital Johor Bahru has been repaved and replanted, has covered up its stinky sewers and is suddenly a really decent place to hang out. Grimy bus stops, ear-piercing traffic and desperate-looking people still congregate along Jln Tun Abdul Razak, but literally one block off this main drag you'll find an atmosphere of bustling food hawkers, interesting old architecture and wide, clean sidewalks. The city is still very edgy compared with most Malaysian towns, but the buzz keeps you on your toes and there are some surprisingly cosmopolitan corners to explore.

JB is connected to Singapore by road and rail across a 1038m-long causeway, across which Singaporeans flood for shopping and excitement on weekends and holidays. However, other than just for changing trains, planes or buses, few foreign travellers linger here. A spiralling crime rate (including bag-snatching and car theft), plus a government crackdown on prostitution, have sent male Singaporeans elsewhere for their paid pleasures.

As one of the five 'economic zones' of the Iskandar development project (see the boxed text above) that will radically change southern Malaysia over the next decade, JB is in for

JOHOR

JOHOR BAHRU

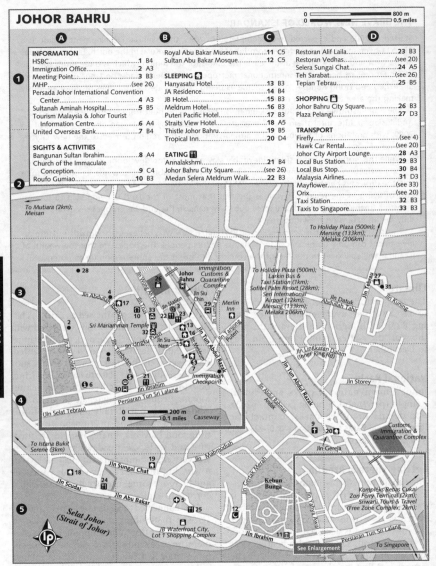

INFORMATION	Royal Abu Bakar Museum..............11 C5	Restoran Alif Laila............................23 B3
HSBC..1 B4	Sultan Abu Bakar Mosque...............12 C5	Restoran Vedhas.........................(see 20)
Immigration Office...........................2 A3		Selera Sungai Chat............................24 A5
Meeting Point.....................................3 B3	**SLEEPING**	Teh Sarabat.................................(see 26)
MHP...(see 26)	Hanyasatu Hotel................................13 B3	Tepian Tebrau....................................25 B5
Persada Johor International Convention	JA Residence.......................................14 B4	
Center...4 A3	JB Hotel...15 B3	**SHOPPING**
Sultanah Aminah Hospital...............5 B5	Meldrum Hotel...................................16 B3	Johor Bahru City Square....................26 B3
Tourism Malaysia & Johor Tourist	Puteri Pacific Hotel...........................17 B3	Plaza Pelangi.....................................27 D3
Information Centre.......................6 A4	Straits View Hotel..............................18 A5	
United Overseas Bank.......................7 B4	Thistle Johor Bahru...........................19 B5	**TRANSPORT**
	Tropical Inn.......................................20 D4	Firefly...(see 4)
SIGHTS & ACTIVITIES		Hawk Car Rental........................(see 20)
Bangunan Sultan Ibrahim................8 A4	**EATING**	Johor City Airport Lounge................28 A3
Church of the Immaculate	Annalakshmi......................................21 B4	Local Bus Station..............................29 B3
Conception...................................9 C4	Johor Bahru City Square..............(see 26)	Local Bus Stop...................................30 B4
Roufo Gumiao.................................10 B3	Medan Selera Meldrum Walk...........22 B3	Malaysia Airlines..............................31 D3
		Mayflower...................................(see 33)
		Orix..(see 20)
		Taxi Station.......................................32 B3
		Taxis to Singapore............................33 B3

Orientation

more than a makeover. The gussied-up waterfront and building of the modern Customs, Immigration and Quarantine (CIQ) complex are just the beginning: Danga Bay is a 720-hectare area, 5km from the Causeway, that is poised to be a financial and commercial centre with the lofty hopes of being as scenic and enticing as Sydney's Darling Harbour.

The road and railway across the Causeway drive straight into the heart of JB. The train station and CIQ complex are just east of the grid of streets that make up the centre of town. West of the Causeway, Jln Ibrahim stretches along JB's waterfront, leading you to the city's colonial district with its parkland, colonial buildings and museum. The Second Link (Linkedua) between Johor and Singapore connects Tanjung Kupang in the southwest of Johor with Tuas in Singapore's west.

The Larkin long-distance bus and taxi station is 5km northwest of the train station. Senai International Airport is 32km northwest of the city centre, in Senai.

Information

Moneychangers infest Jln Wong Ah Fook, and rates are competitive.

HSBC (Jln Timbalan) Has a 24-hour ATM.
Immigration office (☎ 224 4255; 1st fl, Block B, Wisma Persekutuan, Jln Air Molek)
Meeting Point (59 Jln Meldrum; per hr RM3; ◷ 10.30am-10pm) Internet access. Just south of the Gateway Hotel.
MHP (☎ 221 9134; Level 3, Johor Bahru City Square, Jln Wong Ah Fook) Has the best selection of books in English.
Sultanah Aminah Hospital (☎ 223 1666; Jln Skudai)
Tourism Malaysia & Johor Tourist Information Centre (☎ 223 4935; www.johortourism.com.my; 3rd fl, Jotic Bldg, 2 Jln Air Molek; ◷ 9am-5pm Mon-Sat)
United Overseas Bank (2 Jln Wong Ah Fook) Has a 24-hour ATM.

Dangers & Annoyances

Although travelling in JB is generally safe, visitors should be alert to motorcycle-riding bag-snatchers and, as in any city, avoid walking alone down dark alleyways. If you have any troubles call the **police hotline** (☎ 221 2999).

Sights

ROYAL ABU BAKAR MUSEUM

Once the Johor royal family's principal palace, the marvellous Istana Besar was built in Victorian style by Anglophile sultan Abu Bakar in 1866, and is open to the public as the **Muzium Diraja Abu Bakar** (☎ 223 0555; Jln Ibrahim; adult/child $US7/3; ◷ 9am-5pm Sat-Thu, ticket counter closes 4pm). The admission fee is also payable in ringgit (at a bad exchange rate).

The finest museum of its kind in Malaysia, conveying the tremendous wealth and privilege of the sultan and housing his possessions, the museum is arranged much as it was when it served as the palace. The superb exhibits embrace Chinese, Japanese, Indian and Malay carved wooden pieces and a dazzling full-sized crystal-glass table and chairs from France. The hunting room has some bizarre exhibits from *pukka sahib* days when wildlife was there to be shot,

including elephant's-foot umbrella stands and antelope-leg ashtrays.

The 53-hectare palace grounds (free entry) are beautifully manicured and provide a great breathing space in this cramped and messy city.

OTHER SIGHTS

Wandering around the area between Jln Ibrahim and Jln Ungku Puan is a real highlight of JB. Walk past colourful, old shophouses filled with sari shops, barbers, Ayurvedic salons and old-style eateries.

Under construction from 1892 to 1900, the magnificent **Sultan Abu Bakar Mosque** (Jln Ibrahim) is a mixture of architectural styles (principally Victorian). Further out of town, **Istana Bukit Serene** (Jln Skudai) has a 32m stone tower and is the residence of the Sultan of Johor. The palace was built in 1932 and isn't open to the public – you can glimpse it on the waterfront, 5km west of the Abu Bakar museum.

Sitting magnificently atop Bukit Timbalan, designed by Palmer & Turner architects, the imposing **Bangunan Sultan Ibrahim** (State Secretariat Bldg; Bukit Timbalan) is a mighty melange of colonial pomp, Islamic motifs and indigenous design. Completed in 1942, the city landmark was employed as a fortress by the Japanese as they prepared to attack Singapore.

The Catholic **Church of the Immaculate Conception** (☎ 224 3034; 9 Jln Gereja) provides refreshing relief from Johor's searing streets. Try to get here for the Tamil feast of **Pongal** in mid-January, when a colourful harvest festival service is held within the church.

The Chinese **Roufo Gumiao** (Roufo Temple; Jln Trus), near the centre of town, is a shrine dedicated to Hongxian Dadi, Yuantian Shangdi and Weitian Dadi, all Taoist characters whose effigies adorn the temple interior.

Sleeping

Hotel rooms mentioned here include private shower or bath, unless stated otherwise.

BUDGET

The main zone of cheap and low-bracket midrange hotels clusters on and around the relatively ambient Jln Meldrum, in the centre of town. Budget price tags are high for Malaysia, and most places ask for a room deposit of around RM30 that's returned to you when you check out.

JOHOR

Meldrum Hotel (☎ 227 8988; www.meldrumhotel .com; 1 Jln Siu Nam; dm/s/d RM32/64/76) All options here are air-conditioned, clean, spacious and freshly painted, and the rooms have TVs, free drinking water and kettles. It's worth upgrading to a RM88 standard room with attached bathrooms – these are downright plush.

JB Hotel (☎ 223 4989; 80A Jln Wong Ah Fook; r RM70; ☒) Small air-con rooms come with TV, tiled floor and sinks, but bathrooms are shared. It's family-run, helpful and very clean.

Hanyasatu Hotel (☎ 228 8811; hotelhanya1@yahoo .com; 29 Jln Meldrum; s/d RM70/80; ☒ ▣) This place is a touch more stylish than the competition thanks to some bold coloured walls and new tiled floors, but rooms are all small and some lack windows. There's a good internet cafe on site.

MIDRANGE

Hotels in this price bracket inflate prices on Friday, Saturday and Sunday by about 10%.

Straits View Hotel (☎ 224 1400; straitsvhjccg @po.jaring.my; 1-D Jln Scudai; tw/d RM110/135; ☒) Perched facing the Strait of Johor, service here can be rather slack. The ground-floor bar is noisy, but rooms are well furnished and spacious with coffee- and tea-making facilities and TVs. The restaurant here, Marina Seafood Restaurant, is recommended.

Tropical Inn (☎ 224 7888; 15 Jln Gereja; s/d incl breakfast RM130-175; ☒) Standard rooms at the Tropical are slightly tatty, but good value, with coffee- and tea-making facilities, cold water in the fridge, clean bathrooms with long, deep bathtubs, and powerful air-con. Views are excellent.

JA Residence (☎ 221 3000; www.javh.com.my; 18 Jln Wong Ah Fook; r RM130-250; ☒ ▣) Right in the heart of JB, this is a comfortable, clean and modern high-rise hotel offering good value for money. It's getting slightly frayed at the edges, despite the fact that it was recently remodelled, but its cream coloured paint and polished wood interiors do have some design flair. Angle for a room on the upper floors that have views over the causeway.

TOP END

Thistle Johor Bahru (☎ 222 9234; www.thistle.com .my; Jln Sungai Chat; r from RM220; ☒ ▣ ▣ ⍔) At the time of research, the five-star British hotel chain Thistle was refurbishing and rebranding the already excellent old Hyatt Regency. Overlooking the Straits of Johor, the hotel

promises to become the poshest option this side of the Causeway. Quirky extras include rooms designed especially for travelling executive women who can opt to lodge with a pet, which is supplied by the hotel.

Puteri Pacific Hotel (☎ 223 3333; www.puteri pacific.com; Jln Abdullah Ibrahim; r incl breakfast from RM250; ☒ ▣ ⍔) This centrally located hotel has polite staff, a range of fine restaurants and facilities such as tennis and squash courts. Rooms are well kept and have light green carpets with blond wood furniture. It's quite classy for the price.

Mutiara (☎ 332 3800; www.mutiarahotels.com; Jln Dato Sulaiman; r RM420-1000, incl breakfast; ☒ ▣ ▣) Located 2km north of the city centre, rooms here are just as comfortable as you'd hope for the price tag. Junior Club Suites are a great choice for families as they're equipped with toys, PlayStation and board games. The hotel's Chinese restaurant, Meisan (opposite), is recommended and there's live music in the Polo Lounge.

Sofitel Palm Resort (☎ 599 6000; www.sofitel.com; Jln Persiaran Golf; r from €47; ☒ ▣ ▣) Only a three-minute drive from Senai International Airport (28km from Central JB) this resort is a far cry from the city's hubbub. Alongside the very elegant accommodation there are nearly unlimited activities available from very inexpensive golf to paintball, an Olympic-sized pool and ATV trails. Afterwards chill out at the on-site Mandara Spa.

Eating

Whatever you think of JB, you can't complain about the food. The streets here sizzle with some of the country's best seafood, as well as local specialities including a local, curry-heavy version of *laksa*.

RESTAURANTS

Annalakshmi (☎ 227 7400; 39 Jln Ibraham; buffet meals by donation; ⍩ 11am-3.30pm Mon-Fri) An authentic vegetarian Indian buffet run by volunteers of the Temple of Fine Arts, the motto here is 'eat what you want and give as you feel'. There's also an Annalakshmi in Singapore (see p540); donate generously.

Teh Sarabat (Johor Bahru City Square; meals from RM3; ⍩ breakfast, lunch & dinner) Good for those wanting to sample street food in more sterile surrounds, this place at the mall serves up sophisticated versions of all the local favourites at prices similar to those at grittier food stalls. The well-stuffed *masala tosei* (RM3) is fantastic, as is the *Sarabat rojak* (RM5.90).

Restoran Alif Laila (☎ 226 0445; 57 Jln Meldrum; meals RM7; ☺ breakfast, lunch & dinner) With all its food on display so you can see what you are getting, this cheap and friendly outfit offers very good value in its range of roti and curries, and is popular with locals.

Restoran Vedhas (1 Jln Gereja; meals RM10; ☺ lunch & dinner) Reasonably priced southern and northern Indian meals – biryani dishes, dhal curry and tandoori chicken, as well as a selection of meat-free dishes and naan (bread baked in a clay oven).

Meisan (☎ 332 3800; Mutiara Hotel, Jln Dato Sulaiman; meals RM45-50; ☺ lunch & dinner) Meals at this fine Sichuan restaurant are rather expensive, but authentically spicy and full of flavour. Set meals are available for those eager to avoid the pricier à la carte dishes.

HAWKER CENTRES & FOOD COURTS
The shopping malls about town are littered with food courts. The basement of **Johor Bahru City Square** (108 Jln Wong Ah Fook) has good Chinese, Japanese and Western restaurants and cafes; for coffee, Starbucks (wi-fi zone) and Coffee Bean are on the ground floor.

Street food is the highlight of a stay in JB and hawker centres are the best place to let your tastebuds go wild.

Medan Selera Meldrum Walk (meals from RM3; ☺ dinner) Every late afternoon, the little food stalls crammed along this alley (that runs parallel to Jln Meldrum) start frying up everything from *ikan bakar* to the local curry *laksa*. Wash down your meal with fresh sugar-cane juice or a Chinese herbal jelly drink.

our pick **Tepian Tebrau** (Jln Abu Bakar; meals RM7; ☺ breakfast, lunch & dinner) This food centre is celebrated for its excellent *ikan bakar*, other seafood and stalls serving up a catch-all of Malaysian food. It has views overlooking the Straits of Johor.

Selera Sungai Chat (Jln Abu Bakar; meals RM20) One kilometre west of Tepian Tebrau is this other well-patronised seafood centre specialising in *ikan bakar*.

Shopping
JB promotes itself as a major shopping destination. Singaporeans do come across for shopping – petrol and groceries – but for most goods Singapore has better prices and a far better range. Branches of Jusco and Carrefour are in the north of town.

Some major shopping centres:
Holiday Plaza (Jln Dato Sulaiman) Go here for DVDs, mobile phones, music and computer software.
Johor Bahru City Square (Jln Wong Ah Fook) A flashy mall with affordable designer shops and a great food court.
Plaza Pelangi (Jln Tebrau) A mishmash of everything and very popular.
Zon (Kompleks Bebas Cukai; 88 Jln Ibrahim Sultan, Stulang Laut) A five-level duty-free centre catering to Singaporeans. Sells booze, cigarettes, leather and more. The complex also incorporates a ferry terminal (see below).

Getting There & Away
AIR
JB is served by the **Senai International Airport** (☎ 599 4500; www.senaiairport.com) in Senai, 32km northwest of JB.

Airline Offices
AirAsia (☎ 1300 889 933; www.airasia.com) Has low-cost flights to KL, Penang, Kuching, Kota Kinabalu, Sibu and Miri, as well as Bangkok, Jakarta and Surabaya.
Firefly (☎ 603 7845 4543; mezzanine fl, Persada Johor International Convention Center, Jln Abdullah Ibrahim) Flies twice daily to Kuala Lumpur's Subang Airport.
Malaysia Airlines (☎ 334 1011/331 0036; 1st fl, Menara Pelangi Bldg, Jln Kuning, Taman Pelangi) Flights to Kuching and Kuala Lumpur with easy connections to a variety of destinations. Prices are much lower than from Singapore.

BOAT
Ferries leave from the Zon Ferry Terminal, about 2km east of the Causeway. **Sriwani Tours & Travel** (☎ 221 1677; Zon Ferry Terminal, Stulang Laut) handles tickets to most destinations.

There are several daily departures to the Indonesian islands of Batam (one way RM69, 1½ hours) and Bintan (one way RM86, 2½ hours). Additional boats depart from Kukup (p263), southwest of JB, to Tanjung Balai in Sumatra.

BUS
Frequent buses run between Singapore's Queen St bus terminal and JB's Larkin bus station, inconveniently located 5km north of the city (a taxi to/from the Causeway should cost RM10). Most convenient is the Singapore–Johor Bahru Express (from JB/Singapore RM2.40/S$2.10, 6.30am to midnight, every 10 minutes). Another option is the regular SBS (city bus) 170 that runs between Larkin and Ban San terminal (RM1.70/S$1.30) in

Singapore every 10 minutes between 5.21am and 12.44am, departing from stand 13 in Larkin – tickets can be purchased on the bus. If you are going to Singapore from central JB, board any bus after clearing Malaysian immigration just before the Causeway – you can buy a ticket on the bus or at the agents facing the train station on Jln Tun Abul Razak. For any bus, disembark with your luggage as you may not board the same bus after clearing immigration; hang on to your ticket, too, to avoid having to pay for another one.

At Larkin bus station – a frantic sprawl of hawker stalls, restaurants, clothes shops and other outlets – numerous bus companies run services to Melaka (RM19, 2½ hours), KL (RM31.20, four hours, nonstop), Ipoh (RM49, eight hours), Seremban (RM26, 3½ hours), Mersing (RM11.70, two hours), Pekan (RM3.40, 2½ hours), Kuantan (RM31.20, five hours) and Kuala Terengganu (RM27.30, eight hours).

There is a **left-luggage counter** (per bag RM2; 🕑 7am-11pm) at Larkin bus station.

ON FOOT
Walking across the 2km Causeway technically hasn't been allowed since the opening of the new CIQ complex in 2008, but you'll see lots of people doing it anyway. At the time of research plans were being made to open a legal pedestrian route.

TAXI
JB's main **long-distance taxi station** (☎ 223 4494) is at the Larkin bus station (5km north of town); a handier terminal is on Jln Wong Ah Fook near the Sri Mariamman Temple. Regular taxi destinations and costs (share taxi with four passengers) include Desaru (RM160), Kukup (RM80), Melaka (RM250), KL (RM340), Kuantan (RM320) and Mersing (RM150).

Registered taxis to Singapore depart from the **Plaza Seni Taxi Terminal** (Jln Trus) in the centre of town, with taxis to Orchard Rd or Queen St terminal costing around RM40. Local city taxis cannot cross the Causeway.

TRAIN
The sparkling **JB Sentral** (☎ 223 4727; www.ktmb .com.my; 🕑 booking office 8.30am-9pm) train station is in the CIQ complex where you can clear immigration and take a bus or train across the Causeway to Singapore. There's a footbridge that links the station to Johor Bahru

City Square shopping mall – the easiest route on foot if you're heading to Central JB. Three daily express trains run to KL (8.28am, 2.49pm and 11.08pm). The line passes through Tampin (for Melaka), Seremban, KL Sentral, Tapah Rd (for Cameron Highlands), Ipoh, Taiping and Butterworth. The line bifurcates at Gemas so you can board the 'jungle train' for Jerantut (for Taman Negara), Kuala Lipis and Kota Bharu.

KTM trains also run to Singapore (RM2.90, 55 minutes) on a separate lane so are immune to traffic jams, but are still usually slower than the bus – they run infrequently (about six per day). You have to get out and clear customs at Woodlands on the Singapore side.

Getting Around
TO/FROM THE AIRPORT
JB's **Senai International Airport** (☎ 599 4500; www .senaiairport.com), 32km northwest of town, is linked to the city centre by regular shuttle buses (RM8, 45 minutes) that run from the new **City Airport Lounge** (Kotaraya II terminal, Jln Trus). A taxi from the City Airport Lounge to central Singapore costs around RM40; alternatively jump on the Causeway Link Yellow Bus from City Lounge to Kranji MRT (RM1) or the SBS (city bus) 170 from City Lounge to Queen Street or Woodlands Rd in Singapore (RM1.70).

A taxi between the airport and JB is RM45, taking 30 to 45 minutes, depending on traffic.

BUS
Local buses operate from several stops around town, the most convenient being the stop in front of the post office on Jln Ibrahim. From Larkin bus station bus 39 goes into Central JB (RM1.70).

CAR
Car hire in JB is considerably cheaper than in Singapore, but check that the hire firm allows cars to enter Singapore. Car hire prices begin at around RM138 per day (RM3070 per month) for a Proton Wira 1.5L automatic; prices are inclusive of insurance and tax. Many more international rental companies hire cars from Senai International Airport.

Hawk Car Rental (☎ 224 2849; Suite 221, 2nd fl, PanGlobal Plaza, Jln Wong Ah Fook)

Mayflower (☎ 224 1357; www.mayflowercarrental. com.my; Level 2A, Plaza Seni, Jln Trus)

Orix (☎ 224 1215; G9, Tropical Inn, 15 Jln Gereja)

TAXI
Taxis in JB have meters, and drivers are legally required to use them. Flagfall is RM2.50, with an average trip costing RM8. Taxis can be hired at around RM30 per hour for sightseeing.

AROUND JOHOR BAHRU
Kukup
☎ 07
About 40km southwest of JB, on the Strait of Melaka, the fishing village of Kukup is known for its seafood (most notably prawns and chilli crab), which are consumed in open-air restaurants set on stilts over the water. Singaporeans, fired up by the prospect of seafood munchies, arrive en masse at weekends. The food is good, but it's no secluded idyll and the golf course draws a stratum of business types.

To reach Kukup, take bus 3 from JB to Pontian Kecil (RM6, 2½ hours), and then take a taxi (RM12). A chartered taxi (for four persons) all the way to/from JB costs RM70.

JOHOR BAHRU TO MELAKA
Roads north to Melaka run through a productive region of palm oil, rubber and pineapple plantations. The coast road is fairly scenic and passes a series of quaint *kampung* (villages).

Muar
☎ 06
A lethargic riverside town, languorously Malaysian in mood and with the feel of a bustling Chinatown, Muar was historically an important commercial centre but today it's a very sleepy backwater. It makes for an off-the-beaten-path (though not very action-packed) stop between Melaka and Johor Bahru.

There is a HSBC branch with a 24-hour ATM on Jln Maharani, which runs along the Muar Sungai, near the bus station.

The graceful **colonial district** by the river turns up several buildings of note. Walk around the area and look out for the customs house, the courthouse, the high school (built in 1914) and Masjid Jamek, a Victorian fantasy in much the same style as JB's Sultan Abu Bakar Mosque.

SLEEPING & EATING
Muar is known for its Nonya-style *otak-otak* (fish cakes) and satay breakfasts. You'll find hawker stalls on Jln Haji Abu just off Jln Ali.

Hotel Leewah (☎ 952 1605; 44 Jln Ali; d without/with air-con & bathroom RM35/45; ❄) At this clean family-run hotel, the air-con rooms are much brighter than those with fan.

Muar Trader's Hotel (☎ 953 8100; www.muartraders hotel.com; 16 Jln Petrie; r RM95-450; ❄ 💻 🤶) Muar's newest high-rise has monster-sized, blandly decorated rooms with terraces and refrigerators. Ask for a room with a view – the panorama across the Sungai Muar and over the mosque is stunning.

Hotel Classic (☎ 953 3888; 69 Jln Ali; r RM125-250; ❄ 🤶) Classy rooms here have complimentary newspaper, coffee- and tea-making facilities and satellite TV, and are the best in town.

Kampung Nyonya (☎ 954 0088; 39 Jln Sayang; dishes RM3-6; ⏱ 10.30am-3pm & 5.30-10pm) This clean place is the snazziest place in town and serves a range of seafood and Nonya favourites, including Nonya *chap chai* (mixed vegetables) and *tomato telor* (tomato and egg).

GETTING THERE & AWAY
Regular buses to JB (RM15.20, 2½ hours) and KL (RM16, 2½ hours) depart from the Muar long-distance bus station by the river. Less-frequent buses run to Seremban (RM13, two hours), Kuantan (RM23, six hours), Penang (RM17.50, eight hours) and Singapore (RM16, three hours). Buses to/from Melaka (RM5.20, one hour), and Gunung Ledang/Segamat (RM4, one hour) operate from the local bus station. The taxi station is just to the right of the bus station.

Gunung Ledang National Park
According to legend, the highest mountain in Johor, Gunung Ledang (also called Mt Ophir; 1276m), is the fabled home of Puteri Gunung Ledang, a mythical princess whose presence is said to still permeate the jungle slopes. Many visitors climb part-way up the mountain to admire the falls, but a very demanding two-day return trip can take trekkers to the summit. This climb is a good introduction to tropical mountaineering and is recommended for those travellers who don't have time for longer treks in Taman Negara. There's a park entrance fee of RM5 and an additional hiking fee of RM5.

There's a camp site at the base of Gunung Ledang, as well as several along the way up the mountain. Sites are RM10 per night and you'll be asked to show all your food and equipment at the Ranger's Office – you get checked again on the way out to ensure you've packed in your rubbish.

The **Gunung Ledang Resort** (☎ 06-977 2888; www.ledang.com; sales office BT 28, Jln Segamat, Sagil, Tangkak; cabins RM50, standard/deluxe tw RM150/200; 🔀 🖳) at the base of the mountain has accommodation and good facilities, and organises expeditions and programs relating to the mountain, as well as guides.

To get there from Muar, take Segamat-bound bus 65 (RM4, 30 minutes) and ask to be let off at Gunung Ledang (there's a large 'Gunung Ledang' sign near the bus stop). It's a 1km walk in from the main road to the start of the falls. From elsewhere, take a bus or train to Segamat then hop on a local bus to Segil (RM5, 45 minutes), ask to get off at Gunung Ledang and follow the same directions as above.

If staying at the Gunung Ledang Resort you can take the train to Segamat and the resort can arrange transfer from there.

MERSING

☎ 07

Once just a peripheral fishing village on the east coast of Johor, Mersing would be an inconsequential blip on the road to Kuantan were it not the hopping-off point for boats to Pulau Tioman and other islands of the Seribuat Archipelago. Nowadays it's a busy, compact town with everything that travellers passing through on their way to the islands might need: cheap internet, good sleeping options, grocery stores, cold beer and a pharmacy. The river is clogged with colourful fishing boats, but beyond the riverfront there's not much to explore.

Information

Eddy Internet Café (Jln Abu Bakar; per hr RM1.50; 🕙 9am–midnight)

Maybank (Jln Ismail) Can cash travellers cheques.

Mersing Tourist Information Centre (☎ 799 5212; Jln Abu Bakar) Rarely open and no set hours.

Police (☎ 799 2222; Jln Sultanah)

Post office (Jln Abu Bakar)

Public Bank (21-22 Jln Sulaiman) Has a 24-hour ATM that accepts MasterCard, Maestro, Cirrus, Visa and Plus.

Pure Value Travel & Tours (☎ 799 6811; 7 Jln Abu Bakar) Opposite the jetty.

Sights

There is little to see in Mersing itself. At the rear of the 95-year-old Taoist and Buddhist

Hock Soon Temple (Fushun Temple) is a splendid, gilded statue of Guanyin (Goddess of Compassion). To the right of the goddess stands Tianhou (Queen of Heaven) herself, worshipped by fishing folk and those whose lives are connected with the sea. Women hoping for children entreat the effigy of Zhusheng Niangniang, placed to the left of Guanyin.

Tours

Several places around the port work as booking offices for islands in the Seribuat Archipelago and Tioman Island, and can also arrange packages.

Omar's (☎ 799 5096, 019-774 4268; Jln Abu Bakar) at Omar's Backpacker's Hostel (below) is the best option for backpackers. Day-long island-hopping speedboat tours (RM60 per person; minimum four people) take you to several islands of the Seribuat Archipelago and include transport and snorkelling equipment. Omar's Overland Tour (per person RM110; minimum four people) is a day tour to Endau-Rompin National Park, complete with transport, guide, insurance, permit, food and accommodation. Omar also runs a RM60 local trek through jungle with stops at palm oil and rubber plantations.

Sleeping

You may end up spending a night or two in Mersing waiting for ferries (due to weather or the tides).

BUDGET

Omar's Backpackers' Hostel (☎ 799 5096, 019-774 4268; Jln Abu Bakar; dm/d RM10/25) A tiny, clean and social backpacker's pad very near the jetty, Omar's is just as well known for the owner's tours (above). Reservations are recommended during the peak season.

Hotel Golden City (☎ 799 5028; 23 Jln Abu Bakar; s RM15, d RM35-45; 🔀) Rudimentary rooms here have cement floors and saggy mattresses, but it's passably clean and good value. Singles have shared bathrooms and only the most expensive options have air-conditioning.

Ting Merdeka Hotel (☎ 799 3506; 27-A Jln Ismail; r RM35; 🔀) On two floors, the Chinese-run Ting Merdeka is a very basic choice, but the owners are pleasant.

Kali's Guesthouse (☎ 799 3613; Kampung Sri Lalang 12E; d/f RM35/85; 🔀) In a garden setting and near the beach, accommodation here is in

MERSING

0		0.5 km
0		0.3 miles

INFORMATION
Eddy Internet Café.............................**1** B3
Maybank..**2** B4
Mersing Tourist Information Centre...**3** B3
Police Station.....................................**4** B3
Post Office...**5** B3
Public Bank..**6** A3
Pure Value Travel & Tours..................**7** B3

SIGHTS & ACTIVITIES
Hock Soon Temple.............................**8** A4
Omar's...(see 12)

SLEEPING
Hotel Embassy...................................**9** A3
Hotel Golden City.............................**10** A3
Hotel Timotel....................................**11** A3
Omar's Backpackers' Hostel.............**12** B3
Seri Malaysia....................................**13** D4
Ting Merdeka Hotel..........................**14** B3

EATING
Dragon Phoenix Restaurant.........(see 9)
Loke Tien Yuen Restaurant..............**15** A3
Mersing Seafood Restaurant...........**16** A4

Port Café & Bistro............................**17** B2
Restoran Al-Arif................................**18** B4
Seafood Stalls...................................**19** A3

TRANSPORT
Bus Station & Taxi Stand...................**20** A3

To Pulau Besar (13km);
Pulau Rawa (16km);
Pulau Pemanggil (45km);
Pulau Tioman (51km);
Pulau Aur (80km);
Pulau Dayang (80km)

SOUTH CHINA SEA

Jln Abu Bakar
Jln Ibrahim
Jln Hussein
Jln Ahmad

Sungai Mersing
Morning Market
Sports Field
Jln Sulaiman
Jln Sultanah
Jln Abu Bakar
Jln Ismail
Jln Ismail
Jln Endau
Jln Jemaluang
Route 3

Hospital Mersing

To Green House (1.5km);
Kali's Guesthouse (1.5km);
Endau (38km);
Kuantan (191km)

To Johor Bahru (100km);
Singapore (135km)

To Teluk Iskandar
Inn (4.5km)

Jln Nong Yahya

JOHOR

chalets on stilts and bungalows (some neglected and in disrepair). It's 1.5km north of town (reached by taking an Endau-bound bus).

Hotel Embassy (☎ 799 3545; 2 Jln Ismail; d/tr/q RM45/55/65; ✷) This is a fabulously posh-feeling choice compared with the other cheapies in town, and is a great place to clean up and get back to reality after bumming it on island beaches. All rooms are huge, bright, have cable TV, air-con and attached bathrooms.

MIDRANGE
Avoid arriving in Mersing during the Chinese New Year and other holiday periods, as midrange hotels can be booked solid.

Teluk Iskandar Inn (☎ 799 6037; www.iskandarinn .com; 1456 Jln Sekakap; r incl breakfast RM110-140; ✷ ☎) With a lovely garden sloping all the way down to the beach, this well-groomed spot is quiet and secluded, 4.5km south of town. The two-person rooms are large and airy. The owners can prepare Malay meals by arrangement. The hotel is on the left side of the road as you head away from Mersing.

Seri Malaysia (☎ 799 1876; smmsg@serimalaysia .com.my; Lot TTB, 641 Jln Ismail; d RM130-150; ✷ ☎) An average branch of the Seri Malaysia chain, this has a small kidney-shaped pool, karaoke and a shuttle bus service to the jetty, but it's stranded in the east of town.

Hotel Timotel (☎ 799 5888; www.timotel.com.my; 839 Jln Endau; s & d incl breakfast from RM150; ✷ ☎)

Just across the bridge over the river, this is a quality hotel with excellent service. Doubles are clean, well furnished, spacious and have satellite TV. The hotel can arrange early breakfasts if you have an early boat. Promotional rates from RM88 make this place a steal.

Eating

Seafood stalls open up nightly near the bus station along the river.

Restoran Al-Arif (44 Jln Ismail; mains around RM6; 🕑 breakfast, lunch & dinner) Serving up *roti canai* (flaky, flat bread; 60 sen), *roti telur* (roti with an egg; RM1.40) and nasi goreng (fried rice; RM3), there's not much selection but the food is good and vegetarian options are available.

Mersing Seafood Restaurant (56 Jln Ismail; mains RM8; 🕑 lunch & dinner) One of several Chinese restaurants specialising in seafood, this place offers good-value dishes, including fish slice and vegetable soup, prawns with coconut sauce, and spicy Sichuan dishes.

Port Café & Bistro (Jln Abu Bakar; mains RM8-25; 🕑 lunch & dinner) A surprisingly hip little open-air bar and eatery right at the jetty, service and food here are excellent. Western grub like pizzas (from RM22) and grilled chicken salads with balsamic dressing (RM10) are delicious, as are the gourmet Malay specialities like a dolled-up *nasi lemak* (RM9). The bar serves beer, wine and cocktails and there's live music some nights.

For Chinese fare similar to Mersing Seafood Restaurant:

Dragon Phoenix Restaurant (2 Jln Ismail; mains RM10; 🕑 lunch & dinner)

Loke Tien Yuen Restaurant (55 Jln Abu Bakar; mains RM10; 🕑 lunch & dinner) Mersing's oldest Chinese restaurant.

Getting There & Away

Long-distance and local buses as well as long-distance taxis all depart from the bus station near the bridge on the river. Destinations include KL (RM37.70, 5½ hours, four a day), Singapore (RM13.70, three hours, twice daily), Johor Bahru (RM11.70, 2½ hours, two a day), Kuantan (RM16.10, three hours, twice daily), Melaka (RM22.80), Kota Bharu (RM48, 10 hours, twice daily) and Kuala Terengganu (RM34, seven hours, two a day). For buses to Cherating, travel first to Kuantan.

Taxi destinations and costs (per car) include Johor Bahru (RM160), Kuantan (RM200),

Endau (RM24) and Pekan (RM140). Local buses run to Endau (RM4, 45 minutes). For boats to Sibu Island, take a taxi to Tanjung Leman (RM60).

For ferry information to Tioman Island see p282. For the Seribuat Archipelago, see the individual island entries.

SERIBUAT ARCHIPELAGO
☎ 07

A cluster of 64 islands scattered off the east coast of Johor, the Seribuat Archipelago is a constellation of some of Malaysia's most beautiful islands. Most people only know of Pulau Tioman (see p274), the starlet and largest of the group, which is actually a part of Pahang. This leaves the rest of the archipelago (covered in this section) as far less-visited dots of tranquillity.

Divers can expect to see excellent coral and a startling array of marine life, from butterfly fish and parrot fish to young barracudas, giant clams, giant cockles and more. The waters around the archipelago are frequently whipped into foam during the monsoon from November to February, so ferry services can be patchy, especially during the high monsoon (November and December).

In addition to the islands listed below, there are other islands in the archipelago that are harder to reach and subsequently less visited. If you want to see as many islands as possible, join Omar's island hopping tour (p264) in Mersing.

Visitors to the Seribuat Archipelago (and Pulau Tioman) should purchase a **Marine Parks entry ticket** (adult/child RM5/2) at the jetty in Mersing.

Pulau Besar
☎ 07

Easy to get to and perfect for a day or two of serious beach lounging, Pulau Besar's long white-sand beach is fronted by a veritable swimming pool when the sea is calm. If you tire of vegging out, there are trails to more hidden beaches and plenty of dense jungle to explore. That said, the coral isn't great here and there is no dive operator on the island, so you'll have to spend your water time frolicking in the sandy-bottomed turquoise water or snorkelling along the scattered bits of reef. The island is only 4km long and 1km wide and was once known as Pulau Babi Besar (Big Boar Island), but

---

SURVIVING EXPEDITION ROBINSON

It will seem a little ironic while you're sipping your cocktail on a white sand beach, but other visitors to your island paradise might be crunching bugs and scrounging for water. This is because the Seribuat Archipelago is the location of *Expedition Robinson*, the original reality TV show that inspired the popular American version *Survivor*. The program first aired in 1997 and the sets now host several groups (for different versions of the show) from countries such as Belgium, the Netherlands, Denmark and South Africa.

Base camp is on Pulau Besar, while many of the rougher 'survivor' locations are on the smaller, more remote islands. The Robinson TV crew begins setting up around April and filming takes place around June and July. During these two months it can be hard to find a room, especially on Pulau Besar, so book in advance!

---

the wild swine that used to snort and crash through its jungle have vanished.

You can visit Pulau Besar on a day trip by hopping on the resort's shuttle boats or by going with **Seafarest** (☎ 799 8990; Mersing jetty; one way RM45), which makes the trip two to three times a day, with departure times depending on the tides.

SLEEPING & EATING
The island's four resorts are all situated along the beach on the west of the island. All have restaurants and provide transfers to/from Mersing for guests for around RM95 return.

Nirwana Resort (☎ 799 5979/29; r from RM50) Ageing wood shacks are kept very clean and are in a stunning setting just steps from the beach.

our pick **Mirage Island Resort** (☎ 799 2334; mirage islandresort@gmail.com; chalets RM165-345) Cheaper digs are in stylish A-frames while the more expensive options are in huge, louvered wood chalets. All exude a tropical-colonial charm, the staff is young and fun and there's a bar and pool table in the restaurant area.

Aseania Resort (☎ 019-736 1277; www.aseania resortsgroup.com.my; chalets RM180-225; 🔧 🖭) Rooms are big, clean and have dark-wood interiors, while the service is stellar and the jungle pool, surrounded by a stylish wood deck, is a shady alternative to the beach.

D'Coconut Island Resort (☎ 603-4252 6686; www.dcoconut.com; chalets RM200; 🔧 🖭) Paint-chipped exteriors and faded carpet interiors will have you lusting after the rooms at neighbouring resorts.

Pulau Sibu
☎ 07
Apart from Tioman Island, this cluster of several islands (**Pulau Sibu Besar, Pulau Sibu**

Kukus, Pulau Sibu Tengah and **Pulau Sibu Hujung**) is the most popular destination in the archipelago. Pulau Sibu Besar is where the bulk of the accommodation is found. Around 7km and 1km wide, the main reasons to visit is for the good diving and even better beaches. Tiny Pulau Sibu Tengah, which was once a Vietnamese refugee camp, is now home to sea turtles that crawl ashore in July to lay their eggs. The island has some superb coral on its northern side.

Ferries for Pulau Sibu do not depart from Mersing, but from the jetty at Tanjung Leman around 30km south of town. Since there are no public boats you'll have to organise transport with your resort (usually about RM75 return).

SLEEPING & EATING
Sea Gypsy Village Resort & Backpackers (☎ 799 3124; www.siburesort.com; A-frames s/d/t RM50/90/120; chalets incl full board per person RM210) Deservedly popular Sea Gypsy also has a backpacker's section with six fan-cooled A-frames right on the beach. The rest of the resort is also well run, with solid wooden chalets that are a favourite for families. The restaurant serves good food and caters to children and those with special dietary needs.

Twin Beach Resort (☎ 019-700 3769; www.twinbeach .com; chalets incl full board per person RM200; 🔧) Beach shacks with gussied-up kitsch interiors are a good base for a range of activities from wind-surfing to deep-sea fishing. Prices include boat transfer.

Rimba Resort (☎ 010-714 7495; www.malaysia islandresort.com; s/d chalets incl full board RM225/350; 🖭) Rimba has 19 ageing cottages with verandahs looking out over a small beach. There's no dive centre, but snorkelling and fishing trips are available.

Sibu Island Cabanas (☎ 331 7216; www.sibuisland cabanas.com; s/d chalets incl full board RM245/400; ❄ 🤿) The 'cabanas' here have particularly large terraces and real Malaysian style. There's a PADI dive centre, kayaks and massages are available – plus the resort keeps its beach clean and its beers cold.

Sibu Island Resort (☎ 223 1188; www.sibuisland resort.com.my; 2-night packages per person from RM580; ❄ 🖥 🐕) On Pulau Sibu Tengah this plush resort has all the mod-cons and you get a night free if it rains more than five hours in one day! There's a full spa, dive centre, tennis courts and anything else you could possibly need/want on holiday.

Pulau Rawa
☎ 07

Edged by a fine white-sand beach, and luring bands of sunseekers, surfers and snorkellers, the tiny island of Rawa pokes out of the sea 16km from Mersing.

Rawa Safaris Island Resort (☎ 799 1204; www .rawasfr.com; 1-night packages incl full board & boat transfers per person from RM310; ❄) is the island's main resort and has a variety of accommodation scattered over the hillsides and on the beachfront, including a longhouse and chalets. There's a restaurant, dive centre and a wide range of facilities and activities.

More rustic and a favourite with surfers, **Le Club Rawa** (chalets RM180-200) isn't as well liked by other visitors, who complain that the huts are overpriced. Meal prices at both resorts are hefty – count on RM25 or more per meal. Note also that neither resort supplies drinking water (and the well water can get pretty salty) so stock up in Mersing.

Both resorts arrange transport, but you can also get to Rawa with the Tioman Island ferry (RM45) if there are four people or more that need to stop there.

Pulau Tinggi
☎ 07

Thirty-seven kilometres southeast of Mersing, jungle-clad Tinggi is an impressive sight when seen from a distance – it's an extinct volcano (*tinggi* means 'tall').

The island supports three village populations: Kampung Tanjung Balang, Kampung Pasir Panjang and Kampung Sebirah Besar. Accommodation is largely resort-style, although some locals may supply budget accommodation. **Dreamz Tinggi Island**

(☎ in Singapore 65-8103 1319; www.dreamztinggiisland.com; 2-day/1-night packages incl full board per person from S$165; 🐕) has good-quality chalets and bungalows, a jacuzzi and a restaurant. It's next to a turtle hatchery, and boat transfers from Tanjung Leman are included in the package rate.

Pulau Aur & Pulau Dayang
☎ 07

Eighty kilometres from the mainland, Pulau Aur has crystal-clear azure water and excellent coral. With sunken wrecks off its coast, the island boasts good open-water dive sites, including Rayner's Rock, Pulau Pinang and the Pinnacles. Accommodation is almost exclusively Singaporean owned and on the weekends and Singaporean holidays these islands swarm with dive students and seasoned divers from the island city.

On Pulau Aur, several chalet and resort operations include the **Diver's Lodge** (☎ 65-6557 0016; 3-day/2-night dive packages from S$340), which is probably the island's best value on a fantastic beach in Kampung Berhala. A cross-island walk (approximately one hour) takes you to the far side of Pulau Aur.

About 300 beds are available on Pulau Dayang, across the channel from Pulau Aur, at the scenic beach at **Dayang Blues Resort** (1-night packages from S$380) in Kampung Pasir Putih. All prices include boat transfers from Mersing (about 1½ hours). You can also charter a boat from **Seafarest** (☎ 799 8990) at the Mersing jetty for around RM1000 for a day trip.

Pulau Pemanggil

Forty-five kilometres east of Mersing – or around five hours by boat – and capped by the distinctive peak of Batu Buau, beautiful Pulau Pemanggil supports a sparse population divided between three small villages: Kampung Buau, Kampung Pak Kelah and Kampung Pontianak (the last named after a female vampire who feasts on the blood of newborn children). Needless to say, the water is beautiful, enticing snorkellers and sightseers alike.

Pak Mazlan's Chalet (☎ 799 1649; r RM45) offers simple longhouse lodgings (fan and attached shower) at Kampung Pak Kelah. Near Kampung Pak Kelah, **Lanting Resort** (☎ 799 3793; www.lantingresort.com.ny; 3-day/2-night package RM268) has a variety of chalet, longhouse and suite accommodation, and offers lots of fishing adventures. At Kampung Buau, **Dagang Chalets** (dm RM10) has cheap longhouse beds.

ENDAU-ROMPIN NATIONAL PARK

Straddling the Johor–Pahang border, the 260-million-year-old, 870-sq-km Endau-Rompin National Park is the second-largest park on the peninsula after Taman Negara. The park's lowland forests are among the last in Peninsular Malaysia and have been identified as harbouring unique varieties of plant life. Of these are enormous umbrella palms, with their characteristic fan-shaped leaves, and *Livinstona endanensis,* a species of palm with serrated circular leaves.

The park is also Malaysia's last refuge of the Sumatran rhinoceros, although they roam only within the park's remote areas. Endau-Rompin is also a tiger habitat, but they are rarely spotted. Among birds that you are likely to see or hear are the red jungle fowl, the black hornbill and the grey wagtail.

Exploring Endau-Rompin National Park

The majority of travellers arrive on tours arranged by private operators. It is possible to make an independent visit, provided you have your own camping gear, but it won't necessarily work out any cheaper and the isolated location can make transport to the park inconvenient to arrange.

Most visitors explore the park along the banks of Sungai Endau and one of its tributaries, Sungai Jasin. Trips to the park usually involve treks along the banks of these rivers, with stops at two impressive waterfalls along the way and the four-hour return trip up to the Janing Barat plateau, near the Kuala

Jasin base camp. Treks from Lubuk Tapah base camp in the west of the park follow the Sungai Selai to explore waterfalls along the river. It's worth noting there is no way of traversing the forest between Lubuk Tapah base camp or the Selai Entry point and the Kuala Jasin base camp, so you either enter Endau-Rompin at Kampung Peta in the east or at Selai in the west, and stick to the sights in each respective area.

Officials of the **Johor National Parks Corporation** (☎ 07-788 2812; www.johorparks.com .my) generally require that you hire a guide to explore the park. Guides can be hired for RM50 per day at the park headquarters at Kampung Peta, or at its **Selai office** (☎ 07-922 2875) in Kampung Kemidak (which is about a 40-minute drive from Bekok). A park entry permit (RM10) is also required. Further charges include fishing-rod permit (RM20), hiking permit (RM10) and further (daily) permits to travel within the park to destinations including the Buaya Sangkut and Upeh Guling waterfalls, and the Janing Barat plateau.

The park is shut during the rainy monsoon season (November to February). See the boxed text, p86, for advice on preparing yourself for a trek.

Walks

JANING BARAT PLATEAU

The Janing Barat plateau is a 500m-high sandstone plateau southeast of **Kuala Jasin base camp**. The trail starts at the dirt track behind

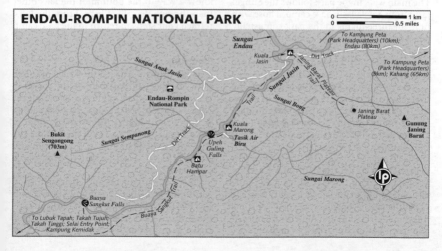

ENDAU-ROMPIN NATIONAL PARK

ON THE TRAIL OF JOHOR'S SNAGGLE-TOOTHED GHOST

Johor's famed *hantu jarang gigi* (Snaggle-toothed Ghost) is a tall, hairy, camera-shy biped that's possibly stuck in the same evolutionary cul-de-sac as the Yeti or Sasquatch. The last major sighting was in 2005 near a river in the jungle around Kota Tinggi, when an entire family of primates was reportedly glimpsed by labourers.

The primate has been tracked unsuccessfully for decades, with regular Orang Asli sightings of the 3m-tall brown-haired 'missing link' – as well as discoveries of oversized footprints. Zoologists have placed motion-sensitive cameras deep within the jungle of Johor and Pahang, but so far expeditions to uncover the woolly hominid have returned empty-handed. Even into 2009 wildlife experts, film crews and adventurers continued to search. There is enough concrete evidence to keep the buzz going.

Frequent sightings have been made on the slopes of Gunung Panti, Gunung Sisek and Gunung Muntaha, while claims by a zoologist that a Bigfoot was shot dead around Taman Negara's Gunung Tahan in 2001 (its remains inconveniently destroyed by loggers) have further fuelled feverish hopes.

So note: if you encounter a fugitive Yeti-like creature stumbling from the bushes, have your camera ready – and *no sudden movements*.

the camp; look for it heading into the woods opposite the path to the camp.

The trail climbs gently for the first 100m or so, then steepens into a challenging uphill slog. Soon after starting the climb, the first *Livinstona endanensis* are visible on either side of the trail. Once on the plateau, the terrain levels out and becomes marshy; keep an eye out for pitcher plants around the forest floor. There is nothing to mark the high point of the trail; simply walk across the plateau for a few hundred metres and then turn around.

TRAIL TO BUAYA SANGKUT FALLS

The main walk in the park follows the Sungai Jasin from Kuala Jasin base camp. Those with time for three nights in the park can usually reach the highest waterfall on the river, Buaya Sangkut; those with time for only two nights must usually turn around at Batu Hampar rocks or the falls at Upeh Guling.

After a night at **Kuala Jasin base camp**, the first day's hike crosses Sungai Jasin to follow the level terrain along the river bank through jungle for two hours to **Kuala Marong** (also known as Lembah Marong), a camp site at the confluence of Sungai Jasin and the much smaller Sungai Marong. The impressive falls at **Upeh Guling** are a further 10-minute hike up Sungai Jasin. From Upeh Guling, it's a gentle 40-minute hike to the flat rocks and camp site of **Batu Hampar**. Along the way you'll see some huge umbrella palms and dipterocarp trees. If you reach Batu Hampar before noon and are

very fit, it's possible to continue on to Buaya Sangkut and return all the way to Kuala Jasin in one day. Otherwise, camp at Batu Hampar or at Buaya Sangkut. Note that it is at least 4km from Batu Hampar to the falls at Buaya Sangkut. Because the path is quite faint, only attempt this hike with a guide.

The hike from Batu Hampar to **Buaya Sangkut** is a challenging three-hour slog over several ridges to the top of the spectacular 40m drop of the main falls. You can work your way down the side of the falls for a better view, but use extreme caution as the rocks can be treacherous. There is room to camp in the clearing above the falls. Your guide may know a way to the bottom of the falls other than the one described here. From the falls, retrace your steps to return to the base camp at Kuala Jasin.

Sleeping

You can camp at Kuala Jasin, Kuala Marong, Batu Hampar and at Upeh Guling for RM5 per night per person. Of these, Buaya Sangkut is the nicest and has the most remote location. A lightweight tent is the preferred option, but you can spread a ground sheet under the covered picnic platforms at Kuala Jasin and Kuala Marong – just be sure to bring some mosquito coils.

There are fan dorms and chalets, in good condition, available in Kampung Peta (dorm bed RM10, chalet RM60 to RM120) and simple A-frames at Kuala Jasin. At Selai, simple chalet accommodation is available at Lubuk

Tapah base camp, with a camping site at Lubuk Merekek.

Getting There & Away

The main entry point to Endau-Rompin from Johor is along Route 50 in Johor to a turn-off 5km east of the small town of Kahang (the turn-off is at mile marker 26 – 'Batu 26' in Bahasa Malaysia – from where it's a 56km drive over rough roads (4WD is advisable) to Kampung Peta, the park's visitor centre. At Kampung Peta, you can hire a boat (RM22 per person for five people or more, RM120 per boat for under five people, 45 minutes) to take you the final 10km upriver to the base camp at Kuala Jasin, or you can walk the 15km (around three hours).

For visitors coming from the west, it is possible to enter a different region of the park via the Selai entry point. Take a train to Kampung Bekok station, followed by transport to the **park office** (☎ 07-922 2875) for registration at Kampung Kemidak, before entering the park at Selai, in the foothills of Gunung Tiong.

If driving, take the exit at Yong Peng on the Lebuhraya (North–South Hwy) and drive to Kampung Bekok via Chaah. From Bekok you can drive onto Selai, but if you want to take your vehicle to the park camp sites at Lubuk Merekek and the base camp at Lubok Tapah, you will need a 4WD.

The park is also accessible from Kuala Rompin in Pahang along a paved road to Seladang, and then by following a 26km dirt track to Kuala Kinchin on the park boundary.

Because of the difficulties in arranging your own transport into the park, most travellers go on a tour. Mersing is the best place to arrange this; **Omar's Backpackers' Hostel** (☎ 07-799 5096, 019-774 4268) can arrange tours (see p264) and permits. Prices per person for all-inclusive two-night trips are around RM400; three-night trips cost around RM500.

JOHOR

Pahang

Holding Peninsular Malaysia's grandest jungles and bordered by 209km of surfable sandy beaches and near-perfect tropical islands, Malaysia's largest state is home to some of the county's most accessible outdoor action. Just three hours from Kuala Lumpur you can reach the primordial national park of Taman Negara, with elusive elephants and tigers hidden in its tracts of virgin jungle. If you're coming from Singapore, the bottle-green peaks and blue waters of Pulau Tioman are only 4½ hours away. Those heading down the east coast from Terengganu shouldn't miss a stop at the super-laid-back surf-bum/artist's haven of Cherating.

In between these tourism starlets you'll find off-the-beaten-path gems offering similar experiences without the crowds. Kenong Rimba National Park sees a fraction of the tourists and is famous for its many waterfalls, while Tasik Chini – a lotus flower–filled lake encircled by small Orang Asli villages – is surrounded by pristine jungles filled with the same wildlife and flora that visitors flock to see at Taman Negara. Those looking for Malaysian culture and architectural treats should go to Kuala Lipis for its charming old gold rush–era Chinatown, or Pekan, the seat of the Pahang Sultanate, with its majestic royal palaces and mosque that contrast with the simple *kampung* (village) houses in the surrounding area.

HIGHLIGHTS

- Hopping from one perfect beach village to the next, diving and jungle trekking on **Pulau Tioman** (p274)

- Getting wet, muddy and covered in leeches, but loving every minute of it in deep, dark and undeniably adventurous **Taman Negara** (p294)

- Staying out half the night at a beach bar then curing the morning's hangover by surfing mellow waves in languorous **Cherating** (p289)

- Being stared at by curious **Pekan** (p283) locals, who find visitors as interesting as we find their regal architecture and quaint *kampung* houses

- Floating around the lakes with the lotus blossoms then trekking the buzzing un-touched jungles around **Tasik Chini** (p288)

- Exploring the pint-sized Chinatown of **Kuala Lipis** (p302) before delving into the wild jungles of **Kenong Rimba State Park** (p303)

- TELEPHONE CODE: 09   - POPULATION: 1.48 MILLION   - AREA: 35,964 SQ KM

PAHANG

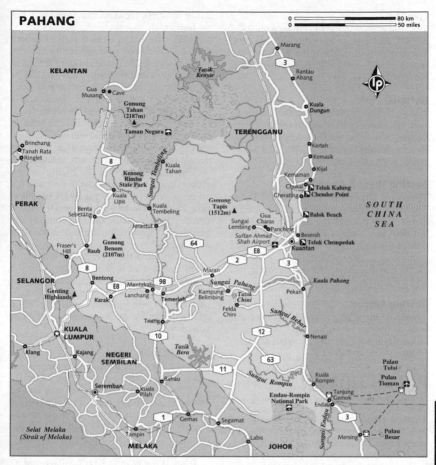

PAHANG

History

Pahang really emerged as a separate political entity when the Melaka sultanate launched an attack against the Siamese (who had held the region as a dependency since the 14th century) in the middle of the 15th century and installed Mohammad, the eldest son of the Melaka sultan, as ruler.

In the 16th century the state became a pawn in the four-way struggle for ascendancy between Johor, Aceh (in Indonesia), the Dutch and the Portuguese. In a period of 30 years it was sacked many times, with its rich, mineral-based economy ruined, its rulers killed or abducted and much of its population murdered or enslaved. After the decline of the Acehnese empire in the

mid-17th century, Pahang was ruled by Johor for 200 years.

From 1858 until 1863 Pahang suffered a civil war brought about by a leadership struggle between two brothers, Wan Ahmad and Mutahir. On the death of their father, the sultan, Wan Ahmad finally won, and in 1887 he became sultan. From then on his role was reduced to a largely symbolic position after the British forced him to sign a treaty bringing Pahang under the control of a British Resident.

In 1896 Pahang was one of the four states that became the Federated Malay States. These eventually formed the Federation of Malaya in February 1948 and finally the Federation of Malaysia, as it is today, in 1963. Kuantan replaced Kuala Lipis as state capital in 1957.

Climate

The temperature in Pahang ranges from 21°C to 32°C and average humidity exceeds 82%. There is rain throughout the year, but the wettest months are during the monsoon, from November to February.

National Parks

Taman Negara (p294), Peninsular Malaysia's greatest national park, overlaps with northern Pahang. Also in Pahang, the smaller 120-sq-km Kenong Rimba State Park (p303) can be accessed via Kuala Lipis.

Getting There & Away

There are airports at Kuantan and Pulau Tioman. The railway network in Pahang slices north–south through the centre of the state, but does not connect with the coast. Route 2 links the state capital Kuantan with Kuala Lumpur (KL). See the Getting There & Away sections in this chapter for details on air, bus and train transport to and from Pahang.

Getting Around

Transport in Pahang is largely by road and boat, as the rail network is limited. See individual destinations for details on bus and train transport within Pahang.

PULAU TIOMAN

☎ 09

Tioman Island has a near-Polynesian feel to it with its heavy-lidded hibiscus flowers, steep green peaks and turquoise, coral-rich waters. At 20km long and 11km wide the island is so spacious, and is home to so many secluded beaches, that your ideal holiday spot is surely here somewhere. But of course this is no secret: the island attracts around 190,000 visitors annually looking for their dream beach. Fortunately holidaymakers are absorbed subtly and the island retains a pristine feel within its plethora of authentic village smiles.

The permanent population on Tioman is small, with just a handful of small *kampung* dotted around the coast. These villagers have retained a wonderfully untainted vibe. Even after all the years of being descended on by hundreds of thousands of tourists, they still extend a warm welcome. The mountainous jungle of the interior is home to a spectacular array of flora and fauna (think flying squirrels, monkeys and fruit bats), but no humans.

Tekek, the island's main hub, is where Tioman steps most wholeheartedly into the modern world. The island is a duty-free zone (cheap beer!) and unsightly duty-free shops selling mostly alcohol, chocolate and cigarettes clutter the town's streets. The airstrip is located here as well as 95% of the island's cars, the only bank and a marina that can hold 36 yachts. The rest of the island remains relatively off the technology radar and even finding a decent internet connection can be taxing.

And did we mention the diving? Many visitors come to Tioman just to dive and it's an economical place to get PADI certification. The underwater world around the island remains largely intact, offering some of the best easily accessible diving and snorkelling in Malaysia.

Bear in mind that everything stocked in shops on Tioman is shipped over from the mainland and tends to be expensive (except beer and tobacco), so stock up on essentials, such as mosquito repellent containing DEET (particularly for pesky sandflies), before you arrive.

ORIENTATION

A short stretch of road runs along the western side of the island from Berjaya Tioman Beach, Golf & Spa Resort to the northern end of Tekek, where it is interrupted by steps before continuing as a path to the end of Air Batang (known as ABC). A 4WD road through the jungle links Tekek with the dozy east coast idyll of Juara.

Tekek is the island's largest village and its administrative centre. The airport is here, as well as well-stocked shops and some pleasant restaurants.

INFORMATION

It is advisable to get money in Mersing before coming to Tioman, although travellers cheques can be cashed at the Berjaya Tioman Beach, Golf & Spa Resort and there's a money-changer at the airport – but rates are poor. There's a small post office not far north of the Babura Seaview Resort in Tekek.

There are numerous public phones at Tekek, Air Batang (ABC) and Salang, but many are in disrepair. Only Telekom cards can be used for calls, on sale at shops around the island.

PAHANG

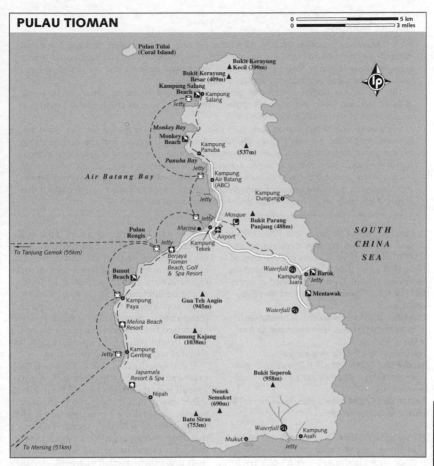

PULAU TIOMAN

0   5 km
0   3 miles

Pulau Tulai (Coral Island)

Bukit Kerayung ▲ Kecil (390m)

Bukit Kerayung ▲ Besar (409m)

Kampung Salang Beach ▲ Kampung Salang

Jetty

Monkey Bay

Monkey Beach

Kampung Panuba

▲ (537m)

Panuba Bay

Jetty

Air Batang Bay

Kampung Air Batang (ABC)

Jetty

Kampung Dungung

Mosque

Marina ▲ Bukit Parang Panjang (488m)

Jetty

Airport

Pulau Rengis

Jetty

To Tanjung Gemok (55km)

Kampung Tekek

SOUTH CHINA SEA

Berjaya Tioman Beach, Golf & Spa Resort

Waterfall

Kampung Juara ▲ Barok Jetty

Bunut Beach

Mentawak

Kampung Paya

Gua Teh Angin (945m)

Waterfall

Melina Beach Resort

Gunung Kajang (1038m)

Jetty

Kampung Genting

Japamala Resort & Spa

Bukit Seperok (958m)

Nipah

Nenek Semukut (690m)

Batu Sirau (753m)

Waterfall

Kampung Asah

Mukut

Jetty

To Mersing (51km)

Bank Simpanan Nasional (Tekek; ☾ 6am-midnight) Has the island's only ATM, which takes Visa and MasterCard.

Poliklinik Komuniti Tekek (☎ 419 1880) For medical services.

Tioman Information Centre (☾ closed 1 Nov-28 Feb) Each beach has an information centre kiosk at the foot of its jetty, but these are rarely open. Even when open they only sell ferry and taxi boat tickets (at poor rates).

SIGHTS & ACTIVITIES
Diving & Snorkelling

Tioman is one of the most popular places for diving in Malaysia as it offers good visibility and a variety of marine life at easily accessible sites (about 20 around the island). It's also one of the few places in the country where you have a good chance of seeing pods of dolphins.

There is good snorkelling off the rocky points on the west coast of the island, particularly those just north of ABC, but the best snorkelling is around nearby Pulau Tulai, better known as Coral Island. Some wreck diving is available at the sites of the famous WWII HMS *Repulse* and HMS *Prince of Wales*. The sea, however, can be very rough during the high monsoon season (November and December).

There are so many dive centres on Tioman (with more opening all the time), it's impossible for us to list every operator. Snorkelling equipment for hire is easy to find (masks and snorkels are typically RM10 per day) at many places around the island. PADI courses are priced competitively (credit cards accepted

FRAGILE PARADISE

Tioman fascinates biologists because its relative isolation has generated flora and fauna that markedly deviate from mainland species. Most creatures are elusive, but you have a good chance of seeing monitor lizards, long-tailed macaques, giant black squirrels and sea eagles, and you may even spot some of the island's reclusive mouse deer.

The sea around Tioman is home to dolphins, occasional migrating whale sharks, shoals of exotic fish, and green and hawksbill turtles. A total of 233 species of fish and 183 species of coral flourish in the waters around Tioman.

Fortunately Tioman is a marine park, with strict rules protecting marine life. The island has, however, long been propelled down the road of commercialisation and the accompanying environmental degradation has been substantial. The huge new marina at Tekek has angered environmentalists who see it as an unnecessary luxury that threatens coral reefs and other marine life. It is also argued that the large visitor numbers can only further alter the personality of Tioman and overstretch its limited resources. However, the most noticeable impact on the island is that of global warming, which has affected the health of some of the corals.

at most) – expect to pay about RM1000 for a four-day PADI open-water course and RM100 for fun dives. It's easy to shop around. Note that some dive schools shut during the monsoon season. Some established centres:

B&J (☎ 419 5555; www.divetioman.com) Has a diving pool in ABC.

DiveAsia (☎ 419 1654; www.diveasia.com.my) Tends to offers the lowest price open-water courses and fun dives; in Salang, Tekek and ABC.

Eco-Divers (☎ 419 1250; www.eco-divers.net)

Sunrise Dive Centre (☎ 419 3102; www.sunrisedive centre.com) In Juara, it has easy access to the less-visited east coast sites.

Tioman Dive Centre (www.tioman-dive-centre.com) At Tekek, it has a stellar reputation.

For information and advice for safe and responsible diving, see p84. Other activities on Tioman include rock climbing; travellers can ask for more information at Sunrise Dive Centre.

Cross-Island Walk

By walking across the island from Tekek to Juara (around 7km), you can really get a feel for the richness of the spectacular interior. While not too strenuous, parts of the walk are steep, and hiking in tropical heat can be taxing. Carry plenty of water.

There are two ways to get across the island, via the paved 4WD track or on a jungle trail. The paved road begins just southwest of the airport and, though relatively shady, you won't see much besides trees and will have to watch out for vehicles. Much better for walking is the hiking trail that starts about 1km north of the main jetty in Tekek (or 200m south of the

second jetty) where a sign says 'Trek ke Kg. Juara 7km'. Follow the concrete path, passing the mosque on your left, and then around a weed-covered cyclone fence, veering to the right and onto a small footpath. Boulder steps continue intermittently for most of the way to the top. You'll cross streams, and go deep into an awesome jungle full of giant trees with buttressed root systems that nearly eat up the path, bright coloured butterflies and, less cheerfully, mosquitos and horse flies.

If you lose the trail, follow the power lines overhead. Near the top of the hill, you pass a small waterfall that's tapped for drinking water so you're not supposed to swim in it. Shortly after making it over the top of the hill, the trail merges with the concrete 4WD track that drops steeply into Juara. About 1km before Juara a small unmarked path on the right leads to another waterfall where you can take a dip. Just watch out for the terrapin – it bites!

You'll see more wildlife here than in most of Malaysia's national parks, including black giant squirrels, long-tailed macaques, brush-tailed porcupines and – if you're incredibly lucky and out at dawn or dusk (with a torch of course) – the endangered, nocturnal binturong (bear cat). Watch out for snakes: 25 species including the king cobra and reticulated pythons have been recorded on the island. The walk takes from 1½ to three hours. A car back from Juara will cost around RM90. If returning or setting out on foot, be wary of entering the jungle after around 4.30pm, as you can get lost in the dark. During the monsoon season, the path can be very slippery, so wear shoes with a good grip.

PAHANG

Other Walks

Much of the west coast is open to walking, but trails can be difficult to follow and are often very overgrown during the low season; again, take lots of water.

The easiest accessible jungle walk of reasonable distance (about 3.5km) is between ABC and Salang. This trail mostly runs inland from the coast (no sea views) and is not well marked so it's easy to get lost, but it does lead to some excellent empty beaches. Climb up to Bamboo Hill Chalets at the northern end of ABC bay for a 10-minute hike over the next headland to Panuba Bay. From there it's another 40 minutes through the rainforest to Monkey Beach, before the trail continues from the far end of the beach across the next headland to the white-sand beach at Monkey Bay. You could stop and turn back here, making it a good day walk, or continue on for the more brutal and long, steep climb over the headland to Salang. This trail should not be attempted during the monsoon season when it's miserably muddy and the trail becomes nearly impossible to follow. The whole route takes about three to four hours if you don't lose the trail.

It's an easy 30-minute walk south from Tekek to Berjaya Tioman Beach, Golf & Spa Resort, either by the road or by rock-hopping around the headland at low tide. From there you can walk through the golf course. Just before the telecommunications tower there is a trail to the deserted beach of Bunut. From the end of the beach, the occasionally faint trail continues over the headland to Paya, from where you can walk south to Genting – the trail is easy to follow and there are houses along the way where you can ask directions.

Heading north from Tekek, you can walk all the way to ABC, and boat transport to the beaches can be arranged at most of the guesthouses in ABC or Salang, if you don't want to walk back.

From Mukut in the south of the island (reached by boat from Genting), a popular trek leads to the waterfalls near Asah.

SLEEPING, EATING & DRINKING

Accommodation on Tioman is largely strung out on the easier-to-reach west coast, with most Western tourists flocking to Berjaya Tioman Beach, Golf & Spa Resort, Tekek, Salang and ABC. Paya and Genting have lots of accommodation that is very popular with Singaporean weekenders, but they get little business during the week. All of the above are serviced by ferries from Mersing.

Trickier places to get to include Juara, a quiet beach community flung out on the east coast, while even more isolated bliss can be found at the luxurious Japamala Resort and Spa on the southwest coast. Budget options are strung out along the remote south and southwestern beaches.

The island is inundated with arrivals from June to August and during Chinese New Year, when accommodation becomes tight. For the rest of the year, it's a buyer's market and during the monsoon season (November to February) the island is almost deserted. You can generally find accommodation from January to February, although some places (especially the pricier options) shut up or undergo repairs for the entire monsoon season.

Budget accommodation largely comprises small wooden chalets and longhouse rooms (all in poor condition), typically with a bathroom, fan and a mosquito net. Air-con rooms with hot showers are more expensive. Most operations have larger family rooms for those with children, and many have restaurants.

Berjaya Tioman Beach, Golf & Spa Resort

This huge **resort** (☎ 419 1000; www.berjayaresorts .com; d RM330-710; 🔀 🖳) has a vast number of rooms, ranging from chalets and blocks of fully furnished suites to entire villas, but retains enough charm to entice repeat visits. Most rooms are chalet-style with air-con, in-house movies and classically designed furnishings, but the facilities and activities are the standout attractions. These include a golf course, tennis courts, a dive centre, a football pitch, children's playground, donkey rides, amusement arcade, a delightful strip of beach (but the swimming dries up at low tide), two swimming pools (one with great water slides), four restaurants and a beach bar. Up to 50% discounts apply during slack months in the monsoon season (November to February). Look for deals in Mersing. This is the only big resort of this kind on the island.

Tekek

Tekek is Tioman's commercial and transport hub. While the central part of town, with its unsightly twin jetties, characterless marina

PAHANG

and shabby duty-free shops isn't scenic, the village is getting gussied up a bit with a large paved waterfront promenade bordered with coconut palms. The best part of Tekek, however, is the beach that runs wide and golden at the far south of town and is arguably one of the island's best.

All accommodation options lie close to each other on the excellent southern beach.

Babura Seaview Resort (☎ 419 1139; d incl breakfast RM60-100, chalets/sea-view d incl breakfast RM152/170; ✖) This very Chinese place offers ageing longhouse fan rooms and a selection of newer, freshly painted rooms and chalets with aircon and hot-water bathrooms. Though right on a lovely stretch of beach, no effort has been made to take advantage of the sea view. The Tioman Reef Divers dive shop (www .tiomanreefdivers.com) is located here, as well as the recommended Babura Seaview Chinese Restaurant, which has fresh seafood (meals RM25) and chilled beer.

ourpick Swiss Cottage Resort (☎ 419 1642; longhouse d RM75-110, chalets RM78-140; ✖) The rooms to nab here are the seaview chalets (RM120) directly on the beach, which have breezy bamboo and wood interiors alongside colourfully painted walls and comfy deck furniture. Other options are nestled in a shady back garden, but all exude a beachy colonial style and are clean and great value. The on-site Tioman Dive Centre (www.tioman-dive-centre.com) has an excellent reputation.

Chinese Sarang Seafood (☎ 013-706 6484; meals RM20; ✖ lunch & dinner) Near Babura Seaview Resort, this spot does a particularly tasty sizzling hotplate bean curd (RM8) and serves beer.

Tioman Cabana (✖ cafe 9am-6pm, bar 8pm-2am) This hotchpotch beach bar at the north of the southern beach also acts as a cafe and tour operator offering bike rentals, internet and a slew of sports activities. Friendly Ray's Dive (☎ 019-330 8062) is right next door.

Ari's Café (✖ 9am-late) A reggae style bar tucked on the mountain side not far from the trailhead to ABC, this friendly place can prepare packed lunches (around RM6) for the trek over to Juara and has a chilled-out atmosphere.

Air Batang (ABC)

ABC is Tioman's main backpacker hangout with a less flashy beach than at Salang, but with a more down-to-earth *kampung*

atmosphere. The beach here is usually best at the southern and northern ends, although the sands are constantly shifting so this is changeable. Most of the beachfront is rocky with little sand.

All the following chalets have attached cold-water bathrooms, fans and mosquito nets unless otherwise noted. Air-con is often available in pricier options.

Internet can be found at **Double Ace Shop** (per hr RM10; ✖ 9am-10.30pm) next to Nazri's II and at a few guesthouses.

Johan's Resort (☎ 419 1359; dm/chalets/f RM15/30/130) The two four-bed dorms here up the hillside are clean and good value, while the chalets are exactly the same as all the other cheapies on the beach. The advantage here is that some of the chalets face the sea and the good beachside restaurant is reliably open from about 8am to 10pm. It's north from the jetty right before Nazri's II.

My Friend's Place (☎ 419 1150; r RM25) Busy, social and priced a hair lower than the competition, this is a clean place with all rooms facing the garden. The restaurant is just as popular and serves good food. It's south of the jetty right before Mokhtar's Place.

South Pacific (☎ 419 1176; chalets RM30) Just north of the jetty, this simple, family-run and clean place offers laundry, shows films in the evening, and has a restaurant and a small library of secondhand books. The pricier chalets are by the sea and all come with a shower and mosquito net.

Mawar Beach Chalets (☎ 419 1153; chalets RM30) Just south of the jetty, the chalets here are the same as everywhere else, but run in a row facing the beach. The restaurant has tables on the sand.

Mokhtar's Place (d RM30-45, tr RM55; ✖ 🖳) There's a very mellow family vibe going on at this quiet spot. Cheaper bungalows are set back from the beach under pleasant shady trees and all rooms are spacious and clean, though ageing. Internet is available (when it's working) for RM10 per hour.

ourpick ABC Bungalows (☎ 419 1154; d chalets RM50-150; ✖) Swing on a hammock overlooking the sea and a lovely section of beach at the north end of ABC. With a couple of chalets almost on the beach, accommodation is spread over pleasant, well-tended grounds. Marked by a huge durian tree, a decent beachfront restaurant out the front rounds it off. The large, pricier air-con chalets come with hot water, sea views, hot shower, freezer and tea- and coffee-making facilities.

our pick Nazri's Place (☎ 419 1329; www.nazris place.com; d incl breakfast RM60-180, f incl breakfast RM250; ⊠ ⚟) At the far southern end of the beach, which has some of ABC's best sand, Nazri's has clean rooms and a wide range of accommodation, from budget rooms with air-con (cross a small river to the cheapies at the rear) to deluxe rooms and family rooms in the brick units. All options are a big step up in comfort from what's available elsewhere, with varnished wood floors and walls and tasteful furniture. The restaurant is right on the water and serves an excellent seafood barbecue at dinner time.

Bamboo Hill Chalets (☎ 419 1339; bamboosu@tm.net .my; chalets RM70-120; ⚟) Perched on rocks overlooking the sea at the northern end of the beach, six well-kept chalets are in a stupendous location surrounded by bougainvillea and humming cicadas alongside a waterfall and pool. They are almost always full, so call ahead. There's no air-con, but the location benefits from cooling sea breezes. Visa and MasterCard are accepted and this place shuts from November to February.

Nazri's II (☎ 419 1375; d with fan/air-con RM80/140; ⊠) Towards the north end of ABC, this place is set in a particularly well-tended garden that spreads up the hillside. The cheaper chalets are essentially the same as elsewhere (just with a higher price tag), but the higher-end options with air-con, hot water and spacious verandahs overlooking the sea are worth a look if you want more comfort. Its Hijau restaurant (below) is our favourite restaurant on Tioman.

Tioman House (☎ 019-704 5096; chalets RM150; ⊠) Between Johan's and Nazri's II, the setting of this place (in a sparse garden right off the main path) is nothing special, but the chalets are the most comfortable in ABC. Walls are painted a happy yellow, and the huge units have air-con, hot-water bathrooms, tea-making facilities and a classic modern hotel decor.

Sunset Corner (pizzas from RM18; ⚟ 2pm-late) Right near Nazri's on the plush southern part of the beach, this is the ideal place to split a pizza and sip a cold beer while watching the sunset. Fresh fruit juices are also available for RM5. Happy hour is from 5pm to 7pm.

our pick Hijau Restaurant (meals RM10; ⚟ breakfast & dinner) This place rocks the tastebuds, serving everything from Indian specialities

including an outrageous vegetarian *aloo ghobi* (potato and cauliflower dish) for RM10 and tandoori prawns for RM26, Chinese dishes (try the excellent ginger fish for RM8) and authentic Western dishes including good breakfasts. It's set on a hillside terrace perfect for sunsets over a bottle of wine (from RM40).

Hallo Café (⚟ 5pm till late) This small beachfront watering hole has music and a 5pm to 7pm happy hour (three beers RM10). It's north of the jetty in front of Nazri's II.

Kampung Panuba

Panuba Inn Resort (☎ 419 1424; www.panubainn.com; d incl breakfast RM50-140, f incl breakfast RM170; ⊠ ⚟) Over the headland from ABC, the peaceful Panuba Inn has a pier and restaurant and 30 chalets built on a hill overlooking the bay. Rooms all face the sea, ranging from simple fan affairs to chalets with hot shower, air-con and plenty of mod-cons. Bali Hai Divers operates from here.

Salang

The small bay at Salang is jam-packed with accommodation, restaurants, tourists of every creed and touts trying to sell taxi-boat tickets and tours. There's more of a party vibe here than elsewhere on the island, as well as plenty of internet cafes, minimarts and anything else a traveller might need. A very wide and inviting white-sand beach is just south of the jetty and is good for swimming, although there's a lot of boat traffic. For many, Salang's star attraction is the monstrous monitor lizards that lurk in the inky river than runs through the village centre.

Salang Indah Resort (☎ 419 5015; www.salangindah .com; d RM30, longhouse tw RM60, hillside/sea-view chalets RM80/90, q RM120; ⊠ ⚟) An expanse of chalets seemingly sprawls forever here, north of the jetty. Most rooms aren't in tip-top condition, but if you look at several you'll probably find one to your liking. The most interesting are the Popeye-like chalets on stilts over the sea (RM120), although the bathrooms in some of these are in such bad shape, they're almost unusable. The mosque-like restaurant acts as a hub of sorts and serves everything from cheeseburgers to cheap local-style seafood (dishes around RM8). There's also a bar, shop and internet access (RM10 per hour).

Ella's Place (☎ 419 5004; chalets RM40-100; ⊠) There's usually a lounge-able patch of sand at this cute-as-a-button family-run place at the quiet northern end of the beach. There are 10 clean chalets (some with air-con) and a small cafe.

Pak Long Island Chalet (☎ 419 5000; enquiry@pak longislandchalet.com.my; chalets with fan/air-con RM50/60; ❄ 🖳) Pak Long has wooden chalets with peeling plastic flooring and OK verandahs, the more expensive of which face the sea. What sets this place apart is the family-run atmosphere that makes it feel like its own mini-village.

Salang Sayang (☎ 419 5020; www.salangsayangresort .com; chalets RM70, sea-view chalets RM80-250, q RM220; ❄) Also called Zaid's Place, this place spreads along the luscious knuckle of beach south of the jetty before trickling up the hill (meaning a handful of the chalets have excellent bay views). The setting is the best on Salang, but unfortunately there were no staff around to show us the interior of the bungalows when we passed (and we passed several times).

Khalid's Place (☎ 419 5317; salangpusaka@yahoo.com; d chalets with fan RM80, with air-con RM90-110; ❄) South of the jetty, behind the Salang Complex and across a festering section of Sungai Salang, this place has 47 cleanish chalets set in a large grassy area. Accommodation is set back from the beach; air-con chalets come with fridge and hot shower.

A few bars and cafes inject vitality into the community: **Four S Cafe** (Tiger/Guinness RM5/6; ☼ 6pm-1am) is north of the jetty, as is **Ng Café**, an odd shack that sells nothing but take-away cans of Tsing Tao beer (four for RM10).

Juara

A world of its own, Juara is the sole place to stay on the east coast of the island and hovers in a constant sleepy state of remote-hideaway bliss. There are two long stretches of wide white sandy beach here (separated by a small hill and boulder outcrop). The northern half of the beach (called Barok) is where most accommodation is found, while the southern strip (known as Mentawak) is near-deserted and kicks up some of the country's best surfing waves during the monsoon (see the boxed text, p291). While the Tekek–Juara road has technically made Juara easily accessible, the exorbitant prices for the half-hour 4WD trip (RM90 to RM120 per vehicle each way, depending on how hard you bargain) has kept the beach relatively secluded. The Mersing ferry might stop here if there are four or more people who want to visit, and a taxi boat to

ABC costs RM150. Another option is to walk from Tekek (see p276).

Turtles nest on both beaches and the area has been proclaimed a 'green zone' by the Sultan of Johor. This means it is protected from development, including the building of any big new resorts. All the places to stay in Juara hover right over magnificent beach and a few places hire out kayaks (RM15 per hour), surfboards (RM20 per hour) and fishing rods (RM15 per hour).

our pick **Beach Hut** (☎ 012-696 1093; camp sites with tent for 2 RM15, dm/chalets RM20/40) This is a bona fide surf shack (on the southern bay) run by a surf pioneer Australian/Malay couple. Chalets have heaps of character via shell mobiles, strategically placed driftwood and even some Bollywood fabrics and fake flowers. Budget warriors can get a tent (which comes with sleeping bags) next to the beach – the site is sublime. After your surf lesson (RM60 per hour) chill out in the social, lounge-able Tube Café for sandwiches, a meal or a cold beer. Dorms were in the works when we passed, but weren't yet completed.

Paradise Point (☎ 419 3145; r incl breakfast RM35) North of the jetty and with a homey vibe, this place offers simple, unnoteworthy rooms in a longhouse and has a small restaurant on the beach.

Mizani's Place (☎ 419 3157; chalets RM40) On the southern section of beach, Mizani's is directly next door to Beach Hut and has simple, old but clean bungalows with fan, mosquito nets and attached bathrooms.

Mutiara Resort (☎ 419 3159; chalets RM40-100; ❄) This is Juara's largest establishment, just south of the jetty, with lots of options that all have relatively high standards. Best are the bungalows right on the beach that are equipped with air-con, tiled hot-water bathrooms, good beds and fresh paint. The two brand-new beach-side fan-cooled bungalows with hot water (for RM50) are the best bargain in Juara. Check out the bats hanging from the coconut trees along the beach here.

Bushman (☎ 419 3109; matbushman@hotmail.com; chalets RM50) Nabbing one of Bushman's three new varnished wood chalets with particularly inviting wicker furniture on their terraces is like winning the Juara lottery – reserve in advance! The location is right up against the boulder outcrop and a small river that marks the end of the northern beach. The little cafe is a wondrously languorous place to chill out.

Rainbow Chalets (☎ 419 3140; d RM50, tw RM60-70) Super-friendly and fittingly colourful, the seven beachfront chalets (all with shower) have an excellent reputation and thus are always full. It's right before Bushman at the southern end of the northern bay. Its Sunrise Café serves some of the best grub on the beach.

Juara Beach (☎ 013-771 1137; www.island.com.my; s/d/tr RM70/80/120; 😠) All the rooms here have air-con, wood floors and hot-water bathrooms and face a grassy garden studded with coconut palms. It doesn't have much character, but service is friendly and there's a good restaurant on stilts over the beach.

Juara Lagoon (☎ 419 3153; www.tatturtlesanctuary .com; chalets & longhouse q RM100) At the very far end of the southern bay, the Juara enjoys sensational views of the entire sweep of the bay. The establishment runs its own turtle sanctuary and you can hang out with Jo, a three-year-old deaf and blind green turtle that the centre cares for. The fan-cooled chalets seem a little pricey for their simplicity, but the location and friendly welcome make up for this.

our pick **Riverview** (☎ 419 3168; d RM150) Run by the same crew as Juara Lagoon, Riverview nabs another prime location at the north end of the northern bay. Relatively chic and vaguely Tudor-style A-frame huts have balconies directly over a lazy jungle river that winds its way to the sea. The large flat area of beach on the restaurant side has an inviting volleyball pitch and the rest of the grounds are covered in soft Japanese grass (go barefoot!).

Santai Bistro (meals around RM10; 🕙 9am-11pm) Smack next to the jetty, this bar/restaurant plays classic rock and serves up everything from sambal prawns (RM18) to mixed vegetable salads (RM6). The beers are cold and the views are hypnotising.

Just north of the jetty there's a modern looking building that houses a handful of local-style restaurants that serve some of the best value food on this beach, with everything from Western breakfasts to *roti canai* and seafood dinner barbecues.

Kampung Paya

Swarming with happy Singaporeans, the short, wide, white-sand beach here is jam-packed with two resorts and a few restaurants and food shacks. The rocky and shallow water makes this a poor choice for swimming.

Paya Resort (☎ in Mersing 07-799 1432; www.paya beach.com; dm incl breakfast RM40, chalets incl breakfast RM200-480; 😠 😠) is the best place to stay at Paya, with most of the spacious modern chalets linked together by wooden bridges over a lily pond. There are also tidy, air-con four-bed dorm rooms (with attached shower), and a restaurant, full spa, dive centre, lounge and a range of activities.

Melina

our pick **Melina Beach Resort** (☎ 419 7080; www .tioman-melinabeach.com; chalets for 4/5/6/8 people incl breakfast RM140/240/400/650; 😠) is the only place to stay at this remote beach of photogenic boulders and white sand. Each sleeping option is unique and creatively designed from wood, thatch and plexiglass to create a certain Crusoe chic – the most interesting is a tree house that hovers right over the beach. The owners have set up a successful turtle hatchery and the laid-back atmosphere attracts lots of families. Meals are served at the resort or you can walk for 20 minutes to Genting and try the restaurants there. Plenty of activities are organised to keep folks entertained.

Genting

Genting is the most built-up beach and caters mostly to the weekend Singapore and KL crowd, but its surrounding local village gives it more authenticity than the others. During the week there are rarely more than a handful of tourists, but you might come across local people practising music for an upcoming ceremony, or you can chat with fishermen about their catch. The long, white beach would be lovely were it not for the unsightly cement breakwater decaying in the sand.

Sun Beach Resort (☎ 419 7069; www.sunbeachresort .com.my; tw RM50-90, tr RM70-100, f RM90-110; 😠) The biggest place in Genting, it has plenty of beachfront chalets.

Golden Dish Café (dishes from RM6; 🕙 10am-midnight) This might be the only place on Tioman serving their own home-grown organic vegetables. There are also plenty of authentic Chinese seafood specialities and healing herbal drinks.

Japamala Resort & Spa

our pick **Japamala Resort & Spa** (☎ 419 6001; www .japamalaresorts.com; tree-top chalets incl breakfast RM390-680, sea-cliff chalets incl breakfast RM480-890; 😠 😠) is the only Relais & Chateau hotel in Malaysia (only 475 'outstanding properties with a truly unique character' around the world have this exclusive membership) and it's as decadent as that entails. The powdery beach is in small patches between rocky outcrops and everything from the over-the-water bar to the spa are draped in fabric, and look like they've come straight off the pages of the *Vogue* travel section. This is a whole lot of luxurious bang for your buck.

Nipah

A great choice for backpackers wanting to bliss out in isolation, Nipah Beach is a long strip of white with an unusual stripe of black sand running through it. A river mouth at the southern end creates an outrageous deep blue swimming hole that's bordered on one side with a large, flat knuckle of sand with a volleyball pitch. There are plenty of walking opportunities from here to small, empty beaches and a jungle waterfall.

You can stay at either **The Nipah Beach Tioman** (☎ 019-735 7853; chalets from RM70), which is run by young and friendly Abbas and offers some rustic chalets on the beach, or at **Bersatu Nipah Chalets** (☎ 07-797 0091; bersatunipah_tioman@yahoo .com; r with fan/air-con RM60/90; ✷), which has clean beachfront longhouse rooms, great service and an excellent riverside restaurant.

Both places can arrange pick up from the ferry stop in Genting for RM20 each way.

Mukut

On the southern tip of Tioman, Mukut is another secluded and tranquil spot with a lovely beach.

Mukut Coral Resort (☎ 07-799 2535/2612; r/chalets RM25/88; ✷) Traditional village-style chalets (all with air-con and hot water, some with TV) are set in a marvellous location. The resort has a sea-view restaurant serving Chinese and Western food.

GETTING THERE & AWAY
Air

Berjaya Air (☎ 419 1303, in KL 03-7846 8228, in Singapore ☎ 02-6481 6302), with offices at Berjaya Tioman Beach, Golf & Spa Resort and at the airstrip, has one daily flight to/from KL (RM228) and Singapore (RM296) from the **airport** (☎ 419 1309) at Tekek.

Boat

Mersing in Johor is the main access port for Tioman. **Bluewater** (☎ 799 2535) runs the regular ferries to the island and departure times vary with the tide – usually the first ferry leaves in the morning and the last mid-afternoon. Ferries (one way RM35, two to three hours) leave from the main jetty and stop at Genting, Paya, Berjaya Tioman, Tekek, ABC and Salang, in that order, picking up from those jetties in the reverse order on the return trip. Decide where you want to get off and tell the ticket inspector. Purchase tickets from one of the many tour operators around Mersing or at the jetty just before departure. For the return trip from Tioman, ask at the place you're staying for the next day's sailing times. There is a car park at the jetty in Mersing where you can leave your vehicle (RM7.50 per day). On weekends and holidays it's a good idea to buy your tickets in advance since the boats fill quickly.

Boat departures during the monsoon season (November to February) can be erratic (and dangerous), although sailings become more regular during the low monsoon months (January and February).

You can also charter a speedboat from the jetty at Mersing with **Seafarest** (07-799 8990; round trip RM1200).

Ferries also depart for Tioman from the **Tanjung Gemok ferry terminal** (☎ 413 1997; one way RM35), 35km north of Mersing near Endau (opposite). Departure times are 9am, noon and 4pm, returning from Tioman at 10am, noon and 4pm. This route is useful if coming from the north and is faster, taking only 1½ hours to the Berjaya Tioman Beach, Golf & Spa Resort, but call ahead and make sure the ferries are running before you arrive. Ferry services dry up between November and April.

GETTING AROUND

In 2009 there was no longer a sea bus, so the only way to beach hop is by sea taxi. Typical sea taxi fares from Telek are: Salang (RM30), ABC/Panuba (RM25), Paya Beach (RM30), Genting (RM30), Nipah (RM75) and Juara (RM105). Most chalets can arrange boat charter, but it is expensive (RM300 to RM400 per day).

If you have the time, you can explore some of the island on foot. Bicycles can be hired at guesthouses on all the main beaches (RM5 per hour).

A lift in a 4WD from Tekek to Juara or from Juara to Tekek costs around RM90 to RM120 (bargain hard) for up to four people.

THE COAST

ENDAU

☎ 09

There's little of interest in Endau, but fast boats speed to Pulau Tioman from nearby **Tanjung Gemok**, which functions as an alternative to Mersing in Johor for reaching Pulau Tioman (see opposite).

Hotel Seri Malaysia (☎ 413 2723; smrom@serimalaysia.com.my; d incl breakfast RM120; ❄ ☁), just across Sungai Endau in Tanjung Gemok, has clean air-con rooms with shower. Also near the jetty in Tanjung Gemok are numerous other small, cheap hotels and restaurants, and a couple of internet cafes – but honestly, it's a much better option to take the ferry to/from more interesting Mersing if you need to spend the night.

PEKAN

☎ 09

The seat of the Pahang Sultanate, Pekan has a regal air and is uncommonly scenic with its wide clean streets, spacious *padang* (city square) and many grand buildings surrounded by expansive pristine lawns. There is also a collection of old Chinese shophouses along a shady river (which is unfortunately filled with rubbish), friendly giggling locals unused to seeing tourists, and some great accommodation at the Chief's Rest House. Around the town centre are acres of traditional *kampung* houses surrounded by livestock and veggie gardens.

Information

There's internet access at **10 Net Cyber Café** (Jln Sultan Abu Bakar; per hr RM3; ❄ 10am-7pm). **CIMB Islamic Bank** (Jln Rompin Lama) has an ATM that accepts foreign cards.

Sights

The stately **Museum Sultan Abu Bakar** (Jln Sultan Ahmad; admission RM1; ❄ 9.30am-5pm Tue-Thu, Sat & Sun, 9am-12.15pm & 2.45-5pm Fri) is housed in a wonderful building constructed by the British in 1929 for the local Resident. Exhibits are largely about the Pahang royal family, such as the sultan's car and his polo achievements, but there are also weapons, pottery (including Chinese porcelain and Arab ceramics unearthed on Pulau Tioman) and exhibits on wildlife in Pahang.

On the river island facing the museum is a display of traditional Malaysian watercraft in **Galeri Pengangkutan Air** (❄ 9.30am-5pm Tue-Thu, Sat & Sun, 9am-12.15pm & 2.45-5pm Fri). Look out for the fabulously carved craft with the head of a mythical beast. Both museums were under renovation in 2009.

To the west of the Museum Sultan Abu Bakar along the river is the blue-domed **Sultan Abdullah Mosque** (Jln Sultan Ahmad), a large, slightly mouldering creation with blue domes dating back to 1932. Behind the mosque stands the old **Pekan Lama**, fashioned from wood and stone. The active **Abu Bakar Mosque** (Jln Sultan Ahmad) is further west, crowned with gold domes.

Walk to the end of the road (Jln Sultan Ahmad), turn the corner and head along the road away from the river, through the memorial archway fashioned like huge tusks, passing the Chief's Rest House (see p284) on your left. Keep walking past the blue-painted **Istana Mangga Tunggal** with its red-tile roof on your right, before continuing to the rural setting of **Kampung Permatang Pauh** and **Kampung Padang Buloh**, where splendid single *kampung* houses line the roads, and cows ruminate by the wayside.

The focus of the litter-free, palm-lined roads of the royal quarter of Pekan is the Regent of Pahang's palace, **Istana Permai**, and further on, the sultan's palace, the **Istana Abu Bakar**, set in vast grounds of cow grass and adjacent to the verdant polo field of the **Royal Pahang Polo Club**. It's worth completing a lazy circuit of the road around the field (Prince Charles reputedly played here) as it's a very well-tended area; sitting on a section of track within the grounds of the polo field is an old steam engine.

TIOMAN SCAMS

For literally years now, the less savoury of Mersing's entrepreneurs have been coming up with a variety of techniques for getting Tioman-bound tourists into their offices. Here they try to sell you ferry tickets (at the going price, no loss to the traveller there) and get you to reserve a Tioman hotel – sometimes at double the real price. Outside of holidays and high season, and particularly for budget chalets, it's best to shop around for a place to stay once you reach your beach. If you want to reserve accommodation in Tioman in advance, call or email the place yourself!

PAHANG

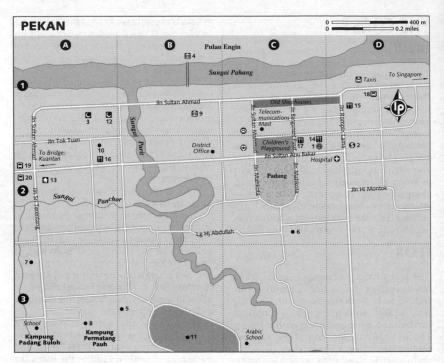

North of the polo field (back towards the river) are attractively coloured, traditional *kampung* houses on stilts. North of the main shopping district and the *padang*, the **Istana Leban Tunggal**, within Kampung Leban Tunggul, is a fine old red-tiled, two-storey building, in need of a lick of paint, with two buff-coloured domes.

Returning to the river, wander past the old shophouses, a row of old family shops, Chinese guildhalls, barbers and restaurants. **Sungai Pahang**, which can be crossed at this town via a lengthy bridge, is the longest river in Malaysia and was the last east-coast river to be bridged.

Sleeping & Eating

Staying a night in Pekan is a great way to shift into the low gear of small-town Malaysia. A few restaurants, food vendors and fruit stalls can be found in the grid of streets in-between the Padang and Sungai Pahang and along the riverfront Jln Sultan Ahmad. Also, a handful of *ikan bakar* and *tom yam* (spicy Thai-style) seafood restaurants open for dinner along Jln Sultan Abu Bakar.

Chief's Rest House (☎ 422 6941; Jln Istana Permai; d RM55-70; ✕) Exuding atmosphere and style, this wooden building (dating from 1929), with a wide verandah, is reason enough to stop in Pekan. All the rooms have wood floors, towering ceilings, TV and air-con. It's nearly 1km from the bus terminal, so let the driver know that you want to get off near the rest house. Alternatively, walk (shadeless and hot) or take a taxi (RM6) from the main bus station.

Umi Café (22 Jln Bangunant Pusat; meals RM5-10; ⏰ 7.30am-9pm) Right across from the shady *padang* this is the most airy and pleasant place to eat in town. There's a Chinese-Malay buffet at lunch and delicious curry *pao* (RM1; steamed bun filled with meat) all day.

Getting There & Away

Regular local buses run to/from Kuantan (RM5.30, one hour), Kuala Rompin (RM6.50, two hours) and to Chini Village (RM5, 1½ hours). Long-distance buses run to Kuala Terengganu (RM22.10) and to KL (RM25).

The taxi station is at the bus station. A taxi to/from Kuantan costs RM40; to Tasik Chini it's RM60.

KUANTAN
☎ 09

The second-biggest port in Malaysia and the capital of Pahang, most travellers only stop in busy Kuantan to break up long bus trips. Until recently there wasn't much to do besides get out of town and out to the nearby beach of Teluk Chempedak, but a few new activities, including a river cruise and walking tour, make stopping in this city for the day a bit more interesting.

Information

Lots of banks (many with 24-hour ATMs) are on or near the aptly named Jln Bank. You'll find wi-fi in most hotels, plus internet cafes at the Berjaya Megamall and East Coast Mall.
Hamid Bros Books (☎ 516 2119; 23-25 Jln Mahkota; ☽ 9am-9pm Mon-Sat, 10am-3pm Sun) A licensed moneychanger; also sells some English-language books.
Mega Tech (2nd fl, Lg Pasar Baru 3; per hr RM2; ☽ 9am-midnight) Next to the long-distance bus station.
Post office (Jln Haji Abdul Aziz) On the continuation of Jln Mahkota, near the soaring Masjid Negeri.
Tourist information centre (☎ 516 1007; Jln Mahkota; ☽ 8am-1pm & 2-5pm Mon-Thu, 8am-12.45pm & 2.45-5pm Fri) Has particularly helpful staff and a range of useful leaflets.

Sights & Activities

Kuantan's major attraction is the beach, Teluk Chempedak (see p287), outside town. The **Masjid Negeri** (State Mosque; Jln Mahkota) is the east coast's most impressive mosque, which presides regally over the *padang*. At night it's a magical sight with its spires and lit turrets.

Ninety-minute **river cruises** (adult/child RM15/8; ☽ 9am, 11am, 2pm & 4pm) run from the jetty to the Sungai Kuantan river mouth, then upriver again through mangroves at the edge of town. You can also take a 90-minute **guided heritage walk** (☎ 012-267 0098; ravee_tg@yahoo.com.au; per person RM40) that explores Kuantan's small collection of colonial architecture, as well as sites of local interest, with tour guide Ravendran.

If you happen to be in town on a Saturday afternoon and want to do something completely out of the ordinary, go check out the **horse races** (Indrah Makota Indo Stadium) where you can sit in the air-con and watch locals go into a betting frenzy.

Sleeping

Budget choices in Kuantan (except one) are grim, so do yourself a favour and splurge on something midrange or better.

Sungai Wang Utama Hotel (☎ 514 8273; 16 Jln Penjara; r RM15-35; ❄) The vibe is a little sleazy but it's cleanish and cheap.

Hotel Makmur (☎ 514 1363; 1st & 2nd fl, B 14 & 16 Lg Pasar Baru 1; r RM30-70; ❄) Totally boring and functional but clean, this is the only cheapy in town we feel absolutely OK about recommending. Reception is friendly and it's very near to the long-distance bus station.

Classic Hotel (☎ 516 4599; chotel@tm.net.my; 7 Jln Besar; d incl breakfast RM90; ❄) An excellent choice, all rooms here (ask for a river view) are spacious and clean, with large bathrooms, free filtered water, tea-making facilities, TVs and air-con. Add the central location, ample Malay-style breakfast and considerate staff and there's no point staying anywhere else.

Seasons Boutique Hotel (☎ 516 3131; seasons boutiquehotel@gmail.com; 2-8 Jln Beserah; r from RM98; ❄) Bright coloured walls and Zen-style furniture makes this the most chic choice in town, but rooms are small and many are window-less. There's a spa offering reflexology and a big restaurant serving Malay and Western food.

Mega View Hotel (☎ 517 1888; Lot 567, Jln Besar; r RM150-350; ❄ 🍴) This high-rise has a bit more atmosphere than the other hotels in town thanks to its direct riverfront position and lots of natural light in the lobby areas, the Alfresco Bar (see p287) and in the rooms. Opt for a standard executive to get

PAHANG

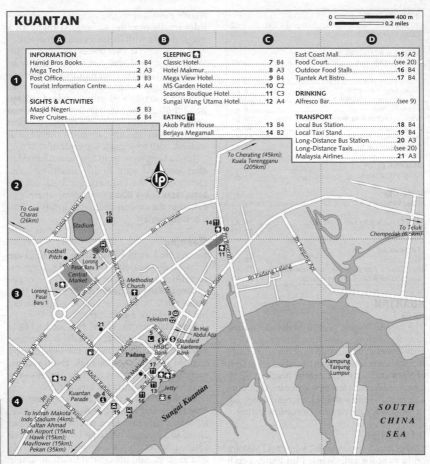

KUANTAN

INFORMATION	
Hamid Bros Books..................................1 B4	
Mega Tech...2 A3	
Post Office...3 B3	
Tourist Information Centre................4 A4	
SIGHTS & ACTIVITIES	
Masjid Negeri...5 B3	
River Cruises...6 B4	

SLEEPING	
Classic Hotel..7 B4	
Hotel Makmur...8 A3	
Mega View Hotel....................................9 B4	
MS Garden Hotel..................................10 C2	
Seasons Boutique Hotel....................11 C3	
Sungai Wang Utama Hotel...............12 A4	
EATING	
Akob Patin House................................13 B4	
Berjaya Megamall.................................14 B2	

East Coast Mall.....................................15 A2	
Food Court...(see 20)	
Outdoor Food Stalls............................16 B4	
Tjantek Art Bistro.................................17 B4	
DRINKING	
Alfresco Bar..(see 9)	
TRANSPORT	
Local Bus Station.................................18 B4	
Local Taxi Stand...................................19 B4	
Long-Distance Bus Station................20 A3	
Long-Distance Taxis........................(see 20)	
Malaysia Airlines..................................21 A3	

a balcony and uninterrupted river view. All the suites were renovated in 2009 and have modern wood furniture as well as two balconies. The RM165 family rooms are a great deal if you're travelling with kids.

MS Garden Hotel (☎ 555 5899; www.msgarden.com.my; Lot 5 & 10, Lg Gambut, off Jln Beserah; r incl breakfast from RM390; 🅿 🖥 🛱) Kuantan's poshest hotel was getting a total remodel throughout 2009. Rooms are big, there's a fitness centre, kid-oriented pool with waterslides, and excellent service. It's conveniently located next to the Berjaya Megamall.

Eating & Drinking

Kuantan's most distinctive dish is *patin* (silver catfish). For more common fare head to the Berjaya Megamall or the East Coast Mall to find everything from Délifrance and Starbucks to Malay-style food courts. Small food stalls can be found dotted along the riverbank, in the central market, on Jln Bukit Ubi and inside the long-distance bus station.

our pick Akob Patin House (☎ 013-931 2709; Jln Besar; 🕑 lunch) Fancy trying *patin*, the local delicacy? This riverfront place serves both wild caught (RM20) and farmed (RM8) *patin* in a *tempoyak* (fermented durian sambal) sauce served buffet style with other Malay style meat and vegetable dishes – the price is per fish. The friendly staff can help explain what's what.

Tjantek Art Bistro (☎ 967 2021; 46 Jln Besar; meals RM30; 🕑 4pm-1am Mon-Sat) Modern art hangs from the walls, jazz issues from the speakers, and the menu – pastas, cooling salads, sizzling steaks, noodles and desserts – is trendy. How weird that it's in Kuantan.

Alfresco Bar (Mega View Hotel, Lot 567, Jln Besar) At the rear of the Mega View Hotel (p285), this sits right next to the river, with a huge TV screen for live sports events. Coupled with ambient music, it's a very relaxing venue.

Getting There & Away

AIR

Malaysia Airlines (☎ 515 6030; Ground fl, Wisma Persatuan Bolasepak Pahang, Jln Gambut) has daily direct flights to KLIA with plenty of onward connections from there. **Firefly** (☎ 03-7845 4543) also has two daily flights to/from Subang Airport in KL and four weekly flights to Singapore. The airport is 15km away from the city – take a taxi (RM15).

BUS

Long-distance buses leave from the station on Jln Stadium. The ticket offices and information counter, as well as a food court, are on the 2nd floor of the building.

There are services to/from the following cities: Kuala Lumpur (RM22, four hours), Singapore (RM26, six hours), Jerantut (RM16, 3½ hours), Mersing (RM16.10, three hours), Kuala Lipis (RM24, six hours), Melaka (RM27, six hours), Seremban (RM22, five hours), Temerloh (RM10, two hours), Butterworth (RM48, eight to nine hours), Kuala Terengganu (RM15, four hours) and Kota Bharu (RM29, six hours).

Buses for Pekan (RM5.30), Balok (RM3), Beserah (RM3) and Cherating (bus 27; RM4) depart from the local bus station on Jln Besar.

CAR

Some car rental offices in Kuantan:

Hawk (☎ 538 5055; www.hawkrentacar.com.my; Sultan Ahmad Shah Airport, Kuantan)

Mayflower (☎ 538 4490; www.mayflowercarrental .com; Lot 1, Terminal Bldg, Sultan Ahmad Shah Airport, Kuantan)

TAXI

The long-distance taxi stand is in front of the long-distance bus station on Jln Stadium. Destinations and costs (per car): Pekan (RM50), Mersing (RM180), Johor Bahru (RM350), Cherating (RM50), Kuala Terengganu (RM180), Jerantut (RM190) and KL (RM230).

AROUND KUANTAN
Teluk Chempedak

A quality slice of white beach blankets this strip of coast, 6km east of Kuantan. Light waves crash on the shore while several **walking tracks** wind along the park jungle area on the rocky promontory from the northern end of the shoreline. From November to around February the beach break here becomes surfable, but there's not much in the way of surfboard rental – try the hut renting kayaks near the Hyatt Regency.

One half of the beach is occupied by a big seafood food court (as well as a beachfront McDonald's heartbreaker) while the other side is taken entirely over by the luxurious Hyatt Regency. A road leading back out to the main road is cluttered with trinket shops (many selling kites since there's often a good wind blowing through) and cheap hotels. In all, Teluk Chempedak is the ideal locale for having alfresco chats over sizzling seafood dinners after a day of frolicking in the surf or hiking the coast.

The **Hyatt Regency Kuantan** (☎ 566 1234; http:// kuantan.regency.hyatt.com; r RM420; 🖭 🖭) is a spacious, breezy and effortlessly luxurious place, with amenable staff, lovely views and a solid list of amenities (including two pools, two very good restaurants, three tennis courts, squash courts, a spa, a children's play area and a water sports centre). Rooms are sumptuous and a whole bevy of activities are on offer, including walks along the cliffs to Methodist Bay.

About 200m from the beach just beyond the McDonald's, the **Pine Beach Hotel** (☎ 940 4458; s/d/f RM50/60/120; 🖭) is unremarkable but clean; its newish rooms all have air-con, TVs and hot-water showers. Ground floor rooms are windowless. Prices rise by around RM10 at weekends.

Traipse the sand and dive into one of the beachfront restaurants and food stalls for a bite to eat, but note that the fiercest drinks served at some places are mocktails (as ever in Malaysia, aim for Chinese-owned restaurants, or the Hyatt Regency if you want beer).

At the time of research there was no public bus service between Kuantan and Teluk Chempedak. A taxi between the two towns costs RM12.

PAHANG

Beserah & Balok Beach

Beserah is a long stretch of *kampung* sand-wiched between the beach and the road, the best part being Balok Beach 15km north of Kuantan. The beach at Balok is long and pleasant, and beachfront accommodation – largely resort-style – is easy to find, as the length of the beach is littered with a variety of lodging options. The **Natural Batik Factory** (☎ 551 0113; www.batikfactory.com; Lot 4898, Jln Kemaman, Lg Chengal Lempong, Balok; ☻ 10am-7pm) offers batik-making lessons for children and adults, and has a wide selection of batik products. The **Swiss Garden Resort & Spa** (☎ 544 7333; www.swiss gardenkuantan.com; 2656-2657 Mukim Sungai Karang, Balok Beach, Beserah; d RM276-351, f RM500; ☒ ☐ ☐ ☒ ☎) is the top pick, boasting a huge pool and a superb restaurant (the Garden Terrace) that serves up fantastic pizza.

Regular buses run from Beserah into Kuantan (RM2).

Gua Charas

Twenty-six kilometres north of Kuantan at Panching, the limestone karst containing **Gua Charas** (Charas Caves/Charah Caves; RM1) towers high above the surrounding palm plantations. The caves owe their fame to a Thai Buddhist monk who came to meditate here about 50 years ago.

It's a steep climb up a stairway to the caves' entrance – be careful. The colossal **Sleeping Buddha Cave** (Wofo Dong) is decorated with small altars to Guanyin, Puxian, other Bodhisattvas and Buddhist idols leading to the sleeping Buddha, a rather modest cement effort at the rear of the cavern.

Take the Sungai Lembing–bound bus 48 (RM2.50, one hour) from the local bus station in Kuantan and get off at the small village of **Panching**, just past the sign read-ing 'Gua Charas 4km'. From the bus stop in town it's a hot 4km walk each way, but you may be able to get someone in Panching to give you a lift on the back of a motorcycle for around RM2. A taxi from Kuantan to the caves costs RM40. You can also see the caves on tours run from Cherating (opposite).

TASIK CHINI

☎ 09

So hard to get to and yet so worth it, Tasik Chini (Lake Chini) is a series of 12 lakes linked by vegetation-clogged channels. Its shores are inhabited by the Jakun people, an Orang Asli tribe of Melayu Asli origin. The surrounding waves of jungle hills are some of the least-visited trekking areas in the country and still hide tigers and elephants, as well as glorious waterfalls and caves. Locals believe the lake is home to a serpent known as Naga Seri Gumum, sometimes translated in tour-ist literature as a 'Loch Ness Monster'. The best time to visit the lakes is from June to September when the lotuses are in bloom.

Sleeping

Tasik Chini Resort (☎ 477 8000; tasikchini@hotmail.com; camp site RM3, dm/d RM15/80) Under renovation in 2009, this place on the southern shore has little cottages strewn across a grassy slope right at the lake's edge. There's a restaurant, and you can arrange boat trips, canoeing, night treks, fishing, an overnight climb up Gunung Chini and other activities.

Rajan Jones Guest House (☎ 017-913 5089; r per person incl breakfast & dinner RM25) Nestled in flower-filled Kampung Gumum, the rustic but clean longhouse rooms (with fan, mos-quito nets and shared bathrooms) are the base camp for host Rajan's excellent jungle and lake adventures. Breakfast, afternoon tea and dinner are served on the lakeside and you can also get lunch for an extra RM5. Rajan speaks perfect English, is close with the Orang Asli, has been leading treks for over 20 years, knows all about local flora and fauna, and can arrange a spectrum of activi-ties from jungle trekking (five-hour trips, RM50 per person), night hikes (RM35), longer treks (RM80 per day) waterfall trips (RM80) and lake trips (RM50 to RM100).

Getting There & Away

Buses run to Kampung Chini four times per day from Kuantan's local bus station (RM5, two hours) and twice a day from Pekan (RM4, 1½ hours). To get to Kampung Gumum ask to be let off at the Chini 2 bus stop. From here you'll have to ask around for a private car to take you the remaining 7.5km – this should cost about RM20. You can also call Rajan Jones and ask him to help arrange a private car. A taxi all the way to Kampung Gumum from Pekan/Kunatan should cost RM70/80. Lake Chini Resort ar-ranges transport for its guests – call them for details.

CHERATING

☎ 09

There is something special about Cherating, but not everyone who visits here gets it – or wants to. Though beautiful, the sweeping white beach bordered by coconut palms doesn't compare to those on the islands and the village itself is just a half-dead strip of guesthouses and shops with more monkeys, monitor lizards and cats walking around than humans. And yet many travellers end up extending their stays here for days, months or even years. There is a lot to do (surfing, horse riding, tours etc) but it's the people that draw the travellers in. This unusual resident band of hipster Malay surfers, musicians, artists and *kampung* folk who shun big city life genuinely want to hang out with you over a beer and share in the holiday spirit. With all these new friends, it's hard to hit the lonely road again.

Information

There are no banks in Cherating, but Travelpost will exchange cash and traveller's checks at poor rates.

Tourist Information Centre (cnr Hwy 3 & Main Rd) A flashy new building with plenty of hand-outs, but it's understaffed and rarely open.

Travelpost (☎ 581 9796; 🕙 9am-11pm) Can organise bus tickets to just about anywhere (takes a commission). There's also a book exchange, bike hire (per hour RM3), internet access (per hour RM4) and tourist information.

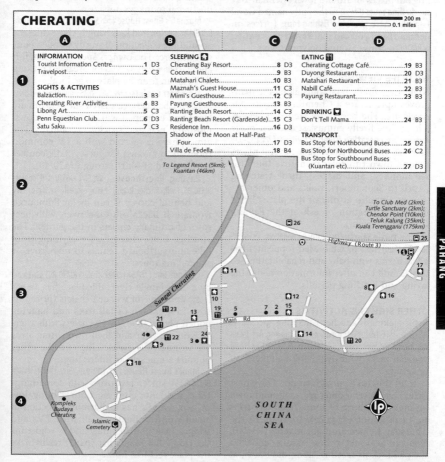

CHERATING

INFORMATION		
Tourist Information Centre..............1	D3	
Travelpost.....................................2	C3	
SIGHTS & ACTIVITIES		
Balzaction......................................3	B3	
Cherating River Activities................4	B3	
Libong Art......................................5	C3	
Penn Equestrian Club......................6	D3	
Satu Saku......................................7	C3	
SLEEPING		
Cherating Bay Resort......................8	D3	
Coconut Inn...................................9	B3	
Matahari Chalets...........................10	C3	
Maznah's Guest House....................11	C3	
Mimi's Guesthouse.........................12	B3	
Payung Guesthouse........................13	B3	
Ranting Beach Resort.....................14	C3	
Ranting Beach Resort (Gardenside)...15	C3	
Residence Inn................................16	D3	
Shadow of the Moon at Half-Past Four..........17	D3	
Villa de Fedella.............................18	B4	
EATING		
Cherating Cottage Café..................19	B3	
Duyong Restaurant........................20	D3	
Matahari Restaurant......................21	B3	
Nabill Café..................................22	B3	
Payung Restaurant........................23	B3	
DRINKING		
Don't Tell Mama...........................24	B3	
TRANSPORT		
Bus Stop for Northbound Buses.......25	D2	
Bus Stop for Northbound Buses.......26	C2	
Bus Stop for Southbound Buses (Kuantan etc)...........................27	D3	

PAHANG

Sights & Activities

Cherating is just as great for lazing around on the beach and hanging out with the friendly locals as it is for its many activities.

WATER SPORTS

Some of Malaysia's best surfing waves pound the beach at Cherating and other surf spots to the north. Several places in town rent out surfboards for around RM20 per hour and you can get surf lessons at **Satu Saku** (Main Rd; ☺ November-March). Right on the beach, **Balzaction** (☺ 9.30am-11pm) rents out windsurfing and kite-surfing equipment from around RM50 per hour and offers classes.

The Cherating beach isn't great for snorkelling but places all around town offer half-day **snorkelling tours** (RM50) to the aptly named Coral Island. There are also **fishing tours** (prices on demand) and you can rent **kayaks** (sea or river, per hr RM20) to cruise around on your own.

WILDLIFE VIEWING

Night-time firefly boat tours along the mangroves upriver are a Cherating activity *par excellence*. The best tours are led by Hafiz, a long-time firefly enthusiast and self-made expert at **Cherating River Activities** (☎ 013-939 9256; Main Rd; tours per person RM20). Several places around town run river mangrove tours (to see monkeys and snakes), turtle-watching (April to September), walks and other activities. Enquire at one of the places listed under Information or ask at the Payung Guesthouse (right).

The **turtle sanctuary** (entry by donation; ☺ 9am-5pm Tue-Sun) next to Club Med (opposite) has a few basins with baby and rehabilitating sea turtles, and can offer information about the laying and hatching periods.

OTHER SIGHTS & ACTIVITIES

Batik-making is another Cherating speciality. Matahari Chalets (right) and **Limbong Art** (Main Rd) both offer courses (from RM25) where you can make your own batik handkerchief or sarong.

If all this isn't enough to do, Travelpost (p289) and several other places around town arrange a plethora of tours from day trips to Tasik Chini (RM178), to visits to the Thursday Kememan night market (RM50). You can also take riding lessons, either in the paddock or trotting along the beach, at the well-kept **Penn Equestrian Club** (☎ 292 9265; Main St; per hr RM100).

Sleeping

BUDGET

Budget digs tend to fill up during the monsoon surf season from November through January, so book in advance.

Shadow of the Moon at Half-Past Four (☎ 016-794 0144; dm/d/tr RM20/35/55) OK, this place is getting pretty rundown and is not for everyone, but it exudes so much shadowy jungle character that we have to keep it in the book. If you don't stay in the ageing bungalows or dark dorms, at least stop by for a stiff drink or a meal of wild boar while listening to tales of the owner's hunting adventures and the squawks of wild nocturnal monkeys outside.

Maznah's Guest House (☎ 581 9072; chalets incl breakfast RM20-35) Spirited kids happily chase chickens around the collection of sturdy wooden bungalows here. The owners speak little English and *nasi lemak* is served for breakfast making this a great, friendly place to go local.

Matahari Chalets (☎ 581 9835; small/large chalets RM25/35) Chalets have shared showers but are clean and equipped with a fridge, windows, mosquito nets and spacious verandahs. The atmosphere is relaxed with a TV common room and a kitchen for guests. Batik courses are also held (T-shirt/sarong RM30/40).

Payung Guesthouse (☎ 581 9658; s/d chalets RM30/35, f with kitchen RM50) This excellent, friendly and helpful choice is run by an Edinburgh woman. It backs onto the river, with neat rows of ordinary chalets in the garden. The attached tour office offers everything from bike and surfboard rentals to mangrove or snorkelling tours.

Coconut Inn (☎ 581 9299; chalets RM30-80) Backed by a dark jungle river, this place has an eclectic ensemble of wooden chalets (priced by size) in a garden of tall trees and hanging potted plants. The RM50 chalets with a terrace on the river and their own sitting areas are wonderfully rustic-chic and the other options are nearly as interesting.

Mimi's Guest House (☎ 012-939 7309; chalets RM40-60; ☒) A surfer favourite with some long-term residents clinging onto a bungalow or two, Mimi's has a charming selection of small wood bungalows, all with TVs and fridges. Ani and her husband – who runs the Don't Tell Mama bar (p292) really make the place feel like home.

SURFING INSIDER: ARIL ZAINAL

Who'd have thought there was surf in Malaysia? But fun waves break along the East Coast during the monsoon months (from around October to April).

Why Cherating? Cherating is a surf hub with accommodation, food, transportation and lots of board rentals. The Cherating point left-hander starts breaking with a 1ft swell, can hold up to 5ft and has a sand bottom good for beginners. Sometimes during low tide it can get really hollow. There are lots of breaks near Cherating, like Chendor point on the Terengganu–Pahang border that was a secret point for us, but now lots of people know it. It can hold up to a solid 5ft swell and is really hollow. It's about 10-minute drive from Cherating and you have to drive a bit off road – a bit tricky. Teluk Kalung is about a 30-minute drive from Cherating. Lots of people surf this beach break, especially beginners.

Beyond Cherating? Juara on Tioman Island in Pahang (p274) has lots of breaks, but for some you need a boat. Mentawak Point, at a small river mouth, starts to break at 2ft to 3ft and can hold to 6ft and even more. It's a right-hander with a rock bottom and some reef. There's also a beach break in Mentawak in front of the Beach Hut (p280) and on the Barok side of the jetty.

The scene? The scene is small but growing every year. It's good for the local businesses, restaurants and guesthouses, especially during monsoon season. Many people come to Cherating to learn to surf and the Pahang Tourism Action Council organises some surf event every December. Last year [2008] was the Billabong Pro Am competition, which was open to anyone that wanted to join in.

To see some of Aril's Malaysia surfing photographs go to www.cheratingpoint.com.

Aril Zainal is a dedicated Malay surfer and surf photographer who follows the swells up and down the coast each year.

MIDRANGE

Midrange choices tend to fill with Malaysian holidaymakers on weekends and holidays, so book in advance during these times.

Ranting Beach Resort (☎ 581 9068; beachfront chalets RM100-150, garden chalets RM50-80; 🅿) The best chalets here are the wooden fan-cooled ones right on the busiest strip of the beach. Concrete air-con beachfront bungalows are also good, though a little musty, while the cheapest garden-side bungalows across the road from the beach were looking worn but were expecting a remodel. Service is near non-existent but the place is kept clean.

ourpick Villa de Fedella (Tanjung Inn; ☎ 581 9081; d/f chalets with air-con RM120/150, d/tr chalets with fan RM55-70; 🅿 💻) The grounds here are stunning. Chalets are clustered around a lotus-filled pond and a grassy lawn that's studded with coconut palms and stretches to the beach. Fan-cooled chalets are in good shape and have terraces overlooking the pond, but it's the massive, colonial feeling air-con chalets with good beds and hot showers that steal the show. It's run by a lovely local family.

Cherating Bay Resort (☎ 581 9988; d/f apt from RM140/260; 🅿 💻) Resembling a southern Californian apartment complex, the tidy apartments here are arranged over two floors, and are all equipped with teapots, sinks, TVs and living areas. The top floor lets in more light. Among other facilities, there's a children's playground, pool with waterslide and restaurant.

TOP END

Residence Inn (☎ 581 9333; www.ric.com.my; r/chalet incl breakfast RM248/268; 🅿 💻 🛜) Surrounding a good swimming pool, the newly remodelled, crisp and modern rooms are the most comfortable choice in town. Skip the chalets, which are old and dark. Service is great, there's a big restaurant and promotional rates from RM180 are often available.

Legend Resort (☎ 581 9818; www.legendsgroup.com; Lot 1290, Mukim Sungai Karang; d/ste incl breakfast RM450/800; 🅿 💻 🛜) Outside Cherating, this luxury resort on the road to Kuantan has huge outdoor pools by the beach, spacious rooms, two restaurants, a lovely section of beach, squash and tennis courts, a convenience store, a bar with a snooker table and tempting discounts.

ourpick Club Med (☎ 581 9133; www.clubmed .sg; all-incl package per night per person from RM550; 🅿 💻) Crafted to look like a particularly beautiful Malaysian *kampung* with wooden buildings on stilts, the resort comes fully equipped with its own stretch of beach, immaculate sprawling lawns, international restaurants, nightclub, kiddies club, nearby turtle sanctuary and sports facilities. Prices are all-inclusive; contact the hotel for standard package deals.

Eating & Drinking

Nabill Café (meals around RM6; ☺ dinner) Eat where the locals do and save a handful of ringgit. Choose your fresh seafood then watch it get grilled in a delicious spicy sambal.

Duyong Restaurant (meals RM15; ☺ lunch & dinner) Raised on stilts at the western end of the beach, this offers unbroken views around the bay. There's a large selection of seafood, steaks, poultry and vegetables, but it's the setting that is superlative. Try the *tom yam* (hot and spicy seafood soup, RM8).

Payung Restaurant (meals from RM17; ☺ breakfast, lunch & dinner) Off the main road against the quiet riverside, this semi-outdoor hang-out serves thin-crust pizzas and a selection of pastas (all from RM17). There's often groovy music playing and a friendly extended family to hang out with.

Most guesthouses run their own restaurants, the best being **Matahari Restaurant** (seafood barbecue from RM10; ☺ breakfast, lunch & dinner) at the west end of town. The **Cherating Cottage Café** (breakfasts around RM5; ☺ breakfast, lunch & dinner) is the first to open in the mornings (around 8am) and serves good breakfasts.

Right on the beach, **Don't Tell Mama** (☺ till late) is the hippest bar in town and is a great place to stop by day or night to make friends over a cold beer. Impromptu barbecues and parties are the norm.

Getting There & Away

From Kuantan's local bus station catch a bus marked 'Kemaman' and ask to be dropped at Cherating (look for a sign by the road that reads 'Pantai Cherating'). Buses leave every 30 minutes (RM4.50, one hour, 6.45am to 8pm). When coming from the north, any bus heading for Kuantan will drop you on the main road. A taxi from Kuantan should cost about RM70.

From Cherating to Kuantan, wave down a Kuantan-bound bus from the bus stop on the highway (Route 3). For taxis from Cherating call the **Cherating Taxi Service** (☎ 581 9355).

Travelpost (☎ 581 9796; ☺ 9am-11pm) can arrange long-distance bus tickets (convenient for those heading north to places like Kuala Terengganu or Kota Bharu), but takes a commission. Your only other option is to try to flag down northbound buses from the bus stop on the highway and hope there's an empty seat.

CENTRAL PAHANG

JERANTUT
☎ 09
Jerantut is the small, slightly dreary gateway to Taman Negara. There are no attractions in this town, but it's easy to manage and most visitors to the park spend at least one night here. Chinese liquor stores line up along Jln Diwangsa hoping you'll want to stock up on booze before heading to dry Kuala Tahan.

Information
Several banks in town can change cash and travellers cheques (change money before heading into Taman Negara). The ATMs do dry up sometimes so it's best to get money before reaching Jerantut.

AM Finance Bank (Jln Diwangsa; ☺ 9.30am-4pm Mon-Fri & 9.30am-noon Sat) Has an ATM that accepts most foreign cards, including Visa.

Bumiputra Commerce (Jln Tahan; ☺ 9.30am-4pm Mon-Fri & 9.30am-noon Sat) The ATM accepts MasterCard and Cirrus.

Internet (1st fl, 11 Jln Tahan; per hr RM3; ☺ 9am-5pm)

Internet Café (NKS Hostel; per hr RM5; ☺ 24hr)

Police (☎ 266 2222; Jln Besar)

Sleeping
Most places offer luggage storage, are open 24 hours and can arrange transport to Taman Negara. Hotels can get very busy around July and August.

Hotel Sri Emas (☎ 266 4499; tamannegara@hotmail .com; 46 Jln Besar; dm/tr/f RM8/21/64, d without shower RM15-35, d with shower RM38; ☒ ⚟) Many people get herded here by the handy NKS minivan that picks up at the bus and train station, and it's not a bad place to end up. Fan doubles with shared hot-water bathrooms have saggy mattresses, but are clean and excellent value (RM15!). Pricier rooms are bigger and have attached bathrooms and air-con. There's an internet terminal downstairs.

Hotel Chet Fatt (☎ 266 5805; 177 Jln Diwangsa; dm/d with shared bathroom RM10/20; ⚟) Stumble across the street from the bus station if you arrive late

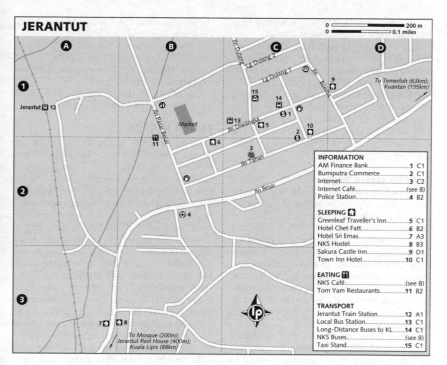

at night to this place with window-lit rooms, internet terminals and free filtered water.

Greenleaf Traveller's Inn (☎ 267 2131; 3 Jln Diwangsa; dm RM10, d RM20-30; 🅿) Run by a sweet lady and her family, this is a quiet choice with simple, clean rooms and dorms.

Town Inn Hotel (☎ 266 6811; www.towninnhotel .com; Lot 3748, Jln Tahan; d/tr/q RM48/65/85; 🅿 🖳 🛜) Bright clean rooms here are a big step-up from the backpacker oriented places. Service is friendly.

NKS Hostel (21-22 Jln Besar; d with/without shower incl breakfast RM50/35) Another arm of Sri Emas (and just across the street) NKS is ever so slightly more upmarket with clean, tiled rooms, although not all RM35 doubles (with TV) have outside-facing windows. NKS buses to Kuala Tahan and Kuala Tembling (for the boat) stop right outside the NKS Café and there's a large internet cafe on the ground floor so you can down your breakfast and check your email right before heading into the wilds of the national park.

Sakura Castle Inn (☎ 266 5200; sakuracastleinn @yahoo.com; 51-52 Jln Bomba; d RM55-85, f RM95; 🅿) This is the classiest place in town (for Jerantut

remember) and has clean, comfortable rooms all with TVs (Astro), hot water and air-con.

Eating

An excellent food court specialising in *tom yam* is on Jln Pasar Besar, while cheap *kedai kopi* (coffee shops) serving Chinese food and Malay favourites can be found scattered around town.

NKS Café (NKS Hostel; 21-22 Jln Besar; meals RM10; ⏱ 7.30am-9pm, closes 6pm low season) Serves mediocre Western breakfasts, Malay staples, *dou fu* (tofu) meals, sandwiches and beer.

Getting There & Away
BUS

Long-distance buses leave from the ticket offices near the taxi stand; local buses depart from the station not far away on the same street.

Four buses depart daily to/from KL's Pekeliling bus station (RM17, three hours, last bus to/from Jerantut 5pm/4pm) via Temerloh. If you miss the bus to KL, buses go every hour to Temerloh (RM5, one hour, last bus 6.30pm), from where there are more connections to KL and other destinations. Three daily buses run to/from Kuantan (RM16.10, 3½ hours). One bus runs daily to Johor Bahru (RM38).

Buses coming through from KL continue to Kuala Lipis; otherwise, take a bus to Benta Seberang (RM6, hourly from 7am to 6pm) and then another to Kuala Lipis.

NKS arranges minibuses and buses to a variety of destinations, including Tembeling jetty (RM5), KL (RM40), Perhentian Island jetty (RM65), Kota Bharu (RM65) and the Cameron Highlands (RM65). They leave from the NKS Café.

To/From Taman Negara

Most visitors prefer to take the wonderfully scenic river trip to the national park from Kuala Tembeling, but the public bus (RM7) all the way to Kampung Kuala Tahan at Taman Negara is a much cheaper way to get there. Buses depart from the bus station at 5.30am, 8am, 1.30pm and 5pm. In the return direction, buses leave Kampung Kuala Tahan for Jerantut at 7.30am, 10am, 3.30pm and 7pm. NKS minibuses from the NKS Hostel also make the trip to Kuala Tahan (RM25) at 8.30am and 1pm; returning 8am and 7.30pm.

Public buses go to the jetty at Kuala Tembeling (RM2, 45 minutes), for the boat to Taman Negara every hour from 7.45am to 5pm, but schedules are unreliable and don't coincide with boat departures. It's better to pay a bit more and take the NKS bus (RM5, 8.30am and 1.30pm; returning at 11.30am and 4.30pm) from in front of the NKS Hostel. These are linked to the boat services. Returning to Jerantut from the jetty, buses come by at around 12.30pm and 4pm, but again, don't count on it. For information on the boats to/from Kuala Tembling and Taman Negara see p301.

Alternatively you can take a taxi (see below) from Jerantut to Kuala Tembeling/Kampung Kuala Tahan, drive or hitchhike (though never entirely safe) to the park.

TAXI

Taxi fares are as follows: Kuala Tembeling (RM20), Kampung Kuala Tahan (RM65), Temerloh (RM50), Cherating (RM240), Kuala Lipis (RM65), KL (RM200) and Kuantan (RM180). A surcharge of RM30 is enforced after 3pm.

TRAIN

Jerantut train station (☎ 266 2219) is on the Tumpat–Gemas railway line (also known as

the jungle railway). All northbound trains go via Kuala Lipis and Gua Musang.

Two express trains run daily to Singapore (2am, 12.30pm), via Johor Bahru. For KL Sentral, take the 12.30am express; there are four trains for Kuala Lipis.

For an up-to-date timetable and list of fares, consult **KTM** (www.ktmb.com.my).

TAMAN NEGARA

The 'green lungs' of the Malay Peninsula, Taman Negara blankets 4343 sq km (from Pahang to Kelantan and Terengganu) in shadowy, damp, impenetrable jungle. Inside this buzzing tangle, ancient trees with gargantuan buttressed root systems dwarf luminescent fungi, orchids, two-tone ferns and even the giant rafflesia (the world's largest flower). Hidden within the flora are Asian elephants, tigers, leopards and rhinos, as well as smaller wonders such as flying squirrels, but these animals stay far from the park's trails and sightings are extremely rare. Even if the animals do come close, the chances are you'll never see them through the dense jungle thicket. What you might see are snakes (dog-toothed cat snakes, reticulated pythons, temple pit vipers and red-headed kraits), lizards, monkeys, small deer and perhaps tapir. Nearly everyone who visits Taman Negara gets an up-close and personal meeting with leeches and an impressive array of flying and crawling insects.

The time scale is as dauntingly massive as the jungle itself (it's 130 million years old), which is claimed to be the oldest in the world. None of the Ice Ages had any effect here, and Taman Negara has eluded volcanic activity and other geological upheavals. The Batek people, one of Malaysia's aboriginal groups (also called Orang Asli), are relative newcomers compared with much of the forest's life. Between 200 and 400 Batek make their home in the park, where they live off hunting and gathering, moving around often to different encampments.

The more you put into a visit to Taman Negara, the more you'll get out of it. Fleeting visits are naturally feasible, but invariably only scratch the surface. Consider an overnight trek or at least a long boat-trip up one of the park's rivers (p298).

The best time to visit the park is during the dry season from February to September. Rainfall is not constant during the rainy

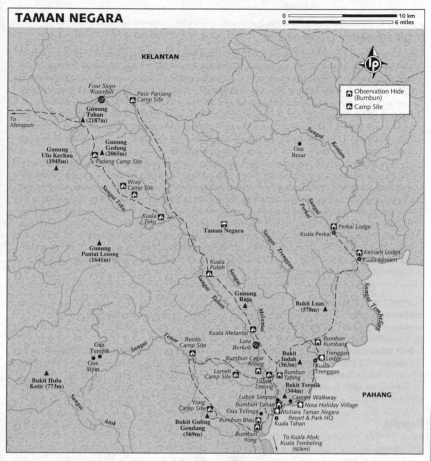

TAMAN NEGARA

season, but when it rains it pours, and trails rapidly transform into treacherous, muddy bogs. The peak tourist season is from April to August.

Orientation

The park headquarters and the privately run Mutiara Taman Negara resort are at Kuala Tahan at the edge of Taman Negara National Park, while all the other accommodation and restaurants are across Sungai Tembing at Kampung Kuala Tahan. River taxis buzz between the two sides of the river (RM1 each way) throughout the day.

Information

Daily **video shows** (🕑 7pm) on Taman Negara are shown in the exhibition hall at the Mutiara Taman Negara resort/park headquarters and at the NKS Restaurant in Kampung Kuala Tahan. The exhibition hall at the Mutiara also has informative displays on the park.

For health care, the Poliklinik Komuniti is adjacent to Agoh Chalets in Kampung Kuala Tahan, opposite the school.

INTERNET

Internet cafe (per 10 min RM1; 🕑 8am-midnight) Just down from the Teresek View Motel.

Internet cafe (per hr RM6) At Agoh Chalets, it has fast connections.

POLICE

Police station (☎ 266 6721) Next to the Teresek View Motel.

PAHANG

THE FUTURE OF TAMAN NEGARA

First established as a preservation area in 1937, Taman Negara is Malaysia's oldest and most prestigious national park. Its relentless promotion as a wildlife haven and *the* place for an experience of the Malaysian jungle, however, has been met by growing numbers of visitors (around 60,000 per year).

Large animals once roamed right up to park headquarters, but sightings are becoming very rare and the effective animal habitat area of the park has shrunk. The busy 5% of the park, through which hiking trails run, is largely shunned by wildlife so the chances of seeing anything at all these days is dismal. Meanwhile, the 631 elephants (the largest population in Southeast Asia) and up to 110 of Malaysia's estimated 300 tigers that call Taman Negara home have been increasingly pushed towards the Kelantan and Terengganu borders.

The visitor boom is not all bad news, though, as the resort provides necessary local employment; and increasing revenues from tourism, along with stiff government penalties, has helped eliminate poaching. Orang Asli are allowed to hunt small animals and continue their traditional nomadic lifestyle, but their impact is relatively low (although the impact of tourism on the Orang Asli is high).

With all the increased traffic putting strains on the park, there has been much talk of how to best preserve Taman Negara and cater to increasing visitor attention. Restricting access, by introducing quotas or raising prices may be unpalatable as Taman Negara is one of Malaysia's major tourist attractions. Not only does it generate foreign income but the park is also an important educational resource for Malaysians, who are increasingly aware of the ecology and natural beauty of their own wilderness areas.

TOURIST INFORMATION
Information Centre (☯ 9am-11pm) Right at the riverside end of the road out of Kampung Kuala Tahan, it offers everything from onward transport info to tours.
Tourist Information Counter (☯ 8am-10pm Sun-Thu, 8am-noon & 3-10pm Fri) In the building behind the reception of Mutiara Taman Negara resort, this is where you must register before heading off into the park. Also offers park information and guide services (below).

Permits

Most people purchase **permits** (park entrance/camera/fishing RM1/5/10) when they buy their bus and/or boat tickets to Kuala Tahan with NKS in Jerantut. Otherwise you'll need to get your permits at the Tourist Information Counter (above) at Mutiara Taman Negara resort. Permits can also be picked up at the office at the Kuala Tembeling jetty. Failure to buy a permit can incur fines of up to RM10,000 (or three years' imprisonment).

Guides

Guides who are licensed by the Wildlife Department have completed coursework in forest flora, fauna and safety. Often the Kuala Tahan tour operators offer cheaper prices than those available at the Tourist Information Counter at Park Headquarters (whose guides are licensed), but talk with these guides first to find out what training they've had. Guides cost RM180 per day (one guide can lead up to

12 people), plus there is a RM100 fee for each night spent out on the trail.

Activities

The major activity at Taman Negara is penetrating the magnificent jungle. There's a wide variety of walking and trekking possibilities – from an hour's stroll to nine arduous days up and down 2187m-high Gunung Tahan. You can shorten your hiking time in most cases by taking river bus services (see p298) or tours that include boat transport. Don't enter the jungle after 6pm (unless on a guided trek), and do pack a torch (flashlight) just in case.

The trails around the park headquarters are convenient but heavily trafficked. Relatively few visitors venture far beyond the headquarters, and longer walks are much less trammelled. A long day-walk will take you away from the madding crowd, but getting well away from it all requires a few days trekking and/or expensive trips upriver by boat.

SHORT WALKS FROM KUALA TAHAN
Easy-to-follow trails around park headquarters are signposted and marked with approximate walking times; enquire at the information office for details on other routes. All these walks can be shortened by taking Nusa Camp's river bus (see p298) one or both ways to the nearest stop.

Canopy Walkway & Around

East from the park headquarters, the Bukit Indah (Indah Hill) trail leads along Sungai Tembeling to the **Canopy Walkway** (adult/child RM5/3; ⊙ 10am-3.30pm Sat-Thu, 9am-noon Fri), 30 minutes away. Queues can get long here as only four people are allowed on each swinging gangplank at one time (show up before 10.30am or around noon to avoid the tour groups), but it allows for closer inspections of the higher forest reaches. The walkway is suspended between huge trees and the entire circuit takes around 40 minutes.

From behind the Canopy Walkway a trail leads to **Bukit Teresik** (344m), from the top of which are fine views across the forest. The trail is steep and slippery in parts, but is easily negotiated and takes about an hour up and back. You can descend back along this trail to the Mutiara Taman Negara resort or, near the Canopy Walkway, take the branch trail that leads across to **Lubok Simpon**, a swimming area on Sungai Tahan. From here it is an easy stroll back to park headquarters. The entire loop can easily be done in three hours.

Past the Canopy Walkway, a branch of the main trail leads to **Bukit Indah** (563m), another steep but rewarding hill-climb offering fine views across the forest and the rapids in Sungai Tembeling.

Kuala Trenggan

The well-marked main trail along the bank of Sungai Tembeling leads 9km to Kuala Trenggan, a popular trail for those heading to the Bumbun Kumbang hide (p298). Allow five hours. Though generally flat, it traverses a few small hills before reaching Sungai Trenggan. From here, boats go back to Nusa Holiday Village and Kampung Kuala Tahan, or it's a further 2km walk to Bumbun Kumbang. An alternative longer trail leads inland, back across Sungai Trenggan from Bumbun Kumbang to the camp site at Lubok Lesong on Sungai Tahan, then back to park headquarters (six hours). This trail is flat most of the way and crosses small streams. Check with park headquarters for river levels – Sungai Trenggan can be forded only when levels are low.

Gua Telinga

From the park headquarters, it's roughly a 1½-hour walk (2.6km). Think wet: a stream runs through this cave (with sleeping bats) and a rope guides you for the strenuous 80m half-hour trek – and crawl – through the cave. Return to the main path through the cave or take the path round the rocky outcrop at its far end. From the main path, it's a 15-minute walk to Bumbun Blau hide or you can walk directly back to Kuala Tahan.

Lata Berkoh

North from park headquarters, the trail leads to Gunung Tahan, but you can do an easy day walk to Lata Berkoh, the cascading rapids on Sungai Tahan. The trail passes the Lubok Simpon swimming hole and Bumbun Tabing, 1¼ hours from Kuala Tahan. There is one river crossing before you reach the falls, which can be treacherous if the water is high; do not attempt the river crossing in high water – you should hail one of the boatmen waiting on the opposite side to ferry you across.

PLANNING

Leeches are everywhere inside the park (but are rarely found in Kampung Kuala Tahan) so boots with gaiters or long socks tucked over your trousers (for that fashionable look) then doused in DEET will make hiking more pleasant. Note that insect repellent with DEET isn't usually available in Taman Negara, so stock up before you get there.

Camping, hiking and fishing gear can be hired at the Mutiara Taman Negara resort shop or at several shops and guesthouses on the Kampung Kuala Tahan side. Asking prices per day are around RM8 for a sleeping bag, RM10 for a rucksack, RM25 for a tent, RM20 for a fishing rod, RM5 for a sleeping pad, RM8 for a stove and RM8 for boots. Prices can be negotiated and it's good to shop around for bargains as well as quality.

Taman Negara: Malaysia's Premier National Park by David Bowden (available in the bigger bookshops of Kuala Lumpur or online) is an excellent book on the park, with detailed route maps and valuable background information.

See the boxed text, p86, for more information on leech protection and preparation for trekking.

PAHANG

LONGER TREKS

Kuala Keniam

A popular walk is the trail from Kuala Trenggan to Kuala Keniam. It's normally done by chartering a boat to Kuala Keniam and then walking back to Kuala Trenggan (six hours). The trail is quite taxing and hilly in parts, and passes a series of limestone caves. This walk can be combined with one of the Kuala Tahan–Kuala Trenggan trails to form a two-day trip, staying overnight in the Trenggan Lodge or at Bumbun Kumbang (see below). It is also possible to walk from Kuala Keniam to the lodge at Kuala Perkai, an easy two-hour walk.

Gunung Tahan

Really adventurous travellers climb Gunung Tahan (2187m), the highest peak in Peninsular Malaysia, 55km from park headquarters. It takes nine days at a steady pace, although it can be done in seven. A guide is compulsory (RM700 for seven days plus RM75 for each day thereafter). With no shelters along the way, you have to be fully equipped. Try to organise this trek in advance so you don't have to hang around park headquarters for a couple of days.

Rentis Tenor

From Kuala Tahan, this trek takes roughly three days. Day one: take the trail to Gua Telinga, and beyond, for about seven hours, to Yong camp site. Day two is a six-hour walk to the Rentis camp site. On day three cross Sungai Tahan (up to waist deep) to get back to Kuala Tahan. It's roughly a six hour walk, or you can stop over at the Lameh camp site, about halfway.

HIDES & SALT LICKS

Animal-observation hides (bumbun) are built overlooking salt licks and grassy clearings, which attract feeding nocturnal animals. You'll need to spend the night in order to see any action. There are several hides close to Kuala Tahan and Kuala Trenggan that are too close to human habitation to attract the shy animals. Your chances of seeing wildlife increase if you head for the hides furthest away from park headquarters. There's a chance of spotting tapir, wild boar or deer, but sightings of elephant and other large game are extremely rare. Even if you don't see any wildlife, the jungle sounds are worth it – the 'symphony' is best at dusk and dawn.

Hides (RM5 per person per night) need to be reserved at the Tourist Information Counter (p296) and they are very rustic with pit toilets. Some travellers hike independently in the day to the hides, then camp overnight returning the next day, while others go to hides that require some form of transport and a guide; the Tourist Information Counter can steer you in the right direction. For overnight trips you'll need food, water and a sleeping bag. Rats on the hunt for tucker are problematic, so hang food high out of reach.

The hides (with distances from park headquarters) are Bumbun Tahan (250m), Bumbun Blau (3.1km), Bumbun Yong (4km), Bumbun Tabing (3.1km), Bumbun Kumbang five hours walk) and Bumbun Cegar Anjing (1½ hours walk). They can be reached on foot and/or by river boat.

FISHING

Anglers will find the park a real paradise. Fish found in the park's rivers include the superb fighting fish known in India as the *mahseer,* but here as the *kelasa.*

Popular fishing rivers include Sungai Tahan, Sungai Keniam (north of Kuala Trenggan) and the remote Sungai Sepia. Simple fishing lodges are scattered through the park and can be booked at park headquarters. The best fishing months are February, March, July and August. Fishing permits are RM10, and hiring a rod costs RM20 per day.

RIVER BUS & BOAT TRIPS

The Mutiara Taman Negara resort has daily boats that go upriver to Kuala Trenggan at 10am and 2.30pm. In the reverse direction, boats leave Kuala Trenggan at 11.15am and 3.15pm. These services are intended for guests only.

Nusa Holiday Village (p300) runs a very useful river bus (not restricted to guests) from the Nusa Riverbus jetty on the Kampung Kuala Tahan side to the following places (prices are one way; return trip prices are about 1½ times the one-way fare):

Bumbun Yong (RM15) Three per day; first boat 8.30am.

Canopy Walkway (RM10) Boats at 10.15am & 12.30pm, returning 11.30am & 1.45pm.

Gua Telinga (RM10) Four boats per day; first boat 8.30am.

Kuala Tembeling (RM25) One boat per day at 9am.

Kuala Trenggan (RM30) Boats at 10.15am & 3.05pm, returning 11am & 3.30pm.

Nusa Holiday Village (guest/nonguest RM6/15) Six boats per day; first boat 8.15am.

The same boat also runs from Nusa Holiday Village to Kuala Trenggan (RM15).

Keep in mind that these regularly scheduled river-boat services run pretty much on time during the peak season, but may be dropped entirely during the rainy season. It's best to ask at Nusa Holiday Village or the Mutiara Taman Negara resort for up-to-the-minute information.

In addition to these boat trips, you can arrange private boat trips at the Tourist Information Counter (p296), or at the restaurants in Kampung Kuala Tahan (the latter are usually 10% cheaper). The following prices are for boats seating four/10 people from Kuala Tahan: Bumbun Tabing RM50 (four-seater), Bumbum Cegar Anjing RM50 (four-seater), Canopy Walkway RM50/65, Gua Telinga RM50/65, Lubok Lesong RM100 (four-seater), Kuala Keniam RM210/260, Kuala Trenggan RM110/150, Kuala Perkai RM320 (four-seater), Lata Berkoh RM160 (four-seater), Nusa Holiday Village RM90/110.

Tours

Everyone in Kuala Tahan wants to take you on a tour. There are popular night tours (RM35), which are on foot or by 4WD. You're more likely to see animals (such as slow loris, snakes, civets and flying squirrels) on the drives, which go through palm-oil plantations outside the park but even these don't guarantee sightings.

Many travellers sign up for tours to an Orang Asli settlement. Tribal elders give a general overview and you'll learn how to use a long blowpipe and start a fire. While local guides insist that these tours provide essential income for the Orang Asli, most of your tour money will go to the tour company. A small handicraft purchase in the village will help spread the wealth.

Sleeping
KUALA TAHAN

Mutiara Taman Negara resort (☎ 266 3500, in KL 03-2145 5585; www.mutiarahotels.com; camp site RM5, dm/guesthouse/chalets/bungalows incl breakfast RM60/300/470/1800; ✷) Conveniently located right at park headquarters, there's a huge range of accommodation here from OK

> ### TOUR WARNING
>
> Before booking a tour, take time to talk to other travellers for their experiences on tours and possible recommendations. For example, sometimes everyone is raving about all the animals they saw on the night 4WD tour while at other times of the year people aren't seeing anything. Some operators promise certain tour features that fail to materialise on the tour itself.
>
> By all means wait till you arrive in Taman Negara and ask around there; it is simple to reach the park under your own steam and find a tour guide there.

---

guesthouse rooms (all with garden terraces) in an older brick building to comfortably palatial (though dark) colonial-style family and honeymoon suites (some with kitchens) in wooden chalets. Clean, eight-person dorms (with air-con, wardrobe and mosquito nets) are good quality, but expensive. Campers are only accepted in groups of 10 or more.

KAMPUNG KUALA TAHAN

Kampung Kuala Tahan, directly across the river from park headquarters, is where most of Taman Negara's lodging, restaurants and shops are found. It's a scruffy place and standards are low, but it's a pleasant enough base. Crossing the river is easy; sampans go on demand throughout the day and the evening (fare RM1).

Try to arrive early in the day or book in advance since the better places fill up quickly.

Liana Hostel (☎ 266 9322; dm RM10) Has barracks-like, four-bed dorm rooms and non-existent service.

ourpick Durian Chalet (☎ 266 8940; dm/d/f RM10/40/50, A-frame RM25) About 800m outside of the village (beyond the Teresek View Hotel) in a flowery garden between rubber and durian plantations, this family-run forest hideaway is a destination in itself. Besides the six-bed dorm, the cheapest options are microscopic, rustic, twin-sized A-frame huts with bathrooms. Better are the well-maintained, large doubles and family rooms painted in bright colours that exude a simple village-style charm. All options have fans and mosquito nets, there's a simple restaurant and you can pitch a tent for RM2.

PAHANG

Tembeling Riverview Hostel (☎ 266 6766; rosnahtrv@hotmail.com; dm RM10, r RM35-50) Straddling the thoroughfare footpath, folks stay here to be close to the action not for privacy, though there are some pleasant communal areas overlooking the river. Rooms are barrack basic.

our pick **Tahan Guesthouse** (☎ 266 7752; dm/d RM10/50) Far enough from 'town' to feel away from it all but close enough to be convenient, Tahan Guesthouse (about 200m from the Teresek View Motel) has excellent four-bed dorms and even better, colourfully painted bright rooms upstairs. The whole place feels like a happy preschool with giant murals of insects and flowers all over the place.

Yellow Guesthouse (☎ 266 4243; dm/d RM10/80; 🗙 🖳 📶) Up and over the top of the hill from the NKS floating restaurant, this quiet new place is cleaner and in better shape than most of the others. The big rooms and dorms have brightly painted walls and new mattresses and the owner is super-friendly and helpful.

Mat Leon Village (☎ 013-998 9517; dm/chalets RM15/60) This boasts a supreme forest location with views over the river (swimming possible) from its restaurant, clean four-bed dorms (shared shower), ageing chalets (with shower) and free boat pick-up from the Mat Leon floating deck at the Kampung Kuala Tahan jetty. On foot go past Durian Chalet for around 350m to the sign at the edge of the forest; follow the forest path for 200m and you will see the chalets on the far side of a small stream.

Teresek View Motel (☎ 019-970 6800; mr8seasons @gmail.com; chalets RM50-60, r RM70-90; 🗙) You can't miss this eyesore of a cement building in the 'centre' of Kuala Tahan. The good rooms in the main building are tiled, clean and have hot-water bathrooms and terraces, but lack the homey feel of the family run places elsewhere. Budget chalets across the street have floors that give way underfoot, but are decent value and well kept. There's a minimart and restaurant here as well.

Agoh Chalets (☎ 266 9570; d/f RM50/80; 🗙 🖳) Chalets here are made from concrete modelled to look like logs and all surround a shady garden in the middle of the village. The interiors are ageing, but are in better shape than many other places.

Woodland Resort (☎ 266 1111; www.woodland.com .my; d/chalets/ste from RM108/160/252; 🗙 🖳 🔊) Just before the Rainforest Resort, this place has

small, musty cave-like standard rooms and much better spacious, well-lit deluxe chalets. Accommodation (all with satellite TV and air-con) is spread over a plain yard and the pool is quite small.

Rainforest Resort (☎ 266 7888; www.rainforest -tamannegara.com; d/ste incl breakfast from RM207/414; 🗙 🖳 📶) Slightly behind town away from the river, the spotless, modern rooms here are the most comfortable in Kampung Kuala Tahan. It's worth upgrading to a deluxe, which gets you much more room as well as a pleasant terrace. Prices include breakfast at the vaguely stylish restaurant and service is friendly and professional. Near-constant promotional rates are about 40% lower than the published rates (making a deluxe room about RM190).

SOUTH OF KAMPUNG KUALA TAHAN

Several peaceful places lie removed from the action west of the main Kampung Kuala Tahan–Jerantut road south of Kampung Kuala Tahan.

Park Lodge (☎ 017-983 2074; www.parklodge .nurnilam.com; fan d incl breakfast RM50) Hidden away down a dirt track around 500m south of Kuala Tahan, this quiet spot has eight chalets and a restaurant. They can drive guests to Kampung Kuala Tahan.

Persona Village Resort (☎ 266-9696; www.persona tamannegara.com; chalets RM145-240; 🗙) This modern, recently constructed chalet resort has pleasant river views, trekking packages and good discounts, but little personality.

our pick **Traveller's Home** (☎ 2667766; www.travellers home.com.my; d incl breakfast RM160, chalet incl breakfast & dinner RM185; 🗙 🖳) Very clean and highly recommended, this bright and airy place, around 1km down a turn-off 2km south of Kuala Tahan (look for the signs), has impeccable, friendly service that will make you feel instantly at home. Rooms here are very new (with balcony) and there's a handy book and DVD library and internet access (per hour RM4), plus all-day free coffee, tea and soft drinks. Chalets are more private and luxurious, and are nestled in the garden's many fruit trees. Free shuttles to Kampung Kuala Tahan are available on demand. This is an excellent choice for families.

NUSA HOLIDAY VILLAGE

About a 15-minute boat ride upriver from park headquarters, **Nusa Holiday Village** (☎ 266 3043, in Jerantut 09-266 2369, in KL 03-4042 8369;

www.tamannegara-nusaholiday.com.my; camp sites RM5, dm/A-frames/cottages/houses RM15/55/90/110) is more of a 'jungle camp' than anything. The isolation paired with the staff's general lack of English skills makes this a difficult place to stay unless you're on a packaged itinerary (three-days and two-nights from RM295 per person). The double cottages are the best value, while the cheaper A-frames are literally falling in on themselves. The restaurant serves good but unexciting food. Camping costs RM15, tent included.

At the time of research Nusa Camp was building an activities-oriented Outward Bound Centre just downriver.

KUALA PERKAI & KUALA KENIAM

Located about an hour upstream from Kuala Trenggan, the Kuala Keniam **lodge** (camp sites per person RM1, r RM100) is without electricity. Four-bed dorms are available at **Kuala Perkai** (camp site per person RM1, dm RM8), also without electricity and a further two hours' walk past Kuala Keniam. If camping at either of these places, bring your own tent. Check with the Mutiara Taman Negara resort to see if these are operational when you arrive in the park.

Eating

Floating barge restaurants line the rocky shore of Kampung Kuala Tahan, all selling the same ol' cheap basic noodle and rice meals plus bland Western fare. These restaurants tend to come and go, but at the time of research the best was **Mama Chop** (meals around RM7; ☺ breakfast, lunch & dinner) at the far northern end of the strip and accessible by a small staircase. Mama's serves Indian vegetarian banana leaf meals at lunchtime and has very good clay-pot dishes for dinner.

For something more high class head to **Seri Mutiara Restaurant** (Mutiara Taman Negara resort; ☺ breakfast, lunch & dinner), which has salads (from RM16), sandwiches/burgers (from RM20), pizza (RM30), local dishes and a small kiddies' menu (from RM10). Breakfast (American/buffet RM30/40) is filling. This is also the only place in the area where you can get a beer.

Getting There & Away

Most people reach Taman Negara by taking a bus from Jenantut to the jetty at Kuala Tembling, then a river boat from here to the park. However, there are also popular private minibus services that go directly to/from several tourist destinations around Malaysia directly to/from Kampung Kuala Tahan. You can also take a bus from Jerantut direct to Kampung Kuala Tahan (see p294 for details), but by doing this you miss the scenic boat trip.

BOAT

The 60km boat trip from Kuala Tembling (18km north of Jenantut) to Kuala Tahan takes two to three hours, depending on the level of the river. Along the river you'll see several Orang Asli *kampung*, local fishing people and domestic animals such as water buffalo. You might also see monkeys, otters, kingfishers and hornbills from the boat. It's a beautiful journey and a highlight for many visitors.

Regular boats (one way RM35) depart daily at 9am and 2pm (9am and 2.30pm Friday). Extra boats are laid on during the busy season, but the service can be irregular during the November to February rainy season. Boats are run by the Mutiara Taman Negara resort and Nusa Holiday Village. At Tembeling, the Mutiara's office is up the steps above the jetty, and Nusa Holiday Village's is near the parking area.

On the return journey, regular boats leave Kuala Tahan at 9am and 2pm (2.30pm on Friday).

BUS & TAXI

For details on buses and taxis from Jerantut to Kuala Tembeling, see p294. A public bus from Kampung Kuala Tahan goes to KL (RM26) every day at 8am via Jenantut. **NKS** (☎ 03-2072 0336; www.taman-negara.com) and **Banana Travel & Tours** (☎ 017-902 5952; Information Centre, Kampung Kuala Tahan) run several useful private services, including daily buses to KL (RM35) and minibuses to Penang (RM120), the Perhentian Islands (RM165 including boat) and the Cameron Highlands (RM95). These minibuses can also drop you off en route anywhere in between.

CAR

A road goes all the way from Jerantut to Kampung Kuala Tahan, traversable in an ordinary car. Hitching is possible, too (though not always safe).

BY FOOT

You can walk into or out of the park via Merapoh, at the Pahang–Kelantan border. The trail from Merapoh joins the Gunung Tahan trail, adding another two days to the Gunung Tahan trek (see p298). Guides are compulsory and can be hired in Merapoh to take you in. Contact the **Kuala Lipis tourist information centre** (☎ 09-312 3277).

KUALA LIPIS

☎ 09

At the confluence of the Lipis and Jelai rivers, Kuala Lipis is a bustling little town with a charming colonial-era centre of Chinese shop-houses. A large percentage of the population is Chinese or Indian, with the common language between them being English, so it's easy to chat with these particularly friendly locals and find your way around.

Lipis was a gold-mining centre long before the British arrived in 1887, but the town's heyday began in 1898 when it became the capital of Pahang. Grand colonial buildings date from this period, and trade increased when the railway came through in 1924. In 1957 the capital shifted to Kuantan and Kuala Lipis went into decline, but now it's on the rise again with people pouring in once again to seek their fortunes in gold mining. The town is rapidly expanding with a newly built modern section known as 'New Town' across the river from the old centre.

Besides being an interesting destination in itself, Kuala Lipis is the major launching pad for visits to the nearby Kenong Rimba State Park.

Information

Hand-drawn maps of Kuala Lipis are available at Appu's Guest House (right). There are a few banks with ATMs on Jln Besar and the post office is east of the train station.

The two private travel agencies at the train station called **Tourist Office** (☎ 312 5032; off Jln Besar; ☽ 9am-5pm Mon-Fri, 9am-1pm Sat) and **Tuah Travel & Tours** (☎ 312 2292; off Jln Besar; tuahtravel @hotmail.com; ☽ 9.30am-2pm Mon-Sat) are equally helpful, organise trips to Kenong Rimba (day trips from RM150 per person) and can answer basic questions.

Sights & Activities

Kuala Lipis has some lovely colonial-era architecture. Maroon and white, and decorated with arches, the noble **District Offices**, located off Jln Lipis, crown a hill 1km south of the centre of town. The offices overlook

the exclusive **Clifford School**, a grand public building that began life as the Anglo-Chinese School in 1913 and was later named after Sir Hugh Clifford, the second British Resident of Pahang. During the occupation, the school served as the headquarters of the Kempetai (the Japanese secret police).

The road next to the school leads up the hill to the black-and-white wooden **Pahang Club**, off Jln Lipis, a stately and dignified bungalow with wide, open verandahs.

A very pleasant **walk** starts on the road behind the Lipis Centrepoint Complex. Follow the road up the hill where the sign says 'Driving Range Lipis'. You will soon pass the **Istana Hinggap** on your right; keep going uphill and the road forks. Take either branch and you will be led to old, wooden built colonial-era houses – some now abandoned and being slowly reclaimed by jungle.

If you're in town on Friday evening, be sure to visit the excellent **night market** held in the parking lot next to the bus station.

A taxi around town for an hour to see the sights costs RM25.

Sleeping, Eating & Drinking

There are busy and popular food stalls on either side of the northern end of the overhead walkway crossing Jln Pekeliling.

Appu's Guesthouse (Hotel Lipis; ☎ 312 3142; jungle appu@hotmail.com; 63 Jln Besar; dm RM10, d RM20-35, q RM60; ☒) Appu's is great for tourist info and guide services, but it's very rundown. Locks on the doors don't work well so lone women may not feel safe here.

Hotel Jelai (☎ 312 1192; 44 Jln Jelai; r RM50-60; ☒ ☜) Clean, newly refurbished rooms are plain, but this is a great location on the riverfront and service is friendly.

Centrepoint Hotel & Apartments (☎ 312 2688; Lipis Centrepoint, Jln Pekeliling; ekonomi s/d RM48/70, standard d from RM108; ☒) One floor of this high-rise hotel is dedicated to mediocre ekonomi rooms, while the rest of the place has more comfortable standard rooms. It's the busiest place in town and has a tour office (specialising in trips to Kenong Rimba), great service and a bustling food court down stairs.

Residence Rest House (☎ 312 2788; r RM60-150; ☒) In a huge, homey colonial hilltop house that once housed the British Resident, rooms here are massive with floral wallpaper, big windows and garden grounds. The restaurant is only open for dinner and a taxi to town costs RM7.

Flash Jack's Bar 55 (☎ 019-966 7903; New Town) Recently moved to 'New Town' near the bus station, this low-key place is run by the affable Jack.

Getting There & Away

Buses run from the **bus station** (Transnasional ☎ 312 5055) in New Town to KL (RM15, four hours, six daily), Kuantan (RM24, six hours, four daily) via Temerloh (RM13.40), Raub (RM5) and Gua Musang (RM11.20, two hours, two daily), from where you can catch onward buses to Kota Bharu.

Daily trains run to Singapore (7.39am, 12.55am) and KL (10.54pm). Trains bound for Singapore, KL or Gemas stop at Jerantut (for Taman Negara). The local ('jungle') train connects with Wakaf Baharu, the closest station to Kota Bharu.

Taxis leave from the bus station for KL (RM180), Jerantut (RM65), Kuala Tahan (RM50), Gua Musang (RM120), Temerloh (RM100) and Kuantan (RM200).

KENONG RIMBA STATE PARK
☎ 09

A sprawling area of lowland forest rising to the limestone foothills bordering Taman Negara, this 120-sq-km forest park can be explored on three- or four-day jungle treks organised from Kuala Lipis. It's a much less-visited alternative to Taman Negara. Sightings of big mammals are rare so monkeys, wild pigs, squirrels, civets and possibly nocturnal tapir are all you should expect to see. The park is also home to the Batek people, an Orang Asli tribe. For information on preparing for the jungle, see the boxed text, p86.

Visitors need to acquire a permit from the **Kuala Lipis District Forest Office** (☎ 312 1373). Guides are compulsory for entry to the park and can be arranged in Kuala Lipis. **Appu** (☎ 312 2619) of Appu's Guesthouse in Kuala Lipis offers cheap tours – RM80 per person per day plus RM200 (minimum three people) for the boat to and from Jeti Tanjung Kiara and a RM2 per-person per-night camping fee. Tours include food, guide and all expenses in the park, but they are no-frills jungle experiences – you camp in the park, with all equipment and meals provided. Trips go when enough people are interested – it's best to get a group together yourself.

You can also book trips through Tourist Office and Tuah Travel (opposite), and

Kiara Holidays (at the Centrepoint Hotel & Apartments, opposite).

There is also simple dorm and chalet accommodation available at the **Persona Rimba Resort** (☎ 312 5032).

Getting There & Away

Access to Kenong Rimba is from Kuala Lipis on southbound local trains to Batu Sembilan (Mile 9). From Batu Sembilan, hire a boat (per person RM25) to Jeti Tanjung Kiara, just across the river from Kampung Kuala Kenong.

TEMERLOH
☎ 09

An old town on the banks of the enormous Sungai Pahang, Temerloh has hints of colonial style and a colourful Sunday market. As the main city of central Pahang, it serves as a transport hub – the chief reason to visit. The train station is 12km away at **Mentakab**, a thriving satellite of Temerloh with a bustling nightly market.

If you get stuck overnight try the **Hotel Semantan** (☎ 296 8111; C-98 Jln Dato Ngau Ken Lock; d RM60-70, f RM100; 🅿 🖳), opposite the Dunhuang Chinese restaurant, which offers clean and spacious rooms.

Buses go to all parts of the peninsula from Temerloh, including Kota Bharu (RM42), Kuala Lipis (RM13.40), Melaka (RM16) and Penang (RM51.30). Regular buses depart to Jerantut (RM7), KL's Pekeliling bus station (RM10) and Kuantan (RM10).

Taxis at the bus station go to Mentakab (RM10), Jerantut (RM38), Kuantan (RM95) and KL (RM150).

AROUND TEMERLOH
Kuala Gandah Elephant Conservation Centre

The **Kuala Gandah Elephant Conservation Centre** (☎ 09 279 0391; www.wildlife.gov.my/webpagev4_en/bhg _ekogandah.html; Kuala Gandah, Lanchang; entry by donation; 🕙 10am-4.45pm) is the base for the Department of Wildlife and National Parks' Elephant Relocation Team, which helps capture and relocate rogue elephants from across Southeast Asia to other suitable habitats throughout the peninsula, such as at Taman Negara. Most of the elephants at the centre are work elephants from Myanmar or Thailand.

Visitors to Kuala Gandah are first shown a **video** (🕙 1pm, 1.30pm & 3.45pm daily, also 12.30pm

PAHANG

Sat & Sun) about the elephant's plight, then can watch and join in while the handlers wash down and feed the big guys fruit (☉2pm Saturday to Thursday, 2.45pm Friday). Next everyone is herded to an elevated hut to line up to ride on an elephant and finally you can line up again to get dumped into the river off an elephant's back and take a swim with a few of the gentle beasts. Public bathrooms with showers are available to rinse off afterwards – bring a change of clothes!

While all of this is good fun and hopes to raise awareness about the elephants' precarious situation in Southeast Asia, animal activists criticise the circus-like activities at the centre, which they claim are not enjoyable for the animals and are not in line with animal welfare principles. The centre also received negative press in 2006 when one elephant died and another was injured due to mishandling by the centre; it remains questionable if the centre has improved its handling practices since this time.

Before heading out this way, it's imperative to call the centre to reserve a ticket (only 120 people are admitted each day) and check on opening times – if you are on a tour this will be taken care of by your operator.

Deerland

About five minutes away on the road to Kuala Gandah, **Deerland** (☎ 013-967 6242; 67 Jln Zabidin; entry adult/child RM10/5; ☉ 10.30am-5.30pm Sat-Thu) is a mini zoo in the forest. The main activity here is petting one of the three Malaysian sun bears. The bored-looking sun bears don't seem to like this much and after watching

one husk a coconut with its massive, sharp claws, you have to wonder if these up-close encounters are safe. The three species of deer (which you can also pet) look happier in their very large enclosure and there are also some caged birds and monkeys. The team here also leads 2½-hour **medicinal herb jungle treks** (RM35 per person; reserve at a least day in advance) that include lunch and an adventurous river crossing along a network of swinging ropes. Similar treks lasting up to three days can also be arranged.

Sleeping & Eating

Accommodation near these two sites is available at **Mr Zukifili's Homestay** (☎ 013-377 3838) in a basic *kampung*-style house on the roadside.

Saudi's Cafe (meals RM4), on the grounds of the Kuala Gandah Elephant Conservation Centre, is a mom-and-pop shack serving simple Malay grub like nasi goreng and mee sup (noodle soup).

Getting There & Away

These two sites are located about 150km east of KL near the town of Lanchang west of Mentakab. Getting to this area independently is difficult without your own wheels. You can get a taxi from Mentakab (RM50) or Temerloh (RM60), but these rates are one way and you might have to pay more if the driver has to wait to take you back from where you came. Most people visit on tours (including a visit to Kuala Gandah and Deerland), available from KL, Jerantut, Cherating and other tourist hubs on the peninsula. Expect to pay around RM180 per person for a day tour from KL.

PAHANG

Terengganu

Some places evoke a colour. In this case Terengganu is, far and away, blue. The rich robin's-egg blue of big skies bending under clear, bright sunlight. The deep, royal blue of the ocean running behind ferries to tropical paradise. The turtle-dotted teal of shallow lagoons and horseshoe bays lapping the sugar sands in Pulau Perhentian (the Perhentian Islands). And the organic, vegetative green-blue of Lake Kenyir, vine-shrouded in its jungle womb.

Blue is a cooling colour, and the general laid-back vibe of Terengganu makes for a cooling escape – something about the slow pace of life makes relaxed sighs some of the most common means of communication here. Most travellers come to the state for an island experience, and they're in the right spot: some of the best beaches in the country can be found on Pulau Perhentian, Pulau Redang and Pulau Kapas. Divers in particular are well cared for here, but if you're up for doing nothing at all, Terengganu will indulge your indolence.

But don't completely dismiss mainland Terengganu from your exploration. This is one of the most ethnically Malay states in the country, and you have the opportunity here to engage the Malay people at, simultaneously, their most traditional, their most evolving – note the waves of modernity replacing the traditional stilt houses of Kuala Terengganu, the capital, with air-con condos – and their most Islamic. They're also, we'd note, at their most friendly when dealing with travellers who've wandered off the beach. So enjoy the sun and sand and their considerable charms, and don't forget to engage the real Malaysia hidden behind the palms.

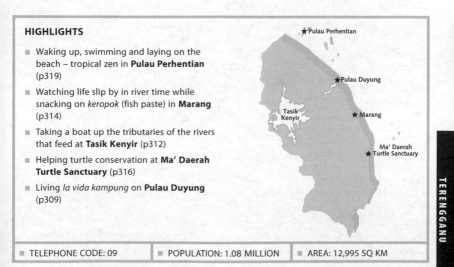

HIGHLIGHTS

- Waking up, swimming and laying on the beach – tropical zen in **Pulau Perhentian** (p319)

- Watching life slip by in river time while snacking on *keropok* (fish paste) in **Marang** (p314)

- Taking a boat up the tributaries of the rivers that feed at **Tasik Kenyir** (p312)

- Helping turtle conservation at **Ma' Daerah Turtle Sanctuary** (p316)

- Living *la vida kampung* on **Pulau Duyung** (p309)

★ Pulau Perhentian

★ Pulau Duyung

Tasik Kenyir

★ Marang

Ma' Daerah
★ Turtle Sanctuary

- TELEPHONE CODE: 09   - POPULATION: 1.08 MILLION   - AREA: 12,995 SQ KM

TERENGGANU

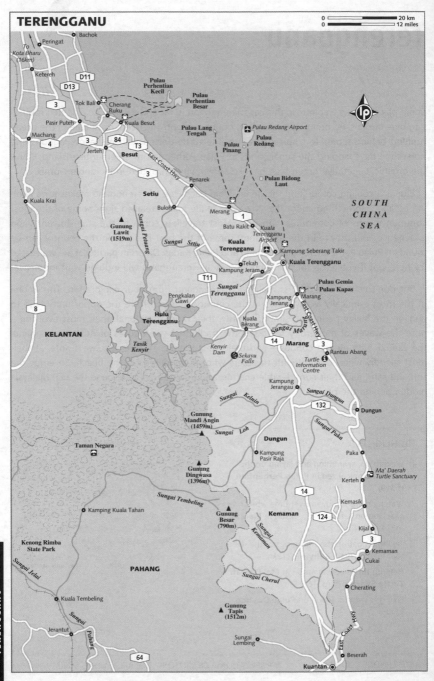

TERENGGANU

0 _____ 20 km
0 _____ 12 miles

To Kota Bharu (16km)

Peringat
Bachok
Ketereh
D11
D13
3
Tok Bali
Cherang Ruku
Kuala Besut
Pasir Puteh
Machang
4
3
84
Jerteh
T3
Besut
3
Setiu
Kuala Krai
Buloh
8
KELANTAN

Pulau Perhentian Kecil
Pulau Perhentian Besar
Pulau Lang Tengah
Penarek

East Coast Hwy

Gunung Lawit (1519m)
Sungai Petuang
Sungai Setiu

Merang
Batu Rakit
1
Kuala Terengganu Airport
Kuala Terengganu
Kampung Seberang Takir
Kuala Terengganu

Pulau Redang Airport
Pulau Pinang
Pulau Redang

Pulau Bidong Laut

SOUTH CHINA SEA

Pengkalan Gawi
Hulu Terengganu
T11
Sungai Terengganu
Tekah
Kampung Jeram

Pulau Gemia
Pulau Kapas
Kampung Jenang
Marang

Tasik Kenyir
Kuala Berang
Kenyir Dam
Sekayu Falls
14
Marang
3
Rantau Abang
Turtle Information Centre

East Coast Hwy

Sungai Marang

Sungai Kelnin
Gunung Mandi Angin (1459m)
Sungai Loh

Kampung Jerangau
Sungai Dungun
132
Dungun

Taman Negara

Dungun
Kampung Pasir Raja

Sungai Paka
Paka
Ma' Daerah Turtle Sanctuary
Kerteh

Gunung Dingwasa (1396m)

Sungai Tembeling

Kamping Kuala Tahan

Gunung Besar (790m)
Kemaman
14
Kemasik
124
Kijal
3
Kemaman
Cukai

Kenong Rimba State Park

PAHANG

Sungai Jelai

Gunung Tapis (1512m)
Sungai Cherul

Cherating

Sungai Kemaman

Kuala Tembeling

Jerantut
Sungai Pahang
Sungai Lembing
64
Kuantan
East Coast Hwy
Beserah

History

An Islamic state, possibly the oldest in Malaysia, is known to have existed in Terengganu from at least the early 14th century, although by the following century it had become a vassal of the expansionist Melaka sultanate. However, Terengganu managed to retain a large degree of independence during the emergence of Riau (in Indonesia) and Johor as partners in the region, and was trading with Siam and China.

Terengganu was formally established as a state in 1724. The first sultan was Tun Zainal Abidin, a younger brother of one of the former sultans of Johor. The close association with Johor was to continue for some years; in the mid-18th century, Sultan Mansur spent 15 years in the state. Later, Mansur turned his attention to Kelantan and, after some fighting and shrewd manoeuvring, had his son installed as ruler of the then-kingdom. The main legacy of Mansur's reign was Terengganu becoming a vassal of the Siamese for the duration of the 19th century. Eventually, Terengganu sultan Baginda Omar managed to keep the Siamese at arm's length and the state flourished under his rule.

In 1909 an Anglo-Siamese treaty saw power pass to the British. It was an unpopular move locally, and in 1928 a peasant uprising erupted. It was quickly put down and the British went about consolidating their power in the state until the Japanese invaded in WWII.

During the Japanese occupation, control of the state was passed back to Thailand, but this was short-lived and Terengganu became a member of the Federation of Malaya in 1948. It remained an undeveloped backwater until oil and gas revenue started to flow into the state in the 1980s. Kuala Terengganu was transformed into a bustling city, and tourist development continues to grow apace. In 2004 the state voted in the Parti Islam se-Malaysia (PAS), but since then the ruling government coalition of Barisan National has reclaimed a three-quarter majority of the state's parliamentary seats. Currently, the sultan of Terengganu serves his country as the King of Malaysia.

Climate

Terengganu has a tropical climate, with daily temperatures ranging between 21°C and 32°C. There is intermittent rain all year, with heavier and more prolonged rainfall during the east-coast monsoon (November to February). Humidity levels hover around 90%.

National Parks

Taman Negara (p294), most of which is within Pahang, includes a small section of western Terengganu, stretching from the Pahang border up towards Tasik Kenyir (p312). Tasik Kenyir, the largest man-made lake in Southeast Asia, is surrounded by virgin rainforest. Protected marine parks include Pulau Perhentian, Pulau Redang and Pulau Lang Tengah.

Getting There & Away

Kuala Terengganu is the state's main transport hub, with bus links to most of Malaysia and Singapore. The East Coast Hwy runs the length of Terengganu, heading north towards Kelantan and the Thai border and south towards Johor Bahru. Kuala Terengganu has an airport, with regular flights to/from KL, while Pulau Redang has air links to KL and Singapore.

Getting Around

Regular buses link the coastal towns, but service is reduced on Fridays. Travelling into the interior is more difficult without your own wheels. Ferries leave from Kuala Besut for Pulau Perhentian, from Merang for Pulau Redang and Pulau Lang Tengah, and from Marang (and sometimes Kuala Terengganu) for Pulau Kapas.

KUALA TERENGGANU

☎ 09 / pop 359,700

Terengganu's capital microcosms the Malaysian economic explosion. It's a Southeast Asian success story: fishing village finds oil, money flows in, modernity ensues. The strict version of Islam practiced here rubs up against the naturally relaxed approach to life most Terengganans seem to possess, making KT's pros and cons manifest in interesting ways. On the plus side, Islamic hospitality and Malay friendliness make this a very welcoming city. The drawback: severe Islam and Malay conservatism means this town can sometimes feel sedate. This isn't helped by new, often sterile-looking buildings created with oil-generated cash. But you can still find an old *kampung* (village) house seemingly hiding among the high-rises, and these glimpses, plus a seafood-heavy local cuisine and good transport links, make Kuala Terengganu worth a few days of exploration.

Information

Jln Sultan Ismail is the commercial hub and home to most banks, which are open 9.30am to 3.30pm, except Friday.

TERENGGANU

KUALA TERENGGANU

0 — 600 m
0 — 0.4 miles

INFORMATION
Golden Wood Internet...........1 B3
Hospital Kuala Terengganu....2 D4
Immigration Office..............3 C3
Mr Dobi Laundry................4 B2
Tourism Information Office....5 B2
Tourism Malaysia Office........6 C3

SIGHTS & ACTIVITIES
Bukit Puteri 7 B2
Central Market....................8 B3
Cultural Centre Stage..........9 D4
Heritage One Stop Travel &
Tours...........................10 C3

Ho Ann Kiong....................11 B3
Istana Maziah....................12 B2
Ping Anchorage..............(see 18)
Zainal Abidin Mosque........13 B3

SLEEPING
Awi's Yellow House.............14 A3
Hotel Mini Indah...............15 C3
Hotel Sri Tanjung...............16 C2
Hotel YT Midtown..............17 B3
Ping Anchorage Travellers'
Inn.............................18 B3
Primula Beach Resort..........19 D3
Seri Malaysia Hotel............20 B3

EATING
Billi Kopitiam....................21 C3
Food Stalls.....................(see 32)
Hawker Centre..................22 B3
Lounge Kuala Kopi.........(see 19)
MD Curry House................23 C3
Night Market....................24 D4
Restoran Golden Dragon.....25 B3
Terapung Puteri................26 B2

SHOPPING
Wanisma Craft & Trading.....27 D3

TRANSPORT
Express Bus Station............28 C2
Ferry to Pulau Duyung.........29 A3
Jetty for Ferries to Pulau
Redang........................30 B2
Local Bus Station.............(see 32)
Long-Distance Taxi Stand....31 B3
Main Bus Station................32 B3
Main Taxi Stand.............(see 32)

Pulau
Duyung

SOUTH
CHINA
SEA

Pantai
Batu Buruk

To Airport (5km);
Pura Tanjung Sabtu (14km);
Merang (38km);
Kota Bharu (159km)

Sultan Mahmud
Bridge

To Taman Tamadu Islam
& Crystal Mosque (2km);
Kompleks Muzium Negeri Terengganu (3km);
Anjung Pantai Seberang (7.5km);
Wan Kay Homestay (14km);
Tasik Kenyir (55km);
Sekayu Falls (56km)

To Masjid Tengku Tengah
Zaharah (2.5km);
Noor Arfa Craft Complex (4.5km);
Kraftangan Malaysia (4.5km);
Suterasemai Silk Gallery (4.5km);
Marang (15km)

Golden Wood Internet (☎ 631 0128; 59 Jln Tok Lam; per hr RM5)

Hospital Kuala Terengganu (☎ 623 3333; Jln Sultan Mahmud)

Immigration office (☎ 622 1424; Wisma Persekutuan, Jln Sultan Ismail)

Mr Dobi Laundry (☎ 622 1671; Jln Masjid Abidin)

Tourism Malaysia Office (☎ 630 9087; No 11 Menara Yayasan Islam Terengganu (Yayasan Islam Terengganu Tower), Jln Sultan Omar; ☾ 9am-5pm Sat-Thu)

Tourist Information Office (☎ 617 1553; Jln Sultan Zainal Abidin; ☾ 9am-5pm Sat-Thu) Brochures on Terengganu. www.tourism.terengganu.gov.my Useful portal.

Sights

The most interesting area to explore is the tiny (but more picturesque for its small size)

Chinatown. There are atmospheric watermarked buildings and faded alleyways clotting this small neighbourhood, which is centred on Jln Kampung Cina (also known as Jln Bandar). The oldest Chinese temple in the state, **Ho Ann Kiong**, is a compact explosion of vibrant red and gold dating from the early 1800s.

For fish so fresh it's still in its death flop, look for the boats docking at the **central market** (Jln Sultan Zainal Abidin). Besides indulging your piscatorial fix, there's a good collection of batik and *kain songket* (cloth brocaded with gold and silver).

Across the road from the market, look for a steep flight of steps leading up to **Bukit Puteri** (Princess Hill; admission RM1; ☾ 9am-5pm Sat-Thu), a 200m-high hill with good views of the city.

On top are the scant remains of a mid-19th-century fort (the legacy of intersultanate warfare), some cannons and a bell.

East of the hill is **Istana Maziah** (Jln Masjid Abidin), the sultan's palace. It's built in semi-tweedy colonial style, but renovations have given the structure a blocky, over-modernist feel. The palace is closed to the public, except for some ceremonial occasions. Nearby, the gleaming **Zainal Abidin Mosque** (Jln Masjid Abidin) dominates the city centre.

Pantai Batu Buruk is the city beach, popular with families and, unfortunately, litter bugs. It's not the best beach in Malaysia given the strong winds and rips, but it's pretty nonetheless. Across the road is the **Cultural Centre stage**; check with the tourist office to see if any shows are lined up.

From the jetty near Seri Malaysia Hotel you can take a 60-sen ferry ride to **Pulau Duyung**, the largest island in the estuary. Fishing boats are built here for both local and international clients, using old-school techniques and tools, and visitors are welcome to look around.

Tours

Popular tours include day trips to Tasik Kenyir (from RM189), river cruises and packages to Pulau Redang. Going in groups reduces individual rates.

Heritage One Stop Travel & Tours (☎ 631 6468; www.heritageonestop.com.my; Blok Teratai, Jln Sultan Sulaiman)

Ping Anchorage (☎ 626 2020; www.pinganchorage.com.my; 77A Jln Sultan Sulaiman)

Sleeping

Homestays are an increasingly popular accommodation option, especially near the beach.

BUDGET

Ping Anchorage Travellers' Inn (☎ 626 2020; www.pinganchorage.com.my; 77A Jln Sultan Sulaiman; dm/r from RM10/26; 🖳) Spread over two floors above the travel agency of the same name, Ping's is a budget standby. Rooms are reasonably clean, but it doesn't have much going for it besides a vaguely social vibe on the rooftop cafe and a central location.

Awi's Yellow House (☎ 624 7363, 622 2080; r RM18-25) Awi's is (or sells itself as) what Terengganu was: a wooden stilt house, the smell of fish paste, salt and chilli, no air-con and nights that stick to you like a wet kiss. Built over the Sungai Terengganu on Pulau Duyung, don't come here if you don't like roughing it a little, but do if you want a taste of *kampung* life.

Hotel Sri Tanjung (☎ 626 2636; Jln Sultan Zainal Abidin; r from RM60; 🖳) This little option is decked out in over-the-top girly shades of pink and white, but it is a well-kept place that's quite comfy and just within the budget bracket.

Hotel Mini Indah (☎ 622 9053; 60 Sultan Zainal Abidin; s/d RM50/65; 🖳) The Mini Indah doesn't exactly drip with character, but it serves a very clean and functional purpose: getting you a pretty room within stumbling distance of the city beach.

MIDRANGE

Hotel YT Midtown (☎ 623 5288; ythotel@streamyx.my; 30 Jln Tok Lam; r/ste from RM90/225; 🖳 🖳) The YT is a big, modern hotel in the centre of town with neat, good-value rooms that come with the regular mod cons such as TVs, minifridges and kettles. There's a decent restaurant downstairs.

Wan Kay Homestay (☎ 019-983 4360; http://wkhomestay.blogspot.com; 1 Taman Abadi, Jln Gong Badak; r/ste from RM100; 🖳 🖳) Wan Kay gives you the opportunity to stay with a friendly Malaysian family in their modest but spacious suburban home. The hosts, Beib and Wan, are happy to integrate you into their extended (and extensive) family, and get rave reviews for their hospitality from travellers.

Seri Malaysia Hotel (☎ 623 6454; www.serimalaysia.com.my; 1640 Jln Balik Bukit; r RM120; 🖳) A popular chain with branches all over Peninsular Malaysia, this is a reliable, squeaky-clean place offering the standard, comfortable, could-be-anywhere set-up. It boasts an attractive riverside terrace restaurant, too.

TOP END

Anjung Pantai Seberang (☎ 013-910 3900, 013-928 2022; www.anjungpantai.co.nr; Pantai Kampung Baru; r 150-480; 🖳) This homestay option consists of several guesthouses ranging from low-slung, somewhat boring bungalows to attractive wooden stilt-style houses. It's a creative alternative that's a little more interesting than the blander corporate high-rise choices in town. About 12 minutes' drive from the city.

Primula Beach Resort (☎ 622 2100; www.primulahotels.com; Jln Persinggahan; s/d/ste from RM250/330/760; 🖳 🖳 🖳) Kuala Terengganu's biggest option is this seafront hotel with spacious, attractively furnished rooms, including some outstanding suites with four-poster beds and multiple balconies. It's perched on a wide stretch of white sand, and is particularly popular with young families. It has a few very good restaurants and the best coffee bar in town.

our pick Pura Tanjung Sabtu (☎ 615 3655, 019-983 3365; www.puratanjungsabtu.com; Kampung Tanjung Sabtu; house from RM800; ❄ 🖳 ☒) It's good, as they say, to be king, yet so rarely can we be. Unless you jaunt near the airport to Pura Tanjung Sabtu, the countryside retreat of a former sultan of Terengganu and, today, the best accommodation option around. Besides being run by the current sultan as a window onto rural Malay life, Pura Tangung Sabtu is headily romantic. Your sleeping choice is one of three traditional Malay houses adorned in silks, crafts and luxury leaking from the sweet-smelling walls. There's a two-person, two-night minimum in each house; your day is plotted out for you though, as guests get meals cooked for them and are treated to an intense tour itinerary.

Eating & Drinking
Naturally enough, fish plays a big role in local cuisine, but the real local specialty is *kerepok*: a grey concoction of deep-fried fish paste and sago, usually moulded into sausages (*lekor*) or crackers (*keping*). Good with hot sauce.

RESTAURANTS
Billi Kopitiam (No 5, Jln Kampung Dalam; mains from RM4; ❄ lunch & dinner) Billi's isn't your average *kopitiam* (coffee house). This smooth little spot, decked out in Chinese vintage movie posters, brews a mean cup of joe (the iced version is divine), but the chef also whips out some interesting variations on standards like *nasi lemak* and anything *goreng* (fried).

MD Curry House (☎ 013-902 6331; Jln Kampung Dalam; mains from RM4; ❄ lunch & dinner) Sometimes, you need a curry and you need it served on a banana leaf by friendly locals. The MD pretty much has you covered in all regards if you fit the above description.

Restoran Golden Dragon (☎ 622 3034; 198 Jln Kampung Cina; mains from RM5; ❄ lunch & dinner) The Golden Dragon seems constantly packed, usually with loud (often drunk) Chinese customers. There's beer aplenty and one of the finest Chinese seafood menus in town – anything steamed or off the fish list should serve you right.

Terapung Puteri (☎ 631 8946; Jln Sultan Zainal Abidin; mains from RM5; ❄ lunch & dinner) This busy Malay restaurant is perched on stilts, *kampung*-style, on the seafront next to the jetty. There's a huge menu, with fish, prawns and crab featuring heavily, as well as local items such as *kerepok* and a few Western dishes.

QUICK EATS
There are cheap **food stalls** inside the main bus station and a beachfront **night market** nearby every Friday evening; the latter is a great place to sample *kerepok*, satay and sweets. Chinatown's outdoor **hawker centre** (off Jln Kampung Cina), is divided into Chinese and Malay sections and sizzles with cooking and socialising at night.

If you need a bean fix, **Lounge Kuala Kopi** (Jln Persinggahan; ❄ 3pm-late) inside the Primula Beach Resort, has an excellent range of coffees, including its unique house blend, *kopi de ganu*.

Shopping
Batik and *kain songket* are particularly good buys in Kuala Terengganu. The following three can be found on the Chendering industrial estate (about 4.5km south of town, not far from the 'Floating Mosque', opposite). Minibus 13 from Kuala Terengganu will drop you outside (90 sen).

Noor Arfa Craft Complex (☎ 617 5700; www.noor-arfa .com; ❄ 9am-7pm Sat-Thu) This is a handicraft centre selling a large stock of batik shirts and dresses, *kain songket*, basketware and glass. Printed cotton batik pieces start at RM15 for 2 sq m.

Kraftangan Malaysia (☎ 622 6458; ❄ 9am-5pm Sun-Thu) This outlet sells high-quality *kain songket* costing as much as RM12,000 for 2.5 sq m. There's also a tiny 'Songket Heritage Exhibition' showing varying designs.

Suterasemai Silk Gallery (☎ 617 1355; http://sute rasemai.blogspot.com; ❄ 8am-6pm Sun-Thu, 9am-4pm Sat) Offers a collection of handwoven silk, with both hand-drawn and printed designs. Hand-painted silk shirts go for around RM250.

Wanisma Craft & Trading (☎ 622 3311; 32 Ladang Sekolah; ❄ 9.30am-6.30pm) Closer to town, this is a batik-dyeing and brass workshop (the largest brass workshop in the country, supposedly) where you can watch the skilled craftsmen at work. The shop here sells their products.

Central market (Jln Sultan Zainal Abidin) Handicrafts are also sold upstairs at the central market. Bargaining is possible here – and necessary to get fair prices.

Getting There & Away
AIR
Malaysia Airlines (☎ 662 6600; airport) and **AirAsia** (☎ 32 171 9333; airport) have direct flights to KL,

with fares going for as low as RM50 if you book in advance. **Firefly** (☎ 7845 4543; airport) offers flights to Singapore.

BUS

The main bus station on Jln Masjid Abidin is a terminus for all local buses. Some long-distance buses depart from here as well, but most use the express bus station in the north of town (ask at your lodgings or when buying your ticket if you're unsure of which station to go to).

At the local bus station there are services to/ from Marang (RM3), Rantau Abang (RM5), Dungun (RM8) and Merang (RM2).

From the express bus station there are regular services running to and from Kuantan (RM13), Johor Bahru (RM34), Singapore (RM36), Melaka (RM34), KL (RM30), Ipoh (RM43), Kuala Besut (RM10) and Kota Bharu (RM11). There are two daily buses to Penang (RM32).

TAXI

Kuala Terengganu's main taxi stand is near the bus station. Regular taxi destinations include Marang (RM15), Kota Bharu (RM80), Kuala Besut (RM60), Rantau Abang (RM40), Merang (RM35) and Tasik Kenyir (RM120). Some long-distance taxis leave from a stand on Jln Masjid Abidin.

Getting Around

A hop on, hop off town bus goes to all of the major sites in town, the State Museum (right), Floating Mosque (right) and Islamic Park (right); it runs through the main bus station on an ostensibly regular basis, but service was down during our research. It should run for an as yet unspecified price (but not likely more than RM3) by the time you read this.

A taxi to the airport costs around RM28. Local buses leave from the main bus station in the town centre. Taxis around town cost a minimum of RM5, but there aren't many about; try at the long-distance taxi stand.

Once the trishaw (bicycle rickshaw) capital of Malaysia, there are still a very few of these pedal-powered numbers around. Prices are highly negotiable.

AROUND KUALA TERENGGANU
☎ 09

Kuala Terengganu is the natural base for exploring Terengganu state. In the southwest and southeast, respectively, are the impressive Kompleks Muzium Negeri Terengganu (Terengganu State Museum) and the distinctive Masjid Tengku Tengah Zaharah (Floating Mosque). Sekayu Falls and Tasik Kenyir are far to the southwest.

Kompleks Muzium Negeri Terengganu

The **Kompleks Muzium Negeri Terengganu** (Terengganu State Museum; ☎ 622 1433; http://museum.teren gganu.gov.my; adult/child RM5/2; 🕑 9am-5pm Sat-Thu) is nothing if not memorable, if only for the fact that it consists of some 26 hectares of Terengganu educational goodness. It's the largest museum in Southeast Asia, and thankfully, quantity and quality aren't too disjointed here. The complex of traditional houses that fronts the grounds is practically worth your custom on its own. On the inside are historical artefacts (such as a Jawi – traditional Malay text – inscription that essentially dates the arrival of Islam to the nation) that are fantastic. That said, a few exhibits are duds; the Petroleum Gallery presents a, shall we say, somewhat one-sided depiction of things (ie 'Petrol is great!'). The Istana Tengku Long, a wooden palace that dates from 1888, contains much of the royal regalia of the Terengganu sultanate, and boat-enthusiasts will love the outdoor maritime gallery recreations of water-borne vessels. To get here, take minibus 10 (90 sen), marked 'Muzium/ Losong', from the main bus station. A taxi from Kuala Terengganu will cost RM12.

Masjid Tengku Tengah Zaharah

The most famous religious structure in the state is the 'Floating Mosque', located 4.5km southeast of Kuala Terengganu. It's not really floating, just set on a man-made island, but its white, traditional Moorish design is beautifully blinding in the strong daylight, and warmly enchanting as the sun sets. Bus 13 from Kuala Terengganu will drop you outside (90 sen).

Taman Tamadu Islam

Touted as the world's first 'Islamic civilisation park,' **Taman Tamadu Islam** (Window on Islam; ☎ 627 8888; www.tti.com.my; adult/child RM20/10; 🕑 10am-7pm Mon-Thu, from 9am Fri-Sun), 2.5km west of Kuala Terengganu, is essentially a series of miniature models of famous Islamic landmarks from across the world. The holistic approach to Islam is interesting – where else can you see the Taj Mahal next to Syria's Aleppo Citadel – but the contextual explanations needed to appreciate the site are a bit lacking. The park also houses the **Crystal Mosque**, opened in 2008. Constructed largely from glass and steel, its one of those buildings that, in an effort to look futuristic, comes off as immediately dated. Still, it is garishly eye-catching at night, when the entire affair is lit from within. Shuttle buses run here from the Kuala Terengganu jetty station for RM2 on a somewhat regular basis; a taxi will cost around RM15.

Sekayu Falls

These waterfalls, 56km southwest of Kuala Terengganu, are part of a large park popular with locals on Friday and public holidays. The falls extend up a mountainside; the main falls are 15 minutes in from the entrance. A further 20 minutes' walk brings you to the more attractive upper falls. There's also an orchard with a huge variety of seasonal tropical fruit.

There are three daily buses from Kuala Terengganu to the park entrance (RM4.40), 2km from the falls. The first leaves at 9am, and the last bus comes back at 3pm. Ping Anchorage (p309) offers day trips taking in the falls and Kenyir Dam from RM99 per person, including lunch.

TASIK KENYIR
☎ 09

The construction of the Kenyir Dam in 1985 flooded some 2600 sq km of jungle, creating Southeast Asia's largest man-made lake, with clumps of wild overgrowth gasping over the water's surface. Today Tasik Kenyir (Lake Kenyir) and its 340 islands constitute Terengganu's most popular inland tourism destination. There are some resorts dotted around the water, all low-key and fairly upscale in terms of cost and service. If you're looking to spend a relatively luxurious night in the local jungle, which houses some 8000 species of flowers, this is the spot for you.

Information

There is a small **tourist information office** (☎ 626 7788; www.ketengah.gov.my/kenyir; ☻ 9am-5pm) near the jetty in Pengkalan Gawi, the lake's main access point. Also at the jetty you'll find a cafe, a shop, and a few kiosks where you can book boat trips, which start from RM600 for a jaunt to the nearest islands to significantly more for day trips and fishing expeditions across the

lake. There's technically a RM1 entrance fee and a RM5 camera fee upon arrival at the lake, but this wasn't collected during our visit.

Sights

Waterfalls and **caves** are high on the list of Kenyir's attractions, as well as a number of fish farms. These are reached by boat (as day trips from the lake's main access point, Pengkalan Gawi), or from the resorts themselves. Perhaps more interesting are trips up the rivers that empty into the lake. Among these, a journey up **Sungai Petuang**, at the extreme northern end of the lake, is a highlight of a Kenyir visit. When the water is high, it's possible to travel several kilometres upriver into beautiful virgin jungle.

Fishing is a popular activity and the lake is surprisingly rich in species, including *toman* (snakehead), *buang* (catfish), *kelah* (a kind of carp), *kelisa* (green arowana) and *kalui* (giant gouramy). You will need a permit (RM10) to fish here; this will be arranged for you if you book onto a fishing trip.

The water level varies considerably, peaking at the end of the rainy season in March or April and gradually decreasing until the start of the next rainy season in November. When the water is high the lake takes on an eerie atmosphere, with the tops of drowned trees poking through the surface; when low the lake is reduced to a series of canals through partially denuded jungle hills. Of the two states, high water is undoubtedly more beautiful so come in late spring or early summer.

At the height of the rainy season there is a risk of flooding, and some areas and communities can become inaccessible as poorly maintained roads and bridges are submerged or damaged by rising water.

Sleeping

Most accommodation is in resort chalets or floating longhouse structures built over the lake. There are no budget options. Resorts usually offer meals and boat transport from Pengkalan Gawi.

Kenyir Sanctuary Resort (☎ 019-824 4360; r from RM85; ☒) Offers some of the cheapest rooms on the lake. There are 40 rustic wooden chalets, including some pricier air-con rooms.

Musang Kenyir Resort (☎ 623 1888; r from RM140; ☒) On the north shore of the lake, Musang consists of several rustic *kampung*-style houses plopped over the waters. Facilities are basic, but the setting is beautiful.

Petang Island Resort (☎ 822 1276; www.pirkenyir.com .my; r RM250; ☒ ☒) On its own little island in the middle of the lake, this is a quiet retreat with a choice of comfortably furnished single- or double-storey chalets and longhouse rooms. Chalets have kitchens if you want to cook for yourself, but there's a good restaurant here, too.

Kenyir Lakeview Resort (☎ 666 8888; www .lakekenyir.com; r/ste from RM380/620; ☒ ☒) The most glamorous property on the lake, this peaceful resort has spacious and well-equipped chalets with balconies overlooking the water or the rainforest. There's a restaurant, tennis courts and a gym, and plenty of organised activities.

Another option is to explore Kenyir by houseboat, which allows you to reach remote regions of the lake, but you'll likely need a large group to make a trip economical.

Most visitors come to Kenyir on all-inclusive packages, which can either be arranged directly with the resort or with a travel agency in Kuala Terengganu, which will probably work out cheaper.

Getting There & Away
Tasik Kenyir is 15km west of Kuala Berang and 55km from Kuala Terengganu. The main access point is the jetty at Pengkalan Gawi, on the northern shore of the lake. To get there, take a taxi from Kuala Terengganu (RM120 per car). There are also buses to Kuala Berang from Kuala Terengganu (RM8); from Kuala Berang a taxi is only about RM80. If you book a package in Kuala Terengganu with an agency it should provide minibus transport and offer day trips to the lake.

Getting Around
Travel around the lake is expensive as you will have to charter a whole boat, either from Pengkalan Gawi or from your resort. Boat hire costs around RM150 to RM200 per hour and a half-day fishing trip costs about RM700. The resorts offer various trips around the lake, but prices depend on the number of passengers, so again this can be rather pricey. Cruises are sometimes included in package deals. An organised day trip (p309) from Kuala Terengganu is your best bet if you just want a quick scout around.

SOUTH OF KUALA TERENGGANU
Besides long stretches of beach and ocean, the most distinctive landmark of this stretch of the Malaysian coast are flaming oil refineries. About 25km north of Cherating, **Cukai** and **Kemaman** are the first towns of any size north of Kuantan, and the first towns you reach in Terengganu state when travelling up the coast. The two towns have merged into one long developed strip, with little of interest to hold passing travellers. **Hotel Tiara** (☎ 859 1802; K-353 Jln Kampung Tengah; r RM45-55; ☒), roughly opposite the bus station (turn at the 'Masjid Jamek' sign), has basic rooms.

Buses from Cherating or Kuantan both cost RM7. Express buses cost RM9 from Marang and RM11 from Kuala Terengganu. Taxis (per car) cost RM30 to Cherating, RM50 to Kuantan, RM60 to Dungun and RM80 to RM100 to Kuala Terengganu.

Kemasik
☎ 09
Kemasik's palm-fringed beach has some of the clearest water on the east coast. The nearest accommodation is at the gargantuan, five-star **Awana Kijal Golf, Beach & Spa Resort** (☎ 864 1188; www.awana.com.my; r/ste from RM280/520; ☒ ☒ ☒) on the beach around 1km south, towards Kijal, stacked with the usual golf courses, tennis courts, spa etc. Discounts are often available, especially if you book over the internet. Take a local bus running between Kemaman-Cukai and Dungun, or if you're driving, turn off Route 3 (East Coast Highway) at the 'Pantai Kemasik' sign.

Paka
☎ 09
The beach here is almost as good as the one at Kemasik, but the view is somewhat marred by the refinery a few kilometres down the coast. The village is a little run-down but quite picturesque.

The modern **Residence Resort** (☎ 827 3366; www .residenceresortpaka.com; r/ste from RM280/500; ☒ ☒ ☒) is a luxurious cluster of airy rooms with smooth white sheets and rattan furniture. The best way to visit Paka is to take a local bus running between Kerteh and Dungun. If you're driving, turn off at the 'Pantai Paka' sign.

Dungun
☎ 09
Dungun and the port of Kuala Dungun form the largest town on the coast between Kemaman-Cukai and Kuala Terengganu. You may need to stay here if no buses are running.

There are a few standard hotels; try **Hotel Kasanya** (☎ 848 1704; 225 Jln Tambun; r from RM98; ❄), a reasonable option, around five minutes' walk from the bus station; cross the sports field and take a left on the main road.

Buses go to Kuala Terengganu (RM8) and Kemaman-Cukai (RM6). Kuala Terengganu-bound buses will drop you at Rantau Abang (RM3); the same bus heading in the opposite direction will stop at Dungan. You can also hop on the bus in Rantau Abang (RM2), from where a taxi shouldn't be more than RM10.

On the coast around 8km east of Dungun is the gorgeous **Tanjong Jara Resort** (☎ 03-2783 3000; www.tanjongjararesort.com; Batu 8 off Jln Dungun; r/ste from RM350/900; ❄ 💻 ☎). It's a peaceful and secluded place set on a long, sandy stretch of beach, with a choice of spacious and luxurious traditional-style chalets, some with private verandahs and sunken baths set in a futuristic yoga-chic-style studio setting.

Rantau Abang
☎ 09

Rantau Abang once attracted flocks of tourists who came to see giant leatherback turtles come ashore to lay their eggs. Now that the focus of turtle conservation is the Ma' Daerah sanctuary (p316) further south, Rantau Abang has taken on the dusty if pleasant ambience of a quiet seaside town gone slightly to seed. The beach is still golden and the water is still blue, although the latter is also plagued by strong undertows.

You can still pop by the **Turtle Information Centre** (☎ 845 8169; ⏰ 8am-4.30pm Sun-Thu, 8am-noon Sat), essentially a small showroom with a few information boards where staff will run a 10-minute film (in English) on request. Otherwise, there's not much to do but nothing, and a good place to do that is **Awang's Beach Resort** (☎ 019-974 9533; r from RM70; ❄), a cluster of sandy chalets inhabited by some laid-back staff, loud pet birds and general Jack Johnson–ambience.

Dungun–Kuala Terengganu buses run in both directions every hour from 7am to 6pm and there's a bus stop near the Turtle Information Centre. To/from Dungun costs RM2; to Kuala Terengganu costs RM5. A taxi to Kuala Terengganu costs RM40.

Marang
☎ 09

Marang is the jump-off point for ferries to Pulau Kapas (see opposite) and a quiet fishing town. It's a little overbuilt by the highway but still pleasant in a rural way, especially in spots like **Kampung Jenang**, where you can observe the weaving of *atap* (roof thatching) and the making of coconut sugar, as well as the gathering of coconuts by trained monkeys. It's especially attractive in summer, when numerous exotic fruit trees are in season. It's possible to visit the village as an easy day trip from Marang or Kuala Terengganu.

If you are in town on Sunday be sure to check out the excellent **market**, which starts at 3pm near the town's jetties.

SLEEPING & EATING
Kamal Guesthouse (☎ 618 2181; No B 283 Jln Kampung Paya; r RM30-70; ❄) This sleepy guesthouse on the main road has some reasonable rooms with attached showers and toilets. Only the pricier ones have air-con.

Marang Guesthouse (☎ 618 1976; www.marang guesthouse.com; Jln Kampung Paya Bukit; r from RM40; ❄) A series of dark, comfy if occasionally musty chalets perch on a hill overlooking the main road down to the jetty. At night, the high-up location and surrounding jungle makes for an agreeably rustic escape.

Angullia Beach House Resort (☎ 618 1322; angul-lia _resort@yahoo.com; r RM75-185; ❄) Across the bridge to the southeast is this peaceful resort. There's a variety of chalets spread out under the palm trees on a stretch of coarse golden sand, with a good view of Pulau Kapas. There are also larger chalets housing up to four people (RM250) and a garden restaurant. It's popular with school groups.

Hotel Seri Malaysia (☎ 618 2889; www.serimalaysia .com.my; 3964 Jln Kampung Paya; r RM150; ❄ ☎) The most upscale spot in town is this bright, modern chain hotel on the coast north of the centre, offering rooms any Western traveller in need of mod-cons will be comfortable with.

There are a couple of basic *kedai kopi* (coffee shops) in the town centre, near the bus ticket office, and you can also find some **food stalls** (Jln Kampung Paya) near the jetties.

GETTING THERE & AWAY
There are regular local buses to Kuala Terengganu (RM3) and Dungun/Rantau Abang (RM6/4). For long-distance buses there's a **ticket office** (☎ 618 2799; Jln Tanjung Sulong Musa) near the town's main intersection. There are two daily buses to KL (RM30.40),

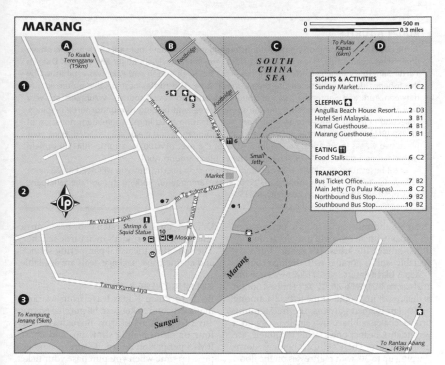

MARANG

SIGHTS & ACTIVITIES
Sunday Market.....................1 C2

SLEEPING
Angullia Beach House Resort.......2 D3
Hotel Seri Malaysia.................3 B1
Kamal Guesthouse..................4 B1
Marang Guesthouse................5 B1

EATING
Food Stalls..........................6 C2

TRANSPORT
Bus Ticket Office....................7 B2
Main Jetty (To Pulau Kapas)........8 C2
Northbound Bus Stop...............9 B2
Southbound Bus Stop..............10 B2

two to Johor Bahru (RM35) and five to Kuantan-Cherating (RM15).

There are four bus stops on the main road. Southbound express buses usually stop in front of the mosque, and northbound services will pick you up just north of the post office. This is not a hard and fast rule, however, and it's best to ask the owner of your guesthouse or someone at the ticket office first.

Pulau Kapas
☎ 09

Pretty Pulau Kapas is an emerald coated in powder-white sand and a general air of take it easy. All accommodation is concentrated on three small beaches on the west coast, but you can walk around the headlands to quieter beaches. Just off the north coast of Kapas is tiny Pulau Gemia; it's not usually possible to visit, unless you're staying at the island's exclusive Gem Wellness Resort (p316).

Pulau Kapas is best avoided during holidays and long weekends, when it is overrun with day-trippers. Outside of these times, the island is likely to be very quiet. It shuts

down during the east-coast monsoon season (November to March).

ACTIVITIES

Kapas is billed as a snorkelling paradise, though coral is scarce on the most accessible beaches facing the coast. Some of the best snorkelling is around the northern end of the island and Pulau Gemia. North of Gemia, a sunken WWII Japanese landing craft, now carpeted in coral, is a popular dive site.

All of the resorts listed here can arrange snorkelling and diving trips.

Aqua-Sport Divers (☎ 019-983 5879; www.divekapas .com), attached to Duta Puri Island Resort, charges RM110/180 for one/two dives, including equipment, and trips out to the Japanese boat (RM150). Snorkelling costs RM30 for a session.

SLEEPING & EATING

Many people staying on Kapas do so through all-inclusive package tours.

Lighthouse (☎ 017-988 9046; dm/r RM20/50) On the southernmost tip of the bay, this is the

TERENGGANU

ADOPT A TURTLE

Turtles were once a common sight all along Terengganu's coastline, but sadly their numbers have diminished significantly. However, green turtles remain relatively abundant and the **Ma' Daerah Turtle Sanctuary** (http://madaerah.org) on the coast between Kerteh and Paka was established by the fisheries department to ensure their survival here. The turtles nest on this protected site between April and September, and although not open to casual tourists, volunteers are very welcome. In the summer months you can spend a weekend helping to monitor turtle landings, collecting eggs for transfer to the hatchery and releasing hatchlings. A minimum donation of RM250 (RM150 for children) is required, and accommodation and meals are provided; book your place two weeks in advance. You could also 'adopt' a nest (RM100) or a turtle (RM150) or help with cleaning up the beach, which usually takes place around April.

Local buses running between Kerteh and Dungan stop nearby, but you will need an advance reservation to visit. Ping Anchorage (p309) in Kuala Terengganu, working through the sanctuary, runs night-time trips here in summer (RM150).

---

cheapest and most atmospheric budget spot on Kapas, with all rooms in one elevated longhouse under the trees. It's rustic, but very sociable, and is popular with diving groups.

Kapas Island Resort (☎ 631 6468; www.kapasislandresort.com; dm RM20, r RM90-200; ✸ ▣) The best option is this resort just south of the jetty. Set among pretty landscaped gardens, the freestanding timber chalets all have two single beds and a verandah. Cheaper ones, facing the jungle, are more secluded. There's also a longhouse dorm sleeping up to 30, with mattresses on the floor; a bargain if you can get it to yourself.

North of the jetty, a stone walkway leads to another beach with a couple more options.

Kapas Beach Chalet (☎ 019-936 0750; r RM40-70) Also known simply as KBC, there's a choice of rooms here, ranging from very basic 'backpacker' rooms with outside (but private) toilets to more comfortable A-frame huts with TVs. The friendly Dutch owner can arrange fishing trips and barbecues.

Mak Cik Gemuk Beach Resort (☎ 624 5120; r RM40-120; ✸) This older place has a variety of unmodernised rooms; take a look at a few before deciding. A few are in need of a good scrub, and a few have received a wash down.

Qimi Chalet (☎ 019-951 8159; r RM80-120) A walkway leads to this small, northernmost collection of huts, on its own beach. Basic indeed, and isolated, but it has a certain castaway charm.

Gem Wellness Spa & Island Resort (☎ 625 2505; information@gemisle.com; r from RM260; ✸) Perched on tiny Pulau Gemia, 800m north of Pulau Kapas, this resort is worth a try for those in search of something more sophisticated. It's a peaceful spot, with airy wooden chalets, a couple of small private beaches and, between May and

October, guests can watch baby green turtles emerging at the resort's own turtle hatchery. The spa offers the usual pampering services, and all-inclusive package deals are available.

GETTING THERE & AWAY
Boats to Pulau Kapas leave from Marang's main jetty and tickets can be purchased from any of the agents nearby. Boats leave when four or more people show up, and charge RM25 per person return. Be sure to arrange a pick-up time when you purchase your ticket. You can usually count on morning departures at around 8am and 9am. The same boats will continue to Pulau Gemia if requested.

NORTH OF KUALA TERENGGANU
North of Kuala Terengganu the main road (Route 3) leaves the coast and runs inland to Kota Bharu, 165km north, via Jerteh. The quiet coastal back road from Kuala Terengganu to Kuala Besut runs along a beautiful stretch of coast and is popular with cyclists.

Merang
☎ 09
Gateway to Pulau Redang, the sleepy little fishing village of Merang (not to be confused with Marang) is one of the few remaining villages of its kind where development hasn't gone ahead in leaps and bounds. There's little of interest in the village, but the beach is attractive if you have to spend some time waiting for ferry connections to Redang.

SLEEPING
Kembara Resort (☎ 653 1770; http://kembararesort.tripod.com; dm RM10, r RM35-60; ✸ ▣) About 500m

south of the village (follow the signs from the main road), this is a friendly place with a range of plain but homely chalets. There are organised activities and a common kitchen.

Merang Inn Village Resort (☎ 624 3435; r RM40-60; ☒) In the centre of the village, this place has decent fan and air-con chalets just across the road from the beach, but the rooms are lacking in character.

Sutra Beach Resort (☎ 669 6200; www.sutra beachresort.com.my; Kampung Rhu Tapai; r/ste from RM185/650; ☒ ☒) About 6km south of Merang, and 35km north of Kuala Terengganu, this big complex is set on a private beach and offers a choice of accommodation. Most attractive are the beach-front rooms with uninterrupted views of the South China Sea. There are numerous organised tours available, and various packages.

Aryani Resort (☎ 653 2111; www.thearyani.com; Jln Rhu Tapai; r from RM369; ☒ ☒) One of Malaysia's most exclusive hotels lies on a secluded stretch of coast 4km south of Merang. The detached chalets are a mix of Malay and Javanese design, and are spread out in tranquil, landscaped grounds just off the beach. All have private gardens and sunken outdoor baths. Best of all is the sumptuous Redang Suite (RM1055), a traditionally furnished 150-year-old Malay house on stilts. The restaurants serve Western and Malay cuisine, while the spa offers indulgent body treatments and massages.

GETTING THERE & AWAY

There are daily buses from the main bus station in Kuala Terengganu to Merang (RM3). Taxis from Kuala Terengganu cost RM35 per car. Coming from the north is more difficult and it is easiest to go south as far as Kuala Terengganu and then backtrack. Otherwise, taxis from Kota Bharu cost RM70.

Pulau Redang
☎ 09

Redang is one of the prettiest east-coast islands and a definite candidate for tropical bliss, but for a few issues. Its position within a marine park lends itself to excellent diving and snorkelling, and you can easily lose yourself in between the golden sunlight, cackling jungle and lapping waves. Unfortunately, it's difficult to visit outside of package tours, which tend to be regimented affairs with arrival lectures, set times for meals, snorkelling and 'leisure'. It's popular with groups of young Malaysians and weekending Singaporeans.

In the past, and to a degree now, debris from construction has lead to coral damage and ugly piles of rubble along the beach, but some folks on the island are starting to both wisen and clean up. There are beautiful bays on the eastern shore, including Teluk Dalam, Teluk Kalong and Pasir Panjang. The huge Berjaya Redang Beach Resort and the airport are on the north shore, while island's main village is in the interior.

Note that Pulau Redang basically shuts down from 1 November to 1 March; the best time to visit is from mid-March to late September. There is a RM5 conservation fee for entering the marine reserve, usually payable at your resort.

SLEEPING

Accommodation on Pulau Redang is best organised as a package in Kuala Terengganu; tour companies such as Ping Anchorage (p309) sell packages for all the resorts, and several of the resorts have offices in Kuala Terengganu too, in particular along Jln Kampung Cina.

Note that package prices given in this section are for three days and two nights and are per person, based on two sharing, and include boat transfer from Merang, all meals and two snorkelling trips. Single occupancy normally carries a minimum surcharge of RM50 per night. Prices rise on school and public holidays. Promotional packages are frequently offered – check hotel websites before visiting.

Pasir Panjang

Most of the small resorts are built on a beautiful stretch of white-sand beach known as Pasir Panjang, on the east coast of the island.

Redang Pelangi Resort (☎ 624 2158; www.redang pelangi.com; r from RM259; ☒) This is a casual, resort-style affair that offers fairly simple two- and four-bed wooden chalets. There's an on-site dive centre, a couple of shops and a beachfront bar. The price here also includes transfer from Kuala Terengganu to the jetty in Merang.

Redang Bay Resort (☎ 620 3200; www.redangbay .com.my; dm/s/d per person from RM310/368/418; ☒ ☒) At the southern end of the beach, this rather characterless resort has a mix of concrete-block-style accommodation and chalets. Rooms are neat and clean, if a little spartan. The karaoke lounge is open till all hours, and there's a 'beach disco' on weekends, so don't come looking for a quiet island retreat.

Redang Holiday Beach Villa (☎ 624 5500; www .redangholiday.com; r from RM329; ⊠) At the northern tip of the beach is this welcoming place, with a series of smart duplex chalets climbing the rocks (chalets S13 and S14 have the best outlooks). Larger chalets sleep up to eight.

Coral Redang Island Resort (☎ 630 7110; www.coral redang.com.my; s/d per person from RM690/485; ⊠) Towards the northern end of the beach, this full-blown resort has slightly overpriced but very pleasant chalets that offer a bit more character than some of the cheaper places. There's a dive centre attached and diving packages start at RM800 per person, which includes four dives.

South of Pasir Panjang

In the bay directly south of Pasir Panjang you will find several more places to stay strung out along an excellent white-sand beach.

Redang Kalong Resort (☎ 03-7960 7163; www.redang kalong.com; r from RM249; ⊠) At the secluded Teluk Kalong is this quiet place, set among the palm trees in a private little bay. Diving packages start at RM589 and include five dives. Turtles often come ashore along here to lay eggs.

Ayu Mayang Resort (☎ 626 2020; www.redangkalong .com; r from RM269; ⊠) In seeming response to the high-rise-type hotels that have taken over much of the seashore, Ayu Mayan consists of wooden chalets, more rustic than regal, that give a good Robinson Crusoe crossed with a *kampung* vibe. Room interiors are a bit plain for the price.

Redang Reef Resort (☎ 622 6181; www.redangreef resort.com.my; r from RM300; ⊠) On the headland, this friendly place is in a great location, though you'll get your feet wet going to and fro at high tide. The two-storey wooden chalets are very basic but popular with student groups. The better chalets on the rocks are more secluded and have fantastic views of the bay. It also has a tiny private beach.

Laguna Redang Island Resort (☎ 630 7888; www .lagunaredang.com.my; r from RM348; ⊠ 🖳 🖳) Redang's biggest resort – a vast, 222-room complex that is still being added to – dominates this beach. It has luxurious sea-view suites with balconies, excellent restaurants, a diving centre and a full program of children's activities. Buildings are in traditional Malay style, designed by the same architect who built the state museum in Kuala Terengganu.

Redang Beach Resort (☎ 623 8188; www.redang .com.my; r from RM369; ⊠ 🖳) This place has an arrangement of modern double-storey chalets and boasts a five-star PADI diving centre, a few shops and a regular beach disco, which makes it a bit intense for a quiet escape.

Berjaya Redang Beach Resort (☎ 630 8866; www .berjayaresorts.com.my; r/ste from RM690/1150; ⊠ 🖳 🖳) Redang's most luxurious resort has a wide choice of sumptuous wooden chalets in delightful, landscaped gardens, and an excellent private beach. This is as close to royalty as you'll get at Redang; some of the chalets really do feel like small palaces.

GETTING THERE & AWAY

Nearly all visitors to Redang purchase packages that include boat transfer to the island. If you go independently, you'll need to hitch a ride on one of the resort boats (adult/child RM100/50), but in the high season (April to September) room-only deals will be scarce. Ferries run from the string of jetties along the river in Merang. Ferries also run from Shahbandar jetty in downtown Kuala Terengganu, but are less frequent and must generally be arranged via your resort. A schedule for all resort ferries can be found at www.redang.org /transport.htm.

Redang's airport is near the Berjaya Redang Beach Resort; **Berjaya Air** (☎ 630 8866; www.berjaya-air.com) has daily flights to KL (Sultan Abdul Aziz Shah Airport; roundtrip RM526) and to Singapore (Seletar Airport; roundtrip RM837).

It's also possible to visit Redang on a dive trip from Pulau Perhentian (see p320).

Pulau Lang Tengah
☎ 09

Tiny, idyllic Lang Tengah lies roughly halfway between Pulau Redang and Pulau Perhentian, and with only three resorts to choose from, it's a much quieter, less-developed place than its better-known neighbours, and there is no resident population. It's a hidden gem, with soft white-sand beaches, clean turquoise waters and some of the best snorkelling in Malaysia just offshore. Like Redang, almost everyone comes on package deals that include ferry transport, snorkelling or diving.

SLEEPING

The island's three resorts are spaced out on the west coast, and offer a bewildering variety of package deals; unless otherwise stated, those listed in this section are for three days and two nights. The prices here are for the high season (June to September).

Islands (☎ 07-235 1216; www.langtengah.com.my), based in Johor Bahru, offers good deals.

D'Coconut Lagoon (☎ 03-4252 6686; www.dcoconut lagoon.com; r from RM225; ☒) The smallest of the resorts has fairly plain but comfy chalets with fridges, TVs and other mod-cons, set around an attractive pool. These prices are per night, but half- and full-board options are also offered.

Redang Lang Island Resort (☎ 623 9911; www .malaysiaislandresort.com; s/d from RM340/420; ☒) Offers basic but neat wooden chalets just a few steps from the beach, with a common TV lounge and karaoke bar. Snorkelling and diving packages are available, and prices are slightly higher from Thursday to Sunday.

Lang Sari Resort (☎ 03-2166 1318; http://langsari.com; s/d from RM348/478; ☒ ☒) Huge wooden chalets look over strings of lanterns, the beach and guests relaxing in hammocks. You can canoe, go turtle or shark watching, or do what your purpose here is: nap in the shade. Amenities are pretty advanced for the rural setting.

GETTING THERE & AWAY
Between April and August, ferries to Lang Tengah leave from the jetty in Merang at 10am and noon, and return from the island at 8.30am and 2pm. From September to March they leave Merang at 12.30pm and depart the island at 2pm. If you're travelling independently, the one-way fare for adults/children is RM80/40.

Kuala Besut
☎ 09
Kuala Besut, on the coast south of Kota Bharu, is a sleepy fishing village that serves as the ferry point to Pulau Perhentian.

ORIENTATION & INFORMATION
Taxis and local buses run to and from the taxi stand in the centre of town, very near the seafront. There are numerous travel agencies around town that can arrange ferries to, and accommodation on, the islands, and all charge identical prices. Several of the resorts have their own agents' offices in town, too. There is a RM5 conservation fee for entering the marine park around the Perhentians; buy your ticket at the jetty before you board.

SLEEPING & EATING
Kuala Besut's few hotels are mostly functional affairs.

Yaudin Guesthouse (☎ 697 4887/611; Jln Pantai; r RM20-40; ☒) This is the cheapest place in town, with a few drab rooms over the travel agency of the same name. Only two rooms have air-con, and bathrooms are communal.

Samudera Hotel (☎ 697 9326; www.kekal -samudera.com; Jln Pantai; r from RM65; ☒) Near the jetty, this renovated place is the best option in town, with large simple rooms and private bathrooms.

There are several *kedai kopi* around town, as well as a few shops where you can buy basic provisions. Around the square formed by the taxi stand are a few small shops and restaurants.

GETTING THERE & AWAY
Kuala Besut is best reached from Kota Bharu to the north. There is no direct bus – you will have to travel via Jerteh or Pasir Puteh for an onward connection. The total fare ends up being between RM5 and RM10. However, as a taxi from Kota Bharu costs RM65 per car, most people choose this easier option. From the south, you can come from Kuala Terengganu by bus (RM8) or taxi (RM80 per car). There are also two daily buses from KL (RM33.80, nine hours).

PULAU PERHENTIAN
☎ 09
The Perhentians are tropical paradise. Full stop. The water is simultaneously electric teal and crystal clear; the jungle is thick, fecund and thrilling; the sand, from a distance, looks like snow. At night bonfires and kerosene lamps on the beach and phosphorescence in the water makes pin holes in the velvety black, the stars soar above you and the real world becomes something like a bad dream. Most people come to snorkel, dive or do nothing at all. These goals are all eminently achievable.

Even Eden must be divvied up. There are two main islands: smaller Kecil ('Small'), popular with the younger backpacker crowd, and Besar ('Large'), with higher standards of accommodation and a quieter, more relaxed ambience. The undecided can cross the strait from island to island for around RM20 (about five to 10 minutes).

Not everyone loves the Perhentians, though. These are quiet islands, and if you're looking for a Thai-style party atmosphere, you're very much in the wrong place. Alcohol is available and during the high season (May to September) you can usually find some kind of impromptu beach party at night, but this isn't full-moon territory by any stretch. Prices quoted here are for the high season. The islands basically shut down during the monsoon (usually from mid-November to mid-February) although some hotels remain open for hardier tourists. That said, some places don't bother opening until April or even later. There are no banks or ATMs on the islands, so bring cash.

Orientation

A narrow strait separates Perhentian Besar from Perhentian Kecil.

On Perhentian Kecil the most popular spot is Long Beach (Pasir Panjang), an excellent white-sand beach with a string of mostly budget chalets, cafes and a few tiny shops. Perhentian Kecil is the administrative centre of the islands and has a fair-sized village with a few *kedai kopi* and shops, as well as a police station and basic clinic, though nothing to entice tourists. Across the narrow waist of the island, Coral Bay (Aur Bay) is a moon-shaped stretch of beach that's arguably prettier than Long Beach, although it's tough to wade here on the shell-strewn sea-floor. There are other isolated bays with private beaches for those in search of solitude.

Over on Besar, most of the accommodation is clustered on the western side of the island along a series of beaches divided by rocky headlands. For those looking to get away from it all, a walk through the jungle, or a five-minute boat ride, leads to the isolated Teluk Dalam (Dalam Bay), which has a wide, palm-fringed beach.

Information

Once more, with feeling: *there are no banks or ATMs on the islands.* Some of the bigger resorts will cash travellers cheques, but at poor rates, and usually only for their own guests. Even the pricey diving schools only occasionally accept credit cards. The nearest bank is in Jerteh, on the mainland – no one wants to spend their tropical vacation bussing to a bank branch.

There are no public telephones. Hotels may allow you to make calls from their mobile phones, but it won't be cheap. Mobile phone numbers for resorts given here may change from one season to the next, and some have no phones, but travel agents in Kuala Besut will have the latest contact details. Where land-line numbers have been given, these are for more reliable resort offices in Kuala Besut. Internet access is limited and expensive; expect to pay around RM20 to RM24 per hour. The cheapest is at **Lazy Buoys** (per hr RM16) on Long Beach.

The only medical facility on the islands is the very basic **clinic** (Perhentian Village). Dive operators and some of the bigger resorts can offer first aid if needed.

There is a RM5 conservation fee for everyone entering the marine park around the Perhentians; this fee will likely be tacked onto the price of your ticket at the jetty in Kuala Besut.

If the tides are low, you may have to board a small fishing boat to get between the ferry and your destination island (and vice versa). This service comes with an unexpected RM3 fee.

Local 'beach boys' are generally harmless, but we have read reports of inappropriate propositions made to female travellers who have been invited on private walks, boat trips, etc. Ask yourself: would you follow this man at home? If the answer is 'No,' best not follow him here either.

Finally, we need to stress: you are still in Malaysia, and topless sunbathing is unacceptable. Locals are too polite to tell people to their face, but you are insulting their sense of modesty (and while we're not making excuses for them, certainly encouraging the sleaziness of the aforementioned 'beach boys') by taking off your top.

Activities

DIVING & SNORKELLING

There are coral reefs off both islands and around nearby uninhabited islands, Pulau Susu Dara in particular. The best bets for snorkelling off the coast are the northern end of Long Beach on Kecil, and the point in front of Coral View Island Resort on Besar. You can wade out to a living coral reef right in front of Tuna Bay Island Resort. Most chalets organise snorkelling trips for around RM40 per person (more or less depending on the size of the group) and also rent out equipment.

For scuba divers there are several operations on both islands, though prices are pretty uniform. At the time of research, open-water certification went from RM850 to RM1100, while dives cost around RM80 to RM125, with discounts for multiple dives. Many of the operators below also run dive excursions out to Pulau Redang.

Alu Alu Divers (☎ 691 1650; www.alualudivers.com) At Bayu Dive Lodge on Besar.

Flora Bay Divers (☎ 691 1661; www.florabaydivers .com) At Teluk Dalam on Besar.

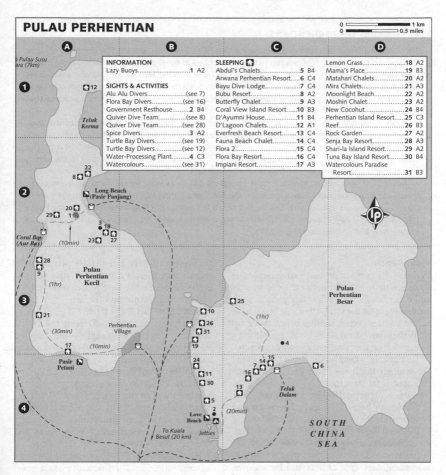

PULAU PERHENTIAN

0 —————— 1 km
0 —————— 0.5 miles

INFORMATION
Lazy Buoys..........................**1** A2

SIGHTS & ACTIVITIES
Alu Alu Divers.....................(see 7)
Flora Bay Divers..................(see 16)
Government Resthouse........**2** B4
Quiver Dive Team...............(see 8)
Quiver Dive Team...............(see 28)
Spice Divers..........................**3** A2
Turtle Bay Divers................(see 19)
Turtle Bay Divers................(see 12)
Water-Processing Plant......**4** C3
Watercolours......................(see 31)

SLEEPING
Abdul's Chalets....................**5** B4
Arwana Perhentian Resort....**6** C4
Bayu Dive Lodge...................**7** C4
Bubu Resort..........................**8** A2
Butterfly Chalet....................**9** A3
Coral View Island Resort....**10** B3
D'Ayumni House..................**11** B4
D'Lagoon Chalets................**12** A1
Everfresh Beach Resort.......**13** C4
Fauna Beach Chalet.............**14** C4
Flora 2...................................**15** C4
Flora Bay Resort..................**16** C4
Impiani Resort......................**17** A3

Lemon Grass.........................**18** A2
Mama's Place........................**19** B3
Matahari Chalets...................**20** A2
Mira Chalets.........................**21** A3
Moonlight Beach..................**22** A2
Moshin Chalet......................**23** A2
New Cocohut........................**24** B4
Perhentian Island Resort......**25** C3
Reef.......................................**26** B3
Rock Garden.........................**27** A2
Senja Bay Resort..................**28** A3
Shari-la Island Resort...........**29** A2
Tuna Bay Island Resort........**30** B4
Watercolours Paradise
   Resort...............................**31** B3

To Pulau Susu
Dara (7km)

Teluk
Kerma

Long Beach
(Pasir Panjang)

Coral Bay
(Aur Bay)   (10min)

Pulau
Perhentian
Kecil   (1hr)

(30min)

Perhentian
Village   (10min)

Pasir
Petani

Pulau
Perhentian
Besar

(1hr)

Teluk
Dalam

Love
Beach

To Kuala
Besut (20 km)   Jetties   (20min)

SOUTH
CHINA
SEA

Quiver Dive Team (☎ 012-213 8885; http://quiver
-perhentian.com) Next to Bubu resort on Kecil; operates as
Senja Mantis in Coral Bay.
Spice Divers (☎ 691 1555; http://spicedivers.net) On
Kecil; offers two dives for RM150.
Turtle Bay Divers (☎ 019-333 6647, 019-910 6647;
www.turtlebaydivers.com) Has offices at D'Lagoon (on
Kecil) and Mama's (on Besar).
Watercolours (☎ 691 1850; www.watercoloursworld
.com) By Paradise Island Resort on Besar. Also has an office
on Impiani Resort on Kecil.

HIKING
On Pulau Kecil, the jungle track between Long
Beach and Coral Bay is signposted and takes
10 to 15 minutes to walk. It's an easy, if humid,
hike; take a torch at night. Longer tracks run

between Coral Bay and Pasir Petani; ask your
guesthouse about conditions and keep in mind
the trail is only half-decently marked. Don't
attempt walking it in anything less than sports
sandals. On Pulau Besar, a jungle track cuts
across the island (and around a water-processing plant) from near Perhentian Island Resort
to Teluk Dalam at Fauna Beach Chalet. Again,
check beforehand if it's clear the whole way.

Sleeping & Eating
PULAU PERHENTIAN BESAR
There are three main beaches on Perhentian
Besar: the northern beach on the western side,
dominated by Perhentian Island Resort; the
main beach on the western side of the island; and
Teluk Dalam, on the island's southern coast.

TERENGGANU

PRESERVING THE PERHENTIANS

The Perhentians are, unfortunately, becoming victims of their own success. The presence of algae on exposed reefs during high season may be attributed to overflowing resort septic tanks. Long-time visitors and expats say some species of fish have become less visible over the years. Boat operators certainly have no qualms about flicking cigarette butts in the ocean and otherwise casually littering, and some will grab sea turtles and bring them to the surface, a practice that is extremely stressful to the turtle.

Rubbish from the Perhentians is stored on offshore pontoons and collected by contractors. Unfortunately, bags of trash are occasionally washed off those pontoons and float their way back to the islands, according to Kuala Lumpur conservation group Wild Asia (www.wildasia.org). The same group says an overtaxed sewage system has added nutrients (ie your waste) to the water, resulting in algal blooms on the fragile reef eco-system.

Never litter, and encourage your boat operators not to as well. Never stand on living coral, which can cause irreparable damage (even the force of a strong flipper kick can damage a reef). Observe the sea life around you, but do not touch it. Contact the **Department of Marine Parks** (☎ 308-886 1111; www.dmpm.nre.gov.my) with information on tour operators and resorts that engage in questionable environmental practices.

Main Beach

Perhentian Besar's main beach stretches to the southern tip of the island, interrupted by several rocky headlands – at low tide you can walk around them on the sand, otherwise you'll have to use a water taxi. A smaller beach taken up by Perhentian Island Resort is accessible via a footbridge on the northern end of the beach.

It's possible to **camp** on the beach south of the Government Resthouse ('Love Beach'), although this area is far from quiet on long weekends. You'll need a permit (RM5 per night) available at a little cafe here, if it's open. The beach and bays here are, to put it lightly, spectacular.

D'Ayumni House (☎ 691 1680, 019-436 4463; http://d-ayumnihouse.blogspot.com; dm RM40, r RM80-200; 🌂 💻) A pretty wooden house rises over a series of low-slung, teak-chic chalets and bungalows. Popular with divers and those seeking a bit of budget backpacker vibe in Besar.

Mama's Place (☎ 019-985 3359; www.mamas chalet.com; r RM60-100) The most southern place on this section of beach has a choice of reasonably comfortable chalets with or without bathrooms.

Watercolours Paradise Resort (☎ 691 1850; www.watercoloursworld.com; r RM70-130; 🌂) This friendly resort has clean chalets operated under the same management as the attached Watercolours dive centre, and is about the best value on Besar. The 'Impiani' expansion is a little more upscale, but more in terms of price (RM150 to RM240) than actual quality of lodging.

Abdul's Chalets (☎ 019-912 7303; s/d from RM70/150) The wooden beach huts at this popular place

are pretty ordinary, but all have private bathrooms and there's a cafe too. Just beyond is the Government Resthouse, reserved for Malaysian government officials.

Reef (☎ 019-981 6762; r RM100-270) Reef's very basic chalets are set back from the beach amidst a gaggle of lounging, flip-flopped staff. There's an equally basic cafe and a lazy, laid-back atmosphere.

Coral View Island Resort (☎ 019-981 3359; r/ste from RM135/295; 🌂 💻) With a great location at the northern end of the beach, Coral View's accommodation runs from simple fan chalets up to rather smart beachfront suites. There are a couple of good restaurants serving Asian and Western dishes (lunch RM30), and shops.

New Cocohut (☎ 691 1811; www.perhentianislandcoco hut.com; r RM140-230; 🌂) Cocohuts has a good choice of rooms including pleasant beachside chalets and a two-storey longhouse, which has some great views from the upstairs balcony. The semi-sea-view rooms' interiors are probably a little nicer than the sea-view rooms.

Tuna Bay Island Resort (☎ 690 2902; www.tunabay .com.my; d/tr/f from RM220/270/370; 🌂 💻) This gathering of pristine chalets perches on a lovely stretch of white sand, with others set in the pretty gardens or facing the jungle behind. You can wade out to a living coral reef just offshore, and afterwards relax in the islands' best restaurant and only authentic cocktail bar – a great place to unwind with a Long Island iced tea.

Perhentian Island Resort (☎ 691 1111; www.per hentianislandresort.net; s/d/tr from RM398/436/614; 🌂 🕭)

Approached via a rickety wooden walkway from behind Coral View Island Resort, this luxurious option overlooks perhaps the best beach on the islands – a beautiful half-moon bay with good coral around the points on either side. There's a huddle of comfortable bungalows and a first-class restaurant.

Teluk Dalam

An easily missed track leads from behind the second jetty near Love Beach over the hill northeast to Teluk Dalam, a secluded bay with a shallow beach, but it's easier to take a boat.

Everfresh Beach Resort (☎ /fax 697 7620; r RM30-80) At the western end of the bay, this is an ageing array of ramshackle A-frames and bungalows set around a pretty garden. It's quiet and just about OK, but has seen better days.

Arwana Perhentian Resort (☎ 778 0888; www .arwanaperhentian.com.my; dm/d/ste from RM30/120/580; 🛇 🖳) This huge upmarket resort occupies the eastern flank of Teluk Dalam, although it has no beach frontage itself. The broad array of rooms includes, surprisingly, two dorm blocks at the very back. The cheaper 'standard' rooms are a bit pokey. Facilities include a snooker room, karaoke booths and a dive centre.

Fauna Beach Chalet (☎ 691 7607; r RM50-140; 🛇) Sitting on an attractive stretch of sand, Fauna has a choice of the usual creaky wooden huts and more comfortable sea-view bungalows. Pricier ones have air-con; there's no hot water.

Bayu Dive Lodge (☎ 691 1650; www.alualudivers .com; r RM60-190) A collection of smart deep-brown chalets situated around a sandy central courtyard, this place is only open during the high season, when it also operates a dive centre.

Flora Bay Resort (☎ 691 1666; www.florabayresort.com; r RM130-215; 🛇 🖳) This big place has a variety of options at the back of the beach, ranging from garden-view fan huts to 'deluxe' air-con beach chalets. Flora 2, an extension of Flora Bay, is a little further along the beach, with a smaller range of pretty much identical chalets.

PULAU PERHENTIAN KECIL

Accommodation on Perhentian Kecil tends to be simpler and prices generally lower, starting at around RM20 to RM30 for a standard hut with two beds and shared bathroom, or as little as RM10 in the low season. Conditions are often much of a muchness. There are a couple of upscale developments if you crave more comfort.

With a picturesque swathe of white sand, Long Beach is the most popular place on the island. Note that swimming here can be very dangerous, though, especially during the monsoon and for a month or two after, when high waves and powerful riptides pose serious threats; there have been a number of near tragedies here. There are no lifeguards and no markers to tell you which sections of the beach are safe.

A signposted jungle trail over the narrow waist of the island leads from Long Beach to Coral Bay on the western side of the island. The beach is quite pleasant and gets good sunsets but, like Long Beach, it can get a little crowded.

There are a number of small bays around the island, each harbouring isolated chalets. Practically, these are only accessible by boat.

D'Lagoon Chalets (☎ 019-985 7089; dm RM10, r RM25-60) On Teluk Kerma, a small bay on the northeastern side of the island. This is one of the better places on Kecil, with good coral and a tranquil, isolated location. There are longhouse rooms and chalets, as well as a more unusual treehouse for all those budding Tarzans and Janes. Tracks lead to a couple of very remote beaches in the northwestern corner of the island.

Senja Bay Resort (☎ 691 1799; www.senjabay.com; dm/r/ste from RM20/105/230; 🛇 🖳) A slight step up from budget blah, the facilities at this cluster of bungalows and huts are a little more polished and pricey than many of the alternatives. Good for travellers who may want a little quiet.

Matahari Chalets (☎ 019-914 2883; www.matahari chalet.com; r RM25-120) Set back among the trees with a walkway to the beach, Matahari is one of the better chalet operations. It has a good range of accommodation, from simple huts with shared bathroom to spacious bungalows. There's also a restaurant, shop and moneychanger.

Mira Chalets (r RM30-70) On the southwest coast, Mira is an adventurous choice, set on a small secluded beach with the jungle right behind. There are eight rickety chalets set amid banana and coconut trees, in a location Robinson Crusoe would've been proud to call home. Meals are offered in the driftwood-bedecked restaurant. Walking tracks lead through the rainforest to Pasir Petani (30 minutes, about 1.5km) and north to Coral Bay (one hour, about 3km).

Mohsin Chalet (☎ 961 1580; r from RM30) Mohsin has some great chalets sprawling into the sand and up a hill. The receptionist is surreally friendly, and the ambience is tropically languid.

Moonlight Beach (☎ 019-926 9441; r RM30-150; 🛇) Moonlight's staff are friendly as hell, their

EAT. DRINK. BE PERHENTIAN.

When it comes to food, there are three options. First: cheap cafes with cookie-cutter menus, all serving the same bland-it-for-the-foreigner Malay and decent-because-you're-on-a-beach-so-no-one's-complaining Western food for roughly RM6 to RM15 per main. Next: nightly beachfront barbecues, which are ubiquitous. Usually a very filling, tasty bit of grilled fish and potatoes will cost around RM18. Finally, the more upmarket resorts like Tuna Bay have kitchens cranking out some pretty good steak, pasta and Malay mainstays.

If you need a party at night, look for the bonfires and listen for the techno that sprouts up along the beach most evenings. Buy yourself some overpriced beer and 'monkey juice,' the nickname for a sickeningly sweet brown liquor that will, after a few pulls, have you face down in the sand.

A-frame huts are fairly spruce and their regular rooms, while a bit blocky, are comfortable enough. It's also likely the only spot on the island partly managed by a lady boy.

Lemon Grass (☎ 012-956 2393; r RM35) At the southern tip of Long Beach, Lemon Grass has 16 no-frills fan huts with shared bathrooms. There are great views from the verandah at reception and nice secluded spots to sit and gaze out to sea.

Rock Garden (r RM40) Steep steps behind Lemon Grass will get you to this vertiginous place on the rocks, which had just come under new ownership during our research and may no longer be called Rock Garden when you read this. The position of the huts, overlooking the, well, long sweep of Long Beach is fabulous.

Butterfly Chalet (r RM45-60) Reached by a steep clamber over the rocks next to Senja Bay, this end-of-the-line place has a series of basic wooden huts perched precariously on the headland. They're all a bit tattered, but the setting, among blooming gardens and with superb views across the bay, is beautiful.

Impiani Resort (☎ 019-981 1852, 013-952 5182; www.impiani.com; r RM150-240; 🌀) This resort is on the south coast at isolated Pasir Petani. It's a peaceful, secluded setting, and the pricier chalets facing the beach have great views out over the open sea. There's an on-site restaurant and diving facilities.

Shari-la Island Resort (☎ 691 1500; www.shari-la.com; r/ste from RM230/350; 🌀 🖳) Situated on the northern end of Coral Bay, and sprawling back into the jungle trail, this is a good, clean and relatively posh option for those needing a little luxury while living the backpacker dream. Has 24-hour electricity.

Bubu Resort (☎ 03 2142 6688; www.buburesort.com.my; r from RM250; 🌀) At the northern end of the bay, this is the sole top-end option on Long Beach. It's a somewhat overpriced, modern three-storey hotel that looks out of scale here, but the rooms

catch the sun, and most have balconies. There's a restaurant, bar and dive centre.

Getting There & Away

Speedboats (adult/child RM70/35 return, 30 to 40 minutes) run several times a day between Kuala Besut and the Perhentians from 8.30am to 5.30pm although you can expect delays or cancellations if the weather is bad or if there aren't enough passengers. There used to be cheaper (and safer) slowboats plying this route, but this wasn't the case during our research. The boats will drop you off at any of the beaches.

In the other direction, speedboats depart from the islands daily at about 8am, noon and 4pm. It's a good idea to let the owner of your guesthouse know a day before you leave so they can arrange a pick-up. Tickets are sold by several travel agents around Kuala Besut (p319). If the water is rough (and on Long Beach in general, where the badly built jetty comes out over shallow water) you may be ferried from the beach on a small boat to your mainland-bound craft; you'll have to pay around RM3 for this.

Boats also run to and from the Perhentians from the tiny port of Tok Bali in Kelantan. There is only one operator (Symphony) on this route and prices are the same as from Kuala Besut, though the journey takes slightly longer. Both readers and Malaysian Tourism authorities have complained about the reliability and condition of these boats; we recommend that travellers only use ferries out of Kuala Besut.

Getting Around

While there are some trails around the island, the easiest way to go from beach to beach or island to island is by boat. Chalet owners can arrange a taxi boat. From island to island, the trip costs RM20 per boat, and a jaunt from one beach to another on the same island usually costs about RM10. Prices double at night.

TERENGGANU

Kelantan

Cities that broadcast chirping competitions between songbirds cooing in lattice cages; ancient cowhide puppets wielding pistols on a paraffin-lit night; a silk half-moon rippling past the blue sky on a sunny day. Really – how is it that so many travellers rush through Kelantan?

Likely as not, it's because they see *Darul Naim* (The Blissful Home) as a waypoint to something else: Thailand or Pulau Perhentian. That's a shame, as those who don't linger are missing out on experiencing both a stronghold of Malay culture and one of Southeast Asia's great cultural blending zones. This is a state that's heady with those things that make Malaysia distinctively Malay: the fire flicker of kerosene and the tinkle of a *gamelan*, blue rice dished out in paper cones, and the graceful kicks and punches, like a warrior's delicate dance, of traditional martial arts.

But seeing as Kelantan borders Thailand, there's a great deal of osmosis occurring here as well. Malaysia's cultural mix is generally realised in its distinctive blend of Chinese, Indian and Malay cultures, but here the mixing component comes from neighbouring Thailand. The graceful arch of Buddhist temples are likely as not to top the jungle treeline as the onion domes of a mosque, and Thai slang is mixed with Malaysian catcalls as the young of Kota Bharu, the state's pretty capital, go cruising in the evening.

This is one of the most Muslim, conservative and poor states in Malaysia. Despite this, and because of this, it's one of the most fascinating. Simultaneously an entrepôt of multi-culturalism and bastion of traditional Malay heritage, Kelantan deserves more from you than a bus transfer.

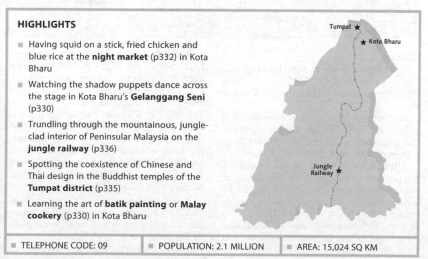

HIGHLIGHTS

- Having squid on a stick, fried chicken and blue rice at the **night market** (p332) in Kota Bharu
- Watching the shadow puppets dance across the stage in Kota Bharu's **Gelanggang Seni** (p330)
- Trundling through the mountainous, jungle-clad interior of Peninsular Malaysia on the **jungle railway** (p336)
- Spotting the coexistence of Chinese and Thai design in the Buddhist temples of the **Tumpat district** (p335)
- Learning the art of **batik painting** or **Malay cookery** (p330) in Kota Bharu

Tumpat ★

★ Kota Bharu

Jungle
Railway ★

| ■ TELEPHONE CODE: 09 | ■ POPULATION: 2.1 MILLION | ■ AREA: 15,024 SQ KM |

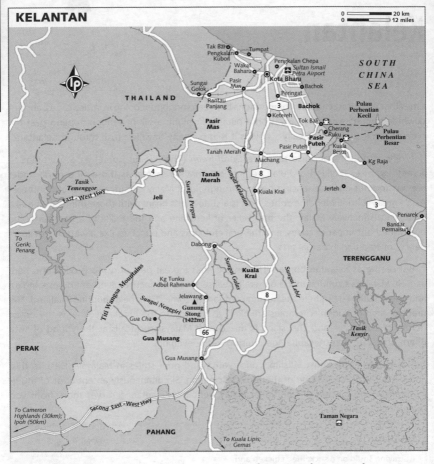

History

Archaeological finds at Gua Musang and Gua Cha have turned up evidence of human settlements dating back to prehistoric times.

In the early Middle Ages, Kelantan was influenced by the Funan kingdom on the Mekong River, and there were strong links with both Siam and the Khmer Empire.

After being a vassal of the Sumatran Srivijaya Empire and then the Siamese, Kelantan came under the sway of the Melaka sultanate in the 15th century. After the demise of the Melaka sultanate in the 17th century, Kelantan was ruled by Johor and then in the following century, Kelantan was ruled by Terengganu.

By the 1820s Kelantan was the most populous state on the Malay Peninsula. It managed to escape the ravages of the disputes that plagued west-coast states and experienced largely unimpeded development. Like Terengganu, Kelantan had strong ties with Siam throughout the 19th century, before control was passed to the British following the Anglo-Siamese treaty in 1909. Kelantan's wealth and importance waned after ties with Siam were cut, the state becoming a northerly backwater of colonial Malaya.

It was the first place in Malaya to be invaded by Japanese troops in WWII. During the occupation, control of the state was passed to Thailand, but in 1948 Kelantan became a member of the Federation of Malaya.

Since 1990 Kelantan has been governed by the Parti Islam se-Malaysia (PAS) and joined at the hip to this state in many Malaysians' minds.

Climate

Kelantan has a tropical climate, with average temperatures between 21°C and 32°C. There is intermittent rain throughout the year, and heavier, more prolonged rainfall during the east-coast monsoon season (November to January). Temperatures in Kota Bharu are often higher than in the surrounding countryside, and cooler temperatures are recorded on the coast. Humidity levels are highest in the jungled interior of the state, rarely dipping below 90%.

Dangers & Annoyances

Newly arrived foreign tourists are regularly approached at Kota Bharu bus stations by unlicensed drivers offering lifts. Besides being illegal, this is potentially dangerous and you're pretty certain to be ripped off. Only get into an official cab, which will display the company name and phone number.

If you're going to Pulau Perhentian, be aware that some taxi drivers, working on commission, will take you to the tiny port of Tok Bali. The ferry service from here is longer and more expensive than the one leaving from the main Perhentian departure port of Kuala Besut.

KOTA BHARU

☎ 09 / pop 425,000

The northernmost major city in Malaysia is also one of its most devoutly Muslim and deeply grounded in Malay heritage. Kota Bharu is supremely pleasant: it has the energy of a mid-sized city, the compact feel and friendly vibe of a small town, superb food and a good spread of accommodation. It's also a logical overnight stop between Thailand and the Perhentians. But you'd be wise to treat Kota Bharu as more than a pit stop. This is a good base for exploring Kelantan on both physical and other levels; the state's villages are within day-tripping distance, and its crafts and culture can be dug through while strolling city streets. The charms of this town reveal themselves slowly, but once you have a taste for it, it's easy to get sucked into KB's languid way of life.

Orientation

The centre of town is a busy area northeast of the clock tower, bounded by Jln Pintu Pong, Jln Kebun Sultan/Jln Mahmud, Jln Hospital and Jln Temenggong. The central bus station is just off Jln Padang Garong, opposite a huge, fenced-off hole in the ground where

---

PAS PERFORMANCE

Thanks in part to its high proportion (95%) of ethnic Malays, Kelantan has long been a stronghold of the Parti Islam se-Malaysia (PAS). PAS is both an Islamic and Islamist party (the difference being the former promotes Muslim interests, while the latter's goal is creating an Islamic state).

Islamic law is enforced more stridently here than anywhere else in Malaysia. Since PAS came into power, supermarket checkout queues have been segregated into lines for single men, women and families; couples have been fined for public 'indecency' (including hand-holding); and women have been fined for not wearing headscarves. Traditional arts like *wayang kulit* (shadow puppetry) have been criticised, boycotted and protested by PAS because of their links to pre-Islamic Hindu and animist belief systems. Muslim missionaries are encouraged to marry and convert Orang Asli (indigenous) women, and Muslims who renounce their religion (apostates) can be detained in 'Islamic rehabilitation centres' – better than being executed, which the State Legislative Assembly called for in 1993.

You may think the above atmosphere would be anathema to non-Muslim Chinese and Indians in Kelantan, yet traditionally these groups have helped keep PAS in power. Partly that's because Kelantanese have a strong sense of linguistic solidarity; locals speak a distinctive dialect of Malay that often unifies across political and ethnic lines. Partly it's because there is more to governance than religious debates; a 2008 article in *The Star* notes many Kelantanese, Muslim or no, simply think PAS does a good job of the day-to-day running of the state.

Travellers are unlikely to experience repercussions related to the above. Non-Muslims are not subject to Muslim ordinances unless they try to convert Muslims, and Chinese women, for example, freely walk around Kota Bharu in short shorts.

KELANTAN

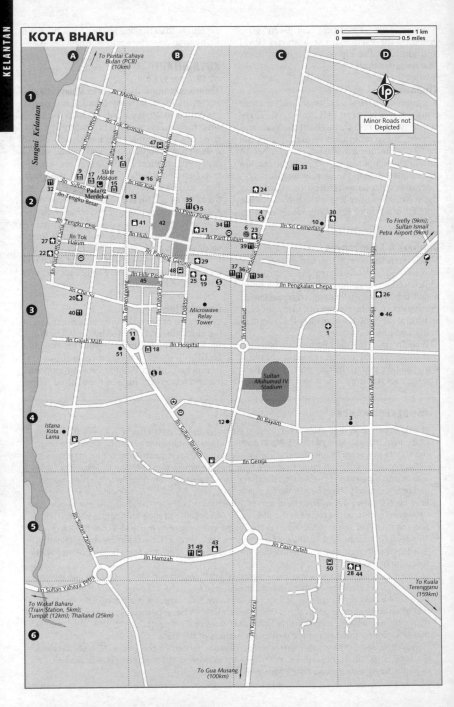

KOTA BHARU

INFORMATION		
General Hospital	1	C3
HSBC Bank	2	B3
Immigration Office	3	D4
Mayban Finance	4	C2
Maybank	5	B2
Multimedia Internet	6	C2
Thai Consulate	7	D3
Tourist Information Centre	8	B4

SIGHTS & ACTIVITIES		
Bank Kerapu	9	A2
Bird-Singing Venue	10	C2
Clock Tower	11	B3
Gelanggang Seni	12	B4
Istana Balai Besar	13	B2
Istana Batu	14	A2
Istana Jahar	15	A2
Kampung Kraftangan	16	B2
Muzium Islam	17	A2
Muzium Negeri Kelantan	18	B3
Zecsman Design	(see 16)	

SLEEPING ⌂		
Azam Hotel	19	B3
Crystal Lodge	20	A3
Denai Lodge	21	B2
Grand Riverview Hotel	22	A2
Hotel Anda	23	C2
Ideal Travellers' House	24	C2
KB Backpackers	25	B3
New Pacific Hotel	26	D3
Pelangi Condominiums	27	A2
Renaissance Hotel	28	D5
Suria Hotel	29	B3
Zeck's Traveller's Inn	30	C2

EATING 🍴		
Food Court	(see 43)	
Food Stalls	31	B5
Food Stalls	32	A2
Medan Selera Kebun Sultan Food Court	33	C2
Muhibah Aneka Cake House	34	B2
Night Market	35	B2
Restoran Golden City	36	C3

Ships	37	C3
Sri Devi Restaurant	38	C3
Sultan Kopitiam	39	C2
UP2U	40	A3

SHOPPING 🛍		
Bazaar Buluh Kubu	41	B2
Central Market	42	B2
KB Mall	43	B5
Kota Seri Mutiara	44	D5
Old Central Market	45	B3

TRANSPORT		
AirAsia	46	D3
Buses to PCB	47	B1
Central Bus Station	48	B3
Jln Hamzah External Bus Station	49	B5
Langgar Long Distance Bus Station	50	C5
Malaysia Airlines Office	51	A3
Taxi Stand	(see 48)	

the 25-storey Kota Bharu Trade Centre was being built during our research – it's been scheduled for completion several times in the past, and may be done by the time you read this.

Information
Banks are open from 10am to 3pm Saturday to Wednesday and 9.30am to 11.30am Thursday, and are closed on Friday.

HSBC Bank (Jln Padang Garong)

Immigration office (☎ 748 2126; Wisma Persekutuan, Jln Bayam)

Maybank (Jln Pintu Pong) Near the night market and usually open to 7pm.

Multimedia Internet (☎ 747 7735; 171 Jln Parit Dalam; per hr RM2)

Tourist information centre (☎ 748 5534; Jln Sultan Ibrahim; ☯ 8am-1pm & 2-4.45pm Sun-Wed, to 4.30pm Thu) Very helpful staff and good reading material.

Sights
PADANG MERDEKA
Padang Merdeka (Independence Sq) is a strip of grass that was established as a memorial following WWI. It is best known as the place where the British exhibited the body of Tok Janggut (Father Beard), a respected elder who was killed at Pasir Puteh in 1915 after leading a 2000-strong uprising against British colonial land taxes.

MUSEUMS
The real attraction of the Padang Merdeka area is the nearby cluster of **museums** (☎ 748 2266; www.kelantan.muzium.net, in Malay), all

contactable by the one phone number. There was talk during our visit of raising ticket prices by a ringgit.

Built in 1912 for the Mercantile Bank of India, the **Bank Kerapu** (WWII Memorial Museum; Jln Sultan; adult/child RM2/1; ☯ 8.30am-4.45pm Sat-Thu) building is a gem of colonial architecture, the first stone structure in Kelantan and, during WWII, HQ of the Kempai Tai, Japan's feared secret police. Today it is also known as the 'War Museum', thanks to its focus on the Japanese invasion and occupation of Malaya and the 1948 Emergency. Exhibits mainly consist of old photography, rusty guns and other miltaria. Upstairs is an uninspired gallery devoted to pre-war Kelantan and a garden interrupted by a reconstruction of a British pillbox.

Muzium Islam (Islamic Museum; Jln Sultan; admission free; ☯ 8.30am-4.45pm Sat-Thu) occupies an old villa once known as Serambi Mekah (Verandah to Mecca) – a reference to its days as Kelantan's first school of Islamic instruction. Nowadays it displays a small collection of photographs and artefacts relating to the history of Islam in the state.

Istana Jahar (Royal Ceremonies Museum; Jln Hilir Kota; adult/child RM3/1.50; ☯ 8.30am-4.45pm Sat-Thu) is the best museum of the bunch, both in terms of exhibits and structure. It's an achingly beautiful chocolate-brown building that dates back to 1887; thanks to its verandah and general sense of breezy space, it's one of the most attractive traditional buildings in the city. The interior displays focus on Kelantanese ritual and crafts, from detailed descriptions of batik-weaving to the elaborate ceremonies that once marked the life of local youth, from circumcision to wedding nights to funerary rights.

The pale yellow **Istana Batu** (Royal Museum; Jln Hilir Kota; adult/child RM2/1; 8.30am-4.45pm Sat-Thu), also known as Muzium Diraja, was constructed in 1939 and was the crown prince's palace until donated to the state. The richly furnished rooms give a surprisingly intimate insight into royal life, with family photos and personal belongings scattered among the fine china and chintzy sofas, and the late sultan's collection of hats.

Kampung Kraftangan (Handicraft Village; Jln Hilir Kota; admission free), a touristy affair opposite Istana Batu, has a one-room **museum** (adult/child RM2/1; 8.30am-4.45pm Sat-Thu) with displays of woodcarving, batik-making and other crafts. The complex includes souvenir shops and (why not?) a good-value lunchtime buffet. Batik classes also take place here (right).

Nearby, surrounded by walls and closed to the public, is **Istana Balai Besar** (Palace of the Large Audience Hall). Built in 1840 as the principal royal residence, it's now used only for formal state functions.

Muzium Negeri Kelantan (State Museum; 748 2266; Jln Hospital; adult/child RM2/1; 8.30am-4.45pm Sat-Thu), next to the tourist information centre, is the official state museum. The exhibits on Kelantan's history and culture are interesting, but the accompanying signage is poor.

GELANGGANG SENI

If you want to see *gasing uri* (top-spinning), *silat* (a Malay form of martial arts), kite-making, drumming, shadow-puppet shows and the like, the **Gelanggang Seni** (Cultural Centre; 744 3124; Jln Mahmud) is the place to go. Free afternoon and evening sessions are held on Monday, Wednesday and Saturday from February to September, currently between 3.30pm and 5.30pm and 9pm and 11pm, but check with the **tourist information centre** (748 5534; Jln Sultan Ibrahim; 8am-1pm & 2-4.30pm Sun-Thu), or your hotel's owners, who should have a full timetable of events.

A note on *wayang kulit* (shadow puppetry): performances are interesting, but can be difficult to appreciate without any prior context. You may want to check out http://discover-indo.tierranet.com/wayang for a primer before catching a shadow-puppet show.

Courses
COOKING

The ever-cheerful Roselan runs popular Malay cookery workshops at his home; prices vary depending on the number of participants and ingredients used, but expect to pay around RM75 per person for a group of four. Contact the **tourist information centre** (748 5534; Jln Sultan Ibrahim; 8am-1pm & 2-4.30pm Sun-Thu) for Roselan's current contact details. You will be invited to a real, middle-class Malay home and see food cooked under middle-class Malay conditions.

Hostels such as Zeck's, KB and Denai Lodge can all hook you up with their own cooking courses, which are offered at similar rates.

BATIK-PAINTING

You can try your hand at a spot of batik-painting at **Zecsman Design** (012-929 2822; zecsman_design@yahoo.com; Kampung Kraftangan, Jln Hilir Kota; 10am-7pm Sat-Thu). Tutored four- to five-hour classes cost RM50 for work on cotton and RM70 on silk, and a full-day course costs RM100. You'll need to book ahead.

Tours

Most hostels organise tours for their guests. Possible tours include two-day/three-night expeditions into the jungle around Gua Musang (RM250 to RM350), boat trips up small local rivers into sleepy fishing villages where silk kites are made by candlelight (RM60 to RM80), and short city tours (RM25 to RM35). Prices will vary based on how many people are going and exactly what sort of service you are demanding; qualified guides should cheerfully meet your demands or provide good explanations for refusing them.

In our experience, and based on conversations with travellers, the guys at KB Backpacker's Lodge (opposite) and Zeck's Traveller's Inn (opposite) run the best operations around.

The **tourist information centre** (748 5534; Jln Sultan Ibrahim; 8am-1pm & 2-4.30pm Sun-Thu) keeps a running list of reputable tour operators, and their former director, Roselan, also conducts excellent private tours, including a two-hour tour of the Tumpat temples (RM65) and a half-day river cruise (RM85). Contact Roselan through the tourist information centre.

Festivals & Events

Kota Bharans love birdsong, to the point where they broadcast the chirping of birds in an abandoned building across loudspeakers set up through the city. Each year around August the city holds a **bird-singing contest**, during which you can see Malay songbirds perform; the ornate cages the birds are housed in are almost as pretty as their songs. Finally, every Friday and Saturday morning there's a bird-singing contest near Zeck's Traveller's Inn, where locals hang decorative bird cages up on long poles, then sit back and listen. Travellers are often invited to watch and even provide a bit of amateur judging.

The spectacular **kite festival** (Pesta Wau) is held in June, and the **cultural carnival** (Karnival Kebudayaan Kelantan), featuring drum and top-spinning contests, takes place in September. The **Sultan's Birthday** celebration (March/April) involves a week of cultural events. The dates vary, so check with the tourist information centre.

Sleeping

The **tourist information centre** (☎ 748 5534; Jln Sultan Ibrahim; ☺ 8am-1pm & 2-4.30pm Sun-Thu) helps arrange homestays in Kota Bharu's suburbs and nearby villages. The program was just getting off the ground during our research, but staying with a local family has the potential to be an ideal way of experiencing Kelantan. Otherwise, Kota Bharu is a popular stop on the backpacker trail, and there's plenty of cheap hostels around town, including several along Jln Padang Garong. Midrange and luxury options are aimed at business travellers and run from bland and big to plain big.

The budget options listed here all have shared bathrooms unless otherwise stated.

BUDGET

KB Backpackers (☎ 748 8841, 019-944 5222; www.kb-backpackers.com.my; 1872-D Jln Padang Garong; dm/r from RM8/20; ☒ ☐) Run by the almost surreally friendly Pawi, KB's actual rooms are only so-so (the bigger the better is the rule). But Pawi is so helpful, and the vibe at his hostel is so internationally chill in that laid-back way that made us love backpacking in the first place, we can't help but declare our love of KB. Long may it reign.

Denai Lodge (☎ 017-370 7781, 019-963 2324; denai_lodge@yahoo.sg; 2984-F Jln Parit Dalam; dm/s/d from RM8/20/35; ☐) Run by former trekking guides, Denai gets high marks for its friendly owners and clean digs. It was new at the time of research, but a lot of thought seemed to be going into making it the sort of sociable spot every backpacker loves to lounge around in from time to time – quiet reading room, TV-centred common room etc.

Zeck's Traveller's Inn (☎ 743 1613; 7088-G Jln Sri Cemerlang; dm/s/d from RM10/18/25; ☒ ☐) Zeck's is a long-standing backpacker favourite in a peaceful nook north of the centre, with an attractive little garden to lounge about in and light meals and drinks always at hand. The friendly owner is a mine of information and travel hook-ups.

Ideal Travellers' House (☎ 744 2246; www.ugoideal.com; 3954-F Jln Kebun Sultan; s/d from RM10/25; ☐) Good for those needing a bit of quiet (there's a midnight curfew), this backpacker pad is located down an alley off Jln Kebun Sultan. There's a pleasant garden for having a laze during the day.

MIDRANGE

Hotel Anda (☎ 744 7920, 747 7600; 2529-A Jln Kebun Sultan; r from RM63; ☒) If you need an upgrade to general midrange levels of cool and comfort with slightly less cleanliness, the Anda is a good option. It offers cold air-conditioning and a private room at almost budget rates.

Crystal Lodge (☎ 747 0888; www.crystal-lodge.com.my; 124 Jln Che Su; s/d from RM75/149; ☒ ☐) This airy place offers the best value in its price range. Rooms are plain but clean and comfortable, and there are free in-house movies and daily newspapers, while the attractive rooftop restaurant has a great view over the river. There is a business centre on site.

Suria Hotel (☎ 743 2255; suria.kb@tm.net.my; Jln Padang Garong; s & d from RM75, tr RM90; ☒) A welcoming though slightly drab hotel set right in the heart of town. The cheapest rooms are windowless but there are some more appealing choices boasting natural light and 'wall to wall carpets', no less. Rooms overlooking the street may be subject to noise.

Azam Hotel (☎ 747 0508; 1872-A Jln Padang Garong; s & d from RM80, f from RM110; ☒) This cosy if boring hotel is set right in the heart of town above the photography shop of the same name. The worst rooms are windowless; better ones have nice, natural lighting. Rooms overlooking the street may be subject to noise

New Pacific Hotel (☎ 745 6555; www.newpacifichotel.com.my; 26 Jln Pengkalan Chepa; r/ste from RM188/330; ☒ ☐ ☒) This towering chain hotel provides a good level of comfort and service, and the spacious rooms come with all the usual mod cons. However, it's awkwardly placed on a very busy junction east of the centre. There are regular promotional prices.

TOP END

Pelangi Condominiums (☎ 980 0996; http://jompergi .com/homestay (in Malay); Jln Post Office Lama; r from RM200; 🟐 🖳) Not a hotel per se, but an agency that rents out luxury (and normal) condos around town on everything from a nightly to weekly to longer basis. This could be a good deal for groups of travellers, who may be able to get low individual rates if they split a property, or anyone needing a little privacy.

Grand Riverview Hotel (☎ 743 9988; www.grh.com .my; 9 Jln Post Office Lama; r/ste from RM215/318; 🟐 🟐) Perched on the river edge, this huge hotel offers high standards at reasonable prices; long-term 'promotions' will shave around 40% off the published rates. Rooms at the back have some fine views across the water, and all have king-sized beds and big bathrooms with both showers and baths.

Renaissance Hotel (☎ 746 2233; www.renaissance hotels.com; Jln Pasir Puteh; r/ste from RM248/352; 🟐 🖳 🟐) Part of the international Marriott chain, this gigantic hotel on the southern fringe of town offers all the business-class comforts and facilities you would expect. It's in the same block as the Kota Seri Mutiara shopping centre, but a long way from anything else.

Eating

Kota Bharu is one of Malaysia's better eating cities, with Malay, Thai, Indian and Chinese cuisine on offer in small hawker stalls and upscale restaurants. No visit is complete without sampling the town's famed night market (right).

If you need beer, head to the Chinese restaurants, which usually happily stay open late to satisfy booze-needy travellers. Note that some restaurants close on Fridays.

RESTAURANTS

Medan Selera Kebun Sultan Food Court (☎ 746 1632; Jln Kebun Sultan; mains from RM3; 🕑 lunch & dinner) A big, bright and bustling Chinese food court with a variety of standard Chinese dishes on offer, such as claypot chicken rice and *kway teow* (rice-flour noodles). Everything's in Chinese, but there are numbered photos you can point at. Beer is also available.

Sultan Kopitiam (Jln Kebun Sultan; mains from RM3; 🕑 24hr) This bustling cafe is ostensibly open around the clock, although it seems to close if no one's around. It has good coffee and free wi-fi for net heads.

UP2U (Jln Sultan Zainab Pong; mains from RM3; 🕑 breakfast, lunch & dinner) This hip 'dessert station' is the perfect antidote to the searing Malaysian heat, with its yummy Oreo milkshakes and sweet fruit juices. Very popular with local teens and tweens.

Muhibah Aneka Cake House (☎ 748 3298; Jln Pintu Pong; mains from RM4; 🕑 breakfast, lunch & dinner) Downstairs there's a nice bakery, while the upstairs restaurant serves decent Chinese vegetarian fare, although some of the stuff can be a bit oily.

Sri Devi Restaurant (☎ 746 2980; 4213-F Jln Kebun Sultan; mains from RM4; 🕑 lunch & dinner Sat-Thu) As popular with locals as it is with tourists, this is a great place for an authentic banana-leaf curry and a mango lassi; the biryani dinners are an especial treat.

Restoran Golden City (Jln Padang Garong; mains from RM5; 🕑 lunch & dinner) This basic but very good Chinese eatery in the centre of town has a big menu, in English, of the usual steamed fish, chicken, bean curd, rice and noodle dishes. At night, they'll serve beer until the last customer stumbles out.

Ships (171-181 Jln Padang Garong; mains from RM15; 🕑 lunch & dinner) Inside the Sabrina Court hotel, this nautically themed restaurant offers a menu of Western dishes including fish and chips, steak, and lamb chops.

QUICK EATS

The best and cheapest Malay food in town is in the **night market** (off Jln Pintu Pong): look for the yellow arch reading 'Medan Selera MPKB'. The stalls are set up in the evening around 5pm, when the sizzle of oil and heat hits the air and magic ensues. They're used to foreigners here and stall owners often tone down the heat without you having to ask; the resulting food is sometimes overtly sweet. Say 'Suka pedas' ('I like it hot') to eat as the locals do. Specialities include *ayam percik* (marinated chicken on bamboo skewers) and *nasi kerabu* (rice with coconut, fish and spices), blue rice, squid-on-a-stick and *murtabak* (pan-fried flat bread filled with everything from minced meat to bananas). Bear in mind, though, that the whole thing closes down for evening prayers between 7pm and 7.45pm, and Muslims and non-Muslims alike must vacate the premises. The market closes around 2am.

The so-called **Chinese night market** (6pm-midnight) takes over much of Jln Kebun Sultan in the evenings, with numerous hawker stalls selling hot snack food.

More food stalls can be found next to the river opposite the Padang Merdeka and by the Jln Hamzah bus station, and there's a modern **food court** (Jln Hamzah; lunch & dinner) inside KB Mall.

Shopping

Kota Bharu is a centre for Malay crafts. Batik, *kain songket* (fabric with gold thread), silverware, woodcarving and kite-making factories and shops are dotted around town.

One of the best places to see handicrafts is on the road north to Pantai Cahaya Bulan (PCB). There are a number of workshops, representing most crafts, stretched out along the road all the way to the beach. Unfortunately, it's hard to visit these without your own transport; an alternative is to join an organised tour (see p330).

One of the most colourful and active markets in Malaysia, the **central market** (Pasar Besar Siti Khadijah; Jln Hulu; 6am-6pm) is at its busiest first thing in the morning, and has usually packed up by early afternoon. Downstairs is the produce section, while upstairs stalls selling spices, brassware, batik and other goods stay open longer.

Near the central market, **Bazaar Buluh Kubu** (Jln Hulu; Sat-Thu) is a good place to buy handicrafts.

The **old central market** (Sat-Thu) consists of a block of food stalls on the ground floor, and a selection of batik, *kain songket* and clothing upstairs. A **street market** (6-10pm) selling clothes, copy watches and DVDs takes over Jln Parit Dalam in the evenings.

Modern chain stores can be found on the city fringes in huge shopping centres such as **KB Mall** (Jln Hamzah) and **Kota Seri Mutiara** (Jln Pasir Puteh).

Getting There & Away

AIR

The **Malaysia Airlines office** (771 4703; Jln Gajah Mati) is opposite the clock tower. There are direct flights to/from Kuala Lumpur (from RM48). **AirAsia** (746 1671) has direct daily flights to KL from RM39. **Firefly** (037-845 4543; airport) has direct daily flights to KL from RM49.

BUS

The state-run bus company **SKMK** (748 3807) operates city and regional buses (and some long-distance buses) from the **central bus station** (off Jln Padang Garong), and most long-distance buses from **Langgar bus station** (Jln Pasir Puteh) in the south of the city. All other long-distance bus companies run from the Jln Hamzah external bus station. On arrival in Kota Bharu some buses will drop you at the central bus station, or just outside, but they don't depart from there.

SKMK has ticket offices at all the bus stations. Ask which station your bus departs from when you buy your ticket, and book as far ahead as possible, especially for the Butterworth and Penang buses.

SKMK has regular buses from the central bus station to Kuala Terengganu (RM10.90, three hours), Kuantan (RM24.20, seven hours), Ipoh (RM25.40, eight hours) and Gua Musang (RM10.20, three hours). The following SKMK buses leave from Langgar bus station: buses to Johor Bahru/Singapore (RM49.10, 10 to 11 hours) leave at 8am and 8pm. Eight buses go to KL (RM30.90, nine hours), leaving from 8:30am to 11pm. 'Business class' buses (with fewer seats) are available for these routes as well, and cost roughly 30% more. Buses to Butterworth/ Penang (RM28.70, eight hours) leave at 9am and 9:30pm. Other destinations include Alor Setar (RM76.60, eight hours), Lumut (RM29.40, eight hours) and Melaka (RM40.20, nine hours).

The other companies cover many of the same routes. Buy your tickets at the Jln Hamzah external bus station or from the numerous kiosks behind the central bus station.

Most regional buses leave from the central bus station. Destinations include Wakaf Baharu (buses 19 and 27, RM1.20), Rantau Panjang (bus 29, RM3), Tumpat (bus 19, RM1.50), Bachok (buses 2B, 23 and 29, RM3.30), Pasir Puteh (bus 3, RM5.10), Jerteh (bus 3.30, RM7.10) and Kuala Krai (bus 5, RM8.30). Note that some of these may be identified by destination rather than number.

Thailand

The Thailand border is at Rantau Panjang (Sungai Golok on the Thai side), reached by bus from Kota Bharu. Bus 29 departs on the hour from the central bus station (RM3.8, 1½ hours).

From Rantau Panjang you can walk across the border; it's about 1km from the station. Share taxis from Kota Bharu to Rantau Panjang cost RM30 per car and take 45 minutes.

An alternative route into Thailand is via Pengkalan Kubor, on the coast. It's more time consuming and transport links aren't as good. The crossing here used to be dodgy due to sectarian violence in southern Thailand, but at the time of research it was safe. You may still want to ask hotel owners about conditions before you depart.

CAR
Travellers can hire cars from **Hawk** (☎ 773 3824; Sultan Ismail Petra Airport).

TAXI
The taxi stand is on the southern side of the central bus station. Avoid the unlicensed cab drivers who will pester you here and elsewhere around town, and take an official taxi as these are cheaper and safer. The **tourist office** (☎ 748 5534; Jln Sultan Ibrahim; ⏰ 8am-1pm & 2-4.45pm Sun-Wed, to 4.30pm Thu) will put you in touch with a reliable taxi driver.

Those who plan to catch an early morning train should arrange for the taxi to Wakaf Baharu the night before they plan to leave, as it can be difficult to find a (licensed) taxi on the street in the early morning.

TRAIN
The nearest station is **Wakaf Baharu** (☎ 719 6986). There is a daily express train all the way to KL (RM38, 13 hours), stopping at Kuala Lipis, Jerantut and Gemas, and a daily express to Singapore (RM41, 16 hours).

A daily local train stops at almost every station to Gemas (RM19.20, 13 hours). There are also two or three local trains a day that go as far as Gua Musang (RM7.20, five to six hours).

KTM has a ticket office (counter 5) at Kota Bharu's Jln Hamzah bus station.

Getting Around
The airport is 9km from town. You can take bus 8 or 9 from the old central market; a taxi costs RM20.

Most city buses leave from the middle of the old central market, on the Jln Hilir Pasar side, or from opposite the Bazaar Buluh Kubu.

Trishaws can still be seen on the city streets, though they are not as common as they once were. Prices are negotiable but reckon on around RM5 and upwards for a short journey of up to 1km.

AROUND KOTA BHARU
Masjid Kampung Laut
Reputed to be the oldest mosque in Peninsular Malaysia, Masjid Kampung Laut was built about 300 years ago by Javanese Muslims as thanks for a narrow escape from pirates. Built entirely of wood, without the use of nails, and with a stacked pyramid appearance, it's a very different mosque to the more Arabic-style structures commonly seen across Malaysia.

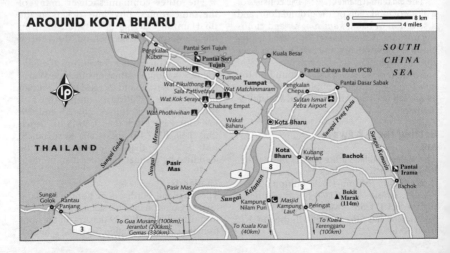

It originally stood at Kampung Laut, just across the river from Kota Bharu, but each year the monsoon floods caused considerable damage, and in 1968 it was moved to a safer location. It now stands about 10km inland at Kampung Nilam Puri, a local centre for religious study. Note that entry is forbidden to non-Muslims.

To get there, take bus 5 or 44 (RM2) from Kota Bharu's central bus station and get off at Nilam Puri. Try to go in the morning, when the mosque is least crowded.

Beaches

PCB beach once had a much better title: Pantai Cinta Berahi, the Beach of Passionate Love. Now, in keeping with Islamic sensibilities, it's **Pantai Cahaya Bulan** (Moonlight Beach), but the same initials apply and everyone calls it PCB.

our pick **Pasir Belanda** (☎ 747 7046; www.kampungstay.com; Jln PCB; s/d/tr RM149/179/199; 🛏) This privately run homestay is one of the nicest accomodation options in Kelantan. Three sizes of traditional Malay homes have been decked out in smooth sheeting and with little luxuries such as coffee makers. You're close to the beach and can lose yourself there, or just watch the stars from under your *kampung*-style awning.

To get there, take bus 10 (RM1.30) from behind Kampung Kraftangan (Handicraft Village) in Kota Bharu. A taxi costs RM30. If you're staying at Pasir Belanda, you may be able to arrange a pick-up from Kota Bharu.

Pantai Irama (Beach of Melody), in isolated, wild and windswept Bachok, is one of the best beaches around. However, swimming here during, or just after, the monsoon period (November to March) is hazardous. **Motel Irama Bachok** (☎ 778 8462; r from RM75; 🛏) has all right chalet-style accommodation. From the central bus station in Kota Bharu, buses 23 and 39 (RM2) run out to Pantai Irama.

Pantai Seri Tujuh (Beach of Seven Lagoons), just 5km from the Thai border, is an undeveloped stretch of sand on a long spit, backed by a quiet bay. It's very serene and lonely; if this appeals, there are rooms at **Chalet Sri Tujuh** (☎ 721 1753; r RM48-150; 🛏) and a few food stalls near the beach.

Tumpat District

Nowhere else in Malaysia is as Thai as Tumpat, a green quilt of rice paddies, villages, mud paths and smooth roads between Kota Bharu and the border. This is a culturally porous hinterland, not quite of one nation or the other. The main attractions here are Buddhist temples that, while Thai in origin, are culturally Malay-Chinese-Thai in execution. Chinese guardian deities and laughing Buddhas often share space with typically fiery, golden Thai religious imagery; if you're into Asian art, it's quite a fascinating culture clash.

Pengkalan Kubor is an exit point for Thailand, while Tumpat town is the terminus of the railway line, although it has no hotels or attractions. The best way to see the temples is on an organised tour from Kota Bharu (p330). Visiting more than one or two places using public transport and walking long distances in the heat is likely to be a trying experience, and with poor signposting, even local drivers sometimes get lost.

TEMPLES

Numerous Buddhist temples are found all over the region, and **Wesak Day** (a celebration of Buddha's life, usually held in April or May) is a particularly good time to visit.

Supposedly one of the largest Buddhist temples in Southeast Asia, **Wat Phothivihan** boasts a 40m-long reclining Buddha statue, erected in 1973. There are some smaller shrines within the grounds, as well as a canteen and a resthouse for use by sincere devotees, for a donation. To get here, take bus 19 or 27 from Kota Bharu to Chabang Empat. Get off at the crossroads and turn left (southwest). Walk 3.5km along this road, through postcard villages and paddies, until you reach Kampung Jambu and the reclining Buddha (about one hour).

At Chabang Empat, if you take the turn to the right (north) at the light in front of the police station, you will come to **Wat Kok Seraya** after about 1km, which houses a modest standing female Buddha. While the temple's architecture is Thai, the female Buddha is more Chinese in origin, which is probably attributable to most Buddhists here being of Chinese origin. Continuing north about 4km towards Tumpat, you will come to **Wat Pikulthong**, housing an impressive gold mosaic standing Buddha. You can get to both wats on bus 19; continue past Chabang Empat and ask the driver to let you off.

Around 4km north of Chabang Empat near the village of Kampung Bukit Tanah is **Wat Maisuwankiri**. A richly decorated dragon

---

THE JUNGLE RAILWAY

Commencing in Tumpat, the so-called jungle railway runs through Kuala Krai, Gua Musang, Kuala Lipis and Jerantut (the access point for Taman Negara), and eventually meets the Singapore–KL railway line at Gemas. The local trains stop almost everywhere and don't strictly adhere to posted schedules; contact the train station for the latest timetable.

---

boat surrounded by a channel of murky water constitutes the 'floating temple', but of more interest may be the preserved body of a former abbot kept on somewhat morbid public display. The bus from Kota Bharu to Pengkalan Kubor stops outside the temple.

Also worth a look is **Wat Matchinmaram** with its magnificent 50m-high seated Buddha (more Chinese than Thai, but also decorated with an Indian-origin dharma wheel), allegedly the largest of its type in Asia. Just across the road from here is **Sala Pattivetaya**, a Thai temple and village complex dotted with colourful statues. They are located about 2km south of Tumpat.

PENGKALAN KUBOR

Right on the Thai border, Pengkalan Kubor is the immigration checkpoint for this little-used back route into Thailand. During the day a large car ferry (RM1 for pedestrians) crosses the river to busy Tak Bai in Thailand. From Kota Bharu, take bus 27 or 43 (RM2.40) from the central bus station.

GUNUNG STONG STATE PARK

The wildest, woolliest area of Kelantan is its southern jungle interior, accessible via the so-called Jungle Railway. This line, which cuts through peninsular Malaysia's mountainous backbone, still evokes a feeling of tropical frontier adventure – the greenery is lush and presses in on all sides, and you generally feel a world away from the comparative modernity of urban, and even agricultural Malaysia. If you're exploring here, head for the savagely beautiful **Gunung Stong State Park**, named for the granite rock formation that dominates the surrounding wilderness. Once known as the 'Jelawang Jungle', the park consists of 21,962 hectares of remote, sparsely inhabited green: sharp mountain

peaks, thickly matted vegetation, the world's largest flower (the rafflesia, see p432) and Stong Waterfalls, reputed to be the highest in Southeast Asia.

Due to infrequent transport links, it can be frustrating to visit this area without your own wheels, unless you do it via a tour organised in Kota Bharu (p330). The main base for exploring is Dabong, located on the jungle railway (it's more scenic to arrive by riverboat from Kuala Krai if you're coming from that direction). There are several caves in the limestone outcrops a few kilometres southeast of town; **Gua Ikan** (Fish Cave) is the most accessible, but the most impressive is **Stepping Stone Cave**, a narrow 30m corridor through a limestone wall that leads to a hidden grotto and on to **Kris Cave**. These latter two should not be attempted by claustrophobics.

From Dabong, cross Sungai Galas for 80 sen and take a minivan (RM3) out to the **falls** on 1422m-high Gunung Stong. The main falls are a 20-minute climb past the forgettable Perdana Stong Resort; a further 45 minutes of climbing brings you to the top of the falls and a camp site. From the base of **Baha's Camp** you can make longer excursions to the summit of **Gunung Stong** and the upper falls; most tour companies divide the trek into three checkpoints. A combination of jungle mist and mountain fog can make for hazy conditions, but on good days you get the sense you're climbing over clouds humming with the screams of animals in the jungle below.

Rumah Rehat Dabong (☎ 09-744 0725; r from RM25; ✿) is a 1980s longhouse and the only decent place for independent travellers to stay in Dabong; ask at the district office opposite the resthouse. There's the usual collection of food stalls near Dabong station. If you come on an organised tour, you'll be directed to your guides' camp sites, which tend to be of good quality.

GUA MUSANG

The town is named after the caves in the limestone outcrop towering above the train station. The *musang* is a native civet that looks like a *cross between* a large cat and a possum, but you're unlikely to see one, as hunters have killed off most of these cave dwellers. It's possible to explore the caves, but it's a very steep, hazardous climb to the entrance, which is above the *kampung* next to the railway line, 150m from the train station (walk south along the train tracks). Don't attempt the climb in wet conditions and be sure to take a torch (flashlight). A guide is recommended.

Once you complete the dangerous climb to the caves, you'll have to shimmy through a narrow opening and do some scrambling to reach the main chamber, which extends some 150m before opening onto the opposite side of the mountain. There are no views, but the chamber is impressive.

There are several hotels on the main road that leads away from the train station. The best of these is **Evergreen Hotel** (☎ 09-912 2273; s/d from RM32/50; ✷) on the left just before the bend in the road. The amusingly named **Fully Inn** (☎ 09-912 3311; r from RM90; ✷) is a little more polished (and has a karaoke lounge!), although some rooms are definitely overpriced.

Bus 57 to/from Kota Bharu costs RM12, and Gua Musang is also on the jungle railway. You can organise tours of Gunung Musang from Kota Bharu; see p330.

Sabah

Malaysia's state of Sabah proves that there is a god, and we're pretty sure that he's some sort of mad scientist. Sabah was his giant test tube – the product of a harebrained hypothesis. You see, on the seventh day, god wasn't taking his infamous rest, he was pondering the following: 'what would happen if I took an island, covered it with impenetrable jungle, tossed in an ark's worth of animals, and turned up the temperature to a sweltering 40°C?'

The result? A tropical Eden with prancing mega-fauna and plenty of fruit-bearing trees. This 'land below the wind', as it's known, is home to great ginger apes that swing from vine-draped trees, blue-hued elephants that stamp along marshy river deltas and sun-kissed wanderers who slide along the silver sea in bamboo boats. Oh but there's more: mighty Mt Kinabalu rises to the heavens, governing the steamy wonderland below with its imposing stone turrets. The muddy Sungai Kinabatangan roars through the jungle – a haven for fluorescent birds and cheeky macaques. And finally there's Sipadan's seductive coral reef, luring large pelagics with a languid, come-hither wave.

In order to make the most of *your* days of rest, we strongly encourage you to plan ahead. Sabah's jungles may be wild and untamed, but they're covered in streamers of red tape. With a bit of patience and a lot of preplanning, you'll breeze by the permit restrictions and booked beds. Independent travellers may find Sabah a bit frustrating, but we promise that the hoop-jumping is well worth it.

HIGHLIGHTS

- Smiling in your scuba mask while doing the backstroke past tranquil turtles, slippery sharks and technicolour coral in the **Semporna Archipelago** (p388)

- Hoofing it over pitcher plants and granite moonscapes for the ultimate Bornean sunrise atop **Mt Kinabalu** (p357)

- Pressing your binoculars tight against your face as you spot soaring hornbills and nest-weaving orang-utans along the mighty **Sungai Kinabatangan** (p379)

- Getting ape close and personal with our ginger-haired cousins at the **Sepilok Orang-Utan Rehabilitation Centre** (p375)

- Enjoying vistas of green as far as the eye can see in the protected old-growth (primary) forest of the **Danum Valley** (p384)

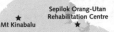

★ Mt Kinabalu

Sepilok Orang-Utan
Rehabilitation Centre ★

Sungai Kinabatangan ★

★ Danum Valley
Conservation Area

★ Semporna
Archipelago

- TELEPHONE CODE: 087, 088, 089
- POPULATION: 3.39 MILLION
- AREA: 76,115 SQ KM

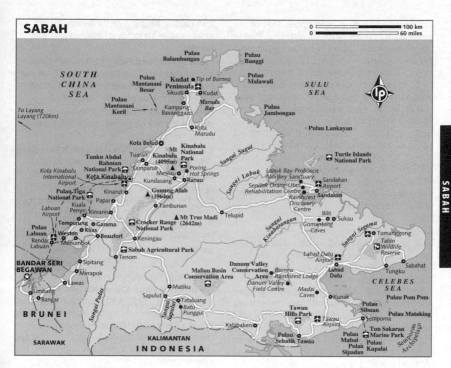

SABAH

0 ─────── 100 km
0 ─────── 60 miles

SOUTH CHINA SEA

To Layang Layang (120km)

Pulau Balambangan

Pulau Banggi

Kudat • Tip of Borneo
Pulau Mantanani Besar
Pulau Mantanani Kecil
Kudat Peninsula
Sikuati • Kudat
Kampung Bavanggazo
Marudu Bay

Pulau Malawali

SULU SEA

Pulau Jambongan

Pulau Lankayan

Kota Marudu

Kota Belud
Tunku Abdul Rahman National Park
Kinabalu National Park
Mt Kinabalu (4095m)
Tuaran
Tamparuli
Poring Hot Springs
Mesilau
Ranau
Kundasang

Sungai Sugut

Turtle Islands National Park

Kota Kinabalu International Airport
Kota Kinabalu
Kinarut
Papar
Gunung Afab (1964m)
Labuk Bay Proboscis Monkey Sanctuary
Sepilok Orang-Utan Rehabilitation Centre
Sungai Labuk
Labuk
Sandakan Airport
Sandakan

Pulau Tiga National Park
Kuala Penyu
Kimanis
Tambunan
Mt Trus Madi (2642m)
Telupid
Rainforest Discovery Centre
Bilit
Sukau

Labuan Airport
Tempurung
Garama
Crocker Range National Park
Sungai Kinabatangan
Gomantong Caves
Sungai Segama
Tomanggong

Pulau Labuan
Bandar Labuan
Weston
Klias
Beaufort
Keningau

Tabin Wildlife Reserve

BANDAR SERI BEGAWAN

Menumbok
Sabah Agricultural Park
Tenom
Lahad Datu

Sipitang
Merapok
Maliau Basin Conservation Area
Danum Valley Conservation Area
Borneo Rainforest Lodge
Danum Valley Field Centre
Lahad Datu

Sabahat

CELEBES SEA

Lawas
Matiku
Madai Caves

Limbang
Bangar
Sapulut
Tataluang
Batu Punggul
Kunak

Pulau Pom Pom

BRUNEI

Sungai Padas
Sungai Sapulut
Tawau Hills Park
Tawau
Tawau Airport

Pulau Sibuan
Pulau Mataking
Semporna

SARAWAK
KALIMANTAN
INDONESIA
Kalabakan
Pulau Sebatik
Tawau
Pulau Mabul
Pulau Sipadan
Tun Sakaran Marine Park
Pulau Kapalai
Sempornan Archipelago

SABAH

History

After centuries as a pawn in various Southeast Asian power games, Sabah was neatly carved up by enterprising British business in the late 19th century, when it was known as North Borneo and administered by the British North Borneo Company. After WWII Sabah and Sarawak were handed over to the British government, and both decided to merge with the peninsular states to form the new nation of Malaysia in 1963.

However, Sabah's natural wealth attracted other prospectors and its existence as a state was disputed by two powerful neighbours – Indonesia and the Philippines. There are still close cultural ties between the people of Sabah and the Filipinos of the nearby Sulu Archipelago and Mindanao, through not always manifested positively: several small islands to the north of Sabah are disputed by the Philippines, there's a busy smuggling trade, Muslim rebels often retreat down towards Sabah when pursued by government forces, and pirates based in the Sulu Sea continue to raid parts of Sabah's coast.

After independence, Sabah was governed for a time by Tun Mustapha, who ran the state almost as a private fiefdom and was often at odds with the federal government in Kuala Lumpur (KL). Even when the Parti Bersatu Sabah (PBS; Sabah United Party, controlled by the Kadazan indigenous group) came to power in 1985 and joined Barisan National (BN), Malaysia's ruling coalition party, tensions with the federal government were rife. In 1990 the PBS pulled out of the alliance with BN just days before the general election. The PBS claimed that the federal government was not equitably returning the wealth that the state generated, and in 1993 it banned the export of logs from Sabah, largely to reinforce this point. The federal government used its powers to overturn the ban, and despite ongoing discussions, to this day nothing has changed – only a small percent of revenue trickles back into state coffers.

As a result of this imbalance and its bad relations with the federal government, Sabah is the poorest of Malaysia's states, with an unemployment rate twice the national average (which is around 3.5%). Although the state is rich in natural resources, 16% of the population lives below the poverty line. Part of the problem is a bizarre rotation system that forces a change of political administration every two years (see the boxed text, p43).

To compound the economic difficulties, Sabah has experienced an extraordinary population boom over the last couple of decades – in 1970 the total number of inhabitants was under 650,000, whereas now it's nearing 3.5 million. The government attributes this to illegal immigrants, claiming that there are around 1.5 million foreigners in the state, but whatever the truth, a solution will need to be found in the next few years for Sabah's stretched resources.

Climate

Like the rest of Malaysia, Sabah's climate is hot and humid. Expect temperatures in the high 20s and low 30s throughout the lowlands. The state's rainfall averages about 300cm annually and though it rains throughout the year, the heaviest rainfall generally occurs between November and April. At higher elevations the temperature is refreshingly cool and downright cold at night. Mt Kinabalu has its own climate and, above 3500m, temperatures can drop to freezing.

Visas & Permits

Sabah is semi-autonomous, and like Sarawak it has its own immigration controls. On arrival most nationalities are likely to be given a visa for three months' stay (on top of any time they had previously spent in Peninsular Malaysia). It is rare to be asked to show money or onward tickets.

Visas can be renewed at immigration offices at or near most points of arrival. If you miss the expiry date you can report to another immigration office, even if it's several days later, and explain your situation to the officials. For information on organising permits, see opposite.

National Parks & Reserves

Sabah's national parks are among the main reasons tourists visit the state. They include:

Crocker Range National Park (139 sq km) Preserving a huge swathe of forested escarpment overlooking the coast, this park has no facilities; see p396.

Kinabalu National Park (754 sq km) Easily accessible from Kota Kinabalu (KK), this is the state's largest and most popular national park. It offers mountain-trekking at Mt Kinabalu, forest walks at the headquarters and Mesilau, and the hot springs at Poring; see p357, p365 and p365.

Pulau Tiga National Park (15 sq km) Three islands 50km southwest of KK: one formed by volcanic mud eruptions, one famous for sea snakes and the third virtually washed away by wave action; see p399.

Tawau Hills Park (29 sq km) Near Tawau in the state's southeast, this park has forested volcanic hills, waterfalls and hot springs; see p394.

Tun Sakaran Marine Park (325 sq km) Protects some of the best reef dive sites in the world; see p388.

Tunku Abdul Rahman (TAR) National Park (49 sq km) A group of five islands, one quite large, a few kilometres west of the capital. Features include beaches, snorkelling and hiking; see p354.

Turtle Islands National Park (17 sq km) Three tiny islands 40km north of Sandakan, protecting the nesting ground of green and hawksbill sea turtles; see p379.

The Sabah Foundation runs two reserves: the **Danum Valley Conservation Area** (p384) and the **Maliau Basin** (p394), and a third area, Imbak Canyon, is currently in the works. The **Tabin Wildlife Reserve** (p386) is managed by both the Forestry and the Wildlife Departments, though a private company manages the visitor facilities.

Tours

Independent travel in Sabah is limited compared to neighbouring Sarawak, and most travellers will have to rely on tour outfits at some point. Sabah has a huge number of tour operators, mostly based in Kota Kinabalu. A good operator can make life easier if you're short on time, and some places are simply too expensive or too much hassle to visit independently. If you run into problems with a tour agency, take your complaint to the **Sabah Tourism Board** (p344).

Getting There & Away

There are regular flights connecting Kota Kinabalu to a variety of international cities including Singapore, Manila, Shenzhen, Bandar Seri Begawan, Hong Kong, Cebu, Guangzhou, Macau, Seoul and Jakarta. Most visitors arrive at the state capital, Kota Kinabalu (KK), by air or boat, but it is possible to travel into Sabah overland from Sarawak via Brunei (see p593), and by boat, from Kalimantan (Indonesia; p393).

SABAH

GAINING ENTRY TO THE WORLD'S BIGGEST THEME PARK

They call Sabah 'The World's Largest Themepark', and like any good attraction, Sabah has lines. You won't see frowning tourists queuing for their turn on the ride – instead you'll find disgruntled adventurers snared by red tape. As we researched our way across the island, we encountered scores of vacationers lamenting booked beds, or bemoaning being barred from national parks. So, we're coming right out and saying it – plan ahead!

The best way to get the most out of a Sabahan sojourn is to develop an itinerary before you arrive. Check out a couple of our suggested routes in the Itineraries section p24 to get a few ideas. Once you have a good sense of the sights you'd like to visit, find out if those destinations require permits. Mt Kinabalu (p359) and Tun Sakaran Marine Park (Sipadan; p388) are the two most popular spots in Sabah that have stringent visitation regulations imposed by the Malaysian government.

For a Kinabalu climb, it is best to book as far in advance as possible – six months is ideal although usually not feasible for most travellers. Head directly to the Sutera Sanctuary Lodges office in KK (p347) if you did not organise your climb before leaving home – sitting in front of the booking agents will increase your chances of finding a cancellation (although you'll probably have to reshape your itinerary once they offer you an inconvenient ascent date). Most of the beds have been gobbled up by tour operators, so if you can't snag a bed with Sutera, chances are you can find a travel agency around town that can sell you one (at a much higher price of course). Adventurers interested in tackling the mountain's *via ferrata* course should contact Mountain Torq (p359).

To delight in a famous Sipadan scuba session, divers must obtain a permit. You can roll the dice and show up in Semporna hoping to find a golden ticket, but remember, as with any game of luck, the house always wins. Permits could be cloaked in frilly vacation packages, or worse, you could be forced to dive every other site in the Celebes Sea before you're allowed to explore Sipadan's walls. In general, most dive centres in the area are very upstanding operations and can cater to your needs if you book well in advance (four weeks is ideal, but the earlier the better).

Swarms of travel agents in KK will try to convince you that Sabah can only be discovered whilst on a tour. This is simply not true. Yes, there are places like the Danum Valley that cannot be accessed by private vehicle, but hotspots like Sepilok, Sandakan or Sungai Kinabatangan can in fact be explored under your own steam.

Although neighbouring Sarawak lends itself more to a 'do it yourself' adventure, you may still encounter a few logistical snags when trying to hit up some of the more popular sights. Lodging at Gunung Mulu (p452) is limited, and although Bario (p458) does not see tonnes of tourism, the puddle-jumper planes have limited seating.

Getting Around

With the advent of cheap airfares, getting around Sabah has gotten a lot easier...well faster at least. A web of flight routes criss-crosses the state, connecting the capital, Kota Kinabalu, to smaller destinations like Sandakan, Pulau Labuan and Tawau. With a little preplanning you could find a flight that rivals the local bus prices.

A paved road makes a frowning arc from KK to Tawau, passing hotspots like Mt Kinabalu, Sepilok, Sandakan, Lahad Datu and Semporna (the gateway to Sipadan) along the way. Daily express buses service all of these places. It takes around ten hours to make this journey. Completing the loop (circling back to KK through the south) is a more difficult task. An infrastructure of public buses does not yet exist here, however the road is mostly paved. If you can get a lift to Keningau, then the rest of the journey is a breeze.

It's important to note that many of Sabah's natural gems are managed by private organisations, so you may find yourself on a tour more times than not.

KOTA KINABALU

pop 579,300

West Malaysia has KL; East Malaysia has KK. Borneo's version of a capital city isn't the most distinguished spot, especially if it's your welcome mat to the island (as it is for most tourists). Dreams of gorgeous

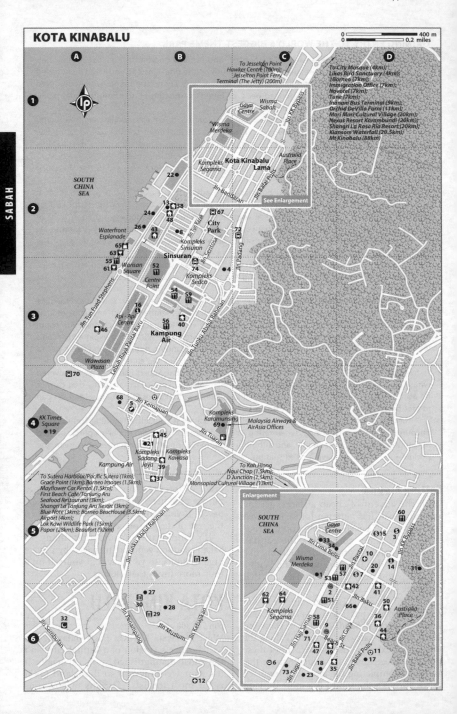

KOTA KINABALU

SABAH

SOUTH CHINA SEA

To Jesselton Point
Hawker Centre (180m);
Jesselton Point Ferry
Terminal (The Jetty) (200m)

To City Mosque (4km);
Likas Bird Sanctuary (4km);
1Borneo (7km);
Immigration Office (7km);
Novotel (7km);
Tune (7km);
Inanam Bus Terminal (9km);
Orchid DeVilla Farm (11km);
Mari Mari Cultural Village (20km);
Nexus Resort Karambunai (20km);
Shangri La Rasa Ria Resort (20km);
Kiansom Waterfall (20.5km);
Mt Kinabalu (88km)

Gaya Centre

Wisma Sabah

Wisma Merdeka

Kota Kinabalu Lama

Kompleks Segama

Australia Place

See Enlargement

City Park

Waterfront Esplanade

Kompleks Sinsuran

Sinsuran

Kompleks Sedco

Warisan Square

Centre Point

Api-Api Centre

Kompleks Sedco

Wawasan Plaza

Kampung Air

KK Times Square

Kampung Air

Kompleks Karamunsing

Malaysia Airways & AirAsia Offices

Kompleks Sadong Jaya

Kompleks Kawasa

To Kah Hiong
Ngui Chap (1.5km);
D Junction (1.5km);
Monsopiad Cultural Village (13km)

To Sutera Harbour/Pacific Sutera (1km);
Grace Point (1km); Borneo Images (1.5km);
Mayflower Car Rental (1.5km);
First Beach Café/Tanjung Aru
Seafood Restaurant (3km);
Shangri La Tanjung Aru Resort (3km);
Blue Note (3km); Borneo BeacHouse (3.5km);
Airport (4km);
Lok Kawi Wildlife Park (15km);
Papar (28km); Beaufort (92km)

Enlargement

SOUTH CHINA SEA

Gaya Centre

Wisma Merdeka

Kompleks Segama

Australia Place

jungles and charming seaside shanties will be quickly abandoned as you glimpse the unattractive grid of concrete structures from your airplane window.

The city is quick to blame its insipid central core on the atrocities of war. Originally founded as Jesselton, KK was razed by the Allies not once but twice during WWII, the first time to slow the Japanese advance and the second time to hasten their retreat. After the war the whole thing was rebuilt from scratch, and renamed Kota Kinabalu in 1963.

You'll end up spending a day or two in KK if you're game to see a number of Sabah's attractions, so make the most of your stay and eat your way across town. Steaming street noodles and fresher-than-fresh seafood beckon the palate, and the bar scene ain't half bad for a Muslim nation. If you're really stuck for things to do, ask the locals what the word 'Kinabalu' means. We're not gonna tell you the answer – namely because

there are a dozen different definitions – but we're pretty sure that you'll find them all rather interesting…

ORIENTATION

Downtown KK is a dense grid of concrete buildings nestled between the waterfront and a range of low, forested hills to the east. It's compact, walkable and easy to navigate – most of the restaurants, markets, accommodation, tourist offices and tour operators are located here. Transport terminals bookend the city on either side. The international airport is in Tanjung Aru, 7km south of central KK, while the Inanam bus station is 9km north.

There is a huge outdoor map at the beginning of Jln Gaya facing City Hall.

INFORMATION
Bookshops
Borneo Books 2 (☎ 088-538077; Ground fl, Phase 1, Wisma Merdeka; www.borneobooks.com ☒ 10am-7pm)

A brilliant selection of Borneo-related books, maps & a small used-book section. Plenty of those useful Lonely Planet guides too. Wink.

Consulates

Indonesian Consulate (☎ 088-218600; Lg Kemajuan, Karamunsing; ☒ 9am-5pm Mon-Fri)

Emergency

Ambulance (☎ 999 or 088-218166)
Fire (☎ 994 or 088-214822)
Police (☎ 999, 088-212092; Jln Dewan)

Internet Access

Every sleeping spot in town also has some form of internet connection, be it dial-up or wi-fi.

Borneo Net (Jln Haji Saman; ☒ 9am-midnight; per hr RM3) Twenty terminals, fast connections and loud headbanger music wafting through the air.

Net Access (Jln Pantai; ☒ 9-2am; per hr RM3) Plenty of connections and less noise than other net places in KK. LAN connections are available for using your own laptop.

Immigration Office

Immigration office (☎ 088-488700; Kompleks Persekutuan Pentadbiran Kerajaan, Jln UMS; ☒ 8am-1pm & 2-5pm Mon-Thu, 8-11.30am & 2-5pm Fri)

Laundry

Hotel laundry service works out to be the same price as buying new clothes at the market – use an outside service instead.

Mega Laundry (☎ 088-238970; Ruang Sinsuran 2; ☒ 8am-8pm; per kilo RM6) This fast and efficient laundry is one of the few in KK open on Sunday. Ask them not to write your name on your laundry.

Maps

The Sabah Tourism Board (right) sells an excellent map of Sabah for RM2. Free maps of central KK are available at almost every hostel or hotel.

Medical Services

Permai Polyclinic (☎ 088-232100; 4 Jln Pantai) Private outpatient clinic.
Queen Elizabeth Hospital (☎ 088-218166; Jln Penampang) Past the Sabah Museum.

Money

Moneychangers are plentiful in KK, particularly in the Wisma Merdeka and Centre Point malls; they are more convenient than banks, and sometimes have better rates.

HSBC (☎ 088-212622; 56 Jln Gaya; ☒ 9am-4.30pm Mon-Thu, 9am-4pm Fri) 24hr ATM.
Maybank (☎ 088-254295; 9 Jln Pantai; ☒ 9am-4.30pm Mon-Thu, 9am-4pm Fri) 24hr ATM.
Standard Chartered Bank (☎ 088-298111; 20 Jln Haji Saman; ☒ 9.15am-3.45pm Mon-Fri) 24hr ATM.

Post

Main Post Office (☎ 088-210855; Jln Tun Razak; ☒ 8am-5pm Mon-Fri) Western Union cheques and money orders can be cashed here. Has an efficient poste restante counter.

Tourist Information

Sabah Tourism Board (☎ 088-212121; www.sabah tourism.com; 51 Jln Gaya; ☒ 8am-5pm Mon-Fri, 8am-4pm Sat, 9am-4pm Sun) Housed in the historic post office building, KK's main tourist office has helpful staff and a wide range of brochures, pamphlets and other information covering every aspect of independent and tour travel in Sabah. Ask about their homestay program.

Tourism Malaysia (☎ 088-248698; www.tourism.gov .my; Ground fl, Api-Api Centre, Jln Pasar Baru; ☒ 8am-4.30pm Mon-Thu, 8am-noon & 1.30-4.30pm Fri) This office is of limited use for travellers, but does offer a few interesting brochures on sights in Peninsular Malaysia.

Sabah Parks (☎ 088-211881; Lot 1-3, Ground fl, Block K, Kompleks Sinsuran, Jln Tun Fuad Stephens; ☒ 8am-1pm & 2-4.30pm Mon-Thu, 8-11.30am & 2-4.30pm Fri, 8am-12.50pm Sat) Good source of information on the state's parks.

Borneo Images (☎ 088-270733; Suite A33A, 3rd fl, Tanjung Aru Plaza; ☒ 9am-5pm Mon-Fri, 9am-1pm Sat) A beautiful and informative gallery inspiring travel throughout the region. Definitely worth stopping by to get a photographer's perspective of Borneo.

SIGHTS
City Centre

For a guided walk of the city's historical centre, try the **KK Heritage Walk** (☎ 012-802 8823; www.kkheritagewalk.com; RM200; ☒ 9am Tue & Thu). The two-hour tour, which can also be booked through several tour operators, explores colonial KK and its hidden delights. Stops include Chinese herbal shops, bulk produce stalls, a *kopitiam* (coffee shop) and Jln Gaya (known as Bond Street when the British were in charge). There's also a quirky treasure hunt at the end leading tourists to the Jesselton Hotel. Guides speak English, Chinese and Bahasa Malaysia.

You can wander up to the UFO-like observation pavilion on **Signal Hill**, at the eastern edge of the city centre, to escape the traffic and to get another take on the squatters' stilt village at Pulau Gaya. The view is best as the sun sets over the islands. From the top, it's also possible to hike down to the bird sanctuary on the other side.

The modest timepiece at the foot of the hill is the **Atkinson Clock Tower**, one of the only structures to survive the Allied bombing of Jesselton in 1945. It's a square, 15.7m-high wooden structure that was completed in 1905 and named after the first district officer of the town, FG Atkinson, who died of malaria aged 28.

SABAH MUSEUM COMPLEX

The **Sabah Museum** (☎ 088-253199; jmuzium@tm.net .my; Jln Muzium; RM15; ◷ 9am-5pm Sat-Thu) is centred on a modern four-storey structure inspired by the longhouses of the Rungus and Murut tribes. It's slightly south of the city centre, on the hilly corner of Jln Tunku Abdul Rahman and Jln Penampang.

In the main building there are good permanent collections of tribal and historical artefacts, including ceramics, and some nicely presented exhibits of flora and fauna. The prehistory gallery even has a replica limestone cave, in case you don't make it to any of the real ones!

In the gardens, the **Heritage Village** offers the chance to wander round examples of traditional tribal dwellings, including Kadazan bamboo houses and a Chinese farmhouse, all nicely set on a lily-pad lake.

The adjoining **Science & Education Centre** has an informative exhibition on the petroleum industry, from drilling to refining and processing. The **Sabah Art Gallery** features regular shows and exhibitions by local artists.

A short walk towards town is another annexe, the **Museum of Islamic Civilisation** (☎ 088-538234; admission included in the Sabah Museum ticket; ◷ 9am-5pm Sat-Thu), devoted to Muslim culture and history.

If you're heading east after KK, keep hold of your admission ticket – it will also allow you entry to Agnes Keith House (p372) in Sandakan.

To get to the museum complex, catch a bus (RM1) along Jln Tunku Abdul Rahman and get off just before the mosque. Bus 13 also goes right round past the Queen Elizabeth hospital and stops near Jln Muzium.

MOSQUES

A fine example of contemporary Islamic architecture, the **State Mosque** (Jln Tunku Abdul Rahman) is set some distance from the heat and noise of central KK. It's south of the city centre past the Kampung Air stilt village, not far from the Sabah Museum; you'll see the striped minaret and Octopussy-style dome on your way to or from the airport. Non-Muslim visitors are allowed inside, but must dress appropriately and remove their shoes before entering.

Heading north out of KK, you can't miss the four minarets and graceful dome of the Kota Kinabalu **City Mosque** (off Jln Tun Fuad Stephens), in Kampung Likas, about 4km north of the city centre. Overlooking the South China Sea, this mosque is more attractive than the State Mosque in terms of setting and design. Completed in 2000, it can hold up to 12,000 worshippers. It can be entered by non-Muslims outside of regular prayer times. To get there, take bus 5A from Wawasan Plaza going toward UMS (RM1.50). Just ask the conductor to drop you off outside the City Mosque after the Tanjung Lipat round about. Taxis are about RM15 each way.

LIKAS BIRD SANCTUARY

Opened in 2000 and protected by the WWF, the **Likas Bird Sanctuary** (☎ 088-246955; kkcbs@tm.net .my; Jln Bukit Bendera Upper; adult/child RM10/5; ◷ 8am-6pm Tue-Sun) sits across from the mosque, covering 24 hectares of mangrove swamp. The preserve attracts a variety of migratory birds, some from as far away as Siberia. To reach the bird sanctuary, see the directions to the City Mosque (above).

MARKETS

KK's brilliant **Night Market** (Jln Tun Fuad Stephens; ◷ late afternoon-11pm) is a place of delicious contrasts: it huddles beneath the imposing Le Meridien as venders hawk their knock-off wares. The market is divided into two main sections: the southwest end is given over mostly to produce, while the northeast end (the area around the main entrance) is a huge hawker centre, where you can eat your way right through the entire Malay gastronomy. If you've never seen a proper Southeast Asian market, this place will be a revelation.

KK's vast **Central Market** (Jln Tun Fuad Stephens; ◷ 6.30am-6pm) occupies a long stretch of waterfront real estate in the middle of town. While it's not as interesting as the Night Market, it's fun to wander the aisles and watch as locals transact their daily business.

Sandwiched between the Central Market and the Night Market, the **Handicraft Market** (Filipino Market; Jln Tun Fuad Stephens; 10am-6pm) is a good place to shop for inexpensive souvenirs. Offerings include pearls, textiles, seashell crafts, jewellery and bamboo goods, some from the Philippines, some from Malaysia and some from other parts of Asia. Needless to say, bargaining is a must!

On Sundays, a lively Chinese street fair takes over the entire length of **Jalan Gaya**. If you're not digging the KK vibe, this manic market will change your mind.

Beyond the City Centre

Some of KK's best attractions are located beyond the city centre, and it's well worth putting in the effort to check 'em out.

MARI MARI CULTURAL VILLAGE

Located about 25 minutes outside of the city centre, the **Mari Mari Cultural Village** (019-820 4921; www.traversetours.com, Jln Kiansom; adult/child RM150/130) is the most interactive centre of its kind in all of Borneo. Visitors are taken on a three-hour show/tour (beginning at 10am, 3pm and 7pm), which winds through the jungle passing various tribal dwellings along the way. At each stop, tourists learn about the indigenous way of life, and can try their hand at a variety of interesting (and fun) activities, like traditional bamboo cooking, rice-wine making (and drinking!), fire starting, tattooing, blowpipe shooting etc. But the most fascinating part of the tour is little tribal titbits offered by your guide. For example, in the Dusun tribe, an immense stone would be placed at the entrance of a longhouse as a testament to the strength of warriors living inside. In the Lundaya tribe a knife must always be kept over the mouth of a rice wine bottle to ensure that no evil spirits mix with the wine. A short dance recital and delicious meal (lunch or dinner depending on the time of visitation) are included in the visit – the centre must be notified of any dietary restrictions in advance. A trip to the cultural village can be combined with a white-water rafting tour (see opposite for more information).

There is also a small chute – **Kiansom Waterfall** (RM1; dawn-dusk) – about 400m beyond the cultural village, which is easily accessible by private transport or on foot. The area around the cascade lends itself well to swimming and it's a great place to cool off after a visit to Mari Mari.

Travellers interested in plant life should consider a visit to the **Orchid DeVilla Farm** (088-380611; orchiddevilla@yahoo.com, www.orchid-de-villa.com.my; Jln Kiansom; 8am-5pm), located halfway between central KK and the cultural village (at 'Km 6'). The farm specialises in rare Bornean orchids, hybrid orchids, cacti and herbal plants, and services all of the five-star hotels in the region.

MONSOPIAD CULTURAL VILLAGE

In the small town of Penampang, about 13km south of KK, this high-quality Kadazan-Dusun **cultural village** (088-761336; www.monsopiad.com; RM65; 8.30am-5pm) on the banks of Sungai Moyog is named after a legendary warrior and headhunter, whose direct descendants established this private heritage centre in 1996. The hefty entrance fee includes a tour, a dance performance and several activities (similar to Mari Mari). The highlight is the House of Skulls, which supposedly contains the ancient crania of Monsopiad's unfortunate enemies, as well as artefacts illustrating native rituals from the time when the *bobolian* (priest) was the most important figure in the community.

Many tour companies include Monsopiad on local itineraries. To get here independently, take a bus from central KK to Donggongon (RM1), where you can catch a minivan to the cultural village (RM1). You can also take a taxi or charter a minivan direct from KK for around RM35.

LOK KAWI WILDLIFE PARK

If you'd like to check out the orang-utans but won't make it out to Sepilok or the Kinabatangan, a visit to **Lok Kawi Wildlife Park** (088-765710; Jln Penampang, Papar Lama; adult/child RM20/10; 9.30am-5.30pm) is highly recommended, especially for those with children in tow. There are plenty of other animals as well, from tarsiers to rhinos. Don't miss the giant aviary at the top of hill, with its ominous warning sign 'beware of attacking birds'!

It's best to arrive by 9.50am at the latest – feedings take place throughout the park at 10am. After the various feedings, an interactive show takes place at the stage around 11.15am everyday. After feeding time, most of the animals take their daily siesta – only the humans are silly enough to stay out in the scorching midday sun.

The 17B minibus goes to Lok Kawi (RM2). Visitors with a private vehicle can access the park via the Papar–Penampang road or the Putatan–Papar road. Travel agents offer half-day tours, or you can hire a taxi, which will cost around RM100, including a two-hour wait.

TOURS

KK has a huge number of tour companies, enough to suit every taste and budget. Head to Wisma Sabah – this office building is full of agents and operators. We've listed tour operators for relevant destinations throughout this chapter, so check each section to scout out the best company for you. The following options have an office in KK and offer a broad range of reputable tours.

Borneo Adventure (☎ 088-486800; www.borneo adventure.com; Block E-27-3A, Signature Office, KK Times Square) Award-winning Sarawak-based company with very professional staff, imaginative sightseeing and activity itineraries and a genuine interest in local people and the environment.

Borneo Authentic (☎ 088-773066; www.borneo -authentic.com) A friendly operation offering a variety of package tours including day-trip cruises on the Klias River.

Borneo Divers (☎ 088-222226; www.borneodivers .info; 9th fl, Menara Jubili, 53 Jln Gaya) Longest-established Borneo dive outfit; can arrange courses and dives just about anywhere and has its own dive shop. It's possible to get discounted rates as a walk-in.

Borneo Eco Tours (☎ 088-438300; www.borneo ecotours.com; Pusat Perindustrian Kolombong Jaya, Mile 5.5 Jln Kolombong) This is a place with a good reputation, arranging tours throughout Malaysian Borneo, including travel to the Kinabatangan area.

Borneo Nature Tours (☎ 088-267637; www.borneo naturetours.com; Block D, Lot 10 Kompleks Sadong Jaya) Professional and knowledgeable operation managing bookings for Danum Valley's beautiful Borneo Rainforest Lodge (p385).

John Nair (☎ 019-811 2117; nair_john@yahoo.com) Not technically a company – John is a freelance guide who helped the BBC produce the orang-utan documentary shown regularly at Sepilok. He offers private guiding services and usually hangs out at Hunter's (p352) in the lobby of the Kinabalu Daya.

Sutera Sanctuary Lodges (☎ 088-243629; www .suterasanctuarylodges.com; Lot G15, Ground fl, Wisma Sabah, Jln Haji Saman; ⏰ 9am-6.30pm Mon-Fri, 9am-4.30pm Sat, 9am-3pm Sun) Make this your first stop in KK if you're planning to climb Kinabalu and didn't book your bed in advance. Go now! Hurry!

Traverse Tours (☎ 088-260501; www.traversetours.com; Lot 227, Wisma Sabah, Jln Tun Fuad Stephens) An excellent and forward-thinking operator with plenty of new products.

SLEEPING
Budget

Although Kuching's backpacker scene is a bit more design oriented, KK delivers with sheer volume. Hostels proliferate faster than horny rabbits in Sabah's gateway city, and intense competition equals lower rates. If you want to window-shop before dropping your rucksack, head to 'Australia Place' when you arrive in town. This area, orbiting the Sabah Tourism Board, is stacked to the brim with pleasant budget options.

Recently, a group of budget hotel and hostel owners have banded together to form the **Sabah Backpacker Operators Association** (SBA; www .sabahbackpackers.com) in an effort to help shoe-string travellers in the region. Check out their website for discount deals on accommodation and tours.

Lucy's Homestay (Backpacker's Lodge; ☎ 088-261495; Lot 25, Lg Dewan, Australia Pl; dm/s/d incl breakfast RM18/45/50) We have a soft spot for lovely Lucy and her homey homestay in the Australia Place. There's loads of charm here, with wooden walls smothered in stickers, business cards and crinkled photographs. If you're looking for a quaint home away from home, you'll find it here. Laundry service starts at RM15 per load.

Akinabalu Youth Hostel (☎ 088-272188; akinabaluyh@ yahoo.com; Lot 133, Jln Gaya; dm/r incl breakfast from RM20/50) Friendly staff, fuchsia accent walls and trickling Zen fountains make this a solid option among KK's hostels, particularly if you find a quiet time to take advantage of the gratis internet and DVDs. Accommodation is mostly in basic four-bed rooms, with windows facing an interior hallway.

Summer Lodge (☎ 088-244499; www.summerlodge .com.my; Lot 120, Jln Gaya; dm/d RM28/65; ✂ 💻) Summer Lodge feels a bit like a bed factory, with mattresses indiscriminately stuffed behind every door. Quality varies so you'll probably have to check out a few rooms before you find a comfy one. The friendly owners also run a hostel (dorm beds/doubles from RM25/60) near the base of Mt Kinabalu (1.5km away). Transport between accommodation costs RM17 (one way).

Step-In Lodge (☎ 088-233519; www.stepinlodge.com; Block L, Kompleks Sinsuran, Jln Tun Fuad Stephens; dm with fan/air-con RM28/38, d with fan/air-con RM70/90; ✂ 💻) This popular spot wins the award for KK's smartest hostel with larger-than-normal bunk beds, comfy mattresses, *real* coffee at breakfast, and an excellent (not to mention knowledgeable) staff. These clever touches make Step-In feel much more homey than some of the factory-style operations nearby. Ask about special rates for families.

Green View Lodging (☎ 088-255872; 1336 Jln Mat Salleh; r with shared bathroom from RM68; ✂ ▣) Green View is trying something new by offering simple private accommodation at the lowest price possible. Beds sit on low-slung box springs and there are mini plasma TVs in the deluxe rooms. To reach central KK, it's a RM10 taxi ride, or jump on bus 16, bus 16A or the Penambang bus – all three stop near the front door. Other backpacker options include:

Borneo Backpackers (☎ 088-234009; www.borneoback packers.com; 24 Lg Dewan, Australia Pl; dm/d incl breakfast from RM20/65; ✂ ▣) This long-running backpackers just got a fresh coat of paint (although it's still a bit cramped).

Borneo BeacHouse (☎ 088-218331; www.borneo beachouse.com; 122 Oorong Ikan Lais, Jln Mat Salleh, Tanjung Aru; dm RM22) Rooms are uber-basic, but it's one of the only options around with self-service kitchen facilities, and there's a supermarket down the street. Located near the airport (15-minute walk).

Borneo Global Backpackers (☎ 088-270976; www.bgbackpackers.com; 29 Karamunsing Godown, Jln Karamunsing; dm/r RM25/58; ✂ ▣) Feels a bit like a warehouse, but nonetheless popular with the budget crowd. Located at the southern end of town. Ask about tours to Semporna and Sungai Kinabatangan.

Hamin Lodge (☎ 088-272008; Lot 19, Block C, Kompleks Sedco; www.haminlodge.com; dm/tw from RM28/62; ✂ ▣) A great find. Ten-bed dorms are cramped, but basic private rooms are good value.

Travellers' Light (☎ 088-238877; Lot 19, Lg Dewan, Australia Pl; www.travellerslight.com; dm/d incl breakfast from RM25/65; ✂ ▣) Only a few rooms here, but they're spick and span.

Midrange

Lately, KK's midrange options seem to be sliding towards either end of the budget spectrum. Although backpacker hangouts and top-end treats are in great proliferation, there are still several spots around town suiting those Goldilockses out there.

Rainforest Lodge (☎ 088-258228; Jln Pantai; www.rainforestlodgekk.com; dm/s/d/ste from RM30/98/128/148; ✂ ▣) Fire-engine-red facades are currently luring curious travellers – it's the newest place in town. The deluxe double rooms are quite attractive, but the windowless ones fall a bit short. There are a few overpriced dorm rooms, but this place has much more of a midrange feel.

One Hotel (☎ 088-233234; www.onehotel.com.my; 1 Kompleks Sadong Jaya, Jln Karamunsing; r RM70; ✂) Just outside the city centre in the Sadong Jaya complex, this newer hotel has a cache of small en suite rooms at record-low prices. It's a RM10 cab ride into town and there's a taxi rank conveniently located near the entrance. Wi-fi available.

Kinabalu Daya (☎ 088-240000; www.kkdayahotel.com; Lot 3-4, Block 9, Jln Pantai; r/ste incl breakfast from RM130/240; ✂) Hallways leading to nowhere and strangely placed elevators give Kinabalu Daya a certain 'ten-year-old's-Lego-project' vibe. Nevertheless, tonnes of tourists swear by this midrange stalwart – and we can see why – it's smack dab in the centre of the action and the Best Western branding ensures a certain amount of familiar comfort. It's your best bet for RM140.

D'Borneo Hotel (☎ 088-266999; www.dborneohotel.com; Block L, Kompleks Sinsuran, Jln Tun Fuad Stephens; r from RM140; ✂) The 'D-apostrophe' gives this downtown option a certain je ne sais quoi, but there's nothing particularly boutique about it. The two biggest draws are the exceptionally friendly staff, and the spacious deluxe rooms that feel larger than most rooms in the same price range. Free wi-fi sweetens the deal.

A 'hypermall' complex, 1Borneo, located about 20 minutes north of the city centre, has a few chain hotel options geared towards business travellers (there are roughly 900 hotel rooms on the grounds). A free shuttle bus connects the development to the city centre. Tourists who seek an international standard of comfort and don't mind being removed from the action should consider staying at one of the following options:

Novotel (☎ 088-529888; www.accorhotels.com; 1Borneo Hypermall, Jln UMS; d from RM160; ✂ ▣) A real stunner, but stunningly far from the city centre.

Tune (☎ 03 7962 5888; www.tunehotels.com; 1Borneo Hypermall, Jln UMS; d from RM50; ✂ ▣) Great for small budgets and business travellers.

Top End

Central KK has several full-facility hotels vying for the lucrative top-end trade. Hefty promotional discounts frequently apply outside high season, so you'll seldom have to pay full price if you're looking for a little luxury.

Jesselton Hotel (☎ 088-223333; www.jesseltonhotel.com; 69 Jln Gaya; r from RM 215; ✂) Mock-colonial wood and marble give the place plenty of character, and the single suite even has its own fishpond! There's also a very good restaurant, coffee shop, business centre and a red London

KK GETAWAY

If you've got the dime (and the time) why not turn your KK layover into a luxury beach vacation? Here are two sexy options located just a few kilometres north of the city:

our pick Shangri La Rasa Ria Resort (☎ 088-792888; www.shangri-la.com; Pantai Dalit, Tuaran; r from RM450; ✷ ▭ ☎) This sister resort of the Shangri La Tanjung Aru Resort in KK occupies a fine stretch of peach-hued dunes about 45 minutes north of the KK airport. It's a sprawling resort complete with its own 18-hole golf course, several fine restaurants, an amoeba-esque pool and a relaxing spa. The resort's best feature is the small nature sanctuary with a few resident orangutans – a well-kept secret amongst the locals. The resort will arrange airport transfer from KKIA when you book, otherwise, it's a RM50 taxi-ride from KK.

Nexus Resort Karambunai (☎ 088-411222; www.nexusresort.com; Jln Sepangar Bay, Tuaran; r from RM430; ✷ ▭ ☎) About seven kilometres north of the Rasa Ria Resort, you'll find this snazzy beach resort on Sabah's west coast. Like the Rasa Ria, it's got a great 18-hole golf course, a good slice of sand, a lagoon-like pool, several restaurants and a spa. The standard rooms are getting a little long in the tooth here, so it's better to splurge for a step up. The resort will arrange airport transfer from KKIA when you book, otherwise, it's a RM50 taxi ride from KK.

cab to shuttle you to the airport. Go for a non-smoking room, even smokers will probably find the puff-friendly rooms too 'fragrant'.

Le Meridien Kota Kinabalu (☎ 088-322250; www.kotakinabalu.lemeridien.com; Jln Tun Fuad Stephens; r from RM300; ✷ ▭ ☎) 'If you can't undercut 'em, outclass 'em' seems to be the motto at KK's most central five-star venture, which just reeks of luxury, from the complimentary internet access to the flatscreen TVs and DVD players. The eye-watering prices come down a little in low season, and may even get as low as RM200 if you catch the right discounts.

Promenade Hotel (☎ 088-265555; www.promenade.com.my; Lg Api Api 3; r from RM300; ✷ ☎) Very popular with international tour groups and Malaysian business travellers, this mammoth hotel near the south of the city is right on the foreshore and commands great ocean views. Amenities are plentiful, and discounts of 30% or more make it a solid bargain.

Shangri La Tanjung Aru Resort (STAR; ☎ 088-225800; www.shangri-la.com; Tanjung Aru; r from 700; ✷ ▭ ☎) The Shangri La is the perfect choice for those who want to combine the attractions of Kota Kinabalu with the features of a tropical resort. It's a sprawling complex, dotted with swaying palms and metal gongs, located in the Tanjung Aru area about 3km south of the city centre.

Sutera Harbour (☎ 088-318888; fax 088-317777; www.suteraharbour.com; 1 Sutera Harbour Blvd; r from RM800, packages & discounts available; ✷ ▭ ☎) While not as 'old-world Asia' as the stunning Shangri La, Sutera caters to big spenders with a cache of five-star amenities orbiting the vaulted lobby. Some of the rooms (especially those with car-

peting) feel a bit tired, so don't hesitate to ask to see a couple of options. A second on-site tower, the Magellan, offers additional rooms.

EATING

KK is one of the few cities in Borneo with an eating scene diverse enough to refresh the noodle-jaded palate. Besides the ubiquitous Chinese *kedai kopi* (coffee shops) and Malay halal restaurants, you'll find plenty of interesting options around the city centre – head to the suburbs if you're looking for some truly unique local fare.

In recent years, the local government has cracked down on shady dining establishments, implementing a health code grading system from 'A' to 'C' ('A' being the best; consider giving restaurants with no grade a miss). Gradings are usually displayed on storefronts or windows. Also, all ice served in eating establishments is privately produced using filtered water.

Restaurants & Cafes

Kedai Kopi Fook Yuen (G33 Ground fl, No 4 Kompleks Asia City; kaya RM2.60; ◷ 6.30am-1am) Cheap and quick, a snack of sweet *kaya* is the perfect energy booster after a morning of sightseeing. And this isn't your standard Singaporean coconut-egg-jam, Sabahans have developed their own version of this tasty confection. Wi-fi available.

Kedai Kopi Fatt Kee (28 Jln Bakau; mains from RM5; ◷ lunch & dinner Mon-Sat) The woks are always sizzlin' at this popular Chinese place next to Ang's Hotel. Long lines are guaranteed, but it's always worth the wait. Their *sayur manis* (p350) cooked in *belacan* (shrimp paste) is

SABAH

MAKAN: KK-STYLE

Kota Kinabalu may be light on sights, and its urban core isn't a stunner, but the city comes up trumps in the food category. KK's veritable melting pot of cultures has fostered a lively dining scene that differentiates itself from the rest of Malaysia with a host of recipes fusing foreign recipes and local ingredients.

KK's four essential eats are:

Sayur Manis

Also known as 'Sabah veggie', this bright green jungle fern can be found at any Chinese restaurant worth its salt. It's best served fried with garlic, or mixed with fermented shrimp paste. The *sayur manis* plant is a perennial and can grow about 3m high. It is harvested year-round so there's a very good chance that your plateful of weeds was plucked from the jungle only a few days prior. Adventurous eaters might want to try other local produce like *tarap*, a fleshy fruit encased in a bristly skin, or *sukun*, sweet-tasting tuber used to make fritters.

Filipino Barbecue

Located at the north end of the KK Night Market, the Filipino Barbecue Market is the best place in town for grilled seafood at unbeatable prices. Hunker down at one of the crowded tables and point to your prey. Once the waitress has sent your order off to the grill, she'll hand you a cup (for drinking), a basin (to wash your hands) and a small plate to prepare your dipping sauce (mix up the chilli sauce, soy sauce, salt and fresh lime for your own special concoction). No cutlery here! Just dig in with your bare hands and enjoy steaming piles of fresher-than-fresh seafood. Figure around RM15 for a gut-busting meal.

Hinava

Perhaps the most popular indigenous appetiser, colourful *hinava* is raw fish pickled with fresh lime juice, chilli padi, sliced shallots and grated ginger. The melange of tangy tastes masks the fishy smell quite well. The best place to try *hinava* is Grace Point, a posh local food court near Tanjung Aru. You'll find it at the 'Local Counter' for around RM2 per plate (the portions are small – the perfect size for a little nibble).

Roti Canai

The ubiquitous *roti canai*, a flaky pancake fried on a skillet, is served from dawn 'til dusk at any Indian Muslim *kedai kopi* around town. Although the dish may appear simple, there's actually a lot of skill that goes into preparing the perfect platter. The cook must carefully and continuously flip the dough (*à la* a pizza parlour chef) to create its signature flakiness. *Roti canai* is almost always served with sauce, usually *dhal* (lentil curry) or another curry made from either chicken or fish.

a classic, and the salt-and-pepper prawns are great.

Kah Hiong Ngui Chap (☎ 019-870 0080; Block A, Ground fl, Kolam Centre Phase 2, Jln Lintas; mains from RM5.50; ☺ 7am-3pm) Head to Kah Hiong if you're craving the ultimate local experience. Tucked away in KK's suburban sprawl, this bustling restaurant specialises in *ngui chap* (beef soup) served with a special chilli sauce. Everyone knows about this spot – it's a local institution and has been featured on the local TV channel as one of the spots in town for a bite.

Shikai (☎ 088-484242; G15-16 Kompleks Asia City, Jln Asia City; mains from RM9; ☺ lunch & dinner) Fancy lanterns dangle above jet-black furniture and swishing Lazy Susans. Lunch specials start at RM9 per dish, although weekend dim sum is the biggest draw. Vegetarians will find plenty of excellent tofu options scattered throughout the pan-Asian menu.

D Junction (☎ 088-703131; Batu 3, Jln Lintas; beer RM7, mains from RM10; ☺ lunch & dinner) Located just beyond the city centre, this small complex has a clutch of high-end franchised eating options including Royal Chino restaurant (serving delicious dim sum on weekends), Indian Spice Garden (specialising in North Indian favourites) and Umai (a Japanese affair overflowing with spicy sushi rolls and saucy karaoke). There's a sociable bar on the ground level with plenty of Tiger on tap, and a surprisingly excellent shrimp wonton soup.

Bella Italia (☎ 088-313366; 69 Jln Gaya; mains RM19; ☙ lunch & dinner) In an attempt to muscle-*ini* their way into the competition, Bella Italia, in the Jesselton Hotel, has started a special 50% discount deal for pasta dinners between 5pm and 7pm.

Little Italy (☎ 088-232231; Jln Haji Saman; mains from RM23; ☙ lunch & dinner) Dear homesick holidaymaker; this is your place. Create your own carbo-lode with a variety of saucey tributes to the Bootland. All things considered, it's a rather pricey endeavour, but it's definitely worth stopping by if you're in desperate need of a rice respite.

Port View Seafood Village (☎ 088-221753; Lot 18, Waterfront Esplanade; dinner from RM50; ☙ lunch & dinner) This cavernous Chinese seafood specialist feels like an aquarium where you can eat the displays – we've never seen such an extravagant array of live fish. Even if you don't eat here, it's worth walking into the foyer to check out the veritable cascade of turquoise tanks.

Kohinoor (☎ 088-235160; Lot 4, Waterfront Esplanade; dinner about RM50; ☙ 11.30am-2.30pm & 5.30pm-11pm) There are several excellent restaurants along the Waterfront Esplanade, including this Indian place offering comfortable indoor seating and a breezy outdoor patio. Take advantage of their authentic tandoori oven and don't forget to grab a side of pillowy garlic naan.

TANJUNG ARU

In the early evening, head to Tanjung Aru at the south end of town near the airport for sunset cocktails and light snacks along the ocean. The area has three beaches – First Beach offers up a few restaurants, Second Beach has steamy local stalls, and Third Beach is a great place to bring a picnic as there are no establishments along the sand. A taxi to Tanjung Aru costs RM20, or you can take public transport (RM1.80) – take bus 16, 16A or city bus 2.

First Beach Café (☎ 088-245158; Aru Drive, Tanjung Aru; drinks RM10, mains RM8-20; ☙ 9am-2am) This restaurant boasts the best sunsets in KK and it's hard to argue: it's right on the beach at Tanjung Aru and you can literally step down from your table onto the sand. This is a good spot for light nibbles and beer in the evening.

Tanjung Aru Seafood Restaurant (☎ 088-245158; Tanjung Aru; dinner from RM60; ☙ 11am-2pm & 5-10pm) It's more about the sunset than the seafood here, but diners never complain (until they see the bill!). While locals prefer scruffy seafood markets around Sinsuran, this spot is a perennial expat fave. There's a cultural show on the weekends starting at 7pm.

Hawker Centres & Food Courts

Night Market (off Jln Tun Fuad Stephens; meals from RM2; ☙ dinner) The night market is the best, cheapest and most interesting place in KK for dinner. Vegetarian options available. For details on the Night Market see p345.

Centre Point Basement Food Court (Basement fl, Centre Point Shopping Centre, Jln Pasar Baru; mains RM3-10; ☙ lunch & dinner) Your ringgit will go a long way at this popular and varied basement foodcourt in the Centre Point mall. There are Malay, Chinese and Indian options, as well as drink and dessert specialists.

Grace Point (Grace Point, Tanjung Aru; mains RM2-8; ☙ lunch & dinner) Take bus 15 out near Tanjung Aru for some local grub at this KK mainstay. The development is actually quite chic compared to the smoke-swathed food courts in the city centre – KKers joke that the public bathrooms here are Borneo's nicest (and it's true!). Go for the Sabahan food stall (located in the far right corner when facing the row of counters) and try *hinava* – see opposite for more info.

Self-Catering

There are a variety of places to stock up on picnic items and hiking snacks, including the centrally located **Milimewa Superstore** (Jln Haji Saman) and **Tong Hing Supermarket** (Jln Gaya). **7-Eleven** (Jln Haji Saman; ☙ 24hr) is conveniently open throughout the evening.

DRINKING & ENTERTAINMENT

Averaging 12 cans of beer a month per capita (not including smuggled goods), Sabahans are big drinkers by Malaysian standards, and KK's nightlife allows plenty of scope for visitors to join the party. The **Waterfront Esplanade** (Jln Tun Fuad Stephens) houses a good number of upscale 'resto-bars', while Beach St, in the centre of town, is a semi-pedestrian street cluttered with bars and eateries. Live music (usually karaoke) takes place almost every night in the latter's central round. Most of KK's larger venues rely heavily on live music to pull in the punters, providing regular employment for a whole flotilla of local and Filipino cover bands. The quality of the performances is often encouragingly high, but drinks are quite pricey.

SABAH

SABAH

KAMPUNG ADIDAS

Malaysia's backwater version of a hiking shoe, '*kampung* Adidas' is the secret ingredient for a stumble-free jungle trek. These flimsy pieces of footwear take the shape of an authentic Adidas soccer cleat, but are made entirely of rubber (kinda like a souped-up Croc). They're everywhere: local guides wear 'em, the porters dashing up Mt Kinabalu have a pair or two – even some of the finalists in the Kinabalu International Climbathon (p362) were wearing them when they crossed the finish line in record time! '*Kampung* Adidas' can be purchased almost anywhere in Malaysia that sells cheap shoes. They cost around RM5 per pair – roughly a hundred times cheaper than those trekking boots you have in your rucksack...

Bed (☎ 088-251901; Waterfront Esplanade) Get those bed puns ready: the space that launched a thousand quips is arguably the fulcrum of KK nightlife, and it's a rare night out that won't see you ending up in Bed at some point. Bands play from 9pm, followed by DJs til closing.

Cocoon (☎ 088-211252; Jln Tun Razak Segama) In the busy corner of town opposite the Hyatt, Cocoon is a smart bar-restaurant that goes all bar in the evening when the live bands emerge. The post-gig DJs have a tendency to talk over the records, but at least their R&B-leaning tunes are danceable.

Shenanigan's (☎ 088-221234; Hyatt Regency Hotel) Following the international 'Irish pub' model, from dodgy draught Guinness to drunk and incapable patrons, this has long been a popular establishment in KK. Live bands perform most nights from 9pm and the place is totally rammed on weekends. Prices are horrendous (up to RM30 for a small beer) but get better during happy hour.

Blue Note (☎ 088-225800; Shangri La Tanjung Aru Resort) If you're staying out of town or just fancy a change, the spacious Blue Note doles out plenty of DJed tunes, though jazz aficionados may feel cheated.

Hunter's (☎ 016-825 7085; Kinabalu Daya Hotel) A favourite for local guides and expats, Hunter's offers up karaoke, sport on the plasma TV and balmy outdoor seating in the heart of the action.

Shamrock (☎ 088-249829; 6 Anjung Samudra, Waterfront Esplanade) Well, the Irish have landed in KK and they've brought everything with them (except the bad weather): Guinness, meat stews and Kelly green decor.

Also worth a look:

Upperstar (Jln Datuk Saleh Sulong) Opposite the Hilton, this pleasant semi-outdoor bar offers cheap booze and decent pub grub.

Rumba (Le Meridien Kota Kinabalu, Jln Tun Fuad Stephens) Upbeat and danceable tunes are spun at this happenin' night spot.

The Loft (Waterfront Esplanade) Yet another option along the pub-lined waterfront. Good place for sunset cocktails.

SHOPPING

Locals love their shopping, and the market-going spirit quickly rubs off on visitors; see p345 for details of the best ones to visit. Soon you'll find yourself bargaining for pearls at the Handicraft Market or haggling for a souvenir T-shirt at Jalan Gaya's Sunday street fair. Upmarket tribal art and souvenirs are available at **Borneo Trading Post** (☎ 088-232655; Lot 16, Waterfront Esplanade, Jln Tun Fuad Stephens).

GETTING THERE & AWAY
Air

In March 2009, **JetStar** (www.jetstar.com) and **Tiger Airways** (www.tigerairways.com) announced a bevy of new flights from Singapore, giving AirAsia some serious competition when it came to Borneo-bound flights. Since then, it has been cheaper than cheap to hop on a flight to KK from various Southeast Asian destinations. These days, flying through Borneo can actually be cheaper than taking a bus (and obviously much less of a time suck). Flights can be purchased online up to 24 hours before the scheduled departure. **Malaysia Airlines** (MAS; ☎ 1-300 883 000, 088-515555; www.malaysiaairlines.com; 1st fl, Departure Hall, KKIA; ☀ 5.30am-7.30pm) has similar flight schedules, although they are usually much more expensive than the budget carriers. MASwings services domestic destinations like Mulu, Miri, Sandakan and Lahad Datu.

Please note that the two terminals at Kota Kinabalu International Airport are not connected to one another, in fact they feel like two different airports. Most airlines operate out of the swankified Terminal 1, with the exception of AirAsia, Tiger Airways and charter flights, which depart from Terminal 2.

AirAsia (within Malaysia ☎ 03-2171 9333; www .airasia.com; Ground fl, Wisma Sabah, Jln Gaya) offers the following international flights to/from KK: Shenzhen, Macau, Jakarta, Manila, and Singapore. Within Malaysia, flights go to/from Johor Bahru, Kuala Lumpur and Penang in Peninsular Malaysia, and Kuching, Labuan, Miri, Sandakan, Sibu and Tawau in Borneo. The AirAsia counter at Terminal 2 of KKIA handles all bookings less than 24 hours prior to departure. It's open from 8am to 7pm.

Boat

All ferries, including taxi boats out to Tunku Abdul Rahman National Park, operate from the Jesselton Point Ferry Terminal, commonly referred to as 'the jetty' by locals and taxi drivers. A lot of construction was underway during our visit, so it's best to get a heads up about departure locations from your local accommodation. All passengers must pay an RM3 terminal fee for ferries departing from Kota Kinabalu.

Passenger boats connect KK to Pulau Labuan twice daily (first/economy class RM39/31), with onward service to Brunei; see p403) and to Tunku Abdul Rahman National Park (see p357), and a schedule is in the works to link the state capital to Pulau Tiga.

Bus & Minivan

You need to know ahead of time where you want to travel because there are several different stations around KK serving a variety of out-of-town destinations. In general, buses heading east depart from Inanam (Utara Terminal; 9km north of the city) and buses heading south leave from Padang Merdeka Bus Station (also called Wawasan or 'old bus station'; at the south end of town). Buses, minivans and private taxis serving destinations on the west coast and northern Sabah operate from the Padang Merdeka Bus Station. Local buses (RM1.80) from Wawasan can take tourists to Inanam if you don't want to splurge on the RM20 taxi. If you're going to Poring Hot Springs, take a minivan to Ranau and switch to a Poring-bound minivan.

Have your hotel call ahead to the bus station to book your seat in advance. Same-day bookings are usually fine, although weekends are busier than weekdays. It's always good to ring ahead because sometimes transport will be halted due to flooding caused by heavy rains.

Taxi

Share taxis operate from the Padang Merdeka Bus Station. Several share taxis do a daily run between KK and Ranau, passing the entrance road to the Kinabalu National Park office. The fare to Ranau or Kinabalu National Park is RM20 or you can charter a taxi for RM80 per car (note that a normal city taxi will charge RM150 to RM200 for a charter).

Train

The North Borneo rail line is currently closed and a reopening date has yet to be confirmed.

GETTING AROUND

Take a deep breath – transport in KK can be a bit of a nuisance, with two unconnected airport terminals (one of which is *still* under construction), taxi drivers that bend the 'standardised cab fare' rules and bus interchange stations situated at the opposite ends of the city. Ask around to find out the best ways to get about town – locals are always up on the cheapest and fastest way to get around.

To/From the Airport

Kota Kinabalu International Airport (KKIA) is 7km southwest of the centre. To reach the airport using public transport, try city bus 2 and bus 16A (RM1; do not take bus 16 as it does not go all the way to the airport). These buses can be boarded at the City Park station downtown. Both of these buses service Terminal 2 (AirAsia's terminal); at the time of research there was no public transport to Terminal 1, although that will no doubt change (look for city bus 1 to access this terminal). Public transport runs from 6am to 7pm daily. Taxis heading from the terminals into town operate on a system of vouchers (RM20), sold at a taxi desk on the terminal's ground floor. Taxis heading to the airport should not charge more than RM20 if you catch one in the city centre. For those taking one of AirAsia's popular late-evening flights, a taxi to/from the airport will cost RM30.

Don't forget to check which airport terminal you are using as the two terminals are not located near one another.

Car

The major car-rental agencies have counters on the first floor at KKIA and branch offices elsewhere in town. Manual cars start at RM100 per day and most agencies can arrange chauffeured vehicles as well.

SABAH

MAIN DESTINATIONS AND FARES FROM KOTA KINABALU

The following bus and minivan transport information was provided to us by the Sabah Tourism Board and should be used as an estimate only: transport times can fluctuate due to weather, prices may change and the transport authority has been known to alter departure points.

Destination	Duration (hr)	Price (RM)	Terminal	Departures
Beaufort	2	10	Padang Merdeka	7am-5pm (frequent)
Keningau	2½	13	Padang Merdeka	7am-5pm (eight daily)
Kota Belud	1	10	Padang Merdeka	7am-5pm (frequent)
Kuala Penyu	2	18	Segama Bridge	8-11am (hourly)
Kudat	3	18	Padang Merdeka	7am-4pm (frequent)
Lahad Datu	8	40	Inanam	7am, 8.30am, 9am, 8pm
Lawas (Sarawak)	4	20	Padang Merdeka	8.30am & 1.30pm
Mt Kinabalu NP	2	15	Inanam & Padang Merdeka	7am-8pm (very frequent)
Ranau	2	15	Padang Merdeka	7am-5pm
Sandakan	6	33	Inanam	7.30am-2pm (frequent) & 8pm
Semporna	9	50	Inanam	7am, 8.30am, 9am, 8pm
Tawau	9	55	Inanam	7.30am, 2pm, 8pm
Tenom	3½	25	Padang Merdeka	8am, noon, 4pm

Adaras Rent A Car (☎ 088-216671, 088-211866; adarasrac@hotmail.com; Lot G-03, Wisma Sabah)
Borneo Express (☎ 088-268009; G25, Wisma Sabah, Jln Tun Fuad Stephens)
Extra Rent A Car (☎ 088-218160, 088-251529; www .e-erac-online.com; 2nd fl, Beverly Hotel, Jln Kemajuan)
Kinabalu Rent A Car (☎ 088-232602; rentcar@ po.jaring.my; Lot 2.47, 2nd fl, Kompleks Karamunsing)
Mayflower Car Rental (☎ 012-803 3020, 088-221244; D3-3A, 3rd fl, Block D, Plaza Tanjung Aru)

Minivan
Minivans operate from several stops in KK, including the Padang Merdeka Bus Station and the parking lot outside Milimewa Superstore. They also circulate the town looking for passengers. Since most destinations within the city are within walking distance, it's unlikely that you'll need to catch a minivan. If you do catch one, most destinations within the city cost RM1.

Taxi
Most of KK's taxis have meters, but few drivers will agree to use them. Set prices rule the roost, but you should always negotiate a fare before heading off. There are several hubs where taxis congregate, including the Milimewa Superstore in the centre of town. Figure on around RM7 to RM10 for a ride in the city centre.

AROUND KOTA KINABALU

TUNKU ABDUL RAHMAN NATIONAL PARK
Just west of Kota Kinabalu, the five islands of Manukan, Gaya, Sapi, Mamutik and Sulug and the reefs in between make up the **Tunku Abdul Rahman National Park** (admission RM10), covering a total area of just over 49 sq km. Only a short boat ride from the KK city centre, they have some nice beaches and the water in the outer areas is usually clear, offering ideal day-trip material for anyone wanting to escape the city and unwind.

Pulau Manukan
Manukan is the most popular destination for KK residents and has plenty of facilities. It is the second-largest island in the group and its 20 hectares are largely covered in dense vegetation. There's a good beach with coral reefs off the southern and eastern shores, a walking trail around the perimeter and a network of nature trails. There's quite a good range of tropical fish, many of which can be seen simply by looking down from the jetty.

Equipment for hire on the island include masks and snorkels (RM15), beach mats (RM5) and bodyboards (RM10); a security deposit is payable.

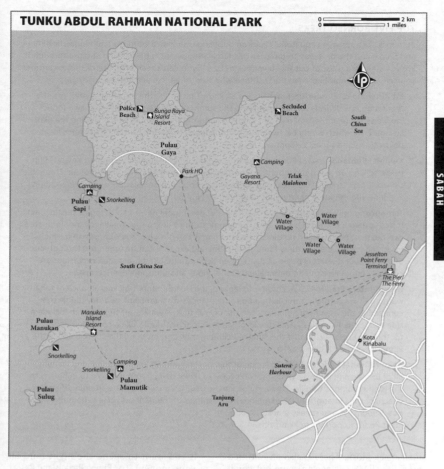

TUNKU ABDUL RAHMAN NATIONAL PARK

SABAH

Manukan Island Resort (☎ 088-302399; www.sutera sanctuarylodges.com; villa RM910; 🏊 🎾), managed by Sutera Sanctuary Lodges, has the only accommodation on the island, comprising 20 villas, a restaurant, swimming pool and tennis courts.

Pulau Mamutik

A mere 300m from end to end, tiny Mamutik offers the best snorkelling in the group with a lovely coral garden and a nice beach that runs up and down the east coast of the island. There's no resort here, but camping (RM5 per person, payable on arrival) is possible. There's also a small store/restaurant/snorkel-rental place, although it's a good idea to bring your own supplies from the mainland.

Pulau Sapi

Dwarfed by nearby Pulau Gaya, pin-sized Pulau Sapi (Cow Island) is another popular and attractive little island that offers snorkelling and attractive beaches (although at the time of research some tourists have complained that the water has been quite filthy). The island is separated from Gaya by a very shallow 200m channel that you can swim across if you feel up to it. Otherwise, the main activities here include wading, relaxing on the beach around the jetty or exploring the trails through the forest. There's a decent coral garden around the southeast point of the island, but it's no match for the coral garden off Mamutik. There are changing rooms, toilets and barbecue pits, as well as a

TOP FIVE BORNEO TREKS

Borneo is like a steaming equatorial cauldron bubbling over with a veritable encyclopaedia of flora and fauna, and the best way to discover this fascinating world is by trekking straight through it. We've assembled a list of our five favourite treks – if you can check off three of these, consider yourself an accomplished adventurer. Those who tick off all five are Borneo superstars.

- **Mt Kinabalu** (opposite) Yes Kinabalu, we all know that you're the big cheese. And, yes, the reputation is well deserved. In addition to the summit's granite spires offering awe-inducing views, there are several pleasant jaunts around the mountain's base, including the 6km Liwagu Trail, which would be swarming with people if it weren't for the fact that it's located below the island's most celebrated climb.

- **Kelabit Highlands** (p458) Borneo's real trekking hotspot is Sarawak's stunning Kelabit Highlands, spiking up along the Indonesian border like the spine of a sleeping dinosaur. This is the closest it gets to Himalayan teahouse treks in Borneo as visitors pass between hidden runes and lonely longhouse communities peppered throughout the region.

- **Temburong** (p590) Due to the surplus of oil and gas, Brunei never had to log its pristine rainforest to earn a few extra bucks. Thus, the jungle in Temburong (the smaller of the sultanate's two puzzle-piece-like land holdings) is a stunning realm of sweltering old-growth (primary) forest. All-inclusive adventures through this emerald expanse can be organised through one of several tour operators based in Bandar Seri Begawan (p581; self-planned excursions are currently impossible due to national park regulations and transport restrictions).

- **Headhunters Trail** (p455) According to legend, the Headhunters Trail was an ancient tribal warpath (it was actually a docile trading route) – today it's a fantastic two-day jungle trek connecting the island's green interior to the crystal coastal waters. Fit trekkers can include a side trip to the Pinnacles – an expanse of jagged stone that looks like a collection of granite toothpicks. But be warned: if the Kinabalu climb is, say, a '7' on the difficulty scale, then the Pinnacles add-on is about a '10'.

- **Bako National Park** (p423) Bako is one of the most rewarding 'do it yourself' destinations in all of Borneo and it proves that you don't have to travel deep into the jungle to mingle with the island's famous wildlife. Try the Telok Limau Trail (12km), ending at a stunning deserted beach, or the Lintang Trail (5.25km), boasting samples of the park's diverse vegetation. Proboscis monkeys and sneaky macaques abound.

See p86 for important trekking tips in Borneo.

---

small snack kiosk. There is also an outfitted camp site (RM5 per person) here but you'll need to bring over most of your supplies from the mainland.

Pulau Gaya

With an area of about 15 sq km, Pulau Gaya is the Goliath of KK's offshore islands, rising to an elevation of 300m. It's also the closest to KK and is covered in virtually undisturbed tropical forest. The bays on the east end of the island are filled with bustling water villages, inhabited by Filipino immigrants (legal and otherwise) who live in cramped houses built on stilts in the shallow water, with mosques, schools and simple shops, also built on stilts. Residents of KK warn against exploring these water villages, saying that incidents of theft and other crimes have occurred.

If you want to spend the night (and all of your money), try **Bunga Raya Island Resort** (☎ 088-442233; www.gayana-eco-resort.com; villas from US$649; 🔀), a stunning property with fresh-faced wooden bungalows on a fertile patch of beachfront.

Pulau Sulug

Shaped like a cartoon speech bubble, Sulug has an area of 8.1 hectares and is the least visited of the group, probably because it's the furthest away from KK. It only has one beach, on a spit of land extending from its eastern shore. Unfortunately, the snorkelling is pretty poor around this island. If you want a quiet getaway, Sulug is a decent choice, but you'll have to charter a boat to get here (see Getting There & Away, opposite), as the normal boats don't stop here. If you want a secluded beach and don't want to lay out for a charter, you'll do better by heading to Manukan and walking down the beach to escape the crowds.

Getting There & Away

Boats to the islands are arranged inside the waiting room at KK's Jesselton Point Ferry Terminal (commonly known as 'the jetty' by locals and taxi drivers). Inquire at the counter for the next available boat. Sign up for your chosen destination and then take a seat until there are enough passengers (usually eight) to depart. Services run from 7am to 6pm daily but it's best to catch a boat in the morning, as it's much harder to make up boat numbers in the afternoon. Boats also run from Sutera Harbour – which is more convenient for those staying near Tanjung Aru (or for those wanting to reach Pulau Gaya). Return fares to Mamutik, Manukan and Sapi hover around RM25. You can also buy two-/three-island passes for RM33/43.

The set fee for boat charter to one island is RM204, but you can negotiate a lower price. Try to deal directly with a boatman if you do this – don't talk to the touts who prowl the area. And don't consider paying until you return to the dock.

Note that there is an RM3 terminal fee added to all boat journeys, and a RM10 entrance fee to the marine park, paid when you purchase your ticket (if you are chartering a boat this is usually included).

NORTHWESTERN SABAH

The biggest draw in northwestern Sabah is, of course, the awesome Mt Kinabalu, ruling over the island with its granite fist. Before darting off to eastern Sabah's cache of superlative sights, why not stick around for a day or two to check out the small coastal towns and stilt villages.

MT KINABALU & KINABALU NATIONAL PARK

Towering above the island with its haunting husk of granite and halo of cotton-puff clouds, 'Borneo's roof' majestically rises over Sabah's swatch book of rainforest greens as if it were shouting 'climb me!' to wandering travellers. And climb it they

do. Mt Kinabalu, or Gunung Kinabalu in Bahasa Malaysia, is the region's biggest tourist attraction.

As far as mountains go, the 4095m peak of Mt Kinabalu may not be as wow-inducing as, say, a Himalayan sky poker, but Malaysia's first Unesco World Heritage Site is by no means an easy climb. Around 60,000 visitors of every ilk make the gruelling trek up Borneo's ultimate Thighmaster each year, returning to the bottom with stories of triumph, pictures of sun-lit moonscapes, and *really* sore legs.

Amazingly, the mountain is still growing: researchers have found it increases in height by about 5mm a year. On a clear day you can see the Philippines from the summit; usually, though, the mountain is thoroughly wreathed in fog by mid-morning.

History

Although it is commonly believed that local tribesmen climbed Kinabalu many years earlier, it was Sir Hugh Low, the British colonial secretary on Pulau Labuan, who recorded the first official ascent of Mt Kinabalu in 1851. Today, Kinabalu's tallest peak is named after him; thus Borneo's highest point is ironically known as Low's Peak.

In those days the difficulty of climbing Mt Kinabalu lay not in the ascent, but in getting through the jungle to the mountain's base. Finding willing local porters was another tricky matter – the tribesmen who accompanied Low believed the spirits of the dead inhabited the mountain. Low was therefore obliged to protect the party by supplying a large basket of quartz crystals and teeth, as was the custom back then. During the subsequent years, the spirit-appeasement ceremonies became more and more elaborate, so that by the 1920s they had come to include loud prayers, gunshots, and the sacrifice of seven eggs and seven white chickens. You have to wonder at what point explorers started thinking the locals might be taking the mickey…

Theses days, the elaborate chicken dances are no more, although climbing the mountain can still feel like a rite of passage.

Check out Mountain Torq's website (www .mountaintorq.com) for more fun facts about Kinabalu's history. They opened Asia's first *via ferrata* course in 2007 (see the boxed text, p359, for details).

SABAH

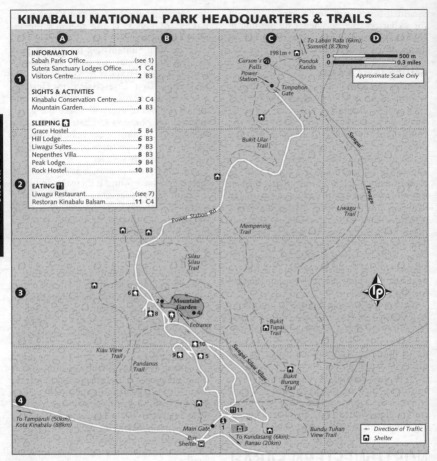

KINABALU NATIONAL PARK HEADQUARTERS & TRAILS

INFORMATION
Sabah Parks Office.............................(see 1)
Sutera Sanctuary Lodges Office.........1 C4
Visitors Centre.......................................2 B3

SIGHTS & ACTIVITIES
Kinabalu Conservation Centre............3 C4
Mountain Garden...................................4 B3

SLEEPING
Grace Hostel...5 B4
Hill Lodge..6 B3
Liwagu Suites...7 B3
Nepenthes Villa.....................................8 B3
Peak Lodge...9 B4
Rock Hostel...10 B3

EATING
Liwagu Restaurant...........................(see 7)
Restoran Kinabalu Balsam.................11 C4

Geology

Many visitors to Borneo assume that Mt Kinabalu is a volcano, but the mountain is actually a huge granite dome that rose from the depths below some nine million years ago. In geological terms, Mt Kinabalu is still very young. Little erosion has occurred on the exposed granite rock faces around the summit, though the effects of glaciers that used to cover much of the mountain can be detected by striations on the rock. There's no longer a snowline and the glaciers have disappeared, but at times ice forms in the rock pools near the summit.

Orientation & Information

Kinabalu National Park HQ is 88km by road northeast of KK and set in gardens with a magnificent view of the mountain. At 1588m the climate is refreshingly cool compared to the coast; the average temperatures are 20°C in the day and 13°C at night. The hike to the summit is difficult – see p360 for detailed information about the climb

On the morning of your arrival, pay your park entry fee, present your lodging reservation slip to the Sutera Sanctuary Lodges office (Map p358) to receive your official room assignment, and check in with the Sabah Parks office (Map p358) to pay your registration and guide fees. See opposite for more on pricing details. Making advance accommodation bookings is *essential* if you plan on climbing the mountain (see p363 for more information).

PERMITS, FEES & GUIDES

OK, this is where things appear to get tricky, but it's actually quite simple: a park fee, climbing permit, insurance and a guide fee are *mandatory* if you intend to climb Mt Kinabalu. All permits and guides must be arranged at the **Sabah Parks office** (Map p358; 7am-7pm), which is directly next door to the Sutera Sanctuary Lodges office, immediately on your right after you pass through the main gate of the park. Pay all fees at park HQ before you climb and don't ponder an 'unofficial' climb as permits (laminated cards worn on a string necklace) are scrupulously checked at two points you cannot avoid passing on the way up the mountain. Virtually every tour operator in KK can hook you up with a trip to the mountain, but it's significantly cheaper to do it on your own – just make sure you plan ahead.

All visitors entering the park are required to pay a **park entrance fee**: RM15 for adults and RM10 for children under 18 (Malaysians pay RM3 and RM1 respectively). A **climbing permit** costs RM100/RM40 for adults/children, while Malaysian nationals pay RM30/RM12. **Climbing insurance** costs a flat rate of RM7 per person. **Guide fees** for the summit trek cost the following: RM85 per small group (one to three climbers) or RM100 per large group (four to six climbers). Climbers ascending Kinabalu along the Mesilau trail will pay an extra RM10 (small group) or RM20 (large group) for their guide. Your guide will be assigned to you on the morning you begin your hike. If you ask, the park staff will try to attach individual travellers to a group so that guide fees can be shared. Couples can expect to be given their own guide. Guides are mostly Kadazan from a village nearby and many of them have travelled to the summit several hundred times. Try to ask for a guide who speaks English – he or she (usually he) might point out a few interesting specimens of plant life. The path up the mountain is pretty straightforward, and the guides walk behind the slowest member of the group, so think of them as safety supervisors rather than trailblazers.

So, the total minimum price for a couple climbing the mountain is (drum roll please) RM164.50 per person, and that does not include the RM360 for room-and-board on the mountain at Laban Rata (that's a grand total of RM524.50 for all of you math whizzes out there).

Optional extra fees include a taxi ride from the park office to the Tempohon Gate

---

VIA FERRATA

In 2007, Mountain Torq dramatically changed the Kinabalu climbing experience by creating an intricate system of rungs and rails crowning the mountain's summit. Known as *via ferrata* (literally 'iron road' in Italian), this alternative style of mountaineering has been a big hit in Europe for the last century and is just starting to take Asia by storm. In fact, Mountain Torq is Asia's first *via ferrata* system, and, according to the Guinness Book of World Records, it's the highest 'iron road' in the world!

After ascending Kinabalu in the traditional fashion (p360), participants use the network of levers to return to the Laban Rata rest camp along the mountain's dramatic granite walls. Mountain Torq's star attraction, the **Low's Peak Circuit** (RM380; minimum age 17 years old), is a four-to-five-hour scramble down metres upon metres of sheer rock face. This route starts at 3800m, passing a variety of obstacles before linking up to the Walk the Torq path for the last part of the journey. The route's thread-like tightrope walks and swinging planks will have you convinced that the course designers are sadistic, but that's what makes it so darn fun – testing your limits without putting your safety in jeopardy. Those who don't want to see their heart leaping out of their chest should try the **Walk the Torq** route (RM300; minimum age ten years old). This two-to-three-hour escapade is an exciting initiation into the world of *via ferrata*, offering dramatic mountain vistas with a few less knee-shaking moments.

No matter which course you tackle, you'll undoubtedly think that the dramatic vertical drops are nothing short of exhilarating. But the best part about the whole adventure actually happens a few weeks later, when you're back home showing off your eye-popping photos to friends: 'yeah, look at that shot of me dangling off the edge…I'm so hardcore…'

Via ferrata may be an Italian import, but Mountain Torq is pure Bornean fun. For more information about Mountain Torq check out www.mountaintorq.com.

(RM16.50 per vehicle, one way, four-person maximum), a climbing certificate (RM10) and a porter (RM102 per trip to the summit or RM84 to Laban Rata) who can be hired to carry a maximum load of 10kg. You'll see scores of porters huffing past you during your ascent as they carry supplies to Laban Rata. In case you're curious (we were!), they get paid RM8 per kilogram lugged in each direction (adult males carry around 30kg on each jaunt), and they often make two or three trips *per day*).

EQUIPMENT & CLOTHING

No special equipment is required to successfully summit the mountain, however a headlamp is strongly advised for the predawn jaunt to the top – you'll need your hands free to climb the ropes on the summit massif. Expect freezing temperatures near the summit, not to mention strong winds and the occasional rainstorm. Check out our tailor-made packing list (below) for more information, and don't

---

KINABALU PACKING LIST

- headlamp (with spare batteries)
- comfortable running shoes or *kampung adidas* (p352)
- wool socks and athletic socks
- hiking shorts or breathable pants
- three T-shirts (one made of lightweight synthetic material)
- fleece jacket
- lightweight shell jacket or rain jacket
- fleece or wool hat
- fleece gloves
- long johns
- hand towel
- water bottle
- light, high-energy snacks
- camera
- money
- earplugs for dorms

The aforementioned items should easily fit into a small waterproof backpack. Apply a dab of sunscreen and insect repellent before you depart. See p86 for more information about trekking in Borneo.

---

forget a water bottle, which can be refilled at unfiltered (but potable) tanks en route.

The Climb to the Summit

Climbing the great Mt Kinabalu is a heart-pounding two-day adventure that you won't soon forget. You'll want to check in at park headquarters at around 9am (8.45am at the latest for *via ferrata* participants; p359) to pay your park fees (p359), grab your guide and start the ascent (four to six hours) to Laban Rata (3272m) where you'll spend the night before finishing the climb. On the following day you'll finish scrambling to the top at about 2.30am in order to reach the summit for a breathtaking sunrise over Borneo.

Although you will see hikers of all ages making the journey, a climb up Kinabalu is only advised for those in adequate physical condition. The trek is tough, and the ascent is unrelenting as almost every step you take will be uphill. You will negotiate several obstacles along the way, including slippery stones, blinding humidity, frigid winds and slow-paced Japanese 50-somethings in Chanel tracksuits. Check out left for information on what to pack for your mountain adventure.

There are two trail options leading up the mountain – the Timpohon Trail and the Mesilau Trail. If this is your first time climbing Kinabalu, we strongly advise taking the Timpohon Trail – it's shorter, easier (but by no means easy!) and more convenient from the park headquarters (an hour's walk or short park shuttle ride; RM16.50 one way per vehicle, four-person maximum). If you are participating in Mountain Torq's *via ferrata*, you are required to take the Timpohon Trail in order to reach Laban Rata in time for your safety briefing at 4pm. The Mesilau Trail offers second-time climbers (or uber-fit hikers) the opportunity to really enjoy some of the park's natural wonders. This trail is less trodden so the chances of seeing unique flora and fauna are higher.

As you journey up to the summit, you'll happen upon signboards showing your progress – there's a marker every 500m. There are also rest shelters (*pondok*) at regular intervals, with basic toilets and tanks of unfiltered (but potable) drinking water. The walking times that follow are conservative estimates – don't be surprised if you move at a slightly speedier pace, and certainly don't

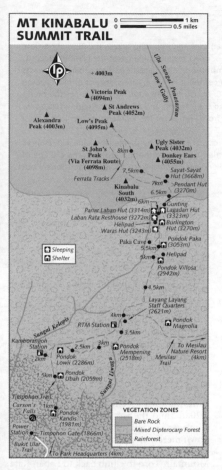

MT KINABALU SUMMIT TRAIL

0 — 1 km
0 — 0.5 miles

+4003m

Ulu Sungei Penataran
Low's Gully

Victoria Peak ▲ (4094m)
▲ St Andrews Peak (4052m)
Alexandra Peak (4003m)
Low's Peak (4095m)
St John's Peak (Via Ferrata Route) (4098m)
8km
Ugly Sister ▲ Peak (4032m)
Donkey Ears ▲ (4055m)
7.5km
Ferrata Tracks
Sayat-Sayat Hut (3668m)
7km
Pendant Hut (3270m)
Kinabalu South (4032m)
6.5km
6km
Gunting Lagadan Hut (3323m)
Panar Laban Hut (3314m)
Laban Rata Resthouse (3272m)
Burlington Hut (3270m)
Helipad
Waras Hut (3243m)
Paka Cave
5.5km
Pondok Paka (3053m)
5km
Helipad
Pondok Villosa (2942m)
4.5km
Layang Layang Staff Quarters (2621m)
4km
Pondok Magnolia
RTM Station
3.5km
Kamborangoh Station
2km
2.5km
3km
Pondok Mempening (2518m)
To Mesilau Nature Resort
Mesilau Trail (4km)
Pondok Lowii (2286m)
Sungei Kolopis
Sungei Liwag
1.5km
Pondok Ubah (2059m)
Timpohon Trail
Carson's Falls
1km
Pondok Kandis (1981m)
Power Station
Timpohon Gate (1866m)
Bukit Ular Trail
To Park Headquarters (4km)

🏠 Sleeping
🏠 Shelter

VEGETATION ZONES
Bare Rock
Mixed Dipterocarp Forest
Rainforest

start, and the forest can be alive with birds and squirrels in the morning. Five *pondok* (shelters) are spaced at intervals of 15 to 35 minutes between Timpohon Gate and Layang Layang and it's about three hours to the Layang Layang (2621m) rest stop. Near Pondok Lowii (2286m) the trail follows an open ridge giving great views over the valleys and up to the peaks.

LAYANG LAYANG TO PONDOK PAKA

'Why did I put all that extra crap in my rucksack?'

This part of the climb can be the most difficult for some – especially around the 4.5km marker. You've definitely made some headway but there's still a long trek to go – no light at the end of the jungly tunnel quite yet. It takes about 1¾ hours to reach Pondok Paka (3053m), the seventh shelter on the trail, 5.5km from the start. You'll welcome the few flat sections near Pondok Paka lying between the seemingly endless steps. This stretch is good for spotting pitcher plants, although you probably won't see any growing by the side of the track – look among the dense vegetation.

PONDOK PAKA TO LABAN RATA

'Why did I pay all that money just to climb a freakin' mountain?!'

Also known as the 'can't I pay someone to finish this for me?' phase, this part of the climb is where beleaguered hikers get a second wind as the treeline ends and the summit starts to feel closer. At the end of this leg you'll reach Laban Rata (3272m), your 'home sweet home' on the mountain (see p363 for more sleeping information). Take a good look at the slender signpost announcing your arrival – it's the propeller of the helicopter once used to hoist the construction materials to build the elaborate rest station. This leg takes around 45 minutes.

LABAN RATA TO SAYAT-SAYAT HUT

'Why am I waking up at the time I usually go to bed back home?'

It's 2am and your alarm just went off. Is this a dream? Nope. You're about to climb the last part of the mountain in order to reach the summit before sunrise. Most people set off at around 2.45am, and it's worth heading out at this time even if you're in great shape (don't forget your torch). The one-hour climb to Sayat-Sayat hut (3668m) involves

be discouraged if you take longer – everyone's quest for the summit is different.

TIMPOHON GATE TO LAYANG LAYANG

'Why am I sweating this much *already?*'

The trip to the summit officially starts at the Timpohon Gate (1866m) and from there it's an 8.72km march to the summit. There is a small bathroom outhouse located 700m before the Timpohon Gate, and a convenience shop at the gate itself for impulse snack and beverage purchases (get a 100-Plus!).

After a short, deceptive descent, the trail leads up steep stairs through the dense forest and continues winding up and up for the rest of the trip. There's a charming waterfall, **Carson's Falls**, beside the track shortly after the

SABAH

ADDING INSULT TO INJURY

As your two-day Kinabalu adventure comes to an end and you limp across the Timpohon Gate a shrivelled bundle of aching muscles and bones, don't forget to glance at the climbing records chart. Every year the **Kinabalu International Climbathon** (http://climbathon.sabahtourism.com) attracts the fittest athletes from around the world for a competitive climb-off as dozens of hikers zoom up the mountain *a la* the Road Runner. In 2008, Agustí Roc Amador from Spain set the men's record by completing the roundtrip (that's up to the summit and back to the gate – just to be clear) in 2 hours and 44 minutes. Corinne Favre from France set the women's record with a total time of 3 hours and 17 minutes.

And it's not just the clock-beaters who put casual trekkers to shame: the oldest person to reach the summit was a Japanese lady who battled her way to the top at the grand old age of 90. So just remember, when you're smugly slinking by slower hikers, there are pensioners out there who would leave you for dead...

a lot of hiker traffic and the crossing of the sheer Panar Laban rock face. There is little vegetation, except where overhangs provide some respite from the wind. It is one of the toughest parts of the climb, especially in the cold and dark of the predawn hours. Thick ropes are used to pull yourself up the granite sheets; it's hard work in places, but it feels great to use arm muscles instead of your weary legs. It's a bit of a mad dash as the jumble of headlamped hikers scurry over jagged rocks and narrow steps.

SAYAT-SAYAT HUT TO SUMMIT
'Why is it so darn cold out?! I'm standing near the equator for Pete's sake!'

After checking in at Sayat-Sayat, the crowd of hikers begins to thin as stronger walkers forge ahead and slower adventurers pause for sips from their water bottle. If you are able to position yourself ahead of the crowd, stop every so often to look back down at the climbers below you – they look like pilgrims on a silent spiritual quest (even the headlamps look like flickering candles). Despite the stunning surroundings, the last stretch of the summit ascent is, of course, the steepest and hardest part of the climb. Some spots are so precarious that you'll be thankful you couldn't see exactly what you were doing as you climbed up!

From just beyond Sayat-Sayat, the summit looks deceptively close and, though it's just over 1km, the last burst will take between one to three hours depending on your stamina. You might even see shattered climbers crawling on hands and knees as they reach out for the top of Borneo.

Once you're motionless at the top – waiting for the sun to rise – the coldness really starts to set in.

THE SUMMIT
[Speechless]

This is it – the million-dollar moment (or the RM600+ moment for those who are keeping score...) Climbers crowd together while jockeying for the essential photograph of the summit sign. Flashbulbs go off like lightning waking up sleepy eyes, and everyone obsesses over trying to nab a seat at the official summit point, forgetting that the sunrise can be glimpsed from anywhere on the mountain.

The summit warms up quickly as the sun starts its own ascent between 5.45am and 6.20am, and the weary suddenly smile; the climb up is a distant memory and the trek down merely an afterthought.

True adventurers should sign up with Mountain Torq to climb back to Laban Rata along the world's highest *via ferrata* (see p359 for details).

THE JOURNEY BACK TO THE BOTTOM
'Why didn't I believe anyone when they said that going down was just as hard as going up?!'

You'll probably leave the summit at around 7.30am and you should aim to leave Laban Rata no later than 12.30pm. The gruelling descent back down to Timpohon Gate from Laban Rata takes between three to four hours (if you're returning to the bottom along the Mesilau Trail it will take more time than descending to the Timpohon Gate). The weather can close in very quickly and, although you probably won't get lost, the granite is slippery even when it's dry. During rainstorms the downward trek feels like walking through a river. Slower walkers often find that their legs hurt more the day after – quicker paces lighten the constant pounding as legs negotiate each descending step. If you participated in the exhilarating *via ferrata* (p359) you will be absolutely knackered during your descent and will stumble into Timpohon Gate just before sunset (around 6pm to 6.30pm).

A 1st-class certificate can be purchased for RM10 by those who complete the climb; 2nd-class certificates are issued for making it to Laban Rata. These can be collected at the park office.

Walks Around the Base

It's well worth spending a day exploring the marked trails around park headquarters; if you have time, it may be better to do it before you climb the mountain, as chances are you won't really feel like it afterwards. The various trails and lookouts are shown on the map on p358.

The base trails interconnect with one another like a tied shoelace, so you can spend the day, or indeed days, walking at a leisurely pace through the beautiful forest. Some interesting plants, plenty of birds and, if you're lucky, the occasional mammal can be seen along the **Liwagu Trail** (6km), which follows the river of the same name. When it rains, watch out for slippery paths and legions of leeches.

At 11am each day a **guided walk** (RM3) starts from the park office and lasts for one to two hours. The knowledgeable guide points out flowers, plants, birds and insects along the way. If you set out from KK early enough, it's possible to arrive at the park in time for the guided walk.

Many of the plants found on the mountain are cultivated in the **Mountain Garden** (Map p358; RM5; ☯ 9am, noon & 3pm) behind the visitors centre.

Sleeping

LABAN RATA (ON THE MOUNTAIN)

Organising your accommodation on the mountain can be the most difficult part of your Kinabalu adventure. Access to the summit is essentially rationed by access to the huts on the mountain at Laban Rata (3272m) and this *must* be booked in advance (the earlier the better). In order to have any hope of clear weather when you reach the summit, you must arrive around dawn, and the only way to do this is by spending a night in one of the huts at Laban Rata. Yes, Sabah Parks will let you attempt a one-day ascent, starting around 7am, but by the time you get to the summit in mid-afternoon, it will almost certainly be clouded over or raining. And, just in case you're thinking about it: a) they won't allow a night climb and b) they will not allow an 'unofficial' climb (permits are carefully checked at several points on the mountain).

Sutera Sanctuary Lodges (see p347) in Kota Kinabalu operates almost all of the accommodation here, but space is very limited. Many travellers report extreme frustration with booking huts on the mountain –

FLORA & FAUNA OF MT KINABALU

Mt Kinabalu is a botanical paradise, designated a Centre of Plant Diversity as well as a Unesco-listed World Heritage Site. The wide range of habitats supports an even wider range of natural history, and over half the species growing above 900m are unique to the area.

Among the more spectacular flowers are orchids, rhododendrons and the insectivorous nepenthes (pitcher plant). Around park HQ, there's dipterocarp forest (rainforest); creepers, ferns and orchids festoon the canopy, while fungi grow on the forest floor. Between 900m and 1800m, there are oaks, laurels and chestnuts, while higher up there's dense, rhododendron forest. On the windswept slopes above Laban Rata, vegetation is stunted, with *sayat-sayat* a common shrub. The mountain's uppermost slopes are bare of plant life.

Deer and monkeys are no longer common around park HQ, but you can see squirrels, including the handsome Prevost's squirrel and the mountain ground squirrel. Tree shrews can sometimes be seen raiding rubbish bins. Common birds are Bornean treepies, fantails, bulbuls, sunbirds and laughing thrushes, while birds seen only at higher altitudes are the Kinabalu friendly warbler, the mountain blackeye and the mountain blackbird. Other wildlife includes colourful butterflies and the huge green moon moth.

they complain that the booking system is disorganised and inefficient, the huts are often full or it's difficult to get a confirmed booking. Bookings can be made online, in person or over the phone. We did a little experiment of our own and had four different people (tourists and locals) contact Sutera Sanctuary Lodges (pronounced 'sutra') to try and book accommodation two weeks before their desired climb time. Each person was offered different climbing date options and a different set of caveats involving accommodation restrictions and pricing.

The most common sleeping option is the heated dormitory (bedding included) in the Laban Rata Resthouse, which sells for RM360 per person. Three meals are included in the price; see right for more information about eating at Laban Rata. Non-heated facilities surrounding the Laban Rata building are also available for RM320 per person (meals included). Yes, the inflated prices feel monopolistic, and to make matters worse, Sutera is trying to force climbers to stay in the park for two nights – one night at Laban Rata and one night at the base.

The other option at Laban Rata is to stay at **Pendant Hut** (Map p361), which is owned and operated by **Mountain Torq** (see the boxed text, p359; pricing is on par with Sutera). All guests sleeping at Pendant Hut take two of three meals at Sutera's cafeteria, and are required to participate in (or at least pay for) the *via ferrata* circuit. Pendant Hut is slightly more basic (no heat – although climbers sleep in uber-warm sleeping bags), however, there's a bit of a summer-camp vibe here while Laban Rata feels more like a Himalayan orphanage. Prices for Pendant Hut are comparable to Sutera.

See p359 for information about additional fees associated with climbing Kinabalu.

PARK HEADQUARTERS (AT THE BASE)

The following sleeping options are located at the base of the mountain and are all operated by Sutera Sanctuary Lodges (p347). As per Sutera's monopolistic reputation, these options are overpriced when compared to the non-affiliated sleeping spots outside the park (p366).

Grace Hostel (Map p358; dm RM120) Clean, comfortable 20-bed dorm with fireplace and drink-making area.

Hill Lodge (Map p358; r RM390) These semi-detached cabins are a good option for those who can't face a night in the hostels. They're clean and comfortable, with private bathrooms.

Liwagu Suites (Map p358; r RM490) These hotel-like rooms (four in total) can be found in the Liwagu Building. While they sleep up to four people, they're best for couples as they contain only one bedroom and one living room.

Nepenthes Villa (Map p358; lodge RM760) These attached two-storey units fall somewhere between hotel rooms and private lodges. They have two bedrooms (one with a twin bed, one with a queen) and verandahs offering limited mountain views.

Peak Lodge (Map p358; lodge RM660) These semi-detached units have two bedrooms (one with a bunk bed and one with two twin beds), pleasant sitting rooms, fireplaces and nice views from their verandahs.

Rock Hostel (Map p358; dm RM120) Somewhat institutional 20-bed hostel with similar facilities to the Grace Hostel. Twin-share rooms are available here as well (RM350 per room).

Eating

LABAN RATA (ON THE MOUNTAIN)

At Laban Rata the cafeteria-style restaurant in the **Laban Rata Resthouse** (Map p361) has a simple menu and also offers buffet meals coordinated with the usual climbing times. Most hikers staying at Laban Rata (either in one of Sutera's huts or at Pendant Hut) have three meals (dinner, breakfast and lunch) included in their accommodation packages (see p363 for sleeping information). It is possible to negotiate a price reduction if you plan on bringing your own food (boiling water can be purchased for RM1 if you bring dried noodles). Note that you will have to lug said food up to Laban Rata. Buffet meals can also be purchased individually – dinner costs RM45. A small counter in the dining area sells an assortment of items including soft drinks (RM5.50), chocolate (RM5), pain relievers and postcards.

PARK HEADQUARTERS (AT THE BASE)

There are two restaurants at park headquarters. Both restaurants open every day at 6am, closing at 10pm on weekdays and 11pm on weekends.

Restoran Kinabalu Balsam (Map p358; dishes RM5–10) The cheaper and more popular of the two is this canteen-style spot directly below the park office. It offers basic but decent Malaysian, Chinese and Western dishes at reasonable prices. There is also a small but well-stocked shop in Balsam selling tinned and dried foods, chocolate, beer, spirits, cigarettes, T-shirts, bread, eggs and margarine.

Liwagu Restaurant (Map p358; dishes RM10-30) In the visitors centre, this is more expensive than the Balsam, but there's a huge range of dishes, including noodles, rice and seafood standards. An 'American breakfast' is pretty ordinary here – the cheaper breakfast at the Balsam canteen is better value.

Getting There & Away
It is highly advised that summit seekers check in at the park headquarters by 9am, which means that if you're coming from KK, you should plan to leave by 7am, or consider spending the night somewhere near the base of the mountain.

A shuttle bus runs from the Pacific Sutera (9am), the Magellan Sutera (9.10am) and Wisma Sabah (9.20am) to Kinabalu National Park HQ, arriving at 11.30am (RM40). In the reverse direction, it leaves Kinabalu National Park HQ at 3.30pm. There is also a shuttle bus from Kinabalu National Park HQ to Poring Hot Springs at noon (RM25) and another at 3.30pm (RM25) to Mesilau Nature Resort.

Express buses and minivans travelling between KK and Ranau (and Sandakan) pass the park turn-off, 100m uphill from the park entrance. Air-con express buses (RM15, three hours) and taxis leave from both Inanam and Padang Merdeka (Wawasan) stations (see p354). A share-taxi from one of these transport junctions is significantly cheaper than hailing a cab in the city centre (RM150).

AROUND MT KINABALU
Kinabalu National Park is home to Borneo's highest mountain and some of the island's best-preserved forest. Most travellers make a beeline for the mountain and the main park headquarters area, but the following spots are also worth exploring.

Mesilau Nature Resort
This lovely slice of country is the trailhead for an alternative approach up Mt Kinabalu, often favoured by trekkers as it's more challenging than the main route and much less crowded than park headquarters. The Mesilau route wanders up the mountain and links up with the Timpohon route to continue the ascent to Laban Rata. Arrange your trip with Sutera Sanctuary Lodges (p347) and your guide will meet you at Mesilau.

See p359 for more information about permits and fees. Mesilau Nature Resort is 30 minutes beyond the entrance to Kinabalu (when driving towards Ranau from KK).

Kundasang Memorial
The junction for the Mesilau Nature Resort on the KK–Ranau Hwy is the site of the **Kundasang War Memorial** (Kundasang; RM10; 8am-5.30pm). There are English and Anzac gardens here, commemorating the prisoners from these countries who died on the infamous Sandakan Death Marches (p373). In the Anzac Garden you can see a full list of the dead and at the back of the gardens there is a viewpoint that offers a stunning view of Mt Kinabalu.

The memorial is in Kundasang, 10km east of Kinabalu National Park headquarters. You'll know you're in Kundasang when you see the market stalls on either side of the road. Take the turn on the left for Mesilau Nature Resort. The memorial is on the right 150m after the turnoff. Look for the flags and the stone fort-like structure above the road.

Ranau
Ranau is a collection of concrete shop blocks on the road between KK and Sandakan. There's a busy Saturday **night market**. While the surrounding valley is quite lovely, the town itself is rather uninspiring. After your epic Kinabalu climb, head to **Tagal Sungai Moroli** (admission RM10) in Kampung Luanti for a truly unique massage experience. The term 'tagal' means 'no fishing' in the local Kadazan-Dusun language, as the fish in the river (a species known locally known as 'ikan pelian') are not to be captured – they are special massage fish. The townsfolk claim that they've trained the little swimmers to gently nibble at weary feet.

Poring Hot Springs
One of the few positive contributions the Japanese made to Borneo during WWII, **Poring Hot Springs** (admission adult/child RM15/10) has become a popular weekend retreat for locals. The complex is actually part of the Kinabalu National Park, but it's 43km away from the park headquarters, on the other side of Ranau.

If you're expecting some kind of natural paradise with rock pools and the like, think again: the setting is real forest but the facilities themselves are quite patently manmade.

SUPER SIZE ME

If Borneo were in the game of stealing slogans, it would probably choose 'super size me'. And it wouldn't take long to figure out why. Everything about Borneo (from its biodiversity to its topography) is on a totally different scale than the rest of the world – it's like the island's taking steroids.

Here are a few examples:

■ The biggest flower on the earth, a parasitic plant known as the rafflesia, blossoms on Borneo to a whopping 1m in diameter (p432).

■ The Sarawak Chamber, the biggest cave chamber a tourist can visit, is located in Gunung Mulu National Park (p452).

■ The Kinabalu giant red leech can grow up to 30cm in length – that's longer than the average foot of an adult human male. (Luckily, it doesn't feed on humans!)

■ Southeast Asia's highest point is Mt Kinabalu (p357), a stunning granite fortress rising 4095m. And let's not forget, Borneo is the third biggest island on the planet (only Greenland and New Guinea are larger).

Steaming, sulphurous water is channelled into pools and tubs where visitors can relax their tired muscles after the trek to the summit of Mt Kinabalu. For some, it's a huge anticlimax, for others it's a perfect playground worth far more than the customary quick stop. Don't forget a towel and your swimming trunks.

A **Tropical Garden** (adult/child RM3/1.50; 9am-4pm), a **Butterfly Farm** (adult/child RM4/2; 9am-4pm Tue-Sun) and an **Orchid Garden** (adult/child RM10/5; 9am-4pm) are also part of the Poring complex. Rafflesia sometimes bloom in the area; look out for signs in the visitors centre and along the road.

Up above the trees and houses, the **Canopy Walkway** (adult/child RM5/2.50; 9am-4pm) consists of a series of walkways suspended from trees, up to 40m above the jungle floor, providing unique views of the surrounding forest. Get there early if you want to see birds or other wildlife.

Sleeping & Eating

It's worth spending a night around the base of Kinabalu before your ascent, and there are plenty of accommodation options suiting everyone's budget. All of the following lodging options have an on-site restaurant.

The accommodation at Mesilau and Poring is run by Sutera Sanctuary Lodges (p347). At forested Mesilau, the Bishop's Head Resthouse has dormitory beds for RM120 per person. Rooms at Crocker Rage Lodges cost RM315. Chalets at Ugly Sister's Peak Lodge start at around RM895 per night, while Low's Peak

Lodge will set you back RM1065. The lodges at Poring fall into the same price range.

There are also plenty of privately owned sleeping options looping around Kinabalu's base. Most of these are located along the road between the park headquarters and Kundasang (6km east of the park's entrance).

Puncak Borneo Resort (012-828 0866; Kundasang; dm/s/d incl breakfast from RM40/168/188;) A respectable choice, Puncak (pronounced 'poon-chak') makes a few worthy attempts at style with lipstick-red accent walls and animal-print rugs. The stairs up to the reception can feel like an impossible obstacle if you've just climbed the mountain.

Cottage Hotel (088-888885; Kundasang; www .thecottagehotel.com.my; r RM126;) Popular with tour operators, this fine option offers prim rooms and great views of the mountain. Backpackers can cash in on slower nights – simply rock up and ask them about their RM60 deal which includes room and full board. Wi-fi available.

Kinabalu Rose Cabin (088-889-233; krc145@yahoo .com; Km 18, Jln Ranau-Tuaran; r RM130-250) Look for the shiny blue-roofed pagoda and you've found Rose Cabin. Rooms are as kitschy as their shimmery brochures, but frequent mid-week discounts sweeten the deal. A minivan from park HQ should cost around RM5.

Kinabalu Pine Resort (088-889388; Kundasang-Ranau Hwy; r from RM150) A paradigm of country club landscaping, this welcoming camp-style resort is extremely popular with Sabahans, who sit on the wooden balconies while enjoying the breezy sunsets. Ask for a room with hardwood floors – the carpeting here is a bit tattered.

Getting There & Around

The area around Mt Kinabalu is easily accessible from KK, with buses running at a high frequency throughout the day (7am to 8pm). KK roundtrip buses stop in front of park headquarters and in Ranau (RM15, two hours).

Shuttle buses and minivans are constantly moving tourists around the base of the mountain and taxis can be hired if you don't have time to wait for public transport. Minivans operate from a blue-roofed shelter in Ranau servicing the nearby attractions (park HQ, Poring etc) for RM5. Opting for a taxi will set you back RM30 (if you negotiate). The national park operates a van service between the headquarters and Poring for RM25 – it leaves the park HQ at noon.

TUARAN

Tuaran, 33km from KK, is a bustling little town with tree-lined boulevard-style streets and a distinctive nine-storey **Chinese pagoda**. There's little point stopping in the town itself unless you happen to pass through on a market day, but the surrounding area conceals a couple of luxury resorts (p349) and two stilt villages.

Mengkabong Water Village, a Bajau (indigenous group) stilt village built over an estuary, was once a very picturesque spot, though it's not very special now. The settlement at **Penimbawan** is much more appealing; to get there, take a minivan to Serusup (RM1.50) and charter a motorboat (RM40). The trip up the river takes about 15 minutes, and the boat will wait while you wander the plankwalks of the village. The villagers are friendly, but you're better off going with someone who speaks Malay, because it can feel a bit intrusive just wandering around.

Given the town's proximity to KK (with its heaps of accommodation options), you probably won't need to stay in town. However, if for some reason you need a room, try **Orchid Hotel** (☎ 088-793789; 4 Jln Teo Teck Ong; r from RM80; ⊠). It's somewhat overpriced but it'll do the trick for a night.

All buses north pass through Tuaran, and minivans shuttle regularly to and from KK (RM5 to RM10, 30 minutes). Minivans to Mengkabong are less frequent and cost RM1. Regular minivans go from Tuaran to Kota Belud (around RM10, 30 minutes).

KOTA BELUD

You might think Kota Belud isn't much to look at, but every Sunday a huge **tamu** takes place on the outskirts of this small, sleepy town. The market is a congested, colourful and dusty melee of vendors, hagglers, browsers, gawpers and hawkers, all brought together by a slew of everyday goods in a bustle that consumes the whole town each and every week. A smaller version takes place on Wednesday.

A *tamu* is not simply a market where villagers gather to sell their farm produce and to buy manufactured goods from traders; it's also a social occasion where news and stories are exchanged. Sadly, tourists now often outnumber buffalo, and the fascinating local Bajau horsemen have mostly moved away from the car park, though some do put on a show for visitors.

Visitors looking for tribal handicrafts and traditional clothing will be disappointed, but the market is certainly lively and you can enjoy a good breakfast at the steaming stalls after looking around. The hilly views from the *padang* (grassy field) may also tempt you to stay a while and do some walking away from the Sunday crowds.

Sleeping & Eating

Most people visit Kota Belud as a day trip from KK, since you can make it there and back with plenty of time for the market. One reason to stay overnight here is the stunning view of Mt Kinabalu at first light. There are several homestays in the area; check out www.sabahtourism.com for details. Try **Kota Belud Travelers' Lodge** (☎ 088-977228; 6 Plaza Kong Guan; dm RM25, r RM60-85; ⊠), a simple affair in the centre of town. It's about 200m southwest of the mosque in a shopping block (it's well marked, so finding it shouldn't be a problem).

Kota Belud is hardly a gastronome's delight, but plenty of tasty snacks can be picked up at the Sunday market. There are plenty of Chinese and halal coffee shops around the municipal offices.

Getting There & Away

Minivans and share-taxis gather in front of Pasar Besar, the old market. Most of these serve the Kota Belud–KK route, (RM5, two hours) or Kudat (RM10, two hours), departing between 7am and 5pm. On Sunday, *tamu* day, the number of vehicles has to be seen to be believed!

To get to Kinabalu National Park, take any minibus going to KK and get off at Tamparuli, about halfway (RM5, 30 minutes). There are several minivans from Tamparuli to Ranau every day until about 2pm, all of them passing the park entrance (RM5, one hour). To go all the way to Ranau costs RM8 (the trip takes just over an hour).

KUDAT

Kudat is a quiet port town in the very north of Sabah, 190km from KK. The surrounding countryside is home to the friendly Rungus people, tribal cousins of the Kadazan, but the town itself displays noticeable Filipino influences, as much of the trade here is with Malaysia's northeastern neighbour.

The town itself is fairly unremarkable, but increasing tourist traffic has been brought to the area by the development of the so-called Tip of Borneo as a tour-bus attraction. There are also some good beaches west of town and homestay opportunities in Rungus longhouses near the highway, but unless you prearrange a tour you'll need a car or taxi to reach them.

Swing by **New Way Car Rental & Souvenir Centre** (☎ 088-625868; 40 Jln Lo Thien Chok) if you want to explore the area under your own steam. They can also book your accommodation on Pulau Banggi (opposite).

Easily the best deal in town, if not the entire region, **Ria Hotel** (☎ 088-622794; 3 Jln Marudu; r RM80-108; 🅿 🖵) hits all the right notes: clean, spacious, well-appointed rooms, nice bathrooms with hot showers, and little balconies (some with scenic views). It's a short walk southwest of the bus station.

our pick **Kudat Riviera** (☎ 088-249276; www.exquisite borneovillas.com; Pantai Kulambu; villa incl breakfast from US$540; 🅿 🖵 🚲) is Borneo's newest attempt at opulence, and boy is it a success. Stunning villas are constructed in a dreamy Balinese style – go for an ocean-facing Rice Barn Villa – the perfect incarnation of 'tribal chic'.

The bus station is in Kudat Plaza, which is in the western part of town, very close to the Ria Hotel. Bus destinations include KK (RM20, three hours) and Kota Belud (RM15, ninety minutes). Minivans also operate from this station and other points in town.

AROUND KUDAT

The area around Kudat is prime package-tour territory, although the area can easily be explored by private vehicle (4WD is always a safe bet for any off-roading). Either way, make sure you take in one of the lovely tropical sunsets – Sabah's west coast is famous for 'em!

Rungus Longhouses

The indigenous people of the Kudat area are known as the Rungus, a subgroup of Sabah's Kadazan-Dusun race. The Rungus inhabit the Kudat Peninsula and the Pitas Peninsula, on the far side of Marudu Bay. The Rungus are famous for their basketry, beadwork and fine longhouses, which house one extended family, rather than several unrelated families, as is the case with other groups in Borneo (see p430 for more information on Borneo's longhouses).

These days, as with many other indigenous people in Borneo, most of the Rungus have abandoned their longhouses in favour of Malay-style wooden or concrete-brick houses. However, the Rungus maintain two fine **longhouses** (Bavanggazo Rungus Longhouses; ☎ 088-621971; per person per night from RM70) in Kampung Bavanggazo.

Make no mistake, these longhouses are primarily set up for display purposes and to attract tourists, but a night here still provides visitors with a good chance to interact with Rungus people and learn about their culture. The rates include dinner and breakfast and simple cultural entertainment. You will sleep in a traditional room in one of the longhouses with insect netting above your bed.

Kampung Bavanggazo is 44km south of Kudat on the north–south highway (look for the milepost reading 'Kudat 44km'). There is a sign off the highway that reads 'Kg. Bavanggazo 'Rungus Longhouse''. Follow this road (Jln Tinangol) down the hill for about 1.5km, cross a bridge and go uphill to the left. You will quickly come to the first longhouse, and the second one is at the top of the hill 800m further on. There is no public transport right to the longhouses. All KK–Kudat buses and minivans will stop at Kampung Bavanggazo if you ask the driver. A taxi from Kudat will cost around RM50.

Tip of Borneo

Sabah's northernmost headland, at the end of a wide bay some 40km from Kudat, is known as Tanjung Simpang Mengayu, or the Tip of Borneo. Magellan reputedly landed here for 42 days during his famous round-the-world voyage. Once a wild promontory, this wind-swept stretch where the cliffs meet the sea has been co-opted as a tourist attraction – there's a large, truncated globe monument dominating the viewpoint. A sign warns visitors not to climb down onto the rocks that form the mainland's actual tip, effectively guaranteeing that tourists will do exactly that – so watch out for crashing waves if you follow suit…

There's no public transport, so you'll need to negotiate for a taxi from Kudat (around RM60, including waiting time upon arrival) or drive yourself (we suggest washing the dust off the car before returning it to the rental agency). **TYH Borneo Tours** (☎ 017-830 1188) and **Exotic Adventure** (☎ 019-589 0719; G-40-3A KK Times Square, Jln Coastal Hwy, Kota Kinabalu) offer guided day trips from KK, which stop at the Rungus longhouses along the way. Figure on around RM250 per person.

OFFSHORE ISLANDS

The real highlights of northwestern Sabah lie offshore – and we're not talking about Tunku Abdul Rahman National Park. The first gem is Pulau Mantanani, perfect tropical islands lying about 40km northwest of Kota Belud. The second is Layang Layang, a diving mecca about 300km northwest of KK – it's basically just an airstrip built on a reef way out in the middle of the South China Sea. Famous for great visibility, seemingly endless wall dives and the occasional school of hammerheads, it's second only to Sipadan (p388) on Malaysia's list of top dive spots.

Pulau Mantanani

Pulau Mantanani Besar (Big Mantanani Island) and **Pulau Mantanani Kecil** (Little Mantanani Island) are two little flecks of land fringed by bleach-blond sand and ringed by a halo of colourful coral, about 25km off the coast of northwest Sabah (about 40km northwest of Kota Belud).

The **Borneo Sea Resort** (☎ 088-230000; www.bornsea .com/mantanani; 3-day/2-night all-inclusive dive packages from RM1900; 🍴) sits on a nice private beach at the west end of the big island. The bungalows here are quite nice, with tile floors, hot-water showers and bathtubs, large double beds, verandahs and air-con. Sea kayaks are available for rent and would allow you to explore the area, but be careful as there are strong currents offshore and you could easily get washed out to sea. KK operators offer day trip diving packages for those who don't want to stay on the island.

Pulau Banggi

Travellers who want to fall off the map, or at least get off the tourist trail for a few days, might want to visit the remote island of Pulau Banggi, which lies some 40km northeast of Kudat. The Banggi people, known locally for their unusual tribal treehouses, are Sabah's smallest indigenous group, and speak a unique non-Bornean dialect. The island is an interesting spot to explore for a day, and the surrounding reef islands can also be visited on dive trips organised from KK.

Accommodation is provided by a small government **resthouse** (r RM40) and the modest **Banggi Resort** (☎ 019-587 8078; r fan/air-con RM35/55, huts RM70; 🍴), which can arrange boat trips and other activities. The small huts have kitchens and twin beds. This place can get fully booked on weekends, so reserve in advance.

Kudat Express (☎ 088-328118; one way RM15) runs a ferry between Kudat and the main settlement on Pulau Banggi. It departs the pier (near the Shell station) at 9am daily. In the reverse direction, it leaves Pulau Banggi daily at around 3pm.

Layang Layang

Some 300km northwest of KK, Layang Layang is a tiny island surrounded by a coral atoll. It's an exclusive **dive location**, well known to scubaholics as part of the famous Borneo Banks. As you would guess from its isolated location, the reef here is healthy and diverse. Although it may not be quite as colourful as the reef at Sipidan, it's likely to be one of the most unspoilt reefs most divers have seen. And the best part is that it just goes on and on, with new surprises waiting up and down its length. The visibility here is usually excellent, sometimes extending to 30m or more. While hammerheads are occasionally sighted, it might be better to consider them a bonus, and to concentrate on the reef fish, which are abundant and varied. There are also plenty of reef sharks in attendance, along with a healthy population of rays.

Layang Layang Island Resort (in Kuala Lumpur ☎ 03-2162 2877; www.myoutdoor.com/layanglayang; 6-day/ 5-night all-inclusive package twin-share per person from US$1250; 🍴 🛫) is the only game in town and it's all about the diving. The five daily meals – that's right, five – are scheduled around the dive times. The standard rooms are very comfortable, with air-con, TV, private verandahs and hot-water showers.

The all-inclusive packages include accommodation, food, twelve boat dives and tank usage. Package rates for non-divers start at US$850. An extra night costs $180/$125 diver/non-diver.

The resort operates its own Antanov 26 aircraft, which flies every Tuesday, Thursday, Friday and Sunday between KK and Layang Layang. The flight over from KK in this barebones Russian prop plane is a big part of the adventure: it feels more like a military transport than a commercial airliner. The return flight costs US$285, which is not included in the accommodation/food/dive package.

EASTERN SABAH

A trip to eastern Sabah is like one giant tongue twister. The names of the towns and rivers sound like meditation mantras or mythical beasts: Kinabatangan, Gomantong, Pinuanakan. Sabahans will spot you a mile away as you fumble over five-syllable words, but don't let these syllabic setbacks deter you from visiting. Once you've crossed Kinabalu off your Bornean to-do list, head here for the remainder of Sabah's world-class sights.

Travel agents will wave fancy brochures in your face encouraging you to link up with a tour, but many of the area's attractions can be done under your own steam. After snagging some snaps of the jolly ginger apes at Sepilok, swing through the roaring Sungai Kinabatangan for a wildlife-watching river cruise. Then go on to the sparkling islands of Semporna Archipelago for some top-notch scuba at Sipadan. Those with a bit more time on their hands (and a sizeable stash of cash) should indulge in a jungle safari around the Danum Valley, or a bone-busting trek-a-thon through the Maliau Basin, commonly called Sabah's Lost World.

SANDAKAN
pop 453,750

Sandakan has been a dot on traders' maps for centuries. After the nearby natural wonders – Sepilok (p375) and an archipelago of idyllic islands (p378) – the city's biggest draw is its turbulent history, retold through religious relics, haunting cemeteries and stunning colonial mansions. Although Sandakan is far less exciting than it used to be, the city has

plenty of character and even a certain down-market charm. Once the shop shutters come down in the evening the centre can feel a bit deserted and creepy, but head to the lively Bandar Indah area: nights are best spent clinking cocktails at sunset, singing karaoke and devouring an aquarium's worth of seafood.

History
At the height of the timber boom Sandakan was said to have had the world's greatest concentration of millionaires. It was perhaps an extravagant claim, but the area has always been renowned for luxury goods such as pearls, sea cucumbers and bird's nests, and so attracted trade from the nearby Philippines and as far away as China.

In the 18th century Sandakan came under the suzerainty of the sultan of Sulu, who ruled the southern islands of what is now the Philippines. In the early 1870s the Scottish adventurer and arms dealer William Clarke Cowie managed to obtain permission to start a settlement at Pulau Timbang, in Teluk Sandakan. The township quickly became known as Kampung German due to the large number of German traders who emigrated here.

In 1879 the settlement relocated to its current position and the city of Sandakan was established by then British Resident William Pryer. The port quickly boomed and many modern advances were seen here even before Hong Kong or Singapore. In 1883 Sandakan became the capital of British North Borneo, a status it held until WWII. Allied bombing and Japanese retaliation in 1945 virtually destroyed the town, and in 1946 the capital was moved to the equally devastated Jesselton, now called Kota Kinabalu.

Orientation
The centre of Sandakan consists of only a few blocks squashed between the waterfront and a steep escarpment from where you can look out over the bay (Teluk Sandakan). In the centre you'll find most of the hotels, restaurants, banks and local transport.

Like many Malaysian towns, Sandakan has suburbs and outlying areas extending considerable distances down the main highway, denoted by their distance from the centre, eg Batu 1 (Mile 1). Check out Batu 4 for additional lodging, eating and drinking options. Express buses to KK and other destinations

SANDAKAN

INFORMATION

Cyber Café	**1** D2
Discovery Tours	(see 5)
HSBC	**2** C3
Main Post Office	**3** A3
MayBank	**4** D2
SI Tours	**5** D2
Standard Chartered Bank	**6** C3
Tourist Information Centre	**7** C2
Wang Liau Chun Mii Moneychanger	**8** C2
Wildlife Expeditions	(see 5)

SIGHTS & ACTIVITIES

Agnes Keith House	**9** C1
Observation Pavilion	**10** C1
Sam Sing Kung Temple	**11** B2
Sepilok Tropical Wildlife Adventure	**12** D2
St Michael's & All Angels Church	**13** B2

SLEEPING

Hotel London	**14** D2
Hotel Sandakan	**15** C2
Nak Hotel	**16** C3
Sandakan Backpackers	**17** D2
Sunset Harbour Botik Hostel	**18** D3
Swiss Inn Waterfront Sandakan	**19** D2

EATING

English Tea House & Restaurant	**20** C1
Fat Cat V	**21** D2
Gentingmas Mall	**22** D3
Harbour Square Complex	**23** D2
Imperial Seafood Restaurant	(see 25)
Milimewa Superstore	**24** C3
New Market	**25** D2
Night Food Stalls	**26** A3
Suntos Supermarket	**27** D2

DRINKING

Balin	(see 16)

TRANSPORT

AirAsia	**28** C3
Local Bus Station	**29** C3
Malaysia Airlines	**30** C3
MASwings	(see 30)
Minibus & Minivan Stand	**31** C3

leave from the long-distance bus station at
Mile 2½, 4km north of the town centre.

Information

INTERNET ACCESS

Cyber Café (3rd fl, Wisma Sandakan, Lebuh Empat; per hr
RM3; ⏰ 9am-9pm)

MEDICAL SERVICES

Duchess of Kent Hospital (☎ 089-219460; Mile 2,
Jln Utara)

MONEY

HSBC (Lebuh Tiga)
MayBank (Lebuh Tiga) In addition to a full-service bank
and ATM, a sidewalk currency-exchange window is open
9am to 5pm daily for changing cash and travellers cheques.

Standard Chartered Bank (Lebuh Tiga)
Wang Liau Chun Mii Moneychanger (Tung Seng
Huat, 23 Lebuh Tiga; ⏰ 8.30am-4.30pm) Cash only.

POST

Main post office (☎ 089-210594; Jln Leila)

TOURIST INFORMATION

Forestry Department (☎ 089-213966; 2nd fl, Jln
Leila) Next to UMW Toyota, 2km west of the main post
office. Get permits for the mangrove forest walk to Sepilok
Bay here (see p376).
Tourist Information Centre (☎ 089-229751; pempt
.j.mps@sabah.gov.my; Wisma Warisan; ⏰ 8am-12.30pm
& 1.30-4.30pm Mon-Thu, 8-11.30am & 2-4.30pm Friday)
Located opposite the municipal offices (known as MPS)
and up the stairs from Lebuh Tiga. The dedicated staff

dispenses advice on everything from regional attractions to local restaurants and can link travellers together for group excursions.

Sight & Activities

Central Sandakan is light on 'must-see' attractions, although history buffs will appreciate the *Sandakan Heritage Trail* brochure available at the tourist office.

The **Puu Jih Shih Temple**, 4km west of the town centre, is a large Buddhist temple perched on a steep hill overlooking Teluk Sandakan. Take a bus to Tanah Merah and ask for directions. Closer to the centre of town, the **Sam Sing Kung Temple** dates from 1887 and fronts the municipal *padang*. Another building of note is the 19th-century **St Michael's & All Angels Church** (off Jln Puncak), one of the few stone buildings in Malaysian Borneo. Prison labourers lugged the stones across the jungle during the church's construction – perhaps not the best example of Christian charity!

For travellers seeking something a bit more obscure, try the **Japanese Cemetery**, located beyond the city's large Chinese cemetery near the Agnes Keith House. A Japanese woman established the cemetery in the 1890s – her name was Kinoshita Kuni, known to the English as Okuni of South Seas. She was a successful madam who ran the lucrative 'Brothel 8', which once stood on Lebuh Tiga. Today the cemetery is quite small, but at one time there were hundreds of buried dead (most of them prostitutes). A monument to the fallen Japanese soldiers of WWII was erected in the cemetery in 1989.

AGNES KEITH HOUSE

On the hill above town, overlooking Teluk Sandakan and the scruffy port itself, is **Agnes Keith House** (Jln Istana; RM15; 9am-5pm), an old two-storey wooden villa now renovated as a museum. Keith was an American author who came to Sandakan in the 1930s with her husband, the Conservator of Forests, and ended up writing several books about her experiences, including the famous *Land Below the Wind*. The Keiths' villa was destroyed during WWII and rebuilt identically upon their return in 1946. The house fell into disrepair during the 1990s, but Sabah Museum restored it as a faithful recreation of Keith's original abode.

The villa documents Sandakan in all its colonial splendour, with detailed displays on the lives of the Keiths. Most poignant are mementos of Agnes' imprisonment by the Japanese during WWII, when she had to try to care for her young son under gruelling conditions. Her book, *Three Came Home,* recounts those years. The admission price includes entry to the various branches of the Sabah Museum in KK (p345) – now didn't we tell you to keep hold of your ticket? Also on the grounds is the English Tea House & Restaurant (p374), conveniently ignoring Keith's US background and the fact that she found Sandakan to be 'too British' when she first arrived!

To reach the museum, follow Jln Singapura from the city centre and turn right up the hill, or head up the shady Tangga Seribu (100 Steps) to Jln Residensi Drive and turn left. Just below the museum gardens is an **observation pavilion** built by the local Rotary Club, which offers more fine views.

SANDAKAN MEMORIAL PARK

Now just a quiet patch of woods, **Sandakan Memorial Park** (Taman Peringatan; admission free; 9am-5pm) was the site of a Japanese POW camp and starting point for the infamous 'death marches' to Ranau. Of the 1800 Australian and 600 British troops imprisoned here, the only survivors by July 1945 were six Australian escapees. See opposite for more information.

Large rusting machines testify to the camp's forced-labour program, and a pavilion at the centre of the park includes accounts from survivors and photographs from personnel, inmates and liberators. In 2006 the original march route was officially reopened as a memorial trail – see www .sandakan-deathmarch.com for details.

To reach the park, take any Batu 8 (or higher-numbered) bus from the local bus terminal in the city centre (RM1.80); get off at the 'Taman Rimba' signpost and walk down Jln Rimba. A taxi from downtown costs about RM15 one way.

Tours

It is possible to visit many of the attractions around Sandakan independently – to see wildlife, however, you'll need a guide, and the easiest way to arrange this is by taking a tour. The town has plenty of general tour operators offering packages to Sepilok, Sungai Kinabatangan, the Gomantong Caves and the Turtle Islands National Park. Hotels

THE SANDAKAN DEATH MARCHES

Sandakan was the site of a Japanese prisoner-of-war camp during WWII, and in September 1944 there were 1800 Australian and 600 British troops interned here. What is not widely known is that more Australians died here than during the building of the infamous Burma Railway.

Early in the war, food and conditions were bearable and the death rate stood at around three per month. However, as the Allies closed in, it became clear to the officers in command that they didn't have enough staff to guard against a rebellion in the camps. They decided to cut the prisoners' rations to weaken them, causing disease to spread and the death rate to rise.

It was also decided to move the prisoners inland – 250km through the jungle to Ranau, on a route originally cut by locals to hamper the Japanese invaders, passing mainly through unin-habited, inhospitable terrain. On 28 January 1945, 470 prisoners set off; 313 made it to Ranau. On the second march, 570 started from Sandakan; just 118 reached Ranau. The 537 prisoners on the third march were the last men in the camp.

Conditions on the marches were deplorable: most men had no boots, rations were less than minimal and many men fell by the wayside. The Japanese brutally disposed of any prisoners who couldn't walk. Once in Ranau, the surviving prisoners were put to work carrying 20kg sacks of rice over hilly country to Paginatan, 40km away. Disease, starvation and executions took a horrendous toll, and by the end of July 1945 there were no prisoners left in Ranau. The only survivors from the 2400 at Sandakan were six Australians who escaped, either from Ranau or during the marches.

As a final bitter irony, it emerged after the war that a rescue attempt had been planned for early 1945, but intelligence at the time had suggested that there were no prisoners left at the Sandakan camp.

in Sandakan and Sepilok can also arrange tours, as can agents and accommodation in KK (p341).

Discovery Tours (☎ 089-274106; www.discoverytours .com.my; 9th fl, Wisma Khoo Siak Chiew, Lebuh Empat) Popular operator servicing the majority of Sabah's major attractions.

MB Permai Tours (☎ /fax 089-671535; 1st fl, Sandakan Airport) Tours and car rental from RM120 per day (4WD from RM380).

Sabah Holidays (☎ 089-671718; www.sabahholidays .com; Ground fl, Sandakan Airport) Tours, rental cars and minivans, with a branch in KK.

Sepilok Tropical Wildlife Adventure (☎ 089-271077; www.stwadventure.com; 13 Lebuh Tiga) Mid-priced tour specialist. Owners of Sepilok Jungle Resort and Bilit Adventure Lodge on Sungai Kinabatangan.

SI Tours (☎ 089-213502; www.sitoursborneo.com; 10th fl, Wisma Khoo Siak Chiew, Lebuh Empat) This full-service agency opened Abai Jungle Lodge in December 2006 as a base for Kinabatangan tours. Also has an airport branch.

Wildlife Expeditions (☎ 089-219616; www.wildlife -expeditions.com; 9th fl, Wisma Khoo Siak Chiew, Lebuh Empat) Tour menu includes its Sukau River Lodge on the Kinabatangan. Has a KK office.

Sleeping

Over the last two years, the number of hotel rooms has doubled in Sandakan despite the decrease in tourists, so spontaneous travellers won't be too hard-pressed to find an available room. If you're only passing through Sandakan to see the orang-utans, it's better to stay at Sepilok itself, since the rehabilitation centre is about 25km from town.

Sunset Harbour Botik Hostel (☎ 089-229875; www.sunsethostels.com; 1E, HS14, Harbour Square Complex; dm/d incl breakfast from RM20/60; 🖸 🖵) The dorm rooms are bit too 'little orphan Annie', but there are excellent kitchen facilities here and a large market around the corner to buy your meal-to-be.

Sandakan Backpackers (☎ 089-221104; www .sandakanbackpackers.com; Lot 108, Block SH-11, Harbour Square Complex; dm/s/d RM25/40/60; 🖸 🖵) Cheap sleeps is the name of the game – the young backpacker crowd seems to congregate here (maybe 'cause they're on a package tour?).

Nak Hotel (☎ 089-272988; www.nakhotel.com; Jln Pelabuhan Lama; dm/r incl breakfast from RM30/88; 🖸 🖵) If you're into architectural anomalies (or Soviet-style riffs) then this concrete behemoth might be the place for you. Picky travellers fear not – the owners have a real *nak* for chic interior decor, outfitting the oddly shaped rooms with clever design details. Don't miss the hotel's kick-ass roof lounge, (Balin; p374) – a must even if you're not staying here.

The Mark's Lodge (☎ 089-210055; themarks@ streamyx.com; Lot 1-7, Block 36, Bandar Indah; r from RM154; ❖ 🖳) The word 'boutique' is written in fogged glass across the front entrance – just in case you didn't get the memo. This business-class hotel, located at Batu 4 (Bandar Indah) is a solid option for a comfortable sleep with no surprises (good or bad). Go for a non-smoking room. It's a RM12 cab ride into town and a RM40 drive to Sepilok.

Hotel Sandakan (☎ 089-221122; www.hotelsandakan .com.my; Lebuh Empat; r/ste incl breakfast RM240/310; ❖ 🖳) A three-star establishment offering comfortable but characterless Western-style rooms. Back in Agnes Keith's time, staying here would have cost you just $8…

Also worth a look:

Hotel London (☎ 089-216371; www.hlondon.com .my; 10 Lebuh Empat; d incl breakfast RM55; ❖ 🖳) Renovated up from its shoestring roots; rooms are clean and comfortable.

Swiss Inn Waterfront Sandakan (☎ 089-240888; www.swissgarden.com; Harbour Square Complex; r from RM120; ❖ 🖳) Fresh-faced with pleasant ocean views. Try negotiating for big discounts – they're never fully booked.

Eating & Drinking

When Sandakan's Old Market was demolished, the stalls were moved to a rather soulless new building along the sea. Although atmosphere is a bit lacking, **New Market** (Jln Pryor) is still a great place for cheap breakfast or lunch. Raw food at ground level includes the only unadulterated ground coffee in town. Upstairs find strictly halal food stalls, with a mix of Chinese and Malay up another level. Try the on-site Imperial Seafood Restaurant (halal).

The city's large Chinese population means that there are excellent homages to the motherland, and the region's port history equals fresher-than-fresh seafood. For an authentic Malay meal, head to the KFC in the new Harbour Square Complex development on the sea – don't eat there! – the restaurants surrounding it are cheap and flavourful.

If you're wondering where everyone goes when Sandakan shuts down in the evening, just hop in a taxi to Bandar Indah, commonly known as Mile 4 or Batu 4. This buzzing grid of two-storey shophouses is the playground of choice for locals and expats alike, and is packed with restaurants, bars, karaoke lounges and nightclubs. It comes alive at night in a way that makes central Sandakan seem deader than the morgue in a ghost town. Bars generally close around 1am or 2am, music venues slightly later.

Sim Sim Seafood Restaurant (dishes RM5; Sim Sim 8; ❖ breakfast & lunch) During a visit to Sandakan, you'll see scores of tour groups passing through, but we guarantee that none of them will stop at this rickety spot hidden amongst a chaotic tangle of driftwood. Located in the heart of a stilt village, Sim Sim Seafood Restaurant is a dockside fishery, where the daily catch is unloaded and sorted. A cluster of red plastic patio furniture huddles in the corner – just grab a seat and point to your prey! Sim Sim is located outside the city centre – ask a cab to drop you off at 'Sim Sim Bridge 8'.

Fat Cat V (☎ 089-216867; 21 Lebuh Tiga; dishes RM3-10; ❖ breakfast & lunch) Forget I to IV, for once the sequel is just as good as the originals. The corpulent kitty proclaims itself a 'Restaurant for Everyone', and the broad menu of Malay, Chinese and fast food, plus juices, shakes and floats, helps justify its popularity. The cake shop next door is equally good.

Kedai Ang Bang Guan (☎ 089-213854; Jln Buli Sim Sim; mains from RM15; ❖ lunch & dinner) Just east of downtown, next to Sandakan's main mosque, Ang Bang Guan is a tasteful and tasty take on Chinese seafood.

our pick **English Tea House & Restaurant** (☎ 089-222544; www.englishteahouse.org; 2002 Jln Istana; mains RM24-40, cocktails RM26.50; ❖ breakfast, lunch & dinner) Soak up the *recherché* colonial atmosphere and elegant food at this exquisitely restored restaurant on the grounds of the historic Agnes Keith House. The manicured gardens are a particular joy, with wicker furniture and a small croquet lawn overlooking the bay, perfect for afternoon tea (RM17.25), a round sunset Pimms, or perhaps some snobbish guffawing.

our pick **Balin** (☎ 089-272988; www.nakhotel.com; Jln Pelabuhan Lama; drinks from RM7, mains from RM15; ❖ lunch & dinner) Bringing a certain LA rooftop sexiness to Sandakan, Balin is your best bet for nightlife in the city centre. The three tiers of uber-chill lounge space are accented by a factory's worth of pillows.

Self-caterers have a few options:

Gentingmas Mall (☎ 089-210010; 26 Jln Pryer)

Milimewa Superstore (☎ 089-235021; Centre Point, Jln Pelabuhan Lama)

Suntos Supermarket (cnr Lebuh Tiga & Jln Dua)

Getting There & Away

AIR

Malaysia Airlines (☎ 089-273966; cnr Jln Pelabuhan Lama & Lebuh Dua) has daily flights to/from KK and KL. **AirAsia** (☎ 089-222737; Jetliner, Lebuh Dua) operates two daily direct flights to/from KL and KK. **MASwings** (☎ 1-300-883000; cnr Jln Pelabuhan Lama & Lebuh Dua) offers one daily flight to/from Tawau and two to/from KK.

BUS

Buses to KK, Lahad Datu, Semporna and Tawau leave from the long-distance bus station in a large parking lot at Batu 2.5, 4km north of town, not a particularly convenient location. Most buses and all minivans leave in the morning. Get the latest schedule from hotels or the tourist office. To reach the bus station, catch a local bus (RM1) from the stand at the waterfront. A taxi from the station to town is around RM10.

Bus companies have booths at the long-distance bus station and touts abound. Most express buses to KK (RM40, six hours) leave between 7.30am and 2pm, with a couple of evening departures. All pass the turn-off to Kinabalu National Park headquarters (RM30).

Buses depart regularly for Lahad Datu (RM20, 2½ hours) and Tawau (RM30, 5½ hours). There's also a bus to Semporna (RM30, 5½ hours) at 8am. If you miss it, head to Lahad Datu, then catch a frequent minivan to Semporna.

Minivans depart throughout the morning from Batu 2.5 for Ranau (RM24, four hours) and Lahad Datu (some of those continuing to Tawau). Minivans for Sukau (RM15) leave from a lot behind Centre Point Mall in town.

Please note that it is impossible to get a ride from KK to Sandakan around Ramadan or Chinese New Year if you have not booked your ticket ahead of time.

Getting Around

TO/FROM THE AIRPORT

The airport is about 11km from downtown. The Batu 7 Airport bus (RM1.80) stops on the main road about 500m from the terminal. A coupon taxi from the airport to the town centre costs RM24; going the other way, a taxi should cost around RM20.

BUS & MINIVAN

The local bus terminal is on Jln Pryer, in front of Gentingmas Mall. Buses run from 6am to about 6pm on the main road to the north, Jln Utara, designated by how far from town they go, ie Batu 8. Fares range from RM1 to RM4.

Local minivans wait behind Centre Point Mall, fares cost from RM2. Use them for the Pasir Putih seafood restaurants and the harbour area.

TAXI

Taxis cruise the town centre, and park near main hotels. Many hotels will steer you toward a preferred driver, not a bad thing. Short journeys around the town centre should cost RM5; it's RM12 to Bandar Indah and RM40 for a lift to Sepilok.

SEPILOK

The little hamlet of Sepilok sees almost as many visitors as the granite spires of Mt Kinabalu. With up to 800 visitors daily, Sepilok's Orang-Utan Rehabilitation Centre (SORC) is the most popular place on earth to see Asia's great ginger ape in its native habitat. Those who have time to stick around will also undercover several scenic nature walks, a sanctuary for the elusive proboscis monkey and a couple of great places to call home for a night or two.

Orientation & Information

Sepilok's main attraction, the Sepilok Orangutan Rehabilitation Centre, is located at 'Batu 14' – 14 miles (23km) from Sandakan. The street connecting the highway to the rehab centre is lined with a variety of accommodation suiting all budget types. The Rainforest Discovery Centre is also along this road. The proboscis monkey sanctuary at Labuk Bay is further up the road (in the direction of KK) and is accessible via taxi or private vehicle. See p378 for details. Banks and medical services are located in Sandakan. Money can be changed at the upmarket sleeping spots (for a hefty change fee).

Sights & Activities

SEPILOK ORANG-UTAN REHABILITATION CENTRE (SORC)

One of only four orang-utan sanctuaries in the world, the Sepilok Orang-Utan Rehabilitation Centre (SORC) occupies a corner of the Kabili-Sepilok Forest Reserve about 25km north of Sandakan. The centre was established in 1964; it now covers 40 sq km and has become one of Sabah's top tourist attractions, second only to Mt Kinabalu.

SABAH

SABAH

WILD MAN OF BORNEO

The term 'orang-utan' literally means 'man of the wild', or 'jungle man' – a testament to the local reverence for these great ginger apes. Traditionally, orang-utan were never hunted like other creatures in the rainforest; in fact, Borneo's indigenous people used to worship their skulls in the same fashion as they did the heads taken from enemy tribesmen.

Orang-utans are the only species of great ape found outside Africa. A mature male is an impressive, not to mention hairy, creature with an armspan of 2.25m, and can weigh up to 144kg. Dominant males also have distinctive wide cheek pads to reinforce their alpha status. It was once said that an orang-utan could swing from tree to tree from one side of Borneo to the other without touching the ground. Sadly this is no longer the case, and hunting and habitat destruction continue to take their toll; it's estimated fewer than 15,000 specimens now exist in the wild.

Orphaned and injured orang-utans are brought to Sepilok to be rehabilitated to return to forest life. When we visited there were only seven primates 'on campus'. It's unlikely you'll see this many at feeding time – three or four is more likely, or maybe none at all.

Feedings are at 10am and 3pm and last for around 30 to 50 minutes. Schedules are posted at the **visitor reception centre** (☎ 089-531180; soutan@po.jaring.my; admission RM30, camera fee RM10; ☯ 9-11am & 2-3.30pm). Tickets are now valid for one day only; in the past, tickets entitled buyers to a pair of feedings, so afternoon arrivals could revisit the next morning on the same ticket. Far more annoying than this (reasonable) change in policy is park staff's angry denials of the change. The feeding platform is a short jaunt over a wooden walkway.

A worthwhile 20-minute video about Sepilok's work is shown five times daily (9am, 11am, noon, 2.10pm and 3.30pm) opposite reception in the **Nature Education Centre** auditorium.

Use the lockers provided for your valuables – orang-utans and macaques have been known to relieve tourists of hats, bags, sunglasses, cameras and even clothing. It's especially important that you don't bring any containers of insect repellent into the reserve,

as these are highly toxic to the apes and other wildlife. Spray yourself before entering.

SORC is supported by a UK-based charity and its orang-utan adoption scheme is a particular hit with visitors: for UK£25 a year you can sponsor a ginger bundle of fun and receive updates on its progress. For details, pick up a leaflet or contact **Sepilok Orang-Utan Appeal UK** (www.orang-utan-appeal.org.uk). If you're really taken with the place Sepilok has one of the most popular overseas volunteer programs in Malaysia. Apply through **Travellers Worldwide** (www.travellersworldwide.com).

If you want to explore further, several **walking trails** (☯ 9am-4.15pm) lead into the forest; register at the visitor reception centre to use them. Trails range in length from 250m to 4km, and different paths are open at different times of year. Guided night walks can be arranged through the centre or at the various lodges. There's also a 10km trail through mangrove forest to **Sepilok Bay**. A permit from the **Forestry Department** (☎ 089-213966; Jln Leila, Sandakan) is required in advance for this route. The department can also arrange basic overnight accommodation at the bay (RM100) or a boat back to Sandakan (RM150). Some travel or tour agencies can assist with the permit and other arrangements.

RAINFOREST DISCOVERY CENTRE (RDC)

The **Rainforest Discovery Centre** (RDC; ☎ 089-533780; adult/child RM10/5; ☯ 8am-5pm), about 1.5km from SORC, offers an engaging graduate-level education in tropical flora and fauna. Outside the exhibit hall, a botanical garden presents varying samples of tropical plant life, with the accompanying descriptions every bit as vibrant as the foliage. There's a 1km lakeside walking trail as well. A series of eight canopy towers are being built – three have been completed. Paddleboats (RM5) are available to ride around the inviting lake near the centre's entrance.

It's best to get there either at 8am or 4pm, as the wildlife tends to hibernate during the sweltering hours in the middle of the day. A proper visit along the trails and towers takes around 1½ hours.

LABUK BAY PROBOSCIS MONKEY SANCTUARY

Proboscis monkeys (*Nasalis larvatus*) are an even more exclusive attraction than orang-utans. After all, you can see orang-utans in

Sumatra but the proboscis is found only on Borneo. These reddish-brown primates, one of nine totally protected species in Sabah, can grow to 72cm with a tail almost as long, and they can weigh up to 24kg. Named for their long bulbous noses, proboscis monkeys are also pot-bellied with white faces, and the males are constantly, unmistakably aroused. With the arrival of Europeans, Malays nicknamed the proboscis *monyet belanda* (Dutch monkey).

An eco-friendly plantation owner has created a private **proboscis monkey sanctuary** (☎ 089-672133; www.proboscis.cc; RM60, camera RM10, video RM20), attracting the floppy-nosed locals with sugar-free pancakes at 11.40am and 4.30pm feedings. A third feeding at 2.30pm often occurs during a ranger-led hike deeper in the sanctuary. An estimated 300 wild monkeys live in the 600-hectare reserve. Animals in the reserve generally steer clear of human contact, except for those mischievous macaques with their 'up in your grill' attitude as they try to snag snacks and sunhats.

The sanctuary offers package trips. A half-day visit costs RM160, including transfers from Sandakan (RM150 from Sepilok). Overnight trips with meals and a night walk start at RM250. Food and accommodation are provided at the Nipah Lodge, on the edge of the oil-palm plantations that surround the sanctuary. Independent travel here is difficult; it's 15km down a rough dirt track off the main highway (see p378 for more information).

Sleeping & Eating

Although most tourists rush in and out of Sepilok faster than the flash of a camera, it's well worth spending the night in this sleepy township. Most accommodation options are scattered along Jln Sepilok, the 2.5km-long access road to the rehabilitation centre. At the time of research the Forestry Department was building staff quarters at the RDC – it's worth getting in touch with the centre to see if those are complete and available to tourists.

Sepilok B&B (☎ 089-534050, 089-532288; www.sepilok bednbreakfast.com; Jln Arboretum; dm/s/d RM23/40/60) The former head of Sabah's reforestation division manages this unpretentious option, which has a palpable summer camp vibe. It's popular with large groups, who pile into the simple dorm rooms accented with pale pastel drapery. Crooked picnic tables and varnished lounge chairs offer backpackers plenty of room to chill out after a sweaty day of orang-u*tanning* under the equatorial sun. The B&B is opposite the forest research centre, about 250m off Jln Sepilok and 1km short of the SORC entrance.

our pick **Paganakan Dii** (☎ 089-532005; www.paganakandii.com; dm/d RM28/98; 🔀 🖳) Hands down the best budget place to stay at in Sepilok (if not all of Sabah), this welcoming and quiet retreat sits deep within a deer preserve on the far side of the highway. Chic design details (made from recycled materials), crisp white linen and friendly staff will have you thinking that the owners surely left a zero off the price tag. Overall, staying in the

---

OLD KING COAL...

...wasn't such a merry old soul. In 2008, TNB, the national energy company, decided to revive a terminated coal fire power plant project. The original construction site was in the port town of Lahad Datu, but planners are now eyeing a site near Sandakan, Sabah's second largest city. The target construction zone is only a few hundred metres from the Kabili-Sepilok Forest Reserve, which is home to Sepilok's beloved orang-utans. This prospective project has greatly angered the local population, who care deeply about their pristine forest preserve and resident apes.

What You Can Do To Help

Anton Ngui, a local environmental activist and owner of Paganakan Dii (above), says 'help us by asking the locals about their views on this impending disaster.' He feels strongly that the promises of 'development' and 'job generation' are insincere and do not outweigh the irreparable damage that the plant will do to the environment. 'Ask your accommodation provider about supporting the local anti-coal campaign and encourage them to play an active part in the fight to preserve the orang-utans' habitat.' Petition forms are widely available – even online (www.savesandakan. com) – encouraging the government to ban 'power'-hungry conglomerates from destroying one of the last vestiges of Sabah's rainforest.

longhouse-inspired dorms or duplex doubles is a great reason to get stuck in Sepilok... oh right, and don't forget to see the orang-utans too... Transfers to the Sepilok Rehabilitation Centre are included in the price.

Sepilok Forest Reserve & Labuk B&B (☎ 089-533190, 089-223100; labukbb@yahoo.com; dm/d/chalet from RM28/65/180; 🖳 🖳) Dorm and double rooms (located in the Labuk B&B portion of the property) are fine – it's the chalets that are the property's *pièce de résistance*. The comfortable cabins are peppered across an obsessively maintained acreage (think golf course). There's a relaxing pool-like jacuzzi on the grounds as well, which is reserved for chalet guests (or backpackers willing to drop an extra RM8).

Sepilok Jungle Resort (☎ 089-533031; www .sepilokjungleresort.com; dm RM28, r 69-130; 🖳 🖳) Everyone seems to stay here but it's hard to see why. Don't trust the snazzy website – the superior rooms are institutional and musty, and the staff is indifferent, except when steering unhappy guests to 'deluxe' (read: pricey) digs. Maybe this place should be renamed 'The Last Resort'...

Uncle Tan's (☎ 089-531639; www.uncletan.com; dm/tw incl all meals RM38/100; 🖳) Uncle Tan built a reputation amongst backpackers for providing great river tours along the Kinabatangan. Now he's set up shop right in the heart of Sepilok with a couple of thatch-roofed gazebos and a stack of backpacker shacks – they're pretty dank but unbeatably cheap.

Sepilok Nature Resort (☎ 089-535001; http://sepilok .com; r RM250; 🖳 🖳) Run by very exclusive Pulau Sipadan Resort and Tours, these rattan-accented chalets are luxuriously furnished and have private verandahs overlooking scrumptious gardens and a shaded lagoon. Breakfast (RM35) and dinner (RM55) are available at the on-site restaurant.

Most accommodation in the Sepilok area serves breakfast – some offer guests three-meal packages. The **SORC cafeteria** (meals from RM5; 🕑 7am-4pm) vends sandwiches, noodle bowls, rice plates, snacks and beverages, though they are known for running out of items during the tourist rush. **Mah Fung Enterprise** (🕑 Mon-Sat), across from the turn-off to the RDC, sells cold drinks, snacks, sunscreen and insect repellent. There's also a small hut with a blue fence at Batu 14 serving bread and cold drinks.

Getting There & Away

If you are coming directly from Sandakan, a taxi should cost no more than RM40 (either from the airport or the city centre). Bus 14 from Sandakan (RM3) departs hourly from the city centre and stops at the RDC. If you are coming from KK, board a Sandakan-bound bus and ask the driver to let you off at 'Batu 14'. You will pay the full RM33 it costs to reach Sandakan (which is only another 23km up the road). Pay no attention to the blue signs on the side of the highway marking the kilometres – they don't correlate to the antiquated 'Batu' system that most locals use.

Taxi 'pirates', as they're known, wait at Batu 14 to give tourists a ride into Sepilok. It's RM3 per person for a lift. Travellers spending the night can arrange a lift with their accommodation if they book ahead of time. Walking to the SORC is also an option – it's only 2.5km down the road.

To reach the Labuk Bay Proboscis Monkey Sanctuary have the KK–Sandakan bus drop you off at Batu 19 (Mile 19; 32km from Sandakan), but note that it's too far from the highway to walk, so you will have to arrange transport from the junction (it's a 15-minute drive). Shared vans from Sepilok/Sandakan to Labuk Bay cost RM110/RM130 per person.

You can usually organise a pick-up (in a shared van from the Kinabatangan operators) from Sepilok after the morning feeding if you are planning to head to Sungai Kinabatangan in the afternoon. Set off around noon to reach the river for the afternoon cruises. Accommodation in Sepilok selling bus tickets back to KK will charge an extra RM10 'agency fee', so it is best to buy your ticket in advance if you can.

SANDAKAN ARCHIPELAGO

Located further north from Sabah's highly promoted Semporna Archipelago, the Sandakan Archipelago, off the coast of its namesake port, is a quieter collection of emerald isles. The diving isn't as stellar as Sipadan, but the vibe is noticeably more laidback. Consider giving Turtle Islands National Park a miss if you're heading to Mabul (p388), you'll probably see a greater number of sea turtles while diving (or snorkelling) around Sipadan.

Lankayan

Lovely Lankayan (Pulau Lankayan) was all the buzz when we visited. A quieter alternative to the dive-centric islands in the Semporna Archipelago, this beautiful bump in the sea has one resort, **Lankayan Island Resort** (☎ 089-673999; www.sipadan-resort.com; Batu 6, Bandar Tyng, Sandakan), a popular spot for young romantics. There are 23 cabins dotted along the sand where jungle meets the sea. All-inclusive four-day/four-night packages start at RM3160/RM2544 for divers/non-divers. The island is located about 1½ hours from Sandakan by boat (included in your accommodation package).

Turtle Islands National Park (Selingan)

Known as Pulau Penyu in Malay, this park 40km north of Sandakan is comprised of three small islands, Pulau Selingan, Pulau Bakungan Kecil and Pulau Gulisan, within swimming distance of nearby islands belonging to the Philippines.

Though numbers have fallen off, two species of marine turtles – the green and hawksbill – come ashore here to lay their eggs at certain times of the year, giving the islands their name. Since the laying seasons for each species are virtually complementary, it's possible to see one or the other at almost any time of year.

Sea turtles are harmless vegetarians that spend most of their lives at sea. They are strong, graceful swimmers that grow to a great age and size. The green turtle commonly lays on Pulau Selingan and Pulau Bakungan Kecil between July and October, while the smaller hawksbill turtle lays its eggs on Pulau Gulisan from February to April. The eggs are collected by permanent staff based on Pulau Selingan and transferred to fenced hatcheries, where they are safe from illegal collection by fishermen who eat or sell them.

The only way to visit the Turtle Islands is on an organised tour. While the income from visitors is undoubtedly important to help finance the conservation program, it's easy to feel that this has turned the whole thing into a bit of a circus – on any one night you can have 30-odd gawping tourists clustered round a single laying turtle. Allowing visitors to handle baby turtles before releasing them seems a highly dubious practice. Photography is allowed without flash, but there's always that one person who can't work out how to adjust their camera, and three accidental discharges will generally result in the ranger banning pictures altogether. Hardcore conservationists and nature lovers may find the whole experience unappealing.

For more information on sea turtles (and how you can make sure you do them no harm), see p77.

Tours can be arranged through a travel agency or directly with **Crystal Quest** (☎ 089-212711; cquest@tm.net.my; Jln Buli Sim Sim, Sandakan), and include air-con chalet accommodation on Pulau Selingan and speedboat transfers. Package prices start from RM220 per person (shared bathroom), going up to RM700 per night for full board with guide. Facilities are limited and tour companies often make block reservations, so it's worth booking ahead to make sure you don't get stuck with the most expensive option.

Most boats leave at 9.30am, so you'll have the whole day to hang around the tiny island before the evening turtle viewing. Swimming and snorkelling help pass the time, and there's a small **information centre** (⏰ 6.30-9pm) above the cafeteria, but you might want to bring a book!

SUNGAI KINABATANGAN

An artist painting a portrait of the mighty Sungai Kinabatangan would need a palette of green, blue, and brown…lots and lots of brown… This mighty muddy river is Sabah's longest, measuring a lengthy 560km from its headwaters deep in the southwest jungle to the marshy delta on the turquoise Sulu Sea.

The Kinabatangan's great menagerie of jungle creatures is an ironic by-product of the rampant logging and oil-palm industries. As plantations and camps continue to gobble up virgin rainforest, the area of unruffled jungle becomes thinner, forcing the animals to seek refuge along the river's flood plains. Dozens of tin boats putter along the shores offering tourists the opportunity to have a close encounter with a rhinoceros hornbill or perhaps a doe-eyed orang-utan. Even if you went ape over Sepilok's crew of ginger beasts, seeing an orang-utan in the wild is a truly magical experience (we saw three!).

Sights & Activities
WILDLIFE RIVER CRUISE

Wildlife is the number one reason to visit Sabah, and a cruise down the Kinabatangan is almost invariably a highlight of any nature-nutter's trip. In the late afternoon and early morning, binocular-toting enthusiasts have a chance of spotting an ark's worth of wildlife – from nest-building orang-utans and nosy proboscis monkeys to stealth samba deer and timid pigmy elephants. Mammals can be seen at anytime of year, moving around in small groups while travelling through plantations. Colourful birds are another main draw. Birdwatchers commonly spot all eight varieties of Borneo's hornbills, plus brightly coloured pittas, kingfishers, and, if you're lucky, you may also come across a Storm's stork or the bizarre Oriental darter (also known as a snake-bird). Avian wildlife is more numerous and varied during rainier months (usually October to late March), which coincides with northern-hemisphere migrations. Though friendly for birds, the rainy season isn't very accommodating for humans. Flooding has been a problem of late and a couple of lodges will sometimes shut their doors when conditions are severe.

The success rate of animal-spotting largely depends on luck and the local knowledge of your guide – don't be afraid to ask hard questions about the specifics of your trip before you sign up. Elephants and other larger animals come and go, as herds often break up to get through the palm plantations.

TREKS
Depending on the location of your lodge, some companies offer short treks (one to three hours) through the jungle. Evening hikes are usually shorter and focus on indigenous insect life. Headlamps should be carried in your hand, rather than worn on your head – bats tend to be attracted to light sources and may fly into them; they also secrete an enzyme causing localised paralysis (it's temporary but nonetheless uncomfortable). Most lodges rent out torches for RM5.

GOMANTONG CAVES
Many Kinabatangan tour packages offer an optional side trip to the Gomatong Caves. These limestone caverns are Sabah's most famous source of swiftlet nests used for the eponymous birds-nest soup. There are two types of soup-worthy birds nests: black nests and white nests. Nests of the black variety are a mix of twigs and spit, while the white nests are purely made from the birds' saliva. The white nests are significantly more valuable and Gomantong's got a whole bunch of 'em. A kilogram of white swiflet spit can bring in over RM2000 – making nest-grabbing a popular profession despite the perilous task of shimmying up bamboo poles to pluck the prized puke.

In the last few years visitation has been restricted due to dwindling bird populations (cash-hungry locals were taking the nests before the newborn birds had enough time to mature). Today, the caves operate on a four-month cycle, with closings at the beginning of the term to discourage nest hunters. It's worth asking around before planning your visit – oftentimes the caves are empty or off-limits to visitors. The four-month cycles are strictly enforced to encourage a more sustainable practice of harvesting.

The forested area around the caves conceals plenty of wildlife and a few good walks. The most accessible of the caves is a 10-minute walk along the main trail near the **information centre** (☎ 089-230189; www.sabah.gov.my/jhl; adult/child RM30/15, camera RM30, video RM50; 🕙 8am-noon & 2-4.30pm). Head past the living quarters of the nest collectors to get to the main cave, **Simud Hitam** (Black Cave). You can venture in, though it involves wading ankle-deep through a bat shit cocktail covered in squirming roaches. A 45-minute uphill trek beyond the park office leads to **Simud Putih** (White Cave), containing a greater abundance of prized white nests. Both trails are steep and require some sweaty rock climbing.

It is possible to visit the caves under one's own steam, usually by private vehicle. The turnoff to the caves is located along the road connecting Sukau to the main highway. Minivans plying the route between Sandakan and Sukau (RM17) can drop you off at the junction, but you'll have to walk the five additional kilometres to the park office. If the world-famous caves at Gunung Mulu or Niah are on your Borneo itinerary then it's probably worth giving Gomatong a miss.

Sleeping & Eating
A few nights along the mightly Kinabatangan can be a fantastic way to unwind. In the last few years, river cruises have become exceedingly popular and these days there are dozens of lodges vying for your precious ringgit.

In Kinabatangan lingo, a 'three-day/two-night' stint usually involves the following: arrive in the afternoon on day one for a cruise at dusk, two boat rides (or a boat/hike combo) on day two, and an early morning departure on day three after breakfast and a sunrise cruise. When booking a trip, ask about pick-up and drop-off prices – this is usually extra. The 'B&Bs' along the Kinabatangan – like the B&Bs

elsewhere in Sabah – do not fit the Western definition of a traditional bed and breakfast. No dainty grey-haired dames serving milk and cookies by a roaring fire – these are basic, budget-friendly sleep spots, many of which don't even include breakfast in the price.

Be wary of travel agents selling a bevy of Kinabatangan options – you might think that they've hooked you up with the lodge of your choice, but then you find out that they 'accidentally' booked you in somewhere else. If you have a sense of which place will suit your fancy, it's best to book with them directly to avoid winding up at a lesser lodge for the same price.

See p382 for information about getting to the Sungai Kinabatangan under your own steam.

SUKAU

Sukau means 'tall tree' in the local dialect, and the name is quite fitting. The tiny town sits on the river amongst the skyscraping branches of a shaded thicket. For many years, Sukau was the only place along the Kinabatangan catering to wildlife enthusiasts. Today, it's still the most popular place to hang one's hat, but the abundance of lodging options means that the town can feel a tad busier than one might expect whilst on a 'safari'. If you are planning to visit Sungai Kinabatangan on your own, then Sukau is your best option for lodging and river tours.

There is a small **internet cafe** (one hr RM1.50; 9am-6pm) in the cream-tinged building along the main road (yes, the town is *that* small that buildings are referred to by their colour).

Sukau B&B (☎ 019-583 5580, 089-565269; www.sukau bnb.com; dm/s/tw incl breakfast RM20/40/40) The road leading into Sukau ends here: a grassy knoll with longhouse-style accommodation and a small cottage in the back. It's a good spot for backpackers, sporting clean (and cheap!) bedrooms and a passable common bathroom that's not as cringe-worthy as a lot of backwater backpacker places in Borneo. Two-hour cruises cost RM80 per boat (six person maximum), night cruises are RM100. If you're arriving on your own, around ask around for a boy named Sue – he'll get you sorted.

Sukau Greenview B&B (☎ 013-869 6922, 089-565266; sukau_greenview@yahoo.com; s/tw RM45/60, meals RM10) Another cheapie in central Sukau, this pleasant option offers nine rooms (all with twin-size beds) in a small cottage-style lodge. It's basic (the floors are made from particle

board) but comfy enough for the price. River cruises cost RM35, night rides are RM45 and trips to Oxbow Lake are RM45 (prices are per person). The friendly owners can organise a Sandakan-bound van (RM30 per person) when you depart – it leaves at 6.30am.

Barefoot Sukau Lodge (☎ 089-235525; www.bare footsukau.com; r per person RM80, meals RM25) Barefoot's best features are the scenic eating area over the river and the super-smiley staff (the English is a bit thin, but they get an 'A' for effort). The rooms are small but covered with thick coats of white paint. A two-day/one-night package costs RM200 and includes accommodation, three meals and one cruise. If you're interested in photography, ask for Mr Cede Prudente…

Last Frontier Resort (☎ 016-676 5922; www.thelast frontierresort.com; 3-day/2-night package RM450) Known throughout the Kinabatangan region for their excellent fusion cuisine, this Belgian/Malaysian-owned crash pad sits high, high up (538 steps!) on a hill overlooking the flood plains. Sadly a Sherpa is not included in the rates.

Kinabatangan Riverside Lodge (☎ 089-213502; www.sitours.com; 3-day/2-night package RM550) The rooms don't get tonnes of natural light, but you'll only be in your room at bedtime. During the day, you'll be snooping around for wild creatures on pleasant river cruises (your seat will have a back rest – a luxury around these parts!) and hikes. There's a looping nature trail in the back and the adorable dining area abounds with stuffed monkeys and faux foliage. Pick-ups can be arranged at Sandakan airport or at Sepilok Orang-Utan Rehabilitation Centre for an extra fee.

Sukau Rainforest Lodge (☎ 089-220210, 088-438300; www.sukau.com; 2-day/1-night package RM850) A swish common space stuffed with gongs, tiki torches and *bubu* (local fish traps) welcomes guests after their riverine adventure. The ambience gets a ten out of ten; we'll give the rooms a six – they're standard fare with simple white walls and token accent sculptures. Don't miss the 440m annotated boardwalk in the back that winds through the canopy.

BILIT

Bilit is the new Sukau, with its own collection of jungle lodges and homestays. All of the accommodation here is located at the end of a *very* rutty road (4WD needed!) or on the far side of the river, which means that independent travel here is not as simple as in Sukau.

Even if you are willing to pay through the nose for a water taxi, most of Bilit's riverine sleeping spots require advanced notification and bookings.

Nature Lodge Kinabatangan (☎ 013 863 6263, 088-230534; www.naturelodgekinabatangan.com; 3-day/2-night package dorm/chalet RM300/335) Located just around the river bend from Bilit, this charming jungle retreat is an excellent choice for backpacker budgets. The campus of prim bungalows is divided into two sections: the Civet Wing caters to penny-pinchers with dorm-style huts, while the spiffed-up Agamid Wing offers higher-end twin-bed chalets. The three-day/two-night packages include three boat tours, three guided hikes *and* all meals!

Proboscis Lodge Bukit Melapi (☎ 088-240584; proboscislodge@sipadandivers.com; 2-day/1-night package twin share per person RM330) Despite the snarky management, Proboscis Lodge has created a sociable ambience with its large bar area and comfy tree-stump seating. The wooden bungalows, strewn along a shrubby hill, have oxidised cooper-top roofs that clink when it rains. The two-day/one-night packages include three meals, one river cruise and a pick up from the Lapit jetty.

Bilit Rainforest Lodge (☎ 089-202399; www.tropicalg .com; 2-day/1-night package from RM350, 3-day/2-night package RM700; 🛇 🖳) One of the more luxurious sleeping spots along the Kinabatangan, this snazzy option caters to an international clientele with huge bungalows, modern bathrooms and generous amounts of gushing aircon. The two-day/one-night packages include three meals, accommodation and a three-hour evening cruise around Oxbow Lake.

Bilit Homestay Program (☎ 013-891 3078, 019-537 8043; bilit2002@hotmail.com; 3-day/2-night package RM360) A twist on the Kinabantangan experience, this cultural program offers accommodation in locals' homes (visitors sleep in a private room). The three-day/two-night packages include meals, accommodation, activities and transfers. It is best to book ahead, however if you don't, this part of Bilit can be accessed by private vehicle or minivan (4WD is a must for the last 5km of rutty road). Look for the wooden advert swinging from the home of the *haji awang* ('chief who has performed the haj') – you can't miss it. Walk-in rates are pricier: RM50 per night (not including meals) plus RM45 for one day of activities.

Kinabatangan Jungle Camp (☎ 089-533190; labukbb@yahoo.com; www.kinabatangan-jungle-camp

.com; 2-day/1-night package RM400) GAP Tours (a popular international tour company) uses the facilities here, and when it isn't booked out, this earth-friendly retreat caters to a niche market of birders and serious nature junkies. Packages include three meals, two boat rides, guiding and transfers. The owners, Robert and Annie, also run the Labuk B&B (p378) in Sepilok, and four out of five travellers opt for a Kinabatangan-Sepilok combo tour.

UPRIVER

The following options are way out in the middle of nowhere.

Mescot (Miso Walai Homestay; ☎ 089-551064; www .misowalaihomestay.com; r RM70) This admirable community eco-tourism initiative is a refreshing alternative to the big lodges, and it's great value to boot – rates include all meals and village transfers. In addition to the usual smattering of river trips and guided hikes, there are also potential volunteer opportunities on the community's wetland restoration project. Definitely one worth supporting.

Abai Jungle Lodge (☎ 089-213502, 013-883 5841; www.sitoursborneo.com; 2-day/1-night packages from US$260) Managed by SI Tours (the same company that runs Kinabatangan Riverside Lodge; p381), Abai Jungle Lodge sits 37km upstream from Sukau just as the river emerges from the secondary forest. Eco-conscious attempts are being made at this jungle-clad hideaway – rainwater is collected in cisterns above the chalets, which run on eco-friendly diesel engine generators. Tree-planting projects and a bird-observation tower will attract nature enthusiasts as well. The lodge also helps facilitate a local homestay program (RM50 per person per night, including meals).

Getting There & Away

Taking a bus instead of tour-operated transport to – or at least near – Sungai Kinabatangan can save quite a bit of cash. To reach Sungai Kinabatangan by bus from KK, board a Tawau- or Lahad Datu-bound bus and ask the driver to let you off at 'Meeting Point' (sometimes called 'Sukau Junction') – the turnoff road to reach Sukau. If you are on a Sandakan-bound bus, make sure your driver remembers to stop at the Tawau-Sandakan junction – it's called 'Batu 32' or 'Checkpoint' (sometimes known as Sandakan Mile 32). The blue signs on the side of the highway mark kilometres and do not correlate to the antiquated 'Batu'

BYE BYE BIRDIE

Palm oil plantation...logging farm...palm oil plantation...logging farm... Seems like some parts of Sabah and Sarawak have turned into a brown-and-green checkerboard of industry. Certain forested areas are well protected by stringent government decrees, however rampant deforestation has become a serious problem for several species of bird that require large swathes of jungle through which to fly. Dwindling rainforest also affects many of the nation's endangered species like the cherished orang-utan. Tourists are quick to raise their raised fists in disapproval, but is it *all* bad? See p78 for the full story.

---

system. It should cost no more than RM30 to reach 'Meeting Point' from KK. From Sepilok or Sandakan, expect to pay around RM15 to reach 'Batu 32', and around RM20 if you're on a Sandakan-Tawau bus and want to alight at 'Meeting Point'. A minivan ride to 'Meeting Point' from Lahad Datu costs RM17. You can arrange transport from these drop-off points with your tour operator or with a local minivan. Don't get on the *Birantihanti* buses – they stop anytime someone wants to get on or off, which could quadruple your travelling time. When buying your bus tickets remember to tell the vendor where you want to get off so you don't get overcharged.

If you are travelling to Sukau or Bilit with your own transport, note that the Shell petrol station on the highway at the turnoff to Sukau is the last place to fill up before arriving at the river. The road is paved all the way to Sukau, so a 4WD is not obligatory. The last five kilometres to Bilit are extremely rutty, so a 4WD is recommended here.

LAHAD DATU
pop 105,200

'Lahad Datu' literally means 'place of princes' in the Sulu dialect, but there's nothing particularly regal about this portly port town. In fact, the city would probably qualify as Sabah's most boring destination if it weren't for the rumours of seafaring pirates, who eschew Johnny Depp romanticism in favour of speedboats and machine guns...

There's no real reason to stop in Lahad Datu, except to arrange a visit to the Danum

Valley, Maliau Basin or Tabin Wildlife Reserve. **Borneo Nature Tours** (☎ 089-880207; www .borneonaturetours.com; Lot 20, Block 3, Fajar Centre), who run the Borneo Rainforest Lodge (BRL), and the **Danum Valley Field Centre** (☎ 089-881092; Block 3, Fajar Centre) have offices next to each other in the upper part of town – known as Taman Fajr, or Fajar Centre. Make sure you enter the correct office – we've heard of several tourists booking their Danum expedition with the wrong company. See p385 for the difference between the two Danum options (and yes, these are your only two options).

Around the block, you'll find the booking office of **Tabin Wildlife Holidays** (☎ 088-267266; www.tabinwildlife.com.my), a secondary forest sanctuary on the other side of Lahad Datu.

Don't be surprised if cars frequently slow down and honk as you walk by. These are private taxis that shuttle people between the upper and lower parts of town (where the bus station is) for RM5.

Sleeping & Eating

Lahad Datu lodging is pretty grim, although when we visited there was construction underway on two new properties (we've got our fingers crossed that they'll open in 2010). They are located two blocks away from the Executive Hotel; the current titleholder for the city's best stay.

If you need a quick bite while waiting for your Danum-bound transport, there's a **MultiBake** (cakes from RM1.80; ☾ 8am-10pm) – Malaysia's franchised patisserie – in Fajar Centre (they have free wi-fi too!). **Dovist** (mains from RM5; ☾ lunch & dinner), also around the corner from the Danum booking offices, is a respectable spot for a more substantial meal. It's worth stopping by one of the convenience stores in Fajar Centre to stock up on a couple of snacks before your trip into the Danum Valley.

Tabin Lodge (☎ 089-889552; Jln Urus Setia Kecil; s/d from RM20/30; ❄) Housed in a conspicuous structure smothered in brown paint, this dowdy option might convince budgeters to splurge on the Executive Hotel. In some rooms the walls, ceiling and floor are covered with tiles, giving off a creepy Chinese water torture vibe.

Executive Hotel (☎ 089-881333; 238-240 Jln Teratai; s/d/ste from RM80/100/295; ❄ ▢) A big 'EH' welcomes guests to Lahad Datu's most upmarket sleeping option. Tuxedoed receptionists move at glacial speeds, but the rooms are good enough for your one-night layover. Go for a superior room – the 'standard' ones don't have windows. There's wi-fi in the lobby.

Getting There & Away

MASwings (☎ 1800-88 3000, outside Malaysia 03-7843 3000) currently operates four daily flights to Lahad Datu from KK. The airport is in the upper part of town near Fajar Centre. You must take the first flight of the day (departing KK at 7am) if you don't want a one-day layover in town before heading to the Danum Valley.

Express buses on the KK–Tawau route stop at the Shell station (Taman Fajr) near the Danum Valley office in the upper part of town. Other buses and minivans leave from a vacant lot near Tabin Lodge in the lower part of town. There are frequent departures for Sandakan (RM35, 2½ hours), Sukau (RM17, two hours), Semporna (RM25 to RM30, two hours) and Tawau (RM25 to RM30, 2½ hours). Transport services slow down at around 2.30pm so it's best to make a move by lunchtime. The last minivans technically depart at 5pm, but if there aren't enough people they'll wait until morning. Charter vehicles and 4WDs wait in an adjacent lot.

DANUM VALLEY CONSERVATION AREA

They say that at any given time, there are over a hundred scientists doing research in the Danum Valley. And we aren't surprised – this steaming old-growth forest overflows with colourful wildlife – it's like owning one of those relaxation machines that coos and caws when you're trying to fall asleep. Except at Danum, you get to see the animals too.

This stunning realm of vivid greens is part of a slice of land known as the Sabah Foundation Concession Area, which is managed by **Yayasan Sabah** (Sabah Foundation; www .ysnet.org.my), a semigovernmental organisation tasked with both protecting and utilising the forest resources of Sabah.

It's effectively impossible to visit Danum as an independent traveller, but if you have the time and the cash, the valley is undoubtedly one of Sabah's highlights. There are two places to stay in the park (opposite) – they are about an hour's drive away from each other, so you'll have to decide where you want to stay before making your way into the jungle.

Sights & Activities

Both the BRL and the Danum Valley Field Centre (see p383 for their details) offer a variety of jungle-related activities. Only the BRL has official nature guides, whereas the Field Centre offers park rangers.

TREKKING

The main activities at the BRL and the Danum Valley Field Centre are walking on the meandering trails. At the BRL, take advantage of the well-trained guides who can point out things you would have never seen on your own. The **Coffincliff Trail** is a good way to start your exploration of the area and get your bearings. It climbs to a cliff where the remains of some Dusun coffins can be seen (although the provenance of the coffins is unclear). After reaching a viewpoint, you can either return the way you've come or detour around the back of the peak to descend via scenic **Fairy Falls** and **Serpent Falls**, a pair of 15m falls that are good for a quick dip. The **Danum Trail**, **Elephant Trail** and **Segama Trails** all follow various sections of the Sungai Danum and are mostly flat trails offering good chances for wildlife spotting. All can be done in an hour or two. The **Hornbill Trail** and **East Trail** have a few hills, but are still relatively easy, with similarly good chances for wildlife sightings. Finally, if you just need a quick breath of fresh air after a meal, the **Nature Trail** is a short plankwalk near the lodge that allows you walk into the forest unmolested by leeches.

There are heaps of fantastic trails weaving around the Field Centre – you must bring a ranger along if you aren't a scientist (note that a guide is better than a ranger though).

BIRD-WATCHING

Danum Valley is very popular with bird-watchers from around the world, who come here to see a whole variety of Southeast Asian rainforest species, including the great argus pheasant, the crested fireback pheasant, the blue-headed pitta, the Bornean bristlehead and several species of hornbill, among many others. Some of the guides at the BRL are particularly knowledgeable about birds, and attempts are made to match birders up with these pros. The access road and canopy walkway are good for early morning bird sightings and you'll likely make a few worthwhile sightings right from the verandah of your cabin.

CANOPY WALKWAY

As you'll probably know, most of the action in a tropical rainforest happens up in the forest canopy, which can be frustrating for earthbound humans. The BRL's 107m canopy walkway provides a good chance to get up in the action. The swinging bridges traverse a nice section of forest, with several fine mengaris and majau trees on either side. Bird-watchers often come here at dawn in hopes of checking a few species off their master list. Even if you're not a keen birder, it's worth rolling out of bed early to see the sun come up over the forest from the canopy walkway – when there's a bit of mist around, the effect is quite magical. It's located on the access road, a 10-minute walk from the lodge.

NIGHT DRIVES

This has to be one of the best ways to see some of the valley's 'night shift', though driving in the forest hardly gets a gold star for eco-friendliness, and sensitive souls might empathise with that 'caught-in-the-headlights' feeling. Expect to see one or two species of giant flying squirrels, sambar deer, civets, porcupines and possibly even leopard cats; lucky sightings could include elephants, slow loris and clouded leopards.

Night drives leave the BRL most evenings; the best trips are the extended night drives, which depart at about 8.30pm and return at 1am or 2am. Things you'll be glad you brought include a light waterproof jacket, camera with flash, binoculars and a powerful torch. Drives can be arranged at the Field Centre as well, although you'll probably have to arrange the vehicle one day in advance.

Sleeping & Eating

There are two lodging options in the Danum Valley, each with their own set of pros and cons. If price is paramount go for the Field Centre – wildlife fanatics who value professionally trained guides should pick the BRL.

The **Borneo Rainforest Lodge** (BRL; ☎ 088-267637; www.borneonaturetours.com; standard/deluxe 3-day/2-night full-board package from RM1890/2750) is a class act deep within the buzzing haze of Sabah's remaining old-growth forest. After a recent refurbishment, both the standard and deluxe rooms offer all the amenities of an international-class hotel. Go for the deluxe if you can – they have private jacuzzis on the wooden verandahs that overlook the quiet ravine – so romantic! Honeymooners should go for Kempas D11 – this room has a secluded jacuzzi in its

own wooden pagoda. Meals are taken on a beautiful terrace also fronting the river. We were pretty impressed with the assortment of dishes at the buffet – especially since it all had to be lugged in by 4WD. The BRL's only downfall is their marketing strategy. Yes, the lodge is lovely and the outdoor jacuzzis in the superior rooms are undoubtedly lavish, but this is by no means a five-star resort. And how could it be? Surrounded by relentlessly encroaching jungle and steamy tropical mist, we're impressed that this much luxury exists so deep in the rainforest. Guests who temper their expectations will adore the ambience and find plenty of creature comforts at their fingertips (no aircon though).

Danum Valley Field Centre (☎ 089-880441, 088-326318; resthouse r & board from RM155; ✪) An outpost for scientists and researchers, the field centre also welcomes tourists. Accommodation at the centre is organised into three categories: hostel, resthouse and VIP. We recommend the resthouse rooms, which are located at arm's length from the canteen (the only place to eat). These rooms are basic but clean, sporting ceiling fans and twin beds. Towels are provided for the cold-water showers. The simple hostel is about a seven-minute walk from the canteen, and the barrack-style rooms are separated by gender. The two VIP rooms have aircon and hot water. All buildings at the field centre run on generated power, which shuts off between midnight and 7am. There are no professionally trained guides at the centre – only rangers who can show you the trails. You might luck out and find a friendly researcher who will point you in the direction of a few cool things, but some of the scientists (especially the birders) are quite reclusive. There is a kitchen on the campus, however it is reserved for the research assistants. Tourists take their meals in the cafeteria-style canteen (veggie friendly).

Getting There & Away

The Danum Valley Conservation Area is only accessible by authorised private vehicle. Travellers staying at the Borneo Rainforest Lodge will depart from the lodge office in Lahad Datu at 9am, arriving at the lodge by lunchtime. If you do not want to spend the night in Lahad Datu, it is recommended that you take the morning MASwings flight from KK arriving in Lahad Datu at 7.55am. If you have pre-booked, the driver will wait should your flight be delayed. Walk-ins should head to the booking office in either KK or Lahad Datu, but be prepared to wait for a few days until there is availability. Guests have the option of chartering a private vehicle into the park for a hefty fee.

Tourists staying at the Danum Valley Field Centre must board one of the two jungle-bound vans that leave the booking office in Lahad Datu at 3.30pm on Mondays, Wednesdays and Fridays. Transport is RM60 per person each way – ask about all-inclusive packages for discounts. Vans return to Lahad Datu from the Field Centre at 8.30am on the same days. There are 12 seats in each van and this is the only way to reach the centre unless you charter a pricey private vehicle.

Figure on at least 2½ hours to make the trip through the rutty jungle roads (it took us five hours – our vehicle got stuck in the mud!).

TABIN WILDLIFE RESERVE

Tabin's patch of jungle is starting to emerge as an alternative to the great Danum Valley. This 1205-sq-km reserve consists mainly of lowland dipterocarp forest with mangrove areas at the northern end. Tabin is mostly secondary forest, but that doesn't seem to trouble the wildlife. The stars here are the elephants and primates – gibbons, red-leaf monkeys and macaques. Bird life is abundant, and there's a herd of the endangered Sumatran rhino, though you're unlikely to see them.

The park is managed by **Tabin Wildlife Holidays** (☎ 088-267266; www.tabinwildlife.com.my; Lot 11-1, Block A, Damai Point, Kota Kinabalu), which runs the on-site Tabin Wildlife Resort, an attractive retreat with a clutch of upscale chalets. At the time of research a hostel was being built on the grounds to attract the penny-pincher crowd. Camping is prohibited. Five trails snake out into the jungle from in front of the resort. Try the Elephant Trail (800m) if you're interested in belching mud pits. The Gibbon Trail (2.8km) leads to the pretty Lipa Waterfall.

An all-inclusive day-trip package to the park (8am to 2.30pm) costs RM210 per person. The three-day/two-night 'Observation 'n' Nature' package will set you back RM1010.

Tabin can be accessed with a rental vehicle (4WD is a must). There are several entrances to the reserve; the easiest one to navigate to is near the junction of Ladan Tungju and Ladang Premai (it's 15km from Lahad Datu airport to Ladang Kajai). Pay the RM5 entry fee at the park's second gate (there are six gates in total).

SEMPORNA
pop 133,000

Semporna is the kind of town that makes tourists want to swear – especially if they're travelling on a tight schedule. As your bumpy ride trundles into this sleepy burg, you'll quickly realise that you haven't reached your oceanic Eden just yet. Semporna is one of those necessary evils – a lacklustre layover that'll snag you for a night on your way to paradise. Several lower-priced scuba centres have set up shop in town, but we highly recommend splurging on the island accommodation nearby (p388).

Orientation & Information

If you're arriving in Semporna under your own steam, leave the bus and minivan drop-off area and head towards the mosque's spiking minaret. This is the way to the waterfront. Follow the grid of concrete streets to the right until you reach 'Semporna Seafront' – a collection of newer structures decked out in primary colours that starkly contrast with the charmless pastels throughout the rest of town. This neighbourhood (which feels more like Havana than Southeast Asia) is home to a cluster of diving outfitters, each stacked one next to the other in a competitive clump. Sleeping and eating options crowd around this area as well.

Although money moves quickly around town as tourists drop some serious ringgit on diving adventures, ATMs are few and far between. The closest bank to the 'Semporna Seafront' is the yellow-bannered **Maybank** (☎ 089-784852) on Jln Jakarullah. Expect small lines and the occasional beggar, especially in the evening. Dragon Inn (opposite) has a small air-conditioned internet lounge for those needing to update their blog.

The local navy base has the closest **decompression chamber** (☎ 089-783100).

Diving

'Diving' is the answer every tourist provides when someone asks them why they're in Semporna, and 'Sipadan' is the answer to 'where do you want to dive?' Scuba is the town's lifeline, and there's no shortage of places to sign up for some serious bubble blowing. Operators are clustered around the 'Semporna Seafront', a newer neighbourhood near the Dragon Inn, while other companies have offices in KK. Due to the high volume of interest, it is best to do your homework and book ahead – diving at Sipadan is limited to 120 persons per day. If time isn't an issue, consider swinging through town to examine your options, book your dive package, and come back a few weeks later to hit the waves.

See p388 for everything you need to know about diving at Sipadan (and at the other sites in the Tun Sakaran Marine Park).

Sleeping

Semporna is no great shakes, but the town offers a lot of passable options at the low end of the budget spectrum. If you've already signed up with a scuba operator ask them about sleeping discounts (and don't be shy about trying to finagle a good deal, especially if you're sticking around for a while). Some dive centres, like Scuba Junkie, offer cheap in-house sleeps, both in Semporna and in the marine park (see below), while others will point you in the direction of Dragon Inn. Keep an eye out for newer spots not mentioned here – high demand means an ever-increasing number of places to crash.

Dragon Inn (Rumah Rehat Naga; ☎ 089-781088; www.dragoninnfloating.com.my; 1 Jln Kastam; dm RM15-20, r incl breakfast RM66-88; ✕ 🖵) The owners are going for a tiki-chic vibe, and although it's a bit more memorable than the other options in town, the decor kinda falls flat. Long rows of dark rooms sit on stilts above the greenish tidewater at the far corner of the town's dive-centric district. Go for the 'standard' private rooms (RM66) – they are identical to the 'front row' rooms (RM88).

Seafest Hotel (☎ 089-782333; www.seafesthotel.com; Jln Kastam; r incl breakfast from RM200; ✕) Six storeys of bay-view, business-class comfort at the far end of the 'Semporna Seafront' neighbourhood. It's affiliated with Seafest fishery, so check the restaurant's catch of the day. Don't be shy about asking for discounts.

Other options include:

Borneo Global Sipadan BackPackers (☎ 089-785088; borneogb@gmail.com; Jln Causeway; dm/tr incl breakfast RM22/90; ✕) Dozens of dorm beds.

Scuba Junkie Backpackers (☎ 089-785372; www.scuba-junkie.com; Lot 36, Block B, Semporna Seafront; dm/r incl breakfast RM30/80; ✕) Sociable spot offering 50% discounts for divers.

Sipadan Inn (☎ 089-782766; www.sipadan-inn.com; Block D, Semporna Seafront; r incl breakfast RM84; ✕) Spotless rooms are light on decor. A better deal that Dragon Inn's RM88 rooms.

Eating

You can't go wrong with any of the options around the 'Semporna Seafront'. Try one of the restaurants at the Seafest Hotel complex for some authentic Chinese cuisine. Scuba Junkie's restaurant specialises in Western fare and claims to have the best pizza in town (not a hard feat when you're one of two places serving slices). If you wanna go native, sample the *nasi lemak* or *korchung* (rice dumplings) – Semporna is well known for these two dishes.

Anjung Paghalian Café (Jln Kastam, mains RM3-5; ☾ dinner) Beside the Tun Sakaran Marine Park entrance sign, this indoor/outdoor place on a pier features fish, prawn, chicken, squid and venison sold by portions (for two or more people) and cooked in your choice of up to 12 different styles. It also has standard Malay hawker stalls and even one which serves burgers.

Mabul Steak House (☎ 089-781785; Semporna Seafront; mains from RM4; ☾ lunch & dinner) This easy-going balcony restaurant's large and glacial 'ice-blended juices' are a soothing antidote for sucking bottled air. For further chilling, there's a leather couch and overstuffed chairs around a huge TV showing movies or sport. The RM4.90 and RM7.90 set meals won't leave you cold – or hungry.

Getting There & Away

The advent of uber-cheap airfares has made Semporna easily accessible from both KK and KL. Flights on AirAsia can cost as little as RM9 from KK, and RM89 from KL – including tax. Planes land at Tawau Airport, roughly 28km from town. Tawau–Semporna buses (RM15) will stop at the airport if you ask the driver nicely. Buses that do not stop at the airport will let you off at Mile 28, where you will have to walk a few (unshaded) kilometres to the terminal. If you are staying at midrange or top-end digs, chances are your accommodation will arrange any necessary airport pick-ups and drop-offs. Remember that flying less than 24 hours after diving can cause serious health issues, even death.

The bus 'terminal' hovers around the Milimewa supermarket not too far from the mosque's looming minaret. Morning and night buses to KK (RM50, 9 hours) leave at around 7am or 7pm. Minivans to/from Tawau (RM10 to RM15, 1½ hours),

SABAH

Lahad Datu (RM20 to RM25, 2½ hours) and Sandakan (RM35 to RM40, 5½ hours) arrive and depart around the grocery store area as well. All run from early morning until 4pm.

Semporna is the gateway to the islands in the Tun Sakaran Marine Park, see p391 for information on accessing the archipelago.

SEMPORNA ARCHIPELAGO

The stunning islets of the Semporna Archipelago freckle the cerulean sea like a shattered earthen pot – each sandy chunk a lonely spot on the ocean's mirror-like surface. Bands of sun-kissed sea gypsies patrol the waters scooping up snapping crabs and ethereal shells. But another world exists deep below – a silent realm inspiring even more wonder and awe. Sipadan's technicolour sea walls reach deep down – 2000m to the distant ocean floor – and act like an underwater beacon luring docile turtles, slippery sharks and waving mantas.

Orientation & Information

The Semporna Islands are loosely divided into two geographical sections: the northern islands (protected as **Tun Sakaran Marine Park**, gazetted in 2004) and the southern islands. Both areas have desirable diving – Sipadan is located in the southern region, as is Mabul and Kapalai. Mataking and Sibuan belong to the northern area. If you are based in Semporna you'll have a greater chance of diving both areas, although most people are happy to stick with Sipadan and its neighbours.

Consider stocking up on supplies (sunscreen, mozzie repellent etc) before making your way into the archipelago. Top-end resorts have small convenience stores although the prices are inflated. ATMs are nonexistent, but all resorts accept credit cards (Visa and Mastercard). Mabul has a small police station near the village mosque, as well as a small pharmacy shack selling basic medical and hygiene supplies in the fishing village. Internet is of the wi-fi variety and is available only at the upmarket sleeping options.

The closest **decompression chamber** (089-783100) is at the naval base in Semporna.

Diving

Maybe the name Semporna doesn't ring a bell – that's because the key word here is 'Sipadan'.

Located 36km off Sabah's southeast coast, **Sipadan** (also called 'Pulau Sipadan') is the shining star in the archipelago's constellation of shimmering islands. The elliptical islet sits like a clay-tinged crown atop a stunning submerged pinnacle with its world famous near-vertical walls. This underwater beacon is a veritable weigh station for virtually all types of sea life, from fluttering coral to school-bus-sized whale sharks. Sea turtles and reef sharks are a given during any dive, and luckier scuba-holics may spot mantas, eagle rays, octopus, even scalloped hammerheads!

Roughly a dozen delineated dive sites orbit the island – the most famous being the aptly named **Barracuda Point**, where streamers of barracuda collide to form impenetrable walls of undulating fish flesh. Reef sharks seem to be attracted to the strong current here and almost always swing by to say hello. **South Point** sits at exactly the opposite end of the island from Barracuda Point and usually hosts the large pelagics (manta magnet!). The west side of the island features technicolour walls that tumble down to an impossibly deep 2000m. The walls are best appreciated from out in the blue on a clear afternoon. The east coast tends to be slightly less popular, but oodles of turtles and sharks are still inevitable.

Although Sipadan outshines the neighbouring sites, there are other reefs in the marine park that are well worth exploring. The macro-diving around **Mabul** (or 'Pulau Mabul') is world-famous. In fact, the term 'muck diving' was invented here. The submerged sites around **Kapalai**, **Mataking** and **Sibuan** are also of note.

While it is technically possible to rock up and chance upon an operator willing to take you to Sipadan the following day, we strongly suggest that you book in advance (the earlier the better; see p341 about preplanning in Borneo). The downside to pre-booking, of course, is that you can't visit each dive centre's storefront to suss out which one you like best, but Johnny-come-latelies might be forced to wait a few weeks before something opens up. The government issues 120 passes (RM40) to Sipadan each day (this number includes divers, snorkellers and day-trippers). Bizarre rules and red tape, like having certain gender ratios, make the permit process even more frustrating. Each dive company is issued a predetermined number of passes per day (usually around eight to 12 tickets for companies based in Semporna) depending on the size of their operation and the general demand for permits. Each operator has a unique way of 'awarding' tickets – some companies place their divers in a permit lottery, others promise a day at Sipadan after a day (or two) of diving at Mabul and Kapalai. No matter which operator you choose, you will be required to do a non-Sipadan intro dive unless you are a Divemaster that has logged a dive in the last six months. Permits to Sipadan are issued by day (and not by dive) so make sure you are getting at least three dives in your package.

A three-dive day trip costs between RM250 and RM450 (some operators include park fees, other do not – make sure to ask), and equipment rental (full gear) comes to about RM50 or RM60 per day. Cameras (around RM100 per day) and dive computers (around RM60 per day) are also available for rent at most dive centres. Snorkellers will drop RM100 for a day of bubble blowing. Top-end resorts on Mabul and Kapalai offer all-inclusive package holidays (plus a fee for equipment rental).

Although most of the diving in the area is 'fun diving', Open Water certifications are available for scuba virgins, and advanced coursework is popular for those wanting to take things to the next level. Diving at Sipadan is geared towards divers with an Advanced Open Water certificate (currents and thermoclines can be strong), although experienced Open Water divers should not have any problems (they just can't go as deep as advanced divers). A three-day Open Water course will set you back between RM750 and RM850. Advanced Open Water courses (two days) cost around RM700 to RM850, and the Divemaster certification runs for around RM1850.

The following dive operators are amongst the growing laundry list of companies in the area. Several operators are based at their respective resorts, while others have storefronts and offices in Semporna and/or KK. No matter where your desired operator is located, it is *highly* recommended that you contact them in advance.

Billabong Scuba (☎ 089-781866; www.billabongscuba .com; Lot 28, Block E, Semporna Seafront) Semporna-based outfit with reasonable prices. Accommodation can be arranged at a rickety 'homestay' on Mabul.

Blue Sea Divers (☎ 089-781322; www.thereefdivers .com; Semporna Seafront) Reputable day-trip operator in Semporna. Request chicken curry for your post-dive lunch.

Borneo Divers (☎ 088-222226; www.borneodivers.info; 9th fl, Menara Jubili, 53 Jalan Gaya, Kota Kinabalu) The original operators in the area, Borneo Divers were the good folks who unveiled Sipadan to an awestruck Jacques Cousteau. They have maintained their high standards throughout the years offering knowledgeable guides and comfy quarters. Their office is located in Kota Kinabalu. See p390 for information about their comely resort on Mabul. Recommended.

Scuba Junkie (☎ 089-785372; www.scuba-junkie.com; Lot 36, Block B, Semporna Seafront) Popular with the young backpacker crowd, Scuba Junkie invented the hard sell in Semporna. Prices are kept low and diving gear is well maintained. Ask about cheap sleeps – they'll hook you up with a budget bed on Mabul or in the hostel across from their storefront (p387). If you're sleepless in Semporna, stop by their restaurant in the wee hours for some greasy pizza.

Sipadan Scuba (☎ 089-784788, 919-128; www .sipadanscuba.com; Lot 23, Block D, Semporna Seafront) Twenty years of Borneo experience and an international staff makes Sipadan Scuba a reliable choice. This is the only PADI 5 Star Instructor Development Centre in Semporna. Recommended.

Sipadan Water Village (☎ 089-784100; www.swv resort.com; Jln Kastam) A private operator based at the Mabul resort with the same name (p390).

SMART (www.sipadan-mabul.com.my) The dive centre operating at Sipadan-Mabul Resort and Mabul Water Bungalow; both are located on Mabul (p390).

Uncle Chang's (Borneo Jungle River Island Tours; ☎ 089-785372; 36 Semporna Seafront) Offers diving and snorkelling day trips, plus stays at its 'lodge' on Mabul (p390) or Maiga (RM80 per person).

Sleeping

From opulent bungalows to ragtag sea shanties, the marine park offers a wide variety of accommodation catering to all budget types. Sleeping spots are sprinkled across the archipelago with the majority of options clustered on the peach-fringed island of Mabul (Sipadan's closest neighbour). All options, regardless of budget type, include three meals per day in the price. Divers and snorkellers can also opt to stay in the town of Semporna (p387), which offers a slightly better bang for your buck, but you'll miss out on post-dive chill sessions along flaxen strips of sand, and fiery equatorial sunsets that plunge into the crystalline sea. Also, Semporna is noticeably farther away from the park's oceanic treasures.

SIPADAN

Although it has been several years since the government banned Sipadan sleepovers, we just wanted to reiterate that it is not possible to stay here. The island is under the control of the Wildlife Department and is patrolled by rangers and local army personnel. Day trips to the island and its house reef are capped at 120 individuals.

MABUL

Beautiful Pulau Mabul is a great place to be based for some serious Sipadan scuba. Mabul itself is also an excellent spot to strap on a mask and check out the world-class macro-diving. This sandy bump in the sea is home to a fishing village and a community of Bajau Bajau (sea gypsies).

Budget

As you've probably noticed, a trip to Sipadan can be a very pricey venture. Mabul has a large clump of cheapies, but remember the old adage – you get what you pay for.

Mabul Beach Resort (☎ 089-784788, 089-919128; www.sipadanscuba.com; per person r RM80-120) Owned and operated by Scuba Junkie, this brand new spot on Mabul is shaking things up for shoe-stringers. No more are the days of dingy 'long-house' accommodation – divers will finally be able to get a good night's sleep. Most of the resort was still under construction when we visited, but we think it looks very promising!

The following options are located within Mabul's 'town' (and we use that term lightly) of sea shanties. The quality is fairly similar at all four places: in need of an upgrade. At the time of research we noticed a couple of renovation attempts underway, but guests should still expect uber-basic digs in wobbly shacks, flimsy mattresses, grim toilet stalls, cold showers, floating pieces of rubbish and roosters crowing in the early morning. The tightest of wallets will appreciate the chilled-out atmosphere and local vibe, but light sleepers and choosier travellers should consider dropping the extra cash to stay elsewhere. All options feature communal bathrooms unless otherwise noted.

Arung Hayat Resort (☎ 089-782526; per person r/ste RM50/80) An autonomous homestay with low-slung beds, baby blue walls and plenty of smiles. Divers with Scuba Junkie can opt to stay here. They also caters to non-divers.

Billabong (☎ 089-781866; per person r RM50) Six basic rooms hovering on stilts above the ebbing tide. Associated accommodation for Billabong Scuba (p389).

Lai's Homestay (per person r RM60) Features a large, wood-planked verandah stretching over the sea. Slightly newer, but still shanty-esque. Affiliated with Big John Scuba.

Uncle Chang's (☎ 089-781002; per person dm/s/d RM50/120/60, per person d with aircon & private bathroom RM90; ✿) A Sipadan backpacking stalwart catering to the like-named dive operator (p389). We've received reports from several travellers that a charming family of rats also calls this place home.

Midrange & Top End

With the noticeable increase in quality comes a noticeable increase in price. Watch out folks, some of these prices are in US dollars!

Seaventures Dive Resort (☎ 088-261669; www.seaventuresdive.com; 4-day/3-night dive package from RM1950; ✿) A worthy attempt at offering tourists something unique, this oceanic eyesore sits just off of Mabul's silky shoreline. The upshot: excellent diving at your toes. The downside: after your daily scuba sesh, you're stuck living aboard an ugly iron oilrig.

Borneo Divers Mabul Resort (☎ 088-222226; www.borneodivers.info; 3-day/3-night dive packages from US$660; ✿ ▢) The oldest dive centre in the region used to have a resort on Sipadan until they closed it down in 2005. Today, they continue to provide top-notch service on Mabul with an earth-friendly focus. The U-shape of accommodation is in semi-detached mahogany bungalows with bright yellow window frames. Open-air pavilions with gauzy netting punctuate the perfectly manicured grounds. Overall this is one of the best bangs for your buck on the island. Ask about on-site camping opportunities to cut back on costs. Wi-fi available in the dining room.

Sipadan-Mabul Resort (SMART; ☎ 088-486389; www.sipadan-mabul.com.my; 3-day/2-night dive package from US$762, non-divers US$503; ✿ ▢) Even though the summer-camp styling suits the tropical landscape, the prices here are a bit out of whack. If you're gonna splurge why not go all the way and snag a room at SMART's sister property (see opposite). Wi-fi is available in the dining area.

Sipadan Water Village Resort (☎ 089-751777; www.swvresort.com; 4-day/3-night package from RM3500; ✿ ▢) Outmoded design details (although when were wooden tarantula ornaments ever in style?) quickly set the tone here – this resort-on-stilts doesn't pull off 'graceful elegance' quite like Mabul Water Bungalow next door despite the idyllic location. If you decide that this is the spot for you, then go for the 'grand deluxe' bungalows.

Mabul Water Bungalow (☎ 088-486389; www.mabul waterbungalows.com; 3-day/2-night dive package from US$1045, non-divers $640; ✖ ▣) The ritzier sister of Sipidan-Mabul Resort (opposite), this floating enclave of temple-like chalets and taupe golf carts is one of the poshest addresses in all of Borneo. The rooms are effortlessly opulent, and the resort's only suite, the Bougain Villa, features a trickling waterfall in the bathroom, its own private dock and glass floors revealing the starfish-strewn sea floor. Wi-fi available.

KAPALAI
Although commonly referred to as an island, Kapalai is more like a large sandbar sitting slightly under the ocean surface. From afar, the one hotel, **Sipadan-Kapalai Resort** (☎ 089-673999; www.dive-malaysia.com; Mile 6, Bandar Tyng, Sandakan; 4-day/3-night package from RM2480; ✖ ▣), looks like it's sitting on palm trunks in the middle of the sea. The resort designers went for a sea-gypsy theme and tacked on an opulent twist, making the sea cabins out of shiny lacquered wood.

MATAKING
Mataking Island (☎ 089-782080; www.matakingisland .com; 3-day/2-night package from US$640; ✖) is the only accommodation on little Mataking. This sandy escape has some beautiful diving, which is usually dwarfed by Sipadan further south.

POM POM
Pom Pom needs no cheerleading – this stunning, secluded haven sits deep within the Tun Sakaran Marine Park, about one hour by boat from Semporna. **Sipadan Pom Pom Island Resort** (☎ 089-781918; http://pompomisland.com; 4-day/3-night package from RM3085; ✖ ▣) runs the only operation on the island. Reed-and-thatch bungalows are spacious and offer seaviews from the spacious balconies.

ROACH REEFS
This network of artificial reefs was once the private underwater playground for a wealthy businessman, but today **Roach Reefs Resort** (☎ 089-779332; www.roachreefsresort.com; 4-day/3-night package from RM3200; ✖ ▣) has opened its doors to tourists.

Getting There & Around
All transport to the marine park is funnelled through the town of Semporna. See p387 for detailed information on how to reach Semporna, and remember, it is a *serious* health risk to fly within 24 hours of your last dive (it's also unsafe to dive directly after flying due to poorly pressurised cabins and dehydration). Tourists who are staying on one of the many offshore islets must book ahead as space is quite limited and there is no public transport to any of the archipelago's islands. Your accommodation will arrange your transport needs from Semporna or Tawau airport (usually for an extra fee), which will most likely depart in the morning (meaning that if you arrive in Semporna in the afternoon, you will be required to spend the night in town before setting off into the park). Transport to Tun Sakaran's breathtaking dive sites (Sipadan!) is always included in your dive package. Chartered boats from Semporna can be scouted – check out the motley crew of bobbing vessels parked outside the Seafest Hotel. Raish (pronounced like 'rice'; ☎ 012-811 0934) offers the cheapest water-taxi service around the marine park at RM200 per ride (eight-person maximum). His English isn't stellar so you might have to recruit a local to help translate.

TAWAU
pop 354,250

If you liked Sandakan's nondescript port vibe, then you'll love Tawau – Sabah's most forgettable spot. Though it's known as a Bugis (ethnic group) city, a massive stilt village east of town houses many of the Filipino and Indonesian immigrants who eke out a living on the waterfront. Patchy street lighting doesn't help the atmosphere, and travellers, especially women, may feel more comfortable in pairs after dark. Locals do seem quite proud of their town, however. Check out www.etawau.com for recommendations.

The only lure for travellers is the border: Tawau is the only crossing point with Kalimantan where foreigners can get a visa to enter Indonesia. The (so far) low-profile Indonesian consulate (see p392), about 200m beyond Tawau Hospital, has remained fast and friendly while foreigners have been few. But even the most successful applicant will have to spend at least one night in town before shipping off. Divers with Sipadan on the brain needn't pass through Tawau.

Information
City Internet Zone (☎ 089-760016; 37 Kompleks Fajar, Jln Perbandaran; per hr RM2-3; ⏰ 9am-midnight)
HSBC (Jln Perbandaran) ATM.

SABAH

SABAH

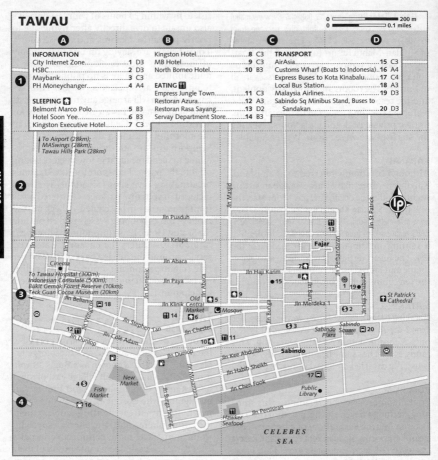

TAWAU

INFORMATION	
City Internet Zone	1 D3
HSBC	2 D3
Maybank	3 C3
PH Moneychanger	4 A4

SLEEPING 🏠	
Belmont Marco Polo	5 B3
Hotel Soon Yee	6 B3
Kingston Executive Hotel	7 C3

Kingston Hotel	8 C3
MB Hotel	9 C3
North Borneo Hotel	10 B3

EATING 🍴	
Empress Jungle Town	11 C3
Restoran Azura	12 A3
Restoran Rasa Sayang	13 D2
Servay Department Store	14 B3

TRANSPORT	
AirAsia	15 C3
Customs Wharf (Boats to Indonesia)	16 A4
Express Buses to Kota Kinabalu	17 C4
Local Bus Station	18 A3
Malaysia Airlines	19 D3
Sabindo Sq Minibus Stand, Buses to Sandakan	20 D3

Indonesian consulate (☎ 089-772052; 089-752969; Jln Tanjong Batu; ☻ 8am-noon, 1-4pm) Efficient one-day service (usually) for visas.
Maybank (☎ 089-762333; Jln Dunlop)
PH Moneychanger (☎ 089-776389; Kompleks Kojasa) Changes cash in harbour area.

Sights

Tawau is pretty light on sights and isn't worth going out of your way to stop by. The **Teck Guan Cocoa Museum** (☎ 089-775566; 5-person guided tour RM100; ☻ 8-11.30am & 1.30-4pm Mon-Fri, 8am-1pm Sat) is a testament to Tawau's burgeoning cocoa industry. A tour includes a 20-minute video, detailed dioramas and hands-on presentations. A taxi from Tawau town to the museum (40 minutes away) costs RM40 each way – the taxi can wait

at no extra charge while you tour the grounds (two hours maximum). The **Bukit Gemok Forest Reserve** (adult/child RM5/1), located 10km from Tawau town centre, is a fantastic park sitting on 445 hectares of protected land. Developed in the early 1990s, the jungle here has only recently become popular with trekkers, Hash runners and tour groups – many consider it to be far better than the trails around Poring Hot Springs. A taxi to the park costs RM20.

Sleeping

Splurge for a midranger if you're stopping through Tawau. They cater to local businessmen and are excellent bang for your buck – miles beyond anything you can get in KK for a similar price.

Hotel Soon Yee (☎ 089-772447; 1362 Jln Stephen Tan; r RM22-38; ✖) No prostitutes, no phones, no hot water (except in shared bathrooms), but lots of value and camaraderie in this guesthouse. Cheaper fan-cooled rooms have shared bathrooms.

North Borneo Hotel (☎ 089-763060; fax 089-773066; 52-53 Jln Dunlop; r RM50-80; ✖) Strategically placed between the Sabindo and Fajar quarters, this older hotel has large rooms, many with terraces overlooking the street, and surprisingly appealing bathrooms, most with bathtubs. Not fancy, but good value.

Kingston Executive Hotel (☎ 089-702288; fax 089-702688; 4581-4590 Jln Haji Karim; d RM87-109; ✖ 💻) The swankier add-on to the old Kingston Hotel across the street, this 'executive' strives for boutique touches, like bucket sinks and trippy art. Some rooms have duvets made from *kain songket* (traditional Malay handwoven fabric with gold threads).

MB Hotel (☎ 089-701333; hotelmayblossom@yahoo .com; Jln Masjid; r from RM110; ✖) MB knows what's important: a comfortable night's sleep. The hallways could use a facelift and the lobby is going for a 'minimal' theme, but who really cares – the rooms are outfitted with modern business amenities (including the fastest wi-fi in Borneo) that edge out the Heritage Hotel nearby, since a sleep here is slightly cheaper.

Belmont Marco Polo (☎ 089-777988; bmph@tm.net .my; Jln Klinik; s/d from RM220/250; ✖) Forestry executives will feel at home with mahogany shutters and other elegant wooden accents at Tawau's luxury leader. For work, there's wi-fi, for play there's transport to the golf course nearby.

Eating

Locals love splurging on the buffet lunch at the Belmont Marco Polo (above) which, for RM14.80 (RM22 on weekends), is a steal considering the variety of tasty bites. The interior courtyard around the Kingston Hotel has a few local haunts serving up tasty dishes, and the seafood in the Sabindo area is top-notch albeit slightly pricey.

Restoran Azura (☎ 012-863 9934; Jln Dunlop; dishes RM3-6; ✖ breakfast, lunch & dinner) Recommended for its tasty South Indian food and snickerworthy menu, Azura serves up a killer fishhead curry and sundry 'tits-bits'. The noodles are pretty good too. There's another branch in Sabindo Sq.

Restoran Rasa Sayang (☎ 089-777042; Jln Haji Karim; dishes from RM5; ✖ lunch & dinner) Part of Tawau's burgeoning restaurant quarter, this is a neat Chinese diner doing good-value set meals (RM15) and novel specials such as prawn mango rice.

Empress Jungle Town (☎ 089-776393; 54 Jln Dunlop; mains RM5.75-30; ✖ lunch & dinner) A rather bizarre new enterprise attempting to recapture the rainforest experience *inside* a restaurant, right down to the semi-convincing fake trees, piped birdsong, cascading water and, um, mirror ball. Unlike most jungles, though, this plastic paradise has a snack bar, a karaoke lounge and a cafeteria-style menu of Chinese and Western dishes.

Self-caterers should try the **Servay Department Store** (Jln Musantara), across from the Old Central Market, for everything from picnic lunches to DVDs of dubious authenticity.

Getting There & Away

AIR

Malaysia Airlines (☎ 089-761293; Jln Haji Sahabudin) has daily flights to both KK and KL. **AirAsia** (☎ 089-761946; Jln Bunga) has two daily direct flights to KK, although the second flight of the day is often cancelled if the plane is empty. **MASwings** (☎ 1300-883 000) flies to Sandakan twice daily, the afternoon flight continuing to KK.

BOAT

Boats for Indonesia leave from the customs wharf near the fish market. Fast ferries *Tawindo* or *IndoMaya* to Tarakan (RM75, 3½ hours) leave every morning except Sunday. Several companies run boats daily to Nunukan (RM40, one hour), an alternative border crossing. Most sailings continue or connect to Tarakan (from RM35), three hours from Nunukan.

BUS

When purchasing your bus ticket to leave KK, it's best to do it in advance to avoid the rush of touts that create a veritable mosh pit before departures. Buses leave around 8am or 8pm – there's nothing in between (so swing by around lunchtime to snag your ticket). Daily express buses for KK (RM75, 9 hours) leave from behind the Sabindo area in a large dusty lot.

Buses to Sandakan (RM30, five hours), depart hourly 7am to 2pm from the stand in Sabindo Sq, one block on a diagonal from the KK terminus, behind the purple Yassin Curry

House sign. That's also the spot for frequent minivans to Semporna (RM8 to RM10, two hours), Kunak (RM8 to RM10, 1½ hours), Lahad Datu (RM17 to RM20, three hours) and Sandakan (RM32 to RM35, six hours).

Getting Around

Tawau's airport is 28km from town along the main highway to Semporna and Sandakan. A shuttle bus (RM12) to the local bus station in Tawau's centre leaves six times daily. A taxi costs RM45.

TAWAU HILLS PARK

Hemmed in by agriculture and human habitation, this small reserve has forested hills rising dramatically from the surrounding plain. The **park** (RM10) was gazetted in 1979 to protect the water catchment for settlements in the area, but not before most of the accessible rainforest had been logged. Much of the remaining forest clings to steep-sided ridges that rise to 1310m Gunung Magdalena.

On a clear day the Tawau Hills Park's peaks make a fine sight. A trail leads to **hot springs** and a **waterfall** three hours' walk north of the park headquarters, and there's a 30-minute walk to **Bombalai Hill** (530m), to the south.

There's accommodation at **Tawau Hills Park headquarters** (Taman Bukit Tawau; ☎ 089-753564; dm/chalet RM20/200). Rates are lower on weekdays.

Tawau Hills is 28km northwest of Tawau. A taxi will cost about RM30 to RM40.

MALIAU BASIN CONSERVATION AREA

Looking down on Sabah with Google Earth, the eye is immediately drawn to what looks like the crater of an giant extinct volcano in the middle of the state, about 45km north of the border with Kalimantan. Zooming in, the heart starts to beat with excitement, for you cannot help but notice one thing: there are no roads here, only winding rivers and lush rainforest. This is the **Maliau Basin Conservation Area** (MBCA; www.ysnet.org.my/Maliau), known very appropriately as 'Sabah's Lost World'.

The Maliau Basin is run by the Sabah Foundation, and is the single best place in Borneo to experience the wonders of an old-growth tropical rainforest. More than that, it is one of the world's great reserves of biodiversity, a dense knot of almost unbelievable genetic richness. As such, it deserves to rank high on the itinerary of anyone interested in the natural world, as well as deserving

the strongest protections afforded by the Malaysian government and world environmental bodies. And a visit to the basin is always a poignant affair, as you'll share the road with a parade of logging trucks hauling trees out of the forest at an astonishing rate.

Unbelievably, there is no known record of human beings entering the basin until the early 1980s (although it is possible that indigenous peoples entered the basin before that time). It is only recently that the area has been opened up to a limited number of adventurous travellers, and it's still an expensive and time-consuming destination that is practically impossible to visit on your own.

Orientation & Information

Maliau Basin is located in the southern part of central Sabah, just north of the logging road connecting Tawau with Keningau, a minimum of five hours' drive from either of these towns by 4WD vehicle. It is part of the Yayasan Sabah Forest Management Area, a vast swath of forest in southeastern Sabah under the management of **Yayasan Sabah** (www.ysnet.org.my), a semigovernmental body tasked with both developing and protecting the natural resources of Sabah. Innoprise Corporation, the commercial arm of Yayasan Sabah, runs tours to the basin through its subsidiary **Borneo Nature Tours** (☎ 088-267637; www.borneonaturetours.com; Lot 10, ground fl, Block D, Kompleks Sadong Jaya, Kota Kinabalu), which also runs Borneo Rainforest Lodge (p385). Other tour operators in Sabah can also arrange tours of the park.

The **MBCA security gate** is just off the Tawau–Keningau Rd. From the gate, it's a very rough 25km journey to the **Maliau Basin Studies Centre**, for researchers, and about 20km to **Agathis Camp**, the base camp for most visitors to the basin.

Independent visits to the basin are difficult: proficient 4WD drivers could probably get there with their own steam with private vehicles, and you could arrange for guides and porters at the security gate, if none are out with tours at that time, but the overall expense would likely be similar to an organised tour, once vehicle rental costs are taken into account. It is likely that as the Tawau–Keningau road improves (it is due to be paved) and interest in the basin increases, independent travel will become easier. Check online for the latest information when you plan your tour.

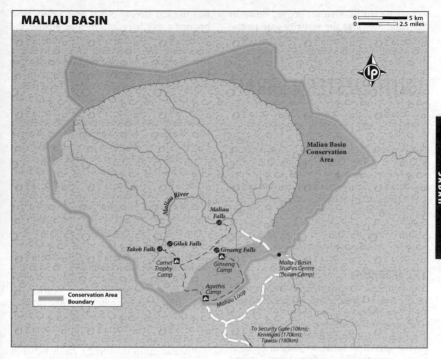

SABAH

Accommodation in Maliau Basin is in the form of simple camps, which range from basic bunkhouses such as Agathis Camp to **Camel Trophy Camp**, a wood-frame two-storey hut with private bedrooms. None of the camps are luxurious, but after a day on the trail fighting leeches, they'll seem like paradise.

Trekking

The trek through the Maliau Basin will undoubtedly be the most memorable hike of your Borneo experience, but it'll be a serious drain on funds. **Borneo Nature Tours** (☎ 088-267637; www.borneonaturetours.com; Lot 10, Ground fl, Block D, Kompleks Sadong Jaya, Kota Kinabalu) is the main operator here offering a five-day/four-night all-inclusive tour of Maliau Basin starting at RM3350. The package is purposefully cost prohibitive to eliminate those who aren't the most die-hard nature fans. The density of the old-growth forest is striking, and as it is more remote than the Danum Valley, the preserved wildlife is even better.

Several treks are possible in the basin, ranging from short nature walks around Agathis Camp to the multiday slog to the rim of the basin via Strike Ridge Camp. The vast majority of visitors to the basin undertake a three-day/two-night loop through the southern section of the basin that we'll call the Maliau Loop. This brilliant route takes in wide swathes of diverse rainforest and four of the basin's waterfalls: Takob Falls, Giluk Falls, Maliau Falls and Ginseng Falls. Do not attempt the trek unless you are in excellent shape (in fact, Borneo Nature Tours will require a letter from a doctor testifying to your ability to undertake the trek). Your tour operator will supply a guide and porters to carry your food. You'll be in charge of your daypack, camera, leech socks, walking clothes and dry kit for the evening.

Getting There & Away

There is no public transport to the park and your transport will be arranged by your tour operator. Access is by 4WD vehicle from either Tawau or Keningau. Most organised tours operate from Tawau, from which the ride takes about five hours under good conditions. There are frequent delays en route as logging trucks often get bogged down in the mud. Once at the security gate to the park, you'll have to take an even narrower dirt track to Agathis Camp.

SOUTHWESTERN SABAH

The Crocker Range is the backbone of southwestern Sabah, separating coastal lowlands from the wild tracts of jungle in the east. Honey-tinged beaches scallop the shores from KK down to the border, passing the turbid rivers of the Beaufort Division. Offshore you'll find Pulau Tiga, forever etched in the collective consciousness as the genesis site for the eponymous reality show *Survivor*, and Pulau Labuan, centre of the region's oil industry and the transfer point for ferries heading onto Sarawak and Brunei.

THE INTERIOR

The southwest interior of Sabah is dominated by the **Crocker Range**, which rises near Tenom in the south and runs north to Mt Kinabalu. The range forms a formidable barrier to the interior of the state and dominates the eastern skyline from Kota Kinabalu down to Sipitang. Once across the Crocker Range, you descend into the green valley of the Sungai Pegalan that runs from Keningau in the south and to Ranau in the north. The heart of the **Pegalan Valley** is the small town of **Tambunan**, around which you'll find a few low-key attractions.

While much of the Crocker Range has been gazetted as **Crocker Range National Park**, there are few facilities for visitors. Likewise, the Pegalan Valley has no real must-see attractions. However, the Crocker Range and the Pegalan Valley make a nice jaunt into rural Sabah and are particularly suited for those with rental cars. As you make your way over the range between KK and Tambunan, you'll be treated to brilliant views back to the South China Sea and onward to Mt Trus Madi. The road itself is a lot of fun to drive, and you might find yourself craving a sports car instead of the Proton rental you're likely to be driving.

Tambunan

Nestled among the green curves of the Crocker hills, Tambunan, a small agricultural service town about 81km from KK, is the first settlement you'll come to in the range. The region

was the last stronghold of Mat Salleh, who became a folk hero for rebelling against the British in the late 19th century. Sadly Salleh later blew his reputation by negotiating a truce, which so outraged his own people that he was forced to flee to the Tambunan plain, where he was eventually besieged and killed.

Near the top of the Crocker Range, next to the main highway 20km from Tambunan, is the **Tambunan Rafflesia Reserve** (☎ 088-898500; RM5; ☼ 8am-3pm), devoted to the world's largest flower. The rafflesia is a parasitic plant that grows hidden within the stems of jungle vines until it bursts into bloom. The large bulbous flowers can be up to 1m in diameter. The 12 or so species of rafflesia here are found only in Borneo and Sumatra; several species are unique to Sabah, but as they only bloom for a few days it's hard to predict when you'll be able to see one.

Tambunan's only tourist accommodation is **Tambunan Village Resort Centre** (TVRC; ☎ 087-774076; 24 Jln TVRC, Kampung Keranaan; r & chalet RM50-90; ▣), about 2km from the tiny town centre. The staff at the centre can help arrange trips up Mt Trus Madi. If you're driving here from KK, the centre is just south of the Shell station on the main road.

Regular minivans ply the roads between Tambunan and KK (RM10, 1½ hours), Ranau (RM12, two hours), Keningau (RM7, 1 hour) and Tenom (RM12, two hours). KK–Tenom express buses also pass through, though you may have to ask them to stop. The minivan shelter is in the middle of Tambunan town. Minivans to KK pass the entrance to the rafflesia reserve; you'll usually be charged for the whole trip to KK.

Mt Trus Madi

About 20km southeast of Tambunan town is the dramatic **Mt Trus Madi**, Sabah's second-highest peak, rising to 2642m. Although logging concessions encircle the mount, the upper slopes and peak are wild and jungle-clad and classified as forest reserve. Ascents are possible, however it's more challenging than Mt Kinabalu, and more difficult to arrange. Independent trekkers must be well equipped and bring their own provisions up the mountain. It is possible to go by 4WD (RM300) up to about 1500m, from where it is a five- to seven-hour climb to the top. There are places to camp halfway up the mountain and on the summit. Before setting off, you are strongly advised to hire a guide (RM200) or at least get maps and assistance from the **Forestry Department** (Jabatan Perhutanan; ☎ 087-774691) in Tambunan. Trekking packages can be booked at agencies in KK (p347).

Keningau

If you have a bent for the bucolic, you'll probably want to skip Keningau – this busy service town has a touch of urban sprawl about it, and most visitors only pass through to pick up transport, use an ATM or stock up on supplies. As far as attractions go, you might check out **Taipaek-gung**, a colourful Chinese temple in the middle of town, or the large **tamu** (market) held every Thursday.

For a sleepover, try **Hotel Juta** (☎ 087-337888; www.sabah.com.my/juta; Lg Milimewa 2; standard/superior d from RM195; 🖭), which towers over the busy town centre. It's convenient to transport, banking and shopping needs. There is a restaurant on the premises.

There are eight daily express buses to/from KK (RM13, 2½ hours) and four to/from Tenom (RM7, 1 hour). These buses stop at the Bumiputra Express stop on the main road across from the Shell station. Minivans and share-taxis operate from several places in town, including a stop just north of the express bus stop. There are services to/from KK (RM25, 2½ hours), Ranau (RM18, three hours) and Tenom (RM7, one hour).

Tenom

This sleepy little town at the southern end of Crocker Range has seen better days but still manages to be more attractive than traffic-choked Keningau. Tenom was closely involved in uprisings against the British in 1915, led by the famous Murut chief Ontoros Antonom, and there's a **memorial** to the tribe's fallen warriors off the main road. Most people pass through Tenom on their way to the nearby Sabah Agricultural Park (right).

If you somehow get stuck in town, spend the night at **Orchid Hotel** (☎ 087-737600; Jln Tun Mustapha; s/d RM35/44; 🖭) – it's the lesser of the town's two evils (there are actually three iffy hotels in town, but 'the lesser of three evils' don't sound quite right).

Minivans operate from the *padang* in front of the Hotel Sri Perdana. Destinations include Keningau (RM6, one hour) and KK (RM20, two to four hours depending on stops). There are also regular services to Tambunan (RM12,

two hours). Taxis congregate at a rank on the west side of the *padang*.

Sabah Agricultural Park

Heaven on earth for horticulturalists: the vast **Sabah Agricultural Park** (Taman Pertanian Sabah; ☎ 087-737952; www.sabah.net.my/agripark; adult/child RM25/10; 🖰 9am-4.30pm Tue-Sun), about 15km northeast of Tenom, is run by the Department of Agriculture and covers about 1500 acres (610 hectares). Originally set up as an orchid centre, the park has expanded to become a major research facility, tourist attraction and offbeat camp site (RM10), building up superb collections of rare plants such as hoyas, and developing new techniques for use in agriculture, agroforestry and domestic cultivation.

Due to the size of the place, a fair bit of walking in the hot sun is involved (bring sunscreen, sun hats and sufficient clothing). Exploring by bicycle would be a good idea, but the fleet of rental bikes here has just about rusted to the point of immobility. There is a free 'train' (it's actually more like a bus) that does a 1½-hour loop of the park, leaving from outside the reception hourly from 9.30am to 3.30pm.

Take a minivan from Tenom heading to Lagud Seberang (RM3). Services run throughout the morning, but dry up in the late afternoon. Tell the driver you're going to Taman Pertanian. The park entrance is about 1km off the main road. A taxi from Tenom will cost around RM60.

Batu Punggul

Not far from the Kalimantan border, Batu Punggul is a jungle-topped limestone outcrop riddled with caves, towering nearly 200m above Sungai Sapulut. This is deep in Murut country and the stone formation was one of several sites sacred to these people. Batu Punggul and the adjacent Batu Tinahas are even traditionally believed to be longhouses that gradually transformed into stone. It can be difficult and expensive to get here, but this is a beautiful part of Sabah that few tourists visit, and it offers a chance to rub shoulders with the jungle Murut.

Batu Punggul is located a 10-minute motorboat ride upstream along the Sungai Sapulut from the Murut longhouse community of Tataluang. To reach Tataluang, take a bus to Keningau (left) where you must charter a jeep for the three-hour drive (figure on around RM275).

BEAUFORT DIVISION

With Borneo's clutch of tongue-twisting tribal names (try saying 'Balambangan' three times fast!), it's a pleasure asking for a bus to Beaufort. This shield-shaped peninsula, popping out from Sabah's southwestern coast, is a marshy plain marked with curling rivers and fringed by golden dunes. Tourists with tight travel schedules should consider doing a wildlife river cruise at Klias or Garama if they don't have time to reach Sungai Kinabatangan. Yes, the Kinabatangan is better, but packs of proboscis monkeys can still be spotted here, and it's only a day trip from KK.

BEAUFORT

Born as a timber town, Beaufort has reinvented itself with the proliferation of palm-oil plantations. A suitable pit stop for tourists travelling between Sabah and Sarawak, this sleepy township is the gateway to white-water rapids on the Padas River and the monkey-filled Klias and Garama areas. The Padas River divides Beaufort into two sections: the aptly named Old Town with its weathered structures, and New Town, a collection of modern shophouses on flood-phobic stilts.

White-water rafting enthusiasts can book a river trip with **Riverbug** (☎ 088-260501; www.traverse tours.com; Wisma Sabah, Jln Haji Saman, Kota Kinabalu), the premiere operator in the area. **Borneo Wavehunters** (☎ 088-432967; www.travelmateholidays. com; Lot 27, Block D, Kuala Inanam, Kota Kinabalu) is another reputable outfitter with a band of cheery guides. Day trips organised out of KK cost around RM200 per person, including transfers by van, and normally require 24 hours' advance notice. Tourists who seek calmer waters can ride the rapids of Sungai Kiulu (bookable through the aforementioned operators) near Mt Kinabalu.

There's really no need to spend the night in Beaufort, but if you must, then try the **MelDe Hotel** (☎ 087-222266; 19-20 Lo Chung Park, Jln Lo Chung; s/d/ste RM60/75/85; ✱). The rooms are a bit crusty in the corners, but it's passable for a night's sleep while in transit. Go for a room on one of the upper floors – they have windows. The Chinese restaurant under the inn is very popular with locals. MelDe is located in Old Town. If you're stopping in town for a bite,

make sure you try a pomelo (football-sized citrus fruit) – Beaufort is famous for 'em.

GETTING THERE & AWAY

Express buses operate from near the old train station at the south end of Jln Masjid (the ticket booth is opposite the station). There are departures at 9am, 1pm, 2.15pm and 5pm for KK. The fare is RM9 and the journey takes 1½ hours. There are departures at 9.10am, 10.30am, 1.45pm and 6.20pm for Sipitang. The fare to Sipitang is RM4.50 and the trip takes 1½ hours. The KK to Lawas express bus passes through Beaufort at around 3pm; the trip from Beaufort to Lawas costs RM13 and takes 1¾ hours.

Minivans operate from a stop across from the mosque, which is at the north end of Jln Masjid. There are frequent departures for KK (RM9, two hours), and less-frequent departures for Sipitang (RM11, 1½ hours), Lawas (RM15, 1¾ hours) and Kuala Penyu (until around 2.30pm, RM6, one hour). To Menumbok (for Labuan) there are plenty of minivans until early afternoon (RM8, one hour).

Taxis depart from the stand outside the old train station, at the south end of Jln Masjid. Charter rates include: KK (RM60), Kuala Penyu (RM50), Sipitang (RM32), Menumbok (RM50) and Lawas (RM100).

Kuala Penyu

Tiny Kuala Penyu, at the northern tip of the peninsula, is the jumping-off point for Pulau Tiga if you are not accessing 'Survivor Island' via the new boat service from KK. From KK, minivans leave from behind Wawasan Plaza (RM10 to RM15, two hours). From Beaufort minivans to Kuala Penyu (RM5 to RM10) leave throughout the morning, but return services tail off very early in the afternoon, so you may have to negotiate a taxi or local lift back. A minivan to/from Menumbok costs RM50 per vehicle.

Tempurung

Set along the quiet coastal waters of the South China Sea, the serene ourpick **Tempurung Seaside Lodge** (☎ 088-773066; 3 Putatan Point; www.borneo-authentic .com; 3-day/2-night package from RM450) is the perfect place for hermits who seek a pinch of style. The main lodge was originally built as a vacation home, but friends convinced the owners that it would be a crime not to share the lovely property with the world. Rooms are scattered between several chalet-style bungalows accented with patches of jungle thatch. The packages include fantastic meals. Nightly rates are also available.

Borneo Express (☎ 012-830 7722) runs buses from KK (departing from Wawasan) at 6.45am, 10am and 12.30pm daily. Ask the driver to let you off at the junction with the large Kuala Penyu sign. The bus will turn left (south) to head towards Menumbok, you want to go right (north) in the direction of Kuala Penyu. If you arranged accommodation in advance, the lodge van can pick you up here (it's too far to walk). Buses pass the junction at 9.30am and 3.30pm heading back to KK. If you're driving, take a right at the junction and keep an eye out for the turnoff on the left side of the road just before Kuala Penyu. We suggest calling the lodge for directions. A charter taxi from Beaufort will cost about RM50.

Klias

The tea-brown Sungai Klias looks somewhat similar to the mighty Kinabatangan, offering short-stay visitors a chance to spend an evening in the jungle cavorting with saucy primates. There are several companies offering two-hour river cruises. We recommend **Borneo Authentic** (☎ 088-773066; www.borneo-authentic .com; package trip RM150), the first operator to set up shop in the region. Trips include a large buffet dinner and a short night walk to view the swarms of fireflies that light up the evening sky like Christmas lights. Cruises start at dusk (around 5pm), when the sweltering heat starts to burn off and animals emerge for some post-siesta prowling.

There is no accommodation in Klias, although Borneo Authentic can set you up with one of their comfy rooms at the Tempurung Seaside Lodge nearby (opposite). Tourists can make their own way to the row of private jetties 20km west of Beaufort, however most trip-takers usually signup for a hassle-free day trip from KK (which ends up being cheaper since you're sharing transport).

Garama

Narrower than the river in Klias, the Sungai Garama is another popular spot for the popular river-cruise day trips from KK. Chances of seeing fireflies are slim, but Garama is just as good as Klias (if not better) when it comes to primate life. Gangs of proboscis monkeys

and long-tailed macaques scurry around the surrounding floodplain offering eager tourists plenty of photo fodder.

Like Klias, the tours here start at around 5pm (with KK departures at 2pm), and after a couple of hours along the river, guests chat about the evening's sightings over a buffet dinner before returning to KK. There are currently four operators in the area, the best being **Only In Borneo** (☎ 088-260506; www.oibtours.com; package tour RM190), an offshoot of Traverse Tours. They have a well-maintained facility along the shores of Sungai Garama and offer an overnight option in prim dorms or double rooms.

While it is technically possible to reach Garama with one's own vehicle, the network of unmarked roads can be tricky and frustrating, especially at night when nothing is lit (and water buffalo start to wander the roads).

Weston

The little village of Weston – a couple shacks clustered around a gold-domed mosque – is the jumping-off point for the surrounding wetlands. The area was bombed beyond recognition during WWII, but recent conservation efforts have welcomed groups of curious proboscis monkeys. **Weston Wetland Paradise** (☎ 019-821 7919; www.westonwetland.com) operates a variety of package tours including river-cruise day trips and sleepovers at their swamp-side lodge, **Borneo Eco-Stay** (all-inclusive package RM230). The dorm facilities are rustic at best, but we've heard that renovations will probably be under way by the time you read this. **Century Proboscis Monkey** (☎ 016-832 2443) is the only other operator to offer river cruises around Weston's estuaries. Day trips to the wetlands cost around RM200 per person (around RM130 if you can arrange your own transport to the jetty).

Menumbok

The tiny hamlet of **Menumbok** is where you catch the ferry to Pulau Labuan (which then provides continuing ferry service to Brunei or Sarawak). A charter taxi from Beaufort costs RM60, minivans from Kuala Penyu cost RM50 per vehicle. The car ferry to Pulau Labuan departs daily at 10.30am and 4.30pm (RM5 per person, RM40 per car). There is a direct bus service connecting Menumbok to KK (see left).

PULAU TIGA NATIONAL PARK

Outwit, outplay and outlast your fellow travellers on what is known throughout the world as 'Survivor Island'. The name Pulau Tiga actually means 'three islands' – the scrubby islet is part of a small chain created during an eruption of mud volcanoes in the late 1890s. Over a hundred years later, in 2001, the island had its 15 minutes of fame when it played host to the smash-hit reality TV series *Survivor*. TV junkies still stop by for a looksee, although the 'tribal council' was destroyed in a storm and the debris was cleared after it turned into a home for venomous snakes. Whatever your viewing preferences though, it's still a great place for relaxing on the beach, hiking in the forest and taking a cooling dip in burping mud pits at the centre of the island.

Nearby, the hard-to-pronounce Pulau Kalampunian Damit is little more than a large rock covered in dense vegetation but is famous for the sea snakes that come ashore to mate, hence the island's nickname, **Snake Island**. On any one day up to 150 snakes can be present, curled up under boulders, among roots and in tree hollows. It's a fascinating phenomenon, made doubly enigmatic by the fact that the snakes are never seen on nearby Pulau Tiga. Pulau Tiga Resort runs boat trips to the island (RM35 per person), with a stop en route for snorkelling.

Sleeping & Eating

The main player on the island, **Pulau Tiga Resort** (☎ 088-240584; www.pulau-tiga.com; per person RM175-330; ❄) was originally built to house the production crew for the *Survivor* series (Jeff Probst stayed in Cabin E). Accommodation is available in dorm-style 'longhouse' rooms (three beds in each), and private cabins have double beds and plenty of air-con. The beach-facing grounds offer amazing views of the sunset. A detailed map is available for those that want to track down the beach where the Pagong Tribe lived (called Pagong Pagong Beach). There's currently only one staff member that was working here when *Survivor* was being filmed – he was friendly enough to entertain all of our dorky questions (we were big fans back in the day).

Sabah Parks (☎ 088-211881; www.sabahparks.org.my; Lot 1-3, Block K, Kompleks Sinsuran, Jln Tun Fuad Stephens, Kota Kinabalu; ☷ 8am-1pm & 2-5pm Mon-Thu, 8am-11.30am & 2-5pm Fri) has more basic lodging on the island for less affluent survivalists. It's right next door to Pulau Tiga Resort, about 10m from where 'Tribal Council' was once held. Facilities here

are limited and there's no restaurant, though a cooking area is provided.

Getting There & Away

Pulau Tiga is 12km north of Kuala Penyu off the Klias Peninsula. The boat ride takes about 20 minutes and can be pretty bumpy if there's any wind about. Boats leave at 10am and 3pm from the south side of the river in Kuala Penyu. Most visitors to Pulau Tiga come as part of a package with one of the resorts, in which case transport all the way to the island from KK will be included in the price. Otherwise, you could try just showing up in Kuala Penyu and asking if you can board one of the day's boats out to the island (we don't recommend this option as priority is given to resort guests with bookings). For Sabah Parks' lodgings try to hop a ride with the Pulau Tiga Resort boat – it'll be way cheaper than chartering your own craft (RM400).

PULAU LABUAN
pop 85,000

Pulau Labuan is Sabah's version of Vegas, but if you're expecting schmancy hotels and prostitutes you're only half-right... The island doesn't feel seedy though; in fact, think of Labuan as a giant airport terminal – everything here is duty free, because politically, it's part of a federal territory governed directly from KL.

The sultan of Brunei ceded Labuan to the British in 1846 and it remained part of the Empire for 115 years. The only interruption came during WWII, when the Japanese held the island for three years. Significantly, it was on Labuan that the Japanese forces in North Borneo surrendered at the end of the war, and the officers responsible for the death marches from Sandakan (see p373) were tried on the island.

Bandar Labuan is the main town and the transit point for ferries linking Kota Kinabalu and Brunei.

Information

Arcade Moneychanger (☎ 087-412545; 168 Jln OKK Awang Besar) Cash and travellers cheques. Inside Labuan Textile shop.

Bertam Mass Money Changer (Jln Bunga Raya) Cash and travellers cheques. Near the ferry terminal.

Harrisons Travel (☎ 087-412557; 1 Jln Merdeka) Handy and reputable travel agency.

HSBC (☎ 087-422610; 189 Jln Merdeka) ATM.

Maybank (☎ 087-443888; Financial Park) ATM.

Labuan Tourism Action Council (☎ 087-422622; Ground fl, Labuan International Sea Sports Complex; 8am-1pm & 2-5pm Mon-Fri) Located about 1km east of the town centre, this is the most useful information office in town. They stock the excellent *Fly Drive Labuan Island & Town Map of Labuan*.

Tourist Information Centre (☎ 087-423445; www .labuantourism.com.my; cnr Jln Dewan & Jln Berjaya; ◷ 8am-5pm Mon-Fri, 9am-3pm Sat) Tourism Malaysia office. Less useful than Labuan Tourism Action Council.

Sights & Activities
BANDAR LABUAN

Labuan's uncharismatic main settlement is light on character but has a couple of passable attractions. The **Labuan Museum** (☎ 087-414135; 364 Jln Dewan; admission free; ◷ 9am-5pm) takes a glossy, if slightly superficial, look at the island's history and culture. The most interesting displays are those on the different ethnic groups here, including a diorama of a traditional Chinese tea ceremony (the participants, however, look strangely Western). There's also an excellent diorama of a water village.

On the coast just east of the centre, the Labuan International Sea Sports Complex houses the **Marine Museum** (☎ 087-425927; Jln Tanjung Purun; admission free; ◷ 9am-5pm). It's a decent little museum with a good shell collection and displays of marine life found in the area. Don't forget to head upstairs where you'll find a 42ft-long skeleton of an Indian fin whale. The real highlight, however, and a guaranteed hit with the kids, is the 'touch pool' opposite reception. This has to be the only shark-petting zoo we've ever seen (fret not: the sharks are less than a metre long).

AROUND PULAU LABUAN

Labuan used to be known for its **diving**, with no fewer than four major wrecks off the coast, but the downturn in tourism has caused operators to suspend all activities since 2004. If visitor numbers improve diving may resume; check with **Borneo Divers** (☎ 088-222226; www .borneodivers.info) in KK.

The **WWII Memorial (Labuan War Cemetery)** is an expanse of lawn with row upon row of headstones dedicated to the nearly 4000 Commonwealth servicemen, mostly Australian and British, who lost their lives in Borneo during WWII. The cemetery is near the golf course, about 2km east of town along Jln OKK Abdullah. A **Peace Park** on the west of the island at Layang Layangan commemo-

rates the place of Japanese surrender and has a Japanese war memorial.

Towards the northern tip of the island, **Labuan Bird Park** (☎ 087-463544; admission free) offers refuge to a wide range of species in three geodesic domes, and a swathe of rainforest. Nearby, the **Chimney**, believed to be part of an old coal-mining station (though strangely it was never actually used as a chimney), is the only historical monument of its kind in Malaysia, and has good views along the coast.

Pulau Kuraman, Pulau Rusukan Kecil and Pulau Rusukan Besar are uninhabited islands lying southwest of Labuan that are now protected as the **Labuan marine park**. The beaches are pristine, but dynamite fishing has destroyed much of the coral. You can hire boats from the jetty at the Labuan International Sea Sports Complex to explore the marine park. A day's charter costs around RM400 to RM600 per group of six people.

Sleeping

ourpick We're stingy with our 'Our Pick' symbols, but **Labuan's Homestay Programme** (☎ 087-422622; www.labuantourism.com; r/2 days incl full board RM65/140) deserves three. This excellent service matches visitors with a friendly local in one of three villages around the island: Patau Patau 2, Kampong Sungai Labu and Kampong Bukit Kuda. Some of the homes are just as grand as one of the international-class hotels on the waterfront! If you want to be near Bandar Labuan, ask for accommodation at Patau Patau 2 – it's a charming stilt village out on the bay. Stay a bit longer and learn how to make *ambuyat*, a Bruneian favourite p584.

A serviced apartment can be a real money saver for families and small groups. **Beta Service Apartment** (☎ 087-453333; johar@fpl.com.may; Financial Park, Jln Merdeka; apt RM155) offers 84 suites, each with a full kitchen.

Note that unlike most urban hotels in Sabah, you must book ahead in Labuan as the city is full of visiting expats in the oil business.

ASV Backpackers (☎ 087-413728; asvjau@yahoo.com; Lot U0101, Jln Merdeka; r with shared bathroom RM28; ▨) We don't know how long this place is going to last, namely because Labuan doesn't have a roaring backpacker scene, but this quiet spot is dirt cheap with the dirt. It's actually better than most of the dingy midrangers around town.

Hotel Mariner (☎ 087-418822; mhlabuan@streamyx .com; 468 Jln Tanjung Purun; r from RM110; ▨ ▣) Pitched at the low-end business-class market, this

SABAH

SABAH

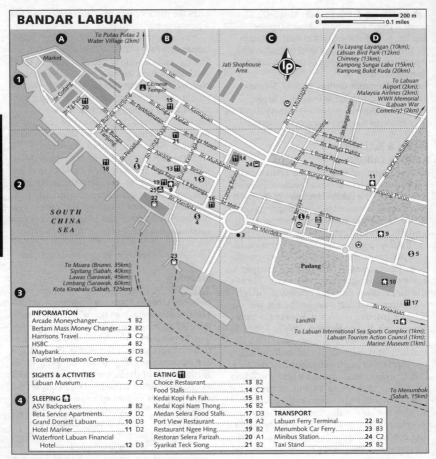

BANDAR LABUAN

0   200 m
0   0.1 miles

South China Sea

To Putau Putau 2
Water Village (2km)

Market

Jln Godang

Jln Tg Pasir

Chinese Temple

Jln Tanjung

Jln Rg-Bunga OKK

Jln Bunga Tanjung

Jln Perpaduan

Jln Perkhidmatan

Jln Bunga Melati

Jln Bunga Raya

Jln Jati

Jln Kemajuan

Jati Shophouse Area

To Layang Layangan (10km);
Labuan Bird Park (12km)
Chimney (13km);
Kampong Sungai Labu (15km);
Kampong Bukit Kuda (20km)

To Labuan
Airport (2km);
Malaysia Airlines (2km);
WWII Memorial
(Labuan War
Cemetery) (2km)

Jln Tun Mustapha

Jln Bunga Mawar

Jln Muhibbah

Jln Bunga Matahari
Jln Bunga Dahlia
Jln Bunga Anggerik
Jln Bunga Anggerik
Jln Bunga Kesuma

Jln OKK Abdullah

Jln Tanjung Purun

Jln Awang

L Bunga Raya

Jln Bunga Kenanga

Jln Bunga Besar

L B Kenanga

Lorong Barat

Jln Merdeka

Jln Melor

Jln Berjaya

Jln Dewan

Jln Merdeka

Padang

Landfill

To Muara (Brunei, 35km);
Sipitang (Sabah, 40km);
Lawas (Sarawak, 45km);
Limbang (Sarawak, 60km);
Kota Kinabalu (Sabah, 125km)

Jln Wawasan

To Labuan International Sea Sports Complex (1km);
Labuan Tourism Action Council (1km);
Marine Museum (1km)

To Menumbok
(Sabah, 15km)

INFORMATION
Arcade Moneychanger.....................1	B2
Bertam Mass Money Changer.........2	B2
Harrisons Travel..............................3	C2
HSBC..4	B2
Maybank...5	D3
Tourist Information Centre.............6	C2

SIGHTS & ACTIVITIES
Labuan Museum.............................7	C2

SLEEPING
ASV Backpackers............................8	B2
Beta Service Apartments................9	D2
Grand Dorsett Labuan..................10	D3
Hotel Mariner...............................11	D2
Waterfront Labuan Financial Hotel..12	D3

EATING
Choice Restaurant.......................13	B2
Food Stalls..................................14	C2
Kedai Kopi Fah Fah......................15	B1
Kedai Kopi Nam Thong................16	B2
Medan Selera Food Stalls............17	D3
Port View Restaurant..................18	A2
Restaurant Ngee Hing.................19	B2
Restoran Selera Farizah...............20	A1
Syarikat Teck Siong.....................21	B2

TRANSPORT
Labuan Ferry Terminal................22	B2
Menumbok Car Ferry..................23	B3
Minibus Station...........................24	C2
Taxi Stand..................................25	B2

smart block offers good facilities for the price. Rooms come with fridges, laminate floors and neat, spacious bathrooms.

Waterfront Labuan Financial Hotel (☎ 087-418111; leslbn@tm.net.my; 1 Jln Wawasan; r RM360-580, ste RM580-2150; ※ ⬛) Not just for merchant bankers – this is a large, luxurious leisure hotel with full facilities and a small marina attached. The rooms are spacious here and some have great sea views. There's a huge outdoor pool and a restaurant. Wi-fi available. All in all, it's a comfortable place to stay.

Grand Dorsett Labuan (☎ 087-422000; www.dorsett hotels.com; 462 Jln Merdeka; r RM473; ※ ⬛ ⬛) The Grand Dorsett (once a link in the Sheraton chain) has everything you would expect from an international hotel, with five-star rooms,

good restaurants and a pub hosting live bands. Weekend room-only (without breakfast) rates are a fraction of the published prices.

Eating

Kedai Kopi Fah Fah (cnr Jln Bunga Raya & Jln Bunga Melati; meals RM3-10; ☽ breakfast, lunch & dinner) With indoor and outdoor seating, an English menu, tasty fresh juice and cheap beer, this simple Chinese restaurant is a good choice. We particularly liked their *kway teow goreng* (fried flat rice noodles).

Other Chinese *kedai kopi* to choose from in town include **Kedai Kopi Nam Thong** (Jln Merdeka; meals from RM3; ☽ breakfast & lunch), which has chicken rice and fried noodle stalls, and **Restaurant Ngee Hing** (Jln Merdeka; meals from RM3;

SABAH

breakfast & lunch), which has a stall that does a good bowl of laksa (it's directly opposite the ferry terminal and serves as a good place to wait for a ferry). If you prefer a Muslim *kedai kopi*, you could try **Restoran Selera Farizah** (Lg Bunga Tanjung; meals from RM3; breakfast, lunch & dinner), which serves roti, curries, *nasi campur*, accompanied by the inevitable pro-wrestling videos.

Choice Restaurant (☎ 087-418086; 104 Jln OKK Awang Besar; dishes RM1.20-10; breakfast, lunch & dinner) Forget false modesty, the Choice simply proclaims 'We are the best', and this seems to be corroborated by the popularity of the authentic Indian meals with the authentic Indian residents who turn out for roti, fishhead curry and *sambal*.

Port View Restaurant (☎ 087-422999; Jln Merdeka; dishes RM15-30; lunch & dinner) An outpost of the successful Chinese seafood franchise in KK, this waterfront restaurant has air-con indoor seating and outdoor seating that affords a nice view over Labuan's busy harbour. It's one of the few proper sit-down restaurants in town (that is, something nicer than a *kedai kopi*). We liked the baby *kailan* (Chinese vegetable) with crab sauce and butter prawns, which had the unusual addition of sesame to the sauce. Beware of a secret hidden charge in the form of 'special napkin' (tell them at the outset that you don't need it). Service can be a little slow and erratic.

In addition, you'll find outdoor **food stalls** at the east end of Jln Bunga Mawar and in the **Medan Selera Complex** near the Grand Dorsett. Self-caterers can do their grocery shopping at **Syarikat Teck Siong** (Jln Bunga Mawar).

Getting There & Away
Malaysia Airlines (☎ 1300-883000; www.malaysiaairlines.com.my; airport) has flights to/from KK (45 min-

utes) and KL (2½ hours), which are usually booked full of oil prospectors.

Passenger ferries (1st/economy class RM39/31, 3¼ hours) depart KK for Labuan from Monday to Saturday at 8am and 1.30pm. On Sunday they sail at 8am and 3pm. In the opposite direction, they depart Labuan for KK from Monday to Saturday at 8am and 1pm, while on Sunday they depart at 10.30am and 3pm. Note that the air-con on these ferries is always turned up to 'arctic' – bring a fleece.

Numerous express boats go to Muara port in Brunei daily (1st/economy class RM40/35, one hour) between 9am and 4.30pm, returning between 7.30am and 3.30pm. From Brunei the cost is B$18/15 for 1st/economy class, with six departures between 7.30am and 4.40pm.

There are also daily speedboats from Labuan to Limbang in Sarawak (RM28, 2.30pm, two hours) and Lawas, also in Sarawak (RM33, 12.30pm, two hours). There are also daily speedboats to Sipitang (RM25, 40 minutes).

Car ferries go to Menumbok (passenger/car RM5/40, two hours, three times daily) from a separate dock to the east. Speedboats (RM10) do the journey in about 30 minutes and leave roughly every hour between 8am and 4pm.

Getting Around
Labuan has a good minibus network, based on a six-zone system. Minibuses leave regularly from the parking lot off Jln Tun Mustapha. Their numbers are clearly painted on the front, and fares range from 50 sen for a short trip to RM2 for a trip to the top of the island.

Taxis are plentiful and there's a stand opposite the local ferry terminal. The base rate is RM6.60 for short journeys, or RM10 to the airport.

Sarawak

While Sabah sees itself as 'nature', Sarawak plays up its cultural counterpoint. With a thriving indigenous population featuring dozens of dialects and tribes, Sarawak's local people are the keepers of Borneo – the ancient storytellers and guardians of lost traditions. Many communities still cling to the longhouse lifestyle, a coveted way of communal life steeped in hundreds of years of myth, legend and lore.

But make no mistake, Sarawak offers oh-so much more than blowpipes, rice wine and sacred dances. The state has its fair share of natural wonders as well. The yawning Niah Caves reveal the island's 40,000 years of human history through haunting burials and cryptic cavern drawings. Caves are super-sized at Gunung Mulu National Park – home to more bats than there are people in the entirety of Sarawak. Don't miss the trek up to the Pinnacles, a curious formation of limestone spikes shooting straight up into the balmy jungle air. Then it's on to the Kelabit Highlands, an earthen kingdom tucked high in the clouds along the dark green borders of Kalimantan. Wild macaques and prowling proboscis monkeys patrol the southern shores as they swing past trekking tourists in Bako National Park.

Ultimately, Sarawak is a land of dreaming – a place where fantasies are fulfilled. If you're imagining a world of steaming jungles, secreted villages, curious beasts and muddy treks into the unknown, then you've come to the right place. Sarawak promises to deliver on all of those magical Bornean stereotypes, and it'll keep you coming back for more.

SARAWAK

HIGHLIGHTS

- Sipping wild teas and crunching savoury pineapple at a wobbly, wooden abode hidden deep within the **Kelabit Highlands** (p458)
- Wandering around catty **Kuching** (p409) *purr*using cluttered markets and colourful Chinese shophouses
- Exploring yawning caverns and trekking to the spiky Pinnacles in **Gunung Mulu National Park** (p452)
- Sharing smiles, stories and sips of cloudy rice wine while staying at a **longhouse** (p430)
- Snapping photographs of languid lagoons, ebbing tides and curious proboscis monkeys at **Bako National Park** (p423)

Gunung Mulu
National Park
★

Kelabit ★
Highlands

Bako
National
Park
★
Kuching

- TELEPHONE CODE: 082, 083, 084, 085, 086
- POPULATION: 2.5 MILLION
- AREA: 124,449 SQ KM

History

Archaeological evidence suggests early humans lived in Sarawak as long as 40,000 years ago, 30,000 years earlier than on the Malay peninsula. The Chinese started arriving around the 7th century, along with other Eastern traders, and from the 11th century Sarawak came under the control of various Indonesian factions. Many of today's indigenous tribes migrated from Kalimantan, including the Iban, who came here around the end of the 15th century and now make up around 33% of the state's population.

From the 15th until the early 19th century Sarawak was under the loose control of the sultanate of Brunei. It was only with the arrival of Sir James Brooke, the first of three so-called white raja, that it became a separate political region.

Brooke, invalided from the British East India Company after being wounded in Burma, eschewed an easy retirement and set off on a voyage of discovery, aided by a sizable inheritance and a well-armed ship. He arrived in Sarawak in 1839, just in time to find the local viceroy under siege, providing the perfect opportunity to ingratiate himself with the ruling class. Brooke duly suppressed the rebellion, and by way of reward the sultan of Brunei installed him as raja of Sarawak in 1842.

When James Brooke died in 1868 he was succeeded by his nephew, Charles Brooke. Through a policy of divide and rule, and the ruthless punishment of those who challenged his authority, Brooke junior extended his control and the borders of his kingdom during his long reign, which lasted until his death in 1917.

The third and last white raja was Charles Vyner Brooke, the second son of Charles Brooke, whose rule was rudely interrupted by the arrival of the Japanese in WWII. After the Japanese surrender in August 1945, Sarawak was placed under Australian military administration until Brooke, who had fled to Sydney, decided to cede his 'kingdom' to the British in 1946. On 1 July Sarawak officially became a British Crown colony, thus putting Britain in the curious position of acquiring a new colonial possession at a time when it was shedding others.

Cession was followed by a brief but bloody anticessionist movement supported chiefly by Anthony Brooke, Vyner Brooke's nephew and heir apparent. About 300 government officers resigned in protest at being excluded from the political process, and the conflict climaxed in late 1949 when the governor of Sarawak was murdered by a Malay student. By 1951, however, the movement had lost its momentum and Brooke urged supporters to give it up.

Along with Sabah (then North Borneo) and Brunei, Sarawak remained under British control when Malaya gained its independence in 1957. In 1962 the British proposed including the Borneo territories into the Federation of Malaya. At the last minute Brunei pulled out, as the sultan (and, one suspects, Shell Oil) didn't want to see the revenue from its vast oil reserves channelled to the peninsula. At the same time, Malaya also had to convince the UN that Philippine claims to North Borneo were unfounded, as was Indonesia's argument that the formation of Malaysia was a British neocolonialist plot. The agreement was finally hammered out in July 1963, and in September of the same year the Federation of Malaysia was born.

This was also when the Indonesian Konfrontasi (Confrontation) erupted, initiated by then Indonesian president Achmed Soekarno, who hoped to destabilise the fledgling state. Paramilitary raids and army attacks across Kalimantan's border with Sarawak and Sabah continued until 1966. At the conflict's height 50,000 British, Australian and New Zealand troops were deployed in the border area, where some horrific confrontations occurred.

Internally, Sarawak also faced conflict during the early 1960s. The state's large population of impoverished Chinese peasant farmers and labourers was courted by the North Kalimantan Communist Party, which supported guerrilla activity. After the collapse of the Indonesian Communist Party in 1965, however, Indonesians and Malaysians combined forces to drive the rebels out of their bases in Sarawak.

Today Sarawak is the most multicultural state in Malaysia, with no outright ethnic majority. Economically it has avoided the pitfalls of unemployment and federal discord that plague its neighbour, Sabah, but the state budget deficit has grown steadily over the last five years and revenue still depends heavily on the much criticised timber industry. Accusations of corruption and cronyism are virtually a daily occurrence, and most people would be surprised to find out if

SARAWAK

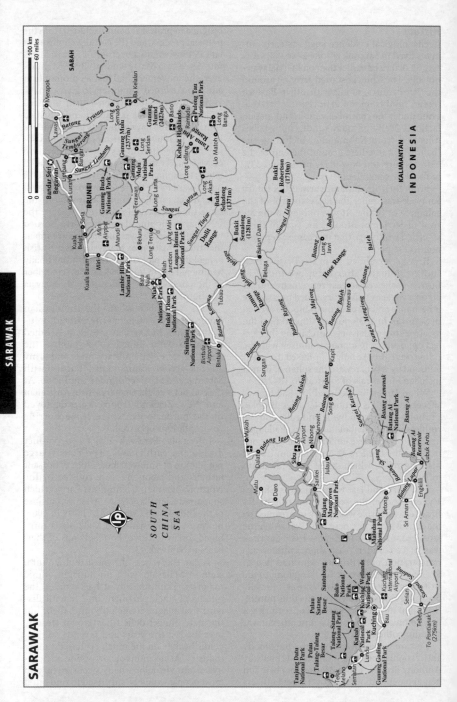

SARAWAK

a major company didn't have some link to a government office.

Despite the strongest showing for opposition parties since 1987, state elections in mid-2006 once again confirmed the ruling government amid widespread rumours of dubious tactics. Chief Minister Abdul Taib Mahmud (now in his eighth term) has described his unchanged cabinet as 'transitional', but exactly what transitions are involved remains to be seen. In 2008, his son won a seat in the Malaysian parliament – he had no previous political experience.

Climate

Sarawak has a hot and humid climate, with temperatures generally between 27°C and 34°C. It's cooler up in the hills, especially in the Kelabit Highlands. The heaviest rainfall occurs with the northeast monsoon from November to February, though it rains throughout the year. There's an average annual rainfall of about 350mm to 450mm.

Visas & Permits

As a semiautonomous state, Sarawak has its own immigration controls designed to protect indigenous people from being swamped by migrants from the peninsula and elsewhere, and to prevent the smuggling of protected plants and animals. You will have to clear immigration every time you cross a border – travelling to or from the peninsula, Sabah, Brunei and, of course, Indonesia.

OFF WITH THEIR HEADS!

Borneo has often been dubbed 'The Land of the Headhunters' – a catchphrase popularised by the Sarawak Tourism Board when they chose it as their promotional slogan (then they promptly abandoned the motto after realising that travellers weren't particularly psyched about the threat of decapitation). Headhunting has been a key facet of Borneo's indigenous culture for over 500 years, yet many of the rites, rituals and beliefs surrounding the gruesome tradition remain shrouded in mystery.

The act of taking heads was treated with the utmost seriousness, and warriors practised two types of premeditated expeditions. The first was known as the *kayo bala* – a group raid involving several warriors – while the second, *kayo anak,* was performed by a lone brave, or a *bujang berani*. In the upper regions of the Batang Rejang, the *kayo anak* was a common method of wooing a prospective bride. Believe it or not, the most valuable heads were those belonging to women and children, who were usually hidden away from marauders near the longhouse hearth. Only the savviest and sneakiest warrior could ambush a child or woman as they bathed or picked berries unattended.

After a successful hunt, the warrior would wander the jungle, wrestling with the taken spirit rather than letting down his guard for a nap. In the morning, he would return to his longhouse where the head would be smoked and strung up for the others to see and honour. Heads were worshipped and revered, and food offerings were not uncommon. A longhouse with many heads was feared and respected by the neighbouring clans.

The fascinating tradition began its gradual decline in 1841 when James Brooke, at the behest of Brunei's sultan, started quashing the hunt for heads in order to attract foreign traders. No one wanted to trade in Borneo due to the island's nasty reputation for harbouring ferocious noggin-grabbing warriors. However, the sultan wasn't interested in importing goods – he wanted to charge traders hefty port taxes (Brunei's cache of black gold hadn't yet been discovered). A nasty skirmish involving a knife-wielding pirate and a Chinese merchant's noodle gave Brooke the opportunity to show the Dayaks that he meant business – he promptly executed the criminal.

Headhunting flew under the radar until WWII when British troops encouraged the locals to start swinging machetes at Japanese soldiers (many of their heads still hang as longhouse cranium ornaments). Today murmurs about headhunting are usually sensationalised to drum up foreign intrigue – the last '*tête* offensive' was during the ethnic struggles in the late 1990s (in Indonesian Kalimantan). As Borneo's indigenous people continue to embrace Christianity over animistic superstition, many longhouses have dismantled their dangling dead. Although, if you ask around, you'll quickly learn that the heads haven't actually been tossed away – that would just be bad luck!

On arrival, travellers of most nationalities will be granted a three-month stay, though at some borders (particularly land crossings) you may only be given 30 days. Since you can easily spend a month exploring Sarawak, you may have to extend your visa. Extensions can be granted at the immigration office in Kuching (p412).

If you plan to visit any of the longhouses above Kapit on the Rejang or Baleh Rivers, you will need a free permit, which can be easily obtained in Kapit (p439).

The **Indonesian Consulate** (☎ 082-421734; 6th fl, Bangunan Binamas, Jln Padungan 93100, Kuching; ☺ 8.30am-noon & 2-4pm Mon-Fri) in Kuching is south of the city centre. Please note that during the time of research, plans were underway to move the office, although a new location has not been chosen. Most nationalities require visas to enter Indonesia, which is accessible from Sarawak by air at Pontianak or by land at Tebedu/Entikong. Visas may take several (usually three) days to process.

National Parks

Many of Malaysia's finest tracts of jungle and coastline lie within Sarawak's verdant borders. The following laundry list includes the state's finest preserves, many of which can be tackled on a day trip from Kuching or Miri.

Always take along your passport (or a photocopy of your passport), as you need to register at the following parks:

Bako National Park (p423) This 27-sq-km park has 17 trails and beaches to explore. It's about 1½ hours north of Kuching.

Batang Ai National Park (p434) This 240-sq-km park, deep in Iban country, is home to wild orang-utans. It's some 250km east of Kuching.

Bukit Tiban National Park A recovered logged area reforested and given park status in 2000, this 80-sq-km park is 50km northeast of Bintulu.

Gunung Buda National Park This 62-sq-km park juts up on the northeast side of Gunung Mulu National Park and contains similar karst formations and caves to those found at Gunung Mulu.

Gunung Gading National Park (p429) On Sarawak's extreme western tip near Sematan, the rafflesia flower is a major attraction at this 54-sq-km park.

Gunung Mulu National Park (p452) Sarawak's most popular national park (529 sq km) is east of Marudi near the Brunei border.

Kubah National Park (p427) This 22-sq-km park has hiking trails in a pristine rainforest and clear rivers to swim in. It's 20km west of Kuching.

Kuching Wetlands National Park (p427) Located a mere 15km from central Kuching, this mangrove reserve is home to a cornucopia of fascinating wildlife including Irrawaddy dolphins.

Lambir Hills National Park (p448) Famous for its diverse plant species, this 69-sq-km park is 32km south of Miri.

Loagan Bunut National Park This 10.7-sq-km park includes Sarawak's largest freshwater lake; it's in the Miri hinterland.

Maludam National Park This 431-sq-km sanctuary, about 70km northwest of Sri Aman, protects the red banded langur monkey and other primates.

Niah National Park (p450) This 32-sq-km park has massive caves and is the source of the raw ingredient for birds-nest soup; it's about halfway between Bintulu and Miri.

Pulong Tau National Park (p458) Sarawak's newest park (598 sq km) was gazetted in 2005 to preserve the rich jungle of the Kelabit Highlands.

Rajang Mangroves National Park This 94-sq-km park, in the Batang Rejang estuary on the coast west of Sarikei, provides a mangrove habitat for a variety of species.

Similajau National Park (p444) A coastal park (75 sq km), it has hiking trails, beaches and rivers – known for estuarine crocodiles – northeast of Bintulu.

Talang-Satang National Park (p432) A large marine park (194 sq km) protecting sea turtles, it includes the several *pulau* (islands) off the coast between Santubong and Sematan.

Tanjung Datu National Park (p432) This small national park (13.8 sq km) on the far southwest coast has beautiful beaches, clear rivers and coral reefs.

Currently, Batang Ai and Tanjung Datu do not have official accommodation or facilities for visitors, though it's possible to visit them through travel agencies or stay at private accommodation nearby.

Entry passes cost RM10 for adults and RM5 for children, and are issued at park entrances. Accommodation charges for national parks have been standardised across Sarawak. Most of the incidental charges are small and go towards upkeep of the park, but they can add up.

It's strongly recommended that you book accommodation in advance either through a tourist information centre or a **National Parks & Wildlife Booking Office** Kuching (☎ 082-248088; ☺ 8am-5pm Mon Fri); Miri (☎ 085-434184, 436637; 452 Jln Melayu; ☺ 8am-6pm Mon-Fri, 9am-3pm Sat & Sun).

Sarawak's **Forest Department** (www.sarawak forestry.com) has an excellent website with national park information, and online bookings are available at http://ebooking.com.my.

Tours

Sarawak has an incredible array of travel agencies and tour operators offering trips to every corner of the state. Some companies cater to special interests, such as photography, natural history and textiles, tattoos or crafts. Kuching has by far the highest number of companies.

The most common packages are centred on Gunung Mulu National Park, Sarawak's biggest attraction. In Kuching, the standard short-stay package will generally involve a city tour and visits to the Sarawak Cultural Village, Semenggoh Orang-utan Rehabilitation Centre and Bako National Park. One- to three-night trips to the longhouses south of Kuching are also big sellers.

As well as trekking tours, there is a growing number of adventure-sports activities, though Sarawak can't yet compete with Sabah in this department. Possibilities include potholing (caving), mountain biking and some reef diving. Almost any itinerary can be tailored to include a longhouse visit or local homestay, which often include cultural performances or communal activities such as cooking and harvesting.

Most tours are priced for a minimum of two people (and often five or six). Trips are often cancelled because of insufficient numbers, particularly with the cheaper tour operators – refunds should be immediate if a trip is cancelled. If you're looking for a group to join, you can leave a contact number with tour operators or the local tourist information centre.

If you found Sabah's rigid infrastructure to be stifling, you'll be able to breathe much easier in Sarawak – Malaysia's largest state is great for independent travel.

Getting There & Away

There are regular flights to Kuching from Kuala Lumpur, Johor Bahru, Kota Kinabalu, Macau, Penang, Hong Kong, Guangzhou, Bangalore, Perth and Singapore.

You can also enter Sarawak by land from Sabah, Brunei or Indonesia. These routes are all served by express buses. Express boats and speedboats run from the northern towns of Limbang and Lawas to Brunei, connecting with services to Sabah.

Getting Around

AIR

The recent advent of uber-cheap airfares has made travel around Sarawak a fair bit easier. Plane tickets are often similarly priced to bus tickets, if you can catch a good deal online.

The best way to reach Gunung Mulu National Park and the Kelabit Highlands (arguably the two best attractions in Sarawak) is by plane. Daily MASwings flights depart from Miri in the morning. We highly recommend booking in advance as there are only a handful of seats on each flight. There are multiple daily flights connecting Kuching and Miri.

BOAT

Transport by boat has long been the traditional way of getting around in Sarawak, though the use of this option has decreased in recent years as roads have improved. War parties and traders used to rely on brute paddling strength to get them up and down Sarawak's rivers; these days travel on larger rivers, such as the Rejang and Baram, is accomplished in fast passenger launches known by the generic term *ekspres* (express). These long, narrow boats carry around 100 people, and look a bit like ex-Soviet jumbo jets with the wings removed. Where and when the express boats can't go, river travel is still mainly by longboat, though these are now motorised.

Hiring a longboat is often your only option for reaching many spots. Be prepared to pay a fair bit for the experience, as fuel isn't cheap in remote areas (ie most of Sarawak). Getting a group together to share costs can be worth the time and effort.

LAND

Travel by road in Sarawak is generally good, and the road from Kuching to the Brunei border is surfaced all the way. Travellers arriving from elsewhere in Malaysia will be pleasantly surprised by the relative sanity of Sarawak drivers. Express buses ply the Kuching–Brunei route all the time, although it should be noted that the boat ride from Kuching to Sibu is significantly faster than the bus route.

KUCHING

pop 632,500

A capital, a kingdom, a cat, a colonial relic – Kuching wears many hats. Sarawak's main

SARAWAK

SARAWAK

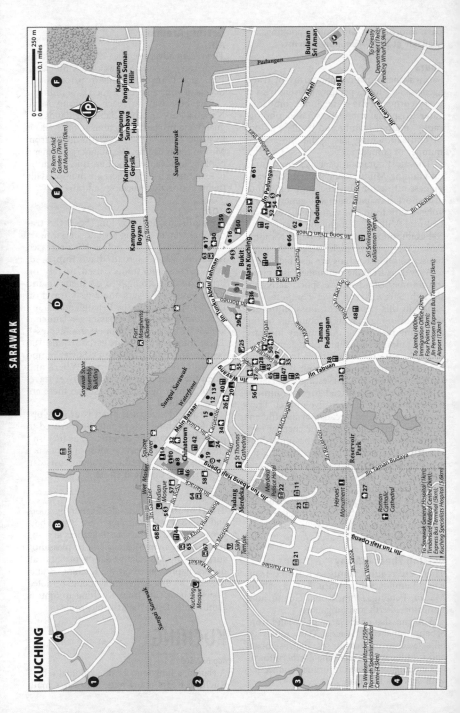

KUCHING

SARAWAK

point of entry plays its romantic *Indochine* card quite well, yet manages to be Borneo's most trendy, forward-thinking destination. There's a certain cosmopolitan *je ne sais quoi* that floats through the air, especially in the evenings as hookah smoke fills the streets amid the clinking of designer cocktails – shaken not stirred, of course. In the daytime the colourful shophouses in Chinatown are abuzz as sweaty tinsmiths hawk their wares and tuxedoed businessmen line up for steamy meat buns on their lunch break.

Kuching means 'cat' in Malay, a mascot exploited at every souvenir stall and highway roundabout. The city was so named by Charles Brooke, one of the white rajas, who must have sensed his capital's feline fierceness. Kuching embodies the spirit of a lion, sitting regally in its wild surrounds as it guards the roaring Sungai Sarawak from other prowlers.

ORIENTATION

The main sights – and most of the city – are on the south bank of the Sungai Sarawak.

The western end of the city is overlooked by the green-and-white Kuching Mosque, and is home to markets, local bus stations and museums. Most useful hotels, places to eat, banks and offices are between the mosque and the Great Cat of Kuching, 2km east. The waterfront is a quiet thoroughfare between the eastern and western parts of town.

Across the river from the wet market is the *istana* (palace). Nearby, Fort Margherita is on a low hill and visible from most points along the waterfront, while the new State Assembly Building looms large like a gilded circus tent.

Almost all attractions are within easy walking distance of each other; public buses or taxis are only needed to reach the Cat Museum (north of the river), the airport (about 12km south of town), the Express Bus Terminal (5km south) and the Pending wharf for the boat to Sibu (6km east). Most of the destinations listed in the Southern Sarawak section are doable as a day trip from Kuching.

INFORMATION

Bookshops

Mohamed Yahia & Sons (☎ 082-416928; Basement, Sarawak Plaza, Jln Tunku Abdul Rahman; ☷ 10am-9pm) Has English-language fiction and books on Borneo, plus Sarawak maps.

Popular Book Co (☎ 082-411378; Level 3, Tun Jugah Shopping Centre, 18 Jln Tunku Abdul Rahman; ☷ 9am-7pm) This is a more modern and spacious bookshop with a good selection of international titles, but fewer local interest books.

Emergency

Ambulance (☎ 999)
Fire (☎ 994)
Police (☎ 999)

Internet Access

Coffee Bean & Tea Leaf in Sarawak Plaza offers free wi-fi to their customers.

Cyber City (☎ 082-243680; www.cybercity.com.my; Taman Sri Sarawak Mall; per hr RM4; ☷ 10am-11pm Mon-Sat, 11am-11pm Sun) A clean, friendly place with printing and scanning services.

Laundry

Mr Clean (Jln Green Hill; per kg RM6; ☷ 8am-6pm Mon-Sat, 8am-4pm Sun) Reliable and economical; in the popular Green Hill area of town.

Medical Services

Kuching Specialist Hospital (KPJ; ☎ 082-365777; Lot 10420, Block 11 Tabuan Stutong Commercial Centre) Good facilities for tourists and English-speaking staff.

Normah Medical Specialist Centre (☎ 082-440055; www.normah.com.my; Jln Tun Abdul Rahman) A private hospital with good facilities and staff, 4.5km west of town. It's favoured by many residents and expats.

Sarawak General Hospital (☎ 082-257555; Jln Ong Kee) For emergencies and major ailments only, 1km south of town.

Timberland Medical Centre (☎ 082-234991; Mile 3, Jln Rock) Private hospital 2km south of town with highly qualified staff.

Money

There is a RHB change counter at the airport. Expect money changers in town to only take large bills (B$50, S$50 etc.)

Everrise Money Changer (☎ 082-233200; 199 Jln Padungan; ☷ 9am-5pm) Cash only. Ever rise? Seriously?

Majid & Sons (☎ 082-422402; 45 Jln India) A licensed moneychanger dealing in cash only.

Maybank (☎ 082-416889; Jln Tunku Abdul Rahman; ☷ 9.15am-4.30pm Mon-Thu, 9.15am-4pm Fri) ATM 6am to midnight daily.

Mohamed Yahia & Sons (☎ 082-416928; Basement, Sarawak Plaza, Jln Tunku Abdul Rahman; ☷ 10am-9pm) Inside the bookshop here.

Standard Chartered Bank (☎ 082-252233; Jln Padungan; ☷ 9.15am-4.30pm Mon-Thu, 9.15am-4pm Fri)

Post

Main post office (Jln Tun Abang Haji Openg; ☷ 8am-4.30pm Mon-Sat) Closed on the first Saturday of every month.

Tourist Information

The excellent **visitors information centre** (☎ 082-410944; www.sarawaktourism.com; Sarawak Tourism Complex, Jln Tun Abang Haji Openg; ☷ 8am-6pm Mon-Fri, 9am-3pm Sat & Sun) is in the old courthouse. The centre's staff can tell you just about everything you need to know about travelling in Sarawak, and there are enough brochures to paper your living room. Maps abound and transport schedules are also readily available if you're unsure about which buses go where. Ask about the invaluable *Official Kuching Guide*.

The **National Parks & Wildlife Booking Office** (☎ 082-248088; Sarawak Tourism Complex, Jln Tun Haji Openg; ☷ 8am-5pm Mon-Fri) is next door to the visitors centre and arranges accommodation at national parks (most people swing by to arrange an overnight stay at Bako National Park; p423).

Visas

Immigration office (☎ 082-245661; 2nd fl, Sultan Iskandar Bldg, Jln Simpang Tiga; ☷ 8am-noon & 2-4.30pm Mon-Fri) Visa extensions 3km south of town centre. From in front of the mosque, take Chin Lian Leong (CLL) bus 11 or 14A/B/C. Get off at Simpang Tiga.

SIGHTS

Like many cities, Kuching is a whole lot greater than the sum of its parts. There are a few interesting museums and historical attractions to keep you occupied, but the main attraction is the city itself. Leave plenty of time to wander aimlessly – try our walking tour (p414) to unveil the city's hidden treasures or pick up the baby-blue *Heritage Trail* pamphlet at the visitors information centre.

Note that the Astana and Fort Margherita, both on the northern banks of the Sungai Sarawak, are not currently open to the public.

SARAWAK

Chinatown

Kuching's Chinatown is centred on Jln Carpenter and runs roughly from Jln Wayang to Jln Tun Abang Haji Openg. This area forms part of our Walking Tour (see p414). It's a collection of beautiful colonial-era shophouses and Chinese temples that is conducive to strolling (if you can take the heat). At the western end you'll find **Harmony Arch**, an ornate arch that marks the official entrance to the district. Continuing east along Jln Carpenter, you'll see **Siang Ti Miao** on your right. Take some time to enter the spotless main hall of this temple to soak up the gaudy brilliance (across the way you'll find a good Chinese hawker centre in case you need to fuel up).

At the very eastern end of Chinatown you'll find the **Hong San Si Temple**, which is easily Kuching's finest Chinese temple. Thought to date back to around 1840, this Hokkien Chinese temple was fully restored in 2003. The new stone carvings, done by stonemasons brought in from mainland China, are superb, as is the Buddhist altar.

There is a big celebration at this temple in April, with a long procession of floats, lion and dragon dancers and other groups winding their way through town following the altar of Kong Teck Choon Ong (the deity at the temple).

Finally, be sure to have a look at **Tua Pek Kong**, the temple on the red wedding-layer-cake structure on Jln Padungan at the end of Main Bazaar. It's the most popular temple in town for local Chinese residents.

Waterfront

The south bank of the Sungai Sarawak has been tastefully developed with a paved walkway, lawns and flowerbeds, a children's playground, cafes and food stalls. It's a quiet, pleasant place to walk or sit and watch the *tambang* glide past with their glowing lanterns. In the evening it's full of couples and families strolling by or eating snacks. While you're strolling, be sure to have a look at the **Brooke Memorial**, in front of the visitors information centre.

Sarawak Museum

Established in 1891 the **Sarawak Museum** (☎ 082-244232; www.museum.sarawak.gov.my; Jln Tun Abang Haji Openg; admission free; 9am-4.30pm) has a fascinating collection of cultural artefacts and is a must-visit for anyone who wants to learn more about the region's indigenous peoples and natural environment. It consists of two wings connected by an ornate footbridge.

On the eastern side of the road is the **old wing**, opened in 1891, which currently contains the Ethnology Museum. Despite the name, displays touch on everything from natural history and geology to archaeology and anthropology; the most interesting exhibits are those dealing with the customs of Borneo's tribal peoples, including Melanau sickness images, Iban tattoos (see the boxed text, p416) and the infamous *palang* (see the boxed text, p438).

Upstairs in the Old Wing you'll find a recreated traditional longhouse display that you can enter and explore. Nearby are good wooden models of the different types of longhouse found in Sarawak. In the basketry section you'll find a beautiful Bidayu door charm, which was used to keep evil spirits out of the longhouse.

While you're at the Sarawak Museum, be sure to have a look at the **Art Museum** and **Natural Science Museum**, both of which are just down the hill from the museum's Old Wing. The former houses both permanent and temporary exhibits, some of which are very good. The latter was not open at the time of writing, but it is expected to open soon.

Islamic Museum

Over the hill from the Sarawak Museum, the **Islamic Museum** (Muzium Islam Sarawak; ☎ 082-244232; Jln P Ramlee; admission free; 9am-6pm) is well worth the walk. It's divided into seven thematically based rooms: weapons; decorative arts and domestic utensils; Qurans; Islamic architecture; science, technology, economy and literature; music and costumes; and the coming of Islam to the Malay Archipelago. Of particular note are the fantastic wooden and metal boxes in the decorative arts section and the fine carved panels in the architecture section.

Weekend Market

Kuching's best and busiest market, known locally as Pasar Minggu, sits along Jln Satok, west of the town centre. The market begins late on Saturday afternoon, when villagers bring in their produce and livestock and start trading. They sleep at their stalls and resume trading at around 5am on Sunday.

KUCHING WALKING TOUR

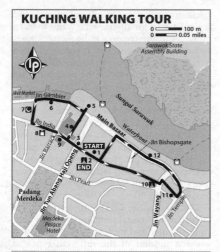

WALK FACTS

Start 43 Jln Carpenter
Finish Siang Ti Miao
Distance 2.2km
Duration 2½ hours (leisurely pace)

Things start to wind down at around noon. The air is heady with the smell of fresh coriander, ginger and herbs, which are stacked among piles of bananas, mangoes, custard apples and obscure jungle fruits sold by the local farmers' association. In the Chinese section of the market you'll find freshly cut-up boar and stinky durian when it's in season (November to February).

Cat Sights

Perched at the eastern end of Jln Padungan, the large white pussycat with the blue eyes, burgundy bow tie and wire whiskers is known as the **Great Cat of Kuching**. Other kitsch cat statues are opposite the Hotel Grand Margherita and on the waterfront. Yet another, at the roundabout at the east end of Jln Pandungan (once considered the centre of the city), features four cats on the bottom and four rafflesia flowers near the top.

Kuching's kitsch one-of-a-kind **Cat Museum** (☎ 082-446688; Bukit Siol, Jln Semariang; admission free, camera/video RM3/5; ☼ 9am-5pm), 11km from the city centre, pays homage to the origins of the city's name. It's all pretty light-hearted, with plenty of trivia, photos, children's art and movie posters featuring cats.

The Cat Museum is in the UFO-shaped DBKU building, north of the river. It's too far to walk, so take a taxi (RM20) or the Petra Jaya bus 2B (RM1).

WALKING TOUR
Undiscovered Kuching

Kuching reveals its charms quite quickly, making the city an instant fave among travellers. Charming Chinese shophouses beckon the click of a camera, rickety tin street stalls attract lunching locals with thick plumes of aromatic steam, and trendy nightspots bounce with the city's giddy glitterati as they sip imported wines. That said, the best thing about this catty capital is the fact that the longer one stays the better things get. We know you don't have oodles of time to let the hidden gems reveal themselves, so we teamed up with Jeremy Tan, a local history buff and photographer, to show you the *real* Kuching – Borneo's multicultural nexus of hot-blooded politicos, outspoken youths and trendsetting artists, all hiding under a glossy holiday veneer.

Start in the morning and skip the jam and toast at your hotel – you're in for the ultimate Bornean breakfast. Head to **43 Jln Carpenter (1)** and grab a seat at one of the rickety tables. Locals call this place Lau Ya Keng (in Hokkien) or Shang Di Miao (in Mandarin), which takes its name from the temple across the street. The stalls in this open-air food court serve up an eclectic assortment of native bites. There's noodles, laksa and, for the adventurous, a 50-year-old stall dishing out *kueh chap* – broth with pork entrails.

Cross the street to check out the colourful **Siang Ti Miao Temple (2**; p413). The temple was completed in 1889 as a shrine to Shang Di (the Emperor of Heaven) and serves a Teochew congregation. The temple is currently under renovation (or restoration); the local Chinese have a hard time differentiating between the two, making preservation a bit tricky round these parts), perhaps to remove the garish figurines put on display in the late 1960s... The temple's most interesting celebration is the Hungry Ghost Festival, held on the 15th day of the seventh lunar month (around mid-August or early September). The Chinese believe that the gates of hell swing open for the entirety of their seventh month and the spirits of the dead are free to roam the earth. On the 15th day, offerings of food, prayer, incense and paper money are made to appease the spirits. A priest blesses the offerings and promptly burns an enormous effigy to the Hell King in a dramatic bonfire. In the evening, parcels of food are doled out in a chaotic lottery, which is undoubtedly the most interesting part of the festival for a tourist to witness.

After leaving the temple grounds, head west down **Jln Carpenter (3)**, which locals called Attap Street. *Attap* is the Malay word for roofs made from *nipah* palm fronds. The street was once lined with *attap*-topped timber structures, all of which were incinerated in the Great Fire of 1884. At the end of Jln Carpenter you'll hit the **Old Court House (4)**, which was the main administrative centre around the time of the Great Fire. Today this unique architectural relic serves as the Sarawak Tourism Complex (stop in and grab some handy brochures!). Don't miss the Brooke Memorial, built in 1924, standing in the middle of the courtyard.

Across the road is the **Square Tower (5)**, which guarded the lazy river against marauders along with its companion bastion, Fort Margherita, across the river (currently closed). Both structures were erected around 1879, and over the last century the tower has served as a prison, a mess and dance hall.

From here, move on towards **Jln Gambier (6)**, named after the ubiquitous vine used for tanning, dyeing, betel chewing, and herbal medicines. After sampling a selection of Indian spices and Chinese herbs, have a look at the empty buildings across the street – this used to be the Old Market, a trading centre that pre-dates the reign of the white rajas. In 2008 the local venders were contentiously evicted to an area outside the city centre after the local government decided to extend the waterfront. Locals are fighting against the redevelopment as it would mean the demolition of several historic structures like the Cheko Market (1924), the Fish Market (1924) and the First Sarawak Museum (1889).

Still on Gambier Street, pay particular attention to a row of shops with distinctive Moorish facades. Don't miss the entrance to the **Indian Mosque (7)** – Kuching's oldest, built before the Brooke Era. Visitors may enter the mosque during non-prayer hours. Duck down the tiny passageway beside the mosque, hidden behind a profusion of spices, to reach **Jln India (8)**, once the main shopping district for imported textiles, brassware and household

goods. Converted into a pedestrian mall in the 1980s, it's a charming place for a stroll, especially Fridays when the young Muslim congregation emerges from their midday prayer.

There are several buildings of historical interest at the intersection of Jln Barrack (no relation to Obama) and Jln Carpenter; the **Round Tower (9)** is perhaps the most intriguing. Constructed in 1886, the building was used by the dreaded *kempeitai* (Japanese military police) during the Occupation. Today the structure hosts the Sarawak Craft Council, although most locals dare not step inside – its haunted (all buildings used by the *kempeitai* are haunted…).

Continue down Jln Carpenter, past your starting point, and head to **Hong San Si Temple (10**; p413), also known by its Hokkien name, Say Ong Kong, at the corner of Jln Wayang. Remember the Great Fire of 1884 that destroyed the *attap* roofs? Well, according to legend, as the flames roared down the street, onlookers spotted a mysterious boy waving a black banner. Suddenly, the wind changed directions and the fire stopped just short of the shrine. Today the Hokkien people worship this child-god with a yearly procession – the largest in Kuching. For a bird's eye view of the city's colonial core, hop on the elevator to the top floor of the **Star Cineplex (11)** across street.

Swing around the corner on to **Main Bazaar (12)** and reward yourself with some retail therapy (see the boxed text, p421). Turn on Jln China and pass the faint clinking of the remaining tinsmith workshops before returning to our starting point – the colourful Siang Ti Miao Temple on Jln Carpenter. By now (around 11am) a nondescript cart on wheels will have set up shop dispensing scrumptious banana fritters, which are undoubtedly the best in town. Let your nose guide you – you can't miss it!

COURSES

There are several places around town that offer Malay and Bidayuh cooking courses. Try **Bumbu Cooking School** (☎ 082-380050; bumbu cookingclass@hotmail.com; 57 Jln Carpenter; per person RM70) or ask about the tailor-made cooking classes at Rom Orchid Garden (p417).

TOURS

Kuching is the main hub of Sarawak's tourist economy. Everything in our Southern

SARAWAK

BEJALAI BODY ART

His reputation preceded him – Ernesto was *the* man to see around town for the best tattoos in all of Borneo. We were invited up to his studio – a saloon-style loft in central Kuching – to learn more about the mythos and mystery behind the coveted Iban *bejalai*. First we hung out among brass skulls and bamboo carvings as the monotonous buzz of the ink gun jittered in the hazy air. Then, over mugs of tepid insta-coffee and mounds of crinkled cigarette butts, we talked with the artist about the cultural significance of his art, and the meaning behind his tribal tattoos.

The *bejalai*, he explained, can loosely be defined as a journey, or a voyage of discovery. After leaving the safety of the village, a warrior-to-be would head out into unfamiliar lands. Lessons were learned and skills were taught, like boat building, hunting, shamanism and even traditional dancing. With each task mastered, the traveller would add a tattoo to their body creating a biographical constellation of swirling designs.

Traditionally an Iban would get their first tattoo around the age of 10 or 11. The initiating tattoo was the eggplant flower, or the *bungai terung,* drawn on each shoulder. The design was rich with symbolism, and commemorated the beginning of one's journey as a man (women were known to get them as well). The squiggly centre of the flower symbolised new life and represented the intestines of a tadpole, visible through their translucent skin. The plant's petals were a reminder that patience was a virtue, and that only a patient man could truly learn life's lessons.

After receiving the eggplant ornaments, the Iban was ready to leave home. Scores of tattoos followed, including the popular crab design, usually inked on a man's arm. The design symbolised strength, and evoked the strong legs and hard shell of the crafty sideways walkers. When animism was more widely embraced, the Iban believed that the design, when drawn with magical ink, could act like the actual shell of a crab, protecting bearers from the blade of a machete. For women, tattoos on the arm meant that they were skilled at craft making.

Sarawak section (national parks, orangutan sanctuaries, longhouses) can be visited by linking up with a tour operator (though most of these can be done on one's own as well). Most of the hotels listed offer their own tours or have links with an operator. Many companies also offer car hire, with or without driver. The visitors information centre has a photocopied list of well-established operators and can make objective recommendations based on your desires.

Reputable operators include but are not limited to:

Borneo Adventure (☎ 082-245175; www.borneo adventure.com; 55 Main Bazaar) Award-winning company that has set the standard for private tours in Borneo. The leader in cooperative projects benefiting Sarawak's indigenous people. Excellent guides.

Borneo Interland Travel (☎ 082-413595; www .bitravel.myjaring.net; 1st fl, 63 Main Bazaar) Offers a wide variety of tours near Kuching and throughout Sarawak at reasonable prices.

FESTIVALS & EVENTS

The three-day **Rainforest World Music Festival** (www.rainforestmusic-borneo.com) unites Borneo's indigenous tribes with international artists for a musical extravaganza in the Sarawak Cultural Village outside Kuching. It's held annually in the middle of July. Check out our website (www.lonelyplanet.com) for an informative podcast about the festival.

SLEEPING
Budget & Midrange

The recent fad in Kuching is trendy budget sleeping spots decked out with generous amounts of hip lounge furniture. These flashpacker dens have quickly overtaken the tired midrange hotels of yore.

Mr D's B&B (☎ 082-248852; www.misterdbnb.com; 26 Jln Carpenter; dm/s/tw/d from RM20/55/65/75; ☒ ▢) 'Tribal chic' is the name of the game here – the hang-out room at the entrance is stuffed with sassy leopard-skin pillows and there are arty black-and-white prints of tribal warriors on the wall. Rooms are quite standard though – they're very clean, but most of 'em don't have windows. Rather than signing a guest book, travellers are invited to doodle their goodbye message on the walls. Thoughtful perks include wi-fi throughout and power points beside everyone's pillow.

Fairview (☎ 082-240017; http://thefairview.com.my; 6 Jln Taman Budaya; dm/s/d RM25/50/70; ☒) An oldie but a goodie, Fairview scores big points for

Later on, the bravest travellers received the coveted throat tattoo as they evolved into a *bujang berani* (literally meaning 'brave bachelor'). The design – a fish body that morphs into a double-headed dragon – wanders up from the soft spot at the centre of the human clavicle, known as the 'life point' to the Iban.

In addition to the intricate rules of design, there were also several tattoo taboos surrounding the *bejalai* tradition. The most important faux pas to avoid was getting a tattoo on the top of one's hands – this area of the body was strictly reserved for those who had taken heads. Also, every animal inked facing inward must have something to eat – dragons were always depicted with a small lizard near their mouths – because if the design was left hungry it would feed on the bearer's soul.

Technically the *bejalai* never stopped during a warrior's life, although when they returned to their village, the tattoos acted like the stamps in a passport; visual aids when recounting stories of adventure. It is only through the *bejalai* that one could collect these veritable merit badges, and the number of tattoos acquired greatly increased one's desirability as a bachelor. It was also believed that a large number of tattoos enabled a soul to shine brightly in the afterlife.

Over the last century the tattooing materials have greatly changed. Traditionally, the ink was made from soot mixed with fermented sugarcane juice, and needles were made from bone or bamboo. Then brass needles were introduced, followed by steel, and in the 1970s household sewing needles were quite popular. Standard surgical steel needles are commonly used today.

The tradition of tattoos has evolved as well. In recent years, fewer Iban are getting inked, and those who do generally get designs commemorating trips to other countries, or military service. Although it is by no means a lost art, the tradition of *bejalai* body art is beginning to fade.

Ernesto K Umpie, 39, is a renowned Iban tattoo artist with a studio in downtown Kuching (p420). Visit www.borneoheadhunter.com to check out his work.

SARAWAK

its unpretentious atmosphere and friendly owners who dispense oodles of information about hidden Kuching gems.

Nomad (☎ 082-237831; www.borneobnb.com; 3 Jln Green Hill; dm/s/tw/d from RM26/55/65/75; ☒ ▣) There's a buzzing backpacker vibe at this Iban-run favourite. Bright patches of paint enliven the rooms, and guests congregate in the common area to hang out with the friendly management or watch the latest episode of Malaysian reality TV. Our favourite thing was the all-day breakfast – swing by the kitchen for toast, fruit and sugary snacks any time you want. If Nomad is full, try Tracks next door – it's owned by the same people (and looks exactly the same, except slightly smaller).

Rom Orchid Garden (☎ 082-447001; kakrom@ tm.net.my; 333A, Lg 5, Jln Siol Kandis; r per person RM30; ☒) Located in a quiet *kampong* on the way to Bako National Park, Rom Orchid Garden is a small campus of traditional Malay homes. There's an on-site orchid garden, as the name would suggest, and thousands of other potted plants scattered throughout. If you want to check out Borneo's version of suburban life, why not give this place a whirl? There's also a great restaurant offering traditional cooking classes, so you won't have to go far for a good bite.

Lodge 121 (☎ 082-428121; www.lodge121.com; 121 Jln Tabuan; dm/s/d/tr RM30/59/79/99; ☒ ▣) Polished concrete abounds at this mod charmer. The owners have transformed a commercial space into a multileveled hang-out for flashpackers. The dorm room is in the attic, and although the lack of bunks is welcoming, the mattresses are on the floor.

Pinnacles (☎ 082-419100, 012-809 6866; www.pinnacles kuching.com; 21 Block G, Jln Borneo; dm/d RM30/60; ☒) As far as dorm rooms go, you'll probably do better at Singgahsana or Kuching Waterfront Lodge, but keep Pinnacles in your back pocket in case the other spots are full.

our pick **Singgahsana Lodge** (☎ 082-429277; www .singgahsana.com; 1 Jln Temple; dm RM30, r RM88-138; ☒ ▣) Tourists can thank Singgahsana for upping the ante in Kuching's budget bed game. The trendsetting owners out-swanked the competition early on with an effective use of colourful accent walls and tribal knick-knacks – now everyone's playing catch-up, though no one has completely caught up just yet. Don't miss the hunting lodge–style bar at the top of the stairwell – it's only open to guests.

Kuching Waterfront Lodge (☎ 082-231111; www .kuchingwaterfrontlodge.com; 15 Main Bazaar; dm/d RM30/110; ☒ ▣) The only spot right in the heart of the

Main Bazaar, this up-and-comer has a large welcoming lobby stacked with lacquered furnishings. Rooms are light on designer details, but they're comfortable enough (ask to see a few options before dropping your bags). The best deal here are the dorm rooms – they're slightly pricier than the competition so you'll usually find yourself with a suite to yourself!

Harbour View Hotel (☎ 082-274666; www.harbourview.com.my; Jln Temple; r from RM170; ⚒ ☐) If it's modern comforts you're after, this is one of Kuching's best bargains – it offers full Western facilities for a thoroughly Southeast Asian price. The tall white building does indeed furnish good river vistas, and the buffet breakfast (RM10) is as lavish as one could wish for. The hotel also has an on-call doctor and bartender (hopefully not the same person). Big discounts are usually available.

Also worth a look-see:

Berambih Lodge (☎ 012-888 5589, 082-238589; 104 Jln Carpenter; dm/s/d RM20/35/45; ⚒ ☐) Bamboo-lined common area feels like a Hawaiian holiday. Rooms could use a designer's touch.

John's Place (☎ 016-894 5592, 082-258329; 5 Jln Green Hill; r from RM55; ⚒ ☐) Simple rooms are fresh and clean. Family suites are bright and spacious.

Top End

Keep an eye out for the white behemoth up the road from the Green Hill area – it's the new Novotel, and should be complete in 2010.

Hotel Grand Margherita Kuching (☎ 082-423111; www.grandmargherita.com/gmh; Jln Tunku Abdul Rahman; r incl breakfast from RM260; ⚒ ☐ ⚑) Kuching's sprawling Grand Margherita occupies a fine piece of real estate right on the river, smack dab in the middle of town. The rooms are of good quality and well kept, and the pool is welcome after a day of sightseeing.

Four Points (☎ 082-280888; www.fourpoints.com/kuching; Jln Lapangan Terbang Baru; r RM265; ⚒ ☐) A new competitor in the upmarket range, Four Points is a Sheraton product that provides sleek suites at competitive rates, 5km south of town.

Hilton Hotel (☎ 082-248200; www.kuching.hilton.com; Jln Tunku Abdul Rahman; r RM419; ⚒ ☐ ⚑) Dominating the waterfront even from across the street, the Hilton towers over Chinatown and offers prim rooms stuffed with the usual factory furnishings.

EATING

Kuching has the best selection of food in Borneo, boasting over a thousand choices, ranging from hawker-stall fare through good seafood to first-class Italian. Cafes serving standard rice and noodle dishes, beef, roti (unleavened flaky bread) and *murtabak* (roti filled with mutton, chicken or vegetables) are everywhere. For good Western fare try the upmarket hotels.

Restaurants & Cafes

Pick up the *Official Guide to Kuching*, available at the tourist information centre, for a veritable laundry list of top eats. Check out http://eatingoutkuching.com for the latest goss on the hot places to eat.

Chin Sa Barbeque Specialist (Jln Padungan; chicken rice from RM3; ☽ breakfast, lunch & dinner) Eat in or take away at this popular Jln Padungan barbecue joint, where savoury chicken or pork slices over rice are the speciality of the house.

Rom Orchid Garden (☎ 082-447001; mains RM3-6) If you're out in the burbs, Rom is a great place for spicy Malay dishes. Stick around to try your hand in the kitchen – you can even spend the night (p417).

Black Bean Coffee & Tea Company (☎ 082-420290; Jln Carpenter; drinks from RM3.90; ☽ 9am-6.30pm Mon-Sat) Serving fresh, fair-trade coffee, this quaint cafe, housed in a converted Chinese shophouse, strikes the guiltless balance between Starbucks and Sarawak.

a-ha Café (☎ 016-889 3622; 38 Jln Tabuan; mains RM6-28; ☽ breakfast, lunch & dinner) a-ha wouldn't look at all out of place in any cosmopolitan European capital, and the emphasis is firmly on healthy eating, with organic produce, all-natural ingredients and no MSG or artificial additives, plus a special 'healthy heart' menu. Whether you treat yourself to Norwegian salmon, ostrich steak or deer kebabs, or just pop in for a fruit 'n' vegetable smoothie, a-ha is a rare treat with virtually zero guilt factor. Wi-fi available.

Little Lebanon (☎ 082-247523; Japanese Bldg, Jln Barrack; mains from RM6, sheesha RM10.50; ☽ breakfast, lunch & dinner) Borneo's only Arabic restaurant sits in an elegant breezeway overlooking colourful Jln India. Belly dancing music wafts through the air as contented customers slurp some muddy Turkish coffee and dip their pita pillows into freshly mashed hummus. Swing by in the evenings for flavourful puffs on a *sheesha* pipe – there's celery and cherry, but mint is the best.

Bla Bla Bla (☎ 082-233944; 27 Jln Tabuan; mains from RM15; ☽ dinner Wed-Mon) Spiffier than a pimp's outfit, Bla Bla Bla brings a splash of Hollywood to Kuching. The tasty fusion food is anything but 'blah', and patrons will adore the koi pond and golden Buddhas.

our pick **Junk** (☎ 082-259450; 80 Jln Wayang; mains from RM15; ☾ dinner Wed-Mon) The coolest car-boot sale you'll ever see, Junk is filled to the brim with…well…junk. But it's all so very chic – when you walk in you'll think, 'Did Amelie explode in here?' A favourite among Malaysian celebs, Bla Bla Bla's sister restaurant offers superb sophisticated Western food with an Italian bias. A word to the wise: don't set your watch by any of the wall clocks…

Living Room (☎ 082-233944; Jln Wayang; mains from RM25; ☾ dinner) Living Room completes Kuching's trendy triumvirate of fusion eats. The menu mixes the top noshes at Junk and Bla Bla Bla and guests dine in breezy open-air *salas*. You will no doubt find yourself wondering where you are: is this Borneo, Bali or Barcelona?

See Good Food Centre (☎ 082-251397; 53 Jln Ban Hock; meals from RM30; ☾ noon-11pm, closed 4th & 18th of the month) Follow the crowds of locals here to try Sarawak specialities such as lobster in pepper sauce, *midin* (crispy jungle fern) and *ambol* (bamboo or finger clam).

Hawker Centres & Food Stalls

Chinese Food Stalls (43 Jln Carpenter; meals from RM3; ☾ breakfast, lunch & dinner) Start your day with a brilliant, old-school Kuching breakfast (see Walking Tour, p414). Note that Chinese locals refer to this hawker centre as Lau Ya Keng in Hokkien.

Hawker Centre (Jln Khoo Hun Yeang; meals from RM3; ☾ breakfast, lunch & dinner) The best hawker centre in town, with both Malay and Chinese sections, is in the west end of town near Kuching Mosque (locals sometimes refer to this as the 'open-air market').

Green Hill Corner (Jln Temple; meals RM3-4; ☾ breakfast, lunch & dinner) Several stalls here crank out a variety of noodle and rice dishes, including a brilliant plate of *kway teow goreng* (fried rice noodles). The problem is that the chef who makes this dish only shows up when he damn well feels like it.

Top Spot Food Court (☎ 082-238730; Jln Padungan; meals RM4-35; ☾ lunch & dinner) The double entendre definitely holds true. This excellent rooftop plaza has acres of tables and a good variety of stalls. Order anything from abalone to banana prawns or numerous varieties of

fish, and chase it down with a cold bottle of Tiger. To get here, climb the stairs leading from Jln Padungan to Tapanga restaurant, and keep heading upstairs from there.

DRINKING & ENTERTAINMENT

Like most places in Borneo, a lively night scene usually focuses on an evening meal, but cosmopolitan Kuching has a clutch of spirited drinking spots as well (pun intended). Bars and other entertainment venues stay open until around 1am, although live music can blare on until later (especially on weekends). Beers cost around RM8 to RM10 (cocktails are a bit more) and keep an eye out for popular two-for-one happy hours. Oh, and just for the record, Fort Margherita does not dispense alcohol (actually, the whole campus is closed).

The *Official Kuching Guide* has a lengthier list for those who plan on sticking around for a while. Check out Kuching's trifecta of trendy restaurants; Bla Bla Bla, Living Room and Junk, for some pre- or post- (or between) dinner carousing (opposite).

The following options are a great place to start.

Jambu (32 Jln Crookshank) Jambu? Crookshank? The names in Kuching are pretty weird, but this local fave in a blazing pink bungalow, south of the city centre, is a hip spot to sling back a few designer cocktails with friends. Closed on Mondays.

Soho (☎ 082-247069; 64 Jln Padungan) This is arguably the hippest bar in the centre – even the name oozes London cool. Local *Gossip Girl*-esque youngsters hobnob to grind-worthy play lists of jazz, dance and latin beats. The atmosphere starts out relaxed but can definitely build up some heat under the red lights as the night draws on!

Mojo (Jln Chan Chin Ann) Wander through to the back of the Denise wine shop and you may think you've entered another world – this is a cocktail lounge every bit as fashionable as you might find in KL or Singapore, with a giggly young crowd trying to live up to the style.

Cottage (Crowne Plaza Riverside, 16 Jln Bukit Mata) Fitted out along the lines of an English pub (albeit one with no walls), proceedings start gently here with lunchtime and evening meals, leading into live music six nights a week.

Also worth a look:

99 (☎ 082-423799; 98-99 Jln Green Hill) Football on the big screen; thumping tracks on the weekend.

Ipanema (66 Jln Padungan) 'Minimal-chic' theme, with trendy tapas snacks.

Ruai (3 Jln Green Hill) Iban-themed pub below Nomad hostel.

SHOPPING

If it's traditional Borneo arts and crafts you're after, then you've come to the right place. Kuching is undoubtedly the best spot in Borneo for collectors and cultural enthusiasts. Traditional handicrafts include Orang Ulu beadwork, Bidayuh basket weaving, traditional wooden carvings and hand-woven rugs, to name just a few. Also, Sarawak pepper can be a unique and inexpensive gift for friends back home – the Malaysian government exports over 25,000 tonnes each year. Check out www.mpb.gov.my for more info about this aromatic spice.

Don't expect many bargains, but don't be afraid to negotiate either – there's plenty to choose from, and the quality varies as much as the price. Overpricing and dubiously 'aged' items are common, so be sure to spend some time browsing to familiarise yourself with prices and range before committing yourself to a purchase. Start on the aptly named **Main Bazaar** – a seemingly unending promenade of souvenir shops, some outfitted like art galleries, others with more of a 'garage sale' appeal. **Jln Carpenter**, a block behind Main Bazaar, has a few shops as well.

Sarawak Craft Council (Sarawak Handicraft Centre; ☎ 082-245652; www.sarawakhandicraft.com; 32 Jln Tun Abang Haji Openg; ☯ 8.30am-4.30pm Mon-Fri) Daily demonstrations by local artists accent the eclectic and authentic assortment of tribal decor here.

ARTrageously Ramsey Ong (☎ 082-24346; www. artrageouslyasia.com; 94 Main Bazaar) Moving away from customary handicrafts, this private gallery exhibits and sells mainly contemporary paintings, and champions local artists, including Mr Ramsey Ong himself, who is also a renowned fashion designer. It's run by the owners of Singgahsana Lodge (p417), who also happen to be amateur photographers.

Sarakraf (☎ 082-232771; Sarawak Plaza, 78 Jln Tabuan) High-end arts and crafts from around the state, with artists receiving 'fair' compensation for their talents. A cache of glossy photographs and coffee table books is also on sale.

our pick Borneo Headhunters Tattoo & Piercing Studio (Ministry of Pain; ☎ 019-856 6317; 47 Jln Wayang) International tattoo all-star Ernesto Umpie inks customers with a variety of intriguing Iban designs. Check out the boxed text (p416) for the full story on Borneo's tribal body art.

Empress Studio (☎ 241009; 1B Jln India) Not much art goin' on here – this electronics boutique specialises in camera supplies, accessories and repairs. A great place to stop if you have any post- (or pre-) jungle camera woes.

GETTING THERE & AWAY

Air

AirAsia (☎ in Malaysia 03-8775-4000, outside Malaysia +60-3-8660-4343; www.airasia.com; ground fl, Wisma Ho Ho Lim, 291 Jln Abell) has numerous daily flights to/from Kuala Lumpur at bargain-basement prices. They also fly to/from Penang and Johor Bahru. Within Borneo, they fly to/from Bintulu, Kota Kinabalu, Miri and Sibu. Check for prices as they constantly change.

Batavia Air (☎ 082-626299; www.batavia-air.co.id; 1, ground fl, Padungan Arcade Garden, Jln Song Thian Cheok) has flights to/from Jakarta (Java) and Pontianak (Kalimantan) for around US$50 one way.

Malaysia Airlines (MAS; ☎ in Malaysia 1300-883-000, 03-7843-3000, in Kuching 082-220618; www.malaysiaairlines. com; 215 Jln Song Thian Cheok) offers flights between Kuching and Kuala Lumpur (RM259) and Johor Bahru (RM199). They also fly between Kuching and Hong Kong and Guangzhou. Within Borneo, MAS flies to/from Bintulu (RM139), Kota Kinabalu (RM229), Miri (RM139) and Sibu (RM89).

Silk Air (☎ 082-256772; www.silkair.com; 7th fl, Gateway Bldg, Jln Bukit Mata) has flights to/from Singapore.

Boat

Express Bahagia (☎ 082-410076) has boats running to and from Sibu (RM45, 4½ hours), departing from the express boat wharf in Pending at 8.30am daily. Note that this is an easier and faster trip to Sibu than the bus, which takes eight hours.

The express-boat wharf is 6.5km east of town in the suburb of Pending. Chin Lian Leong (CLL) bus 1 (RM1.50, 30 minutes) connects the wharf with Kuching. It operates from the STC-CLL bus stand near Kuching Mosque and stops on Jln Tunku Abdul Rahman just west of the Hotel Grand Margherita Kuching. Taxis from town cost RM20.

Bus

Long-distance buses depart from the **Express Bus Terminal** (Jln Penrissen), 5km southeast of the

BRINGING HOME A PIECE OF BORNEO

As you wend your way across the island, you'll happen upon thousands of potential souvenirs – masks, pearls, T-shirts, carpets, tattoos, spices – and sometimes it can be difficult to sort out the goodies from the crap.

Jln Main Bazaar in Kuching is a great place to shop, as is the Sarawak Craft Council (opposite) down the street. Here you'll find objects from all over the region. In Sabah, the markets of KK are filled with little gems like irregular pearls, sold at record low prices. Items made from indigenous materials (like rattan) are generally authentic; however, the masks aren't very Bornean (in fact, the colourful ones are Balinese). Most longhouses in Sarawak also have handicrafts for purchase, but many of these objects were actually produced in Kuching and shipped into the jungle. There's no need the stress about debating the authenticity of that wicker basket – simply ask and the locals will be honest about the product's origin.

If you are looking to bring home something more authentic (antiques, plants etc), make sure you're aware of any relevant regulations affecting your purchase. Most outlets can organise the necessary fumigation of wooden artefacts, as well as shipping. Some antiques such as cannons and jars are difficult to export. You'll need to get permission from the Sarawak Museum *before* you purchase the item. In general, it is illegal to export any plants or seeds without a permit from the Department of Agriculture (Sarawak pepper is OK), and animal parts (like leopard teeth or hornbill feathers) are strictly off limits. Seashells are commonly sold around KK and Semporna – please do not purchase these as it may encourage the pillaging of the ocean for more.

Some countries also restrict the importation of weapons as souvenirs. For example, Australian customs officials seem worried about the safety of suburban cats if blowpipes get in (although they may have a point…). The machete-esque *parang,* once the head-hunting weapon of choice, is another trinket you may have trouble explaining to your postman back home (never mind trying to get past your local customs agent!).

centre. There are regular services to Sibu (RM45, eight hours, 10 departures daily between 6.30am and 10pm), Bintulu (RM60, 10 hours, nine departures daily between 6.30am and 10pm), and Miri (RM80, 14 hours, eight departures daily between 6.30am and 10pm).

Numerous Sarawak Transport Co (STC) buses run between the terminal and city for 90 sen. The buses are 3A, 4B and 6, and leave from either in front of the mosque or on Jln Barrack behind the courthouse. A taxi costs RM20.

Border Crossings

The closest border crossing from Kuching into the Indonesian state of Kalimantan is located at Tebedu, near Serian. Travellers making land crossings into Kalimantan are required to obtain a visa beforehand from the **Indonesian Consulate** (☎ 082-421734; 6th fl, Bangunan Binamas, Jln Padungan; ☯ 8.30am-noon & 2-4pm Mon-Fri) as the border posts at the Kalimantan border do not issue visas on arrival. Fees and requirements differ from country to country (it's usually RM170); contact the consulate for more information. Visas are granted upon arrival at Pontianak airport –

consider flying if you are short on time (around RM184) – overland visas usually take a few days.

GETTING AROUND
To/From the Airport

Kuching International Airport (KCH) is 12km south of the city centre. At the time of research there were no public buses connecting the airport and the city centre. If you don't want to take a cab on arrival, then head left (which will feel counterintuitive as taxis head right) and walk for 500m until you hit the main route. Venture across the road to the bus shelter and flag a bus down (all buses in this direction are heading downtown). It may require a bit of patience, but the ride will only cost RM1.

To get to the airport from Kuching, take a Bau-bound bus and ask the driver to let you off near the airport. If the driver doesn't understand you, ask for 'Batu Sentosa' (or 'Mile 7'), but make sure you get off *before* the bus reaches the junction.

Taxis will cost around RM24. Buy a coupon before you leave at the counter outside the terminal entrance.

AROUND KUCHING

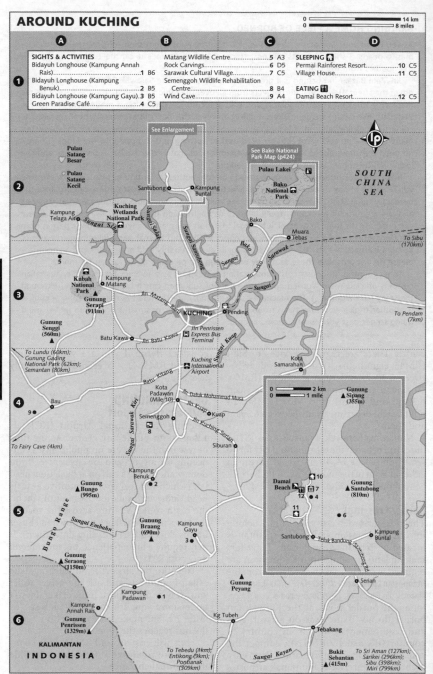

SIGHTS & ACTIVITIES
Bidayuh Longhouse (Kampung Annah
Rais)...1 B6
Bidayuh Longhouse (Kampung
Benuk)...2 B5
Bidayuh Longhouse (Kampung Gayu).3 B5
Green Paradise Café..........................4 C5

Matang Wildlife Centre.....................5 A3
Rock Carvings..................................6 D5
Sarawak Cultural Village..................7 C5
Semenggoh Wildlife Rehabilitation
Centre..8 B4
Wind Cave......................................9 A4

SLEEPING
Permai Rainforest Resort.................10 C5
Village House.................................11 C5

EATING
Damai Beach Resort........................12 C5

Boat

Tambang (small passenger ferries) will ferry you across Sungai Sarawak for destinations such as Fort Margherita and the Astana. The fare is 30 sen, which you pay as you disembark. You can catch *tambang* at several jetties along the waterfront.

Car

There are several car rental agencies in the arrivals hall of Kuching International Airport. Despite the fact that they have different names, most of them are fronts for the same company, and it's very difficult to play one off against another in the hope of getting a better price.

Taxi

There are taxi ranks around the city centre and at the Express Bus Terminal. Most short trips around town cost between RM6 and RM10. Taxis in Kuching do not have meters, so be sure to settle on the fare before setting out. Luckily, most of the drivers are fairly honest and you don't have to bargain too hard.

SOUTHERN SARAWAK

Kuching's biggest asset is its proximity to a dozen natural wonders. The city is a great base for day trips to the coast and into the jungle. Almost all of the destinations in this section are within arm's reach of Kuching.

BAKO NATIONAL PARK

Bako National Park (☎ 082-478011; admission RM10; ✹ park office 8am-5pm) proves that you don't have go too far to find Borneo's signature jungles stuffed to the treetops with wildlife. Sarawak's oldest national park is a 27-sq-km natural sanctuary located on a jagged jade peninsula jutting out into the South China Sea. Although it's only a stone's throw from the capital, it's well worth spending the night here.

Orientation & Information

Register for the park (adult/child RM10/5) upon arrival at the boat dock in Bako Bazaar. From here it's a choppy 30-minute boat ride to **park headquarters** (Telok Assam; ☎ 082-478011), where you'll find accommodation, a cafeteria and the park office. Staff will show you to

your quarters and can answer any questions you have about trails. There's a large trail map hanging outside the office; ask for a free copy. Storage lockers are available for RM5 per day.

There's a good, if slightly weathered, information centre here, with photos and displays on various aspects of the park's ecology. An entertaining video on the proboscis monkey is shown at regular times and also on request – ask at the office.

Sights & Activities

WALKING

Bako has a total of 17 trails ranging from short walks around park headquarters to strenuous day treks to the end of the peninsula. Guides are available upon request at the park office (RM20 per hour), but it's easy to find your way around because all trails are colour-coded and clearly marked with splashes of paint. You don't have to go far to see wildlife (try the Telok Paku trail), and there are walks to suit all levels of fitness and motivation. Plan your route before starting out on longer walks, and aim to be back at Telok Assam before dark (about 6.45pm). Some trails may be closed for maintenance after the wet season – check at the park office before setting out.

If you have only one day in Bako, try to get here early and attempt the **Lintang Trail** (5.25km, four to five hours). It traverses a range of vegetation and climbs the sandstone escarpment up to the *kerangas*, where you'll find many pitcher plants as well as some grand views over the nearby island plateaus.

The longest trail is the **Telok Limau**, a 12km walk that's impossible to do as a return trip in one day. You will need to carry camping equipment or else arrange to be dropped off by boat in the morning and walk back to park headquarters (expect to be charged about RM165, and be sure to let someone know of your plans). A giant wooden billboard near the park office lists all trails and conservative time estimates.

Take adequate water or purification tabs and be prepared for intense sun (with sun hats and sunscreen) as it gets particularly hot in the *kerangas* and there's no shade for long stretches (sun-sensitive folks might consider lightweight long-sleeve shirts and trousers). Mozzie repellent is a good idea as well.

In the evening, park rangers may offer a guided night trek if there is enough interest from guests. This is an opportunity not to be

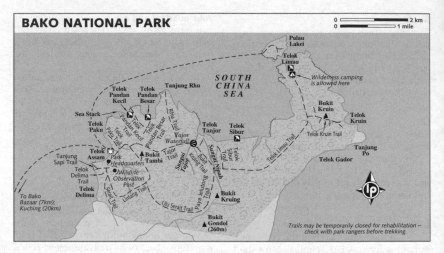

missed, as the wildlife present at night is entirely different from that seen during the day. The rangers are also particularly good at spotting things that an ordinary traveller would miss. Inquire at the welcome desk to see if there is a trek on that night. The trek lasts between 1½ to two hours and costs about RM10 per person.

WILDLIFE
Bako is a storehouse of incredible natural diversity: biologists estimate that the park is home to 37 species of mammals, 24 reptile species and 184 bird species (some of which are migrant species).

Walking trails pass through peat swamp, rainforest and, on the low sandstone plateau behind Telok Assam, *kerangas*. The latter, especially near the intersection of the Lintang and **Ulu Serait** trails, is a fascinating ecosystem where pitcher plants are common.

Animals include long-tailed macaques, silver-leaf monkeys, monitor lizards, palm squirrels and, at night, mouse deer, civets and culago (flying lemur). The best place to look for proboscis monkeys is along the beach at the end of the **Telok Paku Trail**, where they forage around the trees lining the cliff. Walk very quietly and listen for them crashing through the trees – they will see you long before you see them. **Telok Delima** trail offers a more close-up experience: listen for grunts and crashing vegetation and follow the sound with your eyes. You've also got a good chance of seeing them feeding around the mangrove boardwalk just before the park jetty in the late morning.

Bird-watching is best near the park head-quarters, especially in and around the mangroves at Telok Assam.

The large bearded pig that hangs around near the cafeteria is a minor celebrity in the park and a big hit with kids. It often ambles by in the afternoons.

BEACHES
The beach at **Telok Pandan Kecil**, surrounded by spectacular sandstone rock formations, is gorgeous. Around the point is the famous **Bako Sea Stack**, which you have no doubt already seen on countless postcards; to get close to it for a photo, however, you'll have to hire a boat.

The quiet, attractive beach at **Telok Pandan Besar** is only accessible by boat from the park headquarters as the final descent from the cliff top of the trail is closed. The beach at **Telok Sibur** is accessible by foot but hard to reach as the descent is steep, and you have to negotiate through a mangrove swamp, but it is worthwhile as others rarely make it down here.

If you're thinking of hitching a boat ride to or from a beach, boats to beaches near park headquarters will cost around RM25 (one way or return), but to beaches further away it is quite expensive (eg RM80 to Telok Sibur). **Pulau Lakei**, on the park's northeastern tip, is also accessible by boat (RM120).

Sleeping & Eating
Bako's reputation is twofold among tourists: first, the park has amazing trails and wildlife; and second, the park's accommodation

is crap. The rooms at Bako have torn mozzie nets, dank bathrooms and a faint stench of mildew. Fortunately, plans are underway to build a new dormitory complex. Most people opt for a dorm room, although camping is allowed in a designated camping zone.

Bookings can be made at the **National Parks & Wildlife Centre** (☎ 082-248088; www.sarawaktourism. com; Sarawak Tourism Complex, Jln Tun Haji Openg; ☺ 8am-5pm Mon-Fri) in Kuching.

The **cafeteria** (☺ 7am-11.30pm) sells cheap buffet noodle and rice meals. The adjoining shop sells a good variety of reasonably priced tinned and dried food, chocolate, biscuits, film and toiletries, although fresh bread, produce and vegetables are not always available.

Getting There & Away
Arriving and departing Bako is dependent on the tides. Call ☎ 082-431-336 for daily tide information.

To get to Bako from Kuching, first take a bus to Bako Bazaar in Kampung Bako, then charter a boat to the park. Petra Jaya bus 6 leaves from near the Hawker Centre (open-air market) near Kuching Mosque in Kuching every hour (approximately) from 7.20am to 6pm (RM2.50, 55 minutes). The last bus back to Kuching leaves Kampung Bako at 5pm. You can also go by taxi all the way from Kuching (RM35, 45 minutes).

A boat from Bako Bazaar to the park headquarters takes 20 to 30 minutes and costs RM47 each way for up to five people. The chances are high that someone on the bus or at the pier will be looking to share a boat too.

Take note of the boat's number (or ask for the driver's mobile phone number) and be sincere when you agree to a pick-up time. If you do want to share a different boat back, tell park headquarters your boat number – staff are happy to call and cancel your original boat. Boats generally operate between 8am and 5pm, though this is generally weather and tide dependent.

SANTUBONG PENINSULA (DAMAI)
The Santubong Peninsula is like Kuching's Malibu – a stunning seaside strip home to high-end resorts and the private villas of the elite. The main drawcards are the beaches, a golf course, modest jungle trekking and a clutch of seafood restaurants in the small fishing village of Kampung Buntal, at the base of the peninsula.

Sights & Activities
SARAWAK CULTURAL VILLAGE
Surrounding an artificial lake at the foot of Gunung Santubong, the **Sarawak Cultural Village** (☎ 082-846411; www.scv.com.my; adult/child RM60/30; ☺ 9am-5pm) is an excellent living museum. It has examples of traditional dwellings built by different peoples of Sarawak – Orang Ulu, Bidayuh, Iban and Melanau – as well as Malay and Chinese houses.

There are six buildings in all, plus a games centre and a shelter of the type used by the nomadic Penan in the jungle. The dwellings are staffed by tribespeople who demonstrate local arts and crafts, including basketry and weaving, blowpipe shooting, sago processing and bird's-nest goods production.

There's also a twice-daily performance showcasing the traditional dances of the various groups, which include spectacular physical feats such as the Melanau funeral pole dance (plus the corny 'Malaysia: Truly Asia' song). It's all quite touristy, of course, but tastefully done and sincere in intent.

Hotels and travel agencies in Kuching have packages that include admission, lunch and transport ranging in price from RM90 to RM150. If you're planning to get married in Sarawak, you can choose to tie the knot in style here according to Iban, Bidayuh, Orang Ulu or Malay ceremonies.

SARAWAK

MISCHIEVOUS MACAQUES

The long-tailed macaques that hang about the park headquarters are great to watch, but they are cunning and mischievous – an attitude fostered by tourists who insist on offering them food. The monkeys (and some tourists) are opportunists and will make running leaps at anything they think they can carry off. Lock all your doors, close all your bags and do not leave valuables, food or drink unattended, especially on the beaches, at the canteen or on the verandahs. It's wise to leave the monkeys in peace – the males can be aggressive, and once you've seen a macaque tear open a drink can with its teeth you'll be happy that you didn't mess with them. If you get cornered, yell for the park staff. Monkeys are not a problem after dark.

There's no public transport to the village, but a shuttle bus leaves from the Riverfront and from the Hotel Grand Margherita Kuching at 9am and 12.30pm, returning at 1.45pm and 5.30pm (RM10 each way).

JUNGLE WALKING

The Santubong Peninsula offers good jungle walking within easy reach of Kuching, and more adventurous walkers can attempt the ascent of **Gunung Santubong** (910m), a 3.4km trail that takes around five hours one way.

An easy to moderate circular walk (2km, one to two hours) starts near the Damai Beach Resort and ends near the cultural village, passing a pretty **waterfall** on the way. Both trails start at the ramshackle **Green Paradise Café**, where you register and pay a RM1 fee. The trails are well marked so you shouldn't get lost, although it's a good idea to report in at the police box in Santubong village before setting off. If you really wish to put in the hours, there's a camp site near the cafe, but if you want to make an overnight trek you'd be better off investigating somewhere more adventurous like Bako National Park.

ROCK CARVINGS

Although they're a little difficult to find, the Santubong rock carvings on Sungai Jaong are worth seeking out, if you have an interest in archaeology. There's said to be nearly 40 of these artefacts, which are mostly carvings on boulders (including a distinct human figure), though it's unlikely you'll be able to find that many without spending quite a bit of time looking around. An accurate dating of the site hasn't been made yet, but it's thought to be at least a thousand years old. Chinese ceramic pieces from the Tang dynasty and evidence of ironmaking have also been found here, making it one of Sarawak's most important archaeological sites.

To reach the petroglyphs, turn into a gravel road south off the main road going into Santubong, about 3km after the turn-off for Kampung Buntal and near the 6km marker on the road to Damai. The gravel road will take you to two houses and a walking trail to the rock is behind them. You will more than likely need to ask a local for directions. The site is called Batu Gambar in Malay, but don't be surprised if the first local you ask does not know about it – keep trying and you'll find someone who does.

WILDLIFE TOURS

The Santubong area is home to a wide variety of wildlife, and guided wildlife tours are beginning to catch on here. Commonly spotted species include endangered Irrawaddy dolphins, known locally as *pesut*, estuarine monkeys, crocodiles, fireflies and all manner of birds

CPH Travel (☎ 082-242289; www.cphtravel.com.my; per person RM160, minimum 2 people), based in Santubong, runs wildlife tours to the area. See opposite for more information about cruise tours. If you are already in the Santubong-Buntal area, consider going with local Buntal boatman, **Mr Ehwan bin Ibrahim** (☎ 019-826 5680), who offers a selection of tours of the area. Expect to pay around RM450 for a four-person boat for a dolphin-and-mangrove tour, and be sure to book three or four days in advance. **Camp Permai** (☎ 082-846847) offers guided kayaking tours for about RM60 per person.

Sleeping & Eating

Permai Rainforest Resort (☎ 082-846487; www.permai rainforest.com; Damai Beach, Santubong; camp sites/long-houses/treehouses RM10/120/198, cabins RM208-228; ⊠) This excellent ecofriendly nature retreat offers a choice of longhouse dorms, six- to eight-person cabins and luxury treehouse rooms (which include breakfast and minibar), as well as space for camping. Even better, the adjoining Camp Permai training centre (day entry RM5) is the best spot on the peninsula for leisure and adventure activities, with a high-ropes course, rock climbing, kayaking, boat cruises, obstacle course and abseiling to name but a few. This place is good for those travelling with children.

Village House (☎ 082-846166; www.villagehouse. my; Santubong; dm/d RM88/220; ⊠ 🖳 ⚍) The owners of Singgahsana (p417) have done it again. Lipstick-red walls, double-stuffed mattresses, dreamy white linen and fusion cuisine – this is boutique elegance par excellence.

Damai Beach Resort (☎ 082-846999; www. damaibeachresorst; Teluk Bandung, Santubong; r from RM220; ⊠ 🖳 ⚍) The oldest hotel in Santubong, this sprawling resort has two distinct parts; classic ocean rooms and modern hillside suites. The beautiful Barok suites were inspired by traditional Bidayuh homes and have been constructed in a beautiful round structure. There are enough activities on the grounds to make you feel like you're on a cruise ship (in a good way).

There are several restaurants around the resorts in the peninsula. Kampung Buntal, a few kilometres away, boasts a large collection of seafood restaurants with attractive patios on stilts over the beach, all very popular with Kuching locals, the favourite being Lim Hok Ann near the end of the restaurant strip.

Getting There & Away

At the time of research Petra Jaya buses were no longer running between Kuching and Kampung Buntal, although a van service (RM3 to RM4) departing from Jln India has been shuttling passengers. Ask at the tourist information centre for the latest transport updates. For Santubong, take a taxi from Kampung Buntal (around RM10, 15 minutes). If you want to stay for a meal the only option is to take a taxi back to Kuching (around RM25, 45 minutes). There's also a shuttle to Damai that stops in front of Singgahsana Lodge in central Kuching.

A taxi to the resorts costs RM25 to RM45 from Kuching; if you want to be picked up after dinner, expect to pay RM60 for the return trip. A taxi from Kampung Buntal to any of the resorts should cost around RM10. Taxis can also be hired for a trip from the resorts out to Kampung Buntal and Santubong.

KUCHING WETLANDS NATIONAL PARK

Kuching Wetlands National Park makes for a fascinating half-day trip away from the state capital or from the Santubong area. The park is a mere 15km from Kuching proper (and only 5km from Damai), but this riverine realm feels like a whole different world. Although this protected mangrove forest is only 6610 hectares, it is known throughout Malaysia as being one of the top spots in the country to see the Irrawaddy dolphin, which feeds in shallow waters.

The only way to gain access to the park is by boat. Several local tour companies operate within in the park, offering a broad spectrum of half-day experiences. Most boats wander along the lazy Sungai Salak before slinking down one of the shaded tributaries. Some groups pay a brief visit to the Malay fishing village at Pulau Salak. We recommend the lauded dusk wildlife cruise run by CPH Travel, which leaves Santubong at around 4.30pm and returns three hours later. Visitors must book ahead (see opposite for more info).

Kuching Wetlands is located about 55 minutes away from the city central, and about a 30-minute boat ride from Damai. Most tour companies servicing the park depart from either Damai or Santubong and will include hotel transfers (from either Kuching or Damai) in the rates. Access to the park is also available from Samariang or Telaga Air.

KUBAH NATIONAL PARK

Only 15km from downtown Kuching, **Kubah National Park** (☎ 011-225 003; adult/child RM10/5) is yet another good natural retreat within easy striking distance of the city. While Bako has the edge for wildlife, Kubah offers good trekking and the trails are more shaded, which is a plus for the sun-averse. The 22-sq-km park consists of a range of forested sandstone hills that rise dramatically from the surrounding plain to a height of 450m. There are waterfalls, walking trails and lookouts, and the beautiful rainforest is home to a wide variety of palms and orchids. Kubah National Park has also played host to two Hollywood productions: *Farewell to the King*, starring Nick Nolte, and the more recent *The Sleeping Dictionary*, with Jessica Alba.

Park accommodation can be booked through the Kuching **National Parks & Wildlife Booking Office.** (☎ 082-248088; www.sarawaktourism. com; Sarawak Tourism Complex, Jln Tun Haji Openg; ◷ 8am-5pm Mon-Fri) next door to the visitors information centre. The Kubah park headquarters offers hostel, resthouse and double-storey chalet accommodation. There's no restaurant, but a kitchen is supplied with all facilities, including a fridge and utensils.

Matang Transport bus 11 leaves Kuching (from the stand near Kuching Mosque) for Red Bridge, near the turn-off for Kubah, at regular intervals (RM2, 40 minutes); there's no set timetable, but services run roughly every 90 minutes in the morning. Note that at the time of research this bus was not operating and may not be operating during your visit. From Red Bridge, near the Jublee Mas Recreation Park, it's a 4km walk to the park entrance, quite a lot of it uphill. Follow the signs for Matang Family Park, as the signposts for Kubah at the moment look like they're about to fall off. A taxi from town will cost at least RM75 return; arrange with the driver a time to be picked up. You can also try to get a ride on a private van (RM5 per person or RM45 for the whole van one way, leaving near Saujana car park).

MATANG WILDLIFE CENTRE

A short drive beyond Kubah National Park, the **Matang Wildlife Centre** (☎ 082-225012; admission

SARAWAK

RM10; 8am-5.30pm) was set up as a rehabilitation centre for endangered species released from captivity, particularly Borneo's larger mammals. Although it's supposed to recreate natural conditions as closely as possible, there's no denying that it's better described as a zoo located in the jungle.

There are twice-daily feeding programs for orang-utans, sambar deer and crocodiles, as well as rainforest walking trails, including the **Rayu Trail**, which links up with Kubah National Park (three to four hours).

The animals are kept in enclosures, or sometimes even cages, and people who don't like zoos may find it depressing. It is important to remember, however, that the centre is part of an active rehabilitation program and that many of these animals will find themselves being released into the wild in the future.

The only practical options for getting here from Kuching are by taxi (about RM40 one way) or with a tour (around RM130 for an overnight stay). Walking from Red Bridge is not an option as the entrance is another 12km from the entrance to Kubah National Park. Hitching is an option, but we don't recommend it.

SEMENGGOH WILDLIFE REHABILITATION CENTRE

Semenggoh Wildlife Rehabilitation Centre (☎ 082-442180; adult/child RM3/1.50; 8am-12.45pm & 2-4.15pm) is a great place to sneak a peek at our ginger-haired cousins (no, not the Irish). Over 20 of Borneo's great orang-utans live in the centre, and although there isn't sufficient natural forest in the surrounding area to make actual reintroduction into the wild possible, it's still a good opportunity for a photo shoot. Semenggoh is noticeably less touristy (and much, much cheaper) than the widely publicised Sepilok Orang-utan Rehabilitation Centre in Sabah. Note that you're not guaranteed any orang-utan sightings, because the apes are free to come and go as they please. Feeding times are at 9am and 3pm.

Semenggoh is 24km south of Kuching. To get there, take STC bus 6 from Kuching (RM4, 40 minutes). At the time of research there were only two bus services per day, 7.30am and 1.30pm. Ask the bus driver for details on his desired return time. Get off at the Forest Department Nursery, then walk 1.3km down the paved road to the centre. The last return bus passes Semenggoh at

1.30pm, but you should be able to flag down a private van (RM3) or a bus from the main road. A taxi from Kuching to the centre costs around RM40.

Tour companies also operate guided day trips out to the centre for RM50 per person. Note that some tours don't leave sufficient time to explore the gardens and arboretum at the centre (ask before you sign up).

BIDAYUH LONGHOUSES

Longhouses near Semenggoh have been on the tourist circuit for decades. **Kampung Annah Rais** is one of the most commonly visited longhouses. It's an impressive structure with more than 100 doors, and has preserved its traditional look, apart from metal roofs and satellite dishes, that is. Standard price for admission to these longhouses is RM10. There are quite a few homestay options averaging RM300 for a two-day and one-night stay per person, including food and activities, and tourists can be accommodated even if they show up unannounced.

To get to Annah Rais, take a taxi or van from Kuching to Kota Padawan and try to find a shared van from the car park near the hornbill statues at the end of the main street (RM6 and up if there are sufficient passengers to share the ride; it costs RM40 to RM50 to charter the van).

BAU

About 26km southwest of Kuching, the little town of Bau is the access point to two interesting cave systems, which are typical of the caves found all across the island of Borneo. You won't find much to keep you around the town itself, but these jutting limestone caves make for an interesting trip away from the capital, particularly if you won't have the chance to visit the grander caves at Mulu or Niah Caves national parks. Take a picnic lunch, drinks and a good torch (which can also be hired at the entrance to each cave).

About 3km southwest of Bau, the **Wind Cave** (☎ 082-765490; adult/child RM3/1.50; 8.30am-4.30pm) is a network of underground streams on the banks of the Batang Kayan. Slippery, unlit boardwalks run through the caves, allowing you to wander along three main passages with chittering bats swooping over your head. Don't be tempted to leave the boardwalk if you see steps in the rock – this is probably the exit to a subterranean adventure-caving trail.

About 5km further south, **Fairy Cave** is an extraordinary elevated chamber 30m above the ground in the side of a cliff. You can follow the footsteps of generations of Chinese and wander the grotto making up your own names for the 'fairies' seen in the various anthropomorphic cave formations; if you want anything from these stony spirits, though, make sure you bring some incense. Reached by a steep concrete staircase, the cave is quite large and you could spend an hour exploring it.

From Kuching, STC or BTC bus 2 to Bau (RM4, one hour) departs every half-hour between 6.20am and 6pm. You can also take a detour here on your way to or from Gunung Gading National Park; two STC buses (2A) run to Lundu (RM7.80) daily.

To get to Wind Cave, take BTC bus 3 or 3A (RM1, one bus every 90 minutes or so) from Baru and walk the 700m to the entrance. For the Fairy Cave, take BTC bus 3 (RM1.40) and walk the 1.3km from the main road. The last bus back passes through at around 5.30pm. A taxi will cost around RM12 one way.

GUNUNG GADING NATIONAL PARK

There is some good walking in this pleasant little **park** (☎ 082-735714; adult/child RM10/5; 🕑 8am-12.30pm & 2-5pm), but most visitors come to see the rare *Rafflesia tuanmudae* (see the boxed text, p432). These massive flowers, blessed with a spectacular bouquet of rotting flesh, appear year-round but at unpredictable times and in varying locations. Check whether any are in bloom before heading to the park by ringing the park headquarters or the **National Parks Booking Office** (☎ 082-248088; www.sarawaktourism.com; Sarawak Tourism Complex, Jln Tun Abang Haji Openg; 🕑 8am-5pm Mon-Fri, 9am-3pm Sat & Sun); the flowers only last for a few days, so get here as soon as you can if one is in bloom.

The park features a plank-walk built around the area that the flowers are found. If unaccompanied by a ranger, do not step off the plankwalk as the rafflesia flower buds are small, difficult to spot and can easily be crushed underfoot. If a plant is far away from the main boardwalk, a park ranger may be able to guide you. Do not stray from where he walks and follow his instructions. Guiding fees are RM20 per hour (per group). November to January are said to be the peak blooming months.

Few visitors take much time to explore beyond the rafflesia, which is a shame as there are some well-marked **walking trails**.

The **hostel** (dm/r RM15/40) has fan rooms with shared bathroom and fully equipped kitchen. Two three-bedroom **lodges** (r RM150; 🔀) with cooking facilities sleep up to six people. Camping, where permitted, costs RM5 per person. Weekdays are the least busy times.

To get to Gunung Gading, first take STC bus EP07 from the Express Bus Terminal on Jln Penrissen to Lundu (RM10, 1¼ hours, four daily). The park entrance is 2km north of Lundu, on the road to Pantai Pandan; you can either walk there or take a taxi (RM15) from the Lundu bus station. Vans also operate on this route (RM2), but they only leave when full.

SEMATAN

Sematan, 107km northwest of Kuching by road, is a pleasant fishing village on the coast facing the South China Sea. An attractive promenade lines the waterfront, and a long concrete pier affords wonderful washed-out early morning views as mist shrouds the hills and the surf pounds away in the distance. The northern end of the promenade leads to some colourful stilt houses and a park commemorating the early Malay fishermen of the area. The beach here is clean, deserted and lined with coconut palms, but the water is very shallow. In the direction away from town, you can encounter bucolic picture-book kampung scenery set against the dramatic Gunung Gading range, perfect for a hike or a bicycle ride.

The Malay village of **Telok Melano** is about 30km down the coast from Sematan (if you're driving, hug the coast in a north westerly direction). It offers pristine beaches and clear blue water against the backdrop of Gunung Melano. Activities such as nature walks, camping, boat trips and fishing are offered, and homestay accommodation (averaging RM230 to RM300 a night, inclusive of meals, national park entrance, boat rental and other activities) with villagers can be arranged. Contact Mr Hashim at the **Fisheries Development Authority** (☎ 013-824 6785).

Sleeping & Eating

Jln Seacom heading west out of town leads to a few beach resorts. These are usually packed during the weekends, but you'll have the place to yourself on a weekday.

Sematan Hotel (☎ 082-711162; 162 Sematan Bazaar; r RM25-50; 🔀) A friendly place with simple tiled rooms and shared bathrooms, it's on

THE BORNEO LONGHOUSE

Longhouses are the traditional dwellings of the indigenous people of Borneo and the island's most distinctive feature of tribal life. These large communal dwellings, raised on stilts above the forest floor, can contain over a hundred individual family 'apartments' beneath one long, long roof. The most important part of a longhouse is the covered common verandah, which serves as a social area, 'town hall' and sleeping space.

The longhouse lifestyle is by no means a forgotten tradition in Borneo, even in the face of globalisation. Community living is a very sustainable way of life – most youngsters that leave for greener pastures (read: more money) usually keep close ties to their village and return home later on in life. Over time, some longhouse communities have upgraded their building materials from thatch and bamboo to wood and linoleum. But don't let the errant satellite antenna betray your wild Kipling-esque fantasies; a trip to a longhouse is a must for anyone who wants to know the real Borneo.

PLANNING A VISIT

You may be initially surprised to discover that longhouse visits can be a pricey venture. Tours are not cheap, and if you go on your own you'll need to pay for a boat and/or 4WD (figure RM300 to RM800), a guide (RM80 per day, plus RM35 per night) and lodging (usually RM10 per night).

There are two essential ingredients in organising a memorable longhouse visit: finding an excellent guide and choosing the right longhouse (the latter is always a function of the former). A great guide or tour company has a clutch of longhouse options and will always be receptive to the type of experience you desire. When searching for a tour operator or freelance guide, it is best to keep an open mind – after all, they are the experts – but do not hesitate to be upfront about your desires and concerns. Do you require a certain level of sleeping comfort? Might you have any dietary restrictions? Is it a heart-to-heart you're after? Will you be disappointed if you see a satellite dish dangling off the side of the structure? Do you want to be the only traveller at the longhouse, or would you prefer it if there were others?

Sarawak has plenty of tour operators and guides eager to take you (and your money) on Borneo's ultimate cultural adventure. Most operations are based in Kuching, though Miri has a handful as well. Guides in Kuching can plan your visit to the Sri Aman Division (Batang Skrang, Batang Lemanak and Batang Ai). Start in Sibu (try the tourist information centre) for trips along the Batang Rejang, although in the last few years this region has experienced some dubious guiding activity. Trekkers interested in connecting the dots between the longhouses of the Kelabit Highlands should fly to Bario and plan their adventure there.

Scouting a tour locally is significantly cheaper than any pre-departure booking on the internet, and it's well worth spending a day checking out your options – it can mean the difference between spending a sleepless evening with other sweaty tourists, or having a spirited evening (double entendre intended) swapping smiles, stories and shots of rice wine with the local inhabitants. If you want to assemble your own trip, the Sarawak Tourism Board publishes a yearly *Members Directory* listing all registered freelance guides and their contact information. Membership can be expensive and some of the best guides opt to work for tour operators rather than renewing their freelancer's licence. Unregistered freelance guides may be friendly and knowledgeable, but they cannot be held accountable if something goes wrong during your trip.

We cannot overstress the importance of doing your research and finding a great guide. Yes, you could potentially head upriver on your own, but you'll still need to find someone to take you to a longhouse. An invitation is essential, and turning up unannounced is not only bad manners, it also can be a major cultural faux pas. Even if you make your way into a longhouse without a guide, you will find major communication and cultural barriers. Interacting spontaneously with locals isn't always easy as the elders usually don't speak English, and the younger people are often out working the fields or have moved to the 'big city' to earn more money. A great guide usually knows several people at the longhouse (including the chief) and can act as a translator while you try to strike up a conversation. Your guide will always keep you abreast of any cultural differences – like when and where to take off your shoes – so you needn't worry too much about saying or doing the wrong thing.

VISITING THE LONGHOUSE

When you arrive at a longhouse, you may be surprised to find that it's quite modernised, with satellite TV, electric lighting, corrugated iron and other upgrades – after all, even if their manner of living is old-fashioned, the people here are living in the 21st century. A longhouse is a way of life, not just a building. It embodies a communal lifestyle and a very real sense of mutual reliance and responsibility, and it is this spirit rather than the physical building that makes a visit special. Do your best to engage with the inhabitants of any community you are allowed to enter, rather than just wandering around snapping photographs.

Depending on the various goings-on at the longhouse, you may or may not spend time with the *tuai rumah* (chief) – although he (it's always a he) will usually 'show face' as it is impolite for him not to do so. Your guide will usually be the one showing you where to sleep – either on the verandah, in a specially built hut next door or in a resident's living room within the longhouse itself.

If you are travelling with your own guide, he or she will be in charge of organising your meals – whether it's a separately prepared repast, or a feast with some of the longhouse residents. The Iban in particular like to honour their guests by offering meat on special occasions. Vegetarians and vegans should be adamant about their dietary restrictions as vegetable dishes are often served in a chicken sauce. Meals will be plentiful no matter what, and it is not considered rude or disrespectful to bring your own food. Two important things to remember when eating with longhouse residents: don't put your feet near the food (which is always served in a 'family style' communal fashion) and don't step over anyone's plate if you need to excuse yourself from the eating area.

After dinner, when the generators start clicking off, it's time to hunker down with the evening's bottle of milky white broth: rice wine, or *tuak*. You'll be a big hit if you bring a bottle of brand-name liquor – 'Johnny Walker' and 'Southern Comfort' are oftentimes the extent of the locals' English vocabulary. The ceremonial shot glass will be passed from person to person amid chitchat and belly laughter. Drink the shot when it's your turn (you won't really have a choice – those Iban women can be pretty forceful!) and pass the glass along. *Tuak* may taste mild but it is pretty potent stuff, and you can expect a stunning hangover the next day. If you don't want to drink, you can pretend to have a medical condition. When you reach your limit, simply press the rim of the glass with your finger like you're pushing an eject button. If that doesn't work then feign a sudden medical condition. Smiles, big hand gestures and dirty jokes go a long way, even in your native language (and it'll all be second-nature when you're nice and lubricated!).

GIFTS

Gift giving has become rather controversial over the last few years, with locals, tourists and tour operators offering a wide variety of advice on the subject. Longhouse communities do not traditionally require gifts from guests; in fact, some say that the tradition of gift giving actually began when travellers started visiting. Your best bet to avoid any awkward cultural miscommunications is to ask your guide for their opinion. Longhouses set far away from the beaten track could use bulk bags of rice or sugar, while communities that are a bit more in touch with the modern world might appreciate items like pencils, toothbrushes or fishing line. Some travellers bring an item that can be shared over glasses of rice wine. Any way you do it, gifts are never a must, nor are they expected. Many tourists prefer contributing to the longhouse economy by taking a local longboat trip or buying one of the handicrafts for sale. If you are visiting independently, it's polite to bring a small gift for the family of the person who invited you.

the left-hand side of the road just before entering Sematan.

Kampung Pueh (☎ 013-827 4967; 2-day 1-night stays RM105, 3-day 2-night stays RM180) This Bidayuh Salako village about 9km outside of town has a longhouse homestay program. Activities include a trek up Gunung Gading as well as visits to local industries. Contact Mr Jehim Milos.

Sematan Palm Beach Resort (☎ 082-712388, 295 Jln Seacom; weekday/weekend r & chalets for 2 people RM153/180; 🏊) The best of the bunch on Jln Seacom, it has cheerfully painted chalets and a restaurant, and also rents out bicycles and sea kayaks. From the beach, you can walk all the way back to town, fording a small stream near its outskirts.

Sematan has a couple of Chinese *kopitiam* facing the waterfront and some Malay food stalls near the wharf.

Getting There & Away
To get to Sematan from Kuching, take STC bus EP07 to Lundu (RM10, 1¼ hours, four daily), then try to find a private hired van from the area around the Lundu bus station. A full van will cost around RM5 per person, but if you can't find any other fellow travellers, you'll end up paying between RM20 to RM30 for the whole vehicle.

TANJUNG DATU NATIONAL PARK
Located in the far west of the state, abutting the border with Kalimantan, this 14-sq-km park protects rainforest, unpolluted rivers and near-pristine beaches, on which endangered turtles lay their eggs. The park boasts four trails, which include the **Telok Melano Trail** from Telok Melano village and the **Belian Trail**, which makes a steep climb up to the summit of Gunung Melano. The turtle hatchery on the beach is fenced off and strictly off limits.

For park information and permits, inquire at the **National Parks Booking Office** (☎ 082-248088; Sarawak Tourism Complex, Jln Tun Abang Haji Openg; 🕐 8am-5pm Mon-Fri) located next door to the visitors information centre (it's also worth stopping in here!).

Travel here is not recommended between October and March as the sea can get very rough. Snorkelling and scuba diving are allowed in certain areas; divers must be accompanied by an approved guide.

The only accommodation in the park is in the form of a **camp site** (camping per person RM5), for which you can make arrangements at the Kuching visitors information centre. If tenting is not your cup of tea, the Telok Melano homestays (p429) provide a convenient base.

Access for day trips is only possible by boat from Sematan; prices start at around RM450 for up to 10 people. If you visit Gunung Gading on the way, someone at the park office may be able to organise a boat for you; otherwise try the Sematan Hotel (p429).

TALANG-SATANG NATIONAL PARK
Talang-Satang National Park consists of two pairs of islands: Pulau Satang Besar and Pulau Satang Kechil (Big and Small Satang Islands) and Pulau Talang-Talang Besar and Pulau Talang-Talang Kecil (Big and Small Talang-

---

THE EXTRAORDINARY RAFFLESIA

People use words like bizarre, awe-inspiring or enigmatic upon viewing the rafflesia flower. One of the greatest wonders of the botanical world, the 1m-wide flower can elicit both astonishment at its incredible size and revulsion at its scent (it often emits a smell similar to that of rotting flesh). Even more amazing is the fact that this oddity erupts directly from the forest floor, with no visible stems or leaves.

The rafflesia plant is actually a parasite that lives entirely on the roots of a grapelike vine in the genus *Tetrastigma*. The parasite does not produce any food of its own, but instead forms a network of microscopic filaments that penetrate the vine's roots to steal water and nutrients.

In preparation for flowering, the parasitic rafflesia sends up a cabbage-like bud that grows on the forest floor for a year or more before blossoming. The flower itself is a giant succulent creation that is red in colour with white splotches all around. After two or three days the flower begins to deteriorate and within two weeks it is reduced to a blob of black slime.

Seeing a rafflesia is a very special treat. Not only are the flowers themselves fleeting and rarely encountered, but poaching and habitat loss has greatly reduced their numbers. Of the nine species thought to live in Borneo, only six have been spotted in the last 60 years.

IBAN LANGUAGE LESSON

The Iban language is quite similar to Bahasa Malaysia (the Malay language). Often there are simple suffix differences: *jalan* (road) is *jalai* in Iban, *makan* (eat) is *makai*, *salamat datang* (welcome) is *salamat datai* and so forth. The Iban traditionally expressed gratitude through gestures rather than words, so phrases like 'thank you' have been borrowed from Malay. Numbers have also been taken from Malay. The Iban word *nuan* connotes respect, much like *vous* in French or *usted* in Spanish. *Dik* is used among friends, and is the Iban equivalent of the French *tu*.

In general, Iban humour has a reputation for being quite filthy, and locals respond well to chatty visitors even if they are trying to communicate in their native language.

Also note that words can be pronounced slightly differently throughout Sarawak as there are several Iban dialects.

Good morning.	*Salamat pagi.*
Good afternoon.	*Salamat tengah-hari.*
Good night.	*Salamat malam.*
Goodbye.	*Salamat tinggal.*
Thank you.	*Terima kasih.*
How are you?	*Nama brita nuan?*
Are you OK? (relating to health)	*Gerai nuan?*
Pleased to meet you.	*Rindu amat betemu enggau nuan.*
What's your name?	*Sapa nama nuan?*
Can I take a photograph of you?	*Tau aku ngambi gambar nuan?*
How much?	*Brapa?*
See you again.	*Arap ke betemu baru.*
I'm sorry.	*Ampun aku.*
I'm tired.	*Lelak.*

Talang Islands). Together, these islands comprise Sarawak's first marine park, established in 1999 to protect sea turtle egg-laying habitat.

Pulau Satang Besar and Pulau Satang Kecil form the Satang section (9894 hectares), part of which is open to visitors, who must visit under park warden supervision. Permits are available from Kuching's **National Parks Booking Office** (☎ 082-248088; Sarawak Tourism Complex, Jln Tun Abang Haji Openg; ✆ 8am-5pm Mon-Fri) or the **Forestry Department** (☎ 082-348001; www.sarawakforestry.com; Hock Lee Center, Jln Datuk Abang Abdul Rahim). On Pulau Satang Besar visitors can watch fragile eggs being moved from the beach to a hatchery and, if especially lucky, witness baby turtles being released into the wild. Snorkelling and diving are permitted, but only within certain designated areas and divers must be accompanied by an approved guide.

The Talang-Talang section (9520 hectares) is off limits to visitors due to the islands' small size and the sensitivity of the marine turtles. Local villagers and fishermen have retained their right to access the park and continue their traditional activities.

The Sematan Hotel or Palm Beach Resort (see p429) can help arrange transport to the park; boats cost around RM250. **CPH Tours & Travel** (☎ 082-243708; www.cphtravel.com.my) run tours to the area.

SERIAN

Serian is a tiny Bidayuh town 65km southeast of Kuching. Tour groups often stop here to have lunch or pick up gifts on the way to the longhouses located along nearby rivers (see below). Serian boasts a bustling **market**, where people from nearby longhouses come to sell jungle fruits and herbs, snake meat, sago grubs and other unusual produce.

STC bus 3A runs between Kuching and Serian (one way/return RM6/4, one hour, every half-hour between 6.15am and 6.45pm). The bus station is in the centre of Serian, near the market. Vans park behind Electra House and shuttle passengers to/from Kuching (RM6 per person).

SRI AMAN DIVISION

Originally known as Simanggang, Sri Aman is a quiet town on the turbid Batang Lupar, halfway between Kuching and Sarikei. Sri Aman's main claim to fame is the *benak*, a tidal wave that periodically sweeps up the river, scattering all craft in its path; it nearly took the life of writer W Somerset Maugham, an event he recorded in a short story called 'The Yellow Streak'. James Brooke's **Fort Alice**, a little downstream, was built in 1864 and is a prominent landmark.

The Skrang, Lemanak and Ai rivers flow into the Lupar, and visits to the river longhouse communities can be organised in Kuching (either with an operator or with a private guide). See the boxed text, p430, for more on longhouse visits.

Batang Skrang & Batang Lemanak

Lemanak has four longhouse communities, two of which have accommodation set up in a special building for tourists. Both **Serubah** and **Kesit** attract considerable numbers of tourists and evenings are often spent hanging out with your fellow travellers instead of the villagers. Sleeping arrangements are dorm-style, with a sprinkling of paper-thin mattresses, and the bathrooms are…well…we recommend holding it in till you get back to Kuching. If you're OK with sleeping on the longhouse verandah à la *bujang berani* (Iban bachelor warrior), then try a visit at **Kacung** or **Ngemahili**.

Batang Ai

Live out your wildest *Heart of Darkness* fantasies along the muddy Batang Ai. A stunning reservoir acts like the region's welcome mat – its dimpled vales merely a sneak peek of the jungle yet to come. Cruise through thin rivulets that swish past lazy vines. Pass canopies of trees soaring overhead where thirsty branches twist towards the steaming earth as though they were reaching for water. This intricate network of river systems crawls deep into the island's interior until it reaches the **Batang Ai National Park** – a haven for wild orang-utans.

Nanga Sumpa, a local longhouse, has been lauded as one of the most impressive indigenous eco-tourism efforts in Borneo. Funded by Borneo Adventure (p416), the locals here have constructed a small courtyard of huts to accommodate their visitors. You'll pay a little more, but you'll probably be the only traveller sipping rice wine with the friendly villagers. Contract Borneo Adventure for package pricing.

If you crave the longhouse experience but can't live without your evening puffs of air-con, consider staying at the **Hilton Batang Ai Longhouse Resort** (☎ 083-584338; www.batang.hilton.com;

r RM366; ❄ ❄) at the far end of the reservoir. Branding this jungle resort under the Hilton name has been a bit of a double-edged sword. Customers are attracted by the name, but the facility falls a tad short of the reputation. Had the resort gone with something like 'Batang Ai Jungle Lodge' – this place would probably be a big hit. The design scheme here is 'longhouse chic' and they pull it off quite well, although the rooms are beginning to show their age ('70s shag carpeting anyone?). There's a dial-up computer terminal, but it wasn't working when we visited. Transport to the lodge can be arranged at the Hilton Hotel in Kuching.

Although the infamous Batang Rejang is further from Kuching, a visit to Batang Ai's remote longhouses can prove to be far more rewarding. Tourist numbers are significantly smaller, and you don't have to waste your valuable vacation days to reach this realm of green and brown. Trips to Batang Ai should be booked in Kuching, either with a tour operator or with a private freelance guide. See the boxed text (p430) for everything you need to know about planning a longhouse visit.

BETONG DIVISION

The Betong Division has its own constellation of far-flung longhouses. The rural **Bukit Saban Resort** (☎ 082-647178; amab88@gmail.com; r from RM75), near the town of Betong along the Sibu–Kuching highway, is an excellent springboard for launching a multiday visit of off-the-beaten-path communities. There are large on-site obstacle courses for those who feel so inclined. Ask about leech therapy if you're not pressed for time.

CENTRAL SARAWAK

For those making a beeline between Kuching and the wilds of the north, Central Sarawak will merely be a riverine realm glimpsed out the window from an aeroplane seat. From high above, the expanse of deep greens and browns stretches along the horizon as curving waterways slither into the jungle, cutting across the terrain. Overland travellers will delight in sleepy harbour villages dotted along the quiet lowland coast, and those with a bit more time on their hands can head down the roaring Batang Rejang into Borneo's steamy interior.

BATANG REJANG

Carrying the mystic resonance of the exotic interior, the mighty Batang Rejang is Borneo's jugular, and the main trade artery for all of central and southern Sarawak. But if it's an Amazonic tangle of jungle vines you're after, you'll be sorely disappointed. These days, the Rejang feels like a wide, muddy conveyor belt for the insatiable logging industry. Topsoil and logging detritus have been clogging the waters for years, and it's not a pretty sight. And let's not forget the bungled Bakun Dam hydroelectric plant, which has yet to be completed thanks to mismanagement, financial problems and the overambitious scale of the project. The area south of the dam has already been emptied of an estimated 11,000 tribal people to make room for the reservoir – now there is talk of building an aluminium smelting plant.

It's not all bad though – the serpentine tributaries splintering off the main river hide dozens upon dozens of remote longhouse communities. Visiting a longhouse offers travellers the unique opportunity to interact with the island's indigenous people, and it's an experience you won't soon forget. See p430 to learn more about longhouses and planning a visit. Trips to longhouses in the region can be organised in Kapit and Belaga, although it's worth stopping by the tourism offices in Kuching or Sibu to bone up on some useful background info first.

The best time for a trip up the Rejang is in late May and early June. This is the time of **Gawai Dayak**, a harvest festival, when there is plenty of movement on the rivers and the longhouses welcome visitors. There are also plenty of celebrations, which usually involve the consumption of copious quantities of *tuak* and arak.

Along the river, the only hotel accommodation available is in Song, Kanowit, Kapit and Belaga. You are technically required to have a permit (see p439) if you plan to travel beyond Kapit.

Sibu
pop 255,000
While Kuching takes the cat as its mascot, it comes as no surprise that Sibu aspires to

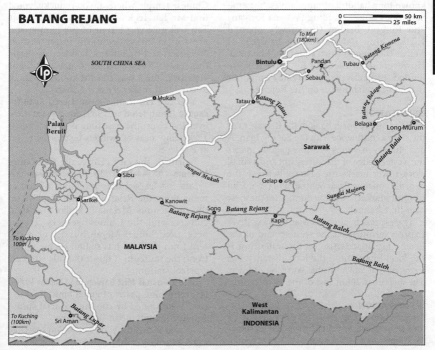

BATANG REJANG

be a swan – the city is, after all, quite the ugly duckling. If you are from your nation's (or region's) 'second city', then you might have a soft spot for Sibu as you wander through the town's bustling markets. Locals are staunchly proud of their roaring burg despite the noticeable lack of attractions.

Sibu was once known as New Foochow, named for the Chinese migrants who came from Foochow (Fujian) province in the early years of the 20th century. Prior to this, the Melanau, then the Malays and the Iban, were the area's inhabitants.

Sibu is the gateway to the Batang Rejang and the centre for trade between the coast and the vast upriver hinterland. The Brookes were happy to let Sibu's capitalists manage the extraction of upriver wealth. Situated 60km upstream from the sea, Sibu is where the interior's raw materials are brought for transhipment and export. The wide, muddy river hosts a motley procession of fishing and cargo boats, tugs, barges laden with timber, express boats and speedboats skipping over their wash.

As well as its hectic waterlife, Sibu is known for a handful of superlatives, boasting Sarawak's tallest building (Wisma Sanyan) and longest bridge (the newly opened 1.22km-long Batang Rejang bridge), as well as the biggest town square in Malaysia. However, its attractions for travellers are limited, and most people only stay a night or two before pushing on up the Rejang.

ORIENTATION

Sibu lies on the north bank of the Rejang, near the river's confluence with the Batang Igan. A graceful seven-storey Chinese pagoda marks the western edge of the waterfront and a small clock tower marks the eastern; between the two, the concrete Pasar Sentral Sibu (PSS; Sibu Central Market) building dominates the view over Jln Channel.

The express boat wharf is at the new River Express terminal on the western end of the Rejang Esplanade. Also on the waterfront is the local bus station; the long-distance bus terminal is at Sungai Antu, 3km west of town. The airport is 20km east of the town centre.

INFORMATION

Greatown Travel (☎ 084-211243, 019-8565041; www.greatown.com; No 6, 1st fl, Lorong Chew Siik Hiong 1A) Reliable inbound tour operator.

ibrowse Netcafé (☎ 084-310717; 4th fl, Wisma Sanyan, 1 Jln Sanyan; per hr RM3; ☽ 8am-10pm) Internet access.

Main post office (☎ 084-332312; Jln Kampung Nyabor; ☽ 8am-4.30pm Mon-Fri, 8am-3pm Sat)

Rejang Medical Centre (☎ 084-330733; www.rejang.com.my; 29 Jln Pedada) A group of private specialist clinics with 24-hour emergency services.

Sibu General Hospital (☎ 084-343333; Jln Abdul Tun Rahman)

Standard Chartered Bank (Jln Tukang Besi) Opposite the visitors information centre; changes travellers cheques and has an ATM. Be prepared to wait for the cheques to go through.

Visitors Information Centre (☎ 084-340980; 32 Jln Tukang Besi; ☽ 8am-5pm Mon-Fri) Has friendly and informative staff (ask for Jessie) who can help with information about upriver trips out of Song, Kapit and Belaga. Has plenty of materials, including maps, bus schedules and brochures on sights and travel to other destinations in Sarawak.

Yewon moneychanger (☎ 084-330577; 8 Jln Tukang Besi) South of the visitors centre; only changes cash.

SIGHTS

Tua Pek Kong Temple (Jln Temple; admission free; ☽ dawn-dusk) is an interesting riverside Chinese temple where, if you're lucky, you'll find Mr Tan Teck Chiang in attendance. Mr Tan will give you a tour of the temple and explain (in lavish detail) his interpretation of Taoism and Buddhism. You can also scale the seven-storey pagoda to get a brilliant view over the town and the muddy Batang Rejang as it makes its way seaward.

You can climb the seven-tiered **Kuan Yin Pagoda** (completed in 1989) for a great view over the river; the best time is sunset, when a wheeling mass of swiftlets buzzes the tower at eye level.

North of the city centre, the **Civic Centre Museum** (☎ 084-331315; Jln Suarah; admission free; ☽ 8am-5pm Tue-Sun) tells the story of settlement along the Rejang through displays on the indigenous Melanau, Malay and Iban cultures and the Chinese settlers. To get here, take Sungei Merah bus 1A or 4 (90 sen) from the local bus station on the waterfront; the museum is down the side street by a petrol station.

The unusual **Mist Garden** (Jln Kampung Nyabor) is a refreshing patch of green amid the busy roads, moistened by cooling artificial sprays and appealingly neon-lit at night.

As well as the many 'no spitting/no sneezing' signs adorning lampposts, Sibu council does

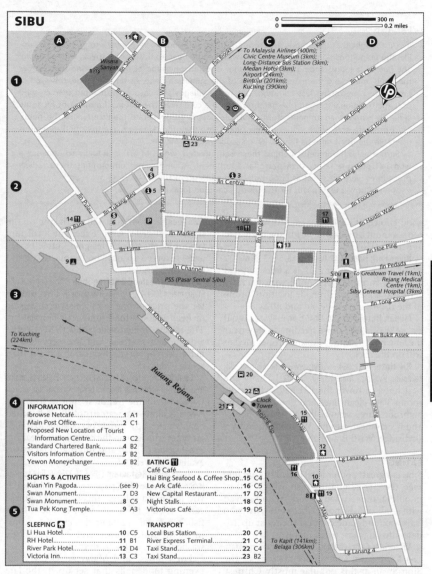

SIBU

0 — 300 m
0 — 0.2 miles

SARAWAK

its bit for civic spirit with a number of borderline kitsch **swan monuments**.

SLEEPING

Most of the budget lodging in Sibu is of a
very low standard and this is a city where
even budget travellers should opt for a midrange option if at all possible.

Li Hua Hotel (☎ 084-324000; Lg Lanang 1; r RM45-80;
🖳) On the riverfront, about 100m south (upriver) of the swan statues, you will find Sibu's
best-value hotel, with spotless tile-floor rooms
and good views from the upper floors.

Victoria Inn (☎ 084-320099; 80 Jln Market; r RM50-
85; 🖳) If the River Park and the Li Hua are
full, this centrally located budget hotel is a

PALANG

If you thought that tribal body art stopped at tattoos, you are very, very wrong. However, unlike the ubiquitous skin ink, you probably won't come head to head, so to speak, with a *palang*. The *palang*, a long-standing Dayak tradition, is a horizontal rod of metal or bone that pierces the penis, mimicking the natural genitalia of the Sumatran rhino. As times change, this type of procedure is becoming less common, but many villages still have an appointed piercer, who uses the traditional method of a bamboo vice in a cold river. The real macho men opt for some seriously extreme adornments, from multiple *palang* to deliberate scarification of the penis. Most bizarrely, some men will even sew beads into their foreskins to make their nether regions resemble the giant rafflesia flower. (Overcompensating? Maybe…)

Surprisingly, the impetus behind these self-inflicted 'works of art' is actually to enhance a woman's pleasure rather than personal adornment. Among some communities these radical procedures were once just as important as lopping off heads.

See the boxed text (p416) for the inside scoop on local ink art.

good choice. It's a tightly packed warren of rooms about a block away from the high-rise Tanahmas Hotel.

River Park Hotel (☎ 084-316688; 51-53 Jln Maju; r RM55-80; 🖳) The River Park is a fairly typical and well-run midrange hotel with friendly staff and a pleasant riverside location. Some of the rooms are a little old and noisy.

Medan Hotel (☎ 084-216161; Jln Pahlawan, Jaya Li Hua; s/d RM65/75) For those needing to stay near the Sibu bus terminal, prim and proper Medan will do the trick.

RH Hotel (☎ 084-365888; www.rhhotels.com; Jln Kampung Nyabor; r from RM260; 🖳 🖳) Easily the best hotel in town, the RH has stylish new rooms with clean lines and good light. The bathrooms are spacious, there's a rooftop pool and it's connected to the Wisma Sanyan by a skybridge. Wi-fi is available.

EATING

Sibu is a great spot for local eats. Try *kam pua mee*, the city's signature dish, which is thin noodle strands soaked in pork fat and served with a side of roast pork. Check out www.sibu .sarawakfoodguide.com for the most up-to-date info on where to eat in town.

Victorious Cafe (Jln Maju; meals RM3-8; 🖳 breakfast, lunch & early dinner) Dine under the gaze of the Sibu Swan at this popular mostly Chinese *kedai kopi* (coffee shop) across the street from the Li Hua Hotel. There's a stall here that makes a smoky and wonderful plate of *kway teow* (rice noodles), which you can wash down with a nice iced lemon tea.

Café Café (☎ 084-328101; 10 Jln Chiew Geok Lin; mains from RM3; 🖳 10am-10pm) Tucked down the street in the shadow of the towering pagoda,

this local hotspot puts a modern spin on the traditional *kedai kopi*. Excellent local fare (and a smattering of designer coffee beverages) is served up amid bodacious decor and flickering candles.

Hai Bing Seafood & Coffee Shop (☎ 321491; 31 Jln Maju; mains RM4-15; 🖳 lunch & dinner) Two outlets for the price of one: go cafe-style streetside or head indoors for Chinese air-con eating. The special mixed vegetables (RM2) come with added seafood and are served in a hefty doughy 'nest'; it's nearer a main than a side order.

Le Ark Café (☎ 084-321813; Rejang Esplande; mains from RM8; 🖳 lunch & dinner, breakfast also Sat & Sun) Undoubtedly the trendiest spot in town, Le Ark sits along the waterfront like a beached boat, serving up a variety of cocktails to trendier types who laze on the comfy patio seating. A selection of local and international eats is available as well.

New Capital Restaurant (☎ 084-326066; Jln Kampung Nyabor; meals around RM25 per person; 🖳 lunch & dinner) If you feel like a splurge, this brilliant Chinese eatery is sure to satisfy, with excellent fresh fish, meat and vegetable dishes. We recommend the butter prawns and stir-fried *midin* washed down with a fresh fruit juice.

For Chinese and Malay snacks, try the evening food stalls that set up in the late afternoon along Jln Market. You'll also find several stalls on the 1st floor of PSS (Pasar Sentral Sibu).

GETTING THERE & AWAY
Air
Malaysia Airlines (☎ 1300-883 000; www.malaysiaairlines .com.my; 61 Jln Tuanku Osman) has several flights daily

from Sibu to Kuching (RM89), Miri (RM139), Kota Kinabalu (RM210) and Kuala Lumpur (RM319). **AirAsia** (☎ 1300-889 933; www.airasia.com; Jln Keranji) has dirt-cheap flights to/from Kuala Lumpur, Johor Bahru and Kuching.

Boat

If you are heading to Sibu from Kuching, check the local newspaper for the most up-to-date speedboat departure times (times to Kapit are published as well). Boats leave from the River Express Terminal at the western end of Jln Bengkel (which is at the southwestern end of town). There is one boat per day at around 11.30am (RM35).

Getting to Kapit is the first leg of the journey up Batang Rejang. Several boats motor the 140km from Sibu to Kapit (RM17 to RM30, three hours, departures between 5.30am and 1pm). Some boats continue up to Belaga, but most terminate in Kapit. All boat companies have booths at the terminal and they display their next departure times with large clocks outside their booths, making choosing your boat a snap. Contact the local branch of the **Sarawak River Board** (☎ 084-339936) for any additional inquiries.

Bus

Bus companies have ticket stalls at the long-distance bus station (Sungai Antu) and around the local bus station on the waterfront. Buses run between the long-distance bus station and Sibu's town centre all day for RM1. A taxi to/from town will cost RM10.

Buses run between Sibu and Kuching (RM40, eight hours, regular departures between 6.30am and 10pm), Miri (RM40, 7½ hours, roughly hourly from 6am to 10pm) and Bintulu (RM20, 3½ hours, roughly hourly from 5.30am to 6pm).

GETTING AROUND

Sibu's airport is about 20km east of town. Bus 3A runs to and from town every 1½ hours from 6.30am to 6pm (RM2.50, about 30 minutes). You could also try flagging down any rural bus that passes by. The coupon taxi fare into town is RM28.

The local bus station is on the waterfront. To get to the long-distance bus station, take Lanang Rd bus 21 (90 sen) from the local bus station. It leaves roughly hourly between

6.30am and 5.30pm. A taxi costs RM10. Taxi stands operate 24 hours a day. Try ☎ 084-320773 or ☎ 084-335787 if you are having a hard time finding service.

Kapit
pop 19,500

After a three-hour journey in what feels like a cramped space shuttle, you'll arrive in the 'kapital' of the mighty, murky Batang Rejang. It's not much to look at, but after a few hours you'll quickly discover that this far-flung trading centre is an important commerce hub for the smattering of long-houses hidden in the nearby jungle. Have a wander through the lively fresh markets and sample savoury jungle ferns. We recommend organising your longhouse visits from Kapit rather than Belaga as there is a wider variety of river systems from which to choose.

Fans of Redmond O'Hanlon's *Into the Heart of Borneo* know Kapit as the starting point of the author's jungle adventures, and if you want to head off up the Batang Baleh to emulate them, this is the place to make arrangements.

INFORMATION

It's important to take note that there's an antiquated permit system in place for those wishing to travel from Kapit and Belaga. However, we've never heard of any authority actually checking these permits, especially since, strangely, a permit is not required for travel in the other direction. The permit office is located in an ultra-modern building called **Resident's Office** (☎ 084-796963, 084-796242; http://www.kapitro.sarawak.gov.my; ⏰ 8am-5pm Mon-Fri, closed for lunch) on Jln Airport, past the old airport on the west side of town. It's a 15-minute walk in each direction.

If you're looking for a wireless internet connection, ask for 'wi-five'.

Good Time Cyber Centre (☎ 084-746303; 354 Jln Yong Chai; per hr RM3) Internet access.

Hua Chiong Travel Service (☎ 084-796681; Jln Koh) Airline tickets and local travel services.

Hyper Link Cyber Station (17 Jln Tan Sit; per hr RM3) Internet access.

KL Ling Moneychanger (☎ 084-796488; Jln Penghulu Gerinang) Changes cash and travellers cheques.

Maybank (☎ 084-790122; 73C Jln Penghulu Atan)

Public Bank (☎ 084-790106; 64 Jln Wharf) Changes cash and travellers cheques.

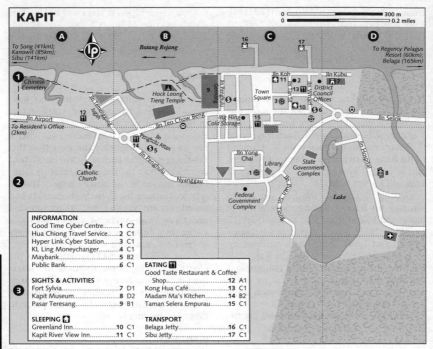

SIGHTS

Another of the wooden fortifications marking the white rajas' progress up the Rejang, **Fort Sylvia** (☎ 799171; Jln Kubu; admission free; ☺ 10am-noon & 2-5pm Tue-Sun) was built as Fort Kapit in 1880 to keep the peace and gain control of the upper Rejang. In 1925 the fort was renamed to honour Ranee Sylvia, wife of the third raja, Charles Vyner Brooke. The *belian* (ironwood) timbers have lasted amazingly well, even after massive flooding in 1934 almost reached the top of the doorway! In 1997 the fort was declared a historical building, and the Tun Jugah Foundation now runs it as a museum and a training centre for artisans, weavers and artists in the Kapit District.

The civic centre (Dewan Suarah) houses the **Kapit Museum** (Jln Hospital; admission free; ☺ 8am-1pm & 2-5pm Mon-Sat, closed 11.45am-2.15pm Fri). It has a couple of cultural displays and there's a relief map showing all the longhouses in the area, perfect for picking at random if you like a bit of spontaneity in your planning. Just opposite the centre is a lake with a network of small pagodas and wooden walkways, good for a stroll or a picnic.

The focus of activity in Kapit is invariably the **waterfront**, which is continually packed with ferries, barges and longboats, all swarming with people. It's fascinating to watch the activity on the water and to see people shouldering (or sometimes 'heading') impossibly heavy loads of every description up the steep steps from the wharf.

Some of these goods will end up in Kapit's colourful daily market, the **Pasar Teresang** (Wet Market). It's a chatty, noisy hive of grass-roots commerce, and the friendly vendors have a lot of fun trying to explain to tourists how to prepare and eat a galaxy of unfamiliar items.

TOURS

If you did not organise a longhouse visit from Kuching, then Kapit will do just fine. Rather than exploring the well-trodden Batang Rejang, ask around for tours that go up into the quieter Batang Belah. Tourists have expressed concern that there are crooked guides in Kapit and Belaga taking large sums of money without providing an adequate product. The Sarawak Tourism Board has strongly encouraged tourists to use licensed guides, as only a licensed guide can be held accountable for any wrongdoings.

One of the most knowledgeable guides in the area is **Joshua Muda** (☎ 019-485 9190; joshuamuda@hotmail.com). He is Iban, and leads a variety of trips to traditional Iban longhouses along the Sungai Mujong, a tributary north of the Batang Baleh. Joshua is not a licensed guide, but he is very experienced and has even led more ambitious expeditions to the Kalimantan border. If you can't get hold of Joshua by phone or email, then head to the Greenland Inn – the receptionist should be able to put you in touch with him. If you want a registered guide try **Alice Chua** (☎ 019-485 9190), a pleasant Chinese woman that can organise a variety of local longhouse visits for around RM75 per person per day.

Although it is the general custom to visit a longhouse with a guide (see p430 for information about the longhouse experience), there are a few longhouse communities orbiting Kapit that are quite accustomed to independent travellers. Kapit's system of buses is quite easy to navigate – destinations are written in large letters on the sides of each van. If you know which longhouse you'd like to visit, simply ask around for the van that goes there. Note that the name of a longhouse is almost always the name of the chief (unless he has recently passed away), so if you know the name of your destination, you'll know the name of the chief when you arrive. Rumah Bundong (10km) is a 45-minute drive from Kapit and welcomes day trippers and overnighters (RM60).

FESTIVALS & EVENTS
Baleh-Kapit Raft Safari A challenging two-day race recreating the experience of Iban and Orang Ulu people rafting downstream with their jungle produce to Kapit. Teams of eight head 50km down the Balleh and Rejang rivers on homemade rafts, overnighting in Iban longhouses. It's usually held the last weekend in April. Check with the Kapit Resident's Office (☎ 084-796963, 084-796242) or the tourist office in Sibu for dates and entrance fees.
Gawai Dayak Beginning on 1 June, Gawai Dayak celebrates the end of the harvest season in Sarawak. This is the best time to visit the region's longhouses, as the Iban people cut loose in a mania of feasting, dancing and *tuak*-drenched celebrations.

SLEEPING
Kapit River View Inn (☎ 084-796310; krvinn@tm.net. my; 10 Jln Tan Sit Leong; s & d RM55-60; 🖳) A good option with – as the name promises – a river view or two. Most rooms don't have windows though…

Greenland Inn (☎ 084-796388; 463-464 Jln Teo Chow Beng; s/d RM80/90; 🖳) Kapit has about as much in common with Greenland as Kuching does with Greenwich, but if you can ignore the geographical misnomer, this is a respectable step up from the budget class.

Regency Pelagus Resort (☎ 084-799051; www. theregencyhotel.com.my/Pelagus; full board s RM320-340, d RM400-440; 🖳 🏊) Inaccessible by road, Pelagus Resort is a unique longhouse-style resort that's a 45-minute boat ride from Kapit, within earshot of the roaring Pelagus Rapids. The two-tiered wooden design blends beautifully into the jungle, but the rooms are starting to look a bit tired and mildewed. Transport to the resort is arranged by the resort when bookings are made.

EATING
Kapit is packed with small restaurants and *kedai kopi*, but the best place to eat in the

---

NABAU: BORNEO'S NESSIE

In traditional Iban lore, the Nabau is a giant snake deity measuring over 30m long. An elusive reptile, the Nabau lives in the turbid waters of the upper Rejang, appearing in dreams but rarely rearing its dragon-like head. Heroes who glimpse the mega-beast are instantly blessed with good fortune.

In early 2009 a local conservation team was analysing the flood plains around the Batang Rejang from a helicopter when suddenly they spotted the Nabau. Out came the cameras and a series of photographs were taken. News of the uber-snake quickly spread on the web. Despite the hubbub surrounding the pictures, most scientists believe that the images were doctored and the Nabau remains purely a myth and local admonition.

Borneo's largest snake (whose existence has actually been proven) is the reticulated python, which can reach up to 10m in length. There are several documented cases of human fatalities – both strangulation and digestion – at the hands (so to speak) of these slithery creatures.

evening has to be the busy **Taman Selera Empurau** (Kapit Bypass Rd; dishes RM0.50-3.50), which is near the centre of town, roughly behind Ing Hing Cold Storage. In contrast to the rest of Kapit's dining scene, which is overwhelmingly Chinese, this market is almost exclusively Malay-Muslim. As such the emphasis is on *satay* and other *halal* dishes.

Kong Hua Café (☎ 084-796459; 1B Jln Wharf; dishes RM3-8; ☺ breakfast & lunch) This is a fine example of the type of old-school Chinese coffee shop that Malaysia does so well. Breakfast here is not much more than sugary snacks though.

Madam Ma's Kitchen (☎ 084-796119; Hotel Meligai, 334 Jln Airport; mains RM5-15; ☺ breakfast, lunch & dinner) Ma's is one of the only places in town with air-con, making it a refuge on a hot day (which is every day). The staff are friendly and speak some English, and the chicken curry is pretty tasty.

Good Taste Restaurant & Coffee Shop (☎ 084-798658; Wisma Ngieng Ping Toh, Jln Teo Chow Beng; dishes RM6-12; ☺ breakfast, lunch & dinner) Diner-style mixed cuisine attracts a loyal following among the office workers in the building above.

GETTING THERE & AWAY
Boats do not travel along the Batang Rejang between dusk and dawn. Express boats leave for Sibu between 6.30am and 2.30pm (for information on boats from Sibu, see p439). Times are posted on the wharf and in the newspaper, although your best bet is simply to ask around, particularly at the hotels.

Boats depart for Belaga (RM30, five to six hours) at 9am. When the river is low, express boats can't get past the Pelagus Rapids, and smaller speedboats are used instead. Fares for these boats start at RM50. If you want to do a day trip to Pelagus, ask around the wharf or at your hotel, as the express boats don't stop there.

Express boats bound for the Batang Baleh depart before noon and go as far as Rumah Penghilu Jambi, Entawau and Balleh; all Iban longhouses. The last boat back to Kapit departs Rumah Penghilu Jambi at 12.30pm.

Belaga
pop 2500
By the time you pull into Belaga after the long journey up the Rejang, you may feel like you've arrived at the very heart of Borneo – in reality you're only about 100km from the coastal city of Bintulu (as the crow flies). Despite this, Belaga certainly feels remote. It's the main bazaar and administrative centre along the upper Rejang.

INFORMATION
Belaga District Office (☎ 084-461339) Can arrange permits and guides. Behind Hotel Sing Soon Huat.
Hasbie Enterprises (☎ 084-461240; 4 Belaga Bazaar) Airline tickets, local travel services and internet.
Residence Office Bintulu (☎ 086-331896)
Residence Office Kapit (☎ 084-796963/796242)

TOURS
The main reason that tourists visit Belaga is to venture deep into the jungle in search of hidden longhouses and secreted waterfalls. But before you can share shots of rice wine with smiling locals, you have to find a tour guide. Unfortunately, we have received a lot of reports from unhappy travellers stating that there are several fraudulent operations in town. The Sarawak Tourism Board encourages tourists to use licensed guides, as only a licensed operator can be accountable for any wrongdoings. In Belaga, the most common form of fraud is overcharging.

We're not going to blacklist anyone here, but we will say this – if a mute girl approaches you, don't follow her. Try tracking down **Hamdani** (☎ 019-886 5770) or **Hasbie** (☎ 084-461 240) to organise your tours. You'll probably be able to find Hasbie at Belaga B&B. For Hamdani, you can swing by the Belaga Hotel and ask the receptionist to put the two of you in touch.

SLEEPING & EATING
Belaga's accommodation is of the cheap and cheerful variety, but if you're doing the longhouse circuit you shouldn't really need to sleep here for more than a night or two.

Belaga B&B (☎ 086-461512; Lot 168, No 2b, Jln Penghulu Hang Nypia; r RM22-28) Affiliated with Sarawak Tourism, this cheapie has basic but clean rooms.

Hotel Belaga (☎ 084-461244; 14 Main Bazaar; r RM30-60; ❄) A convenient location makes up for less-than-perfect standards at Belaga's principal doss house. There's a decent Chinese *kopitiam* downstairs and a free washing machine sweetens the deal.

Hotel Sing Soon Huat (☎ 084-461307; 26-27 New Bazaar; r RM35-45; ❄) The bright-yellow building behind the Hotel Belaga holds this slightly less appealing establishment.

Jea Corner (off Jln Ului Lian; dishes from RM3; ☺ dinner) This tiny stall is literally the only place in Belaga still serving food after 6pm. It serves up a small variety of decent Malaysian rice-based dishes. The friendly proprietor, Albert, will probably find you before you find him. He has a wealth of information about the surrounding area and its people and culture – just don't get him started on politics!

Kafetaria Mesra Murni (Jln Temengong Mat; dishes RM3-5; ☺ breakfast, lunch & dinner) This family-run Muslim restaurant can lay claim to being the only real riverfront dining in Belaga. Try the decent *mee goreng* or the exceptionally refreshing *limau ais* (iced lime juice). It's past the park and playground.

GETTING THERE & AWAY
Boat
Boats leave Kapit for Belaga (RM30, five to six hours) at 9am. When the river is low you'll need to take a speedboat instead; fares start at RM50. Returning to Kapit from Belaga, express boats leave Belaga early (between 6am and 6.30am), from where you can catch onward boats downriver to Sibu. Boats go upriver from Belaga as far as the Bakun Dam area near Rumah Apan (RM10, one hour), from where you can explore the resettled river country north of the Rejang. It's possible to do a loop back to Bintulu this way along a recently paved road.

Land
Instead of backtracking all the way to Sibu, you can cut across country via a concrete logging road, which links up with the main north–south coastal highway. A handful of 4WD pick-ups head to Bintulu (around RM50, 4½ hours) daily, mostly in the morning – check the handwritten signs in Belaga cafes or ask your guide. If you're heading north, you could ask to be dropped at the highway to catch a bus towards Miri. Vehicles wait in front of the Welcome Inn in Bintulu for the return trip.

Upriver from Belaga
About 40km upstream from Belaga, the Rejang divides into several rivers, including the mighty Batang Balui, which winds almost all the way to the Kalimantan border. Sadly, just below this junction is the site of the controversial Bakun Dam project, which was started in 1996 and is near completion. In order to build the dam, the surrounding forest was logged and an estimated 11,000 people were forcibly resettled. Once the reservoir above the dam starts to fill, it will flood a huge stretch of the Balui valley and several other tributaries of the Rejang.

Because of the difficulty of getting boats above the dam, it's now very difficult to travel upriver on the Balui, which is a shame, because the upper reaches promise some of the most exciting river trips in Sarawak.

CENTRAL COAST
Sarawak's central coast is light on attractions, although an afternoon at Similajau National Park and an evening in Bintulu can quickly fill up your time if you have to layover while en route between Miri and the Batang Rejang.

Bintulu
pop 180,000
The name Bintulu means 'place of gathered heads' in an ancient local dialect – the area was prime noggin-nabbing territory until the Brooke era. In 1861 James Brooke set up shop and stamped out the gruesome tradition in order to encourage foreign trade (see the boxed text, p407, for a brief history of headhunting in Borneo). Today, Bintulu is an undistinguished commercial centre servicing offshore oil and gas installations and upriver logging.

ORIENTATION
Bintulu lies along the north bank of the Batang Kemena, within walking distance of the river mouth. All the places to stay and eat, banks and other services are situated in the riverside district south of the old airport. The waterfront just north of the shopping area along Jln Masjid has several busy markets. The long-distance bus station is 5km north of town at Medan Jaya, and the airport is 25km west of the centre.

INFORMATION
Bintulu Hospital (☎ 086-331455; off Jln Lebuh Raya Abang Galau)

HSBC (☎ 086-315928; 25 Jln Law Gek Soon; ☺ 9am-3pm Mon-Fri) The best bank in Bintulu. There's an ATM here.

Standard Chartered Bank (☎ 086-334166; 89 Jln Keppel; ☺ 9am-3pm Mon-Fri) Another useful bank with an ATM.

Star Internet (Jln Law Gek Soon; per hr RM3; ☺ 9am-11pm) Internet access. Noisy with slow machines.

SLEEPING

Bintulu's ultra-budget lodgings can be on the dodgy side, and you may be better off paying a little more for peace of mind.

My House Inn (☎ 086-336399; 161 Jln Masjid; s/d RM35/40; 🌣) Looking at this cheapie from the outside you'd be pretty glad this wasn't your house, but inside it's no worse than grubby in places, with tiled rooms and decent double beds.

Kintown Inn (☎ 086-333666; 93 Jln Keppel; r from RM70; 🌣) These bright, modern rooms, done out in smart linen with some nice touches like big shower heads and fan headboards, are particularly good value. The location's also perfect for quick getaways.

Riverfront Inn (☎ 086-333111; riverf@tm.net.my; 256 Taman Sri Dagang; r from RM90; 🌣) A long-standing favourite with business and leisure visitors alike, the Riverfront is low-key but still classy. It's well worth paying top whack to get a room overlooking the river – the view is pure Borneo. There's a decent cafe on the ground floor and wi-fi in the lobby.

ParkCity Everly Hotel (☎ 086-333666; www.ping anchorage.com.my; Lot 3062 Jln Tun Razak; r RM219; 🌣) If you're looking for a little luxury on your layover, try the plush ParkCity Everly, housed in a modern skyrise.

EATING

Chef (92 Jln Abang Galau; cakes from RM0.90; 🌣 breakfast, lunch & dinner) No chocolate salty balls here: this drool-inducing bakery-cafe can satisfy most sweet and savoury cravings, from local cakes and pastries to a good rendition of tiramisu (RM4.50).

Ban Kee Café (off Jln Abang Galau; meals from RM10; 🌣 lunch & dinner) Run, don't walk, to this brilliant indoor-outdoor Chinese seafood specialist. It doesn't look like much, but the food is so good that you'll consider staying in town for a second night just so you can eat here again. Try the butter prawns or the baby *kailan* (a Chinese vegetable similar to baby bak choi). The food is fresh as can be.

Every evening, a busy **night market** (off Jln Abang Galau; meals from RM1; 🌣 nightly from 5.30pm) sets up in a lot off a backstreet between the old airport and Jln Abang Galau. It's a good place to snack track for Malay dishes and fresh fruit.

Finally, there are several food stalls on the upper floor of the **Pasar Utama** (New Market; Jln Main Bazaar; meals RM2-5; 🌣 breakfast, lunch & early dinner). The stalls at the neighbouring **Tamu Bintulu** (Bintulu Market; meals RM2-5; 🌣 breakfast, lunch & early dinner) sell fresh fruit and jungle produce.

GETTING THERE & AWAY

Air

Bintulu airport is 25km west of the centre. A taxi there costs RM25.

Malaysia Airlines (☎ 1300-883-000, 086-331554; www.malaysiaairlines.com.my; Jln Masjid) flies between Bintulu and Kota Kinabalu (RM148), Kuching (RM139), Miri (RM73) and Sibu (RM81), as well as Kuala Lumpur (RM339).

AirAsia (☎ 1300-889933; www.airasia.com) connects to Kuching.

Bus

The long-distance bus station is 5km north of town. Travel between the two by local bus or taxi (RM10 to RM15).

There are frequent daily services between Bintulu and Kuching (RM60, 10 hours), Miri (RM20, 4½ hours) and Sibu (RM20, 3½ hours).

Van & Long-Distance Taxi

Taxis and vans congregate in front of the markets and alongside the Tua Pek Kong temple. The return-trip taxi fare to Simalajau National Park is RM80 per car.

GETTING AROUND

Taxis (official and unofficial) congregate alongside Tua Pek Kong temple and at the big taxi stand near the markets. Most taxi fares around town are RM5. The trip to the long-distance bus station costs around RM10 to RM15; the airport is RM25 to RM30.

Similajau National Park

Another one of Borneo's hard-to-pronounce destinations, **Similajau National Park** (☎ 086-391284; admission RM10; 🌣 8am-noon & 2-5pm), 30km north of Bintut, is a quiet coastal park with nice white-sand beaches, good walking trails and simple accommodation. While the park does not have the habitat variety of Bako National Park, it's perfect if you want a quiet, relaxing natural getaway as you work your way along the coast of Sarawak.

Similajau occupies a narrow 30km coastal strip between the South China Sea and the typical logged-out secondary forest of

Sarawak. As such, it's one of the only havens for wildlife in this part of the state and a recent survey recorded 230 bird species, making it one of the most diversely inhabited areas in Sarawak. The forest is also home to 24 species of mammal.

The park headquarters occupies the south bank of the mouth of the Sungai Likau, though most of it lies north of the river, and is accessed by a suspension bridge.

You might be able to arrange a boat up the mangrove-lined Sungai Likau for RM50 per hour (one hour should be enough). If you go in the early morning, you'll see a range of birds, including hornbills, and maybe even some gibbons or macaques. Dolphins can occasionally be spotted out at sea, and marine turtles lay their eggs at certain points along the beach.

Note that estuarine crocodiles are found in the rivers of the park and around river mouths. *Do not* swim or wade in the park's rivers or near river mouths, and be careful when walking near the rivers early or late in the day. Three locals were killed by crocodiles in the area in 2002, so this is not a warning to be taken lightly.

WALKING

Similajau has a limited trail network, the backbone of which is a long trail (9.8km from park headquarters) to Golden Beach. It's a long, hot walk so take lots of water.

Trails are well marked and a guide isn't necessary. After crossing the river from headquarters, head left off the boardwalk towards the headland. It's about half an hour's walk to a pavilion from where you can enjoy the view back along the coast towards Bintulu.

Further along the coast, the main trail leads to **Turtle Beach** (7km) and **Golden Beach** (9.8km), two beautiful, deserted spots where turtles come ashore to lay their eggs. Other trails forge into the low hills behind the coast to the **Selunsur Rapids** (6.9km). To get to **Kolam Sebubong**, a natural pool fed by the Sebubong river, you'll have to organise a boat at park headquarters (about RM75 per boat, minimum five people). The trip takes 30 minutes and the pool is a 15-minute walk from the boat drop-off point. If you take the boat, you could also be dropped off at one of the other beaches along the way and walk back.

SLEEPING & EATING

Similajau can be visited as a day trip from Bintulu, but if you want to enjoy the beach, go for a night walk or do the entire length of the coastal trail, you should stay a night or two. Accommodation for the park can be booked through the park headquarters or the **National Parks & Wildlife Centre** (Sarawak Forestry Corporation; ☎ 085-434184) in Miri.

Comfortable accommodation is provided in the air-conditioned **Drive-In Chalets** (RM75), each with two rooms sleeping up to four people. The two **hostels** (dm/r RM15/40) can accommodate 16 and 72 people respectively, all in four-bed bunk rooms. There's also a **camp site** (per person RM5).

The park **cafeteria** (🕒 9.30am-6pm) has decent food and sundry items for sale. There are no stoves in the chalets or hostels, but there are refrigerators.

GETTING THERE & AWAY

Bintulu is the gateway to Similajau National Park. There is no regularly scheduled bus or van transport to the park. A taxi or private car will cost RM40 each way from Bintulu – be sure to arrange a pick-up time when you get dropped off.

NORTHERN SARAWAK

The northern region serves up Sarawak's hat trick of natural beauties: Gunung Mulu National Park, the Kelabit Highlands and the Niah Caves. Use urban Miri as the jumping-off point to explore these treasures.

MIRI
pop 269,380

It's funny: the closer one gets to the Bruneian border, the more one notices shady characters coming out of the woodwork. Is it for the repressed Bruneians stepping over the border for some afternoon delight, or is it for the oil-loving expats who fill up suburban communities with their country club accommodation? (We're pretty sure it's the latter...) Either way, Miri's memorable cast of characters gives the city an interesting bordertown vibe, despite its size and population. Perhaps it's because Miri is the gateway point to a variety of Borneo's oft-travelled destinations. Tourists will have to pass by in order to reach Gunung Mulu National Park, the Kelabit Highlands and, for some, the Niah Caves.

SARAWAK

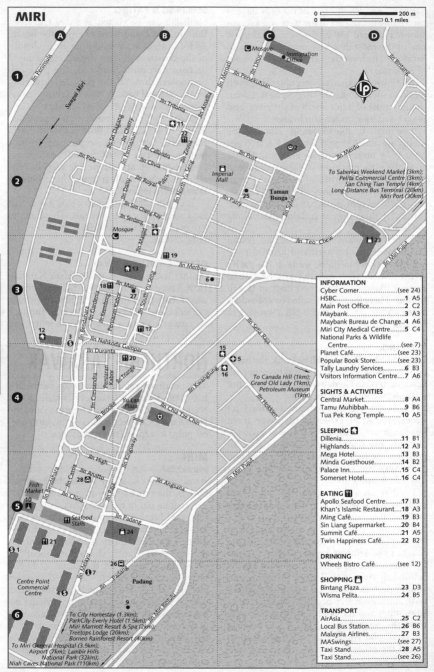

MIRI

0 _____ 200 m
0 _____ 0.1 miles

To Saberkas Weekend Market (3km);
Pelita Commercial Centre (3km);
San Ching Tian Temple (4km);
Long-Distance Bus Terminal (20km);
Miri Port (30km)

To Canada Hill (1km);
Grand Old Lady (1km);
Petroleum Museum
(1km)

To City Homestay (1.3km);
ParkCity Everly Hotel (1.5km);
Miri Marriott Resort & Spa (2km);
Treetops Lodge (20km);
Borneo Rainforest Resort (40km)

To Miri General Hospital (3.5km);
Airport (7km); Lambir Hills
National Park (32km);
Niah Caves National Park (110km)

SARAWAK

INFORMATION
Cyber Corner......................(see 24)
HSBC......................................1 A5
Main Post Office....................2 C2
Maybank.................................3 A3
Maybank Bureau de Change..4 A6
Miri City Medical Centre.......5 C4
National Parks & Wildlife
  Centre...............................(see 7)
Planet Café.........................(see 23)
Popular Book Store..............(see 23)
Tally Laundry Services...........6 B3
Visitors Information Centre....7 A6

SIGHTS & ACTIVITIES
Central Market.......................8 A4
Tamu Muhibbah....................9 B6
Tua Pek Kong Temple..........10 A5

SLEEPING
Dillenia................................11 B1
Highlands............................12 A3
Mega Hotel..........................13 B3
Minda Guesthouse...............14 B2
Palace Inn............................15 C4
Somerset Hotel....................16 C4

EATING
Apollo Seafood Centre.........17 B3
Khan's Islamic Restaurant....18 A3
Ming Café............................19 B3
Sin Liang Supermarket.........20 B4
Summit Café........................21 A5
Twin Happiness Café...........22 B2

DRINKING
Wheels Bistro Café.............(see 12)

SHOPPING
Bintang Plaza......................23 D3
Wisma Pelita.......................24 B5

TRANSPORT
AirAsia.................................25 C2
Local Bus Station.................26 B6
Malaysia Airlines.................27 B3
MASwings.........................(see 27)
Taxi Stand............................28 A5
Taxi Stand..........................(see 26)

Orientation

Miri lies on a narrow plain between the east bank of the Sungai Miri and low hills that were once covered in oil derricks. Most places to stay and eat are within walking distance of each other, spread out between the Centre Point Commercial Centre, local bus station and visitors information centre to the south and the main post office and immigration office to the north.

Travellers will need a bus or taxi to get to the long-distance bus station and the airport.

Information

BOOKSHOPS

Popular Book Store (☎ 085-439052; 2nd fl, Bintang Plaza, 1264 Jln Miri Pujut) Good general selection.

INTERNET ACCESS

Cyber Corner (1st fl, Wisma Pelita, Jln Padang; per hr RM3)
Planet Café (1st fl, Bintang Plaza, 1264 Jln Miri Pujut; per hr RM4)

LAUNDRY

Tally Laundry Services (☎ 085-430322; Jln Merbau; ⏰ 8am-6pm)

MEDICAL SERVICES

Miri City Medical Centre (☎ 085-426622; 918 Jln Hokkien) Private medical centre.
Miri General Hospital (☎ 085-420033; Jln Cayaha) South of town, off the Miri bypass.

MONEY

There are banks and ATMs all over town, and moneychangers are common.
HSBC (Lot 1268, ground fl, Miri Commercial Centre, Jln Melayu) There's an ATM here.
Maybank (☎ 085-412282; Lot 112, Jln Bendahara; ⏰ 9.15am-4.30pm Mon-Thu, 9.15-4pm Fri)
Maybank Bureau de Change (☎ 085-438467; 1271 Centre Point Commercial Centre; ⏰ 9am-5pm) Dedicated exchange and cash-advance facilities. Travellers cheques are changed here for RM10 per transaction plus 15 sen stamp duty per cheque.

POST

Main post office (☎ 085-441222; Jln Post)

TOURIST INFORMATION

The **visitors information centre** (☎ 085-434181; 452 Jln Melayu; ⏰ 8am-6pm Mon-Fri, 9am-3pm Sat & Sun) is at the southern end of the town centre. The helpful staff can provide city maps, transport schedules and information on accommodation and tours. It also produces the useful free *Visitors' Guide to Miri*. You can book accommodation with the **National Parks & Wildlife Centre** (Sarawak Forestry Corporation; ☎ 085-436637, 085-434184) here for Gunung Mulu, Niah, Lambir Hills and Similajau national parks.

There is an information counter at the airport, and further city information is available on www.miri .net.my.

Sights

CITY CENTRE

The atmospheric old part of town begins around the southern end of Jln Brooke; this is the area most worth exploring. There's plenty of lively commerce around the Chinese shophouse blocks, the **Central Market** and the **Tamu Muhibbah**, where local Dayak come to sell their vegetables. Also of note are the **Muslim and Chinese cemeteries** along the coastal road. The wide courtyard of the **Tua Pek Kong Temple**, near the fish market, is a good spot to watch the river traffic float by. During **Chinese New Year**, virtually the whole of this area is taken over by a lively street fair and the crowds cram in under red lanterns and gold foil.

Canada Hill, on the low ridge behind the town centre, is the site of Malaysia's first oil well, the **Grand Old Lady**. Bored in 1910, the well produced around seven barrels a day until it was abandoned in 1972. The **Petroleum Museum** (☎ 085-635516; Jln Canada Hill; admission free; ⏰ 9am-5pm, last admission 4.30pm, closed Mon) has a few interesting displays on the source of the city's wealth. The hill itself is a popular exercise spot with a handful of refreshment kiosks, and it's worth walking up here at sunset just for the views across Miri to the South China Sea.

If you land in Miri on a weekend, don't miss the **Saberkas Weekend Market**, which takes place from Friday evening to midday Sunday, about 3km northeast of Bintang Plaza. It's one of the most colourful and friendly markets in Sarawak and vendors are more than happy to answer questions about the various products displayed.

Not far from the market site, in the suburb of Krokop, the **San Ching Tian temple** is the largest Taoist temple in Southeast Asia. Built in 2000, the design features intricate dragon reliefs brought all the way over from China.

LAMBIR HILLS NATIONAL PARK

Although **Lambir Hills National Park** (☎ 085-491030; admission RM10; ☒ park office 8am-5pm, last entry 4pm) doesn't have the spectacular scenery of Niah and Mulu, it is the closest primary rainforest to Miri (around 30km south) and it makes for a pleasant day trip out of the city. A perennial favourite among the locals, this scenic scrap of jungle offers waterfalls, picnic areas and a clutch of pleasant walking trails through its dipterocarp rainforest.

The national park covers 70 sq km and protects a range of low sandstone hills that reach a height of 465m at Bukit Lambir. Much of the forest was logged before the park was declared, but the secondary forest is beautiful in its own right – any given 50-hectare plot contains an amazing 1100 tree species (including wild bananas and the awesome 'wandering tree', which uses its branch to move around in search of more sunlight!) Indigenous fauna includes gibbons, tarsiers, pangolins and barking deer, though you are unlikely to see any of these close to the park headquarters. Lambir Hills is also home to many species of birds.

The park's main trail follows a small river to **Latuk Waterfall**, which has a picnic area and is suitable for swimming. It takes no more than 25 minutes to walk the 835m from park headquarters. Don't forget to register your name at the trailhead booth, especially if you plan to climb **Bukit Pantu** or **Bukit Lambir**, further afield.

There are no cooking facilities at the park, but a canteen sells rice and noodle dishes, drinks and basic provisions. Opening hours depend on demand but are generally from 8am to about 7pm.

From Miri, any bus (RM3, 35 minutes) bound for Bekenu or Niah Junction can drop you here. A taxi from Miri costs RM40.

Festivals & Events

Miri Cultural Heritage Week (Miri Heritage Centre) A week-long festival of cultural activities, handicrafts and performances, held in September.

Miri International Jazz Festival (www.mirijazz festival.com; the Pavilion, ParkCity Everly Hotel, Jln Te-menggong Datuk Oyong Lawai) Held in May, this growing event brings in an eclectic range of performers from across the international jazz scene.

Sleeping

Although there isn't much to see or do in Miri, its strategic position close to phenomenal tourist attractions (not to mention phenomenal amounts of oil) has made it the most expensive burg in all of Borneo.

BUDGET & MIDRANGE

Choose your budget accommodation wisely – Miri's brothel business booms at some of the shadier by-the-hour digs. The following options are a safe bet.

Highlands (☎ 085-422327, 016-809 0328; www.borneo jungles.com; 1271 Jln Sri Dagang; dm/r RM25/50; ☒ ☐) Highlands styles itself a 'budget tourist and travel information centre', and scores a bull's eye on all counts. Look out for the affable owner, a Twin Otter pilot from New Zealand. If you're allergic to cats you might have to give this place a miss.

Dillenia (☎ 085-434204; dillenia.guesthouse@gmail .com; 846 Jln Sida; dm/s/d RM30/50/80; ☒ ☐) Dillenia is a new backpacker option with eager-beaver management and fresh coats of paint on the walls.

Treetops Lodge (☎ 085-472172; www.treetops -borneo.com; Lot 210, Siwa Jaya; r incl breakfast per person RM35; ☒) Located south of Miri along the coastal road, this family-run option runs a laid-back cluster of cabins.

Somerset Hotel (☎ 085-422777; somerhot@streamyx .com; 12 Jln Kwangtung; r from RM99; ☒) The Somerset is a good Miri midranger in the centre of town. The staff may be light on smiles, but the rooms are clean enough for under RM100 (just barely!). There's wi-fi in the lobby.

Palace Inn (☎ 085-421999; siewpoh@pc.jaring.my; Lot 192 Jln Kwangtung; s/d from RM78/88; ☒) If Somerset is full, try this spot across the street.

Borneo Rainforest Resort (☎ 085-613888; www .borneorainforestresort.com; Km36 Miri-Bintulu Rd; r from RM110; ☒ ☐ ☒) Located 37km south of Miri (7km south of Lambir Hills), this jungly compound is a veritable tropical theme park. Although much of the campus feels like the product of a drunken architect (rooms with slanted floors and labyrinthine paths), it's a good place for some quality family time.

The following backpacker digs are definitely worth checking out:

City Homestay (☎ 085-428118; fax 085-436382; 1st fl Brighton Centre, Jln Temenggong Datuk Oyong Lawai; d from RM78; ☒) Located above the Marine Sea House Bistro near the ParkCity Everly Hotel. Great gusts of air-con pour through the prim rooms. New coats of paint and plasma TVs have spruced things up. The beds are really comfy too.

Minda Guesthouse (☎ 085-411422; www.minda guesthouse.com; 1st & 2nd fl Lot 637 Jln North Yu Seng;

per person dm/tw RM20/25) Great value for money. The sundeck and bright common space sweeten the deal.

TOP END

Miri's top end spots often have discounts that drop the prices into the midrange category.

ParkCity Everly Hotel (☎ 085-440288; www.vhhotels.com; Jln Temenggong Datuk Oyong Lawai; r from RM166; 🐱 🐱) The ParkCity Everly is a large resort-style hotel on the beach about 2km south of Miri city, very close to the Miri Marriott. The sea-view rooms have nice views and the swimming pool is excellent. There's wi-fi on the executive floor and in the lobby. Service can be a bit uneven, but if you can get a good rate here, it's worth considering for those who don't want to stay in the centre of town.

Mega Hotel (☎ 085-432432; www.megahotel.com.my; 907 Jln Merbau; r from RM190; 🐱 🖥 🐱) The aptly named Mega Hotel dominates central Miri with its imposing bulk. Things improve once you get past the busy and somewhat confused reception area. Rooms are clean and well maintained and there's 24-hour room service, a convenience store and wi-fi on the premises.

Miri Marriott Resort & Spa (☎ 085-421121; www.marriotthotels.com/myymc; Jln Temenggong Datuk Oyong Lawai; r from RM327; 🐱 🖥 🐱) Next door to the ParkCity Everly, the Marriott is the nicest place to stay in Miri. It's a large resort with a spa, a swimming pool, several restaurants and good common areas. Rooms are spacious with large bathrooms and balconies. Wi-fi is available on the premises.

Eating & Drinking

Dining in Miri caters to the diverse array of locals. There's something for every palate. For self-catering, the **Sin Liang Supermarket** (☎ 085-413762; Jln Duranta; 🕑 8.30am-9pm) is centrally located and well stocked.

ourpick Summit Café (☎ 019-354 7306; Jln Melayu; mains from RM2; 🕑 breakfast & lunch) Not to be confused with the Summit Café across from the Apollo, this spot, specialising in traditional Kelabit cuisine, is a 10-minute walk southwest of Mega Hotel (in the 'Waterfront Area'; look for a big sign saying 'Tian Tian'). If Bario isn't on your travel itinerary, then a meal here is a must. Try the colourful array of 'jungle food' – *canko manis* (forest ferns), minced tapioca, and wild boar – served on leaves instead of plates. It's best to come for an early lunch, because once the food runs out they close!

Twin Happiness Cafe (☎ 085-421868; 747 Jln Merpati; dishes RM2.50-7; 🕑 breakfast & lunch) We all take our happiness where we can find it, and the twin joys of good Chinese food and cheap prices make this particular pleasure zone worth seeking out. Besides, how can you not love a place that serves 'drunken prawn'?

Ming Café (cnr Jln North Yu Seng & Jln Merbau; dishes from RM3; 🕑 lunch & dinner) Take your pick of Malay, Chinese, Indian and Western food at this ever-busy corner eating emporium. There's a good drink counter here serving fresh juices and signature tapioca teas.

Khan's Islamic Restaurant (229 Jln Maju; mains from RM4; 🕑 breakfast, lunch & dinner) This simple canteen is one of Miri's best Indian eateries, whipping up tasty treats like mouth-watering tandoori chicken and *aloo gobi* (Indian potato and cauliflower dish), as well as the usual *roti canai*. It's opposite Mega Hotel.

Apollo Seafood Centre (4 Jln South Yu Seng; meals from RM30; 🕑 lunch & dinner) This deservedly popular Chinese seafood restaurant is a big hit with ex-pat visitors. Just about anything you order will be delicious, but we recommend the crabs and the fried *midin* with *belacan*. If you are a big spender, you could always go for some lobsters straight from the tank.

Wheels Bistro Café (☎ 085-419859; 1271 Jln Dagang) Underneath the Highlands hostel, this slightly dingy bistro-pub often has live music and is a favourite hang-out for Miri's expat community.

Getting There & Away

Miri is the main access point to reach Gunung Mulu National Park, the Kelabit Highlands and the Niah Caves.

AIR

MASwings (☎ 1300-883 000; www.maswings.com.my; Jln Maju), has flights to Gunung Mulu National Park and the Kelabit Highlands – see the respective destination coverage for more information. Malaysia Airways (the umbrella company of MASwings) also flies to Bintulu (RM73), Kota Kinabalu (RM139), Kuching (RM139), Lawas (RM70), Limbang (RM65), Marudi (RM50), Pulau Labuan (RM50) and Sibu (RM138). Book flights to/from Bario and Mulu as far in advance as possible.

AirAsia (☎ 1300-889933; www.airasia.com) has cheap flights between Miri and KL, Kuching, Kota Kinabalu and Johor Bahru.

SARAWAK

BUS

Most buses operate from the long-distance bus terminal outside of town. Miri Transport Company bus 33A runs there from the downtown local bus station on Jln Melayu (RM1, 15 minutes). A taxi to the long-distance bus terminal costs around RM20. For travel information to Brunei, see the boxed text, p593.

Main destinations:

Batu Junction Any southbound service can drop you at the Batu Niah turn-off (RM10, 1½ hours).

Bintulu Buses go daily to Bintulu (RM20, 4½ hours), departing roughly hourly between 6am and 6pm.

Kuala Baram The Miri Transport Company bus 1A goes to Kuala Baram (RM4.50, one hour) every two hours between 5.50am and 5.30pm. The bus leaves from the local bus terminal in downtown Miri on Jln Melayu in front of Taman Pelita. From Kuala Baram you can catch an express boat to Marudi.

Kuching The major companies each have a couple of direct buses daily (RM80, 15 to 16 hours), with the morning bus leaving at 8.30am and the night bus at 9pm.

Lambir Hills Frequent north-south buses go past Lambir Hills (RM3, 45 minutes).

Mukah There is one bus from Miri to Mukah (RM40, 12 hours) and Dalat (RM45, 12 hours) at 7.30am.

Sibu There are direct buses from Miri to Sibu (RM40, eight hours) leaving every two hours or so with the earliest at 7am and the last bus at 9pm. All buses to Kuching also stop at Sibu.

Getting Around

Miri's city centre is easily negotiable on foot. **Taxis** (☽ 085-432277) from the city to the airport cost RM20; bus fares are RM2. Buses run from 7am to 6pm. There are several taxi stands within arm's reach of the visitor's centre.

NIAH NATIONAL PARK

Near the coast about 115km south of Miri, this small national park (32 sq km) protects one of Borneo's gems, the Niah Caves. Alongside Gunung Mulu National Park, these caves must be the most famous natural attractions in Sarawak – not bad for a bunch of hollowed-out hills. At the heart of the park is the Great Cave, one of the largest caves in the world. Outside, the park is dominated by a 394m-high limestone massif, Gunung Subis, and is covered in dense rainforest.

In 1958 archaeologists discovered evidence of human occupation of the cave area dating back some 40,000 years. Rock paintings were found in what has become known as the Painted Cave, and the discovery of several small canoelike coffins (death ships) indicate that this site was once used as a burial ground. Some of the artefacts found here can be seen in the Sarawak Museum in Kuching (p413).

The Niah Caves are an important nesting site for swiftlets, which supply the vital ingredient for the famous birds-nest soup, and also accommodate a staggering number of bats. Traditionally the Penan are custodians and collectors of the nests, while the Iban have the rights to the caves' other commodity, the gritty 'black gold' of bat guano (no prizes for guessing who got first pick). During the harvesting season, nest collectors live in the caves, and their massive bamboo poles can be seen inside, lashed together and wedged against the cave roof above.

Orientation

The bus from Bintulu or Miri will drop you in the centre of Batu Niah town. It's a 3km walk along the river to the park headquarters (follow the path past the red Chinese temple); you can also go by taxi, by longboat (if one is available) or by private car. The road to the headquarters is behind the town centre to the left of the bus stop, and the boat dock is directly to the right.

Information

Upon arrival you must register at **park headquarters** (☎ 085-737454; adult/child RM10/5; ☽ 8am-5pm) to pay the entrance fee and pick up a trail map.

Booking is advisable for accommodation at the park lodges. You can book accommodation at the Sarawak Forestry Corportation at the **Miri visitors information centre** (☽ 085-434184; Lot 452 Jln Melayu; ☽ 8am-6pm Mon-Fri, 9am-3pm Sat & Sun) or the **National Parks & Wildlife Centre** (☎ 082-248088; Sarawak Tourism Complex, Jln Tun Haji Openg; ☽ 8am-5pm Mon-Fri) located next door to the tourist info centre in Kuching. Make sure you get a receipt to present if requested at Niah. If you're staying at the hostel you can usually turn up without a booking, especially during the week. If it's busy and there's no accommodation, the worst you'll have to do is head the 3km back to Batu Niah, where there are three hotels.

Sights

NIAH ARCHAEOLOGY MUSEUM

A lovely Malay-style building, the **Niah Archaeology Museum** (admission free; ☽ 9am-5pm) houses interesting displays on the geology, archaeology and ecology of the caves. It's in the park, just across the river from the park headquarters.

NIAH CAVES

To get to the caves from park headquarters first take a boat across the Sungai Niah; the jetty is down the path between the office building and the cafeteria. During the day the ferry costs RM1, and from 5.30pm until 7.30pm it costs RM1.50. After 7.30pm the ferry only operates on request and the price is negotiable; arrange with the boatman in advance if you require a late return.

Once across the river, follow the raised boardwalk to the caves. It's 3.1km to the Great Cave and another 1.4km to the Painted Cave. The boards are loose in places, can get very slippery when wet and make a lot of noise, but if you stop for a while you'll hear lots of birds and may also see macaques. As well as the hundreds of beautiful butterflies, wildlife includes squirrels, flying lizards and a striking emerald-green lizard that sometimes sits on the boardwalk.

Approaching the caves, the trail skirts jagged limestone outcrops that look like ancient ramparts festooned with giant vines and creepers. Just before the cave entrance the boardwalk forks; head to the right for the caves. The left fork goes to the village of **Rumah Patrick Libau**, where there are a couple of longhouses. An informal homestay program is available here, call ☏ 019-8052415 for more information. Villagers sometimes sit at the junction selling drinks and souvenirs. The trail goes under the **Traders' Cave**, a large overhang with stout stalactites. As the name implies, this is where early bird's-nest and guano collectors carried on their business. The trail then rounds a corner to enter the vast **Great Cave**.

This impressive cavern measures 250m across at the mouth and 60m at its greatest height. Since you approach the cave from an angle, its enormous size probably won't strike you straight away. It's usually only after descending the steep stairs into the bowels of the cavern for half an hour or so that visitors pause to look back at where they've come.

At one time, some 470,000 bats and four million swiftlets called Niah home. There are no current figures, but the walls of the caves are no longer thick with bats and there are

fewer bird's nests to harvest. Several species of swiftlet nest on the cave walls; the most common by far is the glossy swiftlet, whose nest contains vegetation and is not harvested. For obvious reasons, the species whose nests are edible are far less abundant and can only be seen in the remotest corners of the cavern. Several species of bat also roost in the cave, but they're not in dense colonies and must be picked out in the gloom among the bird's nests – take a powerful torch.

The best time to see the cave wildlife is at dusk during the 'changeover', when the swiftlets stream back to their nests and the bats come hurtling out for the night's feeding, creating a dark swarm to rival any horror movie. If you do come at this time, remember that you'll need to either arrange a late ferry or hurry back to make the 7.30pm boat to park headquarters.

Inside the cave, the boardwalk continues down to the right, but you'll need a torch to explore any distance. The stairs and handrails are usually covered with dirt or guano, and can get very slippery in places. The rock formations are spectacular and ominous by turns as you slip in and out of the gloom, and when the sun hits certain overhead vents the cave is perforated by the kind of dramatic light beams that ought to herald the voice of God, or at least Charlton Heston.

Allow a good hour to explore the Great Cave; the trail branches around a massive central pillar but both branches finish at the same point and it's impossible to get lost if you stick to the boardwalk. There's no need to hire a guide, although you can hire torches (RM5) from the museum office.

After following the walkway through the Great Cave, a short forest path emerges beyond the larger cavern's opening and leads to the **Painted Cave**. It's easy to walk straight past the small fenced-off area by the cave entrance that protects the (now empty) death ships and the ancient paintings. A set of small travel binoculars are useful to make out the red hematite figures, as many have faded to little more than indistinct scrawls along a narrow 30m-strip at the back of the cave.

Alternative trails from the museum or Batu Niah will take you through the jungle to the summit of **Bukit Kasut** (267m), alongside Gunung Subis. A boardwalk has recently been constructed along this route and should now be open to the public. The park headquarters provides a trail map.

SARAWAK

Sleeping & Eating

Niah Caves can be visited as a day trip from Miri or Bintulu, especially if you go by hire car all the way. If you would like to stay at or near the caves, the best choice is the park accommodation. Otherwise, there are a few simple hotels in Batu Niah town, about 3km away.

Niah National Park (☎ 085-737454; camp sites RM5, r from RM45) There are simple and clean hostel rooms and private rooms along with a basic canteen at the park headquarters. Camping is another option.

Niah Cave Hotel (☎ 085-737726; 155 Batu Niah Bazaar; r RM30; ✗) Over a cafe in Batu Niah, the simple rooms here with common bathroom are just barely acceptable.

Niah Cave Inn (☎ 085-737333; 621 Batu Niah Bazaar; economy/standard r from RM64/75; ✗) Despite the unfortunate connotations of its name, this is the best hotel in Batu Niah. The economy rooms aren't worth the price, but the standard rooms are decent.

There are several *kedai kopi* in town, including the **Friendly Café** (Batu Niah Bazaar; meals from RM3; ✆ breakfast, lunch & dinner), which serves the usual coffee-shop fare. It's opposite the Niah Cave Inn.

Getting There & Away

Access to Batu Niah, the town nearest the caves, is by road only. At the time of research, bus services to Batu Niah itself were suspended, with no indication of when they might resume. Express buses on the coastal highway make a brief stop at the Batu Niah turn-off (RM10, two hours), 102km south of Miri, but you'll have to make your own way to the town itself, 13km west of the main road, and then get to the park headquarters.

Private cars often hang around the junction offering transport to Batu Niah and the park gate; the going rate is RM10, though it can be harder finding a lift on the way out. For convenience, though, you may be better off organising return-trip transport from Miri, especially if you're only coming for the day. At RM20 each way, unless you're on your own it should be no more expensive and much quicker than doing the journey in stages. Ask at **Highlands** (☎ 085-422327; http://borneojungles.com; 1271 Jln Dagang) or the **visitors information centre** (☎ 085-434181; vic-miri@sarawaktourism.com; 452 Jln Melayu; ✆ 8am-6pm Mon-Fri, 9am-3pm Sat & Sun), both in Miri.

Coming from Bintulu, you can also charter a minivan or private vehicle, but this could cost around RM100 per car each way, which is hardly viable without a group.

Getting Around

Transport to the park headquarters from Batu Niah is usually by taxi or boat. A short but exhilarating journey past jungle-clad limestone cliffs, the boat trip costs RM10, plus RM2 per person for more than five people. Taxis also cost RM10. Boats do most of their business in the morning; in the afternoon it's usually quicker to get a taxi, a few of which are always waiting next to the bus stand.

MARUDI & BATANG BARAM

Marudi is a quiet town some 45km inland from Miri. This sleepy spot sits on the sluggish Batang Baram, which, like the Rejang further south, is a vital artery for Sarawak's interior. After Marudi, the river runs deep into Kayan and Kenyah territory, while its tributary (Batang Dapur) continues right up into the Kelabit Highlands.

The town has a **bank** (☎ 085-756235; 59 Jln Cinema) and plenty of *kedai kopi* around the square and along the main street at the western end of town. Try **Grand Hotel** (☎ 085-755711; Lg Lima; r from RM40-50; ✗) if you need to spend the night.

Marudi is accessible by a short flight from Miri on **Malaysia Airlines** (☎ 1300-883 000; Jln Maju; www.malaysiaairlines.com.my), which offers a service five times a week (no flights on Wednesdays and Fridays) starting at around RM30.

Express boats (RM30, 2½ hours) run between Miri Port (also known as Kuala Baram) and Marudi. To get to Miri Port, you can take a taxi for RM25. The last boat leaves about 3pm daily in both directions. For details on continuing upriver to Gunung Mulu National Park by boat, see p458.

GUNUNG MULU NATIONAL PARK

Hey, remember on BBC's *Planet Earth* documentary when that poor cameraman had to wade through thick steaming mounds of bat shit? Well, they filmed that here in Mulu! The park's intricate systems of underground haunted houses are stuffed to the brim with braids of stalactites, armies of alien insects and over two million bats, plus their noxious piles of roach-ridden excrement. Even if you haven't seen the show, we're pretty sure you can imagine that seething mountain of bat dung – you'll love it, we promise.

It comes has no surprise that the park's yawning caverns had a cameo in this documentary of superlatives – these caves are the biggest on earth. In fact, several years ago a team of local explorers discovered the world's largest chamber, the Sarawak Chamber, reputed to be the size of 16 football fields.

Mulu's most famous attractions, however, are the Pinnacles, a forest of razor-sharp limestone peaks clustered 45m above the rainforest; and the so-called Headhunters Trail, which follows an old tribal warpath through vine-draped jungle. If you're planning on doing any serious trekking in Sarawak, this park should be your first port of call.

Orientation & Information

On arrival, head to the **park headquarters** (HQ; ☎ 085-792300; www.mulupark.com; adult/child RM10/5; ☽ 8am-5pm) to pay the entry fee and receive your room or bed allocation.

Sights & Activities

Gunung Mulu's world-class sights really pack a punch – a one-two punch, in fact: steaming cavern openings reveal a mysterious underworld like a yawning beast, while thick ribbons of rainforest squiggle across the jagged landscape offering trekkers an unexplored Jurassic Park.

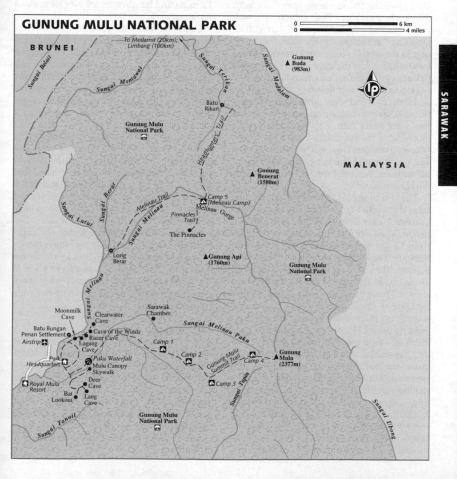

GUNUNG MULU NATIONAL PARK

CAVES

Mulu's caves are the park's most popular attraction. Five of these are open to all and are easily visited from park HQ: Deer Cave, Lang Cave, Clearwater Cave, Cave of the Winds and Lagang Cave, which was just opening its doors while we were researching. It costs RM10 per day (per person) to 'enter' the park, and an additional RM10 to tour two show caves at a time. The Lagang Cave is viewed on its own for RM55 (which includes boat fare). Bring some tiger balm or put a dab of deodorant on a hanky if you are sensitive to sharp smells.

Deer Cave & Lang Cave

An easy 3km walk along a boardwalk separates Deer Cave and the adjoining Lang Cave from the park headquarters. Both are very safe, with walkways and wooden steps. In March 2009, Deer Cave was eclipsed as the largest cave passage in the world (a bigger one was discovered in Vietnam), but the cave is still the biggest passage on the globe that a traveller can visit.

Lang Cave has countless jagged stalagmites and stalactites and some other strange formations. Water cascades from openings in the roof after heavy rain. You enter the cave on one side of the mountain after a 3km walk (allow 50 minutes) to reach the cave entrance. The tour through the Lang Cave takes about 30 minutes. A strong torch is useful for the darker areas.

The star of the lot is **Deer Cave**, which contains the world's largest cave passage open to tourists – over 2km in length and 174m in height. The Deer Cave is located a mere 100m from Lang Cave, and takes about an hour to navigate. Tours depart park HQ at 1.45pm and 2.30pm (the caves are lit from 2pm to 5pm). Once inside the cave, take a deep breath – stinky! That's the guano of over two million bats you're smelling – they cling to the roof, a seething black mass gearing up for their evening prowl. Hope you brought a hat! (Just kidding – airborne dung isn't a threat.)

After visiting the caves, your guide will take you to the 'bat observatory' viewing area with informal, amphitheatre-like seating facing the gaping mouth of Deer Cave. Between 5pm and 6.30pm an endless stream of bats (which kinda looks like a cartoon swarm of bees) emerges from the cave to search the jungle for tasty insects. This dramatic parade is not to be missed. If it's very overcast or raining, the bats will not come out, but fear not, the park has set up a hidden camera in the heart of the cave so you can still sneak a couple glances.

Cave of the Winds & Clearwater Cave

Next on the Mulu menu are two more so-called 'show caves': Cave of the Winds and Clearwater Cave. Tours depart at 9.45am and 10.30am from the entrance to the Cave of the Winds. **Cave of the Winds**, first on the tour, contains several chambers filled with phantasmagorical forests of stalactites and stalagmites.

To reach the caves, you'll pass a small settlement along the river called Batu Bungan. These people were settled along the banks of the stream as part of a government effort to discourage the nomadic lifestyle of the Penan. Trinkets and handicrafts are for sale under a canopied area.

Clearwater Cave, another 400m away by river or plankwalk, is said to be the longest cave in Southeast Asia (the tour only visits a tiny segment of the cave near one of its mouths). The real highlight of Clearwater Cave is the underground river that runs through the chambers. Bring a swimsuit: there's a wonderful swimming hole outside the entrance to Clearwater Cave.

If you like, you can walk back from these caves to park HQ via a concrete path and plankwalk that winds through the narrow passage of **Moonmilk Cave**, but be warned that there is a steep climb en route, and you'll need a headlamp for the cave. When you get to the cave, keep an eye out for the jungle creeper that winds its way into the cave – like a giant octopus tentacle exploring the darkness. After a rain, you may encounter clouds of brilliant black and green Brooke's birdwing butterflies. The total distance from Cave of the Winds to park HQ is 3km. A guide is not necessary for Moonmilk Cave or the walk to/from the cave.

Lagang Cave

The brand new tour of the Lagang Cave was all the buzz during our visit to Mulu. This special tour follows a 1500m-long plankwalk while focusing on the origin of the local limestone and the formation of the region's caves. Subterranean wildlife is also a major focus here. Tours (RM55 including return boat fare) last between two and three hours and can accommodate a maximum of 12 individuals.

Adventure Caves

Hungry for more? Mulu's advanced caves will be sure to satisfy. Around 10% of Mulu's visitors dabble in adventure caving before departing and 99% of 'em are glad they did – there's always that one dude who suddenly gets claustrophobic... And speaking of phobias, travellers with confinement issues or a severe dislike for creepy crawlies should probably cap their caving at the show caves.

Caves and routes are graded beginner, intermediate and advanced. If you have no previous spelunking experience, you will be encouraged to try an intermediate cave (usually Racer Cave) before moving on to advanced. Minimum ages for adventure caving are eight years for beginner caving, 12 for intermediate and 16 for advanced.

The park offers guides for adventure caving and it's best to book in advance. Only the guides employed by the park are licensed to lead advanced caving trips. Prices range from RM200 to RM500 for groups of up to five people. The park produces a brochure called *The Adventure*, which details the seven main caving routes, including the **Sarawak Chamber**, a 12-hour voyage to the centre of the earth to see the world's biggest cave chamber.

MULU CANOPY SKYWALK

In between visits to the show caves, why not try the **Mulu Canopy Skywalk**, easily one of Borneo's best. The park requires that you traverse it as part of a guided walk (RM30 per person; tours depart at 7am, 8.30am, 10.30am, 1pm, 2pm and 2.15pm; night walks are also available). Despite the relatively steep cost, we urge you not to skip this attraction – every bit of its 480m length is unforgettable. Climbing to the canopy is really the only way to see what a tropical rainforest is all about, so it's well worth the splurge. Also, it's fun to shake the wobbly bridges when scaredy-cats crawl across – but don't tell the park management we said that...

BIRD-WATCHING

Birders will enjoy the park's newest feature; the 'Tree Top Tower', which has been specifically designed and constructed to give visitors the opportunity to venture 30m up into the canopy and glimpse the surrounding wildlife. Access is free during the day time, although numbers are strictly controlled. A key deposit is refunded upon a timely return to park HQ. Avian enthusiasts can reserve exclusive access to the tower for a flat rate of RM40 per hour.

TREKKING

If you thought the caves were amazing, wait until you hit the trails! Mulu offers some of the best and most accessible jungle trekking in all of Borneo. The forest here is in excellent condition, and there are trails for every level of fitness and skill, ranging from the easy plankwalks around park HQ to the legendary four-day slog up Gunung Mulu (2377m).

The three main treks in the park are the Headhunters Trail, the Pinnacle Route and the hike to the Gunung Mulu summit. An attempt at any of them will involve some expense, and it's best to go with a group to reduce the cost of both transport and guide. All three trips are multiday affairs. Ask around when you get to the park to see if anyone's interested in sharing costs – it may even be worth trying to scout out travel buddies in Miri. You should not attempt any of these trails without a guide – and you won't be permitted to anyway. Expect rain, leeches, slippery and treacherous conditions, and a very hot workout – carry lots of water. For more general information on trekking see p85.

Guides can be arranged at the park HQ. Although only a fraction of visitors attempt these trails, it's best to book in advance as the park officials cap the number of daily hikers for conservation purposes.

The Headhunters Trail

This back-door route from Gunung Mulu to Limbang can be done in either direction, though most organised trips start in the national park for convenience. The trail is named after the Kayan war parties that apparently marched their way up the Sungai Melinau to the Melinau Gorge, then dragged their canoes overland to the Sungai Terikan to raid the peoples of the Limbang region.

Starting from Mulu's park HQ, hikers first take a boat to **Long Berar** (Kuala Litut), then walk along the **Melinau Trail** to Camp 5 (about four hours) and overnight there at the end of the first day. From here you can delay your trip down the legendary warpath and opt to spend the next day climbing up to the Pinnacles lookout (see p456).

Everyone else will follow a flat but fascinating 11.3km walk through deep jungle to the **Sungai Terikan** (four to five hours), where you could spend the night at the rangers station (Mentawai) or proceed to an Iban longhouse, **Rumah Bala Lesong**, another three or four hours away by boat. After overnighting in the longhouse, the boat trip continues downriver to **Medamit**, and from there it is possible to travel by minivan to Limbang.

The boat ride from to Long Berar (Kuala Litut) from park HQ is RM220 (one to four people; RM55 for each additional passenger). Accommodation at Camp 5 is RM25 per person. The guide fee for the Headhunters route is RM220 per group of one to five people (RM40 more for each additional hiker). The boat from the Kuala Terikan to Medamit costs RM565 for a group of one to four people (a fifth person costs an additional RM100) – groups of six to 10 people must pay RM1055 for two boats. A night at the Iban longhouse costs approximately RM20, and meals (RM15/RM8 for dinner/breakfast) are also on offer. The minivan from Medamit to Limbang Airport costs RM85 (five person maximum) or you can catch the public bus for RM5 per person. Thus, a couple travelling with their own guide (skipping the Pinnacles add-on) should budget around RM610 per person.

Extra costs include food for the stay at Camp 5, gifts for the longhouse and a tip for your guide if you feel it is warranted.

The Pinnacles

Hello trekkers – this is why you came to Borneo. Like bristles on a craggy toothbrush, the Pinnacles are an uncanny collection of sharp limestone spikes that is undoubtedly the world's worst parachute drop zone. These incredible stone towers (some 45m high) protrude from the cloud-swathed forest on the flanks of mysterious Gunung Api, or 'Fire Mountain'.

The trek to the Pinnacles starts with a two- or three-hour boat trip (depending on the level of the river) from park HQ to **Long Berar** (Kuala Litut). From here it is an 8km trek along the Melinau Trail to **Camp 5** (also called 'Melinau Camp') by the Sungai Melinau. Camp 5 has hostel-style accommodation with running water, cold showers, a cooking area, and covered sleeping quarters. You sleep overnight at this picturesque spot before climbing **Gunung Api** (1760m).

The three- to four-hour climb up to the Pinnacles is unrelentingly steep and taxing,

and you may have to unleash your inner gymnast to hobble through the final stage. You'll have to climb the entire distance to see the **Pinnacles** – there's no easy way out. Start early in the morning to ensure that you can make it up and back in one day. If you have not reached a signposted point by 11am, your guide will not allow you to continue to the top (this is for your own safety – if you're having trouble before the signpost, the chances are the final parts of the climb will be too difficult). Camping at the Pinnacles is forbidden. Going downhill takes just as long as coming up and can be twice as wearying.

Although you may hear whispers about forging forward upon returning to Camp 5, the national park has packaged the Pinnacles trek as a three-day/two-night excursion. You'll sleep at Camp 5 for a second evening before finishing the trip, either by heading down the Headhunters Trail, or by returning to Mulu's park HQ. (You may find freelance guides promising to turn the hike into a two-day/one-night combo – hardly a pleasurable experience.)

Guiding fees are RM400 per group (one to five people) for a three-day, two-night trek. The rate for boat hire to Long Berar (Kuala Litut) from park HQ is RM220 each way (one to four people, plus RM55 for each extra person). Accommodation at Camp 5 is RM25 per person each night. So, for a couple travelling with their own guide up to the Pinnacles and back to Mulu's park HQ, the total cost comes out to be roughly RM470 per person. Note that you are also required to bring three days' worth of rations.

Gunung Mulu

The most strenuous of Mulu's extended treks, the climb to Gunung Mulu is normally done as a four-day trek. You must carry enough food for the entire trip, as well as your own cooking utensils and a sleeping bag (it gets quite cold at night). It's not unusual for it to rain every day, so you could find yourself wallowing in mud all the way. Good walking shoes are a must. The guide fees are RM1000 per group.

There are several camps (basic wooden huts) along the trail; Camps 1, 3 and 4 are the ones usually used for overnight stops. The most common schedule involves an easy first day (about three or four hours' walking) and overnighting at **Camp 1** beside a beautiful river. On day two you're faced with a long (four or five hours), hard and extremely steep climb to **Camp 4**. If it hasn't rained, there won't be any water at Camp 4, so carry some up from Camp 3.

On day three you leave your pack at Camp 4 and climb to the summit of **Gunung Mulu**. On your descent, spend another night at Camp 3 before returning to the park headquarters on day four.

The guide fee for a group of one to five people is a healthy RM1000.

Shorter Trails

If you aren't up for a multiday trekking adventure, there are several easier walks around the park HQ.

The **Moonmilk Cave Trail** leaves from park HQ and parallels the river heading upstream to Moonmilk Cave. It's mostly flat for 1.5km until it reaches the steep steps up to the cave. No guide is required and it's paved with concrete, which means easy walking and no leeches – a very pleasant way to check out the Borneo rainforest. Note that the concrete path is pressure cleaned every three months, so for the few weeks before its scheduled cleaning the path can be very slippery. If you don't feel like the sweaty climb up to the cave, a there-and-back to the base of the steps is a good idea.

About 600m along the Moonmilk Cave Trail, a **plankwalk** branches off on the right and continues through the forest for about 1km, eventually coming out along the main plankwalk to the show caves, near the park accommodation. This is another fun and easy way to experience the jungle.

The **plankwalk** to Deer and Lang caves leaves from just beyond the park accommodation, past the second longhouse block. It's about 1500m to the junction that leads on the left to the Mulu Canopy Skywalk and on the right to Deer and Lang Caves. If you just walked out to this junction and turned around, you'd probably find the time well spent.

Just before this junction, the Gunung Mulu Summit branches off (marked Summit Trail) on the left. This is also the **Paku Waterfall Trail**. This flat trail works through the jungle to Paku Waterfalls, an interesting set of three waterfalls that come right out of a limestone cliff face. There's good swimming here. The total distance from park HQ to the falls is about 3km and the return trip takes about three hours at a leisurely pace. Note that the ground can become a swamp after rain. The best advice: don't fight it – just take the plunge and get muddy early on. No guide is required for this route, but let the folks at park HQ know before you set out and when you expect to return.

Sleeping & Eating

Given Mulu's popularity and penchant for tour groups, you must book your accommodation in advance with **Mulu Park** (☎ 085-792300; enquiries@mulupark.com; www.mulupark.com).

Park accommodation takes the form of a 21-bed **hostel** (dm RM40), which is a clean, spacious room sleeping both men and women. Hot showers and lockers are available. Comfortable private rooms are available as well, including simple Rainforest rooms (from RM110) and the charming Deluxe Longhouse rooms (from RM170). Camping is permitted at the park HQ for RM7.50 per night. See the website for images and additional info.

There are no cooking facilities in park accommodation. Simple but tasty meals are served at **Café Mulu** (The Canteen; meals RM10-15; ☻ breakfast, lunch & dinner) – try the Mulu laksa, a staff favourite. There are a couple of low-key eating spots peppered around the main road back to the airport.

You'll see the inviting swimming pool at **Royal Mulu Resort** (☎ 085-792388; www.royalmulu resort.com; ☒ ☒) from your aeroplane window as you land. If you're staying at the park, you might be initially sad that you didn't splurge, but after exploring this self-proclaimed luxury resort, you'll be happy you didn't. The setting is lovely though – a sprawling campus built around limestone bluffs – but the rooms, stocked with dated furnishings, don't do a good job of fending off the oppressive jungle moistness. Nonguests are welcome at the pleasant spa, which just might be the perfect reward after a Pinnacles trip. It's best to ask about promotional rates (there always seems to some sort of discount scheme going on) – a three-day/two-night package including four meals and two cave tours is RM1370 per couple.

Getting There & Away
AIR
The most practical way to reach Gunung Mulu is by taking a direct flight between Miri and Mulu. **MASwings** (☎ 1300-883 000;

SARAWAK

www.maswings.com.my), a branch of Malaysia Airlines, operates at least two flights per day (usually in the morning). The flight takes around 30 minutes and costs about RM300 round trip.

BOAT

It's possible to travel to Mulu from Miri by river, but it's a long, long journey and it actually costs more than flying.

First, you must take a taxi from Miri to Kuala Beram to catch the 8am river express to Marudi (RM30, 2½ hours). From Marudi, take the noon boat upriver to Long Terawan (the destination plate reads 'Tutoh'; RM20, six hours). Once there, you must charter a boat for the final three-hour journey upriver to the park (RM250). It's best to call ahead to the park to make sure that a boat will be available to take you from Long Terawan to the park. If no boat is available, be prepared to spend the night in Long Terawan unless you want to charter a boat from the park (you will then pay double the price to have a boat sent from the park to pick you up).

OVERLAND

Gunung Mulu National Park can be the finish line of the awesome Headhunters Trail. The overland trekking route begins in Limbang and incorporates several boat rides. See p455 for more information.

Getting Around

The park HQ is a 1km walk from the airport, along the road that leads to the Royal Mulu Resort. Royal Mulu picks up its customers after every flight, and those staying at the national park can grab a ride on one of the circulating vans (RM6 or RM7 depending on the driver's mood).

BARIO & THE KELABIT HIGHLANDS

A land of sacred stones, of muddy longhouse pilgrimages, of wispy clouds thumbing thick greens like lazy fingers – the Kelabit Highlands is a faraway land indeed. Snuggled up against the Indonesian border like a sleeping leviathan, this kingdom of earth and sticks rests quietly under the rain as time tiptoes by oh-so slowly.

Bario, a gathering of wooden cabins and quaking rice paddies, is the region's largest community and unofficial capital. You wouldn't

think it now, but this simple village has seen its share of action, during both WWII and the Konfrontasi with Indonesia in the early 1960s.

Today, however, it's the widespread logging that poses the biggest problem. Large swathes of primary forest have been flattened by industry, and acres more lie waiting to be taken. Fortunately, several areas, including Bario's dimpled plateau and the greenbelt around Gunung Murud, are now protected by the cross-border **Pulong Tau National Park**, fully gazetted in 2005.

Orientation & Information

The Kelabit Highlands ride the Indonesian border in the easternmost part of Sarawak. Bario, in the region's centre, is essentially the Highland's capital. The village's collection of humble structures is flung across an emerald valley dotted with juicy rice fields and marshes.

Bario is the best place to base yourself for your trip through the Highlands. The airport in Bario is about a 30-minute walk south of the shophouses. You're bound to be offered a lift on arrival, as seemingly everyone in town turns up to meet the daily flights.

A recently installed communications tower has made it possible for locals to use mobile phones. Only Celcom SIM cards will work in the Highlands (and callers must be relatively close to Bario). There are no bank, ATM or credit-card facilities in the whole Kelabit Highlands. Travellers should bring plenty of small-denomination cash for accommodation, food and guides, plus some extra ringgit in case you get stranded.

Check out www.ebario.com and www.kelabit.com to help prepare for your trip to the region.

Sights & Activities
BARIO
The **Bario Asal longhouse** is one of the oldest in the area, built in the traditional style with a separate fireplace for each family on the wide verandah. Nearby the secondary school has a small collection of rare orchids.

DAY TRIPS
The Kelabit Highlands offer many opportunities for exploration even if you aren't of the intense trekker variety. Short day trips from Bario include **fishing**, **bird-watching**, trekking to **Prayer Mountain** (two hours return) and visits to the nearby villages of **Pa' Umor** and **Pa' Ukat**. You can also hike up to **Bario Gap** (half-day return), a visible notch that was cut in the rainforest on a ridge above town to celebrate the millennium and two thousand years of Christianity. Coordinated by local character and guide Peter Matu, this *kawang* (human-made natural monument) follows the Kelabit tradition of altering their surroundings to mark important events. The intriguing settlement of **Pa' Tik** lies several kilometres beyond 'the gap'. The local Kelabits warned us that there is a potential threat of malaria among Pa' Tik's migratory Penan, although the high altitude means that mozzies are few and far between.

Those interested in food and agriculture might appreciate a short trip to the local **main tudah** (salt lick). This cemented salt collector is a great place to learn about the local method of salt processing, which is done in giant vats over a roaring fire. The high-iodine salt goes perfectly with local specialities such as deer and wild boar, but the production technique is beginning to die out.

A variety of intriguing tribal **megaliths** is strewn throughout the quiet landscape – many are within a day's reach; see p461. For information on longer treks, see below. Note that portions of the following hikes can be altered for intensive day-trip experiences as well.

Standard guiding fees apply for day trippers (a minimum of RM80), even if you only require a tour leader for a half-day trek. Recommended guides around Bario include (but are not limited to) Joshua, Florence, Stuart, Ridi and Sylvester.

TREKKING
Hikers, gird those loins: this is why you came to Borneo. The temperate, forested highlands around the Indonesian border offer some of the best jungle trekking on the island, taking in

---

PUN TUMID: THE KELABIT BOGEYMAN

Half-man, half-ghost, Pun Tumid is the jungle spirit of the Kelabit Highlands. His name literally means 'grandfather heel' – a moniker earned because of his oversized paw-like feet and staggered gait (think Sasquatch). Pun Tumid features prominently in Kelabit oral history and many tribal elders claim to have encountered the spectre on their jungle treks. It is believed that he patrols the region, toeing the mountain ridges and punishing those who do not follow the rules of the jungle. There are three faux pas that will incur his wrath:

■ Never hang your wet clothes over the fire.

■ Never throw your fruit skins in the fire.

■ Never put your machete in the fire.

Pun Tumid was not fond of those who didn't obey his requests and would punish dissenters by blowing out their campfires, causing long-lasting insomnia, and moving lit logs to create unwanted flames.

Young Kelabits lived in fear of this Bornean bogeyman until they embraced Christianity. Then the wraith mysteriously disappeared…

farming villages, rugged peaks and supremely remote Kenyah and Kelabit longhouses along the way. While the Highlands are certainly cooler than Borneo's coastal regions, it's still hard work trekking up here and you should be in pretty good shape to consider a multiday trek. See p85 for detailed information about trekking in the tropics.

Guided treks range from overnight excursions to one-week slogs into the wilds of Kalimantan. Bario is a great place to begin your journey – every homestay in town can arrange guides and accommodation, as well as transport to trailheads if necessary. It's certainly possible to just turn up and make arrangements after you arrive, especially if you don't mind waiting a day or two in Bario before the start of your trek. If you're in a hurry though, consider making arrangements in advance by email or (preferably) phone. The region's topography is constantly in flux due to marauding loggers, so consider chatting with a local before choosing your route. At the time of research, treks between Bario and Ba Kelalan were still possible; however, trails from Bario to Long Lellang were closed.

Going rates for guides (and porters, if needed) start at RM80 per day, plus an extra RM20 per night on multiday trips. If you are connecting the dots between rural longhouses, expect to pay RM50 per person for a night's sleep plus three meals (you can opt out of lunch and save RM10). If you are trekking in one direction only (perhaps Bario to Ba Kelalan; see right) you will be asked to continue paying the guiding fee while your guide returns home through the jungle (in this scenario, it would take the guide two days to make the journey back to Bario from Ba Kelalan).

The Kelapang Loop
During your visit to the Highlands, you might hear locals wax nostalgic about the great Bario Loop. Sadly the circuit no longer exists as loggers continue to gobble up the virgin jungle. Today the Kelapang Loop (a three- to five-day trek) is one of the most popular routes in the Highlands, taking in three of the main longhouses south of Bario: Pa' Dalih, Ramadu and Pa' Mada. 'Loop' is something of a misnomer as it's more of an oar-shaped trek – an out-and-back trail with an oblong circuit at the tip. All three longhouses en route are welcoming, friendly places where you'll get a good glimpse into Kelabit life.

One possible itinerary is as follows: day one – Bario to Pa' Mada via deserted Pa' Main (eight hours); day two – Pa' Mada to Pa' Dalih (two hours); day three – Pa' Dalih to Ramadu (three hours); day four – Ramudu to Pa' Mada (three hours); day five – Pa' Mada back to Bario (eight hours). Trekkers can snip a day off the itinerary by combining day two and day three.

Travellers on a tight schedule can do a one- or two-day abridged version of the trip by driving to Pa' Mada along the logging roads (four hours). After lunch (RM10) at the longhouse, hike to Pa' Dalih, then take a boat (RM40 per person) back to Pa' Mada and return to Bario by car. An overnight at Pa' Mada can be easily arranged in order to get the full longhouse experience, and trekkers can walk back to Bario rather than drive (although the route isn't particularly scenic). Figure RM250 (one way) for the car ride between Bario and Pa' Mada (maximum of five people).

Alternatively, you can extend the journey for as long as you'd like by staying at some of the longhouses for a few days or altering your route to include the deserted Pa' Berang on your return trip to Bario, although unsightly logging roads have consumed parts of the trails in this western area. Parts of the Kelapang Loop can also be combined with an invigorating overland hike to Ba Kelalan.

Bario to Ba Kelalan
The three-day trek from Bario to the village of Ba Kelalan is a good route for those who don't want to cover the same ground twice (you can arrange to fly out of Ba Kelalan so that you don't have to return to Bario). It covers a variety of mostly gentle terrain and gives a good overview of the Kelabit Highlands.

The typical itinerary is as follows: day one – Bario to Pa' Lungan (four hours); day two – Pa' Lungan to Pa' Rupai (eight hours); day three – Pa' Rupai to Ba Kelalan (three hours). Note that this route takes you through part of Kalimantan, which is technically illegal, although blurred tribal boundaries mean that the governments usually turn a blind eye. Have a chat with your guide about whether this route is possible at the time you attempt the route.

It is also possible to combine part of the Kelapang Loop with a trek to Ba Kelalan by connecting the dots from Bario through deserted Pa' Main, down to Pa' Mada, over to Pa'

Dalih, then cross the border into Kalimantan, stay at Long Layu, move onto Long Bawan, then loop around to Ba Kelalan. This route takes three to five days depending on how quickly you reach Long Layu.

Note that if you journey in one direction you will be required to pay an additional guiding fee as your guide returns home through the jungle.

Batu Lawi

If you were sitting on the left side of the plane from Miri to Bario, you probably caught a glimpse of the twin granite fingers known as Batu Lawi (the largest rising to 2040m). While an ascent of the higher rock formation (known as the 'male peak' of the mountain) is only for expert technical rock climbers, ascending the lower 'female peak' is possible for fit trekkers without any special technical skills. It's a three-day return trip from Bario and hiring a porter is highly recommended.

Those wanting to loop back to Bario do the following: day one – Bario to Base Camp via Pa' Ukat (eight hours); day two – Base Camp to summit to Base Camp (10 hours); day three – Base Camp to Bario (eight hours).

Gunung Murud

Sarawak's highest mountain (2423m) is just begging to be climbed, but very few visitors make the effort to put the trip together. The mountain can be reached from both Ba Kelalan and Bario; from Bario, the more common starting point, a typical return trip takes six days. This adventure is only for the fittest of the fit, and it's highly recommended that you hire a porter.

The typical itinerary from Bario is as follows: day one – Bario to Pa' Lungan (four hours); day two – Pa' Lungan to Long Rapung (four hours); day three – Long Rapung to Church Camp (eight hours); day four – Church Camp to summit and back to Church Camp (seven hours); day five – Church Camp to Long Rapung (eight hours); day six – Long Rapung to Bario (eight hours).

MEGALITHS

Megaliths play an important part in Kelabit and Kayan culture – stone carvings, *dolmen* (stone burial markers) and runes are hidden throughout the landscape – but if you're expecting Stonehenge you'll be sorely disappointed. At the time of research, local guides were getting ready to signpost some of the more impressive megaliths orbiting Bario. Due to the logging in the southern part of the highlands, megalith enthusiasts should stick to the region's northern region.

There are two interesting day-trip loops from Bario that cover an eclectic collection of stones. From Bario, head to Pa' Umor (1½ hours) passing the Bario 'salt lick' along the way. From Pa' Umor, continue on (15 minutes) to Arur Bilit Farm, which is home to **Batu Navit**, an impressive stone carving featuring a human in the spread-eagled position among its design. This stone was used as a tally for every head taken. It was also used to tally sexual conquests. From the farm, use the log bridge to cross a small river (15 minutes) in order to reach **Batu Ipak**. According to local legend, this stone formation was created when an angry Kelabit hunter pulled out his machete and took a wrathful swing at the rock, cutting it in two. Head back to Pa' Umor for lunch before returning to Bario. This entire excursion will take approximately four or five hours – maybe a tad longer if your guide is a good storyteller.

The other option is to head towards Pa' Lungan from Bario (four hours) stopping halfway at **Batu Arit**, a large stone featuring bird carvings and humanoid figures with heart-shaped faces. From Pa' Lungan it's a two-minute walk to **Batu Ritung**, a seven-foot stone table (probably a burial site), although no one is quite sure as the site was created outside of living memory. Also near Pa' Lungan (15 minutes away) is **Perupun**, a huge pile of stones. This type of rock pile was assembled to bury the valuables of the dead who had no descendants to receive their belongings. Those with a bit more time could consider basing themselves in Pa' Lungan for a day or two to visit additional burial sites, including one with a collection of mysterious jars. There is also a vine-cluttered 'jungle trail' between Pa' Lungan and Bario reserved for those with a bit more stamina and spirit. A scenic (but expensive; prices negotiable) boat ride can be arranged between the two villages for those seeking something more relaxing.

Sleeping & Eating

BARIO

Little Bario is a great place to base oneself during a visit to the Highlands. There are several

---

IT'S A BIRD... IT'S A PLANE... IT'S TOM HARRISON...?

Whoosh! A loud swishing sound scraped across the sky. A strange contraption hovered high above the lazy clouds in the valley. Suddenly, a small creature emerged, a monkey perhaps, falling towards the earth with an umbrella overhead. Farmers left their rice paddies. Some moved towards the flying object, some slunk back into the jungle shade, others stood motionless, eyes fixed on the dropping mass.

It was a man. And he landed in a marsh with a great thud. Dressed in jungle colours, the young man with fair skin regained his footing and slowly moved towards an inquisitive farmer and his awestruck son. The man from the sky unveiled a small brown item wrapped in foil. He broke off a piece and placed it in his mouth, offering the remaining part to the farmer's son. The child nibbled off a small amount with a slight smile. It was surprisingly sweet. The fair-skinned man promptly fired a gunshot into the clouds signalling for others from the sky to drop down to earth.

The year was 1945, and the man from the sky was Tom Harrison. He came with his cadre of soldiers to warn the locals that the Japanese were quickly approaching. The enemy forces had reached Ba Kelalan on the other side of the ridge, and it was time to turn the Kelabits into crafty guerrilla fighters.

After the British put the kibosh on the Japanese invasion, Tom decided to stick around. He offered the locals special pills that cured malaria, constructed lavatories in an attempt to encourage hygiene, and eventually built a school (without the permission of the British government). The Kelabit people were keen students and embraced his foreign teachings. Tom's mythic debut proved quite telling – he is now remembered and honoured as a demigod throughout the region.

Check out *The Most Offending Soul Alive*, a biography by Judith M Heimann, to learn more about the adventures of this colourful character – he is remembered quite differently in his native England.

---

cosy options, with most offering bed-and-board services for a flat per-person rate. You don't need to book ahead in Bario – internet connections are limited and tourist traffic isn't exactly bustling. Check out www.ebario.com for more information about accommodation, including a longer list of homestays and an online booking system. If you decide that you are unhappy with your accommodation choice, simply return to the airport around 9am and take a ride to a different homestay after the new batch of tourists lands on the morning flight.

Bariew Backpackers Lodge (☎ 014-892 3431, 019-859 0937; bariewlodge@yahoo.com; r RM20, full board package RM65-70) The quietly affable Raddish runs this excellent family-run guesthouse near the centre of Bario. He knows everyone in town and has an intimate knowledge of the trails and longhouses scattered throughout the highlands – his large collection of hand-drawn maps are regularly updated to reflect the region's changing geography. Rooms are simple but well kept – there's no need for fans as it is pleasantly cool in the evenings. If you aren't booking accommodation ahead of time (and you don't really have to in Bario), someone from the 'lodge' will always be at the airport to scoop up backpackers after each incoming flight.

Tarawe's Lodge (liantarawe@yahoo.com; r per person RM20) The oldest place to hang your hat in Bario does not pretend to be anything grand, and although this honesty is refreshing, the property is a tad ragtag. The four basic rooms (located on the 2nd floor) have three single beds (orphanage-style) and there's a dusty living room on the ground level with a bumpin' sound system hooked up to an iPod. Guests can cook their own meals in the on-site kitchen.

Labang's Longhouse (ncbario@yahoo.com; r per person RM20, with 2/3 meals RM43/58) A friendly place owned by a retired Sarawak Forestry employee, this longhouse-style establishment offers prim twin-bed rooms and plenty of comfy common space decked with posters, world flags and cowboy hats. It's a great place for large groups.

Gem's Lodge (gems_lodge@yahoo.com; r RM60) Bario itself is hardly a bustling burg, but this welcoming guesthouse, just 6km southeast of town near the longhouse village of Pa' Umor, is tranquillity incarnate. The owner, Jaman, is one of Bario's nicest and most informative guides. He offers a wide array of treks, tours and excursions based on his own formidable local knowledge. There are four pleasant private rooms and a cosy common area. Email ahead to arrange a pick-up – it's pretty far from the airport.

Jungle Blues Dream (☎ 019-884 9892; jungleblues dream@gmail.com; r & board per person RM60) Owned by local artist Stephen Baya and his lovely Danish wife, this lodge-cum-gallery is a fantastic place to call home during your Highlands visit. Rooms are lofted above the gallery and have subtle touches of Western comfort. Stephen's art hangs on all of the walls and guests are encouraged to leave an artistic message on a wooden plaque before departing. Bathrooms are in outhouse-like stalls on the ground floor. Those who book ahead can arrange an airport pick-up, and mountain bikes are available for rent (RM30 per day). Stephen's grandfather runs the Ngimat Homestay (also RM60) nearby.

HIGHLAND LONGHOUSES

It is not required to bring gifts when staying at the longhouses scattered across the Kelabit Highlands, especially if you are trying to minimise the weight in your rucksack on a week-long trek. If you have time in Miri before your arrival, consider stopping by a supermarket to grab a bag of sugar crystals, noodles, salt, (healthy) biscuits or individually wrapped items that can be passed out by the chief. Expect to pay around RM50 for one night's rest, which includes three meals (you can skip lunch and save RM10 if cash is tight). Handicrafts, like woven rattan baskets, are available for purchase at most longhouses. The longhouse communities that are more *on* the beaten track in the Kelabit region include Pa' Mada, Pa' Umor, Pa' Dalih and Ramadu.

BA KELALAN

Bario is a metropolis when compared with Ba Kelalan. This collection of nine Lun Bawang communities is known throughout Borneo for two things: apple orchards and genuine hospitality. Homestay accommodation is readily available, or trekkers can opt to stay at Apple Lodge, a friendly place at the edge of the airstrip run by the Tagal family. Pre-booking is not a must.

Getting There & Away

The most practical way to reach the Kelabit Highlands is by direct flight between Miri and Bario. **MASwings** (☎ 1300-883 000; www.mas wings.com.my), a branch of Malaysia Airlines, operates at least one flight per day (always in the morning) on their Twin Otter aircraft. The flight takes one hour and costs RM98. Four weekly flights connect Miri to Ba Kelalan (RM93, one hour) and Long Lellang (RM94, one hour). Online bookings at the MASwings website can be temperamental (the site may incorrectly announce that a flight is full) so it is best to swing by their office in Miri. Planes are small and demand is high, so it's best to book as far in advance as possible.

It is also possible to reach Bario overland. The trip between Miri and Bario (RM900 per vehicle – four person maximum) takes more than a day, and passes several remote longhouses along the snaking network of logging roads.

Once in Bario it's roughly a 30-minute walk into the central part of the village (turn left at the T-junction), although the chances are high that you'll be greeted like a celeb when you get off the plane. Local lodging operators often swing by to scoop up trekkers when the planes land.

BARIO BITES

Bario is famous throughout Malaysia for two things: rice and pineapple. The town sits in a breezy valley lofted high in the clouds, and this privileged position has fostered the perfect soil conditions for growing flavourful grains and sweeter-than-sweet citrus. The subtle differences in taste might not be obvious to an undiscerning Western palate, but locals are quick to point out that their rice is smaller and more aromatic, and the local pineapple lacks a certain tart zing found in lowland plantations.

The area's coveted produce is markedly more expensive than the crops from other regions – at the markets in Miri, a kilogram of Bario rice costs a whopping RM20 (it's RM6 or RM7 if purchased in Bario).

The Kelabit also collect their own salt deposits, making this far-flung community completely self-reliant.

LIMBANG DIVISION

Limbang

If you've only seen Limbang on the map, you may be in for a surprise when you rock up expecting a backwoods outpost and find a prosperous, bustling river town. Tourism is pretty much an irrelevance in these parts, so there are few reasons to stay over, but trekkers coming from the Headhunters Trail might well appreciate an evening here to relax before hitting the road again.

ORIENTATION & INFORMATION

The main part of Limbang sits along the east bank of the Sungai Limbang, which loops across a forested plain before emptying into Brunei Bay. The older part of town is only a couple of hundred metres square and is bordered on the riverbank by the two-storey, blue-roofed main market.

Boats to Brunei and Labuan leave from the wharf below the blue-roofed market, and taxis park just outside. Boats to Lawas tie up at the jetty a few hundred metres downstream. Buses leave from a stand a couple of blocks east of the river, behind the old part of town. The airport is about 4km south of town.

SIGHTS

A **tamu** (weekly market) is held on Friday in the car park in front of the main market. Bisayah villagers, many of whom still speak the Brunei Malay dialect, come in from all around the district to attend.

The small but informative **Limbang Regional Museum** (Muzium Wilayah; admission free; ⊙ 9am-6pm Tue-Sun) is upstairs in another of Charles Brooke's forts, built in 1897. The collection is well presented and features exhibits on archaeology, culture and crafts of the region. To get here, follow the riverbank upstream (south) past the police station and look for the replica totem pole.

SLEEPING & EATING

Decent places are mostly midrange, air-con hotels, some of which accept credit cards.

Royal Park Hotel (☎ 085-212155; Lot 1089 Jln Buagsiol; r from RM60; 🏵) Much better value than the budget fleabags in the centre of town, this clean, well-run hotel is worth the walk to get to it. From the town centre, walk north (downstream) 400m along the river.

Purnama Hotel (☎ 085-216700; Jln Buangsiol; r RM150; 🏵) A four-star hotel with friendly staff, the Purnama has large, adequate rooms, a cafe, lounge bar, spa and fitness centre, as well as all the consumerist delights of Limbang Plaza. Discounts make it particularly good value.

There are food stalls on the 1st floor of the waterfront market, at the bus station and along the river. Basic Malay food, roti and *murtabak* are served in halal cafes around the centre.

GETTING THERE & AROUND

For information about Brunei border crossings, see the boxed text, p593.

AIR

MASwings (☎ 1300-883 000; www.malaysiaairlines.com.my) has flights to Miri (RM65) and Kota Kinabalu (KK; RM75). The airport is 4km south of the town centre, a RM10 taxi ride away.

BOAT

The express boat to Pulau Labuan in Sabah leaves at 8.30am daily (RM25, two hours). Speedboats go to Bandar Seri Begawan in Brunei (RM15, 30 minutes) and Lawas in Sarawak (RM25, one hour) when sufficient passengers turn up (you may find yourself waiting quite a while). Boats leave from the jetty outside the immigration hall on the river, just upstream from the large pink building housing the market (Bengunan Tamu Limbang).

BUS

There are buses to Kuala Lurah, at the border with Brunei, that depart at 9.30am, 1pm and 5pm (RM5.50, one hour). There are buses to Medamit (RM5) but none to the Temburong District of Brunei (you'll have to take a taxi). Buses depart from the stand a few blocks east of the river in the centre of town. There is also a daily bus from Limbang across Brunei to Miri (RM40, three hours, departs Limbang at 9am).

CAR

A taxi to Kuala Lurah, at the border with Brunei, will cost RM40. Most taxi drivers will refuse to continue over the border to Bandar Seri Begawan (BSB) due to the time it takes to clear immigration. You can walk across the border and catch another taxi onward to BSB for about B$10. A taxi from Limbang to the border with the Temburong District of Brunei will cost RM15, and, once again, taxi drivers will usually refuse to cross. Once across, you'll have to hitch or arrange a private car (which will not be easy). Consider heading to Temburong (Bangar) from BSB or negotiate with a taxi driver from Limbang to take you all the way.

Lawas

Lawas is a transit point in the sliver of Sarawak pinched between Sabah and the Temburong district of Brunei. There is little of interest to travellers. A branch of Maybank can be found in the centre of town.

Hotel Perdana (☎ 085-285888; Lot 365 Jln Punang; r from 46; 🔀) is the best economy hotel in town, although it's a little frayed round the edges. To get there, start with your back to the main market (Pasar Baru Lawas) and go left, following the main road out of town. It will be on your right after about 300m.

There are several **Malaysia Airlines** (☎ 1300-883 000; www.malaysiaairlines.com.my) flights each week to/from Miri (RM70). The airport is 2km from town.

A boat to Limbang (RM28, one hour) leaves at 9am every day except Thursday. A boat to Labuan (RM33, two hours) leaves at 7.30am every day except Tuesday and Thursday. Boats leave from the jetty on the west side of town, just downstream from the Shell petrol station. Buses head to Kota Kinabalu in Sabah (RM20) at 7am and 1pm daily.

Malaysia Directory

CONTENTS

ACCOMMODATION

Malaysia's accommodation possibilities range from rock-bottom flophouses to luxurious five-star resorts. Outside the peak holiday seasons (around major festivals such as Chinese New Year in January/February) big discounts are frequently available – it's always worth asking about special offers.

Budget places are those indicated with prices under RM70 per room (under RM100 in Kuala Lumpur); at such hotels and guesthouses don't expect much in the way of comfort, although most will offer a choice of rooms with or without air-conditioning and with or without attached bathrooms.

Midrange (in KL, RM100 to RM400; elsewhere RM70 to RM200) hotels will offer pleasant extras such as swimming pools, nicely designed rooms, and facilities such as restaurants and business centres. Top-end hotels charge over RM200 (in KL over RM400) per room.

Top end and a few midrange places often quote prices exclusive of tax (5%) and service charge (10%) – these charges are represented as ++ (called plus-plus), for example RM120++ for a double. Net means that tax and any service charges are included – these are the prices quoted in practically all budget and many midrange places. Tax and service charges are also applied to food, drinks and services in top hotels and the more expensive restaurants. We quote net prices for all budget and midrange places.

Warning: bed bug infestations are common in Malaysia's hotels and are a particular problem at the budget end of the market; see p603 for more details.

Camping

Many of Malaysia's national parks have official camping grounds and will permit camping in nondesignated sites once you are deep in the jungle. There are also many lonely stretches of beach that are ideal for camping. Likewise, it is possible to camp on uninhabited bays on many of Malaysia's islands. A two-season tent with mosquito netting is ideal. A summer-weight sleeping bag is OK, but the best choice is a light-weight bag-liner, since even the nights are warm.

BOOK YOUR STAY ONLINE

For more accommodation reviews and recommendations by Lonely Planet authors, check out the online booking service at www.lonelyplanet.com/hotels. You'll find the true, insider low-down on the best places to stay. Reviews are thorough and independent. Best of all, you can book online.

PRACTICALITIES

- Connect to the reliable electricity supply (220V to 240V, 50 cycles) with a UK-type three-square-pin plug.

- Read the English-language newspapers the *New Straits Times,* the *Star* and the *Malay Mail.* In Malaysian Borneo you'll also find the *Borneo Post,* the *Eastern Times* and the *New Sabah Times.*

- Listen to Traxx FM (www.traxxfm.net; 90.3FM), HITZ FM (www.hitz.fm; 92.9FM) and MIX FM (www.mix.fm; 94.5FM) for pop music and Fly FM (www.flyfm.com.my; 95.8FM) for news (these frequencies are for the KL area). In Sabah, listen to Traxx FM (90.7FM) or Muzik FM (88.9FM); in Sarawak tune in to Traxx FM (89.9FM), or Wai FM (101.3FM) for tribal music.

- Watch Malaysia's two government TV channels (TV1 and TV2), four commercial stations (TV3, NTV7, 8TV and TV9) as well as a host of satellite channels.

- Use the metric system for weights and measures.

Homestays

Staying with a Malaysian family will give you a unique experience many times removed from the fast-paced and largely recognisable life of the cities and towns. It's worth enquiring with **Tourism Malaysia** (www.tourism malaysia.gov.my) and each of the state tourism bodies about the homestay programs operating throughout the country in off-the-beaten-track *kampung* (villages). Also see p201 about a homestay program in Penang.

Hostels & Guesthouses

At beach resorts and in the main tourist cities you will find a variety of cheap hostels and guesthouses. These options may be huts on the beach, private homes or houses divided by partition walls into a number of rooms. Dormitory accommodation is usually available. Rooms are spartan, but this is the cheapest accommodation option around and often the nicest, with a real family atmosphere. These places often cater only to foreign travellers and offer their customers lots of little extras to outdo the competition, such as free tea and coffee, bicycles and transport. You'll normally pay around RM6 to RM30 for a dorm bed or RM15 to RM70 for a hotel-style room with air-con.

Hotels

Standard rooms at top-end hotels are often called 'superior' in the local parlance. Most hotels have slightly more expensive 'deluxe' or 'club' rooms, which tend to be larger, have a better view and include extras such as breakfast or free internet access. Many also have suites.

At the low end of the price scale are the traditional Chinese-run hotels usually offering little more than simple rooms with a bed, a table and chair, and a sink. The showers and toilets (which will sometimes be Asian squat-style) may be down the corridor. Note couples can sometimes economise by asking for a single, since in Chinese-hotel language 'single' means one double bed, and 'double' means two beds. Don't think of this as being tight; in Chinese hotels you can pack as many into one room as you wish.

The main catch with these hotels is that they can sometimes be terribly noisy. They're often on main streets, and the cheapest ones often have flimsy walls that stop short of the ceiling – great for ventilation but terrible for acoustics and privacy.

Longhouses in Malaysian Borneo

These communal homes, the traditional dwellings of the indigenous peoples of Borneo, may contain up to 100 individual family 'apartments' under one long roof. These days there are two main types of longhouse: tourist longhouses and authentic longhouses. While a visit to (or a stay overnight in) a tourist longhouse is easy enough, it's unlikely to be of much interest. A visit to an authentic longhouse can be a magical experience, but is tricky to arrange and there's a very specific etiquette; see p430 for details.

Resthouses

A few of the old British-developed resthouses in Malaysia are still operating. These were set up during the colonial era to provide accommodation for travelling officials, and later provided comfortable shelter for all types of travellers. Many of the resthouses are still government owned but are privately operated. Some have been turned into modern mid-range resorts, others retain old colonial decor. The average price for a room in a resthouse is between RM70 and RM100, and this usually includes air-con and attached bathroom.

ACTIVITIES

See the Outdoor Activities chapter (p83).

BUSINESS HOURS

Government offices are usually open from 8am to 4.15pm Monday to Friday. Most close for lunch from 12.45pm to 2pm, and on Friday the lunch break is from 12.15pm to 2.45pm for Friday prayers at the mosque.

Bank hours are generally 10am to 3pm on weekdays and 9.30am to 11.30am on Saturday.

Shop hours are variable, although a good rule of thumb for small shops is that they're open from 9am to 6pm Monday to Saturday. Major department stores, shopping malls, Chinese-run emporiums and some large stores are open from around 10am until 9pm or 10pm, seven days a week.

Restaurants generally serve breakfast 7am to noon, although a Malaysian breakfast is something that you could just as well eat for lunch and most places serving such food will be open straight through from early morning to late night. Unless mentioned otherwise the restaurants listed are open daily for lunch (noon to 2.30pm) and dinner (6pm to 10.30pm).

Most of Malaysia follows this working week: Monday to Friday, with Saturday a half-day. But in the more Islamic-minded states of Kedah, Perlis, Kelantan and Terengganu, government offices, banks and many shops are closed on Friday and on Saturday afternoon. These states have declared Friday the holiday, and their working week is from Saturday to Thursday, which is a half-day. However, federal government offices follow the same hours as the rest of the country.

CHILDREN
Practicalities

Travelling with the kids in Malaysia is generally a breeze. For the most part, parents needn't be overly concerned, but it pays to lay down a few ground rules – such as regular hand-washing –

to head off potential problems; see p604 for more on health issues. Children should especially be warned not to play with animals, as rabies occurs in Malaysia.

Lonely Planet's *Travel with Children* contains useful advice on how to cope with kids on the road and what to bring along to make things go more smoothly, with special attention paid to travelling in developing countries. Also useful for general advice is www.travelwithyourkids.com.

There are discounts for children for most attractions and for most transport. Many beach resorts have special family chalets. Chinese hotels can also work out a bargain as they charge by the room rather than the number of people. Cots, however, are not widely available in cheap accommodation. Public transport is comfortable and relatively well organised, although pushing a stroller around isn't likely to be easy given there are often no footpaths and kerbs are high.

Baby formula, baby food and nappies (diapers) are widely available. However, it makes sense to stock up on these items before heading to remote destinations or islands.

Sights & Activities

Some beach destinations suitable for families with younger children include Pulau Perhentian (p319), Pulau Kapas (p315) and Tunku Abdul Rahman National Park (p354). Those with older children might enjoy some of the jungle parks of the country, including Taman Negara (p294) and, over in Sarawak, the Bako (p423) and Gunung Mulu (p452) national parks. For more animal encounters also consider the Sepilok Orang-Utan Rehabilitation Centre (p375) in Sabah and the Kuala Gandah Elephant Conservation Centre (p303) in central Pahang.

For several ideas on how to entertain the kids in Kuala Lumpur see p108.

CLIMATE

The tropics can take some adjusting to. It's hot and humid year-round in Malaysia with temperatures rarely dropping below 20°C, even at night, and usually climbing to 30°C or more during the day. Take it easy when you first arrive and avoid running around in the heat of the midday sun.

Rain tends to arrive in brief torrential downpours, providing a welcome relief from the heat. At certain times of the year it may

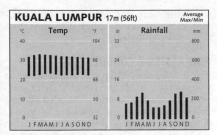

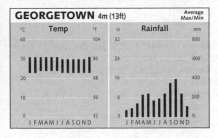

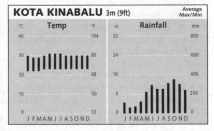

rain every day, but it rarely rains all day. Although the region is monsoonal, it's only the east coast of Peninsular Malaysia that has a real rainy season – elsewhere it's just a time of year when the average rainfall is higher than at other times of the year.

Throughout the region the humidity tends to hover around the 90% mark, but on the peninsula you can always escape from heat and humidity by retreating to the delightfully cool hill stations.

For current weather forecasts check the website of the **Malaysian Meteorological Department** (www.kjc.gov.my/english /weather/weather .html).

For tips on the best times to visit, see p20.

COURSES

The best place to look for interesting courses is KL (p108). Elsewhere in Malaysia, travel to Balok Beach in Pahang to study batik (p288), and to Kota Bharu for cookery and batik courses (p330).

CUSTOMS REGULATIONS

The following can be brought into Malaysia duty free: 1L of alcohol, 225g of tobacco (200 cigarettes or 50 cigars) and souvenirs and gifts not exceeding RM200 (RM500 when coming from Labuan or Langkawi). Cameras, portable radios, perfume, cosmetics and watches do not incur duty.

The list of prohibited items is: counterfeit currency, weapons (including imitations), fireworks, drugs and 'obscene and prejudicial articles' (pornography, for example, and items that may be considered inflammatory, or disruptive to Malaysia's ethnic harmony).

Visitors can freely carry only RM1000 in and out of Malaysia; there's no limit on foreign currency. When you enter Malaysia, you must fill out a Currency Declaration Form on which you are required to declare both the amount of ringgit notes, if the figure exceeds RM1000, and any amount of foreign currency you are carrying. Keep this form in your passport as you must produce it when leaving Malaysia.

Drug trafficking in Malaysia carries the death penalty.

DANGERS & ANNOYANCES

Operators mentioned in this book have been personally checked by the authors and should be reliable. However, you should always check terms and conditions carefully.

Animal Hazards

Rabies occurs in Malaysia, so any bite from an animal should be treated very seriously. Snakes are probably the thing you'll encounter most in the jungle; see p604 for details on how to deal with snake bites.

Scams

Like any big city Kuala Lumpur has its share of scams. A popular one is from people who claim to have a relative studying abroad and need money for them; these always start with the scammer asking you where you come from – the best answer is none at all. Guys dressed as Buddhist monks can often be found around Jln Sultan Ismail in the Golden Triangle – they'll offer you a 'free' good luck charm then expect you to pay a big donation; just try to avoid them.

For details of a scam at the Malaysia–Thailand border see p208.

Theft & Violence

Theft and violence are not particularly common in Malaysia and compared with Indonesia or Thailand it's extremely safe. Nevertheless, it pays to keep a close eye on your belongings, especially your travel documents (passport, travellers cheques etc), which should be kept with you at all times.

Muggings do happen, particularly in KL and Penang, and physical attacks have been known to occur, particularly after hours and in the poorer, run-down areas of cities. We've been told that thieves on motorbikes particularly target women for grab raids on their handbags. Also keep a watch out for sleazy local 'beach boys' in Langkawi and the Perhentians.

Credit-card fraud is a growing problem in Malaysia. Use your cards only at established businesses and guard your credit-card numbers closely.

A small, sturdy padlock is well worth carrying, especially if you are going to be staying at any of the cheap chalets found on Malaysia's beaches, where flimsy padlocks are the norm.

DISCOUNT CARDS

A Hostelling International (HI) card is of limited use in Malaysia, as only a handful of places accept it (see ww.hihostels.com/dba/country-Malaysia-MY.en.htm for the list). The card can also be used to waive the small initial membership fee at some YMCAs and YWCAs. Bring it if you have one.

An international student identity card (ISIC) is worth bringing. Many student discounts, such as for train travel, are

---

TRAVEL ADVISORIES

For the latest travel advisories check the following websites:

Australia (www.smartraveller.gov.au)
Canada (www.voyage.gc.ca)
New Zealand (www.safetravel.govt.nz)
UK (www.fco.gov.uk/en/travelling-and-living-overseas)
USA (www.travel.state.gov/travel)

---

available only for Malaysian students, but some places do offer discounts for international students.

EMBASSIES & CONSULATES

For a full list of Malaysian embassies and consulates outside the country check out www.kln.gov.my. Unless mentioned all the following foreign embassies are in Kuala Lumpur and are generally open 8am to 12.30pm and 1.30pm to 4.30pm Monday to Friday.

Australia (Map p96; ☎ 03-2146 5555; www.australia.org.my; 6 Jln Yap Kwan Seng)

Brunei (Map pp92-3; ☎ 03-2161 2800; Level 19, Menara Tan & Tan, 207 Jln Tun Razak)

Canada (Map pp92-3; ☎ 03-2718 3333; Level 18, Menara Tan & Tan, 207 Jln Tun Razak)

France (Map pp92-3; ☎ 03-2053 5500; 196 Jln Ampang)

Germany (Map pp92-3; ☎ 03-2142 9666; www.kuala-lumpur.diplo.de; Level 26, Menara Tan & Tan, 207 Jln Tun Razak)

Indonesia Georgetown (Off Map p180; ☎ 04-227 5141; 467 Jln Burma, Georgetown, Penang); Kota Kinabalu (Map p342; ☎ 088-218600; Lg Kemajuan, Karamunsing; ❤ 9am-5pm Mon-Fri); Kuala Lumpur (Map pp92-3; ☎ 03-2116 4100; 233 Jln Tun Razak) Visas (RM170) ready in one day; Kuching (Map p410; (☎ 082-421734; 6th fl, Bangunan Binamas, Jln Padungan; ❤ 8.30am-noon & 2-4pm Mon-Fri); Tawau (Off Map p392; ☎ 089-772052; Jln Apas, Tawau, Sabah)

Ireland (Map pp92-3; ☎ 03-2161 2963; Ireland House, The Amp Walk, 218 Jln Ampang)

Netherlands (Map pp92-3; ☎ 03-2168 6200; www.netherlands.org.my; 7th fl, The Amp Walk, 218 Jln Ampang)

New Zealand (Map p96; ☎ 03-2078 2533; Level 21, Menara IMC, 8 Jln Sultan Ismail)

Singapore (Map pp92-3; ☎ 03-2161 6277; 209 Jln Tun Razak)

Thailand Georgetown (Off Map p180; ☎ 04-226 8029; 1 Jln Tunku Abdul Rahman, Georgetown, Penang); Kota Bharu (Map p328; ☎ 09-744 0867; 4426 Jln Pengkalan Chepa, Kota Bharu, Kelantan); Kuala Lumpur (Map pp92-3; ☎ 03-2148 8222; 206 Jln Ampang)

UK (Map pp92-3; ☎ 03-2148 2122; www.britain.org.my; 185 Jln Ampang)

USA (Map pp92-3; ☎ 03-2168 5000; http://malaysia.usembassy.gov; 376 Jln Tun Razak)

FESTIVALS & EVENTS

With so many cultures and religions, there's an amazing number of occasions to celebrate in Malaysia. Although some of them have a fixed date, the Hindus, Muslims and Chinese

---

RAMADAN & ASSOCIATED FESTIVALS

The major Islamic events each year are connected with Ramadan, the month during which Muslims do not eat or drink from sunrise to sunset. Fifteen days before the start of Ramadan, on Nisfu Night, it is believed the souls of the dead visit their homes. During Ramadan Lailatul Qadar (Night of Grandeur), Muslims celebrate the arrival of the Quran on earth, before its revelation by Mohammed. A Quran-reading competition is held in KL (and extensively televised) during Ramadan.

Hari Raya Puasa marks the end of the month-long fast, with two days of joyful celebration. This is the major holiday of the Muslim calendar and it can be difficult to find accommodation in Malaysia, particularly on the east coast. During this time everyone wears new clothes, homes are cleaned and redecorated, and everyone seems to visit everyone else.

---

all follow a lunar calendar, so the dates for many events vary each year. Tourism Malaysia publishes a Calendar of Events pamphlet with specific dates and venues of various festivals and parades – state tourist offices have more detailed listings.

Apart from Ramadan (see above) the other major Islamic event is Hari Raya Haji, marking the successful completion of the hajj (pilgrimage to Mecca). It's a two-day holiday in many of the peninsula states, and is marked by the consumption of large amounts of cakes and sweets. For the Chinese community the major event of the year is Chinese New Year; the major Indian celebration is Deepavali.

There are many other special events, ranging from fun runs, kite-flying and fishing competitions to the Malaysian Grand Prix – see the destination chapters for details of events specific to particular towns and cities.

January–February

Thai Pongal A Hindu harvest festival marking the beginning of the Hindu month of Thai, considered the luckiest month of the year. This Tamil celebration is always held on 14 January.

Chinese New Year Dragon dances and pedestrian parades mark the start of the new year. Families hold open house, unmarried relatives (especially children) receive *ang pow* (money in red packets), businesses traditionally clear their debts and everybody wishes you *kong hee fatt choy* (a happy and prosperous new year). The New Year is celebrated on 14 February 2010, 3 February 2011 and 23 January 2012.

Birthday of the Jade Emperor Nine days after New Year, this Chinese festival honours Yu Huang, the supreme ruler of heaven, with offerings at temples.

Chap Goh Meh 15 days after Chinese New Year, the celebrations officially end.

Thaipusam Dramatic Hindu festival (now banned in India), in which devotees honour Lord Subramaniam with acts of amazing physical resilience – see p52.

Prophet Mohammed's Birthday Muslims pray and religious leaders recite verses from the Quran. In 2010 it will be held on 26 February, in 2011 on 15 February and in 2012 on 4 February.

March–April

Malaysian Grand Prix Formula One's big outing in Southeast Asia is held at the Sepang International Circuit in Selangor (see p138) either at the end of March or early April.

Panguni Uttiram The marriage of Shiva to Shakti and of Lord Subramaniam to Theivani is celebrated on the full-moon day of the Tamil month of Panguni.

Birthday of the Goddess of Mercy Offerings are made to the very popular Kuan Yin at her temples across the region.

Cheng Ming On Cheng Ming, Chinese traditionally visit the tombs of their ancestors to make offerings and to tend, clean and repair the tombs.

Sri Rama Navami A nine-day festival held by those of the Brahmin caste to honour the Hindu hero of the Ramayana, Sri Rama.

Birthday of the Monkey God The birthday of T'se Tien Tai Seng Yeh is celebrated twice a year. Mediums pierce their cheeks and tongues with skewers and go into trances during which they write special charms in blood.

April–May

Songkran Festival A traditional Thai Buddhist New Year festival in which Buddha images are bathed.

Chithirai Vishu The start of the Hindu New Year.

Birthday of the Queen of Heaven Ma Cho Po, the queen of heaven and goddess of the sea, is honoured at her temples.

Wesak Day Buddha's birth, enlightenment and death are celebrated with various events, including the release of caged birds to symbolise the setting free of captive souls and processions in KL, JB, Melaka and Penang. It's celebrated on 27 May 2010, 17 May 2011 and 6 May 2012.

June

Gawai Dayak Annual Sarawak Dayak Festival on 1 and 2 June to mark the end of the rice season, with war dances, cockfights and blowpipe events.

Festa de San Pedro Christian celebration on 29 June in honour of the patron saint of the fishing community; notably celebrated by the Eurasian-Portuguese community of Melaka.

Birthday of the God of War Kuan Ti, who has the ability to avert war and to protect people during war, is honoured on his birthday.

Dragon Boat Festival Commemorates the death of a Chinese saint who drowned himself. In an attempt to save him, the local fishing community paddled out to sea, beating drums to scare away any fish that might attack him. To mark the anniversary, this festival is celebrated from June to August, with boat races in Penang and other places.

July–August
Birthday of Kuan Yin The goddess of mercy has another birthday!

Sri Krishna Jayanti A 10-day Hindu festival celebrating popular events in Krishna's life is highlighted on day eight with celebrations of his birthday. The Laxmi Narayan Temple in KL is a particular focus.

Rainforest World Music Festival Held annually either in July or August for three days at the Sarawak Cultural Village (p425), this wonderful music and arts festival features musicians from around the world and highlights indigenous music from Borneo.

August–September
Festival of the Seven Sisters Chinese girls pray to the weaving maid for good husbands.

Festival of the Hungry Ghosts The souls of the dead are released for one day of feasting and entertainment on earth. Chinese operas and other events are laid on for them and food is put out. The ghosts eat the spirit of the food, but thoughtfully leave the substance for mortal celebrants. Mainly in Penang.

National Day (Hari Kebangsaan) Malaysia celebrates its independence on 31 August with events all over the country, but particularly in KL where there are parades and a variety of performances in the Lake Gardens.

Vinayagar Chaturthi During the Tamil month of Avani (around August and September), prayers are offered to Vinayagar, another name for the popular elephant-headed god Ganesh.

Moon Cake Festival The overthrow of the Mongol warlords in ancient China is celebrated by eating moon cakes and lighting colourful paper lanterns. Moon cakes are filled with bean paste, lotus seeds and sometimes a duck egg-yolk.

September–October
Navarathri In the Tamil month of Purattasi, the Hindu festival of 'Nine Nights' is dedicated to the wives of Shiva, Vishnu and Brahma. Young girls are dressed as the goddess Kali.

Festival of the Nine Emperor Gods Nine days of Chinese operas, processions and other events honour the nine emperor gods. Fire-walking ceremonies are held on the evening of the ninth day at the Kau Ong Yah Temples in KL and Penang.

Puja Ketek Offerings are brought to Buddhist shrines (ketek) in the state of Kelantan during this festival in October. Traditional dances are often performed.

October–November
Thimithi (Fire-Walking Ceremony) Hindu devotees prove their faith by walking across glowing coals at temples in Melaka.

Kantha Sashti Subramaniam, a great fighter against the forces of evil, is honoured during the Hindu month of Aipasi.

Deepavali Later in the month of Aipasi, Rama's victory over the demon king Ravana is celebrated with the Festival of Lights, when tiny oil lamps are lit outside the homes of Hindu people, as it's believed that Lakshmi, the goddess of wealth, will not enter an unlit home. For business people, this is the time to start a new financial year, and for the family a predawn oil bath, new clothes and lots of sweets is the order of the day. In 2010 Deepavali is celebrated on 5 November, in 2011 on 26 October and in 2012, 13 November.

Birthday of Kuan Yin This popular goddess of mercy gets to celebrate her birthday for the third time in the year.

Kartikai Deepam Huge bonfires are lit to commemorate Shiva's appearance as a pillar of fire following an argument with Vishnu and Brahma. The Thandayuthapani Temple in Muar is a major site for this festival.

Guru Nanak's Birthday The birthday of Guru Nanak, founder of the Sikh religion, is celebrated on 22 November.

December
Winter Solstice Festival A Chinese festival to offer thanks for a good harvest.

FOOD
The region's food and drink offerings are simply terrific, with unbeatable variety, high quality and pleasantly low costs. For a complete description, see p60.

Restaurant and cafe listings in this guide give an indication of how much you'll pay for a main course or meal (including starter and soft drink). In general, for a budget meal you'll be looking at under RM10, from RM10 to RM39 for a midrange meal, and RM40 and above for a top-end meal.

GAY & LESBIAN TRAVELLERS
The level of gay tolerance in Malaysia is directly related to its status as a predominantly conservative Muslim country. It's illegal for men of any age to have sex with other men.

In addition, the Islamic *syariah* laws (which apply only to Muslims) forbid sodomy and cross-dressing. Outright persecution of gays and lesbians is rare but not unknown.

Gay and lesbian travellers should avoid behaviour that attracts unwanted attention. Malaysians are conservative about displays of public affection; women, and straight Indian men, can get away with same-sex hand-holding, but an overtly gay couple doing the same would attract attention. It is highly unlikely, however, that you will encounter vocal or aggressive homophobia.

Given all this, you may be surprised to hear there's actually a fairly active and visible gay scene in KL; see p120. The lesbian scene is less obvious but, naturally, exists for those willing to seek it out. Start looking for information on www.utopia-asia.com or www.fridae.com, both of which provide good coverage of gay and lesbian events and activities across Asia.

The **PT Foundation** (www.ptfmalaysia.org) is a voluntary nonprofit organisation providing sexuality and HIV/AIDS education, care and support programs for marginalised communities.

HOLIDAYS

In addition to national public holidays, each state has its own holidays, usually associated with the sultan's birthday or a Muslim celebration. Muslim holidays move forward 10 or 11 days each year. Hindu and Chinese holiday dates also vary, but fall roughly within the same months each year.

Public Holidays

January–February

New Year's Day 1 January (except in Johor, Kedah, Kelantan, Perlis and Terengganu)
Thaipusam Variable (in Johor, Negeri Sembilan, Perak, Penang and Selangor only)
Federal Territory Day 1 February (in KL, Labuan and Putrajaya only)
Sultan of Kedah's Birthday 7 February (in Kedah only)
Chinese New Year Variable, two days in late January/early February (one day only in Kelantan and Terengganu)
Prophet Mohammed's birthday Variable, February/March
Hari Raya Haji Variable, February/March

March

Sultan of Selangor's Birthday Second Saturday of March (in Selangor only)
Anniversary of Installation of Sultan of Terengganu 21 March (in Terengganu only)

Muslim New Year Variable
Sultan of Kelantan's Birthday 30 and 31 March (in Kelantan only)

April

Sultan of Johor's Birthday 8 April (in Johor only)
Good Friday Variable (in Sarawak and Sabah only)
Melaka Historical City Day 15 April (in Melaka only)
Sultan of Perak's Birthday 19 April (in Perak only)
Sultan of Terengganu's Birthday 29 April (in Terengganu only)

May

Labour Day 1 May
Raja of Perlis' Birthday Variable, April/May (in Perlis only)
Wesak Day Variable
Harvest Festival Variable (in Sabah and Labuan only)

June

Yang di-Pertuan Agong's (King's) Birthday First Saturday in June
Dayak Festival 1 and 2 June (in Sarawak only)
Prophet's Birthday Variable

July

Governor of Penang's Birthday Second Saturday in July (in Penang only)
Governor of Negeri Sembilan's Birthday 19 July (in Negeri Sembilan only)

August

Malaysia's National Day (Hari Kebangsaan) 31 August

September

Malaysia Day 16 September (in Sabah only)
Hari Raya Puasa Variable September/October (two day celebration of end of Ramadan)

October–November

Governor of Melaka's Birthday Second Saturday in October (in Melaka only)
Sultan of Pahang's Birthday 24 October (in Pahang only)
Israk Mikraj (Ascension of the Prophet) Variable (in Kedah and Negeri Sembilan only)
Deepavali Variable (no holiday in Sarawak and Labuan)
Awal Ramadan (Beginning of Ramadan) Variable (in Johor and Melaka only)

December

Nuzul Al-Quran Variable (in Kelantan, Pahang, Perak, Perlis, Selangor and Terengganu)
Hari Raya Puasa Variable
Christmas Day 25 December

School Holidays

Schools in Malaysia break for holidays five times a year. The actual dates vary from state to state but are generally in January (one week), March (two weeks), May (three weeks), August (one week) and October (four weeks).

INSURANCE

It's always a good idea to take out travel insurance. Check the small print to see if the policy covers potentially dangerous sporting activities such as diving or trekking, and make sure that it adequately covers your valuables. Health-wise, you may prefer a policy that pays doctors or hospitals directly rather than your having to pay on the spot and claim later. If you have to claim later, make sure that you keep all documentation. Check that the policy covers ambulances or an emergency flight home.

A few credit cards offer limited, sometimes full, travel insurance to the holder.

For information on health insurance, refer to p595 and for info on car insurance see p487.

INTERNET ACCESS

You'll have to be deep in the jungle to be off-line in Malaysia. KL is as wired a city as they come with ubiquitous hot spots for wi-fi connections (often free; see p94) and cheap internet cafes typically charging RM3 per hour for broadband access. In the remote reaches of the peninsula and Malaysian Borneo don't expect the internet to be fast though.

Digital warriors should equip themselves with a three-pronged, square-pin plug (as used in the UK) or adaptor for their computer. If your computer is not wi-fi enabled, check whether the internal or card modem is enabled to work outside your home country – not all are.

If you intend to rely on cybercafes, you'll need to carry three pieces of information with you to enable you to access your internet mail account: your incoming (POP or IMAP) mail server name, your account name and your password. Your internet service provider (ISP) or network supervisor will be able to give you these.

Among the internet providers in Malaysia are **Jaring** (www.jaring.my) and **Telekom Malaysia** (www.tm. com.my).

LEGAL MATTERS

In any dealings with the local police it will pay to be deferential. You're most likely to come into contact with them either through reporting a crime (some of the big cities in Malaysia have tourist police stations for this purpose) or while driving. Minor misdemeanours may be overlooked, but don't count on it, and be careful about offering anyone a bribe – Malaysia is not that sort of country.

Drug trafficking carries a mandatory death penalty. A number of foreigners have been executed in Malaysia, some of them for possession of amazingly small quantities of heroin. Even possession of tiny amounts can bring down a lengthy jail sentence and a beating with the *rotan* (cane). Just don't do it.

MAPS

Periplus (https://peripluspublishinggroup.com) have maps covering Malaysia, Peninsular Malaysia and KL. Tourism Malaysia's free *Map of Malaysia* has useful distance charts, facts about the country and inset maps of many major cities.

For accurate maps of rural areas contact the **National Survey & Mapping Department** (Ibu Pejabat Ukur & Pemetaan Malaysia; Map pp92-3; ☎ 03-2617 0800; www.jupem.gov.my; Jln Semarak, Kuala Lumpur; ⊙ 7.30am-5.30pm Mon-Fri).

MONEY

See the Quick Reference page on the inside front cover for currency exchange rates.

ATMs & Credit Cards

MasterCard and Visa are the most widely accepted brands. Banks will accept credit cards for over-the-counter cash advances, or you can make ATM withdrawals if you have your PIN. Many banks are also linked to international banking networks such as Cirrus (the most common), Maestro and Plus, allowing withdrawals from overseas savings accounts.

Maybank (www.maybank2u.com.my), Malaysia's biggest bank with branches everywhere, accepts both Visa and MasterCard. HSBC accepts Visa, and the Standard Chartered Bank accepts MasterCard. If you have any questions about whether your cards will be accepted in Malaysia, ask your home bank about its reciprocal relationships with Malaysian banks.

Contact details for credit card companies in Malaysia:

American Express (☎ 2050 0000; www.american express.com/malaysia)

Diners Card (☎ 2161 1055; www.diners.com.my)

MasterCard (☎ 1800 804 594; www.mastercard .com/sea)

Visa (☎ 1800 802 997; www.visa-asia.com)

Currency

The ringgit (RM) is made up of 100 sen. Coins in use are 1 sen, 5 sen, 10 sen, 20 sen and 50 sen; notes come in RM1, RM5, RM10, RM50 and RM100.

Malaysians sometimes refer to ringgit as 'dollars', which is the old name used for the country's currency. Unless someone makes it clear that they are talking about US dollars, you can be sure they mean ringgit.

Be sure to carry plenty of small bills with you when venturing outside cities – in most cases people cannot change bills larger than RM10.

Taxes & Refunds

There is no general sales tax but there is a government tax of 5% at some midrange and all top-end hotels and many larger restaurants (in addition to an establishment's 10% service fee).

Travellers Cheques & Cash

Banks in the region are efficient and there are plenty of moneychangers. For changing cash or travellers cheques, banks usually charge a commission (around RM10 per transaction, with a possible small fee per cheque), whereas moneychangers have no charges but their rates vary more – so know what the current rate is before using moneychangers. Compared with a bank, you'll generally get a better rate for cash at a moneychanger – it's usually quicker too. Away from the tourist centres, moneychangers' rates are often poorer and they may not change travellers cheques.

All major brands of travellers cheques are accepted across the region. Cash in major currencies is also readily exchanged, though like everywhere else in the world the US dollar has a slight edge.

PHOTOGRAPHY

Malaysians usually have no antipathy to being photographed, although, of course, it's polite to ask permission before photographing people and taking pictures in mosques or temples. For advice on taking better photos, Lonely Planet's *Travel Photography: A Guide to Taking Better Pictures* is written by travel photographer Richard I'Anson.

Burning digital photos to a disk can easily be arranged at photo development shops across the country; it will cost around RM10 per disk. Print film is also commonly available – a 36-exposure roll is around RM9. Slide film is a little harder to come by and more expensive – a 36-exposure roll of Fuji Velvia averages RM30. Professional slide film can be found only in the biggest cities – if you're a serious photographer, you may want to bring your own slide film.

Processing prices for a 36-exposure roll of slide film range from RM15 to RM18 (mounted), and 60 sen to 70 sen per exposure for print film. In bigger cities like KL, you'll find photo shops with a decent range of equipment at reasonable prices.

POST

Pos Malaysia Berhad (☎ 1300 300 300; www.pos.com. my) runs an efficient postal system with good poste restante at the major post offices. Post offices are open daily from 8am to 5pm, and closed on Sunday and public holidays (closed on Fridays and public holidays in Kedah, Kelantan and Terengganu).

Aerograms and postcards cost 50 sen to send to any destination. Letters weighing 20g or less cost 90 sen to Asia, RM1.40 to Australia or New Zealand, RM1.50 to the UK and Europe, and RM1.80 to North America. Parcel rates range around RM20 to RM60 for a 1kg parcel, depending on the destination.

Main post offices in larger cities sell packaging materials and stationery.

TELEPHONE

Landline services are provided by the national monopoly Telekom Malaysia (TM; www.tm .com.my).

Fax

Fax facilities are available at TM offices in larger cities and at some main post offices. If you can't find one of these try a travel agency or large hotel.

International Calls

If you have your mobile phone with you, once you've sorted out a local SIM you should have no problem dialling overseas. Otherwise our advice is to buy a cheap local mobile phone to avoid the frustration of having to deal with the neglected and run-down public phone system.

International direct dial (IDD) calls and operator-assisted calls can be made from any private phone. The access code for making international calls to most countries is ☎ 00. Call ☎ 108 for the international operator and ☎ 103 for directory enquiries. You'll get the best rate if you buy an international prepaid telephone card, available from 7-Elevens and other small grocery stores and newsagents.

To make an IDD call from a payphone, you'll have to find a TM payphone marked 'international' (with which you can use coins or TM phonecards; dial the international access code and then the number). Sadly, there are very few regular payphones that allow IDD calls, apparently because of a rash of counterfeit phonecards.

The third option is to go to a TM office, where you can make IDD or operator-assisted international calls.

If you're making a call to Malaysia from outside the country, dial ☎ 60, drop the 0 before the Malaysian area code, then dial the number you want. See individual destination chapters for specific area codes.

Local Calls

Making domestic telephone calls in Malaysia is usually a simple matter, provided you can find a working payphone (try train stations, shopping malls and big hotels). You can direct-dial long-distance between all major towns in Malaysia. Local calls cost 10 sen for three minutes.

Although there are a few private operator payphones dotted around, they're so rare that they are sure to become extinct. Less rare – although hardly common – are TM payphones which take coins or prepaid cards which are available from TM offices, post offices and some shops such as 7-Eleven. Here you'll also find a range of calling cards in amounts ranging from RM10 to RM60 in value.

Mobile Phones

As long as you have arranged to have 'global-roaming' facilities with your home provider, your GSM digital phone will automatically tune into one of the region's digital networks.

If not, and you have your phone with you, the simplest way to go mobile is to buy a prepaid SIM card for one of the services on arrival in the country.

Even if you've not brought a phone with you it's far simpler to buy a cheap mobile on arrival and use that to make your calls while in Malaysia rather than deal with the dilapidated public phone network.

The three main mobile-phone service providers are **Celcom** (www.celcom.com.my; numbers beginning with 013 or 019), **DiGi** (www.digi.com.my; numbers beginning with 016), and **Maxis** (www.maxis.com.my; numbers beginning with 012 or 017). If you're sticking to Peninsular Malaysia any of the three are fine, but if you're heading into the remoter parts of Malaysian Borneo then get Celcom, which has the largest coverage of the three (it works in distant regions like Bario and Mulu).

Rates for a local call are around 40 sen per minute and an SMS is 10 to 15 sen. Top-up cards for prepaid SIM cards are available at all 7-Elevens and, if you're planning on calling overseas a lot, it's probably worthwhile getting a calling card too; a good one is TM's **iTalk** (www.i-talk.com.my).

TIME

Malaysia is 16 hours ahead of US Pacific Standard Time (San Francisco and Los Angeles), 13 hours ahead of US Eastern Standard Time (New York), eight hours ahead of GMT/UTC (London) and two hours behind Australian Eastern Standard Time (Sydney and Melbourne). Thus, noon in the region is 8pm in Los Angeles and 11pm in New York (the previous day), 4am in London, and 2pm in Sydney and Melbourne.

TOILETS

Although there are still some places with Asian squat-style toilets in Malaysia, you'll most often find Western-style ones these days. At public facilities toilet paper is not usually provided. Instead, you will find a hose which you are supposed to use as a bidet or, in cheaper places, a bucket of water and a tap. If you're not comfortable with this, remember to take packets of tissues or toilet paper wherever you go.

TOURIST INFORMATION

Tourism Malaysia (www.tourismmalaysia.gov.my) has an efficient network of overseas offices, which are useful for predeparture planning.

Unfortunately, its domestic offices are less helpful and are often unable to give specific information about destinations and transport. Nonetheless, they do stock some decent brochures as well as the excellent *Map of Malaysia*.

Within Malaysia there are also a number of state tourist-promotion organisations, such as KL's **Malaysian Tourist Centre** (p95) and the office of **Tourism Melaka** (p242), which often have more detailed information about specific areas.

Where there are representatives, Tourism Malaysia and state tourism offices are listed in individual destination entries.

Tourism Malaysia maintains the following offices overseas:

Australia Melbourne (☎ 03-9654 3177; 355 Exhibition Street, Melbourne, VIC 3000); Perth (☎ 08-9481 0400; MAS Bldg, 56 William St, Perth, WA 6000); Sydney (☎ 02-9299 4441; Level 2, 171 Clarence St, Sydney, NSW 2000)

Canada (☎ 604-689 8899; www.malaysiantourism.ca; 1590-111 West Georgia St, Vancouver BC V6E 4M3)

France (☎ 01-4297 4171; www.ontmalaisie.com; 29 rue des Pyramides, 75001 Paris)

Germany (☎ 069-460 923 420; www.tourismmalaysia .de; Weissfrauenstrasse 12-16, D-60311 Frankfurt-am-Main)

Japan Osaka (☎ 06-6444 1220; 10F Cotton Nissay Biru, 1-8-2 Otsubo-Honmachi, Nishi-ku, Osaka 550-0004); Tokyo (☎ 03-3501 8691; www.tourismmalaysia.or.jp; 5F Chiyoda Biru, 1-6-4 Yurakucho, Chiyoda-ku, Tokyo 100-0006)

Singapore (☎ 02-6532 6321; 01-01 B/C/D, 80 Robinson Rd, Singapore 068898)

Thailand (☎ 02-631 1994; Unit 1001 Liberty Sq, 287 Silom Rd, Bangkok 10500)

UK (☎ 020-7930 7932; 57 Trafalgar Sq, London WC2N 5DU)

USA Los Angeles (☎ 213-689 9702; 818 West 7th St, Suite 907, Los Angeles, CA 90017); New York (☎ 212-754 1114; 120 East 56th St, Suite 810, New York, NY 10022)

TRAVELLERS WITH DISABILITIES

For the mobility impaired, Malaysia can be a nightmare. In most cities and towns there are often no footpaths, kerbs are very high, construction sites are everywhere, and crossings are few and far between. On the upside, taxis are cheap and both Malaysia Airlines and KTM (the national rail service) offer 50% discounts on travel for travellers with disabilities.

Before setting off get in touch with your national support organisation (preferably with the travel officer, if there is one). For general travel advice in Australia contact **Nican** (☎ 02-

---

> ### VISA STAMPS
>
> We've heard of travellers having problems when they leave Malaysia after having entered the country by train from Singapore – this is because the Malaysian immigration officials at Singapore's railway station, which is the southern termination point for Malaysia's Keretapi Tanah Melayu (KTM), do not stamp your passport. This shouldn't be a problem as long as you keep your immigration card and your train ticket to show how you entered the country. Your details will have been input into the Malaysian immigration computer and should come up when you exit. Stand your ground if anyone asks you to pay a fine.

6241 1220; www.nican.com.au); in the UK contact **Tourism For All** (☎ 0845 124 9971; www.tourismforall .org.uk); and in the USA try **Accessible Journeys** (☎ 800-846 4537; www.disabilitytravel.com), an agency specialising in travel for those with disabilities, or **Mobility International USA** (☎ 541-343 1284; www.miusa.org).

VISAS

Visitors must have a valid passport or internationally recognised travel document valid for at least six months beyond the date of entry into Malaysia. The following gives a brief overview of other requirements – full details of visa regulations are available on the website www.kln .gov.my.

Commonwealth citizens (except those from India, Bangladesh, Sri Lanka and Pakistan), and citizens of the Republic of Ireland, Switzerland, the Netherlands, San Marino and Liechtenstein do not require a visa to visit Malaysia.

Citizens of Austria, Belgium, the Czech Republic, Denmark, Finland, France, Germany, Hungary, Iceland, Italy, Japan, Luxembourg, Norway, the Slovak Republic, South Korea, Sweden, the USA and most Arab countries do not require a visa for a visit of less than three months.

Citizens of Greece, South Africa and many South American and African countries do not require a visa for a visit of less than one month. Most other nationalities are given a shorter stay-period or require a visa.

Citizens of Israel cannot enter Malaysia.

Nationals of most countries are given a 30- or 60-day visa on arrival, depending on the expected length of stay. As a general rule, if you arrive by air you will be given 60 days automatically, though coming overland you may be given 30 days unless you specifically ask for a 60-day permit. It's possible to get an extension at an immigration office in Malaysia for a total stay of up to three months. This is a straightforward procedure that is easily done in major Malaysian cities (immigration offices are listed under Information in the relevant destination chapters).

Sabah and Sarawak are treated like separate countries. Your passport will be checked on arrival in each state and a new-stay permit issued. You are usually issued with a 30-day permit on arrival in Sarawak or Sabah. Travelling directly from either Sabah or Sarawak back to Peninsular Malaysia, however, there are no formalities and you do not start a new entry period, so your 30-day permit from Sabah or Sarawak remains valid. You can then extend your initial 30-day permit, though it can be difficult to get an extension in Sarawak. For more information see the Sabah (p340) and Sarawak (p407) chapters.

VOLUNTEERING

Opportunities include:

All Women's Action Society Malaysia (www.awam.org.my) Aims to improve the lives of women in Malaysia by lobbying for a just, democratic and equitable society with respect and equality for both genders.

Amnesty International (www.aimalaysia.org) Help out the local branch of the human rights organisation on their various campaigns.

LASSie (www.langkawilassie.org.my) Dog and cat lovers may want to help out at the Langkawi Animal Shelter & Sanctuary Foundation, next to Bon Ton Resort (see p222).

Ma' Daerah Turtle Sanctuary In Terengganu (p316).

Malaysian AIDS Council (www.mac.org.my) Assist in their campaigning work.

Malaysian Nature Society (www.mns.org.my) Check their website or drop them a line to find out ways you can get involved in helping preserve Malaysia's natural environment.

Miso Walai Homestay Program (http://misowalai homestay.com) Gets travellers involved with local wetlands restoration projects.

PAWS (www.paws.org.my) Animal rescue shelter near KL's Subang Airport.

Real Gap (www.realgap.com) Arranges trips that involve environmental project and community work in Sabah, or work as an assistant at Zoo Negara near KL.

Regional Environmental Awareness Cameron Highlands (Reach; www.reach.org.my) Take part in reforestation and recycling programs in the Cameron Highlands.

Sepilok Orang-utan Rehabilitation Centre (p375) Has one of the best established volunteer programs for animal lovers.

Travellers Worldwide (www.travellersworldwide.com) Offers a range of programs including working on wildlife reserves, with disabled children, teaching English and scuba-diving work experience.

Trekforce (www.trekforce.org.uk) Offers a 10-week course working with the Kelabit people on community projects in Sarawak's Kelabit Highlands

Wild Asia (www.wildasia.org) Check this organisation's website for a variety of volunteer options generally connected with the environment and sustainable tourism in the region.

World Challenge (www.world-challenge.co.uk) Brings a lot of (mainly UK) volunteers to Malaysia for conservation and other projects.

Zoo Negara (p132) Help the zookeepers feed and care for their charges.

WOMEN TRAVELLERS

The key for women travelling with minimum hassle in Malaysia is to blend in with the locals, which means dressing modestly and being respectful, especially in areas of stronger Muslim religious sensibilities, such as the east coast of Peninsular Malaysia. Regardless of what local non-Muslim women wear, it's better to be safe than sorry – in the past we've had reports of attacks on skimpily-clad women ranging from minor verbal aggravation to full-on physical assault.

Be proactive about your own safety. Treat overly friendly strangers, both male and female, with a good deal of caution. In cheap hotels check for small peepholes in the walls and doors. You could always plug the holes with tissue paper or try asking to change rooms, but if you're on a budget you may not have much of a choice in some towns. On island resorts, stick to crowded beaches, and choose a chalet close to reception and other travellers.

No matter how limited your budget, it sometimes pays to upgrade – take taxis after dark or in seedy areas of town, and treat yourself to a midrange hotel if all your other options are brothels or the equivalent. We've also had reports of women being targeted in busy city areas by thieves on motorbikes who snatch handbags – make sure you walk with your bag slung across your body, away from the road.

In conservative Muslim areas, consider tying a bandanna over your hair as a minimal concession to the headscarf worn by most Muslim women. When you're visiting mosques, cover all limbs, and either borrow a headscarf at the entrance to the mosque or buy one of the cheap silk ones that are available on the street. At the beach, most Malaysian women swim fully clothed in T-shirts and shorts, so don't even think about going topless.

Tampons and pads are widely available in Malaysia, especially in the big cities, and over-the-counter medications for common gynaecological health problems (like yeast infections) are also fairly easy to find.

WORK

There are possibilities for those who seek them out, from professional-level jobs in finance, journalism and the oil industry to temporary jobs at some guesthouses and dive centres in popular resort areas. Those with teaching credentials can find English-teaching jobs in Malaysia, though pickings are slim compared to Japan and Korea. Teachers can check some of the many TEFL sites, including Edufind Jobs (www.jobs.edufind.com).

Depending on the nature of your job, you'll need either an Expatriate Personnel Visa or a Temporary Employment Visa. For details and requirements, check the Immigration Department of Malaysia's website (www.imi. gov.my).

For details of volunteer work see opposite.

Malaysia Transport

CONTENTS

GETTING THERE & AWAY

ENTERING MALAYSIA

The main requirements are a passport that's valid for travel for at least six months, proof of an onward ticket and adequate funds for your stay, although you will rarely be asked to prove this. Sabah and Sarawak have additional entry procedures; see p407 and p340.

For details of visa and other entry requirements, see p477. Flights, tours and rail tickets can be booked online at www.lonelyplanet.com/travel_services.

AIR

Airports & Airlines

Kuala Lumpur International Airport (KLIA; Map p130; www.klia.com.my) at Sepang, 75km south of Kuala Lumpur (KL), is the main gateway. Near KLIA is the Low Cost Carrier Terminal (LCC-T), from which **AirAsia** (www.airasia.com) operates. Together both of these terminals handle the bulk of international flights, with the exception of a few flights from Asia and Australia, which come via Penang, Kuching, Kota Kinabalu and a few other cities (see the relevant chapters for specific airport details).

For airline offices in KL and other cities see the regional chapters.

THINGS CHANGE...

The information in this chapter is particularly vulnerable to change. Check directly with the airline or a travel agent to make sure you understand how a fare (and ticket you may buy) works and be aware of the security requirements for international travel. Shop carefully. The details given in this chapter should be regarded as pointers and are not a substitute for your own careful, up-to-date research.

AIRLINES FLYING TO/FROM MALAYSIA
AirAsia (www.airasia.com)
Batavia Air (www.batavia-air.co.id)
Berjaya Air (www.berjaya-air.com)
Cathay Pacific (www.cathaypacific.com)
Emirates (www.emirates.com)
Eva Air (www.evaair.com/html/b2c/english/)
Firefly (www.fireflyz.com.my)
Kartika Airlines (www.kartika-airlines.com)
Malaysia Airlines (www.malaysiaairlines.com)
Qantas (www.qantas.com)
Royal Brunei Airlines (www.bruneiair.com)
Silk Air (www.silkair.com)
Singapore Airlines (www.singaporeair.com)

Tickets

When shopping for a ticket, you should compare the cost of flying into Malaysia versus the cost of flying into Singapore. From Singapore you can travel overland to almost any place in Peninsular Malaysia in less than a day, and Singapore also has direct flights to Malaysian Borneo and Brunei. KL and Singapore are also good places to buy tickets for onward travel.

To research and buy a ticket on the internet, try these online booking services:

www.cheapflights.com Really does post some of the cheapest flights, but get in early to get the bargains.

www.dialaflight.com Offers worldwide flights out of Europe and the UK.

www.expedia.com A good site for checking worldwide flight prices.

www.kayak.com Great search engine for flight deals with links through to its selections.

www.lastminute.com Start here and choose sites specifically for Australia, the US and the UK, as well as a variety of other European countries.

www.statravel.com STA Travel's US website. There are also UK and Australian sites (www.statravel.co.uk and www.statravel.com.au).

www.travel.com.au A good site for Australians to find cheap flights.

Australia

Discounted fares from Melbourne or Sydney to Kuala Lumpur range from around A$800 to A$1300 return, although purchase your ticket far enough in advance with AirAsia and you can get deals as low as A$391 from Perth, A$630 from Brisbane and AS$646 from Melbourne. **Malaysia Airlines** (MAS; www.malaysiaairlines.com), **Singapore Airlines** (www.singaporeair.com) and **Qantas** (www.qantas.com) all offer good deals; also check some of the Middle Eastern airlines that fly between Europe and Australia.

Two well-known agencies for cheap fares, with offices throughout Australia, are **Flight Centre** (☎ 133 133; www.flightcentre.com.au) and **STA Travel** (☎ 1300 733 035; www.statravel.com.au).

Brunei

Royal Brunei Airlines (www.bruneiair.com), Malaysia Airlines and AirAsia have direct flights between Bandar Seri Begawan and KL: advance purchase tickets on AirAsia go for as little as B$91. For more details on flights into and out of Brunei see p593.

Canada

There are no direct flights between Canada and Malaysia; the cheapest fares are going to be on an airline like **Eva Air** (www.evaair.com/html/b2c/english/) via Taiwan. For flights to Malaysia, low-season return fares from Vancouver average C$1200; from Toronto C$1350.

Travel CUTS (☎ 866 246 9762; www.travelcuts.com) is Canada's national student travel agency.

China & Hong Kong

AirAsia return flights to KL from Shenzhen start from around Y1000; the company also has budget services to Guangzhou, Guilin, Haikou, Hangzhou (for Shanghai) and Tianjin. For other options check the Chinese site of **STA Travel** (www.statravel.com.cn).

Return flights from Hong Kong start from around HK$1175 with AirAsia. Cathay Pacific also has direct flights from Hong Kong to Penang and Kota Kinabalu.

MALAYSIA TRANSPORT

The Tsim Sha Tsui area is Hong Kong's budget travel-agency centre. Try **Hong Kong Student Travel** (☎ 2730 2800; www.hkst.com) or **Traveller Service** (☎ 2375 2222; www.taketraveller.com).

Continental Europe

There's not much variation in fares from the main European cities. All the major airlines as well as travel agencies are usually offering some sort of deal, so shop around. From Paris to KL costs as little as €720 return with **Emirates** (www.emirates.com).

Specialising in youth and student fares **Nouvelles Frontières** (☎ 0825-000 747; www.nouvelles-frontieres.fr) has branches across France. Also try **Anyway.com** (☎ 0892-302 301; http://voyages.anyway.com) and **Lastminute** (☎ 0892-705 000; www.fr.lastminute.com).

Recommended agencies in Germany include **STA Travel** (☎ 069-7430 3292; www.statravel.de) and **Travel Overland** (☎ 01805-276 370; www.travel-overland.de).

In Italy try **CTS Viaggi** (☎ 06-441 1166; www.cts.it), in the Netherlands **Airfair** (☎ 0900-771 7717; www.airfair.nl) and in Spain **Bacelo Viajes** (☎ 902-200 400; www.barceloviajes.com).

Indonesia

AirAsia has direct connections between KL and 15 destinations in Indonesia, including Jakarta (one way from 219,000Rp/RM96), Medan (145,000Rp/RM72.50), Padang (240,000Rp/RM168) and Denpasar (639,000Rp/RM163). Malaysia's other budget airline **Firefly** (☎ 03-7845 4543; www.fireflyz.com.my) connects KL (Subang) with Medan, Pekanbaru, Batam and Padang; and Penang with Banda Aceh and Medan. Malaysia Airlines has services to Jakarta, Surabaya, Medan, Denpasar and Jogyakarta and has fares comparable to the budget carriers if you book far enough in advance. Indonesian budget carrier **Kartika Airlines** (www.kartika-airlines.com) flies between Medan and Penang.

From Kuching **Batavia Air** (www.batavia-air.co.id) flies to Pontianak (see p420 for details).

A reliable Jakarta-based agency is **Smailing Tours** (☎ 350 8080; www.mysmailing.com).

Japan

Direct return flights to KL cost between ¥50,000 and ¥70,000, although with one stop you can find fares for as low as ¥32,000. One-way tickets average around ¥50,000.

It's usually around ¥10,000 cheaper to fly to/from Tokyo, rather than Osaka/Kansai International Airport.

Reliable discount agencies in Japan include **No 1 Travel** (☎ 03-3205 6073; www.no1-travel.com), **Across Travellers Bureau** (☎ 03-5467 0077; www.across-travel.com) and **STA Travel** (☎ 03-5391 2922; www.statravel.co.jp).

New Zealand

Return fares range from NZ$1200 to NZ$1600 between Auckland and KL on Emirates. Round-the-World (RTW) and Circle Pacific fares for travel to/from Malaysia are often good value.

Flight Centre (☎ 0800 243 544; www.flightcentre.co.nz) and **STA Travel** (☎ 0800 474 400; www.statravel.co.nz) have branches in Auckland and elsewhere in the country; check the websites for complete listings.

Singapore

AirAsia, Firefly, Malaysia Airlines and Singapore Airlines operate frequent flights between Singapore and KL as well as several other destinations in Malaysia, including Ipoh, Kuala Terengganu, Kuantan, Langkawi, Melaka and Penang. AirAsia one-way tickets start at S$40 from Singapore (RM48.50 from KL).

Silk Air (www.silkair.com), Singapore Airlines' regional wing, has daily flights between Singapore and Langkawi. **Berjaya Air** (www.berjaya-air.com) flies from Selatar Airport (p567) to Pulau Tioman in Malaysia.

With the considerable difference in the exchange rate, it's much cheaper to buy tickets in Malaysia. So rather than buying a return fare to Malaysia from Singapore, buy a one-way ticket and then buy the return leg in Malaysia.

Thailand

AirAsia (www.airasia.com) has one-way/round-trip flights from Bangkok to KL from around 1535/2645B. Check its website for similarly cheap fares to another 11 Thai destinations. Firefly connects KL (Subang) with Koh Samui and Phuket, as well as Penang with Phuket. For advance purchases Malaysia Airlines also has good deals for direct services to Bangkok and Phuket.

Bangkok has a number of excellent travel agencies, but there are also some suspect ones; you should ask the advice of other travellers before handing over your cash. **STA Travel** (☎ 662-236 0262; www.statravel.co.th) is a reliable place to start.

UK

From London you can take your pick from a wide range of carriers, one of the cheapest being AirAsia with fares as low as UK£413 return, although Malaysia Airlines also has deals from UK£435 return.

Reputable agencies in London:

ebookers (☎ 0871 223 5000; www.ebookers.co.uk)
Flight Centre (☎ 0870-499 0040; www.flightcentre .co.uk)
STA Travel (☎ 0871-230 0040; www.statravel.co.uk)
Trailfinders (☎ 0845-058 5858; www.trailfinders.com)

USA

Malaysia Airlines has fares of around US$800 from New York or US$1170 from Los Angeles to KL. Cheaper fares may sometimes include a stopover.

If you are going to be travelling the region, you could always look into the Circle Pacific pass offered by **Oneworld** (www.oneworld .com) carriers.

Good deals on tickets can also be found in San Francisco, Los Angeles, New York and other big cities. A good place to start is **STA Travel** (☎ 1-800-781 4040; www.statravel.com), which has a wide network of offices.

LAND
Brunei

See p593 for details of border crossings into Brunei from Sarawak.

Indonesia

Several express buses run between Pontianak in Kalimantan and Kuching and Miri in Sarawak, and Kota Kinabulu in Sabah. The bus crosses at the Tebedu/Entikong border. See p421 for details.

Singapore

The Causeway linking Johor Bahru with Singapore handles most traffic between the countries. Trains and buses run from all over Malaysia straight through to Singapore, or you can take a bus to JB and get a taxi or one of the frequent buses from JB to Singapore (p261). For further information see p565 and p124.

Trains linking Singapore and KL cost between S$30/RM34 and S$130/RM130 depending on what class of ticket you buy and whether you go for a berth or not. The journey takes about seven hours. For more details see p566.

A good website with details of express buses between Singapore, Malaysia and Thailand is the **Express Bus Travel Guide** (www.myexpress bus.com).

There is also a causeway linking Tuas, in western Singapore, with Geylang Patah in JB. This is known as the Second Link, and some bus services to Melaka and up the west coast head this way. If you have a car, tolls on the Second Link are much higher than those on the main Causeway.

Thailand
BUS & CAR

You can cross the border by road into Thailand at Padang Besar (p227), Bukit Kayu Hitam (p226), Rantau Panjang (Sungai Golok on the Thai side) and Pengkalan Kubor (p333).

TRAIN

The rail route into Thailand is on the Butterworth–Alor Setar–Hat Yai route, which crosses into Thailand at Padang Besar. You can take the **International Express** (☎ 03-2267 1200; www.ktmb.com.my) from Butterworth all the way to Bangkok. Trains from KL and Singapore are timed to connect with this service.

From Butterworth to Hat Yai the 2nd-class fare is upper/lower berth RM65/73, to Bangkok RM95/103, from Alor Setar to Hat Yai RM58.40/66.40 and to Bangkok RM88.40/96.40.

From Alor Setar there is an additional daily northbound train to Hat Yai (from RM12, three hours). And from KL there is one through service daily (the Senandung Langkawi) to Hat Yai (seat/upper berth/lower berth RM44/52/57).

From Hat Yai there are frequent train and bus connections to other parts of Thailand.

The opulent **Eastern & Oriental Express** (www .orient-express.com) also connects Singapore and Bangkok (p566) making stops in KL and Butterworth (for Penang).

SEA
Brunei

Boats connect Brunei to Lawas and Limbang in Sarawak, and to Pulau Labuan, from where boats go to Sabah. With the exception of speedboats for Limbang, all international boats now depart from Muara, 25km north-east of Bandar Seri Begawan, where Brunei immigration formalities are also handled.

See p594 for more information and details on boat services.

Indonesia

The following are the main ferry routes between Indonesia and Malaysia:

- Bengkalis, Sumatra, to Melaka (see p252)
- Batam to Johor Bahru (p261)
- Dumai, Sumatra, to Melaka (see p252)
- Medan, Sumatra, to Penang (see p196)
- Pekanbaru, Sumatra, to Melaka (see p252)
- Tanjung Pinang, Bintan, to Johor Bahru (p261)
- Tanjung Balai, Sumatra, to Pelabuhan Klang (see p140) and Kukup (see p261)
- Tarakan, Kalimantan, to Tawau (see p393)

Singapore

Singapore has a number of regular ferry connections to Malaysia and the Indonesian islands of Batam and Bintan. Cruise trips in the region are also very popular with locals. For more details see p566.

Thailand

Ferries connect Kuah on Pulau Langkawi with Satun on the Thai coast and, from November to mid-May, with Ko Lipe (see p225); make sure you get your passport stamped going in either direction.

GETTING AROUND

AIR
Airlines in Malaysia

The two main domestic operators are **Malaysia Airlines** (MAS; ☎ 1300-883 000, outside Malaysia ☎ 03-2161 0555; www.malaysia-airlines.com.my) and **AirAsia** (☎ 1300-889 933, outside Malaysia ☎ 603 8660 4343; www.airasia.com).

The MAS subsidiary **Firefly** (☎ 03-7845 4543; www.fireflyz.com.my) has flights from KL (Subang) to Penang, Kota Bharu, Kuala Terengganu, Kerteh, Langkawi, Johor Bahru, Alor Setar and Kuantan, and from Penang to KL (Subang), Johor Bahru and Langkawi.

Berjaya Air (☎ 03-7847 8228; www.berjaya-air.com) flies between KL (Subang), Pulau

Tioman, Pulau Pangkor and Pulau Redang in Peninsular Malaysia, as well as Singapore and Koh Samui in Thailand.

Over in Malaysian Borneo, MAS's subsidiary **MASwings** (☎ 1300-88 3000, outside Malaysia 03-7843 3000; www.maswings.com.my) offers local flights within and between Sarawak and Sabah. These services are very much reliant on the vagaries of the weather. In the wet season (October to March in Sarawak and on Sabah's northeast coast; May to November on Sabah's west coast), places like Bario in Sarawak can be isolated for days at a time, so don't venture into this area if you have a very tight schedule. These flights are completely booked during school holidays. At other times it's easier to get a seat at a few days' notice, but always book as far in advance as possible.

DISCOUNTS & SPECIAL FLIGHTS

All the airlines offer discounts tickets on the internet, depending on how far in advance you book – in some cases you might only pay for the airport taxes. A variety of other discounts (typically between 25% and 50%) are available for flights around Malaysia on Malaysia Airlines, including for families and groups of three or more – it's worth inquiring when you book tickets in Malaysia. Student discounts are available, but only for students enrolled in institutions that are in Malaysia.

Air Passes

Malaysia Airlines' Discover Malaysia pass costs US$199 (not including airport taxes) and travellers can take five flights anywhere in Malaysia within a 28-day period. It also has a US$99 pass for five flights with any one province. You must have flown into Malaysia on a Malaysia Airlines flight to qualify for this pass, though.

For flying around the region the **Asean Air Pass** (www.visitasean.travel) needs to be bought at the same time as a ticket from your home country to the region on one of the following airlines: Singapore Airlines, Malaysia Airlines, Thai, Garuda, Silk Air, Philippine Airlines, Air Vietnam, Laos Airlines and Myanmar Airlines. You can buy a minimum of three coupons (US$420) covering three flights, up to a maximum of six coupons (US$600).

For more details on these and a host of other air passes that are useful for travellers covering the region at speed, check out www.airtimetable.com/airpass_asia.htm.

BICYCLE

Bicycle touring around Malaysia and neighbouring countries is an increasingly popular activity. The main road system is well engineered and has good surfaces, but the secondary road system is limited. Road conditions are good enough for touring bikes in most places, but mountain bikes are recommended for forays off the beaten track.

KL has plenty of bicycle shops. Top-quality bicycles and components can be bought in major cities, but generally 10-speed (or higher) bikes and fittings are hard to find. Bringing your own is the best bet. Bicycles can be transported on most international flights; check with the airline about extra charges and shipment specifications.

KL Bike Hash (www.bikehash.freeservers.com) has a whole load of useful information and links to other cycling-connected sites in Malaysia. Also see **David's Cycling Adventure** (www.bicycle touringmalaysia.com), run by a local guy who also offers homestays at his home in the state of Perak. It's a mine of information about cycling around the region.

BOAT

There are no services connecting Peninsular Malaysia with Malaysian Borneo. On a local level, there are boats and ferries between the peninsula and offshore islands, and along the rivers of Sabah and Sarawak – check the relevant chapters for details. Note that some ferry operators are notoriously lax about observing safety rules, and local authorities are often nonexistent. If a boat looks overloaded or otherwise unsafe, *do not board it* – no-one else will look out for your safety.

BUS

Bus travel in Malaysia is economical and generally comfortable, and seats can be reserved. It's also fast – sometimes too fast. In a bid to pack in as many trips as possible, some bus drivers speed recklessly, resulting in frequent, often fatal, accidents. There's even an online petition (see http://buscrashnomore.blogspot.com) aimed at getting the government to do something about it.

Konsortium Transnasional Berhad (www.ktb.com.my) is Malaysia's largest bus operator running services under the **Transnasional** (☎ 1300-888 582; www.transnasional.com.my), **Plusliner** (www.plusliner.com) and **Cityliner** (www.cityliner.com.my) brands. Its services tend to be slower than rivals, but not that much safer, as its buses have also been involved in several major accidents. They have competition from a variety of privately operated buses on the longer domestic routes including **Aeroline** (www.aeroline.com.my) and **Supernice** (www.supernice.com.my). There are so many buses on major runs that you can often turn up and get a seat on the next bus.

On main routes most private buses have air-con (often turned to frigid so bring a sweater!) and cost only a few ringgit more than regular buses.

In larger towns there may be a number of bus stations; local/regional buses often operate from one station and long-distance buses from another; in other cases, KL for example, bus stations are differentiated by the destinations they serve.

Bus travel off the beaten track is relatively straightforward. Small towns and *kampung* (villages) all over the country are serviced by public buses, usually non-air-conditioned rattlers. Unfortunately, they are often poorly signed and sometimes the only way for you to find your bus is to ask a local. These buses are invariably dirt cheap and provide a great sample of rural life. In most towns there are no ticket offices, so buy your ticket from the conductor after you board.

CAR & MOTORCYCLE

Driving in Malaysia is fantastic compared with most Asian countries. There has been a lot of investment in the country's roads, which are generally of a high quality. New cars for hire are commonly available and fuel is inexpensive (RM1.80 per litre).

It's not all good news. Driving in the cities, particularly KL, can be a nightmare, due to traffic and confusing one-way systems. Malaysian drivers aren't always the safest when it comes to obeying road rules – they mightn't be as reckless as those you might see elsewhere in Southeast Asia, but they still take risks. For example, hardly any of the drivers keep to the official 110km/h speed limit on the main highways and tailgating is a common problem.

The Lebuhraya (North–South Hwy) is a six-lane expressway that runs for 966km along the length of the peninsula from the Thai border in the north to JB in the south. There are quite steep toll charges for using the expressway

MALAYSIA TRANSPORT

ROAD DISTANCES FOR PENINSULAR MALAYSIA (KM)

	Alor Setar	Fraser's Hill	Butterworth	Ipoh	Johor Bahru	Klang	Kota Bharu	Kuala Lumpur	Kuala Terengganu	Kuantan	Melaka	Mersing	Pelabuhan Klang	Port Dickson	Seremban
Alor Setar															
Fraser's Hill	443														
Butterworth	93	350													
Ipoh	257	186	164												
Johor Bahru	830	467	737	573											
Klang	495	132	400	236	401										
Kota Bharu	409	406	386	391	689	507									
Kuala Lumpur	462	99	369	205	368	33	474								
Kuala Terengganu	521	453	498	503	521	488	168	455							
Kuantan	684	253	591	427	325	292	371	259	209						
Melaka	606	243	513	349	224	177	607	144	508	292					
Mersing	815	436	722	558	134	386	568	353	401	191	255				
Pelabuhan Klang	503	140	410	246	409	8	515	41	496	300	185	394			
Port Dickson	552	189	459	295	318	115	564	90	503	291	94	321	123		
Seremban	526	163	433	269	304	97	538	64	471	259	80	289	105	32	
Taiping	183	272	90	86	659	322	369	291	481	513	435	644	332	387	355

and these vary according to the distance travelled. As a result the normal highways remain crowded while traffic on the expressway is light. Many other highways are in excellent condition and many are under construction.

You can join the **Automobile Association of Malaysia** (Map p96; ☎ 03-2162 5777; www.aam.org.my; 7-4 Megan Ave 1, 189 Jln Tun Razak, 50400 Kuala Lumpur) if you have a letter of introduction from your own automobile association.

Bring Your Own Vehicle

It's possible to bring your vehicle into Malaysia, but the cost and hassle of shipping it here makes it an unrealistic proposition for all but the most determined.

Driving Licence

A valid overseas licence is needed to rent a car. An International Driving Permit is usually not required by local car-hire companies, but it is recommended that you bring one.

Hire

Major rent-a-car operations include **Avis** (www.avis.com.my), **Hertz** (www.simedarbycarrental.com),

Mayflower (www.mayflowercarrental.com) and **Orix** (www.orixcarrentals.com.my); there are many others, though, including local operators only found in one city. Unlimited distance rates for a 1.5L Proton Wira, one of the cheapest and most popular cars in Malaysia, are posted at around RM176/1155 per day/week, including insurance and collision-damage waiver. The Proton is basically a Mitsubishi assembled under licence in Malaysia.

You can often get better deals, either through smaller local companies or when the major companies offer special deals. Rates drop substantially for longer rentals, and if you shop around by phone, you can get wheels for as little as RM2500 per month, including unlimited kilometres and insurance. The advantage of dealing with a large company is that it has offices all over the country, giving better backup if something goes wrong and allowing you to pick up in one city and drop off in another (typically for a RM50 surcharge). Mayflower is one local company with offices all over and some competitive rates.

The best place to look for car hire is KL (p126), though Penang is also good (p198). In Sabah and Sarawak there is less competition and rates are higher, partly because of road conditions.

Most rental companies also require that drivers are at least 23 years old.

Insurance

Rental companies will provide insurance when you hire a car, but always check what the extent of your coverage will be, particularly if you're involved in an accident. You might want to take out your own insurance or pay the rental company an extra premium for an insurance excess reduction.

Road Rules & Hazards

Driving in Malaysia follows many of the same rules as in Britain and Australia – cars are right-hand drive, and you drive on the left side of the road. The only additional precaution you need to take is to be aware of possible road hazards: stray animals and the large number of motorcyclists. And take it easy on the *kampung* back roads.

Wearing safety belts is compulsory. Although most drivers in Malaysia are relatively sane, safe and slow, there are also a fair few who specialise in overtaking on blind corners and otherwise trusting to divine intervention. Malaysian drivers also use a curious signalling system, where a flashing left indicator means 'you are safe to overtake' or 'I'm about to turn off'. Giving a quick blast of the horn when you're overtaking a slower vehicle is common practice and helps alert otherwise sleepy drivers to your presence.

HITCHING

Hitching is never entirely safe in any country in the world, and we don't recommend it. Travellers who decide to hitch, particularly single women, should understand that they are taking a small but potentially serious risk. People who do choose to hitch will be safer if they travel in pairs and let someone know where they are planning to go.

This said, Malaysia has long had a reputation for being a great place for hitchhiking, and it's generally still true, though with inexpensive bus travel most travellers don't bother.

On the west coast of Malaysia, hitching is generally quite easy, but it's not possible on the main Lebuhraya expressway.

On the east coast, traffic is lighter and there may be long waits between rides. The same applies to hitching in Malaysian Borneo.

LOCAL TRANSPORT

Local transport varies widely from place to place. Large cities in Malaysia have local taxis (as opposed to long-distance taxis, see below). These taxis usually have meters, but there are exceptions to this rule (usually in smaller towns like Kuantan in Pahang). For metered taxis, rates are as follows: flagfall (first 2km) is RM2; 10 sen for each 200m or 45 seconds thereafter; 20 sen for each additional passenger over two passengers; RM1 for each piece of luggage in the boot (trunk); plus 50% on each of these charges between midnight and 6am. Drivers are legally required to use meters if they exist – you can try insisting that they do so, but sometimes you'll just have to negotiate the fare before you get in.

In major cities there are also buses, which are extremely cheap and convenient, provided you can figure out which one is going your way. KL also has commuter trains (p127), and a Light Rail Transit (LRT; p128) and monorail system (p127).

Bicycle rickshaws (trishaws) have died out in KL, but they still exist in such places as Georgetown and Melaka, and are definitely handy ways of getting around the older parts of town, which have convoluted and narrow streets.

In the bigger cities across Malaysian Borneo, such as Kuching and Kota Kinabalu, you will find taxis, buses and minibuses. Once you're out of the big cities, though, you're basically on your own and must either walk or hitch. If you're really in the bush, of course, riverboats and aeroplanes are the only alternatives to lengthy jungle treks.

Long-Distance Taxi

Long-distance taxis make Malaysian travel – already easy and convenient even by the best Asian standards – a real breeze. In almost every town there will be a *teksi* stand where the cars are lined up and ready to go to their various destinations.

Taxis are ideal for groups of four, and are also available on a share basis. As soon as a full complement of four passengers turns up, off you go.

If you're travelling between major towns, you have a reasonable chance of finding other

---

THE EVOLUTION OF MALAYSIA'S RAILWAY

Malaysia's first railway line was a 13km route from Taiping to Port Weld that was laid in 1884, but it's no longer in use. By 1903 you could travel all the way from Johor Bahru to near Butterworth; the line was extended to the Thai border in 1918 and across the Causeway to Singapore in 1923. In 1931 the east-coast line was completed, effectively bringing the railway system to its present state.

Keppel Railway Station in Singapore, built in 1932, is actually still part of Malaysia, as is the land on which the tracks run up to the Causeway. This was part of the deal done at the time of federation, and it's one that Singapore, with its hungry eye on the local development possibilities of this corridor of Malaysian land, is keen to have revised.

The success of the high-speed rail link between KL and the Kuala Lumpur International Airport (KLIA) has encouraged Keretapi Tanah Melayu to increase its investment in extending this rapid and modern system. A high-speed service between KL and Ipoh is scheduled to start in 2011.

---

passengers to share without having to wait too long, but otherwise you will have to charter a whole taxi, which is four times the single-fare rate (in this book we generally quote the rate for a whole taxi).

As Malaysia becomes increasingly wealthy, and people can afford to hire a whole taxi, the share system is becoming less reliable. Early morning is generally the best time to find people to share a taxi, but you can inquire at the taxi stand the day before as to the best time.

Taxi rates to specific destinations are fixed by the government and are posted at the taxi stands; usually the whole-taxi rate is listed. Air-con taxis cost a few more ringgit than non-air-con, and fares are generally about twice the comparable bus fares. If you want to charter a taxi to an obscure destination, or by the hour, you'll probably have to do some negotiating. As a rule of thumb, you should pay around 50 sen per kilometre.

Taxi drivers often drive at frighteningly high speeds. They don't have as many head-on collisions as you might expect, but closing your eyes at times of high stress certainly helps! You also have the option of demanding that the driver slow down, but this can be met with varying degrees of hostility. Another tactic is to look for ageing taxis and taxi drivers – they must be doing something right to have made it this far!

TOURS

Reliable tours of both Peninsular Malaysia and Malaysian Borneo are run regularly by international operators, including **Exodus** (www .exodus.co.uk), **Explore Worldwide** (www.explore.co.uk), **Peregrine Adventures** (www.peregrineadventures.com) and **Intrepid Travel** (www.intrepidtravel.com). Such tours are often a good way to see the best of Malaysian Borneo in a short period of time and without having to worry about possibly problematic transport connections.

In contrast, getting around the peninsula under your own steam is rarely difficult, making a tour less necessary.

Also see the destination chapters for listings of local tour operators.

TRAIN

Malaysia's privatised national railway company is **Keretapi Tanah Melayu** (KTM; ☎ 03-2267 1200; www.ktmb.com.my). It runs a modern, comfortable and economical railway service, although there are basically only two lines and for the most part services are slow.

One line runs up the west coast from Singapore, through KL, Butterworth and on into Thailand. The other branches off from this line at Gemas and runs through Kuala Lipis up to the northeastern corner of the country near Kota Bharu in Kelantan. Often referred to as the 'jungle train', this line is properly known as the 'east-coast line'.

In Sabah the **North Borneo Railway** (www.north borneorailway.com.my), a small narrow-gauge line running through the Sungai Padas gorge from Tenom to Beaufort, was out of action at the time of research; check the website to see if tourist trips are up and running again.

Services & Classes

There are two main types of rail services: express and local trains. Express trains are air-conditioned and have 'premier' (1st class), 'superior' (2nd class) and sometimes 'economy' (3rd class) seats. Similarly on overnight trains you'll find 'premier night deluxe' cabins (upper/lower berth RM50/70 extra), 'premier night standard' cabins (upper/lower berth RM18/26), and 'standard night' cabins (upper/lower berth RM12/17). Local trains are usually economy class only, but some have superior seats.

Express trains stop only at main stations, while local services, which operate mostly on the east-coast line, stop everywhere, including the middle of the jungle, to let passengers and their goods on and off. Consequently local services take more than twice as long as the express trains and run to erratic schedules, but if you're in no hurry they provide a colourful experience and are good for short journeys.

Train schedules are reviewed biannually, so check the **KTM website** (www.ktmb.com.my), where you can make bookings and buy tickets.

Train Passes

KTM offers a Tourist Railpass for five days (adult/child US$35/18), 10 days ($55/28) and 15 days (US$70/35). This pass entitles the holder to unlimited travel on any class of train but does not include sleeping-berth charges on night express services.

Railpasses are available only to foreigners and can be purchased at Sentral KL, JB, Butterworth, Port Klang, Padang Besar, Wakaf Baharu and Penang train stations, as well as at Singapore station.

MALAYSIA TRANSPORT

Singapore

PHIL WEYMOUTH

Singapore

Love it or loathe it, Singapore is hard to ignore. It's a long-haul-stopover favourite, and yes, it's guilty on all counts of pandering to hordes of package tourists who get shepherded around on air-conditioned buses.

But stay for more than a few days and you'll find an intriguing brew of Chinese, Malay, Indian and Western cultures all blended into a diverse cultural melting pot. And it's anything but boring. Sure, the graffiti-free trains run on time, and on top of being bilingual (English is the first language here), everyone looks clean-cut and wholesome, but who needs pollution, poverty and chaos?

Food and shopping are the two main preoccupations of Singaporeans. And why not? There are thousands of food outlets serving every conceivable cuisine to suit every budget. Broke? Pull up a plastic chair at a hawker centre and order a Tiger beer and whatever Asian delight the next table is having. Flush? Splash out on a 10-course degustation with paired wines at one of the region's top restaurants. And the shopping? Mall after mall of all the top brands, at reasonable prices too.

But Singapore is never one to rest on its laurels. Two new 'integrated resorts' will lure tourists with glam casinos, theme parks and big-ticket attractions. And the Formula 1 night race and inaugural 2010 Youth Olympics has helped put Singapore on the international sporting stage.

Singapore is the perfect antidote to the brashness, dust and grime of the rest of Asia. Go on, tack on a couple of extra days to your trip and stop by for some pampering and deserved downtime.

HIGHLIGHTS

- 'Bolly' jamming with the teeming masses in **Little India** (p500) over the weekend
- Immersing yourself in the cultural complexities of Straits Chinese culture at the **Peranakan Museum** (p496) or the **Asian Civilisations Museum** (p495)
- Giving thanks to the gods at the busy **Kuan Im Thong Hood Cho Temple** (p497), or spending time on quiet reflection at **St Andrew's Cathedral** (p497)
- Cooing and gushing at the animals in the **Singapore Zoo** (p504) and at the **Night Safari** (p504)
- Rampaging through greenery at **Bukit Timah Nature Reserve** (p505), **MacRitchie Reservoir** (p505), **Pulau Ubin** (p504) and the **Southern Ridges** (p507)

- POPULATION: 4.8 MILLION
- AREA: 710 SQ KM

SINGAPORE IN...

Two Days

Start your day with a stroll at the idyllic **Singapore Botanic Gardens** (p501). After a *kopi* (coffee) and *kaya* (coconut jam) toast breakfast, hit the **Orchard Road** (p557) shops or spend the afternoon museum-hopping. The **Singapore Art Museum** (p496), **National Museum** (p494), **Peranakan Museum** (p496) and **Asian Civilisations Museum** (p495) are all within striking distance of each other. Break up the gallery crawl with a circuit through **Fort Canning Park** (p496). Find time for an afternoon tipple with a Singapore Sling at the **Raffles Hotel** (p496) and make your way along the Singapore River for **dinner** (p539). End your night with a drink at the **New Asia Bar** (p547) on the 70th floor of Swissôtel, the Stamford.

Day two begins with an MRT (Mass Rapid Transport) trip out to **Little India** (p500). Do some shopping at the massive **Mustafa Centre** (p557), have some delish Indian feed for lunch and do some temple-spotting. Grab a taxi to the **Singapore Zoo** (p504) for some daytime animal action and stay on for nocturnal animal action at the **Night Safari** (p504). If animals aren't your thing, make it out to **Kampong Glam** (p500) for a hit of Malay culture, and stay for kebabs and *sheesha*. Wind yourself down or rev yourself up with revellers at **Clarke Quay** (p549).

Four Days

If you're staying a couple more days, kick off day three with a cable-car ride from **Mt Faber** (p507), then cross to **Sentosa Island** (p509) – at least a day's frivolous indulgence. Retreat to the all-night bustle of the **Maxwell Road Food Centre** (p542) in Chinatown for dinner before boogieing on down at the **St James Power Station** (p551).

Go green on day four – make it out to the treetop walk at the **MacRitchie Reservoir** (p505), blitz through the snaking trails of the **Southern Ridges** (p507) or just take a bumboat out to **Pulau Ubin** (p504) for some cycling and mangrove boardwalks.

On the way back from Ubin, pay your respects at the **Changi Museum & Chapel** (p503) or drop by **Chinatown** (p498) for temples and shopping before a show at the **Esplanade** (p495) or a slap-up pepper-crab feast at the **East Coast Seafood Centre** (p542) as the ships of the world bump and sway in the Straits of Singapore.

HISTORY

Singapore has hardly looked back since Sir Thomas Stamford Raffles stepped into the mud in 1819 hell-bent on making the island a bastion of the British Empire (see p34). Despite a few ups and downs – invasion by the Japanese in WWII (p36) and getting booted out of the nascent federation of Malaysia in 1965 (p39) – the island has prospered in its role as a free-trade hub for Southeast Asia.

The downturn in the worldwide economy in 2009 had its effect on Singapore. Exports shrunk, unemployment increased and the government announced a S$20 billion economic-stimulus package. Despite all this, to the casual spectator, Singaporeans' love of shopping and dining out continues unabated.

In March 2009, a move by the elections department to update registers and adjust polling-district boundaries sparked election talk – might the People's Action Party (PAP) be planning to call a snap election before the fear of further worldwide recession caused the electorate to turn to new leadership? As of September 2009, there was no news. The next elections are due by February 2011.

ORIENTATION

Singapore is a city, an island and a country all rolled into one. It's about 45km west to east, 25km north to south. While there are built-up, high-density areas all around the island, the main city area is in the south.

The City

Downtown Singapore nestles around the Singapore River in the south, which, after decades of decline, has re-established itself as the city's watery heart. South of the river are the stalagmites of the CBD and the tourist epicentre of Singapore's cultural life, Chinatown. Immediately north of the river is the Colonial (also referred to as the Civic) District, dappled with elegant colonial architecture, museums galore, gargantuan shopping malls and the iconic Raffles Hotel.

Lining the river itself are Boat Quay, Clarke Quay and Robertson Quay, once swampy, nefarious warehouse districts, now progressive entertainment and eating precincts. The Marina Bay area at the river mouth is being heavily redeveloped – expect a mass of building sites that will only be fully cleared up by 2011.

Most of Singapore's tourist action revolves around Chinatown and along the mall-littered Orchard Rd, just north of the Colonial District. Heading slightly northeast, one will find the unfettered, colourful Little India district, and the gracious Kampong Glam, Singapore's Muslim quarter.

Singapore Island

To the island's west are the predominantly industrial areas of Jurong and Tuas, which are peppered with tourist attractions, many surprisingly family-oriented. Heading south you'll bump into Sentosa Island – Singapore's recreational playground. Within sight of Sentosa are the southern islands: St John's, Kusu and Lazarus.

East Coast Park stretches east from the city – imported sand on reclaimed land. Inland from here are the unpolished Geylang and Katong areas, with the *lorongs* (alleys) off Geylang Rd harbouring Singapore's surprisingly saucy (some say sleazy) red-light district. The much-lauded Changi Airport occupies the eastern corner of the island. Changi Village and Pulau Ubin are north of here. Not far from Changi is Pasir Ris, home to a quiet strip of beach and family-friendly amusement parks.

The central north of the island has much of Singapore's undeveloped land, tracts of primary and secondary rainforest, reservoirs, the Singapore Zoo and Night Safari, and the Sungei Buloh Nature Park.

Addresses

Singapore is well laid-out, with signposted streets and logically numbered buildings. Most addresses are preceded by the number of the floor and then the shop or apartment number. Addresses do not quote the district or suburb. For example, 05-01, the Heeren, 260 Orchard Rd, is outlet No 01 on the 5th floor of the Heeren building at 260 Orchard Rd.

SIGHTS

COLONIAL DISTRICT

The Colonial District owes its name and location to the British. Not long after Sir Stamford Raffles 'discovered' Singapore in 1819, he found that the area had all the necessities of a place of governance – it was central and close to the ports – and made Fort Canning Hill a base of operations. Squalid warehouses eventually made way for an ordered city grid. Most of these colonial elements were left in place even after Singapore gained independence in 1965. Like the rest of Singapore the district is constantly being tinkered with. The government has pumped millions of dollars into revitalising the waterfront for the Formula 1 motorcar night race and the building of the Marina Bay Sands integrated resort. The area is also home to the Marina Barrage, a 10,000-hectare freshwater reservoir that doubles as a park. An intriguing mix of colonial architecture and ubermodern sights, the Colonial District is a perfect introduction to Singapore.

At the river mouth is Singapore's water-spouting mascot, the funky 1960s **Merlion** (Map p517) – half-fish, half-lion. The local media went into a frenzy when the statue took a lightning bolt to the dome in early 2009. Repairs were made in double-quick time, much to the relief of locals who were sick of reading about it on the front page of local rags.

National Museum of Singapore

A facelift in 2006 has turbocharged this once-dull **museum** (Map p517; ☎ 6332 5642; www.national museum.sg; 93 Stamford Rd; adult/child S$10/5, Living Gallery free 6-9pm; ✆ History Galleries 10am-6pm, Living Galleries 10am-9pm). The colonial-era facade is deceptive – through the huge rotunda, the building opens up to a cavernous modern extension stretching towards Fort Canning Hill.

The basement hosts classy travelling exhibitions such as the costumes of Christian Lacroix and is a great starting point. The engaging 'Singapore Story' exhibition begins on the top floor and spirals down over two floors. Visitors are greeted upon entry by a stunning two-storey-high *Koyaanisqatsi*-esque video installation. Every conceivable slice of Singaporean life, from opium pipes (!)

VIVA LAS SINGAPORE...OR HOW SINGAPORE IS GETTING A CASINO OR TWO!

That constant hammering and drilling you hear around the Marina Bay area isn't from your hangover. There are several huge projects set to finish in 2010. The biggest and most controversial being the construction of the massive Marina Bay Sands casino...oops...we mean Integrated Resort (IR; the government's preferred euphemism for casino). Once completed, the **complex** (Map p517; www.marinabaysands.com) will span three wedge-shaped buildings. The crowning glory will be a rooftop swimming pool the size of three football fields, which connects across all three buildings. Singaporeans can now trade their casino cruises for a post-gambling swim.

In addition to the Sands complex, the government has spent millions sprucing up the flora in the area. **Gardens by the Bay** (Map p517; www.gardensbythebay.org.sg) is a 101-hectare space comprising three parks that connect the Marina Bay area.

Not to be outdone, the Genting Group is building another IR on Sentosa. Also set to open in 2010, **Resorts World Sentosa** (Map pp514-15; www.rwsentosa.com) will include a Universal Studios theme park (hurrah, parents have a place to dump their kids while feeding money into the slot machines), six accommodation options and several other attractions.

The introduction of the IRs was not without controversy. Debate about the social ills of gambling raged in the local rags. There was constant assurance that checks such as phone help lines and hefty casino entry charges would be put in place to address these issues. In the end commercial sense prevailed and the IRs were given the green light.

Singaporeans seem to have come round to the idea, though: in the latest 2009 recruitment drive, over 2000 people applied for jobs at Marina Bay Sands. Some Singaporeans have even quit their day jobs and spent astronomical sums on casino-dealer courses. Social ills? I'll see your $10 and raise you $50.

---

to grainy videos of a young Lee Kuan Yew at a rally, is on display.

Try to book a meal at Chef Chan's (p537) before you start your visit.

Asian Civilisations Museum

Inside a grand old Empress Place building (1865) named in honour of Queen Victoria, this **museum** (Map p517; ☎ 6332 7798; www.acm.org .sg; 1 Empress Pl; adult/child S$8/4, free after 7pm Fri; ☺ 1-7pm Mon, 9am-7pm Tue-Thu, Sat & Sun, Fri 9am-9pm) is a must for any Singapore visit – escape the humidity, put your watch in your pocket and enter a timeless realm. Ten thematic galleries explore traditional aspects of pan-Asian culture, religion and civilisation, with exquisite, well-displayed artefacts from Southeast Asia, China, India, Sri Lanka and even Turkey. The exploration of Islam and its influence in the region is particularly compelling, though the boys might be more interested in the large display of *krisses* (daggers).

Esplanade – Theatres on the Bay

Architecturally out of this world, Singapore's S$600-million **Esplanade – Theatres on the Bay** (Map p517; ☎ 6828 8377; www.esplanade.com; 1 Esplanade Dr; admission free, guided tours adult/child S$10/8; ☺ 10am-6pm, box office noon-8.30pm) is the poster-boy for contemporary Singapore. Architects wanted to challenge ingrained conservatism, and they succeeded – the centre has been compared to flies' eyes, melting honeycomb and two upturned durians, and called a whole lot of rude words we can't repeat here. The controversial aluminium shades reference Asian reed-weaving geometries and maximise natural light. Eight years on, the building has been accepted as part of the local landscape. There's a nonstop program of international and local performances, some great restaurants and free outdoor performances. Book tickets through **SISTIC** (☎ 6348 5555; www.sistic.com.sg).

Singapore Flyer

People in cities around the world are paying money to get into a gigantic Ferris wheel for glorious views. Why not? The **Singapore Flyer** (Map p517; ☎ 6333 3311; www.singaporeflyer.com .sg; 30 Raffles Ave; adult/child S$29.50/20.65) is an expensive 30-minute ride with views towards the Colonial District, CBD, Marina Bay, the high-rise housing landscape to the east and out to the South China Sea. You're better off going on a clear day than at night, if only to avoid the annoying flashing neon lights outside the cabin.

SINGAPORE

Raffles Hotel

An adored Singaporean institution and architectural landmark, **Raffles Hotel** (Map p517; ☎ 6337 1886; www.raffleshotel.com; 1 Beach Rd) was opened in December 1887 by the Sarkies brothers, immigrants from Armenia. At first a modest 10-room bungalow, the main building followed in 1899 and the hotel soon became synonymous with Oriental opulence, attracting the British elite and literary luminaries such as Somerset Maugham. The Singapore Sling was invented here by bartender Ngiam Tong Boon, and (far less gloriously) the last Singaporean tiger, which escaped from a travelling circus nearby, was shot beneath the Billiard Room in 1902.

By the 1970s, Raffles was a shabby relic, dodging the wrecking ball in 1987 with National Monument designation. In 1991 it reopened after a S$160-million facelift. If you want to stay here, rooms start at S$750 a night. The lobby is open to nonguests, but dress sharp – no shorts or sandals. There are some top-notch restaurants, and high tea is served in the Tiffin Room, or sip a Singapore Sling and throw peanut shells on the Long Bar's floorboards.

You could easily dismiss the **Raffles Museum** (Map p517; 3rd fl, Raffles Hotel Arcade; admission free; ☼ 10am-10pm) as an exercise in self-aggrandisement, but it's actually interesting. Old photos, memorabilia and advertisements sit alongside 'thank you' notes from celebrity guests such as Somerset Maugham and Noël Coward.

Peranakan Museum

Singapore's newest **museum** (Map p517; ☎ 6332 7591; 39 Armenian St; adult/child S$6/3; ☼ 1-7pm Mon, 9.30am-7pm Tue-Sun, to 9pm Fri) stands as a testament to the Peranakan (Straits-born Chinese) cultural revival in the Lion City. Opened in 2008, it has 10 thematic galleries featuring over 1200 artefacts and a variety of multimedia exhibits designed to introduce visitors to historical and contemporary Peranakan culture.

In addition to featuring traditionally crafted, beaded Peranakan clothing and exquisitely carved antique furniture, the museum also has a number of interactive exhibits. Our favourite is the diorama displaying a traditional Peranakan home complete with two video-mounted portraits of elders who argue with each other about whether or not their descendents are leading culturally appropriate lives.

Singapore Art Museum & 8Q SAM

The **Singapore Art Museum** (Map p517; ☎ 6332 3222; www.singart.com; 71 Bras Basah Rd; adult/child S$8/5; ☼ 10am-7pm Sat-Thu, 10am-9pm Fri) occupies the former St Joseph's Catholic boys' school. The gallery champions the arts in an economics-obsessed nation, with exhibitions ranging from classical Chinese calligraphy to electronic arts, though it seems content to hide away its permanent collection. The exhibition spaces are in a constant state of flux, always closed for maintenance or in preparation for the next show. You might get lucky and chance upon some of the S$70-million worth of Wu Guangzhong's donated art.

Round the corner from SAM, the art museum's new extension, **8Q SAM** (Map p517; ☎ 6332 3200; www.singart.com/8qsam; 8 Queen St; adult/child S$3/1.50; ☼ 10am-7pm Sat-Thu, 10am-9pm Fri), is named after its address and has a revolving-door focus on quirky installations, interactivity and contemporary art.

There's free admission to both spaces from noon to 2pm daily and 6pm to 9pm Fridays.

Fort Canning Park

Mall-crazy Singaporeans often overlook this gem of a **park** (Map p517; ☎ 6332 1200; www.nparks.gov.sg; entry via Hill St, Canning Rise, River Valley Rd, Canning Walk; ☼ 24hr). Fourteen sights are crammed into this 18-hectare space, the centre being **Fort Canning Centre** (Map p517), a 1926 barracks.

When Raffles rolled into Singapore and claimed it for the mother country, locals steered clear of Fort Canning Hill, then called Bukit Larangan (Forbidden Hill), out of respect for the sacred shrine of Sultan Iskandar Shah, ancient Singapura's last ruler. Raffles built a modest *atap* (thatched roof) residence on the summit in 1822, which acted as Government House until the military built Fort Canning. The latter was named in honour of Viscount Canning, first viceroy of India.

Visitors are greeted by the comforting call of crickets, and mossy paths criss-cross the grounds tempting visitors to veer from sight to sight. Stop at the spice garden and take in the scents of tamarind and cinnamon.

Visit the **Battle Box Museum** (Map p517; ☎ 6333 0510; 2 Cox Terrace; adult/child S$8/5; ☼ 10am-6pm Tue-Sun), the former command post of the British during WWII, and get lost in the eerie and deathly quiet 26-room underground complex. War veterans and Britain's Imperial War Museum helped recreate the authentic bunker environs; life-sized models re-enact the fateful surrender to the Japanese on 15 February 1942. Japanese Morse codes are still etched on the walls.

Over the weekend, you can gawk at newlyweds melting in the sun as they pose for wedding photos (the Registry of Marriages is located in the park). The entire park circuit can be completed in a few leisurely hours.

The hill hosts several outdoor events and concerts each year including WOMAD (August to October) and Ballet under the Stars (July).

Churches & Cathedrals

The peaceful **St Andrew's Cathedral** (Map p517; ☎ 6337 6104; www.livingstreams.org.sg; 11 St Andrew's Rd; ⏰ visitors centre 9am-5pm Mon-Fri, 9am-7pm Sat, 9am-1.30pm Sun) stands in stark contrast against the cityscape.

Completed in 1838 but torn down and rebuilt in its present form in 1862 after lightning damaged the original building (twice!), the cathedral has a 63.1m tall tower, towering naves and lovely stained glass above the west doors.

Dedicated to St Gregory the Illuminator, Singapore's oldest church (1836) is the neoclassical **Armenian Church** (Map p517; ☎ 6334 0141; 60 Hill St), designed by eminent colonial architect George Coleman. Pushing up orchids in the graveyard is Agnes Joaquim, discoverer of Singapore's national flower – the *Vanda Miss Joaquim* orchid.

All of these churches are open during the day, with the usual Sunday services.

Kuan Im Thong Hood Cho Temple

In the heart of Waterloo St (which we swear has more vibrancy and soul than glossy Chinatown), **Kuan Im Thong Hood Cho Temple** (Map p517; 178 Waterloo St; admission free) is lively and colourful. Dedicated to Guan Yin, the Goddess of Mercy, it's usually busy. Flower sellers and fortune tellers swarm around the entrance. Devotees stream into the temple daily, offering joss sticks and shaking *kau cim* (fortune telling) sticks, all under the gaze of the magnificent golden Buddha.

Next door is the polychromatic Hindu **Sri Krishnan Temple** (Map p517; 152 Waterloo St; admission free), which has a magnificent silver-and-gold shrine. Pragmatic worshippers from the Kuan Im Temple also burn joss sticks here for extra insurance.

THE QUAYS

Splitting the Colonial District from the CBD is the Singapore River, the site of British landfall and Singapore's main trade artery for over a century. Once the dirty commercial hub that was the lifeline of Singapore's flourishing trade, a determined government clean-up in the 1980s saw the many *godowns* (warehouses), bumboats and commercial craft moved and the Singapore River 'cleaned up'. With the area now shiny and sparkly, the government quickly admitted that it lacked 'soul' and immediately embarked on yet another initiative to fill the area with bars and restaurants.

Boat Quay

Closest to the river mouth, **Boat Quay** (Map p517) was once Singapore's centre of commerce, and remained an important economic area into the 1960s. By the mid-1980s, many of the shophouses were in ruins, businesses having shifted to hi-tech cargo centres elsewhere on the island. Declared a conservation zone by the government, the area has become a major entertainment district filled with colourful restaurants and bars. You'll find riverfront restaurants serving all manner of Singaporean delicacies, though the restaurant touts are aggressive. Parallel with Boat Quay one block to the south is **Circular Road** (Map p517), where there are dozens of bars. After work thirsty businessmen swarm here from the CBD.

Clarke Quay

Clarke Quay (Map p517) has had more comebacks than John Travolta and Mickey Rourke. This quay, named after Singapore's second colonial governor, Sir Andrew Clarke, was developed into a dining and shopping precinct in the early 1990s and most recently revamped with a slew of bars and clubs in 2006.

It's on this stretch of riverfront that Singapore's most whimsical designers have been given carte blanche to bring their dreams to life. Among the high (or low) lights: lilypad umbrellas straight out of a Dr Seuss colouring book, and many once-dignified shophouses now painted in ultrabright shades.

On the western end of Clarke Quay is the **Royal Selangor Pewter Gallery** (Map p517; ☎ 6268 9600; www.royalselangor.com.sg; 01-01 Clarke Quay; ⏰ 9am-9pm). Walk through the back where pewter-casting demos are run, then

SINGAPORE

STREET SCULPTURE

Singapore is dappled with a healthy collection of public sculpture by acclaimed local and international artists. Check out these babies:

Abundance (Map p517; Suntec City) By Sun Yu Li.

Between Sea & Sky (Map p517; Marina Mandarin Hotel, 6 Raffles Blvd) By Olivier Strehelle.

Bird (Map p517; UOB Plaza, Boat Quay) By Fernando Botero.

First Generation (Map p517; Cavenagh Bridge) By Chong Fat Cheong.

Homage to Newton (Map p517; UOB Plaza, Boat Quay) By Salvador Dalí.

Love (Map p517; near Dhoby Ghaut station on Penang Rd) By Robert Indiana.

Millennium (Map p517; Empress Pl) By Victor Tan.

Reclining Figures (Map p517; OCBC Bldg, Chulia St) By Henry Moore.

Seed (Map p517; Esplanade waterfront garden) By Han Sai Por.

Six Brushstrokes (Map p517; Millenia Walk, 9 Raffles Blvd) By Roy Lichtenstein.

---

gawp at or buy the shiny stuff in the retail cabinets. It also runs pewtersmithing courses (p529).

Robertson Quay

The most remote and thus least visited of the Quays, **Robertson Quay** (Map p517) features a desultory collection of restaurants, hotels, bars, a really garish bridge and a club selling cheap drinks (accounts for its popularity with the young 'uns). This area was once used for storage of goods that had come west up the Singapore River.

The white-walled, polished concrete spaces of the **Singapore Tyler Print Institute** (Map p517; ☎ 6336 3663; www.stpi.com.sg; 02-41 Robertson Quay; admission free; ⏰ 10am-6pm Tue-Sat) hosts international and local exhibits, showcasing the work of resident print- and paper-makers. Exhibitions often have a 'how to' component, and there's an impressive program of visual arts courses year-round.

Officially known as the Sri Thandayuthapani Temple, the open-walled, blue-green **Chettiar Hindu Temple** (Map p517; ☎ 6737 9393; 15 Tank Rd; admission free; ⏰ 8am-noon & 5.30-8.30pm) was completed in 1984, replacing a temple built by Indian *chettiars* (moneylenders). Dedicated to the six-headed Shaivite god, Lord Subramaniam, it's at its most active during the Thaipusam festival.

Undergoing massive renovations at the time of research, the **Hong San See Temple** (Map p517; 31 Mohamed Sultan Rd; admission free; ⏰ 6am-7pm) was completed in 1913 and set up on a hill. The temple is built in a southern Chinese fashion, with sloping tiled roofs and ornamented columns.

THE CBD

Immediately south of the Singapore River is the central business district (CBD), Singapore's financial hub. **Raffles Place** (Map pp526–7) is a rare slice of green above the MRT (Mass Rapid Transit) station, surrounded by gleaming towers of commerce. There are some great sculptures (see above) around here and along the river nearby.

Strewn among the high-rise landscape are a few colonial relics. The **Fullerton Hotel** occupies the former general post office and is no less elegant than the Raffles Hotel. Further south is **Lau Pa Sat** (p539), a popular hawker centre beneath an elaborate wrought-iron structure imported from Glasgow in 1894.

Also check out the Taoist **Wak Hai Cheng Bio Temple** (Map pp526–7; cnr Phillip & Church Sts; admission free; ⏰ 7.30am-5.30pm), which translates as Calm Sea Temple. Dating from 1826, it's an atmospheric place – giant incense coils smoulder over an empty courtyard while a village of tiny plaster figures populates the roof.

CHINATOWN

Singapore's celebrated cultural heart is Chinatown, roughly bounded by Church St to the north, New Bridge Rd to the west, Maxwell Rd to the south and Cecil St to the east. It's a strange mix of ebullient commerce and slightly rough nightlife, tempered with memories of more desperate times when impoverished immigrants survived on their wits, hard work, prayers and good fortune. Restoration projects and numerous clean-ups have created pockets of artificiality, and some locals are of the opinion that the 'soul' of Chinatown has been lost. Wandering off the main thoroughfares, away from the busloads of tourists, is probably the best way to catch a glimpse of the Chinatown that still endears itself to locals.

Buddha Tooth Relic Temple

The massive and jaw-dropping five-storey **Buddha Tooth Relic Temple** (Map pp526-7; ☎ 6220 0220; www.btrts.org.sg; 288 South Bridge Rd; admission free; ◐ 4.30am-9pm) opened to great fanfare in 2008, its main drawcard being what is believed to be a sacred tooth of the Buddha (dental experts have expressed doubts over its authenticity).

The main worship hall greets visitors at the entrance: swirling joss smoke and all-day chanting combine in hypnotising fashion. The tooth relic itself sits on a pedestal in a stupa made with 420kg of gold donated by worshippers. Want to see the tooth? It's only brought out on the first day of the Chinese New Year and on Wesak day.

The top floor opens into a peaceful garden with a revolving prayer wheel and the other floors house exhibits and a comprehensive display on the history and building of the temple. There's a teahouse serving a wide range of teas and vegetarian food on the second level. This is also the only temple that – to our knowledge – has its own underground parking garage.

Thian Hock Keng Temple

Also known as the Temple of Heavenly Happiness, **Thian Hock Keng Temple** (Map pp526-7; ☎ 6423 4616; 158 Telok Ayer St; admission free; ◐ 7.30am-5.30pm) is one of Singapore's oldest and most eye-popping temples. Dedicated to Ma Cho Po, Goddess of the Sea, it was built by early Chinese Hokkien immigrants in gratitude for safe passage to Singapore.

Declared a National Monument in 1973 and renovated in 2000, the temple's twin rooftop dragons represent the principles of yin and yang. Stone lions guard the door, and as security back-up, fierce-looking portraits of door gods prevent evil spirits from entering. Inside, gilded ceilings feature intricate carvings of Chinese folkloric stories and heroes. Locals favour the Wak Hai Cheng Bio Temple (opposite).

Sri Mariamman Temple

Paradoxically cast in the middle of Chinatown, the **Sri Mariamman Temple** (Map pp526-7; ☎ 6223 4064; 244 South Bridge Rd; admission free; ◐ 7.30am-8.30pm) is the oldest Hindu temple in Singapore, originally built in 1823, then rebuilt in 1843. The

S$3 fee for taking photos is a rip-off, but tourists still descend in droves – and many trigger-happy snappers ignore the fees.

You can't miss the incredible technicolour 1930s *gopuram* (tower) above the entrance, key to the temple's South Indian Dravidian style. Sacred cow sculptures graze the boundary walls, while the *gopuram* is covered in over-the-top plasterwork images of Brahma the creator, Vishnu the preserver and Shiva the destroyer. In October each year the temple hosts the Thimithi Festival – devotees queue along South Bridge Rd to hot-foot it over burning coals. Wander around the back for great views of the temple structure set against the skyscrapers of the CBD.

Chinatown Heritage Centre

Set on three floors of an old shophouse, the **Chinatown Heritage Centre** (Map pp526-7; ☎ 6325 2878; www.chinatownheritagecentre.sg; 48 Pagoda St; adult/child S$10/6; ◐ 9am-8pm) is an engaging museum focusing on the arduous everyday lives of Singapore's Chinese settlers. Reconstructed living environments are festooned with artefacts. The cramped quarters of shophouse living are decked out with startling reality (right down to the fake poop inside the bucket toilet – thankfully, scent-emitting technology won't be invented until 2050). The oral and video histories of local people are genuinely moving…if the projectors and screens decide to work.

Singapore City Gallery

The Urban Redevelopment Authority's **Singapore City Gallery** (Map pp526-7; ☎ 6321 8321; www.ura.gov.sg/gallery; URA Bldg, 45 Maxwell Rd; admission free; ◐ 9am-5pm Mon-Sat) provides a rather compelling insight into the government's resolute and much-admired policies of high-rise housing and land reclamation. Highlights include an 11m x 11m scale model of the city, and a voyeuristic bird's-eye-view roof camera. Would-be property investors would do well to visit for the displays detailing future plans for suburbs in Singapore.

Baba House

You've got to ring and book a visit to the **Baba House** (Map pp526-7; ☎ 6227 5731; babahouse@nus.edu .sg; 157 Neil Rd; admission by appointment S$10; ◐ Wed & Thu), but the one- to two-hour guided tour of this pre-war terrace house built in the elaborate Peranakan style is worth every cent.

Built in the 1890s and formerly home to shipping tycoon Wee Bin, the house was donated to the National University of Singapore. A two-year restoration was completed in September 2008. Every detail, from the carved motifs on the blue facade of the building down to the door screens, has been attended to. The house is a living museum and is furnished as it was in the 1920s. Knowledgeable tour guides weave tales of Peranakan life with every detail: secret peepholes behind screens allowed shy Nonya ladies to spy on visitors in the central hall.

The no-photos-and-video policy is a little draconian but is enforced with the intention of creating a mysterious allure to the place.

LITTLE INDIA

Worlds apart from the rest of Singapore, Little India (Map p522) was originally a European enclave, blooming into an Indian cultural centre after a Jewish-Indian businessman started farming buffalo here. Today Little India teems with men on two-year contracts from India, Bangladesh and Sri Lanka doing the dirty construction jobs that Singaporeans won't stoop to. The weekends are truly an eye-opener for locals and tourists alike. Produce, spices and other trinkets spill onto the streets and crowd the five-foot walkways. Many businesses operate late into the night (some even run 24 hours) and traffic slows to a messy crawl.

Sri Veeramakaliamman Temple

Dazzlingly colourful, the bustling Shaivite **Sri Veeramakaliamman Temple** (Map p522; ☎ 6293 4634; 141 Serangoon Rd; admission free; 🕐 8am-noon & 4-8.30pm) is dedicated to Kali, bloodthirsty consort of Shiva. Kali's always been big in Bengal, birthplace of the labourers who built this temple in 1885. Inside, Kali is pictured draped with a garland of skulls, disembowelling victims, and also sharing peaceful moments with her sons Ganesh and Murugan.

Sri Srinivasa Perumal Temple

Dedicated to Vishnu, the **Sri Srinivasa Perumal Temple** (Map p522; ☎ 6298 5771; 397 Serangoon Rd; admission free; 🕐 5.45am-noon & 5-9pm) dates from 1855, but the 20m-tall *gopuram* is a S$300,000 1966 addition. Inside is a statue of Vishnu (aka Perumal), his sidekicks Lakshmi and Andal, and his bird-mount Garuda. Sri Srinivasa Perumal is the starting point for the parade to the Chettiar Hindu Temple (p498) during the Thaipusam festival.

Sakaya Muni Buddha Gaya Temple (Temple of 1000 Lights)

In 1927 a Thai Buddhist monk founded the **Sakaya Muni Buddha Gaya Temple** (Map p522; ☎ 6294 0714; 366 Race Course Rd; admission free; 🕐 8am-4.30pm), usually called the Temple of 1000 Lights. The entrance is flanked by a leopard and tiger, the latter in midleap, snarling jaws open. Inside is a 15m-high, 300-tonne Buddha alongside an eclectic collection of deities including Guan Yin (Chinese Goddess of Mercy) and the Hindu deities Brahma and Ganesh. At the base of the Buddha's back is a low door into a small prayer room. Around the Buddha's base are 'Buddha – This Is Your Life!' models and, of course, at least 1000 electric lights.

Leong San See Temple

Across the road from the Temple of 1000 Lights (above) is the gorgeous Taoist **Leong San See Temple** (Dragon Mountain Temple; Map p522; ☎ 6298 9371; 371 Race Course Rd; admission free; 🕐 6am-6pm), dedicated to Guan Yin, Goddess of Mercy. Built in 1917 using traditional joinery and intricately carved ceiling beams in a style similar to that of Thian Hock Keng (p499), this temple has an effervescent, happy atmosphere. The smiling Buddha welcomes you at the door; to promote good feng shui, walk around clockwise.

KAMPONG GLAM

Neatly self-contained Kampong Glam, roughly bounded by Victoria St, Jln Sultan and Beach Rd, all immediately northeast of Bugis MRT, is Singapore's Muslim centre. Its name derives from the Malay for village *(kampung)* and *gelam,* a type of tree that once grew here. By day, the area is a great place for visiting mosques and shops selling clothing, raw cloth and dry goods. By night, hip youths come out and smoke *sheesha* at one of the many Middle Eastern joints. The offbeat Haji Lane has cool boutiques and eateries.

Sultan Mosque

Kampong Glam's gold-domed epicentre is **Sultan Mosque** (Map p522; ☎ 6293 4405; 3 Muscat St; admission free; 🕐 5am-8.30pm), named after Raffles' buddy Sultan Hussein Shah. Originally built in 1825 with a grant from Raffles and the East India Company, it was replaced 100 years later with the current edifice. The prayer hall can accommodate 5000 worshippers; a glaring red digital clock compromises the atmosphere a little, but at least everybody knows when to pray. The massive rug on the prayer hall (no entry to non-Muslims) is a gift from a Saudi Prince, whose emblem is woven onto it.

Malay Heritage Centre

This dignified terracotta-tiled **heritage centre** (Map p522; ☎ 6391 0450; www.malayheritage.org.sg; 85 Sultan Gate; adult/child S$4/3, performances S$11; ☼ 10am-6pm Tue-Sun, 1-6pm Mon) is set back against a large garden and was once the Malay royal *istana* (palace), built in 1843 for Singapore's last sultan, Ali Iskandar Shah. An agreement allowed the palace to stay in the sultan's family as long as they continued to live there. This was repealed in 1897, but the family stayed on for another century, the palace gradually sliding into ruin.

The restored building opened as a museum in 2004, celebrating Singapore's Malay heritage with a reconstructed *kampung* house upstairs, spare but wordy displays throughout and cultural performances (available by website-booking only).

Other Mosques

Painted cream and brown, the **Hajjah Fatimah Mosque** (Map p522; ☎ 6297 2774; 4001 Beach Rd; admission free; ☼ 7am-8pm) was built in 1846 and named after the mosque's wealthy Malaccan-born Malay benefactor. Equally curious is its 'Leaning Tower of Kampong Glam' – a European-style minaret tilting about 6 degrees off-centre. The outbuildings are also well out of kilter.

Located on a busy street corner, the sky-blue hexagonal-tiled **Malabar Muslim Jama-Ath Mosque** (Map p522; ☎ 6294 3862; 471 Victoria St; admission free; ☼ 7.30am-7pm) is hard to miss. Malabar Muslims from the southern Indian state of Kerala have worshipped here since 1963. Overgrown with time and tree roots, the **Royal Cemetery** is behind the mosque, its shambolic tombstones slowly succumbing to gravity.

ORCHARD ROAD

Singapore's premier shopping strip is really a massive shrine devoted to the Gods of Retail. And locals flock here in droves to pay homage and make offerings. It's a far cry from the verdant and ordered nutmeg and pepper plantations found here in the 19th century.

Orchards have been replaced with towering malls and ubiquitous five-star hotels that induce some tourists to scream with delight and others to run screaming. Shopping aside, there are several pockets that still delight.

Singapore Botanic Gardens

If Singapore's urban planners could manufacture paradise, it wouldn't look too different from the **Singapore Botanic Gardens** (Map p524; ☎ 6471 7361; www.sbg.org.sg; 1 Cluny Rd; admission free; ☼ 5am-midnight). The front entrance leads to an idyllic koi pond. On weekends, laughing children feed the multicoloured fish. Right behind, a waterfall gurgles and birds hop around the water's edge, at ease with the locals.

Established in 1859 and covering 52 hectares, the gardens were originally a testing ground for potential cash crops such as rubber. Today they host a herbarium, a library of archival materials dating back to the 16th century, wide-open spaces, manicured gardens and a 4-hectare patch of the primary rainforest that once blanketed the island.

The **National Orchid Garden** (Map p524; ☎ adult/child S$5/2.50; ☼ 8.30am-7pm) is also here, with over 60,000 plants and a cool house showcasing pitcher plants and orchids from cooler climes. Don't miss the *Vanda Miss Joaquim*, Singapore's national flower, which Agnes Joaquim discovered in her garden in 1893.

The gardens are at their busiest on Sunday mornings. Domestic helpers congregate here on their day off for impromptu small-group church services. Families come out in full force and share the pavement with joggers and pet owners being dragged by leashed dogs. Free open-air concerts are held on the last Sunday of the month at the Shaw Foundation Symphony Stage – call or check the website.

Buses 7, 77, 105, 106, 123 and 174 all run to the gardens from the Orchard MRT exit on Orchard Blvd.

Cathay Gallery

Film buffs will go ga-ga at the **Cathay Gallery** (Map p524; www.thecathaygallery.com.sg; 02-16 the Cathay, 2 Handy Rd; admission free; ☼ noon-8pm Mon-Sat), housed in Singapore's first high-rise building. The displays here trace the history of the Loke family, early pioneers in film production and distribution in Singapore and founders of the Cathay Organisation. Check out old movie posters, cameras, and programs that capture the golden age of local cinema.

SINGAPORE

Istana

Constructed between 1867 and 1869 by Indian convicts transported from Bencoolen on Sumatra, the Istana (Map p524; ☎ 6737 5522; www.istana.gov.sg; Orchard Rd) is where Singapore's President SR Nathan hangs out. The neo-Palladian structure, set 750m back from Orchard Rd in beautifully maintained grounds, was originally Government House, built at great expense to impress the visiting Duke of Edinburgh. It's only open to the public on selected holidays (eg New Year's) – bring your passport to get past the gun-toting guards. Call, or check the website, for details.

Emerald Hill Road

Take some time out to wander through the pedestrianised Peranakan Pl to residential Emerald Hill Rd (Map p524), where original Peranakan terrace houses reside in states that run the gamut from glamorous decay to immaculate restoration. The quiet atmosphere around here feels a million miles from shop-till-you-drop Orchard Rd. All the walking will mean you need to grab a beer from one of the many bars at the Orchard Rd end of Emerald Hill (p549).

EASTERN SINGAPORE

Heading east of the city centre, the sleazy red-light Geylang district is also home to temples, mosques, churches and some of the best eating spots in Singapore. It connects up to Geylang Serai, a largely Malay district rarely frequented by foreign visitors. Further on is the popular East Coast Park. Next door, the Katong district is a gentrified neighbourhood, once filled with old Peranakan homes, now a hotbed of condominiums. Further east is Pasir Ris Park, the Changi Museum and Chapel; and snoozy Changi Village, the jumping-off point for leafy Pulau Ubin.

Geylang

Nowhere else in Singapore are food, commerce, religion, culture and sleaze more at ease with each other than in Geylang (Map pp514–15). It's nothing more than a vaguely busy road during the day, but once night falls, it transforms.

You might see a crowd rubbing shoulders with prostitutes after spilling out onto the streets from evening prayer at a mosque. And if the sights haven't yet gotten to you, the smell of food soon will. You'll see hordes of

---

> **HARRY LEE KUAN YEW'S HUMBLE ABODE**
>
> If you're planning a jaunt down Orchard Rd, make a short detour along **Oxley Road** (off Map p524). The father of modern Singapore, Harry Lee Kuan Yew, lives along this street. In order to keep out the plebs and crazies, car gantries are installed at either end of the road. Pedestrians are free to walk through, but expect to be hurried along by heavily armed Gurkhas. Go on, walk on the side of the guards for a closer look. We dare you.

---

people sweating over plates of fried beef *hor fun* and frogs' leg porridge.

Come see the circus. Take the MRT to Kallang. Cross the road and head south towards all the lights across the street.

Geylang Serai

Geylang Serai is a Malay residential area, but you're not going to see any traditional *atap* houses or sarong-clad cottage-industry workers. This is strictly high-rise country.

Trundle out to Paya Lebar MRT station, from where it's a short walk along Sims Ave to the temporary home of **Geylang Serai Wet Market** (Map pp514–15; Sims Ave; ⊙ 7am-10pm). The original market across the street is getting a facelift and has already missed its 2008 reopening deadline. Expect a crowded, traditional Asian wet market with meat hanging on hooks, baskets of sloshing fish, squirming frogs, slippery eels and people haggling over the produce. Watch your step! There's a **food centre** next to the wet market that achieved some notoriety in April 2009 after more than 100 people got food poisoning from eating contaminated Indian *rojak* (salad with peanut-sauce dressing). If you push further into the complex, you'll find textiles and clothes – a perfect place to pick up traditional Malay dress.

Katong

Down Joo Chiat Rd from the Malay Cultural Village is the Katong district. Along Koon Seng Rd just east of Joo Chiat Rd are some of the finest **Peranakan terrace houses** (Map pp514–15) in Singapore, decorated with plaster stucco columns, dragons, birds, crabs and brilliantly glazed tiles. *Pintu pagar* (front saloon doors) are also typical, letting the breezes in and keeping peering eyes out.

Joo Chiat Rd and traffic-plagued East Coast Rd have some top-notch Peranakan restaurants (see p541). Also in this area is the **Katong Antique House** (Map p528; ☎ 6345 8544; 208 East Coast Rd; admission free; ☾ 11am-6pm). Owner Peter Wee will show you his large collection of Peranakan antiques including beautifully beaded slippers, wedding costumes and traditional ceramics and furniture.

Further along East Coast Rd are **Kim Choo's Kitchen** (Map p528; ☎ 6741 2125; 208 East Coast Rd; admission free; ☾ 11am-6pm) and **Rumah Bebe** (Map p528; ☎ 6247 5781; 113 East Coast Rd; admission free; ☾ 9.30am-6.30pm). You can catch demonstrations of how to make *bak chang* (rice dumplings) at the former. Both places also sell traditional *kebayas* (Nonya-style blouses with decorative lace) and beaded shoes, and run beading classes. Don't forget to buy some *bak chang* or *kueh* (bite-sized titbits) before you go.

The nearby **Sri Senpaga Vinayagar Temple** (Map p528; 17 Ceylon Rd; admission free; ☾ 11am-6pm) is stunning, with its intricate yet understated facade. The temple eschews colour on the exterior and instead stuns visitors with its devotional art inside.

Heading west back to the city, East Coast Rd becomes **Mountbatten Road** – there are some grand old bungalows around here, dating from the early 20th century. From East Coast Rd, buses 12 and 32 head into the Colonial District, while bus 14 goes down Stamford Rd and then Orchard Rd.

East Coast Park

This waterside park (Map p528), stretching for 10km along East Coast Parkway (ECP), is where Singaporeans come to take a dip in the soupy Straits of Singapore, windsurf, cable-ski, eat, cycle, in-line skate and chill out on the sand. The beach is built on reclaimed land – it won't win any tropical-paradise awards, but it's popular with families, and the park has some great seafood restaurants (p542) and a busy hawker centre (p542). Bikes and in-line skates can be rented from kiosks that line the busiest areas of the park. You can also camp in the park (see p532).

Bus 401 runs from Bedok MRT station to Mountbatten Rd and stops along the park's service road.

Pasir Ris Park & Downtown East

Paris Ris Park (Map pp514–15) is a 71-hectare waterside park with family-friendly activities

galore. Rent a bike or in-line skates to get around. Or hoof it and explore the 6-hectare **mangrove boardwalk** – go during low tide to see little crabs scurrying in the mud. Speaking of hooves, kids will love the pony rides at **Gallop Stables** (Map pp514-15; ☎ 6583 9665; www.gallop stable.com; 61 Pasir Ris Green; rides S$10; ☾ 8am-noon & 2-7pm Tue-Sun).

Head to **Downtown East E! Hub** (Map pp514-15; www.downtowneast.com.sg; cnr Pasir Ris Dr 3 & Pasir Ris Close). It's the building with the Ferris wheel built inside (rides S$6.50). The standouts here are the **Escape Theme Park** (Map pp514-15; ☎ 6583 9665; www .escapethemepark.com; admission adult/child S$17.70/8.90; ☾ 8am-8pm Sat, Sun, public & school holidays) and **Wild Wild Wet** (Map pp514-15; ☎ 6583 9665; www.wildwild wet.com; admission adult/child S$15.50/10/50; ☾ 1-7pm Mon & Wed-Fri, 10am-7pm Sat, Sun, public & school holidays). Price of admission allows access to unlimited rides: go-kart, slide, ride and splash around till you're wrinkled, sunburnt and sore.

There are lots of restaurants and food stalls to keep the energy levels up. To get here, take the MRT to Pasir Ris and walk to the park. A free shuttle bus serves Downtown East. Or take bus 12, 354, 358 or 403.

Changi Museum & Chapel

The **Changi Museum & Chapel** (Map pp514-15; ☎ 6214 2451; www.changimuseum.com; 1000 Upper Changi Rd Nth; admission free; guided tour adult/child S$8/4; ☾ 9.30am-5pm) poignantly commemorates the WWII Allied POWs who suffered horrific treatment at the hands of the invading Japanese. Stories are told through photographs, letters, drawings and murals; tales of heroism and celebration of peace temper the mood. There are also full-sized replicas of the famous **Changi Murals** painted by POW Stanley Warren in the old POW hospital. The originals are off limits in what is now Block 151 of the nearby Changi Army Camp.

The museum's centrepiece is a replica of the original Changi Chapel built by inmates as a focus for worship and as a sign of solidarity and strength.

Bus 2 from Victoria St or Tanah Merah MRT will take you past the entrance. The bus terminates at Changi Village.

Changi Village

On the far northeast coast of Singapore, **Changi Village** (Map pp514–15) is an escape from the city mayhem. The low-slung buildings are modern, but there's still a village atmosphere;

SINGAPORE

the lively hawker centre next to the bus terminus is the focal point. Changi Beach (where thousands of Singaporean civilians were executed during WWII), lapped by the polluted waters of the Straits of Johor, is lousy for swimming, but there's a good stretch of sand. The ferry terminal for catching a bumboat to Pulau Ubin is located opposite the hawker centre. Bus 2 from Tanah Merah MRT runs here.

Pulau Ubin

A chugging 10-minute bumboat ride (one way S$2.50, trips between 7am and 8pm) from Changi Point Ferry Terminal at Changi Village lands you on the shores of Pulau Ubin (Map pp514–15). There's no timetable; boats depart when 12 people are ready to go.

Singaporeans like to wax nostalgic about Ubin's *kampung* atmosphere, and it has thus far resisted the lure of cashed-up developers. It remains a rural, unkempt expanse of jungle full of fast lizards, weird shrines and cacophonic birdlife. Tin-roofed buildings bake in the sun, chickens squawk and panting dogs slump in the dust.

The best way to get around is by mountain bike (rental per day S$2 to S$10). Don't bother with the cheaper clunkers as your bum will appreciate proper suspension. Veer right from the jetty to the **Pulau Ubin information kiosk** (Map pp514-15; ☎ 6542 4108; www.nparks .gov.sg; ☉ 8.30am-5pm), pick up a map, and sniff around the exhibition on Ubin's culture, history and wildlife.

Trundle off on your bike and see where the road takes you. For those keen on scraping their knees, there's **Ketam Mountain Bike Park** (Map pp514–15), with over a dozen trails of varying difficulty. You can also take a trip to the **Chek Jawa Wetlands** (Map pp514-15; ☉ 8.30am-6pm) in the island's east. A 1km coastal boardwalk takes you out to sea and loops back through the mangrove swamp and the 20m-high **Jejawi Tower** offers stunning views of the area.

There are plenty of places to eat near the ferry terminal – complete your island adventure with some chilli crab and Tiger beer as the Bee Gees wail shamelessly from the stereo.

For those inclined to stay on the island, you can rent a basic but comfortable **chalet** (☎ 6385 6166; marinacountryclub.com.sg; 1-/2-bedroom chalets S$120/240; ⊠) run by the Marina Country Club. Rates plunge on weekdays.

NORTHERN & CENTRAL SINGAPORE

Apart from the major sights listed below you'll also probably find yourself visiting **Dempsey Hill** (Map pp520-1; Tanglin Village, Dempsey Rd), a once-crumbling army barracks now packed with several very 'see and be seen' restaurants and bars as well as furniture stores and even an art gallery. The nearby busy expat enclave of **Holland Village** (Map pp514–15) is also a prime dining destination.

Singapore Zoo

Set on a peninsula jutting into the Upper Seletar Reservoir, the **Singapore Zoo** (Map pp514-15; ☎ 6269 3411; www.zoo.com.sg; 80 Mandai Lake Rd; adult/child S$18/9; ☉ 8.30am-6pm) is world class. Its 28 landscaped hectares and open concept (no cages) are a far cry from the sad concrete confines some zoos retain.

There are more than 2530 residents here and most of them, with the possible exceptions of elephants used in a ride, seem pretty happy. Attractions such as the 'The Great Rift Valley of Ethiopia' enclosure convey entire ecosystems: animal, mineral, vegetable and human. Visitors can stand behind a window in 'Ethiopia' and watch 50 shameless red-bummed baboons doing things that Singaporeans still get arrested for. The popular proboscis monkeys sit on tree branches in two different enclosures, scratching and swinging more than their arms.

Children will be entertained by the list of shows and feeding sessions that seem to require a PhD to decipher. You can get around the zoo on foot or by tram (adult/child S$5/2.50). To get here take bus 138 from Ang Mo Kio MRT or bus 927 from Choa Chu Kang MRT. A taxi to/from the city costs around S$18.

Night Safari

Next door but completely separate from the zoo is the **Night Safari** (Map pp514-15; ☎ 6269 3411; www.nightsafari.com.sg; 80 Mandai Lake Rd; adult/child S$21/11; ☉ 7.30pm-midnight). You can walk around the three trails in the 40-hectare forested park but the best experience is via the tram (adult/child S$10/5), even though we think it's a little cheeky (and greedy) that you have to pay for the atmospheric 45-minute jungle tour past a parade of 120 different spot-lit nocturnal species.

The tram takes you past tigers, elephants, anteaters and lions, and some species, like the sambar deer, often sidle up close to the side of the tram. It's best to come early as the animals would have just been fed and are happy to come out to play. Don't use the flash on your camera, as it unsettles the animals.

The impressive and humorous 'Creatures of the Night' show (7.30pm, 8.30pm, 9.30pm and, on weekends, 10.30pm) will make you wonder why we ever bothered to evolve. You can save some money with a combined Zoo and Night Safari ticket (adult/child S$32/16).

After the Night Safari catch a return bus by 10.45pm to ensure you make the last train from Ang Mo Kio (11.30pm) or Choa Chu Kang (midnight). There's a taxi rank at the zoo entrance.

Mandai Orchid Gardens & Orchidville

Cultivating orchids is big business in Singapore – **Mandai Orchid Gardens** (Map pp514–15; ☎ 6269 1036; www.mandai.com.sg; 200 Mandai Lake Rd; adult/child S$3/1; ☼ 8.30am–7pm), four flowery hectares near the zoo, is the place to see them. **Orchidville** (Map pp514–15; ☎ 6552 7003; www.orchidville .com.sg; 10 Lg Lada Hitam, Mandai Agrotechnology Park; admission free; ☼ 8am–6pm Mon-Fri, 8am-9.30pm Sat & Sun) is similar to the Mandai Orchid Gardens, but has the bonus of a fantastic on-site restaurant, **Forrest** (mains from S$12; ☼ lunch & dinner). To get to these two sights, see the transport details on the zoo (opposite).

Bukit Timah Nature Reserve

Singapore's steamy heart of darkness is **Bukit Timah Nature Reserve** (Map pp514–15; ☎ 1800-468 5736; www.nparks.gov.sg; 177 Hindhede Dr; admission free; ☼ 6.30am–7pm), a 164-hectare tract of undeveloped primary rainforest clinging to Singapore's highest peak, Bukit Timah (163.63m). Established as a reserve in 1883, Bukit Timah has never been logged.

Guffawing British naturalist David Bellamy once noted that the reserve holds more tree species than the entire North American continent. The unbroken forest canopy of the reserve also shelters what remains of Singapore's native wildlife, including long-tailed macaques (monkeys), pythons and literally dozens of bird species.

There are four well-established **walking trails** through the reserve, which take from 20 minutes to one-hour return. The most popular and easiest is the concrete-paved route straight to the summit, though you should leave time to explore the less busy side trails. The steep

paths are sweaty work, so take plenty of water, embalm yourself in mosquito repellent, and don't feed the monkeys no matter how politely they ask. There is also 6km of **cycling trails** circumnavigating the forest – pick up a trail map from the **visitors centre** (☼ 8.30am-6pm).

To get here catch bus 171 from Orchard MRT, bus 75 from the CBD or bus 170 from Queen St Bus Terminal. Get off at the Bukit Timah Shopping Centre; the park's entrance is about 1km north along Hindhede Dr.

MacRitchie Reservoir

Bring lots of water and wear good walking shoes…this ain't no ordinary hike in the park. In the middle of the 2000-hectare Central Catchment Nature Reserve is the **MacRitchie Reservoir** (Map pp514–15; ☎ 6256 4248; www.nparks .gov.sg; Lornie Rd; admission free; ☼ 6.30am-6pm). The mirror-surfaced reservoir is surrounded by a 12km, five-hour, circular jungle trail. Though less popular, the six trails here are no less beautiful than the Bukit Timah Nature Reserve walks and provide more of a challenge. Pick up a map from the rangers' office along Lornie Rd or at the start of the Pierce Track.

The standout attraction here is the **treetop walk** (☼ 9am to 5pm Tue-Fri, 8.30am to 5pm Sat & Sun). Yes, it's a hard slog to get here, but once you're standing in the middle of the narrow 250m suspension bridge, all tiredness will fade. You can see glimpses of Lower Seletar Reservoir, and if you look down at the forest canopy, your naked eye alone will easily be able to spot at least nine different species of flora.

For those not inclined to walking up rocky trails, you can also hire a kayak (p513) or go fishing.

Kids will delight at the monkeys that appear along the trails…but don't feed them, no matter how cute they look.

Bus 157 runs here from Toa Payoh MRT station.

Sungei Buloh Wetland Reserve

Attention bird-nerds! The 87-hectare **Sungei Buloh Wetland Reserve** (Map pp514–15; ☎ 6794 1401; www.sbwr.org.sg; 301 Neo Tiew Cres; admission free Mon-Fri, adult/child S$1/0.50 Sat & Sun; ☼ 7.30am-7pm Mon-Sat, 7am-7pm Sun) overlooks the Straits of Johor in the far northwest of the island. The park sustains 140 bird species, most of which are migratory, and features mangrove boardwalks, walking trails enclosed by thick foliage, observation huts and guided tours on Saturdays (9am,

---

TOTO, WE'RE NOT ON ORCHARD ROAD ANY MORE...

After years of being overshadowed by the commerce of Orchard Rd, the farm owners in Kranji decided to form a collective, **Kranji Countryside Association** (www.kranjicountryside.com) to promote awareness of their existence. Thus far, they've done a great job considering they don't have the multimillion-dollar advertising budgets of retail heavies, but hey, anyone who decides to make a living selling goats' milk deserves special mention.

These **farms** (Map pp514–15) are open to the public, so you'll get a chance to sample and purchase organic vegetables, fruit and, yes, even goats' milk. Other farms specialise in seafood (consumable) and koi (not consumable), pottery, frogs and wheatgrass. There are cafes and restaurants located on some farms. To complete the 'out of Orchard' experience, stay in a plush villa at **D'Kranji Resort** (Map pp514-15; ☎ 6862 9717; www.dkranji.com.sg; d/tr from S$230/330).

The best way to check out the farms is via a shuttle bus (adult S$2/1) that runs every 1½ hours daily from outside the Kranji MRT. The bus stops at 12 farms along the return loop.

10pm, 3pm and 4pm). Audiovisual shows on the park's flora and fauna are held at 9am, 11am, 1pm, 3pm and 5pm (hourly between 9am and 5pm on Sunday). BYO binoculars and mosquito repellent.

Take bus 925 from Kranji MRT to the Kranji Reservoir bus stop – it's a 15-minute hike from here. The bus stops at the park entrance on Sundays. There's also a shuttle bus from Kranji MRT that does rounds past Kranji farms (see the boxed text, above).

Lian Shan Shuang Lin Monastery

Nestled in a corner of the Toa Payoh HDB housing estate, the photogenic **Lian Shan Shuang Lin Monastery** (Map pp514-15; ☎ 6259 6924; 184E Jln Toa Payoh; ☺ 7am-5pm), aka Siong Lim Temple, is a little out of the way, but well worth the journey. The original temple structure at the back of the compound is rather blah, no thanks to the many Frankenstein renovations done through the years. The sprawling mass built up around it, though, is something out of *Crouching Tiger, Hidden Dragon*.

Shaded pathways connect massive halls covered in gold, red and blue. A massive white reclining Buddha greets visitors in one room. Look for 12 large mythical-style paintings telling the story of the temple's founding abbots.

Next door, the **Cheng Huang Temple** (☺ 9am-5pm) is constantly buzzing with locals paying their respects. Dedicated to a god who administers justice in the netherworld (must explain the crowd), the atmospheric interior of the 1912 structure soars up to red- and ochre-hued ceilings, thick beams stained with decades of incense smoke.

The monastery and temple is about 1km east of Toa Payoh MRT station – follow the signs down Kim Keat Link off Lg 6 Toa Payoh, or take bus 238 three stops from Toa Payoh bus interchange.

Kong Meng San Phor Kark See Monastery

Take a few hours to explore the **Kong Meng San Phor Kark See Monastery** (Map pp514-15; ☎ 6453 5300; www.kmspks.org; 88 Bright Hill Rd; admission free; ☺ gates 6am-9pm, halls 8am-4pm), Singapore's largest (12 buildings) and most stunning. 'Don't speak unless it improves the silence' is the creed here, the resultant quiet a surreal counterpart to dragon-topped pagodas, shrines, plazas and lawns linked by Escher-like staircases.

On the premises is a large columbarium, several different halls devoted to various guises of the Buddha and even a dining hall that serves up free vegetarian meals to devotees. Finish your visit by reflecting under a bodhi tree beside the Hall of Precepts (the tree is claimed to be a descendant of the sacred bodhi tree at Buddha Gaya).

Buses 52 and 410 (white plate) run here from Bishan MRT station.

Kranji War Memorial

Near the Causeway off Woodlands Rd, the austere white structures and rolling lawns of the **Kranji War Memorial** (Map pp514-15; ☎ 6269 6158; www.cwgc.com; 9 Woodlands Rd; admission free; ☺ 24hr) contain the WWII graves of thousands of Allied troops. It's hard to believe that this area was once a hospital and ammunitions dump.

Headstones (more than a few simply inscribed with 'A Soldier of the 1939–1945 War') are lined in neat rows across manicured grass. Walls are inscribed with the names of 24,346 men and women who lost their lives in Southeast Asia. Row 262 has the name of a suspected (but never convicted) Japanese spy, Patrick Balcombe Heenan. Register books are available for inspection. The bodies of Singapore's first two prime ministers are interred at the front. To get here catch the MRT to Kranji then walk 10 minutes, or take bus 170 two stops west.

SOUTHERN & WESTERN SINGAPORE
Mt Faber & the Cable Car

Mt Faber (Map pp520–1) stands proud (if not tall) at 116m on the southern fringe of the city, opposite the HarbourFront Centre, VivoCity and not far from Sentosa Island. From the summit, the strange splendour of Singapore rolls away to the horizon in all directions. To the south are scenes of Keppel Wharves and industrial Pasir Panjang. Turn around to the north and the landscape does a 180. The sheer density and homogeneity of Singapore's high-rise buildings are set in a perfect panorama.

To get to the top, ride the spectacular **cable car** (Map pp520-1; ☎ 6270 8855; www.mountfaber.com.sg; 109 Mt Faber Rd; adult/child 1-way S$18.90/9.50; ⏰ 8.30am-9pm) from the HarbourFront Centre or take bus 409. Walking is difficult but rewarding, a maze of steep trails taking you through twisted copses of dense, buzzing forest, with strategically positioned seats, pavilions, lookouts and colonial-era black-and-white bungalows along the way. The summit is also part of the Southern Ridges span of parks (see below).

Impress the pants off the object of your desires with **Sky Dining** (Map pp520-1; ☎ 6377 9688; per couple S$115-198; ⏰ 6.30-8.30pm) in the cable car – a romantic three-course dinner with plummeting 60m-high views. An interesting spot to get steamy; a bad place to break up.

Southern Ridges – Kent Ridge Park to HortPark

Mt Faber is connected to Kent Ridge Park via HortPark in a 9km-long chain known as the Southern Ridges. Set aside a day, pack lots of water and start at **Kent Ridge Park** (Map pp514-15; Vigilante Dr; ⏰ 24hr). This park commands views over the port and the southern islands and is nearly always deserted. The walk will take you through a treetop boardwalk with the call of crickets your only companion. Look out for signs directing you to HortPark. Don't forget

to visit Reflections at Bukit Chandu (below) en route.

The idyllic leafy shade of Kent Ridge quickly gives way to the wide-open gardens of…don't laugh…**HortPark** (Map pp514-15; 33 Hyderabad Rd; free admission; ⏰ 24hr). This Hort(icultural) Park has more than a horrid name and a lack of shelter from the merciless sun. Walk past prototype glasshouses (sadly not open to the public) filled with all manner of flora. There are interactive displays for kids to learn about exciting gardening methods (hydroponics is cool kids!). Buy gardening tools and supplies at the **HortMart** before stopping for a Thai lunch at Kha.

Cross the leaf-like Alexander Arch bridge from HortPark and follow the gently ascending walkways up to the stunning **Henderson Waves**. This undulating sculptural pedestrian bridge is Singapore's highest, suspended at 36m above ground. It connects pedestrians to Telok Blangah Hill Park. If you're really keen on further testing the limit of your sweat glands, you could walk on through to Mt Faber (left).

The nearest bus stops to Kent Ridge Park (for buses 10, 30, 51 and 143) are on Pasir Panjang Rd, from where it's a steep hike up the hill. A taxi from the nearest MRT station, at Queenstown, will cost around S$6. You can also take bus 61, 93, 97, 100, 166, 408 or 963 from HarbourFront MRT station to HortPark.

Reflections at Bukit Chandu

Atop Bukit Chandu (Opium Hill), this WWII **interpretive centre** (Map pp514-15; ☎ 6375 2510; www .s1942.org.sg; 31K Pepys Rd; admission S$2; ⏰ 9am-5pm Tue-Sun) is set inside a tiny renovated villa. The focus is on the 1st and 2nd Battalions of the Malay Regiment, who bravely (and unsuccessfully) defended the hill against the 13,000 Japanese in the Battle of Pasir Panjang in February 1942.

The nearest bus stops (for buses 10, 30, 51 and 143) are on Pasir Panjang Rd, from where it's a steep hike up the hill. A taxi from Orchard Rd will cost around S$10. Combine this sight with a walk through the Southern Ridges (left).

Labrador Nature Reserve & Labrador Secret Tunnels

Believe it or not, this was an overgrown patch of jungle, slated to be turned into a theme park in the late '80s. Some locals had the sense to protest, and the discovery of WWII gun batteries put a stop to dreams of Disneyland. A lush **park** was carved into the hillside instead.

In addition to old gun placements on top of casemates, there's the intriguing **Labrador Secret Tunnels** (Map pp514-15; ☎ 6339 6833; Labrador Villa Rd; admission adult/child S$8/5; ⏰ 9am-5pm Tue-Sun). This series of storage and armament bunkers leads to the base of a 9.2in-circumference gun emplacement. Look for the buckled and caved-in walls from a direct hit from a Japanese bomb. Ring before visiting, as the tunnels aren't regularly manned.

Bus 408 from HarbourFront MRT takes you here. A taxi from HarbourFront costs S$6.

Haw Par Villa

There's no accounting for taste, really. Millionaire philanthropist and co-inventor of the Tiger Balm, Aw Boon Haw, certainly didn't hold back when he built the **Haw Par Villa** (Map pp514-15; ☎ 6872 2780; 262 Pasir Panjang Rd; admission free; ⏰ 9am-7pm), an unbelievably weird (some say tacky) and undoubtedly kitsch theme park.

Inspired by Chinese literature and mythology, the park is filled with thousands of statues set in dioramas depicting scenes from disparate sources including *Romance of the Three Kingdoms* and Confucianism. The park's crowning glory is the 'Ten Courts of Hell', where grotesque statues depict sinners' fates in gory detail (impaling seems to be a popular form of punishment). Recompose yourself and calm your now-disturbed children at the nearby laughing Buddha.

Located on a hill within the compound is the **Hua Song Museum** (Map pp514-15; ☎ 6872 2780; adult/child S$8.60/5.35; ⏰ 9am-6pm). As classy as the villa is tacky, this museum offers visitors a glimpse into the lives, enterprises and adventures of Chinese migrants around the world in a more studious fashion than those in Haw Par Villa.

Bus 200 from Buona Vista MRT runs here as well as buses 10, 30 and 143 from HarbourFront MRT.

NUS Museums

Ask any local about the trio of small **art museums** (Map pp514-15; ☎ 6516 4617; www.nus.edu.sg/museums; 50 Kent Ridge Cres; admission free; ⏰ 10am-7.30pm Tue-Sat, 10am-6pm Sun) in the National University of Singapore (NUS) campus and you'll probably get a blank stare before they reply, 'Huh? NUS has got a museum?' Which is a shame, as these galleries are top-notch and house a more exciting collection than the heavily advertised Singapore Art Museum (p496).

On the ground floor is the **Lee Kong Chian Art Museum** with artefacts and works spanning 7000 years of Chinese art. Look out for ceramic pillows (ouch) and delicate funerary jars from the Song dynasty. The concourse level features the **South & Southeast Asian Gallery** with art from across the region, including textiles and sculptures, all expertly curated. When we visited, there was a huge display of art by Jendela, an Indonesian collective.

Upstairs is the **Ng Eng Teng Gallery**, displaying 1106 paintings, drawings and sculptures by Ng Eng Teng (1934–2001), one of Singapore's foremost artists, specialising in imaginative, sometimes surreal, bodily depictions. There's a human, sometimes self-deprecating, element to the work, perhaps best seen in a display of bloodied cotton balls (the artist had tuberculosis).

Visit the Raffles Museum of Biodiversity Research (below) while you're on campus. Catch bus 95 from Buona Vista MRT to get here.

Raffles Museum of Biodiversity Research

If examining stuffed animals and creatures preserved in large jars gets your pulse racing, the small **Raffles Museum of Biodiversity Research** (Map pp514-15; ☎ 6874 5082; www.rmbr.nus.edu.sg; Block 56, Level 3, NUS Faculty of Science, Science Dr 2, Lower Kent Ridge Rd; admission free; ⏰ 9am-5pm Mon-Fri), on the NUS campus, will give your adrenal glands a workout.

There are stuffed and preserved examples of rare and locally extinct creatures, including a 4.42m king cobra (clubbed to death when it slithered into the Singapore Country Club) and a banded leaf monkey (mauled by dogs… do we sense a theme here?) eerily floating in a tank, arms held up by strings.

It's not exactly on the tourist trail, but it's worth the trip if you combine it with the NUS Museums (left) nearby. Catch bus 95 from Buona Vista MRT.

Jurong Bird Park

This ageing attraction is still popular with school kids, families and nature photographers. The **Jurong Bird Park** (Map pp514-15; ☎ 6265 0022;

SINGAPORE'S LAST KAMPUNG (VILLAGE)

As if willed into existence from an old black-and-white photograph from the 1950s, Lg Buangkok's *kampung* (Map pp514–15), in an urbane corner of Singapore, is mainland Singapore's last little blip of resistance against the tide of modern development.

Hidden behind a wall of trees, this little swath of land houses a ramshackle collection of wooden houses, many with zinc roofs. The few residents live an idyllic existence not unlike how many Singaporeans did before the development frenzy. Chickens roam the grounds, dogs flick flies away with a flap of their ears, crickets and birds hum and chirp in the background, and the 28 families here have carefree sensibilities not common in the general populace (the cheap S$30 per month rents must help). The *kampung* is busiest during the weekend when curious locals and photo clubs descend for a slice of nostalgia.

Sadly, the owner of the land, Sng Mui Hong, might not be able to preserve this family legacy. Master plans by the Urban Redevelopment Authority of Singapore have revealed that the land the *kampung* stands on is slated to be, what else, redeveloped into housing and schools.

To get here, either catch a taxi from the city (roughly S$15) or take bus 88 from Pasir Ris or Toa Payoh and get off on Ang Mo Kio Ave 5 just after Yio Chu Kang Rd. Go north up Yio Chu Kang Rd and turn right onto Gerard Dr. Continue until you find Lg Buangkok. Look for an unpaved road leading into the village. Good luck, for it might have been bulldozed by the time this goes to print.

www.birdpark.com.sg; 2 Jurong Hill; adult/child S$18/9, panorail S$5/2.50; 🕑 8am-6pm) is home to 8000 birds – 600 species, 30 of them endangered. Visitors walk through themed enclosures along 1.7km worth of trails: pelicans gawp at passers-by along a boardwalk, leggy pink flamingos stand proud by a lake, penguins nosedive through water in air-conditioned comfort and cutting through it all is the escapable scent of bird poop.

Other highlights include the penguin feedings at 10.30am and 3.30pm, the Waterfall Aviary (with its 30m-high man-made waterfall, the highest in the world), and the nocturnal World of Darkness. There are various flappy-bird shows throughout the day and a 'panorail' to shunt you around if you're feeling lazy.

To get here take bus 194 or 251 from Boon Lay MRT.

Singapore Science Centre

The endearingly geeky **Singapore Science Centre** (Map pp514-15; ☎ 6425 2500; www.science.edu.sg; 15 Science Centre Rd; adult/child S$6/3; 🕑 10am-6pm Sat-Thu, 10am-9pm Fri) is chock-full of exhibits covering a variety of themes, from optical illusions to maths (ugh), the human body and even climate change. Many displays are of a push/pull/twist-and-see-what-happens variety but our favourite is the gi-normous Tesla coil that frenetically shoots up sparks to the ceiling. No touching, kids!

Outside is the free **Kinetic Garden**, an interactive scientific sculpture garden. Next door, the **Omni-Theatre** (Map pp514-15; adult/child S$10/5; 🕑 11am-8pm) projects films (of the nature-documentary variety) onto a 23m hemispheric screen and blasts your eardrums with 20,000 watts of sound.

Jurong East is the nearest MRT station – take the left-hand exit, walk through a row of stores and across Jurong Town Hall Rd. A taxi from Orchard Rd costs around S$18.

SENTOSA ISLAND

Five hundred metres off the south coast of Singapore is **Sentosa Island** (Map pp514-15; ☎ 6736 8672; www.sentosa.com.sg; adult/child S$2; 🕑 7am-midnight), the city's unfailingly popular resort getaway. The Brits turned the island into a military fortress in the late 1800s. In 1967 it was returned to the Singaporean government, who developed it into a holiday resort. These days, a concerted effort to transform the island from tacky second-rate to tacky world-class is under way. By 2010, the entire northern front will be home to a Universal Studios Theme Park and a casino (see the boxed text, p495).

Like its beaches with imported sand, fake boulders and piped tin-drum renditions of 'Girls Just Wanna Have Fun' and 'Summer Holiday', Sentosa is an almost entirely synthetic attraction, but kids love the flashy rides and there are some substantial museums and outdoor activities for adults to chew on.

SINGAPORE

There's easily enough here for a full day's entertainment; if that's not enough time, you can stay overnight (see p534). The improving crop of restaurants and bars will keep you fed and watered.

Most attractions cost extra, which really adds up if you want to see them all. Ticket packages are a solid option at adult/child S$38.90/26.90. The Singapore Tourism Board (STB) branches have all the details. Free stuff on the island includes the buses and beaches.

Underwater World

Sentosa's saving grace, Gracie the dugong is the star performer at **Underwater World** (Map pp514-15; ☎ 6275 0030; www.underwaterworld.com.sg; adult/child S$22.90/14.60; ☏ 9am-9pm). Leafy sea dragons and wobbling Medusa jellyfish are mesmeric, while stingrays and 10ft sharks cruise inches from your face as the travellator takes you through the Ocean Colony's submerged glass tubes. Watch divers feeding the fish, or muster some nerve for the 30-minute *Dive with the Sharks* experience ($120 per person; call for details and bookings). The lights are turned off after 7pm and the aquarium takes on an eerie torchlit atmosphere.

Entry includes admission to **Dolphin Lagoon** (Map pp514-15; ☏ 10.30am-6pm) at Palawan Beach, where Indo-Pacific humpbacked dolphins (aka pink dolphins) dutifully perform at 11am, 1pm, 3.30pm and 5.30pm. For S$150 you can swim with the dolphins (call or check the website for bookings).

Fort Siloso

Dating from the 1880s, when Sentosa was called Pulau Blakang Mati (Malay for 'island behind which lies death'), is **Fort Siloso** (Map pp514-15; adult/child S$8/5; ☏ 10am-6pm). Three self-guided tours lead you around the various gun emplacements, tunnels and buildings, with waxwork recreations and voice-overs. When it came to the crunch in the WWII Japanese invasion, Siloso's guns were all pointing the wrong way (you can see the view from the southernmost gun emplacement). The Japanese used the fort as a POW camp.

From 1989 until 1992, Siloso housed Sentosa's most unusual 'attraction', political prisoner Chia Thye Poh. Arrested in 1966 for alleged communist sympathies, Chia served 23 years in jail before being placed under house arrest in Siloso – Sentosa's holiday delights sprang up around him.

Images of Singapore

This diverting historical and cultural **museum** (Map pp514-15; adult/child S$10/7; ☏ 9am-7pm) kicks off with Singapore as a Malay Sultanate then takes you through its consolidation as a port and trading centre, WWII and the subsequent Japanese surrender. Scenes are recreated using lifelike wax dummies, film footage and dramatic light-and-sound effects. Recreations of local customs and tradition are particularly interesting. A well-worn attraction on the school-excursion trail.

Beaches

Sentosa's three southern beaches – **Siloso** to the west, **Palawan** in the middle and **Tanjong** to the east – will never match the beaches in Malaysia or Indonesia, but that doesn't seem to matter to the Singaporeans who flock here. The sandy coconut vibe is soporific, even if the muddy Straits of Singapore are a little uninviting.

Other Attractions

Songs of the Sea (Map pp514-15; admission S$10; ☏ 7.40 & 8.40pm) is set out on *kelongs* (offshore fishing huts) and nightly combines musical gushings with a spectacular S$4-million sound, light and laser extravaganza – worth hanging around for.

You'll be fluttered by more than 50 species of butterfly inside the **Butterfly Park & Insect Kingdom** (Map pp514-15; adult/child S$16/10; ☏ 9am-6.30pm). The Insect Kingdom museum has thousands of mounted butterflies, rhino beetles, Hercules beetles (the world's largest), scorpions, and other critters and varmints – kids stare wide-eyed while adults feign disinterest.

Among the trashier of Sentosa's attractions is the **Merlion** (Map pp514-15; adult/child S$8/5; ☏ 10am-8pm), a 37m hybrid lion-mermaid statue towering over the island; the view is great but it's better from the cable car.

Cineblast, **4D Magix** and **Desperadoes** (Map pp514-15; adult/child S$18/11; ☏ 10am-9pm) offer different 4-D virtual-reality thrill rides and shows per admission – the 'fourth' dimension being the water sprayed at you (how rude!). There are several nature trails including the **Dragon Trail Nature Walk**, which has been typically livened up with plaster dragons and fossils. There are also plenty of long-tailed macaques about – keep your food hidden!

The 'over too quickly' **Sentosa Luge** (Map pp514-15; per ride & chairlift S$11; ⊙ 10am-6pm) is a 650m downhill blitz on a wheeled toboggan.

Make like a dotcom dork on a Segway ride with **Gogreen Segway Eco Adventure** (Map pp514-15; rides from S$10; ⊙ 10am-9.30pm). Get perpendicular on this two-wheeled vehicle and scoot round a circuit (10 minutes, S$10) or opt for a longer jaunt to Tanjong or Siloso Beach (45 minutes, S$35).

Resembling a camembert impaled on a carrot, the former Carlsberg Sky Tower has had a fresh coat of paint and been rebadged the **Tiger Sky Tower** (Map pp514-15; adult/child S$12/8; ⊙ 9am-9pm). Take the slow ride up the 110m column for magical Singapore views. Thankfully, the Carlsberg Float – a beer and ice-cream monstrosity at the bar – was not replaced with a Tiger version.

Getting There & Away

The easiest way to get to Sentosa is via shuttle bus (S$3) from HarbourFront Bus Interchange, running every 15 minutes from 7am to 11pm Sunday to Thursday, and until 12.30am on Friday and Saturday.

You can also catch the Sentosa Express rail link (Map pp514-15; return ticket S$3; ⊙ 7am-midnight) from the 3rd floor of the mammoth VivoCity mall, next to HarbourFront MRT.

For a more memorable trip, take the cable car to Sentosa from the top of Mt Faber or HarbourFront Tower Two (see p507). Standard cabins cost S$18.90/9.50 for adults/children one way; the cable car operates between 8.30am and 11pm.

Getting Around

Transport on the island is included in the admission price. There are three colour-coded bus lines zooming between attractions, and motorised trams connecting the beaches. The island is small enough to walk around but some parts are steep. You can also hire bikes and in-line skates from S$5 to S$10 per hour at Palawan and Siloso Beaches – very tempting when weekend bus queues start to burgeon.

SOUTHERN ISLANDS

Three other islands popular with castaway-fantasising locals are St John's, Kusu and Lazarus. On weekends they're mildly crowded but during the week they can be almost deserted…unless your visit clashes with a school camp – still, they're great for fishing, swim-ming, a picnic and guzzling BYO six-packs. St John's and Kusu Islands have changing rooms and toilets.

St John's Island (Map pp514-15) is the largest of the three. It was once a quarantine station for immigrants, a drug-rehabilitation centre and a detention centre. These days, there isn't much there except retro-looking low-lying bungalows, a swimming lagoon and local flora. Bring a fishing rod and expect to snag some snappers or groupers – just as well, because the culinary offerings here are nonexistent.

You can stay overnight in air-conditioned colonial-style bungalows (from S$53.50 per night) – contact the **Sentosa Development Corporation** (☎ 1800-736 8672) for details. You could also camp for free along the beach.

Lazarus Island (Map pp514-15) is now connected to St John's via a concrete walkway. If St John's is quiet, then Lazarus is a ghost town. It's popular with anglers and local campers. At night, it's pitch black except for the twinkling of lights from shipping boats moored not far off the coast.

Kusu Island (Map pp514-15) is more culturally interesting; devotees coming to pray for health, wealth and fertility at its Taoist temple and Malay *kramat* (shrine). There's a turtle sanctuary (awww) and the Tua Pek Kong Temple next to the ferry jetty. Entering the temple is akin to entering someone's home: a lazing resident dog stares at you, fishing nets and laundry lie drying in the sun, and a mango tree out the back tempts you with its juicy fruit (no, don't try).

A canary yellow–painted *kramat* is at the top of some steep steps on a small hill. Strangely enough, there's a Chinese altar at the front of the *kramat* and the caretaker offers you Chinese-style joss sticks for S$2. Pray for wealth and pick a 4D lottery number.

You can visit both temple and shrine in less than an hour, leaving you the rest of the day to loll around on the beach. Kusu is also home to the only place in Singapore with sea water that's actually clear! The swimming lagoon that faces Indonesia is pure joy and most visitors spend most of their time frolicking here. BYO food and drinks. The 'hawker centre' marked on the map is empty.

The liveliest time to visit Kusu is during the annual pilgrimage of Taoists in the ninth lunar month (around October).

SINGAPORE

Getting There & Away

The ferry from **Marina South Pier** (Map pp520-1; ☎ 6275 03888; www.islandcruise.com.sg; 31 Marina Coastal Dr; adult/child return S$15/12; ☑ 10am & 2pm Mon-Fri, 9am, noon & 3pm Sat, every 2hr 9am-5pm Sun) runs to St John's, stopping for 20 minutes before heading to Kusu. You can spend a few hours at each island by getting the first ferry to St John's, getting off and catching the next one on to Kusu before getting the last one back to Marina South. To get to Marina South Pier, take bus 402 from outside the Marina Bay MRT station.

Some harbour cruises also pass St John's Island and stop at Kusu for 20 minutes or so (see p529).

ACTIVITIES

ADVENTURE SPORT

If you like your highs quick, intense and somewhat brutal, the **G-max Reverse Bungy** (Map p517; ☎ 6338 1146; www.gmax.com.sg; 3E River Valley Rd; per ride S$45; ☑ 1pm-1am Mon-Thu, 1pm-2am Fri, noon-2am Sat, noon-1am Sun) might be for you. You are strapped into padded chairs inside a metal cage, which is propelled skyward to a height of 60m at speeds exceeding 200km/h before being pulled back down by gravity.

A relatively more gentle high ('relatively' is the key word here) is offered right next door on the **GX-5** (Map p517; ☎ 6338 1146; www.gmax.com.sg; 3E River Valley Rd; per ride S$40; ☑ 1pm-1am Mon-Thu, 1pm-2am Fri, noon-2am Sat, noon-1am Sun). The GX5 swings riders up and over the Singapore River at a less nauseating velocity. Many patrons sign up in a fit of alcohol-fuelled courage, as these rides are located next to the bar-filled Clarke Quay.

CYCLING

You can hire a bike and trundle along the foreshore at East Coast Park (p503), at Pasir Ris Park (p503) or on Pulau Ubin (p504) for between S$5 and S$10 per hour, depending on the quality of the bike. There are tandem bikes.

There's a 5.7km **bicycle track** looping around Sentosa Island that takes in most of its attractions. Hire a bike at Siloso or Palawan Beaches – see p511.

For a more challenging workout tackle the mountain-bike trails around Bukit Timah Nature Reserve (p505) and at Pulau Ubin (p504).

Two Wheel Action (☎ 6471 2775; www.twa.com .sg) organises Sunday rides in collaboration with the Singapore chapter of the Hash House Harriers. You bring your own bike, meet at a prearranged point, then propel yourself into it. It costs S$10 per session.

GOLF

Golf is big business in Singapore, and big status too.

There are two 18-hole golf courses at the **Sentosa Golf Club** (Map pp514-15; ☎ 6275 0022; 18 holes S$305-425).

Most other clubs are members only, but the following courses will let you tee-off for S$30 to S$50 for nine holes on weekdays, or S$50 to S$180 on weekends:

Executive Golf Course (Map pp514-15; ☎ 6556 0600; Upper Seletar Reservoir, Mandai Rd)
Jurong Country Club (Map pp514-15; ☎ 6560 5655; 9 Science Centre Rd)
Marina Bay Golf Course (Map pp520-1; ☎ 6345 7788; 80 Rhu Cross)

GYMS

Most big hotels have gyms, or gym junkies can head to **Fitness First** (Map p524; ☎ 6737 7889; 05-01 Paragon, 290 Orchard Rd; ☑ 6.30am-10.30pm Mon-Sat, 8am-10pm Sun), **California Fitness** (Map p524; ☎ 6834 2100; Orchard Bldg, 1 Grange Rd; ☑ 6am-midnight Mon-Sat, 8am-10pm Sun) or **True Fitness** (Map p517; ☎ 6820 9000; 07-0011 Suntec City Mall, 3 Temasek Blvd; ☑ 6am-11pm Mon-Thu, 6am-10pm Fri, 6am-9pm Sat, 8am-8pm Sun).

POOL & SNOOKER

Singaporeans *love* to play pool. Chalk your cue at **Pool Fusion** (Map p517; ☎ 6339 9225; 01-04 Beach Centre, 15 Beach Rd; per hr S$12; ☑ noon-3am), or bend elbows with raucous teens at **SuperCue** (Map p517; ☎ 6334 1000; www.superbowl.com.sg; 03-200 Marina Sq, 6 Raffles Blvd; per hr S$12; ☑ 10am-1am Sun-Thu, 10am-3am Fri & Sat).

ROCK CLIMBING

Dairy Farm Quarry (Map pp514-15; Dairy Farm Rd) near Bukit Timah is the only legal place to climb in Singapore. Most of the 20-plus routes are bolted and can be tackled with a 50m rope; bring your own gear. Groups of climbers come here regularly on weekends – check www.indoorclimbing.com/singapore.html for details.

SPAS & MASSAGE

Massage, beauty treatments and reflexology are regulation Singaporean indulgences – everyone seems to have clear skin, clean nails and lustrously flowing hair. Every mall seems to have a spa or massage joint of some sort, so you're never too far from an overhaul!

Willow Stream Spa (Map p517; ☎ 6432 5600; www .willowstream.com; 06-01 Fairmont Singapore, 80 Bras Basah Rd; ☺ 10am-10pm) covers all the bases – massages, facials, wraps, manicures pedicures, waxing – and keeps you relaxed for hours. Prices start at S$40 and go sky high.

With branches scattered throughout the city, **Kenko Wellness Boutique** (Map pp526-7; ☎ 6223 0303; www.kenko.com.sg; 211 South Bridge Rd; ☺ 10am-10pm) is the McDonald's of Singapore's spas, but there is nothing drive-thru about its foot reflexology (30 minutes S$33).

Spa Botanica (Map pp514-15; ☎ 6371 1318; www .spabotanica.com; Sentosa Resort & Spa, 2 Bukit Manis Rd, Sentosa; ☺ 10am-10pm) was Singapore's first indoor/outdoor spa. The signature Galaxy Steam Bath (S$95) is a 30-minute wallow in medicinal chakra mud in a specially designed steam room.

SWIMMING

Given the polluted waters, Singapore's beaches aren't particularly swim-friendly, although there are safe swimming areas at East Coast Park and on Sentosa and the southern islands. Alternatively, Singapore's 50m public swimming pools (per adult S$1 to S$1.30, child S$0.50 to S$0.70, open from 8am to 9.30pm) are winners:

Delta Swimming Complex (Map pp520-1; ☎ 6474 7573; 900 Tiong Bahru Rd)

Jalan Besar Swimming Complex (Map p522; ☎ 6293 9058; 100 Tyrwhitt Rd)

Katong Swimming Complex (Map p528; ☎ 6344 9609; 111 Wilkinson Rd)

River Valley Swimming Complex (Map p517; ☎ 6337 6275; 1 River Valley Rd)

TENPIN BOWLING

Just what the government ordered – good, clean family fun! **SuperBowl** (Map p517; ☎ 6334 1000; www.superbowl.com.sg; 03-200 Marina Sq, 6 Raffles Blvd; per game S$4-4.30; ☺ 10am-1am Sun-Thu, 10am-3am Fri & Sat) has 16 lanes of bowl-o-rama.

WATER SPORTS

Aquabikes, canoes, kayaks and sailboards are available for hire on Sentosa's beaches for around S$15 per hour.

Water-Venture (off Map p528; ☎ 6444 0409; www .water-venture.org.sg; 1390 East Coast Parkway; ☺ 9am-6.30pm Tue-Sun) offers windsurfing classes (S$35) and courses (S$55 to S$150).

The **Singapore Waterski & Wakeboard Federation** (Map pp526-7; ☎ 6348 9943; www.swwf.org.sg; Water Sports Centre, 269A South Bridge Rd) runs waterskiing and wakeboarding lessons (from S$90 per hour on weekdays, S$120 on weekends).

Ski360° (Map p528; ☎ 6442 7318; www.ski360degree .com; 1206A East Coast Parkway; per hr Mon-Fri S$32, per hr Sat & Sun S$42; ☺ 10am-10pm Mon-Fri, 9am-10pm Sat & Sun) is a daredevil cable-ski installation at East Coast Lagoon where, if you can master the launch technique, you're dragged around the lagoon on a wakeboard by a circular cable system.

The Singapore Canoe Federation rents kayaks from the **Paddle Lodge** (Map pp514-15; ☎ 6258 0057; Lornie Rd, MacRitchie Reservoir; 1/2hr rental S$12/15; ☺ 9am-6pm Tue-Sun) at MacRitchie Reservoir.

YOGA

The **Shambhala Yoga Centre** (Map p524; ☎ 6735 2163; www.comoshambhala.bz; 06-05 Forum, 583 Orchard Rd; 1½hr class S$34; ☺ 9am-9pm Mon-Fri, 9.30am-5pm Sat & Sun) has Hatha, Iyengar, Vinyasa and Ashtanga classes, and Pilates. It sometimes offers a free class for first-time visitors.

Absolute Yoga (Map pp520-1; ☎ 6732 6007; www .absoluteyogasingapore.com; 02-01 Valley Point, 491 River Valley Rd; 1½hr class S$34; ☺ 7am-9pm Mon-Fri, 8.30am-6pm Sat & Sun) offers 'Hot Yoga', Hatha and Iyengar classes along with Pilates.

COURSES

COOKING

You've eaten the food, now learn how to cook it yourself, Singapore-style! Cooking classes generally run from two to four hours. Many are hands-on; some are instruction only. Check websites or call for bookings and schedules.

at-sunrice (Map p517; ☎ 6336 3307; www.at-sunrice .com; Fort Canning Centre, Fort Canning Park; classes from S$107) Banish your dinner-party woes. Half-day classes with a spicy hands-on emphasis equip you with the skills to prepare a three-course meal.

(Continued on page 529)

SINGAPORE

SINGAPORE

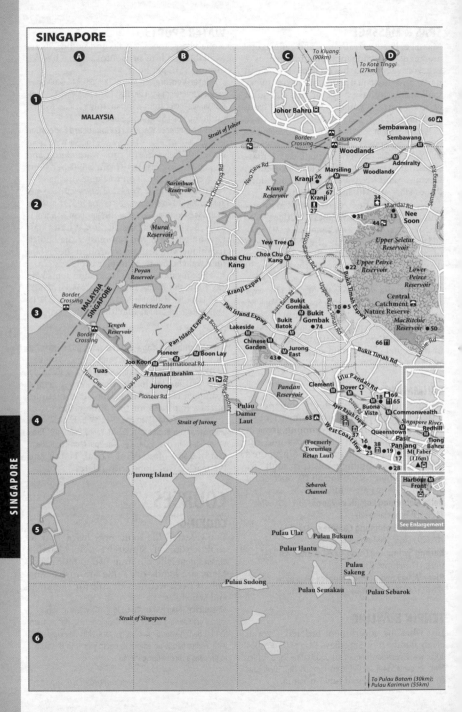

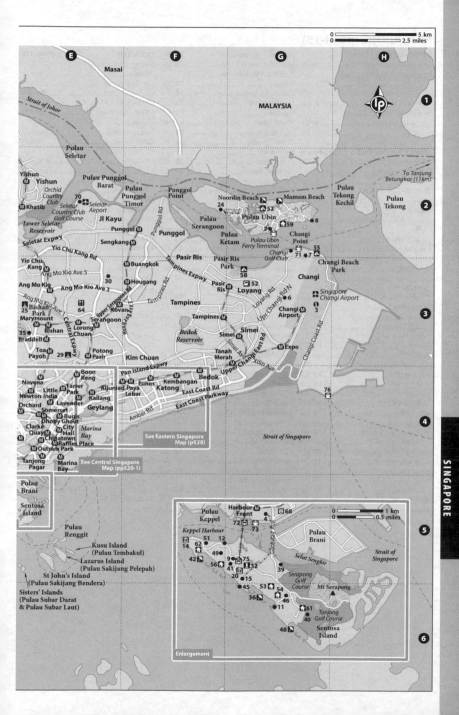

SINGAPORE (p514-15)

SINGAPORE

COLONIAL DISTRICT & THE QUAYS

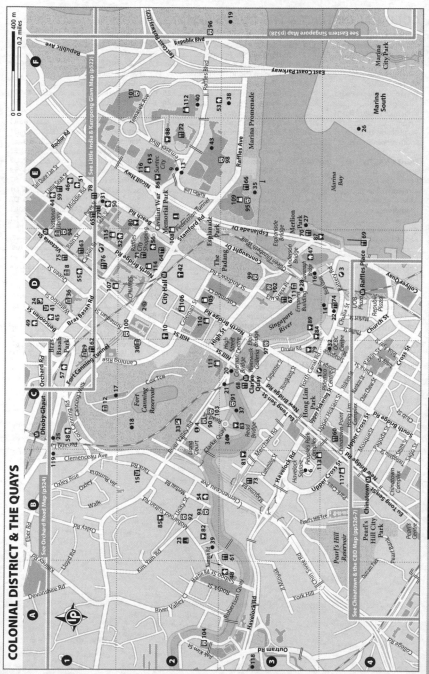

COLONIAL DISTRICT & THE QUAYS (p517)

COLONIAL DISTRICT & THE QUAYS (p517)

SINGAPORE

CENTRAL SINGAPORE

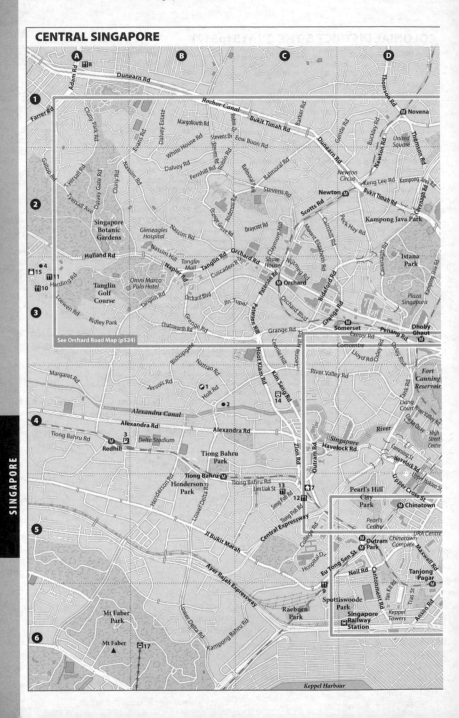

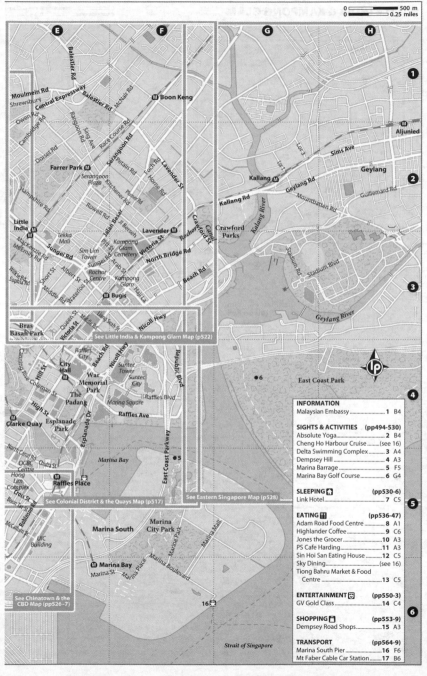

SINGAPORE

INFORMATION
Malaysian Embassy **1** B4

SIGHTS & ACTIVITIES (pp494–530)
Absolute Yoga................................ **2** B4
Cheng Ho Harbour Cruise ....(see 16)
Delta Swimming Complex **3** A4
Dempsey Hill **4** A3
Marina Barrage **5** F5
Marina Bay Golf Course **6** G4

SLEEPING (pp530–6)
Link Hotel **7** C5

EATING (pp536–47)
Adam Road Food Centre **8** A1
Highlander Coffee **9** C6
Jones the Grocer **10** A3
PS Cafe Harding **11** A3
Sin Hoi San Eating House **12** C5
Sky Dining .... (see 16)
Tiong Bahru Market & Food
Centre **13** C5

ENTERTAINMENT (pp550–3)
GV Gold Class **14** C4

SHOPPING (pp553–9)
Dempsey Road Shops **15** A3

TRANSPORT (pp564–9)
Marina South Pier **16** F6
Mt Faber Cable Car Station **17** B6

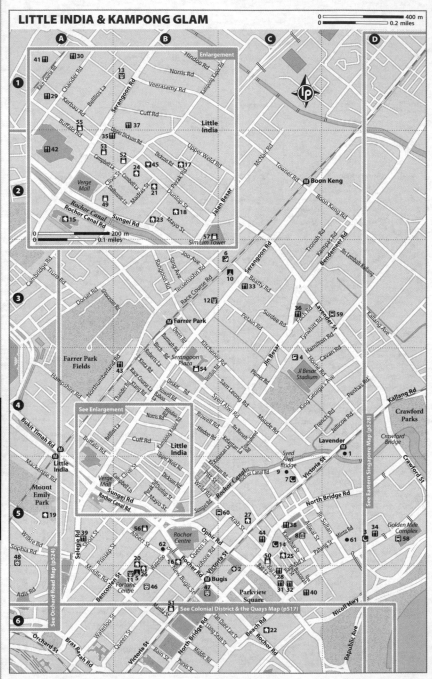

LITTLE INDIA & KAMPONG GLAM

LITTLE INDIA & KAMPONG GLAM (p522)

SINGAPORE

ORCHARD ROAD

ORCHARD ROAD (p524)

SINGAPORE

CHINATOWN & THE CBD

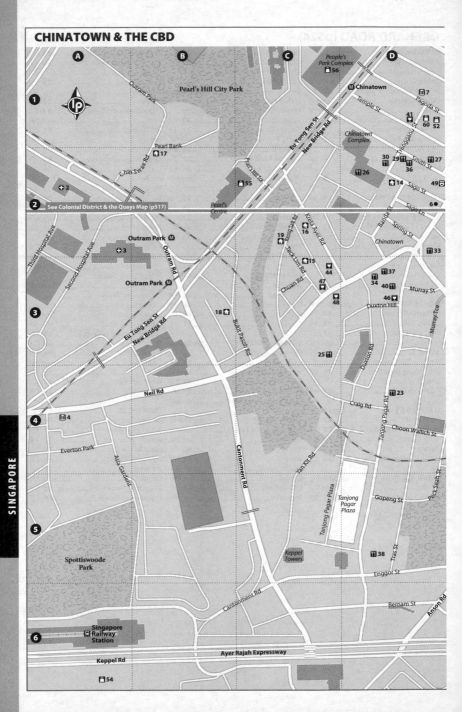

See Colonial District & the Quays Map (p517)

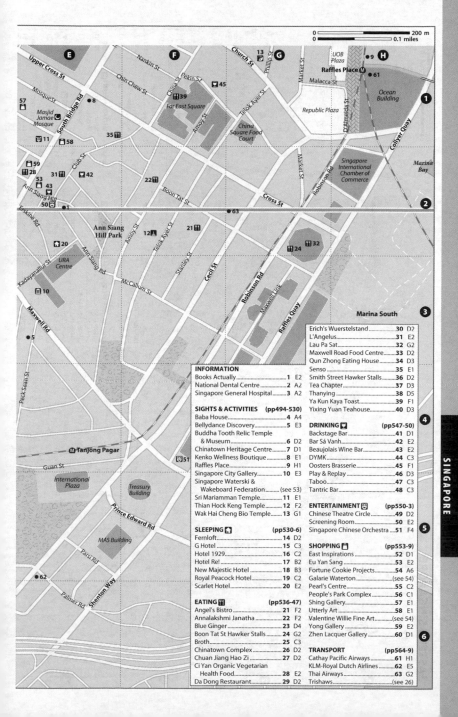

SINGAPORE

EASTERN SINGAPORE

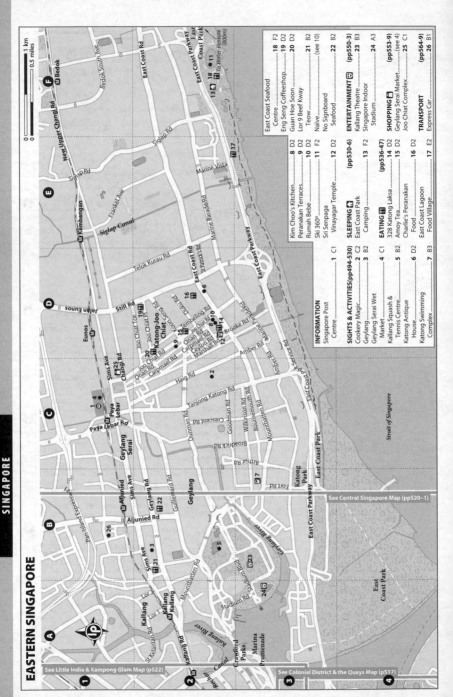

INFORMATION		
Singapore Post		
Centre	**1**	C1
SIGHTS & ACTIVITIES	(pp494–530)	
Cookery Magic	**2**	C2
Geylang	**3**	B2
Geylang Serai Wet		
Market	**4**	C1
Kallang Squash &		
Tennis Centre	**5**	B2
Katong Antique		
House	**6**	D2
Katong Swimming		
Complex	**7**	B3
Kim Choo's Kitchen	**8**	D2
Peranakan Terraces	**9**	D2
Rumah Bebe	**10**	D2
Ski 360°	**11**	F2
Sri Senpaga		
Vinayagar Temple	**12**	B2
SLEEPING	(pp530–6)	
East Coast Park		
Camping	**13**	F2
EATING	(pp536–47)	
328 Katong Laksa	**14**	D2
Amoy Tea	**15**	B2
Charlie's Peranakan		
Food	**16**	D2
East Coast Lagoon		
Food Village	**17**	E2
East Coast Seafood		
Centre	**18**	F2
Eng Seng Coffeeshop	**19**	D2
Guan Hoe Soon	**20**	D2
Lor 9 Beef Kway		
Teow	**21**	B2
Naïve	(see 10)	
No Signboard		
Seafood	**22**	B2
ENTERTAINMENT	(pp550–3)	
Kallang Theatre	**23**	B3
Singapore Indoor		
Stadium	**24**	A3
SHOPPING	(pp553–9)	
Geylang Serai Market	(see 4)	
Joo Chiat Complex	**25**	C1
TRANSPORT	(pp564–9)	
Express Car	**26**	B1

(Continued from page 513)

Cookery Magic (Map p528; ☎ 6348 9667; www
.cookerymagic.com; Haig Rd, Katong; classes S$65-130)
Ruqxana conducts standout Asian-cooking classes in her
own home. She also conducts classes on an ecofarm (harvest
your own veggies before cooking!) and on Pulau Ubin (in an
old *kampung* home). Splash out for the hands-on classes.
Raffles Culinary Academy (Map p517; ☎ 6412 1256;
www.raffleshotel.com; 03-03/04 Raffles Hotel, 1 Beach
Rd; sessions S$95-140) Take cues from the Raffles chefs
and cook up a storm at the academy's new digs. Hands-on
courses cover an international range of cuisines…pastries
too!
Shermay's Cooking School (Map pp514-15; ☎ 6479
8442; www.shermay.com; 03-64 Block 43 Jln Merah Saga,
Chip Bee Gardens; classes S$89-159) Singaporean, Thai,
Peranakan, chocolate and guest chefs are Shermay's faves!
Hands-on classes cost more. Catch bus 7, 61 or 77.
Spice Queen (Map p522; ☎ 6255 2440; www.spice
-queen.com; 24 Race Course Rd; classes from S$40) Local
celebrity chef Devagi Sanmugam conducts Indian cooking
demos in a kitchen above her restaurant. Shopping trips
are a highlight.

DANCING

Belly Dance Discovery (Map pp526-7; ☎ 9879 9980;
www.bellydance.com.sg; 03-00, 20 Peck Seah St) Master
the Middle Eastern art of booty shaking. The S$5 introduc-
tory classes are popular. Eight-lesson courses cost S$175.
Guys will have to continue nursing their belly-dancer
aspirations; strictly female-only.
Jitterbugs Swingapore (Map p517; ☎ 6887 0383;
www.jitterbugs.com; 03-02 Millenia Walk, 9 Raffles Blvd)
Beautiful teachers instruct participants in the art of shimmying and shaking (there's even pole dancing). Walk-in
classes are S$20 and eight-week classes are S$160.

PEWTERSMITHING

Royal Selangor (p497) runs the **School of Hard
Knocks** (Map p517; ☎ 6268 9600; www.royalselangor.com

SCARE YOUR PANTS OFF

For the last few years, **Singapore Paranormal Investigators** (www.spi.com.sg/news/
tours/index.htm) have been supplementing
their work by taking groups of people
around Singapore's 'haunted' sites and
generally frightening the wits out of them.
This is no theme-park haunted-house thrill
trip, though – these guys are serious. Email
ghoulish@spi.org.sg for upcoming trips.

.sg; 01-01 Clarke Quay), at which groups of 12 bash
pewter into malleable masterpieces. Thirty-
minute courses cost S$30; you get to keep
the inscribed dish you make and your natty
SOHN apron.

TOURS

The Singapore Tourism Board (p563) books
a range of tours and publishes a handful of
free, self-guided walking-tour brochures.
The SIA Hop-On, CityBuzz, City Hippo
and Singapore Trolley tourist buses (p568)
traverse Singapore's most-loved sites. See
also the Trishaws boxed text (p567).

FOOD TOURS

Food Safari Tours (☎ 6438 4038; www.makansutra
.com) Runs four-hour foodie tours (from S$160), usually
including three pit-stops. Options include the North-
South-East-West Tour (street food), Multicultural Tour
(Little India, Chinatown, Geylang and Katong), Uniquely
Singapore Tour (*bak kut teh*, fish-head curry, chicken rice
etc) and Midnight Tour (duh!).
I Eat, I Shoot, I Post Makan Sessions (http://ieat
ishootipost.sg) Not strictly a food tour. Leslie Tay is a
doctor by day and a foodie by life. He organises monthly
makan (eating) sessions. These are usually reasonably
priced multicourse meals at great local restaurants. Check
the blog and forums for details. There are also impromptu
eating sessions organised by forum members.

HARBOUR CRUISES

Cheng Ho Harbour Cruise (Map pp520-1; ☎ 6533
9811; www.watertours.com.sg) A 2½-hour tour on the
Cheng Ho, a gaudy Ming-dynasty-junk replica, bobbing
around the harbour, port and Kusu Island. Tours leave
Marina South Pier at 10.30am (adult/child S$27/14) and
3pm (S$32/16 with afternoon tea). Its two-hour dinner
cruise (adult/child S$55/29) leaves at 6.30pm and loops
past Sentosa.

Duck Tour (Map p517; ☎ 6338 6877; www.ducktours .com.sg; adult/child S$33/17) A one-hour romp in the 'Wacky Duck', a Vietnam War amphibious curio, departing from Suntec City. Check out the city's sites from the road then hit the water for a harbour cruise. A good one for the kids! Adults will be comprehensively embarrassed.

RIVER CRUISES

A super way to get a feel for central Singapore and its history is to take a river cruise. Bumboat cruises depart from various jetties along the Singapore River including Clarke Quay, Raffles Landing and Boat Quay, as well as Merlion Park and the Esplanade Jetty on Marina Bay, generally running between 9am and 11pm.

Hippo River Cruise (Map p517; ☎ 6338 6877; www .ducktours.com.sg) This is a 30-minute open-top boat ride (adult/child S$13/9) departing from Clarke Quay every 25 minutes. You can opt for a day pass (adult/child S$23/13), which allows ticket holders to hop on/off at nine stops along the Singapore River.

Singapore Explorer (Map p517; ☎ 6339 6833; www. singaporeexplorer.com.sg) Offers trips up and down the river in a glass-top boat (adult/child S$15/6, 45 minutes) or traditional bumboat (adult/child S$12/6, 30 minutes). Commentary ensures you know what you're looking at.

Singapore River Cruises (Map p517; ☎ 6336 6111; www.rivercruise.com.sg) Offers bumboat tours (adult S$13-18, child S$8-10, 30 to 45 minutes) from the Merlion at the river mouth upstream to Robertson Quay, plus everything in between.

SPECIAL INTEREST TOURS

Original Singapore Walks (☎ 6325 1631; www .singaporewalks.com; tours from adult/child S$25/15) Conducts irreverent but knowledgeable off-the-beaten-track walking tours through Chinatown, Little India, Kampong Glam, the Colonial District and war-related sites. Rain-or-shine tours last from two to three hours; check its website for a schedule.

Geraldene Lowe-Ismail (☎ 6737 5250; geraldenes tours@hotmail.com) Offering a wealth of information, Singapore-born Geraldene has been conducting Singapore walking tours for more than 40 years. Her various private tours (starting from S$90 per hour) lend a unique insight into Singapore's history, architecture, religions, botany and culture. She will happily tailor a tour to suit your particular interests. Group tours start from S$40.

Diana Chua (☎ 9489 1999; dianachua1999@yahoo .com.sg) Another recommended walking-tour guide, Diana charges S$90 an hour and offers similar tours to Geraldene, often aligning tours with festivals. She also touches upon more esoteric and less touristy areas such as feng shui and cemeteries.

FESTIVALS & EVENTS

With so many cultures and religions, there are an astounding number of colourful celebrations in Singapore. Some have fixed dates, but Hindus, Muslims and Chinese follow a lunar calendar that varies annually. Check out www.visitsingapore.com.sg for exact dates and full listings of other events.

Thaipusam (see the boxed text, p52) A procession from Sri Srinivasa Perumal Temple to Chettiar Hindu Temple marks this dramatic Hindu festival usually held in February.

Chingay (www.chingay.org.sg) Singapore's biggest street parade is held on the 22nd day after the Chinese New Year.

Mosaic Music Festival (www.mosaicmusicfestival.com) A 10-day feast of music in March held at the Esplanade theatre that includes many free events.

Singapore Food Festival (www.singaporefoodfestival .com.sg) A month-long celebration of eating held in March/April that also includes the World Gourmet Summit (www.worldgourmetsummit.com).

Singapore International Film Festival (www.film fest.org.sg) This showcase of world cinema, usually held in early April, is a rare chance to see movies from somewhere other than Hollywood.

Singapore Arts Festival (www.singaporeartsfest.com) June sees the National Arts Council organise this premier arts festival.

Singapore National Day (www.ndp.org.sg) A nationalistic frenzy of military and civilian parades followed by fireworks. 9 August.

Formula One Grand Prix (Map p517; ☎ 6728 6738; www.singaporegp.sg; tickets from S$38-1388) Singapore has bragging rights for hosting the first Formula 1 race held at night…though ironically, the track is flooded with bright lights. From 25 to 27 September.

SLEEPING

Singapore's hotel accommodation is some of the most expensive (and competitive) in Southeast Asia. Though the published hotel rates we supply are high, a mind-boggling array of discounts from 25% to 50% are common. The best deals mean you often get top-end hotels at midrange prices. For the nitty gritty on hotel pricing, see p559.

Until quite recently, Singapore's budget accommodation was unspeakably ordinary – cubicle-like, cramped, windowless – but a new breed of hostel around Little India and Kampong Glam has raised the bar…if

---

YMCA (IT'S FUN TO STAY AT THE...)

Singapore has two YMCAs and a YWCA providing consistent midrange accommodation. They're not the bargain they used to be but they remain popular. Non-YMCA members pay an additional S$3 for temporary membership.

The cheapest rooms at the rather dated **YMCA Metropolitan** (Map p524; ☎ 6839 8333; www .mymca.org.sg; 60 Stevens Rd; dm incl breakfast S$45, d incl breakfast S$200-270; 🖾 🖳 🛜 🏊) don't have windows, but they're spacious and well appointed. Dorms have air-con and are single-sex only. It's a good 1km walk north of Orchard Rd; take bus 105, 132 or 190, or there's a morning shuttle bus to Orchard Rd from Monday to Saturday.

YMCA International House (Map p517; ☎ 6336 6000; www.ymcaih.com.sg; 1 Orchard Rd; dm/d/f incl breakfast S$35/180/215; 🖾 🖳 🛜 🏊) has a fantastic location at the start of Orchard Rd. Rooms have been upgraded with LCD TVs, birch-coloured walls, and carpets the colour of streaky bacon. Roomy four-bed dorms have an attached bathroom. It has a restaurant, a fitness centre, a rooftop pool, squash and badminton courts and a billiard room. Staff attitudes have markedly improved since we last visited.

The **YWCA Fort Canning Lodge** (Map p517; ☎ 6338 4222; www.ywcafclodge.org.sg; 6 Fort Canning Rd; dm/d/f incl breakfast from S$80/200/380; 🖾 🖳 🏊) has a similar list of facilities to the YMCA International House albeit with higher prices (and a trek up Fort Canning too). There are only four female-only dorm beds; standard rooms are just that...standard.

---

only slightly. Most budget places offer both air-con and cheaper (and less common) fan rooms.

Solid midrange options line the Singapore River, while Orchard Rd groans under the weight of high-end chain hotels. Boutique midrange hotels in old shophouses convene around Chinatown. Some shophouse rooms don't have windows, and some shophouse hotels don't have lifts. If you want to be close to the beach, head to Sentosa (see the boxed text, p534).

With most hotels, weekend rates and occupancy levels are higher than midweek. Rates are also higher during holidays and during large international events such as the Formula 1 night race. Unless otherwise indicated, budget rooms have shared bathrooms; midrange and above have private bathrooms.

BUDGET
Colonial District & the Quays

Note that the midrange YMCAs and YWCA (see the boxed text, above) also have dorm beds.

Backpackers Cozy Corner (Map p517; ☎ 6339 6128; www.cozycornerguest.com; 490 North Bridge Rd; dm S$12-17, d incl breakfast S$36-60; 🖾 🖳) Yes, we'll say it – this place can get a little too cosy when it's busy (and it usually is). The location is a huge plus, though rooms are dark and a little cramped. Ask for a dorm facing away from North Bridge Rd unless you like the noise of

heavy traffic and merrymakers from the street. Expect to wait for internet access.

Bugis Backpackers Hostel (Map p522; ☎ 6338 5581; www.bugisbackpackers.com; 162B Rochor Rd; dm/s/d S$20/45/59; 🖾 🖳) Barely four years old, this busy place 50m from Bugis MRT started out clean and has managed to stay that way. It has good security (lockers and key pads), mixed and single-sex dorms, and a relaxed vibe. Shower facilities are limited and the kitchen is basic, but who wants to cook in Singapore?! The only way to book a room or bed is via the website.

Summer Tavern (Map p517; ☎ 6338 2381; www .summertavern.com; 87 Victoria St; dm/s/d incl breakfast S$40/90/180; 🖾) Still among the most popular hostels in Singapore despite the high dorm-bed price, Summer Tavern offers fine dorm beds, medium-sized rooms good for one or two, and a rooftop beer lounge. A recent expansion includes a second building across the street, in which you'll find deluxe rooms with queen-sized beds and attached bathrooms.

Chinatown

our pick **Fernloft** (Map pp526-7; ☎ 6225 6696, www .fernloft.com; 02-82, 5 Banda St; dm/d incl breakfast S$20/60; 🖾 🖳) Fernloft is set in a traditional Singapore housing development block and offers visitors a chance to live like a local. Chinatown, with all its food and sights, opens up down a flight of stairs. The dressed-up common corridor is not a bad place to chill with a beer, gaze across

---

CAMPING IT UP

The **National Parks Board** (Map p522; ☎ 6391 4488; www.nparks.gov.sg; 18-01/08 Gateway West, 150 Beach Rd) maintains five camp sites around Singapore: **Changi Beach** (Map pp514–15), **East Coast Park** (Map p528), **Sembawang Park** (Map pp514–15), **West Coast Park** (Map pp514–15) and the east end of **Pasir Ris Park** (Map pp514–15). You need a permit to camp during the week. Get a permit online (www.axs.com.sg) or from the AXS (ATM-like) machines found in most malls. You can camp a maximum of eight days per month.

Permits are S$1 and there's a small fee to use the barbecue pits and shower facilities. On Pulau Ubin you can camp at **Noordin** or **Maman Beach** (Map pp514–15) on the island's north coast. The sites are free, but very basic. There's no drinking water, so bring your own. You can also camp on the **southern islands** (Map pp514–15) for free. BYO drinking water too.

---

the open field towards South Bridge Rd, and share stories with fellow travellers. There are limited beds and only two large (windowless) private air-con rooms, so book in advance. There's only one shower.

G Hotel (Map pp526–7; ☎ 6225 6696, www.ghotel .com.sg; 22 Teck Lim Rd; s & d from S$80; ☒ ▣) Formerly the stodgy Tropical Hotel, it's amazing what a renovation, mood lighting and a name change does for a place. This converted shophouse is now one of the more attractive sleeping options in the area. Rooms have slate floors and comfy beds. Some singles are windowless; larger balcony rooms go for S$140. Renovations were still under way during research but ask for a renovated room just in case plans stall.

Kampong Glam

Sleepy Sam's (Map p522; ☎ 9277 4988; www.sleepysams .com; 55 Bussorah St; dm/s/d incl breakfast S$29/59/89; ☒ ▣) Prices at this budget hostel mainstay have gone steadily upwards over the years. But the ambience is more boutique hotel than hostel. Expect lots of woody, earthy tones, little nooks, chairs and cushions in the common areas. The location, on a pedestrianised street, is right in the middle of a bohemian district and steps away from the imposing Sultan Mosque.

Superb Hub (Map p522; ☎ 6299 0993; superbhub@ yahoo.com.sg; 1148 Arab St; s & d from S$50-70; ☒) Positioning itself in between a full-fledged dorm and a motel, Superb Hub offers small-ish, windowless one-, two- or three-bed rooms with ample privacy but an uncongenial atmosphere. Where are the people lounging on common couches and watching bad cable TV? Owner Ronnie is extremely helpful and is ready to dispense bottled water and tourist information.

Little India

InnCrowd (Map p522; ☎ 6296 9169; www.the-inn crowd.com; 73 Dunlop St; dm/d/tr incl breakfast S$20/59/79; ☒ ▣ ⊚) As close to a typical backpacker hostel as you'd find in Singapore. Clean accommodation, living areas where travellers like to hang and saccharine-sweet staff. The atmosphere's decidedly convivial, with free lockers and internet, discounted tickets to sights and cheap Tiger draft beer on tap.

Prince of Wales (Map p522; ☎ 6299 0130; www.pow .com.sg; 101 Dunlop St; dm/d S$20/60; ☒ ▣ ⊚) This Australian-style pub and hostel has a raucous beer-and-sawdust rock bar downstairs (p552) and clean, high-ceilinged dorms upstairs. The two private rooms share a bathroom. Not everyone wants to rock-out, but it's a lively place in an ace location.

Fragrance Backpackers Hostel (Map p522; ☎ 6295 6888; www.fragrancebackpackers.com.sg; 63 Dunlop St; dm S$22-25; ☒ ▣) The evergrowing midrange Fragrance chain has sniffed out a sweet-smelling niche in the budget market. Its Little India outfit is sparklingly clean, with leather couches in the (small) TV lounge, great security, chunky mattresses and backpack-sized lockers. Avoid the basement dorms, which are sans windows.

Footprints Backpacker Hostel (Map p522; ☎ 6295 5134; www.footprintshostel.com.sg; 25A Perak St; dm S$22-30, d S$70-80, tw S$80; ☒ ▣) This recent addition to the swath of backpacker joints in the area is also one of the largest. Dorms are narrow but clean, and the communal area is decorated like the set of a bad Hong Kong movie: bright colours, chunky leather couches and, oh my god, the chandelier. Breakfast is included in the rates.

hangout@mt.emily (Map p522; ☎ 6438 5588; www .hangouthotels.com; 10A Upper Wilkie Rd; dm/d/tr incl breakfast S$40/100/200; ☒ ▣ ⊚ ☒) Prices for the comfy seven-bed dorms are a relative bargain considering the location, nestled in Mt Emily's leafy glades. Private rooms were a little ordinary and cramped, though the the place is undergoing renovations, which should freshen these up. You'll find a lovely rooftop terrace with a 'standing pool', a library, a cafe, free internet and cosy lounge areas with a large plasma TV.

MIDRANGE
Colonial District & the Quays

South-East Asia Hotel (Map p522; ☎ 6338 2394; www.seahotel.com.sg; 190 Waterloo St; d/tr/f incl breakfast S$100/118/140; 🞸 🖳) Right next to one of Singapore's busiest temples, this cash-only 'mom and pop' hotel is perfect for visitors who want to live smack bang in the middle of one of Singapore's liveliest streets. Rooms are a little dated but spacious. The bathrooms are akin to upright coffins. Breakfast is served at the great vego restaurant downstairs.

Hotel Bencoolen (Map p517; ☎ 6336 0822; www .hotelbencoolen.com; 47 Bencoolen St; s/d incl breakfast S$110/178; 🞸 🖳 🞲) Rooms at the 'Uncoolen' are far from stylish, but they've been recently renovated and decked out in somewhat uninspired shades of green and cream. The single rooms are tiny with a shower to match. Larger double rooms will get you an LCD TV and a bathtub. The outdoor spa pool is almost big enough for a soak.

Beach Hotel (Map p517; ☎ 6336 7712; www.beach hotel.com.sg; 95 Beach Rd; r S$140-170; 🞸 🖳) Just down the block from the Park View Hotel (which views no park) is the Beach Hotel (which has no beach). Rooms, prices and amenities are much the same here as there, though online discounts of up to 35% make this hotel a bargain.

Ibis Singapore on Bencoolen (Map p522; ☎ 6593 2888; www.ibishotel.com; 170 Bencoolen St; r S$150; 🞸 🖳 🞲) With brand-spanking new rooms decked out in pine and orangey hues, and with LCD TVs, comfy beds and great city views, the Ibis group probably hopes visitors extend their stay to match the length of the hotel's name.

Bayview Hotel (Map p517; ☎ 6337 2882; www.bay viewhotels.com/singapore; 30 Bencoolen St; r incl breakfast S$176-235; 🞸 🖳 🞲 🞲) The Bayview won't get your knickers in a knot – thanks to recent renovations, rooms are swisher and more modern than most midrangers in this lot. There's a self-serve laundry on the roof be-

side the pool, so you can cool off while your unknotted knickers are in the wash.

Robertson Quay Hotel (Map p517; ☎ 6735 3333; www.robertsonquayhotel.com.sg; 15 Merbau Rd; s & d S$200; 🞸 🖳 🞲) Probably the best-value hotel along the river, this medieval castle–like circular tower has immaculate but unadventurous rooms with cheesy wallpaper and throwaway wall art, and a surprisingly pretty palm-fringed rooftop swimming pool. Internet discounts of up to 35% are often available.

Park View Hotel (Map p517; ☎ 6338 8558; www .parkviewhotel-singapore.com.sg; 81 Beach Rd; s & d incl breakfast S$220-280; 🞸 🖳) Park View is centrally located to the Bugis shopping area. All rooms have bathtubs but some of the cheaper rooms are windowless. Don't be scared off by the high rack rate. When we last checked, rooms cost S$140 to S$180.

Gallery Hotel (Map p517; ☎ 6849 8686; www.gallery hotel.com.sg; 1 Nanson Rd; d incl breakfast from S$320; 🞸 🖳 🞲 🞲) Its grey fascia studded with primary-coloured window boxes, the Gallery remains one of Singapore's truly boutique hotels. Sure, guests have to switch elevators on the 4th floor to get to the rooms but knockdown online deals bring you top-end rooms at midrange prices. Rooms feature retro furnishings, steel beams and frosted-glass bathroom walls. The glass rooftop pool and free internet access are bonuses.

Chinatown

Royal Peacock Hotel (Map pp526-7; ☎ 6223 3522; www .royalpeacockhotel.com; 55 Keong Saik Rd; s/d incl breakfast S$135/155; 🞸 🖳 🞲) Beautiful lobby and peacock-palette rooms with gilt-edged mirrors and cramped bathrooms are the order of the day here. Cheaper rooms are windowless and some have sloping ceilings. Management assured us that renovations would refresh rooms by 2010.

Hotel 1929 (Map pp526-7; ☎ 6347 1929; www .hotel1929.com; 50 Keong Saik Rd; s/d/ste S$200/230/350; 🞸 🖳) The rooms at this groovy boutique hotel border on diminutive (even the suites are a bit tight), but the architects have maximised limited space, cheerily festooning rooms with vintage designer chairs (look out for reproduction Eames and Jacobson) and technicolour mosaics. Rooftop suites have private terraces and outdoor clawfoot baths. Online promos yield 30% discounts.

Link Hotel (Map pp520-1; ☎ 6622 8585; www .linkhotel.com.sg; 50 Tiong Bahru Rd; s & d S$200-300;

SENTOSA NIGHTS

If you feel like bunking down on Sentosa Island (p509) after a day basking on the beach, there are several (mainly top end) options to choose from, each newer addition outdoing the last in terms of design and comfort. The opening of Resorts World in 2010 will add six hotels to the fray.

The midrange **Costa Sands Resort** (Map pp514-15; ☎ 6275 1034; www.costasands.com.sg; 30 Imbiah Walk; huts from S$80, d from S$150; 🛇 🖳 🖭) is Sentosa's cheapest option, with motel-style rooms and 15 small wooden huts sleeping up to four (air-conditioned, with shared bathrooms). Rates soar and availability dips over the weekend and during school-holiday season. The cliff-top pool is good for those who want to avoid the crowded beach.

ourpick **Siloso Beach Resort** (Map pp514-15; ☎ 6722 3333; www.silosobeachresort.com; 51 Imbiah Walk; r incl breakfast from S$230; 🛇 🖳 🖭) is a sanctuary unto itself and designed with lots of ecofriendly touches (the natural spring-fed pool has its own filtration system, gardens on top of buildings lower ambient temperatures and some rooms are built around trees). Rooms are comfortable enough to tempt you into staying in, but the landscaped grounds, 95m-long pool and nearby Siloso Beach will ensure you get your fix of the sun.

The salubrious five-star **Sentosa Resort & Spa** (Map pp514-15; ☎ 6275 0331; www.thesentosa.com; 2 Bukit Manis Rd; r from S$260; 🛇 🖳 🖭) is a low-rise cliff-top belle, replete with contemporary furnishings, the romantic Cliff restaurant, Singapore's only garden spa – Spa Botanica (p513) – and peacocks wandering aimlessly underneath frangipani trees. Check the website for promo deals.

Singapore's only beachfront resort, **Shangri-La's Rasa Sentosa Resort** (Map pp514-15; ☎ 6275 0100; www.shangri-la.com; 101 Siloso Rd; d incl breakfast from S$290; 🛇 🖳 🖭) is shaped like a bent cruise ship and is immensely popular with families. There is a huge swimming pool if you don't fancy swimming in the murky Straits of Singapore. Splash out for sea-facing rooms, all of which have spacious balconies.

The five-star **Amara Sanctuary** (Map pp514-15; ☎ 6825 3888; www.amarasanctuary.com; 1 Larkhill Rd; r/ste/villa from S$280/450/950; 🛇 🖳 🖭) looks like it was transported direct from the pages of a *Wallpaper* magazine spread with its infinity pool, glass walls and furniture in every shade of 'resort brown'. Stunning (and expensive) villas have outdoor baths and plunge pools or opt for suites housed in former British army barracks for a touch of colonial-style living

The **Capella** (Map pp514-15; ☎ 6275 0331; www.capellasingapore.com; 1 the Knolls; r from S$550, villa from S$1800; 🛇 🖳 🖭) resort is probably the crème de la crème of Sentosa's, possibly even Singapore's, accommodation options. Visitors will be greeted by the majestic whitewashed colonial 'Tanah Merah' building as they crest the driveway. Walk through to the cleverly hidden modern extension. Pools and gardens are organically spread down along the ridgeline of the hill. Guests will be delighted, as rooms offer every conceivable comfort and the mighty Capella gives even the Raffles Hotel a run for its money.

🛇 🖳) What else do you do with abandoned art-deco housing development flats? Why, you turn them into a boutique hotel, of course! Rooms in these former walk-up apartments are compact, with wooden floors and views of suburban Singapore. It's far from a train station but extremely close to great local food joints and Singapore's best club, Zouk (p551).

Hotel Re! (Map pp526-7; ☎ 6827 8288; www.hotelre.com.sg; 175A Chin Swee Rd; d from S$320-350; 🛇 🖳 🛜 🖭) Whoa! Groovy baby. Austin Powers would approve of this hotel – but we're not entirely sure that's a good thing. This is a '60s/'70s-themed hotel decorated in loud tones, with silhouettes of Travolta, Abba and the Bee Gees on the walls. The only thing missing are the disco balls and waterbeds (oh wait, the suites have them). Ignore ridiculous published rates and check online for whopping 50% discounts!

Little India

Perak Hotel (Map p522; ☎ 6299 7733; www.peraklodge .net; 12 Perak Rd; s & d incl breakfast S$148-168; 🛇 🖳 🛜) The Peranakan-style Perak Hotel (formerly Perak Lodge) is deservedly popular. Interiors feature lashings of natural timber and ceramics, and a bubbling fountain eases you through breakfast. There are many nooks and spaces for sitting and meditation. Cheaper rooms don't have windows, but they're well-furnished and have cable-TV access. No lifts, so you'll be hefting luggage up the stairs.

Albert Court Hotel (Map p522; ☎ 6339 3939; www .albertcourt.com.sg; 180 Albert St; s & d from S$200-220; 🌌 🖳) At the southern fringe of Little India, this is a slightly dated colonial-era hotel in a shophouse redevelopment that now shoots up eight storeys. An external glass elevator takes you to your room. Rooms are quiet and have the usual mod cons and charming ceiling fans. Promotional rates almost nudge budget levels.

Orchard Road

Lloyd's Inn (off Map p524; ☎ 6737 7309; www.lloydinn .com; 2 Lloyd Rd; s & d S$100-120; 🌌 🛜) You'll find Orchard Rd's cheapest rooms at Lloyd's, a sprawling California-style motel surrounded by crumbling mansions. Sure, rooms are in need of a revamp, but at these prices they fill up quick. Ask for one with a garden view. On your way to town, head northeast up Oxley Rd and go past the gun-toting guards outside Lee Kuan Yew's ancestral home (see the boxed text, p502).

Hotel Grand Central (Map p524; ☎ 6737 9944; www .ghihotels.com; 22 Cavenagh Rd; r from S$160; 🌌 🖳 🌉) This large (hence Grand) 390-room hotel buzzes with tourist and business traffic. Its low pricing, central location and inoffensive rooms decked out in the earth tones so popular in Singapore must account for its popularity. Corridors smell of Chinese medicine and some rooms are a little musty. Fingers crossed you get a room with a renovated bathroom. Premium rooms come with LCD TVs.

Elizabeth Hotel (Map p524; ☎ 6885 7888; www.the elizabeth.com.sg; 24 Mt Elizabeth Rd; r from S$160; 🌌 🖳) One of a cluster of three hotels located in a quiet nook off Orchard Rd, the Elizabeth is old but has aged gracefully. Rooms are warm and welcoming, with lots of wooden furniture and soft lighting. Guests can chomp on excellent wood-fired pizzas at in-house Modesto's, which has an extremely soothing waterfall-side dining room.

our pick Quincy (Map p524; ☎ 6738 5888; www.quincy .com.sg; 22 Mt Elizabeth Rd; r from S$268; 🌌 🖳 🛜) Many middle-of-the-rung hotels have started dubbing themselves 'boutique' in order to stand out. Many don't. The Quincy does. It impresses with its sleek, ultramodern sensibilities, slightly gimmicky three cooked meals

per day (with Orchard Rd at the doorstep, who has three meals at a hotel restaurant?), free wi-fi and, best of all, free-flowing drinks from 6pm to 8pm daily.

TOP END
Colonial District & the Quays

Naumi (Map p517; ☎ 6403 6000; www.naumihotel.com; 41 Seah St; r from S$400; 🌌 🖳 🛜 🌉) Lying in the shadow of the Raffles Hotel, Naumi is dressed so sharp in glass and steel you could get cut just by looking. It balances cool looks with lots of silk and leather and fluffy pillows. Its infinity pool offers jaw-dropping views across to Raffles Hotel and the Swissôtel.

Swissôtel the Stamford (Map p517; ☎ 6338 8585; www.swissotel-thestamford.com; 2 Stamford Rd; d from S$450; 🌌 🖳 🌉) Everyone raves about IM Pei's iconic Swissôtel, the tallest hotel in Southeast Asia. It boasts one of Singapore's hippest dining complexes (Equinox), the views are sublime, and service standards are as elevated as the building. Rooms are predictably decked out in corporate-friendly hues and patterns. Yep, lots of cream and brown.

Ritz-Carlton (Map p517; ☎ 6337 8888; www.ritzcarlton .com; 7 Raffles Ave; r from S$550; 🌌 🖳 🌉) No expense was spared, no feng shui geomancer went unconsulted and no animals were harmed in the building of this six-star establishment. Guests will be torn between taking a romantic soak in the bath (oh, the unimpaired views!) or taking a self-guided audio tour to view the in-house art collection (oh, the Hockney, Warhol, Stella and Chihuly pieces!).

Raffles Hotel (Map p517; ☎ 6337 1886; www.raffles hotel.com; 1 Beach Rd; r/ste from S$750/850; 🌌 🖳 🌉) The grand old dame of Singapore's Colonial District has had many facelifts in her 121 years and is looking as spritely as ever. She's seen many a famous visitor in her time, from Somerset Maugham to Michael Jackson, and it's easy to see what the fuss is about (cost be damned). Rooms are all class – expect a spacious parlour, rattan furniture, verandahs, lazily swirling ceiling fans and a Singapore Sling from the Long Bar.

Chinatown

New Majestic Hotel (Map pp526-7; ☎ 6511 4700; www .newmajestichotel.com; 31-37 Bukit Pasoh Rd; r from S$280-550; 🌌 🖳) Its terrazzo-tiled open lobby is dressed like a 1940s Shanghai movie set and oozes boutique sleekness. Designer-themed rooms are fun! Local theatre legend

---

WHAT? YOU HAVEN'T BOOKED A ROOM?

The Singapore Hotel Association 24-hour desks at Changi Airport **Terminal 1** (☎ 6542 6966), **Terminal 2** (☎ 6545 0318) and **Terminal 3** (☎ 6542 0442) can help you book a hotel across all ranges for S$10. You can also book hotels on the association's website: www.stayinsingapore.com.sg.

If you're only in Singapore for a short time or have an endless wait between connections, try the **Ambassador Transit Hotel** (Map pp514-15; ☎ Terminal 1 6542 5538, Terminal 2 6542 8122, Terminal 3 6507 9788; www.airport-hotel.com.sg; s/d S$58/65; 🗙 🖭). Rates quoted are for the first six hours and each additional hour block thereafter is S$13; rooms don't have windows and there are budget singles (S$35) with shared bathrooms. The Terminal 1 branch has a sauna, gym and outdoor pool.

The only swish option at Changi Airport is Terminal 3's **Crowne Plaza Hotel** (Map pp514-15; ☎ 6823 5300; www.cpchangiairport.com; r from S$250; 🗙 🖳 🖭). The business-oriented focus shows through its sleek lines, geometric-patterned carpets and (over)use of wood panels.

Glen Goei's room is awash in red silk, hanging lanterns and Chinese motifs. Other highlights include private balconies and voyeuristic portals in the restaurant ceiling looking up into the swimming pool (skinny-dip at your peril).

Scarlet Hotel (Map pp526-7; ☎ 6511 3333; www.thescarlethotel.com; 33 Erskine Rd; d/ste from S$320/780; 🗙 🖳) Sexy Scarlet has seduced Singapore's boutique hotel market. Occupying a string of gorgeous 1924 shophouses, 84 (smallish) rooms are lustily decorated with deep velvet, gilt-framed mirrors, ebony timbers and plush Arabic cushions – you'd think you had walked into a boudoir. Dizzying corridors to the rooms are like walking down Alice's rabbit hole. The rooftop bar, Breeze, is perfect for predinner drinks.

Orchard Road

Goodwood Park Hotel (Map p524; ☎ 6737 7411; www.goodwoodparkhotel.com.sg; 22 Scotts Rd; r from S$385; 🗙 🖳 🖭) Dating from 1900, this Tudor-inspired remnant was here when tigers roamed Orchard Rd's pepper plantations. Old-world opulence strays into slightly schizo territory here and there (dark bathrooms, mazy building extensions and naff greyish-green paint), but it's worth tolerating for the history whispering from the walls. Poolside suites are the pick of the plantation.

EATING

Singaporeans are food-crazy. Over 6500 restaurants and more than 12,000 food stalls are packed into a country that's a mere pinprick on the map. All kinds of international cuisine lines Singapore's collective stomach, but Chinese, Indian, Malay and regional Peranakan (Malay-style sauces with Chinese ingredients) dishes are what you're here for.

Be adventurous. Looking out for the long queues at hawker centres and joining in is a sure way to partake in the familiar Singaporean ritual of food worshipping. Each ethnic group has its own food rules; if unsure, look around to see what others are doing. It's OK to ask for a fork!

Reservations are essential for upmarket eateries; a smart-casual dress code usually applies. A service charge will be added to your bill (10% + 7% GST); additional tipping is optional. All restaurants (except hawker stalls) are nonsmoking.

Most restaurants serve lunch from around 11.30am to 2.30pm and dinner from 6pm to 10.30pm. If a place opens for breakfast, it's usually from around 10am till noon. Hawker centres listed under Quick Eats sections are generally open from 10am until late (some 24 hours); most hawker dishes range from S$3 to S$6.

COLONIAL DISTRICT
Cafes

Ah Chew Desserts (Map p517; ☎ 6339 8198; 01-10/11, 11 Liang Seah St; desserts S$1.50-4.50; 🕑 12.30-11.30pm Mon-Thu, to 12.30am Fri, 1.30pm-12.30am Sat, 1.30-11.30pm Sun) Packed with locals wanting a sweet post-dinner fix, this place boasts a massive menu featuring a variety of Chinese desserts. If you've never had honeydew sago or sesame paste before, now is your chance to go Ah Chew! Bless you!

Chinese

YY Kafei Dian (Map p517; ☎ 6336 8813; 37 Beach Rd; meals from S$3; 🕑 breakfast, lunch & dinner) This modern coffee shop pays homage to the Hainanese eateries of days past, with its ceiling fans, linoleum floors, round marble-top tables and wooden chairs. For breakfast, order the soft *kaya* (coconut jam) buns, half-boiled eggs (go nuts with the condiments) and a thick, sweet *kopi* (coffee). For lunch, try the Hainanese chicken rice. There's an extensive á la carte menu at dinner, so order with abandon.

Yet Con (Map p517; ☎ 6337 6819; 25 Purvis St; mains S$8-24; ⊙ lunch & dinner) We doubt that much has changed in the 50-odd years that Yet Con has been in business. The chicken rice and steamboat are popular dishes at this retro eatery… just look around. The air-con is the only modern (and welcome) addition to this joint.

Empire Café (Map p517; ☎ 6337 1886; Raffles Hotel, 2 Stamford Rd; mains S$10-20; ⊙ 11am-11pm) Not everyone wants to get sweaty at a hawker centre over a plate of *char kway teow* (broad noodles, clams and eggs fried in chilli and black-bean sauce), Hainanese chicken rice or other local delights. Those people should visit the faux-1920s-style coffee house Empire Café. For those who want to get sweaty, there are al fresco seats facing busy North Bridge Rd.

Space @ My Humble House (Map p517; ☎ 6423 1881; 02-25 Esplanade Mall, 8 Raffles Ave; mains S$10-25; ⊙ lunch & dinner) Serves up humble, affordable, local favourites with just a touch of flair from the same kitchen as My Humble House. Try chef Sam Leong's chicken rice the way his mum cooks it or the wagyu beef *hor fun*.

Wah Lok Cantonese Restaurant (Map p517; ☎ 6311 8188; Level 2, Carlton Hotel, 76 Bras Basah Rd; mains from S$18; ⊙ lunch & dinner) Long-running Cantonese restaurant popular with families. Staff are happy to offer suggestions if you're unable to make a decision past the exquisite Peking Duck and dim sum selections.

My Humble House (Map p517; ☎ 6423 1881; 02-27/29 Esplanade Mall, 8 Raffles Ave; mains S$30-45; ⊙ lunch & dinner) The irony of the restaurant's name is quite apparent when diners are seated in the *Alice in Wonderland*–meets–Phillipe Starck dining room. Chow down on subtly flavoured abalone, truffles, wagyu and seafood from an elaborate menu that changes weekly. Dress snazzy; reservations essential.

Chef Chan's Restaurant (Map p517; ☎ 6333 0073; 01-06 National Museum of Singapore, 93 Stamford Rd; meals from S$80; ⊙ lunch & dinner) Eponymous chef gets sick of cooking for over 200 people in his large restaurant, closes shop and opens tiny restaurant with seven tables, serving from a daily changing set menu. The restaurant is decked out with Chef Chan's exquisite antique

---

ALL DAY DINING, SINGAPORE STYLE

Do as the locals do and dine on the cheap at hawker centres and roadside coffee shops. Just go with an empty stomach and expect to pay an average of S$3 to S$6 per dish.

For breakfast, head out to **Tiong Bahru Market & Food Centre** (Map pp520-1; 30 Seng Poh Rd; ⊙ 7am-11pm). Go up to the 2nd floor, park yourself at a bench, look out for any stall selling coffee and order a *kopi* or *teh* (thick coffee or tea sweetened with condensed milk) and *kaya* toast (a heady coconut jam slathered with butter over thin charcoal-toasted bread). When you've polished that off, look for Jian Bo Shui Kueh (a market stall) and order some *chee kueh* – S$1 will get you four steamed rice cakes topped with *chai poh* (fried preserved radishes) and chilli.

Come lunchtime, take a taxi to **328 Katong Laksa** (Map p528; 216 East Coast Rd; ⊙ lunch & dinner). The namesake dish is a bowl of thin rice noodles in a light curry broth made with coconut milk and Vietnamese coriander and topped with shrimps and cockles. Order some *otah-otah* (spiced mackerel cake grilled in a banana leaf) to accompany the laksa.

For dinner, make your way to **Lor 9 Beef Kway Teow** (Map pp514-15; 237 Geylang Lg Nine; ⊙ dinner-late). Once you've stopped gawking at the street-walkers across the road in this red-light district, order the beef *hor fun* (flat rice noodles wok-fried with tender slices of beef in black-bean sauce) and some *tian ji zhou* (frog's leg porridge). The frog is cooked in a claypot with dried chilli, spices, spring onion and soy sauce. It tastes like chicken, only crunchier. Wash it all down with copious amounts of Tiger beer.

If you think that's gross, we'll leave you with these words by local food guru KF Seetoh: 'There's nothing I will not try. Whale sperm? Been there done that. It's like a savoury jelly. Fried scorpions, shark's liver, snake skin, the list goes on. If it's good, I don't care what it is. There's only good food and bad food.'

SINGAPORE

furnishings, which still pale in comparison to the food. Book ahead.

French

Gunther's (Map p517; ☎ 638 8955; www.gunthers.com.sg; 36 Purvis St; mains from S$38, lunch sets S$38; ☺ lunch & dinner) The dining room is akin to a museum crossed with a tomb but the service (immaculate), presentation (classy) and the food (tasty) will soon distract you from the sombre environs. If you can't decide what to order, the maître d' does a very good show and tell using the day's produce.

Indian

Rang Mahal (Map p517; ☎ 6333 1788; 3rd fl, Pan Pacific Hotel, 7 Raffles Blvd; mains S$16-40; ☺ lunch Sun-Fri, dinner daily) Much-praised Indian in sophisticated stone and teak subcontinental surrounds. The vegetarian selection offers silky dhals, and the lunch buffets are perfect for stuffing your face – it's a holiday right?

International

7atenine (Map p517; ☎ 6338 0789; 01-10/12 Esplanade Mall, 8 Raffles Ave; tapas from S$12; ☺ lunch & dinner) Euro-Asian tapas (think dishes such as crisp *kurobuta* pork belly with iberico cheese) accompany the long list of drinks at this popular bar-cum-restaurant. Sit outside and watch the bartenders twist and hurl cocktails into the air with careless abandon.

Equinox (Map p517; ☎ 6837 3322; 70th fl, Swissôtel the Stamford, 2 Stamford Rd; mains S$25-50; ☺ lunch & dinner) Adjectives struggle to describe the jaw-dropping views from this 70th-floor restaurant. Soaring ceilings, Asiatic wall hangings and plush fabrics are mere backdrops. The view rates a 10, the food a little less. Book early for a window seat.

Italian

Garibaldi (Map p517; ☎ 6837 1468; www.garibaldi.com.sg; 01-02, 36 Purvis St; mains S$28-48; ☺ lunch & dinner) Swish, sequestered Garibaldi is the pick of Singapore's Italian crop (and Singapore tries hard): Italian chefs and debonair staff, and over 150 Italian wines. The menu is *classico*; try the antipasti, then the homemade *tortellini di granchio e cozze* (handmade crab tortellini with mussels, zucchini and saffron sauce).

Japanese

Ichiban Boshi (Map p517; ☎ 6423 1151; 02-14 Esplanade Mall, 8 Raffles Ave; sushi from S$2.50; ☺ noon-10.30pm

Sun-Thu, to 11pm Fri & Sat) Conveyor-belt sushi at reasonable prices in the sassy Esplanade Mall complex. It's a couple of rungs up from others of its ilk in Singapore.

Kuriya (Map p517; ☎ 6883 2020; 01-07, Raffles City Shopping Centre, 252 North Bridge Rd; mains from S$25; ☺ lunch & dinner) Singaporeans are more accustomed to the ubiquitous 'conveyor-belt' sushi bars, and Kuriya is a sneering 'up yours' to such plebian Japanese dining experiences. Seasonal seafood and vegetables are flown in from Japan and diners are charmed by waiters in a classy setting.

Shiraishi (Map p517; ☎ 6338 3788; 03-01/02 the Ritz-Carlton, 7 Raffles Ave; dishes S$30-100; ☺ lunch & dinner Mon-Sat) Don't let the casual *izekaya* appearance fool you. This restaurant is strictly for those seeking an exquisite Japanese dining experience (and who have the cash to spare). Prop yourself at the sushi bar and watch sushi chefs bark orders before proceeding to make masterpieces from hunks of raw fish.

Quick Eats

Colonial District food courts and hawker centres fill with a strange mix of suits and locals during lunch time. Come evening, locals fill up on beer and are content to watch English Premier League on large-screen TVs.

Victoria Street Food Centre (Map p517; 143 Victoria St; ☺ 10am-3am) Seemingly manifested to fill a space between high-rises, and with its small shrine outside, this is a great fallback when every other place is closed. Locals wheel and deal, friends neck bottles of beer, solo guys read books.

Coffee Express 2000 Food Court (Map p517; 01-79 Bras Basah Complex, 232 Victoria St; ☺ 24hr) Has over 10 stalls serving up a range of Chinese, Malay and Indian food and is air-conditioned.

Glutton's Corner (Map p517; ☺ lunch & dinner) Food celebrity KF Seetoh took the hard work out of finding great hawker food by inviting the best ones here, beside the Esplanade Mall. You can't go wrong with dishes such as oyster omelette, satay and barbecued stingray. You have to try the divine *kaya* fondue.

For an ultracheap feed, pull up a table at one of several **steamboat restaurants** (Map p517; cnr Beach Rd & Liang Seah St; ☺ dinner), where S$15.50 to S$19 will buy you an 'all you can eat' spread of meats, seafood and veggies.

Toss it all into the large steamboat in the middle of the table.

The basement and 3rd floor of **Raffles City** (Map p517; 252 North Bridge Rd; ☺ 11am-10pm) and the basements of **Funan DigitaLife Mall** (Map p517; 109 North Bridge Rd; ☺ 10.30am-8.30pm) and **Bugis Junction** (Map p522; 200 Victoria St; ☺ 9am-10pm) have fluoro-lit, hygienic food courts.

CBD & THE QUAYS
Asian Fusion
IndoChine Waterfront (Map p517; ☎ 6339 1720; 1 Empress Pl; mains from S$16; ☺ lunch Mon-Fri, dinner daily) The IndoChine cartel's riverside operation boasts Boat Quay views and sumptuous surrounds – dark leather chairs and glittering chandeliers. The menu is a sophisticated collation of Vietnamese-, Cambodian- and Laotian-inspired dishes. No MSG, colouring or preservatives are used in cooking. You'll have a similar experience (at cafe prices) at Siem Reap II (☎ 6338 7596) next door.

Cafes
Epicurious (Map p517; ☎ 6734 7720; 01-02 the Quayside, 60 Robertson Quay; mains S$4-20; ☺ lunch & dinner Tue-Fri, 9am-10pm Sat & Sun) The worn coffee-shop tables and breakfast bench here are a result of diners frantically shovelling down walnut bread French toast with orange butter, *laksa* pesto and other delights. Weekend breakfast single-handedly breathes life into this largely ignored quay.

Chinese
One on the Bund (Map p517; ☎ 6221 0004; Clifford Pier; 80 Collyer Quay; mains S$15-38; ☺ lunch & dinner) The Marina Bay waterfront is hardly like the real Bund, but that's not stopping restaurateurs from calling it so. Housed in the former Clifford Pier, One on the Bund has replaced boat services with Shanghainese food service. The cavernous atmosphere is a little too art gallery/mausoleum but the smoked duck helps warm you up.

Si Chuan Dou Hua Restaurant (Map p517; ☎ 6535 6006; 60-01 UOB Plaza 1, 80 Raffles Pl; mains S$17-35; ☺ lunch & dinner) Order with haste so you can start enjoying 60th-floor views. Standout dishes like braised abalone with mushrooms and smooth beancurd with wolfberries will temporarily tear your eyes away from the windows. Ask for a tea performance: tea masters assume martial-arts stances while pouring the drink out of a long-spouted tea-

pot. There's a branch at Parkroyal Beach Rd (Map p522).

French
Saint Pierre (Map p517; ☎ 6438 0887; 01-01 Central Mall, 3 Magazine Rd; mains from S$40; ☺ lunch & dinner Mon-Fri) While we're naturally sceptical of self-styled 'celebrity' chefs, the peroxide blond Mr Stroobant has earned his fame. The modern French menu is often inspired, and though the six types of foie gras might test the patience of animal lovers, it pulls in the crowds.

Japanese
Bon Goût (Map pp520-1; ☎ 6732 5234; 01-01 the Quayside, 60 Robertson Quay; mains S$6-17; ☺ lunch & dinner) This eccentric place (not to be misread as 'Bong Out') is weird enough to be straight out of Tokyo. It's a second-hand bookshop/CD store/restaurant full of students and literati, reading, laughing and slurping *ramen* (noodle soups), Japanese curries and Tiger beer (sometimes all at once).

Marutama Ramen (Map p517; ☎ 6534 8090; 03-90/91 the Central, 6 Eu Tong Sen St; ramen S$12; ☺ 11.30am-10pm) When the *ramen* stock runs out, the restaurant closes up for the day. It does happen because it's that good. Sadly, ingredients are on the skimpy side and you'd best shell out extra for side dishes (S$1 to S$8) or risk succumbing to McDonald's later. There's a branch at Liang Court (Map p517).

Seafood
Palm Beach Seafood (Map p517; ☎ 6227 2332; 01-09 One Fullerton, 1 Fullerton Rd; mains S$12-60; ☺ lunch & dinner) There's not a palm or a beach in sight (name inherited from its parent branch at East Coast Parkway), but the bay views from this split-level diner are pretty good. Groups of suits spin the lazy Susan, enjoying baked, steamed and fried crabs.

Vegetarian
Angel's Bistro (Map pp526-7; ☎ 6220 4344; www.angelsbistro .com.sg; 28 Stanley St; meals from S$6; ☺ lunch) Diners here leave with uplifted spirits thanks to the organic, vegetarian produce at this no-frills restaurant. Watch the spritely 'aunties' behind the counter whip into action…must be the food.

Quick Eats
Lau Pa Sat (Map pp526-7; 18 Raffles Quay; ☺ 24hr) Originally used for a market (Lau Pa Sat

SINGAPORE

THE ART OF TEA APPRECIATION

Taking time out in a Chinatown teahouse is a great way to relax and to learn about local teas and customs. Start at **Yixing Yuan Teahouse** (Map pp526-7; ☎ 6224 6961; 30/32 Tanjong Pagar Rd; ⓨ 10am-10pm), where reformed corporate banker Vincent Low explains everything you need to know about sampling different types of tea. Demonstrations with tastings last around 45 minutes to two hours (S$20 to S$40). The dim sum lunch is popular.

Once you know your green tea from your oolong, duck around the corner to **Tea Chapter** (Map pp526-7; ☎ 6226 1175; 9-11 Neil Rd; ⓨ 10am-11pm), where Queen Elizabeth dropped by for a cuppa in 1989. If you don't know the tea-making drill, the waiter will give you a brief demonstration. Downstairs, all manner of tea paraphernalia are precariously balanced on display shelves and can be purchased.

If you're out in Katong, check out **Amoy Tea** (Map pp528; ☎ 6346 0929; 331 Joo Chiat Rd; ⓨ 9am-6pm), which imports a huge range of ready-packed and loose-leaf Chinese teas.

---

means 'old market' in Hokkien), this handsome wrought-iron canopy was freighted out from Glasgow in 1894 and lays claim to being the most popular hawker centre. Wander the aisles and take pleasure in picking out your food.

Boon Tat Street hawker stalls (Map pp526-7; ⓨ 7pm-3am Mon-Fri, 3pm-3am Sat & Sun) In the evenings, additional hawker stalls specialising in satay set up along this street beside Lau Pa Sat. Satays go for 80¢ a pop; the chilli crab is excellent too.

Ya Kun Kaya Toast (Map pp526-7; 01-01 Far East Sq, 18 China St; ⓨ 7.30am-7pm Mon-Fri, 9am-5pm Sat & Sun) Though a chain of outlets have mushroomed across Singapore, this outlet most closely matches the original 1940s stall selling strong coffee, runny eggs and *kaya* toast, which so many Singaporeans love.

CHINATOWN
Chinese
Da Dong Restaurant (Map pp526-7; ☎ 6221 3822; 39 Smith St; yum cha S$2.80-4.80, mains from S$12; ⓨ 11am-10.45pm Mon-Fri, 9am-10.45pm Sat & Sun) One of Chinatown's longest lasting restaurants first opened its doors in 1928. These days, it still serves up some of the best dim sum in town. Longevity hasn't equated to great service, but with *char siew* (barbecue pork) buns this good, who cares?

Chi Yan Organic Vegetarian Health Food (Map pp526-7; ☎ 6225 9026; 2 Smith St; mains S$5-10; ⓨ noon-10pm) Organic, 100% vegetarian food cooked sans garlic and onion is surprisingly delish. Tiny wooden tables and chairs and the spiritual book selection give this place

a schoolhouse atmosphere to complement your rising sense of worthiness.

Qun Zhong Eating House (Map pp526-7; ☎ 6221 3060; 21 Neil Rd; mains S$8-10; ⓨ lunch & dinner Thu-Tue) Lunchtime queues conga onto the street for seafood, pork and vegetable dumplings expertly rolled by a crew of old ladies up the back of this shophouse. The red-bean pancake is a knock-out dessert.

Sin Hoi San Eating House (Map pp520-1; 01-59, 55 Tiong Bahru Rd; mains S$12-45; ⓨ 5pm-5am) The pre- and post-clubbing crowd love to pile onto the plastic chairs and load up on a variety of *sze char* (cooked to order) dishes. If you want to splash out, try the chilli crab. Yes, the crabs and seafood are taken from one of the many aquarium tanks that line the walls of the restaurant.

Chuan Jiang Hao Zi (Map pp526-7; ☎ 6225 1518; 12 Smith St; steamboats from S$25; ⓨ lunch & dinner) Look around. You're not the only one choking on the fiery broth at this Sichuan steamboat restaurant. Still, locals flock here for what is arguably the best hot pot in town. Two tips: don't put veggies into the chilli stock; and do order lots of beer.

French
L'Angelus (Map pp526-7; ☎ 6225 6897; 85 Club St; mains from S$16; ⓨ lunch & dinner Mon-Sat) Comfort-food staples at this unpretentious Provençal bistro make it one of Singapore's better French eateries. Launch into the cassoulet, escargots and the famous hot chocolate cake.

Indian
Annalakshmi Janatha (Map pp526-7; ☎ 6223 0809; 104 Amoy St; meals S$5-10; ⓨ 11am-3pm Mon-Sat) No-frills

'pay what like' Indian eatery whose profits are donated to various charities. The range of vegetarian curries and dhals are served in all-you-can-eat buffet style and are popular with the white-collar lunch crowd. There's another branch in Chinatown Point (Map p517; B1-02 Chinatown Point, 133 New Bridge Rd).

International

Broth (Map pp526-7; ☎ 6323 3353; 21 Duxton Hill; mains from S$20; ☒ lunch & dinner Mon-Fri, dinner only Sat) In a leafy oasis atop sleepy Duxton Hill, past a row of sleazy KTV bars, this welcoming bistro has friendly staff, bentwood chairs, ceiling fans and a wall of wine and cookbooks. The menu is typically modern with dishes such as lamb loin, steaks and risottos.

Italian

Senso (Map pp526-7; ☎ 6224 3534; 21 Club St; mains S$24-38; ☒ lunch Mon-Fri, dinner daily) Grab a drink from the bar before retreating to the courtyard for dinner. Get a senso(ry) overload with the homemade pasta with superfresh lobster (live from in-house tanks) and pan-roasted king prawns in saffron cream sauce.

Peranakan

Blue Ginger (Map pp526-7; ☎ 6222 3928; 97 Tanjong Pagar Rd; mains S$10-28; ☒ lunch & dinner) Blue Ginger serves traditional Peranakan cuisine in a homely shophouse, enlivened by local artist Martin Loh's striking contemporary paintings. Its claim to fame is the *ayam panggang* (grilled chicken in coconut milk and spices).

Thai

Thanying (Map pp526-7; ☎ 6222 4688; 2nd fl, Amara Hotel, 165 Tanjong Pagar Rd; mains S$18-32; ☒ lunch & dinner) Thanying is one of Singapore's best Thai restaurants. Meticulously prepared Royal Thai curries and stir-fries are shuffled out by efficient, unintrusive staff in a slightly ostentatious setting. There's a recently opened branch in Sentosa (Map pp514–15).

Quick Eats

Highlander Coffee (Map pp520-1; 49 Kampung Bahru Rd; sandwiches from S$3.90; ☒ 9am-11pm Mon-Sat) If you're tired of the weak coffee they call lattes at Starbucks, head here for your fix. Highlander blends and roasts its own beans and the owners, Phil and Cedric, are happy

to talk coffee all day. Have a smoked duck ciabatta to accompany the brew. Or sign up for a coffee-making class.

Chinatown Complex (Map pp526-7; cnr Sago & Trengganu Sts; ☒ 9am-11pm) As you'd expect, the large, eternally busy hawker centre here has some great Chinese food stalls. The choice is vast, the smoky atmosphere appropriately unkempt.

Eric's Wuerstelstand (Map pp526-7; Stall 2 & 3 Trengganu St; ☒ 10am-8pm) Eric, an eccentric Austrian, hawks low-priced sausages and sauerkraut from a street stall.

Smith Street Hawker Stalls (Map pp526-7; Smith St; ☒ 4-11pm) Some vendors have also set up along this street, beneath red umbrellas – rivulets of water run down unwitting shirt backs when it rains. It's very touristy, but locals eat here too.

Maxwell Road Food Centre (Map pp526-7; cnr Maxwell & Neil Rds; ☒ 24hr) Generally esteemed as one of Singapore's best hawker centres, this is in an open-sided food barn with over 100 stalls under the roof. Don't miss the raw fish congee (Zhen Zhen, stall 54). Can't decide what to eat? Look for the stall with the longest queues and get to the end of the line pronto.

EAST COAST
Chinese

Eng Seng Coffeeshop (Map p528; 247/249 Joo Chiat Pl; mains from S$15; ☒ 5-9pm) The definitive Singapore dish – black-pepper crab – is so good here that locals are 1) willing to queue over an hour to order and 2) be rudely told how many crabs they can order by the proprietress. The sticky honeylike peppery sauce makes it worth arriving at 4.30pm for an early dinner.

Peranakan

Guan Hoe Soon (Map p528; ☎ 6344 2761; 214 Joo Chiat Rd; mains from S$8; ☒ lunch & dinner Wed-Mon) This modest brick-fronted restaurant is the oldest Peranakan restaurant in Singapore (established 1953). Lee Kuan Yew gets his takeaway here. The definitive Peranakan *ayam buah keluak* (chicken with black nut) is a standout. Ask for the *babi panggang* (charcoal grilled pork) on weekends.

Charlie's Peranakan Food (Map p528; ☎ 6344 8824; 205 East Coast Rd; mains S$10-18; ☒ lunch & dinner) When chef Charlie Tan retired over 10 years ago, people kept begging him to cook for them – so he went back into business! The essential Peranakan staple is *ayam buah keluak* – Charlie's version is brilliant.

MAGNIFICENT SEVEN HAWKER CENTRES

Essential to any Singapore visit is at least one hawker-centre meal, washed down with a cold bottle of Tiger beer. Here are seven of the best:

Adam Road Food Centre (Map pp520-1; cnr Adam & Dunearn Rds; ☺ 6am-3am) Try the *char kway teow* (broad noodles, clams and eggs fried in chilli and black-bean sauce) or barbecued stingray.

Chinatown Complex (Map pp526-7; Smith St; ☺ 9am-11pm) One hundred and fifty cheap, grungy and magically authentic stalls. Lubricate some roast duck and rice with a *kopi*.

Chomp Chomp (Map pp514-15; Kensington Park Rd; ☺ 6pm-1am) Wander the smoky aisles to see what takes your fancy. It's out of the way in the north of the island – you'll probably be the only tourist in sight.

Lau Pa Sat (Map pp526-7; 18 Raffles Quay; ☺ 24hr) Steamed dim sum, chilli crab and sizzling satay under a magnificent wrought-iron structure.

Lavender Food Centre (Map p522; cnr Jln Besar & Foch Rd; ☺ 11am-3am) Much less touristy than most and stays open until the wee smalls. The won-ton noodles are worth queuing for.

Maxwell Road Food Centre (Map pp526-7; cnr Maxwell & Neil Rds; ☺ 24hr) A breezy open-sided food hall with 103 stalls. Locals rack up empty beer bottles next to chubby school kids, who obviously spend too much time here.

Tekka Centre (Map p522; cnr Bukit Timah & Serangoon Rds; ☺ 10am-late) A hectic, malodorous wet market with Indian, Muslim, Keralan, Sri Lankan and vegetarian food stalls; don't miss the *roti prata* (unleavened flaky bread).

Gd O' Times (Map pp514-15; ☎ 6542 2382; 01-2017, 5 Changi Village Rd; mains from S$10; ☺ lunch & dinner Wed-Mon) A relatively late player in the Peranakan food game, but boy has this restaurant got game. Its *ayam buah keluak* and Assam fish head are family recipes and stand toe to toe with the best of them.

Seafood

No Signboard Seafood (Map p528; ☎ 6842 3415; 414 Geylang Rd; mains S$15-30; ☺ noon-1am) The irony of the 30ft crustacean-emblazoned neon signboard seems to escape the diners here – they're too busy munching plates of white-pepper crab with spring onions and garlic under a fluoro-lit marquee. There's another branch at the East Coast Seafood Centre (below).

East Coast Seafood Centre (Map p528; 1202 East Coast Parkway; mains S$15-55; ☺ dinner) Overlooking the Straits of Singapore in the salty breeze, this renowned seafood centre boasts several excellent Chinese and Thai restaurants, all with outdoor seating. Don't miss the chilli crabs and the intoxicating 'drunken' prawns. Standout places include Jumbo, Long Beach, No Signboard and Red House.

Vegetarian

Naïve (Map p528; ☎ 6348 0668; 99 East Coast Rd; mains from S$10; ☺ lunch & dinner) The cosy dining room has communal tables, so you can rub shoulders with other diners enjoying a feel-good vegetarian fix. The menu features meatless variations on local favourites such as Golden Oat, where tofu (instead of prawns) is deep fried and coated with sweet oats. Portions are a little small.

Western

Charlie's Corner (Map pp514-15; ☎ 6542 0867; 01-08 Changi Village Hawker Centre; dishes S$10-15; ☺ lunch & dinner Tue-Sun) Charlie's Corner is something of an institution, run by an old fella who's been a fixture here for years. The endless varieties of beer and the fish and chips are the main draws. The prices are a little high for a hawker-centre stall, but after a few beers you won't notice.

Quick Eats

East Coast Lagoon Food Village (Map p528; East Coast Park Service Rd; dishes S$3-15; ☺ 10.30am-11.30pm) There are few hawker centres with a better location. Tramp barefoot off the beach, order up some satay, seafood, or the uniquely Singaporean *satay bee hoon* (rice vermicelli) from Meng Kee at stall 17. Expect to queue. Cheap beer available.

Changi Village Food Centre (Map pp514-15; Lg Bekukong; dishes S$3-6; ☺ 10.30am-11.30pm) This small but extremely popular food centre is home to various stalls selling *nasi lemak* (p61). Stall 157 is the most popular but the surrounding ones are just as good minus the long queues.

HOLLAND VILLAGE & BUKIT TIMAH
French
Au Petit Salut (Map p524; ☎ 6475 1976; 40C Harding Rd; mains S$30-50; ☯ lunch & dinner Mon-Sat) Au Petit serves up familiar French fare in peaceful environs. Down tenderly cooked beef cheeks, the speciality dish, to the chirping of crickets. An extensive wine list tops the experience off. The set menu (typically three courses) offers similar food to the à la carte menu but with better value.

Indian
Samy's Curry Restaurant (Map p524; ☎ 6472 2080; Civil Service Club, 25 Dempsey Rd; mains from S$10; ☯ lunch & dinner) For 25 years the ceiling fans have spun above Samy's munificent curries in this leafy, open-walled, timber-shuttered colonial throwback. Recent renovations have removed some of the charm but the fish-head curry is still sublime. Come early for a verandah table.

Italian
Michelangelo's (Map pp514-15; ☎ 6475 9069; 01-60 Chip Bee Gardens, 44 Jln Merah Saga; mains S$24-45; ☯ lunch & dinner) Michelangelo's offers an artistic selection of pastas (penne sambuca and penne vodka help uninhibit conversations), salads and meat-oriented mains. Choose between the fan-cooled streetside terrace or the romantic dining room with its Sistine Chapel–esque ceiling efforts.

Vegetarian
Original Sin (Map pp514-15; ☎ 6475 5605; 01-62 Chip Bee Gardens, 43 Jln Merah Saga; mains S$24-32; ☯ lunch & dinner) The originally (and strictly vegetarian) sinful menu ranges from towering ricotta cakes to melt-in-your-mouth moussaka and excellent risottos, not to mention an expansive/expensive Antipodean wine list. Book a mosaic-topped outdoor table.

Quick Eats
Holland Village Food Centre (Map pp514-15; Lg Mambong; meals from S$3; ☯ 10am-late) Avoid the raft of expat locals dining at pricey restaurants across the street and join the in-the-know locals for cheap Singapore grub. A small clutch of stalls sell chicken rice, prawn noodles and other classics. Walk off the calories with a visit to the wet market behind.

Da Paolo Gastronomia (Map pp514-15; ☎ 6475 1323; 01-74 Chip Bee Gardens, 43 Jln Merah Saga; meals from S$6;

☯ 9am-9pm) Have your travelling companion nab one of the precious few stone stables outside while you nip inside this deli for gourmet-topped pizza slices, black-truffle tagliatelle and made-to-order sandwiches.

Riders Cafe (Map pp514-15; ☎ 6466 9819; 51 Fairways Dr; mains S$10-35; ☯ 8am-10pm) It's a S$10 taxi ride to get here from Orchard Rd but where else in Singapore can you chow down on eggs Benedict while watching horses being groomed and trained? The nonair-conditioned setting, in an utterly charming retro black-and-white colonial bungalow, completes the experience.

Jones the Grocer (Map pp520-1; ☎ 6476 1512; 9 Dempsey Rd; mains from S$20; ☯ 9.30am-11pm) This rather trendy deli also serves up a decent feed. Or is it a restaurant with a full-service deli? It's hard to tell, as Jones has craftily blended the two into a beautiful high-ceilinged, airy space. The cheese room is a delight, as is the open-faced wagyu burger. The espresso-based coffees are top-notch too.

KAMPONG GLAM
Indian & Malay
Zam Zam (Map p522; ☎ 6298 7011; 699 North Bridge Rd; meals S$4-8; ☯ breakfast, lunch & dinner) These guys have been here since 1908, so we figure they know what they're doing. Tenure hasn't bred complacency – the touts try to herd passers-by through the door as frenetic chefs whip up *murtabaks* (flaky, flat bread filled with mutton, chicken or vegetables).

Pariaman Warong Nasi (Map p522; ☎ 6292 2374; 738 North Bridge Rd; meals S$6-10; ☯ 7.30am-3.30pm) Cars roll up for quick takeaways at lunchtime at this corner coffee shop, where you'll smell the food before you see the crowd waiting to order the Malay dishes. The *beef rendang* (dry beef curry) and *sambal goreng* (long beans, tempeh and fried bean curd) are dishes to try.

Middle Eastern
Cafe Le Caire (Map p522; ☎ 6292 0979; 39 Arab St; meals S$8-17; ☯ lunch & dinner) This casual Egyptian hole-in-the-wall comes to life at night and attracts a multinational crowd hellbent on devouring the best kebabs and dips in town. Puff on *sheesha* pipes (S$15) and dissect the day.

Al-Tazzag (Map p522; ☎ 6295 5024; 24 Haji Ln; mains from S$8; ☯ 11.30am-4am Mon-Sat, 4pm-4am Sun) Tiny, colourfully painted Egyptian cafe full of atmosphere, *sheeshas*, dips and kebabs. The tables spill out under the five-foot ways at

SINGAPORE

night and the merriment goes on into the wee hours.

Quick Eats

Golden Mile Food Centre (Map p522; 505 Beach Rd; ✿ 10am-10pm) Promotes the government's 'Ask for Healthier Changes' policy (less oil, syrup, fat etc), but the famous *tulang* soup (S$5) from basement stalls 4, 15 and 28 doesn't really comply – meaty bones stewed in a rich, spicy, blood-red tomato gravy. Gnaw off the flesh, suck out the marrow, and sop up the sauce with bread. Seedy karaoke bars and Thai food stalls proliferate in the Golden Mile Complex across the road.

BluJaz Cafe (Map p522; ☎ 6292 3800; 11 Bali Ln; meals S$8-18; ✿ noon-midnight Mon-Thu, noon-2am Fri, 4pm-2am Sat) Live jaz (sic) is only played here on Saturday nights and on the first Monday each month. This bohemian-decorated eatery is popular for its wide range of Asian and Western dishes and the belly dancer on the first and third Friday of each month.

LITTLE INDIA
French

French Stall (Map p522; ☎ 6299 3544; 544 Serangoon Rd; mains S$10-22; ✿ drinks & dessert 3-6pm Tue-Sun, dinner Tue-Sun) A cross-cultural gem! French chef Xavier Le Henaff married a Singaporean and set up this place for regular folks – the best of France (good wine, great food, better desserts and lilting accordion music) merged with Singaporean affordability and no-frills outdoor dining. No reservations; cash only.

Indian

Madras New Woodlands (Map p522; ☎ 6297 1594; 12-14 Upper Dickson Rd; mains S$5-10; ✿ 7.30am-11.30pm) This enduring vegetarian family favourite is nothing flash to look at, but sometimes you need a break from all that Bolly schmaltz. The banana-leaf *thalis* (veggie curries, dhal and condiment) are more than generous; the service is gracious, unintrusive and helpful to confused foreigners.

Komala Vilas (Map p522; ☎ 6293 6980; 76-78 Serangoon Rd; meals S$6.50-10; ✿ breakfast, lunch & dinner) This McDonald's of Indian fare serves decent, cheap vegetarian meals all day long. Try some spicy samosas (stuffed pastries), or order the *thali*. Its outlet at 82 Serangoon Rd sells sugary Indian sweets.

Andhra Curry (Map p522; ☎ 6293 3935; 41 Kerbau Rd; meals from S$7; ✿ lunch & dinner) No-frills restaurant

that prides itself on fiery recipes from the Indian state of Andhra Pradesh. Order up some Hyderabadi biryani (oven-baked rice with vegetables and meat). Masala tea helps quell the fire in your belly. On Sunday nights it's mayhem!

our pick Spice Queen (Map p522; ☎ 6255 2240; 24/26 Race Course Rd; mains S$8-20; ✿ lunch & dinner) Self-taught celebrity chef Devagi Sanmugam serves Indian dishes with a distinctly Singaporean twist in the heart of Little India. The staff are ultrafriendly and happy to make recommendations. Fish-head curry is a must. Take home recipe books or sign up for a cooking class (see p513).

Banana Leaf Apolo (Map p522; ☎ 6293 8682; 54 Race Course Rd; mains S$10-20; ✿ lunch & dinner) Supremely tourist-friendly restaurant famed for its fish-head curry (dig into the delish meat on those fishy cheeks!). Can't face a fish face? Standards like rogan josh (tomato and red-pepper lamb curry) and lamb vindaloo (spicy Central or South Indian curry) are less confronting.

Quick Eats

Tekka Centre (Map p522; Race Course Rd; ✿ 10am-late) Unfortunately, at the time of writing, the original Tekka Centre was being renovated and tarted up. Sadly, these temporary premises only house 60% of the original stalls and 0% of the original atmosphere.

Lavender Food Centre (Map p522; cnr Jln Besar & Foch Rd; ✿ 11am-3am) Much less touristed than most and stays open until the wee hours. The wonton noodles (the queues start before the stall opens and persist all day) and Hong Kong dim sum are worth queuing for.

Rochor Original Beancurd (Map p522; 2 Short St; ✿ noon-midnight) Grab a plastic stool and order these items: bean curd, soy-bean milk and *yu tiao* (fried dough fritters). If it's too crowded, try the same dishes at the competition next door.

ORCHARD ROAD
Cafes

Killiney Kopitiam (Map p524; ☎ 6734 9648; 67 Killiney Rd; meals S$3-10; ✿ breakfast, lunch & dinner) The original local coffee joint, which spawned a whole host of imitators and an empire of franchisees, is still *the* place for breakfast. The waiter yells your order at ear-splitting volume and the coffee – shaken by the resulting seismic disturbance – inevitably arrives erupted into the saucer.

Freshly Baked (Map p524; ☎ 6735 3298; 57 Killiney Rd; sandwiches S$7; ☺ 8am-8pm Mon-Fri, 8am-6pm Sat) Office workers drop by for the excellent sandwiches but the proverbial icing on the cake is the selection of sweets and pastries. Gorge on cheesecake and éclairs and diet later.

Casa Verde (Map p524; ☎ 6467 7326; Visitors Centre, Singapore Botanic Gardens, 1 Cluny Rd; meals S$14-28; ☺ breakfast, lunch & dinner) Pet-friendly restaurant seeks pooch-loving diners for culinary fun. Smashing wood-fired pizzas attracts hordes of families and pet lovers (pets in tow). Good luck trying to get a seat. Pets optional.

PS Cafe Palais (☎ 9834 8232; 02-09 Palais Renaissance Shopping Centre, 390 Orchard Rd; mains from S$18; ☺ breakfast, lunch & dinner) Beautiful people blend easily into the equally gorgeous 'industrial grit meets colonial charm' surrounds. Slug back a cocktail under swirling ceiling fans and tear into the fish pie (fish, scallops and prawns cooked with chutney and pesto, enveloped in delicate pastry). There are two less-glamorous branches: the ProjectShop Cafe (Map p524; ☎ 6735 6765; 02-20 Paragon, 290 Orchard Rd) and PS Cafe Harding (Map pp520–1; ☎ 6479 3343; 28B Harding Rd).

Chinese

Din Tai Fung (Map p524; ☎ 6836 8336; B1-03 Paragon, 290 Orchard Rd; dishes from S$6; ☺ lunch & dinner) The queues at this Taiwanese restaurant are a testament to its excellent food. While waiting, watch chefs at work through 'fishbowl' windows; they painstakingly make 18 folds in the dough used for the *xiao long pao* (steamed pork dumplings). Delicate dumplings are served steaming fresh in bamboo baskets and explode with flavour in your mouth.

Crystal Jade La Mian Xiao Long Bao (Map p524; ☎ 6238 1661; 04-27 Ngee Ann City, Takashimaya Shopping Centre, 391 Orchard Rd; mains S$8-20; ☺ lunch & dinner) The Lanzhou handmade noodles and *xiao long pao* keep bringing people back. It has an extensive numbered 'I want that one' menu (lots of dim sum) and several set menus. There are branches at Suntec City (Map p517) and Holland Village (Map pp514–15).

Chatterbox (Map p524; ☎ 6831 6291; Level 38 Orchard Wing, Mandarin Singapore, 333 Orchard Rd; mains from S$20; ☺ 5am-1am) Chatterbox has ditched its old dull lobby digs for floor-to-ceiling 38th-floor views of the city. Its chicken rice is still legendary (both for its taste and high cost). Boiled chicken is plunged into ice then served cold

with warm broth, fragrant rice, rich soy, chilli and freshly ground ginger. Singaporeans still flock here to pay 10 times what they'd pay at a hawker centre.

French

Au Jardin (Map p524; ☎ 6466 8112; EJH Corner House, Singapore Botanic Gardens, 1 Cluny Rd; degustation S$175, brunch S$78; ☺ dinner daily, lunch Fri, brunch Sun) The dinner degustation is filled with wagyu, Alaskan crab, foie gras and all the good things in life. The genteel garden-house setting helps calm the nerves when the bill arrives. Come for Sunday brunch. Why? Your mind and stomach will turn to mush with the choice of 14 Provençal-inspired buffet dishes.

Indonesian

Rice Table (Map p524; ☎ 6835 3788; 02-09/10 International Bldg, 360 Orchard Rd; buffet lunch/dinner S$18/29; ☺ lunch & dinner) An uninspired building in Orchard Rd is saved by a restaurant serving *rijsttafel* (rice table) – a free-flowing buffet of 11 to 20 small Dutch-influenced Indonesian dishes such as *daging rendang* (spicy beef stew) and *gado gado* (tofu and beansprouts in peanut sauce).

International

our pick **Oriole Cafe & Bar** (Map p524; ☎ 6238 8348; 01-01 Pan Pacific Serviced Suites, 96 Somerset Rd; mains S$10-18; ☺ lunch & dinner) Stuck at the back of a service hotel, Oriole's modern bistro sensibilities are reflected in a wide-ranging menu guaranteed to induce dining indecision. Do you go with the beef-cheek tagliatelle, good old fish and chips or a Philly steak and cheese? Singapore's barista champion, John Ting, pulls perfect espressos behind the impressive La Marzocco machine.

The Canteen (Map p524; ☎ 6738 2276; 01-01B Shaw Centre, 1 Scotts Rd; mains S$13-16.50; ☺ lunch & dinner) The office-white furnishings and flooring don't deter shoppers from stopping by for local delights cooked with a twist: *laksa udon*, crab *mee pok* (flat egg noodles), curry chicken ramen, black-pepper beef spaghetti and handmade noodles with truffle oil.

Iggys (Map p524; ☎ 6732 2234; Level 3, the Regent Singapore, 1 Cuscaden Rd; set menus S$50-250; ☺ lunch & dinner Mon-Fri, dinner Sat & Sun) Singapore's best restaurant. Period. The surpisingly casual dining room is forgiven when the courses hit the table. Japanese and European sensibilities are meshed together in a tasting menu of epic

---

CELEBRITY CHEF EXTRAORDINAIRE: DEVAGI SANMUGAM

How did you get involved in the food industry? I'm a self-taught chef and have been in the food business for 27 years. My parents thought it was taboo for a girl to work as a chef. Their image of one was of guys flipping *roti prata* over an oily griddle! But food runs in the family. My brother is a chef in Chennai. My sister ran a food stall in River Valley.

I was a school clerk and would bring food for my colleagues to sample. People started encouraging me to run cooking classes and I finally put an ad in the papers…three people turned up for my first class. I got five family members to make up the numbers.

When did a breakthrough in your career eventuate? My break came when a *Her World* (a women's magazine) food writer gave my class a glowing review. Classes ballooned from five to 25. I had to move out of my housing development board flat to a larger landed property. I also ended up providing recipes to *Her World* for 12 years. I wrote my first cookbook in 1995. All the publishers I wrote to rejected it but my husband self-published it in Tamil and English. The 3000 copies sold out in three years. Since then I have published 16 books across many cuisines.

In 2002, I was invited by Mediaworks (now defunct) to do a TV show, *Chef on Call*. The show was about being called up by various celebrities to prepare dinner parties for their friends. Then I did a second series where I was working on a different cuisine every episode. My next TV show was *Cooking for Love*, where I taught people how to cook meals to surprise loved ones.

So you went from being teacher to restaurateur? I opened a fine-dining Indian restaurant for four years in Upper Thompson. I decided to move to casual dining and opened up a 150-seat restaurant in Little India (Spice Queen; see p544). Frankly it's frightening opening an Indian restaurant in Little India. I get criticised for not being 'authentic'. But my food is prepared to my own recipes. They are authentically mine and cater to local palates.

I'm popular but I'm not rich. It's hard work, as I run classes in the day and have to do promotion for the restaurant at night. My dream would be to open a fine-dining restaurant serving South Indian cuisine and to do a cooking show in India.

Tell us what your favourite spices are? My top three spices would be: cardamom – it's a fragrant spice and used for both savoury and sweet dishes. A little bit goes a long way! Cinnamon – this international spice is used in many cuisines. It lasts forever and can even be used as a preservative. Use it whole or ground up. Black mustard seeds – used widely in Indian cooking in meat and veg dishes.

---

proportions (eight courses for dinner). The wine list is as impressive as it is extensive.

Japanese

Wasabi Tei (Map p524; 05-70 Far East Plaza, 14 Scotts Rd; dishes S$5-15; ☼ noon-3pm & 5.30-9.30pm Mon-Fri, noon-4.30pm & 5.30-9.30pm Sat) Join the queue snaking out of this 20-seat mom-and-pop sushi bar. The chef is Chinese but he sure can slice raw fish. You'd better make your choices before you sit because seconds and postorder amendments are not allowed. Nazi-like, you say? Nineteen other people will gladly take your place.

Sun with Moon (Map p524; ☎ 6733 6636; 03-15 Wheelock Place, 501 Orchard Rd; mains from S$15; ☼ 11.30am-11pm Sun-Thu, 11.30am-midnight Fri & Sat) If Japanese novelist Haruki Murakami opened a restaurant, it would look exactly like Sun with Moon. The cavernous interior has light-filled seats (sun?) and dark little nooks (moon?),

hanging Japanese lanterns and shag carpets. *Kamameshi* (rice dish cooked in an iron pot) is delicate and the desserts taste as good as they look (the tofu cheesecake is playfully served in a bird cage).

Nagomi (Map p524; ☎ 6732 4300; 02-22 Cuppage Plaza, 5 Keok Rd; meals S$40-80; ☼ 6pm-midnight Mon-Sat) The stunning but dark atmosphere at this eatery is so moody you just want to nurse sake all night. Thankfully, the food will lift your spirits. Ingredients are flown from Japan four times a week, and meals are prepared *omakase* (there's no menu and the chef prepares seasonal specialities) and served in beautiful Japanese earthenware.

Russian

Shashlik (Map p524; ☎ 6732 6401; 06-19 Far East Shopping Centre, 545 Orchard Rd; mains S$10-26; ☼ lunch & dinner) Ooookay, a Russian coffee house in Singapore? Thumbs up for uniqueness. Additional points for doing a brave borscht and tender beef/chicken/pork shashliks. The interior is as dated as the waiters who shuffle around behind food trolleys, expertly igniting bombe Alaskas. Fun!

Quick Eats
Burrow into the basements of most Orchard Rd malls and you'll find great-value food courts.

Lucky Prata (Map p524; 01-42 Lucky Plaza, 304 Orchard Rd; 11am-9pm) You'd have to be extremely lucky to get a table at this joint during lunchtime. If you do, thank your lucky stars, roll up your sleeves and tuck into *roti prata* and *teh tarik* ('pulled' tea).

Takashimaya Food Village (Map p524; B2 Takashimaya, Ngee Ann City, 391 Orchard Rd; 10am-9.30pm) A crazy (but oh so good) mishmash of stalls selling everything from Japanese pancakes to *bibimbap* (mixed rice and meat over rice), ice cream and sweet cream puffs.

Food Republic (Map p524; Level 4 Wisma Atria Shopping Centre, 435 Orchard Rd; 10am-10.30pm) A cornucopia of local food. Muck in with the rest of the crowd for seats before joining the longest queues. Roving 'aunties' push around trolleys filled with drinks and dim sum.

Newton Food Centre (Map p524; 500 Clemenceau Ave Nth; 5pm-late) Near Newton MRT, this food centre gets a bum rap thanks to aggressive touts and overcharging. Still, the atmosphere is lively. Make sure to check prices before you confirm your order. Try the oyster omelette at Hup Kee (stall 73).

SENTOSA & AROUND
Imperial Herbal Restaurant (Map pp514-15; 6337 0491; 03-08, Lobby G, VivoCity; mains from S$22; lunch & dinner) Located in new premises, it still retains the scorpions on the menu and the in-house Chinese physician who checks your pulse, examines your tongue and then prescribes something on the menu to rebalance your yin and yang. Boost your libido, lose the zits, or stop the grey-hair onslaught – something tasty will save the day!

Il Lido (Map pp514-15; 6866 1977; Sentosa Golf Club, 27 Bukit Manis Rd; mains S$28-68 lunch & dinner) Starry-eyed lovers and suits on corporate accounts share the simple al fresco dining space for stunning views of the South China Sea while twirling squid-ink fettuccine on

their forks. Alcoholics rejoice for there's a S$98 champagne brunch on Sundays.

DRINKING
Despite ludicrously high alcohol prices, high disposable incomes and relaxed licensing laws fuel a lively bar scene in Singapore – you'll always find somewhere to suit your mood. Hit the bars early to cash in on happy hours, typically stretching from 5pm to 9pm, when you'll often get two-for-one drinks. On Wednesday nights some bars have cheap or free drinks for women. Watch out for higher age limits at some bars (usually 18 for most, though some require men to be 21 or 23).

The main party places are Circular Rd, Boat Quay, Mohamed Sultan Rd, Chijmes in the Colonial District, Club St in Chinatown, Emerald Hill off Orchard Rd, and Holland Village. Unless otherwise stated, bars have free entry, most opening around 5pm until at least midnight Sunday to Thursday, and through to 2am or 3am on Friday and Saturday.

If you don't want to go home broke and don't mind plastic tables and fluoro lights, bottles of Tiger, Heineken and Tsingtao cost S$6 to S$8 at hawker centres and coffee shops.

COLONIAL DISTRICT
Chijmes (Map p517; 30 Victoria St) Perennially popular Chijmes is a high-density collection of bars and chilled-out patio areas.

New Asia Bar (Map p517; 6831 5681; Swissôtel The Stamford, Lvl 71, Equinox Complex, 2 Stamford Rd; cover Fri & Sat incl 1 drink S$25; 3pm-late) Save the S$30 you would have spent on the Singapore Flyer and spend it on drinks here instead! The 70th floor and panoramic views help your drinks go down a little easier. Come early for sundowners, and once you tire of the views, shake it on the dance floor.

Loof (Map p517; 6338 8035; www.loof.com.sg; 03-07 Odeon Towers Bldg, 331 North Bridge Rd; 5pm-1.30am Sun-Thu, 5pm-3am Fri & Sat) This rooftop bar gets its name from the Singlish (local slang) mangling of the word 'roof'. Ambient beats soothe away the city noise and comfy leather-clad seats are scattered around the deck…perhaps these are to blame for the mellow crowd. For privacy (and air-con), ask for one of the seven semi-enclosed seating areas.

Orgo (Map p517; nick@orgo.sg; 4th fl Esplanade Roof Tce, 1 Esplanade Dr; 5pm-2am) Yawn. Yet another

---

GAY & LESBIAN SINGAPORE

Although male homosexuality remains illegal (and lesbianism doesn't officially exist!), when some 2500 Singaporeans of all sexual persuasions dressed in pink and met in Hong Lim Park in May 2009 to form a pink dot (www.pinkdot.sg), it was hailed a defining moment in the island's long march to freedom of sexual expression. Every August for the past few years, the island's gays have also rallied round for the pride celebration **Indignation** (www.plu.sg/indignation).

Chinatown's Tanjong Pagar Rd area has an active gay and lesbian bar scene and welcomes drinkers regardless of their sexuality. Apart from the following also check out the listings at www.utopia-asiacom and www.fridae.com, and see p560.

DYMK (Map pp526-7; ☎ 6224 3565; www.dymk.sg; 9 Kreta Ayer Rd; ☾ 7pm-midnight Tue-Thu, to 1am Fri, 8pm-2am Sat) Standing for Does Your Mother Know, this cute yellow-and-red-painted shophouse is a chilled and friendly place to start or wind down your night.

Backstage Bar (Map pp526-7; ☎ 6227 1712; www.backstagebar.moonfruit.com; 13A Trengganu St; ☾ 7pm-2am Sun-Thu, 7pm-3am Fri & Sat) The entrance to this long-running bar with a breezy balcony is on Temple St; it attracts an older set and their acolytes.

Tantric Bar (Map pp526-7; 78 Neil Rd; ☾ 8pm-3am Sun-Fri, Sat 8pm-4am) With a spacious multilevel courtyard, this bar is the place to see and be seen, catch up on the latest goss and scope out potential playmates.

Taboo (Map pp526-7; ☎ 6225 6256; www.taboo97.com; 65-67 Neil Rd; ☾ 8pm-2am Wed & Thu, 10pm-3am Fri, 10pm-4am Sat) It may keep moving location but Taboo remains a tried and trusted venue for late-night dancing and frolicking – release your inner Madonna on that podium.

Play & Replay (Map pp526-7; ☎ 6227 7400; http://playclub.com.sg; 21 Tanjong Pagar Rd; admission incl 1 drink S$15; ☾ 9pm-3am Wed-Fri, 9pm-4am Sat) Spacious and popular club with all sexes; the attached bar Replay is a sophisticated space catering to the stylish gay set and playing a more progressive, 'eclectric' range of sounds.

---

rooftop bar with stunning views. But this one has the added bonus of Japanese mixologist Tomoyuki Kitazoe crafting crazy drinks such as soursop calamansi martinis in addition to panoramic views of Marina Bay. Air-conditioned glass enclosures available for wilting patrons. Let's orgo to Orgo!

Paulaner Bräuhaus (Map p517; ☎ 6883 2572; 01-01 Times Square@Millenia Walk, 9 Raffles Blvd; ☾ noon-1am Sun-Thu, noon-2am Fri & Sat) A brassy, three-storey German microbrewery bar and restaurant serving up brothy tankards of Munich Lager and Munich Dark and platters of sausage and cheese 'knacker'. There's live music in the evenings.

Raffles Hotel (Map p517; ☎ 6337 1886; 1 Beach Rd; ☾ 10am-late) Yeah, we know it's a cliché, but a visit to Singapore is practically incomplete without a drink at Raffles (p496). The Bar & Billiard Room has two billiard tables and a verandah perfect for postcolonial posturing. The courtyard Gazebo Bar is a tasty spot for a tipple below rattling palms. Sipping a Singapore Sling in the Long Bar and throwing peanut shells on the floor is a quintessential Singapore experience…just go in the day to avoid the horrid evening cover band. A frosty glass of the sweet, cherry-red intoxicator will set you back S$25. Cheers.

THE QUAYS

Over Easy (Map p517; ☎ 6423 0503; 01-06 One Fullerton, 1 Fullerton Rd) The egg dishes on the menu aren't anything to shout about but the drinks are easily done over, given the stunning Marina Bay views and one-for-one happy-hour specials (6pm to 8pm).

Boat Quay & Circular Road

Penny Black (Map p517; ☎ 6538 2300; 26/27 Boat Quay; ☾ 11am-1am Mon-Thu, 11am-2am Fri & Sat, 11am-midnight Sun) Fitted out like a 'Victorian' London pub (without the tuberculosis and dodgy gin), Penny Black specialises in hard-to-find English ales for the swaths of expat Brits that work in the area (who keep one eye on their pints and another on the Premier League matches screened on TVs).

Archipelago Brewery (Map p517; ☎ 6327 8408; 79 Circular Rd; ☾ 3pm-1am Mon-Thu & Sun, 4pm-3am Fri & Sat) Asia Pacific Breweries (makers of Tiger) decided to jump on the microbrewery bandwagon with their line of yummy Asian-accented beers. This is their flagship pub on a Y-junction on mildly seedy Circular Rd.

Molly Malone's (Map p517; ☎ 6536 2029; 53-56 Circular Rd; ☾ 11am-midnight Sun & Mon, to 1am Tue-Thu, to 2am Fri & Sat) Molly Malone's has moved to larger premises. Well-travelled drinkers will have seen the Irish interior and the genuine Irish stew and fish-and-chip menu 100 times before, but that doesn't make it any more appealing.

Harry's Bar (Map p517; ☎ 6538 3029; 28 Boat Quay; ☯ 11am-1am Sun-Thu, 11pm-2am Fri & Sat) Harry's has spawned an empire of bars across the island but the original is still the best. This financial-district hang-out gained infamy as the haunt of Barings-buster Nick Leeson. Grab a pint and toast his misdeeds.

Clarke Quay

Brewerkz (Map p517; ☎ 6438 7438; 01-05 Riverside Point Centre, 30 Merchant Rd; ☯ noon-midnight Sun-Thu, noon-1am Fri & Sat) Across the river from Clarke Quay, this large microbrewery (the irony doesn't escape us) brews eight beers on site, including an Indian Pale Ale, Pilsener and Golden Ale. Happy hours run from opening to 9pm, with prices escalating throughout the day (pints S$4 to S$15, jugs S$10 to S$37).

Cuba Libre (Map p517; ☎ 6338 8982; Block B, 01-03 Clarke Quay, 3B River Valley Rd; ☯ 6pm-1am Sun-Thu, 6pm-3am Fri & Sat) The live Cuban music surges with energy and will compel even the most wooden of legs to start moving. If you can resist the siren of salsa, nurse drinks and watch students go through the motions.

Robertson Quay & Mohamed Sultan Road

Next Page (Map pp520-1; ☎ 6235 6967; 17 Mohamed Sultan Rd; ☯ 3pm-3am) This is where Hunter S Thompson would have hung out if he'd been a journo in Singapore. Dark timber bar, red lanterns, exposed brickwork, booths, pool table, Carlsberg on tap and quirky bartenders – sit down and write the next page of your novel.

Brussels Sprouts Belgian Beer & Mussels (Map pp520-1; ☎ 6887 4344; 01-12 Robertson Quay, 80 Mohamed Sultan Rd; ☯ 5pm-midnight Mon-Thu, noon-1am Fri & Sat, noon-midnight Sun) Cute restaurant bar that lays it heavy on the Belgian theme with mussels, trappist ales galore and Tintin murals on the wall (the whole gang's there down to Thompson & Thompson).

CHINATOWN & THE CBD

The following Chinatown bars are closed on Sundays unless otherwise specified.

Bar Sá Vánh (Map pp526-7; ☎ 6323 0145; 49 Club St; ☯ 5pm-2am Mon-Thu, to 3am Fri & Sat) Gorgeous svelte things flit through Sá Vánh's dusky candlelight

as expats sink into sunken lounges and Asian tapas while ambient tunes snake into the night – all under the gaze of Buddha himself.

Beaujolais Wine Bar (Map pp526-7; ☎ 6224 2227; 1 Ann Siang Hill; ☯ 11am-midnight Mon-Thu, 11am-2am Fri, 6pm-midnight Sat & Sun) A *très* cute shophouse bar with chequered Montmarte tablecloths, bentwood chairs, slate floors and low-key jazz. It's a welcome relief from the raft of *très* chic industrial-looking bars now dotting the city.

Oosters Brasserie (Map pp526-7; ☎ 6438 3210; 01-04 Capital Sq Three, 25 Church St; ☯ noon-midnight Mon-Fri, 5.30pm-midnight Sat) Grab a seat at one of the booths or on a bar stool and order from an extensive list of Belgian beers (Leffe on tap!) and trappist ales (expect Orval and Chimay). Get some mussels cooked any way you like. There's a branch at Suntec City (p517; ☎ 6334 2889; 01-39 Suntec City Galleria; open noon to midnight Monday to Saturday).

Helipad (Map p517; ☎ 6327 8118; 05-22 the Central, 6 Eu Tong Sen St; ☯ 6pm-2am Mon-Thu, to 3am Fri & Sat) Yes, this bar's claim to fame is its position on top of a helicopter pad. Well, a faux one at least. The vibe is decidedly partylike and there are one-for-one housepours from 6pm to 9pm.

LITTLE INDIA

Zsofi Tapas Bar (Map p522; ☎ 6297 5875; 68 Dunlop St; ☯ 4pm-1am Mon-Thu, 4pm-2am Fri & Sat) Inspired by their travels through Spain, two mates decided to open a tapas bar named after a travelling companion. Chill out at the eclectic bar downstairs; sit down on the floor on the 2nd level or at a table on the rooftop. All drinks come with a tapas dish of your choice. Now that's choice!

ORCHARD ROAD

Alley Bar (Map p524; ☎ 6738 8818; 2 Emerald Hill Rd; ☯ 5pm-2am Sun-Thu, 5pm-3am Fri & Sat) Sky-high ceilings, dark timbers, candlelight and slick stylings paint this alleyway bar with restrained melodrama. Yuppies and expats converse in shadowy, cushioned nooks, quaffing wine and on-tap Belgian beers.

No 5 (Map p524; ☎ 6732 0818; 5 Emerald Hill Rd; ☯ 5pm-2am Sun-Thu, 5pm-3am Fri & Sat) Not much imagination went into naming this long-running boozer in a 1910 Peranakan shophouse. Expect retro-Asiatic touches, vats of chilli vodka and smoky snooker vibes. It's damned touristy around here, but the cool evening ambience is sweet relief from Orchard Rd.

SINGAPORE

Que Pasa (Map p524; ☎ 6235 6626; 7 Emerald Hill Rd; ⊗ 5pm-2am Sun-Thu, 5pm-3am Fri & Sat) Next door to No 5, this is a classy wine and tapas bar.

Ice Cold Beer (Map p524; ☎ 6735 9929; 9 Emerald Hill Rd; ⊗ 5pm-2am Sun-Thu, 5pm-3am Fri & Sat) It's back to raucous international beer-swilling (to rock tunes) at this spot.

Dubliners (Map p524; ☎ 6735 2220; 165 Penang Rd; ⊗ 11.30am-1am Sun-Thu, to 2am Fri & Sat) Dubliners gains kudos for its whitewashed plantation architecture and quality pub food. No sign of James Joyce, but you can toast his efforts with a pint of the black stuff on the verandah.

HOLLAND VILLAGE

Wala Wala (Map pp514-15; ☎ 6462 4288; 31 Lg Mambong; ⊗ 4pm-1am Mon-Thu, 3pm-2am Fri & Sat, 3pm-1am Sun) This extremely popular bar is loud, raucous and friendly. Seating downstairs is open and breezy while the live-music bar upstairs focuses on danceable, singable, air-punchable tunes.

2AM Dessert Bar (Map pp514-15; ☎ 6291 9727; 21A Lg Liput; ⊗ 6pm-2am Mon-Sat) Chef-owner Janice Wong opened this brave venture in her mid-20s in 2007. Here, the chic bar concept is taken to a whole new level with the focus being 13 drool-worthy desserts, each paired with a wine recommendation. Where else can you satisfy your chocolate cravings at two in the morning?

SENTOSA ISLAND

Sentosa has recently shaken off its tacky image and become something of a fashionable hang-out, especially at weekends, when its beach bars are busy day and night with the tanned and scantily clad. Beach parties are held fairly regularly. **Coastes** (Map pp514-15; ☎ 6274 9668; Siloso Beach), **Bikini Bar** (Map pp514-15; ☎ 6274 9668; Siloso Beach) and **Cafe del Mar** (Map pp514-15; ☎ 6235 1296; Siloso Beach) are all Ibiza-inspired restaurant-bars.

ENTERTAINMENT

Singapore's nightlife gets a bum rap (mainly from Singapore Sling–swilling package tourists) but there's really no excuse for an early night in Singapore.

Clubs generally close at 3am and are strictly drug-free; get your kicks instead from local acts and touring DJs who regu-

larly stop off in Singapore. Dress is smart casual – no shorts or sandals.

In contrast, the live music scene is pretty dismal; cover bands, tinkling Richard Clayderman piano classics and karaoke bars rule the roost. Thankfully, there are several bars that actually hire decent local artists.

Singaporeans adore the cinema – mainstream US blockbusters are standard fodder. The city's theatre scene is surprisingly vibrant, staging everything from experimental originals to repertory standards. You'll also find some quality classical and tourist-friendly opera performances.

Tickets for most events are available through **Sistic** (☎ 6348 5555; www.sistic.com.sg) or **Tickets.com** (☎ 6296 2929; www.tdc.com.sg). Check websites for the nearest outlets. The *Straits Times*, *I-S Magazine* and *Time Out* have listings for movies, theatre and music. For nightlife, pick up the free street mags *I-S Magazine* and *Juice* at cafes, hotels and music stores.

COMEDY & MAGIC

Howl at the Moon (Map p524; ☎ 6838 0281; www.1nitestand.com; Level 2 Peranakan Place, 180 Orchard Rd; admission free; ⊗ 6pm-2am Tue-Sun) This rock bar also hosts monthly comedy nights with mostly UK, US and Australian stand-ups hamming it up. Check the website for schedules.

Arena (Map p517; ☎ 6338 3158; 01-08 Clarke Quay, 3B River Valley Rd; adult/child S$55/27.50) Watch local magician JC Sum and his 'babe' (their words) assistant Ning channel David Copperfield nightly. The venue also hosts music acts and DJs, so call before you head down.

CHINESE OPERA

Chinese Theatre Circle (Map pp526-7; ☎ 6323 4862; www.ctcopera.com.sg; 5 Smith St; ⊗ box office noon-5pm Tue-Thu, noon-5pm & 7-9pm Fri & Sat, 2-10pm Sun) Every Friday and Saturday night at 8pm there's a brief talk (in English) about Chinese opera, followed by a short excerpt performed by professional actors in full costume. Lychee tea and cakes are included in the S$20 price. For S$35, turn up at 7pm and enjoy a full Chinese meal beforehand. Bookings recommended.

CINEMA

Movie-going is huge in Singapore, and at around S$9 per ticket it's good value. Films are mainly Hollywood blockbusters and Chinese, Korean and Japanese crowd-pleasers, plus a few art-house hits from around the

---

PARTY AT THE ST JAMES POWER STATION

The latest and greatest posterboy of Singapore's night scene, **St James Power Station** (Map pp514-15; ☎ 6270 7676; www.stjamespowerstation.com; 3 Sentosa Gateway) is a 1920s coal-fired power station ingeniously converted into an entertainment complex. All the bars and clubs are interconnected, so one cover charge (men/women S$12/10, Wednesday men S$30) gets access to all of them. Some bars – Gallery Bar, Lobby Bar and Peppermint Park – have no cover charge at all. Minimum age is 18 for women and 23 for men at all except Powerhouse, where the age is 18 for both.

The bars include **Dragonfly** (☻ 6pm-6am), a Mandopop and Cantopop club; **Movida** (☻ 6pm-3am), a Latin live-band dance club; **Powerhouse** (☻ 8pm-4am Wed, Fri & Sat), a large dance club aimed at the younger crowd; and the **Boiler Room** (☻ 8.45pm-3am Mon-Sat), a mainstream rock club featuring live bands. There's also French bordello–inspired **Mono** (☻ 6pm-6am), a karaoke bar for those inclined towards belting out their own tunes.

---

world. Non-English films are subtitled; admission prices vary according to session times. Weekend screenings sell out (even midnight sessions) so book ahead. Check the *Straits Times* for session details. Dress warmly – Singaporean cinemas are notoriously chilly.

The **Singapore International Film Festival** (www.filmfest.org.sg), held each April, brings an enormous collection of independent films to the country.

There are multiplex cinemas around the Colonial District at Bugis Junction (Map p522) and Iluma (Map p522), Suntec City and Marina Sq (all on Map p517). Around Orchard Rd you'll find cinemas at Cathay Cineleisure Orchard and Plaza Singapura, Lido cinema at Shaw House and the Picturehouse at the Cathay (all on Map p524).

GV Gold Class (www.gv.com.sg; ☎ 1900 912 1234); Great World City (Map pp520-1; 1 Kim Seng Pde); VivoCity (Map pp514-15; 1 HarbourFront Walk) These swanky cinemas feature plush carpeting and single and double reclining seats complete with footrests, table service and a reasonable menu. Tickets cost S$28.

Sinema (Map p522; ☎ 6337 9707; www.sinema.com .sg; B1-12 Old School, 11B Mt Sophia Rd; tickets S$8-10; ☻ 11am-11pm Tue-Fri, 2-11pm Sat) Started off as a local-movie theatre and soon ran out of steam (erm, someone doing the business plan should have realised there are like, what, five local films?). Has since expanded its repertoire to 'Asian' cinema.

Screening Room (Map pp526-7; ☎ 6221 1694; www .screeningroom.com.sg; 12 Ann Siang Rd; food & movie from S$55; ☻ noon-2.30pm & 6pm-late) Get your ticket, order some food and drinks and settle down on a comfy sofa for a movie. After the film, wander out onto the rooftop bar for views of Chinatown.

CLUBS

Most clubs have cover charges of around S$15 to S$35, often including at least one drink; women usually pay less (or even nothing!). Clubs are forever folding and revamping; check *I-S Magazine* and *Juice* for reviews.

Zouk (Map p517; ☎ 6738 2988; www.zoukclub.com; 17 Jiak Kim St; admission incl 2 drinks S$35; ☻ Zouk & Phuture 7pm-4am Wed, Fri & Sat, Velvet Underground 9pm-3am Tue-Sat, Wine Bar 6pm-3.30am daily) Nineteen going on one, Ibiza-inspired Zouk is still Singapore's hottest club. It features five bars, with the capacity to hold 2000, and a roomy dance floor with plenty of space to cut the rug – it's a world-class contender and a regular destination for globe-trotting DJs. You'll also find the alfresco Zouk Wine Bar, avant-garde Phuture and the Moroccan-inspired Velvet Underground hung with Keith Haring and Andy Warhol originals. Be prepared to queue.

Butter Factory (Map p517; ☎ 6333 8243; www .thebutterfactory.com; 02-02 One Fullerton, 1 Fullerton Rd; admission incl 2 drinks from S$21; ☻ 7pm-1am Tue, 7pm-3am Thu, 8pm-3am Wed & Fri, Sat 8pm-4am) At over 700 sq metres, Butter Factory's new digs is double the size of its old premises and slick as hell. Street art on the walls of Bump, the hip-hop and R&B room, betrays its young crowd. Fash is its chilled-out 'art' bar, and walls are plastered with colourful pop-art reminiscent of underground comics (yes, the ones you hid from mum).

Zirca Mega Club (Map p517; ☎ 6235 2292; www .zirca.sg; 01-02 Block 3C River Valley Rd, the Cannery, Clarke Quay; admission incl 2 drinks men S$25-28, women S$20-25; ☻ 9.30pm to late Wed-Sat) After the Ministry of Sound Singapore was shut down owing to contractual issues, licensee Lifebrandz quickly rebranded the club into Zirca. Mash with the mainly 20-somethings in Zirca (dance

SINGAPORE

club), Rebel (hip-hop arena) or Yellow Jello (retro disco).

dbl O (Map p517; ☎ 6735 2008; www.dbl-o.com; 01-24, 11 Unity St, Robertson Walk; admission S$15; ☷ 8pm-3am Tue-Fri, 8pm-4am Sat) An outrageous three-bar dance club, popular with young clubbers wearing very little and older people who like to look at them. Music ranges from Top 40 on Thursdays, house on Fridays and retro on Saturdays. The reason for its popularity? S$3 house pours.

LIVE MUSIC
Classical

Singapore Symphony Orchestra (☎ 6348 5555; www .sso.org.sg) The 1800-seater state-of-the-art concert hall at the Esplanade – Theatres on the Bay (p495) is home to this respected orchestra, which also graces the Victoria Theatre & Concert Hall (opposite). It plays at least once weekly; check the website for details and book in advance. Half-price student and senior (60-plus) discounts are available; kids under six years old are unceremoniously banned.

Singapore Chinese Orchestra (Map pp526-7; ☎ 6440 3839; www.sco.com.sg; Singapore Conference Hall, 7 Shenton Way) Performs regular classical Chinese concerts throughout the year, featuring traditional instruments, including the *liuqin, ruan* and *sanxian*. There are occasional collaborations with Japanese, jazz and Malay musicians.

Rock

Crazy Elephant (Map p517; ☎ 6337 7859; www.crazy elephant.com; 01-03/04 Clarke Quay; admission free; ☷ 5pm-2am Sun-Thu, to 3am Fri & Sat) Anywhere that bills itself as 'crazy' should set the alarm bells ringing, but you won't hear them once you're inside. This touristy rock bar is beery, blokey, loud, graffiti-covered and testosterone-heavy – rock on!

Prince of Wales (Map p522; ☎ 6299 0130; www.pow .com.sg; 101 Dunlop St; admission free) This Aussie-hewn pub has backpacker accommodation upstairs. Rub shoulders with resident surfy beer-boffins effusing over acoustic rock on week nights and original indie bands on weekends. Harley riders take over the place on Saturday nights. Music is from 9pm most nights.

Timbre@Old School (Map p522; ☎ 6338 0800; 11 Mt Sophia Rd; ☷ 6pm-midnight) At night, groups of art-school types hang out and bob heads to live acoustic sets while downing pints of Erdinger, their hands oily from one too many buffalo wings. It's quite a hike up a hill, so take a cab.

Howl at the Moon (Map p524; ☎ 6838 0281; Level 2 Peranakan Place, 180 Orchard Rd; admission free; ☷ 6pm-2am Tue-Sun) The superbly talented band can play any song request you fling at them (no matter how obscure) and the duelling pianists bashing away on the ivories are entertaining.

Jazz & Blues

Jazz@Southbridge (Map p517; ☎ 6327 4671; www .southbridgejazz.com.sg; 82B Boat Quay; admission free, touring acts from S$20; ☷ 5pm-1am Tue-Thu, to 2am Fri & Sat) This intimate jazz bar sets plush sofas in front of a small stage. In-house crooner Alemay Fernandez ably entertains, and famous internationals often take to the stage (Pat Metheny did an impromptu jam once). Sets kick off around 9.30pm.

Bellini Grande (Map p517; ☎ 6336 7676; 01-01 The Foundry, Clarke Quay, 3B River Valley Rd; ☷ 6pm-3am Sun-Thu, to 4am Fri & Sat) The swing and jazz band at the St James Power Station was such a huge hit they moved their three lead singers, 14-piece band and backup dancers to a swanky larger place. The crowd seems to agree with the move.

SPECTATOR SPORTS

Singapore Indoor Stadium (Map p528; ☎ 6348 5555; www.sis.gov.sg; 2 Stadium Walk; ☷ box office 10am-10pm Mon-Sat, noon-8pm Sun) Most of Singapore's big-ticket sports and entertainment events – from international bands to celebrity wrestling – are played out here; check the website, the *Straits Times* or www.singaporesports.com.sg for details. To get here take bus 11 from Kallang MRT or bus 16 from Orchard Rd.

Singapore Turf Club (Map pp514-15; ☎ 6879 1000; www.turfclub.com.sg; 1 Turf Club Ave) The website claims 'It's more exciting with horses!' We're not sure what 'it' entails, but the races sure are rousing. Seats range from grandstand (S$3) up to Hibiscus Room (S$20). Dress code is collared shirt and pants for men; closed shoes for women. Betting is government controlled; check the website for race schedules (usually Friday nights and all day weekends); Kranji MRT station is right outside. Giddy-up.

THEATRE & DANCE

Singapore's more dynamic and contemporary theatre groups produce edgy but accessible home-grown and international work at various venues around town. Look out for shows by **Theatreworks** (www.theatreworks.org.sg), **Toy Factory Ensemble** (www.toyfactory.org.sg), **Action Theatre** (www.action.org.sg), **Necessary Stage** (www.necessary.org) and Singapore's sexiest theatre company, **Wild Rice** (www.wildrice.com.sg).

Singapore Repertory Theatre (Map p517; ☎ 6733 8166; www.srt.com.sg; DBS Drama Centre, 20 Merbau Rd) The bigwig of Singapore's theatre scene, producing Shakespeare and other mainstream standards. Their Little Company stages plays to entertain the young 'uns.

Nrityalaya Aesthetics Society (Map p522; ☎ 6336 6537; www.nas.org.sg; 155 Waterloo St) For classical Indian dance and vocal and instrumental music check out this company. It even stages Shakespeare in Kathakali (Indian story form)!

Singapore Dance Theatre (Map p517; ☎ 6338 0611; www.singaporedancetheatre.com; 02 Fort Canning Centre, Cox Tce) Produces traditional ballet favourites alongside contemporary works. Don't miss July's 'Ballet Under the Stars' season at Fort Canning Park (S$25).

Apart from the Esplanade (p495), other venues include the following:

Drama Centre (Map p517; ☎ 6837 8400; Level 3, National Library, 100 Victoria St)

Jubilee Hall (Map p517; ☎ 6331 1732; 3rd fl, Raffles Hotel, 1 Beach Rd)

Kallang Theatre (Map p528; ☎ 6345 8488; www.nac.gov.sg; 1 Stadium Walk)

Substation (Map p517; ☎ 6337 7535; www.substation.org; Substation, 45 Armenian St) Space for performance arts and classes.

Victoria Theatre & Concert Hall (Map p517; ☎ 6338 1230; www.vch.org.sg; 11 Empress Pl)

SHOPPING

Shopping is locked in an age-old struggle with eating and movie-going for the title of Singapore's national hobby. Nary a year goes by without a new retail monolith flinging its doors open to slavering hordes nor does a day go by without slick advertising adding fuel to the raging pyre that is hard-core capitalism – failure to participate is not an option!

Compared with Thailand, Indonesia and Malaysia, Singapore is no bargain-hunter's paradise, and prices are usually fixed except at markets and in tourist areas (don't start bargaining if you don't have any interest in purchasing). Still, electronics, computers, clothes and CDs are cheaper than in most Western countries. Most shops open at 10am or 11am and close around 9pm or 10pm.

The STB-endorsed **Great Singapore Sale** (www.greatsingaporesale.com.sg) storms from late May through to late July every year – discount shopping coinciding with various arts

---

BUYER BEWARE!

Singapore has stringent consumer laws and actively promotes safe shopping. You'll rarely have any problems, but still be wary when buying, particularly in smaller shops, where a salesperson may accept a low offer but not give you an international guarantee (important for watches, cameras etc) or the usual accessories. Ensure international guarantees are filled out correctly, including the shop's name and the item's serial number.

Make sure you have exactly what you want before leaving the shop. Check the voltage and cycle of electrical goods: Singapore, Australia, New Zealand, Hong Kong and the UK use 220V to 240V at 50 cycles; Canada, Japan and the US use 110V to 120V at 60 cycles. Most shops will attach the correct plug for your country if you ask. There are two main types of TV systems: PAL in Australia and Europe, and NTSC in the USA and Japan – video equipment must be compatible with your system. If you're buying a DVD or Bluray player or a gaming system, check that it'll play your home country's discs.

When buying antiques, ask for a certificate of antiquity, required by many countries to avoid paying customs duty.

Serious issues with retailers are unlikely (the worst you'll probably get is lethargic service), but if you've been ripped off or taken for a ride, contact the **Singapore Tourism Board** (STB; ☎ 1800-736 2000; www.visitsingapore.com) or the **Small Claims Tribunal** (Map p517; ☎ 6435 5994; www.smallclaims.gov.sg; Subordinate Courts, 1 Havelock Sq; ☯ 8.30am-1pm & 2-6pm Mon-Thu, 8.30am-1pm & 2-5.30pm Fri, 8.30am-1pm Sat). Tourist complaints are usually heard within two or three days.

and food festivals. Best bargains are had during the first week.

GST

Most goods and services incur a 7% goods-and-services tax (GST). See p562 for information on the GST Tourist Refund Scheme.

ART, CRAFTS & ANTIQUES

Too often driven by perceived market opportunity rather than artistic vision, the Singapore gallery scene is nonetheless vibrant. Many galleries are closed on Sundays and/or Mondays. The free fortnightly *Arts Beat* magazine lists all the art shows. Download a PDF version at www.nac.gov.sg/eve/eve07print.asp. Head to Chinatown for Chinese crafts and antiques, Little India for Indian crafts, and Kampong Glam's Arab St for fabrics, cane ware and leather goods.

Colonial District

Chijmes (Map p517; 30 Victoria St) is a serene place to sniff around for crafts. Among the outlets presently operating at Chijmes, **Olathe** (Map p517; ☎ 6339 6880; 01-05) sells a commercial range of batik clothing, bags and ceramics, and **Empress Myanmar** (Map p517; ☎ 6335 5366; 01-25) stocks jewellery and crafts from where else but Myanmar.

Ode to Art (Map p517; ☎ 6250 1901; 01-36 Raffles City Shopping Centre, 252 North Bridge Rd) displays and sells sculptures and paintings from a variety of Asian artists and are happy to ship worldwide.

The Raffles Hotel Arcade is home to **Artfolio** (Map p517; ☎ 6334 4677; 02-25 Raffles Hotel Arcade, 328 North Bridge Rd), which specialises in Southeast Asian art, and **Tomlinson Antique House** (Map p517; ☎ 6338 1700; 02-35/36 Raffles Hotel Arcade, 328 North Bridge Rd), which sells Indian, Burmese and Chinese artefacts dating back to the Tang dynasty. Prices hit the many thousands.

The rainbow-shuttered colonial **MICA Building** (Map p517; 140 Hill St) houses a clutch of quality galleries, including **Art-2 Gallery** (Map p517; ☎ 6338 8719; www.art2.com.sg), **Cape of Good Hope Art Gallery** (Map p517; ☎ 6733 3822; www.capeofgoodhopegallery.com), **Gajah Gallery** (Map p517; ☎ 6737 4202; www.gajahgallery.com), **Art Mosaic** (Map p517; ☎ 6336 4606; www.artmosaic.com) and **Soobin Art Gallery** (Map p517; ☎ 6837 2777; www.soobinart.com.sg), which showcases the best of China's vibrant avant-garde scene.

Chinatown

The classy **Shing Gallery** (Map pp526-7; ☎ 6224 4332; 26 Pagoda St) stocks beautiful wooden screens, lamps, sculptures and antique furniture. **East Inspirations** (Map pp526-7; ☎ 6224 2993; 33/33A Pagoda St) is jam-packed with antique figurines, trinkets and some furniture.

The **Zhen Lacquer Gallery** (Map pp526-7; ☎ 6222 2718; 1/1A/1B Trengganu St) is generally kitsch but sometimes stylish, selling shiny lacquered hand-painted jewellery boxes, placemats, utensils, plates and photo albums.

Mr Yong will carve a Chinese stamp with your name on it at **Yong Gallery** (Map pp526-7; ☎ 6226 1718; 260 South Bridge Rd). He also stocks masterful calligraphic works and jade carvings

Utterly Art (Map pp526-7; ☎ 6226 2605; 229A South Bridge Rd) has exhibitions that change monthly

---

TANJONG PAGAR ARTS ENCLAVE

A clutch of art galleries have sprung up in the most unglamorous of places – Tanjong Pagar Distripark. This warehouse area is more used to hosting pallets of goods than the art elite, but large spaces with high ceilings and reasonable rent have seen three notable art galleries move in.

The **Fortune Cookie Projects** (Map pp526-7; www.fortunecookieprojects.com; 02-04 Tanjong Pagar Distripark, HT Contemporary Space, 39 Keppel Rd) got lucky when it exhibited Julian Schnable's US$275,000 paintings in March 2009. Check its website for future shows.

Valentine Willie Fine Art (Map pp526-7; ☎ 8133 4760; www.vwfa.net; 02-04 Tanjong Pagar Distripark, HT Contemporary Space, 39 Keppel Rd; ☷ 11am-7pm Tue-Sat, 11am-3pm Sun) seeks out and displays the hottest Southeast Asian artists. Ditto at **Galarie Waterton** (Map pp526-7; ☎ 9738 2144; www.galariewaterton.com; 02-01 Tanjong Pagar Distripark, HT Contemporary Space, 39 Keppel Rd; ☷ 11am-7pm Tue-Sat, 11am-3pm Sun) next door.

Take bus 145 from outside St Andrew's Cathedral. A taxi from Orchard Rd will cost S$8.

and sells reasonably priced Southeast Asia art. It specialises in Filipino artists.

Little India

Pick your way through a staggering display of subcontinental knick-knacks at **Celebration of Arts** (Map p522; ☎ 6296 0769; 2/2A Dalhousie Lane) – everything from statues and carved wooden screens to cashmere scarves, saris, bedspreads and lampshades.

Orchard Road

Level two of the **Tanglin Shopping Centre** (Map p524; 19 Tanglin Rd) is Singapore's one-stop shop for antiques, arts and crafts. Treasure-hunt your way through the centre's **Antiques of the Orient** (Map p524; ☎ 6734 9351; 02-40), **Tomlinson** (Map p524; ☎ 6733 1221; 02-11), HaKaren (Map p524; ☎ 6733 3382; 02-43/45) and more.

The offbeat **Pagoda House** (Map p524; ☎ 67332 2177; Tudor Court, 143/145 Tanglin Rd) is packed to the rafters with restored antique furniture.

Polar Arts of Asia (Map p524; ☎ 6734 2311; 02-16 Far East Shopping Centre, 545 Orchard Rd) is a bizarre conglomeration of artefacts, skulls and tribal jewellery among golf shops.

Along Dempsey Road (Map pp520–1), an abandoned former British Army barracks, is now a shopping precinct specialising in Kashmiri carpets, teak furniture and antiques.

Holland Village

Holland Village Shopping Centre seems to be happy to buck the facelift trend. This complex is a warren of independent stores with decor stuck in the '80s. Ladies can enjoy a manicure or pedicure while guys zip off to **Lim's Art & Living** (Map pp514-15; ☎ 6467 1300; 02-01 Holland Rd Shopping Centre, 211 Holland Ave) to rummage for Asian vases, teak furniture, cushions and glassware of all heights and girths.

CAMERAS & ELECTRONIC EQUIPMENT

In Singapore you buy electronics on one basis only – price. Hi-tech goods are the same as you'd get back home. Most stores offer competitive duty-free prices, but haggle if there's a discrepancy between the shelf price and what the item is actually worth (do some homework). See also the boxed text, p553. Lucky Plaza (p558), Sim Lim Square (p557), Sim Lim Tower (p557) and the Mustafa Centre (p557) are good places to start.

For cameras, try the extensively stocked **Cathay Photo** (Map p517; ☎ 6337 4274; 01-11 Peninsula Plaza, 111 North Bridge Rd) or the family-run **John 3:16** (Map p517; ☎ 6337 2877; 05-46 Funan DigitaLife Mall, 109 North Bridge Rd).

If bargaining isn't your bag, decent prices can be had at **Best Denki** (Map p524; ☎ 6835 2855; 05-01/05 Ngee Ann City, 391 Orchard Rd) and **Harvey Norman** (Map p517; ☎ 6311 9988; 2nd Level Millenia Walk, 9 Raffles Blvd).

Hardwire yourself into six floors of big-brand computers at **Funan DigitaLife Mall** (Map p517; ☎ 6336 8327; 109 North Bridge Rd) or the legendary **Sim Lim Square** (Map p522; ☎ 6338 3859; 1 Rochor Canal Rd). For Macintosh equipment head to the **Epicentre** (Map p524; ☎ 6238 9378; 02-20/23 Wheelock Place; 501 Orchard Rd). There are also Apple retailers in Funan DigitaLife Mall.

CHINESE MEDICINE

The venerable **Eu Yan Sang** (Map pp526-7; ☎ 6223 6333; 269 South Bridge Rd) has been revamped to look like a Western chemist – but check out the traditional remedies on the shelves! Get some deer's tail pills to invigorate the kidneys or instant bird's nest to tone the lungs or consult a herbalist for S$17; most remedies come with English instructions.

FASHION

Singapore is a hub of international fashion brands to suit all budgets. You'll find European brands such as Zara, Mango, Massimo Dutti and Topshop sitting not far from upmarket Gucci, Prada, Louis Vuitton and D&G. Sadly, local brands come and go (even the good ones), as they can't compete with the huge budgets of Asian brand powers such as G2000, U2 and Uniqlo.

For up-to-the-nanosecond clubbing gear, head to levels four and five of the **Heeren** (Map p524; ☎ 6733 4725; 260 Orchard Rd; ☽ 10.30am-10pm), or the basement and levels three and four of **Far East Plaza** (Map p524; ☎ 6235 2411; 01 Far East Plaza, 14 Scotts Rd; ☽ 10am-10pm). Haji Lane (Map p522) in Kampong Glam has a series of eclectic and arty stores selling cool clothes…assuming they haven't shut down because of soaring rents.

M)phosis (Map p524; ☎ 6737 2190; B1-10 Ngee Ann City, 391 Orchard Rd) carries the wispy, slinky designs of Singaporean Colin Koh, while **Project Shop Blood Brothers** (Map p524; ☎ 6735 0071; 03-41/44 Paragon, 290 Orchard Rd) stocks lots of funky bags, belts and wallets.

THE IT CRUSH

There is no better place to witness Singaporeans' bottomless patience than at four Information Technology (IT) fairs that dot the yearly calendar – the March **IT Show** (www.itshow.com.sg), the June **PC Show** (www.thepcshow.com.sg), the August **COMEX** (www.comexshow.com.sg) and the November **SITEX** (www.sitex.com.sg). The 2009 IT show was visited by 768,000 Singaporeans, who spent S$58.5 million.

Queues start waaaayyyy before the site opens, and once the doors are flung wide, thousands of Singaporeans flood the aisles, dragging portable shopping trolleys, making a beeline for the deals (earmarked in advance thanks to massive ads in local papers). Lines for the best deals stretch on for ages...all in a bid to save a few bucks on LCD TVs, laptops and every electronic item available to mankind.

There are freebies galore and you'll soon be weighed down with pamphlets and have sales materials shoved in your face. If you have no idea what you're after, you'll be spending your time getting bumped around by irate Singaporeans who are pushing after the next deal on the list.

We say don't bother. Electronics stores are usually willing to match IT show prices – just show the sales advertisements from the local newspapers. If they aren't, walk on to the next store.

For men's designer threads, **Blackjack** (Map p524; ☎ 6735 0975; 01-10 Forum, 583 Orchard Rd) is a fashion ace up your sleeve. Another local label to look out for is **Daniel Yam** (Map p524; ☎ 6733 7220; 01-34/36 Wisma Atria, 435 Orchard Rd).

For saris, sari material and Punjabi suits, head to Serangoon Rd in Little India and Arab St in Kampong Glam. A deluxe gold-threaded silk sari from **Nalli** (Map p522; ☎ 6299 8676; 32 Buffalo Rd) can cost anything from S$200 to S$1000. Get traditional Malay dress from the **Geylang Serai Market** (Map p528) or the **Joo Chiat Complex** (Map p528; 1 Joo Chiat Rd).

MUSIC

Mainstream chains dominate Singapore's music shopping scene: **HMV** (Map p524; ☎ 6733 1822; the Heeren, 260 Orchard Rd) and **Borders** (Map p524; ☎ 6235 7146; 01-00 Wheelock Pl, 501 Orchard Rd; ⏰ 9am-11pm) are the big players.

Cheaper deals are available at **Sembawang Music Centre** (Map p524; ☎ 6884 9628; 03-05 Plaza Singapura, 68 Orchard Rd), **Gramophone** (Map p524; ☎ 6235 3105; 01-21/23 Cathay Bldg, 1 Handy Rd) and **That CD Shop** (Map p524; ☎ 6238 6720; 01-01/02 Pacific Plaza, 9 Scotts Rd).

As well as Indian music CDs, the **Indian Classical Music Centre** (Map p522; ☎ 6291 0187; 26 Clive St) sells sitars, tabla, bells – everything the aspiring Sergeant Pepper requires. **Jothi Music Centre** (Map p522; ☎ 6299 5528; 01-77 Campbell Block, Little India Arcade) pumps sexy Indian dance music into the street.

SHOPPING MALLS & DEPARTMENT STORES

Colonial District

Raffles City (Map p517; 252 North Bridge Rd) has a cavernous atrium and a range of upmarket shops, including Robinsons department store, a food court and a basement loaded with food outlets. It's linked to the enormous **Suntec City** (Map p517; 3 Temasek Blvd) by the underground CityLink Mall (accessed from the City Hall MRT station), which has some good speciality shops.

From Suntec City an underpass leads into **Millenia Walk** (Map p517; 9 Raffles Blvd), which is full of classy jewellers and boutiques under a series of wacky pyramid roofs. There's also an underground link to the **Esplanade Mall** (Map p517; 8 Raffles Ave), mainly a dining destination with a slew of interesting shops like Frank Brothers Violins (for all your cello requirements) and the Cookie Museum (upmarket cookie store).

Audiophiles listen up! The **Adelphi** (Map p517; 1 Coleman St) is the place to visit.

Attached to the Raffles Hotel is the swish **Raffles Hotel Arcade** (Map p517; 328 North Bridge Rd), which, as you'd expect, is firmly highbrow – designer clothes, galleries, gift shops and beauty salons.

Chinatown

Mobile phones, gaming consoles, watches, jewellery and cameras line the shelves at the **People's Park Complex** (Map pp526-7; 1 Park Rd). On the next corner, **People's Park Centre** (Map p517; 110 Upper Cross St) has four levels of luggage shops, travel agents and budget fashion boutiques selling loud Chinese shirts.

Yue Hwa Chinese Products (Map p517; 70 Eu Tong Sen St) is six storeys of products from the Motherland including medicine, furniture, silks, food, tea, arts and crafts. The chaotic, claustrophobic **Pearl's Centre** (Map pp526-7; 100 Eu Tong Sen St) is brimming with electronics stalls, Chinese medicine shops and a cinema showing saucy flicks.

Little India, Bugis & Kampong Glam

Bugis Junction (Map p522; 200 Victoria St) comprises the large BHG department store, the Hotel InterContinental, a cinema and shophouse recreations covered by an atrium. Expect lots of trendy 'here today gone tomorrow' fashion stores. Diagonally opposite Victoria St, brand-new **Iluma** (Map p522; cnr Victoria St & Middle Rd) has a nine-screen cinema and smaller fashion stores.

Sim Lim Square (Map p522; 1 Rochor Canal Rd) is renowned for computers and electronics. Across the road, **Sim Lim Tower** (Map p522; 10 Jln Besar) has everything from capacitors to car stereos. The bustling **Mustafa Centre** (Map p522; 145 Syed Alwi Rd; 24hr) is an improbably crammed

---

WALK FACTS

Start Dhoby Ghaut MRT
Finish Somerset MRT
Distance 3km
Duration Four hours

---

place with electrical and everyday goods at honest prices.

Orchard Road Mall Crawl

Orchard Rd has a mind-boggling array of megamalls. Prices here aren't necessarily the best, but the range of high-quality, big-brand items is superb. The following (by no means exhaustive) walking tour separates the best from the rest.

Start at **Plaza Singapura** (**1**; 68 Orchard Rd), where teens go to the movies and gaming arcades and ride the slowest-moving travelators in the known universe. Parents shop at the Carrefour hypermart.

Head up Orchard Rd past the old-school **Le Meridien Shopping Centre** (**2**; 100 Orchard Rd) – missable unless you're craving Doc Martens boots. Equally unexceptional are Orchard Plaza and Orchard Point – keep walking. At **Centrepoint** (**3**; 176 Orchard Rd) you can get measured for a shirt at Robinsons, or pick up sundry home furnishings. Across the road, **Orchard Central** (**4**; cnr Orchard & Killiney Rds) is one of two malls to be opened in Orchard Rd in the last decade. This one is 12 (yes, count them!) storeys of retail mayhem.

Give Orchard Emerald a miss, but duck into **Midpoint Orchard** (**5**; 220 Orchard Rd) for some camera haggling and reflexology. The **Heeren** (**6**; 260 Orchard Rd) is teen heaven, with a massive HMV and two levels of cutting-edge microboutiques.

Paragon (**7**; 290 Orchard Rd) is sassiness defined, with Salvatore Ferragamo, Jean-Paul Gaultier,

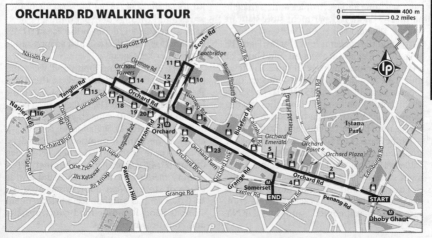

ORCHARD RD WALKING TOUR

PRACTICALITIES

Electricity
You'll need the UK-type three-square-pin plug to connect to the region's reliable electricity supply (220V to 240V, 50 cycles).

Newspapers & Magazines
Singapore's broadsheet is the state-run *Straits Times* (and *Sunday Times*); afternoon tabloid *New Paper* and the free *Today* are popular. International English-language publications like *Time* and *Newsweek* are readily available. For entertainment see *8 Days*, *I-S* and *Juice* magazines. The international listings magazine *Time Out* now has a Singapore edition. Lifestyle magazines include *Her World* and the stylish *Men's Folio*. Gourmands should check out Tatler's *Singapore's Best Restaurants* and *Wine & Dine,* or *Makansutra* for hawker stalls. Oddly, the *Far Eastern Economic Review* was banned after displeasing the government but racy lads' magazines *FHM* and *Maxim* are readily available.

Radio
English-language radio stations include the BBC World Service (88.9FM), Gold (90.5FM), Symphony (92.4FM), NewsRadio (93.8FM), Class (95FM) and Perfect 10 (98.7FM). Passion (99.5FM) features arts and world music; Power (98FM) aims pop at 18s to 35s. International Channel (96.3FM) broadcasts in French, German, Japanese and Korean. Most radio stations have web streaming if you want to get a taste before you come. See www.podcast.net for private broadcaster listings.

Television
Singapore has seven free-to-air channels: Channel 5 (English); Channel 8 (Mandarin); Suria (Malay-language programs); okto (the arts channel in English, plus children's broadcasts); Channel News Asia (news and information channel); Vasantham (Tamil-language programing) and Channel U, a Mandarin-language channel. You can watch TV Mobile in most public buses.

Weights & Measures
Singapore uses the metric system.

Gucci, Versace and YSL, among others. Entirely more downmarket is **Lucky Plaza (8**; 304 Orchard Rd), teeming with cheap clothing, luggage, perfume and electronics outlets (haggle hard). Next door is department-store stalwart **Tangs (9**; 320 Orchard Rd).

Around the corner is funky **Far East Plaza (10**; 14 Scotts Rd) – get a suit, a second-hand book or a tattoo. The basement, level three and level four have 80-plus local fashion outlets. Take the overhead bridge to **DFS Galleria (11**; 25 Scotts Rd), brimming with swanky cosmetics and bag shops: Louis Vuitton, Fendi, Gucci, Salvatore Ferragamo, Burberry, Dior and Prada.

Pacific Plaza (12; 9 Scotts Rd) is the place for street/surf wear and CDs; the **Shaw House (13**; 350 Orchard Rd) enshrouds a huge Isetan department store and the Lido cinema.

Turn right and continue along to **Palais Renaissance (14**; 390 Orchard Rd), which is cool, serene and unpeopled, and has DKNY and Prada.

Cross Orchard Rd to the **Tanglin Shopping Centre (15**; 19 Tanglin Rd), which boasts a selection of Asian arts outlets. Continue down Tanglin Rd to **Tanglin Mall (16**; 163 Tanglin Rd) for homewares amid throngs of expat mums, or head back along Orchard Rd to the **Forum (17**; 583 Orchard Rd) for Toys 'R' Us and a snappy range of designer kids' gear.

Gucci, Armani, Paul Smith and Valentino huddle together, like-minded, in the **Hilton Shopping Gallery (18**; 581 Orchard Rd). Next door is the **Far East Shopping Centre (19**; 545 Orchard Rd), a poky, outmoded mall with nine (!) golf shops.

Wheelock Place (20; 501 Orchard Rd) is next – a classy, cone-domed number with Borders, Nike, Apple and Birkenstock. New **Ion Orchard (21**; 430 Orchard Rd) has a shimmery 21st-century media wall, an art space and a wide range of stores. Next door, **Wisma Atria (22**; 435 Orchard Rd) has another Isetan department store, a Food Republic food court upstairs and countless boutiques.

Finish up at the megalithic **Ngee Ann City** (**23**; 391 Orchard Rd) – the grandmamma of all malls, with the glitzy Takashimaya department store, Kinokuniya, scores of fashion shops including Louis Vuitton, Chanel and Cartier, and oodles of places for noodles.

DIRECTORY

ACCOMMODATION

Accommodation classifications are based on the following: budget is up to S$99 per night; midrange is from S$100 to S$250; while top end is more than S$250. In major hotels, a 7% goods-and-services tax, 1% government tax and 10% service charge are added to your bill – this is the 18% 'plus-plus-plus' that follows the quoted price (eg S$150+++). Prices quoted are net prices ('net' includes taxes and the service charge). Some places are ++, which means 7% GST and the 10% service charge. Hotels stipulate that you shouldn't tip when a service charge applies. GST and government taxes also apply in cheaper hotels but they're usually included in the quoted price.

The **National Parks Board** (Map p522; ☎ 6391 4488; www.nparks.gov.sg; 18-01/08 Gateway West, 150 Beach Rd) administers several camp sites around the island (see the boxed text, p532).

BOOKSHOPS

Books Actually (Map pp526-7; ☎ 6221 1170; www .booksactually.com; 5 Ann Siang Rd) A charming little bookstore with an excellent and eclectic selection of literary fiction (think Burroughs and Murakami), toys, cameras, objets d'art and the prerequisite shelf of Moleskines. Its imprint, Math Paper Press, publishes local poets.

Borders (Map p524; ☎ 6235 7146; 01-00 Wheelock Pl, 501 Orchard Rd; ☽ 9am-11pm)

Kinokuniya (Map p524; ☎ 6737 5021; 03-09/15 Ngee Ann City, 391 Orchard Rd; ☽ 10.30am-9.30pm Sun-Fri, 10am-10pm Sat) Singapore's best bookstore.

MPH Bookstores CityLink Mall (Map p517; ☎ 6835 7637; B1-26A CityLink Mall, 1 Raffles Link; ☽ 10am-10pm); Raffles City (Map p517; ☎ 6336 4232; B1-24-26 Raffles City Shopping Centre, 252 North Bridge Rd; ☽ 10am-10pm)

Select Books (Map p524; ☎ 6732 1515; www.select books.com.sg; 03-15/17 Tanglin Shopping Centre, 19 Tanglin Rd) Specialises in Southeast Asian titles; check its website for local literary happenings.

Sunny Books (Map p524; ☎ 6733 1583; 03-58/59 Far East Plaza, 14 Scotts Rd; ☽ 10am-8pm Mon-Sat, 11.30am-7pm Sun) Also stocks second-hand books and comics.

BUSINESS HOURS

Restaurants serve lunch 11.30am to 2.30pm, often closing until dinner, which is 6pm to 10.30pm. Breakfast hours are generally 9am until noon. Shops open at 10am until 9pm, often later, and night time is the right time for eating – hawker centres kick on until the wee hours, some run 24 hours. Many small shops, except those in Little India, close on Sunday. Government office hours are generally 9am to 6pm Monday to Friday, and 10am to 1pm Saturday. Reviews in this chapter only list opening hours where they differ from standard.

For post-office opening hours, see p562. For bank opening hours, see p562.

CLIMATE

Hot and humid. Practically on the equator, Singapore's temperature never drops below 20°C, usually climbing to 30°C during the day. Rainfall and humidity are steady year-round. Rain arrives in torrential downpours, but is soon replaced by sunshine. It may rain every day during the wet season. The wettest months are November to January, the driest May to July.

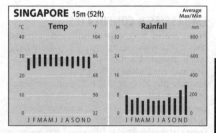

CUSTOMS

Drugs (trafficking carries the death penalty), guns, firecrackers, toy currency and coins, pornographic or seditious material, gun-shaped cigarette lighters, endangered species and their by-products, pirated recordings and publications, and retail quantities of chewing gum are prohibited; but visitors can bring in as much cash as they like!

Electronic goods, cosmetics, watches, cameras, jewellery, footwear, toys, arts and crafts are not dutiable; the usual duty-free concession for personal effects, such as clothes, applies. Singapore does not allow duty-free concessions for cigarettes or tobacco.

SINGAPORE

Take a letter from your doctor if you carry prescription medication.

Visitors can bring in 1L each of duty-free wine, beer and spirits to Singapore, providing visitors are over 18 years of age, are not arriving from either Malaysia or Indonesia and have been away from Singapore for at least 48 hours.

DANGERS & ANNOYANCES

Singapore is a very safe country with low crime rates. Pickpockets aren't unknown, but in general, crime isn't a problem – unsurprising, given the harsh penalties handed out to offenders. Drug trafficking carries the death penalty, which is regularly executed (pardon the pun).

DISCOUNT CARDS

Visitors over 55 are eligible for discounts at many attractions and for tours. Present your passport or ID with your date of birth on it. Travellers on Silk Air or Singapore Airlines get discounts at places by presenting their boarding passes. See www.singaporeair.com/boardingpass for more information.

EMBASSIES & CONSULATES

For a list of Singaporean missions abroad check out www.visitsingapore.com, where you'll also find a full list of foreign embassies and consulates in Singapore.

Australia (Map p524; ☎ 6836 4100; www.australia.org .sg; 25 Napier Rd)

Canada (Map p517; ☎ 6854 5900; www.dfait-maeci .gc.ca/asia/singapore; 11-01 One George St)

France (Map p524; ☎ 6880 7800; www.france.org.sg; 101-103 Cluny Park Rd)

Germany (Map p517; ☎ 6533 6002; www.singapur .diplo.de; 12-00 Singapore Land Tower, 50 Raffles Pl)

Indonesia (Map p524; ☎ 6737 7422; www.kbri singapura.com; 7 Chatsworth Rd)

Ireland (Map p524; ☎ 6238 7616; www.embassyof ireland.sg; 08-00 Liat Towers, 541 Orchard Rd)

Italy (Map p524; ☎ 6250 6022; www.ambsingapore .esteri.it; 27-02 United Square, 101 Thomson Rd)

Malaysia (Map pp520-1; ☎ 6235 0111; www.kln.gov .my/perwakilan/singapore; 301 Jervois Rd)

Netherlands (Map p524; ☎ 6737 1155; www.mfa .nl/sin; 13-01 Liat Towers, 541 Orchard Rd)

New Zealand (Map p524; ☎ 6235 9966; www .nzembassy.com/Singapore; 15-06/10 Ngee Ann City, 391A Orchard Rd)

South Africa (Map p517; ☎ 6339 3319; www.dfa .gov.za/webmissions; 15-01/06 Odeon Towers, 331 North Bridge Rd)

Thailand (Map p524; ☎ 6737 2475; www.thaiembassy .sg; 370 Orchard Rd)

UK (Map p524; ☎ 6424 4200; www.britishhigh commission.gov.uk; 100 Tanglin Rd)

USA (Map p524; ☎ 6476 9100; http://singapore.us embassy.gov; 27 Napier Rd)

EMERGENCY

Useful emergency numbers:
Fire/Ambulance (☎ 995)
Police (☎ 999)
SOS Helpline (☎ 1800-221 4444)

GAY & LESBIAN TRAVELLERS

Homosexuality is illegal in Singapore but authorities generally turn a blind eye to the scene. For more detail on local attitudes, read *People Like Us – Sexual Minorities in Singapore*, edited by Joseph Lo and Huang Gouqin, an upfront look at queer issues; and the blog **Yawning Bread** (www.yawningbread.org).

Singaporeans are conservative about displays of public affection; women and newly arrived straight male Indian and Bangladeshi workers can get away with same-sex hand holding, but an overtly gay couple doing the same would attract attention. That said, vocal or aggressive homophobia is unlikely to rear its ugly head.

HOLIDAYS
Public Holidays
New Year's Day 1 January
Chinese New Year January/February (three days)
Good Friday April (variable)
Labour Day 1 May
Wesak Day May (variable)
National Day 9 August
Deepavali October (variable)
Hari Raya Puasa October/November (variable)
Christmas Day 25 December
Hari Raya Haji December/January (variable)

School Holidays

In Singapore there's a week's holiday towards the end of March, four weeks in June, one week in early September, and a long break from the end of November until the beginning of January.

INSURANCE

For general information on insurance, see p474.

INTERNET ACCESS

In this chapter the internet symbol (🖥) is used where hotels have business centres or dedicated computers for guest use. The wi-fi symbol (🛜) is used for places where wireless internet is available.

Internet Cafes

Internet cafes are a rare breed in Singapore. High rents and free wi-fi access have caused the demise of many joints. Those that remain make their money from doubling as gaming centres. However, many hotels/hostels provide internet access in lobbies, rooms or business centres; at Changi Airport it's free! The following places charge around S$5 per hour:

Chills Cafe (Map p517; ☎ 6883 1016; 01-07 Stamford House, 39 Stamford Rd; ⊙ 9.30am-midnight)

E-Max (Map p524; ☎ 6235 9249; 9th fl Cathay Cineleisure Orchard, 8 Grange Rd; ⊙ noon-midnight)

i-surf (Map p524; B1-25 Orchard Towers, 400 Orchard Rd; ⊙ 10.30am-10.30pm)

Wi-Fi Access

There are free wi-fi hotspots in almost every mall. Anyone with a mobile phone (local sim card or global roaming) can register for a three-year account with **Wireless@SG**. Check www.infocomm123.sg/wireless_at_sg for details.

INTERNET RESOURCES

Asia One (www.asiaone.com.sg) The company that owns Singapore's newspapers; has links to the *Straits Times,* the *New Paper* and the *Business Times.*

Mr Brown (www.mrbrown.com) Website of blogger and podcaster Lee Kim Mun, who achieved infamy when his column in the *Today* newspaper was axed after he was too frank about local politics. That very podcast is still on the website.

Singapore Tourism Board (www.visitsingapore.com) The Singapore Tourism Board's site, with plenty of links to things to see and do.

Sistic (www.sistic.com.sg) Handles bookings to almost all concerts, plays and performances, with a useful events calendar.

Stomp (www.stomp.com.sg) Community site run by the official mouthpiece media company SPH, embodying the kind of carefully monitored 'open society' the government is trying to foster. For an insight into issues that preoccupy Singaporeans, check the 'Singapore Seen' section.

Talking Cock (www.talkingcock.com) The original satirical website that was actually debated in parliament. Ironic takes on the news of the day, plus the priceless Coxford Singlish Dictionary.

LAUNDRY

Singapore gets sweaty, but there are plenty of laundries to help travellers cope. Laundries are found listed in the *Yellow Pages;* most midrange and top-end hotels do laundry. Expect to pay around S$6 to have a skirt, blouse or a pair of trousers washed, S$8 for a dress, S$12 for a suit.

LEGAL MATTERS

The law is extremely tough in Singapore, but also relatively free from corruption. Don't expect special treatment for being a foreigner.

Singapore is notorious for being a 'fine' country. In reality, you'd have to be unlucky to be caught and fined. Smoking in all public places earns a S$500 fine. You can smoke at food stalls and on the street (as long as you put your butt in the bin). Jaywalking (crossing the road within 50m of a designated crossing) could cost you S$50. Littering could set you back S$1000. Possession of drugs means a long jail term and a caning, with trafficking punishable by death. If you are arrested, you will be entitled to legal counsel and contact with your embassy.

MAPS

Various free maps are available around Singapore, including *The Official Map of Singapore,* from the Singapore Tourism Board (p563), as well as from many hotels. Of the commercial maps, Nelles and Periplus maps are good. You'll need the *Mighty Minds Singapore Street Directory* (SG$12.90) if you're driving.

MEDICAL SERVICES

There are private medical clinics in most neighbourhoods in Singapore. Treatment is of high Western standard.

Gleneagles Hospital (Map p524; ☎ 6473 7222; www.gleneagles.com.sg; 6A Napier Rd; ⊙ 24hr)

International Medical Clinic (www.imc-healthcare.com; Jelita Clinic Map pp514-15; ☎ 6465 4440; 02-08 Jelita Cold Storage, 293 Holland Rd; ⊙ 9am-5.30pm Mon-Fri, 9am-1pm Sat; Orchard Clinic (Map p524; ☎ 6733 4440; 14-06 Camden Medical Centre, 1 Orchard Blvd; ⊙ 9am-5.30pm Mon-Fri, 9am-1pm Sat)

Mount Elizabeth Hospital (Map p524; ☎ 6737 2666; www.mountelizabeth.com.sg; 3 Mt Elizabeth Rd; ⊙ 24hr)

National Dental Centre (Map pp526-7; ☎ 6324 8910; www.ndc.com.sg; 5 Second Hospital Ave; ⊙ 8am-5pm Mon-Fri)

Raffles Hospital (Map p522; ☎ 6311 1111; www
.raffleshospital.com; 585 North Bridge Rd; ☾ 24hr)
Singapore General Hospital (Map pp526-7; ☎ 6222
3322; www.sgh.com.sg; Level 2, Block 1, Outram Rd;
☾ 24hr)

MONEY

The major banks are found in the CBD, along
Orchard Rd and in most malls. Opening hours
are 9.30am to 3pm Monday to Friday, and
9.30am to 1pm on Saturday.

ATMs accept MasterCard, Visa and cards
with Plus or Cirrus. ATMs are everywhere,
including shopping centres and MRT stations.
Larger department stores accept foreign cash
and travellers cheques at lower rates than
you'll get from moneychangers. See the Quick
Reference page (inside the front cover) for
currency exchange rates.

Credit Cards

Major credit cards are widely accepted. The
tourism authorities suggest that if shops insist on adding a credit-card surcharge (which
they shouldn't do), contact the relevant credit
company in Singapore. For 24-hour card cancellations or assistance:
American Express (☎ 6396 6000)
Diners Club (☎ 6571 0128)
JCB (☎ 6734 0096)
MasterCard (☎ 1800-1100 113)
Visa (☎ 6437 5800; 1800-1100 344)

Currency

The unit of currency is the Singapore dollar (comprising 100¢). There are 5¢, 10¢,
20¢, 50¢ and S$1 coins, while notes come
in S$2, S$5, S$10, S$50, S$100, S$500 and
S$1000 denominations.

Moneychangers

For changing cash or travellers cheques,
banks usually charge a commission (around
S$3). You'll generally get a better rate for
cash at moneychangers, who don't charge
fees and are located in most shopping centres. Rates are openly displayed, though you
can sometimes haggle if you're changing a
large quantity.

Taxes & Refunds

A 7% goods-and-services tax (GST) is applied
to all goods and services. See p559 for the tax
and service charges that apply to room rates.

Restaurants charge 17% extra on top of listed
prices (7% GST, 10% service charge and a 1%
CESS charge).

Visitors purchasing goods worth S$300
or more through a shop participating in the
GST Tourist Refund Scheme (look for the
'Tax-Free Shopping' logo) can apply for a
GST refund. When you purchase an item,
fill in a claim form and show your passport.
You'll receive a global refund cheque –
present it with your passport and goods at
the Customs GST inspection counter in the
departure hall at Changi *before* you check in.
Customs stamps your cheque, which you then
cash at counters inside the airport, or have
credited to your credit card or bank account.
Pick up a *How to Shop Tax-free in Singapore*
brochure at the airport or visitors centres for
more information.

POST

Singapore's postal system is predictably
efficient, with plenty of outlets. Call ☎ 1605
for the closest branch or see www.singpost
.com.sg. Generally, post-office hours are 8am
to 6pm Monday to Friday, and 8am to 2pm
Saturday. Airmail postcards to anywhere
in the world cost S$0.50; letters cost from
S$1.50 to S$2.50. Handy outlets include
the following:
Changi Airport (Map pp514-15; ☎ public 6542 7899,
transit 6543 0048; ☾ 24hr) At Terminal 2.
Killiney Road (Map p524; ☎ 6734 7899; 1 Killiney Rd)
Takashimaya (Map p524; ☎ 6738 6899; 04-15 Ngee
Ann City, 391 Orchard Rd)

Letters addressed to 'Poste Restante' will end
up at the **Singapore Post Centre** (Map p528; ☎ 6841
2000; 10 Eunos Rd).

TELEPHONE & FAX

You can make local and international calls
from public phone booths (local calls cost 10¢
for three minutes). Most phone booths take
phonecards, and some take credit cards, while
old-school coin booths are rare. For inquiries,
see www.singtel.com.

Fax

Faxes can be sent from all post offices, SingTel
centres and hotels.

Mobile Phones

Singaporean mobile phone numbers usually
start with a ☎ 9 or 8. If you have global roam-

ing facilities with your home provider, your GSM 900/1800 digital phone will automatically lock onto one of Singapore's three digital networks (M1-GSM, ST-GSM or StarHub). There's complete island coverage, and phones also work underground on the MRT.

You can buy SIM cards, from post offices and 7-Eleven stores, for local mobile-phone services (SingTel, StarHub and M1) for around S$10.

Phone Codes

To call Singapore from overseas, dial your country's international access number and then ☎ 65 (Singapore's country code) before entering the telephone number. To call overseas from Singapore dial ☎ 001. There are no area codes within Singapore; telephone numbers are eight digits unless you're calling toll-free (1800).

Phonecards

Local phonecards are widely available from 7-Eleven stores, post offices, SingTel centres, stationers and bookshops. The large migrant-worker population has led to the availability of a wide array of international phonecards. Check which countries they service before you buy.

Useful Numbers

Some helpful telephone numbers include the following:

International directory inquiries (☎ 104, 1635)
Local directory inquiries (☎ 6777 7777, 100)
STB 24-hour Touristline (☎ 1800-736 2000)
Weather (☎ 6542 7788)

TIME

Singapore is 16 hours ahead of US Pacific Standard Time (San Francisco and Los Angeles), 13 hours ahead of US Eastern Standard Time (New York), eight hours ahead of GMT/UTC (London) and two hours behind Australian Eastern Standard Time (Sydney and Melbourne).

TIPPING

Tipping is prohibited in the airport and not expected in major hotels and restaurants, where a 10% service charge is included in the bill. Elsewhere a thank-you tip for good service is discretionary.

TOILETS

Toilets in Singapore are Western-style. Public toilets in the main tourist area are nice enough

to make you want to stay a while. They're plentiful in shopping malls (and hotel lobbies if you're desperate).

TOURIST INFORMATION

The **Singapore Tourism Board** (STB; ☎ 1800-736 2000; www.visitsingapore.com) provides the widest range of services, including tour bookings, event ticketing and a list of Singapore Tourism offices around the world. There are visitors centres at the following locations:

Changi Airport (Map pp514-15; ☼ 6am-2am) Terminals 1,2 and 3.
Liang Court (Map p517; Level 1, Liang Court Shopping Centre, 177 River Valley Rd; ☼ 10.30am-9.30pm)
Little India (Map p522; 73 Dunlop St, InnCrowd Backpackers Hostel; ☼ 10am-10pm)
Orchard Road (Map p524; cnr Cairnhill & Orchard Rds; ☼ 9.30am-10.30pm)
Suntec City (Map p517; Level 1, Suntec City, 3 Temasek Blvd; ☼ 10am-6pm)

TRAVELLERS WITH DISABILITIES

Facilities for wheelchairs used to be nonexistent in Singapore, but in recent years a large government campaign has seen ramps, lifts and other facilities progressively installed around the island. The pavements in the city are nearly all immaculate, MRT stations all have lifts and there are even some buses equipped with wheelchair-friendly equipment. Check out *Access Singapore*, which is a free guidebook by the Disabled Persons Association of Singapore; it has a complete rundown on services and other information, and can be found online at www.dpa.org.sg. The booklet is also available from STB offices (see above) or from the **National Council of Social Services** (☎ 6210 2500; www.ncss.org.sg). The **Disabled People's Association** (☎ 6899 1220; www.dpa.org.sg/access/contents.htm) has an online accessibility guide to the country.

Also see p477 for a few international organisations that have useful information for travellers with disabilties.

VISAS

Citizens of most countries are granted 30-day visas on arrival by air or overland (though the latter may get 14-day visas). The exceptions are the Commonwealth of Independent States, India, Myanmar, China and most Middle Eastern countries. Visitors must have a valid passport or internationally recognised travel document valid for at least six months beyond

SINGAPORE

the date of entry into Singapore. Extensions can be applied for at the **Immigration & Checkpoints Authority** (Map p522; ☎ 6391 6100; www.ica.org.sg; 10 Kallang Rd). This can also be done online. Applications take at least a day to process.

VOLUNTEERING

Singapore serves as a base for many nongovernmental organisations (NGOs) working throughout Southeast Asia, but most of these recruit skilled volunteers from their home countries. In Singapore itself the **National Volunteer & Philanthropy Centre** (www.nvpc.org.sg) coordinates a number of community groups, including an extensive database of grassroots projects, such as education, environment and multiculturalism.

WOMEN TRAVELLERS

Singaporean women enjoy a high degree of autonomy and respect, and the city is one of the safest destinations in Southeast Asia – though women might be a little uncomfortable in Little India during the weekends, when tens of thousands of male migrant workers throng the area. Tampons, over-the-counter medications and contraceptive pills are readily available.

WORK

Singapore has a large expatriate European/US community, a reflection of the large representation of overseas companies here. There are also masses of migrants from mainland China, India, and several neighbouring countries who work in a variety of roles, mainly unskilled. The vacancies pages of the *Straits Times* are often crammed with job notices, mostly for domestic servants and unskilled labourers.

Business experience, marketable job skills and impressive qualifications are your best bet – like many places, Singapore often places a higher value on your paperwork than your experience. **Contact Singapore** (www.contactsingapore.org.sg) has job postings, though there are also dozens of headhunting firms on the lookout for skilled foreigners.

TRANSPORT

GETTING THERE & AWAY

For general border crossing details, see p483.

Air

AIRPORTS & AIRLINES

Singapore's slick **Changi International Airport** (Map pp514-15; ☎ 6542 1122; www.changiairport.com) is about 20km east of the city centre. It has three terminals. Changi's facilities include a 24-hour medical centre, a post office, a transit hotel, free showers, free internet access, free local phone calls, left luggage (between S$3.15 and S$10.50 per day depending on the item's size) and a children's playground for transit passengers. Pick up the free booklets, maps and other guides (including the airport's own magazine) from information stands.

AIRLINES FLYING TO/FROM SINGAPORE

The major airline offices in Singapore:

Air New Zealand (Map p524; ☎ 6734 5595; www.airnewzealand.com; 05-05 Wellington Bldg, 20 Bideford Rd)

Berjaya Air (Map pp514-15; ☎ 6481 6302; www.berjaya-air.com; Block 13, 01-13 Old Birdcage Walk, Seletar Airbase)

British Airways (Map p524; ☎ 6622 1747; www.britishairways.com; 06-05 Cairnhill Place, 15 Cairnhill Rd)

Cathay Pacific Airways (Map p526-7; ☎ 6533 1333; www.cathaypacific.com; 25-07 Ocean Towers, 20 Raffles Place)

Garuda Indonesia (Map p524; ☎ 6250 2888; www.garuda-indonesia.com; 12-03 United Sq, 101 Thomson Rd)

KLM Royal Dutch Airlines (Map p526-7; ☎ 6823 2220; www.klm.com; 06-01/02/03 79 Anson Rd)

Lufthansa Airlines (Map p524; ☎ 6835 5944; www.lufthansa.com; 05-01 Palais Renaissance, 390 Orchard Rd)

Malaysia Airlines (Map p517; ☎ 6433 0220; www.malaysiaairlines.com; 02-09 Singapore Shopping Centre, 190 Clemenceau Ave)

Qantas (Map p524; ☎ 6415 7373; www.qantas.com; 06-05 Cairnhill Place, 15 Cairnhill Rd)

Silk Air (Map p522; ☎ 6223 8888; www.silkair.com; 17-08 Keypoint, 371 Beach Rd)

Singapore Airlines (Map p524; ☎ 6223 8888; www.singaporeair.com; 02-38/39 Paragon, 290 Orchard Rd)

Thai Airways (Map pp526-7; ☎ 6210 5000; www.thaiair.com; 02-00 the Globe, 100 Cecil St)

TICKETS

Compare the costs of flying into Singapore versus Malaysia. You can travel overland to Singapore from almost anywhere in Peninsular Malaysia (and vice versa) in less than a day.

SINGAPORE-TO-MALAYSIA TRAIN ISSUES

Some travellers have had problems leaving Malaysia if they've entered the country by train from Singapore. Malaysian immigration officials at Singapore's railway station sometimes don't stamp your passport – not a problem as long as you keep your immigration card and your train ticket to show how you entered Malaysia. Your details will have been put into the Malaysian immigration computer and should come up when you exit. Stand your ground if you're asked to pay a fine!

The Malaysian railway system also cunningly charges precisely the same figure in Singapore dollars for fares from Singapore to Malaysia as it does in Malaysian ringgit from Malaysia to Singapore. The Singapore dollar is worth more than twice as much as the ringgit – what a rip-off! To beat the system out of Singapore, buy a ticket only as far as the first train station across the border (Kempas Bahru), then another ticket from Kempas Bahru to wherever you're going in Malaysia.

The following budget airlines operate out of Singapore. They are changing their networks all the time, so check websites for details. Bookings are made almost entirely online.

AirAsia (☎ 6307 7688; www.airasia.com)
Cebu Pacific (☎ agents 6735 7155, 6737 9231, 6220 5966; www.cebupacificair.com)
Firefly (☎ 03-7845 4543; ww.fireflyz.com.my)
Jetstar Asia (☎ 1800-6161 977; www.jetstarasia.com)
Tiger Airways (☎ 6538 4437; www.tigerairways.com)

For other internet bookings, see p480.

MALAYSIA
For details of flights between Singapore and Malaysia, see p482.

LAND
The Causeway linking Johor Bahru (JB) with Singapore handles most traffic between the countries. Trains and buses run from all over Malaysia straight through to Singapore, or you can get a taxi or bus to/from JB. There's also a crossing called the Second Link linking Tuas, in western Singapore, with Geylang Patah in Malaysia – some buses to Melaka and Malaysia's west coast head this way. If you have a car, tolls on the Second Link are much higher than the Causeway.

BUSES
Buses run frequently from Singapore into Malaysia, some continuing to Thailand.

From Singapore, both the Causeway Express and Singapore–Johor Express air-con buses (S$2.40) and the public SBS bus 170 (S$1.70) depart for JB every 15 minutes between 6.30am and 11pm from the **Queen**

Street Bus Terminal (Map p522; cnr Queen & Arab Sts). Bus 170 can be boarded anywhere along the way, such as on Rochor, Rochor Canal or Bukit Timah Rds. Yet another, quicker, option is to go to Kranji MRT station by train and catch bus 170 (S$1.20) or to Marsiling MRT and catch bus 950 ($1.20).

In all cases, when you get to the Singapore checkpoint, take all your belongings and get off. After clearing immigration you have to wait for the next bus (but don't have to pay again, as long you have your ticket). Repeat the process at the Malaysian side or, once you've cleared immigration, simply take a two-minute walk into JB city centre. The public bus stops at Komtar Shopping Centre and then the Larkin terminal 5km north of the Causeway. The coach terminates at the terminal. If at all possible, avoid crossing at weekends, when it gets infernally busy.

If you're travelling beyond JB, it's easier to catch a long-distance bus straight from Singapore, but there's a greater variety of bus services from JB and the fares are cheaper.

Long-distance buses to Melaka (S$25, 4½ hours) and east-coast Malaysian cities Kuantan (S$35, seven hours) and Kuala Terengganu (S$40, 10 hours) leave from and arrive at the **Lavender Street Bus Terminal** (Map p522; cnr Lavender St & Kallang Bahru). The terminal is 500m from Lavender MRT station, or get there on buses 61, 107, 133 or 145.

Buses leave from outside the **Golden Mile Complex** (Map p522; Beach Rd) for Kuala Lumpur (S$40, five hours) and other northern Malaysian destinations, including Ipoh, Butterworth and Penang. There's a string of bus agents in the Golden Mile Complex – shop around. Lavender MRT station is about

500m away. Get a one-way ticket if you're planning on returning to Singapore – tickets are cheaper in Malaysia.

TAXI

There are shared long-distance taxis to JB from Singapore's **Queen Street Bus Terminal** (Map p522; cnr Queen & Arab Sts). Share taxis to JB are about S$10 per person, with a maximum of four passengers per taxi, though prices vary depending on the queue at the immigration checkpoint.

TRAIN

From Singapore there are three air-conditioned express trains daily to Malaysia (about seven hours to Kuala Lumpur) with continuing services to Thailand. Contact **Keretapi Tanah Melayu** (KTM; ☎ 6222 5165; www .ktmb.com.my) or its booking office at the **Singapore Railway Station** (Map pp526-7; ☎ 6222 5165; Keppel Rd; ☺ 8.30am-2pm, 3-7pm) for information. Depending on the carriage class and whether you ride in a seat or a sleeper, a Kuala Lumpur fare will be between S$19 and S$110. For a tricky immigration issue when travelling by train, see p565.

The luxurious **Eastern & Oriental Express** (☎ 6392 3500; www.orient-express.com) departs Singapore on the 42-hour, 1943km journey to Bangkok before heading onwards to Chiang Mai and Nong Khai (for Laos). Don your linen suit, sip a gin and tonic, and dig deep for the fare: from S$3000 per person in a double compartment to S$5500 in the presidential suite. You can go as far as KL or Butterworth for a lower fare.

SEA
MALAYSIA FROM SINGAPORE

Regional cruise trips depart for Malaysia from the **HarbourFront Centre** (Map pp514-15; ☎ 6513 2200; www.singaporecruise.com.sg), next to HarbourFront MRT station; a host of agents here handle bookings.

Ferries depart the **Changi Point Ferry Terminal** (Map pp514-15; ☎ 6546 8518) for Tanjung Belungkor, east of JB. This is primarily a service for Singaporeans going to Desaru. The 11km journey takes 45 minutes and costs S$18/22 one way/return. There are usually three services daily in each direction. From the Tanjung Belungkor jetty, buses operate to Desaru and Kota Tinggi. Ferries also sail for Pengerang (one way S$6), across the Straits of Johor in Malaysia. This is an interesting back-door route into Malaysia. There's no fixed schedule; ferries leave between 7am and 4pm when full (12 people). The best time to catch one is before 8am. Clear Singapore immigration at the small post in the terminal. To get to Changi Ferry Terminal, take the MRT to Tanah Merah, then bus 2 to Changi Village (or just a taxi).

INDONESIA FROM SINGAPORE

No direct ferries run between Singapore and Indonesia's main ports, but you can travel between the two countries via Pulau Batam, Pulau Bintan, Tanjung Balai and Tanjung Batu in the Riau Archipelago.

Pulau Batam, Tanjung Balai & Tanjung Batu

Ferries depart for Pulau Batam, Tanjung Balai and Batu, all about 20km away, from the **HarbourFront Centre** (Map pp514-15; ☎ 6513 2200; www.singaporecruise.com.sg), taking about 30 minutes to get to Sekupang, or 45 minutes to Batu Ampar. The main agents are **Penguin** (☎ 6377 6335), **Dino/Batam Fast** (☎ 6270 0311) and **Berlian** (☎ 6546 8830), all with offices at HarbourFront. Between them they have

---

THE EZ-LINK AROUND TOWN

If you're staying in Singapore for longer than a week, the easiest way to pay for travel on public transport is via the EZ-Link card. You'll save money and find it more convenient to buy an EZ-Link card from an MRT station. This card allows you to travel by train and bus by swiping it over sensors as you enter and leave a station or bus. Cards cost S$15: S$10 worth of travel, and a S$5 nonrefundable charge. You can top-up cards at ATM-style machines at stations. Fares using an EZ-Link card are 20% less than using cash.

If you don't use the EZ-Link, buses take cash (exact change only) and you have to buy a single-trip ticket for trains (ticket include a S$1 refundable deposit you redeem by feeding it back into the machine).

dozens of departures every day, at least every half-hour from 7.30am to 8pm. Tickets cost between S$30 and S$34 return. Ferries dock at Sekupang, where you can take a boat to Tanjung Buton on the Sumatran mainland. From there it's a three-hour bus ride to Palembang. This is a popular travellers' route to Sumatra.

Pulau Bintan & Batam

The same companies that operate ferries from Batam also have several ferries a day from **Tanah Merah Ferry Terminal** (Map pp514-15; ☎ 6542 4369; 50 Tanah Merah Rd) to Tanjung Pinang, the main city on Bintan, or Teluk Sebong on the island's north coast as well as to Nongsapara on Batam. The 45km journey takes about an hour and costs between S$38 and S$48 return, ferries departing from 9am to 8pm.

GETTING AROUND

Singapore has fantastic public transport, with a tangled web of bus and train (Mass Rapid Transit; MRT) routes taking you to the doorsteps of most sights. The MRT is easy to navigate, but stops are sometimes far apart (walking in 30°C humidity is sweaty work!). Pick up a free MRT-system map at any MRT station, and the useful *Transitlink Guide*, which details all bus and MRT routes, from bookshops (S$2.50). Due to car-ownership limitations, taxis are also considered public transport. For public transport information, see www.sbstransit.com.sg.

To/From the Airport

CHANGI AIRPORT

Taxi or train (MRT) are the best ways to reach the city. Trains depart Changi from below Terminals 2 and 3 for the CBD from 5.30am to 12.06am (adult/child S$2.70/1.50, 35 minutes, every 12 minutes). Trains to Changi from City Hall station (Map p517) run from 6am to midnight. In both directions you'll have to change trains at Tanah Merah station (just cross the platform).

The most convenient bus is the airport shuttle service (adult/child S$9/6) that will take you to any hotel, except those on Sentosa and in Changi Village. Shuttles operate daily from the arrivals halls of all terminals roughly every 15 minutes from 6am to midnight and every 30 minutes all other times. Book and pay at arrival-hall counters.

TRISHAWS

Trishaws peaked just after WWII when motorised transport was practically nonexistent and trishaw drivers could make a tidy income. Today there are only around 250 trishaws left in Singapore, mainly plying the tourist routes. Trishaws congregate in the pedestrian mall at the junction of Waterloo and Albert Sts (Map p522), outside Raffles Hotel (Map p517) and outside the Chinatown Complex (Map pp526–7). Always agree on the fare beforehand: we were quoted S$40 for half an hour, but you can haggle.

Public bus 36 leaves the airport for the city approximately every 10 minutes between 6am and midnight (adult/child S$2/1). It takes around an hour to reach the city centre, passing through the Colonial District and on to Orchard Rd. Heading to the airport, pick up bus 36 on Orchard or Bras Basah Rds.

Taxis to the city cost around S$20, plus surcharge. From Friday to Sunday the surcharge is S$5 from 5pm to midnight and 50% of the fare from midnight to 6am; at all other times the surcharge is S$3. Alternatively, there's a 24-hour limousine taxi service (S$45) available to any destination in Singapore.

SELETAR AIRPORT

You might find yourself at the small, modern Seletar Airport (Map pp514–15) catching a **Berjaya Air** (☎ 6481 6302; www.berjaya-air.com) flight to Pulau Tioman in Malaysia. Seletar is in the north of the island; taxi is the easiest way to get there. Otherwise bus 103M from Serangoon MRT will take you to the gates of the Seletar Air Force base, from where you change to a local base bus to the airport terminal.

Bicycle

Singapore's roads are not for the faint-hearted. It's furiously hot, and drivers tend to be fast, aggressive and not particularly sympathetic to the needs of cyclists. Fortunately, there's a large network of parks and park connectors and a few excellent dedicated mountain-biking areas – at Bukit Timah Nature Reserve (p505), Tampines and Pulau Ubin (p504). Cycling up to Changi Village and then taking the

SINGAPORE

bike over to Pulau Ubin is an excellent adventure. Other excellent places for cycling include East Coast Park (p503), Sentosa (p509), Pasir Ris Park (p503) and the route linking Mt Faber Park, Telok Blangah Hill Park and Kent Ridge Park.

If you haven't brought your own, pick up some wheels at **Treknology Bikes 3** (Map p524; ☎ 6466 2673; www.treknology3.com; 01-02, 91 Tanglin Place; 24hr hire S$35-50; ☺ 11am-7.30pm). Bikes can also be rented cheaply at several places in East Coast Park and on Sentosa Island and Pulau Ubin.

Boat & Ferry

There are regular ferry services from **Marina South Pier** (Map pp520-1; ☎ 6275 03888; 31 Marina Coastal Dr) to other southern islands (p511), and from Changi Village to Pulau Ubin (p504). You can also take river cruises (p530) or harbour cruises (p529).

Bus

Singapore's bus service should be the envy of the world. You rarely have to wait more than a few minutes for buses, and they'll take you almost anywhere. Most are air-conditioned and even have TVs!

Fares range from 90¢ to S$1.80 (less with an EZ-Link card, see the boxed text p566); there are also a few flat-rate buses. When you board the bus, drop the exact money into the fare box (no change is given) or swipe your EZ-Link card. You need to swipe your card again when you disembark – if you forget, you'll be charged the maximum fare for the bus journey! Contact **SBS Transit** (☎ 1800-287 2727; www.sbstransit.com.sg) for details.

TOURIST BUSES

Singapore Airlines runs the **SIA Hop-On** (☎ 9457 2896; www.siahopon.com) tourist bus, departing from Raffles Blvd and traversing the main tourist arteries (Orchard Rd, Bugis Junction, Suntec City, the Colonial District, Clarke Quay, Boat Quay, Chinatown and the Botanic Gardens) every 30 minutes daily from 9am to 9pm. A Sentosa shuttle runs from 10am to 9pm. Tickets are available from the driver: S$12/6 per adult/child for a day pass; S$6/3 with a Singapore Airlines or SilkAir boarding pass or ticket.

Nutty and garish, the **City Hippo** (☎ 6228 6877; www.ducktours.com.sg) offers a confusing array of tour options round all the major

sites. Two-day tickets including a river cruise cost adult/child S$33/17. It boasts live commentary and an open-top deck. There are numerous pick-up points around town.

Car & Motorcycle

Singaporeans drive on the left-hand side of the road; it's compulsory to wear seat belts. Unlike in most Asian countries, traffic is orderly. But expect local drivers to display true *kiasu* (Hokkien for 'afraid to lose') spirit in the form of aggressive driving, tailgating, speeding and wild lane-changing sans signalling. The profusion of one-way streets and streets that change names (sometimes several times) can make things tricky. The *Mighty Minds Singapore Street Directory* is essential for negotiating the city. See also opposite for zoning and parking issues. Don't bother riding a motorcycle around Singapore, as drivers have little regard for bike safety.

DRIVING LICENCE

A valid overseas licence is needed to rent a car. An International Driving Permit isn't usually required, but bring one. Most rental companies also require that drivers are at least 23 years old.

HIRE

If you want a car for local driving only, smaller rental operators usually quote rates that are slightly cheaper than the major companies. Rental rates are cheaper in Malaysia – if you want to drive around Malaysia, it's better value to hire the car from Johor Bahru.

Rates start from around S$100 a day, while a collision-damage waiver will cost about S$20 per day for a small car. Special deals may be available for longer-term rental.

All major car-hire companies have an office at Changi Airport. There are other offices around Singapore:

Avis (Map p517; ☎ 6737 1668; www.avis.com.sg; 01-07, Waterfront Plaza, 390 Havelock Rd)

Express Car (Map p528; ☎ 6842 4992; www.express car.com.sg; 1 Sims Ln)

Hawk (Map pp514-15; ☎ 6469 4468; www.hawk rentacar.com.sg; 32A Hillview Terrace)

Hertz (Map p524; ☎ 6734 4646; www.hertz.com.sg; 01-01 Thong Teck Bldg, 15 Scotts Rd)

Premier (Map p524; www-singapore.com/premier; 03-05 Balmoral Plaza, 271 Bukit Timah Rd)

RESTRICTED ZONES & CAR PARKING

Between 7.30am and 7pm weekdays, and from 10.15am to 2pm Saturdays, the area encompassing the CBD, Chinatown and Orchard Rd becomes a restricted zone. Cars may enter as long as they pay a toll. Vehicles are automatically tracked by sensors on overhanging ERP gantries that prompt drivers to insert a cashcard (available from 7-Elevens and petrol stations) into their in-vehicle unit. The same system is also in operation on certain major highways. Rental cars are subject to the same rules.

Anyone who doesn't pay the entry toll is automatically photographed by cameras on gantries and a fine will soon arrive at the car owner's address.

Parking in many places (especially in residential areas) in Singapore is operated by a coupon system; buy a booklet at parking kiosks, post offices and 7-Elevens. Display coupons in your car window with holes punched out to indicate the time, day and date you parked. Many car parks are now run using the same in-vehicle unit and cashcard and ERP gantries instead of the coupon system.

Mass Rapid Transit (MRT)

The ultraclean, safe and efficient Singapore MRT (☎ 1800-336 8900; www.smrt.com.sg) subway and light-rail system is the most comfortable and hassle-free way to get around. Trains run from around 5.30am to midnight, departing every three to four minutes at peak times and every six to eight off-peak. Single-trip tickets cost from 90¢ to S$2.70, less with the EZ-Link card (see the boxed text, p566).

Most of the MRT's tracks run underground in the inner-city area, emerging overground out towards the suburban housing estates. The system connects with the Light Rapid Transit (LRT) trains at Bukit Panjang, Punggol and Sengkang.

Construction is under way on a central loop line (ETA 2010) that will link the city centre with Holland Village, Suntec City and the Singapore Indoor Stadium area in Kallang.

Taxi

You can usually flag a taxi on the streets or grab one from the many taxi stands. The fare system is also complicated, but thankfully it's all metered, so there's no haggling over fares. The basic flagfall is S$2.80 to S$3.20, then 20c for every 385m.

These are the taxi companies:

Comfort and CityCab (☎ 6552 1111)
Premier Taxis (☎ 6363 6888)
SMRT Taxis (☎ 6555 8888)

There are a whole raft of various surcharges to note:

- 50% of the metered fare from midnight to 6am.
- 35% peak-hour charges between 7am and 9am, and 5pm and 8pm.
- S$3.50 for telephone bookings; for advance bookings you'll pay S$5.20.
- S$3 on all trips from the CBD between 5pm and midnight, Monday to Saturday. You may also have to pay another surcharge if you take the taxi into the CBD during restricted hours (see Restricted Zones, left).
- S$5 surcharge from 5pm to midnight Friday to Sunday; S$3 all other times for journeys from the airport.

Confused? We are too. Just follow the meter and ask for a receipt to check charges.

SINGAPORE

Brunei

HOLGER LEUE

Brunei

'Where is Brunei?' is usually the first question travellers ask – a query that can easily be solved with a map. 'What is Brunei?' – now that's a much more difficult question to answer. It may seem like nothing more than a bucktoothed bite mark nibbled off the Bornean coast, but there is a lot more to this wee sultanate than meets the eye, and that's where things get tricky.

So perhaps it's best to start with the things that Brunei is not. Brunei is not an ubermodern emirate bustling with a Vegas-like energy, nor is it an uptight Muslim stronghold ruled with an iron fist. This may surprise visitors at first – especially when they discover that the serene capital city (10 points if you can name it without looking at the highlights!) seems to prefer ramshackle stilt villages to architectural allegories for world domination. But make no mistake, Brunei isn't a backwater oil rig either. In fact, for many centuries the sultan's power extended across the entirety of Borneo and over to the Philippines.

But far more interesting than the tall tales of erstwhile power is watching how this micronation grapples with its modern identity. Youngsters memorise names of popular recordings with the same alacrity as historical minutia, while higher up in the ranks, princes ride the waves of 'black gold', erecting myriad monuments to misguided spending. Day trippers will barely peer beyond the very staid mosques, markets and museums, so it's well worth hanging around as the Napoleonic bravado melts away to reveal a spellbinding saga of one sultan and his faithful people.

HIGHLIGHTS

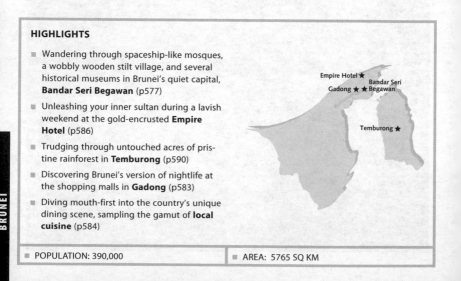

- Wandering through spaceship-like mosques, a wobbly wooden stilt village, and several historical museums in Brunei's quiet capital, **Bandar Seri Begawan** (p577)

- Unleashing your inner sultan during a lavish weekend at the gold-encrusted **Empire Hotel** (p586)

- Trudging through untouched acres of pristine rainforest in **Temburong** (p590)

- Discovering Brunei's version of nightlife at the shopping malls in **Gadong** (p583)

- Diving mouth-first into the country's unique dining scene, sampling the gamut of **local cuisine** (p584)

- POPULATION: 390,000
- AREA: 5765 SQ KM

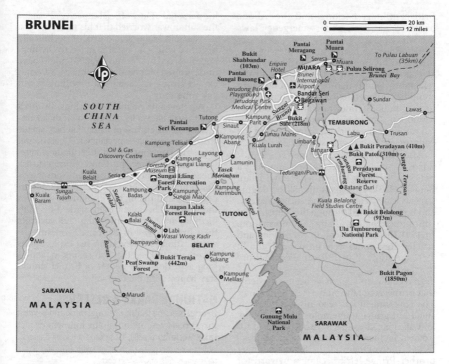

BRUNEI

0 ——— 20 km
0 ——— 12 miles

SOUTH CHINA SEA

Bukit Shahbandar (103m)
Pantai Sungai Basong
Empire Hotel
Pantai Meragang
Pantai Muara
Serasa
MUARA
Muara
To Pulau Labuan (35km)
Pulau Selirong
Brunei Bay
Brunei International Airport
Bandar Seri Begawan
Sundar
Lawas

Jerudong Park Playground
Jerudong Park Medical Centre
Tutong
Kampung Parit
Bukit Saie (218m)
TEMBURONG
Pantai Seri Kenangan
Sinaut
Limau Manis
Limbang
Labu
Trusan
Kampung Telisai
Kampung Abang
Kuala Lurah
Bangar
Bukit Peradayan (410m)
Oil & Gas Discovery Centre
Lumut
Layong
Kampung Sungai Liang
Lamunin
Bukit Patoi (310m)
Sungai Peradayan Forest Reserve
Forestry Museum
Tasek Merimbun
Tedungan/Puni
Sungai Temburong
Batang Duri
Kuala Belait
Seria
Sungai Liang Forest Recreation Park
Kampung Merimbun
Kuala Balalong Field Studies Centre
Kuala Baram
Sungai Tujuh
Kampung Badas
Kampung Sungai Mau
Sungai Belait
Sungai Tuiong
Sungai Limbang
Sungai Terusan
Batang Duri
Bukit Belalong (913m)
Luagan Lalak Forest Reserve
TUTONG
Sungai Mau
Uiu Temburong National Park
Miri
Kuala Balai
Sungai Damit
Labi
Wasai Wong Kadir
Rampayoh
BELAIT
Bukit Teraja (442m)
Kampung Sukang
Kampung Melilas
Bukit Pagon (1850m)
Peat Swamp Forest
SARAWAK
MALAYSIA
Marudi
Gunung Mulu National Park
SARAWAK
MALAYSIA

HISTORY

The earliest recorded references to Brunei's presence relate to China's trading connections with 'Pu-ni' in the 6th century, during the Tang dynasty. Prior to the region's embrace of Islam, Brunei was within the boundaries of the Sumatran Srivijaya Empire, then the Majapahit Empire of Java. By the 15th and 16th centuries, the so-called Golden Age of Sultan Bolkiah (the fifth sultan), Brunei Darussalam had itself become a considerable power in the region, with its rule extending throughout Borneo and into the Philippines.

The Spanish and Portuguese were the first European visitors, arriving in the 16th century, but failing to make inroads by force. In the early 19th century, the more subtle approach of the British, in the guise of Sarawak's first raja, James Brooke, spelled the end of Brunei's power. A series of 'treaties' was forced upon the sultan as Brooke consolidated his hold over the town of Kuching. In 1888 Brunei became a British protectorate and was gradually whittled away until, with a final dash of absurdity, Limbang was ceded to Sarawak in 1890, dividing the crippled sultanate into two parts.

In 1929, just as Brunei was about to be swallowed up entirely, oil was discovered, turning the tiny state into an economic power overnight. The present sultan's father, Sultan Omar Saifuddien, kept Brunei out of the Malayan confederacy, preferring that the country remain a British protectorate and the oil money remain on home soil. He's credited with laying the foundations for Brunei's solid development.

In 1962, in the lead up to amalgamation with the new state of Malaysia, the British pressured Brunei to hold elections. The opposition Ra'ayat Party, which wanted to keep Brunei independent and make the sultan a constitutional monarch within a democracy, won an overwhelming victory. When the sultan refused to allow the new government into power, an armed rebellion broke out, supported by the Indonesian government. The uprising was quickly crushed with

BRUNEI

British military backing, and the 'Abode of Peace' has been under emergency laws ever since.

Saifuddien abdicated in 1967, leaving the throne to his popular son and heir, Sultan Hassanal Bolkiah. Early in 1984 the new ruler reluctantly led his tightly ruled country into complete independence from Britain. As a former public-school boy and graduate of Sandhurst Royal Military Academy, the sultan rather enjoyed British patronage and the country still has close ties to Britain.

After independence, Brunei veered towards Islamic fundamentalism, adopting a national ideology known as Melayu Islam Beraja (MIB). This institutionalised dogma stresses Malay culture, Islam and monarchy, and is promulgated through the ministries of education, religious affairs and information. In 1991 the sale of alcohol was banned and stricter dress codes were introduced, and in 1992 the study of MIB became compulsory in schools.

In recent years signs have begun to emerge that Brunei is not the model state it once was. The government has recognised a relatively small but growing unemployment problem, and disaffected youths have been blamed for isolated incidents of crime. The most disaffected youth of them all, the sultan's younger brother Prince Jefri, became a byword for extravagance both in his private life and, rather more seriously, in his role as finance minister (see the boxed text, p587). The sultan sacked Jefri in 1997, but the damage had been done, and Brunei found itself with seriously depleted financial reserves.

Perhaps as a result of these factors, the prevailing climate in Brunei today seems to be one of controlled reform as the sultan struggles to keep pace with the modern world. In 2004 the legislative council was finally restored after 20 years of 'emergency' law. So far the 29 incumbents are all royal relatives or cronies, but the constitution has been amended to allow the council to grow up to 45 members in the future, with 15 of them elected by the public. In another significant step, former radical leader Muhamad Yasin Abdul Rahman, who was once jailed for his part in the 1962 rebellion, has been allowed to form a new opposition party, the National Development Party.

The mere mention of the words 'election' and 'opposition' must have brought the sultan out in a sweat, as he promptly hedged his bets by adding another clause to the constitution stating that he 'can do no wrong in either his personal or any official capacity'. Perhaps the sultan was worried that his marriage to a 27-year-old Malaysian journalist (technically his third wife – he's still married to the first, and divorced his second in 2003) might have undermined his popularity. Either way, don't expect to see Bruneians at a polling booth any time soon.

Whatever its political waverings, Brunei's wealth still allows its citizens to enjoy an unprecedented standard of living. Literacy stands at 94%, average life expectancy is 77 years, and there are pensions for all, free medical care, free schooling, free sport and leisure centres, cheap loans, subsidies for many purchases (including cars), short working weeks, no income tax and the highest minimum wages in the region. The sultan even marked his 60th birthday in 2006 by awarding civil servants their first pay rise in 20 years. Economic diversification and new deep-sea explorations for oil aim to keep the cash rolling in, and as long as it does, the people of Brunei should stay happy with their lot.

NATIONAL PARKS & RESERVES

Brunei has one major national park and several forest reserves, including the following:

Lake Merimbun (p588; 1.2 sq km) Centred on Brunei's largest lake, this park, 27km inland south of Tutong, has trails and nature observation posts.

Peradayan Forest Reserve (p589; 10.7 sq km) A section of the Peradayan Forest Reserve in Brunei's Temburong district; treks through the jungle lead to the summits of Bukit Patoi (310m) and Bukit Peradayan (410m).

Ulu Temburong National Park (p590; 500 sq km) An untouched expanse of forest, with trails and a canopy walk; accessible by longboat only.

BANDAR SERI BEGAWAN

pop 258,000

If you're expecting some kind of lavish mini-Dubai, think again – Brunei may fancy itself an oil state, but there's no nouveau-riche ostentation here, and the country's capital is as polite and unassuming as its people, wearing its wealth almost prosaically in places. For visitors on a layover, BSB's wide, quiet streets will form the entirety of their Bruneian experience. And while there's plenty to keep you occupied for a couple of days, the city itself is unlikely to inspire any great devotion. However, if you take the time to slow down and talk with the locals, you may find

BRUNEI IN...

One Day (just passing through, or on a layover)
Start in Bandar Seri Begawan (BSB) and test out our tailor-made **walking tour** (p579), which tackles the capital's clutch of spaceship-like mosques and historical museums. Then cross the river in a water taxi to visit the wobbly wooden homes in **Kampong Ayer** (Water Villages; p578), the world's largest floating city. Break for high tea at the **Empire Hotel** (p586), a lavish bastion of Italian marble and gold plating plunked down on the jungle-like seafront. If you're still around in the evening, head to **Gadong** (p583) for some serious shopping (DVDs!) and dare your tastebuds with a dinner of **ambuyat** (p584) – Brunei's most Bruneian dish.

One Week
Take your time exploring downtown BSB, spreading our 'one day' itinerary over two leisurely afternoons and tossing in a search for proboscis monkeys on a **wildlife boat cruise** (p581) down the Sungai Brunei.

After absorbing Bandar's version of city living, it's time to head to Temburong – Brunei's version of the Wild West. Join up with a tour for a lazy longboat ride deep into the virgin rainforests of **Ulu Temburong National Park** (p590). Spend the night among cawing hornbills and giggling macaques before making your way to **Bangar** (p589) for a glimpse of village life.

Two days of sweaty jungle-trekking warrants a big reward: three blissful days at the **Empire Hotel** (p586), Brunei's infamous 'seven-star' luxury resort. Enjoy poolside virgin daiquiris (remember, no alcohol here!), gut-busting buffet dinners, a golf course and a visit to **Jerudong Park Playground** (p585) – the sultanate's unofficial monument to reckless spending.

---

that there's more than meets the eye in this modest metropolis.

ORIENTATION
The central core of BSB is an easily navigable grid facing south towards the busy Sungai Brunei (Brunei River). Stilt villages sprawl on the opposite side of the shore and are connected to the centre by bridges and water taxis. Buildings in central Bandar are spread out and there isn't a lot of shade, so hats and sunscreen are advised. Although the downtown is relatively quiet, there are plenty of sights, restaurants and shops, many of which are located around the Yayasan Complex. The main bus station is also located near the waterfront on Jln Cator. The airport is 5km from the city centre.

INFORMATION
Bookshops
Paul & Elizabeth Book Services (☎ 222 0958; 2nd fl, Block B, Yayasan Complex, Jln Pretty) A small range of English-language paperbacks, including some ancient LP guides!

Emergency
Ambulance (☎ 991)
Fire (☎ 995)
Police (☎ 993)

Internet Access
Paul & Elizabeth Cyber Café (☎ 222 0958; 2nd fl, Block B, Yayasan Complex, Jln Pretty; per hr B$1; ☒ 8am-9.30pm) On the 2nd floor overlooking the central atrium in the northern building of the complex. Decent connections, bad soundtrack.

Internet Resources
For detailed information about visiting Brunei, visit www.tourismbrunei.com. Lately, blogging has become quite popular – check out the boxed text on p585 for local perspectives on the sultanate.

Medical Services
Jerudong Park Medical Centre (☎ 261 1433; Tutong-Muara Hwy; ☒ 24hr) Private medical facility with high standards of care.
RIPAS Hospital (☎ 224 2424; Jln Tutong; ☒ 24hr) A fully equipped, modern hospital across the Edinburgh Bridge on the western side of Sungai Kedayan.

Money
HSBC (☎ 225 2222; cnr Jln Sultan & Jln Pemancha; ☒ 9am-3.30pm Mon-Fri, 9-11am Sat) Charges a fee of B$15 to change most travellers cheques. There's also an ATM.
Rupiah Express (ground fl, Britannia House, 1 Jln Cator; ☒ 8am-5.30pm Mon-Sat, 8am-3pm Sun) Exchanges cash only.

BRUNEI

BANDAR SERI BEGAWAN

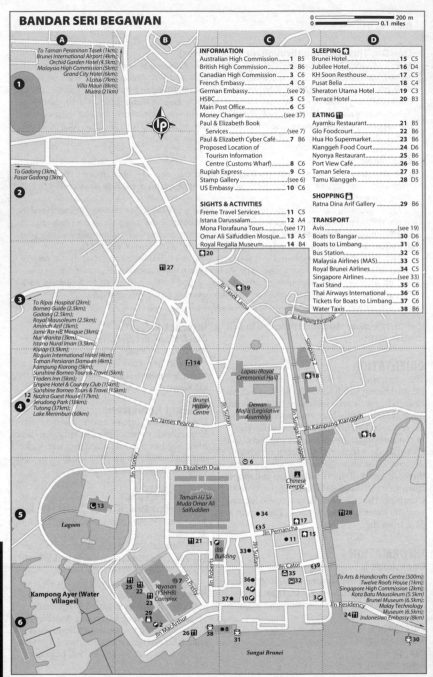

0 -------- 200 m
0 -------- 0.1 miles

INFORMATION

Australian High Commission	**1** B5
British High Commission	**2** B6
Canadian High Commission	**3** C6
French Embassy	**4** C6
German Embassy	(see 2)
HSBC	**5** C5
Main Post Office	**6** C5
Money Changer	(see 37)
Paul & Elizabeth Book Services	(see 7)
Paul & Elizabeth Cyber Café	**7** B6
Proposed Location of Tourism Information Centre (Customs Wharf)	**8** C6
Rupiah Express	**9** C5
Stamp Gallery	(see 6)
US Embassy	**10** C6

SIGHTS & ACTIVITIES

Freme Travel Services	**11** C5
Istana Darussalam	**12** A4
Mona Florafauna Tours	(see 17)
Omar Ali Saifuddien Mosque	**13** A5
Royal Regalia Museum	**14** B4

SLEEPING

Brunei Hotel	**15** C5
Jubilee Hotel	**16** D4
KH Soon Resthouse	**17** C5
Pusat Belia	**18** C4
Sheraton Utama Hotel	**19** C3
Terrace Hotel	**20** B3

EATING

Ayamku Restaurant	**21** B5
Glo Foodcourt	**22** B6
Hua Ho Supermarket	**23** B6
Kianggeh Food Court	**24** D6
Nyonya Restaurant	**25** B6
Port View Café	**26** B6
Taman Selera	**27** B3
Tamu Kiangggeh	**28** D5

SHOPPING

Ratna Dina Arif Gallery	**29** B6

TRANSPORT

Avis	(see 19)
Boats to Bangar	**30** D6
Boats to Limbang	**31** C6
Bus Station	**32** C6
Malaysia Airlines (MAS)	**33** C5
Royal Brunei Airlines	**34** C5
Singapore Airlines	(see 33)
Taxi Stand	**35** C6
Thai Airways International	**36** C6
Tickets for Boats to Limbang	**37** C6
Water Taxis	**38** B6

To Taman Peranian Tasek (1km);
Brunei International Airport (4km);
Orchid Garden Hotel (4.5km);
Malaysia High Commission (5km);
Grand City Hotel (6km);
I-Lotus (7km);
Villa Maun (8km);
Mudra (21km)

To Gadong (3km);
Pasar Gadong (3km)

To Ripas Hospital (2km);
Borneo Guide (2.5km);
Gadong (2.5km);
Royal Mausoleum (2.5km);
Aminah Arif (3km);
Jame Asr HB Mosque (3km);
Nur Wanita (3km);
Istana Nural Iman (3.5km);
Kiulap (3.5km);
Rizqun International Hotel (4km);
Taman Persiaran Damuan (4km);
Kampung Kiarong (5km);
Sunshine Borneo Tours & Travel (5km);
Traders Inn (5km);
Empire Hotel & Country Club (15km);
Sunshine Borneo Tours & Travel (15km);
Nazira Guest House (17km);
Jerudong Park (18km);
Tutong (37km);
Lake Merimbun (60km)

Jln Tasek Lama

Jln Kampung Berangah

Jln Kampung Kianggeh

Sungai Kianggeh

Lapau (Royal Ceremonial Hall)

Dewan Majlis (Legislative Assembly)

Brunei History Centre

Jln James Pearce

Jln Sultan

Jln Stoney

Jln Elizabeth Dua

Chinese Temple

Taman HJ Sir Muda Omar Ali Saifuddien

Jln Pemancha

Lagoon

Jln Roberts

Jln Pretty

IBB Building

Yayasan (YSHHB) Complex

Jln Sultan

Jln Cator

Kampong Ayer (Water Villages)

Jln MacArthur

To Arts & Handicrafts Centre (500m);
Twelve Roofs House (1km);
Singapore High Commission (2km);
Kota Batu Mausoleum (5.5km);
Brunei Museum (6.5km);
Malay Technology Museum (6.5km);
Indonesian Embassy (8km)

Jln Residency

Sungai Brunei

BRUNEI

Post

Main post office (cnr Jln Sultan & Jln Elizabeth Dua; ☯ 8.30am-4.30pm Mon-Thu & Sat, 8.30-11.30am & 2-4pm Fri) Be sure to stop in to the adjoining Stamp Gallery (same hours as post office).

Tourist Information

At the time of research there was no tourist-information centre in Bandar's CBD; however, word is that a visitors centre and adjoining art gallery will be opening in the Old Custom Building along the riverfront. See p592 for information about Brunei's tourism board.

SIGHTS

Sprawling Bandar doesn't lend itself to wandering tourists, especially under the tropical sun. The Royal Regalia Museum, Omar Ali Saifuddien Mosque and Kampong Ayer (Water Village) are located in the city centre (and are included in our tailor-made **walking tour**, p579), while the remaining sights orbit central BSB several kilometres away. Small sights, like the Kota Batu Mausoleum, have been woven into our walking/taxi tour. Buses, taxis and private vehicles are the best ways to explore these spots. The main bus and taxi terminals are located on Jln Cator (pronounced 'kay-tor'), two blocks from the waterfront.

If you intend to visit a mosque, please dress appropriately. (Preferably long pants and polo shirt for men, and covered shoulders and knees for women. A full-length gown and scarf are provided to women at mosque entrances.) Also note that places of worship are not open to tourists during prayer times. The best times of day for a visit are between 8am and 11am, 1.30pm and 3pm, and 4pm and 5.30pm. Visits on Thursdays and Fridays are usually forbidden.

Royal Regalia Museum

A celebration of the sultan and all the trappings of Bruneian royalty, the **Royal Regalia Museum** (☎ 222 8358; Jln Sultan; admission free; ☯ 8.30am-4.30pm Sun-Thu, 9-11am Fri) belongs at the top of any Brunei itinerary. The 1st floor is dominated by a recreation of the sultan's coronation day parade, including a huge gilded royal cart, on which the newly crowned sultan was pulled through the streets of BSB.

On the mezzanine floor of the museum you'll find a selection of gifts received by the sultan. Of course, when you are called upon to give a gift to the Sultan of Brunei, you must inevitably confront the question: what do you give the man who has everything? Here you'll see how various heads of state and royalty have answered this question (hint: you'll never go wrong with priceless gold and jewels). We particularly like the mother of all beer mugs given by Queen Elizabeth, the fine abalone-shell chest given by the Philippines, and the Benjarong porcelain from Thailand.

Visitors must remove their shoes before entering and photography is strictly prohibited beyond the main foyer.

Omar Ali Saifuddien Mosque

Named after the 28th sultan of Brunei (the late father of the current sultan), the **Omar Ali Saifuddien Mosque** (☎ 222 2623; admission free; ☯ 8am-noon, 2-3pm, 5-6pm & 8-9pm Sat-Wed) was built in 1958 at a cost of about US$5 million, and stands next to Sungai Kedayan in its own artificial lagoon. The 44m minaret makes it the tallest building in central BSB, and woe betide anyone who tries to outdo it – apparently the Islamic Bank of Brunei building nearby originally exceeded this height, and consequently had to have its top storey removed by order of the sultan. Listen for the call to prayer that echoes throughout the city centre, starting before dawn or at dusk.

The interior is simple but tasteful, though it's no match for the stunning exterior. The floor and walls are made from the finest Italian marble, the stained-glass windows were crafted in England and the luxurious carpets were flown in from Saudi Arabia and Belgium. Jigsaw enthusiasts can admire the 3.5 million-piece Venetian mosaic inside the main dome. The ceremonial stone boat sitting in the lagoon is a replica of a 16th-century *mahligai* (royal) barge.

The external compound is open between 8am and 8.30pm, and non-Muslims may enter the mosque itself outside prayer times. Remember to dress appropriately and to remove your shoes before entering. You may also be able to take the elevator to the top of the minaret or walk up the winding staircase (ask permission from staff first). The view over the city and Kampong Ayer is excellent.

Jame'Asr Hassanil Bolkiah Mosque

The largest mosque in the country, **Jame'Asr Hassanil Bolkiah Mosque** (☎ 223 8741; Jln Hassan Bolkiah, Gadong; admission free; ☯ 8am-noon, 2-3pm, 5-6pm & 8-9pm Sat-Wed), was built in 1992 to

BRUNEI

WHAT'S IN A NAME?

Hassanal Bolkiah Mu'izzaddin Waddaulah, the current sultan of Brunei, is named after two of his great-great-great-great-great-(etc)-grandfathers. The first, Bolkiah, was Brunei's fifth sultan, ruling from 1485 to 1524. His reign was known as Brunei's Golden Age, as it was during this time that the sultanate expanded to dominate the Malay region and the Philippines. After adding a Sulu princess to his coterie of wives, Bolkiah mysteriously died (some say he was poisoned by a golden needle) leaving the ever-expanding empire to his son.

The sultan takes the name Hassanal from Brunei's ninth sultan, Muhammad Hassan. Considered to be another of Brunei's great rulers, Hassan was instrumental in re-establishing links to lands lost by the previous sultans. He sent his second son to Sulu, where he became sultan – Sulu's sultanate still traces its ancestry to Hassan. Hassan is also credited with passing down a code of law, which is still used in today's courts.

Needless to say, when Hassanal Bolkiah ascended to the throne, he had some pretty big shoes to fill…

---

celebrate the 25th year of the current sultan's reign. While some prefer the facade of the Omar Ali Saifuddien Mosque, the interior here is best described as jaw-dropping. The sheer volume is in itself amazing, not to mention the myriad woven rugs scattered across the men's prayer hall. At the grand opening, the sultan gave every attendee a gold-embroidered prayer rug.

The structure's four main minarets and two golden domes are a fantastic sight when illuminated in the evening and can be photographed from several locations around town. Oh, and yes, it's Hassan*il* and not Hassan*al* like the sultan (we asked around – no one knew why!)

It's located en route to Gadong, about 2.5km northwest of the city centre. To get to the mosque, take bus 22 or 1 (Circle Line) from the bus station in BSB centre.

Kampong Ayer

Housing an estimated 20,000 people, Kampong Ayer is made up of 28 water villages built on either side of Sungai Brunei. This jumble of wooden planks and shacks is considered to be the biggest water village in the world, and the locals love calling it 'Asia's Venice' (there's really no resemblance, though – well, other than the turbid water part).

If you've never visited a water village before, now's your chance. A new **Kampong Ayer Cultural and Tourism Gallery** was just opening its door when we visited. This brand new information centre will focus on the history, lifestyle and crafts of the Kampong Ayer people. A viewing tower offers panoramic views of the bustling scene below. Walk across one of the planks west of the Yayasan Complex and you'll find yourself in the heart of the action. Or, you can charter a water taxi for B$30 (a bit of negotiating is a must) to have a look-see from the river. Finding a taxi won't be a problem, as the boatmen will have spotted you before you spot them. Afternoon rides are ideal, especially if you'd like to check out the Istana Nurul Iman (opposite) as well .

Brunei Museum

Sitting on a bluff overlooking Sungai Brunei, the **Brunei Museum** (☎ 222 3235; Jln Kota Batu; admission free; ⊗ 9.30am-5pm Sun-Thu, 9-11.30am & 2.30-4.30pm Fri) is 4.5km east of central BSB. The main building contains the excellent **Islamic Art Gallery**, which has some wonderful illuminated (decorated) copies of the Quran, as well as an incredible model of the Dome of the Rock, executed in mother of pearl and abalone shell.

In the same building, the **Oil and Gas Gallery** is surprisingly interesting. It answers all of your questions about how they get the stuff from under the ground to your nearest gas pump. Finally, don't miss the **Brunei Traditional Culture Gallery**, also in the main building. It's got good exhibits on all aspects of Bruneian culture, from circumcision (ouch!) to the invigorating sport of grass sledding (?).

Descend the stairs from the car park behind the museum, then turn right to reach the **Malay Technology Museum** (admission free; ⊗ 9.30am-5pm Sun-Thu, 9-11.30am & 2.30-4.30pm Fri) A pair of rooms here have interesting life-sized recreations of stilt houses with accompanying information on traditional cultures. Gallery 1 features water villages and includes reconstructions

BRUNEI

of how *kampung* (village) architecture has evolved over the last 150 years. Gallery 2 has exhibits of handicrafts and fishing techniques practised by the people of the water villages. Gallery 3 shows the tools and techniques used by the indigenous tribes of the interior for food gathering, agriculture and hunting.

To get to the museum, take bus 39 from the bus station in central BSB.

Istana Nurul Iman

The best way to measure the grandeur of a structure is by counting the bathrooms. The sultan's **Istana Nurul Iman** (Jln Tutong) has 257, making it the largest residential palace in the world. With a price tag of over US$350 million, this 1788-room behemoth is, if you can believe it, more than four times the size of the Palace of Versailles and three times larger than Buckingham Palace.

Designed by Filipino architect Leandro Locsin, the design aesthetics of the palace draw heavily on an airport terminal concept. From an art-historical perspective it feels more like a Monet – from far away it's quite a sight, but from up close the whole thing doesn't really make sense.

Those who want to get inside the palace will have to time their visit with the Hari Raya festivities at the end of Ramadan – the sultan only opens the palace doors for three days in September, shaking hands and giving out goodies to his faithful subjects.

If you're visiting Brunei during the other 362 days of the year, then the best way to check out the palace is from Taman Persiaran Damuan – a large landscaped park along the riverbank just beyond the palace when travelling from the city centre. The palace's backyard can also be viewed from a water taxi along the river. Your boatman can also take you past **Pulau Ranggu**, in the middle of the river, which is home to a large colony of proboscis monkeys. The best time to head out is late afternoon, so you can catch the monkeys around sunset and then get dropped off at the park to see the palace in the evening. Asking prices will probably start at B$40, but you should be able to hire a boat for B$28.

Arts & Handicrafts Centre

Built to help develop local craftwork, the **Arts & Handicrafts Centre** (☎ 224 0676; Jln Kota Batu; admission free; ⏱ 7.45am-12.15pm & 1.30-4.30pm Mon-Thu & Sat, 8.30am-2.30pm Fri & Sun) sits on the waterfront

towards the Brunei Museum like an aged Floridian timeshare. It's visible from town and within easy walking distance. While the concept of such a centre is a marvellous idea, it's a little disappointing if you're interested in traditional crafts; only new silverwork and weaving produced by the students are available, and some items are very expensive. If you're really serious about investing some cash, you can pick up the *Directory of Handicraft Entrepreneurs* here.

WALKING TOUR
Bandar In Brief

If you're short on time, most of Bandar's main attractions can be tackled in a single morning. Start at the **Royal Regalia Museum** (1; p577) for a lesson in Bruneian Sultans 101. If you're captivated by the country's well-documented history, then check out the taxi tour add-on below. After perusing rooms full of priceless (and useless) artefacts, head down Jln Sultan passing **Dewan Majlis (2)**, home of the legislative assembly. In Brunei, criminal indiscretions, like petty theft, are handled by the so-called English Court, while the Muslim Court controls religious matters, including divorce, and

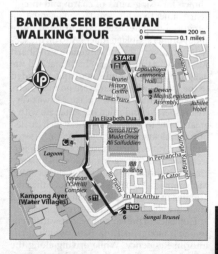

WALK FACTS

Start Royal Regalia Museum
Finish Kampong Ayer
Distance 1.4km
Time Two hours

BRUNEI

ne'er the two courts shall meet. Pass the **Tugu Clock (3)**, the 'ground zero' from which all distances in Brunei are measured, as you head to the stunning **Omar Ali Saifuddien Mosque** (4; p577). Next, walk to the **Yayasan Complex (5)** for an obligatory food break. Stop in the Hua Ho Supermarket to sample Brunei's best-known sweets (p584).

If you have more time, hop on a water taxi and head across the busy Sungai Brunei to check out **Kampong Ayer** (6; p578), the world's largest stilt village. See p578 for more information about the floating city.

Taxi Tour Add-on: In the Footsteps of the Sultans

If you have a bit more time, and a few extra Brunei bucks to burn, consider adding on the following taxi tour, which details the colourful and fascinating history of Brunei's sultans – the world's longest bloodline.

Start at the **Kota Batu Mausoleum**, on Jln Kota Batu just before the Brunei Museum. Here you'll find the final resting place of Brunei's greatest sultan, Bolkiah, who at the height of his reign, pulled all of Borneo and part of the Philippines under Bruneian rule. He was known for using a mix of charm and intelligence rather than his sword when negotiating territorial disputes. See p578 to learn more about Brunei's 'Golden Ruler'. Also on the sacred grounds are the buried remains of Sharif Ali, Brunei's third sultan. Sharif married the daughter of the second sultan and ascended to the throne when there were no male heirs to take his father-in-law's place. He was very well respected, and ruled his sultanate with a great deal of religious discipline, which earned him the nickname *Sultan Berkat*, or 'Blessed Sultan'. Brunei's first mosque and stone fortress are also among his accomplishments. He was a direct descendant of the prophet Mohammed. Archaeologists believe that the remains of Brunei's first sultan, Muhammad Shah, are also buried at this riverfront site.

Hop back in the car and head towards central BSB along Jln Kota Batu, which turns into Jln Residency. While driving along the waterfront you'll pass the gabled **Twelve Roofs House** (Bumbungan Dua Belas; admission free; ✆ 9am-4.30pm Mon-Thu & Sat, 9-11.30am & 2.30-4.30pm Fri), which was once the residence of the British High Commissioners. Today the complex displays photos illustrating British involvement in Brunei and the 'special relationship'

between the two countries. After centuries as a local hegemony, Brunei gradually lost its grip and was taken over the British. The sultanate gained complete autonomy in 1984, but keeps close ties with Queen Elizabeth II.

Follow Jln Tutong over the Edinburgh Bridge towards the **Royal Mausoleum**, the final resting place of several sultans, including Omar Ali Saifuddien III, known as the 'Architect of Modern Brunei' for the significant advances that were made during his reign. Conspicuously absent from the deceased is the 22nd sultan, Muhammad Alam, who enjoyed the kind of reputation usually reserved for a Mongolian warlord. Dubbed the 'King of Fire', Alam finally realised his unpopularity and surrendered to his siblings, and when mercifully given a choice of execution, opted to be publicly garrotted…

Continue on to **Istana Nurul Iman** (p579), the sultan's palace. The palace guards get a bit flustered if you slow down to take pictures at the gate, so it's best to continue on and grab a couple of snaps from Taman Persiaran Damuan – a quiet picnic area along the river with great views back to the palace.

Back in the city centre, it's worth stopping by **Istana Darussalam**, the birthplace of the current sultan. The traditional Malay home sits rather inconspicuously beside a makeshift car park in desperate need of some weeding, but the structure itself is quite elegant. Access is not allowed, although its worth a glimpse from the outside, as it is a lot smaller and humbler than one might think an old *istana* would be.

Head down the aptly named Sultan Hassanal Bolkiah Highway to Brunei's biggest roundabout (the country has more roundabouts than people!), home of the stunning **Jame'Asr Hassanil Bolkiah Mosque** (p577).

Take a few minutes to drive around **Kampung Kiarong**, just south of the mosque. This community, sandwiched between the mosque and the royal palace, is home to a variety of distinguished locals – most are relatives of the sultan.

TAXI TOUR FACTS

Start Kota Batu
Finish Empire Hotel
Distance 23km
Time Two hours
Taxi per hour B$40 to B$50
Rental car per day B$130 to B$150

Head back onto the highway passing several buildings sprouting up from the tropical floor. These are some of the recent billion-dollar blunders made by the sultan's brother, Prince Jefri (see boxed text, p587). Brunei's two biggest white elephants sit at the end of the road: the erstwhile amusement centre, **Jerodung Park Playground** (p585) and the sultanate's seven-star resort, the **Empire Hotel** (p586).

TOURS

It's a cinch to get around Bandar under your own steam, but for a trip to beautiful Temburong, or for a 'night safari' along Sungai Brunei, we recommend linking up with a tour.

Major tour operators in the city include the following:

Borneo Guide (☎ 876 6796; www.borneoguide.com; Block B 1st fl, Warisan Mat Mat, Gadong) Excellent service and a variety of eco-programs around Brunei and Borneo.

Freme Travel Services (☎ 223 4280; www.freme .com; 403B-407B Wisma Jaya, Jln Pemancha) Offers a variety of tours, including the city and Kampong Ayer, and trips to Ulu Temburong and Pulau Selirong.

Mona Florafauna Tours (☎ 223 0761; www.i-s-d-s .com/mona; 209 1st fl, Kiaw Lian Bldg, Jln Pemancha) Specialises in outdoor and wildlife tours around Brunei.

Sunshine Borneo Tours & Travel (☎ 244 6509; www.exploreborneo.com; No 2, Simpang 146, Jln Kiarong) Runs tours of the city and at the Ulu Ulu Resort in Temburong. They also have a counter at the airport, an office at the Empire Hotel and an office in Kiarong.

SLEEPING

A sleepover in the sultanate is a pricier endeavour than in nearby Malaysia. Most of Brunei's accommodation abides by the old 'special price for you' market mantra, meaning that rack rates are usually much higher than what you'll actually pay. Unlike other Southeast Asian countries, the best lodging deals can usually be scouted on the internet. The Empire Hotel (p586), Brunei's most luxurious sleeping spot, sometimes offers bargain-basement deals that can rival the midrange options – check its website for details.

During our visit we heard murmurs about homestays and B&B establishments starting up in Kampong Ayer. Check with the tourism board (p592) or Borneo Guide (above) for details.

Budget

Budget prices in Brunei are more like midrange options in the rest of Malaysia, and there's only one truly 'cheap' option in town.

Pusat Belia (Youth Centre; ☎ 222 2900, 8765515; Jln Sungai Kianggeh; dm B$10; 🏊 🖳) No backpacker comforts here: this is the kind of classic youth hostel that should remind you of school trips or summer camps, and still caters to exactly that kind of local clientele. The single-sex four-bed bunkrooms are basic but adequate, with rather iffy bathrooms; reception is only sporadically staffed, but hang around and someone should find you. And no, that symbol's not a misprint – the youth centre really does have its own swimming pool (B$1, open 9am to 7pm).

KH Soon Resthouse (☎ 222 2052; http://khsoon -resthouse.tripod.com; 140 Jln Pemancha; s/d B$35/39, with shared bathroom B$30/35; 🏊) It's quite a step-up in price from the hostel to this simple Chinese-run place, but you don't get a whole lot for your extra 25 bucks apart from more space, better service and plenty of local information. Still, it's the only other budget option anywhere near the centre, and the bus station's almost right opposite.

Nazira Guest House (☎ 261-2053; hmarzuqo@brunet .bn; Spg 730-34 Kampong Jerudong; r from B$40; 🏊) Located near the Jerudong area, about 15 minutes from central BSB, Nazira is a homey (albeit slightly musty) option set on a residential block. Fully furnished apartments are also available.

Midrange

If you're watching the pennies, the jump from budget to midrange accommodation can seem pretty brutal, though at least all rooms have air-con, TV, hot water and IDD phones.

Terrace Hotel (☎ 224 3554; www.terracebrunei.com; Jln Tasek Lama; r B$60-80; 🏊 🖳 🖳) Even if you're on a tight budget, consider spending a little more to enjoy the comforts of this excellent midrange hotel. Rooms are clean and well taken care of, and there's a great little swimming pool and wireless internet access. Deluxe rooms cost about B$10 more than standard rooms, but are well worth the price.

Jubilee Hotel (☎ 222 8070; www.jubileehotelbrunei .com; Jln Kg Kianggeh; r from B$70; 🏊 🖳) Not quite as appealing as the Terrace, the Jubilee offers simple and clean standard rooms (the deluxe rooms aren't worth the extra price). On-site facilities include a Thai restaurant and billiards. Rates include airport pick-up and breakfast.

Traders Inn (☎ 244 2828; tradersinn@brunet.bn; Lot 11620, Jln Gadong, Gadong-Beribi; r B$80-120; 🏊 🖳) If you want to stay out of the centre, this comfortable business hotel is usefully located within easy reach of the Gadong shops. The bathrooms could use a bit of spiffing up, though – they are currently the colour of dirty teeth.

Brunei Hotel (☎ 224-2372; www.quanix.com/business/bruhotel; 95 Jln Pemancha; r B$176-220, ste B$242-440; 🍽 🖭) Hovering at the upper end of midrange, the Brunei is an earnest business hotel used to train hospitality workers. Huge humidifiers and slightly mentholated air-con help you breathe, and you even get a minibar (dry, of course). It's the closest midrange option to the bus station.

Also recommended:

Grand City Hotel (☎ 245 2188; grandcity@brunei.net; Jln Batu Bersurat, Kg Pengkalan Gadong; r B$88; 🍽 🖭) Good value and near the shops in Gadong.

Orchid Garden Hotel (☎ 233 5544; www.orchid gardenbrunei.com; Jln Berakas, Kg Anggerek Desa; r B$180; 🍽 🖭 🌊) Unmemorable but clean. Popular with tour packages. Free shuttle service links guests to Gadong and central BSB.

Top End

For those whose wallets overfloweth, and need to be in the city centre (usually business travellers), Bandar has a couple of solid options. If you're going to drop some serious bling, we highly recommend hanging your hat at the opulent Empire Hotel (p586).

Rizqun International Hotel (☎ 243 3000; reservation@rizquninternational.com; Abdul Razak Complex, Gadong; r from B$320; 🍽) The premier tourist hotel in the Gadong district is much more sophisticated than you'd expect for something growing out of a shopping mall.

Sheraton Utama Hotel (☎ 224 4272; www.sheraton .com/utama; Jln Tasek Lama; r from B$400; 🍽 🖭 🌊) Brunei's only Western chain hotel flies the flag for international standards on the edge of the town centre. Amenities are rife, and the lounge bar has live music on Saturday, a rare treat in BSB.

EATING

Eating: the only thing Bruneians like to do more than shop. Most of Bandar's top noshes are located beyond the small city centre. See the boxed text on p584 for everything you need to know about local cuisine.

Restaurants

Ayamku Restaurant (Jln Permancha; meals from B$3.50; 🌙 lunch & dinner) Brunei's answer to KFC, this is one of the cheapest places in town to get a meal. You can get a big piece of fried chicken,

some rice and a drink for about B$3. And the chicken is surprisingly good. One note: this may be purely coincidental, but many of the diners here seemed remarkably plump for Southeast Asians.

Nur Wanita (☎ 242 6789; Unit 10 Block B, Kiarong Complex; dishes B$4-10; 🌙 lunch & dinner) A fantastic new restaurant in the Kiarong area, this chic venue serves authentic dishes from Northern Thailand. It's exceptionally popular during lunch when nearby office monkeys swing by to transport their tastebuds.

I-Lotus (☎ 242 2466; No 20 Simpang 12-26, Kg Rimba, Jln Tunku Link; dishes B$5-15; 🌙 lunch & dinner) You'll need a cab or a very keen sense of direction to find this posh Chinese restaurant, but you'll be glad you put in the effort.

Nyonya Restaurant (☎ 223 1236; Yayasan Complex; mains B$6.80-18.80; 🌙 lunch & dinner) The wide-ranging menu and bistro-style air-con chic accentuate the appeal of this popular place on the Yayasan's central courtyard. As well as steak, soup, sandwiches, seabass, and Indian, Chinese and Malay dishes, there's a good-value selection of pasta (B$3 to B$7.80).

Port View Café (☎ 223 1467; Jln MacArthur; mains B$7-10.50; 🌙 lunch & dinner) Not the most original name, but sure enough, the split-level Port View does indeed gaze out over the water towards Kampong Ayer. The downstairs cafe menu includes simple Western, Chinese and Malay dishes, while upstairs is a little more expensive and features Thai, Chinese and Japanese food.

Villa Mauri (☎ 233 5585; Spg 369, Jln Muara, Kpg Sungai Tilong; dishes B$8.80-16; 🌙 breakfast, lunch & dinner) Brunei's best tribute to the Bootland, Villa Mauri's menu reads like a poem: *risotto Milanese, linguine alla pugliese, farfalle al salmone affumicato*. Chequered tablecloths further enhance the Mediterranean vibe – too bad there's no wine list…

Aminah Arif (☎ 223 6198; Unit 2-3 Block B Rahman Bldg, Spg 88, Kiulap; meals B$22; 🌙 breakfast, lunch & dinner) Aminah Arif is synonymous with *ambuyat* (p584) – Brunei's signature dish. If you're up for trying a bowl of wiggly white goo, then this is the place. Aminah's daughter has opened up her own restaurant, Seri Balai Food House, next door, and uses the same family recipe.

Food Courts, Markets & Hawker Stalls

Informal eating is the cornerstone of BSB's food scene, and every major shopping centre has its own air-conditioned food court. The

Yayasan Complex and Gadong's Mall shopping centre are some of the larger specimens.

Taman Selera (Jln Kumbang Pasang; dishes B$1-8) It's not much to look at, but this night-time food spot, across from the Terrace Hotel, offers everything from burgers and noodles to seafood and traditional Muslim dishes (halal, curries etc). The 'smooters' (B$2) at stall four are a damn good approximation of a real ice-cream milkshake.

Kianggeh Food Court (Jln Residency; dishes B$2; breakfast, lunch & dinner) Take in the sunset views over Kampong Ayer while devouring scrumptious local dishes like savoury satay sticks and a big bowl of *soto* (noodle soup) with chicken and yellow noodles. Swing by in the morning for some *roti canai* (flaky flat bread).

Glo Food Court (2nd fl, Yayasan Complex; dishes from B$3; lunch & dinner) Strut past large plastic aquariums full of the daily catch and choose from an array of food stalls – each one with plate polaroids for the uninitiated. Grab a chair amid the cafeteria-style seating and enjoy your cheap grub while taking in the views of the royal barge.

Pasar Gadong (Lr Sultan, Gadong) Brunei's most famous night market, Pasar Gadong is a bustling marquee of munch parked near the big shopping centres in Gadong. Vendors offer every cooked comestible imaginable, from satay and barbecued fish to chicken wings and *kueh melayu* (sweet pancakes filled with peanuts, raisins and sugar), though quality varies widely. Annoyingly there's nowhere to sit, so you will either have to eat on your feet or take your grub elsewhere.

Self-caterers can walk across the canal to the local produce market, **Tamu Kianggeh** (Jln Sungai Kiangggeh; breakfast, lunch & dinner), for a handful of fresh snacks. The large **Hua Ho Supermarket** (☎ 223 1120; Yayasan Complex; 10am-10pm) is a good place for self-catering and has a bunch of Bruneian treats (p584).

SHOPPING
Shopping is Brunei's national sport. Seriously – we might as well label this section 'Entertainment'. Locals bop through the shopping malls scouting out the best deals while bemoaning the fact that their micro-nation doesn't have enough variety. Things can get pretty hectic at the markets – the combination of food and shopping (Brunei's two biggest delights) can be a total bloodbath!

Escape the oppressive heat at the ritzy Yayasan Complex located in the city centre near the mosque. Here you'll find everything from the big brand names (Versace, Guess etc) to a variety of high-end local boutiques selling fabrics and jewellery. There are several great places to eat (see opposite), and don't miss the Hua Ho Department Store, with its cache of traditional Bruneian treats in the basement (p584). There is a small art studio, called **Ratna Dina Arif Gallery** (☎ 866 6934; admission free; 2-4pm Mon, 10am-4.30pm Tue, Thu & Sat, 10am-5pm Fri & Sun) located on the 2nd floor of Yayasan exhibiting a slew of paintings by local artists.

The country's only traffic jam occurs nightly in Gadong, a suburb of BSB, as locals eagerly clog the streets while trying to find a parking space. This is Brunei's main shopping district and features several large complexes including Centrepoint and The Mall, each one a large air-conditioned bastion of commerce. And, just for the record, Brunei's only McDonald's is in Gadong. The Kuilap area, next door, also has a couple of window-shopping-worthy malls, including Seri Q-Lap, which houses Brunei's most popular Cineplex.

As far as souvenirs are concerned, the boxes of *keropol udang* (prawn crackers) are a local fave, and they transport quite well. Textiles are also quite popular – silk is sold at very reasonable prices. For something a bit more upscale, try *jong sarat*, a hand-woven cloth made from gold and silver threads. It can be found at the Arts and Handicrafts Centre in Kota Batu, around 1km east of central Bandar. And don't forget about those DVDs, sold almost everywhere. Make sure you acquaint yourself with the system of coloured dots representing the quality of each recording.

GETTING THERE & AWAY
Bandar Seri Begawan is Brunei's capital city and air hub. See p592 for information about getting to/from BSB.

GETTING AROUND
This section offers information on getting around the capital. See p594 for information on getting around Brunei.

To/From the Airport
Buses 23, 24, 36, and 38 will get you to/from the airport, about 4km northwest of the city, for B$1. Leaving the terminal, keep to the right and walk south for about 300m to the bus stop.

BRUNEI

MAKAN: THE BRUNEIAN REMIX

If there's one word you should learn during a visit to Brunei, it's *makan*, meaning 'food' in Bahasa Malaysia. *Makan* isn't just a word, it's a way of life (because, the locals joke, there's nothing else to do!) This micro-nation really knows how to chow down.

Ambuyat

If Brunei had a national dish, it would be *ambuyat*. Remember that kid in kindergarten who used to eat paste? Well, this comes pretty darn close. Made from the pith of the sago tree, which is ground to a powder and mixed with water, this glutinous mass was popularised during WWII, when the Japanese invaded Borneo and cut off the rice supply.

To eat *ambuyat*, begin by jabbing your chopsticks into the bowl of quivering white goo. Now these aren't your usual chopsticks – Bruneian chopsticks are attached at the top (so don't snap them in two!) making it easier to curl up the gelatinous globs before dunking the contents into a flavourful sauce. *Ambuyat* itself doesn't have a taste – it's the sauce that gives it its zing. Shrimp-and-chilli mixes are the most popular, although you can technically dip the dish in anything you'd like (we've heard of people using vanilla ice cream!) After your *ambuyat* is sufficiently drenched, place the dripping mass in your mouth and swallow – don't chew – just let it slide down your throat...

Ambuyat is widely available throughout Brunei – stop by the famous Aminah Arif (p582) or Seri Balai, both well known throughout the country for perfecting their recipes.

Snacks

Three meals a day? Hardly! Bruneians will always find an excuse for a quick nosh and, as a result, they've perfected some delicious 'tween-meal treats. *Chakoi* is our favourite – it's the Bornean version of a *churro* chopped into bite-sized bits. Go for the *kawin chakoi* (*kawin* means marriage), which is flavoured with a scrumptious mix of butter and kaya. The Hua Ho Supermarket in Yayasan serves up some of the best *chakoi* in town – it's lightly fried and always made to order. A generous helping costs a wallet-busting B$1.

If you are invited to a Bruneian home, you'll probably be served *bualulu* with your tea. This simple dessert is made from eggs, flour and sugar. *Kuripit sagu*, a biscuit-like version of *buahulu* is jazzed up with mild coconut flavours.

Wash it all down with *cendol* (pronounced like 'chendol'), a murky coconut beverage with floating bits of green and brown (kinda like boba tea, although not as sweet). The taste is indefinable (you'll agree with us when you try it), but it's surprisingly refreshing after a long day of sightseeing. Ask around for *cendol Temburong* – a special provincial brew available only around Ramadan.

Tell the driver where you are headed – if it's on the route to the central bus station then he'll let you off. Taxis will charge around B$20 for trips between the airport and city centre (the price goes up by at least B$5 after 6pm); taxis are unmetered, so agree on the price before getting in. For a cheaper alternative, many hotels offer free or inexpensive pick-up service from the airport, so enquire when you book.

Bus

The government bus network covers most sights in and around the city, and the international ferry terminal at Muara. Routes for local buses are displayed at the bus station, beneath the multistorey car park on Jln Cator, and numbers are displayed on each bus. Apart from the 40-minute Muara express service

(B$2), all fares are B$1. Buses to the Gadong area run every 15 minutes; other routes are less frequent (there's usually one bus per hour to Muara terminal). Public transport operates daily between 6.30am and 6pm.

Some useful routes:

Airport Buses 23, 24, 36, and 38.

Brunei Museum and Malay Technology Museum Bus 39.

Gadong Buses 1, 22 and 55.

Jame'Asr Hassanal Bolkiah Mosque Buses 1 and 22.

Jerudong Park Playground Buses 55 and 57.

Muara Buses 37, 38 and 39.

Car & Taxi

Hiring a car is a good way to explore Brunei, and there's definitely some gratification in saying you did a cross-country road trip (in under two hours!). Prices start at around B$130 per day. Rental agencies can arrange pick-ups/drop-offs at your hotel. Drivers can be arranged for an additional fee. See p594 for additional information about renting a car.

If you're staying within the city centre, taxis are a fine option. Negotiate the price before setting off. Trips around town cost around B$10; it's about B$35 to the Muara ferry terminal. Rates can climb by 50% after 6pm.

AROUND BANDAR SERI BEGAWAN

The sights strewn beyond the capital make a strong case for spending more than a day in Brunei.

JERUDONG

Jerudong's two white elephants – the Empire Hotel and the Jerudong Park Playground – should rank high on your to-do list if you want to uncover the real Brunei.

Jerudong Park Playground

Perhaps the biggest birthday gift ever, **Jerudong Park Playground** (☎ 261-1894; Jerudong; admission & unlimited rides B$15, or admission B$1 & individual rides B$3; ◷ 5pm-midnight Wed-Fri & Sun, 5pm-2am Sat) is a sprawling amusement park that was once a private playground for the royal family. Divided into two sections, one for teens and adults, and one for the youngsters, it's now in a semidormant state – most of the rides have been sold to other amusements and those that remain are 'closed for maintenance'. This gives the park a rather bizarre air – a mix of locals and tourists meander around slightly aimlessly, looking at the defunct attractions with a mixture of awe and bewilderment, like inhabitants of the *Planet of the Apes* discovering a postapocalyptic Manhattan.

A DJ'S SPIN ON BRUNEI: JENNY MALAI ALI

Jenny Malai Ali, a well-known radio personality, gives us her spin on what makes Brunei really tick. Born in Brunei to a British mother and Bruneian father, Jenny has lived all over the world, returning to Brunei several years ago to settle down and start a family. We stopped by the radio station for a chat – here's what she had to say:

'Hm…where to begin!? Well, I love Brunei and I think it's quite an appealing place for a visitor, even if they don't have oodles of time to explore. Obviously we're a small country, so there aren't a million things to see, but we have all of the creature comforts one would want, not to mention genuine Bruneian hospitality.

It's funny, though, as much as I love it here, Brunei really is a land of strange contradictions. We are all so proud to be Bruneian, but we readily embrace the country's imminent globalisation. Everyone adds a faux French prefix like Le or D' to their establishment's name, and the hippest restaurants serve American or Japanese food – sushi is so 'in' right now. We're really into food here, namely because alcohol is prohibited…

Right now we are entering an MTV generation – we love acronyms and catchy bumper stickers. Teenagers dress to be noticed and everyone buys cars they can't afford. Actually, there are a lot of people living an alternative lifestyle – quite a few lesbians and transgender individuals – but I think that's more a function of living in a sexually repressed society. It's hard sometimes, you can't even hold hands with your partner.

Bruneians are obsessed with the internet – chatting, Facebook-ing etc – but blogging has really taken our country by storm. Bloggers are our local heroes. If you're interested, I'd check out: www.ranoadidas.com, he's an adopted member of the royal family. And the writer of www.anakbrunei.blogspot.com is a former government employee – he's quite patriotic.

Ultimately, we desperately want to be a modern Islamic nation, but for some reason we haven't quite pulled it off. We have a beautiful country – a scenic shoreline and an untouched rainforest – but every time we build something, like Jerudong for example, it doesn't quite work out! Dubai's pulled it off – I don't know why we aren't there yet…but we'll get there…

Jenny Malai Ali is well-known TV presenter and radio personality. She lives in Bandar Seri Begawan with her husband and son.

BRUNEI

SMS: SIX MUST-SEES

After our interview with radio celeb Jenny Malai Ali (boxed text, p585), she quickly turned the tables, pointing the microphone in our direction for a pop quiz about life on the road. As we chatted about our impressions of Brunei, Jenny encouraged her listeners to send in ideas for our guidebook via SMS. Who better than a smattering of locals to give excellent insider travel tips, right? Well, we received over 50 text messages during our 30-minute interview; these were our six favourites:

■ Go rafting from Taman Negera to Batang Duri in Temburong

■ Take a boat safari through Kampong Ayer, then down Sungai Brunei to see the monkeys and palace

■ Pusat Belia is the cheapest place to sleep in the whole country

■ The best time to visit is during Hari Raya – don't forget to stop by the Istana Nurul Iman!

■ Spend the night at a homestay in Kampong Ayer

■ Visit Serasa Spit and Pulau Pilongpilongan at the easternmost tip of Brunei

---

When the big rides aren't working, admission is discounted to B$5. Sleeveless blouses or shirts are not allowed and proper footwear is required. On Saturdays the park is open until 2am, and there are food and drink stalls in the car park.

It's rumoured that the park will be reopening many of the rides in the near future and revitalising the grounds. We're not holding our breath...

Empire Hotel

Imagine a zillion-tonne hunk of Italian marble dipped in gold and tossed into the rainforest – you've just pictured the fanciful **our pick** **Empire Hotel & Country Club** (☎ 241 8888; www.theempirehotel.com; Muara-Tutong Hwy, Kampung Jerudong; r incl breakfast from B$250; ❄ ☐ ☒). Built on the same scale as a Las Vegas casino, the resort was commissioned by Prince Jefri (see the boxed text, opposite) as – get this – lodging for guests of the royal family. Construction costs were estimated at a whopping US$1.1 billion, an astronomical sum considering the Petronas Towers in KL cost US$1.9 billion to build! The property was quickly transformed into an upscale resort in order to recover some of the construction costs (they still have a *long* way to go). Among the resort's spoils are two camel-shaped lamps made from pure Baccarat crystal, topped with solid gold accoutrements. They cost over US$500,000 each, and one of them lives in the Emperor Suite (B$22,000 per night), home to the world's most opulent indoor swimming pool. Rooms for more conservative wallets have hand-woven carpets, gold-plated power points, and enormous bathrooms with marble floors.

Getting There & Away

It's easy to get to the playground on buses 55 or 57 from the bus station, but the last bus leaves at 5.30pm and getting back to town can be a problem. Major hotels have shuttle services for about B$20 per person. A taxi back to BSB will cost about B$35. Taxis can be organised at a moment's notice from reception at the Empire Hotel.

MUARA

While technically located within the same district as Bandar Seri Begawan (officially called the Brunei-Muara District), rural Muara feels like a different world.

Beaches

Not many people come to Brunei for a sun 'n' sand experience, but if you do have some spare time to stretch out on the dunes, there are a couple of options around the small port of Muara.

Two kilometres from town, **Pantai Muara** (Muara Beach) is a popular weekend retreat. The white sand is clean, but like many beaches in Borneo, it's littered with driftwood and other flotsam that comes in with the tide. It's quiet during the week and has food stalls, picnic tables and a children's playground.

Other beaches include **Pantai Serasa**, a thin bit of beach on an equally thin spit of land jutting out into the sea. The Royal Brunei Yacht Club is here, as well as a water-sports centre and lots of food stalls on the weekend. About 4km west of Muara along the Muara-Tutong highway, **Pantai Meragang** (Crocodile Beach) is another beach that's pleasant and not quite as crowded as the others on weekends. There are a couple of food stalls and it's a good place for a picnic, but it's difficult to get to without your own transport.

Pulau Selirong

Known as 'Mosquito Island', this small island (25 sq km) off Brunei Bay, about one hour by boat from Muara, is on the itinerary of some tour companies for day trips – see p581 for operator listings. The island is a good example of mangrove ecology, with 2km of wooden walkways and an observation tower. A guide is necessary and caution is advised because of venomous snakes. A permit from the Forestry Department must be obtained in advance (which can be arranged by a travel agency within one working day).

Getting There & Away

Buses 37, 38 or 39 go from BSB to Muara town (B$2); bus 33 will take you from there to Pantai Muara or Pantai Serasa (B$1).

TUTONG & BELAIT DISTRICTS

The Tutong and Belait districts form the bulk of the big western section of Brunei. Most travellers merely pass through the region en route between Miri (Sarawak) and BSB, but there are a few mildly diverting attractions for those who have several days to spend in the country. Buses ply the coastal highway, but if you want to see the sights, the best way is to take a tour or rent a car.

TUTONG
pop 19,150

About halfway between Seria and BSB, Tutong is the main town in central Brunei. The town itself is unremarkable, but the area is famous in Brunei for two things: white sand and pitcher plants. Tutong has six species of pitcher plants and the locals cook a variety of dishes in their insect-catching sacs. The local sand (seen in patches along the side of the highway) is so white that Bruneians will often take pictures with it while pretending that it's snow. There's a great beach a couple of kilometres outside Tutong town near Pantai Seri Kenangan, often simply referred to as **Pantai Tutong**. Set on a spit of land, with the ocean on one side and the Sungai Tutong on the other,

---

LAND OF THE WHITE ELEPHANTS...

...sounds so romantic, but we're not talking about pale pachyderms.

Any of Brunei's buildings mentioned in the same breath as Prince Jefri tend to come with a sigh and a seven-digit price tag. The ultimate bored little rich boy, Jefri's appointment as finance minister was like putting a kid in charge of all the candy in the candy store, and his financial flights of fancy were truly epic. His acquisitions through the Amedeo Development Corporation included five luxury hotels overseas, not least the Beverly Hills Hotel in Los Angeles, and by the time the sultan cut him off, the prince had spent almost US$4 billion on himself, with personal possessions including 2000 cars, nine private jets, multiple lavish residences (including an apartment at the opulent Place Vendôme in Paris) and some much-discussed gold-plated toilet brushes.

Prince Jefri left Brunei for London on a 'limited' US$500,000-a-year allowance in 2004, barely enough to support his five wives and 35 children, but continued to enjoy an outlandish lifestyle, prompting the sultan and the Brunei Investment Agency (BIA) to pursue him again through the courts for an estimated US$16 billion in missing funds. In early 2006 things got even more confusing: the British press reported that the sultan ended the veritable battle royale, and had unexpectedly agreed to drop the charges. Attempts have been made to mend the serious dent in the sultan's bank account – most of the rides at Jerudong were sold to other amusement parks and Jefri's ultimate beachside guest house was turned into a hotel (the Empire Hotel no less!), but there are dozens upon dozens of buildings around Brunei that sit empty and unkempt as they are slowly reclaimed by the unrelenting jungle.

BRUNEI

the casuarina-lined beach is arguably the best in Brunei. The royal family clearly agrees, as they have a surprisingly modest palace here for discreet getaways. Us plebeians, sadly, have to make do with picnic tables, a simple restaurant and food hawkers at weekends. The turn-off to the beach is near the Tamu Tutong, where a **market** is held every morning.

TASEK MERIMBUN

The 7800-hectare **Merimbun Heritage Park** is 27km inland from Tutong, gazetted as an ASEAN Heritage Park to protect Tasek Merimbun, Brunei's largest lake. The blackwater habitat is unique in Borneo, dyed a distinctive tea colour by tannin from leaves falling in the water, and supports a wide variety of birds, mammals and snakes. It's a pretty, tranquil spot surrounded by forest and rarely troubled by large groups. It is possible to pitch a tent along the lake, as there are bathroom facilities, but make sure you ask the local chief if you can stay on his land first. He'll say yes, but it's good manners to double check. A wander around the lake will set you back a whopping B$1.

The only way to get there on your own is by car or as part of a tour from BSB (see p581). If you drive, note that the road gets pretty rough between Lammuni and the lake; drive through the *kampung* and stick to the main road.

JALAN LABI

As you enter the Belait district, east of Seria, a road branches inland to Labi, taking you past some prime forest areas. This *jalan* is the easiest way into the interior of Brunei and it offers the chance to see some Iban longhouses, most of which come complete with car parks and mod-cons (see the boxed text, p430 for details about the longhouse lifestyle). Nothing on this road is a must see, but if you've got a few extra days in Brunei, it makes for a good day away from BSB.

The **Forestry Museum** (admission free; 8am-12.15pm & 1.30-4.30pm Mon-Thu & Sat) is located down the Simpang 50 turn-off. It's a simple place that makes for a good leg-stretch on the way to Kuala Belait or into the interior further down Jln Labi. There are cleared walking trails through primary forest and a small museum detailing the history of logging and conservation in the region. The collection of insects is a sneak preview of what's to come on a trip down to Labi.

More than 50km south of the coastal road, the *kampung* of **Labi** is a small Iban settlement with a few fruit orchards. Note that there is a fork in the road just before Labi (as you head south, away from the main coastal road). Take the left fork to reach Labi and Teraja; don't take the right fork, which is marked Jln Labi Lama (Old Labi Rd). Several 'drive-up' longhouses are located beyond Labi.

From the end of Jln Labi, one can make a day hike all the way to Gunung Mulu National Park (p452). A guide and proper border-crossing paperwork are required – ask a tour operator (p581) in BSB for more information.

If you are trying to access Jln Labi without a vehicle, take a bus from BSB towards to Sarawak border and ask the bus driver to let you off at 'Junction to Labi'. After getting off, grab a coffee at the pistachio-coloured building on the side of the road and ask around for a ride into the interior (don't pay more than B$10).

SERIA
pop 30,097

Seria, a company town spread out along the coast between Tutong and Kuala Belait, is a transit stop on the road to Sarawak. This is where Shell Brunei has its major installations, and the low bungalows accommodate company staff and the Gurkha troops brought in to protect their work.

The coastal plain between here and Kuala Belait is the main centre for oil production in Brunei, and at a beach just outside town the curvy **Billionth Barrel Monument** commemorates (you guessed it) the billionth barrel of oil produced at the Seria field. From the beach, oil rigs are visible, jutting up on the horizon.

If that's just not enough hydrocarbons for you, the flashy new **Oil & Gas Discovery Centre** (☎ 337 7200; www.shell.com.bn/ogdc; off Jln Tengah; adult/child/teenager B$5/1/2; ☻ 9am-5pm Tue-Thu, 10am-noon & 2-6pm Fri, 10am-6pm Sat & Sun) aims to put an 'edutainment' spin on the industry, appealing particularly to young science buffs. The complex includes an exhibition hall, a gallery, a theatre, an education centre and even a playground with a skate park to keep any disaffected youths happy. The Discovery Centre is opposite the town centre, on the foreshore. You could walk to it from the bus station, but it will be a hot 500m indeed. It's clearly signposted.

The only place to stay in Seria is the passable **Hotel Koperasi** (☎ 322 7589; Jln Sharif Ali Seria; s/d B$55/65; ✖) about 150m from the bus station.

About 10 buses a day run between Seria and BSB (B$6, two hours). There are regular local buses between Seria and Kuala Belait (B$1, every 30 minutes between 6.30am and 7.30pm), where you can catch buses onward to Miri and Kuching. Brunei transport are now running buses to Tutong and Belait from the main bus station, no longer from Tamu Kianggeh. Private vehicles should note that there is a toll (B$3) located 18km before the Malaysian border.

KUALA BELAIT
pop 31,178

The last stop before Sarawak, Kuala Belait is the main town in Belait district and the place to get buses to Miri. 'KB' has colonial shophouses in the town centre, the **Silver Jubilee Park** (Jln Maulana) and a reasonable beach, though most travellers just hustle through on their way to or from Sarawak. The HSBC bank has an ATM, diagonally opposite the bus station on Jln McKerron.

If you're looking for a bite, take a stroll down **Jalan Pretty**, where you'll find a variety of simple restaurants and Chinese *kopitiam*. Spend the night at the well-run **Hotel Sentosa** (☎ 333 4341; www.bruneisentosahotel.com; 92-93 Jln McKerron; r B$85-95; ✖ ▢), conveniently situated near the bus station.

TEMBURONG DISTRICT

While Malaysia has plundered its cache of lush jungle to keep its economy afloat, Brunei has surfed the waves of 'black gold', leaving its rainforest untouched. Temburong, the smaller of Brunei's puzzle-piece land claims, is plunged deep into the heart of neighbouring Sarawak like an emerald dagger.

For information on getting to/from Temburong, see right of the Bangar section.

BANGAR
pop 3500

The 'capital' of Temburong, quiet Bangar is but a three-street town on the banks of Sungai Temburong. The speedboat trip to reach Bangar is a highlight in itself, roaring down Sungai Brunei and slapping through the open sea of Brunei Bay, then tilting and weaving through dense mangroves into the mouth of Sungai Temburong. Bangar can be visited as a day trip if you catch an early boat, but you'll get more out of it if you stay over and explore the area more thoroughly.

At the time of research, there were plans to reopen the tourism office – hopefully renovations will be well under way by the time you read this. Escape the balmy air at **Restoran Hijrah** (☎ 522 1522; Kedai 8; dishes B$2.50-12; ☽ breakfast, lunch & dinner), a *kedai kopi* (coffee shop) up the road from the boat wharf. The menu offers a good mix of Chinese and Malay flavours, including the region's famous *udang gallah* (river prawns) and steamboat meals (B$12 to B$16, minimum two people).

Spend the evening at **Bangar Guest House** (Jln Batang Duri; r B$20; ✖), a great find located several kilometres from the pier. Rooms are immaculate and there's always service with a smile.

Boats to Bangar (B$6, 45 minutes, about one per hour from 7am to early afternoon) operate from the jetty just east of the riverfront satay stalls, along Jln Residency. The last boat back to BSB leaves Bangar at 4pm.

Temburong has two main roads; both are sealed but traffic is light. One leads south to Batang Duri and the other runs between the east and west borders with Sarawak. Private and unofficial taxis are the only form of transport in the district, and drivers congregate near the wharf. They don't have meters, and prices must be negotiated.

BATANG DURI

The **Sumbiling Eco Village** (www.sumbiling.blogspot .com) is a new ecofriendly project in the Batang Duri area. Borneo Guide (p581) runs this rustic camp in cooperation with the local Iban.

PERADAYAN FOREST RESERVE

Fifteen kilometres southeast of Bangar and protected within the **Peradayan Forest Reserve** (admission free) are the peaks of **Bukit Patoi** (310m) and **Bukit Peradayan** (410m), which can be reached along walking tracks (bring your own water and trail food). For those who can't be bothered with the trouble or the expense of Ulu Temburong National Park (p590), this is a fine and easy alternative.

The 330m trail up to the top of Bukit Patoi is a steep and sweaty climb that starts at the

---

PRACTICALITIES

- The *Borneo Bulletin* is Brunei's English-language daily newspaper.

- English radio broadcasts can be heard on the FM bands Pilihan Network and Pelangi Network.

- State television channel RTB can be received on Channel 5.

- Electricity in Brunei is 220V to 240V, 50 cycles, with UK-type three-square-pin plugs

- Brunei uses the metric system.

---

entrance to the park. It's very much worth the trek as the scenery is breathtaking. Keep an eye out for hornbills, even if you can't spot one, you will likely hear their distinctive calls. Every year, the Bukit Patoi Challenge tests the endurance of willing participants with a 15km dash through the jungle.

Most walkers descend back along the same trail, but it's possible to continue over the other side of the summit and around to Bukit Peradayan. The trail eventually rejoins the road some 12km from Bangar near the Labu Km 5 marker. Allow at least three hours for the walk from Bukit Patoi to Bukit Peradayan and back to the road. This trail is harder and indistinct in parts.

A private car (the only means of getting there) will cost about B$10 each way. Hitchhiking is also an option. The road to the Peradayan Forest Reserve – and Lawas (Sarawak) – is across the bridge from Bangar wharf, on the east side of the river.

ULU TEMBURONG NATIONAL PARK

Beautiful Ulu Temburong National Park is tucked inside the larger Batu Apoi Forest Reserve, a wild expanse of primary rainforest that covers most of southern Temburong. In the last few years, this stunning realm of green has become the most promoted attraction in the wee sultanate. Tourists and locals have been flocking here ever since.

The main feature at the park is the 60m canopy walkway, which is reached by a 1200-step climb up a shiny brass tower. The apparatus itself looks like a carpenter's scaffolding, but the views from the walkway are breathtaking (if you can get over the vertigo, as the tower wobbles in the wind).

The only accommodation in the park is the **Ulu Ulu Resort** (www.uluuluresort.com), managed by Sunshine Borneo Tours (p581). Accommodation prices start at B$248 and include transport and guided treks. Rooms vary in quality – we liked the private doubles the most.

The park is not accessible by independent travellers, as longboat hire is necessary. The vessels along the river service tour groups – and even if you convinced a boatswain to take you, it would cost almost B$200. Tour packages are available with several companies, and start at around B$180 for a day trip.

DIRECTORY

ACCOMMODATION

There are about 2800 rooms in Brunei spread across 35 establishments. Accommodation in Brunei is significantly more expensive than in neighbouring Malaysia. Budget places are under B$60, midrange is B$60 to B$200, and top end is over B$200. Most prices quoted are net, inclusive of 10% service charge. If you are unsure if your room rate is all-inclusive, simply ask if the amount is 'plus-plus' – a 'yes' means that the service charge has *not* been included. See p581 for more information about sleeping in the sultanate.

BUSINESS HOURS

Government offices are open from 7.45am to 12.15pm and 1.30pm to 4.30pm (closed on Friday and Sunday); non-government offices are generally open from 8am to 5pm Monday to Friday and from 8am to noon on Saturday. Most shops in the central area of Bandar Seri Begawan open daily around 10am and are closed by 6pm. Shops and shopping malls generally open around 9am or 10am and close around 9.30pm (some may close earlier on Sunday). Hours are usually shorter during the fasting month of Ramadan. Eateries generally serve breakfast from 7am to 11am, lunch from noon to 2.30pm, and dinner from 6pm to 11pm. For post-office opening hours, see p592. For bank opening hours, see opposite.

CLIMATE

Like the rest of Borneo, Brunei experiences high average temperatures, humidity and rainfall. Temperatures consistently fall

BRUNEI

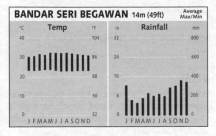

BANDAR SERI BEGAWAN 14m (49ft)

between 24°C and 31°C, with an average humidity of 79%. Average annual rainfall is about 3295mm. Although Brunei doesn't really have marked wet and dry seasons, the wettest months are from September to January, during the northeast monsoon, and the driest period is February to April.

CUSTOMS REGULATIONS

Duty-free allowances for persons over 17 years of age are 200 cigarettes or 250g of tobacco, 60ml of perfume and 250ml of eau de toilette. Non-Muslims may import two bottles of liquor and 12 cans of beer, which must be declared upon arrival.

The importation of drugs carries the death penalty.

EMBASSIES & CONSULATES

Countries with diplomatic representation in Bandar Seri Begawan:

Australia High Commission (Map p576; ☎ 222 9435; www.bruneidarussalam.embassy.gov.au; Jln Pemancha)

Canada High Commission (Map p576; ☎ 222 0043; www.dfait-maeci.gc.ca/Brunei; Bldg 1 Jln McArthur)

France (Map p576; ☎ 222 0960; www.ambafrance-bn.org; Unit 301-305 51-55 Kompleks Jalan Sultan, Jln Sultan)

Germany (Map p576; ☎ 222 5547; www.bandar-seri-begawan.diplo.de; 2nd fl, Unit 2.01, Block D, Yayasan Complex)

Indonesia (Off Map p576; ☎ 233 0180; www.indonesia.org.bn; 4498 Simpang 528, Jln Muara, Kampung Sungai Hanching Baru)

Malaysia High Commission (Off Map p576; ☎ 238 1095; mmalbrnei@kln.gov.my; 61 Simpang 396, Jln Kebangsaan, Kampung Sungai Akar)

Singapore High Commission (Off Map p576; ☎ 226 2741; www.mfa.gov.sg/brunei; 8 Simpang 74, Jln Subok)

UK High Commission (Map p576; ☎ 222 2231; http://ukinbruni.fco.gov.uk/en; 2nd fl, Block D, Yayasan Complex)

USA (Map p576; ☎ 222 0384; amembassy_bsb@state.gov; 3rd fl, Teck Guan Plaza, Jln Sultan)

HOLIDAYS

Brunei has many of the same holidays as Malaysia, based on the Islamic calendar but including Chinese New Year, Christmas Day and New Year's Day.

Brunei National Day 23 February; parades and processions in downtown BSB to celebrate Brunei's independence.

Hari Raya Aidiladha Variable February/March.

Muslim New Year (Hizrah) Variable.

Royal Brunei Armed Forces Day 31 May.

Prophet's Birthday Variable (in Malaysia and Brunei only).

Sultan of Brunei's Birthday 15 July; a lively event marked by fireworks, processions and yet more parades in downtown BSB and around Brunei. Festivities continue through the entire month of July.

Hari Raya Aidilfitri Variable around September/October; the sultan opens the palace to visitors.

LEGAL MATTERS

The sale of alcohol is illegal in Brunei, and drinking in public is strictly prohibited. For being caught in homosexual acts you can be jailed for up to 10 years and fined B$30,000.

MAPS

A tome of maps printed by Brunei Press, known simply as *Brunei Darussalam Street Directory*, is the best source for any of your road queries. Most hotels in central Bandar Seri Begawan have cartoon maps highlighting the city's main attractions.

MONEY

The official currency is the Brunei dollar (B$), available in denominations of $1, $5, $10, $50, $100, $500 and $1000. Singapore dollars can be used within Brunei (exchanged at an equal rate); however, Brunei dollars will usually not be accepted as legal tender in Singapore.

Banks are generally open from 9am to 4pm during the week, and from 9am to 11am on Saturdays. A couple of banks cater to late shoppers by staying open into the evening (especially in the Gadong area). On Fridays, banks close for midday prayer between 11am and 2.30pm.

There is no sales tax in Brunei. Some hotels add a 10% service charge, though this is mostly included in the published price. Tipping after a meal is not widely practiced in Brunei.

Major credit cards (Visa, MasterCard and American Express) are widely accepted.

BRUNEI

PHOTOGRAPHY

Bruneians are quite camera friendly, but it's always polite to ask before clicking – and don't be surprised if they ask to snap your picture as well! Note that photography is strictly prohibited inside mosques, museums and military installations.

Photo shops can be found in Bandar's major shopping centres, while digital cameras and memory cards can also be purchased in mobile phone stores. Photographs can be burned on to CDs at most internet cafes and computer shops. For parts and repairs, it is best to consult the Yellow Pages or stop by a photo shop.

POST

Post offices open from 8am to 4.30pm Monday to Thursday and on Saturday, and 8am to 11am and 2pm to 4pm on Friday.

TELEPHONE

To call Brunei from outside the country, the country code is ☎ 673; from Brunei, the international access code is ☎ 00. Within Brunei, there are no area codes.

Hello card (hallo kad), Netcard (netcad) and Payless are the most common phonecards and can be purchased from most retail stores in denominations of B$5, B$10, B$20 and B$50. These can be used in public booths to make international calls. Most hotels have IDD phones with reasonable local rates.

Prepaid SIM cards from DST and b.mobile, the two major mobile service providers, are available for purchase from authorised dealers in popular shopping areas.

Note that if you have a Malaysian SIM card, it will not work within Brunei unless you use a special dial-out access code. Access rates are astronomical.

TOURIST INFORMATION

At the time of research, Brunei did not have a tourism information centre; however, the government's tourism authority, known simply as **Brunei Tourism** (☎ 238-2822; www.tourismbrunei .com; Ministry of Industry & Primary Resources, Jln Menteri Besar) has a wonderful website with oodles of information on accommodation, sights, local festivals, transport, photographs and maps. Plans are under way to open a small visitors centre in central BSB at the customs wharf.

For additional information on Brunei, check out the following websites:

www.brudirect.com Up-to-date news and current affairs.

www.brunei.gov.bn Brunei's official government website.

VISAS

All visitors must have a valid passport or internationally recognised travel document valid for at least six months beyond the date of entry into Brunei.

Everything you need to know about entering Brunei can be found in the Brunei Border Crossings boxed text (opposite).

There are 49 nationalities that do not require a visa. Citizens of Malaysia, Singapore, the UK, Luxembourg, Ireland, Denmark, Austria, Belgium, Finland, the Netherlands, Germany, Sweden, Italy, France, Spain, Slovenia, Greece, Cyprus, Malta, the Czech Republic, Portugal, Hungary, Estonia, Slovakia, Lithuania, Poland, Latvia, South Korea, Norway, New Zealand, Iran, Oman, the UAE and Iceland do not require a visa for visits of 30 days or less. Citizens of Indonesia, Thailand, the Philippines, Canada, Japan, Switzerland, the Maldives, Vietnam, Laos, Myanmar, Cambodia, Peru and Ukraine get 14 days or less. US citizens get 90 days before having to renew their visa. Citizens from Australia, Bahrain and Kuwait entering by air can get a 30-day multi-entry visa on arrival for B$30; citizens of China and Qatar qualify for 14 days (also B$30). Israeli nationals are barred from entering Brunei.

WOMEN TRAVELLERS

As Brunei is a conservative Muslim society, dressing modestly is highly advised. Muslim women usually do not shake hands with men, thus a hand may not be extended to travellers of the opposite gender.

TRANSPORT

GETTING THERE & AWAY

To enter Brunei, many travellers will need to obtain a visa in advance; however, citizens of visa-restricted nations can get a 72-hour transit permit upon arrival at the international airport if they can supply proof of departure. For detailed information about border controls, please consult the Brunei Border Crossings box (opposite).

BRUNEI

BRUNEI BORDER CROSSINGS

Fancy a stopover in Brunei to check off another country on your list? Before you make the trip, check out www.mfa.gov.bn/visainformation/visaarrangements.htm or www.immigration.gov .bn/002/html/melawat.html for the most up-to-date information about visas (also listed on opposite). The sites list all countries whose citizens do not require visas or who can obtain them upon arrival. Automatic entry permits are awarded in increments of 14 or 30 days depending on your nationality (Americans score 90 days). Citizens of countries not on the list must apply for their visas in advance (Israeli citizens are barred from entering Brunei). Visitors who require a visa can get a 72-hour transit pass if they are arriving by air and their onward destination is different from their origin.

Brunei has five other entry points besides the airport: Sungai Tujuh (Miri-Brunei), Kuala Lurah (Brunei-Limbang), Puni (Limbang-Temburong), Labu (Temburong-Lawas), and Serasa Ferry Terminal. Crossings open at 6am and close around 10pm, but note that the Puni border closes for noon prayer on Friday, and traffic at Kuala Lurah has been known to cause three-hour delays, so plan accordingly.

The Serasa Ferry Terminal in Muara links passengers to Pulau Labuan (Sabah), Limbang (Sarawak) and Lawas (Sarawak). A car-ferry service is in the works and will provide service to Menumbok on mainland Sabah.

When travelling overland from Miri (Sarawak) to Kota Kinabalu (Sabah) you'll rack up a whopping 10 chops in your passport (make sure you have a couple of blank pages!):

- Exit Malaysia at Sungai Tujuh (Miri)
- Enter Brunei at Sungai Tujuh (Belait)
- Exit Brunei at Kuala Lurah
- Enter Malaysia at Kuala Lurah (Limbang, Sarawak)
- Exit Malaysia at Tedungan
- Enter Brunei at Puni
- Exit Brunei at Labu
- Enter Malaysia at Lawas
- Exit Sarawak
- Enter Sabah at Sindumin
- Continue on to Kota Kinabalu

In the last few years, regular bus service from Miri to Bandar and Bandar to Kota Kinabalu has made this adventure through the jungle of red tape a lot easier on the nerves. Note that if you are passing through with your own transport, the Puni (Brunei) crossing is at the side of the road. There are proper border control posts everywhere else now, except for the one in Lawas as you enter from Temburong, where, at the time of research, you still have to stop by the roadside (but this post should be open soon). When the bridge being built across the Trusan river in Lawas is complete there will be only one ferry crossing left.

Oh, and while travelling between Bandar and Temburong don't forget to carry your passport, as you'll technically be passing through Malaysian waters.

Air

Brunei International Airport (☎ 233 2531, flight enquiries 233 1747) is about 4km from the centre of Bandar Seri Begawan.

Royal Brunei Airlines (Map p576; ☎ 221- 2222; www.bruneiair.com; RBA Plaza, Jln Sultan) flies to 20 major cities scattered throughout Asia, Australia, the Middle East and Europe.

Stopover flights go to London and Frankfurt for connections throughout Europe and further afield.

Four other airlines offer services to regional destinations:

Malaysia Airlines (MAS; ☎ 222 4141; www.malaysia airlines.com; 144 Jln Pemancha)

Philippines Airlines (www.philippinesairlines.com; no office in Brunei)

Singapore Airlines (☎ 224-4901; www.singaporeair
.com; 1st fl, Wisma Raya Bldg, 49-50 Jln Sultan).
Thai Airways (☎ 224 2991; www.thaiair.com; 4th fl,
Kompleks Jln Sultan, 51-55 Jln Sultan)

Land

In the last few years, express buses have
started to link Brunei's capital, Bandar Seri
Begawan, with Miri (Sarawak, Malaysia) and
Kota Kinabalu (Sabah, Malaysia). Brunei
transport are now running buses to Tutong
and Belait from the main bus station, no
longer from Tamu Kianggeh. The bus to Kota
Kinabalu (with possible stops in Limbang and
Lawas) and the bus to Pontianak (with possible stops in Miri and Sibu, not Kuching) leave
from across the street from Tamu Kianggeh.
The bus to Kuching was not in operation at
the time of research, but it is in the pipeline.
The price for a one-way ticket to KK is B$45,
to Pontianak one way it's B$80. The same
rates apply if people want to stop along the
way (as they are supposed to be point to
point routes).

Boat service between Malaysian Borneo
and Brunei can be much more convenient
for those travelling overland between Sabah
and Sarawak – crossing through Brunei will
add ten stamps to your passport (and you're
likely to wait in line for each one!) See p593
for detailed border information, especially if
you are planning to use a private vehicle.

Car rentals are much more economical than
taxi service. See right for information about
rental-car operators (almost all are located in
BSB or at the airport).

Sea

Most boats to/from BSB operate from the
Muara Ferry Terminal, in Muara, about
25km northeast of the city (a B$2 bus ride
and a B$40 taxi ride to/from BSB). Arrive
45 minutes before your boat, just in case
there's a line at customs. There are regular
ferries between Muara and Pulau Labuan
in Sabah, (B$15, 1½ hours, six departures
between 7.30am and 4.40pm), Lawas and
Limbang. From Pulau Labuan, there are
two ferries a day onward to Kota Kinabalu,
Sabah. Passengers are charged B$1 departure
tax at the ferry terminal.

Another way to get to Limbang or Lawas in
Sarawak is to go via Pulau Labuan (see p403).

GETTING AROUND

Transport around Brunei is by bus, rental car
or taxi. The public bus system is easy and reliable, but only operates in and around Bandar
Seri Begawan between 6am and 6pm daily.
Taxis are a fine way of exploring central BSB.
At the time of research there was no cen-
tralised taxi service number, all taxis can be
found at the central bus station and in front
of the Sheraton Utama. Ask your hotel for a
contact if you need a cab – there are only 42
drivers in the country! For longer distances
it is more cost-effective to rent a vehicle or
take a bus. Boats to/from Bangar (B$6, 45
minutes, about one departure per hour from
BSB from 7am to 4.30pm) operate from the
jetty along Jln Residency. Boats generally
don't depart until they've got enough passengers to warrant the trip, so you'll probably
have to wait. Temburong has a limited road
network, and taxis are the only way to get
around independently.

Intra-Brunei buses connect BSB's central
bus terminal on Jln Cator to the towns of
Seria (B$6, two hours) and Kuala Belait ($7,
2½ hours). However, if you are making your
way between BSB and Sarawak, it is quicker to
take a direct bus to Miri. Seria and KB aren't
the most interesting destinations if you're on
a tight travel schedule…

Hiring a car is the most cost-effective way
of exploring Brunei. All-inclusive rentals start
at around B$130; surcharges may apply if the
car is taken into Sarawak. Petrol is cheap (fun
fact: there are only Shell stations in Brunei)
and the main roads are in good condition;
some back roads require a 4WD. An international driver's permit is required for driving
in Brunei, and remember, Bruneians drive on
the left side of the road.

If you will be driving your own vehicle,
note that the usage of mobile phones while
driving is strictly prohibited and punishable
by hefty fines. Cameras and radars monitor
phone usage, speed limits and buckled belts,
so even if you don't see a cop, you could still
find yourself with a hefty bill when returning
your rental.

Rental operators in BSB include the follow-
ing (all are located at the airport):
Avis (☎ 242 6345)
Budget-U-Drive (☎ 234 5573)
Hertz (☎ 245 2244)

Health Dr Trish Batchelor

CONTENTS

Health issues and the quality of medical facilities vary depending on where and how you travel in the region. The major cities are now well developed, but travel to rural areas can expose you to a variety of health risks and inadequate medical care. Travellers tend to worry about contracting infectious diseases when in the tropics, but infections rarely cause serious illness or death in travellers. Pre-existing medical conditions, such as heart disease, and accidental injury (especially traffic accidents) account for most life-threatening situations. Becoming ill in some way, however, is relatively common. Fortunately most common illnesses can either be prevented with some common-sense behaviour or be treated easily with a well-stocked traveller's medical kit.

The following advice is a general guide only and does not replace the advice of a doctor trained in travel medicine.

BEFORE YOU GO

Pack medications in their original, clearly labelled containers. A signed and dated letter from your physician describing your medical conditions and medications, plus generic names, is also a good idea. If carrying syringes or needles, be sure to have a physician's letter documenting their medical necessity. If you have a heart condition, bring a copy of your ECG taken just prior to travelling.

If you take any regular medication, bring double your needs in case of loss or theft, and carry these extra supplies separately. You should be able to buy some medications over the counter in Malaysia without a doctor's prescription, but it can be difficult to find some of the newer drugs, particularly the latest antidepressants, blood pressure medications and contraceptive pills.

INSURANCE

Even if you are fit and healthy, don't travel without health insurance – accidents do happen. Declare any existing medical conditions you have – the insurance company will check if your problem is pre-existing and will not cover you if it is undeclared. You may require extra cover for adventure activities such as rock climbing. If your health insurance doesn't cover you for medical expenses abroad, consider getting extra insurance. If you're uninsured, emergency evacuation is expensive; bills of over US$100,000 are not uncommon. Find out in advance if your insurance plan will make payments directly to providers or reimburse you later for overseas health expenses. (Doctors may expect payment in cash.)

RECOMMENDED VACCINATIONS

Specialised travel-medicine clinics are your best source of information; they stock all available vaccines and will be able to make specific recommendations for you and your trip. The doctors will take into account factors such as past vaccination history, the length of your trip, activities you may be undertaking and underlying medical conditions.

Most vaccines don't produce immunity until at least two weeks after they're given, so visit a doctor four to eight weeks before departure. Ask your doctor for an International Certificate of Vaccination (otherwise known

REQUIRED & RECOMMENDED VACCINATIONS

The World Health Organization recommends the following vaccinations for travellers to Malaysia, Singapore and Brunei:

Adult diphtheria and tetanus Single booster recommended if none in the previous 10 years. Side effects include a sore arm and fever.

Hepatitis A Provides almost 100% protection for up to a year; a booster after 12 months provides at least another 20 years' protection. Mild side effects such as headache and sore arm occur in 5% to 10% of people.

Hepatitis B Now considered routine for most travellers. Given as three shots over six months. A rapid schedule is also available, as is a combined vaccination with hepatitis A. Side effects are mild and uncommon, usually headache and sore arm. In 95% of people, lifetime protection results.

Measles, mumps and rubella (MMR) Two doses of MMR are required unless you have had the diseases. Occasionally some people develop a rash and flu-like illness a week after receiving the vaccine. Many young adults require a booster.

Polio There have been no recently reported cases of polio in the region. Only one booster is required as an adult for lifetime protection. The inactivated polio vaccine (IPV) is safe during pregnancy.

Typhoid Recommended unless your trip is less than a week and only to developed cities. The vaccine offers around 70% protection, lasts for two to three years and comes as a single shot. Tablets are also available; however, the injection is usually recommended as it has fewer side effects. Sore arm and fever may occur.

Varicella If you haven't had chickenpox, discuss the vaccination with your doctor.

These immunisations are recommended for longer-term travellers (more than one month) or those at special risk:

Japanese B encephalitis Three injections in all. Booster recommended after two years. Sore arm and headache are the most common side effects. Rarely, an allergic reaction comprising hives and swelling can occur up to 10 days after any of the three doses.

Meningitis Single injection. There are two types of vaccination. The quadravalent vaccine gives two to three years' protection. Meningitis group C vaccine gives around 10 years' protection. Recommended for long-term backpackers aged younger than 25.

Rabies Three injections in all. A booster after one year will then provide 10 years' protection. Side effects are rare; a headache or a sore arm.

Tuberculosis (TB) A complex issue. Adult long-term travellers are usually recommended to have a TB skin test before and after travel, rather than vaccination. Children may be recommended to have the vaccination; only one is necessary in a lifetime.

as the yellow booklet), which will list all the vaccinations you've received.

Proof of vaccination against yellow fever will be required only if you have visited a country in the yellow fever zone (parts of Africa and South America) within six days prior to entering Southeast Asia. If you're coming from Africa or South America, check to see if you require proof of vaccination.

MEDICAL CHECKLIST

Recommended items for a personal medical kit:

- For diarrhoea consider an oral rehydration solution (eg Gastrolyte), diarrhoea 'stopper' (eg Loperamide) and anti-nausea medication (eg Prochlorperazine)
- Antibiotics for diarrhoea – Norfloxacin or Ciprofloxacin or Azithromycin for bacterial diarrhoea; Tinidazole for giardiasis or amoebic dysentery
- Laxative, eg Coloxyl
- Antispasmodic for stomach cramps, eg Buscopan
- Indigestion tablets, eg Quick-Eze, Mylanta
- Throat lozenges
- Antihistamine – there are many options, eg Cetrizine for daytime and Promethazine for night
- Decongestant, eg pseudoephedrine
- Paracetamol
- Ibuprofen or another anti-inflammatory
- Your personal medicine if you are a migraine sufferer
- Sunscreen and hat

- Antiseptic, eg Betadine
- Antibacterial cream, eg Muciprocin
- Steroid cream for allergic/itchy rashes, eg 1% to 2% hydrocortisone
- Antifungal cream, eg Clotrimazole
- For skin infections, antibiotics such as Amoxicillin/Clavulanate or Cephalexin
- Contraceptive method
- Thrush (vaginal yeast infection) treatment, eg Clotrimazole pessaries or Diflucan tablet
- Ural, or equivalent, if prone to urinary-tract infections
- DEET-based insect repellent
- Mosquito net impregnated with a substance like permethrin
- Permethrin to impregnate clothing
- Iodine tablets (unless you are pregnant or have a thyroid problem) to purify water
- Basic first-aid items such as scissors, sticking plasters, bandages, gauze, thermometer (but not mercury), sterile needles and syringes, safety pins, tweezers.

INTERNET RESOURCES

There's a wealth of travel-health advice on the internet. For further information:

Centres for Disease Control and Prevention (CDC; www.cdc.gov) Has good general information.

MD Travel Health (www.mdtravelhealth.com) Provides complete travel health recommendations for every country and is updated daily.

World Health Organization (www.who.int/ith) Publishes a superb book called *International Travel and Health*, which is revised annually and is available online at no cost.

FURTHER READING

Lonely Planet's pocket-sized *Healthy Travel Asia & India* is packed with useful information including pretrip planning, emergency first aid, immunisation and disease

information and what to do if you get sick on the road. *Travel with Children* from Lonely Planet includes advice on travel health for young children.

Other recommended references include *Traveller's Health* by Dr Richard Dawood (Oxford University Press), and *Travelling Well* by Dr Deborah Mills, available at www.travellin gwell.com.au.

IN TRANSIT

DEEP VEIN THROMBOSIS (DVT)

Blood clots forming in the legs during plane flights, chiefly because of prolonged immobility, is known as deep vein thrombosis (DVT). The longer the flight, the greater the risk of DVT occurring. Even though most blood clots are reabsorbed uneventfully, some may break off and make their way through the blood vessels to the lungs, where they may cause life-threatening complications.

The chief symptom of DVT is swelling or pain of the foot, ankle or calf, usually but not always on just one side.

When a blood clot travels to the lungs, the clot may cause chest pain and difficulty breathing. Travellers with any of these symptoms should immediately seek medical attention.

To prevent the development of DVT on long flights you should walk around the cabin, perform isometric compressions of the leg muscles (ie contract the leg muscles while sitting), drink plenty of fluids, and avoid alcohol and tobacco.

JET LAG & MOTION SICKNESS

Jet lag is common when crossing more than five time zones; it results in insomnia, fatigue, malaise or nausea. To avoid jet lag try drinking plenty of fluids (nonalcoholic) and eating light meals. Upon arrival, seek exposure to natural sunlight and readjust your schedule (for meals, sleep etc) as soon as possible.

Antihistamines such as dimenhydrinate (Dramamine) and meclizine (Antivert, Bonine) are usually the first choice for treating motion sickness. Their main side effect is drowsiness. A herbal alternative is ginger, which works like a charm for some people.

HEALTH

IN MALAYSIA, SINGAPORE & BRUNEI

AVAILABILITY & COST OF HEALTH CARE

In Malaysia the standard of medical care in the major centres is good, and most problems can be adequately dealt with in Kuala Lumpur.

Singapore has excellent medical facilities and acts as the referral centre for most of Southeast Asia. You cannot buy medication over the counter without a doctor's prescription in Singapore.

In Brunei, general care is reasonable. There is no local medical university, so expats and foreign-trained locals run the health care system. Serious or complex cases are better managed in Singapore, but adequate primary health care and stabilisation are available.

Clinics catering specifically to travellers and expatriates are usually more expensive than local medical facilities, but they offer a superior standard of care to the traveller and are aware of the best local hospitals and specialists. These clinics can also liaise with insurance companies should you require an evacuation.

Recommended clinics are listed under Information in the capital city sections in this book. Your embassy and insurance company are also good contacts.

It can be difficult to find reliable medical care in rural areas.

Self-treatment may be appropriate if your problem is minor (eg traveller's diarrhoea), you are carrying the appropriate medication and you cannot attend a recommended clinic. If you think you may have a serious disease, especially malaria, don't waste time. Travel to the nearest quality facility to receive attention. It's always better to be assessed by a doctor than to rely on self-treatment.

INFECTIOUS DISEASES
Cutaneous Larva Migrans

Found in Malaysia and Brunei, and caused by the dog hookworm, the rash symptomatic of cutaneous larva migrans starts as a small lump, then slowly spreads in a linear fashion. It's intensely itchy, especially at night, but is easily treated with medications; it should not be cut out or frozen.

Dengue Fever

This mosquito-borne disease is becoming increasingly problematic throughout Asia, including Malaysia, Singapore and Brunei, especially in the cities. As there's no vaccine available, it can only be prevented by avoiding mosquito bites. The mosquito that carries dengue bites both day and night, so use insect avoidance measures at all times. Symptoms include high fever, severe headache and body ache (dengue was previously known as 'breakbone fever'). Some people develop a rash and experience diarrhoea. The southern islands of Thailand are particularly high-risk. There's no specific treatment, just rest and paracetamol – don't take aspirin as it increases the likelihood of haemorrhaging. See a doctor to be diagnosed and monitored.

Filariasis

Occurring in Malaysia and Brunei, filariasis is a mosquito-borne disease, very common in local populations, yet very rare in travellers. Mosquito-avoidance measures are the best way to prevent this disease.

Hepatitis A

This food- and water-borne virus infects the liver, causing jaundice (yellow skin and eyes), nausea and lethargy. There's no specific treatment for hepatitis A, you just need to allow time for the liver to heal. All travellers to Malaysia, Singapore and Brunei should be vaccinated against hepatitis A.

Hepatitis B

The only sexually transmitted disease that can be prevented by vaccination, hepatitis B is spread by body fluids, including sexual contact. In some parts of Asia up to 20% of the population are carriers of hepatitis B, and usually are unaware of this. The long-term consequences can include liver cancer and cirrhosis.

Hepatitis E

Hepatitis E is transmitted through contaminated food and water. It has similar symptoms to hepatitis A, but is far less common. It's a severe problem in pregnant women and can result in the death of both mother and baby. There is currently no vaccine, and prevention is by following safe eating and drinking guidelines while you're travelling in Malaysia, Singapore and Brunei.

HEALTH

HIV

HIV remains a problem through much of Southeast Asia, including Malaysia, Singapore and Brunei, with heterosexual sex now the main method of transmission.

Influenza

Present year round in the tropics, influenza (flu) gives you a high fever, muscle aches, a runny nose, a cough and sore throat. Flu can be very severe in people over the age of 65 or in those with underlying medical conditions such as heart disease or diabetes. Vaccination is recommended for these high-risk individuals travelling in Malaysia, Singapore and Brunei. There's no specific treatment, just rest and paracetamol.

Japanese B Encephalitis

Rare in travellers, this viral disease transmitted by mosquitoes is found in Malaysia and Brunei. Most cases of Japanese B encephalitis occur in rural areas and vaccination is recommended for travellers spending more than one month outside cities. There is no treatment, and a third of infected people will die, while another third will suffer permanent brain damage.

Leptospirosis

Present in Malaysia, leptospirosis is most commonly contracted by travellers after river rafting or canyoning. Early symptoms are very similar to the flu and include headache and fever. It can vary from very mild to fatal. Diagnosis is through blood tests and it is easily treated with Doxycycline.

Malaria

For such a serious and potentially deadly disease, there is an enormous amount of misinformation concerning malaria. You must get expert advice as to whether your trip actually puts you at risk, especially if travelling in Malaysia. Many areas, particularly city and resort areas, have minimal to no risk of malaria, and the risk of side effects from the tablets may outweigh the risk of getting the disease. For some rural areas, however, the risk of contracting the disease far outweighs the risk of any tablet side effects. Remember that malaria can be fatal. Before you travel, seek medical advice regarding the right medication and dosage for you.

Malaria is caused by a parasite transmitted through the bite of an infected mosquito. The most important symptom of malaria is fever, but general symptoms such as headache, diarrhoea, cough or chills may also occur. Diagnosis can be made only by taking a blood sample.

Two strategies should be combined to prevent malaria – mosquito avoidance and antimalarial medications. Most people who catch malaria are taking inadequate or no antimalarial medication.

Travellers are advised to prevent mosquito bites by taking these steps:

- Use a DEET-containing insect repellent on exposed skin. Wash this off at night, as long as you are sleeping under a mosquito net treated with permethrin. Natural repellents such as citronella can be effective, but must be applied more frequently than products containing DEET.
- Sleep under a mosquito net impregnated with permethrin.
- Choose accommodation with screens and fans (if not air-con).
- Impregnate clothing with permethrin in high-risk areas.
- Wear long sleeves and trousers in light colours.
- Use mosquito coils.
- Spray your room with insect repellent before going out for your evening meal.

There are a variety of antimalarial medications available:

Artesunate Artesunate derivatives are not suitable as a preventive medication. They are useful treatments under medical supervision.

Chloroquine & Paludrine The effectiveness of this combination is now limited in most of Southeast Asia. Common side effects include nausea (40% of people) and mouth ulcers. Generally not recommended.

Doxycycline This daily tablet is a broad-spectrum antibiotic that has the added benefit of helping to prevent a variety of tropical diseases, including leptospirosis, tick-borne diseases, typhus and melioidosis. The potential side effects include photosensitivity (a tendency to sunburn), thrush in women, indigestion, heartburn, nausea and interference with the contraceptive pill. More-serious side effects include ulceration of the oesophagus – you can help prevent this by taking your tablet with a meal and a large glass of water, and never lying down within half an hour of taking it. Must be taken for four weeks after leaving the risk area.

Lariam (Mefloquine) Lariam has received much bad press, some of it justified, some not. This weekly tablet suits many people. Serious side effects are rare but include depression, anxiety, psychosis and having fits. Anyone with a history of depression, anxiety, other psychological disorders or epilepsy should not take Lariam. It's considered safe in the second and third trimesters of pregnancy. It's around 90% effective in most parts of Asia, but there's significant resistance in parts of northern Thailand, Laos and Cambodia. Tablets must be taken for four weeks after leaving the risk area.

Malarone This new drug is a combination of atovaquone and proguanil. Side effects are uncommon and mild, most commonly nausea and headache. It is the best tablet for scuba divers and for those on short trips to high-risk areas. It must be taken for one week after leaving the risk area.

A final option is to take no preventive medication but to have a supply of emergency medication should you develop the symptoms of malaria. This is less than ideal, and you'll need to get to a good medical facility within 24 hours of developing a fever. If you choose this option, the most effective and safest treatment is Malarone (four tablets once daily for three days). Other options include mefloquine and quinine but the side effects of these drugs at treatment doses make them less desirable. Fansidar is no longer recommended.

Measles

Occurring in Malaysia, this highly contagious bacterial infection is spread via coughing and sneezing. Most people born before 1966 are immune, as they had the disease in childhood. Measles starts with a high fever and rash and can be complicated by pneumonia and brain disease. There is no specific treatment.

Rabies

This fatal disease, present in Malaysia, is spread by the bite or lick of an infected animal – most commonly a dog or monkey. You should seek medical advice immediately after any animal bite and commence post-exposure treatment.

Having pretravel vaccination means the postbite treatment is greatly simplified. If an animal bites you, gently wash the wound with soap and water, and apply an iodine-based antiseptic. If you are not prevaccinated you will need to receive rabies immunoglobulin as soon as possible.

SARS

Standing for Severe Acute Respiratory Syndrome, the respiratory illness SARS seems to have been brought under control since its major outbreak in 2003. The symptoms of SARS are identical to many other respiratory infections, namely high fever and cough. There's no quick test for SARS but certain blood-test and chest X-ray results offer support for the diagnosis. There's also no specific treatment available, and death from respiratory failure occurs in about 10% of patients. Fortunately, it appears it's not as easy to catch SARS as was initially thought. Wearing masks has a limited effect and is not generally recommended.

STDs

Among the most common sexually transmitted diseases in Southeast Asia, including Malaysia, Singapore and Brunei, are herpes, warts, syphilis, gonorrhoea and chlamydia. People carrying these diseases often have no signs of infection. Condoms will prevent gonorrhoea and chlamydia but not warts or herpes. If after a sexual encounter you develop any rash, lumps, discharge or pain when passing urine, seek immediate medical attention. If you've been sexually active during your travels, have an STD check on your return home.

Tuberculosis

While TB is rare in travellers in Malaysia and Brunei, medical and aid workers and long-term travellers who have significant contact with the local population should take precautions. Vaccination is usually given only to children under the age of five, but adults at risk are recommended to have TB testing both before and after travelling. The main symptoms are fever, cough, weight loss, night sweats and tiredness.

Typhoid

This serious bacterial infection is spread via food and water and is found in Malaysia, Singapore and Brunei. It causes a high, slowly progressive fever, and a headache, and may be accompanied by a dry cough and stomach pain. It's diagnosed by blood tests and treated with antibiotics. Vaccination is recommended for travellers spending more than a week in the region, or travelling outside major cities. Note that vaccination is not 100% effective so you must still take care with what you eat and drink.

Typhus

Murine typhus is spread by the bite of a flea, whereas scrub typhus is spread via a mite.

Although present in Malaysia, these diseases are rare in travellers. Symptoms include fever, muscle pains and a rash. You can prevent typhus by following general insect-avoidance measures. Doxycycline will also prevent it.

TRAVELLER'S DIARRHOEA

Traveller's diarrhoea is by far the most common problem affecting travellers – between 30% and 50% of people will suffer from it within two weeks of starting their trip. In over 80% of cases, traveller's diarrhoea is caused by a bacteria (there are numerous potential culprits), and therefore responds promptly to treatment with antibiotics. Treatment with antibiotics will depend on your situation – how sick you are, how quickly you need to get better, where you are etc. Traveller's diarrhoea is defined as the passage of more than three watery bowel-actions within 24 hours, plus at least one other symptom such as fever, cramps, nausea, vomiting or feeling generally unwell. Treatment consists of staying well hydrated; rehydration solutions like Gastrolyte are the best for this. Antibiotics such as Norfloxacin, Ciprofloxacin or Azithromycin will kill the bacteria quickly.

Loperamide is just a 'stopper' and doesn't get to the cause of the problem. It can be helpful, for example if you have to go on a long bus ride. Don't take Loperamide if you have a fever, or blood in your stools. Seek medical attention quickly if you do not respond to an appropriate antibiotic.

For food and water precautions see p602.

Amoebic Dysentery

Amoebic dysentery is very rare in travellers but is often misdiagnosed by poor-quality labs in Asia. Symptoms are similar to bacterial diarrhoea, ie fever, bloody diarrhoea and generally feeling unwell. You should always seek reliable medical care if you have blood in your diarrhoea. Treatment involves two drugs – Tinidazole or Metronidazole to kill the parasite in your gut and then a second drug to kill the cysts. If left untreated, complications such as liver abscess and abscess in the gut can occur.

Giardiasis

Giardia is a parasite that is relatively common in travellers. Symptoms include nausea, bloating, excess gas, fatigue and intermittent diarrhoea. 'Eggy' burps are often attributed solely to giardia, but work in Nepal has shown that they are not specific to giardia. The parasite will eventually go away if left untreated but this can take months. The treatment of choice is Tinidazole, with Metronidazole being a second-line option.

ENVIRONMENTAL HAZARDS
Air Pollution

Air pollution, particularly vehicle pollution, is an increasing problem in most of Asia's major cities. If you have severe respiratory problems, speak with your doctor before travelling to any heavily polluted urban centres. Air pollution can cause minor respiratory problems such as sinusitis, dry throat and irritated eyes. If troubled by the pollution, leave the city for a few days to get some fresh air.

Diving

Divers and surfers should seek specialised advice before they travel to ensure their medical kit contains treatment for coral cuts and tropical ear infections, as well as the standard problems. Divers should ensure their insurance covers them for decompression illness – get specialised dive insurance through an organisation such as **DAN** (Divers Alert Network; www.danseap.org). Have a dive medical before you leave your home country – there are certain medical conditions that are incompatible with diving, and economic considerations may override health considerations at some dive operations in Asia.

DRINKING WATER

- Never drink tap water (although in Singapore it's considered safe).

- Bottled water is generally safe – check the seal is intact at purchase.

- Avoid ice.

- Avoid pre-prepared 'fresh' juices – they may have been watered down.

- Boiling water is the most efficient method of purifying it.

- The best chemical purifier is iodine. It should not be used by pregnant women or those with thyroid problems.

- Water filters should also filter out viruses. Ensure your filter has a chemical barrier such as iodine and a small pore size, ie less than 4 microns.

HEALTH

THAT CLINGING FEELING

On any rainforest walk, the subject of leeches invariably comes up. You may not encounter any of these slimy little vampires while walking through the Malaysian jungle, but if the trail is leafy and it's been raining, chances are you'll be preyed upon.

The local leeches are maddeningly tiny – so small, in fact, they can squeeze through tight-knit socks. They don't stay tiny for long, however, since once a leech has attached to your skin, it won't let go until it has sucked as much blood as it can hold. Only then will the bloated, sated little parasite release itself and make its way back to the forest floor. Your souvenir of the experience will be bloody, but consider it a flesh wound.

Two species are common: the brown leech and the tiger leech. The tiger leech is recognisable by its cream and black stripes, but you'll probably feel one before you see it. Unlike the brown leech, whose suction is painless, tiger leeches sting a bit. Brown leeches hang around on, or near, the forest floor, waiting to grab onto passing boots or pants. Tiger leeches lurk on the leaves of small trees and tend to attack between the waist and neck, and that can mean any orifice there and around. Keep your shirt tucked in.

Leeches are harmless, but bites can become infected. Prevention is better than the cure and opinion varies on what works best. Insect repellent on feet, shoes and socks works temporarily; loose tobacco in your shoes and socks also helps – Kelabit hunters swear by it. Better yet, invest in some leech-proof socks, which are a kind of tropical gaiter that covers the foot and boot heel and fastens below the knees.

Safe and effective ways to dislodge leeches include flicking them off sideways (pulling a leech off by the tail might make it dig in harder), burning them with a cigarette (though you may burn yourself as well), or sprinkling salt on them. Tiger balm, iodine or medicated menthol oil (a common brand is the Axe Brand Universal Oil) will also get leeches off. High-pitched screaming doesn't seem to affect them much. Succumb to your fate as a reluctant blood donor and they will eventually drop off.

Food

Eating in restaurants or at hawker stalls is the biggest risk factor for contracting traveller's diarrhoea. Ways to avoid it include eating only freshly cooked food and avoiding shellfish and food that has been sitting around in buffets – in this respect, open-air hawker stalls where you can see exactly what the cook is doing and everything is freshly made are likely to be safer places to eat. Peel all fruit, cook vegetables, and soak salads in iodine water for at least 20 minutes. Eat in busy restaurants with a high turnover of customers.

Heat

Most people take at least two weeks to adapt to the hot, humid climate. Swelling of the feet and ankles is common, as are muscle cramps caused by excessive sweating. Prevent these by avoiding dehydration and too much activity in the heat. Take it easy when you first arrive. Don't eat salt tablets (they aggravate the gut), but drinking rehydration solution or eating salty food helps. Treat cramps by stopping activity, resting, rehydrating with double-strength rehydration solution and gently stretching.

Dehydration is the main contributor to heat exhaustion. Symptoms include feeling weak, headache, irritability, nausea or vomiting, sweaty skin, a fast, weak pulse and a slightly elevated body temperature. Treatment involves getting the victim out of the heat and/or sun, fanning them and applying cool wet cloths to the skin, laying the victim flat with their legs raised and rehydrating with water containing a quarter of a teaspoon of salt per litre. Recovery is usually rapid although it's common to feel weak for some days afterwards.

Heatstroke is a serious medical emergency. Symptoms come on suddenly and include weakness, nausea, a hot dry body with a body temperature of over 41°C, dizziness, confusion, loss of coordination, fits, and eventual collapse and loss of consciousness. Seek medical help and commence cooling by getting the sufferer out of the heat, removing their clothes, fanning them and applying cool, wet cloths or ice to their body, especially to the groin and armpits.

Prickly heat is a common skin rash in the tropics, caused by sweat being trapped under the skin. The result is an itchy rash of tiny lumps. If you develop prickly heat, treat it by moving out of the heat and into an air-conditioned area for a few hours and by having cool showers. Creams and ointments clog the skin so they should be avoided. Locally bought prickly heat powder can be helpful.

Tropical fatigue is common in long-term expatriates based in the tropics. It's rarely due to disease but is caused by the climate, inadequate mental rest, excessive alcohol intake and the demands of daily work in a different culture.

Insect Bites & Stings

Bedbugs don't carry disease but their bites are very itchy; see the boxed text, below. Lice inhabit various parts of your body but most commonly your head and pubic area. They can be difficult to treat and you may need numerous applications of an anti-lice shampoo such as permethrin. Transmission is via close contact with an infected person. Pubic lice are usually contracted from sexual contact.

Ticks are contracted after walking in the bush. Ticks are commonly found behind the ears, on the belly and in armpits. If you have had a tick bite and experience symptoms such as a rash at the site of the bite or elsewhere, a fever, or muscle aches you should see a doctor. Doxycycline prevents tick-borne diseases.

Leeches are generally found in humid rainforest areas. They do not transmit any disease but their bites are often intensely itchy for weeks afterwards and can easily become infected. Apply iodine-based antiseptic to any leech bite to help prevent infection (for other details see also the boxed text, opposite).

Bee and wasp stings mainly cause problems for people who are allergic to them. Anyone with a serious bee or wasp allergy should carry an injection of adrenaline (eg an EpiPen) for emergency treatment. For others, pain is the main problem – apply ice to the sting and take painkillers.

Most jellyfish in Southeast Asian waters are not dangerous, just irritating. First aid for jellyfish stings involves pouring vinegar onto the affected area to neutralise the poison. Don't rub sand or water onto the stings. Take painkillers, and anyone who feels ill in any way after being stung should seek medical advice. Take local advice on whether there are dangerous jellyfish around, and keep out of the water.

DON'T LET THE BEDBUGS BITE

They live in the cracks of furniture and walls and then migrate to the bed at night to feed on you – yes, those bedbugs really do bite and according to your reports and our own research they seem to do it with particular relish in Malaysia. Bedbugs are more likely to strike in high-turnover accommodation, especially backpackers, though they can be found anywhere. The room may look very clean but they can still be there.

What can you do to protect yourself?

■ Ask the hotel or hostel what they do to avoid bed bugs. It's a common problem and reputable establishments should have some type of pest-control procedure in place.

■ In any room keep your luggage elevated off the floor to avoid having the critters latch on – this is one of the common ways bedbugs are spread from place to place.

■ Check the room carefully for signs of bugs – you may find their translucent light brown skins or poppy-seed-like excrement. Pay particular attention to places less likely to have seen a dusting from cleaning staff.

If you do get bitten:

■ Treat the itch with antihistamine.

■ Thoroughly clean your luggage and launder all your clothes, then seal them in plastic bags to further protect them.

■ Be sure to tell the management – if they seem unconcerned or refuse to do anything about it complain to the local tourist office and write to us.

TRADITIONAL & FOLK MEDICINE

Throughout Asia, traditional medical systems are widely practised. There is a big difference between these traditional healing systems and 'folk' medicine. Folk remedies should be avoided, as they often involve rather dubious procedures with potential complications. In comparison, traditional healing systems, such as traditional Chinese medicine, are well respected, and aspects of them are being increasingly utilised by Western medical practitioners.

All traditional Asian medical systems identify a vital life force, and see blockage or imbalance as causing disease. Techniques such as herbal medicines, massage and acupuncture bring this vital force back into balance or maintain balance. These therapies are best used for treating chronic disease such as chronic fatigue, arthritis, irritable bowel syndrome and some chronic skin conditions. Traditional medicines should be avoided for treating serious acute infections such as malaria.

Be aware that 'natural' doesn't always mean 'safe', and there can be drug interactions between herbal medicines and Western medicines. If you are using both systems, ensure you inform both practitioners as to what the other has prescribed.

Parasites

Numerous parasites are common in local populations in Southeast Asia; but, most of these are rare in travellers. The two rules to follow to avoid parasitic infections are to wear shoes and to avoid eating raw food, especially fish, pork and vegetables. A number of parasites are transmitted via the skin by walking barefoot, including strongyloides, hookworm and cutaneous larva migrans.

Skin Problems

Fungal rashes are common in humid climates. There are two common fungal rashes that affect travellers. The first occurs in moist areas that get less air, such as the groin, armpits and between the toes. It starts as a red patch that slowly spreads and is usually itchy. Treatment involves keeping the skin dry, avoiding chafing and using an antifungal cream such as Clotrimazole or Lamisil. Tinea versicolour is also common – this fungus causes small, light-coloured patches, most commonly on the back, chest and shoulders. Consult a doctor.

Cuts and scratches become easily infected in humid climates. Take meticulous care of any cuts and scratches to prevent complications such as abscesses. Immediately wash all wounds in clean water and apply antiseptic. If you develop signs of infection (increasing pain and redness), see a doctor. Divers and surfers should be particularly careful with coral cuts as they become easily infected.

Snakes

Southeast Asia is home to many species of poisonous and harmless snakes. Assume all snakes are poisonous and never try to catch one. Always wear boots and long pants if walking in an area that may have snakes. First aid in the event of a snake bite involves pressure immobilisation via an elastic bandage firmly wrapped around the affected limb, starting at the bite site and working up towards the chest. The bandage should not be so tight that the circulation is cut off; the fingers or toes should be kept free so the circulation can be checked. Immobilise the limb with a splint and carry the victim to medical attention. Don't use tourniquets or try to suck out the venom. Antivenin is available for most species.

Sunburn

Even on a cloudy day, sunburn can occur rapidly. Always use a strong sunscreen (at least factor 15), making sure to reapply after a swim, and always wear a wide-brimmed hat and sunglasses outdoors. Avoid lying in the sun during the hottest part of the day (10am to 2pm). If you're sunburnt, stay out of the sun until you've recovered, apply cool compresses and take painkillers for the discomfort. Applied twice daily, 1% hydrocortisone cream is also helpful.

TRAVELLING WITH CHILDREN

There are specific issues you should consider before travelling with your child.

All routine vaccinations should be up to date, as many of the common childhood diseases that have been eliminated in the West are still present in parts of Southeast Asia. A travel-health clinic can advise on specific vaccines, but think seriously about rabies vaccination if you're visiting rural areas or travelling for more than a month, as children are more vulnerable to severe animal bites.

Children are more prone to getting serious forms of mosquito-borne diseases such as malaria, Japanese B encephalitis and dengue fever. In particular, malaria is very serious in children and can rapidly lead to death – you should think seriously before taking your child into a malaria-risk area. Permethrin-impregnated clothing is safe to use, and insect repellents should contain between 10% and 20% DEET.

Diarrhoea can cause rapid dehydration and you should pay particular attention to keeping your child well hydrated. The best antibiotic for children with diarrhoea is Azithromycin.

Children can get very sick very quickly so locate good medical facilities at your destination and make contact if you are worried – it's always better to get a medical opinion than to try to treat your own children.

WOMEN'S HEALTH

Pregnant women should receive specialised advice before travelling. The ideal time to travel is in the second trimester (between 16 and 28 weeks), when the risk of pregnancy-related problems is at its lowest and pregnant women generally feel at their best. During the first trimester there's a risk of miscarriage and in the third trimester complications such as premature labour and high blood pressure are possible. It's wise to travel with a companion. Always carry a list of quality medical facilities available at your destination and ensure you continue your standard antenatal care at these facilities. Avoid travel in rural areas with poor transport and medical facilities. Most of all, ensure travel insurance covers all pregnancy-related possibilities, including premature labour.

Malaria is a high-risk disease in pregnancy. The World Health Organization recommends that pregnant women do not travel to areas with malaria resistant to chloroquine. None of the more effective antimalarial drugs is completely safe in pregnancy.

Traveller's diarrhoea can quickly lead to dehydration and result in inadequate blood flow to the placenta. Many of the drugs used to treat various diarrhoea bugs are not recommended in pregnancy. Azithromycin is considered safe.

In urban areas, supplies of sanitary products are readily available. Birth-control options may be limited so bring adequate supplies of your own form of contraception. Heat, humidity and antibiotics can all contribute to thrush. Treatment is with antifungal creams and pessaries such as clotrimazole. A practical alternative is a single tablet of Fluconazole (Diflucan). Urinary-tract infections can be precipitated by dehydration or long bus journeys without toilet stops; bring suitable antibiotics.

Language

CONTENTS

Bahasa Malaysia (also known simply as Malay, and as *bahasa Melayu* in Malay) and Bahasa Indonesia are virtually the same language; only accents and a few differences in vocabulary distinguish the two. Many of these differences are in the loan words – English-based for Malay and Dutch-based for Indonesian. If you're coming from Indonesia and have developed some proficiency in the language, you may initially be confused by Malay pronunciation. Bahasa Indonesia is a second language for most Indonesians – pronunciation is learnt in schools and thus tends to remain fairly standard. Bahasa Malaysia, however, is subject to a greater degree of regional variation in pronunciation and slang – so much so that a Malaysian from Negeri Sembilan may have difficulty understanding someone from Kelantan.

In many ways, Malay is very simple. Verbs aren't conjugated for tense; the notion of time is indicated by the use of adverbs such as 'yesterday' or 'tomorrow'. For example, you can change any sentence into the past tense by simply adding *sudah* (already). Many nouns are pluralised by simply saying them twice – thus *buku* is 'book', *buku-buku* is 'books'; *anak* is 'child', *anak-anak* is 'children'. There are no articles ('a', 'an', 'the'). Thus 'a good book' or 'the good

book' is simply *buku baik* (literally 'book good'). There is no verb 'to be', so again it would be *buku baik* rather than 'the book is good'. Malay is, however, a very poetic and evocative language – 'the sun', for example, is *matahari*, literally 'eye of the day'.

Many Malay terms have found their way into the everyday English of Malaysia. You'll often see the word *bumiputra* (literally 'sons of the soil') in English-language newspapers, usually in ads for positions vacant; it's a term used to indicate that the job is open only to 'native' Malays, not Indian Malaysians or Chinese Malaysians. Similarly, you may see English-language articles about *jaga keretas*, the people who operate car-parking rackets – pay them to 'protect' your car while it's parked or you'll wish you had. Another expression is *khalwat* (literally 'close proximity') – unmarried Muslim couples definitely do not wish to find themselves suspected of *khalwat*!

For a more comprehensive guide to the language, get hold of Lonely Planet's *Malay Phrasebook*.

PRONUNICATION

Most letters are pronounced the same as their English counterparts, although a few vowels and consonants differ.

Vowels

a   as the 'u' in 'hut'
e   a neutral vowel like the 'a' in 'ago' when unstressed, eg *besar* (big); when the stress falls on **e** it's more like the 'a' in 'may', eg *meja* (table). Unfortunately, there's no single rule to determine whether **e** is stressed or unstressed.
i   as in 'hit'
o   as in 'note'
u   as in 'flute'
ai   as in 'aisle'
au   'ow', as in 'cow'
ua   each vowel is pronounced, as 'oo-a'

Consonants

c   as the 'ch' in 'chair'
g   hard, as in 'go'
ng   as in 'singer'

SINGLISH

One of the most intriguing things the visitor to Singapore will notice is the strange patois spoken by the locals. Nominally English, it contains borrowed words from Hokkien and Malay, such as *shiok* (delicious) and *kasar* (rough). Unnecessary prepositions and pronouns are dropped, word order is flipped, phrases are clipped short, and stress and intonation are unconventional, to say the least. The result is known locally as Singlish. Singlish is frowned upon in official use, though you'll get a good idea of its pervasive characteristics of pronunciation if you listen to the news bulletins on TV or the radio.

There are a number of interesting characteristics that differentiate Singlish from standard English. First off, there's the reverse stress pattern of double-barrelled words. For example, in standard English the stress would be *'fire*-fighter' or *'theatre* company' but in Singlish it's 'fire-*fighter*' and 'theatre *company*'. Word-final consonants – particularly **l** or **k** – are often dropped and vowels are often distorted; a Chinese-speaking taxi driver might not understand 'Perak Road' since they pronounce it 'Pera Roh'. The particle *lah* is often tagged on to the end of sentences as in, 'No good, *lah*', which could mean (among other things) 'I don't think that's such a good idea'. Requests or questions will often be marked with a tag ending since direct questioning is considered rude. So a question such as 'Would you like a beer?' might be rendered as 'You want beer or not?', which, ironically, might come across to speakers of standard English as being extremely rude. Verb tenses tend to be nonexistent; future, present or past actions are all indicated by time phrases, so in Singlish it's 'I go tomorrow' or 'I go yesterday'.

The following are some of the most frequently heard Singlishisms:

ah beng – unsophisticated person with no fashion sense or style; redneck

Aiyah! – 'Oh, dear!'

Alamak! – exclamation of disbelief, frustration or dismay, like 'Oh my God!'

ayam – Malay word for chicken; adjective for something inferior or weak

blur – a slow or uninformed person

buaya – womaniser, from the Malay for 'crocodile'

Can? – 'Is that OK?'

Can! – 'Yes! That's fine.'

char bor – babe, woman

cheena – old-fashioned Chinese in dress or thinking (derogatory)

go stan – to reverse, as in 'Go stan the car' (from the naval expression 'go astern'; pronounced 'go stun')

heng – luck, good fortune (from Hokkien)

hiao – vain

inggrish – English

kambing – foolish person, literally 'goat' (from Malay)

kena ketuk – ripped off, literally 'get knocked'

kiasee – scared, literally 'afraid to die'; a coward

kiasu – selfish, pushy, always on the lookout for a bargain, literally 'afraid to lose'

lah – generally an ending for any phrase or sentence; can translate as 'OK', but has no real meaning; added for emphasis to just about everything

looksee – take a look

malu – embarrassed

minah – girlfriend

Or not? – general tag for questions, as in 'Can or not?' (Can you or can't you?)

see first – wait and see what happens

shack – tired

shiok – good, great, delicious

steady lah – well done, excellent; expression of praise

Wah! – general exclamation of surprise or distress

ya ya – boastful, as in 'He always *ya ya*'

ngg	as 'ng' plus 'g' (as in 'anger')
j	as in 'join'
r	pronounced clearly and distinctly
h	as the English 'h' but slightly stronger (like a sigh); at the end of a word it's almost not audible
k	as English 'k', except at the end of the word, when it's more like a glottal stop (the 'nonsound' created by the momentary closing of the throat before each syllable as in the expression 'oh-oh!')
ny	as in 'canyon'

Word Stress

In Malay words, a good rule of thumb is to put stress on the second-last syllable. The main exception is the unstressed **e** in words such as *besar* (big), pronounced 'be-*sar*'.

ACCOMMODATION

I'm looking for a ...	*Saya mencari ...*
bed	*katil*
guesthouse	*rumah tetamu*
hotel	*hotel*
youth hostel	*asrama belia*

LANGUAGE

MAKING A RESERVATION

For phone or written inquiries:

To ...	Ke ...
From ...	Daripada ...
I'd like to book ...	Saya nak tempah ... (see the list under 'Accommodation' for bed and room options)
for the nights of ...	untuk malam ...
in the name of ...	atas nama ...
credit card	kad kredit
type	jenis
number	nombor
expiry date	tempoh tamat
Please confirm availability and price.	Tolong sahkan tempahan dan harga.

Where is a cheap hotel?
Di mana ada hotel yang murah?
What is the address?
Apakah alamatnya?
Could you write the address, please?
Tolong tuliskan alamat itu?
Do you have any rooms available?
Ada bilik kosong?
I'd like to share a dorm.
Saya nak berkongsi bilik hostel.

I'd like a ...	Saya hendakkan ...
single room	bilik untuk satu orang
double room	bilik untuk dua orang
room with two beds	bilik yang ada dua katil
room with air-con	bilik dengan alat hawa dingin
room with a fan	bilik dengan kipas
room with a bathroom	bilik dengan bilik mandi

How much is it ...?	Berapa harga ...?
per night	satu malam
per week	satu seminggu
per person	satu orang

May I see it?
Boleh saya lihat biliknya?
Where is the bathroom?
Bilik mandi di mana?
I (don't) like this room.
Saya (tidak) suka bilik ini.
I'm/We're leaving today.
Saya/Kami nak mendaftar keluar hari ini.

CONVERSATION & ESSENTIALS

Hello.	Helo.
Good morning.	Selamat pagi.
Good day. (said around midday)	Selamat tengah hari.
Good afternoon.	Selamat petang.
Good night.	Selamat malam.
Goodbye. (said by person leaving)	Selamat tinggal.
Goodbye. (said by person staying)	Selamat jalan.
Yes.	Ya.
No.	Tidak.
Please.	Tolong/Silakan.
Thank you (very much).	Terima kasih (banyak).
That's fine/ You're welcome.	Boleh/Sama-sama.
Excuse me, ...	Maaf, ...
Sorry/Pardon.	Maaf.
I'm sorry. (forgive me)	Minta maaf.
How are you?	Apa khabar?
Fine, thanks.	Khabar baik.
What's your name?	Siapa nama kamu?
My name is ...	Nama saya ...
Where are you from?	Dari mana asal saudara?
I'm from ...	Saya dari ...
How old are you?	Berapa umur saudara?
I'm (20) years old.	Umur saya (dua puluh) tahun.
I like ...	Saya suka ...
I don't like ...	Saya tidak suka ...
Just a minute.	Sebentar/Sekejap.
Good/Very nice.	Bagus.
Good/Fine.	Baik.
No good.	Tidak baik.

DIRECTIONS

Where is ...?	Di mana ...?
Which way?	Ke mana?
Go straight ahead.	Jalan terus.
Turn left.	Belok kiri.
Turn right.	Belok kanan.
at the corner	di simpang
at the traffic lights	di tempat lampu isyarat
at the T-junction	di simpang tiga
behind	di belakang
in front of	di hadapan
next to	di samping/di sebelah
opposite	berhadapan dengan
near	dekat
far	jauh
here	di sini
there	di sana

SIGNS

Ada Bilik Kosong	Rooms Available
Bahaya	Danger
Balai Polis	Police Station
Buka	Open
Di Larang Merokok	No Smoking
Dilarang	Prohibited
Keluar	Exit
Masuk	Entrance
Panas	Hot
Penuh/Tak Ada Bilik Kosong	Full/No Vacancies
Pertanyaan	Information
Polis	Police
Sejuk	Cold
Tandas	Toilets
Lelaki	Men
Perempuan	Women
Tarik	Pull
Tolak	Push
Tutup	Closed

north	*utara*
south	*selatan*
east	*timur*
west	*barat*

beach	*pantai*
bridge	*jambatan*
island	*pulau*
mosque	*masjid*
museum	*muzium*
palace	*istana*
ruins	*runtuhan*
sea	*laut*
square	*dataran*

HEALTH

Where is a ...?	*Di mana ada ...?*
chemist/pharmacy	*apotik/farmasi*
dentist	*doktor gigi*
doctor	*doktor*
hospital	*hospital*

I'm ill.	*Saya sakit.*
It hurts here.	*Sini sakit.*

I'm allergic to ...	*Saya alergik kepada ...*
antibiotics	*antibiotik*
aspirin	*aspirin*
bees	*lebah*
nuts	*kacang*
penicillin	*penisilin*

I'm ...	*Saya ...*
asthmatic	*sakit lelah*
diabetic	*sakit kencing manis*
epileptic	*sakit gila babi*
pregnant	*hamil*

antiseptic	*antiseptik*
condoms	*kondom*
contraceptive	*kontraseptif/pencegah hamil*
diarrhoea	*cirit-birit*
fever	*demam panas*
headache	*sakit kepala*
medicine	*ubat*
pill/tablet	*pil/tablet*
quinine	*kina/kuinin*
sanitary napkins	*tuala wanita*
sleeping pills	*pil tidur*
sunblock cream	*krim pelindung cahaya matahari*
tampons	*tampon*

EMERGENCIES

Help!	*Tolong!*
There's been an accident.	*Ada kemalangan.*
I'm lost.	*Saya sesat.*
Go away!	*Pergi!*
Stop!	*Berhenti!*
I've been robbed.	*Saya dirompak.*
Call ...!	*Panggil ...!*
a doctor	*doktor*
an ambulance	*ambulans*

LANGUAGE DIFFICULTIES

Do you speak English?
Bolehkah anda berbicara bahasa Inggeris?/
Adaka anda berbahasa Inggeris?
Does anyone here speak English?
Ada orang yang berbahasa Inggeris di sini?
How do you say ... in Malay?
Macam mana cakap ... dalam Bahasa Melayu?
What does ... mean?
Apa ertinya ...?
I understand.
Saya faham.
I don't understand.
Saya tidak faham.
Please write it down.
Tolong tuliskan.
Please write that word down.
Tolong tuliskan perkataan itu.
Please repeat it.
Tolong ulangi.

LANGUAGE

NUMBERS

0	kosong/sifar
1	satu
2	dua
3	tiga
4	empat
5	lima
6	enam
7	tujuh
8	delapan/lapan
9	sembilan
10	sepuluh
11	sebelas
12	dua belas
13	tiga belas
14	empat belas
15	lima belas
16	enam belas
17	tujuh belas
18	lapan belas
19	sembilan belas
20	dua puluh
21	dua puluh satu
22	dua puluh dua
30	tiga puluh
40	empat puluh
50	lima puluh
60	enam puluh
70	tujuh puluh
80	lapan puluh
90	sembilan puluh
100	seratus
200	dua ratus
1000	seribu
2000	dua ribu

PAPERWORK

name	nama
nationality	bangsa
date of birth	tarikh lahir
place of birth	tempat kelahiran tempat lahir
sex/gender	jantina
passport	pasport
visa	visa

QUESTION WORDS

Who?	Siapakah?
What?	Apa?
When?	Bilakah?
Where?	Di mana?
How?	Berapa?
Which?	Yang mana?

SHOPPING & SERVICES

I'd like to buy ...	Saya nak beli ...
How much (is it)?	Berapa (harganya)?
I don't like it.	Saya tak suka ini.
May I look at it?	Boleh saya lihat barang itu?
I'm just looking.	Saya nak tengok saja.
It's cheap.	Murah.
It's too expensive.	Mahalnya.
Can you lower the price?	Boleh kurang sedikit?
No more than ...	Tak lebih daripada ...
That's a good price.	Harganya dah murah.
I'll take it.	Saya nak beli ini.
Do you accept ...?	Boleh bayar dengan ...?
credit cards	kad kredit
travellers cheques	cek kembara
more	lebih banyak
less	kurang
big	besar
bigger	lebih besar
small	kecil
smaller	lebih kecil
this	ini
that	itu

I'm looking for a/the ...	Saya nak cari ...
bank	bank
barber	tukang cukur
bookshop	kedai buku
chemist/pharmacy	apotik/farmasi
city centre	pusat bandar
... embassy	kedutaan besar ...
grocery	kedai makanan
market	pasar
night market	pasar malam
police station	stesen polis
post office	pejabat pos
public telephone	telepon umum
public toilet	tandas awam
shop	kedai
shopping centre	pusat membeli-belah
telephone centre	pusat telefon
tourist office	pejabat pelancong

I want to change ...	Saya nak tukar wang ...
money (cash)	wang tunai
travellers cheques	cek kembara

What time does it open/close?
Pukul berapa buka/tutup?
I want to call ...
Saya mau menelefon ...

TIME & DATES

What time is it?	*Pukul berapa?*
It's (seven) o'clock.	*Pukul (tujuh).*
When?	*Bila?*
in the morning	*pagi*
in the afternoon	*tengahari*
in the evening	*petang*
at night	*malam*
today	*hari ini*
tomorrow	*besok/esok*
yesterday	*semalam*
How long?	*Berapa lama?*
hour	*jam*
day	*hari*
week	*minggu*
year	*tahun*

Monday	*hari Isnin*
Tuesday	*hari Selasa*
Wednesday	*hari Rabu*
Thursday	*hari Khamis*
Friday	*hari Jumaat*
Saturday	*hari Sabtu*
Sunday	*hari Minggu*

January	*Januari*
February	*Februari*
March	*Mac*
April	*April*
May	*Mei*
June	*Jun*
July	*Julai*
August	*Ogos*
September	*September*
October	*Oktober*
November	*November*
December	*Disember*

TRANSPORT
Public Transport

What time does the ... leave?	*Pukul berapakah ... berangkat?*
boat	*bot*
bus	*bas*
plane	*kapal terbang*
ship	*kapal*
train	*keretapi*

I'd like a ... ticket.	*Saya nak tiket ...*
one-way	*sehala*
return	*pergi-balik*
1st class	*kelas satu*
2nd class	*kelas dua*
economy class	*kelas ekonomi*

ROAD SIGNS

Bahaya	Danger
Beri Jalan	Give Way
Dilarang Letak Kereta	No Parking
Dilarang Masuk	No Entry
Jalan Sehala	One Way
Jalan Tol	Toll Way
Keluar	Exit
Kosongkan	Keep Clear
Lencongan	Detour
Masuk	Entrance
Perlahan-Perlahan	Slow Down
Plaza Tol	Toll Gate
Tidak Boleh Memotong	No Overtaking

I want to go to ...
Saya nak ke ...
How can I get to ...?
Bagaimana saya pergi ke ...?
How many kilometres?
Berapa kilometer?
The (train/bus) has been delayed.
Keretapi/bas itu telah terlambat.
The (train/bus) has been cancelled.
Keretapi/bas itu telah dibatalkan.

the first (bus)	*(bas) pertama*
the last (train)	*(keretapi) terakhir*
airport	*lapangan terbang*
bus station	*stesen bas*
bus stop	*perhentian bas*
platform number	*nombor platform*
rickshaw/trishaw	*beca*
ticket office	*pejabat tiket*
ticket window	*tempat/kaunter tikit*
timetable	*jadual*
train station	*stesen keretapi*

Private Transport

I'd like to hire a ...	*Saya nak menyewa ...*
4WD	*4WD*
bicycle	*basikal*
car	*kereta*
motorbike	*motosikal*

Is this the road to ...?	*Inikah jalan ke ...?*
Where's a service station?	*Stesen minyak di mana?*
Please fill it up.	*Tolong penuhkan tangki.*
I'd like (30) litres.	*Saya nak (30) liter.*

petrol	*minyak/petrol*
diesel	*disel*
leaded petrol	*petrol plumbum*
unleaded petrol	*tanpa plumbum*

(How long) Can I park here?
(Beberapa lama) Boleh saya letak kereta di sini?
Where do I pay?
Di mana tempat membayar?
I need a mechanic.
Kami memerlukan mekanik.
The car/motorbike has broken down (at ...).
Kereta/motosikal saya telah rosak (di ...).
The car/motorbike won't start.
Kereta/motosikal saya tidak dapat dihidupkan.
I have a flat tyre.
Tayarnya kempis.
I've run out of petrol.
Minyak sudah habis.
I've had an accident.
Saya terlibat dalam kemalangan.

TRAVEL WITH CHILDREN

Do you have a/an ...?	*Ada ...?*
I need a/an ...	*Saya perlukan ...*
baby change room	*bilik salin bayi*
car baby seat	*tempat duduk bayi*
child-minding service	*penjagaan anak*
children's menu	*menu kanak-kanak*
(disposable) nappies/diapers	*(pakai buang) kain lampin*
(English-speaking) babysitter	*penjaga anak (yang tahu bercakap dalam Bahasa Inggeris)*
formula (milk)	*(susu) rumusan bayi*
highchair	*kerusi tinggi*
potty	*bekas najis*
stroller	*kereta tolak bayi*

Are children allowed?
Adakah kanak-kanak dibenarkan masuk?

Also available from Lonely Planet:
Malay Phrasebook

Glossary

See p71 for culinary terms.

adat – Malay customary law
adat temenggong – Malay law with Indian modifications, governing the customs and ceremonies of the sultans
air – water
air terjun – waterfall
alor – groove; furrow; main channel of a river
ampang – dam
ang pow – red packets of money used as offerings, payment or gifts
APEC – Asia-Pacific Economic Cooperation
arak – Malay local alcohol
arrack – see *arak*
Asean – Association of Southeast Asian Nations
atap – roof thatching

Baba-Nonya – descendants of Chinese immigrants to the Straits Settlements (namely Melaka, Singapore and Penang) who intermarried with Malays and adopted many Malay customs; also known as Peranakan, or Straits Chinese; sometimes spelt Nyonya
Bahasa Malaysia – Malay language; also known as Bahasa Melayu
bandar – seaport; town
Bangsawan – Malay opera
batang – stem; tree trunk; the main branch of a river
batik – technique of imprinting cloth with dye to produce multicoloured patterns
batu – stone; rock; milepost
belukar – secondary forest
bendahara – chief minister
bendang – irrigated land
bomoh – spiritual healer
British Resident – chief British representative during the colonial era
bukit – hill
bumboat – motorised *sampan*
bumiputra – literally, sons of the soil; indigenous Malays
bunga raya – hibiscus flower (national flower of Malaysia)

dadah – drugs
dato', datuk – literally, grandfather; general male nonroyal title of distinction
dipterocarp – family of trees, native to Malaysia, that have two-winged fruits
dusun – small town; orchard; fruit grove

genting – mountain pass
godown – river warehouse

gua – cave
gunung – mountain

hilir – lower reaches of a river
hutan – jungle; forest

imam – keeper of Islamic knowledge and leader of prayer
istana – palace

jalan – road

kain songket – traditional Malay handwoven fabric with gold threads
kampung – village; also spelt kampong
kangkar – Chinese village
karst – characteristic scenery of a limestone region, including features such as underground streams and caverns
kedai kopi – coffee shop
kerangas – distinctive vegetation zone of Borneo, usually found on sandstone, containing pitcher plants and other unusual flora
khalwat – literally, close proximity; exhibition of public affection between the sexes, which is prohibited for unmarried Muslim couples
kongsi – Chinese clan organisations, also known as ritual brotherhoods, heaven-man-earth societies, triads or secret societies; meeting house for Chinese of the same clan
kopitiam – coffee shop
kota – fort; city
kramat – Malay shrine
KTM – Keretapi Tanah Melayu; Malaysian Railways System
kuala – river mouth; place where a tributary joins a larger river

laksamana – admiral
langur – small, usually tree-dwelling monkey
laut – sea
lebuh – street
Lebuhraya – expressway or freeway; usually refers to the North–South Highway, which runs from Johor Bahru to Bukit Kayu Hitam at the Thai border
lorong – narrow street; alley
LRT – Light Rail Transit (Kuala Lumpur)
lubuk – deep pool

macaque – any of several small species of monkey
mandi – bathe; Southeast Asian wash basin
masjid – mosque
MCP – Malayan Communist Party

Melayu Islam Beraja – MIB; Brunei's national ideology
merdeka – independence
Merlion – half-lion, half-fish animal; symbol of Singapore
MRT – Mass Rapid Transit (Singapore)
muara – river mouth
muezzin – mosque official who calls the faithful to prayer

negara – country
negeri – state
nonya – see *Baba-Nonya*

orang asing – foreigner
Orang Asli – literally, Original People; Malaysian aborigines
Orang Laut – literally, Coastal People; Sea Gypsies
Orang Ulu – literally, Upriver People

padang – grassy area; field; also the city square
pantai – beach
PAP – People's Action Party
parang – long jungle knife
PAS – Parti Islam se-Malaysia
pasar – market
pasar malam – night market
Pejabat Residen – Resident's Office
pekan – market place; town
pelabuhan – port
pencak silat – martial-arts dance form
penghulu – chief or village head
pengkalan – quay
Peranakan – literally, half-caste; refers to the *Baba-Nonya* or Straits Chinese
PIE – Pan-Island Expressway, one of Singapore's main road arteries
pua kumbu – traditional finely woven cloth
pulau – island
puteri – princess

raja – prince; ruler
rakyat – common people
rantau – straight coastline
rattan – stems from climbing palms used for wickerwork and canes
rimba – jungle

rotan – cane used to punish miscreants
roti – bread

sampan – small boat
samsu – Malay alcohol
sarong – all-purpose cloth, often sewn into a tube, and worn by women, men and children
seberang – opposite side of road; far bank of a river
selat – strait
semenanjung – peninsula
silat – see *pencak silat*
simpang – crossing; junction
songkok – traditional Malay headdress worn by males
Straits Chinese – see *Baba-Nonya*
sungai – river
syariah – Islamic system of law

tambang – river ferry; fare
tamu – weekly market
tanah – land
tanjung – headland
tasik – lake
teluk – bay; sometimes spelt *telok*
temenggong – Malay administrator
towkang – Chinese junk
tuai rumah – longhouse chief (Sarawak)
tuak – local 'firewater' alcohol (Malaysian Borneo)
tunku – prince

ujung – cape
UMNO – United Malays National Organisation

warung – small eating stalls
wayang – Chinese opera
wayang kulit – shadow-puppet theatre
wisma – office block or shopping centre

yang di-pertuan agong – Malaysia's head of state, or 'king'
yang di-pertuan besar – head of state in Negeri Sembilan
yang di-pertuan muda – under-king
yang di-pertuan negeri – governor

The Authors

SIMON RICHMOND   Coordinating Author, Kuala Lumpur, Selangor

Simon has been travelling frequently to this region since the early 1990s when he first crashed at Singapore's Majestic Hotel – it was anything but Majestic, and certainly not as New as it is today. The experience didn't put him off – on the contrary he's kept on coming back for repeat infusions of Malaysian and Singaporean culture, landscapes, adventure and, crucially, the fantastic range of food. This is the third time the award-winning travel writer and photographer (catch him at www.simonrichmond .com) has helmed this guide, one of several he writes for Lonely Planet as well as other publishers.

CELESTE BRASH   Negeri Sembilan, Melaka, Johor, Pahang

Celeste first visited Malaysia while she was studying at Chiang Mai University, Thailand, in 1993 and she later moved to Singapore to teach English. The more of Malaysia she's visited over the years, the more she's fallen in love with it. Malaysian food is her favourite in the world and the country just seems to get better and better with every visit. When not desensitising her taste buds with *sambal*, Celeste lives on Tahiti in French Polynesia with her husband and two children. She's contributed to over a dozen Lonely Planet guidebooks including *Travel with Children,* and her award-winning travel writing has appeared in numerous publications from the *LA Times* to *Islands Magazine.*

ADAM KARLIN   Perak, Penang, Kedah & Perlis, Terengganu, Kelantan

Adam Karlin has gotten lucky with Lonely Planet assignments in the past, but *damn*. Really? The Perhentians? And Penang? *And* Langkawi? Adam's first trip to Southeast Asia was in 1997 as a high school senior; he returned in 2003 to work as a subeditor at the *Vientiane Times* and the *Nation* (Bangkok). He's since gotten an MA from the School of Oriental and African Studies in London with a partial focus on Southeast Asian politics and history. He tries to make it back to this region whenever Lonely Planet isn't sending him around Africa or his native USA.

THE AUTHORS

SHAWN LOW   Singapore

After 23 hot, sticky and sweaty years in Singapore, Shawn made for the cooler but more temperamental climes of Melbourne in 2001. He found his way into Lonely Planet as a book editor in 2006 (and still constantly pinches himself to see if he's dreaming). Since then, he's done a stint as a commissioning editor and has constantly (sometimes successfully) flirted with the Lonely Planet TV department. Authoring has always been on his 'to do' list and if being paid to return home to write the 'definitive' guide to Singapore sounds like a dream job, it probably is. Note: bruises on his arms are from the constant pinching. OW!

BRANDON PRESSER   Sabah, Sarawak, Brunei

Dreams of Borneo started early for Brandon – long before his first trip to Malaysia over a decade ago. He fondly recalls cutting up a tattered *National Geographic* for a grade school project on Iban warriors. Those fanciful magazine memories were brought to life as he scaled granite summits, swam with schools of sharks, stepped in steaming piles of bat guano and downed shots of cloudy rice wine – all in the name of research, of course. Brandon spends most of the year writing his way around the globe, and has contributed to over a dozen Lonely Planet titles, including *Thailand, Thailand's Islands & Beaches* and *Southeast Asia on a Shoestring*.

CONTRIBUTING AUTHORS

Dr Trish Batchelor is a general practitioner and travel medicine specialist who currently works in Canberra, and is Medical Advisor to the Travel Doctor New Zealand clinics. She has just returned from working in Vietnam and has previously worked in Nepal and India. Trish teaches travel medicine through the University of Otago, and is interested in underwater and high-altitude medicine, and the impact of tourism on host countries. She has travelled extensively through Southeast and East Asia.

Robyn Eckhardt has called KL home for the last four of her 13 years in Asia. When not reporting on food and travel for publications like *Travel + Leisure, Wall Street Journal Asia* and *Time Out Kuala Lumpur*, she can often be found enjoying a cuppa at her favourite *kopitiam*. Robyn wrote the Food & Drink chapter for this edition of *Malaysia, Singapore & Brunei*.

Behind the Scenes

THIS BOOK

This 11th edition of *Malaysia, Singapore & Brunei* was researched and written by Simon Richmond (coordinating author), Celeste Brash, Adam Karlin, Shawn Low, Brandon Presser and Robyn Eckhardt. The Health chapter was based on research supplied by Dr Trish Batchelor.

This guidebook was commissioned in Lonely Planet's Melbourne office, and produced by the following:

Commissioning Editors Shawn Low, Tashi Wheeler
Coordinating Editor Nigel Chin
Coordinating Cartographer Peter Shields
Coordinating Layout Designer Kerrianne Southway
Managing Editors Sasha Baskett, Katie Lynch
Managing Cartographer David Connolly
Managing Layout Designer Sally Darmody
Assisting Editors Janet Austin, Pete Cruttenden, Kate Daly, Barbara Delissen, Tasmin McNaughtan, Maryanne Netto, Simon Williamson
Assisting Cartographers Enes Basic, Owen Eszeki, Mick Garrett, Corey Hutchison, Khanh Luu, Ross Macaw, Marc Milinkovic, Jacqueline Nguyen, Brendan Streager
Cover Naomi Parker, lonelyplanetimages.com
Project Managers Craig Kilburn, Sarah Sloane
Language Content Robyn Loughnane
Thanks to Lucy Birchley, Jessica Crouch, Paul Iacono, Trent Paton, Dianne Schallmeiner, Saralinda Turner

THANKS
SIMON RICHMOND

Cheers to Shawn for getting the ball rolling, my fine band of coauthors, and to Tashi for picking the project up and managing it with laudable pragmatism and humour. In KL, it was delightful as ever to hang out with Chris and Eddy and their merry band of friends. Hugs to Princess Kim for braving the fish spa with her Dad and cheers to Matt for driving me to Bukit Fraser and back. A huge thank you to Alex Yong for his expert assistance and connections, to Christopher Wong for showing me around Lok Mansion, and to all the people who spared time in their busy schedules for interviews, in particular: Eli Wong, Reshmonu, Anju Sahadevan, Brian Kwan, Steven Gan, Andrew Sebastian, Elizabeth Cardosa, Fahmi Fadzil, Mei Lim and Dr Reza Azmi. For foodie tips contributing author Robyn Eckhardt was the best, as were the peerless Adly Rizal and Honey Ahmad from Fried Chillies. In KKB, Larry and Anna helped smooth the way enormously. On Langkawi and Penang Narelle and her fantastic staff's hospitality was very welcome. Also on Penang a big thanks to Chris Ong, Karl Steinberg and Sek Thim. Rounding it all out in style was Ray Norris, my gracious host in Singapore.

THE LONELY PLANET STORY

Fresh from an epic journey across Europe, Asia and Australia in 1972, Tony and Maureen Wheeler sat at their kitchen table stapling together notes. The first Lonely Planet guidebook, *Across Asia on the Cheap*, was born.

Travellers snapped up the guides. Inspired by their success, the Wheelers began publishing books to Southeast Asia, India and beyond. Demand was prodigious, and the Wheelers expanded the business rapidly to keep up. Over the years, Lonely Planet extended its coverage to every country and into the virtual world via lonelyplanet.com and the Thorn Tree message board.

As Lonely Planet became a globally loved brand, Tony and Maureen received several offers for the company. But it wasn't until 2007 that they found a partner whom they trusted to remain true to the company's principles of travelling widely, treading lightly and giving sustainably. In October of that year, BBC Worldwide acquired a 75% share in the company, pledging to uphold Lonely Planet's commitment to independent travel, trustworthy advice and editorial independence.

Today, Lonely Planet has offices in Melbourne, London and Oakland, with over 500 staff members and 300 authors. Tony and Maureen are still actively involved with Lonely Planet. They're travelling more often than ever, and they're devoting their spare time to charitable projects. And the company is still driven by the philosophy of *Across Asia on the Cheap*: 'All you've got to do is decide to go and the hardest part is over. So go!'

BEHIND THE SCENES

CELESTE BRASH

Thanks to my family for putting up with my absences, to Peck Choo Ho and all her limes, Yaksa, Aril Zainal and Mania, Amy Wan for being so hardcore, Alex Ageev for putting up with Amy and me; Rajan Jones, Appu, Omar, Kara and Max for the best company; Veloo the taxi driver who saved me in Lipis; Hilary Chiew, Elizabeth Cardosa, and Brandon Presser for endless phone support, Shawn Low for hiring me and for wonderful Singapore; Simon Richmond for KL, elephants and for being so damned detail oriented and to Tashi Wheeler for steady support and clarity.

ADAM KARLIN

What a trip. Thanks: Dommy, Jenny, Fnuggi and Zali: the Kota Bahru and beyond crew. Susann, Nicole, Afton, Colin, Fam and Chris in the Perhentians for much Monkey Juice. The Slovenian Army, particularly Soba and Bego: we broke the walls. Johanna and Riika, my fine Finnish friends. Robbie, Lukas, Anders, Nik, Kat and Katherine and anyone else who played The Game. And Simon Richmond for being a patient, responsive and all-around excellent head author.

SHAWN LOW

Where do I begin? Thanks to Marg and Errol for graciously picking me for this gig and to Tashi for taking over. Tip of the hat to Martin, Melanie and Sasha for dealing with constant changes to my schedules (that damn TV gig!). I'm grateful to the many Singaporeans who showed me a softer side to local life (including an 'auntie' who heaped her food into my bowl. God bless you!). Thanks to Simon for taking a good, hard look at my text. Brandon and Celeste – you two make fab travel buddies and even better friends. Mum for being mum and for always believing there was an author in me. And Wency for letting me play for months away from home and appreciating my presence in absence. I love you.

BRANDON PRESSER

Thanks to Shawn for commissioning the title and for dragging my food-poisoned body up the mountain (and back!); to Celeste (Tyler Durden) for being the best phone buddy one could ever have; to Simon and Tashi for doing an awesome job of helming the ship (the HMS *MSB?*); and to the all-star production staff at LP HQ for putting the finishing touches on a great new edition. Thanks also to the colourful cast of characters that helped me along my eventful journey down the yellow-brick road (there are too many of you

to name!): Chris Rowthorn, Karen Chin, Lillian ('Mama Borneo'), Anton & Linn, Frankie & Yanti, I-Gek, Auther, Papa Bear, Lloyd Jones, BigHeadJer, Melintan, Matty G, Raddish, Jerome, Philip Yong and everyone else at BA. In Brunei, thank you to Irman, Leslie Chiang, Jenny, Amali, Chris and Faten. *Terima kasih!*

OUR READERS

Many thanks to the travellers who used the last edition and wrote to us with helpful hints, useful advice and interesting anecdotes:

A Shaukani Abbas, Joe Alvaro, Laura Ambrey, Claire Andrews, Nick Askew, Ravi Aswani, Mick Atkinson **B** Jie Bao, Andre Barbarin, Julie Barber, Alison Barham, Kim Barnett, Jane Barnett, Michael Barrett, John Barton, William Beavitt, Alexandra Bello, Emma Bennett, Daniela Bischof Boesch, Howard Block, Michele Boillod, Nicolas Bontoux, Julie Booth, Michael Borkan, Vesna Borovnik, Debbie Bradshaw, Karin Branzell, Jeremy Bright, Ben Brocherie, Jared Brubaker, Jake Brumby, Helen Brunt, Ross Buncle, Lee Butler **C** Stuart Calvin, Jack Carey, Antoine Casteignau, Tom Catha, Gordon Cavanaugh, William Chambers, Jenny Cheung, Alicia Choo, Colin Chow, Claudia Christl, Adrian Cole, Anthony Cole, Sara Consigli, Bob Cooper, Simon Cox, Adam Cragg, Laura Cunningham **D** David Daddario, Rod Daldry, Monica Dashen, Daniel De Vries, Sue Deakin, Cathy Degaytan, Mark Degaytan, Ruth Dittmann, Dorothy Doughty **E** Samuel Eberhardt, Afshin Eftekhar, George Elliston, Brenda Engberts **F** Rainer Faus, Carolin Flohr, Buisson

---

SEND US YOUR FEEDBACK

We love to hear from travellers – your comments keep us on our toes and help make our books better. Our well-travelled team reads every word on what you loved or loathed about this book. Although we cannot reply individually to postal submissions, we always guarantee that your feedback goes straight to the appropriate authors, in time for the next edition. Each person who sends us information is thanked in the next edition and the most useful submissions are rewarded with a free book.

To send us your updates – and find out about Lonely Planet events, newsletters and travel news – visit our award-winning website: **lonelyplanet.com/contact**.

Note: we may edit, reproduce and incorporate your comments in Lonely Planet products such as guidebooks, websites and digital products, so let us know if you don't want your comments reproduced or your name acknowledged. For a copy of our privacy policy visit lonelyplanet.com/privacy.

Florence, Marc Forster, Gaye French, Roger Frost, Jack Fry **G** Alan Gale, Michael Gandy, Robinson Gaong, Catherine Garratt, Jolanta Glabek, Katherina Goh, Inge Gommers, Paul Govaerts, Emanuel Graca, William Green, Desiree Groen, Lynette Groszmann **H** Tom Halliday, Eric Hansen, Stephen Harris, Tony Hatwell, Sue Headlam, Daniel Hein, Maria Herrman, Timo Hoffmann, Thomas Hohn, Adrian Holloway, Fiona Holmes, Anouk Horstink, Thys Hovenkamp, Wayne Hsu, Lisa Huffman, Gary Husler, Kristoffer Hvatum **J** Judy Janssen, Olivier Jaumont, Vivien Lee Jensen, Marielle Jippes, Alanna Jorde **K** Hidemitsu Katsura, Webb Keane, Bradley Kendal, Hans Klamer, Silvia Knaus, Ute Kolbeck, Elisabeth Koppelberg, Krzysztof, Saskia Kuijpers **L** William Lamack, Eliana Lamas, Julie Lawson, Anna Lech, Max Lee, Christina Leitner, Alan Leo, Julie Lerat, Jason Letteboer, Barbara Lettner, Guy Lichter, Gisela Liebscher, Annabelle Lincoln, Peter Linssen, Giorgia Liviero, Christian Löhrer, Peter Lovejoy, Judy Lucas **M** Kati M, Cathy Macqueen, Paul Malone, Pierre-Henri Manderscheid, Alessandro Manigrasso, Andrea Mann, Schoch Thomann Maria, Alan Marriott, Nick Martin, Sarah Mason, Michael McCudden, John Mcleod, John Mcmartin, Tjasa Medved, Ann-Mari Michaels, Jayne & Patrick Michel, Karolina Michniuk, Gordon Millar, Jan Mulder **N** Jonathan Newton, Vincent Ng, Maria Nobleza **O** Glen Op Den Brouw, Nicolas Otis, Sander Oudkerk **P** Patricia Park, Kunden Patel, Kirsti Pateman, Mario Pavesi, Barry Peacock, Michal Pelikan, Matt Pepe, Jonathan Phun, Kate Porter, Ludwig Pregernig, Peter Price **R** Linda Rae, Petra Rautenberg, Rupert Reed, Thomas Reichmann, Wayne Richardson, Alexa Ridgway, Rafael Riera Martinez, Juan Rodriguez, Helge Rognaas, Teresa Roque, Nigel Rose **S** Javier San Jose, Saskia Sano, Chiara Satta, Michel & Annemiek Savelkoul, Michael Schlicht, Stephen Scott, Leonie Semmens, Barb Shaw, Steven Shaw, Abraham Silverzweig, Chris Skelley, Nathan Slowinski, Di Smale, Mike Smith, Sandy Smith, Martijn Smits, Floris Snuif, Damian Spellman, Joseph Stimpfl, Morten Stuhr Svensson **T** Derek Tanner, Peter Taylor, Kris Terauds, Michael Todd, Markus Toepler, Marianne Toll, Jessica Toop, Ditch Townsend, Jon Tullett **V** Simon Van Der Putten, Jaap Van Der Stelt, Sylvia Van Dooren, Anneloes Van Erp, Brigitte Van Kessel, John Van Leeuwen, Dennis Van Raalte, Lois Vander Waerdt, Vera Vanderboom, Erik & Lenneke Veldman, Bjoern Viehweger **W** Claudette Wadsworth, Sharon Walsh-Grieve, Kai Walther, Yong Wang, Chris Waters, Geert-Jaap Welsing, Mark Wheeler, Philip Whittick, Sampo Widmann, Thomas Wieser, Timothy Willish, Jan Willoughby, Renske Wink, Paul Wood, Eleanor Woodcock **Y** Karen Young **Z** Manuele Zunelli

ACKNOWLEDGMENTS

Many thanks to the following for the use of their content:

Globe on title page ©Mountain High Maps 1993 Digital Wisdom, Inc.

Index

000 Map pages
000 Photograph pages

000 Map pages
000 Photograph pages

GreenDex

The following is an index of the businesses, events and organisations in Malaysia, Singapore and Brunei that are doing their bit for the environment, sustainable travel and enabling greater cultural understanding. Our decisions about what to include were informed by the work of regional bodies such as Wild Asia (www.wildasia.org) and the opinions of local experts. The index is not exhaustive but does provide a place to start for those who like to make informed choices in how they spend their vacation time and money.

Choosing sustainable travel products, just like running a business that is eco-friendly, is not an exact science and is also a continuous process. We know we haven't got it 100% right yet! We very much welcome feedback on our selection via lonelyplanet.com/contact as well as recommendations for anything that we should be including in this list the next time around. For more information on travelling responsibly see p21 and lonelyplanet.com/responsibletravel.

ecotourism
 KOPEL 201

PERAK
accommodation
 Belum Rainforest Resort 169
attractions
 Zoo Taiping & Night Safari
  170

SABAH
accommodation
 Borneo Divers Mabul Resort 390
 Borneo Rainforest Lodge 385
 Danum Valley Field Centre 385
 Nak Hotel 373
 Paganakan Dii 377
 Tempurung Seaside Lodge 398
activities
 Borneo Divers 389
 Borneo Images 344
 KK Heritage Walk 344
attractions
 Labuk Bay Proboscis Monkey
  Sanctuary 376-7
 Maliau Basin Conservation Area
  394-6, **395**
 Mari Mari Cultural Village 346
 Rainforest Discovery Centre (RDC)
  376
 Sabah Agricultural Park 397
 Sepilok Orang-Utan Rehabilitation
  Centre (SORC) 375-6, 9
 Tambunan Rafflesia Reserve 396
 Tun Sakaran Marine Park 388

ecotourism
 Borneo Adventure 347
 Borneo Authentic 347
 Borneo Divers 347
 Borneo Nature Tours 394
 Kinabatangan Jungle Camp 382
 Mescot 382
 Traverse Tours 347

SARAWAK
accommodation
 Nanga Sumpa 434
 Permai Rainforest Resort 426
attractions
 Bako National Park 356, 423-5,
  424
 Gunung Gading National Park 429
 Gunung Mulu National Park 452-8,
  453, 11
 Kubah National Park 427
 Niah National Park 450-2
 Similajau National Park 444-5
 Talang-Satang National Park
  432-3
 Tanjung Datu National Park 432
drinking
 a-ha Café 418
 Black Bean Coffee & Tea Company 418
ecotourism
 Borneo Adventure 416
shopping
 Sarawak Craft Council 420
wildlife rehabilitation
 Semenggoh Wildlife Rehabilitation
  Centre 428

SELANGOR
accommodation
 Sekeping Serendah Retreat
  134
 Taman Alam Kuala Selangor
  Nature Park 141
attractions
 Chiling Waterfall 133
 Dark Cave 131
 Forestry Research Institute of
  Malaysia (FRIM) 132
 Fraser's Hill (Bukit Fraser) 134-6,
  135
 Kampung Kuantan 140-1
 Kampung Sungai Bumbon
  140
 Orang Asli Museum 132
 Rimbun Dahan 132
 Taman Alam Kuala Selangor
  Nature Park 141
 Taman Botani 137
 Taman Wetland
  137
 Zoo Negara 132

SINGAPORE
ecotourism
 Kranji Countryside Association
  farms 506

TERENGGANU
accommodation
 Pura Tanjung Sabtu
  310
 Wan Kay Homestay 309

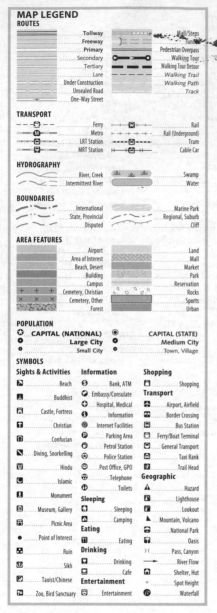

MAP LEGEND

ROUTES

- Tollway
- Freeway
- Primary
- Secondary
- Tertiary
- Lane
- Under Construction
- Unsealed Road
- One-Way Street
- Mall/Steps
- Tunnel
- Pedestrian Overpass
- Walking Tour
- Walking Tour Detour
- Walking Trail
- Walking Path
- Track

TRANSPORT

- Ferry
- Metro
- LRT Station
- MRT Station
- Rail
- Rail (Underground)
- Tram
- Cable Car

HYDROGRAPHY

- River, Creek
- Intermittent River
- Swamp
- Water

BOUNDARIES

- International
- State, Provincial
- Disputed
- Marine Park
- Regional, Suburb
- Cliff

AREA FEATURES

- Airport
- Area of Interest
- Beach, Desert
- Building
- Campus
- Cemetery, Christian
- Cemetery, Other
- Forest
- Land
- Mall
- Market
- Park
- Reservation
- Rocks
- Sports
- Urban

POPULATION

- ☸ CAPITAL (NATIONAL)
- ● Large City
- ○ Small City
- ◉ CAPITAL (STATE)
- ● Medium City
- ○ Town, Village

SYMBOLS

Sights & Activities
- Beach
- Buddhist
- Castle, Fortress
- Christian
- Confucian
- Diving, Snorkelling
- Hindu
- Islamic
- Monument
- Museum, Gallery
- Picnic Area
- Point of Interest
- Ruin
- Sikh
- Taoist/Chinese
- Zoo, Bird Sanctuary

Information
- ☒ Bank, ATM
- Embassy/Consulate
- Hospital, Medical
- ❶ Information
- Internet Facilities
- Parking Area
- Petrol Station
- Police Station
- Post Office, GPO
- Telephone
- Toilets

Sleeping
- Sleeping
- Camping

Eating
- Eating

Drinking
- Drinking
- Cafe

Entertainment
- Entertainment

Shopping
- Shopping

Transport
- Airport, Airfield
- Border Crossing
- Bus Station
- Ferry/Boat Terminal
- General Transport
- Taxi Rank
- Trail Head

Geographic
- ▲ Hazard
- Lighthouse
- Lookout
- ▲ Mountain, Volcano
- National Park
- Oasis
-)(Pass, Canyon
- River Flow
- Shelter, Hut
- + Spot Height
- Waterfall

LONELY PLANET OFFICES

Australia
Head Office.
Locked Bag 1, Footscray, Victoria 3011
☎ 03 8379 8000, fax 03 8379 8111
talk2us@lonelyplanet.com.au

USA
150 Linden St, Oakland, CA 94607
☎ 510 250 6400, toll free 800 275 8555
fax 510 893 8572
info@lonelyplanet.com

UK
2nd fl, 186 City Rd,
London EC1V 2NT
☎ 020 7106 2100, fax 020 7106 2101
go@lonelyplanet.co.uk

Published by Lonely Planet Publications Pty Ltd
ABN 36 005 607 983

© Lonely Planet 2009

© Photographers as indicated 2009

Cover photograph: vegetables and fruit baskets in Chinatown, Singapore, Michael Yamashita/Aurora Photos. Many of the images in this guide are available for licensing from Lonely Planet Images: lonelyplanetimages.com.

Printed by Hang Tai Printing Company, Hong Kong.
Printed in China.

Mixed Sources
Product group from well-managed forests and other controlled sources
www.fsc.org Cert no. SGS-COC-005002
© 1996 Forest Stewardship Council